MAN'S IMPACT ON ENVIRONMENT

McGRAW-HILL SERIES IN GEOGRAPHY

Edward J. Taaffe and John W. Webb, *Consulting Editors*

MAN'S IMPACT ON ENVIRONMENT

THOMAS R. DETWYLER

Department of Geography
University of Michigan

McGraw-Hill Book Company

NEW YORK   ST. LOUIS   SAN FRANCISCO
DÜSSELDORF   JOHANNESBURG   KUALA LUMPUR   LONDON   MEXICO   MONTREAL
NEW DELHI   PANAMA   RIO DE JANEIRO   SINGAPORE   SYDNEY   TORONTO

*This book was set in Times Roman, and
was printed on permanent paper and
bound by George Banta Company, Inc.
The designer was J. E. O'Connor.
The editors were Janis Yates and David Dunham.
Robert R. Laffler supervised production.*

MAN'S IMPACT ON ENVIRONMENT

Library of Congress Catalog Card Number 78-139551

07-016592-0

4 5 6 7 8 9 0 B A B A 7 9 8 7 6 5 4 3 2

FOR LAURA'S WORLD

CONTENTS

PREFACE

The environmental revolution is upon us. Increasing repercussions on man of his own environmental alterations will surely force enlightened action during the 1970s. However, recent substantial information concerning man's impact on environment largely remains scattered in the professional journals of many fields (geography, engineering, ecology, biology, meteorology, etc.). A broad, coherent book treating the facts of man's present impact on environment at a level suitable for college students and intelligent laymen has been greatly needed.

Man's Impact on Environment substantiates the wide spectrum of environmental changes wrought by man, focusing on major *processes* of change, immediate and extended *effects* on the environment, and *trends* in time and space of processes and effects. Taken together, and put into context by synthesizing editorial comments, these articles provide a meaningful overview of the present quality of man's environment and the causes for this condition.

I have tried to select articles and write editorial comments on a level suitable for the beginning college student, although the subject matter creates some difficulty in this regard. As one of my manuscript reviewers has commented, "The heterogeneity of subject matter is so striking that everybody is going to be a beginner with some of the articles. One article roots itself in chemical complexity, the next in genetics, then zoology, demography, mining engineering, and even a touch of comparative economies." The inclusion of such different subjects is not only necessary for showing the breadth and interrelatedness of man's environmental impacts but also advantageous. From my experience, students have been stimulated by this variety and by the case study approach, which presents problems in enough depth to reveal their complexity and involves the methodology of ecological inquiry. Further, many of the studies appropriately present more questions than answers—— and the many environmental crises we face attest to the shortage of real answers.

I hope that *Man's Impact on Environment* will prove useful as a principal text in courses on conservation, natural resources, natural science, physical geography, ecology, environmental science, and environment and man. New courses in the latter two subjects are burgeoning; perhaps this book can serve as a core for their formation. In addition, this book may have value as a supplementary text and resource book in a wide variety of fields —including biology, earth science, cultural geography, engineering, geology, climatology, anthropology, and contemporary issues. Finally, I hope that laymen will find the book enlightening and stimulating.

To accomplish my purpose, I have included case studies and analyses—herein called "selections"—by expert authors and put them in context by means of editorial comments of several kinds. I have provided introductory and concluding chapters, as well as editorial introductions to each "part" (or collection of selections) and to each of the fifty selections by other authors. My aims in these editorial commentaries have been to: weave a fabric of integration between the selections; emphasize important points; discuss important alternative approaches or interpretations; elucidate technical passages; and extend the coverage by presenting additional (sometimes newer) information. In addition to these explicit comments, I have tried to provide context by the careful arrangement of topics and articles. I have edited several of the selections, to various degrees; in each case this is noted at the beginning of the selection. Unlike many books of "readings," all references cited in the original papers are included (except in a few cases where the references were to portions of the text that are deleted here). As a further aid to the reader, especially to increase the book's usefulness for research and reference, nearly every part and selection is supplemented with a list of Further Readings and Additional References. Additional editorial features of the book are: a biographical sketch of each author; a glossary of environmental terms; several new or redrawn illustrations; and a lengthy index.

Selections were chosen using these criteria: contribution to the defined purpose, college-level presentation, factuality (including expertness of the author), clarity of expression, English language and currency (thirty-six of the selections were first published within the past four years).

Man's Impact on Environment may be readily adapted for various college courses. As a central text in courses that are short or use a great deal of other material, coverage can be abbreviated, while retaining much breadth, by using all of Parts 1, 2, and 10, the editorial introductions to other parts, and some selections from each of the other parts. Since the opening selection in most parts is more general and broader than the other selections, the opening selections, along with other preferred selections, may be used.

Earth science courses may concentrate on Parts 1 to 5 and 10, biology courses on Parts 1, 2, and 6 to 10, and so forth. However, the complex nature of man's alterations of environment has precluded strict segmentation of the book along the lines of traditional disciplines; so, for example, the biologist may also find relevant articles in the parts focused on water (e.g., Selections 19 to 21) or land and soil (e.g., Selections 28 to 30). The numerous supplementary references should be helpful to instructors in preparing lecture and discussion notes and to students in investigating topics for papers or discussions.

Both my classroom need for this book and my plans for it evolved from my course at the University of Michigan, "Modification of the Earth by Man" (now called "Man's Impact on Environment" and taught jointly with Donald Gray, an engineer). I am grateful to the students in this course for helping me find appropriate material and for the stimulating discussions that have helped me to define an approach to the subject.

I want to acknowledge here the help I have had in preparing *Man's Impact on Environment*. I thank the publishers and many authors who have granted me permission to reproduce their work. The advice of my colleagues, especially Donald Gray and Melvin Marcus, has been valuable. I am grateful to Cheryl Lougeay, Cecilie Pletcher, and Pat Bosma, all of whom ferreted information and typed correspondence and manuscript while cheerfully enduring my working habits. Joan Enerson drew the several original figures. Finally, for the help that is beyond measurement, to my wife, Sharon: thanks.

Thomas R. Detwyler

Eroded bank. Photo from God's Country and My People *by Wright Morris (*Harper & Row, *1968*).

ONE INTRODUCTION

"Man will destroy himself if he thoughtlessly and violently upsets the complex and delicate web of life of which he is a part."

Selection 1: Modern Man and Environment

Selection 2: Man's Use of the Earth: Historical Background

1
SELECTION

MODERN MAN AND ENVIRONMENT
THOMAS R. DETWYLER

Our Present Plight: The Widening Gap between Change and Understanding

Despite increasing public interest in environmental quality, there is not yet an integrated science of the environment, with established principles or even many substantiated generalizations. This lack of a conceptual framework for understanding how man and environment interact results in part from our fragmented, piecemeal study of the problem. This book focuses on one side of the man-environment relationship—how man affects environment. Because every element of the environment is adjusted to every other (although often distantly), a change induced by man usually sets off a chain of repercussions, of indirect and extended effects. A number of examples, many adversely influencing our health or our economy, come quickly to mind—the effects of air pollution, to cite one. But the details of man's impact on environment are not well understood.

In general, however, the variety, intensity, and geographical spread of environmental change by man is accelerating. And as problems of pesticide contamination, climatic change, or water pollution worsen, they demand our attention. But reaction to crisis is not enough, for technology may not be able to save man from the repercussions of his own actions. The critical question is:

Can we overcome our ignorance and apathy concerning our environmental actions soon enough? There is a race between onrushing environmental catastrophe and enlightened treatment of our environment. Put another way, our present plight is the widening gap between environmental change and environmental understanding.

One might well ask how this state of affairs has arisen. What are the reasons for accelerated change on the one hand and for lagging understanding on the other? The first of these—accelerating environmental change induced by man—is the theme of this book. Some underlying causes for these changes are explicitly discussed in Part 2 and repeatedly illustrated by examples throughout the book.

I believe that our general lack of true concern (including effective action) must largely be due to ignorance, because the facts, when known, are provoking. This book of readings will not only inform the reader but also, I hope, implant a sense of responsibility for action. Although our ultimate interest is to change our harmful environmental actions, we must first clearly recognize what those actions are. Wise recommendations for change can only proceed from an understanding of how man is, in fact, modifying the environment.

The reasons for our poor understanding and harmful treatment of environment merit further discussion here. Our ignorance can be traced to three basic and long-standing faults of science that persisted into the mid-nineteen-sixties. These defects are:

1. *Most of the natural sciences have treated their subjects as though man did not exist and alter nature, when in fact he is a major force of change.* The overwhelming predominance of this orientation can easily be seen by referring to available textbooks—biology, geology, soil science, climatology, and physical geography. In most, man's influence is either seldom (if at all) mentioned or it is tacked on as an unnatural afterthought in a closing chapter.

2. *The environment is artificially divided into separate components for study.* These environmental aspects generally coincide with academic disciplines. Such categorization usually (through specialty of interest or ignorance) tacitly assumes that environmental changes caused by man are more or less restricted to one part of the environment. In fact, they almost never are. There remains a grave paucity of interdisciplinary, broadly integrative studies of the environment, in part because of increasing specialization in science. The greatest, but still only partial, exceptions to this situation are found in the fields of ecology and physical geography (discussed later).

3. *Man-environment research has been neglected since the 1930s,* when the flaws of "environmental determinism" became widely recognized. For the preceding several decades the occurrence of many of man's cultural characteristics were largely attributed to the nature of the environment where they were found, often without much evidence. This idea, promulgated by Friederich Ratzel, Ellsworth Huntington, Ellen Semple, and others, became firmly entrenched in anthropology and geography before it was gradually discredited and replaced by other explanations. The important point here is that in reaction to environmental determinism these disciplines dampened all kinds of environmental investigation, including that of physical geography.

To these three scientific shortcomings should be added the lack of interest and incentive by applied and technical professions. The economic orientation of these groups has dictated an interest in short-run gains to be made from the environment, without consideration of long-term consequences, which are conveniently dismissed as "social costs" (see Selections 5 and 6).

Toward an Integrated Science of Environment

It is essential that man develop an integrated science of environment if he is to solve his worsening plight. To aid this development we may define some primary requisites for this science and draw useful concepts from existing sciences.

REQUISITES

Known facts of environmental change (many of them presented in this book) force a science of environment to incorporate three features that have heretofore been neglected. First, the *dynamics,* or *processes,* of environmental interaction must be accounted for. Second, *extended environmental effects,* or *interdisciplinary repercussions,* of a given action should be recognized and explained; most environmental impacts trigger chains of cause-and-effect relations which cut across established disciplines. And third, the importance and nature of *man's actions* must be appropriately recognized. No single scientific movement has yet integrated these features, and hence there is no explanatory or predictive *environmental science.*

Processes of environmental interaction. The physics of Newton, the geology of Lyell, and the biology of Darwin provide early examples of scientific breakthroughs that resulted from looking beyond the *what* and *where* of nature to inquire into the *why* and *how,* or dynamics, of nature's operation. Within a discipline, this shift from description to dynamics is almost always preceded by scientific specialization and extensive collection of facts. Significantly, the shift is usually initiated by men with broad interests and understanding as well as specialized knowledge. But the modern explosion of scientific knowledge has promoted increased specialization at the expense of breadth of outlook.

An interdisciplinary, integrated viewpoint. Repercussions through the environment of such actions as air pollution and contamination by pesticides make clear the need for an approach that cuts across the grain of established disciplines. The "problem approach," or "mission-oriented research," to environmental difficulties has further emphasized the breadth of expertise that must be effectively combined to understand and manage man-environment relations.

Man as a critical force. While technologists have adapted environment *for* man, scientists have shunned the effects *of* man on environment. Social science has emphasized the impact of environment on man, because the focus of social science is man. But natural scientists, whose interests are on aspects of the environment, have been loath to recognize the complicating factor of man in any corresponding manner—theirs are sciences of *things,* not of people; hence the neglect of man's environmental effects has developed and must be overcome in any meaningful science of environment.

CONTRIBUTIONS OF ECOLOGY AND GEOGRAPHY

It is instructive to look more closely at several of the so-called environmental sciences to see what contributions of value they are capable of making.

Ecology. Ecology has many advocates as *the* science of man-environment. Certainly the most common definition of the field would make it appear to be so: "The study of relationships between organisms and their environments." *In practice,* however, ecology has conformed much more closely to Pierre Dansereau's narrower definition as "The study of the reaction of plants and animals

to their immediate environment, to their habitat" (Dansereau, 1957, p. 323). Ecological studies have usually concentrated on the relations between organisms themselves (with little serious regard for the physical environment) and usually at the scale of the woodlot or the single field. Furthermore, man's place in the ecosystem has been of scarce concern, although applied ecology and human ecology now appear to be developing.

Hence, it is not surprising that many of the principles of ecology do not apply to man in the environment. Some others do, however, and aid understanding of environment; but such existing ecological propositions are certainly not sufficient, and a science of environment must be more broadly, yet more precisely, defined.

Of Dansereau's twenty-seven "ecological laws" (1966, pp. 459–460), seven appear to have special applicability to man in environment:

1. *Law of the inoptimum.* "No species encounters in any given habitat the optimum conditions for all of its functions." Hence, man tends to modify his habitat to satisfy his short-run environmental needs and desires. Further, man draws to given places many desired resources from elsewhere, affecting the distribution of materials, including wastes.

2. *Law of aphasy.* "Organic evolution is slower than environmental change on the average, and hence migration occurs (Cain, 1944, in op. cit.)." Environmental change wrought by man now is probably outstripping man's genetic (i.e., evolutionary) ability to adapt. This is not true for some other organisms—for example some insects (see Selection 50). There are numerous examples of man-induced environmental changes that have led to migration (e.g., see Selection 28); but there are many cases where even migration has been ineffective in providing suitable environments for survival, and extinction has resulted (see Selections 45 and 46).

3. *Law of tolerance.* "A species is confined, ecologically and geographically, by the extremes of environmental adversities that it can withstand." Modifications of environ-

ment by man have surpassed the tolerances of numerous species (see Selection 46), and the extreme danger, of course, is that man's tolerance may soon be exceeded and man will become extinct.

4. *Law of persistence.* "Many species, especially dominants of a community, are capable of surviving and maintaining their spatial position after their habitat and even the climate itself have ceased to favor full vitality." Modern cities are cores of human persistence (see Selection 8 and 11).

5. *Law of factorial control.* "Although living beings react holocenotically (to all factors of the environment in their peculiar conjunction), there frequently occurs a discrepant factor which has controlling power through its excess or deficiency." Such "discrepant controlling factors" as air pollution or pesticides may drastically and inadvertently alter plant or animal populations (e.g., see Selections 37 and 41). Many claimed threats of eco-catastrophe for man are similarly based upon an excess or deficiency of certain environmental factors.

6. *Law of irreversibility.* "Some resources (mineral, plant, or animal) do not renew themselves, because they are the result of a process (physical or biological) which has ceased to function in a particular habitat or landscape at the present time." To such *non*renewable resources can be added resources that are renewed so slowly (compared with consumption of them) that they are essentially subject to the same principle (e.g., ground-water withdrawals in some regions— see Part 5). One might also include here the strict irreversibility of some of man's environmental impacts (e.g., induced extinctions of animals—see Selection 46) and, again because of the slow rate of operation, the essential irreversibility of other changes (e.g., see Selections 27 and 31).

7. *Law of domestication.* "Plants and animals whose selection has been more or less dominated by man are rarely able to survive without his continued protection." Through his culture man has increasingly "domesticated" himself, too, by devising ever more elaborate protection against environmental

influences. In the face of increasing environmental deterioration, how long can man continue this self-protection and, with it, survival?

Two additional principles, advocated by other ecologists, also are pertinent here. One, which Barry Commoner calls the first law of ecology, is that everything in the environment is related to everything else. Physical geographers call this the principle of environmental unity. A second law pertains to the lessened stability of simplified ecosystems. Man's activities tend to reduce the complexity of ecosystems—for example by planting extensive fields of only one or several crops where formerly complex systems of many different wild organisms grew. The latter ecosystems generally are much better buffered against drastic changes than are the former (see Part 6). Many more ecological principles (e.g., nutrient cycling, food chains), discussed in most introductory ecology texts, may also be useful when considering man and environment.

The bulk of recent research in ecology appears to have added little to our understanding of man-environment relations, partly because so often "pristine nature" is sought out for study and in part because of the arbitrary, often minute, scale of most investigations.

Geography. Geography is the study of the relations of man and his environment, with emphasis on the spatial manifestations of this relationship. Unlike ecologists, geographers have tended to study broad spatial patterns and relations between man and landscape. Often their investigations have suffered from overgeneralization because of this. But the traditions of considering man's influence and of relating numerous varied aspects of the environment to one another are longstanding, going back to the work of Alexander von Humboldt and Karl Ritter early in the nineteenth century.

The greater European emphasis on geography generally and physical and "landscape" geography in particular assure this discipline a central place in the development there of a true science of environment. In contrast, in the United States these fields now are sparsely manned (see p. 3).

Geographers should provide the emerging science of environment with an appreciation of scale and valuable methods of spatial analysis, as well as the integrative, interdisciplinary viewpoints mentioned above.

The contributions of other natural sciences such as biology, geology, and meteorology have generally been limited by their narrow disciplinary approach and their avoidance of considering man's effects, although this situation is now changing.

Man's Impact on Environment

To counter existing neglect, this book squarely focuses on answers to the question "What is man doing to environment?" —revealing the wide spectrum of environmental changes wrought by man.

Two prior treatments of the subject stand out: *Man and Nature; or Physical Geography as Modified by Human Action* by George Perkins Marsh, published in 1864, and a monumental collection of original symposium essays, *Man's Role in Changing the Face of the Earth,* edited by William L. Thomas, Jr., 1956. The latter contains a valuable review of the history of man's concern about his influence on nature (pp. xxviii–xxxviii; also see Lacey, 1970).

Decisions concerning what material to include in this book have been based upon the goal of providing a broad, coherent treatment of the facts of man's present impact on environment. More specifically, readings have been selected and commentaries presented which especially consider the following aspects of man's impact on environment:

1. *Present processes of change.* What human activities cause environmental change, and how? What are the basic and detailed causes for different changes? Which are deliberate and which inadvertent?

2. *Environmental effects of man's activities.* Solutions to problems arising from such activities are treated only incidentally be-

cause (a) solutions must follow awareness and understanding of the problems (and there is not room to treat both adequately, and (b) feasible solutions to most environmental problems are a complex blend of environmental understanding, politics, economics, social attitudes, and technological capability.

3. *"Detrimental" effects which cause or probably will cause problems for man.* A claim might be made that coverage is one-sided. However, in general, "good" effects are publicized and well known; "detrimental" effects are not, and they merit attention because of possible grave consequences for man. Of course, "good" and "detrimental" are relative terms and have forced me to be subjective about what to include.

4. *Complexity of change within systems.* Man's initial actions commonly trigger a chain of cause-and-effect relations and synergistic feedbacks within the total environmental system. These second-, third-, and higher-order effects are usually unanticipated and often threatening to man. This book does not treat man's direct effects on man (e.g., effects of smoking), but many indirect effects on man's health, economy, and culture are discussed.

5. *The scale of man's impact varies from the molecular to the global* (see Dansereau, 1966, pp. 449–452). How do processes occurring at different scales in space and time interact?

6. *The temporal and spatial trends of environmental modification are important.* Many of man's effects are intensifying and spreading (e.g., lead pollution from auto exhaust, now detectable on the Greenland icecap).

Many selections are detailed case studies; others are reviews of man's impact on specific environments or reviews of the effects of a given human activity. Such documented case studies and limited reviews are the best material we have at present. Given more examples, generalizations should flow from them and valid principles may become evident. Meanwhile, the specifics of examples are enlivening and suggestive, and hopefully they will stimulate further research.

The complexity and interdisciplinary nature of the subject prohibit any organization from being wholly satisfactory. I have broadly classified man's environmental impacts into parts (each consisting of several selections) according to the environmental sphere that is primarily affected: the atmosphere (Part 3), the hydrosphere (Part 4), the geosphere (Part 5), and the biosphere (Parts 6 through 9). Within these parts individual selections (readings) may be oriented toward a specific process (e.g., surface mining—Selection 26) or a more specific kind of environment (e.g., estuaries—Selection 21). Preceding this survey some underlying basic causes which stimulate environmental change are discussed in Part 2 and the evolving history of man's impacts are recounted in Selection 2.

It must be emphasized that this or any other arrangement* is more or less arbitrary because changes transcend classificatory boundaries. Attempted ease of understanding has been my guide.

Taken together, the selections that follow provide an overview of the present quality of man's environment and the immediate causes for its condition. Today, man's overall impact is greater than at any time in history. The force of man now rivals the strongest of nature's other forces. With this power comes the responsibility to understand the extended consequences of man's actions if his children are to have a life worth living.

* Several alternative approaches have recently been used. Dansereau (1966, pp. 449–452) has defined nine cultural levels or scales of human interference in the landscape, and Nicholson (1970, pp. 308–335) has classified the human impacts on the British countryside according to human activity or operation.

References

Arthur, D. R. 1969. *Man and his environment.* New York: American Elsevier. 218 pp.

Bates, Marston. 1969. The human ecosystem. Pp. 21–31 in *Resources and man.* National Academy of Sciences/National Research Council. San Francisco: Freeman.

Benarde, M. A. 1970. *Our precarious habitat.* New York: Norton. 362 pp. A medical scientist's view of a number of man's environmental actions.

Bouillenne, Raymond. 1962. Man, the destroying biotype. *Science* 135:706–712.

Burton, Ian. 1968. Quality of the environment: A review. *Geograph. Rev.* 58(3): 472–481.

Burton, Ian, and R. W. Kates, eds. 1965. *Readings in resource management and conservation.* Chicago: The University of Chicago Press.

Ciriacy-Wantrup, S. V., and J. J. Parsons, eds. 1967. *Natural resources—quality and quantity.* Berkeley: University of California Press.

Cole, LaMont C. 1958. The ecosphere. *Sci. Am.,* April, pp. 83–92.

Cole, LaMont C. 1970. Playing Russian roulette with biogeochemical cycles. Pp. 1–14 in *The environmental crisis,* ed. by H. W. Helfrich, Jr. New Haven and London: Yale University Press.

Committee on Resources and Man, Division of Earth Sciences, National Academy of Sciences/National Research Council. 1969. *Resources and man.* San Francisco: Freeman. 259 pp.

Commoner, Barry. 1966. *Science and survival.* New York: Viking. (Also Viking Compass Book C212.)

Cox, G. W., ed. 1969. *Readings in conservation ecology.* New York: Appleton-Century-Crofts. 595 pp.

Curtis, Richard, and Elizabeth Hogan. 1969. *Perils of the peaceful atom: The myth of safe nuclear power plants.* Garden City, New York: Doubleday.

Dansereau, Pierre, ed. 1970. *Challenge for survival; Land, air, and water for man in megalopolis.* New York and London: Columbia University Press. 235 pp.

Dansereau, Pierre. 1966. Ecological impact and human ecology. Pp. 425–462 in *Future environments of North America,* ed. by F. F.

Darling and J. P. Milton. Garden City, New York: Natural History Press.

Darling, F. F., and J. P. Milton, eds. 1966. *Future environments of North America.* Garden City, New York: Natural History Press. 767 pp.

Dasmann, R. F. 1965. *The destruction of California.* New York: Macmillan.

The David Davies Memorial Institute of International Studies. 1968. *Principles governing certain changes in the environment of man.* London. 35 pp.

Dorst, Jean. 1970. *Before nature dies.* (Translated from French by C. D. Sherman.) Boston: Houghton Mifflin. 352 pp.

Editors of Ramparts. 1970. *Eco-catastrophe.* San Francisco: Canfield Press (Harper & Row). 128 pp.

Ehrlich, P. R., and A. H. Ehrlich. 1970. *Population/Resources/Environment.* San Francisco: Freeman. 383 pp.

Fosberg, F. R., ed. 1963. *Man's place in the island ecosystem.* Honolulu: Bishop Museum Press. 264 pp.

Glacken, C. J. 1956. Changing ideas of the habitable world. Pp. 70–92 in *Man's role in changing the face of the earth,* ed. by William L. Thomas, Jr. Chicago and London: The University of Chicago Press.

Glikson, Arthur. 1963. Man's relationship to his environment. Pp. 132–152 in *Man and his future,* G. Wolstonholme, ed.; a Ciba Foundation Volume. London: J. & A. Churchill.

Goodman, G. T., et al. 1965. *Ecology and the industrial society.* New York: Wiley.

Graubard, Stephen R., ed. 1967. America's changing environment. *Daedalus* (Journal of American Academy of Arts and Sciences) 96(4):1003–1234.

Hersh, S. M. 1969. *Chemical and biological warfare: America's hidden arsenal.* Garden City, New York: Doubleday.

Jennings, B. E., and J. E. Murphy, eds. 1966. *Interactions of man and his environment.* New York: Plenum Press.

Johnson, H. D., ed. 1970. *No deposit—no return; Man and his environment: A view toward survival.* Reading, Massachusetts: Addison-Wesley. 351 pp.

Kalliola, R. 1961. Man's influence on nature in Finland. *Fennia* 86:9–23.

Kates, Robert. Winter 1966–67. The pursuit of beauty in the environment. *Landscape* 16(2): 21–25.

Kormondy, E. J. 1969. *Concepts of ecology.*

Englewood Cliffs, New Jersey: Prentice-Hall. 209 pp.

Lacey, M. J. 1970. Man, nature, and the ecological perspective. *American Studies* 8(1–3): 13–27.

Leinwand, Gerald, ed. 1969. *Air and water pollution.* New York: Washington Square Press.

Leopold, L. B. 1969. Landscape esthetics; how to quantify the scenics of a river valley. *Natural History,* October, pp. 37–44.

Linton, Ron M. 1970. *Terracide; America's destruction of her living environment.* Boston: Little, Brown. 376 pp.

MacDonald, G. J. F. 1969. The modification of planet Earth by man. *Technology Review,* October/November.

McGauhey, P. H. 1968. Living with our wastes. *Man and the quality of his environment,* ed. by J. E. Flack and M. C. Shipley. Boulder: University of Colorado Press.

McHarg, Ian L. 1969. *Design with nature.* Garden City, New York: Natural History Press, for the American Museum of Natural History. 198 pp.

Marsh, G. P. 1864. *Man and nature; or, Physical geography as modified by human action.* New York: Scribners; London: Sampson Low. 560 pp.

Middleton, J. T. 1965. Man and his habitat: Problems of pollution. *Bulletin of the Atomic Scientists* 21:5.

Milton, John, and Taghi Farvar, eds. 1969. *The ecologic boomerang.* Garden City, New York: Doubleday (for Conservation Foundation and the Center for the Biology of Natural Systems).

Mumford, Lewis. 1956. The natural history of urbanization. Pp. 382–398 in *Man's role in changing the face of the earth,* ed. by William L. Thomas, Jr. Chicago and London: The University of Chicago Press.

Murray, E. G. D. 1954. The place of nature in man's world. *Am. Sci.* 42:130–135, 142.

Nash, Roderick, ed. 1968. *The American environment; Readings in the history of conservation.* Reading, Massachusetts: Addison-Wesley.

Nelson, J. G., and A. R. Byrne. 1966. Man as an instrument of landscape change: Fires, floods, and national parks in the Bow Valley, Alberta. *Geograph. Rev.* 56(2):226–238.

Newbigin, M. I. 1912. *Man and his conquest of nature.* London: A. & C. Black. 183 pp.

Nicholson, Max. 1970. *The environmental revo-*

lution; A guide for the new masters of the world. New York: McGraw-Hill. 366 pp.

Northrop, F. S. C. 1956. Man's relation to the earth in its bearing on his aesthetic, ethical, and legal values. Pp. 1052–1067 in *Man's role in changing the face of the earth,* ed. by William L. Thomas, Jr. Chicago and London: The University of Chicago Press.

Novick, Sheldon. 1969. *The careless atom.* New York: Delta. 225 pp.

Nystuen, John D. 1963. Identification of some fundamental spatial concepts. *Papers Mich. Acad. Sci.* 48:373–384. Also in Bobbs-Merrill Reprints in Geography, C–171.

Odum, E. P. 1959. *Fundamentals of ecology.* 2d ed. Philadelphia and London: W. B. Saunders. 546 pp.

Osborn, Fairfield. 1948. *Our plundered planet.* Boston: Little, Brown.

Osborn, Fairfield. 1953. *The limits of the earth.* Boston: Little, Brown & Co.

Ottersen, S. R. 1967. *Readings on natural beauty: A selected bibliography.* U.S. Dept. of Interior Library, Bibliography No. 1.

Perry, John. 1967. *Our polluted world; Can man survive?* New York: F. Watts. 213 pp.

Prokayev, V. I. 1966. Man-induced differentiation of natural conditions as a factor in physical-geographic regionalization. *Soviet Geography, Review and Translation,* 7:32–40.

Pruitt, W. O., Jr. 1963. Lichen, caribou and high radiation in Eskimos. *Audubon Magazine* 65:284–287.

Reinow, R., and L. T. Reinow. 1967. *Moment in the sun.* New York: Dial.

Ritchie-Calder, Lord. 1969. Polluting the environment. *The Center Magazine* 2(3), May.

Robertson, J. C. 1970. Man's place in the ecological pattern. *Geographical Magazine* 42(4):254–265.

Rockefeller, L. S., and others. 1965. *The White House Conference on Natural Beauty: Report to the President.* Washington, D.C.: U.S. Government Printing Office.

Roslansky, J. D., ed. 1967. *The control of en-vironment.* Amsterdam: North-Holland. 124 pp.

Russell, R. J. 1956. Environmental changes through forces independent of man. Pp. 453–470 in *Man's role in changing the face of the earth,* ed. by William L. Thomas, Jr. Chicago and London: The University of Chicago Press.

Sears, P. B. 1956. The processes of environmental change by man. Pp. 471–484 in *Man's role in changing the face of the earth,* ed. by William L. Thomas, Jr. Chicago and London: The University of Chicago Press.

Shaler, N. S. 1905. *Man and the earth.* New York: Duffield. 240 pp.

Shepard, Paul. 1967. *Man in the landscape: A historic view of the esthetics of nature.* New York: Alfred Knopf.

Shepard, Paul, and Daniel McKinley, eds. 1969. *The subversive science: Essays toward an ecology of man.* Boston: Houghton-Mifflin. 453 pp.

Sherlock, R. L. 1923. The influence of man as an agent in geographical change. *Geograph. J.* 61(4):258–273.

Sherlock, R. L. 1931. *Man's influence on the earth.* London: Home University Library of Modern Knowledge. 256 pp.

Spoehr, Alexander. 1956. Cultural differences in the interpretation of natural resources. Pp. 93–102 in *Man's role in changing the face of the earth,* ed. by William L. Thomas, Jr. Chicago and London: The University of Chicago Press.

Storer, J. H. 1953. *The web of life.* New York: Signet. 128 pp.

Thomas, William L., Jr., ed. 1956. *Man's role in changing the face of the earth.* Chicago: University of Chicago Press. 1193 pp.

Wilkinson, H. R. 1963. *Man and the natural environment.* Hull, England: Department of Geography, University of Hull. 35 pp.

Wilson, B. R., ed. 1968. *Environmental problems—Pesticides, thermal pollution, and environmental synergisms.* Philadelphia: J. B. Lippincott. 183 pp.

MAN'S USE OF THE EARTH: HISTORICAL BACKGROUND

MAX NICHOLSON

How has man's power to modify his environment evolved? And how is this evolution important today? This selection traces the development of culture and tools and, very generally, the environmental changes they have allowed man to create.

Man initially shaped the environment to his individual advantage or to the advantage of his small group. The repercussions of his actions, on the environment and indirectly on himself, were relatively insignificant. Through time man's power grew, and the variety, intensity, and extent of his environmental impacts grew. An understanding of this growth greatly facilitates an understanding of present man-environment relations.

If man's path to the present has been a history of continual adaptation of environment to his needs, so too has environment shaped man. This past relationship has molded every human being, and it explains a measure of our present predicament: We may now be changing the environment at a rate that exceeds our biological ability to adapt. Our culture too—including attitudes, economics, and technology—generally lags behind the environmental changes we have wrought. Our survival as a species depends on our ability to adapt to the accelerating stresses that we ourselves have largely created.

(Editor's comment)

Max Nicholson (b. 1904) has long been an international leader in conservation. He was director-general of the Nature Conservancy from 1952 to 1966 and has directed the conservation section of the International Biological Program since 1963. Nicholson has been an active member of numerous professional societies and was the first medalist of the International Union for the Conservation of Nature and Natural Resources. Educated at Oxford, he has received an honorary LL.D. from Aberdeen. Among his many publications are *Birds in England* (1926), *Birds and Men* (1951), *Britain's Nature Reserves* (1958), and *The System* (1967).

Man's impact on his environment goes back far beyond the beginning of history. As human numbers increased, people colonised new lands so that a larger and larger area was affected. Before reviewing the earth, its vegetation and its animal life, it is important to consider the emergence and growth of human demands and impacts. It is relevant also to indicate something of the evolution of beliefs, attitudes, policies and practices arising from those demands and impacts, from as far back as our knowledge extends to the present time. Without such historical background, however sketchy, the complex environmental problems now facing us cannot be understood.

Imprint of Early Man

Recent discoveries have produced significant evidence of a very long period of co-existence and competition between rival species of early hominid, ending only relatively recently in the elimination of all except the ruthless and cunning form *Homo sapiens*, to which the author and his readers belong. This knockout victory over his simpler cousins left all the other species on the planet defenceless in face of the most formidable breed of the most formidable animal ever to tread the earth.

According to present knowledge man's earliest ancestors were forest-dwellers whose evolution gradually led them out into the savanna and the open plains. With this change of habitat would be associated some change of diet, since food-gathering would no longer be confined to wild fruits and vegetable sources, while dead meat, fishes and large insects would be picked up often enough to substitute an omnivorous for a vegetarian pattern. Such a more diversified, opportunist existence would lend enhanced survival value to cunning, learning and mobility, and would inevitably lead to conflicts with other scavenging and eventually predatory animals with rival claims to prey. Thus killing and being killed or injured would

become a normal contingency of living, with all the far-reaching evolutionary consequences involved—physical, psychological and social.

Starting probably with crudely concerted drives by families or small tribes working together, the threshold of an identifiable hunting pattern would eventually be crossed. Use of convenient topography such as precipices, torrents and morasses would lead to the contrivance of rich harvests of game, which however could not be too often repeated at the same spot without depletion of stocks or adoption of successful evasive expedients by the quarry. Intermittent hunger and primitive mental processes would thus lead naturally to the adoption of such artefacts as stone tools or weapons, the artificial construction of such aids to hunting as stone barriers or dug pitfalls, and the improvement of cave or other troglodyte shelters, supplemented by rough structures made with branches, leaves and treestumps, to serve as more secure resting-places and bases in otherwise open country.

Throughout such protracted early stages of evolution the natural environment would continue virtually unaffected by human influences. On the other hand the influence of that environment on early man would be immense. It would amount to the direct opposite of the situation today, in terms of conscious experience. Man would feel himself not the lord of creation but its naked slave and butt. The shift, however gradual, from a close perpetually covered forest habitat to the open plains; the accompanying change from a vegetarian to an omnivorous diet; the resulting compulsion to participate in the game of killing and being killed; the enhanced pressures and opportunities for exploiting artefacts and for developing group mobility over distances; the need for seeking or making cover and shelter rather than being able to take it for granted—all these would demand a rapid physical, psychological and social evolution, without which the breakthrough away from the dark forest would be doomed to eventual failure.

While numbers remained small and localised early pressures through food gathering and primitive hunting and fishing can have made no appreciable impact on the environment. The emergence of added demands for clothing, shelter and tools appears significant only as the first clear indication of the eventually insatiable demands which man was destined to make upon natural resources.

Early gathering of food and of materials for clothing, shelter and eventually tool-making put a survival value on capacities for observation, identification, testing and experiment, memory of sites and routes, awareness of ecosystems and of seasons, exploration and powers to communicate and cooperate, all ante-dating coherent speech and of course reading and writing. Outstanding significance must be accorded to the emergence of capabilities, independent of words, for recognising and relating broad visible configurations of stars, of weather and of vegetation. Such word-free perceptions of recurrent or related forms are among the springs of scientific discovery and of aesthetic creation to this day. Unfortunately the inevitable near-monopoly of cultural transmission acquired by those who write has enabled them greatly to exaggerate and distort the creative role of writing in social evolution, and to depreciate the resources of knowledge, perception and wisdom developed by man long before writing was invented.

At present, unfortunately, our knowledge of our remote ancestors, although lately much improved by the splendid efforts of such investigators as the Leakeys in East Africa, is inevitably limited to handfuls of tangible remains which tell us next to nothing about their aspirations, emotions and mental equipment. From such far later relics as the talented cave pictures of Altamira, Lascaux and the Saharan crags we obtain some insight into the profound emotional bond between hunters and hunted, and the insatiable yearnings which lent motive force to the evolution of primitive religion and art. It was again the natural environment which afforded the stimulus and the subject-matter for these transcendental emotions, long before the human figure and human activities or ideas emerged as a rival area of interest.

Hunting in particular took men into the wilderness, and exposed them to the wonders, mysteries and dreads of the closed forest from which they had originally broken out. The uncertainty and arbitrariness of its yield aroused a vivid sense of good and bad fortune, and of the possibility of supernatural powers swaying it, perhaps arbitrarily or perhaps in vindication of a sense of guilt or righteousness becoming uncomfortably perceptible in the consciousness of the early human society. From storms and natural catastrophes, sacred beasts, trees, groves and mountains, and tabus linked with hunting and exploration, it was an easy step to imagine quasi-human or godlike beings lurking invisibly in the background. Thus may have been initiated the transference of faith and reverence from the natural to the specifically human realms of religion and philosophy.

Even when man became capable of leaving some mark on his environment that mark long remained insignificant, owing to the fewness of his numbers, his localised distribution and the feebleness of his technology. Considering the impressive traces imprinted by fairly modest concentrations of elephants and hippopotamuses on their haunts in Africa, and the widespread and drastic mark left on many parts of Britain even by rabbits (before myxomatosis hit them) the impact of man upon nature must for many thousands of years have appeared insignificant even among biotic influences. Incapable of colonising the earth's major deserts, ice-caps, mountain ranges, seas or unbroken forests, early men were largely confined to open plains, steppes and savannas and to river banks, accessible coastlines of seas and lakes, and certain types of wetland and valley. Such habitats were in any case liable from time to time to be much more drastically changed by natural disasters such as floods, earth movements and marine transgression than by man. Indeed it is partly owing to this circumstance that the petty traces left behind by early man have been preserved under covering deposits and can be dated by modern science. As we have lately become aware, there was a significant coincidence in time between some of the more dramatic geomorphological and climatic changes of geologically recent ages and certain vital stages in man's prehistoric evolution and distribution.

Fire: The Pretechnical Tool

Multiplier effects sufficient to begin affecting ecosystems were first developed by men with the deliberate use of fire as a means of clearing forests.

With the attainment of capacity to use and to create fire the mischief-making capability of the species, and its tendency to embark upon the use of destructive instruments without understanding the necessary restraints, became manifest.

Fire brought three kinds of effect which were quite new in comparison with earlier impacts on the natural environment with the exception of major sudden natural catastrophes such as earthquakes and volcanic eruptions. It was, at least in some cases, widespread, affecting sizeable areas of forest or grassland. It was inherently a repetitive process, able to hit the same areas at fairly frequent intervals. It was also highly selective, exterminating locally some species and communities while indirectly encouraging others gifted with rapid powers of recovery or an inbuilt fire resistance.

For these and other reasons command and use of fire must be rated as the first advance in human technology which struck the natural environment hard wherever it was practised. It remains to this day the only case in which the capacity of modern man to inflict large-scale damage upon the natural environment is matched by that of pretechnical man. It was however mainly confined to tropical, sub-tropical and temperate forests and grasslands, excluding humid forests but including certain wetlands. Deserts and semi-deserts, what we used to call rainforests, most mountain ranges, most boreal and subarctic forests, tundra and many less widespread habitats remained relatively immune.

Man as Agriculturalist

While no doubt to some extent fire was employed as a tool for assisting hunting success this could not be repeated often. The main incentive for its use was as a rapid means of clearing forest and stimulating growth of plants suitable for grazing and browsing. It was therefore a favorite tool, first of man as pastoralist and then of man as agriculturalist. It acquired significance largely with the discovery and advance of techniques for domesticating livestock, together with animals valuable in managing them, notably the dog and the horse, followed by the development of methods of growing and improving crops of food plants and raw material.

Activity in finding, identifying and testing wild species for such purposes must have been prolonged and intense, as is shown by the very high proportion of all currently exploited species which were already familiar and widely used in neolithic times, more than 7,000 years ago. The great value of these discoveries was that they opened potentialities for massive quantitative increases in the supply of food and raw materials for mankind, and thus for a multiplication of human numbers and division of labour. They also, however increased human energy requirements beyond the capacity of aggregate muscle-power, and thus demanded a build up of draught and transport animals, and of systems of irrigation and waterpower.

The stage was accordingly set for a rise of concentrations of human population involving for the first time a substantial takeover of land from natural to artificial forms of productive use. We know that this takeover began in such areas as the Anatolian uplands, with the adjoining Fertile Crescent of south-west Asia, parts of the great river valleys of the Far East, the lower Nile Valley and later in parts of Central and western South America. It soon gave rise to very extensive modification of the natural environment.

Important as were the direct repercussions of these advances their indirect repercussions were equally so. The need for tending flocks, and still more for growing crops demanded a more highly organised and also often a permanently settled pattern of living. Although in areas of precarious climatic suitability nomadism maintained itself, as it still does, wherever practicable settlement was preferred.

This stage of human existence in settled communities vastly altered the relationship between man and the natural environment. First it created a more or less continuously occupied site, or cluster of sites, on which arose structures for shelter and living, middens of refuse such as shells and bones, crude workplaces and primitive latrines, and stockades or other peripheral barriers against animal or human raiders. Such sites formed the first nuclei for the growth and spread of pollution, disease and erosion, and the first regular targets for the incipient art of warfare, which itself has so greatly contributed to injuring the natural environment, and to distracting human effort from the task of growing in harmony with it.

Around such sites, and among them, were created herds of domestic animals and plots sown with primitive crops of useful plants, involving the disturbance or replacement of natural ecosystems by modified or impoverished plant and animal communities. Elimination of dangerous animals, clearance of forest, and removal or partial treatment of obstacles to movement extended the radius of human impact. From the earliest days an assured source of potable water was essential to a settlement. The need to cope with fluctuations of drought and flood, and to secure convenience of availability and transport must not only have led to much primitive consideration and argument regarding site selection, but also have triggered off a good deal of inventive effort. Man's perennial need for water, and the perennial mystery of water's ways, must be assumed to have been one of the most important focal

areas of the application of early man's new-found mental powers. It also provided, as we now know, a main basis for the subsequent rapid and intensive development towards cities and organised states associated with the hydraulic civilisations.

The Rise of Sedentary Civilisations

Settlement and the development of a primitive economy dictated a new pattern of distribution of human population in terms of early technology. Gradual increases were easiest and best assured either in the areas of origin of wild plants cultivated for food, or in areas of good rainfall and favorable opportunities for clearance and tillage. As the most suitable food plants became better disseminated, and methods of husbandry better understood, it became apparent that the valleys of certain great rivers such as the Nile, Tigris and Euphrates, and the Indus could sustain relatively large populations given sufficient knowledge of their seasonal water regimes, and a capacity to divert part of the flood for irrigating crops. The necessary calculations, techniques and regulations gave rise more than five thousand years ago to the arts and sciences of writing, of mathematics, of engineering and construction and of administration, which grew up together in Mesopotamia, the Nile Valley, the Indus Valley and along the Yellow River in China. Sustenance and government of mass populations had arrived.

One of the first problems confronting the early river civilisations was management of the environment. Our knowledge of how they fared at it is scanty, but they undoubtedly made serious mistakes, although apparently not so grave as in themselves to undermine the communities concerned. Of their areas of operation the Nile and the Yellow River continue to perform similar roles for populations not even now sufficiently richer or denser to contrast unduly with results achieved in very early times. Only, perhaps, in Mesopotamia are there indications that erosion and other misuse of the land may have contributed towards rendering beneficial use of certain community sites impossible. Not so much directly as by encouraging excess growth and concentration of population over wide surrounding areas, which became deforested, overgrazed or overcropped and eroded, did the new cities and states become an instrument for severely degrading their natural environment.

As settled communities developed and reached out their claims to land use it became inevitable that conflicts between them should also develop, becoming less sporadic or random and more chronic, violent, tense and systematic. In this situation embryonic states of warfare must quickly have led to three revolutionary new requirements; for looking ahead beyond the immediate present, for a process of rapid and effective decision-making on behalf of the community, and for securing authoritative personal leadership to carry out decisions and to safeguard the interests and survival of the community in emergency.

Reinforced and underpinned by the economic potential of pastoralism, agriculture and the winning of minerals, this early political evolution must be regarded as a moment of breakthrough from the situation of man as essentially one among the animals benefiting from the natural ecosystems, to his present role of dominating, exploiting and where necessary replacing them. It had by this time become possible to undertake purposeful collective action on a locally significant scale to modify the environment. Such grand examples as the Pyramids, Stonehenge, Easter Island and others show how much could be achieved by the skilful and ruthless concentration of manpower. No doubt many smaller demonstrations of this were undertaken with less enduring results in earlier periods. The sheer bigness and uninhibited ambition of such megalithic exercises suggest a tremendous emotional drive to repudiate the tradition of man's helpless subordination to nature, and to substitute a crude full-blooded and enduring demonstration of superiority and power.

This propaganda was confronted with two immense obstacles—the inconvenient and undeniable fact that even the most powerful men must die, and the overriding and awesome destructive forces of nature exhibited in great storms, floods, volcanic eruptions, landslides, and earthquakes, beyond the powers of men to anticipate or to counter. It was doubtless the need for rationalising and ritualising these contradictions to man's mounting self-confidence which fostered the growth of religion, and the emergence of priesthoods. With these early history, medicine, mathematics, astronomy and magic were often intimately connected.

Through the conception of invisible gods, to whom man stood in a remote and precarious relation, it became possible to explain away the apparent and true natural limitations upon man's powers over nature, and to substitute for the painful man/nature dialogue a new triangular communication between man, god and nature, in which priests and leaders with priestly functions exercised a mediating role.

Another equally serious indirect effect of the rise of cities was their role in promoting warfare to higher levels of destructiveness, partly by internecine quarrels but perhaps more by the tempting target which they offered to raiding troops and hosts. For the growth of larger settlements had created the beginnings of the vast contrasts and inequalities which have ever since characterised the varying levels of human development, and which have enabled favored groups and peoples to enjoy conspicuously higher standards of life, greater power and more mobility and range of choice than the rest.

Impacts of Mobile Man

Safeguarded by Sinai and the Sahara, and by the continued primitiveness of human cultures in the earlier nurseries of mankind in eastern and southern Africa, the great early Egyptian civilisation was able to survive for a remarkably long period. The corresponding civilisations in south-western Asia were less fortunate, especially those based in the area of modern Iran, Iraq, and Turkey. In addition to common difficulties and hazards they found themselves threatened by a new rival and opposite type of culture which had spread throughout the broad steppe zone of central Asia and South East Europe between the Altai mountains and the delta of the Danube. After discovering the vast potential of this zone for breeding cattle and horses the neighboring peasant and hunting tribes boldly uprooted themselves, abandoned their fixed settlements and crops, adopted a horseback and tented life, bringing their women, children and bulkier possessions after them in oxcarts. By exploiting their new mobility as well-equipped nomads they soon created a homogeneous culture of vast extent and formidable energy. Their authoritarian but flexible social system and their massive forces of horseborne archers, practised and skilful, proved more than a match for the more sedentary and rigid major states of the settled richer regions to the south.

For reasons not yet fully understood, probably partly related to climatic change in Central Asia and partly to this social and technological revolution, there occurred roughly three thousand years ago a series of explosive population movements over large parts of Asia and eastern Europe. Its indirect repercussions may arguably be said not even yet to have fully worked themselves through. Although three thousand years may appear a long time in human history it represents much less than one per cent of the period of man's evolution on earth. There is no reason to regard what we call historical times as any more normal or typical of what is to come than the totally different pattern which prevailed earlier.

From the standpoint of relations between man and nature this outbreak of major long-distance population movements is particularly significant since it ended the era of purely localised impacts on each natural environment by human groups who had long been acclimatised to it and grown experienced in its limitations. Henceforth the arbitrary decisions and actions of great intruders, of absentee rulers far away from the scene, began to play the ever-increasing role which they have since maintained in overriding or over-persuading people on the spot to adopt practices and programs which, left to themselves, they would have refrained from. In few traceable cases have these imposed or infiltrated practices proved favorable to conservation, and in many they have ignored it, often with very bad results.

In those early days of the historical period it is already possible to trace a deepening division of mankind into three contrasting elements, empire-builders, nomads and simpler peoples, which are still conspicuous to this day. In a belt of favored land then extending from the Aegean and the Nile (with considerable interruptions) to India and China, advanced technology and intensive settlement had lifted large localised populations to the level of organised states and empires using division of labor and exerting widespread influence, but for that very reason frequently colliding and suffering severe instability. Neighboring this belt were temporarily less developed regions, inhabited by restless and resourceful peoples, uncommitted to the ways of the earlier advanced cultures. The settled peoples proved very easily challenged by the nomads, once these were given the necessary tools to confer on them greatly improved mobility and power of rapid concentration at a distance.

The first of these tools was the rearing of horses, cattle and sheep in large numbers on the Euro-Asian steppelands, which triggered off the upheavals already mentioned. The second was the domestication and breeding of camels, supplemented by horses and the consequential stimulation of the desert cultures of Arabia and North Africa, which was to come to a head in the great Arab conquests of the 7th and 8th centuries AD. The third was the development of shipping and navigation leading in Greek and Roman times to the partial, and in recent times the almost complete substitution of seapower for landpower as an ultimate instrument of domination. In contrast to the very latest advances of rail, road and air transport and of airborne strike forces, those early developments of mobility arose among and favored the expansion of peoples hitherto outside the ranks of the leading states and empires of their times. These empires accordingly found their previously strong positions rendered untenable, by the "hordes of barbarians" who over some three thousand years overcame all the earlier empires from the Hittites to the Romans, Byzantines and Hindus, leaving only China and Egypt intact.

In broad historical terms the English, Dutch, Portuguese and Spaniards rank with the Persians, Scythians, Mongols, Arabs, and others in this new wave of expanding and aggressive cultures. One common effect which it had was enormously to widen and gravely to intensify the impact of man upon natural environments. The mistakes and the desert-making activities of some of the earlier settled cultures, although serious, were at least much more localised. They were partly offset by the interest of these cultures in and care for water yields, crops and pasturage, as exemplified by their reservoirs, aqueducts and wells, their hillside terraces and their irrigation schemes.

The third more primitive and passive great element in mankind, which is only now shrinking rapidly under the influence of technical and economic development, is formed by the innumerable tribes in Africa, Asia, South and Central America and the Pacific which never entered the major technological, economic and political race, retaining cultural patterns more akin to that of mankind before the rise of states and empires. Inevitably and increasingly in course of time the lands of such peoples have become a theater for activities inspired from the more advanced and restless westernised cultures. In many cases these activities are, judged from a conservation standpoint, more destructive than the traditional practices which they brusquely supersede.

The new dynamic, mobile, innovating civilisations which have become paramount during the past three thousand years, at the expense of both the more primitive cultures and of the early sedentary civilisations, have

unfortunately been inclined to extend to their treatment of nature the aggression, arrogance and impatience which has so often characterised their relations with their fellow-men. As heirs to these newer cultures we have to face and resolve this problem, which is both objective and subjective.

It took the newer civilisations some two thousand years to establish between them a loose hegemony over virtually the entire then known world except China. After a pause of some seven hundred years there began, with the age of the fifteenth-century navigators, a systematic extension of this hegemony to all the hitherto unexplored parts of the planet, which, on its virtual completion in the twentieth century, has now been further extended into outer space.

At this point we are concerned with that part of the background consisting of the development of human attitudes and actions; at a later stage the record of successive impacts on and modifications of the natural environment resulting from these actions will also need to be reviewed.

Modern Man and Indirect Impacts

Until modern times major influences exerted by man on the environment were almost all direct and concrete, such as burning and cutting forests, converting land to grazing areas or crop-growing, diverting streams and so forth. Indirect, unintended and unrecognised interferences were relatively insignificant. When occasional local conflicts gradually developed into organised warfare as a general and recurrent expression of many cultures, defence became the first dominant human activity with strong incidental rather than direct effects upon land use.

DEFENCE

Perhaps the most serious impact of defence has been through a tendency to select islands, peninsulas, crags and other readily defensible points which man would find unattractive for production and other purposes, and which are often the base of special ecosystems and the habitat of rare species. The concentration in such areas of forces of able-bodied men, with little to occupy them except beating up the wild life, has been a threat to conservation from early times right up to the present day. Compensating benefits have been few, although as competition for land and disturbing uses become more frequent the virtual sterilisation of certain areas in the interests of secrecy or military training have sometimes brought limited side benefits.

RECREATION

The other main indirect influence going back to early times is recreation. There is room for argument over the precise stage at which the necessity for hunting as a condition of being able to eat first became qualified by an element of hunting for sport, but there are indications pointing to some fairly early date. No doubt proven risks of overcropping local game and causing local exterminations gave impetus long ago to increasingly sophisticated and drastic regulation of hunting activities. While among certain peoples such as the Eskimos and the American Indians the function of hunting seems to have fallen to the most suitable and skilful males, in many other cultures it became partly or wholly reserved to the higher social groups, and especially to royalty, wherever the scarcest and most desirable game were concerned. In Christian Europe, where scarcity arose early, the promulgation of extremely detailed and rigorously enforced controls of hunting antedated by at least a century similarly detailed attention to the conduct of such basic social institutions as local government or marriage. In England recreation as an officially recognised form of land use in the shape of royal forests is already more than a thousand years old.

The first widespread and profound impact of recreation on the land in Britain was, however, during the late 17th and 18th centuries, with the rise of the sporting estate and of a large wealthy group of landowning families who combined development of agriculture, forestry and at times of local industry with the systematic use of their lands for enjoyment and outdoor sports. Not wholly content with this outlet a minority of these privileged persons indulged in what we now know as tourism, identifying and indeed creating the first health and seaside resorts, cultural shrines, and beauty spots, where miniature but often elegant facilities grew up for them. It proved possible and attractive for the leaders of growing affluent classes to follow in their footsteps, and in those of such poets as Wordsworth, Shelley and Byron.

The rapid growth of improved communications, and the period of peace after Waterloo set in hand an expansion of tourism which continues to escalate with no sign of slackening. The great importance of this movement lies in its direct and intense relationship to appreciation of the natural environment, and in the emergence for the first time of a large human group interested in that environment for its own sake, and not merely as a site or quarry for exploitation to satisfy some other requirement. Unfortunately most of the potential benefit has so far been missed, owing to the concentration of so much of the resulting revenue in the hands of ignorant and uninterested commercial or local government bodies, and to the sluggishness of educationists in recognising its vast educational potential.

OTHER INDIRECT INFLUENCES

In very recent times a number of other strong and pervasive indirect influences have begun to play a part in relation to the natural environment. On the positive side the world conservation movement, lately forged from a blending of the interests of naturalists, scientists, countrylovers, specialists in natural resources and a large sentimentally inclined public, now contrives with some difficulty to keep most of the earth under review, and to intervene with increasing effectiveness at a number, still far too small, of threatened points.

Fairly closely related to this is the growth

of regional and land planning, linked with the development and economic plans which are rapidly becoming common form among governments. The researchers, designers and executive officers for such plans vary from country to country in their background and training, their priorities and emphases, and their interest in conservation of the environment. But the trend, although disappointingly slow and patchy, is towards embodying and implementing conservation objectives in the course of such plans, or at least of discouraging projects plainly incompatible with such objectives.

Negative influences are, however, growing at an even greater rate. Among these are the enormously expanding demands upon land for many purposes, the rapid spread and widespread penetration of permanent or temporary human occupancy to innumerable hitherto uninhabited places, and the growing range, intensity and scale of such accompanying nuisances as pollution of air, water and soil, noise, disturbance and erosion.

Eight Horizons of Expanding Technology

In considering the impact of modern man upon the land we must always bear in mind, in addition to his growing requirements and ambitions, his vastly expanding capabilities which have recently enabled him to achieve a breakthrough so complex that eight distinct thrusts are identifiable in it.

Of these the most spectacular confer fresh types of mobility—on the land surface through all kinds of wheeled and tracked mechanical vehicles from landrovers or jeeps to snocats and amphibians; on the water surface from hydrofoils and hovercraft to monster tankers and aircraft carriers; under the water from long-range fast nuclear submarines to bathyspheres and submerged dwellings accommodating subaqua explorers; in the air through fixed-wing and VTOL to almost wingless aircraft, helicopters, gliders and individual backpack propulsion units; and beyond the stratosphere through a series of rocket-driven spacecraft and space plat-

forms. This immense and fast-developing range of new vehicles, accompanied by new forms of protective equipment or clothing and controlled internal environments, now gives almost unlimited access to the many hitherto impenetrable regions of the earth and its neighbouring planets. Only the deeper waters continue for the time being inaccessible to man.

Armed with these new capacities man is confronted with the problem of using them not only economically and efficiently but wisely and with restraint. Yet these are not all. Added to these five main types of mobility for man and his belongings is a sixth of a more tactile and indirect nature—the capacity through powered drills, boring and tunnelling equipment and controlled explosions, conventional or nuclear, to probe deep into the earth's mantle and even beneath its outer crust, and to bring about major changes in its geographic forms through canals, dams, drainage and removal of rock and soil. A complementary new capacity for managing and modifying the earth's surface is through chemical additives to soil and water.

Finally, the most comprehensive and pervasive of these eight new human capabilities is that for systematically exploring and surveying every aspect of the environment and for constructing intellectual models, assembling, processing and using complex data, and for the first time enabling the human mind to grasp and consciously influence the interplay of countless factors which go to make nature tick.

Such, in highly condensed form, is the picture of man's cumulative efforts to date as they bear upon the natural environment. In this record certain points have emerged which should be emphasised as of special importance to our subject.

Current Problems of Adaptation

No other animal species to our knowledge has ever made such immense and hasty shifts of habitat within a very brief period, looked at against the scale of evolution, as man has from the forest to the plains and from the open plains to urban living. There is a very strong presumption that this precipitate double switch must have created gross maladjustments, especially psychologically and socially, which a more leisurely evolution might have avoided. Thus posed, the problem is to use man's resourcefulness at social evolution to buffer for an indefinite period the harmful psychological and social impacts upon him of his sudden breakthrough as the dominant animal species on earth. Assuming that any curbing of man's adventurousness is undesirable and impracticable the requirement appears to be to develop some kind of environmental and social base for balancing and refreshing him to mitigate the distortions and stresses otherwise inherent in his strained and exposed situation.

Man has suddenly emerged from the period of intense struggle against stronger adverse forces, through which his outlook and makeup have been moulded, to a position of immense power and responsibility for which his background has done little to fit him. Some of the most prominent inclinations which he has developed to an extreme degree, such as philoprogenitiveness and addiction to large scale warfare, are in conspicuous conflict at present with the elementary requirements for human survival. Others such as obsession with material development and a blind eye for the environment are less dramatic but may well be equally detrimental.

A further point of great importance is the series of shifts of the main social evolutionary initiative from one part of mankind to another. From the earliest primitive groups which emerged from forest living this initiative passed to omnivorous food-gatherers, hunters, domesticators of animals, farmers, irrigators, and thence to hierarchical chiefs, priests and kings, with their growing corps of administrators and advisers until irruptions of less sophisticated cavalrymen, and traders commanding economic resources, ports and shipping took over the leading role.

It is now a commonplace that we are currently experiencing another of these decisive shifts of initiative and power, in which the technocrat is progressively, although gropingly and hesitantly, stepping into the shoes of earlier ruling types. This replacement is essential and indeed badly overdue. Even in relation to environmental management alone the capability of a classically educated group of administrators and politicians for handling the new forces and tools here outlined is little better than that of a band of apes faced with the task of devising an agricultural system.

The problem of educating new technocratic masters in the full breadth and depth of these issues is nevertheless acute, since the narrowness and inadequacy of their existing education is currently so serious as to create something near a deadlock in the process of changeover. Technologists of broader and deeper formation, with complex and well-balanced professional training, will alone be capable of successfully handling the immense problems of adaptation now facing us, and of using wisely the concentrations of power which will inevitably for good or ill be thrust into their hands. As a counterpoise, means must simultaneously be found for enabling a larger fraction of the citizens to learn and digest the main outlines of these problems of adaptation, and to exercise a sufficient check and supervision over the policies and actions of authorities concerned with government in its various aspects.

It will not be possible to harmonize human development with the natural environment on the necessary grand scale until those in charge, the politicians, administrators, managers, technologists and others are educated afresh so that they learn to see problems as a whole. At present their education has taught them to think about the environment only spasmodically and in unrelated compartments. Indeed modern man has been artificially conditioned not to see his environment as a whole.

But the great tool which should enable us to overcome the piecemeal approach most rapidly is the computer. With its need for careful programming it should ensure that questions are fully thought out and comprehensively related to the activities they purport to handle. This in turn should eliminate many of the omissions, ambiguities and inconsistencies which have hitherto got by, and provide a more adequate flow of statistics and information.

Reinforcing this discipline of the computer is the revitalising influence of television, the film and the other pictorial mass media.

These media are far better able than the older entirely verbalised channels to help mankind to perceive and understand how nature functions. They carry no literary and rhetorical traditions, no ancient dogma and no strong but unfounded assumptions and they can therefore permit the public to see for themselves without the interposition of false or confusing noises into the messages direct from nature.

ADDITIONAL REFERENCES

Crowe, Sylvia. 1963. Civilization and the landscape. *Smithsonian Annual Report*, 1962: 537–544.

Evans, E. E. 1956. The ecology of peasant life in western Europe. Pp. 217–239 in *Man's role in changing the face of the earth*, ed. by William L. Thomas, Jr. Chicago and London: The University of Chicago Press.

Glacken, C. J. 1967. *Traces on the Rhodian shore: Nature and culture in western thought from ancient times to the end of the eighteenth century.* Berkeley: University of California Press. 763 pp.

Heichelheim, F. M. 1956. Effects of classical antiquity on the land. Pp. 165–182 in *Man's role in changing the face of the earth*, ed. by William L. Thomas, Jr. Chicago and London: The University of Chicago Press.

Huth, Hans. 1957. *Nature and the American: Three centuries of changing attitudes.* Berkeley: University of California Press. 250 pp.

Iversen, J. 1949. The influence of prehistoric man on vegetation. *Danmarks Geologiske Undersøgelse*, Series IV, vol. 3, no. 6, Copenhagen.

Lee, R. B., and Irene DeVore, eds. 1968. *Man the hunter*. Chicago: Aldine. 415 pp.

Narr, K. J. 1957. Early food-producing populations. Pp. 134–151 in *Man's role in changing the face of the earth*, ed. by William L. Thomas, Jr. Chicago and London: The University of Chicago Press.

Nash, Roderick. 1967. *Wilderness and the American mind.* New Haven: Yale University Press.

Pfeifer, Gottfried. 1956. The quality of peasant living in central Europe. Pp. 240–277 in *Man's role in changing the face of the earth*, ed. by William L. Thomas, Jr. Chicago and London: The University of Chicago Press.

Sauer, C. O. 1956. The agency of man on the earth. Pp. 49–69 in *Man's role in changing the face of the earth*, ed. by William L. Thomas, Jr. Chicago and London: The University of Chicago Press.

Stewart, Omer C. 1956. Fire as the first great force employed by man. Pp. 115–133 in *Man's role in changing the face of the earth*, ed. by William L. Thomas, Jr. Chicago and London: The University of Chicago Press.

Teilhard de Chardin, Pierre. 1956. The antiquity and world expansion of human culture. Pp. 103–113 in *Man's role in changing the face of the earth*, ed. by William L. Thomas, Jr. Chicago and London: The University of Chicago Press.

von Wissmann, Hermann, et al. 1956. On the role of nature and man in changing the face of the dry belt of Asia. Pp. 278–303 in *Man's role in changing the face of the earth*, ed. by William L. Thomas, Jr. Chicago and London: The University of Chicago Press.

Wittfogel, K. A. 1956. The hydraulic civilizations. Pp. 152–164 in *Man's role in changing the face of the earth*, ed. by William L. Thomas, Jr. Chicago and London: The University of Chicago Press.

Yarnell, R. A. 1963. Reciprocity in cultural ecology. *Econ. Bot.* 17:333–337.

Los Angeles houses.   Photo by William A. Garnett.

TWO SOME BASIC CAUSES

"We shall continue to have a worsening ecologic crisis until we reject the Christian axiom that nature has no reason for existence save to serve man. Since the roots of our trouble are so largely religious, the remedy must also be essentially religious, whether we call it that or not. We must rethink and refeel our nature and destiny."

INTRODUCTION

Our increasing environmental predicament is forcing some change in our attitudes toward environment. Such change is a necessary second step, after initial recognition of problems, toward mending our ecological ills. Hopefully, with knowledge and new will we can correct other basic causes for environmental deterioration.

I can identify *six basic causes* for the deterioration of man's environment: ignorance, attitude, population, technology, economics, and synergism. This whole book is primarily addressed to curing the first of these basic causes, ignorance about the extent and consequences of man's impact on environment. Each of the next four basic causes is dealt with in a separate selection in this part of the book.

To summarize, in Selection 3 an eminent historian, Lynn T. White, Jr., discusses the prevalent attitude in Western culture that man is controller of the created world in its entirety, rather than a dependent part of nature.

John D. Durand, a noted demographer, analyzes the facts and trends of world population growth in Selection 4. The unprecedented expansion of mankind which began about two centuries ago has multiplied man's environmental effects. More people means more land for production and living, more resources used, more wastes discharged.

Technology, while creating a "better life" for man, has created more environmental change per capita, thus escalating man's impact. Also, technology yearly becomes a more and more powerful tool, amplifying our ability to change nature. In Selection 5 an outstanding biologist, Barry Commoner, surveys some encounters between technology and environment. Technological advancement has furthermore spurred urbanization, with its especially intensive impacts.

The major existing economic systems in the world, including private enterprise and socialism, have largely failed to assign the social costs of environmental disruption. In Selection 6 an economist of note, Marshall I. Goldman, dispels the widespread notion that a strongly centralized and socialized economy is inherently better able to cope with environmental decay. Industrial countries with various economies all need to develop economic mechanisms to force paying the price of wise resource use.

Synergism, the final basic cause for the worsening condition of our environment, is not discussed in a separate selection. Hence, it merits some consideration. *Synergism* is the cooperative action of separate agencies such that the resulting effect is greater than the sum of the independent effects. Two environmental disciplines in which the phenomenon has heretofore been studied are atmospheric chemistry (e.g., Goetz, 1961; Pilat, 1968) and pesticide toxicology (e.g., Hewlett,

1968).   One well-known example from the former field is the complex production of photochemical smog by the reaction in sunlight of organic gases and oxides of nitrogen (See Selections 7 and 10).   Similarly, but from a standpoint of physiological effect upon organisms, the potency of a combination of pesticides frequently is greater than might be expected from the potencies of the separate components.   The expanding multitude of man's environmental effects now demands that we consider synergistic reactions between them in a much broader interdisciplinary sense than to date.   For example: Human activities have led to the nutrient enrichment of many lakes and streams (see Selection 19).   In a separate action man may introduce foreign kinds of plants into the enriched waters.   Lacking local ecological checks (diseases, for instance), rampant growth may burst forth, with serious consequences for man (see Selection 20), whereas just the enrichment of water or solely the introduction of plants might very well be inconsequential.

It is interesting to note that the phenomenon of synergism (but not identified as such) has also been studied in cybernetics.   Cybernetics has generally been identified as a science of self-regulating and equilibrating systems.   However, some attention has also been paid to systems in which mutual causal effects are "deviation-amplifying" (Maruyama, 1963).   These are systems which are loosely termed "vicious circles" or "compound interests."   In short, mutual causal processes diverge from the initial condition and continue to build up deviation.   A deviation-amplifying system can be said to have positive feedback loops.   In contrast to equilibrating systems in which the elements tend to stabilize, like a heating unit with a thermostat, the positive feedback loops in a deviation-amplifying system are disruptive.   Thus, cybernetics now provides an additional conceptual framework for considering environmental synergisms.   The approach has recently been applied to ecosystems (Margalef, 1968).

Regardless of the name applied, the phenomenon is at work amplifying man's disruption of the environment.   And with the present proliferation of man's effects we cannot hope to predict all the magnified impacts resulting from synergistic, or deviation-amplifying, interactions.   There are too many possible mixtures, and our understanding of the interactions is poor.   We must begin to realize, though, the increasing threat of environmental synergism.

These six basic causes are, of course, closely related.   The relationships merit books of discussion and cannot be more than mentioned here.   The selections which follow do partly integrate some causes, however.   Advancements in technology and their effects on environment, for instance, are closely tied to our attitudes and economics.   Such connections must be recognized by anyone interested in improving the quality of our environment. Changes in one cause entail changes in others. Ignorance and attitudes probably present the greatest obstacles to constructive change. Man must *understand* environmental problems and *want* to correct them in order to limit population growth, control technological power, and assess environmental costs in economic systems.

Further Readings

Glacken, C. J. 1970. Man against nature: an outmoded concept. Pp. 127–142 in *The environmental crisis*, ed. by H. W. Helfrich, Jr. New Haven and London: Yale University Press.

Goetz, A. 1961. On the nature of the synergistic action of aerosols. *Intern. J. Air Water Pollution* 4:168–184.

Hewlett, P. S. 1968. Synergism and potentiation in insecticides. *Chem. Ind.* June 1, 1968, pp. 701–706.

Lodge, J. P., Jr. 1968. Environmental synergisms: the problem defined. Pp. 146–159 in *Environmental problems*, ed. by B. R. Wilson. Philadelphia & Toronto: J. B. Lippincott Company.

Margalef, Ramon. 1968. The ecosystem as a cybernetic system. Pp. 1–25 in *Perspectives in ecological theory.* Chicago and London: The University of Chicago Press. 111 pp.

Maruyama, Magoroh. 1963. The second cybernetics: deviation-amplifying mutual causal processes. *Am. Scientist* 51:164–179. (Also in *General systems yearbook*, Vol. 8, 1963.)

Pilat, M. J. 1968. Application of gas-aerosol absorption data to the selection of air quality standards. *Air Pollution Control Assoc. J.* 18:751–753.

Radford, J. 1968. Biological aspects of synergisms. Pp. 160–173 in *Environmental problems*, ed. by B. R. Wilson. Philadelphia & Toronto: J. B. Lippincott Company.

Symposium on pesticide interaction phenomena. 1966. *J. Agr. Food Chem.* 14:540–565. November.

Wagar, J. A. 1970. Growth versus the quality of life. *Science* 168:1179–1184.

THE HISTORICAL ROOTS OF
OUR ECOLOGIC CRISIS

LYNN WHITE, JR.

Man's attitude toward nature is the subject of this modern classic. White gives profound insight into the dominant Western tradition of arrogance toward nature. The roots of our environmental troubles are largely religious, he explains. The attitudes and actions of modern technological man contradict the reality that man is *part* of nature, not rightful master over nature: "Despite Copernicus, all the cosmos rotates around our little globe. Despite Darwin, we are *not*, in our hearts, part of the natural process. We are superior to nature, contemptuous of it, willing to use it for our slightest whim."

White concludes that "What we do about ecology depends on our ideas of the man-nature relationship. More science and more technology are not going to get us out of the present ecologic crisis until we find a new religion, or rethink our old one." The author includes Marxism and Islam as part of the Judeo-Christian tradition, and hence sharing the blame.

It should be noted that some other authors take issue with White's implied absolution of Oriental attitudes and actions. Yi-Fu Tuan (1968, 1970), for example, argues that the inconsistency and paradox between man's treatment of environment and his own well-being is a characteristic of all human existence, not just of Western cultures. He points out that the highminded *ideals* of Eastern cultures are frequently not practiced. He believes that at the level of actual impress of man on environment, both constructive and destructive, the pagan world and Oriental

Lynn T. White, Jr. (b. 1907), is professor of history and director of the Center for Medieval and Renaissance Studies at the University of California, Los Angeles. Educated at Stanford, Union Theological Seminary, and Harvard (Ph.D., 1934), he has served on the faculties of Princeton and Stanford and was president of Mills College from 1943 to 1958. White has received several honorary doctorates and numerous professional awards. He is a Fellow of the American Academy of Arts and Sciences, the American Philosophical Society, and the American Association for the Advancement of Science. Among his books are *Frontiers of Knowledge in the Study of Man* (1956), *Medieval Technology and Social Change* (1962), *The Transformation of the Roman World* (1966), and *Machina ex Deo: Essays in the Dynamism of Western Culture* (1968).

societies had as much impact as did European Christians, until the beginning of the modern period. Rhoads Murphey (1967) has shown that in contemporary China ideals are now being adjusted to this reality. With Western technology, China (like Japan and other Asian countries before her) is replacing the traditional notions of harmony with nature with the attitude that man is properly lord over the environment.

(Editor's comment)

A conversation with Aldous Huxley not infrequently put one at the receiving end of an unforgettable monologue. About a year before his lamented death he was discoursing on a favorite topic: Man's unnatural treatment of nature and its sad results. To illustrate his point he told how, during the previous summer, he had returned to a little valley in England where he had spent many happy months as a child. Once it had been composed of delightful grassy glades; now it was becoming overgrown with unsightly brush because the rabbits that formerly kept such growth under control had largely succumbed to a disease, myxomatosis, that was deliberately introduced by the local farmers to reduce the rabbits' destruction of crops. Being something of a Philistine, I could be silent no longer, even in the interests of great rhetoric. I interrupted to point out that the rabbit itself had been brought as a domestic animal to England in 1176, presumably to improve the protein diet of the peasantry.

All forms of life modify their contexts. The most spectacular and benign instance is doubtless the coral polyp. By serving its own ends, it has created a vast undersea world favorable to thousands of other kinds of animals and plants. Ever since man became a numerous species he has affected his environment notably. The hypothesis that his fire-drive method of hunting created the world's great grasslands and helped to exterminate the monster mammals of the Pleistocene from much of the globe is plausible, if not proved. For 6 millennia at least, the banks of the lower Nile have been a human artifact rather than the swampy African jungle which nature, apart from man, would have made it. The Aswan Dam, flooding 5000 square miles, is only the latest stage in a long process. In many regions terracing or irrigation, overgrazing, the cutting of forests by Romans to build ships to fight Carthaginians or by Crusaders to solve the logistics problems of their expeditions, have profoundly changed some ecologies. Observation that the French landscape falls into two basic types, the open fields of the north and the *bocage* of the south and west, inspired Marc Bloch to undertake his classic study of medieval agricultural methods. Quite unintentionally, changes in human ways often affect nonhuman nature. It has been noted, for example, that the advent of the automobile eliminated huge flocks of sparrows that once fed on the horse manure littering every street.

The history of ecologic change is still so rudimentary that we know little about what really happened, or what the results were. The extinction of the European aurochs as late as 1627 would seem to have been a simple case of overenthusiastic hunting. On more intricate matters it often is impossible to find solid information. For a thousand years or more the Frisians and Hollanders have been pushing back the North Sea, and the process is culminating in our own time in the reclamation of the Zuider Zee. What, if any, species of animals, birds, fish, shore life, or plants have died out in the process? In their epic combat with Neptune have the Netherlanders overlooked ecological values in such a way that the quality of human life in the Netherlands has suffered? I cannot discover that the questions have ever been asked, much less answered.

People, then, have often been a dynamic element in their own environment, but in the present state of historical scholarship we usually do not know exactly when, where, or with what effects man-induced changes came. As we enter the last third of the 20th century, however, concern for the problem of ecologic backlash is mounting feverishly. Natural science, conceived as the effort to understand the nature of things, had flourished in several eras and among several peoples. Similarly there had been an age-old accumulation of technological skills, sometimes growing rapidly, sometimes slowly. But it was not until about four generations ago that Western Europe and North America arranged a marriage between science and technology, a union of the theoretical and the empirical approaches to our natural environment. The emergence in widespread practice of the Baconian creed that scientific knowledge means technological power over nature can scarcely be dated before about 1850, save in the chemical industries, where it is anticipated in the 18th century. Its acceptance as a normal pattern of action may mark the greatest event in human history since the invention of agriculture, and perhaps in nonhuman terrestrial history as well.

Almost at once the new situation forced the crystallization of the novel concept of ecology; indeed, the word *ecology* first appeared in the English language in 1873. Today, less than a century later, the impact of our race upon the environment has so increased in force that it has changed in essence. When the first cannons were fired, in the early 14th century, they affected ecology by sending workers scrambling to the forests and mountains for more potash, sulfur, iron ore, and charcoal, with some resulting erosion and deforestation. Hydrogen bombs are of a different order: a war fought with them might alter the genetics of all life on this planet. By 1285 London had a smog problem arising from the burning of soft coal, but our present combustion of fossil fuels threatens to change the chemistry of the globe's atmosphere as a whole, with consequences which we are only beginning to guess. With the population explosion, the carcinoma of planless urbanism, the now

geological deposits of sewage and garbage, surely no creature other than man has ever managed to foul its nest in such short order.

There are many calls to action, but specific proposals, however worthy as individual items, seem too partial, palliative, negative: ban the bomb, tear down the billboards, give the Hindus contraceptives and tell them to eat their sacred cows. The simplest solution to any suspect change is, of course, to stop it, or, better yet, to revert to a romanticized past: make those ugly gasoline stations look like Anne Hathaway's cottage or (in the Far West) like ghost-town saloons. The "wilderness area" mentality invariably advocates deep-freezing an ecology, whether San Gimignano or the High Sierra, as it was before the first Kleenex was dropped. But neither atavism nor prettification will cope with the ecologic crisis of our time.

What shall we do? No one yet knows. Unless we think about fundamentals, our specific measures may produce new backlashes more serious than those they are designed to remedy.

As a beginning we should try to clarify our thinking by looking, in some historical depth, at the presuppositions that underlie modern technology and science. Science was traditionally aristocratic, speculative, intellectual in intent; technology was lowerclass, empirical, action-oriented. The quite sudden fusion of these two, towards the middle of the 19th century, is surely related to the slightly prior and contemporary democratic revolutions which, by reducing social barriers, tended to assert a functional unity of brain and hand. Our ecologic crisis is the product of an emerging, entirely novel, democratic culture. The issue is whether a democratized world can survive its own implications. Presumably we cannot unless we rethink our axioms.

The Western Traditions of Technology and Science

One thing is so certain that it seems stupid to verbalize it: both modern technology and modern science are distinctively *Occidental*. Our technology has absorbed elements from all over the world, notably from China; yet everywhere today, whether in Japan or in Nigeria, successful technology is Western. Our science is the heir to all the sciences of the past, especially perhaps to the work of the great Islamic scientists of the Middle Ages, who so often outdid the ancient Greeks in skill and perspicacity: al-Rāzī in medicine, for example; or ibn-al-Haytham in optics; or Omar Khayyám in mathematics. Indeed, not a few works of such geniuses seem to have vanished in the original Arabic and to survive only in medieval Latin translations that helped to lay the foundations for later Western developments. Today, around the globe, all significant science is Western in style and method, whatever the pigmentation or language of the scientists.

A second pair of facts is less well recognized because they result from quite recent historical scholarship. The leadership of the West, both in technology and in science, is far older than the so-called Scientific Revolution of the 17th century or the so-called Industrial Revolution of the 18th century. These terms are in fact outmoded and obscure the true nature of what they try to describe—significant stages in two long and separate developments. By A.D. 1000 at the latest—and perhaps, feebly, as much as 200 years earlier—the West began to apply water power to industrial processes other than milling grain. This was followed in the late 12th century by the harnessing of wind power. From simple beginnings, but with remarkable consistency of style, the West rapidly expanded its skills in the development of power machinery, labor-saving devices, and automation. Those who doubt should contemplate that most monumental achievement in the history of automation: the weight-driven mechanical clock, which appeared in two forms in the early 14th century. Not in craftsmanship but in basic technological capacity, the Latin West of the later Middle Ages far outstripped its elaborate, sophisticated, and esthetically magnificent sister cultures, Byzantium and Islam. In 1444 a

great Greek ecclesiastic, Bessarion, who had gone to Italy, wrote a letter to a prince in Greece. He is amazed by the superiority of Western ships, arms, textiles, glass. But above all he is astonished by the spectacle of waterwheels sawing timbers and pumping the bellows of blast furnaces. Clearly, he had seen nothing of the sort in the Near East.

By the end of the 15th century the technological superiority of Europe was such that its small, mutually hostile nations could spill out over all the rest of the world, conquering, looting, and colonizing. The symbol of this technological superiority is the fact that Portugal, one of the weakest states of the Occident, was able to become, and to remain for a century, mistress of the East Indies. And we must remember that the technology of Vasco da Gama and Albuquerque was built by pure empiricism, drawing remarkably little support or inspiration from science.

In the present-day vernacular understanding, modern science is supposed to have begun in 1543, when both Copernicus and Vesalius published their great works. It is no derogation of their accomplishments, however, to point out that such structures as the *Fabrica* and the *De revolutionibus* do not appear overnight. The distinctive Western tradition of science, in fact, began in the late 11th century with a massive movement of translation of Arabic and Greek scientific works into Latin. A few notable books—Theophrastus, for example—escaped the West's avid new appetite for science, but within less than 200 years effectively the entire corpus of Greek and Muslim science was available in Latin, and was being eagerly read and criticized in the new European universities. Out of criticism arose new observation, speculation, and increasing distrust of ancient authorities. By the late 13th century Europe had seized global scientific leadership from the faltering hands of Islam. It would be as absurd to deny the profound originality of Newton, Galileo, or Copernicus as to deny that of the 14th century scholastic scientists like Buridan or Oresme on whose work they built. Before the 11th century, science scarcely existed in the Latin West, even in Roman times. From the 11th century onward, the scientific sector of Occidental culture has increased in a steady crescendo.

Since both our technological and our scientific movements got their start, acquired their character, and achieved world dominance in the Middle Ages, it would seem that we cannot understand their nature or their present impact upon ecology without examining fundamental medieval assumptions and developments.

Medieval View of Man and Nature

Until recently, agriculture has been the chief occupation even in "advanced" societies; hence, any change in methods of tillage has much importance. Early plows, drawn by two oxen, did not normally turn the sod but merely scratched it. Thus, cross-plowing was needed and fields tended to be squarish. In the fairly light soils and semiarid climates of the Near East and Mediterranean, this worked well. But such a plow was inappropriate to the wet climate and often sticky soils of northern Europe. By the latter part of the 7th century after Christ, however, following obscure beginnings, certain northern peasants were using an entirely new kind of plow, equipped with a vertical knife to cut the line of the furrow, a horizontal share to slice under the sod, and a moldboard to turn it over. The friction of this plow with the soil was so great that it normally required not two but eight oxen. It attacked the land with such violence that cross-plowing was not needed, and fields tended to be shaped in long strips.

In the days of the scratch-plow, fields were distributed generally in units capable of supporting a single family. Subsistence farming was the presupposition. But no peasant owned eight oxen: to use the new and more efficient plow, peasants pooled their oxen to form large plow-teams, originally receiving (it would appear) plowed strips in proportion to their contribution. Thus, distribution of land was based no longer on the needs of

a family but, rather, on the capacity of a power machine to till the earth. Man's relation to the soil was profoundly changed. Formerly man had been part of nature; now he was the exploiter of nature. Nowhere else in the world did farmers develop any analogous agricultural implement. Is it coincidence that modern technology, with its ruthlessness toward nature, has so largely been produced by descendants of these peasants of northern Europe?

This same exploitive attitude appears slightly before A.D. 830 in Western illustrated calendars. In older calendars the months were shown as passive personifications. The new Frankish calendars, which set the style for the Middle Ages, are very different: they show men coercing the world around them—plowing, harvesting, chopping trees, butchering pigs. Man and nature are two things, and man is master.

These novelties seem to be in harmony with larger intellectual patterns. What people do about their ecology depends on what they think about themselves in relation to things around them. Human ecology is deeply conditioned by beliefs about our nature and destiny—that is, by religion. To Western eyes this is very evident in, say, India or Ceylon. It is equally true of ourselves and of our medieval ancestors.

The victory of Christianity over paganism was the greatest psychic revolution in the history of our culture. It has become fashionable today to say that, for better or worse, we live in "the post-Christian age." Certainly the forms of our thinking and language have largely ceased to be Christian, but to my eye the substance often remains amazingly akin to that of the past. Our daily habits of action, for example, are dominated by an implicit faith in perpetual progress which was unknown either to Greco-Roman antiquity or to the Orient. It is rooted in, and is indefensible apart from, Judeo-Christian teleology. The fact that Communists share it merely helps to show what can be demonstrated on many other grounds: that Marxism, like Islam, is a Judeo-Christian heresy. We continue today to live, as we have lived for about 1700 years, very largely in a context of Christian axioms.

What did Christianity tell people about their relations with the environment?

While many of the world's mythologies provide stories of creation, Greco-Roman mythology was singularly incoherent in this respect. Like Aristotle, the intellectuals of the ancient West denied that the visible world had had a beginning. Indeed, the idea of a beginning was impossible in the framework of their cyclical notion of time. In sharp contrast, Christianity inherited from Judaism not only a concept of time as nonrepetitive and linear but also a striking story of creation. By gradual stages a loving and all-powerful God had created light and darkness, the heavenly bodies, the earth and all its plants, animals, birds, and fishes. Finally, God had created Adam and, as an afterthought, Eve to keep man from being lonely. Man named all the animals, thus establishing his dominance over them. God planned all of this explicitly for man's benefit and rule: no item in the physical creation had any purpose save to serve man's purposes. And, although man's body is made of clay, he is not simply part of nature: he is made in God's image.

Especially in its Western form, Christianity is the most anthropocentric religion the world has seen. As early as the 2nd century both Tertullian and Saint Irenaeus of Lyons were insisting that when God shaped Adam he was foreshadowing the image of the incarnate Christ, the Second Adam. Man shares, in great measure, God's transcendence of nature. Christianity, in absolute contrast to ancient paganism and Asia's religions (except, perhaps, Zoroastrianism), not only established a dualism of man and nature but also insisted that it is God's will that man exploit nature for his proper ends.

At the level of the common people this worked out in an interesting way. In Antiquity every tree, every spring, every stream, every hill had its own *genius loci*, its guardian spirit. These spirits were accessible to men, but were very unlike men; centaurs, fauns, and mermaids show their ambivalence. Before one cut a tree, mined a mountain, or dammed a brook, it was important to placate the spirit in charge of that particular situation, and to keep it placated. By destroying pagan animism, Christianity made it possible to exploit nature in a mood of indifference to the feelings of natural objects.

It is often said that for animism the Church substituted the cult of saints. True; but the cult of saints is functionally quite different from animism. The saint is not *in* natural objects; he may have special shrines, but his citizenship is in heaven. Moreover, a saint is entirely a man; he can be approached in human terms. In addition to saints, Christianity of course also had angels and demons inherited from Judaism and perhaps, at one remove, from Zoroastrianism. But these were all as mobile as the saints themselves. The spirits *in* natural objects, which formerly had protected nature from man, evaporated. Man's effective monopoly on spirit in this world was confirmed, and the old inhibitions to the exploitation of nature crumbled.

When one speaks in such sweeping terms, a note of caution is in order. Christianity is a complex faith, and its consequences differ in differing contexts. What I have said may well apply to the medieval West, where in fact technology made spectacular advances. But the Greek East, a highly civilized realm of equal Christian devotion, seems to have produced no marked technological innovation after the late 7th century, when Greek fire was invented. The key to the contrast may perhaps be found in a difference in the tonality of piety and thought which students of comparative theology find between the Greek and the Latin Churches. The Greeks believed that sin was intellectual blindness, and that salvation was found in illumination, orthodoxy—that is, clear thinking. The Latins, on the other hand, felt that sin was moral evil, and that salvation was to be found in right conduct. Eastern theology has been intellectualist. Western theology has been voluntarist. The Greek saint contemplates; the Western saint acts. The implications of

Christianity for the conquest of nature would emerge more easily in the Western atmosphere.

The Christian dogma of creation, which is found in the first clause of all the Creeds, has another meaning for our comprehension of today's ecologic crisis. By revelation, God had given man the Bible, the Book of Scripture. But since God had made nature, nature also must reveal the divine mentality. The religious study of nature for the better understanding of God was known as natural theology. In the early Church, and always in the Greek East, nature was conceived primarily as a symbolic system through which God speaks to men: the ant is a sermon to sluggards; rising flames are the symbol of the soul's aspiration. This view of nature was essentially artistic rather than scientific. While Byzantium preserved and copied great numbers of ancient Greek scientific tests, science as we conceive it could scarcely flourish in such an ambience.

However, in the Latin West by the early 13th century natural theology was following a very different bent. It was ceasing to be the decoding of the physical symbols of God's communication with man and was becoming the effort to understand God's mind by discovering how his creation operates. The rainbow was no longer simply a symbol of hope first sent to Noah after the Deluge: Robert Grosseteste, Friar Roger Bacon, and Theodoric of Freiberg produced startlingly sophisticated work on the optics of the rainbow, but they did it as a venture in religious understanding. From the 13th century onward, up to and including Leibnitz and Newton, every major scientist, in effect, explained his motivations in religious terms. Indeed, if Galileo had not been so expert an amateur theologian he would have got into far less trouble: the professionals resented his intrusion. And Newton seems to have regarded himself more as a theologian than as a scientist. It was not until the late 18th century that the hypothesis of God became unnecessary to many scientists.

It is often hard for the historian to judge, when men explain why they are doing what they want to do, whether they are offering real reasons or merely culturally acceptable reasons. The consistency with which scientists during the long formative centuries of Western science said that the task and the reward of the scientist was "to think God's thoughts after him" leads one to believe that this was their real motivation. If so, then modern Western science was cast in a matrix of Christian theology. The dynamism of religious devotion, shaped by the Judeo-Christian dogma of creation, gave it impetus.

An Alternative Christian View

We would seem to be headed toward conclusions unpalatable to many Christians. Since both *science* and *technology* are blessed words in our contemporary vocabulary, some may be happy at the notions, first, that, viewed historically, modern science is an extrapolation of natural theology and, second, that modern technology is at least partly to be explained as an Occidental, voluntarist realization of the Christian dogma of man's transcendence of, and rightful mastery over, nature. But, as we now recognize, somewhat over a century ago science and technology—hitherto quite separate activities—joined to give mankind powers which, to judge by many of the ecologic effects, are out of control. If so, Christianity bears a huge burden of guilt.

I personally doubt that disastrous ecologic backlash can be avoided simply by applying to our problems more science and more technology. Our science and technology have grown out of Christian attitudes toward man's relation to nature which are almost universally held not only by Christians and neo-Christians but also by those who fondly regard themselves as post-Christians. Despite Copernicus, all the cosmos rotates around our little globe. Despite Darwin, we are *not*, in our hearts, part of the natural process. We are superior to nature, contemptuous of it, willing to use it for our slightest whim. The newly elected Governor of California, like myself a churchman but less troubled than I, spoke for the Christian tradition when he said (as is alleged), "When you've seen one redwood tree, you've seen them all." To a Christian a tree can be no more than a physical fact. The whole concept of the sacred grove is alien to Christianity and to the ethos of the West. For nearly 2 millennia Christian missionaries have been chopping down sacred groves, which are idolatrous because they assume spirit in nature.

What we do about ecology depends on our ideas of the man-nature relationship. More science and more technology are not going to get us out of the present ecologic crisis until we find a new religion, or rethink our old one. The beatniks, who are the basic revolutionaries of our time, show a sound instinct in their affinity for Zen Buddhism, which conceives of the man-nature relationship as very nearly the mirror image of the Christian view. Zen, however, is as deeply conditioned by Asian history as Christianity is by the experience of the West, and I am dubious of its viability among us.

Possibly we should ponder the greatest radical in Christian history since Christ: Saint Francis of Assisi. The prime miracle of Saint Francis is the fact that he did not end at the stake, as many of his left-wing followers did. He was so clearly heretical that a General of the Franciscan Order, Saint Bonaventura, a great and perceptive Christian, tried to suppress the early accounts of Franciscanism. The key to an understanding of Francis is his belief in the virtue of humility—not merely for the individual but for man as a species. Francis tried to depose man from his monarchy over creation and set up a democracy of all God's creatures. With him the ant is no longer simply a homily for the lazy, flames a sign of the thrust of the soul toward union with God; now they are Brother Ant and Sister Fire, praising the Creator in their own ways as Brother Man does in his.

Later commentators have said that Francis preached to the birds as a rebuke to men who would not listen. The records do not read so: he urged the little birds to praise God, and in spiritual ecstasy they flapped their wings and chirped rejoicing. Legends of saints, especially the Irish saints, had long told of their dealings with animals but always, I believe, to show their human dominance over creatures. With Francis it is different. The land around Gubbio in the Apennines was being ravaged by a fierce wolf. Saint Francis, says the legend, talked to the wolf and persuaded him of the error of his ways. The wolf repented, died in the odor of sanctity, and was buried in consecrated ground.

What Sir Steven Ruciman calls "the Franciscan doctrine of the animal soul" was quickly stamped out. Quite possibly it was in part inspired, consciously or unconsciously, by the belief in reincarnation held by the Cathar heretics who at that time teemed in Italy and southern France, and who presumably had got it originally from India. It is significant that at just the same moment, about 1200, traces of metempsychosis are found also in western Judaism, in the Provençal *Cabbala*. But Francis held neither to transmigration of souls nor to pantheism. His view of nature and of man rested on a unique sort of pan-psychism of all things animate and inanimate, designed for the glorification of their transcendent Creator, who, in the ultimate gesture of cosmic humility, assumed flesh, lay helpless in a manger, and hung dying on a scaffold.

I am not suggesting that many contemporary Americans who are concerned about our ecologic crisis will be either able or willing to counsel with wolves or exhort birds. However, the present increasing disruption of the global environment is the product of a dynamic technology and science which were originating in the Western medieval world against which Saint Francis was rebelling in so original a way. Their growth cannot be understood historically apart from distinctive attitudes toward nature which are deeply grounded in Christian dogma. The fact that most people do not think of these attitudes as Christian is irrelevant. No new set of basic values has been accepted in our society to displace those of Christianity. Hence we shall continue to have a worsening ecologic crisis until we reject the Christian axiom that nature has no reason for existence save to serve man.

The greatest spiritual revolutionary in Western history, Saint Francis, proposed what he thought was an alternative Christian view of nature and man's relation to it: he tried to substitute the idea of the equality of all creatures, including man, for the idea of man's limitless rule of creation. He failed. Both our present science and our present technology are so tinctured with orthodox Christian arrogance toward nature that no solution for our ecologic crisis can be expected from them alone. Since the roots of our trouble are so largely religious, the remedy must also be essentially religious, whether we call it that or not. We must rethink and refeel our nature and destiny. The profoundly religious, but heretical, sense of the primitive Franciscans for the spiritual autonomy of all parts of nature may point a direction. I propose Francis as a patron saint for ecologists.

ADDITIONAL REFERENCES

Bouillenne, R. 1962. Man, the destroying biotype. *Science* 135:706–712.

Glacken, C. J. 1956. Changing ideas of the habitable world. Pp. 70–92 in *Man's role in changing the face of the earth*, ed. by William L. Thomas, Jr. Chicago and London: The University of Chicago Press.

Glacken, C. J. 1967. *Traces on the Rhodian shore.* Berkeley, California: University of California Press. Monumental history of man-nature relationships in Western thought.

Glacken, C. J. 1970. Man against nature: An outmoded concept. Pp. 127–142 in *The environmental crisis*, ed. by H. W. Helfrich, Jr. New Haven and London: Yale University Press.

Matley, I. A. 1966. The Marxist approach to the geographical environment. *Annals Assoc. Am. Geograph.* 56:97–111.

Murphey, R. 1967. Man and nature in China. *Modern Asian Studies* 1(4):313–333.

Murray, E. G. D. 1954. The place of nature in man's world. *Am. Scientist* 42:130–135, 142.

Northrop, F. S. C. 1956. Man's relation to the earth in its bearing on his aesthetic, ethical, and legal values. Pp. 1052–1067 in *Man's role in changing the face of the earth*, ed. by William L. Thomas, Jr. Chicago and London: The University of Chicago Press.

Shepard, P. 1967. *Man in the landscape: A historic view of the esthetics of nature.* New York: Knopf. 290 pp.

Tuan, Y. 1966. Man and nature. *Landscape* 15(3):30–36. An extensive overview of literature on the subject of man in relation to nature.

Tuan, Y. 1968. Discrepancies between environmental attitude and behaviour: examples from Europe and China. *Canadian Geographer* XII(3).

Tuan, Y. 1970. Our treatment of the environment in ideal and actuality. *Am. Scientist.* 58(3):244, 247–249.

THE MODERN EXPANSION OF WORLD POPULATION

JOHN D. DURAND

It is axiomatic that at the present population level more people means more environmental problems. This selection focuses on the characteristics of population growth itself, largely detached from explicit environmental considerations. Durand examines the modern expansion of the human population—"a unique episode in the growth of the species since its origin."

Two phases in the modern growth trend are recognizable: a phase of moderate growth (though much faster than earlier) from 1750 to 1900, and a phase of sharply accelerated growth since 1900. At its present rate of increase, the world's population will double in thirty-five years! Despite this, Durand believes that "The modern expansion of population in the world is far from having run its course."

What is the significance to man and to environment of this growth? One expert has suggested that the earth's ultimate "carrying capacity," or ability to support man, is probably about 30 billion people, but at a level of near starvation for the great majority (Keyfitz, 1969). This is only about three doublings from the present population and at the current growth rate would be attained in about 100 years. However, the distribution of food and other resources is uneven and hence widespread famine appears imminent (e.g., Borgstrom, 1967, 1969; Paddock and Paddock, 1967; Ehrlich, 1968a,b). There is an increasing consideration of the quality of human existence and a search for a definition of *optimum* population. After a rather detailed consideration of this

John D. Durand (b. 1913) is professor of economics and sociology and associated with the Population Studies Center at the University of Pennsylvania. He earned a bachelor's degree from Cornell University and a doctorate in economics from Princeton University in 1939. Durand was formerly associated with the Population Division of the U.S. Census Bureau (1939–1946) and the United Nations Bureau of Social Affairs (1947–1965). He is currently continuing research in world demographic history and, with Dr. Ann R. Miller at the Population Studies Center, studying the growth and changing structure of the labor force in the postwar world as related to economic development and population growth.

This selection is reprinted with permission of the author and the American Philosophical Society from the society's *Proceedings,* Vol. 111, No. 3, pp. 136–145, 1967.

matter, Paul Ehrlich has concluded that the planet earth, as a whole, is *already overpopulated* (1970, p. 201).

Many of the selections in this book demonstrate a positive correlation between population size and magnitude of environmental impact. The more populous a city is, for example, the greater is its influence on local climate (Selection 11). Likewise, the degree of pollution in the various Great Lakes is causally related to the number of people residing on a lake's watershed (Selection 19). There are a number of other recent articles and books which have specifically examined the environmental effects of population levels; many of these are listed as additional references at the end of this selection.

In addition, Max Nicholson (Selection 2) and Paul Martin (Selection 45) have extended our consideration of population and environment into the prehistoric past. Martin relates the prehistoric growth in population to man's geographical expansion and his effects on environment, especially on populations of other animals.

From a global standpoint, population will certainly continue to implode, with increasing harm to man, for some time to come. Besides the demographic reasons cited in this selection, the "growth cult" attitude is an important stimulus to continued population growth. The value of economic growth in market societies is widely accepted. Our attitudes and policies are strongly geared to short-run economic gains (see Selection 6 and its commentary; also Ehrlich, 1968a, who proposes some interesting policies to reverse existing population growth). "Growth" is equated with "progress." To most of us it does not matter *now* that unlimited growth is not suited to man's survival on a finite planet. Thus, problems of population, and also related environmental problems, are closely tied to economics and attitudes.

(Editor's comment)

The extraordinary proliferation of the human species which is going on in the world at present is part of a trend which began about two centuries ago and which has been gathering momentum since the beginning of the present century. This cannot fail to be recognized as one of the principal features of modern world history.[1] In historical perspective, it appears as a unique episode in the growth of the species since its origin; it has no parallel in previous history or prehistory for the speed and magnitude of expansion of numbers, and it seems highly unlikely that a comparable expansion would occur again in the future after the present trend has run its course.

The purposes of this paper are to portray the dimensions of the modern growth of world population against the background of previous long-range trends, to show how the trend has evolved during the last two centuries in the world as a whole and its major areas, and to consider some possibilities with regard to its continuation in the future.

Magnitude of World Population Growth During the Last Two Centuries

Population estimates for the world and major areas since 1750 are shown in Tables 4.1 and 4.2 along with projections to the year 2000. The figures in Table 4.1 are "medium" estimates, intended to represent the center of

TABLE 4.1 "Medium" estimates of population of the world and major areas, 1750–1950, and projections to 2000

Areas	Population (millions)						Annual rate of increase (per cent)				
	1750	1800	1850	1900	1950	2000	1750–1800	1800–1850	1850–1900	1900–1950	1950–2000
World total	791	978	1,262	1,650	2,515	6,130	0.4	0.5	0.5	0.8	1.8
Asia (exc. U.S.S.R.)	498	630	801	925	1,381	3,458	0.5	0.5	0.3	0.8	1.9
China (Mainland)	200	323	430	436	560	1,034	1.0	0.6	0.0	0.5	1.2
India and Pakistan	190	195	233	285	434	1,269	0.1	0.3	0.4	0.8	2.2
Japan	30	30	31	44	83	122	0.0	0.1	0.7	1.3	0.8
Indonesia	12	13	23	42	77	250[a]	0.2	1.2	1.2	1.2	2.4
Remainder of Asia (exc. U.S.S.R.)	67	69	87	118	227	783	0.1	0.5	0.7	1.3	2.5
Africa	106	107	111	133	222	768	0.0	0.1	0.4	1.0	2.5
North Africa	10	11	15	27	53	192	0.2	0.5	1.2	1.4	2.8
Remainder of Africa	96	96	96	106	169	576	0.0	0.0	0.2	0.9	2.5
Europe (exc. U.S.S.R.)	125	152	208	296	392	527	0.4	0.6	0.7	0.6	0.6
U.S.S.R.	42	56	76	134	180	353	0.6	0.6	1.1	0.6	1.4
America	18	31	64	156	328	992	1.1	1.5	1.8	1.5	2.2
Northern America	2	7	26	82	166	354	—	2.7	2.3	1.4	1.5
Middle and South America	16	24	38	74	162	638	0.8	0.9	1.3	1.6	2.8
Oceania	2	2	2	6	13	32	—	—	—	1.6	1.8

[a] Calculated by assuming that Indonesia's share in the projected total for South-East Asia would be the same in 2000 as in 1980.

TABLE 4.2 Range of "low" and "high" variants of estimates of population of the world and major areas, 1750–1950, and projections to 2000

Areas	Population (millions)					
	1750	1800	1850	1900	1950	2000
World total	629–961	813–1,125	1,128–1,402	1,550–1,762	2,479–2,599	5,449–6,994
Asia (exc. U.S.S.R.)	408–595	524– 721	711– 893	853–1,006	1,353–1,453	3,103–4,067
China (Mainland)	180–234	290– 360	390– 480	385– 494	540– 620	882–1,333
India and Pakistan	160–214	160– 214	215– 242	285	434	1,163–1,464
Japan	30	30	31	44	83	115– 139
Indonesia	7– 17	9– 17	19– 27	40– 45	77	227– 267[a]
Remainder of Asia (exc. U.S.S.R.)	31–100	35– 100	56– 113	99– 138	219– 239	716– 864
Africa	60–153	69– 142	81– 145	115– 154	213– 233	684– 864
North Africa	6– 18	8– 18	12– 21	26– 30	53	166– 205
Remainder of Africa	54–135	61– 124	69– 124	89– 124	160– 180	518– 659
Europe (exc. U.S.S.R.)	115–135	147– 157	208	296	392	491– 563
U.S.S.R.	31– 52	46– 66	66– 85	127– 140	180	316– 403
America	14– 23	26– 36	60– 68	153– 160	328	826–1,062
Northern America	2– 3	6– 7	26	82	166	294– 376
Middle and South America	12– 20	20– 29	34– 42	71– 78	162	532– 686
Oceania	1– 3	1– 3	2– 3	6	13	28– 35

[a] Calculated by assuming that Indonesia's share in the "low" and "high" projected totals for South-East Asia in 2000 would be the same as in the 1980 projections shown on page 140 of the United Nations report, *World Population Prospects as Assessed in 1963.*

a range of plausible figures for each area and date. The "low" and "high" variants given in Table 4.2 are not intended to define absolute limits but to indicate the width of estimated ranges of relative plausibility without excluding the possibility that the true numbers might have been outside these ranges. No variants are shown where it seems possible to rely on the "medium" estimate for accuracy within relatively narrow margins of error. Estimates which lack a firm foundation are shown in italics. For the period 1750 to 1900, the estimates are the author's; their basis is stated briefly in the appendix. In the "medium" series, they differ from the well-known estimates by Willcox and Carr-Saunders,[2] slightly at some points and more considerably at others, mainly because they take account of new information which has become available since Willcox's and Carr-Saunders' works were published. The 1950 estimates (except the "low" and "high" variants shown for certain areas) and the projections to 2000 are United Nations figures.[3]

In round numbers, the world population in the middle of the eighteenth century is estimated at about 800 million, plus or minus about 150 million. Compared with the United Nations estimate of 3,281 million for 1965 (which also has margins of error, possibly exceeding 100 million in either direction[4]), the "low" estimate for 1750 indicates a five-fold increase and the "high" estimate an increase of more than three-fold during the last two centuries. By either measure, the growth during this period has been mammoth compared with that of earlier periods of history and prehistory.

Comparison with Population Growth in Earlier Periods

If we wish to trace the trend of world population back to ancient and prehistoric times, of course we have to be content with gross orders of magnitude, but these are sufficient to define the general form of the long-range growth curve. Over the last ten thousand years, the curve has taken approximately the form shown in Figure 4.1.

This has been charted with reference to the "medium" estimates in Table 4.1 for dates since 1750 and the following "medium" estimates of world population at the birth of Christ and about 8000 B.C., prior to the appearance of the earliest known farming communities:

	A.D. 1	8000 B.C.
"Medium" estimates (millions)	300	5
Range of "low" and "high" variants (millions)	200–400	2–10

The estimate as of 8000 B.C. is based on what is known about the population densities of primitive non-agricultural societies.[5] For the estimate as of A.D. 1, the principal bases are the records of the ancient Chinese censuses, Beloch's painstaking estimate of the population of the Roman Empire at the death of Augustus, and Pran Nath's calculations with regard to the possible number of India's inhabitants in Açoka's time.[6] Substitution of different estimates within the ranges of the "low" and "high" variants for each date would make little difference in the shape of the long-range growth curve.

It is interesting to calculate what share of the total increase of the human species since its origin is represented by the growth during the modern epoch. If we define the total increase as a net figure, disregarding whatever gains were canceled out by subsequent losses, of course the measure of it is the present number of the population, estimated at 3,281 million in 1965. Approximately three-fourths of this increase has taken place since 1750 according to the "medium" estimates (or 70 per cent if the "high" estimate of the 1750 population is taken as a basis). In speed as well as magnitude, the modern growth contrasts strongly with that of earlier times. Between 8000 B.C. and A.D. 1, according to the "medium" estimates, the population doubled not quite six times (multiplication of sixty-fold, whereas six doublings

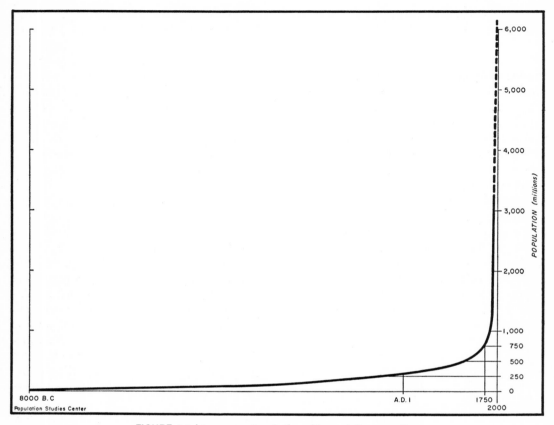

POPULATION (millions)

6,000

5,000

4,000

3,000

2,000

1,000

750

500

250

0

8000 B.C

A.D. I

1750

2000

Population Studies Center

FIGURE 4.1 Long-range trend of world population growth.

would multiply by sixty-four); in other words, the average doubling time was more than a thousand years. Again for the interval between A.D. 1 and 1750, the growth rate indicated by the "medium" estimates corresponds to a doubling time of more than a thousand years. This is the pace of a horse and buggy compared with the racing-car speed of the modern growth—doubling in approximately 150 years after 1750 and again in about 65 years after 1900, according to the "medium" estimates.[7]

It should be noted that the trend in past epochs was far from steady. If reliable measures of the world population could be obtained century by century since the birth of Christ and before, they would show some periods of growth at rates considerably exceeding the long-term average and other periods of relatively stationary or decreasing numbers. It is highly unlikely, though, that the speed of the modern growth was matched, in the world as a whole, during any previous period of considerable length.

It is not possible to fix exactly the date when the extraordinary growth of the modern epoch began: i.e., the date since when the rate of population growth in the world as a whole has been distinctly and consistently above the average of previous centuries. Willcox and Carr-Saunders carried their estimates back to 1650 and both estimated a considerable increase in world population between 1650 and 1750, but the basis of estimates for that period is very weak. The author has refrained from attempting to extend the estimates in Tables 4.1 and 4.2 back beyond 1750 in view of the poverty of information about earlier trends in almost every part of the world. Available data do suggest, though, that accelerated growth probably began somewhat before 1750 in parts of

Europe, Russia, and America and possibly before 1700 in China.

Phases of World Population Growth Since 1750

When the growth of world population during the modern epoch is analyzed in terms of the trend of the growth rate over time and the variations in different areas, it is important to pay attention to the basis of estimates and their margins of error. Unguarded use of Willcox's and Carr-Saunders' estimates for such purposes has led many writers to dubious conclusions. With regard to the annual growth rates shown in Table 4.1, which refer to the "medium" estimates, it should be emphasized that at many points they merely reflect assumptions adopted in making these estimates and that many of the rates would be changed considerably by selecting different, plausible combinations of population estimates for successive dates, within the ranges of the variants.

With due regard for these cautions, two phases of the world population trend since the eighteenth century can be distinguished: from 1750 to 1900, a phase of growth at relatively moderate speed (though much more rapid than that of earlier epochs), and since 1900, a phase of sharply accelerated growth. In the earlier phase, the "medium" estimates show steady growth of the world total at the rate of about ½ of 1 per cent per annum during each fifty-year period. The estimated growth between 1900 and 1950 was at almost twice this rate, and United Nations estimates indicate a marked acceleration since 1920 with an impressive jump of the growth rate in the 1950's (see Table 4.3).

It is commonly asserted that the rate of world population growth has been accelerating steadily during the last two or three centuries (and during all previous history as well, according to some writers). The present estimates do not bear out this idea; but neither do they disprove it, as there is ample room within the limits of the variants for either a rising or a falling trend of the growth

rate between 1750 and 1900. Some acceleration of growth during that period is indicated by available data or else has been assumed in constructing the estimates for a majority of the areas, but this is counterbalanced by an opposite trend in the estimates for China's large population.

Trends in Major Areas During the Initial Phase (1750–1900)

Variations of the population trend in different parts of the world are depicted in Figure 4.2, where the "medium" estimates for each major area are charted on a logarithmic scale, so that the geometric rates of growth are reflected by the slopes of the curves. Where the estimates have a relatively weak basis, the curves are drawn with broken lines, and it will be noticed that these occupy a large share of the chart, especially for the period before 1900. The picture for that period may be badly distorted, yet some of its broad outlines are probably representative of historical reality.

It seems to be commonly taken for granted that the European nations, as leaders in the Industrial Revolution, also took the lead in the modern population expansion and that they were responsible for most of the increase of the world total during the initial phase; but this is not apparent in the present estimates. Either in the chart or in the tabulation of estimated annual growth rates (Table 4.1), Europe does not stand out among the major areas for speed of population growth at any time in the last two centuries. Europe's growth appears more remarkable

TABLE 4.3 Estimates of world population growth, 1900–1960

Date	Population (millions)	Annual rate of increase since preceding date (per cent)
1900	1,650	—
1920	1,860	0.6
1930	2,069	1.1
1940	2,295	1.0
1950	2,515	1.0
1960	2,998	1.8

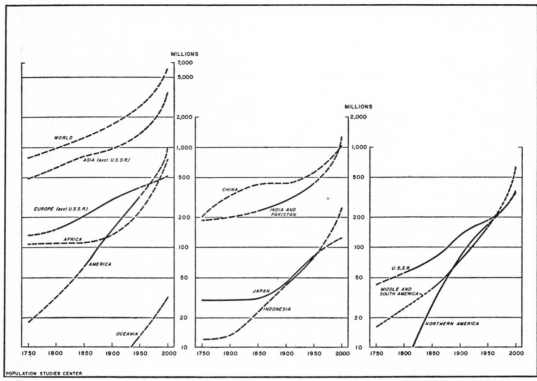

FIGURE 4.2 Growth of population in the world and major areas, "medium" estimates, 1750–1950, and projections to 2000.

for steadiness than for speed. It is true that the expansion of the European peoples is reflected partly in the figures for America and other areas to which tens of millions of Europeans emigrated during the last two centuries. In Table 4.2, the estimates for America, Oceania, and the Soviet Union are added to those for Europe to make a total for the principal areas of European settlement and culture, and the growth rate of this total is found to have been appreciably higher than the rate for Europe along in each period. By this measure, the European peoples appear to have had more than their proportionate share in the expansion of world population during the nineteenth century (though it is doubtfully warranted to say that their growth dominated the trend of the world total at that time). Between 1750 and 1800, on the other hand, it is not clear that the Europeans outpaced the rest of the world in population growth, and their increase since

1900 appears to have been nearly parallel with the trend of the world total.

There is some question whether it is appropriate to include in these totals the whole population of Middle and South America, much of which was of non-European or mixed stock. (This applies with less force to Northern America, the U.S.S.R., and Oceania.) If Middle and South America are excluded, the share of the European peoples in the growth of world population appears more modest, as shown by the figures in the lower panel of Table 4.4.

In the case of western Europe, it may be true as postulated in the theory of the "demographic transition," that the cause of the population expansion in the initial phase was an improvement of economic conditions thanks to industrialization, which made for a reduction of death rates.[8] This explanation does not apply so well to eastern Europe or to the area of the present Soviet Union, where there was little industrialization and economic conditions remained relatively poor until a much later time, yet population grew as much or more than it did in the West from the middle of the eighteenth century onward. The case of China, which appears as one of the areas of greatest expansion of population in the eighteenth century, again calls for a different explanation. In the world-wide picture as represented by the present estimates, little consistent relationship can be seen between the developments connected with the Industrial Revolution and the expansion of population in the initial phase.

What is the explanation, then, for the apparent, approximately simultaneous up-turn of the population trend during the eighteenth and early nineteenth century, in widely separated regions of the earth where economic conditions and developments were so diverse? It is hardly likely to be entirely a figment of errors in the estimates, and it is hardly credible that this rough parallel of trends in different areas could have been merely a coincidence of chance. The operation of some common causal factor or factors is strongly suggested, but the identification of the common causes is a puzzle which research in demographic history has yet to solve. Until a key to this puzzle is found, there cannot be much assurance in explanations for the trend in any area which only fit the history of that particular area.

This question calls for some new directions of research, and one direction which can be suggested is the study of world-wide epidemiological as well as economic repercussions of the European voyages of discovery and conquest from the fifteenth century onward. On the economic side, it is apparent that one of the most important early consequences was strengthening of agriculture, both in the Old and the New World, by the exchange of food plants, which made both for expansion of productive capacity and stabilization of agricultural output. The positive relation of this factor to the growth of population in the eighteenth century and later has been demonstrated, particularly as regards the in-troduction of the Irish potato in Europe and of maize and the sweet potato in China.[9] On the epidemiological side, the effects of the intrusion of Europeans into far regions of the globe have been considered mainly with regard to the epidemics and depopulation which ensued in some of the areas where they intruded, particularly in America and Oceania. In parts of America, depopulation seems to have continued for nearly two centuries after Columbus' voyages, before the indigenous peoples gained enough power of resistance through exposure to new diseases, to begin recouping their losses. But the exchange of diseases, like the exchange of food plants, was surely not only a one-way traffic. Rather little attention seems to have been given to the study of possible repercussions on health and mortality in Europe and other areas, such as China, with which the Europeans were in contact. The hypothesis suggested for study is that the potential stimulus to population growth resulting from the strengthening of agriculture was counteracted during the sixteenth and seventeenth centuries, in varying degrees in different areas, by the transmission of diseases around the globe; and that in the eighteenth century

TABLE 4.4 Growth of population in principal areas of European settlement: "medium" estimates, 1750–1950, and projections to 2000

Date	Population (millions)	Share of world total (per cent)	Increase since preceding date	
			Annual rate (per cent)	Share of world increase (per cent)
A. Including Middle and South America				
1750	187	23.6	—	—
1800	241	24.6	0.5	28.9
1850	350	27.7	0.7	38.4
1900	592	35.9	1.1	62.4
1950	913	36.3	0.9	37.1
2000	1,904	31.1	1.5	27.4
B. Excluding Middle and South America				
1750	171	21.6	—	—
1800	217	22.2	0.5	24.6
1850	312	24.7	0.7	33.5
1900	518	31.4	1.0	53.1
1950	751	29.9	0.7	26.9
2000	1,266	20.7	1.1	14.2

growing natural resistance to the new diseases opened the way for an up-turn of the population trend in several areas.

To be sure, no single formula is likely to be found which would account for all the varieties of the trend in different parts of the world. For instance, the hypothesis just suggested does not very well fit the case of India, where population is thought to have been increasing in the sixteenth and seventeenth centuries and to have made little gain in the eighteenth. But for the sake of orderly historical interpretation of the initial phase of the world population expansion, it would be enough to find a formula which (modified as necessary to suit the circumstances of each area) would explain the curious parallel of apparent trends in Europe, the U.S.S.R., China, and America. With this object, it would be useful to formulate other hypotheses as well, for testing by historical studies in each area.

Divergent Trends in the Second Phase (Since 1900)

Since the beginning of the present century, the former ambiguous relationship between economic development and population in different areas has been transformed into a strong inverse relationship. This is shown by the comparison in Table 4.5, where the "medium" estimates for Europe, the U.S.S.R., Northern America, Japan, and Oceania are combined to form a total for the areas which are relatively well developed economically at present, while the figures for the remainder of the world are taken to represent the trend in less developed areas.[10] It can be seen that since 1900 the less developed areas have forged far ahead in population growth; in fact, they have borne almost the whole responsibility for speeding up the expansion of world population in the second phase, while the growth in more developed areas has proceeded at a relatively steady if not slackening pace.

The cause of this divergence of trends is well known. Great progress has been made since the beginning of the present century, and especially since World War II, in developing knowledge of the causes, cure, and prevention of diseases and means of applying such knowledge for the prevention of premature death. While all the world has shared the benefit in the form of decreasing mortality, the main beneficiaries in the recent phase have been the peoples of the less developed areas, whose mortality rates were relatively high before. With increasing efficiency of life-saving techniques, the relative disadvantage in mortality of the economically handicapped nations has diminished, although they are still more or less far from equality with the wealthier nations in this respect. While death rates have decreased, the birth rates in less developed countries have generally shown little change, with the result that their rates of population growth have accel-

TABLE 4.5 Growth of population in more developed and less developed areas of the World, 1850–2000

	"Medium" estimates				Projections to 2000	
	1850	1900	1950	1965	"Low"	"High"
Population (millions)						
More developed areas	343	562	834	999	1,245	1,516
Less developed areas	919	1,088	1,682	2,281	4,204	5,478
Annual rate of increase since preceding date (per cent)						
More developed areas	—	1.0	0.8	1.2	0.6	1.2
Less developed areas	—	0.3	0.9	2.1	1.8	2.5
Share of world total increase since preceding date (per cent)						
More developed areas	—	56	31	22	11	14
Less developed areas	—	44	69	78	89	86

TABLE 4.6 Percentages of population increase in successive decades, 1960–2000, according to variants of the United Nations projections

Decade	World total			Less developed areas[a]			More developed areas[a]		
	Medium	Low	High	Medium	Low	High	Medium	Low	High
1960–1970	19.8	18.2	22.0	24.1	22.4	26.5	10.8	9.6	12.9
1970–1980	20.6	17.0	24.4	25.0	21.0	29.3	10.3	7.8	12.9
1980–1990	19.8	15.3	25.0	23.4	18.6	29.7	10.4	7.0	12.6
1990–2000	18.2	13.9	22.9	21.2	17.1	26.4	9.3	4.8	12.3

[a] Calculated from the totals for more developed and less developed areas shown in tables A3.2, A3.3, and A3.4 of the United Nations report, *World Population Prospects as Assessed in 1963.* The definitions of the two groups of areas differ slightly from those used for Table 4.5.

erated progressively. In more developed areas, on the other hand, the decrease of mortality in the second phase has been counteracted by tightening control of births.

In some of the more developed areas, the death rate has decreased rather more than the birth rate since the end of the nineteenth century so that the rate of natural increase has risen to some extent in spite of the restriction of births. In other cases, the natural increase rate has been lowered considerably; but an equilibrium of births and deaths has not become established in any country of considerable population size (except temporarily in some European countries during the economic depression of the 1930's).[11] On the average for the group of more developed areas, the population growth rate during 1900–1950 dropped slightly below the estimated level of 1850–1900, but it rose again slightly above that level during 1950–1965, as shown in Table 4.5.

Prospect for Continuing Population Expansion

Evidently the modern expansion of population in the world as a whole is far from having run its course as yet. While it may soon reach its climax so far as the geometric rate of growth is concerned, in all likelihood it is not yet near the halfway mark of absolute numerical increase. If the assumptions of the latest United Nations projections are borne out, world population will rise into the range of approximately 5,500 to 7,000 million

by the year 2000 and will still be growing vigorously at that time. Decade by decade, the rates of growth would follow the trends shown in Table 4.6, according to the variants of the projections.

Both the "medium" and the "low" projections imply that the second phase of the modern population expansion—the phase of growth at an accelerating rate in the world as a whole—is now terminating and a third phase is about to begin: a phase in which the rate of growth will diminish, gradually at first and more rapidly later on. By the "medium" projection, the peak rate of growth would occur in the 1970's but the subsequent drop of the rate would be slow, so that the population would still be increasing in the 1990's almost as rapidly as it did in the 1950's. According to the "low" projection, the growth in the 1990's would be well below the present level but still far above the average for the first half of the present century. If the future trend should follow the "high" projection, on the other hand, the world growth rate would go on rising until the 1980's and would not drop below the present level before the close of the century.

Even the "high" projection may be regarded from a certain point of view as a rather conservative one so far as the less developed areas are concerned, since it incorporates an assumption that considerable decreases of fertility will take place during the next few decades in a majority of those areas, although there are only a few areas where such a trend appears already to have set in. Earlier and more widespread fertility reductions in less developed areas are assumed for the "medium" and "low" projections. The growth which might be expected in the absence of any such change in fertility, but with continuing reductions of mortality rates, is represented by another variant of the projections, designated "constant fertility, no migration." According to this, the rate of growth in the world as a whole would speed up progressively throughout the projection period and the population in the year 2000 would reach a figure of approximately 7,500 million.

What of the farther future? It is idle to calculate how many human beings the earth would hold at some far future date if growth should continue at any specified rate, and it is not a much more useful occupation to try to estimate how many could be supported on the planet if all its resources (and perhaps those of the moon and more distant heavenly bodies as well) were fully exploited with the unknown technologies of the future. Without wandering away into those trackless fields, it may be of some value to consider the prospect for continuation and possible termination of the population expansion in the twenty-first century, supposing that the trend would go on evolving along the general lines assumed in the United Nations "medium" projection.

Of course, the main question relates to what may happen in the presently less developed areas. The United Nations projections are founded on the expectation that the population in these areas will undergo a process of demographic transition, associated with future economic and social developments and helped along by population policy measures, such that they would eventually arrive at a demographic position comparable to that of the more developed areas at present. Upon completion of the transition, it is assumed that they would have expectation of life at birth approximating 75 years and fertility rates at about half the present levels in the various less developed areas. The transition would begin sooner and proceed faster in some areas than in others; some would be

far along in the process by the year 2000 whereas others would scarcely have entered it by that time, so far as the decreasing fertility trend is concerned. In the group of less developed areas as a whole, according to the "medium" projection (Table 4.6), the per decade rate of population would reach a peak of 25 per cent in the 1970's and subside by the 1990's to 21 per cent. One may suppose that upon completion of the transition in all areas, the per decade growth rate for the group as a whole would be somewhere around 10 per cent, corresponding roughly to the current level in the more developed group. Supposing further that the decreasing trend of the growth rate would speed up to some extent after 2000, one may imagine the 10 per cent rate being reached perhaps about the year 2040. If so, the total population in the group of less developed areas would increase from the figure of 4,742 million projected for 2000 to something over 8,500 million by 2040, and the world total would then easily have reached the range of 10,000 million—well over ten times the number with which the modern expansion began two centuries ago.

If the third phase is regarded as completed when the world growth rate comes down to the present average for more developed areas, one still has to reckon with the question of a fourth phase. This would be the phase of transition to the world-wide equilibrium of births and deaths which must ultimately be achieved if the end is not to be a catastrophe. Experience up to the present time affords little basis for estimating how long this final achievement might take and how many more thousands of millions might be added in the process. Enough may have been said, though, to illustrate the point that the expansion of world population is not likely to spend its momentum very shortly. It is apparent that the twenty-first century might well surpass the twentieth for magnitude of its addition to the number of the earth's inhabitants, unless so great an increase should exceed possibilities of expanding production of the necessities of healthy life.

Notes and References

1. The importance of this feature has not escaped the attention of historians. Witness, for instance, the inclusion of a chapter on "World Population, 1800–1950," by D. V. Glass and E. Grebenik, in a prominent place in *The Cambridge Economic History of Europe, Volume VI. The Industrial Revolution and After* (H. I. Habakkuk and M. Postan, editors, Cambridge, 1965), part I, chap. 2.

2. See Table A in the appendix [not reprinted here] and the sources cited there.

3. United Nations, *World Population Prospects as Assessed in 1963* (New York, 1966). The population estimates for various dates since 1920, quoted hereinafter, are also from this source.

4. The possibility of an error of about 100 million in the estimate of world population as of 1959 was indicated by calculations presented in the United Nations *Demographic Yearbook* (1960), pp. 1–9. The error margins about the 1965 estimate are likely to have been wider because of increasing uncertainty as to the amount of increase of China's population since the 1953 census. An error of 100 million in the 1965 population estimate for China alone is not out of the question.

5. The estimate of 5 million implies an average density of about 15 persons per 100 square miles of land in regions of favorable climate for habitation by primitive nonagricultural peoples. This corresponds approximately to estimates of average density of the aboriginal population at times of early European contacts, in the non-desert regions of Australia and temperate zones of North America where agriculture was not practiced (with the exception of the very populous northwestern coastal region). Several writers have made similar estimates of the order of magnitude of world population just before the beginnings of agricultural economies. For example, see Julian Huxley, "Population and Human Destiny," *World Review* (January, 1950) and *Harper's Magazine* (September, 1950); Edward S. Deevey, Jr., "The Human Crop," *Scientific American* (September, 1960).

6. John D. Durand, "The Population Statistics of China, A.D. 2–1953," *Population Studies* 13 (1960): pp. 209–256; Julius Beloch, *Die Bevölkerung der Griechisch-Römischen Welt* (Leipzig, 1886), and "Die Bevölkerung im Altertum," *Zeitschrift für Socialwissenschaft*, II. Jahrgang (1899): pp. 505–514, 600–621; Pranatha Vidyalamkara, *A Study in the Economic Condition of Ancient India* (London, 1929), chap. V. On the basis of these indications, the combined population of China, the Roman Empire, and India at the beginning of the Christian Era would seem to have been in excess of 150 million by a conservative assessment, and it might have been twice that number. Information on the contemporary population in other parts of the world is poor, but in view of what is known about the forms and levels of development of economy, it is safe to presume that the total for China, the Roman Empire and India represented a substantial majority of the earth's inhabitants at the beginning of the Christian Era. A range of 200 to 300 million for the world population at that time was suggested in United Nations, *The Determinants and Consequences of Population Trends* (New York, 1953), p. 8. Estimates below 200 million, which have been proposed by some writers, are more difficult to reconcile with the indications given in the works cited above.

7. The contrast remains strong when the calculations are made with combinations of the "low" and "high" variants which minimize the doubling time for the earlier periods and maximize it for the period since 1750. Taking the "low" variant for 8000 B.C. with the "high" for A.D. 1, one obtains an average doubling time slightly in excess of 1,000 years, and a like calculation for the interval from A.D. 1 to 1750 yields a doubling time of slightly less than 800 years. The combination of the "high" variant for 1750 with a "low" estimate of 3,150 million for 1965 gives a doubling time of 122 years.

8. Historians are not agreed, however, either on the causal relationship between economic developments and accelerated population growth in western Europe during the eighteenth and the early nineteenth century, or on the question, whether the growth of population accelerated primarily through falling death rates or rising birth rates.

9. B. H. Slicher van Bath, *The Agrarian History of Western Europe, A.D. 500–1850* (translated from Dutch by Olive Ordish, New York, 1963); Ho Ping-ti, *Studies on the Population of China, 1368–1953* (Cambridge, Mass., 1953) and "The Introduction of American Food Plants into China," *American Anthropologist* 57 (1955): No. 2, Part 1.

10. This division between less developed and more developed areas is a crude one. Within Middle and South America, for instance, Argentina and Uruguay should be placed in the category of more developed areas, while the minority of Oceania's population outside Australia and New Zealand belongs in the less developed category. Such refinements require a more detailed areal classification of historical estimates than the author has attempted. In the United Nations estimates, the totals given for more developed and less developed regions are 1,032 and 2,249 million, respectively, as of 1965.

    It should also be noted that the low estimated growth rate in less developed areas during 1850–1900 is much influenced by the estimates for China, which show almost no net increase of population during this period. Without China, the annual growth rate during 1850–1900 derived from the "medium" estimates for the less developed areas is 0.6 per cent.

11. In the comparison of crude birth and death rates, the balance between the forces of mortality and fertility is obscured by effects of variations in age

structure of the population. A better measure of this balance is provided by the net reproduction rate, which represents the numerical ratio between successive female generations which would obtain if current age-specific rates of mortality and fertility should continue. Among more developed countries at present, net reproduction rates range from slightly less than unity in Hungary and Japan to approximately 1.8 in Canada (1962) and New Zealand (1964). The net rate for the United States in 1963 was 1.56; i.e., such as to increase numbers by slightly more than one-half in a generation. A compilation of these rates will be found in *Population Index,* April issue of each year.

ADDITIONAL REFERENCES

Ackerman, E. A. 1959. Population and natural resources. Pp. 621–648 in *The study of population,* ed. by P. M. Hauser and O. D. Duncan. Chicago: University of Chicago Press.

Ackerman, E. A. 1967. Population, natural resources, and technology. *Annals of the American Academy of Political and Social Science* 369:84–97.

Borgstrom, Georg. 1967. *The hungry planet.* London: Collier-Macmillan Limited. 507 pp.

Borgstrom, Georg. 1969. *Too many; A story of earth's biological limitations.* New York: Macmillan.

Borgstrom, Georg. 1970. The harvest of the seas: how fruitful and for whom? Pp. 65–84 in *The environmental crisis,* ed. by H. W. Helfrich, Jr. New Haven and London: Yale University Press.

Calhoun, J. B. 1962. Population density and social pathology. *Sci. Am.* 206(2):139–148.

Clark, Colin. 1967. *Population growth and land use.* New York: St. Martin's Press. 406 pp.

Day, L. H., and A. T. Day. 1965. *Too many Americans.* New York: Delta.

Deevey, E. S., Jr. 1960. The human population. *Sci. Am.* 203:195–204.

Demko, G. J., H. M. Rose, and G. A. Schnell, eds. 1970. *Population geography: A reader.* New York: McGraw-Hill. 526 pp.

Dickinson, R. E. The Process of Urbanization. Pp. 463–478 in *Future environments of North America,* ed. by F. F. Darling and J. P. Milton. Garden City, New York: The Natural History Press.

Ehrlich, P. R. 1968a. Population, food, and environment: is the battle lost? *Texas Quarterly* 11(2):43–54.

Ehrlich, P. R. 1968b. *The population bomb.* New York: Ballantine. 223 pp.

Ehrlich, P. R., and Anne H. Ehrlich. 1970. *Population, resources, environment—Issues in human ecology.* San Francisco: W. H. Freeman and Company. 383 pp.

Ginsburg, Norton. 1957. Natural resources and economic development. *Annals of the Association of American Geographers* 47:196–212.

Hardin, Garrett, ed. 1969. *Population, evolution, and birth control.* 2d ed. San Francisco: W. H. Freeman and Company. 386 pp.

Hauser, P. M. 1969. *The population dilemma.* 2d edition. Englewood Cliffs, New Jersey: Prentice-Hall, Inc. 211 pp.

Hoagland, Hudson. 1964. Mechanisms of population control. *Daedalus,* Summer, pp. 812–829.

Horsfall, J. G. 1970. The green revolution: agriculture in the face of the population explosion. Pp. 85–98 in *The environmental crisis,* ed. by H. W. Helfrich, Jr. New Haven and London: Yale University Press.

Kennedy, T. F. 1961. Land, food, and population in the kingdom of Tonga. *Economic Geography* 37:61–71.

Keyfitz, Nathan. 1966. Population density and the style of social life. *BioScience* 16(12):868–873. Differences in urbanization in developed and underdeveloped countries.

Keyfitz, Nathan. 1969. United States and world populations. Pp. 43–64 in *Resources and man,* by Committee on Resources and Man, Division of Earth Sciences, National Academy of Sciences/National Research Council. San Francisco: Freeman.

Mudd, Stuart, H. Bokyo, and others, eds. 1964. *The population crisis and the use of world resources.* Bloomington: Indiana University Press. 562 pp.

Osborn, Fairfield, ed. 1962. *Our crowded planet: Essays on the pressures of population.* Garden City, N.Y.: Doubleday. 240 pp.

Paddock, William, and Paul Paddock. 1967. *Famine—1975! America's decision: Who will survive?* Boston: Little, Brown. 276 pp.

Russell, Sir E. J. 1954. *World population and world food supplies.* London: Allen & Unwin. 513 pp.

Sears, Paul B.   1960.   Pressures of population: An ecologist's point of view. *Atlantic Naturalist* 15:80–86.

Stamp, L. D.   1960.   World resources and technology. *Law and Contemporary Problems* 25(3):389–396.

Sukhatme, P. V.   1961.   The world's hunger and future needs in food supplies. *J. Royal Statistical Soc.* 124(4):463–525.

Taeuber, C.   1967.   Population and food supply. *Annals of the American Academy of Political and Social Science* 369:73–83.

Thompson, W. S.   1956.   The spiral of population. Pp. 970–986 in *Man's role in changing the face of the earth,* ed. by William L. Thomas, Jr.   Chicago and London: The University of Chicago Press.

Thompson, W. S., and D. T. Lewis.   1965.   *Population problems.*   5th edition.   New York: McGraw-Hill.   593 pp.

Wagar, J. A.   1970.   Growth versus the quality of life.   *Science* 168:1179–1184.

Williamson, F. S. L.   1969.   Population pollution.   *BioScience* 19(11):979–983.   Stresses impacts of population, especially urbanization.

Zelinsky, Wilbur.   1966.   The geographer and his crowding world; cautionary notes toward the study of population pressure in the "developing lands."   *Revista Geografica,* No. 65, pp. 7–28.

5
SELECTION

EVALUATING THE BIOSPHERE

BARRY COMMONER

Technology works hand in hand with population growth and other basic causes to intensify man's total influence on nature. The per capita consumption of many resources—air, water, some minerals, space, energy—is increasing in industrial and developing countries alike, thus multiplying the impact of growing numbers of people.

Technological developments work on the environment in two ways. Through machines and energy conversion, technology amplifies man's power to change the environment, and science and technology have created entirely new substances and introduced them into nature. Let's look at our increased power first. An exceptional example is the development of devices for war, especially nuclear weapons. Atomic power has brought with it a host of environmental effects—for example, thermal pollution (see Selection 17) and excavation at a new scale (see Selections 31 and 35). Even the more conventional power sources have promoted development of shovels that can move 115 cubic yards of earth at a scoop (see Selection 26) and tanker ships forty times larger than they were forty years ago (see Selection 22). Selection 2 traced man's early technological development and its consequences, but one more example from the past is of interest. Of the 100 or so species of whales, only five were hunted a century or more ago. All five of these threatened animals were hunted because they do not swim too fast to be overtaken by oarsmen and because they float after they are killed. Needless to say, the development of ship engines broadened the extermination to include other species of whales (McVay, 1966).

The increased conversion of energy by man throughout history has

Barry Commoner (b. 1917) is director of the Center for Biology of Natural Systems and is also professor of plant physiology (since 1947) at Washington University, St. Louis, Missouri. He was educated at Columbia University and Harvard University (Ph.D. in cellular physiology, 1941). For six years he was chairman of the Committee on Science in the Promotion of Human Welfare of the American Association for the Advancement of Science. Commoner's research includes studies on physiochemical processes in biological systems and on mechanisms of virus reproduction. In recent years he has published widely concerning the social and ecological consequences of technology, including the book *Science & Survival* (1963).

This article first appeared in *Science Journal*, Vol. 5A, No. 4, pp. 67–72, 1969. Copyright 1969 by Syndication International.

been fundamental to the increasing development and impact of technology (Mesthene, 1970; Ubbelohde, 1963; U.S.D.A., 1960). The biological minimum energy consumption per person, provided by food, is about 100 watts per hour, or 850 kilowatt-hours annual average. As other sources of energy were added, especially firewood, per capita consumption rose and stabilized at about 500 watts per hour. Then, only a few centuries ago, the curve of energy use accelerated as coal, wind, and water were exploited. At present the curve is nearly vertical and Hubbert (1969, p. 237) estimates that the average per capita conversion of energy in the United States is about 10,000 watts hourly, or 85,000 kilowatt-hours per year—a figure several times higher than Commoner's estimate given in this selection. Much of this energy is derived from fossil fuels, and this essentially fixed resource is rapidly being depleted (*op. cit.;* Ayres, 1956). Alternative sources of energy (including nuclear power, of course) must be sought and developed (see, for example, Scarlott, 1956; Daniels, 1967; and Glaser, 1969).

Many chemical pesticides, radioactive materials, and other substances introduced by man into the environment are entirely new. The medical and ecological casualties of such new substances often do not become apparent for some time (Ford, 1970). Unfortunately, our political systems usually allow new technologies to operate before ultimate hazards are known, for "economic" reasons (see Selection 6).

In this selection Barry Commoner shows some effects of technology on the biosphere. He concludes that "Modern technology has so stressed the web of processes in the living environment at its most vulnerable points that there is little leeway left in the system." Our entire system of biological and economic productivity is seen to be severely threatened.

Change must be deep-seated, for evidence demonstrates that "The faults of our new technologies . . . are fundamental, in the sense that they arise from the very success of the new technologies themselves." Again, it is *attitudes* towards the natural world on which our technology intrudes that need to be changed.

Commoner discusses several problems which result through complex chains of reactions from technological developments (e.g., lead pollution, and the increasing resistance of insects to insecticides—see Selection 50 also). Such repercussions, which are common in examples throughout this book, suggest the importance of this phenomenon. In sum, another icon must be shattered: the faith that technology is an undiluted good.

(Editor's comment)

The biosphere—the Earth's thin skin of air, water and soil—is the habitat of man, as it is of all other living things. Like every other living organism, man depends for his life on what the biosphere provides: water, oxygen, food and shelter. Unless the biosphere continues to provide these necessities of life, man and all his works cannot survive. This much is true of man, seen only as an animal.

But man is much more than an animal that requires water, breathes air, gathers food and seeks shelter. His intelligence has given him the power to acquire resources from the biosphere which are far in excess of those involved in bodily maintenance. For example, human beings expend in bodily energy roughly 1000 kilowatt-hours per year; in a highly developed country such as the United States, the actual expenditure of energy per capita is between 10,000 and 15,000 kilowatt-hours per year. This extension of the impact of human beings on the biosphere is, of course, the consequence of technology.

Technology, therefore, powerfully amplifies the effect of human beings on the biosphere. Prehistoric man withdrew from the atmosphere only the oxygen required for respiration; technological man consumes a far greater amount of oxygen to support fires, power plants and chemical processes. The carbon dioxide produced by technological processes has measurably altered the carbon dioxide concentration of the atmosphere.

Apart from the amplification of such natural processes in the biosphere, technology has introduced into the biosphere substances wholly new to it: man made radioisotopes and a wide array of synthetic materials, such as plastics, insecticides, herbicides and numerous industrial materials. These, too, alter the biosphere.

We speak of the collective change in the nature of the biosphere which has been produced by human activity as environmental pollution. In recent years this has become a matter of great public concern. Although the issue has become most intense in highly developed nations, it is now world-wide. The United Nations has recently undertaken to hold an international conference on the problem in 1972.

Public interest in recent changes in the environment has largely been motivated by concern with the resultant assault on the senses, on bodily functions and to a lesser degree on certain economic values. More fundamental, however, is the question of how the deterioration of the environment affects the resources in the biosphere on which human beings and human society depend for their very survival.

In this article I shall try to show, from an evaluation of some of the effects of modern technology on the biosphere, that our tech-nology as it is currently construed forms an intrinsically unstable relationship with the biosphere. Since the stability and integrity of the biosphere are essential for the continued operation of technology, the present situation represents a threat to the survival of our present system of technology—and, indeed, of man himself.

Fundamental Faults in Technology

We are all aware that there is something very wrong with the relationship between technology and the environment—that there is an urgent lesson to be learned from the growing intensity of air pollution, from the continued deterioration of our surface waters, from the proliferating problems of the urban environment. What is less clear is what that lesson is.

A prevalent view is that environmental deterioration is a consequence of relatively minor faults in our technology—the lack of adequate scrubbers on smokestacks, of insufficient treatment of sewage, of the absence of proper fume traps on motor car exhausts. However, there is strong evidence which shows that the environmental deterioration that we are now experiencing is not due to minor faults in our technology, but to major ones.

One example is the fact that much of our present water pollution problem is not due to inadequate utilization of the present technology of sewage disposal, but rather to the very success of that technology. Present sewage treatment procedures were designed to relieve the burden of organic wastes on the self-purifying biological system of surface waters, by converting these wastes to supposedly innocuous inorganic products. This sewage treatment system is quite successful in achieving its aim. The system is failing, however, because its inorganic products are themselves reconverted to organic materials by the green plants that participate in the aquatic biological system, thereby frustrating the initial aim of the treatment process.

Another example is provided by modern agricultural technology, which is largely based on replacing the dwindling natural supply of plant nutrients in the soil by the massive use of inorganic fertilizers, especially nitrogen. These fertilizers do greatly increase the immediate crop yields; but, at the same time, the impoverishment of soil organic matter, by altering the physical character of the soil (especially its porosity to oxygen), sharply reduces the efficiency with which the added fertilizer is taken up by the crop. As a result, unused nitrogen fertilizer drains out of the soil into rivers and lakes, where it joins with the nitrate imposed on the water by the effluent of sewage treatment plants—causing overgrowths of green plants and the resultant organic pollution. The drainage of nitrogen from fertilizer has already destroyed the self-purifying capability of nearly every river in Illinois. In the Midwest and California fertilizer drainage has raised the nitrate level of drinking water supplies above the safe limit recommended by public health authorities.

A third example which is—surprisingly—closely related to the previous ones is the matter of air pollution due to motor car exhaust fumes. This problem originates with the production of nitrogen oxides by gasoline engines; released to the air these oxides, upon absorption of sunlight, react with waste hydrocarbon fuel to produce the noxious constituents of smog. This problem is the direct outcome of the technological improvement of petrol engines; the development of the modern high compression engine. Such engines operate at higher temperatures than older ones; at these elevated temperatures the oxygen and nitrogen of the air taken into the engine tend to combine rapidly, with the resultant production of nitrogen oxides.

In the air nitrogen oxides are readily converted to nitrates, which are then brought down by rain and snow to the land and surface waters. There they add to the growing burden of nitrogen fertilizer, which, as shown in the previous examples, is an important aspect of water pollution. What is surprising is the amount of nitrogen oxides that are generated by our motor traffic: it now amounts to more than one third of the nitrogen contained in the fertilizer currently employed on United States farms. One calculation shows that farms in New Jersey receive about 10 kg of nitrogen fertilizer per year (a significant amount in agricultural practice) from the trucks and cars that travel the New Jersey highways. Another recent study shows that in the heavily populated eastern section of the United States, the nitrate content of local rainfall is proportional to the local rate of petrol consumption. Thus, the emergence of a new technology—the modern petrol engine—is itself responsible for most of the smog problem and for an appreciable part of the pollution of surface waters with nitrate.

As a final example of the intrinsic failure of a technology which bears a considerable responsibility for the present pollution of the environment, we may look at the current status of the insecticide problem. Recent reports from Asia, Africa and Latin America show that the massive use of synthetic insecticides to control pests of cotton, cocoa and other crops has been characterized by serious ecological hazards. With awesome regularity, major outbreaks of insect pests have been induced by the use of modern contact killing insecticides, because such insecticides kill the natural predator and parasitic insects which ordinarily keep the spread of insect pests under control. At the same time there is now increasing evidence that synthetic insecticides are responsible for declining populations of birds and fish. Because of such hazards, and the still poorly understood danger to man, DDT has just been banned in Sweden, and its official registry is being withdrawn in Michigan and other states in the United States.

I have cited these examples in order to illustrate the point that major problems of environmental pollution arise, not out of some minor inadequacies in our new technologies, but because of the very success of these technologies in accomplishing their designed aims. A modern sewage treatment plant causes algal overgrowths and resultant pollution *because* it produces, as it is designed to do, so much plant nutrient in its effluent. Modern, highly concentrated, nitrogen fertilizers result in the drainage of nitrate pollutants into streams and lakes just *because* they succeed in the aim of raising the nutrient level of the soil. The modern high compression petrol engine contributes to smog and nitrate pollution *because* it successfully meets its design criterion—the development of a high level of power. Modern synthetic insecticides kill birds, fish and useful insects just *because* they are successful in being absorbed by insects, and killing them, as they are intended to do.

Other pollution problems arise as the result of a kind of chain reaction from the initial choice of the aim of a new technology. Thus, once the technology of the petrol engine became dominated by the aim of achieving high power, tetraethyl lead was introduced to smooth out the knock in the high powered cylinder explosions—with the resultant spread of near toxic levels of lead into the environment. Another concomitant of the choice of the internal combustion engine over less powerful external combustion techniques for automotive transport is the massive production of carbon monoxide—an increasingly dangerous pollutant of air.

In a sense these results are testimony to the often praised single minded thrust of modern technological development—the progress towards ever more powerful engines or increasingly concentrated fertilizers. This same concentration on the immediate purpose of a technology often leads to blind spots which generate further pollution problems. Thus, in the development of synthetic detergents 30 years ago, the research effort was concerned with cleansing power, economy and other features attractive to the consumer who was to buy them. What the research neglected was the ultimate consumer of anything that goes down the drain—the bacteria in sewage treatment plants and surface waters that must break down the new detergents. As a result, detergents accumulated

in water supplies to the point that they had to be taken off the market in 1965.

Clearly we have compiled a record of serious failures in recent technological encounters with the environment. In each case the new technology was brought into use *before* the ultimate hazards were known. We have been quick to reap the benefits and slow to comprehend the costs.

Costs of Technology

An important question about new technology is: "Does it pay?" Whether we ask this question in the direct language of profit and loss or in the more abstract language of social welfare, the question is crucial. For, sooner or later, every human endeavour —if it is to continue—must pass this simple test: "Is it worth what it costs?"

It might appear that this question has already been answered. After all, power companies are eager to build plants for nuclear fuels rather than fossil ones; farmers rapidly adopt new insecticides, fertilizers and machines. Apparently their cost accounting tells them that the new technologies yield the best available margin between income and costs. I should like to suggest, however, that these calculations are not complete—that certain costs have not yet been taken into account.

For example, what are the true costs of operating a coal fired power plant in an urban area? The obvious costs—capital outlay, maintenance, operating costs, taxes—are of course well known. These costs are always less than the income derived from selling the power, given the requirements of our system of investment. But we have recently discovered that there are other costs and have even begun to put a value upon them.

We now know that a coal burning power plant produces not only electricity but also a number of less desirable things: smoke and soot, oxides of sulphur and nitrogen, carbon dioxide, a variety of organic compounds and heat. Each of these is a *non*-good and costs someone something. Smoke and soot increase the householder's laundry and cleaning bills; oxides of sulphur increase the cost of building maintenance; for organic pollutants we pay the price—not only in dollars or pounds but in human anguish—of some number of cases of lung cancer.

Some of these costs can be converted to economic values. The U.S. Public Health Service estimates the overall cost of air pollution at about $60 per person per year. A reasonable assessment of the overall costs of air pollution to power production from fossil fuels is about one third. This means that we must add to the cost of such power production, for each urban family of four, about $80 per year—an appreciable sum relative to the annual bill for electricity.

What are the costs of pollution from nuclear power plants? Although nuclear power plants are free of chemical pollutants, radioisotopes may be released by these plants and their associated fuel processing installations. Investigators at the University of Nevada, who studied the iodine-131 content of cattle thyroids during the period 1959–61 (in which there were only rare environmental intrusions of iodine-131 from nuclear tests), found that cattle thyroids always contained some iodine-131—about one picocurie per gramme of thyroid. They concluded: "This constant level in the absence of testing indicates that all the iodine-131 in the biosphere is not from nuclear explosions. Some other process(es) must be producing iodine-131 at a reasonably constant rate and in copious quantities. The principal known source of iodine-131 that could contribute to this level is exhaust gases from nuclear reactors and associated fuel processing plants".

Recent results, reported by the U.S. Public Health Service for the period January–March 1968, are even more striking. During this period of time, in which there were no nuclear explosions capable of nationwide dispersal of radioactive iodine, such radioactivity was found in cattle thyroids in Georgia, Iowa, Kansas, Louisiana, North Carolina, Oklahoma, South Carolina, South Dakota, Tennessee and Texas. Average concentrations ranged from 1–68 picocuries of radioiodine

per gramme in the thyroid gland. From comparative studies of the uptake of environmental iodine-131 by cattle and human thyroids it can be estimated that in the foregoing areas human thyroids would be exposed to 0.2–13.6 rads of radiation on a lifetime basis (assuming a constant exposure to the indicated levels).

For iodine-131 the most recent Federal Radiation Council (FRC) guideline states that the average lifetime exposure to the thyroid should not exceed 10 rads. In 1967 the U.S. Atomic Energy Commission (AEC) projected for 1980 a national level of nuclear power production more than 100 times greater than the 1960–61 output; for the year 2000, the AEC projects more than a 1000-fold increase over the 1960–61 level. In simple economic terms this means that, if we are to stay within the present FRC radiation protection guide, the nuclear power industry will need to include in its projected costs of future power development at least a 20-fold improvement in the technique for restricting the release of iodine-131 into the environment. Obviously this will add to present projections of the cost of producing nuclear power, if indeed such an improvement is technically feasible.

The FRC also tells us that there is a human cost associated with the acceptance of its guideline—10 rads of radioactive exposure to the thyroid. It states that "*any* radiation exposure involves some risk". There is indeed some risk associated with a 10 rad exposure. One calculation suggests that a 10 rad dose to the thyroid would increase the national incidence of thyroid cancer about tenfold; another estimate suggests only a 50 per cent increase. In any case, if we accept as the price of nuclear power that citizens of the United States shall accumulate a radiation exposure of 10 rads to their thyroids for however long that industry endures, we must reckon with the knowledge that some people, at some time, will pay that price with their health.

Another example which illustrates the huge economic problem resulting from the environmental failure of modern technology is given by the paper pulp industry. It has been calculated that if the U.S. paper industry were required to meet present water pollution standards, it would need to spend $100 million for each of 10 years. The total profit in the paper industry is $300 million per year, so that, as a minimum, the bill represented by the pollution caused by the paper industry, if paid, would reduce the industry's profit by one third for 10 years.

The total cost of bringing water pollution control up to present standards has been calculated at $100,000 million over the next 10–20 years. The total economic loss from air pollution has been estimated at $11,000 million annually. These sums loom large, even against the U.S. total gross national product. More important, in certain industries they may represent amounts which are so large relative to the profits as to constitute a serious threat to the industry's viability—if it were required to pay the full bill for the hidden costs of operation.

The foregoing evidence shows that the faults in our new technologies which are revealed by environmental pollution are fundamental, in the sense that they arise from the very success of the new techniques themselves. It is also apparent that technology induced pollution considerably reduces the total economic value of a number of technological processes. Far more serious, however, is evidence which indicates that the environmental failures of our major technological innovations constitute a threat to the continued availability of essential resources provided by the biosphere, and therefore to the survival of our entire system of productivity.

Self-Destruction of Modern Technology

All living things including man, and all human activities on the surface of the Earth, including all of our technology, industry and agriculture, are dependent on the great interwoven cyclical processes followed by the four elements that make up the major portion of living things and the environment: carbon,

oxygen, hydrogen and nitrogen. All of these cycles are driven by the action of living things: green plants convert carbon dioxide into food, fibre and fuel; at the same time they produce oxygen so that the total oxygen supply in our atmosphere is the product of the plant activity. Plants also convert inorganic nitrogen into protein, a critical foodstuff. Animals, basically, live on plant produced food; in turn, they regenerate the inorganic materials—carbon dioxide, nitrates and phosphates—which must support plant life. Also involved are myriads of microorganisms in the soil and water. Altogether this vast web of biological interactions generates the very physical system in which we live: the soil and the air; they maintain the purity of surface waters and, by governing the movement of water in the soil and its evaporation into the air, they regulate the weather.

This makes up a huge, enormously complex living machine—the biosphere—and on the integrity and proper functioning of that machine depends every human activity, including technology. Without the photosynthetic activity of green plants there would be no oxygen for our smelters and furnaces, let alone to support human and animal life. Without the action of plants and animals in aquatic systems, we can have no pure water in our lakes and rivers. Without the biological processes that have gone on in the soil for thousands of years, we would have neither food crops, oil nor coal. This machine is our biological capital, the basic apparatus on which our total productivity depends. If we destroy it, our most advanced technology will come to naught and any economic and political system which depends on it will founder. Yet, the major threat to the integrity of this biological capital is technology itself.

Again, it is the effect on the environment which reveals the self-destructive nature of much of modern technology. For instance our reliance on an agricultural technology which is so heavily based on the massive use of inorganic nitrogen fertilizer grossly disrupts the natural nitrogen cycle and threatens to break it down completely. Relying on inorganic nitrogen for crop productivity, we no longer return enough organic matter to the soil. Organic nitrogen in the crops, used as food, appears ultimately in the sewage which waste technology imposes on surface waters—with the disastrous results that have already been described. Moreover, many modern agricultural systems have increasingly cut down on the use of legumes (such as clover) which, with their associated bacteria, are capable of restoring the organic nitrogen content of the soil through fixation of nitrogen taken from the air. Recent studies, especially of tropical areas, suggest strongly that microbial nitrogen fixation is far more important in maintaining the nitrogen cycle than believed previously. There appear to be numerous bacteria, not only in legumes, but widely associated with many different species of plants that are capable of rapid conversion of air nitrogen into useful soil materials. When this subject has been more fully investigated, it is likely to be found, I believe, that such widespread bacterial nitrogen fixation has been a major factor in maintaining the natural fertility of soil not only in the tropics but in temperate zones too.

What is particularly alarming is that this natural process of nitrogen fixation is seriously disrupted by inorganic nitrogen fertilizers. It has been known for some time, from laboratory experiments, that when nitrogen fixing bacteria are exposed to excessive amounts of nitrate, the process of nitrogen fixation stops, and certain of these bacteria may even be unable to survive in such conditions. Some recent experiments indicate that this same inhibitory effect of inorganic fertilizer on nitrogen fixation also occurs in the soil. Thus in one experiment, the investigators were able to achieve a 55 per cent increase in the yield of a rice crop by developing a special strain of nitrogen fixing bacteria that were adapted to a close association with the roots of the rice plant. However, when nitrate fertilizer was added to the system, the crop yield *declined*, apparently because of the inhibitory effect of nitrate on nitrogen fixation.

By depriving the soil of organic forms of nitrogen, from animal wastes, and by suppressing through choice of crops and the excessive use of nitrogen fertilizer the natural processes of nitrogen fixation which sustain the soil's organic nitrogen store, agricultural productivity becomes increasingly *dependent* on heavy use of inorganic nitrogen fertilizer. Under these circumstances we inevitably pollute the surface waters. But worse than that, this process itself makes recovery from the present disrupted state of the nitrogen cycle increasingly difficult.

As the organic nitrogen store of the soil is depleted its ability to support crops *without* excessive use of inorganic fertilizer deteriorates, and any effort to use the soil effectively for crop growth must await an increasingly longer period of restoration. It is probable, as well, that the widespread use of inorganic nitrogen fertilizer is depleting the natural population of microbial nitrogen fixers, upon which we would have to rely in any program to restore the natural efficiency of the soil. This may be a particularly crucial factor, because current research shows that the effectiveness of these organisms depends on the association of a particular species of plant with a very special variety of bacteria. Therefore in any future effort to restore the natural fertility of the soil we shall need to rely on the availability, in the soil, of a wide variety of nitrogen fixing bacteria for successful association with different plant crops. As we continue to use excessive nitrogen fertilizer, we run the risk of wiping out varieties of nitrogen fixing bacteria, upon which any effort at recovery will depend. Thus we are not merely using up the resource represented by the biological system of the soil, we are destroying its capability to recover.

A similar self-destructive course is evident in the consequences of modern insecticide technology. What has happened in attempts to control cotton pests—where the great bulk of synthetic insecticide is used—shows how we have broken down these natural relations and allowed the normal pest regulating machinery to get out of hand. Here the massive use of the new insecticides has killed off some of the pests that once attacked cotton. But now the cotton plants are being attacked instead by new insects that were never previously known as pests of cotton. Moreover, the new pests are becoming increasingly resistant to insecticide, through the natural biological process of selection, in the course of inheritance, of resistant types.* In the Texas cotton fields, for example, it took 50 times as much DDT to control insect pests in 1963 as it did in 1961. The tobacco budworm, which now attacks cotton, has been found to be nearly immune to methylparathion, the most powerful of the widely used modern insecticides.

In certain important cotton growing areas, the insecticides kill off insect predators and parasites, which are often more sensitive to the insecticide than the pest itself. The result: insecticide induced outbreaks of pests. Finally, birds and fish which take up insecticide residues turn out to be sensitive to insecticides, and their populations are reduced.

The technology of insect control by means of synthetic insecticides appears to be nearing the end of the line. If we continue to rely on it, recovery of the natural forms of control will become increasingly difficult. Where restoration of natural biological control has been successful, it has depended on a natural reservoir of insects which are predatory or parasitic towards the pests; if, through widespread dissemination of insecticides, species that make up this natural reservoir are lost, biological control may be difficult to re-establish.

Man's Dependence on Nature

No optimistic assurances, no government guidelines, can give us release from a profound fact of modern life—that the environment exacts a price for the technological intrusions upon it.

The powerful illusion that we can avoid payment of this price is fostered by the enormous accomplishments of technology. Technology is widely credited with many of the good things in modern life: rising agricultural productivity, new sources of power, automated industries, enormously accelerated travel, a vast increase in the volume and speed of communication, spectacular improvements in medicine and surgery. Technology has greatly magnified the wealth that is produced by human labour; it has lengthened our lives and sweetened the fruits of living. All this encourages a faith that technology is an undiluted good.

In a sense, this faith is justified. The modern motor car or the nuclear reactor is indeed a technological triumph. In each is embodied the enormous insights of modern physics and chemistry and the exquisite skills of metallurgy, electronics and engineering. Our success is in the construction of these machines; our failure is in their operation. For once the motor car is allowed out of the factory and into the environment it is transformed. It then reveals itself as an agent which has rendered urban air carcinogenic, burdened human bodies with nearly toxic levels of carbon monoxide and lead, embedded pathogenic particles of asbestos in human lungs, and contributed significantly to the nitrate pollution of surface waters. Similarly, the design and construction of a nuclear reactor epitomizes all the skills of modern science and technology. However, once it begins to operate, it threatens rivers and lakes with its heated waters and human bodies with its radiation.

We have already paid a large price for our illusions. For the advantages of motor transport, we pay a price in smog induced deterioration and disease. For the powerful effects of new insecticides, we pay a price in dwindling wildlife and unstable ecological systems. For nuclear power, we risk the biological hazards of radiation. By increasing agricultural production with fertilizers, we worsen water pollution.

If we are to succeed as inhabitants of a world increasingly transformed by technology, we need to reassess our attitudes to-

* See Selection 50.

wards the natural world on which our technology intrudes. For in the eager search for the benefits of modern science and technology, we have become enticed into a nearly fatal illusion: that we have at last escaped from the dependence of man on the rest of nature.

The truth is tragically different. We have become, not less dependent on the balance of nature, but more dependent on it. Modern technology has so stressed the web of processes in the living environment at its most vulnerable points that there is little leeway left in the system. Time is short. We must begin, now, to learn how to make our technological power conform to the more powerful constraints of the living environment.

References

Science and Survival, Barry Commoner (Viking Press, New York, 1966; Victor Gollancz, London, 1966).

Restoring the Quality of our Environment, President's Science Advisory Committee (Government Printing Office, Washington, D.C., 1965).

The Killing of a Great Lake, Barry Commoner in *Year Book* of *World Book Encyclopedia*, 1968).

Lake Erie, Aging or Ill? Barry Commoner in *Scientist and Citizen* 10:10.

ADDITIONAL REFERENCES

Ackerman, E. A. 1967. Population, natural resources, and technology. *Annals of the American Academy of Political and Social Science* 369:84–97.

Ayres, Eugene. 1956. The age of fossil fuels. Pp. 367–381 in *Man's role in changing the face of the earth,* ed. by William L. Thomas, Jr. Chicago and London: The University of Chicago Press.

Berkner, L. V. 1966. Man versus technology. *Population Bulletin* 22:83–94.

Boffey, P. M. 1970. Energy crisis: Environmental issue exacerbates power supply problem. *Science* 168:1554–1559.

Brown, Harrison. 1956. Technological denudation. Pp. 1023–1032 in *Man's role in changing the face of the earth,* ed. by William L. Thomas, Jr. Chicago and London: The University of Chicago Press.

Committee for Environmental Information. 1970. The space available. *Environment* 12(2):2–9. Discussion of the trends and consequences of electric power production in the United States.

Daniels, Farrington. 1967. Direct use of the sun's energy. *Am. Sci.* 55:15–47.

Ford, A. B. 1970. Casualties of our time. *Science* 167:256–263.

Glaser, P. E. 1969. Beyond nuclear power—the large-scale use of solar energy. *Trans. N. Y. Acad. Sci.* 31(8):951–967.

Hubbert, M. K. 1969. Energy resources. Pp. 157–242 in *Resources and man,* by Committee on Resources and Man, Division of Earth Sciences, National Academy of Sciences/National Research Council. San Francisco: Freeman.

Konecci, E. B., A. W. Petrocelli, and A. J. Shiner, eds. 1967. *Ecological technology; Space-earth-sea.* Transference of Technology Series No. 1, College of Business Administration, University of Texas, Austin. 300 pp. A wide and varied look for technological solutions to spectrum of ecological problems.

McVay, Scott. 1966. The last of the great whales. *Sci. Am.* 215(2):13–21.

Meier, Richard L. 1966. Technology, resources, and urbanism—the long view. Pp. 277–288 in *Future environments of North America,* ed. by F. Fraser Darling and John P. Milton. Garden City, New York: The Natural History Press.

Mesthene, E. G. 1970. *Technological change; Its impact on man and society.* New York and Toronto: New American Library. 127 pp.

National Academy of Sciences, Ad Hoc Panel on Technology Assessment. 1969. *Technology: Processes of assessment and choice.* (Prepared for Committee on Science and Astronautics, U.S. House of Representatives.) Government Printing Office.

Ordway, S. H., Jr. 1956. Possible limits of raw-material consumption. Pp. 987–1009 in *Man's role in changing the face of the earth,* ed. by William L. Thomas, Jr. Chicago and London: The University of Chicago Press.

Rickover, H. G. 1965. A humanistic technology. *Nature* 208:721–726.

Scarlott, C. A. 1956. Limitations to energy use.

Pp. 1010–1022 in *Man's role in changing the face of the earth,* ed. by William L. Thomas, Jr. Chicago and London: The University of Chicago Press.

Stamp, L. D. 1960. World resources and technology. *Law and contemporary problems* 25(3):389–396.

Ubbelohde, A. R. 1963. *Man and energy.* Revised edition. Baltimore: Penguin Books. 224 pp.

U.S. Department of Agriculture. 1960. Power to produce. *Yearbook of agriculture, 1960.* Washington, D.C.: U.S. Government Printing Office. 480 pp.

Weinberg, A. M., and R. P. Hammond. 1970. Limits to the use of energy. *Am. Sci.* 58:412–418. ("The limit to population set by energy is extremely large, provided that the breeder reactor is developed or that controlled fusion becomes feasible.")

6
SELECTION

ENVIRONMENTAL DISRUPTION IN THE SOVIET UNION

M. I. GOLDMAN

Economics, as widely practiced in the world, is another major perpetrator of environmental degradation. Most economic systems not only allow detrimental impacts on nature but also provide incentives for them. Minimization of costs is a fundamental goal of these economies. And, as pointed out in the previous selection, the cost accounting of new technologies does not generally take into account environmental costs. For example, producers shunt the real costs of the effects of air pollution to society (and, increasingly, to the world society).

Most economic decisions are short-run decisions that neglect the future. Hence, we push the costs of our environmental actions onto future generations, as well as onto other contemporary peoples. J. A. Wagar (1970) has discussed this practice and believes that "At some point we must admit that future people are just as important as present people and that we cannot justly discount the value of their environment. Unless we use the environment responsibly, we will greatly reduce the range of opportunities and alternatives available to our decendants."

The basic fault of existing economies has been pinpointed by Kenneth Boulding (in Jarrett, 1966). He characterizes most existing economies as open "cowboy economies," where resources are considered infinite and nature is assumed to be perpetually self-cleansing. We must switch to closed "spaceman" economies which recognize—just as inhabitants of a space capsule do—that the earth has finite amounts of resources and a finite capability to buffer man-made changes. The problem is one of maintaining adequate capital supplies with the *least* possible production and consumption. But this is heresy!

Marshall I. Goldman (b. 1930) is professor of economics at Wellesley College, Wellesley, Massachusetts, and associate of the Russian Research Center, Harvard University. He has a Ph.D. degree in economics from Harvard (1961) and a bachelor's degree from the University of Pennsylvania. His research interests concern marketing and distribution of goods in the Soviet Union, Soviet foreign aid and economic reform, and the economics of pollution. He has authored and edited several books: *Soviet Marketing: Distribution in a Controlled Economy* (1963), *Soviet Foreign Aid* (1967), and *Controlling Pollution: The Economics of a Cleaner America* (1967).

This, of course, harks back to our attitudes about man and nature. The closed, or "spaceman," economic system demands that man consider himself as a part of, not apart from, nature.

This selection evaluates the impact of one particular economy, that of the Soviet Union, on our treatment of environment. Other examples could have been chosen (see Additional References), but this one reveals and explains failures in a centralized and planned economy, a system which is sometimes proposed as a better alternative than capitalism from an environmental standpoint. Goldman compares these two major economies and concludes that at present neither system does much to solve the problems of environmental disruption, which he attributes mainly to technology and industrialization.

Indeed, the Soviet Union's environmental problems, whose scope and magnitude are briefly surveyed here, are much like those in Western Europe and North America. These kinds and causes of environmental decay have recently been confirmed and elaborated on by a Soviet viewer (Bogdanov, 1970). Selection 23, which details a grand Soviet water plan, sheds further light on the consideration of environment in the U.S.S.R.

It is clear that we must reverse our economic policies, including the treadmill pattern of growth, before they strangle us. Economics *should* provide a mechanism for wise environmental management.

(*Editor's comment*)

Introduction

For most political and economic theorists, it comes as something of a surprise to learn that environmental disruption is as serious a concern in the U.S.S.R. as it is in the United States. In theory, environmental disruption is usually regarded as a function of selfish private enterprise where the public good and social costs are ignored. Presumably the absence of private enterprise in socialist and communist societies means that they will not be troubled by environmental disruption.

Typical of such reasoning is Oscar Lange's statement, "The other feature which distinguishes a socialist economy from one based on private enterprise is the *comprehensiveness* of the items entering into the price system. What enters into the price system depends on the historically given set of institutions. As Professor Pigou has shown, there is frequently a divergence between the private cost borne by an entrepreneur and the social cost of production" (17, p. 103). Most economists agree with Lange and Pigou that if under

socialism individual factories were made to include in their pricing calculations the social costs they have caused, environmental disruption would be a much less serious matter.

Whatever the theoretical implications about how socialism should be able to avoid environmental disruption, it is a major problem in the U.S.S.R. and the Russians seem as puzzled as the rest of us that they should be so affected. As the editor of the journal *Soviet Life* has stated: "Why, in a socialist country whose constitution explicitly says the public interest may not be ignored with impunity, are industry executives permitted to break the laws protecting nature" (38, August, 1966, p. 3). Similarly, Academician Innokenty Gerasimov asks, "What is it in our society with its consistent progress in all spheres of life that interferes with a rapid advance in such an extremely important field as the rational exploitation of nature?" (7, p. 75).

To obtain some conception of the magnitude of the problem, we will begin by considering briefly some examples of environmental disruption in the U.S.S.R. The bulk of the study will then be devoted to an analysis of why environmental disruption exists in a state-owned, centrally planned economy. While many of the explanations apply as well to the U.S.S.R. as they do to the rest of the world, we will devote special attention to some factors which seem to be unique to a country like the Soviet Union. Finally we will discuss certain situations where Soviet methods and procedures for coping with environmental disruption seem to be more effective than those of the capitalist countries.

The Dimensions of the Problem in the Soviet Union

Like the United States, the Soviet Union is a vast country. There are enormous areas where population and industry are sparse and where no serious instances of environmental disruption have been recognized. But like the United States, there are also regions where the ecological balance has been severely affected. We will concentrate on how and where the Russians have misused three of their major resources: the air, water and land.

AIR

Most major Soviet cities have an air pollution problem. Tbiliski, like Los Angeles, has air inversions and smog about half of the year (43, May 23, 1968). Leningrad has 40 percent less daylight than nearby Pavlosk (24, p. 73). The level of carbon monoxide in several Armenian cities such as Kirov exceeds the maximum of 6 mg/m^3 at any one time established by the Ministry of Health (12, December 1, 1969, p. 4). A lead paint factory was shuttered in Krasnogorski; 300 boilers and a zinc and lacquer factory were shut down in Cheliabinsk (18, August 9, 1967, p. 10; 4, January, 1968, p. 40). In Sverdlosk and Magnitogorsk, however, there were complaints that several of the factories remained open because the public health authorities had yielded to pleadings and pressures from factory directors (28, June 27, 1969, p. 4).

For some reason, Shchkino, a major chemical complex was erected within view of Leo Tolstoy's historic country estate at Yasnaya Polyana. The estate with its museum and magnificent forests has long served as an internationally known tourist attraction. Because of the air pollutants from the factory, however, some of the forests are dying (18, March 20, 1965, p. 2; 37, May 13, 1968, p. 2). Initially, an oak forest was reported to be threatened. I was told during a visit in the summer of 1968 that a pine forest had also been affected.

The Russians generally have been slow to deal with air pollution. V. Shkatov reports with some concern that of all the factories acknowledged to be a source of air pollution, only 14 percent are fully equipped and only 26 percent partially equipped with purification facilities (29, p. 67).

WATER

There is a variety of misuse of water resources in the Soviet Union. There are persistent complaints in the Soviet press about massive fish kills. Hundreds of millions of rubles' worth of fish reportedly have died needlessly in the Gulf of Finland, the Caspian Sea, and the Volga and Don Rivers (29, p. 67; 28, December 15, 1967, p. 4). At Ashkabad near the mouth of the Volga, destruction of the fish population upset the ecological balance. With most of the fish gone, the mosquito population grew rapidly and there is now a malaria peril in the area (42, September 6, 1969, p. 3).

Oil disposal is a particular menace. Oil discharge from Latvia and Estonia along with that from other non-Soviet areas is not readily dispersed because of the quiescent nature of the Baltic Sea. Until 1965, the oil refineries at Baku along the Caspian Sea had no waste treatment facilities; waste oil was dumped directly into the water. Nor until recently was any effort made to prevent oil tankers from discharging their ballast overboard. However, harbor treatment plants have now been constructed and it is claimed that 40 percent of the oil waste is now prevented from flowing into the Caspian Sea. Nonetheless, complaints still are made about the ineffectiveness of the new treatment plants (2, June 12, 1968, p. 2).

A spectacular illustration of how seriously water courses can be abused occurred in Sverdlosk in 1964. By accident, the oil-covered Iset River was ignited (3, December 21, 1966, p. 15). Substitute Cuyahoga for Iset and Cleveland for Sverdlosk and we could be describing what happened in Ohio in June, 1969 (23, June 29, p. 38).

Another complaint in the Soviet Union about water usage is that water is squandered. The Soviet Union has built a massive system of dams, reservoirs, and irrigation canals. This has led to the diversion of a large enough quantity of water so that there is now serious concern for the future of the Aral and Caspian Seas. The Caspian Sea has dropped 2½ meters over the past twenty years. This had reduced the spawning areas for the Caspian Sea sturgeon by about one-third (4, February 27, 1968, p. 19; 3, October 12, 1966, p. 15). The combined effect of the oil and the smaller spawning area reduced the fish catch in the Caspian from 1,180,400 centners (1 centner equals 125 pounds) in 1942 to 586,300 centners in 1966 (5, p. 110; 3, February 27, 1968, p. 19). The disappearance of the sturgeon has drastically reduced the output of caviar, and the Russians are now talking about producing artificial caviar (30, p. 3). Shrinkage of the Aral Sea has been just as serious. Beginning in 1961, the Aral Sea began to disappear, and by 1969 it had dropped 5½ feet (23, February 16, 1969, p. 15). The average depth of the sea is 50 feet, which suggests that by about 2030 the sea will have turned into a salt marsh.

Indicative of the scope of the water problem in Soviet cities is the fact that as of the 1960 census, 62 percent of the units in the urban housing fund had no running water (16, p. 130). Since at the same time 65 percent of the homes were not connected to any sewage system, there probably was con-

siderable contamination of ground water and hence well supplies. During the past decade, the urban situation has improved markedly but it is likely that the figures are still high in rural areas. However, major cities like Vladimir, Orenburg, Tiumen, Sukhimi, and Voronezh still lacked adequate drinking water as of 1967 (4, no. 4, January 1967, p. 37; 25, June 28, 1969, p. 3). Over 65 percent of the factories in the Russian Republic discharge their sewage without treatment, and 60 percent of the cities and suburbs lack water treatment facilities.

The building of two paper and pulp mills on Lake Baikal is another water issue that has attracted international attention. This unique lake contains more fresh water than any other lake in the world (it has almost twice the volume of Lake Superior, and it is five times as deep). Despite widespread protests that industrialization near the lake would destroy the quality of its water, two paper mills were built and plans for additional mills have been discussed. Stringent controls have been imposed on the mill at Baikalsk (which is already in operation). The second mill (located on the Selenga River, a tributary of Lake Baikal) was ordered to refrain from production until purification equipment had been completely installed and tested (8, February 8, 1969, p. 2). Yet complaints persist about the drinkable, but nonetheless tainted mixture, that is being returned to the lake. As might be expected, this water pollution has had a deleterious effect on the biota of Lake Baikal. The Limnological Institute of the Soviet Academy of Sciences reported that the number of animals and plants has recently decreased by one-half to one-third in the zone where effluent from the Baikalsk plant is discharged (25, February 16, 1969, p. 1).

Many Soviet conservationists argue that no waste at all from the paper plants should be permitted in Lake Baikal. Toward that end, a proposal has been made that a 42-mile-long sewage conduit be built over the mountains to the Irkut River that flows away from the lake. So far, this has not been approved, primarily because it would cost at least 35 million rubles to build. It is unlikely, however, that even the construction of such a bypass would prevent a deterioration in the quality of the lake's water, since the operation of the paper plant affects the water quality in other ways as well. To supply the paper plants with raw material, logs are rafted across the lake. It is estimated that 10 percent of the logs sink and never reach their destination. These sunken logs form a covering over the natural bed of the lake which disrupts the breeding of the fish; they also consume oxygen from the water in the process of decay. Furthermore, the cutting of the timber accelerates erosion on the watershed and siltation in the lake. Some ecologists (such as Gregory Galazi, the director of the Limnological Institute) point out that it is not just the lake which is threatened, but the whole taiga region. Just a few miles from Lake Baikal is Mongolia and the Gobi Desert. The trees serve to hold the desert dunes in check, and there is fear that with deforestation the desert will spread. Some scientists already report that there has been an extension of the dunes area (38, p. 44).

LAND

Environmental disruption in the Soviet Union is not limited to just air and water. As in other industrial societies, there have been severe abuses of other natural resources. In particular there has been concern over the fate of the Black Sea Coast, a good portion of which is resort area. The shoreline is rapidly eroding landward. From 1956 to 1966, much of the seacoast retreated 5 to 16 meters, and, in some places, 40 meters (25, May 10, 1967, p. 2). As the seacoast disappears, so have buildings, such as a sanitarium, fish processing plants, and hospitals. The main rail line from Tuapse to Adler is also on the verge of dropping into the sea.

Similar erosion takes place in the United States, of course, especially during hurricanes. Thus 2,400 homes were destroyed in New Jersey in 1962 because too many people built their homes in the dunes. The Black Sea Coast however is not only menaced by

construction too close to the seashore. Contractors freely avail themselves of coastal sand and pebbles for construction inland; it is estimated that each year they remove as much as 120,000 cubic meters of beach material (8, March 8, 1967, p. 2). Furthermore, natural replenishment of these materials is blocked by the construction of dams and reservoirs along the streams feeding into the Black Sea (25, May 10, 1967, p. 2). Without the pebbles and sand, there is little to cushion the immense impact of the waves as they crash against the coast and erode it.

There have been other recent examples of resource abuse. Kislovodsk, one of the most popular health resorts in the Soviet Union, may have been destroyed because of the economic planners' failure to recognize the uniqueness of the resort's location. High in the Caucasus, Kislovodsk has long been noted for its pure air. A natural protective barrier around the city was denuded recently when it was discovered that the hills around the city were rich in lime. Eight lime kilns were built to process the material; now the city is not only full of smoke from the kilns, but the mountain barrier which blocks the northern blasts of winter is being removed (8, July 13, 1966, p. 5).

Soviet geographers and ecologists are beginning to worry that the entire climatic pattern of Siberia may have been disrupted by man's activities (7, p. 68). The construction of the impressive network of hydroelectric stations and irrigation reservoirs and canals has altered the flow of water to their traditional water bodies. At the same time it has resulted in a significant loss of water through evaporation and seepage into the ground through unlined irrigation canals. On the one hand this has disrupted the traditional moisture patterns so that even rainfall cycles have been changed (7, p. 68). On the other, it has facilitated salination of the soil because seepage from the unlined canals has caused a rise in the water table in what are generally very dry areas (25, July 21, 1969, p. 3). Moreover, the damming up of water bodies has had a pronounced effect on the ground water flow which has been cut off in some instances. It is feared that this may have consequences that are as yet unknown in areas which obtain their drinking water from wells (8, September 10, 1968, p. 3). It is also feared that this restructuring of nature may result in the creation of new desert areas and a disruption of the Arctic Ocean as Russia's northflowing rivers are diverted to the more populous South.

Factors Responsible for Environmental Disruption in the U.S.S.R.

UNIVERSAL CAUSES OF ENVIRONMENTAL DISRUPTION

Just as many of the examples of environmental disruption in the U.S.S.R. could be duplicated in almost any of our countries, so many of the explanations for it are similar. Like the United States, the Russians have had their own population explosion, and more importantly, there has been a marked migration from the countryside to the city. The urban population almost doubled from 69 million in 1950 to 134 million in 1969 (41, p. 7). As ecologists point out today, the dense gathering of population leads to a concentration of waste deposits in the form of nitrates and phosphates which are not as easily absorbed by the land as they once were when people were more widely dispersed.

The inhabitants of industrialized societies may soon be contending with something like a quasi-Malthusian principle. Malthus worried about the population growing faster than the output of food. When the population exceeded the food supply, population growth would be checked in a variety of ways. Perhaps a more appropriate concern for us today should be not so much with the relatively slower growth of food but with the adequacy of our air and water. At least our food supplies can be increased—our water and air supplies are fixed. Unfortunately these fixed resources have to be spread thinly not only because the population is growing larger but because each person in that population consumes a larger and larger amount of air and water each year as industrialization grows in quantity and complexity. The quasi-Malthusian principle suggests that population growth may be checked not so much by a shortage of food but by a shortage of air and water.

Basic to the whole process of industrialization is the transformation of natural resources. Environmental disruption results when too many of the resources are taken from their natural state and subjected to a production or transformation process. Because some by-products in the production process have no value, they are either discarded into the air or water or left on the ground as solids. In addition the produced product is also likely to be discarded after a time, and it too is likely to end up by being put into the water or air or discarded as a solid. The more production there is, the more there is to discard; and as our cities grow, these discarded products become more concentrated. Again excessive concentration places an undue burden on the digestive powers of nature and it becomes harder and harder to convert these wastes properly back into their natural state. The task is made all the more difficult because industrialization has been accompanied by technological innovations which have brought about the use of new and often synthetic compounds. Items such as plastics and detergents which are just appearing in the Soviet Union are not easily decomposed, reprocessed, or recycled.

In addition to the usual technological explanations, there are also political and economic factors that affect all societies. Even though the hazards of environmental disruption are recognized and laws are passed to preserve or protect various natural resources, the laws are often violated. This happens in the U.S.S.R. as well as elsewhere. At Lake Baikal various promises were made, and 50 ruble fines were imposed for infractions of the law by the paper plants. The law was violated because the penalties imposed were obviously not nearly enough of a deterrent to the paper plants. It was much cheaper to pay the fine than improve the machinery or close down the whole operation (3, January 10, 1968, p. 12). In other instances, the law is not enforced. For example, in 1960, the Supreme Soviet of the Ukranian Council of Ministers passed a law prohibiting further deterioration of the republic's natural resources. But deterioration of the air and water in most regions of the Ukraine has become considerably worse since that time (26, November 21, 1968, p. 2). The same kind of law exists in Kirgizia, but no one has ever brought legal action in support of the law (33, July 26, 1969, p. 4).

The problem of law enforcement is hampered because the Soviet Union like other nations has not established clear lines of authority over the different forms of pollution. In the republic of Moldavia, for instance, there are seven different ministers or agencies that are responsible for the quality of the water (36, June 11, 1969, p. 2). These include the Ministries of Land Reclamation and Water Usage, Household Services, Agriculture, Fisheries, Water Power, Merchant Marine, and the Chief Administration for Geology. With so many different agencies involved, the orders that are issued often contradict one another and no one knows who is ultimately in charge.

The temptation to violate the law is facilitated by the fact that the violator faces only his private costs and may be spared the social costs of his action, especially if the law is poorly enforced or if the penalties are minor in scope. Oscar Lange, in the excerpt quoted at the beginning of this selection, assumed this would not happen in a socialist economy. Presumably each government factory would automatically include in its price an amount equal to the social costs it is responsible for. While the Russian accounting system of Khozraschet does involve charging for the direct cost of factors used in consumption, the Russians have been no more successful than other countries in making explicit the social costs arising from an enterprise's activities and in including them in the cost of production. Moreover, as in most societies, the Russians feel the air and water are free goods and therefore there is a reluctance to attach any value to them. This would appear to be an especially inappropriate step in a socialist country. Even if they wanted to, of course, the Russians would find it hard to measure the consumption and discharge of the air and water by a particular user—a difficult task for every country in the world. For a variety of reasons, then, air and water are generally treated as free or undervalued goods. Inevitably this leads to some misallocation. An example of this that can be readily appreciated, especially by Americans, is the overuse of water in irrigation. At best, the Russians make a minor charge for the water and very often it is free. It is estimated that this practice leads to a 25 percent overuse of water (5, pp. 108–9). Not only does this lead to excessive use of water, but the use of excessive water for irrigation often leads to salination of the soil.

The Russians seem to be contending with the same factors that bring about environmental disruption in almost all the other developing countries of the world. Despite Lange's assumption, they have not been able to assign social costs. In fact there are some causes of environmental disruption which seem unique to an economic system like the Soviet Union. We shall examine these factors next.

UNIQUE CAUSES OF ENVIRONMENTAL DISRUPTION IN A SOCIALIST COUNTRY

Although the preceding causes of environmental disruption in the U.S.S.R. are no different from those that exist in the other developed countries, the following explanations are probably different because of the unique nature of the Soviet political and economic system and its relatively recent drive toward industrialization. It is possible to identify at least seven factors unique to an economic society like the Soviet Union.

1. The Soviet Union has only recently become industrialized. Even though the U.S.S.R. produces the world's second largest gross national product, there are some economists who feel the Soviet Union has a long way to go before it is industrially on a par

with the industrialized countries of Western Europe, Japan, and North America. Given their desire to catch up industrially, the Russians place a heavy premium on continued investment for future growth. One consequence is that the Russians are usually reluctant to divert funds from productive to nonproductive uses. Unfortunately, expenditures on pollution control tend to be nonproductive. These funds could otherwise be used to expand production. This dichotomy between pollution control and increased economic growth is even reflected in the words normally used to describe what is being done. "Conserve" for the conservation of nature generally seems to stand in opposition to "produce" for the production of a higher GNP. Although this dilemma is of primary concern to the developing countries, there are also factions within developed countries that struggle over the same issue.

2. Since the Soviet government is the sole owner of all the country's productive resources, it is usually unable to stand aside as an impartial referee between industry and the citizen consumer. Since the state *is* the manufacturer, there is usually an identity of interests between the factory manager and local government officials. Given the traditional success criteria in the Soviet system, the most applauded government official is the one who facilitates the most rapid growth in the region under his jurisdiction. The most important question is How much has production increased in your region? and not How much cleaner are your rivers this year? Therefore, government officials are as anxious as factory managers to increase production with the resources at their disposal. Again this tends to militate against the nonproductive diversion of resources for pollution control. If anything, there is pressure to exploit to the utmost all the natural resources of an area. There is almost an economic imperative to utilize idle resources. What greater temptation could there be for Gosplan and other government organizations which are striving to increase their output or profits than the virgin timber growing on the shores of Lake Baikal.

At one time many of the capitalist countries were under many of the same pressures. Now as more people have become aware of the issues involved, private industrial interests are frequently offset by a variety of diversified and often anti-industrial interests. No governor or prime minister wants economic depression in his area, but to the extent that he has to appeal to the voting power of conservation-minded groups, he is more likely to serve as an impartial mediator. In any case, he is under more and more pressure to divorce himself from the views of the manufacturers which at one time were often shared by many government officials. In contrast, however, as long as increased production remains the prime success criteria for government officials in the Soviet Union, local administrators will be reluctant to worry about anything else than expanding production.

3. Because of the planned and controlled nature of economic growth in the Soviet Union, Soviet economic activity often lurches suddenly and massively in new and sometimes unexpected directions. One of the best examples of this was the decision to expand chemical production in the early 1960s. Another was the effort to triple the output of automobiles from 1970 to 1971. In economic shifts of this nature, it is usually impossible to anticipate all the possible side effects, especially in terms of the consequences on the existing balance in the environment. Gradual change and pilot projects are not always the superior method, but they often make it possible to perceive the hazards of a particular action and, more important, to take preventive measure at an early stage. This is very difficult to do when all attention is focused on the challenges of implementing a vast reorientation of productive effort.

As an illustration of this kind of problem, there are some Russians who have perceived the dangers inherent to air quality in the rapid increase in the number of automobiles on Russian streets. Even though the increased production of automobiles is scheduled for 1970, only recently has the need for automobile exhaust controls been considered (33, December 22, 1068, p. 4; 2, January 30, 1968, p. 2). And even though the problem has been perceived, nothing is apparently being done to provide for the production of exhaust controls. Evidently none of the automotive planners have time for anything but trying to assure the successful operation of the new automobile plant.

4. There is another aspect of the Soviet planning system which affects environmental disruption. Although the Russians are experimenting with more flexible and decentralized forms of managerial initiative and plant operation, essentially tight controls continue to be exercised centrally from Moscow. This commitment to centralized control together with the fact that supervision must be conducted over such a large country tend to make the Russians insist on uniformity in whatever they do. The effect of such a decision is that often no provision is made for the peculiarities of local conditions. Thus one writer complains that the standardized rock wool manufacturing plant the Russians use may be perfectly suitable for most of the country, but not for Moscow (18, March 15, 1966, p. 2). Nonetheless the Izolit Rock Wool Plant with the standardized equipment was built in Moscow and disbursed phenols in the air throughout the neighborhood. K. Bukovsky complained that no provision existed for varying such factories to take account of varying needs (18, March 15, 1966, p. 2).[1]

This restraint on local initiative has also hindered the establishment of pollution control industries. Presumably this might not happen in other socialist societies nor need it be a permanent condition in the U.S.S.R. But as of this writing, there do not seem to be any enterprises in the U.S.S.R. devoted to the development and production of various forms of pollution control equipment. Such lacunae often exist in the Soviet system. The usual reason is that the central planners and allocators of capital simply have not yet decided that such plants are needed. Since almost all decisions of this sort in the U.S.S.R. must await a determination at the center to finance and approve such a project, it often

happens that some areas of development are neglected or come slower than in other societies where there are more autonomous decision-making units. When a decision is made in the Soviet Union, the operation may be a large-scale one with several plants being constructed at once. In the meantime, however, a good deal of sometimes irreparable damage may already have been done. It is very difficult for individuals or a factory enterprise to innovate and anticipate future needs by themselves. In other economic systems, private entrepreneurs or corporate entities with access to their own sources of capital often seek to anticipate existing or projected needs. If they predict correctly, they profit; if they are wrong, they risk the loss of their capital. But this ability to take a risk and the existence of private and decentralized sources of capital generally facilitate the process of innovation and the production of these new products.

The Russians recognize that their system does not provide for such decentralized forms of innovation. Because they regard this as a handicap, one of the goals of their current economic reforms is to make it easier to innovate and produce new products in a decentralized manner.

At the present, the Russians lack not only factories devoted to the production of pollution control decisions but also an adequate number of specialists who can cope with the problems. There have been numerous complaints that many factory managers have nowhere to turn for advice about what to do on those occasions when they are ordered to improve the quality or reduce the quantity of their effluent (12, December 1, 1968, p. 4; 26, February 5, 1969, p. 2; 26, September 20, 1969, p. 1). Moreover in the absence of specialized production facilities, anything that is produced is usually built on a custom basis by a firm specializing in something else. This often results in inefficient equipment and much duplication of effort.

5. An unexpected consequence of our age of rampant technology is that we occasionally find that a well-intentioned program may create unanticipated by-products which have

disastrous consequences for the environmental status quo. One example of this kind of situation is the discovery that individual use of DDT may be destroying whole species of fish and bird life. This is a hazard which confronts all our societies, but when the state gathers all the economic power in its hands, the likelihood of a major disruption seems all the greater since there are no private interests which might challenge government proposals. There are some Soviet scientists who fear that a fundamental disequilibrium in the climatic balance of Siberia has already been set off. This is not to say that similar situations could not occur in nations with private enterprise. Usually, however, the more diverse the economic interests and power, the more difficult it is to move easily toward some massive reconstruction of nature. An exception was the TVA project in the United States, but such an undertaking would probably be much more difficult to arrange in a nondepression period.

An illustration of the kind of fundamental change that is occurring in the U.S.S.R. is described by Academician Innokenty Gerasimov (7, p. 68). He is particularly concerned about the diversion and redirection of rivers in Central Asia and Siberia. As indicated earlier, this has led to a radical change in the moisture cycle. New areas of evaporation have been set up as dams and reservoirs are built while old evaporation basins are reduced because of the diversion of inflowing streams. This has resulted in a disruption of the entire moisture circulation pattern in Central Asia and Siberia. New dust bowls are being created and Gerasimov fears the entire climatic pattern may be affected. Again all of this is also possible in private economics as the American dust bowl experience indicates; but if economic power is highly concentrated, the likelihood of trouble is all the greater today as our technological capabilities increase so rapidly.

6. Another peculiarity of the Soviet system is that until July 1, 1967, all raw materials in the ground were treated as free goods (1, p. 10). This was largely a by-product of the labor theory of value which maintains that land has no value. In addition, private own-

ership of natural resources was prohibited. In effect, this meant to the mine operator that all mine sites were free. Whenever the mine operator had finished extracting the richest ore from one site, he was prepared to move on if he could find another site where he could extract more material at a lower average variable cost. Given this set of circumstances, mine operators did not care much about intensive exploitation of their mine deposits. K. E. Gabyshev states that some mines and oil wells in the U.S.S.R. had only a 50 percent recovery rate (6A, p. 18). A by-product of these extensive mining processes was that large quantities of salvageable raw materials were often discarded which naturally increased the amount of waste to be disposed of. This will happen as long as the mine operator attempts to economize on his use of labor and machinery and not on his use of raw materials. If mine operators and oil drillers in other societies pay rent for their mining and drilling sites, the tendency to move to a new site may be even higher than in the U.S.S.R. if the total average cost of the new site is lower than the marginal cost per unit of output at the old site. However to the extent that mine operators and oil drillers either buy the mineral rights or the property itself, there will be a more intensive exploitation of the minerals if moving to a new location is only possible after the payment of a new purchase price.

In partial recognition of the distortions generated by the refusal to acknowledge the value of unmined minerals, the Russians introduced rent charges as of July, 1967. It is not entirely clear how these rent fees will be applied. Obviously it is intended that miners and drillers will work their raw material deposits more intensively so that there will be less waste. However as indicated earlier, it is possible that unless the charges are properly scaled, rental charges on mining land may actually accelerate rather than retard mine abandonment.

7. In the first few paragraphs of this selection, Oscar Lange was quoted to show how private property owners and producers tend to abuse the social well being. This happens

since private property owners and producers find it very easy to push many of the costs arising from their operations on to the public at large because it is usually very difficult to identify and assign such social costs and because we have accepted through tradition that it is proper that society at large should assume certain private burdens. What normally happens is that the private property owner determines he can make a profit by putting his land to a certain use. He does this by comparing *only* the private benefit he will obtain from this prospective (and possibly destructive) use with the private cost or loss he will bear by not being able to utilize the land in its original state. In other words, the private owner calculates that the price he is offered for the land is greater than the value he presently enjoys from using the land as it is. So he agrees to sell the land and allow it to be used in some new way. This is purely a calculation of private benefit versus private cost. Any social costs in this new use of the land which exceed the expected social benefits are normally not the concern of the private landowner. There are few if any economists today who would dispute that this happens. Even Milton Friedman acknowledges the inability of the private market system to prevent pollution and he deplores this shortcoming (6, p. 30).

As we have seen, however, the inability to assign social costs is a problem not limited to private enterprise economies alone. The Soviet Union shares this inability. The Soviet factory manager tends to react in the same way as the private property owner described above.

Strangely enough, however, there appear to be some instances where an absence of private property may actually lead to environmental disruption that a system of private property might have prevented. This happens when a private property holder calculates that his private benefit from converting the land to some new destructive use is *not* greater than the private cost he would bear from yielding the land. For example, a resort owner or a landowner might feel that he would prefer to keep his beach as a swimming area for himself or even preserve it for

future sale at a much higher price to a larger resort owner rather than sell it to a contractor who would tear up the beach and use the sand and pebbles for construction purposes.

The absence of private property and a failure to make such a calculation seems to be the major explanation for the erosion of the Black Sea Coast. Because no one could lay claim to the pebbles on the shorefront, they were a free good for anyone who could cart them away. Consequently, there was no need to worry about infringing on the rights of the Black Sea Coast resort and estate owners who, if they existed, might have been willing to pay somewhat more for the sand and pebbles as a beach resort than the contractors who would have been willing to pay for the pebbles for use in construction. This should have been a simple case of private cost and private benefit measurement.

Of course, it often happens that private landowners decide that it is to their benefit to sell their land to some mineral exploiter (especially if the mineral is oil instead of sand and pebbles). Then, despite the fact that the social costs may be greater than the private costs or social benefits, the land may still be abused. Yet the existence of private costs does afford some protection and until the day comes when social costs can be assigned, the absence of private cost calculation may actually cause some forms of environmental disruption in a socialist society that might be avoided in a capitalist society.

Advantages

Having categorized many of the reasons why environmental disruption exists in the U.S.S.R., let us now examine in what ways the Soviet system is better able to prevent or cope with it. We shall see that some of the factors we previously regarded as intensifying environmental disruption may in other ways diminish it.

One of the points made earlier was that the unbalanced nature of Soviet growth in some respects retarded the production of goods for the consumer. This may result in less environmental disruption. If fewer synthetic or exotic compounds have been developed, there are likely to be fewer noxious by-products. For example, the Russians were criticized for many years because of their seeming inability to provide high-test ethyl gasoline for use in their automobiles. Now it turns out that they may have done the right thing. The Soviet Union is the only country in the world that does not put ethyl lead in most of the gasoline used in its automobiles (8, February 15, 1967, p. 3). (The question remains, however, as to how much this was a case of foresight and how much it was a case of where failure turned out to be success.) Similarly, for a long time, one of the reasons given for the decision not to produce more automobiles was the desire to avoid the increase of air pollution.

To the extent that the Russians have deemphasized the production of consumer goods, there is less waste to discard. In the same sense, the absence of private enterprise has meant less innovation for pollution control, but it has also meant less product proliferation, especially of those items that have been designed for easy disposal. Consequently, the Russians do not have to contend with disposable bottles, nor with disposable diapers. Again, what may appear to be a fortuitous circumstance to a conservationist may have been an entirely unintended by-product of an emphasis on heavy industry.

The Russians are also fortunate that their labor costs are relatively low. (This is not necessarily a built-in characteristic of their economic system.) This helps to explain the inordinate amount of manpower devoted to clearing the sidewalks and streets. The cheap cost of labor helps to explain why there are few empty bottles on Russian streets. Bottles are in short supply, and their deposit value is high. Therefore it pays to devote labor to picking up and sorting a valuable commodity. Cheap labor also explains why so many societies including the Soviet Union can handle their sanitation problems despite the absence of a sewer system. The cost of collecting night soil is often offset by the value it has as a fertilizer.

In the same way, the junk business in the Soviet Union is still a vital industry. In the United States where the price paid for waste paper, metal, oil, or used clothing has trouble keeping up with the rise in the price of unskilled labor, it has simply become unprofitable to collect certain kinds of scrap. This disrupts the recycling process which most ecologists view as one of the best solutions for environmental disruption. In most American cities, the owner must pay a junk man to haul away an old car. In 1969, over 50,000 cars were abandoned on the streets of New York City. Because of the completely reversed set of relative values in the U.S.S.R., no one would ever dream of abandoning a car on a Moscow street. It would be repaired and used even if it were an antique, or it would be cannibalized and reused as a set of spare parts.

As reflected in the previous paragraph a traditional complaint about the Soviet price system is that it is arbitrary and frequently bears no relationship to relative scarcity values or market clearing prices. While this creates all kinds of other difficulties, conceivably some day it could be used to advantage in contending with environmental disruption. Just as the Russian prices in the past have not reflected land and capital costs, so some future Russian pricing officials might decide that all Russian products henceforth will include some specified markup intended to reflect social costs. It would be still hard to determine just what social costs are attributable to which products, but implementation of this decision in the U.S.S.R. should be easier to carry out than it would be in other societies.

Because government agencies own the utilities as well as most of the buildings, it is relatively easy for the Russians to avail themselves of certain economies of scale in dealing with environmental disruption. For example the Russians make extensive use of a system of centrally supplied heat (4, no. 24, June 1966, p. 13). In densely populated urban areas, this eliminates the need for each building to have its own furnace and hot water heater. In most large Russian cities, heat and hot water are supplied to an entire neighborhood by the Teplovaia Elektrotsentral' or TETs. Of all heat consumption in the U.S.S.R., 50 percent is provided centrally and 65 percent of this central heat is supplied by a network of TETs stations (15, November 1967, p. 9). Similar systems exist in most large American cities, but individual landlords are not compelled to participate in the system. Consequently some of the advantages are lost. Since a TETs-type system normally makes possible a hotter fire and better smoke-control equipment, there is a more efficient form of combustion and less air pollution. The installation of such a system in Alma Ata made it possible to eliminate 436 individual building furnaces and boilers (10, December 16, 1969, p. 4).

Occasionally there are drawbacks to such a system. Some Russian engineers have complained about the difficulty of providing for the varying heat needs of different buildings and rooms in many of the TETs operations (19, September, 1969, p. 21). It also happens that sometimes the gains derived from concentrating the combustion in one large furnace and boiler are offset by the need to send steam and hot water long distances. There is a tradeoff point where the loss of heat necessitates so much extra combustion that the effluent is actually increased by not having individual boilers and furnaces.

The enormous power of the state in the U.S.S.R. can also be an advantage. Thus when a law is passed, even though enforcement is sometimes weak, it can frequently be very effective. Moreover the state can simply decree the establishment of a natural preserve. In other countries with private property, this can be a very expensive and time-consuming process. It is necessary to overcome numerous court suits and protests and to compensate private property holders, as happened when the American government tried to establish a national park on Cape Cod. Usually there is no such concern in the U.S.S.R. although there may nonetheless be problems of poachers and even industrial exploitation of some of the raw materials on the preserves. As of 1969, the U.S.S.R. had 80 such preserves encompassing 6,400,000 hectares (7, p. 78).

Conclusion

The existence of environmental disruption in the U.S.S.R. comes as a disappointment to those who hope that somehow there will be societies which will be able to avoid it. If the study of the U.S.S.R. demonstrates anything, it shows that industrialization, not private enterprise, is the primary cause of environmental disruption. The question remains, Can there be industrialization without environmental disruption in any society? Since the answer seems to be no, it should come as no surprise that despite the differences in the economic systems, the solutions for environmental disruption in the U.S.S.R. seem to be no simpler than they are in the United States. It is with some disappointment that an American reads statements by M. Loiter implying that the Russians should adopt American methods to solve the Russian problems (20, p. 80). My study was motivated in large part by the hope that a study of the Russian experience would suggest solutions for environmental disruption in the United States.

Currently the proposals for the solution of environmental disruption in the U.S.S.R. seem to be no more advanced than they are in the United States. One thing does seem clear, however: unless the Russians change their ways, there seems little reason to believe at this point that a strong centralized and planned economy has any notable advantages over other economic systems in solving its environmental disruption.

NOTE I am grateful to Leonard Kirsch of the University of Massachusetts, Boston, for his many suggestions and to Elena Vorobey of the Library of the Russian Research Center, Harvard University, for her valuable bibliographical help. This paper was presented at the Conference on Environmental Disruption in Tokyo, March 8–14, 1970, sponsored by the Standing Committee on Environmental Disruption of the International Social Science Council.

[1] This incident involved standards that were too low. Of course the standards could have been set at a high level to satisfy Moscow's needs. Then they would have exceeded the requirements for the rest of the country.

References Cited

1. Allakhverdian, D. "Ekonomicheskaia Reforma i Voprosy Khozrascheti", *Voprosy Ekonomiki*, November 1968, pp. 3–15.
2. *Bakinskii Rabochii.*
3. *Current Digest of the Soviet Press.*
4. *Ekonomicheskaia Gazeta.*
5. "Ekonomicheskaia Otsenka Prirodnykh Resursov," *Voprosy Ekonomiki*, January 1969, pp. 108–110.
6. Friedman, Milton. *Capitalism and Freedom*, Chicago: University of Chicago Press, 1962.
6A. Gabyshev, K. E. "Ekonomicheskaia Otsenka Prirodnykh Resurov i Rentnye Platezhi," *Vestnik Moskovskogo Universiteta Seriia Ekonomika*, No. 5, 1969, pp. 17–23.
7. Gerasimov, I. "Nuzhen General'nyi Plan Preobrazovanikh Prirody Nashei Strany," *Kommunist*, No. 2, January 1969, pp. 68–79.
8. *Izvestiia.*
9. Kadulin, V. "Primor'e—Krai Bogateishikh Bozmozhnostei," *Kommunist*, No. 11, July 1967, pp. 81–91.
10. *Kazakstanskaia Pravda.*
11. Khachaturov, T. "Ob Ikonomicheskoi Otsenke Prirodnykh Resursov," *Voprosy Ekonomiki*, January 1969, pp. 66–74.
12. *Kommunist.*
13. *Kommunist Tadzhikistana.*
14. *Komosomolskaia Pravda.*
15. Kop'ev, S. F. "Razvitie Teplosnabzheniia v SSSR," *Vodosnabzhenie i Sanitarnaia Tekhnika*, November 1967, p. 9.
16. Kriazhev, V. G. *Vnerabochee Vremia i Sphera Obslyzhivaniia*, Moscow, Ekonomika, 1966.
17. Lange, Oscar. Taylor, Fred M. *On the Economic Theory of Socialism*, Minneapolis: University of Minnesota Press, 1938.
18. *Literaturnaia Gazeta.*
19. Livchak, F. Kop'ev, S. F. "Puti Dalneishego Sovershenstvovaniia Tekaniki Otopleniia i Teplosnabzheniia," *Vodosnabzhenie i Sanitarnaia Tekhnika*, September 1969, p. 21.
20. Loiter, M. "Ekonomischeskiia Mery Po Ratsional'nomu Ispol'zovaniiu Vodnykh Resursov," *Voprosy Ekonomiki*, December 1967, pp. 75–86.
21. *Meditsinskaia Gazeta.*
22. Nekresov, V. "Nauchnye Problemy Razrabotki General'noi Skhemy Razmeshchenie Proiz Voditel'Nykh Sil SSSR." *Voprosy Ekonomiki*, September 1966, pp. 3–14.
23. *New York Times.*
24. Petrianov, I. "Vodoushnaia Sreda Problemy i Persecktivy Ee Zaschity," *Kommunist*, No. 11, July 1969, pp. 71–80.
25. *Pravda.*
26. *Pravda Ukrainy.*
27. *Pravda Vostoka.*
28. *Rabochaia Gazeta.*
29. Shkatov, V. "Tseny Na Prirodnye Bogatstva i Sovershenstvovanie Planovogo Tsenoobrazovanuia," *Voprosy Ekonomiki*, September 1968, pp. 67–77.
30. *Sotsialisticheskaia Industriia.*
31. *Sovetskaia Belorussia.*
32. *Sovetskaia Estonia.*
33. *Sovetskaia Kirgiziia.*
34. *Sovetskaia Latviia.*
35. *Sovetskaia Litva.*
36. *Sovetskaia Moldaviia.*
37. *Sovetskaia Rossiia.*
38. *Soviet Life.*
39. *Soviet News.*
40. Sukhotin, I. U. "Ob Otsenkakh Prirodnykh Resursov," *Voprosy Ekonomiki*, December 1967, pp. 87–98.
41. Tsentral'noe Statisticheskoi Upravlenie, *Narodnoe Khoziaistvo V SSSR V 1967 Gody*, Moscow, Statistika, 1968.
42. *Turkmenskaia Iskra.*
43. *Zaria Vostoka.*

ADDITIONAL REFERENCES

Bogdanov, B. 1970. *Conservation and economics.* Ekonomika Selskovo Khozyaistva [Agricultural Economics], No. 2, pp. 7–11. English translation in *Current Digest of the Soviet Press* 23(19):7–9.

Boulding, Kenneth. 1966. Economics and ecology. Pp. 225–234 in *Future environments of North America*, ed. by F. Fraser Darling and John P. Milton. Garden City, New York: The Natural History Press.

Burke, A. E. 1956. Influence of man upon nature—the Russian view: a case study. Pp. 1035–1051 in *Man's role in changing the face of the earth*, ed. by William L. Thomas, Jr. Chicago and London: The University of Chicago Press.

Clawson, Marion. 1966. Economics and environmental impacts of increasing leisure activities. Pp. 246–260 in *Future environments of North America*, ed. by F. Fraser Darling and John P. Milton. Garden City, New York: The Natural History Press.

Dale, E. L., Jr. 1969. The economics of pollution. *The New York Times Magazine,* April 19, pp. 27–29 + .

Ginsburg, Norton. 1957. Natural resources and economic development. *Annals of the Association of American Geographers* 47:196–212.

Goldman, M. I. 1967. *Controlling pollution: The economics of a cleaner America.* Englewood Cliffs, N. J.: Prentice-Hall.

Herfindahl, O. C., and A. V. Kneese. 1965. *Quality of the environment: An economic approach to some problems in using land, water, and air.* Baltimore: The Johns Hopkins Press for Resources for the Future, Inc. 96 pp.

Jarrett, Henry, ed. 1966. *Environmental quality in a growing economy.* Baltimore: Johns Hopkins Press for Resources for the Future. 173 pp.

Matley, I. A. 1966. The Marxist approach to the geographical environment. *Annals Assoc. Amer. Geogr.* 56:97–111.

Meier, R. L. 1966. Technology, resources, and urbanism—the long view. Pp. 277–288 in *Future environments of North America,* ed. by F. Fraser Darling and John P. Milton. Garden City, New York: The Natural History Press.

Rose, Sanford. 1970. The economics of environmental quality. Pp. 65–87 in *The environment,* by the Editors of Fortune. New York: Perennial Library.

Ross, C. R. 1970. The federal government as an inadvertent advocate of environmental degradation. Pp. 171–187 in *The environmental crises,* ed. by H. W. Helfrich, Jr. New Haven and London: Yale University Press.

Shul'ts, V. L. 1968. The Aral Sea problem. *Transactions of the Central Asian Hydrometeorological Scientific Research Institute* (Trudy SANIGMI), No. 32(47), pp. 3–7. English translation in *Soviet Hydrology: Selected Papers,* Issue No. 5, 1968, pp. 489–492.

Wagar, J. A. 1970. Growth versus the quality of life. *Science* 168:1179–1184.

Smog over New York. Photo by Aero Service Corporation, Division of Litton Industries.

THREE MAN'S IMPACT ON ATMOSPHERE AND CLIMATE

"Air pollution continues to grow. Its growth has more or less paralleled man's increasing use of technology, with the result that the most technologically advanced areas of the world are also, with few exceptions, the areas of most severe air pollution. This is due to the overuse of air for waste disposal."

INTRODUCTION

Air is man's most vital resource. But we are spoiling our atmospheric environment with alarming speed, with consequences largely unknown. Philip A. Leighton has remarked (in Selection 10) on this anomalous situation: "The physical requirements of life are limited and their use must be regulated. Since earliest history man has been devising systems for the ownership, protection and use of land and food, and, more recently, of water. Last of all to become subjected to regulation is air. Here the tradition of free use is still dominant. This . . . does not parallel the urgency of man's needs or his ability to adapt his surroundings to meet those needs. He can live indefinitely away from land, he can go several weeks without food and several days without water, but . . . his need for air is never further away than his next breath."

Hence, we look first at man's impact on the atmosphere and on climate. We are changing the air mainly by using it for waste disposal. Pollution may be defined as the process of contaminating a medium with impurities to a less desirable level of quality. The selections in this part focus on air pollution in its many aspects, including its ramifications. Such understanding is requisite background for wise management of air resources. The central concept of wise management is to determine desirable levels of air quality and then restrict emissions correspondingly. However, the determination of allowable levels of pollution depends on an understanding of the relationship between pollutant concentrations and their environmental effects.

Selection 7 begins by examining air conservation and discussing the major kinds of air pollutants, their origin, dispersal, and fate.

The primary sources of pollution and the annual amounts emitted in the United States from each are discussed in Selection 8. The per capita amounts, now a ton yearly, are growing as a result of increased industrialization and combustion of fuel.

Selection 9 proceeds to describe what happens to pollutants after they are emitted into the atmosphere. Various meteorological factors, as well as the nature of the source, determine how fast and to where contaminants will diffuse. Dilution of continuous pollution by fresher air is essential, or pollutants will accumulate, causing disasters such as those in London in 1948, 1952, and 1962.

Further geographical aspects of air pollution are discussed in Selection 10, using the outstanding example of air contamination from use of hydrocarbon fuels, particularly by automobiles. The emission trends and prospects for control are not bright.

Pollution by automobiles is but one of many causes of the

artificial climate of cities, the subject reviewed in Selection 11. Man's urban structures and activities have wrought numerous and pronounced changes in city climate.

These urban effects on climate are no longer confined to the city itself. Selection 12 examines a fascinating case where urban pollution has changed the weather a considerable distance away—the controversial La Porte weather anomaly.

Man is almost surely modifying climate on a global scale now. The complex causes of such changes are considered in Selection 13, demonstrating that the whole earth ecosystem must be recognized as one integrated system and that man is a potent force in the system.

The final article in this part (Selection 14) surveys the important modern problem of noise in the environment.

FURTHER READINGS

American Association for the Advancement of Science. 1965. *Air conservation.* AAAS Publication No. 80.

Battan, L. J. 1962. *Cloud physics and cloud seeding.* Science Study Series. New York: Doubleday. 144 pp.

Battan, L. J. 1969. *Harvesting the clouds; Advances in weather modification.* Garden City, New York: Doubleday. 148 pp.

Bryson, R. A., and J. E. Kutzbach. 1968. *Air pollution.* Association of American Geographers, Commission on College Geography, Resource Paper No. 2. Washington, D.C. 42 pp. Excellent resumé of the sources, spread, and significance of air pollution.

Cooper, C. F., and W. C. Jolly. 1969. *Ecological effects of weather modification.* University of Michigan, School of Natural Resources, Department of Resource Planning and Conservation. 159 pp. A comprehensive review of demonstrated and potential effects.

Esposito, J. C. 1970. *Vanishing air; The Ralph Nader Study Group report on air pollution.* New York: Grossman. 328 pp.

Evelyn, John. 1961. *Fumifugium: Or, the inconvenience of the aer and smoak of London dissipated.* London: W. Godbed for G. Bedel. 26 pp. (Reprinted by the National Society for Clean Air, 1961, 41 pp.)

Fletcher, J. E. 1967. Weather modification. *Science* 158:276–277.

Gates, D. M. 1970. Weather modification in the service of mankind: promise or peril? Pp. 33–46 in *The environmental crisis; Man's struggle to live with himself,* ed. by H. W. Helfrich, Jr. New Haven and London: Yale University Press.

Goldsmith, J. R. 1962. Effects of air pollution on humans. In *Air pollution,* ed. by A. C. Stern. New York: Academic Press.

Haagen-Smit, A. J. 1958. Air conservation. *Science* 128: 869–878.

Heimann, H. 1967. Status of air pollution health research. *Archives of Environmental Health* 14:488–503.

Iglauer, Edith. 1968. The ambient air. *The New Yorker* 44:51–52 + (April 13).

Kahan, A. M. 1968. Weather modification effects on environment. Pp. 81–89 in *Man and the quality of his environment,* ed. by J. E. Flack and M. C. Shipley. Boulder: University of Colorado Press. Treats effects of international weather modification.

Larson, R. I. 1966. Air pollution from motor vehicles. *Annals New York Academy of Science* 136:277 ff.

Lave, L. B., and E. P. Seskin. 1970. Air pollution and human health. *Science* 169:723–733.

McDermott, W. 1961. Air pollution and public health. *Scientific American,* October, p. 206 ff.

Malone, T. P. 1967. Weather modification: Implications of the new horizons in research. *Science* 156:897–901.

Middleton, J. T. 1967. Air quality as a controlling factor in life processes. Pp. 67–79 in *Biometeorology,* ed. by W. P. Lowry. Corvallis, Oregon: Oregon State University Press.

NAS-NRC. 1966. *Weather and climate modi-*

fication, problems and prospects. Final report of the Panel on Weather and Climate Modification to the Committee on Atmospheric Sciences. National Academy of Sciences–National Research Council. Washington, D.C.

Neiberger, Morris. 1970. *Artificial modification of clouds and precipitation.* World Meteorological Organization, Technical Note No. 105. 33 pp. Scales and status of weather modifications; physical basis; evaluation of attempts to increase precipitation and reduce fog, heat, and lightning by cloud seeding.

Ridker, R. G. 1967. *Economic costs of air pollution.* New York: Praeger. 214 pp.

Schaefer, V. J. 1956. Artificially induced precipitation and its potentialities. Pp. 607–618 in *Man's role in changing the face of the earth,* ed. by W. L. Thomas. Chicago: University of Chicago Press. Summarizes the status of rainmaking in the mid-1950s.

Sewell, W. R. D., ed. 1966. *Human dimensions of weather modification.* University of Chicago, Department of Geography, Research Paper 105. 423 pp.

Smith, Alan R. 1966. *Air pollution; A survey, carried out for the society of chemical industry, into the causes, incidence, and effects of air pollution.* New York: Pergamon Press. 203 pp.

Stern, A. C., ed. 1968. *Air pollution.* 2d edition. New York: Academic Press. 3 Vol.

Thornthwaite, C. W. 1956. Modification of rural microclimates. Pp. 567–583 in *Man's role in changing the face of the earth,* ed. by W. L. Thomas, Jr. Chicago: University of Chicago Press. Includes an historical review of man's influence on climate.

Wolman, A. 1968. Air pollution: Time for appraisal. *Science* 159:1437–1440.

World Health Organization. 1961. *Air pollution.* New York: Columbia University Press. 442 pp. A dated, but still useful, collection of authoritative papers on various aspects of air pollution.

AIR CONSERVATION AND THE KINDS OF AIR POLLUTANTS

AIR CONSERVATION COMMISSION

What are the major types of air pollutants produced by man? What is the nature of these substances? Knowledge of answers to these questions should precede consideration of the sources, distribution, and effects of pollution in later selections. This selection provides these answers, and also introduces some fundamentals of air conservation. Finally, the transport and the fate of pollutants are treated briefly.

First, what is the chemical composition of "normal" air, the quality standard against which atmospheric pollution is measured? The four major gases of the air are nitrogen, oxygen, argon, and carbon dioxide. Together they comprise 99.99 percent of the gaseous mixture. Following are estimates of the concentrations in parts per million of gases in the earth's normal dry atmosphere at sea level (after Tebbens, 1968):

GAS	CONCENTRATION (PPM)
Nitrogen	780,900
Oxygen	209,400
Argon	9,300
Carbon dioxide	315
Neon	18
Helium	5.2
Methane	1.0–1.2
Krypton	1
Nitrous oxide	0.5
Hydrogen	0.5
Xenon	0.08
Nitrogen dioxide	0.02
Ozone	0.01–0.04

The Air Conservation Commission was established by the American Association for the Advancement of Science (AAAS) to study air conservation in relation to public policy, including control, legal, socioeconomic, and urban aspects. The chairman of the commission was James P. Dixon, M.D., president of Antioch College.

Water vapor, also commonly present as 1 to 3 percent of the atmosphere, is important in relation to the effects of air contaminants. For example, as sulfur trioxide joins water vapor it is converted to dilute sulfuric acid. It can be seen that some of man's effluents, such as carbon dioxide and oxides of nitrogen, are normal constituents of the atmosphere; they are considered to be pollutants only when they exist in abnormally high concentrations. Other pollutants, such as carbon monoxide and sulfur dioxide, are absent (or nearly so) from "normal" air.

Most air pollution is a direct product of man's deliberate conversions of energy. Other atmospheric modifications by man are also occurring. One interesting and threatening process that has recently come to light involves the possible reduction, rather than increase, of a vital air constituent—oxygen. Photosynthesis by some marine phytoplankton is drastically reduced by only minute amounts of DDT in the water (Wurster, 1968). Thus, a primary source of the earth's atmospheric oxygen supply is now being affected, although there have been no detectable changes in the percent by volume of atmospheric oxygen since 1910 (Machta and Hughes, 1970). Our oxygen supply is not in danger of serious depletion (Broecker, 1970); other environmental changes, including numerous kinds of air pollution, are much more threatening.

Two more kinds of air pollutants related to modern, technological man are treated only briefly in this selection. Evidence is accumulating that particles of biological poisons—insecticides, herbicides, etc.—are commonly found in the atmosphere and are carried throughout the world by air currents (Risebrough and others, 1968; Frost, 1969; also see Selection 39). Radioactive gases and particles from nuclear power plants and especially from nuclear weapons also contaminate the atmosphere (e.g., Holland, 1969; Jammet, 1969; and Slade, 1968). Like biocides, radioactive material is dispersed widely in the atmosphere. The biological accumulation of both types of substances and their effects on organisms are dealt with in Parts 7 and 8.

(Editor's comment)

Introduction

The initial evolution of man took place in an environment that, whatever its other hazards, was characterized by the virtually unlimited availability of what we now refer to as "pure air." That is, man's respiratory apparatus was evolved to breathe a mixture of nitrogen, oxygen, water vapor, and small traces of carbon dioxide, the rare gases, and a few other simple substances. Although there were natural outbreaks of pollution from volcanoes and the like, the usual response was migration; there was not enough

preference for one area over another to hold a tribe in an uncomfortable location. Then mankind began to build or seek shelter for itself, and discovered the use of fire—the deliberate release of stored energy to modify the local environment.

The discovery of how to control fire also marked the start of air pollution. As tribes settled in villages, and villages grew into cities, the levels of concentration of the combustion products, and of the other by-products of human living, increased. This early urbanization was accompanied by the first evidences of industrialization, which further added to the general pool of atmospheric substances to which man was not genetically accustomed. However, since the average human life span was only a few decades, the slow chronic workings of airborne toxicants probably did not have time to seriously affect the human system before death claimed it.

The past century has seen a radical change in man's existence. Improvements in nutrition, agriculture, communication, hygiene, and medicine have extended the human life span tremendously. During this same period, improvements in heating methods and standards of sanitation were so great that the level of insult to the organism probably decreased substantially. As industry continued to introduce new substances into the air, it also put into effect improved industrial hygiene practices, which further decreased the exposure of the individual to high concentrations of many toxic materials.

This environmental improvement, however, much as it may have ameliorated conditions inside homes and factories, was accomplished in most cases by removing the objectionable substances to the outside air. This process, accompanied by rapid industrial development and concentration, began producing, in the outdoor air of the cities, the phenomena that had previously occurred indoors. There were even a few catastrophic, acute pollution episodes, such as the one at Donora, Pennsylvania.

Meanwhile, increasing population and increasing longevity, together with a high standard of living, generated pressure from all population groups for cleaner air. The youngest, the oldest, and those whom medicine had spared without fully curing make up groups who are especially sensitive to pollutants. The younger adults, with long lives ahead, object to any threat to longevity. All ages and conditions have become intolerant of discomfort and annoyance.

Finally, the enormous increase in world population now taking place, an increase apparently destined to continue, raises an entirely new kind of problem. The oxygen in our atmosphere is not a permanent feature, but is rather the result of a delicate balance between its formation in the photosynthetic process and its removal by animals, by combustion, and principally by the slow oxidation of minerals on the earth's surface. This balance completely renews the oxygen supply in the atmosphere in the course of a very small number of millenia. A change of a few percent in the rate of either production or removal could well result in an enormous change in the steady oxygen level.

Although it is unlikely that man or his machines could "breathe" enough oxygen to seriously contribute to upsetting this balance, he could, either through nuclear war or through sheer numbers, destroy enough green plants to seriously decrease the renewal rate of atmospheric oxygen. At present there are no data on which to base a quantitative statement; however, the possibility seems very real. It has also been postulated that the amount of carbon dioxide that human activities are injecting into the atmosphere may be sufficient to upset the global balance.*

These considerations suggest that the time has come for man to stop regarding the atmosphere as unlimited and to undertake its conservation.

It may be worthwhile at the outset to restate the fundamental nature of atmospheric pollution. All creatures live by a process of converting one form of energy into another. Man has raised himself above the animal level to the extent that he deliberately converts this energy by processes outside the limitations of his body. All extensions of the human senses, of the human frame, and of the human muscle, which is to say, our tools and the trappings of civilization, use this energy. Energy conversion has certain material by-products. When they become airborne, in sufficient concentrations to be troublesome to man, we call the resulting airborne material "air pollution." At a very high stage of technology, pollution may also occur from by-products of processes other

* The carbon dioxide content of the atmosphere has increased 11 percent since 1870. Selection 13 discusses postulated effects of this change. (*Editor's note*)

than the liberation of energy, but they are seldom as widespread as the energy by-products.

Some material by-products from this process of energy conversion are inevitable. The only choices are the relative proportions of the various by-products and the way in which they will be removed. Nothing is gained by removing them from the air if we thereby pollute the waters of nearby streams and make them unusable, or contaminate the soil to the extent that it will not support vegetation. In some respects, the problem resembles the old one of attempting to bury a pile of dirt.

In order to obtain an optimum balance of benefit and risk for ourselves and for our posterity, the problem of air conservation is to select the appropriate means for either disposing of or using these by-products and to employ appropriate forms of energy. The definition of such an optimum—the risks we are prepared to take for the benefits we enjoy—is not a matter of scientific judgment, but rather one of moral and ethical judgment; hence, it will not be discussed here. Mankind will probably face enough moral decisions during the next decade to keep occupied; probably the precise setting of an optimum balance will not receive a great deal of attention. However, mankind must ultimately make such a decision; it must decide what the balance of risk and benefit will be. We cannot abandon our technology without relapsing into savagery. But we cannot continue our present course of technological development without the risk of making the earth unfit for human habitation.

The Pollutants

The sources, then, of air pollutants are anywhere that energy is converted under human direction. From the smallest hearth fire to the latest factory, all contribute their share. The pollutants are even greater in number than the sources. However, a small number of groups of substances comprise the vast bulk of human emissions to the atmosphere

and they have been singled out for special attention in this report.

The greatest single product of the energy conversion processes is of least concern here—water. Only in very rare instances can it qualify as a pollutant. Occasionally, the vapor from the stack of a large factory may reduce visibility on a nearby highway. But normally, water vapor does not represent an air pollution problem.

GASES

Carbon dioxide. Carbon dioxide is next in quantity of the waste products produced by our use of organic fuels. It is naturally abundant in the atmosphere, and mankind is well adapted to living with widely varying levels of it. However, while water vapor precipitates out of the atmosphere to join the oceans, carbon dioxide normally remains in a gaseous state for a long time. The liberation of this gas has been so great that we have already increased the global concentration by a substantial figure. This increase has had no effect on any known living organism. However, carbon dioxide is intimately involved in the mechanism that maintains the overall temperature of the earth. Although so many factors are involved in this overall atmospheric heat balance that it is impossible to evaluate the effect of any given increase in atmospheric carbon dioxide, a continued increase over a long period could possibly change the global climate. And, if such a change were to involve an increase of the earth's temperature, thereby causing a large portion of the global ice caps to melt and the oceans to rise, available land area would be reduced at precisely the time when more land is needed for an increasing population. In the light of this possibility, the use of fossil fuels as the principal source of our energy should be continually evaluated.

Carbon monoxide. The complete combustion of carbonaceous fuels produces carbon dioxide; the incomplete combustion, characteristic of many processes involving the conversion of energy, yields carbon monoxide.

In American cities, the primary source of this gas is the automobile. Carbon monoxide begins to be hazardous to most human beings at concentrations of about 100 parts per million (ppm) if experienced over a period of several hours. Particularly susceptible individuals may be affected at lower levels. Although the toxic level seems very high when compared with other pollutant gases, this level has actually been reached occasionally in areas where traffic is heavy; more frequent occurrences may be expected unless automotive emissions can be effectively controlled.

Sulfur dioxide. In addition to substances emitted in massive amounts, there are a variety of materials that normally occur in much lower concentrations. However, these materials are much more toxic. Sulfur dioxide and the sulfuric acid that forms when the gas comes in contact with air and water seldom reach levels above a few parts per million. However, the present consensus is that these two substances have been principal factors in all the air pollution disasters of recent history, including the London smog of 1952 in which some 4000 persons died. (There are many scientists who believe that factors as yet undiscovered contributed materially to these deaths, but most of them would identify sulfur dioxide and sulfuric acid as the major causative agents, perhaps combined with soot or other particles.) Sulfur dioxide results primarily from the combustion of coal or oil, both of which contain substantial percentages of sulfur in various chemical forms. To some extent in the combustion itself, and to a greater extent in the external atmosphere, sulfur dioxide is converted by the action of atmospheric oxygen and water to sulfuric acid. Sulfur dioxide by itself is extremely irritating to the upper respiratory tract in concentrations of a few parts per million. Sulfuric acid appears as a fine mist that can be carried deep into the lungs to attack sensitive tissues. In addition, droplets of sulfuric acid carry absorbed sulfur dioxide far deeper into the system than the free gas alone could penetrate, thus spreading the effect of this irritant over the entire respiratory tract. On the other hand, because of the ease with which sulfur dioxide is converted into sulfuric acid and sulfates, its lifetime in the atmosphere is seldom more than a few days. Consequently, it would not be expected to accumulate in the atmosphere.

Hydrogen sulfide. Hydrogen sulfide can result from a variety of industrial and other processes, but it usually enters the atmosphere as a result of the accumulation of industrial wastes in stagnant waters. Here bacterial action reduces the sulfur-containing compounds to hydrogen sulfide, which is relatively insoluble in water. It has the well-known odor of rotten eggs and it is highly objectionable. In high concentrations, it is also rapidly lethal. However, there are only a few cases in which concentrations of hydrogen sulfide in the open atmosphere exceeded the level of mere nuisance. (In one such case, a score of deaths resulted from an accidental release from a refinery in Poza Rica, Mexico.) The bacterial processes described constantly occur in nature, and by far the bulk of the total sulfur found in the atmosphere comes from natural causes. However, concentrations at any one place are usually not sufficient to be detected by the senses, or, in fact, by any but the most delicate measuring devices.

Nitrogen oxides. There are six known oxides of nitrogen, and there is presumptive evidence for a seventh. However, only two are normally considered as pollutants: nitric oxide and nitrogen dioxide. These are what might be called "status symbol" pollutants. Only a highly mechanized and motorized community is likely to suffer serious pollution from them. Nitric oxide, the primary product, is formed when combustion takes place at a sufficiently high temperature to cause reaction between the nitrogen and oxygen of the air. Such temperatures are reached only in highly efficient combustion processes or when combustion takes place at high pressure. A great deal of nitrogen is fixed in the latter way in automobile cylinders. Electrical power plants and other very large energy-conversion processes will also fix nitrogen in this fashion. However, in most cities, automobiles are the largest single source.

Nitric oxide is generally emitted as such into the atmosphere. However, a complex of processes, some of them photochemical in nature, may convert a substantial portion of the nitric oxide to nitrogen dioxide, a considerably more toxic gas and the only important and widespread pollutant gas that is colored. As a result, nitrogen dioxide can significantly affect visibility. Nitrogen oxides are also liberated from a variety of chemical processes, such as in the manufacture of guncotten and nitric acid. In large-scale pollution, these sources are usually less significant than the broad area source represented by vehicular traffic.

Ozone. There is little or no ozone emitted as such into the atmosphere. However, this gas, which is extremely toxic, is formed in the atmosphere on sunny days as a result of the interaction of nitrogen oxides with certain organic compounds.

Hydrogen fluoride. In addition to the inorganic gases just mentioned, nearly any other objectionable inorganic gaseous material that is used in industry can become a pollutant if it escapes into the atmosphere. However, these are not the general emissions of what might be called the metabolic processes of civilization and they are likely to be restricted to a few locations. Consequently, only one of them, hydrogen fluoride, deserves separate attention. Because of its extreme toxicity for some living organisms, it is likely to be an acute problem wherever materials containing fluorides are processed. Hydrogen fluoride is apparently taken up from the air by nearly all plants, and certain species are damaged by concentrations as low as 1 part per billion. Furthermore, since vegetation tends to concentrate the fluoride that it receives, continuing low atmospheric levels of fluoride can produce toxic levels in forage and probably in some leafy vegetables as well. The manufacture of phosphate fertilizer, the smelting of certain iron ores, and the manufacture of aluminum are all sources of hydrogen fluoride gas as well as of some particulate fluoride.

Organic gases. The organic gases are very numerous. The chemical process industries inevitably release into the atmosphere some of almost everything they manufacture. However, only a few general classes need separate consideration since a number of the organic materials that can be identified in the atmosphere appear to have no adverse effects.

Probably the simplest organic substance significant to air pollution is ethylene. Aside from its participation in the "smog" reaction, it is a potent phytotoxicant (plant damaging agent) in its own right. Concentrations of a few parts per billion, for example, are extremely damaging to orchids, and only slightly higher concentrations adversely affect the growth of tomatoes. Ethylene, like the bulk of other simple hydrocarbons, emanates in part from industrial sources, but it is primarily a product of automotive exhaust.

The higher members of the series to which ethylene belongs, the olefins, appear to have no direct effect upon vegetation or animal life. However, when they (together with several other classes of organics) are exposed to sunlight in the presence of nitrogen dioxide or nitric oxide, an extremely complex reaction sequence ensues. The end products appear to be ozone, aldehydes, and a variety of organic compounds that contain nitrogen. In adequate concentrations, this mixture injures plants and irritates the eyes and mucous membranes in human beings. There is some indication that animals are also affected. This reaction was first noticed in Los Angeles, and is therefore popularly referred to as the "Los Angeles smog reaction." The substances needed for this reaction can be produced by the right combination of industries, but they are present in almost ideal concentrations in automotive exhaust. Consequently, the presence of this type of pollution is characteristic of areas having a high density of automobile traffic.

Some of the aldehydes characteristic of the Los Angeles smog can also arise from other sources. Formaldehyde and acrolein, which are particularly irritating to the eyes and nose, are found in the smoke of poorly operating incinerators and also in stockyards and a number of other sources.

Mercaptans, which are organic substances related to hydrogen sulfide, are among the most odorous materials known. Aside from chemical processes that directly employ or produce these compounds, they are undesired by-products of Kraft paper mills and of some petroleum refineries.

Finally, there is a large class of organic vapors generally referred to as "solvents." They escape from such processes as dry cleaning and painting. They are very diverse chemically, and some of them can probably participate in the smog reaction. Others have objectionable odors. Most of them are toxic to some degree, although it would be difficult to produce toxic concentrations over any period of time in the open air.

PARTICULATE MATTER

Aside from these gases and vapors, large quantities of more or less finely divided particulate matter are put into the air or are formed there as a result of human activities. The largest single particle in nearly all urban atmospheres is dust. This word is used here to denote soil from areas denuded of vegetation, whipped up by natural wind, by the passage of vehicular traffic, or by agricultural activities. For the most part it is without physiological effect, but it is a very substantial nuisance. The particle sizes are usually large, so that, under most circumstances, such dust will not travel great distances. Obvious exceptions occur during times of high winds, as was demonstrated during the dust storms of the middle 1930's.

In many cities, the next most prevalent substance among the airborne particles is soot. Soot is very finely divided carbon clumped together into long chains and networks. Because the individual particles are so fine, they present an enormous surface per unit weight. This surface is extremely active, and it can absorb a large variety of substances from its environment. Soot generally carries with it a substantial load of heavy hydrocarbons that are formed simultaneously with it in smoky flames. These hydrocarbons include organics that are either known or are suspected causes of environmental cancer on sufficiently prolonged contact. Soot can also act under some circumstances in the same manner as sulfuric acid mist; that is, it can absorb vapors that would normally be removed in the upper respiratory tract and carry them deep into the lungs. In addition to all the known or suspected physiological effects, soot is a nuisance because it obscures visibility and soils buildings and clothing. The fall of combined soot, dust, and other particulate materials on a single square foot of horizontal surface in a city may easily exceed a pound per year.

Another variety of fine particles is one of the end results of the photochemical smog reaction. The nature of the particulate matter formed is not understood, but it is oily, not easily wetted, and of a size that is highly effective in obscuring visibility.

The typical urban atmosphere also contains particles caused by practically every process carried on within the city. There are lead salts from the combustion of leaded gasoline and particles of airborne ash from all the solid and liquid fuels burned in the area. The metallurgical industries, the manufacture of fertilizer, the storing of grain, and the milling of flour all add particles that are characteristic of their own processes.

Finally, there is a quantity of material generally referred to as "resuspended matter," refuse dropped into the streets or onto the ground, there to be slowly pulverized and blown into the air. Bits of newspaper, residue of plant matter, particles of glass and tire rubber, all go to make up the complex found suspended in the atmosphere of a typical city.

There are two additional classes of particulate matter which, while not of peculiarly urban origin, have had a substantial impact on human well-being and have received a great deal of attention recently. The first of these are the economic poisons. They include insecticides, herbicides, and other chemicals used by man. A number of them are normally disseminated through the air, and some portion may well find its way substantial distances from the intended site of application. While many of them are toxic to man, they can also harm other forms of life not intended as their targets.

The second category is radioactive material. There are three major sources of radioactive gases and particles. The first is research, which is generally not an important source of contamination except in the case of a major accident. The second is nuclear power plants, which almost continuously give off some gaseous materials. There is no evidence to date that their accumulation in the atmosphere is a major hazard. The nuclear power industry is said to be one of the most carefully controlled of all industries on the face of the earth. However, an accidental discharge can distribute highly toxic concentrations over a rather large area. The final source is, of course, nuclear weapons. They belong in a special category, not because of any chemical or physiological difference in the compounds involved or in their effects, but because the political and economic considerations that govern their use are so special.

Transport of Pollutants

Once a pollutant, or a group of pollutants from a given source, has been ejected into the air, its movement with the air will depend upon a number of factors.

Particles larger than approximately 1 micron are significantly affected by gravity. They tend to settle out from the air and are eventually deposited, the distance from the source usually depending on the size of the particle. In addition to gravity, the movement of pollutants is affected by turbulent diffusion. The wind contains many eddies, ranging in size from millimeters to miles, and these eddies tend to disperse the cloud of pollutants.

Less important over short distances, but of crucial importance on a large scale, are the effects of aggregation and growth. Particles in a pollution cloud tend to increase in size, sometimes by collisions that form larger aggregates, and sometimes by the condensation of vapors on them, with or without chemical reaction. This process may occur in and under water clouds, where the water droplets may form on the particles, thereby increasing their size, or falling raindrops may collide with the particles, thereby carrying them to the ground.

At substantial wind speeds, pollutants are rapidly removed from the point of origin and turbulent diffusion usually dilutes them below the level of significant effect within a short distance. However, under some conditions, turbulence can bring the plume from a stack to the ground in great loops at a point quite close to the source and before extensive dilution has occurred, resulting in brief exposure to extremely high concentrations. Thus, a period of strong winds is likely to be characterized by low mean values of pollutants, with occasional high peaks of short duration near the point of origin. When the air is still, both horizontally and vertically, all pollutants tend to stay near their source and to blend in slowly with other sources in the same area. Generally the result is a very high average level of pollution with a few abrupt short-term variations.

While the horizontal travel of pollutants is largely controlled by wind velocity, the primary factor that regulates the vertical dispersal of pollution is the vertical profile of temperature. The rate of temperature change with height is referred to as the "lapse rate." In the lower atmosphere the temperature usually decreases with increasing height.

A substantial amount of misinformation has been disseminated concerning the effect of lapse rate on pollution. The facts are rather simple. According to well-established physical law, if a parcel of air is carried from a low altitude to a high one, it will expand with the decreasing pressure and its temperature will decrease, provided there is no exchange of heat with its surroundings. By the same token, if the parcel of air is taken to a lower altitude without gaining or losing heat, its temperature will increase. For a given change of altitude, the corresponding temperature change is constant and determinable. This rate of change is referred to as the "adiabatic lapse rate."

If the actual lapse rate is greater than this theoretical rate, a parcel of surface air that begins to rise will continue to do so. This situation is called "unstable." If, on the other hand, the change in temperature with height is less than the adiabatic rate, surface air that begins to rise will tend to sink back to the surface; this is called a "stable" lapse rate. If there is no change in temperature with altitude, or an increase, the atmosphere will be particularly stable. The difference between this and the unstable situation is one of degree, not of kind. An increase in temperature with altitude, a so-called inversion, is not a unique phenomenon.

During unstable conditions, there is a great deal of vertical mixing, in addition to whatever horizontal dispersion the wind may induce, and so the dilution of pollutants takes place in three dimensions. On the other hand, under conditions of high stability, vertical dispersion will be greatly inhibited; if this is accompanied by low winds, a layer of highly polluted air may build up over a large area, such as an entire city or an entire basin.

Shifts from stable to unstable conditions and back are set in motion by three major forces. Since winds tend to have vertical eddies, and since rapid vertical air motions tend to be adiabatic, the wind helps to establish a precisely adiabatic lapse rate. The sun, by heating the surface more than the air, tends to steepen the lapse rate and thus acts as a force for instability. Conversely, at night the ground loses more heat by radiation than the air does, which tends to make the surface colder than the layer overlaying it. This cooling of the ground is a force working for stability. Under most circumstances, there is a continuous diurnal cycle from stability to instability and back. When, for a variety of reasons, this cycle is broken, a serious accumulation of pollutants is possible.

The Fate of Pollutants

For virtually every known pollutant, there are natural processes that tend to remove it from the atmosphere, thus preventing man from smothering in his own by-products.

Reference was made earlier to the tendency of particulate pollutants to coagulate, to increase in size, and to fall. Rain and snow carry large amounts of both particulate and gaseous pollutants out of the atmosphere and into the soil and the water of the earth. Trees and grasses act like the fibers of an enormous filter mat to collect particles and some gases.

The oxygen of the air combines with many pollutants, either directly or indirectly, gradually changing them into forms that are more readily removed. In many cases, sunlight plays a role in this reaction, and frequently particulate matter is formed from gases. These particles can then enter the cycle of filtration, aggregation, and washout, and can thus be removed from the atmosphere. It is worth noting that the droplets of sulfuric acid that have been implicated by many as contributing to the death toll in London, and the photochemical smog that is characteristic of the West Coast, are actually steps in the atmosphere's own process of self-purification. The misfortune is that these intermediate products are physiologically active and that they frequently form in heavily inhabited areas.

A few miscellaneous substances do not participate rapidly enough in the reactions of photochemical oxidation to be removed by that process. The outstanding examples are methane and a few of its relatives and carbon monoxide. They are ultimately destroyed by oxidation, entirely in the gas phase, and become carbon dioxide, although the rate of destruction is not known. Carbon dioxide appears to be removed effectively by direct solution in the ocean, the disposal point for most of the soluble inorganic substances. The capacity of the ocean to ultimately consume such materials by dilution is enormous. However, our rapid production of carbon dioxide seems to be outstripping the ocean's ability to remove it from the atmosphere. It appears that roughly one-third of the carbon dioxide put into the air by combustion remains there and, as noted earlier, it may have an effect on the world's weather.

Thus, the atmosphere has tremendous powers to dilute, disperse, and destroy a large variety of substances that man, for one reason or another, elects to discharge into it. Pollution occurs when these processes cannot keep up with the rate of discharge, and when this happens, only one more factor is needed to constitute pollution—a susceptible receptor, such as man.

Man removes some of the pollutants from the air, for if he did not, the pollutants would not affect him. (The only exception is when pollution is manifested by loss of visibility. This can have economic repercussions in delaying aircraft schedules, in increasing automobile accidents, and by making a location less favorable to paying tourists, or its effect may be purely aesthetic.)

Pollutants collect on, and may affect, buildings, plants, and animals, including man. They enter the lungs of creatures that breathe the air. With the pollution density of the atmosphere increasing rapidly, the possibility of any pollutant leaving the atmosphere without contacting man, his property, plants, or animals is becoming increasingly small. Although it is certainly necessary to use the atmosphere as one of the places to dispose of our wastes, it is going to become more and more difficult to find a parcel of air that can be used for waste disposal and that can adequately detoxify its load of pollutants before it is needed again.

ADDITIONAL REFERENCES

Alexander, Peter. 1965. *Atomic radiation and life*. 2d edition. Baltimore: Penguin Books. 296 pp.

American Chemical Society. 1969. *Cleaning our environment: The chemical basis for action*. Washington, D.C.

Broecker, W. S. 1970. Man's oxygen reserves. *Science* 168:1537–1538.

Cohen, J. M. and C. Pinkerton. 1966. Widespread translocation of pesticides by air transport and rain-out. Pp. 163–176 in *Organic pesticides in the environment*. Advances in Chemistry, Number 60. Washington, D.C.: American Chemical Society.

Frost, J. 1969. Earth, air, water. *Environment* 11(9):14–33. Reviews evidence for atmospheric transport of chlorinated hydrocarbons.

Holland, J. Z. 1969. Radioactive pollution of the atmosphere. Pp. 125–132 in *Biological implications of the nuclear age*. Washington, D.C.: U.S. Atomic Energy Commission, Division of Technical Information.

International Atomic Energy Agency. 1968. *Assessment of airborne radioactivity*. 776 pp. Proceedings of 1967 Symposium, including fifty-six papers.

Jammet, H. P. 1961. Radioactive pollution of the atmosphere. Pp. 381–432 in *Air pollution*, by World Health Organization. New York: Columbia University Press.

Machta, L., and E. Hughes. 1970. Atmospheric oxygen in 1967 to 1970. *Science* 168:1582–1584.

Risebrough, R. W., R. J. Huggett, J. J. Griffin, and E. D. Goldberg. 1968. Pesticides: Trans-Atlantic movements in the Northeast trades. *Science* 159:1233–1236.

Slade, D. H. 1968. *Meteorology and atomic energy 1968*. Washington, D.C.: U.S. Atomic Energy Commission. 445 pp.

Tebbens, B. D. 1968. Gaseous pollutants in the air. Pp. 23–46 in *Air pollution*, 2d edition, Volume 1, ed. by A. C. Stern. New York: Academic Press.

Woodwell, G. M. 1968. Radioactivity and fallout: the model pollution. *Garden Journal* 18(4):100–104. (Also pp. 159–169 in *Challenge for survival*, ed. by P. Dansereau. New York: Columbia University Press.)

World Meteorological Organization. 1970. *Meteorological aspects of atmospheric radioactivity*. Technical Note, No. 106. 169 pp.

Wurster, C. F. 1968. DDT reduces photosynthesis by marine phytoplankton. *Science* 159:1474–1475.

SOURCES OF AIR POLLUTION

**U.S. DEPARTMENT OF HEALTH,
EDUCATION, AND WELFARE**

Where does the garbage in the sky come from? Knowledge of the sources, and the amounts of various pollutants from each, is necessary before air pollution can be controlled. Generally it is easiest to control atmospheric pollutants at their source, because, once emitted, they typically become widely dispersed.

The amounts, given here for the United States alone, are staggering—a ton (of the five types of pollutants discussed here) per person each year. Automobiles are the greatest source of pollution, producing nearly two-thirds of the carbon monoxide and over one-half of the hydrocarbons. Fuel combustion in stationary sources, especially electric power plants, yields two-thirds of the sulfur oxides. Industry, too, adds nearly 30 million tons of waste to the air annually.

Toxic levels of carbon monoxide frequently occur on busy downtown streets in American cities, causing measurable impairment of physiological functions such as vision and psychomotor performance. Daytime levels in Manhattan often soar to between 25 and 30 ppm—an impact on the body equivalent to that of two packs of cigarettes a day. It has been suggested that the celebrated surliness of some New York City taxi drivers and policemen may actually be a symptom of carbon monoxide exposure (*Wall Street Journal*, May 26, 1970). Details of air pollution by the automobile have been discussed by a U.S. Department of Commerce publication (1967).

Mechanization is not the only cause of atmospheric pollution, however. The world's deserts typically produce blankets of dusty air. Forest fires, especially from slash-and-burn agriculture in the tropics, may fill the air with dense clouds of smoke. Volcanic eruptions are a natural source of dust; the atmospheric effects of Mt. Agung on Bali persisted

This selection is extracted from two United States government publications: (1) "Progress in the Prevention and Control of Air Pollution." 1970. Third Report of the Secretary of Health, Education, and Welfare to the Congress of the United States. Senate Document No. 91–64. U.S. Government Printing Office, Washington. 39 pp. (2) "The Sources of Air Pollution and their Control." 1968. U.S. Department of Health, Education, and Welfare. Consumer Protection and Environmental Health Services, Public Health Service (PHS Publ. No. 1548). U.S. Government Printing Office, Washington. 15 pp.

for nearly three years following its eruption in 1963 (see Bryson, Selection 13).

This selection also mentions the existing and planned air quality standards by the United States government.   Sulfur dioxide is one of the first pollutants for which levels have been set.   Average annual concentrations of SO_2 above 0.04 ppm adversely affect health—yet this level has long been exceeded in Chicago, Philadelphia, Washington, St. Louis, and other large cities (Tebbens, 1968).   As realistic standards are set for other atmospheric pollutants it will similarly be shown that harmful levels of other poisons already occur widely.   For example, studies of the effects of atmospheric levels of trace metals have suggested a causal relationship between lead dust fall (mainly derived from gasoline additives) in residential areas of seventy-seven cities and cardiovascular mortality (Third Report of the Secretary of HEW to Congress, 1970). The need for standards and for enforced control of the sources of air pollution is urgent.

(Editor's comment)

The pollution of the air we breathe, ironically enough, is an indirect result of our pursuit of an ever-higher standard of living. Air pollution derives from the burning of fuel for heat and power, from the processing of materials, and from the disposal of wastes. Air pollution, in short, comes from those everyday activities which are so integral a part of modern, technologically advanced societies.

We have available today the technological means of controlling most sources of air pollution.   But we are not applying that technology in anything like adequate measure, and the problem of air pollution continues to grow.

Estimates of total emissions in the United States of sulfur oxides, nitrogen oxides, carbon monoxide, hydrocarbons, and total particulates are made annually.   The most recent estimates are presented in Table 8.1.

Motor Vehicles

The 90 million motor vehicles in the United States today constitute one of the principal sources of air pollution.   Nearly all of each amount attributed to transportation in Table 8.1 is contributed by motor vehicles.

Most of our motor vehicles (99 percent) are powered by the gasoline engine.   Most of the gasoline engine vehicles in operation today discharge pollution from four points. Gasoline is highly volatile, and the gas tank and the carburetor lose hydrocarbons through evaporation.   The gasoline engine is imperfect, and large amounts of unburned and partly burned hydrocarbons discharge from the tailpipe; smaller amounts blow by engine pistons to the crankcase, which vents to the air through a tube.   Carbon monoxide, fuel impurities, and fuel additives discharge from the tailpipe.

Automobiles, primarily passenger cars, are by far the nation's largest source of carbon monoxide, and they are also the major source of hydrocarbons and nitrogen oxides, the two types of air pollutants most involved in the formation of photochemical smog.   In addition, vehicles discharge to the atmosphere chemicals that have been added to improve the quality of fuels (if not the environment), such as tetra-ethyl lead.   To deal with the problem of pollution from vehicles, the Department of Health, Education, and Welfare is authorized to establish and enforce national standards applicable to new motor vehicles at the time of their original sale. Standards for carbon monoxide and hy-

TABLE 8.1 Amounts of air pollutants, by kind and source, produced in the United States, 1966. (From U.S. Department of Health, Education, and Welfare, 1970, p. 9.)

SOURCE	CARBON MONOXIDE	PARTICULATES	HYDRO-CARBONS	NITROGEN OXIDES	SULFUR OXIDES[1]	TOTAL
			[MILLIONS OF TONS PER YEAR]			
Transportation	64.5	1.2	17.6	7.6	0.4	91.3
Fuel combustion in stationary sources	1.9	9.2	.7	6.7	22.9	41.4
Industrial processes	10.7	7.6	3.5	.2	7.2	29.2
Solid waste disposal	7.6	1.0	1.5	.5	.1	10.7
Miscellaneous	9.7	2.9	6.0	.5	.6	19.7
Total	94.4	21.9	29.3	15.5	31.2	192.3
Forest fires	7.2	6.7	2.2	1.2	([2])	17.3
Total	101.6	28.6	31.5	16.7	31.2	209.6

[1] For the year 1967.
[2] Negligible.

drocarbon emissions from new passenger cars and light trucks first went into effect in the 1968 model year. Successively tighter restrictions have been imposed for the 1970 and 1971 model years (see Table 8.2).

In 1970 national standards applicable to heavy-duty motor vehicles went into effect for the first time. Gasoline-fueled vehicles are not permitted to exhaust more than 5.4 grams of hydrocarbons per vehicle mile or

more than 50.0 grams of carbon monoxide per vehicle mile. New diesel-powered, heavy-duty vehicles are also affected; they must be equipped to comply with limitations on smoke emissions.

Though the standards already established will reverse the upward trend in total emissions of carbon monoxide and hydrocarbons from motor vehicles, this effect will be rather short-lived. The number of vehicles in use

TABLE 8.2 United States limits on air pollution from light-duty vehicles.[1]

	1963 model year car:[2,3] Grams per vehicle mile	1968 NATIONAL STANDARDS Grams per vehicle mile	Percent reduction[4]	1970 NATIONAL STANDARDS Grams per vehicle mile	Percent reduction[4]	1971 NATIONAL STANDARDS Grams per vehicle mile	Percent reduction[4]
Exhaust:							
Hydrocarbons	12.2	3.4	71.8	2.2	81.9	2.2	81.5
Carbon monoxide	79.0	35.1	55.6	23.0	70.9	23.0	70.9
Crankcase Hydrocarbons	3.7	0	100.0	0	100.0	0	100.0
Evaporation Hydrocarbons	2.8	[5]2.8	0	[5]2.8	0	.5	82.3
Total:							
Hydrocarbons	18.7	6.2	66.9	5.0	73.5	2.7	85.6
Carbon monoxide	79.0	35.1	55.6	23.0	70.9	23.0	70.9

[1] Vehicles with a gross weight of 6,000 pounds or less.
[2] Tested according to Federal LDV test procedures.
[3] At 2,000 miles.
[4] Percent reduction below 1963 emissions.
[5] No standard in effect; number represents uncontrolled emissions.

is increasing and so is the yearly use made of each one. These trends, if they continue, will in another decade more than offset the effects of the standards established thus far. Then, total emissions of carbon monoxide and hydrocarbons will again begin to rise.

To prevent this from happening, further tightening of the standards will be necessary. In addition, standards should be set for motor vehicle pollutants not already covered, such as nitrogen oxides and particulate matter. Accordingly, the National Air Pollution Control Administration (NAPCA) is in the process of establishing long-term emission reduction standards, as well as intermediate goals to be reached by the mid-1970's.

However, there presently is a serious problem in regard to compliance with the motor vehicle emission standards. The current program for determining whether new motor vehicles comply with standards rests mainly on testing of prototype vehicles in advance of actual production. On the basis of passing this test, manufacturers may receive certificates which are valid for at least one year and which presume that vehicles from the assemblyline will perform like the prototypes insofar as air pollution is concerned. But there is evidence that air pollution control systems installed in mass-produced vehicles often lose some of their effectiveness more rapidly than prototype systems do.

Assuming that the upward trend in vehicle population continues, add-on devices and engine modifications may fail to achieve the needed control; power sources that are fundamentally pollution free may be required.

Fuel Combustion in Stationary Sources

Stationary sources of air pollution include electric generating plants and space heating systems, discussed in this part, as well as industrial operations, incinerators, and so on (discussed later).

In 1966 the United States consumed roughly 1,250 billion kilowatt hours of electricity. More than 95 percent of this energy was generated by burning coal and oil, which contain elemental sulfur as an impurity.

When these fuels are burned the sulfur also burns to form sulfur oxides, which are one of the most serious and prevalent forms of air pollution today.

SULFUR OXIDES

The problem of air pollution by sulfur oxides is growing faster than was estimated by previous estimates by the NAPCA. There also is a widening gap between the steeply rising trend of sulfur oxides emissions and our technological capability for bringing the problem under control. Of particular importance is the need for practical techniques applicable to electric generating plants. These power plants accounted for about 18 million of the 31.2 million tons of sulfur oxides emitted in 1967. Electric generating plants are expected to emit about 43 million tons of sulfur oxides by 1980 if no control measures are taken. Even with rapid application of the control techniques now under development, it is unlikely that sulfur dioxide emissions in 1980 will be reduced even to the 1968 level. The rapid growth of the electric utility industry (from 300,000 megawatts in 1969 to an anticipated 600,000 megawatts by 1980) and slower-than-predicted growth of nuclear electric generating capacity are compounding the problem. Processes must be developed that can be applied not only to electric plants already in existence but also to the many large (more than 500 megawatts) new plants now being planned or built.

There are two general approaches to the control of sulfur oxides pollution arising from fuel combustion—removal of sulfur oxides from stack gas before the effluent escapes into the air and use of low-sulfur fuels.

STACK GAS DESULFURIZATION

Processes involving the use of limestone to react with sulfur oxides are the most likely to be ready for application to electric generating plants in the near future. There are two types of limestone processes—dry and wet. In the dry limestone process, injection of limestone into the boiler results in the formation of sulfurous particles that can be removed from the stack gas by electrostatic precipitators or other particulate control equipment. This process is expected to remove about 50 to 60 percent of the sulfur oxides. In the wet limestone process, limestone is injected either into the boiler or into stack gas scrubbers, and the scrubbers remove the sulfurous material. This process is expected to remove about 90 percent of the sulfur oxides; in addition, it would remove virtually all the particulate matter, thereby making the use of precipitators unnecessary. The limestone processes would be applicable to existing, as well as new, electric generating plants.

FUEL DESULFURIZATION

Removal of sulfur from fuels before they are burned can make only a limited contribution to solving the sulfur oxides pollution problem. Techniques have been developed for removing sulfur from residual fuel oil, a low-grade fuel used by electric utilities. Very little residual fuel oil is produced in the United States; most of what is used in this country is imported. A number of companies are building fuel oil desulfurization plants to process imported fuel and thus supply low-sulfur oil to electric utilities, but the high cost of transporting residual fuel oil by land limits its economical use to areas accessible by water. Electric utilities currently use only about one-tenth as much fuel oil as coal.

Much of the nation's coal has a relatively high sulfur content. Through coal-cleaning techniques, some of the sulfur can be removed from coal, but generally not enough can be removed to produce coal which, from the standpoint of abatement of sulfur oxides pollution, would be of sufficiently low sulfur content.

NITROGEN OXIDES CONTROL

Nitrogen oxides emissions from stationary sources, mainly electric generating and space heating plants, amounted to 7.9 million tons in 1966. Formation of nitrogen oxides is highly dependent on flame temperature and oxygen concentration. Efforts to deal with the problem are centered on developing combustion processes which minimize the formation of nitrogen oxides and techniques for removal of the pollutant after it has been formed. Combustion process modifications may prove relatively easy to achieve, but they may also reduce combustion efficiency. Removal of nitrogen oxides poses a much more difficult problem. Some basic approaches for removal of nitrogen oxides from stack gas have been identified, but none has been developed sufficiently to apply to a pilot-scale or commercial-scale operation.

Industrial Processes

The people of the United States have been so intent on reaping the benefits of the industrial revolution that they have failed to give enough attention to the by-product problems the successes have created. The very industries that provide the materials of the good life also contribute a major share of the gases and particulates that contaminate the air we breathe.

The major industrial contributors to air pollution in the United States are pulp and paper mills, iron and steel mills, petroleum refineries, smelters, inorganic chemical manufacturers (such as fertilizer producers), and organic chemical manufacturers (such as synthetic rubber makers).

Industries discharge into the atmosphere more than 20 percent of the nation's emissions of sulfur oxides and particulate matter, and more than 10 percent of the carbon monoxide and hydrocarbons (Table 8.1).

Refuse Disposal

The production of solid wastes by residues, commerce, and industry now exceeds 350 million tons per year in the United States and is increasing at an annual rate of 4 percent. An increasing portion, already more than half, of this total is collected by local agencies for disposal. Faced with critical waste disposal problems as available landfill areas decrease, local authorities are turning to municipal incinerators to dispose of the debris. However, many municipal incinerators are of inadequate basic design and lack pollutant emission controls, resulting in serious air pollution, especially by carbon monoxides.

Air Quality Standards

Comprehensive knowledge of the effects of air pollution on human health is a prerequisite to the establishment of meaningful air quality standards. The National Air Pollution Control Administration is responsible for developing and publishing air quality criteria documents which summarize available scientific information on the extent to which individual air pollutants or combinations of pollutants are hazardous to public health and welfare.

NAPCA published the first air quality criteria documents in 1969. These documents deal with two of the most common air pollutants—sulfur oxides and particulate matter. The sulfur oxides study reviews and summarizes the results of over 300 studies and indicates that: "Under the conditions prevailing in areas where the studies were conducted, adverse health effects were noticed when 24-hour average levels of sulfur dioxide exceeded 300 micrograms per cubic meter (0.11 parts per million) for three to four days. Adverse health effects also were noted when the annual mean level of sulfur dioxide exceeded 115 micrograms per cubic meter (0.04 parts per million). Visibility was reduced to about five miles at sulfur dioxide levels of 285 micrograms per cubic meter (0.10 parts

per million); adverse effects on materials were observed at an annual mean of 345 micrograms per cubic meter (0.12 parts per million); and adverse effects on vegetation were observed at an annual mean of 85 micrograms per cubic meter (0.03 parts per million)."

The particulate matter criteria document reviews and summarizes results of approximately 350 studies of the effects of particulate air pollution and indicates that: "Under the conditions prevailing in areas where the studies were conducted, adverse health effects were noted when the annual mean level of particulate matter exceeded 80 micrograms per cubic meter; visibility was reduced to about five miles at concentrations of 150 micrograms per cubic meter; and adverse effects on materials were observed at an annual mean exceeding 60 micrograms per cubic meter."

NAPCA planned to publish air quality criteria for carbon monoxide, photochemical oxidants, and hydrocarbons in 1970. Air quality criteria for nitrogen oxides, lead, fluorides, and polynuclear organic compounds are scheduled for publication in 1971. NAPCA intends to publish criteria for odors (including toxological and corrosion aspects of hydrogen sulfide), asbestos, hydrogen chlorides, beryllium, and chlorine gas in 1972. Scheduled for publication in 1973 are criteria documents on arsenic, nickel, and vanadium and their compounds. Criteria scheduled for issuance in 1974 will cover barium, boron, chromium (including chromic acid), mercury, and selenium and their compounds. Air quality criteria for pesticides and radioactive substances are scheduled for publication in 1975.

ADDITIONAL REFERENCES

Alexander, Tom. 1970. Some burning questions about combustion. Pp. 115–129 in *The environment,* by the Editors of Fortune. New York: Perennial Library. Popular discussion of the growing demand for electric power and its effects.

Goldsmith, J. R., and S. A. Landaw. 1968. Carbon monoxide and human health. *Science* 162:1352–1359.

Haagen-Smit, A. J. 1964. The control of air pollution. *Sci. Am.,* January.

Hilst, G. R. 1967. What can we do to clear the

air?   *Bulletin of the American Meteorological Society* 48(9):710–713.

Middleton, J. T., and W. Ott.   1968.   Air pollution and transportation.   *Traffic Quarterly,* April.

Tebbens, B. D.   1968.   Gaseous pollutants in the air.   Pp. 23–46 in *Air pollution,* 2d edition, ed. by A. C. Stern.   New York: Academic Press.

U.S. Department of Commerce.   1967.   *The automobile and air pollution: A program for progress.   Part II.   Subpanel reports to the panel on electrically powered vehicles.*   Washington, D.C.   160 pp.   This detailed report examines the present effects of automobiles and explores alternative systems of transportation for the future; 328 references.

METEOROLOGY OF AIR POLLUTION

DONALD H. PACK

What happens to pollutants once they are discharged into the air? We depend on atmospheric turbulence to bring fresh air in and to carry pollutants away. But we cannot continue to regard the atmosphere as a topless sewer which will endlessly absorb our wastes without repercussion on us. Preservation of adequate air resources challenges our understanding of the atmosphere's capacities.

In this selection Donald H. Pack discusses the atmosphere's role in influencing the distribution of materials which cause air pollution and some uses to which an understanding of meteorological factors can be put in air pollution control. Different meteorological factors are important depending on whether the pollution comes from point, line, or area sources, and whether the ejection is instantaneous or continuous. Vertical turbulence and horizontal turbulence operate differently at various scales and in different situations. The net effect of turbulence is to diffuse pollutants. Pollution from urban areas, however, covers such large areas and is so dense that special approaches are required to understand and predict its diffusion.

Although much remains to be learned about how the atmosphere acts to dilute materials and eventually rid itself of them, progress has been rapid in the few years since this article was written (e.g., see Panofsky, 1969). However, we still need to know much more about the geochemistry of air pollutants and their effects on climate and organisms before we can define tolerable limits of pollution under specified meteorological conditions.

(Editor's comment)

Donald H. Pack (b. 1919) is deputy director of the Air Resources Laboratory, Environmental Science Services Administration, U.S. Department of Commerce. He was educated at New York University and George Washington University. He has served on National Academy of Science committees studying pollution and biological effects of radiation and on World Meteorological Organization working groups on lower tropospheric soundings and plant injury. His recent work has concentrated on wind field perturbations caused by cities, including nighttime effects of Columbus, Ohio, and the complex air flow in the Los Angeles Basin. Pack's current research centers on the use of a "Lagrangian" tracer technique through radar-tracking of balloons with attached transponders.

Reprinted by permission of the author and *Science* from volume 146, pp. 1119–1128, November 27, 1964. Copyright 1964 by the American Association for the Advancement of Science.

The obvious solution to our widely discussed air-pollution problem is to prevent all the pollutants from reaching the atmosphere. Ultimately we may have the technical ability and legal authority to accomplish this in an economical fashion. However, it is quite logical and reasonable to use the atmosphere for the disposal of gaseous and particulate wastes, if we know the effects of this use and keep them within acceptable limits. The layer of air (about 10 kilometers thick) which is readily available for the dilution of pollution represents an enormous reservoir, about 5×10^{18} cubic meters, which can be used for this purpose.

Character of the Pollution Source

Atmospheric diffusion is ultimately accomplished by the wind movement of pollutants, but the character of the source of pollution requires that this action of the wind be taken into account in different ways.

These sources can be conveniently grouped into three classes: point sources, line sources, and area sources. In practice, the first two classes must be further divided into instantaneous and continuous sources.

POINT SOURCES

The instaneous point source is essentially a "puff" of material created or ejected in a relatively short time, as by a nuclear explosion, the sudden rupture of a chlorine tank, or the bursting of a tear-gas shell. The wind of immediate importance is, of course, that occurring at the place and time at which the pollutant is created. Since the wind is highly variable, the initial direction of movement of the puff is also variable and difficult of prediction; a soap-bubble pipe and five minutes' close observation of the initial travel of successive bubbles will convincingly demonstrate the difficulty of predicting the exact trajectory of the next bubble. In addition, dilution of a puff source is a very strong function of time after its release. At first, the small-scale fluctuations of the wind cause it to grow rather slowly and the larger-scale wind variations simply carry it along on erratic paths. But as the puff grows, larger-scale motions can get a "hold" on it to tear it apart and dilute it more rapidly. Thus, the unique feature of the instantaneous point source is its increasing dispersion rate with time, whence the necessity to consider successively larger scales of meteorological phenomena in calculating its spread.

Continuous point sources (the smoke plume from a factory chimney, the pall from a burning dump) are the most familiar, the most conspicuous, and the most studied of pollution sources. The meteorology of the continuous source must take into account the time changes of the wind at the point of emission. The behavior of a plume from a factory chimney is very much like that of water from a hose being played back and forth across a lawn. It is evident that if the hose is steady the same area will be continually exposed to the water. But if the hose (wind) moves back and forth in an arc, the water (pollution) will be distributed over a wider area, hence the concentration will be less. For a truly continuous source there are other changes of great importance—primarily the diurnal and seasonal cycles.

LINE SOURCES

The isolated line source is less common and therefore of less general interest, with two important exceptions—heavily traveled highways, and the swath of chemicals emitted by crop-dusting apparatus. In both these examples, if the line of pollutant is uniform and is long enough, the dispersion of the pollution must be attained in only two dimensions, along the wind and in the vertical. If the line source is a continuous one, as might be the case of a freeway in rush hours, spreading in the downwind direction becomes ineffective (at a particular downwind location), so that only the vertical dimension is left to provide dilution. This behavior of the continuous line source has been exploited by meteorologists in field experiments with controlled tracers to permit the detailed study of vertical diffusion, uncomplicated by effects in the other two coordinates.

AREA SOURCES

The area source can vary enormously in size. It may be distributed over several square kilometers, as in an industrial park, over tens or hundreds of square kilometers, as in a city, or over thousands of square kilometers, exemplified by the almost continuous strip city (the "megalopolis" or "megapolitan area") along the eastern seaboard of the United States. These area sources usually include combinations of all the single-source configurations. A large city will include many thousands of home chimneys, thousands of factories and shops, hundreds of kilometers of streets, open dumps, burning leaves, evaporating fumes from gasoline storage or from cleaning plants and paint factories, and everywhere the automobile. The weather problem of the city area source becomes, in the aggregate, quite different from that of a single source. Here we are concerned not with the increasing rate of wind dispersion with increasing scale, or with the behavior of wind with time at a single point, but rather with the replenishment rate of the air over the city. We must consider the total movement of a large volume of air as it "ventilates" the city. Anything that reduces this ventilation rate, whether it be the confining effect of surrounding mountains or the reduced velocities of a slow-moving anticyclone, is of concern.

In the construction of cities man has modified the weather.* The volume of effluent injected into the air has reduced the solar radiation. The absorption characteristics of cement and asphalt instead of grass and trees create urban "heat islands." These effects must be considered in the meteorology of urban air pollution.

Diffusion of Pollutants

The atmosphere disperses pollutants because, like the sea, it is in constant motion, and this motion is always turbulent to some degree.

*See Selections 11 and 12.

There is as yet no fully accepted definition of turbulence, but empirically it can be described as random (three-dimensional) flow. There is as yet no complete explanation for the complexities even of controlled wind-tunnel turbulence, hence it is not surprising that the understanding of turbulent diffusion in the atmosphere has progressed largely through empirical treatments of controlled tracer experiments. It would be an injustice to the reader and to a fascinating and challenging subject to try to condense turbulent-diffusion theory to a few paragraphs. The current tendency is to deal with turbulence through statistical concepts derived from aerodynamics and fluid dynamics. This treatment, with its emphasis on the detailed properties of the turbulence, is in contrast to earlier theories which centered around a virtual-diffusivity concept based on analogy with molecular diffusion. In the practical application of computing pollution concentrations, it is more usual to employ the statistical method for distances to perhaps 150 kilometers from the source, and equations based on virtual-diffusivity ("K") theory for longer distances, particularly for calculations on a hemispheric or global scale.

VERTICAL TURBULENT DIFFUSION

To all intents and purposes rapid atmospheric diffusion in the vertical is always bounded: on the bottom by the surface of the earth and at the top by the tropopause. The tropopause—the demarcation between the troposphere, where temperature decreases with altitude, and the stratosphere, where the temperature is relatively constant or increases with altitude—is lowest over the poles, at about 8 kilometers, and highest in the tropics, about 20 kilometers. The detection of radon products throughout the troposphere is conclusive evidence of the eventual availability of the full depth of the troposphere for vertical dispersion, since the radon source is exclusively at the earth's surface. Utilization of this total vertical dimension can take place at very different rates, depending on the thermally driven vertical wind. These rates are intimately related to the vertical temperature profile. On the average (and if we neglect the effects of the phase change of water in the air), enhanced turbulence is associated with a drop in temperature with height of 10°C per kilometer or greater. (This is the dry adiabatic rate.) If the temperature change with height is at a lesser rate, turbulence tends to be decreased, and if the temperature increases with height (an "inversion"), turbulence is very much reduced. The temperature profile, particularly over land, shows a large diurnal variation (Figure 9.1). Shortly after sunrise the heating of the land surface by the sun results in rapid warming of the air near the surface; the reduced density of this air causes it to rise rapidly. Cooler air from aloft replaces the rising air "bubble," to be warmed and rise in turn. This vigorous vertical interchange creates "superadiabatic" lapse rate—a temperature decrease of more than 10°C per vertical kilometer—and vertical displacements are accelerated. The depth of this well-mixed layer depends on the intensity of solar radiation and the radiation characteristics of the underlying surface. Over the deserts this vigorous mixing may extend well above 3 kilometers, while over forested lake country the layer may be only one or two hundred meters thick. Obviously, this effect is highly dependent on season; in winter the lesser insolation and unfavorable radiation characteristics of snow cover greatly inhibit vertical turbulence.

In contrast, with clear or partly cloudy skies the temperature profile at night is drastically changed by the rapid radiational cooling of the ground and the subsequent cooling of the layers of air near the surface. This creates an "inversion" of the daytime temperature profile, since there is now an increase in temperature with height. In such a situation the density differences rapidly damp out vertical motions, tend to reduce vertical turbulence, and stabilize the atmosphere. The longer hours of winter darkness favor the formation and maintenance of inversions. In the polar regions, in areas relatively unaffected by storms, inversions of

20°C or more may persist for weeks. Under such extreme circumstances, vertical mixing is very slow and the surface layers of the atmosphere can almost be considered as decoupled from the air above. Such a situation may also occur in middle latitudes, but surprisingly winter is not the time of most intense and persistent surface-based inversions. The greater frequency and intensity of large-scale storm systems, with their higher wind speeds and extensive cloud cover, tend to prevent the frequent formation of this very stable situation. It is in autumn, with its combination of relatively long nights and fewer storms, that inversions are most frequent and persistent.

Two other temperature configurations, on very different scales, have important effects on vertical turbulence and the dilution of air pollution. At the smaller end of the scale, the heat capacity of urban areas and, to a lesser extent, the heat generated by fuel consumption act to modify the temperature profile. The effect is most marked at night, when the heat stored by day in the buildings and streets warms the air and prevents the formation of the surface-based temperature inversion typical of rural areas. Over cities it is rare to find inversions in the lowest 100 meters, and the city influence is still evident 200 to 300 meters above the surface. The effect is a function of city size and building

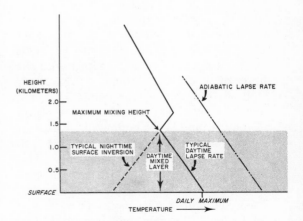

FIGURE 9.1 Schematic representation of the effect of vertical temperature gradient on atmospheric mixing.

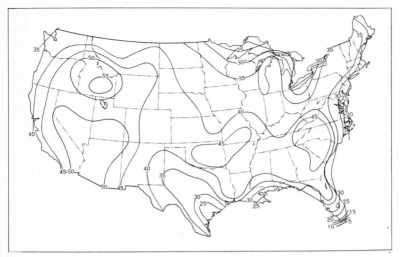

FIGURE 9.2 Frequency of low-level (surface to 150 meters) inversions in the fall season. Isopleths are average percentage of hours of inversion per day.

density, but not enough observations are yet available to provide any precise quantitative relations. Although the effect even for the largest cities is probably insignificant above a kilometer, this locally produced vertical mixing is quite important. Pollution, instead of being confined to a narrow layer near the height of emission, perhaps only 100 meters in thickness, can be freely diluted in more than double the volume of air, the concentrations being reduced by a similar factor.

On a much larger scale the temperature profile can be changed over thousands of square kilometers by the action of large-scale weather systems. In traveling storm systems (cyclones) the increased pressure gradients and resulting high winds, together with the inflow of air into the storm, create relatively good vertical mixing conditions. On the other hand, the flat pressure patterns, slower movement, and slow outflow of surface air in high-pressure cells (anticyclones) result in much less favorable vertical mixing. This is primarily due to the gradual subsidence of the air aloft as it descends to replace (mass-continuity requirement) the outflow at the surface. During this descent the air warms adiabatically, and eventually there is created a temperature inversion aloft inhibit-ing the upward mixing of pollution above the inversion level. As the anticyclone matures and persists, this subsidence inversion may lower to very near the ground and persist for the duration of the particular weather pattern. This pattern is typically associated with the beautiful weather of "Indian summer" (Figure 9.2), but it has also been associated with all the major air-pollution disasters (Donora, Pennsylvania, in 1948, London in 1948, 1952, and 1962, and others).

The action of mechanical turbulence in the vertical requires rather less discussion. It is obvious that if a moving mass of air reaches an obstacle it cannot penetrate, it must go over or around the obstacle. If the obstacles are numerous (blades of grass, rows of trees, or streets of buildings) the air will be constantly rising and falling. Thus, vertical mechanical turbulence is the response to the roughness of the underlying surface and has the most effect in the first few hundred meters above the surface.

HORIZONTAL TURBULENT DIFFUSION

The most important difference between the vertical and horizontal dimensions of diffusion is that of scale. In the vertical, rapid diffusion is limited to about 10 kilometers. But in the horizontal, the entire surface of the globe is eventually available. Even when the total depth of the troposphere is considered, the horizontal scale is larger by at least three orders of magnitude, and the difference, say during a nocturnal inversion which might restrict the vertical diffusion to a few tens of meters, is even greater since the lateral turbulence is reduced less than the vertical component. Mechanically produced horizontal turbulence is, on a percentage basis, much less important than the thermal effects; its effects are of about the same order of magnitude as the vertical mechanical effects.

The thermally produced horizontal turbulence is not so neatly related to horizontal temperature gradients as vertical turbulence is to the vertical temperature profile. The horizontal temperature differences create horizontal pressure fields, which in turn drive the horizontal winds. These are acted upon by the earth's rotation (the Coriolis effect) and by surface friction, so that there is no such thing as a truly steady-state wind near the surface of the earth. Wind speeds may vary from nearly zero near the surface at night in an anticyclone to 100 meters per second under the driving force of the intense pressure gradient of a hurricane. Perhaps the absolute extreme is reached in the thermally driven vortex of a tornado, where speeds of 200 meters per second or more (they have never been accurately measured) may occur. The importance of this variation, even though in air pollution we are concerned with much more modest ranges, is that for continuous sources the concentration is inversely proportional to the wind speed. Consider a source emitting one unit of pollution per second in a wind of one meter per second. If the wind increases to two meters per second, the volume of air passing the source is doubled; hence the concentration is halved. It is not quite so simple for multiple emissions in a large area source, but the variation of wind speed is still a fundamental factor in the dilution of air pollution.

The variation of turbulence in the lateral direction is perhaps the most important factor of all and certainly one of the most interesting. In practice this can best be represented by the changes in horizontal wind direction. We have the basic wind currents of the globe—the polar easterlies, the mid-latitude westerlies, the easterly trades of the subtropics, and so on. These are manifested in the semipermanent pressure systems with a superposition of traveling cyclones and anticyclones. Within each of these systems, which may be several thousand kilometers across, the wind is not steady but is varied by the temperature contrasts between ocean and land, mountain and plain, city and field. These create local land-sea breezes, up- and downslope flows, and even in special cases rural-to-city drifts of air. The situation is succinctly described in a parody of a verse by Swift attributed to the meteorologist L. F. Richardson: "Great whirls have little whirls, that feed on their velocity; And little whirls have lesser whirls, and so on to viscosity."

The net effect of these systems is a constantly varying wind direction (Figure 9.3). Within a few minutes, the wind may fluctuate rapidly through 90 degrees or more. Over a few hours it may shift, still with much short-period variability, through 180 degrees, and in the course of a month it will have changed through 360 degrees numerous times. Over the seasons, preferred directional patterns will be established depending upon latitude and large-scale pressure patterns. These patterns may be very stable over many years, and thus establish the wind climatology of a particular location.

The emitted pollution travels with this ever-varying wind. The high-frequency fluctuations spread out the pollutant (Figure 9.4), and the relatively steady "average" direction carries it off—for example, toward a suburb or a business district. A gradual turning of direction transports material toward new targets and gives a respite to the previous ones. Every few days the cycle is repeated, and over the years the prevailing winds can create semipermanent patterns of pollution downwind from factories or cities.

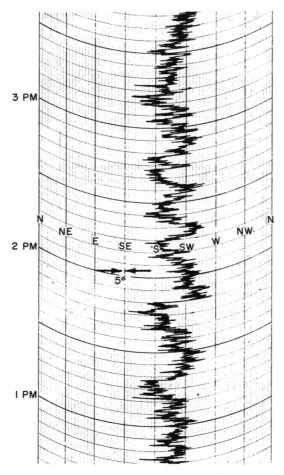

FIGURE 9.3 Typical wind-direction variability. Data are an analogue trace of a conventional wind vane.

Atmospheric Transport

It is convenient to distinguish the turbulent diffusion of pollution from the bulk transport of pollution away from its source. In fact, the statistical theories of diffusion speak of a steady mean flow and the turbulent fluctuations about this mean. This separation, however, is very dependent on the time and space scale of interest. Five hours of south-west wind may become only statistical fluctuations about a mean monthly northwesterly flow, which is in turn a portion of the annual wind frequency distribution. Nevertheless, this division of wind behavior into turbulent fluctuations and mean flow is of practical value, because it permits the use of average wind statistics (the mean flow) to describe the "ventilation" of an area. Certain features of the physiography and meteorology of particular areas can seriously reduce this transport or ventilation. Two of the most effective mechanisms for this reduction are topographical barriers and semipermanent subsidence inversions.

Topographical barriers are best described by examples. The semicircular ring of hills and mountains around the Los Angeles Basin slows the flow of air in and out of the area and acts to form a catch basin for pollutants. On a much larger scale, the Great Basin of Utah and Nevada functions in the same way, particularly in winter, providing a huge bowl which can contain a stagnating air mass with very light winds of variable direction. The narrow valleys of western Pennsylvania also act to slow the flow, but in this instance air movement is constrained to follow the contours of the valley, so that the natural variability of the wind is largely ineffective and pollution repeatedly follows the same path. Again on a larger scale, the San Joaquin Valley of California has much the same effect. The persistent surface fogs of the winter season attest to the reduced air transport in the surface layers of air in this area.

The semipermanent inversion is a feature of west coasts of continents throughout the world; Africa, the Iberian Peninsula, South America, and the southwestern coast of the United States all have this typical vertical-turbulence lid created by the subsidence associated with the semipermanent high-pressure areas of the eastern subtropical oceans. If, as in the case of southern California and

FIGURE 9.4 Effect of averaging time in "smoothing" concentration variability. The source of the smoke is a military smoke pot (extreme right in each picture). Averaging is obtained by time-exposure photography. The smoke has been outlined for clarity. (Top) 1/100-second exposure; (middle) 10-second exposure; (bottom) 8-minute exposure.

Chile, there is also a mountain barrier, the meteorological stage is set for man and his technology to create a persistent air-pollution problem.

Applications of Air-Pollution Meteorology

It was a military weapons system, in this instance the use of gas in World War I, that led to the early quantitative meteorological studies on the dilution of pollutants by the atmosphere. Application to military technology has continued and has provided much valuable information for application to more general and widespread civilian problems.

The major U.S. effort in the meteorology of air pollution began with the Manhattan Engineering Project and the construction of the Hanford Works in the state of Washington. It is a credit to the acumen of this predecessor of the Atomic Energy Commission that it recognized, at a very early stage, the need to study atmospheric dilution near such plants. A group of meteorologists, under the direction of Phil E. Church of the University of Washington, set the pattern by measuring, in detail, the variations, wind speed, and direction throughout the Hanford area, and used a 125-meter instrument tower to measure vertical wind and temperature profiles. This early program was followed by similar efforts at the National Laboratories at Brookhaven, Oak Ridge, and Argonne, at the National Reactor Testing Station, and at the Nevada Test Site. Other nuclear sites have had similar meteorological studies.

Such a study usually begins with recording the small scale (1-to-50-kilometer) variation of the dilution in order to identify diurnal and seasonal patterns and any combination of meteorological parameters that would complicate effluent releases (for example, a persistent wind direction occurring simultaneously with a persistent inversion). The various data are organized as background statistics for engineering design. A model compendium of the type was ORO-99, "A

Micrometeorological Study of the Oak Ridge Area," prepared by J. Z. Holland and collaborators in 1953. It remains a useful guide.

Most of the larger installations have supplemented the measurements of meteorological parameters with direct measurements of atmospheric diffusion through the analyses of concentration measurements from "sources of opportunity." Intensive measurements of argon-41 from the stack of the Brookhaven air-cooled reactor and of iodine isotopes from the chemical processing plants at Hanford and the National Reactor Testing Station, combined with the concurrent meteorological data, have been used to determine average long-period concentration patterns around such installations and the quantitative relation between concentration and averaging time. This latter information, the "peak-to-mean" concentration ratio, is of great practical importance in evaluating biological effects of acute versus chronic exposures to pollutants, and also makes possible the extrapolation of sampling data taken over fixed, and usually short, times to a wide variety of conditions.

As understanding of the diffusion process has become more exact, meteorological information has been used more frequently in the design of experiments involving the release of radioactivity, both in order to optimize safety and to increase the efficiency of the experiment. Knowledge of the seasonal and diurnal frequency of necessary wind directions and trajectories helps in scheduling experiments so as to minimize weather delays (Figure 9.5). Knowledge of the existing meteorology during experiments is often indispensable for the correct evaluation of test results. This requirement was particularly pertinent in the determination of fallout from atmospheric nuclear detonations. Comparison of fallout from different devices, with different yields, and perhaps exploded under different conditions, required the "normalization" of the meteorology. The intensive system developed for the Nevada Test Site of measuring and forecasting wind and temperature profiles was designed to provide not only operational

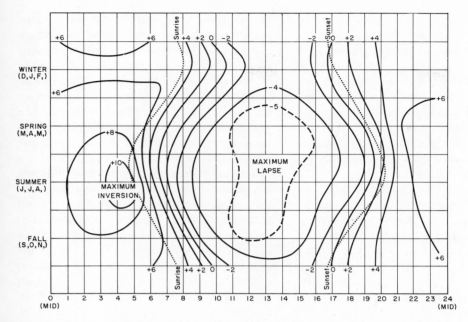

FIGURE 9.5 Diurnal and seasonal variation in temperature profile (between 1.2 and 120 meters) at the National Reactor Testing Station. Isopleths are temperature differences (degrees Fahrenheit). Abscissa is time of day.

data for safety purposes but also the documentation needed to evaluate the scientific experiments.

On a much larger scale, knowledge of global circulation patterns, long-range diffusion, and atmospheric removal processes, part of it gained by using the radioactive debris of previous tests as wide-ranging meteorological tracers, has permitted accurate forecasts of the time and space distribution of global fallout to be expected in various parts of the world.

Still another use of air-pollution meteorology is in the analysis of an accident, particularly in the determination of the amount of material released. In the two major reactor accidents that have occurred, one at Windscale, England, in 1957 and the other at the National Reactor Testing Station in 1961, perhaps the best estimates of the amount of radioactivity released to the air were obtained by calculating the diffusion equations backward, from the observed concentrations through the existing meteorological conditions to the source strength. These results were particularly interesting

because they required spatial and temporal integration of observed concentrations, extrapolation of weather information from only a few points, and the use of reasonable models of diffusion.

There is a very strong motivation to deduce generalized information, as well as empirical results, from these essentially "free" sources of opportunity, and very useful results have been obtained. Useful as such analyses have been, they cannot, however, entirely substitute for well-designed experiments where the atmospheric conditions can be selected with care, the source is controlled, and the sampling procedures are commensurate with the experimental goals. Thus, most of the advances in understanding diffusion have been due to careful field experiments with gaseous or aerosol tracers, concurrent with elaborate measurements of atmospheric turbulence, wind, and temperature gradient. The technology that has developed around these tracers, which range from natural spores to Kleenex lint and soap bubbles, is an interesting one. One of the more recent developments is the use of alpha-particle excitation of the filter samples of a fluorescing particulate to permit automated analysis of the sample concentration. Free balloons have traditionally been used as meteorological tracers. This technique has been given new impetus by the use of new materials and low-cost electronics to provide a nearly-constant-volume balloon and a lightweight radar beacon system, the position of which can be continuously measured by radar to ranges of more than 100 kilometers.

The information thus developed facilitates one of the most important uses of air-pollution meteorology, the planning of the location of pollution sources in relation to sensitive areas (people, animals, and vegetation). Proper site selection makes possible the use of the average features of the weather to minimize the effects of air pollution. Preplanning can be applied to problems of all sizes—choice of location for a rendering plant, selection of a site for a nuclear or coal-fired power plant, urban industrial zoning. The meteorology involved can be as simple as determining the direction of the most prevalent wind or so complex as to require three-dimensional wind statistics, temperature profiles to several kilometers, and data about air trajectories for tens of kilometers from the site. The most efficient solutions must take into account not just meteorology alone, but the entire process, including the economics.

Meteorology and Urban Air Pollution

In the applications previously discussed, the pollution source is usually discrete, readily identifiable, and, with sufficient effort, amenable to individual study and analysis. In fact, most diffusion theory and experiment have been directed to such sources. These problems are important and will remain so. Air pollution meteorology is being increasingly applied, however, to the growing problem of urban air pollution, and here the number and variety of pollution sources prohibit individual study. Indeed,

one of the major sources, the automobile, does not even stay put. Another complication and one of the most interesting features of this entire problem is that, while in the short term the meteorology of diffusion shows great variation and pollution emissions stay relatively constant, over periods of several years it is the meteorology that becomes stable and the pollution sources that vary.

To deal with these factors, two different approaches have been used. For the short term—and to answer such questions as: What is the statistical distribution of pollutant concentrations? Do different pollutants behave differently in the atmosphere? What are the effects of pollution on weather?—the meteorologist has inverted the problem; instead of calculating the field of concentration from a known source (source-oriented approach), he examines the measured field of concentration and the concurrent weather, and through standard statistical techniques relates the two (receptor-oriented approach). This technique has produced interesting results concerning the atmospheric "half-life" of pollutants, the seasonal variability of pollution, the role of sunlight in the production of photochemical smog, the reduction of solar radiation in cities, to mention only a few examples.

In fact, one of the most recent applications of meteorology completely ignores the source. Several years ago the Weather Bureau, on the basis of a statistical evaluation of the concurrent relation of high air-pollution values and large-scale meteorology, found that persistent high values of air pollution were associated with large areas of light wind, at the surface and aloft (slow horizontal ventilation), and sufficient atmospheric stability to inhibit vertical motion. These conditions are most often associated with a slowly moving or stagnant anticyclone (Figure 9.6); hence the designation of this condition as a "stagnation" model. In 1963, after several years of successful testing, the Weather Bureau began issuing "Air Pollution Potential Forecasts" for the United

States when meteorological conditions satisfy the stagnation model and are expected to persist for at least 36 hours. These are area forecasts and are currently limited to situations where at least 90,000 square kilometers are affected. This limitation is necessary because of the significant role played by very local meteorological variations such as sea breezes or mountain-valley winds and local pollution emissions, neither of which can be adequately predicted from the large-scale meteorology. In particular the designation "Pollution Potential" is required. If a stagnation area occurs in the Great Plains (as has happened) the air pollution levels should be very different from those in a similar weather pattern over the industrialized Atlantic States (and they have been). These forecasts, by making advance preparation possible, provide unique opportunities for examining high pollution levels through medical studies, special sampling programs, and so on. Eventually they may contribute to the reduction of pollution levels through control of emissions during these unfavorable periods.

Other applications require a "source-oriented" viewpoint for answers to the questions: What is the origin of this particular pollutant? What are the effects of new pollution controls? Given a specific growth rate, what are the likely future concentrations of pollution? In this approach the sources within a city might be grouped into, for example, industrial, domestic, transportation; then subdivided according to constituents—sulfur dioxide, carbon monoxide, and so on; and further divided by allocation to specific geographical areas. One of the most promising developments of recent years has been the success of mathematical models of urban diffusion, which can accept such source information and calculate the field of urban pollution concentration. The initial field test of such a model was carried out in Nashville, Tennessee, in conjunction with an intensive program of pollution measurements and medical surveys conducted by the Public Health Service and Vanderbilt University. City-wide concentrations of sulfur dioxide were computed for periods as short as 2 hours, and these values were summed to obtain average daily levels. The model, which incorporated an SO$_2$ "half-life" and

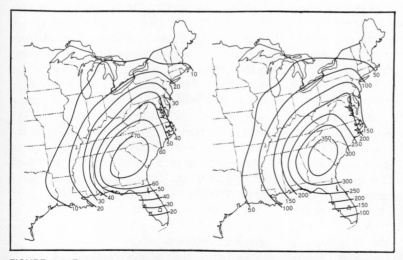

FIGURE 9.6 Frequency of large-scale slow dilution (stagnating anticyclones). Isopleths at left are average number of occurrences of stagnation "cases"—4 days or more—in the period 1936–1960. Isopleths at right are average number of days of stagnation in the same period.

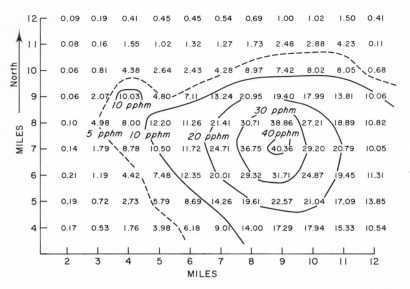

FIGURE 9.7 Computer calculations of sulfur dioxide concentrations for Nashville, Tennessee. Solutions of a multiple-source meteorological diffusion model compare favorably with measured values. Abscissa and ordinate are city dimensions (miles); isopleths are concentration values in parts per hundred million (pphm).

treated all the sources within a 2.5-square-kilometer source area as if they were centered in the middle of this area, was not very sophisticated meteorologically, although it did, by virtue of the two-hour time step, allow for diurnal variability. Crude as this first attempt at prediction was, it gave results that were very similar to the observed values and that in fact had a smaller variability than the sampling values with which the computations were compared (Figure 9.7). Source inventories are under way which will permit testing and refinement of the model in other locations. At the same time additional measurements of the diffusion within cities and studies of the best way to measure city ventilation rates will enable the meteorological portion of this and other models to be more sophisticated and more realistic. This work was, as one would expect, performed on a high-speed computer. As in so many other scientific problems, the required calculations (about 10^6 for the 24-hour average concentration field) became feasible only with such assistance.

The use of mathematical models for computer solution appears to promise much in the quantitive determination of pollution concentrations. As we learn more about the meteorology of cities and the distribution of pollutant emissions, it may be possible to predict expected concentrations routinely and to take into account the changes in the patterns that would occur if the emissions were changed. The auto-exhaust pollution from the Sunday-driver pattern could be differentiated from that of the weekday rush-hour regardless of the variation in the atmospheric dilution. On a larger scale, it is expected that computer-produced "Air Pollution Potential Forecasts" will replace the present techniques, which require both manual data analysis and personal judgment, and will extend both the time period and detail of these forecasts.

Future Problems

Much remains to be learned about how the atmosphere acts to dilute materials and eventually to rid itself of them. The problem is particularly acute within cities, since there now exists no adequate model to describe, in quantitative terms, the movement of air through such a complex structure as an entire city, and since most industrial pollution originates within the city itself. In the near future a major effort will be required to determine the cumulative effect on air purity of the complex of cities that are expanding and combining to create the megalopolis. Here the problem requires consideration of weather patterns over several days and hundreds of kilometers, if we are to determine the extent to which pollution from "foreign" sources 100 to 500 kilometers upwind adds to the locally emitted pollution. On this scale, chemical interactions of pollutants and their "half-lives," the effects of sunlight and humidity, the effects of depletion of pollutants due to deposition, and so on, must be known. None of these problems appears to defy practical solution, but a program of research, probably culminating in extensive, long-range tracer experiments, will be required.

In the longer, and larger, view perhaps the most important future problem is to achieve better understanding of the geochemistry of atmospheric pollutants. It has been pointed out that there are probably no undisturbed atmospheric conditions left in any of the mechanized areas of the world. The possible "greenhouse" effect of carbon dioxide is not known precisely, yet extrapolation of present measurements indicates a global increase in this constituent of about 40 percent by the turn of the century. Sulfur is emitted to the atmosphere in ever-increasing amounts, but we know neither its fate nor its rate of addition with any precision. We cannot be certain whether massive additions of air pollutants could affect our climate and, if they can, in what fashion. A careful, long-term program of measurement, probably of global extent, of the most important pollutants, additional research to increase our understanding of the self-cleansing mechanisms of the atmosphere, and more knowledge about the relation between air pollution and climate are required if we are to safeguard the air reservoir in which we live and breathe.

Bibliographical Notes

In lieu of internal references, I have listed selected material for the interested reader. The first four items cover turbulence theory and its modification for atmospheric application; the next two deal with practical meteorological relations to pollution; the last three, primarily with urban pollution.

Batchelor, G. K. *The Theory of Homogeneous Turbulence* (Cambridge Univ. Press, Cambridge, 1956).

Hinze, J. O. *Turbulence* (McGraw-Hill, New York, 1959).

Pasquill, F. *Atmospheric Diffusion* (Van Nostrand, London, 1962).

Sutton, O. G. *Micrometeorology* (McGraw-Hill, New York, 1953).

Magill, P. L., Ed., *Air Pollution Handbook* (McGraw-Hill, New York, 1956).

U.S. Atomic Energy Commission, *Meteorology and Atomic Energy* (Government Printing Office, Washington, D.C., 1955).

"Air over Cities," *R. A. Taft Sanitary Engineering Center, Cincinnati, Publ.* (1962).

Leighton, P. A., *Photochemistry of Air Pollution* (Academic Press, New York, 1961).

Stern, A. C., ed., *Air Pollution* (Academic Press, New York, 1962).

Picture credits: Figure 9.1, D. H. Pack and C. R. Hosler, in *Proc, UN Intern, Conf. Peaceful Uses At. Energy, 2nd Geneva 1958*, 18, 265 (1958). Figure 9.2, C. R. Hosler, *ibid.* **89**, 319(1961). Figure 9.3, W. M. Culkowski, "Time exposure photography of smoke plumes," *Oak Ridge Office Tech. Inf. Publ. ORO-359* (1961). Figure 9.4, U.S. Atomic Energy Commission, Idaho Falls, Idaho. Figure 9.5, D. H. Pack and J. K. Angell, *Monthly Weather Rev.* 91, 385 (1963). Figure 9.6, J. Korshover, "Synoptic climatology of stagnating anticyclones east of the Rocky Mountains in the United States for the period 1936–1960" (U.S. Weather Bureau, unpublished). Figure 9.7, D. B. Turner, "A simple diffusion model for an urban atmosphere," in preparation.

ADDITIONAL REFERENCES

Holzworth, G. C. 1967. Mixing depths, wind speeds and air pollution potential for selected locations in the United States. *Journal of Applied Meteorology* 6:1039–1044.

Panofsky, H. A. 1969. Air pollution meteorology. *Am. Sci.* 57(2):269–285.

Slade, D. 1967. Modelling air pollution in the Washington, D.C., to Boston megalopolis. *Science* 157:1304–1307.

Slade, D. H. 1968. *Meteorology and atomic energy 1968.* Washington, D.C.: U.S. Atomic Energy Commission. 445 pp.

Wexler, H. 1961. The role of meteorology in air pollution. Pp. 49–61 in *Air pollution,* by World Health Organization. New York: Columbia University Press.

World Meteorological Organization. 1970. *Meteorological Aspects of Air Pollution.* Technical Note, No. 106. 69 pp.

World Meteorological Organization. *Meteorological aspects of atmospheric radioactivity.* Technical Note, No. 68. 194 pp.

GEOGRAPHICAL ASPECTS OF AIR POLLUTION

PHILIP A. LEIGHTON

The previous selection showed that the supply of air available for waste disposal is at times severely limited by certain meteorological factors, including temperature inversions and low winds. In this selection Philip A. Leighton uses specific examples to expand on these causes and, in addition, to show the importance of topography. He then ties these geographical factors to increasing yearly emissions of pollutants to demonstrate the growing danger and dimmer prospects for control of our foul air.

In heavily populated and technologically advanced areas the discharges of many pollutants are increasing faster than the population, so that in spite of efforts at control some kinds of air pollution continue to grow. An outstanding example, created by the increasing use of hydrocarbon fuels, particularly by automobiles, is photochemical air pollution. Nitrogen oxides and hydrocarbons are the emissions chiefly responsible for this. If these emissions continue to grow at present rates, partial control measures such as the installation of exhaust control devices on automobiles will bring at best only temporary relief.

Yet, concerning the prospects presented here for the near future, in 1970 (less than five years after this article was written) Leighton said that "Although these projections were pessimistic, they weren't quite pessimistic enough. In updating the hydrocarbon and nitrogen oxide emissions curves in Figures 10.11 and 10.12, I find that the actual emissions are running higher than the projections in those figures."

Philip A. Leighton (b. 1897) is professor of chemistry, emeritus, at Stanford University. He received an A.B. from Pomona College, and masters and doctoral degrees from Harvard. His current research interests are chiefly in environmental photochemistry, including photochemical air pollution, the photochemical evolution of the atmosphere, and the photochemical origin of life. Leighton remarks, "There are some fascinating speculative relationships here; for example one may draw a parallel between the photochemical particulates which are now formed in the air over our cities and the photochemical coacervates, the forerunners of life which are thought to have been formed eons ago in the shallow waters of the earth. Eventually, it is supposed, the coacervates went on to gain the power of reproduction, which fortunately for us the smog particles haven't done—yet."

Reprinted from the *Geographical Review*, volume 56, pp. 151–174, 1966, copyrighted by the American Geographical Society of New York.

Besides the general year-to-year intensification of air pollution in cities, this selection reveals the tremendous spread of photochemical pollution. By the mid-1960s in California, eye-irritation areas included about 70 percent of the people, plant damage areas 80 percent, and areas of general visibility reduction about 97 percent.

(Editor's comment)

. . . this most excellent canopy, the air,
look you, this brave o'erhanging firmament, this
majestical roof fretted with golden fire, why, it appears
no other thing to me
than a foul and pestilent congregation of vapours.
                                        —Hamlet, Act II, Scene ii.

It is reasonable to suppose that man originally evolved with few if any inhibitions regarding the use of that part of his environment which he was able to capture and hold from his competitors. Only with experience, as his knowledge and numbers increased, did he come to realize that the physical requirements of life are limited and that their use must be regulated. Since earliest history he has been devising systems for the ownership, protection, and use of land and food, and, more recently, of water. Last of all to become subject to this realization and regulation is air. Here the tradition of free use is still dominant. We respect rights of ownership in land, food, and water, but except as a medium of transportation we recognize none for air.

Curiously, this divergence in attitude, or in the stage of modification of attitude, does not parallel either the urgency of man's needs or his ability to adapt his surroundings to meet those needs. He can live indefinitely away from land, he can go several weeks without food and several days without water, awake he normally eats and drinks only at intervals, and asleep he does neither, but awake or asleep his need for air is never further away than his next breath. As for ability to adapt, he can when he so wishes improve the land, he can improve and transport food and water, but except on a small scale, as in air conditioning in dwellings and other buildings or the use of wind machines

in orchards, he cannot yet improve or transport air. Outdoor air in the main he only contaminates.

Although the realization that air also is a limited resource has been slow in developing, the recognition that its contamination may easily exceed acceptable limits is not new. The first ancient who kicked a smoking ember out of his cave was taking an air-pollution control step more effective than many that are taken today, and the first air-pollution control laws on record, designed to reduce the burning of coal, were enacted in England more than six centuries ago. These attempts at control have expanded until there are now in the United States alone some 360 government agencies—local, state, and federal—partly or entirely concerned with the problem.[1]

Despite the unremitting work of such agencies, for the most part air pollution continues to grow. Its growth has more or less paralleled man's increasing use of technology, with the result that the most technologically advanced areas of the world are also, with few exceptions, the areas of most severe air pollution. This is due, of course, to the overuse of air for waste disposal, and an excellent example, which very much involves the tradition of free use of air, is the automobile. Automobiles emit carbon monoxide, nitrogen oxides, and hydrocarbons, all of which must be diluted in air if they are not to reach adverse concentrations. The undesirable effects of nitrogen oxides begin to appear at concentrations of about 0.05 parts per million (ppm). Cruising at 60 miles per hour, the average "full sized" American automobile emits, at 25°C and 1000 mb, about 3 liters of nitrogen oxides per minute. To dilute these below 0.05 ppm requires, for the one automobile, more than 6×10^7 liters of air per minute, a rate which is enough to supply the average breathing requirements, over the same period of time, of five to ten million people.

As a result of such prodigal uses of air for waste disposal, the employment of technology has contributed far more to the production of air pollution than to its abatement, and it is clear that the ratio must be reversed if man as a breathing organism is to retain a compatible environment. But to define the extent to which the uses of air must be regulated, we must first know something about how much is available. As with man's other needs, it is a simple matter of supply and demand.

The Supply of Air

The height of the troposphere in the middle latitudes, 10–14 km, is about one five-hundredth of the earth's radius. This is a thin skin indeed, yet it contains about four-fifths of all the air in the atmosphere, and to man on the surface of the earth the layer of air available for waste disposal is usually only a fraction—and sometimes only a very small fraction—of the troposphere. The air supply at the surface is limited to an extent that varies with place and time, and the factors contributing to the limited surface ventilation are both meteorological and topographic.

The most common meteorological factors are inversions that limit vertical mixing of air and low winds that limit its lateral transport. An inversion is a reversal of the normal tropospheric lapse rate, or decrease in air temperature with increasing altitude above the surface, which for the United States and international standard atmospheres is 0.65°C per 100 meters (Figure 10.1). A parcel of air ascending in the atmosphere expands with the decreasing pressure and is thereby cooled, and when this process occurs adiabatically, the rate of cooling, or the adiabatic lapse rate, in unsaturated air is about 1°C per 100 meters. When the atmospheric lapse rate is

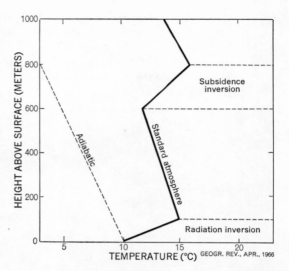

FIGURE 10.1 **Temperature profile through two inversion layers.**

less than this, as it is in the standard atmosphere, an ascending air parcel becomes cooler, and hence denser, than the surrounding air, and work is required to lift it against the downward force produced by the density difference. Similarly, a parcel of air being lowered in a subadiabatic temperature gradient becomes warmer and less dense than the surrounding air, producing an upward force against which work is again required. When the temperature gradient is inverted, the amount of work required to move a parcel of air across the inversion layer usually exceeds the supply available through turbulence and other atmospheric processes, and there is, in consequence, little or no mixing through the layer (Figure 10.2).

Inversions occur both at the surface and aloft. Surface inversions are most commonly produced by cooling of the ground by radiation loss, which in turn cools the surface air, and their depth, intensity, and duration are functions of the wind velocity, the nature of the surface, the transparency of the air above the surface to the emitted radiation, and the amount of insolation during the following day. The chief absorbers, in air, of the long-wave infrared emitted by a surface at ordinary temperatures are water and carbon dioxide. Hence radiative cooling is most

FIGURE 10.2 A low inversion prevents the upward diffusion of pollutants over San Francisco and the east bay.

marked when the air is dry and pure, and it increases with altitude as the amount of air overhead is reduced.

The commonest source of inversions aloft is the subsidence that normally accompanies high-pressure systems, but overhead inversions may also be produced, both on a local scale and on an air-mass or frontal scale, by the intrusion of cold air under warm or by the overrunning of cold air by warm. In the middle latitudes subsidence inversions are most marked in the anticyclonic gradients on the easterly sides of high-pressure cells and approach closer to the surface with increasing distance from the cell center.[2] For this reason the west coasts of the continents are subject to relatively low overhead inversions from the semipermanent marine highs, and these inversions may last for many days. Along the Southern California coast, for example, inversions below 762 m (2500 ft), mostly due to subsidence associated with the Pacific high, exist 90 percent or more of the time during the summer months. The variations in average height and frequency of these inversions with season and location[3] are summarized in Table 10.1.

The effect of high-pressure systems in limiting surface ventilation through subsidence inversions is enhanced by the low winds that usually accompany these systems, and also by clear skies, which promote the formation of radiation inversions. The occurrence of these conditions can be forecast, and since August 1, 1960, for the eastern United States and October 1, 1963, for the western United States the Division of Air Pollution of the United States Public Health Service has issued advisories of high air pollution potential, based on forecasts of the simultaneous occurrence, for periods of 36 hours or more over minimum areas equivalent to a 4° latitude-longitude square, of subsidence below 600 mb, surface winds below 8 knots, no winds above 25 knots up to 500 mb, and no precipitation.[4] The number and regional distribution of forecast days from the initiation of the program through December, 1964, are shown on Figure 10.3.

For the eastern United States, these fore-

TABLE 10.1 Frequency and average height of inversions below 2500 ft. along the California coast* (Base height in m)

SEASON	SAN DIEGO		SANTA MONICA		OAKLAND	
	% of days	Av. base height	% of days	Av. base height	% of days	Av. base height
Jan–Mar	38	382	47	270	22	386
Apr–June	69	465	77	323	59	327
July–Sept	90	434	92	296	85	253
Oct–Dec	55	353	61	243	45	296
Annual	63	408	69	283	53	315

* Estimated from radiosonde observations taken daily at 1600 PST from June, 1957, to March, 1962 (Holzworth, Bell, and De Marrais, *op. cit.* [see text note 3]).

cast frequencies may be compared, if the differences in time period are kept in mind, with Korshover's estimates[5] of the number of periods of four or more successive days of low wind resulting from stagnating anticyclones (Figure 10.4). Both studies agree on the absence of such conditions in the Great Plains region—perhaps to the surprise of residents of Denver—and on increasing frequency east of the Mississippi, with a maximum, though here the two charts differ, in the vicinity of eastern Tennessee. The Great Smokies, it would appear, are aptly named.

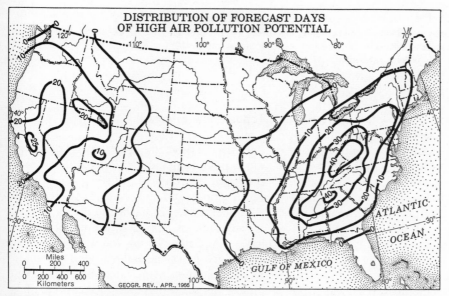

FIGURE 10.3 The air pollution potential advisory forecasts of the Division of Air Pollution, United States Public Health Service, began August 1, 1960, for the eastern United States, and October 1, 1963, for the western United States. The numbers shown on the contours indicate the number of forecast days from the initiation date in each case through December, 1964. Source: data from R. A. McCormick (see text note 4).

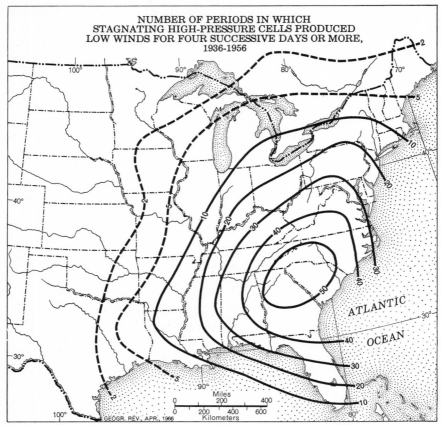

NUMBER OF PERIODS IN WHICH
STAGNATING HIGH-PRESSURE CELLS PRODUCED
LOW WINDS FOR FOUR SUCCESSIVE DAYS OR MORE,
1936-1956

FIGURE 10.4 Number of periods in which stagnating high-pressure cells produced low winds for four or more successive days in the eastern United States, 1936–1956. Source: J. Korshover (see text note 5 for reference).

For the western United States, the forecasting program has been in operation for too short a time to permit more than tentative conclusions, but it does indicate a frequency considerably higher, in days per year, than that in the eastern states. A maximum appears in central California and perhaps another maximum in the Great Basin, extending northwest from Salt Lake City. It should be borne in mind, however, that these forecasts, like Korshover's study, are based on synoptic data and do not take local topographic effects into account; for this reason areas where local effects are important may have a much higher stagnation frequency than the charts seem to indicate.

Topographic Effects

Perhaps the most important effects of topography in limiting the supply of surface air are produced by drainage. Just as water drains down slopes and gullies to form rivers in valleys and lakes in basins, so the air, cooled by radiation loss, drains down those slopes at night. And like flowing water, these density or gravity flows of cold air tend to follow regular channels, which may be marked out almost as definitely as the course of a stream. The volume of air drainage, however, is much larger than that of water drainage; hence the aircourses are broader, and if the valley or basin is not too wide the flows soon collect to reach across it. The layers thus formed, further cooled by radiation loss in the valley or basin itself, become so stable that they often completely control the surface wind direction and velocity and thus control the air supply; the gradient wind is blocked out, and even the gravity flows from the surrounding slopes tend to overrun the air in the bottom (Figure 10.5). After sunrise thermal upslope flow soon sets in on slopes exposed to the sun, but gravity flow may continue until late morning on shady slopes, and even all day on steep northern slopes.[6]

The cold layers accumulated by this process during the long nights of winter may become so deep, with inversions so intense, that they are not broken up by insolation during the short days; and when this happens, severely limited ventilation will persist until a change in weather produces gradient winds high enough, or a cold wedge strong enough, to sweep out the valley or basin. For any particular combination of topography there is usually a fairly critical gradient or synoptic wind velocity below which the local flows are dominant and above which the gradient wind is dominant. The smaller the relief, the lower is this critical velocity; for relief differences of 300–600 m it is of the order of 10–15 knots.[7]

A classic example of the consequences of unrestricted pollution in an air supply limited by both synoptic and topographic effects is found in the Copper Basin around Ducktown in the southeast corner of Tennessee. This basin, with an area of about 100 square km, lies between the Blue Ridge and the Unaka Mountains and has relief differences of as much as 600 m above its floor. It drains into the Ocoee River to the south and slopes gently upward to the northeast, and it lies in a region of maximum occurrence of synoptic conditions favoring low gradient winds (Figure 10.4). The local air circulation, which is dominant a large part of the time (as much as 60 percent in winter), consists of a low level flow that follows the drainage pattern upstream by day and downstream by night; superimposed on this is a gentle gravity flow from the periphery of the basin toward the center on clear nights, which results in pooling with strong inversions up to depths of 50–100 m.[8]

Smelting of copper ore, releasing all the sulfur and arsenic in the ore to the air as the corresponding oxides, began in the basin shortly after the Civil War and reached a maximum in 1890–1895. As a result, by the turn of the century an area of about 30 square km in the center of the basin had been completely denuded of vegetation and the remaining 70 square km had been largely denuded. Although open-hearth smelting has

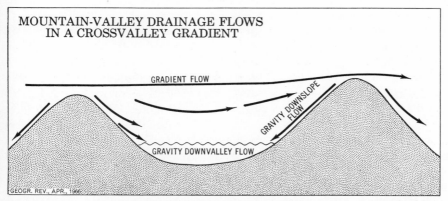

FIGURE 10.5 In the case diagramed, the gradient wind is blocked out of the valley by the bordering mountains, and the air supply on the valley floor is limited to that in the lower part of the gravity downvalley flow.

long since been abandoned, these areas remain bare today. Moreover, the basin has been severely eroded since it was denuded, and the bare areas are therefore still expanding.[9]

Another classic example, but with a happier outcome, is the international transport of polluted air by gravity flow down the Columbia Valley. The Columbia River flows from Canada into the United States in a rather narrow valley, with sides rising steeply 600–800 m above the valley floor. In 1896 a lead-zinc smelter was established in the valley at Trail, British Columbia, some 10 km north of the border, and by 1930 this smelter was emitting as much as 600–700 tons of sulfur dioxide a day. At night this sulfur dioxide was carried downstream by the gravity flow. The resultant damage to agricultural crops in the state of Washington led to international litigation, which in turn led to the formation in 1928 of an International Joint Commission and in 1935 of an Arbitral Tribunal with the dual responsibility of assessing damage and seeking a permanent solution.

The study conducted by the Arbitral Tribunal[10] showed that during the growing season surface concentrations of sulfur dioxide were highest rather regularly about 8:00 a.m., which is about the time of day when growing plants are most sensitive. Moreover, these concentrations developed almost simultaneously at all the measuring stations, which were located from 10 to 55 km downstream from the smelter. The explanation, applicable also to somewhat similar behavior observed in the basinlike Salt Lake and Tooele valleys of Utah, is that during the preceding nights the valley or basin becomes filled with stable air, in which the gases rising from the smelter stacks soon level off to form a shallow but concentrated overhead layer. This layer is carried downstream as a long ribbon in a narrow valley or spreads out over a broader valley or basin. After sunrise, surface heating produces a superadiabatic lapse rate with strong vertical mixing, and when this turbulent layer reaches the polluted layer aloft,

the pollutants are rapidly brought to the surface, producing sudden and almost simultaneous high concentrations over the areas concerned.

Both at Trail and in Utah these studies led to the adoption of methods of meteorological control, under which by continuous monitoring the hazardous periods could be anticipated and the smelter operations curtailed. In Utah the judge under whom this control method was adopted remarked on his retirement many years later that this was, to him, the most satisfactory outcome of all the cases he had tried in forty years on the bench. At Trail the need for control was reduced by recovering the sulfur dioxide and converting it to marketable products, a procedure that has since materially changed the nature of the industrial operation.

In coastal areas diurnal warming and cooling of the land, while the water temperature remains fairly constant, produce the familiar pattern of land-sea breezes, which are usually thought of as improving ventilation but which may under certain conditions restrict it. An example is found in the Los Angeles basin, where the Santa Monica Mountains to the northwest and the Sierra Madre to the north furnish shelter to the extent that local air flow is usually dominant under the subsidence inversion. This local flow consists chiefly of a gentle seaward drainage at night and a more rapid landward movement by day. But the mountains rising above the inversion layer retard the sweeping out of the basin by the landward movement, and the diurnal reversal in direction tends to move air back and forth in the basin. As a result of this entrapment, there is often some carry-over of pollutants from the day before, and pollutants emitted at night move toward or out over the sea, only to be swept back over the land the next morning. On occasion this polluted air is carried back over a neighboring area, even a fairly distant one; thus eye irritation came to Santa Barbara for the first time in January, 1965, partly as the result of this process.

These effects are enhanced by a cold upwelling in the ocean along most of the California coast, which produces surface-water temperatures lower than the temperatures farther out to sea. As the surface layer of air moves over this cold water it also is cooled. One result is the familiar coastal fog of California, but a more important result, with respect to air pollution, is the additional stability the cooling imparts to the landward-moving air.

The airflow patterns in the San Francisco Bay Area illustrate another mechanism by which water may limit the air supply. During the extensive season of the semipermanent Pacific high, air cooled by the offshore ocean upwelling flows through the Golden Gate and between the hills of San Francisco to the inner bay (Figure 10.6). Part of this air crosses the bay and is deflected to the north and south by the east-bay hills, and part travels south and southeast over the bay itself. Meanwhile, another flow of air reaches the south-bay area by moving inland across the mountains to the west. This air, having traveled farther over land, is warmer than the air that comes down the bay, and when the two flows intersect, the warmer overrides the cooler and produces a local overhead inversion that around Palo Alto may be less than 100 m above the ground. Although the existence of this effect was demonstrated twenty years ago, its contribution to the severity of air pollution in the south-bay area remains to be determined.

Many other instances of the increase of air pollution by local topography could be cited. Winter air pollution in the Salt Lake valley is due as much to the pooling of drainage air from the Wasatch Range as it is to Utah and Wyoming coal. Air pollution at Denver, as has already been hinted, is attributed more to topographic than to synoptic

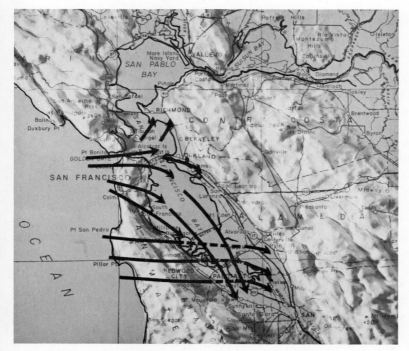

FIGURE 10.6 Daytime airflow patterns in the San Francisco Bay Area. In the southern part of the Bay Area, wind coming over the mountains to the west overrides the colder air coming down the bay, producing an overhead inversion that may contribute to the severity of air pollution in the Palo Alto-San Jose area.

limitations on the air supply. St. Louis, Pittsburgh, and Cincinnati have faced up to difficult problems created in part by local topography. In New York City the Hudson Valley and the surrounding water contribute to the problem. Mexico City suffers from pooling in the Valley of Mexico. The west coast of South America, backed by the Andes, is subject to periods of topographically limited ventilation, which increases air pollution in Santiago and Lima. In Australia the Sydney basin resembles, in a number of respects, the Los Angeles basin. The air-pollution disasters in the Meuse Valley in Belgium and at Donora, Pennsylvania, were the result of the entrapment of air in valleys. Even the chronic problem and the repeated disasters in London may be assigned in part to topography in that the terrain offers no opportunity for drainage, and under a strong surface inversion with no gradient wind the air simply stagnates.

As urbanization and industrialization expand over the world it is interesting, and possibly beneficial, to attempt some assessment of the local air supply in areas that are still relatively empty. Although aero-geographical surveys would be required for an adequate assessment, tentative indications may be obtained merely by consulting maps and weather data. For instance, topography alone suggests that the Granby basin in Colorado would be a poor location in which to build a smelter, and both topography and weather data suggest that such places as the Santa Ynez valley in California and the Sous plain in Morocco should certainly be surveyed before any large industrial or urban development is undertaken. But one does not have to go far in this search to find that most of the unfavorable locations are already occupied. The factors that limit local ventilation are also factors conducive to habitation, and it is ironic that the areas of the world in which the air supply is on occasion most limited are often the areas in which man has chosen to build his cities.

Fortunately, poor ventilation, whether produced by general inversions and low winds or by local conditions, does not exist all the time. The sparkling clarity still enjoyed on days of good ventilation, even over large urban areas, serves to emphasize the great effect of limited air supply on the poor days, and the extent to which it increases the problems of air pollution.

Increase of Photochemical Air Pollution

The contaminants which man introduces into the surface air are of many forms; each creates its own problems, and to a large extent each problem is a case unto itself. Perhaps the least difficult of these problems are those caused by pollutants that come from only one or a few specific sources that can be pinpointed and readily controlled. Sulfur dioxide from smelters, stack dust from cement plants, fluorides from aluminum and phosphate plants, industrial smoke, and various exotic industrial gases and particulates are examples of emissions from specific sources, and control of some of them began more than half a century ago.

A more difficult group of problems, most of which remain for future solution, arise when the sources of pollution, although specific, are not fixed or for other reasons cannot be easily controlled. In this category are such things as agricultural dust, smoke from agricultural burning, airborne insecticides, and hydrogen sulfide and other obnoxious gases from sewage and organic industrial wastes.

The most difficult problems occur when the effects result from a general merging of pollutants from many diverse sources. Historically, the combustion of coal has been a major cause of general air pollution, but in the United States since World War II the overall contribution of coal to air pollution has diminished with its decreasing use, while the contributions of the hydrocarbon fuels have grown with their increasing use (Figure 10.7). Outstanding among the new problems created by the shift in fossil fuels is photochemical air pollution. The emissions chiefly responsible for this form of pollution are nitric oxide, together with some nitrogen dioxide, and hydrocarbons. The nitrogen oxides come from virtually every operation using fire, including internal-combustion engines, steam boilers, various industrial operations, and even home water heaters and gas stoves.

Not all the hydrocarbons emitted to the air take part in the photochemical reactions. Methane, the chief component of natural gas, is inactive. Acetylene, benzene, and the simple paraffins such as propane and butane are nearly inactive. On the other hand, all the olefins, the more complex aromatics, and the higher paraffins are reactive, though they differ widely both in rate and in products. These reactive hydrocarbons come from motor vehicles, from the production, refining, and marketing[11] of petroleum and petroleum products, and from the evaporation of solvents. Other emissions that may play some part in photochemical air pollution are aldehydes, which come chiefly from the incomplete combustion of organic materials, and sulfur dioxide. When these emissions are mixed, diluted in air, and exposed to sunlight, they undergo photochemical reactions that lead to the conversion of the nitric oxide to nitrogen dioxide, which has a brown color and may have adverse effects on plants and animals if its concentration becomes high enough. This is followed, and sometimes accompanied, by the formation of particulates that reduce visibility, of ozone and peroxyacyl nitrates (PAN) that damage plants, and of formaldehyde and other products that, along with the peroxyacyl nitrates, cause eye irritation.

An increasing intensity of pollution is required to produce these symptoms of photochemical air pollution, lowest for visibility reduction, intermediate for plant damage, and highest for eye irritation. Accordingly, the first symptom to appear in any particular area is visibility reduction, the next is plant damage, then follows eye irritation. Simi-

larly, the areas affected are largest for visibility reduction, intermediate for plant damage, and smallest for eye irritation. An estimate of these areas in California is shown in Figure 10.8. The magnitude of the problem is emphasized by the fact that the eye irritation areas comprise about 70 percent of the people of California, the plant damage areas 80 percent, the areas of general visibility reduction about 97 percent.

One of the most challenging aspects of photochemical air pollution is the rate at which it has grown and is growing. For example, photochemical damage to plants was first observed in an area of a few square km in Los Angeles County in 1942. In less than twenty years this area had expanded to more than 10,000 square km and new areas had appeared, bringing the total for California to nearly 30,000 square km. Photochemical pollution has now been observed in more than half the states in the United States and in an increasing number of other countries.[12]

This remarkable spread may be traced to two factors, the first of which is that nitrogen oxide and hydrocarbon emissions have increased faster than the population. The largest source of both nitrogen oxides and hydrocarbons is the automobile; in California at the present time about 60 percent of the

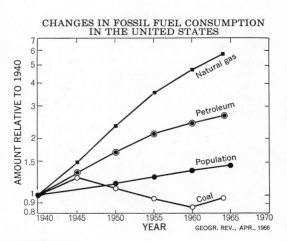

CHANGES IN FOSSIL FUEL CONSUMPTION IN THE UNITED STATES

GEOGR. REV., APR., 1966

FIGURE 10.7

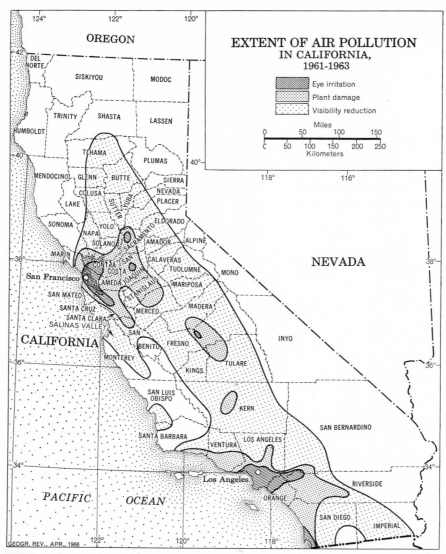

FIGURE 10.8 Extent of general air pollution in California, 1961–1963. The plant-damage areas are specific, but the eye irritation and visibility reduction may be due in part to forms of general pollution other than photochemical. Sources: for plant damage, J. T. Middleton: California against Air Pollution (California Department of Public Health, Sacramento, 1961); for eye irritation and visibility reduction, local reports and personal observations up to December, 1963.

nitrogen oxides and 75 to 85 percent of the reactive hydrocarbons, depending on how these are estimated, come from motor vehicles. Between 1940 and 1965 the population of California increased 2.7 times and gasoline use by motor vehicles in the state increased 4.3 times (Figure 10.9). The growth in elec-tric-power generation, now 9.2 times what it was in 1940, has been another contributor to increasing nitrogen oxide emissions; roughly 16 percent of the present nitrogen oxide emissions in California come from steam-electric power plants. Hydrocarbon emissions, on the other hand, over the state as a whole have probably increased more in accordance with gasoline use.

The second factor contributing to the growth of photochemical air pollution is the relation between emission rate and the area covered by a given concentration as the pollutants are carried by the wind. This may be illustrated, for idealized conditions, by use of the box model, which assumes uniform mixing to a constant height such as an overhead inversion base, with dilution by lateral diffusion beneath that ceiling. The isopleths for a given concentration, calculated from this model[13] for various emission rates in a uniform square source (that is, an idealized city), under constant wind direction and velocity are shown in Figure 10.10. Starting, by definition, with the given concentration appearing at only a single point when the emission rate is unity, the areas within the isopleths are seen to increase much faster than the corresponding emission rates.

When a specific symptom of pollution has expanded to fill a geographical area, as is the case with plant damage in the Los Angeles basin and the San Francisco Bay Area, further increase may be expected to be in intensity rather than in extent. However, the movement of pollutants from one airshed to another is not excluded (Figure 10.8); the fingers of plant damage extending north and east from the Los Angeles region and southeast and east from the Bay region show that these areas are still growing, and if photochemical air pollution is not abated it may be assumed that the present visibility-reduction area is a shadow of the coming plant-damage area, and the present plant-damage area forecast of the coming eye-irritation area.

Some of the hydrocarbons emitted to the air react much more slowly with the nitrogen oxides than others; these less reactive hydrocarbons, such as ethylene and some of the paraffins, produce ozone but little or no PAN. Accordingly, if ozone but not PAN plant damage is observed in an area, it may be taken as evidence that the pollutants have been airborne for some time and may have traveled some distance.[14] Thus PAN damage

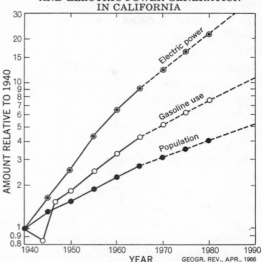

GROWTH OF POPULATION, GASOLINE USE, AND ELECTRIC POWER GENERATION IN CALIFORNIA

FIGURE 10.9 With the exception of the war years, the increase in gasoline use and, to a small extent, that of electric power generation relative to population have followed the exponential relation $A/A_{1940} = P/P_{1940}{}^{n}$, where A/A_{1940} is the amount of gasoline use or power production relative to 1940 and P/P_{1940} is the corresponding ratio for population. The indicated average values of n are 1.5 for gasoline use and about 2.2 for electric power, and the projections were made on this basis. Source: population projection to 1980, Financial and Population Research Section, California State Department of Finance.

is found in and around Washington, D.C., while ozone damage is observed much farther away, in areas that are in agreement with meteorological information on the trajectories of the air that has passed over Washington.[15] Similarly, ozone damage to tobacco

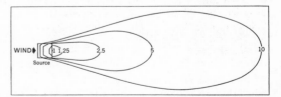

FIGURE 10.10 Area coverage by a pollutant as a function of emission rate. The figures are relative emission rates, and the curves are the corresponding isopleths of given concentration. Estimated for a uniform square source with constant wind direction and velocity under an overhead inversion at constant height.

plants in the upper Delaware Valley, with no concomitant PAN damage, suggests that the pollutants may have been transported some distance, perhaps from the Philadelphia-Trenton or New York metropolitan areas. The same situation with respect to tobacco damage in the Connecticut Valley may be due to the transport of pollutants from any of a number of centers in the Boston–New York conurbation.

The Prospects for Control

Although photochemical air pollution is well on its way to becoming the number one form of general air pollution in the United States, a broad attack against it has thus far been mounted only in California. However, the passage by Congress on October 1, 1965, of a bill requiring the installation after September, 1967, of exhaust control devices on new automobiles of domestic manufacture will expand this attack to a national scale, and in view of this prospect the California program merits examination in some detail.

In an assessment of the prospects for the abatement of photochemical air pollution by automobile controls, three factors are pertinent: the time delay or lead time; the growth in emissions over that lead time; and the degree of control likely to be achieved. To go back in time, we may now say that the visibility reduction which had become widespread in the Los Angeles basin as early as 1920 was due, in part at least, to photochemical air pollution. Reduction in the sizes of oranges and the cracking of rubber products, now known to be due to photochemical air pollution, were reported at least as early as 1930, specific plant damage was first observed in 1942, and eye irritation had appeared by 1945. The first step toward control was taken in 1948 with a California legislative act establishing air pollution control districts, and the control program in Los Angeles County was initiated shortly thereafter. Not until 1952 was the first evidence obtained that what was then known as "smog" was primarily photochemical and that the emis-

sions chiefly responsible for it were nitrogen oxides and hydrocarbons.

The first control steps directed specifically at photochemical air pollution were applied to hydrocarbon emissions from stationary sources in the Los Angeles basin, and by 1960 these sources were about 60 percent controlled. In 1957–1958 the elimination of home incinerators and the restriction of fuel-oil burning during the smog season achieved about a 45 percent control of nitrogen oxide emissions from stationary sources in the basin. The attack on hydrocarbon emissions from motor vehicles was initiated on a statewide basis in 1959. Roughly 75–80 percent of the reactive hydrocarbons emitted by automobiles come from the exhaust, 14–17 percent from the crankcase, and 7–8 percent from carburetor and fuel-tank evaporation. Installation of crankcase control devices on new cars began in 1961, but their installation on used cars has encountered complex difficulties and delays. Moreover, experience has shown that in the hands of individual owners the actual control achieved by these devices falls considerably short of the theoretical, and judgments of the degree of crankcase hydrocarbon control that will eventually be achieved range from less than 70 percent to about 90 percent.

A standard for exhaust hydrocarbons and carbon monoxide, which specifies that the hydrocarbon content under a given cycle of operation shall not exceed an average of 275 ppm, was adopted in 1960, and the installation on new automobiles of devices intended to meet this standard is beginning with the 1966 models of domestic makes. Revised standards now scheduled to take effect in 1970 will reduce the allowed exhaust hydrocarbon content to 180 ppm and will also require a reduction in evaporation losses. If the installation of devices to meet these 1970 standards is limited to new cars it will be at least 1980 before the exhaust control program as it now stands is fully effective, and judgments of the degree of exhaust hydrocarbon control that may be achieved range from 50 percent to 80 percent, the latter being the theoretical value. A standard of 350 ppm for exhaust nitrogen oxides, which is now in process of adoption, will require devices that produce a theoretical 65 percent control of these emissions.

What this attack has accomplished and may be expected to accomplish must be assessed in relation to the growth in sources and emissions that has occurred and may be expected over the time periods concerned.[16] An assessment on this basis for Los Angeles County is shown in Figure 10.11. Examination of the hydrocarbon curve indicates that neither the controls of emissions from stationary sources initiated after 1950 nor the crankcase controls initiated in 1961 have been sufficient to counteract the overall increase in emissions that accompanied population growth in the county. It would appear that the automobile exhaust and evaporation controls now scheduled will indeed reduce hydrocarbon emissions, even in the face of prospective growth, but if no further steps are taken, the upward climb will be resumed after the program is completed. According to the nitrogen oxide curve the controls of stationary sources initiated in 1957–1958 achieved some reduction, but by about 1963 the gains had been wiped out by the process of growth. The projection indicates that the prospective control of nitrogen oxides from motor vehicles will reduce the overall emissions slightly between 1965 and 1980, but the growth after 1980, if no further steps are taken, will soon carry these emissions to new highs.

The level of emissions in 1940 has often been taken as the value that should be regained to eliminate photochemical plant damage and eye irritation in the Los Angeles basin. To the extent that the projections in Figure 10.11 are valid, it would appear that unless supplemented by other measures the California motor-vehicle control program as it now stands offers little hope of returning photochemical air pollution to its 1940 level in the basin. The program will gain some ground, but further steps will be required to

hold the gain, and if such steps are not taken the situation will again deteriorate.

In the more rapidly growing areas of California the prospects of the motor-vehicle control program, taken alone, are still less optimistic. An excellent example is offered by the Salinas Valley in Monterey County. This immensely rich valley is one of the last major agricultural areas of California to be free of photochemical plant damage, but it is already suffering from visibility reduction (Figure 10.8), and measurements of ozone concentration indicate that the plant-damage level is being approached. The population of the valley is expected to double between 1965 and 1980, and to reach more than three times its 1965 value by 1990. Industrial expansion is being encouraged. In an industrial area at the mouth of the valley a large steam-electric power plant is now in operation, a threefold expansion of this plant has

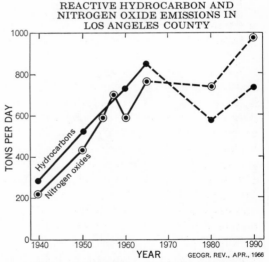

REACTIVE HYDROCARBON AND NITROGEN OXIDE EMISSIONS IN LOS ANGELES COUNTY

GEOGR. REV., APR., 1966

FIGURE 10.11 The projections assume that the population predictions of the California State Department of Finance will be realized; that emissions will continue to increase relative to population as they have since 1940; that motor vehicle crankcase emissions will be 80 percent controlled, exhaust and evaporation hydrocarbons 70 percent controlled, and exhaust nitrogen oxides 60 percent controlled by 1980; and that no other controls will be adopted. Source for emissions to 1965: P. A. Leighton (see text note 16 for reference).

been scheduled, and the construction of an oil refinery has recently been approved. As a result of these and other industries in the valley, the contributions of stationary sources to overall pollution are high; at present, for example, about 75 percent of the nitrogen oxide emissions come from stationary sources, and in view of the prospective industrial growth coupled with the motor-vehicle control program this amount may be expected to increase, perhaps reaching 90 percent by 1980. When these factors and the predicted population increase are taken into account, the projections in Figure 10.12 indicate that the present California motor-vehicle control program in itself will not be sufficient to arrest the growth of photochemical pollution in the Salinas Valley.

The experience and prospects of the Cali-fornia control program illustrate the limitations, and the increasing challenge, that the attack on general air pollution must face in an era of growing population and increasing emissions per capita. With multiple sources and multiple types of sources in all kinds of use, controls at best are incomplete, and most of the steps regarded as practicable provide only a temporary respite from the inexorable pressure of growth. A succession of ever more severe controls is required merely to keep the situation from deteriorating, and if these are not effectively imposed the problem must eventually become one of survival.

In its broader aspects, the challenge is not limited to the air supply in specific geographical areas; it extends to the pollution of the entire atmosphere. Here the outstanding problem is the possibility of self-destruction through atmospheric radioactive contamination as the result of nuclear explosions. However, other problems also loom. There are indications, for example, that the atmospheric lead content in the Northern Hemisphere has increased with man's use of lead and its compounds until it is now about a thousand times what it probably was when our physiological responses to lead were evolved.[17] The carbon dioxide content of the atmosphere has increased 9 percent since 1890, and is reported to be currently increasing by about 0.2 percent a year; and it has been estimated that by the time the known reserves of fossil fuel have been burned the resultant temperature increase on earth, due to the absorption of infrared radiation by atmospheric carbon dioxide, will be sufficient to melt the polar icecaps, inundate present coastal areas, and annihilate many life forms.[18]

In essence these ultimate problems of general air pollution may be stated in simple terms. Whether applied to a local area or to the entire atmosphere it is a matter of maintaining the relation

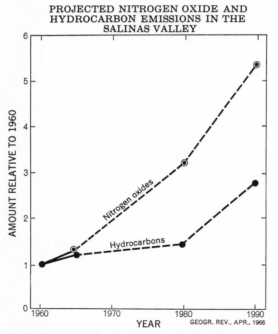

PROJECTED NITROGEN OXIDE AND HYDROCARBON EMISSIONS IN THE SALINAS VALLEY

GEOGR. REV., APR., 1966

FIGURE 10.12 The projections assume that hydrocarbon emissions before controls will increase with gasoline use; that nitrogen oxide emissions from stationary sources will triple between 1965 and 1980 and will increase with population between 1980 and 1990; that vehicular nitrogen oxides will increase with gasoline use to the 1.1 power; and that the controls applied will be the same as in Figure 10.11.

$$\frac{\text{Emissions per capita} \times \text{number of persons}}{\text{Air supply}} < X,$$

where X is the maximum value to which we can accommodate. The means of maintaining this relation, however, are another matter. There is little prospect of increasing the local supply of air and none of increasing the overall supply. The per capita emissions may be reduced by controls, but, as we have seen, with increasing population the steps required become successively more severe, and the end of the process is the elimination of the sources. The accommodation coefficient X, as far as direct physiological effects are concerned, could be increased by the use of protective methods through which we breathed only purified air, but this would not help unprotected life forms or retard the other effects that must be taken into account. The remaining factor in the equation is the number of persons, and it may well be that the resource which eventually forces man to adopt population control as a requirement for survival will not be land, food, or water, but air.

Notes and References

1. *1965 Directory*, Governmental Air Pollution Agencies, Air Pollution Control Association, Pittsburgh, Pa.
2. M. Neiburger, D. S. Johnson, and Chen-wu Chien: Studies of the Structure of the Atmosphere over the Eastern Pacific Ocean in Summer, *Univ. of California Publs. in Meteorol.*, Vol. 1, No. 1, 1961, pp. 1–94.
3. G. C. Holzworth, G. B. Bell, and G. A. De Marrais: Temperature Inversion Summaries of U. S. Weather Bureau Radiosonde Observations in California (U.S. Weather Bureau, Los Angeles, and State of California, Department of Public Health, 1963).
4. Personal communication, R. A. McCormick, Chief, Meteorology Section, Laboratory of Engineering and Physical Sciences, Robert A. Taft Sanitary Engineering Center, Cincinnati.
5. J. Korshover: Synoptic Climatology of Stagnating Anticyclones East of the Rocky Mountains in The United States for the Period 1936–1956, *Rept. SEC TR–A60–7*, Robert A. Taft Sanitary Engineering Center, Cincinnati, 1960.
6. Rudolf Geiger: The Climate near the Ground (translated by Milroy N. Stewart and others; Cambridge, Mass., 1950), pp. 204–230; Friedrich Defant: Local Winds, in *Compendium of Meteorology* (edited by T. F. Malone; American Meteorological Society, Boston, 1951), pp. 655–672; P. A. Leighton: Cloud Travel in Mountainous Terrain, *Quart. Repts. 111-3 and 111-4*, Department of Chemistry, Stanford University, 1954–1955 (Defense Documentation Center AD Numbers 96571, 96486, 96487).
7. Leighton, *op. cit.* [see footnote 6 above], *Quart. Rept. 111-3*, pp. 115–118.
8. *Ibid.*, pp. 54–58.
9. C. R. Hursh: Local Climate in the Copper Basin of Tennessee As Modified by the Removal of Vegetation, *U.S. Dept. of Agric. Circular 774*, 1948.
10. R. S. Dean, R. E. Swain, E. W. Hewson, and G. C. Gill: Reported Submitted to the Trail Smelter Arbitral Tribunal, *U.S. Bur. of Mines Bull. 453*, 1944; E. W. Hewson: The Meteorological Control of Atmospheric Pollution by Heavy Industry, *Quart. Journ. Royal Meteorol. Soc.*, Vol 71, 1945, pp. 266–282.
11. Marketing emissions include such things as losses from tank trucks and service stations, evaporation losses during the filling of automobiles, and so on. In Los Angeles County alone it is estimated that these losses contributed an average of 120 tons of hydrocarbons a day to the air during the year 1963.
12. J. T. Middleton and A. J. Haagen-Smit: The Occurrence, Distribution, and Significance of Photochemical Air Pollution in the United States, Canada, and Mexico, *Journ. Air Pollution Control Assn.*, Vol. 11, 1961, pp. 129–134; J. T. Middleton: Air Conservation and the Protection of Our Natural Resources, in Proceedings of National Conference on Air Pollution (United States Department of Health, Education, and Welfare, Washington, D.C., 1963), pp. 166–172.
13. Personal communication, R. W. McMullen, Metronics Associates, Inc., Palo Alto, Calif.
14. Middleton and Haagen-Smit, *op. cit.* [see footnote 12 above], pp. 132–133.
15. R. C. Wanta and Howard E. Heggestad: Occurrence of High Ozone Concentrations in the Air near Metropolitan Washington, *Science*, Vol. 130, 1959, pp. 103–104.
16. P. A. Leighton: Man and Air in California, in Proceedings of Statewide Conference on Man in California, 1980's (University of California Extension Division, Berkeley, 1964), pp. 44–77.
17. C. C. Patterson: Contaminated and Natural Lead Environments of Man, *Archives of Environmental Health*, Vol. 11, 1965, pp. 344–360.
18. "Implications of Rising Carbon Dioxide Content of the Atmosphere" (Conservation Foundation, New York, 1963).

ADDITIONAL REFERENCES

Garnett, A. 1957. Atmospheric pollution: geographical factors. In *Air pollution,* ed. by M. W. Thring. London: Butterworths Scientific Publications. 248 pp.

Stern, A. C. 1967. The changing pattern of air pollution in the United States. *Amer. Indust. Hyg. Assn. Journal* 28:161–165.

CLIMATE OF THE CITY

JAMES T. PETERSON

In this and the next few selections we turn our consideration from air pollution and its effects to additional kinds of atmospheric modifications wrought by man. We also shift emphasis from man-induced changes in *weather* (defined as the condition of the atmosphere over a short time period, as described by various meteorological phenomena) to changes in *climate* (defined as the combination of weather conditions which characterizes a place or region over a season or longer).

It is natural to look first at the impact of cities on climate. Here the impact of man is greatest, as it is on a number of other aspects of the environment as well. The climatic influence of cities is important because urbanization is increasing and because the intensity and geographic spread of the influence is growing too.

Though the meteorological consequences of urbanization have long been noted, there were only a few detailed descriptions before this century. The present selection, however, indicates the wealth of recent studies in urban climatology. This research is spawning substantive theory and predictive models to explain the nature and ramifications of urban atmospheres.

Pollution and other urban characteristics complexly affect the climate of the city. Every city is unique in the chemistry of its atmosphere, and these differences may cause climatic variations. Wind is the basic parameter of urban climates; tall buildings increase friction and hence reduce the speed of moderate and strong winds, but increase turbulence during light wind situations. Four factors contribute to the excessive

James T. Peterson is a research meteorologist assigned to the National Air Pollution Control Administration by the Air Resources Laboratory, Environmental Science Services Administration. He earned a Ph.D. degree in meteorology from the University of Wisconsin (1968). The author's research is centered on the effects of atmospheric pollutants on radiative transfer, on statistical relations between meteorological factors and pollutant concentrations, and on urban climatology. His interests also include inadvertent weather modification resulting from man's activities and the effects on the environment of waste heat from cooling towers.

This selection is reprinted, with minor editing by permission of the author, from *The Climate of Cities: A Survey of Recent Literature*, 1969, National Air Pollution Control Administration Publication No. AP–59, 48 pp.

heat of towns: changes that buildings and roads cause in the thermal characteristics of the surface; changes in airflow patterns due to reduced diffusion of heat; lower evaporation rates and heat loss; and heat added by man's activities. Precipitation in cities is altered by three major factors: the presence of pollutants that serve as condensation nuclei; increased turbulence caused by buildings; and convective airflow because of higher temperatures. Other climatic factors, too, are affected—humidity, visibility, and radiation. All are discussed in some detail in this selection.

(Editor's comment)

As metropolitan areas expand, they exert a growing influence on their climate. An increasing amount of scientific literature is being devoted to analyses of urban climates, often comparing urban data with data from nearby rural areas to show the differences between "natural" conditions and those influenced by man. These studies also contribute to such areas as the effects of urban environment on health, the influence of meteorological parameters on urban diffusion, and the possible global climatological consequences of increased atmospheric pollution.

The standard review of urban climate consists of the paper by Dr. H. Landsberg (1956) and his supplementary articles in 1960 and 1962; his results, which were presented in tabular form in his latter articles, are summarized in Table 11.1. The purpose of this report is to review the recent literature in

TABLE 11.1 Climatic changes produced by cities (After Landsberg, 1962)

ELEMENT	COMPARISON WITH RURAL ENVIRONS
Temperature	
Annual mean	1.0 to 1.5 °F higher
Winter minima	2.0 to 3.0 °F higher
Relative humidity	
Annual mean	6% lower
Winter	2% lower
Summer	8% lower
Dust particles	10 times more
Cloudiness	
Clouds	5 to 10% more
Fog, winter	100% more
Fog, summer	30% more
Radiation	
Total on horizontal surface	15 to 20% less
Ultraviolet, winter	30% less
Ultraviolet, summer	5% less
Wind speed	
Annual mean	20 to 30% lower
Extreme gusts	10 to 20% lower
Calms	5 to 20% more
Precipitation	
Amounts	5 to 10% more
Days with < 0.2 inch	10% more

this field, primarily that in English, to note the areas of agreement and difference with Landsberg's earlier summaries and to point out the aspects of urban climatology for which more detailed information is now available. This survey concentrates on the most frequently discussed aspects of city-country climatic differences: temperature, humidity, visibility, radiation, wind, and precipitation. Also included is a discussion on urban particulate concentrations. A review of urban concentrations of various gaseous pollutants has recently been published by Tebbens (1968) and thus will not be discussed in this report.

Previous summaries of literature on urban climates include an extensive article by Kratzer in 1937 (revised in 1956 and translated into English), containing references to 533 works, and a bibliography by Brooks (1952) listing 249 references. Books by Geiger (1965), on microclimatology and Chandler (1965) on the climate of London, from which several examples are included herein, also refer to a number of other urban studies. Chandler is currently compiling a bibliography on urban climate under the auspices of the World Meteorological Organization (WMO); this bibliography will reference well over 1,000 articles.

Temperature

Of all the urban-rural meteorological differences, those of air temperature are probably the most documented. That the center of a city is warmer than its environs, forming a "heat island," has been known for more than a hundred years and continues to receive considerable attention in the literature. Many aspects of a heat island have been studied, such as possible reasons for its occurrence; diurnal, weekly, and seasonal variations; relation to city size; and dependence on topography.

NIGHTTIME DIFFERENCES

The fact that a city is warmer than its environs is seen most readily in a comparison of daily minimum temperatures. As Landsberg (1956) pointed out, such comparisons often show temperature differences of 10°F and occasionally differences as great as 20°F. However, since nocturnal temperatures are dependent on topography, a fraction of these differences, sometimes a large fraction, can often be ascribed to terrain features.

Numerous measurements of urban heat islands have been made, frequently by use of automobiles to obtain many observations within a short time period. An example of a London temperature survey associated with clear skies, light winds, and anticyclonic conditions is presented in Figure 11.1 (Chandler, 1965). This figure shows certain features common to most heat islands. The temperature anomalies are generally related to urban morphology. The highest temperatures are associated with the densely built-up area near the city center; moreover, the degree of warming diminishes slowly, outward from the city's heart, through the suburbs and then decreases markedly at the city periphery. The effect of topography is also evident in this example. Urban warming is reduced along the Thames River, in the smaller non-urbanized valleys, and near the city's higher elevations.

Steep temperature gradients at a city's edge have been measured during clear, calm conditions at Hamilton, Ontario (Oke and Hannell, 1968), and Montreal, Quebec (Oke, 1968). These investigators found temperature changes of 3.8 and 4.0°C · km⁻¹, respectively, which they regarded as typical values for moderate to large cities.

Some recent studies have indicated that the mean annual minimum temperature of a large city may be as much as 4°F higher than that of surrounding rural areas. Chandler (1963, 1966) reported on two studies of London, which showed differences of 3.4 and 4.0°F in mean minimum temperatures at urban and rural sites. The first study was based on data from 1921 to 1950 for several stations in and around London; the second compared 1959 data for one downtown and one rural location and applied a correction for the difference in elevation at the stations.

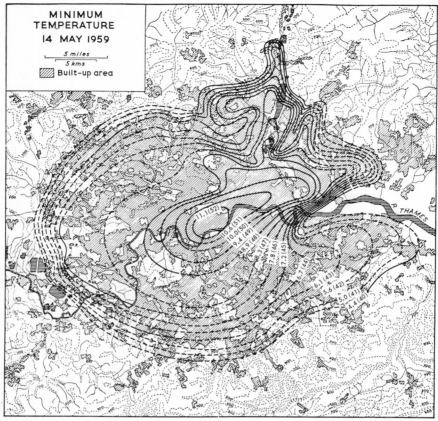

FIGURE 11.1 Minimum temperature distribution in London, May 14, 1959, in °C with °F in brackets (from Chandler, 1965, by permission of the author).

In another study, Woollum (1964) and Woollum and Canfield (1968) presented data for several stations in the vicinity of Washington, D.C., for a 20-year period; mean minimum temperatures for each season were approximately 4°F higher in downtown areas than in outlying regions.

Although the city heat island as indicated by minimum temperatures can be readily detected year-around, the investigations in London by Chandler (1963, 1966) and in Reading, England, by Parry (1966) indicated that the greatest temperature differences occur in summer or early autumn. Woollum (1964) also found that the mean differences between the warmest and coldest stations of his network were greatest in fall and summer, but that the greatest extreme differences be-

tween these stations occurred in winter (see also Landsberg, 1956).

DAYTIME DIFFERENCES

The heat island of a city can be detected during the day, but much less readily than during the evening. The slight daytime temperature differences observed are often difficult to distinguish from those due to the effects of topography. In some instances daytime city temperatures may even be lower than those of the suburbs. For example, Landsberg (1956) presented 1 year of data from city and airport observations in Lincoln, Nebraska, a location essentially free from complicating terrain factors. Daily maxima in the cold season showed little difference between the two sites. During the warm season, however, the airport was more frequently warmer than the downtown site. Such results are not the rule, however, and Landsberg also points out cases of daily maxima that are higher in the city. Similar examples have been given by Chandler (1963, 1966); his data showed that the annual average maximum temperatures of London were 0.6 and 1.1°C higher than those in the outlying areas. Munn et al. (1969) also readily detected a daytime heat island at Toronto, Canada, using daily maximum temperatures.

A recent report by the Stanford Research Institute (Ludwig, 1967; Ludwig and Kealoha, 1968) presents perhaps the most comprehensive documentation of urban daytime temperatures to date. The authors made about twelve auto traverses each at San Jose, California; Albuquerque, New Mexico; and New Orleans, Louisiana, during daytimes in the summer of 1966. Although the temperature anomalies resulting from topographical influences in these cities were greater than those from the heat island, the downtown areas were approximately 0.5°C warmer than the suburbs despite the effects of topography.

In the summer of 1967 SRI extended the study to Dallas, Ft. Worth, and Denton, Texas (population 35,000), where they made 20, 4, and 2 surveys, respectively. When the 1966 and 1967 data were combined with data from three surveys each at Minneapolis, Minnesota, and Winnipeg, Canada (Stanford U. Aerosol Laboratory, 1953a, 1953d, 1953e),[1] and one at London, the investigators found that for these 67 cases the city's warmest part near the downtown area averaged 1.2°C above the typical areas of its environs, with a standard deviation of about 1.0°C. This average value is higher than that observed by other studies, and Ludwig and Kealoha pointed out two possible reasons why investigations of the daytime heat island may underestimate its magnitude. First, they noted that at ground level the highest temperatures of a city do not occur in the central area of tall buildings but rather near that

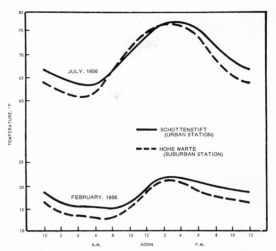

FIGURE 11.2 Diurnal variation of temperature in Vienna for February and July for both an urban and suburban station (from Mitchell, 1962).

part of the downtown area with "densely packed three- to five-story buildings and parking lots." Second, they noted that temperatures observed at suburban airports were higher than those of a true rural environment, either grass-covered or forested.

The diurnal and seasonal heat island variations discussed above are illustrated in Figure 11.2, taken from Mitchell (1962). This figure shows hour-by-hour monthly averages of temperature at an urban and a suburban site in Vienna, Austria. The temperature of the city is higher at night during both February and July, but this urban-rural difference is greater in July. In the daytime, however, the city-rural temperature differences are small during July and consistently small and positive during winter.

ANNUAL DIFFERENCES

The average annual temperatures of a city and its environs, calculated from the daily maxima and minima, also reflect the presence of the urban heat island. Table 11.2 (Landsberg, 1960) lists the average annual urban-rural temperature differences for several large cities. To this can be added the average value for London of 1.3°C based on the

TABLE 11.2 Annual mean urban-rural temperature differences of cities, °C

Chicago	0.6	Moscow	0.7
Washington	0.6	Philadelphia	0.8
Los Angeles	0.7	Berlin	1.0
Paris	0.7	New York	1.1

two studies by Chandler (1963, 1966). Although Woollum and Canfield (1968) do not state a specific number for the mean annual urban-rural temperature differences of Washington, D. C., their recent data for that city indicate that it should be at least 1.0°C, after consideration of the elevation changes of more than 200 feet within the area.

EFFECTS OF CITY SIZE

Several urban studies have considered the effect of city size on the magnitude of the heat island. For example, Mitchell (1961, 1962) showed that during this century most major U.S. metropolitan areas have been both expanding and warming. While the temperature increase may be partly due to global climatic conditions, the amount of warming is well correlated with city growth rate. Dronia (1967) compared temperature trends from 67 paired locations around the world, each pair representing an urban and a rural site, usually separated by several hundred kilometers. He found that in the first five decades of this century the urban areas warmed by 0.24°C more than the rural locations. Similarly, Lawrence (1968) noted that from the late 1940's to early 1960's mean daily minimum temperatures at the Manchester, England, airport increased by about 2.0°F relative to nearby rural stations as the urban area expanded beyond the airport. Landsberg's paper (1960) gave 30 years of data for Los Angeles and San Diego which showed that as the difference in population between those cities increased so did the difference between their mean temperatures.

The relation between city size and urban-rural temperature difference is not linear, however; sizeable nocturnal temperature contrasts have been measured even in relatively small cities. For example, in more than 20 surveys of Palo Alto, California (population 33,000), Duckworth and Sandberg (1954) found that the maximum temperature difference of the survey area was 4 to 6°F. Hutcheon et al. (1967) measured the temperature distribution in Corvallis, Oregon (population 21,000), on two occasions and noted a definite heat island, with maximum temperature differences of 13 and 10°F. Sekiguti (1964) observed a heat island in Ina, Japan (population 12,000). Finally, a heat island effect resulting even from a small, isolated building complex after sunset has been detected (Landsberg, 1968). In contrast, during the two daytime surveys at Denton, Texas, Ludwig and Kealoha (1968) reported no appreciable difference in the maximum temperatures at the center of town and at its outskirts.

Although general relationships have been developed between heat island magnitude and some parameter representing city size, be it area, population, or building density, Chandler (1964, 1966, 1967b) has emphasized that the heat island magnitude at a given location often depends strongly on the local microclimatic conditions. He noted (1968) that data from several English towns showed that the strength of the local heat island was strongly dependent upon the density of urban development very near the observation point, sometimes within a circle as small as 500 meters radius. During nights with strong heat islands, the correlation between the heat island and building density was usually greater than 0.9.

VERTICAL TEMPERATURE
PROFILE DIFFERENCES

Investigators need detailed knowledge about the vertical distribution of temperature near urban areas to accurately determine the dispersion of pollutants. In two recent investigations, one over New York City (Davidson, 1967; Bornstein, 1968) and one over Cincinnati (Clarke, 1969) helicopters have been used to measure the three-dimensional, nocturnal temperature patterns over a city. Besides recording multiple elevated inversions over New York City, Davidson and Bornstein observed that a ground-based inversion was present over the outlying areas, while over the city temperatures were generally higher than those over the countryside from the surface up to about 300 meters. At heights around 400 meters temperatures over the city were generally lower than those of the surrounding area. This finding is similar to those of Duckworth and Sandberg (1954), who noted a "crossover" of the urban and rural temperatures on about half of their wiresonde data.

Clarke has studied vertical temperature distributions in Cincinnati both upwind and downwind of the city. Figure 11.3 shows an example from one of his surveys. On clear evenings, with light consistent surface winds, he found a strong surface-based inversion upwind of the urban area. Over the build-up region, lapse conditions occurred in the lowest 200 feet, while downwind of the urban area a strong inversion was again observed at the surface. Above this inversion, weak lapse conditions prevailed, which Clarke interpreted as the downwind effect of the city. This "urban heat plume" was detectable by vertical temperature measurements for several miles in the lee of the city.

Other authors have investigated the vertical distribution of nighttime urban temper-

atures with tower-mounted instruments. DeMarrais (1961) compared lapse rates in Louisville between 60 and 524 feet with typical rural profiles. During the warm half of the year, while surface inversions were regularly encountered in the country, nearly 60 percent of the urban observations showed a weak lapse rate and another 15 percent showed weak lapse conditions above a super-adiabatic lapse rate. Munn and Stewart (1967) instrumented towers at 20 and 200 feet in central Montreal, suburban Ottawa, and a rural location near Sarnia, Canada. They noted that inversions occurred more frequently and were stronger over the country than over the city. Both DeMarrais, and Munn and Stewart, however, found little difference between rural and urban daytime temperature profiles.

In another study of the vertical distribution of temperature, Hosler (1961) compiled statistics on the frequency of inversions based below 500 feet above station elevation for selected United States localities and discussed the dependence of these data on season, cloud cover, wind speed, time of day, and geographic location. Since he used radiosonde data, which are usually taken at an airport on the outskirts of a city, his results are generally representative of suburban locations and thus underestimate the inversion frequencies of rural sites and overestimate those of cities.

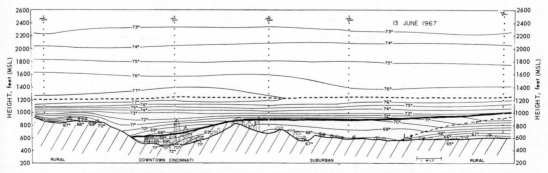

FIGURE 11.3 Cross section of temperature (°F) over metropolitan Cincinnati about 1 hour before sunrise on June 13, 1967. The heavy solid line indicates the top of the urban boundary layer and the dashed lines indicate a temperature discontinuity with less stable air above. Wind flow was from left to right (from Clarke, 1969).

IMPORTANCE OF METEOROLOGICAL FACTORS

In addition to city size the magnitude of the urban heat islands has been shown to depend upon various meteorological parameters. An early study of this type was made by Sundborg (1950), who investigated the relation between the temperature difference between Uppsala, Sweden, and its rural surroundings and meteorological variables measured at the edge of the city. He derived two equations by regression analysis for daytime and nighttime conditions at Uppsala, based on more than 200 sets of data. Correlation coefficients between observed and calculated temperatures were 0.49 and 0.66 for day and night, respectively. At night, wind speed and cloud cover were the most important variables for determining the heat island magnitude.

Chandler (1965) made a similar study based on temperature differences of daily maxima and minima at city and country sites for London and meteorological data observed at London airport. The multiple correlation coefficients for the four equations are 0.608, 0.563, 0.286, and 0.114 for nighttime (summer and winter) and daytime (summer and winter), respectively, an indication that the equations are much better estimators for nocturnal than for daytime conditions. The magnitude of the heat island was shown to depend on wind speed and cloud amount at night, whereas no meteorological variables were found to be particularly significant during the day.

Ludwig and Kealoha (1968) estimated the magnitude of a city's heat island by using the near-surface temperature lapse rate, which was usually measured in the environs of the city or at a radiosonde facility of a nearby city. They found this single variable to be highly correlated with the heat island magnitude and thus provided a simple, accurate method for predicting urban-rural temperature differences. These investigators compiled data from 78 nocturnal heat island surveys from a dozen cities and estimated the heat island magnitude by subtracting a typical rural temperature from the highest temperature in the city's center. Examples of their results, stratified by city population, are as follows:

$$\Delta T = 1.3 - 6.78\,\gamma \quad \text{population} < 500{,}000 \qquad (1)$$
$$\Delta T = 1.7 - 7.24\,\gamma \quad 500{,}000 \text{ to 2 million} \qquad (2)$$
$$\Delta T = 2.6 - 14.8\,\gamma \quad \qquad\quad > 2 \text{ million} \qquad (3)$$

where the lapse rate, γ, is the temperature change with pressure ($°C \cdot mb^{-1}$), i.e., a surface-based inversion is represented by negative γ. Correlation coefficients between ΔT and γ for the three cases are -0.95, -0.80, and -0.87, and the root mean square errors are ± 0.66, ± 1.0, and $\pm 0.96°C$, respectively. Thus, the resulting equations of this example will usually predict ΔT to within $\pm 2.0°C$.

Another meteorological parameter that influences heat island development is wind speed. When the regional wind speed is above a critical value, a heat island cannot be detected. Table 11.3, taken from Oke and Hannell (1968), summarizes several reports on the relation between city population (P) and this critical wind speed (U). Log P and

TABLE 11.3 Critical wind speeds for elimination of the heat island effect in various cities

CITY	AUTHOR	YEAR OF SURVEY	POPULATION	CRITICAL WIND SPEED, $m \cdot s^{-1}$
London, England	Chandler (1962[a])	1959-61	8,500,000	12
Montreal, Canada	Oke, et al.[a]	1967-68	2,000,000	11
Bremen, Germany	Mey	1933	400,000	8
Hamilton, Canada	Oke, et al.[a]	1965-66	300,000	6-8
Reading, England	Parry (1956)	1951-52	120,000	4-7
Kumagaya, Japan	Kawamura	1956-57	50,000	5
Palo Alto, California	Duckworth, et al.	1951-52	33,000	3-5

[a] Unpublished.

U are highly correlated (0.97), and their relationship is described by the regression equation:

$$U = -11.6 + 3.4 \log P \qquad (4)$$

The authors used this equation to estimate the smallest-sized city that would form a heat island. When $U = O$, equation (4) yields a population of about 2500. Although they had no data to test this estimate, they recognized that the scatter of their data points increased at the smaller populations and that sometimes even small building complexes produced measurable heat island effects.

The location of the highest city temperatures also depends on local meteorology. Munn et al. (1969) noted that at Toronto, Canada, the position of the daytime heat island was strongly influenced by the regional and lake breeze windflow patterns of the area and was often displaced downwind of the city center.

CAUSES OF THE HEAT ISLAND

It is generally accepted that two primary processes are involved in the formation of an urban heat island, both of which are seasonally dependent (see, for example, Mitchell, 1962). First, in summer the tall buildings, pavement, and concrete of the inner city absorb and store larger amounts of solar radiation (because of their geometry and high thermal admittance) than do the vegetation and soil typical of rural areas. In addition, much less of this energy is used for evaporation in the city than in the country because of the large amount of run-off of precipitation from streets and buildings [see Selection 16]. At night, while both the city and countryside cool by radiative losses, the urban man-made construction material gradually gives off the additional heat accumulated during the day, keeping urban air warmer than that of the outlying areas.

In winter a different process dominates. Since the sun angle at mid-latitudes is low and lesser amounts of solar radiation reach the earth, man-made energy becomes a significant addition to the solar energy naturally received. Artificial heat results from: combustion for home heating, power generation, industry, transportation, and human and animal metabolism. This energy reaches and warms the urban atmosphere directly or indirectly, by passing through imperfectly insulated homes and buildings. This process is most effective when light winds and poor dispersion prevail.

Many authors have investigated the magnitude of man-made energy in metropolitan areas. In two often-cited older studies for Berlin and Vienna (see Kratzer, 1956), the annual heat produced artificially in the built-up area equalled 1/3 (for Berlin) and 1/6 to 1/4 (for Vienna) of that received from solar radiation. More recently, Garnett and Bach (1965) estimated the annual average man-made heat from Sheffield, England (population 500,000), to be approximately 1/3 of the net all-wave radiation available at the ground. Bornstein (1968) reported results from a similar study of densely built-up Manhattan, New York City. During the winter the amount of heat produced from combustion alone was 2-1/2 times greater than that of the solar energy reaching the ground, but during the summer this factor dropped to 1/6.

In addition to the two seasonal primary causes of heat islands, other factors are important year-around. The "blanket" of pollutants over a city, including particulates, water vapor, and carbon dioxide, absorbs part of the upward-directed thermal radiation emitted at the surface. Part of this radiation is re-emitted downward and retained by the ground; another part warms the ambient air, a process that tends to increase the low-level stability over the city, enhancing the probability of higher pollutant concentrations. Thus, airborne pollutants not only cause a more intense heat island but alter the vertical temperature structure in a way that hinders their dispersion.

Reduced wind speed within an urban area, a result of the surface roughness of the city, also affects the heat island. The lower wind speeds decrease the city's ventilation, inhibiting both the movement of cooler outside air over the city center and the evaporation processes within the city.

Tag (1968) used a numerical model of the energy balance at the atmosphere-ground interface to investigate the relative importance of albedo, soil moisture content, soil diffusivity, and soil heat capacity on urban-rural temperature differences. The author found that during the day the lower city values of albedo and soil moisture caused higher urban temperatures, whereas the higher diffusivity and heat capacity of the city surface counteracted this tendency. At night, however, the relative warmth of the city was primarily the result of the higher urban values of soil diffusivity and heat capacity.

Humidity

Even though little research on humidity has been done, the consensus of urban climatologists is that the average relative humidity in towns is several percent lower than that of nearby rural areas whereas the average absolute humidity is only slightly lower in built-up regions. The main reason to expect differences in the humidity of urban and rural areas is that the evaporation rate in a city is lower than that in the country because of the markedly different surfaces. The countryside is covered with vegetation, which retains rainfall, whereas the floor of a city is coated with concrete, asphalt, and other impervious materials that cause rapid run-off of precipitation [see Selection 16]. Although the city's low evaporation rates result from the shortage of available water and the lack of vegetation for evapotranspiration, some moisture is added to urban atmospheres by the many combustion sources.

Variations of relative humidity within metropolitan areas resemble those of temperature, since the spatial temperature changes of a city are significantly greater than those of vapor pressure. Thus, because of the heat island, relative humidities in a city

are lower than in the suburbs and outlying districts. The humidity differences are greatest at night and in summer, corresponding to the time of greatest heat island intensity (Chandler, 1967a). Other studies have yielded similar findings. Sasakura (1965) reporting on 1 year of data from Tokyo showed that the mean relative humidity in the city center was 5 percent lower than that in the suburbs, a value that concurs with Landsberg's average figure. Chandler (1965) also found a 5 percent difference in the relative humidity of a downtown and a rural site near London. In other work (1962b, 1967a) he has presented nocturnal relative humidity profiles across London and maps of spatial distribution for Leicester, England. These show the dependence of relative humidity variations on the form of the city's heat island, which in turn depends upon the density of the built-up complex. Typical humidities of 90 to 100 percent were noted in rural areas during conditions favorable to heat island formation, whereas in the heart of the city humidity values were approximately 70 to 80 percent. Because of the temperature dependence, when the magnitude of the heat island was small, the urban-rural humidity differences were also small.

Although Chandler (1965) found that the mean annual vapor pressure in London was slightly lower (0.2 mb) than that at a nearby rural location, he (1962b, 1967a) frequently observed that at night the urban absolute humidity was higher than in the outlying regions. Furthermore, variations of humidity within the city often directly corresponded to building density, especially when the meteorological conditions were conducive to heat island formation. Typically under these conditions urban vapor pressures were about 1.5 to 2.0 mb higher than those in the country. The corresponding relative humidities were about 80 and 90 percent for the city and country, respectively. Chandler attributed these higher urban absolute humidities to the low rate of diffusion of air near ground level between tall city buildings during nights with light winds. This air with its high daytime moisture was trapped in the city canyons and remained there into the evening, keeping the absolute humidity high.

The summer surveys at Dallas by Ludwig and Kealoha (1968) recorded slightly lower values of absolute humidity within Dallas than outside it, with the greatest differences measured in the afternoon. During the morning hours the observed patterns were not well developed and could not be related to the urban complex.

Visibility

The atmosphere of metropolitan areas is usually characterized by increased concentrations of pollutants, which cause a difference between the visibilities of urban and rural regions. In this section, the effect of cities on atmospheric particulates is discussed first, followed by examples of visibility contrasts between city and country, with emphasis on the effects of fog. Readers interested in further information on these subjects should consult Robinson (1968), who presents a comprehensive review of practical and theoretical aspects of visibility, or the summary by Holzworth (1962), which also discusses visibility trends and their analysis.

ATMOSPHERIC PARTICULATES

A consequence of metropolitan areas is increased concentrations of atmospheric particles, such as smoke and combustion products. Landsberg (1960) stated that on the average the number of particulates present over urban areas is 10 times greater than that over rural environs. A more recent study by Horvath (1967), who measured the number and size distribution of submicron particles over Vienna and a nearby mountainous region, concurred with this figure. Although the particulate concentrations in Vienna varied considerably, often because of differing meteorological conditions, the general shapes of the size distribution curves of

both the urban and rural samples were similar.

Summers (1966) also showed that the number of particles in an urban atmosphere depends on industrial activity. In central Montreal the soiling index (Hemeon et al., 1953) was approximately 20 percent lower on Saturday and Sunday than on weekdays. Futhermore, in midwinter, the time of maximum heating requirements, this index was 2 to 3 times that of midsummer. Similar weekly and annual variations were also found by Weisman et al. (1969) for Hamilton, Ontario. In addition to industrial sources, urban particulate concentrations depend on meteorological conditions, particularly ventilation. In a summary of the relation between smoke density over Montreal and various weather factors, Summers (1962) showed that winter snow cover was particularly important in that it produced low-level atmospheric stability and frequent temperature inversions.

As a result of air pollution and the associated high aerosol concentrations, visibilities are lower and occurrences of fog are higher in a city than outside the metropolitan area. Fog is more frequent within urban regions because many atmospheric particulates are hygroscopic (Byers, 1965). Thus water vapor readily condenses on them and forms small water droplets, the ingredients of fog. An analogous example was described by Buma (1960), who analyzed visibility data at Leeuwarden on the Netherland coast. For similar relative humidities the visibility was much lower when the wind was from the continent (with high concentrations of condensation nuclei) than when the wind was from the sea (with low concentrations of nuclei). An example of the relationship between air pollution and visibility has been given by Georgii and Hoffman (1966), who showed that for two German cities low visibilities and high concentrations of SO_2 were highly correlated when low wind speeds and low-level inversions prevailed. McNulty (1968) pointed out that between 1949 and 1960 the occurrence of haze as an obstruction

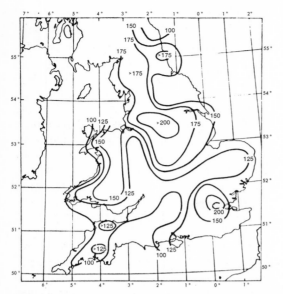

FIGURE 11.4 Average number of days per year with afternoon visibilities less than 6¼ miles in England and Wales (from Smith, 1961, by permission of Meteorological Magazine).

to visibility at New York City increased markedly as a result of increased air pollution.

URBAN-RURAL VISIBILITY CONTRASTS

As part of his general summary Landsberg (1956) presented visibility data from Detroit Municipal Airport (6 miles from downtown) and the Wayne County Airport (17 miles from town). During conditions conducive to the formation of city smogs (winds of 5 miles per hour or less) visibilities less than 1 mile were observed an average of 149 hours per year at the Municipal Airport but only 89 hours at the rural site. The cause of these low visibilities was listed as smoke in 49 of the observations at the Municipal Airport but

in only 5 at the County Airport; most of the occurrences of low visibility were during the late fall and winter. Landsberg (1960) summarized urban-rural fog differences by noting that metropolitan areas had 100 percent more fog in winter and 30 percent more in summer. In another study, Smith (1961) compiled the number of occurrences of visibilities less than 6¼ miles for locations throughout England in the afternoon, the time of least likelihood of fog (Figure 11.4). He found that industrial areas reported low visibilities on two to three times more days than did the rural areas.

Although fog generally occurs more frequently in metropolitan areas, this is not true for very dense fog. Chandler (1965) attributed the high frequencies of fog within a city to atmospheric pollution and relatively low wind speeds, but the extra warmth of a city often prevents the thickest nocturnal fogs from reaching the densities reported in the outlying districts. Table 11.4, presented by Chandler from data of Shellard (1959), shows the estimated hours per year of various density fogs in the vicinity of London, based on four observations per day. The high frequency of fog and the low frequency of very dense fog in the city center are evident. These same general relationships were also detected by Brazell (1964) using similar London data.

EFFECTS OF AIR POLLUTION CONTROL

A few recent reports indicate that the visibility in many locations has improved during the last two decades. The better visibilities of major U.S. cities have been associated with local efforts at air pollution abatement and substitution of oil and gas for soft coal in

TABLE 11.4 Fog frequencies in London

	HOURS PER YEAR WITH VISIBILITY LESS THAN			
	40 m	200 m	400 m	1000 m
Kingsway (central)	19	126	230	940
Kew (inner suburbs)	79	213	365	633
London Airport (outer suburbs)	46	209	304	562
Southeast England (mean of 7 stations)	20	177	261	494

production of heat (see Holzworth, 1962; Beebe, 1967). Brazell (1964), Wiggett (1964), and Freeman (1968) have suggested that London's improved visibility may be due to enforcement of the air pollution ordinances of 1954 and 1956. Similarly, Atkins (1968) and Corfield and Newton (1968) found that visibility has also improved near other English cities as a result of air pollution legislation. In another study of London, Commins and Waller (1967) compiled data showing that the particulate content of that city's atmosphere has decreased. Measurements from downtown London showed that the average smoke concentration from 1959 to 1964 was 32 percent lower than that from 1954 to 1959.

Visibility is not improving at all United States cities. A study by Green and Battan (1967) has shown that from 1949 to 1965 the frequency of occurrence of poor visibility at Tucson, Arizona, definitely increased and was significantly correlated with that city's population.

Radiation

The blanket of particulates over most large cities causes the solar energy that reaches an urban complex to be significantly less than that observed in rural areas. The particles are most effective as attenuators of radiation when the sun angle is low, since the path length of the radiation passing through the particulate material is dependent on sun elevation. Thus, for a given amount of particulates, solar radiation will be reduced by the largest fraction at high-latitude cities and during winter. Landsberg (1960) summarized the average annual effect of cities on the solar radiation they received as follows: the average annual total (direct plus diffuse) solar radiation received on a horizontal surface is decreased by 15 to 20 percent, and the ultraviolet (short wavelength) radiation is decreased by 30 percent in winter and by 5 percent in summer.

De Boer (1966) based a recent study on this topic on 2 years of global solar radiation measurements at six stations in and around Rotterdam, Netherlands. The study showed that the city center received 3 to 6 percent less radiation than the urban fringe and 13 to 17 percent less than the country. Chandler (1965), also reporting on the solar energy values in the heart of smoky urban areas, observed that from November to March solar radiation at several British cities was 25 to 55 percent less than in nearby rural areas. In addition, the central part of London annually received about 270 hours less of bright sunshine than did the surrounding countryside because of the high concentration of atmospheric particulates.

Further emphasizing the dependence of the transfer of solar radiation on the air's smoke content, the study of Mateer (1961) showed that the average annual energy received in Toronto, Canada, was 2.8 percent greater on Sunday than during the remainder of the week. Moreover, the Sunday increase during the heating season, October through April, was 6.0 percent but was only 0.8 percent in all other months.

The investigations of atmospheric turbidity by McCormick and Baulch (1962) and McCormick and Kurfis (1966), which were based on aircraft measurements of the intensity of solar radiation, provided data on the variation of solar energy with height over Cincinnati. These authors observed that pollutants over the city, which often had a layered structure and were dependent on the vertical temperature profile, significantly reduced the amount of solar energy that reached the city surface. In addition, they discussed changes of the vertical variation of turbidity (or solar radiation) from morning to afternoon, from day to day, and from clean air to polluted air. Roach (1961) and Sheppard (1958) have also studied attenuation of solar radiation by atmospheric dust particles. They concurred that most radiation scattered by these particles is directed forward and thus attenuation of total solar radiation is primarily due to absorption. Roach estimated that over "heavily polluted areas" absorption of solar energy by the particles was of sufficient magnitude to cause atmospheric heating rates in excess of 10° C per day. A discussion of optical properties of smoke particles is presented in a report by Conner and Hodkinson (1967).

The introduction of smoke controls in London during the mid-1950's has afforded an opportunity to check the radiation-smoke relation. Monteith (1966) summarized data on particulate concentration and solar energy at Kingsway (central London) for the years 1957 to 1963. During this time smoke density decreased by 10 μg $\cdot$ m^{-3} while total solar radiation increased by about 1 percent. The average smoke concentration of 80 μg $\cdot$ m^{-3} at Kew (inner suburbs) represents an energy decrease of about 8 percent, and in the center of town, where smoke concentrations average 200 to 300 μg $\cdot$ m^{-3}, the income of solar radiation is about 20 to 30 percent less than that in nearby rural areas. Similarly, Jenkins (1969) reported that the frequency of bright sunshine in London also increased in recent years after implementation of the air pollution laws. During the period 1958 to 1967, the average number of hours of bright sunshine from November through January was 50 percent greater than that observed from 1931 to 1960.

Measurements of ultraviolet radiation in downtown Los Angeles and on Mt. Wilson (Nader, 1967) showed its dependence on the cleanliness of the atmosphere. Attenuation of ultraviolet radiation by the lowest 5350 feet of the atmosphere averaged 14 percent on no-smog days; when smog was present, attenuation increased to a maximum of 58 percent. Reduced values of ultraviolet radiation in Los Angeles were also measured by Stair (1966). He presented an example in which the effect of smog was to decrease the amount of ultraviolet radiation received at the ground by 50 percent, and he also noted that on "extremely smoggy days" the decrease may be 90 percent or more.

Wind

The flow of wind over an urban area differs in several aspects from that over the sur-

rounding countryside. Two features that represent deviations from the regional wind flow patterns are the differences in wind speeds in city and country and the convergence of low-level wind over a city. These differences occur because the surface of a built-up city is much rougher than that of rural terrain—exerting increased frictional drag on air flowing over it—and because the heat island of a city causes horizontal thermal gradients, especially near the city periphery. The excess heat and friction also produce more turbulence over the urban area. These general ideas were discussed by Landsberg (1956, 1960); he stated that the annual mean surface wind speed over a city was 20 to 30 percent lower than that over the nearby countryside, that the speed of extreme gusts was 10 to 20 percent lower, and that calms were 5 to 20 percent more frequent. Since then several investigations have refined and expanded the studies summarized by Landsberg. Readers interested in a comprehensive and detailed review of wind flow over a city are directed to a recent paper by Munn (1968).

A difficulty in estimating urban-rural wind differences is selecting representative sites within the city from which to take measurements. Most observations of urban wind flow have been taken either from the roofs of downtown buildings, usually several stories high, or from parks or open spaces, whereas very few data have been obtained at street level in the city center, that place where most human activity occurs. However, these conventional measurements are generally representative of the gross wind flow patterns over a city, and as long as their limitations are recognized they can be useful for urban-rural comparisons.

WIND SPEED

Although recent reports have concurred that the average wind speed within a city is lower than that over nearby rural areas (Frederick, 1964; Munn and Stewart, 1967; Graham, 1968), the study reported by Chandler (1965) for London shows significant variation from this general rule. Although his analysis is based on only 2 years of data, it indicates that differences in urban and rural wind speeds depend on time of day, season, and wind speed magnitude. Some of these relations are brought out in Table 11.5 (taken from Chandler, 1965), which summarizes the mean wind speeds at London Airport (on the fringe of the city) and indicates their excess over the values recorded at Kingsway (in central London). The data show that when the regional wind speeds are light (typically at night) the speeds in downtown London are higher than those at the airport, whereas when wind speeds are relatively high, higher speeds are recorded at the airport. This is evident in comparison of the daytime and nighttime wind speeds given in Table 11.5.

Chandler (1965) attributes this diurnal variation of urban influence to the diurnal differences of regional wind speed and atmospheric stability. At night when surface winds are relatively calm, the stability is much greater in the country, where inversions are common, than in the metropolitan area, where lapse conditions may prevail. This relative instability in the city, combined with the greater surface roughness, enhances turbulence and allows the faster moving winds above the urban area to reach the surface more frequently; thus at night the average city wind speeds tend to be greater than those of the country. During the day, however, with faster regional winds, the frictional effect of the rough city surface dominates the turbulence effect, and lower wind speeds are observed within the built-up area.

The critical value of wind speed that determines whether the urban winds will be faster or slower than those of the country is highest during summer nights and during both day and night in winter (about 5.0 to 5.5 m · s⁻¹). These are times of relatively high atmospheric stability. The lowest values of critical speed (about 3.5 m · s⁻¹) occur during summer and fall days. Moreover, the magnitude of the decrease in urban wind speeds is greatest during spring days and least during spring nights.

Chandler (1965) summarized the wind speed statistics for London by noting that the annual average urban and suburban speeds were lower than those of the outlying regions but only by about 5 percent. However, the annual differences between wind speeds in the center of London and in the outlying areas were somewhat greater. For these locations, when speeds were more than 1.5 m · s⁻¹ the average difference was about 13 percent, whereas for speeds greater than 7.9 m · s⁻¹ the mean difference was only 7 percent. In summer, little difference between average city and rural wind speeds was evident. Light regional winds (1.5 m · s⁻¹ or less), which increase in speed over the city, occur more frequently in summer and compensate for the occurrences of strong rural winds, which decrease over the city. Finally, in contrast to the earlier figures reported by Landsberg, the London data showed that fewer calms and light winds occurred in the city center than in rural regions.

WIND DIRECTION

Past research on the direction of wind flow over urban areas has been primarily concerned with detecting and measuring a sur-

TABLE 11.5 Average wind speeds at London Airport and differences from those at Kingsway, m · s⁻¹

	0100 GMT		1300 GMT	
	Mean speed	Excess speed	Mean speed	Excess speed
December - February	2.5	-0.4	3.1	0.4
March - May	2.2	-0.1	3.1	1.2
June - August	2.0	-0.6	2.7	0.7
September - November	2.1	-0.2	2.6	0.6
Year	2.2	-0.3	2.9	0.7

face flow in toward the urban complex. It has been surmised for some time that if a city is warmer than its environs the warm city air should rise and be displaced by cooler rural air. However, this inflow is weak and occurs only in conjunction with well-developed heat islands, which in turn are dependent on certain meteorological conditions. Since direct measurements of the inflow require a coordinated set of accurate observations, few such investigations have been made.

Pooler (1963) analyzed wind records from the Louisville local air pollution study and determined that there was indeed a surface inflow of air toward the city. This inflow was the dominant feature of the surface wind flow pattern when the regional winds were weak, a situation that could result, for example, from a weak large-scale pressure gradient. Georgii (1968) reported on urban wind measurements in Frankfort/Main, Germany. During clear, calm nights an inflow toward the city center was detected, with a convergent wind velocity of up to 2 to 4 m · s⁻¹. He also noted that when the large-scale surface geostrophic wind speed reached 3 to 4 m · s⁻¹ a local city circulation

was prevented from becoming established, although the increased roughness of the city was still affecting the wind regime.

Measurements of the wind flow around an oil refinery in the Netherlands have been reported by Schmidt (1963) and by Schmidt and Boer (1963). Although the area involved (4 km²) was much smaller than that of a moderate-sized city and the heat produced by the refinery per unit area was considerably greater than that of a city, the general relationships are of interest. A cyclonic circulation occurred around the area, with convergence toward the center. Furthermore, ascending air was detected over the center of the area, with descending currents over the surroundings. The greatest vertical velocities measured in the vicinity of the maximum heat production were about 15 cm · s⁻¹.

Vertical wind velocities were obtained from low-level tetroon flights over New York City by Hass et al. (1967) and Angell et al. (1968). They observed an upward flow over densely built-up Manhattan Island and downward motion over the adjacent Hudson and East Rivers. They ascribed this flow pattern to the urban heat island, to the barrier effect of the tall buildings, and to the relatively cool river water. Low-level convergence over a city has also been detected by Okita (1960, 1965), who applied two novel techniques. For one study he utilized the fact that rime ice formed on the windward side of tree trunks and the thickness of the ice was proportional to wind speed. For the other, (Figure 11.5), he observed the smoke plumes from household chimneys. By observing these features around the periphery of Asahikawa, Japan, he deduced the local wind flow patterns and determined that when the large-scale wind flow was weak there was a convergence over the city.

As a final consideration of urban wind flow, Chandler's observations (1960, 1961) on the periphery of London and Leicester are of interest. Chandler noted that when a well-developed nocturnal heat island formed with a strong temperature gradient near the edge of the built-up area, winds flowed inward toward the city center, but the flow was

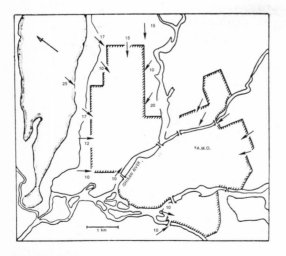

FIGURE 11.5 The direction of wind flow around Asahikawa, Japan, February 26, 1956, as deduced from formation of rime ice on tree branches (from Okita, 1960, by permission of the editor, Jour. of Meteor. Soc. of Japan).

not steady. Rather, movement of cold air from the country toward the city occurred as pulsations, the strongest winds occurring when the temperature gradient was strongest.

Precipitation

A city also influences the occurrence and amount of precipitation in its vicinity. For several reasons an urban complex might be expected to increase precipitation. Combustion sources add to the amount of water vapor in the atmosphere, higher temperatures intensify thermal convection, greater surface roughness increases mechanical turbulence, and the urban atmosphere contains greater concentrations of condensation and ice nuclei. Since no continuous, quantitative measurements of these various parameters have been made in conjunction with the few urban precipitation studies, the relative significance of these factors is not easy to establish. Landsberg (1956, 1958) gave several European examples of urban-rural comparisons and concluded that the amount of precipitation over a city is about 10 percent greater than that over nearby country areas. More recent studies have shown that his conclusion may be an oversimplification and that the greatest positive anomalies occur downwind of the city center.

THE EFFECTS OF CITIES

The effects of cities on precipitation are difficult to determine for several reasons. First, very few rural areas remain undisturbed from their natural state. Second, there is a lack of rain gauges in metropolitan areas, especially instruments with long-term records and uniform exposure throughout the record. Third, many cities are associated with bodies of water or hilly terrain, and these also affect the patterns of precipitation. Finally, the natural variability of rainfall, particularly the summer showers of mid-America, further complicates the analysis of urban-rural precipitation differences. An example of the difficulty of rainfall analysis is the study of

Spar and Ronberg (1968). They observed that the record from Central Park, New York City, showed a significant decreasing trend of precipitation of 0.3 inch per year from 1927 to 1965. This trend was not substantiated by data from other nearby sites; at Battery Place, the nearest station, a small rainfall increase was observed during the period.

A very striking example of the effect of the Chicago urban region on local precipitation has been documented by Changnon (1968a [Selection 12]). He showed that at La Porte, Indiana, some 30 miles downwind of a large industrial complex between Chicago and Gary, Indiana, the amount of precipitation and the number of days with thunderstorms and hail have increased markedly since 1925. Furthermore, the year-to-year variation of precipitation at La Porte agrees generally with data on the production of steel and number of smoke-haze days at Chicago [see Figure 12.2]. During the period from 1951 to 1965, the positive anomalies at La Porte were 31 percent for precipitation, 38 percent for thunderstorm days, 246 percent for hail days, and 34 percent for days with precipitation ≥ 0.25 inch. These results are summarized in Table 11.6. Changnon concluded that these observed differences were a real effect of the industrial area and that they represent the general size of precipitation increase that is possible as a result of man's activities. However, because of the effect of Lake Michigan and its associated lake breeze in channeling the pollutants around the south end of the lake toward the La Porte area and inhibiting dispersion, the large differences detected in this study probably are not representative of American cities in general.

Changnon (1961, 1962, 1968b, 1969) has summarized precipitation data for several other midwestern cities and detected positive increases, but not nearly as pronounced as those at La Porte. In St. Louis, Chicago, Champaign-Urbana, Illinois, and Tulsa, Oklahoma, the city precipitation was 5 to 8 percent higher than the average of nearby rural stations. At St. Louis and Champaign-Urbana the rainfall maxima were

TABLE 11.6 Summary of urban area increases in precipitation and related conditions (expressed as a percent of rural values)

	CHICAGO	LA PORTE	ST. LOUIS	TULSA	CHAMPAIGN-URBANA
Annual precipitation	5	31	7	8	5
Warmer half-year precipitation	4	30	a	5	4
Colder half-year precipitation	6	33	a	11	8
Rain days ≥ 0.01 or 0.1 inch					
Annual	6	0	a	a	7
Warmer half-year	8	0	a	a	3
Colder half-year	4	0	a	a	10
Rain days ≥ 0.25 or 0.5 inch					
Annual	5	34	a	a	5
Warmer half-year	7	54	a	a	9
Colder half-year	0	5	a	a	0
Annual number of thunderstorm days	6	38	11	a	7
Summer number of thunderstorm days	13	63	21	a	17

[a] Data not sufficient for comparison.

downwind of the urban center. The increase of 5 percent at Chicago proper represents a relative maximum over the city and is distinct from the higher precipitation rates downwind of Chicago at La Porte. Spatial data were not available for Tulsa. Table 11.6 (from Changnon, 1968b) shows that the percentage precipitation increase is greater during the cold season and that increases in the warm season result from more days of moderate rain and thunderstorms.

Authors do not totally agree on the distribution of precipitation over cities. The rainfall minimum over the Missouri half of metropolitan St. Louis detected by Changnon (1968b) was also noted by Feig (1968), who observed that a map of isohyets of annual precipitation over the eastern United States showed that minimum precipitation areas occur around most cities having no obvious geographic influences. The annual precipitation pattern at Washington, D.C. (Woollum and Canfield, 1968), also shows low values downtown along the Potomac River, with the greatest amounts of precipitation on the north to northwest side of town and with relative maxima in both the eastern and western suburbs (Figure 11.6). On the other hand, Dettwiller (1968) has indicated that the effect of a city is to increase precipitation. He showed that from 1953 to 1967 the average rainfall in Paris was 31 percent greater on weekdays than on Saturdays and Sundays.

Another reason for believing that more precipitation falls over metropolitan districts is that heavy thundershowers sometimes occur over an area that roughly coincides with the urban complex (Staff, 1964; Chandler, 1965; Atkinson, 1968). However, it is

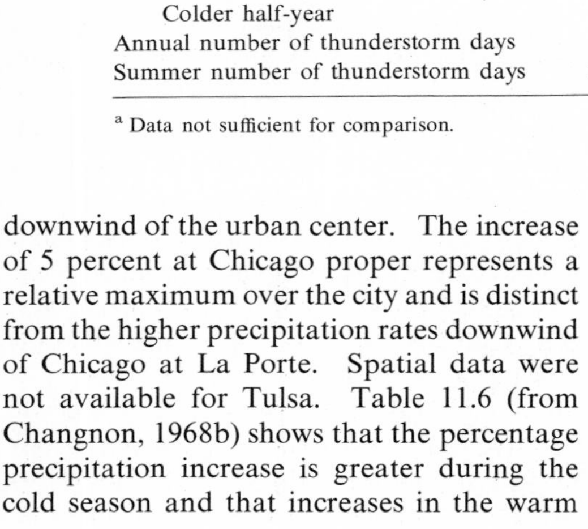

FIGURE 11.6 Mean annual precipitation (inches) over the Washington, D.C., metropolitan area (from Woollum and Canfield, 1968).

always difficult to determine whether a thundershower was a natural event or whether the city actually influenced it in any way.

THE IMPORTANT URBAN FACTORS

Although it is hard to determine the relative importance of the several urban factors that affect precipitation, the extensive studies by Changnon (1968b) led him to the following conclusions about the city-precipitation relationship. Two factors were probably most effective in enhancing precipitation at La Porte—high concentrations of ice nuclei from nearby steel mills and added heat from local industrial sources. Because of the high frequency of nocturnal thunderstorms and hailstorms at La Porte, he concluded that the thermal and frictional effects were probably the most significant. In addition, the precipitation maximum associated with Champaign-Urbana, an area with little industry and a minimum of nuclei sources, also indicated that the thermal and frictional factors could produce significant differences.

Many recent studies have concentrated on measuring condensation and ice nuclei and determining their possible influence on cloud development and precipitation. Measurements showing that cities are an important source of nuclei were reported by Mee (1968). Typical concentrations of cloud droplets and condensation nuclei at the convective cloud base near Puerto Rico were 50 cm^{-3} in the clean air over the ocean, about 200 cm^{-3} over the unpolluted countryside, and from 1000 to 1500 cm^{-3} immediately downwind of San Juan. Abnormally high concentrations were detected for at least 100 miles downwind of the city. In another study, Squires (1966) pointed out that measurements of condensation nuclei over Denver showed that the concentrations of these nuclei produced by human activities were similar to the natural concentration there. Moreover, Telford (1960), Langer (1968), and Langer et al. (1967) observed that industrial areas, and in particular steel mills, are good sources of ice nuclei. Finally,

Schaefer (1966, 1968a) and others (Morgan, 1967; Morgan and Allee, 1968; Hogan, 1967) have shown that lead particles in ordinary auto exhaust form effective ice nuclei when combined with iodine vapor.

Even though cities are generally recognized as good sources of nuclei, the net effect of such nuclei cannot be definitely determined. For example, a few ice nuclei added to supercooled clouds may enhance rainfall, a principle used by commercial cloud seeders. On the other hand, rain that falls from warm clouds is dependent on a number of large drops within a cloud so that coalescence may be effective. If large numbers of condensation nuclei are introduced into a warm cloud, many small drops will form and thus rainfall may be inhibited (Gunn and Phillips, 1957; Squires and Twomey, 1960).

Many examples in the literature show that rainfall can be artificially increased, whereas only a few show decreases. Fleuck (1968) statistically analyzed results of the Missouri seeding experiments by the University of Chicago group and concluded that seeding of clouds in that area suppressed precipitation. In addition, reports of an investigation of the trend of rainfall in eastern Australia (Warner and Twomey, 1967; Warner, 1968) concluded that as the amount of smoke from burning sugar cane in the area increased during the past 50 years, rainfall correspondingly decreased by 25 percent. Therefore, an accurate determination of the effect of a city on precipitation in its neighborhood requires knowledge not only of the number and type of nuclei being introduced by the city but also of such factors as the concentration of natural nuclei and vertical temperature profiles over the city.

Recent findings have further documented Landsberg's statement that it is becoming increasingly difficult to find undisturbed rural areas with which to compare cities to determine urban-rural meteorological differences. Both direct (Schaefer, 1968b) and indirect (Gunn, 1964; McCormick and Ludwig, 1967; Peterson and Bryson, 1968; Volz, 1968) measurements have shown that the particulate content of the atmosphere, even in remote areas, is increasing as a result of greater human activity.

OTHER PRECIPITATION ELEMENTS

Two other precipitation elements of interest are hail and snowfall. Changnon's study (1968b) of the La Porte anomaly found that from 1951 to 1965 the number of hail days was 246 percent greater than that of surrounding stations. Results from similar investigations at other midwestern cities were not definitive. Landsberg (1956) cited a few instances in which snowfall over an urban area was lighter than that at nearby rural locations, presumably because of higher temperatures over the cities. Potter (1961) found similar results for Toronto and Montreal, Canada.

Suggested Future Research

Although this review indicates that a large volume of research has been conducted in urban climatology, several areas warrant emphasis in the future. Among the following suggestions for further study, many were brought out at the recent international conference on the climate of cities at Brussels.

Few studies have been made of the vertical structure of the urban atmosphere, which includes such features as the variation with height of temperature, wind flow, pollutants, and radiation. More such information is needed for a better understanding of the transport and diffusion of pollutants over metropolitan areas. Likewise, additional urban wind measurements are needed at a variety of sites with different exposures, to delineate the fine structure of wind flow throughout a city.

Several aspects of urban-rural radiation differences should be further investigated. In several studies of the effects of a polluted atmosphere on ultraviolet radiation in Los Angeles, the effects were found to be significant. Observations from other cities are now needed to show the amount of attenuation of ultraviolet radiation at different locations. Similarly, studies should be conducted to determine the net effect of a polluted city atmosphere on the total radiation balance of a city, including visible and thermal infrared wavelengths, since net radiation comprises a major fraction of a city's energy budget. In particular, urban-rural differences of infrared radiation should be measured to determine whether reduced values of solar radiation at the city surface resulting from atmospheric pollution are compensated for by an increase in infrared energy.

A cause-and-effect relationship between a city and precipitation has not yet been found. Although several factors are believed to be important, the role of anthropogenically produced dust particles is of special interest. The influence of these particles on the physics of precipitation and the optimum concentration for modifying precipitation have not yet been determined. Also, investigations should be undertaken to ascertain whether city-induced precipitation anomalies of a size similar to that at La Porte, Indiana, are widespread or whether this example is primarily the result of local influences, such as Lake Michigan.

Further research should be directed toward determining exactly upon which parameters urban-rural temperature differences depend. For example, the relative importance of the type and density of local buildings and gross city size on the temperature at a given city location has yet to be definitely established. Similarly, the local cooling produced by parks and greenbelts and the extent of this cooling into nearby neighborhoods should be measured. Such information would be useful in city planning and land use studies, for example.

Finally, these two questions should be studied: How far downwind does a city influence climate, and to what extent does a city in the tropics modify its climate? The former question has implications in larger-scale studies of inadvertent weather modification; the latter is important since nearly all research in urban climatology has been done at cities in temperate climates.

Note

These reports are part of a series (1952, 1953a, 1953b, 1953c, 1953d, 1953e) which were recently declassified (1963) and describe a number of detailed observational surveys of urban temperature and diffusion.

References

Angell, J. K., D. H. Pack, W. A. Hass, and W. H. Hoecker, 1968: Tetroon flights over New York City. Weather **23**, 184.

Atkins, J. E., 1968: Changes in the visibility characteristics at Manchester/Ringway Airport. Meteor. Mag. **97**, 172.

Atkinson, B. W., 1968: The reality of the urban effect on precipitation—a case study approach. Presented at W. M. O. Symp. on Urban Climates and Building Climatology. Brussels, Belgium. October 1968.

Beebe, R. G., 1967: Changes in visibility restrictions over a 20 year period. Bull. Amer. Meteor. Soc. **48**, 348.

Bornstein, R. D., 1968: Observations of the urban heat island effect in New York City. J. Appl. Meteor. **7**, 575.

Brazell, J. H., 1964: Frequency of dense and thick fog in central London as compared with frequency in outer London. Meteor. Mag. **93**, 129.

Brooks, C. E. P., 1952: Selective annotated bibliography on urban climate. Meteor. Abstracts Bibliog. **3**, 734.

Buma, T. J., 1960: A statistical study of the relationship between visibility and relative humidity of Leeuwarden. Bull. Amer. Meteor. Soc. **41**, 357.

Byers, H. R., 1965: *Elements of cloud physics.* University of Chicago Press. 191 pp.

Chandler, T. J., 1960: Wind as a factor of urban temperatures—a survey in north-east London. Weather **15**, 204.

Chandler, T. J., 1961: Surface effects of Leicester's heat-island. E. Midland Geographer No. 15, 32.

Chandler, T. J., 1962a: London's urban climate. Geog. J. **128**(3),279–298.

Chandler, T. J., 1962b: Temperature and humidity traverses across London. Weather **17**, 235.

Chandler, T. J., 1963: London climatological survey. Int. J. Air Water Poll. **7**, 959.

Chandler, T. J., 1964: City growth and urban climates. Weather **19**, 170.

Chandler, T. J., 1965: *The climate of London.* London, Hutchinson & Co. 292 pp.

Chandler, T. J., 1966: London's heat island. in *Biometeorology II,* Proc. of Third Int. Biometeor. Congr., Pau, France, September 1963. London, Pergamon Press, p. 589–597.

Chandler, T. J., 1967a: Absolute and relative humidity of towns. Bull. Amer. Meteor. Soc. **48**, 394.

Chandler, T. J., 1967b: Night-time temperatures in relation to Leicester's urban form. Meteor. Mag. **96**, 244.

Chandler, T. J., 1968: Urban climates: inventory and prospect. Presented at W.M.O. Symp. on Urban Climates and Building Climatology. Brussels, Belgium. October 1968.

Changnon, S. A., 1961: Precipitation contrasts between the Chicago urban area and an offshore station in southern Lake Michigan. Bull. Amer. Meteor. Soc. **42**, 1.

Changnon, S. A., 1962: A climatological evaluation of precipitation patterns over an urban area. in *Symposium: Air over Cities,* U.S. Public Health Service, Taft Sanitary Eng. Center, Cincinnati, Ohio, Tech. Rept. A62–5, p. 37–67.

Changnon, S. A., 1968a: The La Porte weather anomaly—fact or fiction? Bull. Amer. Meteor. Soc. **49**, 4.

Changnon, S. A., 1968b: Recent studies of urban effects on precipitation in the United States. Presented at W.M.O. Symp. on Urban Climates and Building Climatology. Brussels, Belgium. October 1968.

Changnon, S. A., 1969: Recent studies of urban effects on precipitation in the United States. Bull. Amer. Meteor. Soc. **50**, 411.

Clarke, J. F., 1969: Nocturnal urban boundary layer over Cincinnati, Ohio. In press. Mon. Wea. Rev.

Commins, B. T., and R. E. Waller, 1967: Observations from a ten-year study of pollution at a site in the city of London. Atm. Env. **1**, 49.

Conner, W. D., and J. R. Hodkinson, 1967: Optical properties and visual effects of smoke-stack plumes. Publ. No. 999–AP–30, Public Health Service, U.S. Dept. Health, Education, and Welfare, Cincinnati, Ohio.

Corfield, G. A., and W. G. Newton, 1968: A recent change in visibility characteristics at Finningley. Meteor. Mag. **97**, 204.

Davidson, B., 1967: A summary of the New York urban air pollution dynamics research program. J. Air. Poll. Contr. Asso. **17**, 154.

De Boer, H. J., 1966: Attenuation of solar radiation due to air pollution in Rotterdam and its surroundings. Koninklijk Nederlands Meteorologisch Institute, Wetenschappelijk Rapport W. R. 66–1, de Bilt, Netherlands. 36 pp.

DeMarrais, G. A., 1961: Vertical temperature difference observed over an urban area. Bull. Amer. Meteor. Soc. **42**, 548.

Dettwiller, I., 1968: Incidence possible de l'activite industrielle sur les precipitations a Paris. Presented at W.M.O. Symp, on Urban Climates and Building Climatology. Brussels, Belgium. October 1968.

Dronia, H., 1967: Der Stadteinfluss auf den Weltweiter Temperaturtrend. Meteorologische Abhandlugen, **74**, 1.

Duckworth, F. S., and J. S. Sandberg, 1954: The effect of cities upon horizontal and vertical temperature gradients. Bull. Amer. Meteor. Soc. **35**, 198.

Feig, A. M., 1968: An evaluation of precipitation patterns over the metropolitan St. Louis Area. in *Proceedings First Nat. Conf. on Wea. Mod.,* Albany, N. Y., Amer. Meteor. Soc., p. 210–219.

Flueck, J. A., 1968: A statistical analysis of Project Whitetop's precipitation data. in *Proceedings First Nat. Conf. on Wea. Mod.,* Albany, N. Y., Amer. Meteor. Soc., p. 26–35.

Frederick, R. H., 1964: On the representativeness of surface wind observations using data from Nashville, Tennessee. Int. J. Air Water Poll. **8**, 11.

Freeman, M. H., 1968: Visibility statistics for London/Heathrow Airport. Meteor. Mag. **97**, 214.

Garnett, A., and W. Bach, 1965: An estimation of the ratio of artificial heat generation to natural radiation heat in Sheffield. Mon. Wea. Rev. **93**, 383.

Geiger, R., 1965: *The Climate near the Ground.* Cambridge, Mass., Harvard U. Press. 611 pp.

Georgii, H. W., and L. Hoffman, 1966: Assessing SO_2 enrichment as dependent on meteorological factors. Staub, Reinhaltung der Luft (In English) **26** (12), 1.

Georgii, H. W., 1968: The effects of air pollution on urban climates. Presented at W.M.O. Symp. on Urban Climates and Building climatology. Brussels, Belgium. October 1968.

Graham, I. R., 1968: An analysis of turbulence statistics at Fort Wayne, Indiana. J. Appl. Meteor. **7**, 90.

Green, C. R., and L. J. Battan, 1967: A study of visibility versus population growth in Arizona. J. Ariz. Acad. Sci. **4**, 226.

Gunn, R., 1964: The secular increase of the world-wide fine particle pollution. J. Atm. Sci. **21**, 168.

Gunn, R., and B. B. Phillips, 1957: An experimental investigation of the effect of air pollution on the initiation of rain. Meteor. **14**, 272.

Hass, W. A., W. H. Hoecker, D. H. Pack, and J. K. Angell, 1967: Analysis of low-level, constant volume balloon (tetroon) flights over New York City. Q. J. Roy. Meteor. Soc. **93**, 483.

Hemeon, W. C. L., G. F. Haines, Jr., and H. H. Ide, 1953; Determination of haze and smoke concentrations by filter paper samplers. J. Air Poll. Contr. Assoc. **3**, 22.

Hogan, A. W., 1967: Ice Nuclei from direct reaction of iodine vapor with vapors from leaded gasoline. Science **158**, 800.

Holzworth, G. C., 1962: Some effects of air pollution on visibility in and near cities. In *Symposium: Air Over Cities.* U.S. Public Health Service, Taft Sanitary Eng. Center, Cincinnati, Ohio, Tech. Rept. A62–5, p. 69–88.

Horvath, H., 1967: A comparison of natural and urban aerosol distribution measured with the aerosol spectrometer. Env. Sci. Technol. **1**, 651.

Hosler, C. R., 1961: Low-level inversion frequency in the contiguous United States. Mon. Wea. Rev. **89**, 319.

Hutcheon, R. J., et al., 1967: Observations of the urban heat island in a small city. Bull. Amer. Meteor. Soc. **48**, 7.

Jenkins, I., 1969: Increase in averages of sunshine in central London. Weather **24**, 52.

Kawamura, T., 1964: Analysis of the temperature distribution in Kumagaya city—a typical example of the urban climate of a small city. Geog. Rev. Japan **27**, 243.

Kratzer, P., 1956: *Das Stadtklima.* Braunschweig, Friedrich Vieweg and Sohn. (English trans. available through ASTIA, AD 284776).

Landsberg, H. E., 1956: The Climate of Towns. In *Man's role* in *changing the face of the earth.* Chicago, Ill., University of Chicago Press, p. 584–606.

Landsberg, H. E., *1960: Physical Climatology,* 2nd Revised Ed., DuBois, Penn., Gray Printing Co. 446 pp.

Landsberg, H. E. 1962: City air—better or worse. In *Symposium: Air over Cities,* U.S. Public Health Service, Taft Sanitary Eng. Center, Cincinnati, Ohio, Tech. Rept. A62–5, p. 1–22.

Landsberg, H. E., 1968: Micrometeorological temperature differentiation through urbanization. Presented at W.M.O. Symp. on Urban Climate and Building Climatology. Brussels, Belgium. October 1968.

Langer, G., 1968: Ice nuclei generated by steel mill activity. In *Proceedings First Nat. Conf. on Wea. Mod.,* Albany, N. Y., Amer. Meteor. Soc., p. 220–227.

Langer, G., J. Rosinski, and C. P. Edwards, 1967: A continuous ice nucleus counter and its application to tracking in the troposphere. J. Appl. Meteor. **6**, 114.

Lawrence, E. N., 1968: Changes in air temperature at Manchester Airport. Meteor. Mag. **97**, 43.

Ludwig, F. L., 1967: Urban climatological studies. Interim Rept. No. 1, Contr. OCD–PS–64–201. Stanford Res. Inst., Menlo Park, Calif. (AD 657248).

Ludwig, F. L., and J. H. S. Kealoha, 1968: Urban climatological studies. Final Rept., Contr. OCD–DAHC–20–67–C–0136. Stanford Res. Inst., Menlo Park, Calif.

Mateer, C. L., 1961: Note on the effect of the weekly cycle of air pollution on solar radiation at Toronto. Int. J. Air Water Poll. **4**, 52.

McCormick, R. A., and D. M. Baulch, 1962: The variation with height of the dust loading over a city as determined from the atmospheric turbidity. J. Air Poll. Contr. Asso. **12**, 492.

McCormick, R. A., and K. R. Kurfis, 1966: Vertical diffusion of aerosols over a city. Q. J. Roy. Meteor. Soc. **92**, 392.

McCormick, R. A., and J. H. Ludwig, 1967: Climate modification by atmospheric aerosols. Science **156**, 1358.

McNulty, R. P., 1968: The effect of air pollutants on visibility in fog and haze at New York City. Atm. Env. **2**, 625.

Mee, T. R., 1968: Microphysical aspects of warm cloud. Presented at ESSA Atm. Phys. Chem. Lab. Symp. on Wea. Mod., Sept. 1968. Boulder, Colorado.

Mey, A., 1933: Die stadteinfluss auf den tempera-turgang. Das Wetter **50,** 293.

Mitchell, J. M., Jr., 1961: The temperature of cities. Weatherwise **14,** 224.

Mitchell, J. M., Jr., 1962: The thermal climate of cities. In *Symposium: Air over Cities,* U.S. Public Health Service, Taft Sanitary Eng. Center, Cincinnati, Ohio, Tech. Rept. A62–5, p. 131–145.

Monteith, J. L., 1966: Local differences in the attenuation of solar radiation over Britain. Q. J. Roy. Meteor. Soc. **92,** 254.

Morgan, G. M., Jr., 1967: Technique for detecting lead particles in air. Nature **213,** 58.

Morgan, G. M., Jr., and P. A. Allee, 1968: The production of potential ice nuclei by gasoline engines. J. Appl. Meteor. 7, 241.

Munn, R. E., 1968: Airflow in urban areas. Presented at W.M.O. Symp. on Urban Climates and Building Climatology. Brussels, Belgium. October 1968.

Munn, R. E., and I. M. Stewart, 1967: The use of meteorological towers in urban air pollution programs. J. Air Poll. Contr. Asso. **17,** 98.

Munn, R. E., M. S. Hirt, and B. F. Findlay, 1969: A climatological study of the urban temperature anomaly in the lakeshore environment at Toronto. In press. J. Appl. Meteor.

Nader, J. S., 1967: Pilot study of ultraviolet radiation in Los Angeles October 1965. Public Health Serv. Publ. 999-AP-28. U.S. Dept. HEW, Nat. Cent. for Air Poll. Contr., Cincinnati, Ohio.

Oke, T. R., 1968: Some results of a pilot study of the urban climate of Montreal. Climat. Bull. (McGill Univ.) No. 3, 36.

Oke, T. R., and F. G. Hannell, 1968: The form of the urban heat island in Hamilton, Canada. Presented at W.M.O. Symp. on Urban Climates and Building Climatology. Brussels, Belgium. October 1968.

Okita, T., 1960: Estimation of direction of air flow from observation of rime ice. J. Meteor. Soc. Japan **38,** 207.

Okita, T., 1965: Some chemical and meteorological measurements of air pollution in Asahikawa. Int. J. Air Water Poll. **9,** 323.

Parry, M., 1956: Local temperature variations in the Reading area. Q. J. Roy. Meteor. Soc. **82,** 45.

Parry, M., 1966: The urban heat island. In *Biometeorology II,* Proc. of Third Int. Biometeor. Congr., Pau, France, Sept. 1963. London, Pergamon Press, p. 616–624.

Peterson, J. T., and R. A. Bryson, 1968: Atmospheric aerosols: Increased concentrations during the last decade. Science **162,** 120.

Pooler, F., Jr., 1963: Air flow over a city in terrain of moderate relief. J. Appl. Meteor. **2,** 446.

Potter, J. G., 1961: Changes in seasonal snowfall in cities. Canad. Geog. **5,** 37.

Roach, W. T., 1961: Some aircraft observations of fluxes of solar radiation in the atmosphere. Q. J. Roy. Meteor. Soc. **87,** 346.

Robinson, E., 1968: Effect on the physical properties of the atmosphere. In *Air Pollution,* ed. by A. C. Stern. Vol. 1, 2nd Ed., New York, Academic Press. 694 pp.

Saskura, K., 1965: On the distribution of relative humidity in Tokyo and its secular change in the heart of Tokyo. Tokyo J. of Climat. **2,** 45.

Schaefer, V. J., 1966: Ice nuclei from automobile exhaust and iodine vapor. Science **154,** 1555.

Schaefer, V. J., 1968a: Ice nuclei from auto exhaust and organic vapors. J. Appl. Meteor. **7,** 148.

Schaefer, V. J., 1968b: New field evidence of inadvertant modification of the atmosphere. In *Proceedings First Nat. Conf. on Wea. Mod.,* Albany, N. Y., Amer. Meteor. Soc., p. 163–172.

Schmidt, F. H., 1963: Local circulation around an industrial area. Int. J. Air Water Poll. **7,** 925.

Schmidt, F. H., and J. H. Boer, 1963: Local circulation around an industrial area. Berichte des Deutschen Wetterdienstes, No. 91, 28.

Sekiguti, T., 1964: City climate in and around the small city of Ina in central Japan. Tokyo Geog. Papers **8,** 93.

Shellard, H. C., 1959: The frequency of fog in the London area compared with that in rural area of east Anglia and south-east England. Meteor. Mag. **88,** 321.

Sheppard, P. A., 1958: The effect of pollution on radiation in the atmosphere. Int. J. Air Poll. **1,** 31.

Smith, L. P., 1961: Frequencies of poor afternoon visibilities in England and Wales. Meteor. Mag. **90,** 355.

Spar, J., and P. Ronberg, 1968: Note on an apparent trend in annual precipitation at New York City. Mon. Wea. Rev. **96,** 169.

Squires, P., 1966: An estimate of the anthropogenic production of cloud nuclei. J. Rech. Atmos. **2,** 299.

Squires, P., and S. Twomey, 1960: The relation between cloud drop spectra and the spectrum of cloud nuclei. In *Physics of Precipitation,* Amer. Geophys. Union Monog. No. 5, p. 211–219.

Staff, River Forecast Center (Tulsa) and Dist. Meteor. Office (Kansas City), 1964: Cloudburst at Tulsa, Oklahoma, July 27, 1963. Mon. Wea. Rev. **92,** 345.

Stair, R., 1966: The measurement of solar radiation, with principal emphasis on the ultraviolet component. Int. J. Air Water Poll. **10,** 665.

Stanford University Aerosol Laboratory and The Ralph M. Parsons Co., 1952: Behavior of aerosol clouds within cities. Jt. Quart. Rept. No. 2, Oct.–Dec. 1952. 100 pp. (AD 7261)

Stanford University Aerosol Laboratory and The Ralph M. Parsons Co., 1953a: Behavior of aerosol clouds within cities. Jt. Quart. Rept. No. 3, Jan.–Mar. 1953. 218 pp. (AD 31509)

Stanford University Aerosol Laboratory and The Ralph M. Parsons Co., 1953b: Behavior of aerosol clouds within cities. Jt. Quart. Rept. No. 4, Apr.–June 1953. 196 pp. (AD 31508)

Stanford University Aerosol Laboratory and The Ralph M. Parsons Co., 1953c: Behavior of aerosol clouds within cities. Jt. Quart Rept. No. 5, July–Sept. 1953. 238 pp. (AD 31507)

Stanford University Aerosol Laboratory and The Ralph M. Parsons Co., 1953d: Behavior of aerosol clouds within cities. Jt. Quart. Rept. No. 6, Vol. I, Oct.-Dec. 1953. 246 pp. (AD 31510)

Stanford University Aerosol Laboratory and The Ralph M. Parsons Co., 1953e: Behavior of aerosol clouds within cities. Jt. Quart. Rept. No. 6, Vol. II, Oct.-Dec. 1953. 187 pp. (AD 31711)

Summers, P. W., 1962: Smoke concentrations in Montreal related to local meteorological factors. In *Symposium: Air over Cities*, U.S. Public Health Service, Taft Sanitary Eng. Center, Cincinnati, Ohio, Tech. Rept. A62–5, p. 89–113.

Summers, P. W., 1966: The seasonal, weekly, and daily cycles of atmospheric smoke content in central Montreal. J. Air Poll. Contr. Asso. **16**, 432.

Sundborg, A., 1950: Local climatological studies of the temperature conditions in an urban area. Tellus **2**, 222.

Tag, P. M., 1968: Surface temperatures in an urban environment. M. S. Thesis, Dept. of Meteor., The Pennsylvania State Univ., University Park, Penn. 69 pp.

Tebbens, B. D., 1968: Gaseous pollutants in the Air.

In *Air Pollution*, ed. by A. C. Stern. Vol. 1, 2nd Ed., New York, Academic Press, 694 pp.

Telford, J. W., 1960: Freezing nuclei from industrial processes. J. Meteor. **17**, 676.

Volz, F. E., 1968: Turbidity at Uppsala from 1909 to 1922 from Sjostrom's solar radiation measurements. Meddelanden, Ser. B, No. 28. Sver. Meteor. Hydrolog. Inst., Stockholm.

Warner, J., 1968: A reduction in rainfall associated with smoke from sugar-cane fires—an inadvertent weather modification? J. Appl. Meteor. **7**, 247.

Warner, J., and S. Twomey, 1967: The production of cloud nuclei by cane fires and the effect on cloud droplet concentration. J. Atm. Sci. **24**, 704.

Weisman, B., D. H. Matheson, and M. Hirt, 1969: Air pollution survey for Hamilton, Ontario. Atm. Env. **3**, 11.

Wiggett, P. J., 1964: The year-to-year variation of the frequency of fog at London (Heathrow) Airport. Meteor. Mag. **93**, 305.

Woollum, C. A., 1964: Notes from a study of the microclimatology of the Washington, D. C., area for the winter and spring seasons. Weatherwise **17**, 262.

Woollum, C. A., and N. L. Canfield, 1968: Washington metropolitan area precipitation and temperature patterns. ESSA Tech. Memo. WBTM–ER–28. Garden City, N. Y. 32 pp.

ADDITIONAL REFERENCES

Landsberg, H. E. 1966. Air pollution and urban climate. *Biometeorology* (Proceedings of 3rd International Biometeorological Congress) 2:648–656.

Lowry, W. P. 1967. The climate of cities. *Sci. Am.* 217(2):15 ff.

World Meteorological Organization. 1970. *Urban Climates.* Technical Note, No. 108. 390 pp.

THE LA PORTE WEATHER ANOMALY—
FACT OR FICTION?

STANLEY A. CHANGNON, JR.

The effects of cities and their industries on climate can extend far beyond the city itself. Selections 9, 10, and 11 treated these regional effects somewhat incidentally. This selection discusses in detail a specific case where a city has caused sizable climatic change a considerable distance away.

La Porte, Indiana, is 30 miles east of the large complex of industries at Chicago. Since 1925 La Porte has had a notable and anomalous increase in total precipitation, number of rainy days, number of thunderstorm days, and number of days with hail. The size of the changes and the absence of such change at surrounding weather stations led to widespread public attention (e.g. Lear, 1968, Newsweek Editors, 1968) and also to charges that the increases are fictional results due to observer error. After a careful assessment of all available climatological data, Stanley A. Changnon, Jr., has concluded that the climatic changes at La Porte are factual. The changes probably are a consequence of the outpouring of heat, nuclei, and vapor from distant steel plants and related industries.

Subsequent studies by the same author (Changnon, 1969) have revealed similar but less pronounced effects downwind from other urban areas. Another investigation (Schaefer, 1969) has traced clouds of inadvertently produced ice crystals for hundreds of miles downwind from cities; he attributes the clouds mainly to lead compounds, which serve as ice-condensation nuclei, produced from the combustion of leaded automobile gasoline.

(Editor's comment)

Stanley A. Changnon, Jr. (b. 1928), is principal scientist in the Atmospheric Sciences Section of the Illinois State Water Survey, Urbana, for which he has worked since 1955. He holds bachelor's and master's degrees from the University of Illinois. The subject of this selection is the author's primary research interest, the effects on precipitation of urban-industrial centers. He currently is investigating the climatic influence of eight major cities and conducting an extensive field program in the St. Louis area. A second topic of interest is the study of hail, including hailstorm mechanics, radar hail-detection methods, and design of hail suppression projects.

This article is reprinted by kind permission of the American Meteorological Society and the author from *Bulletin of the American Meteorological Society*, 49(1):4–11, 1968.

Introduction

Among the long-term records of thousands of U. S. Weather Bureau cooperative substations is at least one very interesting and certainly significant historical record of precipitation increase during the past 40 years. The record at La Porte, Ind., exhibits a 30 to 40% increase in precipitation and other related conditions since 1925, and the change compares favorably with the production curve of the Chicago iron-steel industrial complex located 30 miles west. Therefore, the question arises—is this localized large increase factual and related to industrial effects, or is it fictional and a result of observer bias or exposure changes?

If real, the La Porte anomaly represents an interaction between two major problem areas of meteorology: weather modification and atmospheric pollution. Falconer and Vonnegut (1948) and Stout (1962) have reported that industrial effects may lead to increases in precipitation, and Landsberg (1956) has noted that large urban areas produce 5 to 15% increases in precipitation, frequencies of rainy days, and numbers of thunderstorm days. If the La Porte increase is fictional, it reflects some of the large errors that may exist in our long-term climatological records, and thus poses a problem for those making climatological analyses.

La Porte is located 11 miles southeast of the southern end of Lake Michigan and is in a zone experiencing heavy snowfall due to lake effects (Changnon, 1967a). The city also sits astride the Valparaiso Moraine, which parallels the lake shore in this area and has an elevation ranging from 100 to 200 ft higher than the lake plain to the north and the flat lands to the south.

A climatological investigation of the La Porte anomaly has been made to ascertain the reality of the increases found in the precipitation amounts and in rain-day frequencies, days with thunderstorms, and days with hail. Seasonal and annual precipitation values from 1901 through 1965 for La Porte and surrounding stations were analyzed to determine the time and degree of change at La Porte. Weather stations in the area of investigation are shown in Figure 12.1. The La Porte precipitation data also were compared with observer and site changes. Frequencies of days of precipitation of different intensities were similarly investigated. Monthly and annual frequencies of thunderstorm days and hail days were analyzed on a spatial and temporal basis to discern the degree and time of increases in these conditions. Cases of thunderstorms and hail occurring at La Porte and not in surrounding areas were carefully studied to determine their reality and possible causes.

If the change at La Porte is due to man's inadvertent activities and therefore real, it is indicative of the sizeable precipitation increases that man could purposely achieve. If real, it also offers a unique laboratory for the study of the specific causes of the increase (added nuclei, heat, or moisture) as well as further analysis of precipitation processes. Furthermore, the La Porte anomaly is an excellent example of how climatological records can be used to detect and study significant mesoscale precipitation variations which may be due to man-made effects or to natural (site) causes.

Precipitation

The annual precipitation values at La Porte were combined to form 5-yr running totals, and these were compared with 5-yr values at the Valparaiso and South Bend stations. Since most precipitation systems in this area move from the southwest, west, or northwest, the Valparaiso station is usually 20 miles upwind of La Porte and the South Bend station 24 miles downwind.

The temporal fluctuations in the 5-yr values at these three stations are revealed in Figure 12.2. The shapes of the time-series curves and the amounts are quite homogeneous from the beginning of their records through the 5-yr period ending in 1930. Thereafter, the two surrounding stations exhibit a general decrease up to 1940, whereas the La Porte curve has a gentle increase through 1940. During 1931–1940, La Porte averaged 46.3 inches per year, whereas Valparaiso had 38.4 inches and South Bend 34.4. From 1941 through 1951 La Porte averaged 55.8 inches, which was 43% more than that at Valparaiso and 61% more than that at South Bend. After this period of maximum departure the differences became less, except for the 5-yr periods ending in 1960 and 1961. Although the Valparaiso values from 1930 through 1965 are considerably less than those at La Porte, the shape of the two curves are alike and they fulfill the criterion of the Helmert test for relative homogeneity (Conrad and Pollak, 1950).

Shown as a curve in Figure 12.2 are the 5-yr running totals for the number of days with smoke and haze at Chicago. This measure of atmospheric pollution has a temporal distribution after 1930 rather similar to the La Porte precipitation curve. A notable increase in smoke-haze days began in 1935, becoming more marked after 1940 when the La Porte precipitation curve began its sharp increase. The diminishment of smoke-haze-day frequencies after the peak reached in 1947 also generally matches the decline of the La Porte curve since 1947.

Stout (1961) has shown that the shape of the time-series curve for La Porte precipitation generally matched a time-series curve for annual steel production (tons) in the Chicago industrial complex. Peaks in steel production occurred in 1923–1929, 1935–1937, 1940–1945, 1950, 1951, 1956–1958, and 1960–1962, and all of these were associated with highs in the La Porte precipitation curve. Of course, these were periods of greater activity and production in most industries, and the association with steel output may be entirely accidental. A change in the method of steel production using the basic oxygen furnace began in 1959, and by 1965 was responsible for about 25% of the steel production. The adoption of this new process, which produces steel in only 7% of the time required for the open hearth process, might relate to the considerably lower La Porte value for the 5-yr period ending in 1965. Telford (1960) in a study of freezing

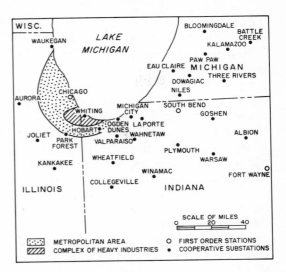

FIGURE 12.1 Location of weather stations.

nuclei produced by industrial sources in Australia found that the smoke from steel furnaces was a prolific source of nuclei, increasing counts by a factor of 50 over those in nearby clean air, and he concluded that there should be increased rainfall occurring downwind of such industrial concerns.

Also shown in Figure 12.2 are marks which indicate changes in cooperative observers at La Porte. Eight different observers served between 1901 and October 1927, but the observer who began in 1927 continued to

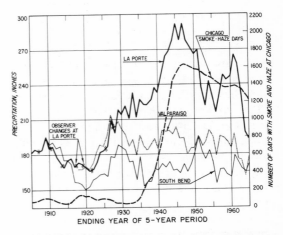

FIGURE 12.2 Precipitation values at selected Indiana stations and smoke-haze days at Chicago, both plotted as 5-yr moving totals.

serve through 1965. The large positive departure of the La Porte values from those at nearby stations began within four years after this last observer change which indicates the possibility that the new raingage site or the observer may have introduced an increase. The station has been in the same location since 1927, and inspection of the site in 1962 and again in 1967 revealed that it had a representative exposure equivalent to those of most substations.

The precipitation anomaly was examined further by plotting the 5-yr amounts for the cold season (November–March) and warm season (April–October), shown in Figure 12.3. La Porte has an average annual snow-

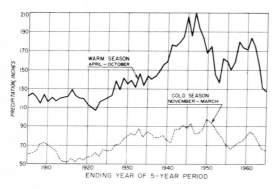

FIGURE 12.3 Warm and cold season precipitation values for 5-yr periods at La Porte.

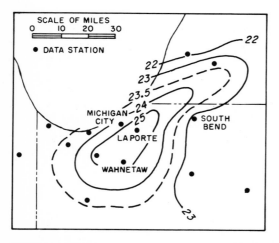

FIGURE 12.4 Average warm season precipitation (inches) based on 1961–1966 data.

fall of 66 inches, which produces nearly 40% of the cold season precipitation, and thunderstorm rainfall is 58% of the warm season total (Changnon, 1967a). The good relationship between the annual curve in Figure 12.2 and the warm season curve in Figure 12.3 illustrates that most of the total increase came from rainfall increases in this season. If gage exposure were the principal cause for the La Porte increase, snowfall would have been affected much more than rainfall (Kurtyka, 1953), and therefore the major increase would have occurred in the cold season. Occurrence of most of the increase in the warm season suggests that the increase has been related to convective type rainfall.

In support of the representativeness of the La Porte warm season precipitation measurements are those of two nearby weather stations established in 1960. The 1961–1966 warm season average at Michigan City was 24.63 inches, that at Wahnetaw was 25.02 inches, and the La Porte average was 25.5 inches. Using these averages and those calculated for the other stations around La Porte, an average pattern was drawn (Figure 12.4). Although for a short period, the pattern suggests that the area of increase is centered at La Porte and that the La Porte value is real. Furthermore, the area of localized increase, as defined by the 24-inch isohyet, is oriented NE–SW and covers about 650 sq mi.

As another examination of the anomaly, the frequencies of rain days with 0.01 inch or more and those with 0.25 inch or more at La Porte, based on data for 1940–1965, were compared with those at South Bend and Valparaiso. The annual average number of days with 0.01 inch or more was 125 at La Porte, 130 at South Bend, and 137 at Valparaiso. The averages for days with 0.25 inch or more were 62 at La Porte, 46 at South Bend, and 46 at Valparaiso. These frequencies suggest that the greater precipitation at La Porte did not result from rainfall production on days with no rain at nearby stations, but came as a result of local intensification of rainfall on days when rain was occurring in the area.

Thunderstorm Days

Data on thunderstorm days were obtained from Weather Bureau first-order stations in the area (Chicago for 1901–1965 and South Bend for 1937–1965), and from cooperative substations in the immediate area. Since substations are operated by volunteer observers, these thunderstorm records had to be evaluated to find what portions, if any, contained quality thunderstorm-day reports. The evaluation method used (Changnon, 1967b) revealed that 14 nearby substations had quality records of at least 15 years' length. South Bend data for 1901–1936, when a substation was in operation there, also were evaluated.

Since the precipitation analysis indicated the La Porte increase was in convective rainfall (warm season), comparable temporal increases should be expected in thunderstorm activity. Figure 12.5 contains curves showing the temporal change in thunderstorm-day frequencies at La Porte and three other stations plotted as 5-yr running totals. Quality thunderstorm records at La Porte began in 1924, and through 1950 the values were quite comparable with those at south Bend. Both stations exhibited notable increases beginning after 1940, and this matched a considerable increase in precipitation (Figure 12.2). The Chicago station did not exhibit the great thunderstorm increase from 1940 through 1945. After 1950 La Porte had another increase in frequencies which maximized in the 5-yr period ending in 1955. The nearby Ogden Dunes station (Figure 12.1), which has good thunderstorm records for the 1949–1965 period, had thunderstorm-day frequencies that are higher than those at South Bend and Chicago, but not as high as those at La Porte. The third peak in the La Porte curve centers on 1961–1963, which again matches peaks in the annual and warm season precipitation curves.

The average annual pattern of thunderstorm days based on 1949–1965 data is shown in Figure 12.6. La Porte, with an average of 54 days per year, has 38% more than the mean value determined from the 9 stations

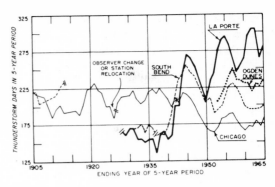

FIGURE 12.5 Temporal changes in thunderstorm days illustrated by 5-yr moving totals.

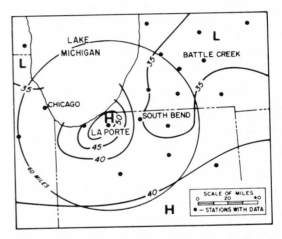

FIGURE 12.6 Pattern of average annual number of thunderstorm days based on 1949–1965 data.

within 60 miles. Ogden Dunes, with an average of 45 days and a location also favorable for realizing industrial effects, supports the reality of the La Porte value. In personal communication, the weather observer at Ogden Dunes (Mr. Robert Ward, a charter member of the American Meteorological Society) reported that he has frequently observed cumulus congestus and thunderstorm development to the east and southeast of his station.

Thunderstorms at La Porte only. During 1951–1964, days with thunderstorms at La Porte and none reported at any station within 60 miles were determined and defined as "solo" thunderstorm days. Obviously, these

TABLE 12.1 Solo thunderstorm days at La Porte, 1951–1964

	JAN.	FEB.	MAR.	APR.	MAY	JUNE	JULY	AUG.	SEP.	OCT.	NOV.	DEC.	ANNUAL
Number	4	4	11	17	24	21	28	35	31	9	6	3	193
Per cent of total thunder days	45	36	24	22	24	17	22	30	33	24	37	43	25
Number with distant lightning at SBN	0	0	0	0	2	3	3	3	2	0	1	0	14
Rain on thunder days													
0 or T	3	2	0	4	10	6	6	16	15	2	0	1	65
.01–.09	0	0	2	4	5	12	8	6	9	1	2	0	49
.10–.50	1	2	7	5	5	2	9	7	5	4	2	1	50
$\geq.51$	0	0	2	4	4	1	5	6	2	2	2	1	29

solo days were largely responsible for the higher frequencies at La Porte during this period, and a clearer understanding of their causes and reality was desired. Table 12.1 shows the number of solo days per month; the 14-yr total was 193, or 14 days per year. These values were expressed as a per cent of the total number of thunderstorm days in the 14-yr period. The solo days represented more than 20% of the total occurrences in all months except June, and the highest percentages occurred in the winter and late summer months.

The possibility that the La Porte observer was reporting thunder when only lightning was viewed was checked using the South Bend first-order station records of distant lightning. As shown in Table 12.1, only 14 of the 193 solo days were days when South Bend reported distant lightning, and most of these occurred in the warm season.

The amount of rainfall on the solo days also was determined, and the values are shown in Table 12.1. Nearly 60% of the 193 days were associated with daily totals of less than 0.1 inch, whereas a study of thunderstorm precipitation in Illinois showed that only 31% of all thunderstorm days produced daily totals of less than 0.1 inch (Changnon, 1957). Thus, the solo thunderstorm days at La Porte frequently produced relatively light precipitation, and inspection of the monthly values in Table 1 shows that these light rains were quite frequent in May, June, August and September. Nearly 50% of the 66 solo days in August and September were associated with no measurable precipitation.

The time of thunder occurrence on the solo thunderstorm days could be determined from the records for 115 of the 193 days, and the frequencies for 6-hr and 12-hr periods are shown in Table 12.2. On 65 of the 115 days, occurrence time was known to the nearest 6-hr period, and the frequencies in each of the four 6-hr periods were expressed as a per cent of 65. Also shown in Table 12.2 are similar percentages for Chicago (U. S. Department of Commerce, 1957), and comparisons showed that a relatively large number of the solo cases occurred in the morning hours, and especially during the

TABLE 12.2 Time of occurrence of solo thunderstorms at La Porte

TIME, CST	NUMBER	PER CENT	PER CENT OF ALL THUNDERSTORMS AT CHICAGO
Unknown	78	—	—
00–06	24	37[1]	21
06–12	12	18[1]	15
00–12	26		
	—	—	—
Morning total	62	54[2]	36
12–18	17	27[1]	35
18–24	12	18[1]	29
12–24	24		
	—	—	—
Afternoon total	53	46[2]	64

[1] Based on 65 cases when 6-hr period of occurrence could be identified.

[2] Based on 115 cases when time of occurrence could be identified.

0000–0600 CST period. This indicates that the La Porte observer was very alert for thunderstorm occurrences.

As a further check on the reliability of the solo thunderstorm days, the synoptic weather conditions on the 103 solo thunderstorm days in the 1956–1964 period were identified. A skilled forecaster was given a list of 150 dates and times including those for the 103 solo cases and asked to discern whether there was an apparent reason for thunderstorm activity in northwestern Indiana, and if so, what was the condition. As shown in Table 12.3, only 16 of the 103 solo days were with conditions under which the analyst could find no apparent reason for thunderstorm activity. However, on 14 of these 16 days measurable rain fell at La Porte. On 87 solo days, however, definite thunderstorm-producing conditions were present in the area, but thunderstorms developed only around La Porte.

Analysis of the surface low-level wind conditions, air mass types, and pressure gradients existing in the La Porte area on solo thunderstorm days revealed that 48% occurred when very flat pressure gradients existed, and only 15% occurred with steep gradients present. Thus, low wind speeds were common and the general low-level wind directions prior to the advent of the solo thunderstorms at La Porte were from westerly azimuths (SW–W–NW) 80% of the time. Prior surface winds were less than 10 mph on 70% of the solo days, and the thunderstorms developed most frequently in cP air masses.

Discussion. Since 1949 there have been 38% more thunderstorm days at La Porte than expected on the basis of surrounding data. The reality of the thunderstorm increase at La Porte is reflected in several findings. The preponderance of early morning solo reports suggests that the observer was quite conscientious. Observer bias is not evident since the increase did not begin until 1940, which was 13 years after he had become the local observer. Only 10% of the 193 solo cases were days with distant lightning at South Bend, which meant that the La Porte observer was not reporting distant lightning as thunder. Nearly 85% of the solo cases had an associated synoptic condition which could be expected to produce thunderstorms, and on 14 of the 16 days with no apparent synoptic reason, measurable rain fell. The high average value at Ogden Dunes agrees with the high value at La Porte, and more importantly, the temporal distribution of thunderstorm days at La Porte exhibits homogeneity with those at nearby stations and with the annual and warm season precipitation distributions at La Porte.

The thunderstorm-day pattern for the 1949–1965 period reveals the high incidence area is localized around La Porte and Ogden Dunes which suggests the increase is related to the adjacent industrial area. The diurnal distribution of the solo thunderstorm days indicated a preference for early morning occurrences when convection due to local heating is at a minimum, suggesting that if a

TABLE 12.3 Synoptic weather conditions associated with solo thunderstorm days, 1956–1964

CONDITION	WINTER (D-J-F)	SPRING (M-A-M)	SUMMER (J-J-A)	FALL (S-O-N)	TOTAL
Cold front		9	17	7	33
Warm front	1	11	4	3	9
Stationary front		2	6	3	11
Occluded front	1	4		1	6
Squall line		5	3		8
Convergence zone			2		2
Wave-small low		5	10	3	18
No apparent reason		5	7	4	16
Total	2	31	49	21	103

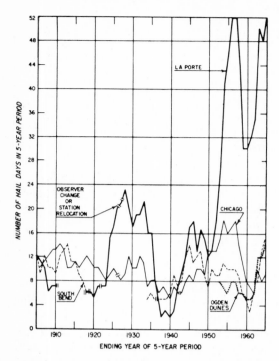

FIGURE 12.7 Temporal changes in hail days illustrated by 5-yr moving totals.

man-made effect was responsible, it aided nocturnal convection. A relatively large number of solo days occurred with small low pressure-wave systems when instability is generally less than with frontal conditions. Again, amplification of convection by local sources appears to be a plausible explanation. Light, westerly low-level winds were the prevalent conditions prior to the solo thunderstorm developments, indicating the presence of conditions generally favorable for realizing the industrial effects upwind of La Porte.

Hail Days

Data on hail days were derived from 247 Weather Bureau stations in Illinois, Indiana, Michigan, and Wisconsin. This included 23 first-order stations, the La Porte substation data, and that for 223 other cooperative sub-stations with most acceptable hail data in the 1920–1965 period (Changnon, 1967a). These substation records were evaluated using the same technique employed for thunderstorm data (Changnon, 1967b). Fifteen stations within a 60-mi radius of La Porte had 20-yr or longer acceptable hail records. La Porte had quality hail records in the 1901–1910 and 1914–1965 periods.

Time-series curves of hail-day incidences for La Porte, Chicago, South Bend, and Ogden Dunes appear on Figure 12.7. The curves at La Porte and Ogden Dunes are based on periods of acceptable records, and dates of observer changes or station reloca-tion are indicated on the 5-yr running total curves of all stations. The La Porte curve shows a marked increase from 1924 through 1928, which agrees with the precipitation increase during this same period (Figure 12.2). This increase occurred during the tenure of three different observers, which tends to dispel an explanation related to single observer bias or error. For the 5-yr periods ending in the 1936–1942 period, La Porte and the other stations had low hail-day values, and their curves remained homoge-neous through 1951. Beginning with the 5-yr period ending in 1952, the La Porte inci-dences of hail increased dramatically, reach-ing a peak of 52 days for the 5-yr periods ending in 1956 and 1957. The high fre-quency of hail days in 1952–1957 is supported by crop-hail insurance data for Indiana which shows that this was the highest 6-yr period of loss in the 1947–1965 period. After di-minishing during the 1956–1960 period, the La Porte hail frequencies increased to a max-imum in 1965. Homogeneity in the shapes of the curves persists in the 1951–1965 period, but the La Porte curve does not exhibit a close relationship with its precipitation curve for this period. During the 1951–1965 period, the South Bend station had 30 hail days, Ogden Dunes had 27, Chicago had 33, and La Porte had 128. The La Porte total was 246% more than the 15-yr mean of the 9 nearest surrounding stations.

Using the total period of quality hail

records at each station, a frequency of hail days was computed for an average 20-yr base period. In the resulting hail-day pattern (Figure 12.8) a high is shown centered at La Porte with elongations extending to stations northeast and southeast of La Porte. These higher values and the shape of the pattern support the reality of the high hail frequency at La Porte. The La Porte long-term average value is 59% greater than the mean of the averages of the stations immediately surrounding La Porte.

Hail at La Porte only. During 1951–1965 all days with hail at La Porte and with none at any station in Illinois, Indiana, Michigan and Wisconsin were identified and labeled as "solo" hail days. Since hail is usually a much more infrequent event over an area than thunderstorms, the 4-state area was used to delineate the solo hail days rather than the area within 60 miles which was used to delineate solo thunderstorm days. There were 30 solo hail days in the 15-yr period under study and all were thunderstorm days with 17 of these being solo thunderstorm days. The number of solo hail days by month are shown in Table 12.4, and the monthly numbers are also expressed as a percentage of the total hail days. All but one of the solo days occurred in the nonwinter months, and one month, July, had a very high frequency.

Associated weather conditions on the solo hail days at La Porte were also investigated. High, damaging winds were reported on 14 of the 30 days, and daily rainfall amounts on the solo days were generally moderate. Four days had only a trace; three had between 0.01 and 0.09 inch; 12 days had between 0.1 and 0.5 inch; and on 11 days the totals were 0.51 inch or more.

The general time of occurrence of the hail on most of the solo days could be determined and 80% of the timed hailfalls occurred in the 0000–1200 CST period. Normally, only 15% of all hailfalls in this area occur in that 12-hr period (Huff and Changnon, 1960), illustrating a marked preference for the solo hailfalls in the early morning, a condition also noted for the solo thunderstorm cases.

As a further check of the validity of the solo hail cases, the synoptic weather conditions on each day were determined by an independent analyst. The condition on one solo day was classed as not capable of hail production, but potential hail-producing conditions were found on the other 29 solo days. Slightly more than 50% of the solo days came with surface lows-waves (no distinct fronts), whereas studies of a large number of hailstorms in Illinois showed that

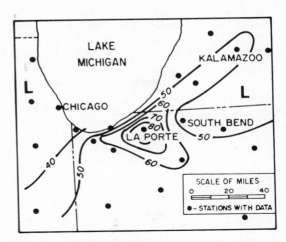

FIGURE 12.8 Number of hail days in an average 20-yr period.

TABLE 12.4 Solo hail days at La Porte, 1951–1965

	JAN.	FEB.	MAR.	APR.	MAY	JUNE	JULY	AUG.	SEP.	OCT.	NOV.	DEC.	TOTAL
Number of solo hail days	1	0	1	6	2	2	13	1	1	3	0	0	30
Per cent of total hail days	50	0	14	22	10	22	43	10	11	25	0	0	23

TABLE 12.5 Difference between average La Porte weather values for 1951–1965 and the means at surrounding stations expressed as a per cent of the means

Annual precipitation	31
Warm season precipitation	28
Annual number of days with precipitation ≥ 0.25 inch	34
Annual number of thunderstorm days	38
Annual number of hail days	246

only 19% of all hail incidences occur with these conditions (Huff, 1960). Ten per cent of the solo cases came with warm front-stationary front conditions, as compared with 22% in the big Illinois sample; and 36% came with cold front-squall line conditions as compared with 59% in the Illinois sample.

Discussion. The long-term average hail-day value at La Porte is 59% higher than those at surrounding stations, but in the 1951–1965 period it was 246% higher. Most of the hail-day findings could be interpreted as meaning that the hail increase was factual. The long-term average hail-day pattern shows a localized high at La Porte, but other areas of relatively high hail-day values exist northeast and southeast of La Porte. Other supporting findings include the fact that all solo days were thunderstorm days; many solo hail days were days of moderate rainfall and high damaging winds; the 1924–1928 increase was associated with 3 different observers; and the temporal distribution of hail days at La Porte was homogeneous with those at other stations and with the thunderstorm distribution at La Porte. Furthermore, the preponderance of solo days in warm season months shows that the observer was not confusing sleet with hail, and the many early morning occurrences indicates considerable diligence by the observer. Two indications of unreality in the La Porte hail data are associated with the hail-day frequencies in the 1951–1965 period. The values are tremendously higher than those at surrounding stations, and the time distribution of hail days in this 15-yr period is not homogeneous with that of precipitation.

Conclusions

Five precipitation conditions at La Porte all indicated generally similar temporal distributions with increases of the same general magnitude for four conditions. The differences between these values and the means of surrounding stations are shown in Table 12.5. The percentage values for annual and warm season precipitation, moderate rain days, and thunderstorm days are of the same general magnitude indicating that if the increase is real, the effects producing the increase were rather uniformly realized in the convective processes. The hail frequencies in the 1951–1965 period were exceptionally high, 246% greater than the mean of the 9 surrounding stations with data.

In the discussions pertaining to precipitation, thunderstorm days, and hail days various reasons supporting the claims of either fiction or fact have been expressed. The more important of those findings that support a claim of an increase due to exposure changes and observer error (fiction) are that: 1) the increases have largely occurred during the service of only one observer who could have systematically altered his reporting; 2) precipitation in the 1931–1940 period showed a slight but steady increase, whereas that at other nearby stations decreased; and 3) 16% of the solo thunderstorm days were associated with synoptic weather conditions which are not conducive to thunderstorm development.

The more significant findings which support a factual conclusion for the La Porte increases include: 1) the temporal agreement between precipitation, thunderstorm, and hail-day distributions is so good that observer bias seems unlikely; 2) the solo cases of thunderstorm and hail days have morning maxima indicating alert observing; 3) a majority of the precipitation increase is in the warm season when a gage exposure-effected result is less likely than in winter, indicating a lack of any significant time change in the raingage exposure; 4) La Porte is located downwind of a major industrial complex capable of sizeable increases in heating, moisture content, and condensation nuclei and freezing nuclei, and the temporal fluctuations in smoke days and steel production compare favorably with those of the precipitation conditions; 5) the average regional patterns of thunderstorm days and hail days both have shapes that support the high values at La Porte; and 6) the time distributions for annual precipitation, thunderstorm days, and hail days at La Porte are homogeneous with those at nearby stations.

The points supporting a factual increase certainly outweigh those for a fictional increase, and the answer to the question posed by this study is that the anomaly is fact. Man has inadvertently produced sizeable increases in precipitation largely by intensification of precipitation when it is occurring. Increases in warm season rainfall, thunderstorm-day frequencies, and hail-day frequencies are substantial proof that the precipitation increase is related largely to added convective activity.

The industrial complex west of La Porte increases the number of condensation and freezing nuclei, the amount of water vapor, and the air temperature, but the effectiveness of each of these additives is not easily assessed. The output of nuclei, vapor, and heat can be considered to have little diurnal variation because the steel plants and related industries generally operate either on a 24-hr basis or not at all. The thunderstorm and hail analyses have shown that the enhancement process is quite frequent in the normally stable morning hours, indicating a diurnal variation in the effectiveness of one or more of the additives. The normal diurnal variations of condensation nuclei and water vapor in unmodified air are not too large but that for temperature is. Therefore, it appears that the thermal island created by heat added to the atmosphere would have a relatively great effect in the cool morning hours. Without further data or field studies, it appears that the addition of heat may be the primary cause for the La Porte anomaly in convective storm activity.

Lake Michigan, which during much of the warm season produces a dome of cold air above it, may assist in the overall process.

With westerly and southwesterly flow, a convergence zone located parallel and a few miles inland from the southern lake shore can be created (Lyons and Wilson, 1967). This condition would keep the industrial effects from being dispersed over the lake, and thus would act to channel the effects towards the La Porte area.

The conclusion of reality for the La Porte anomaly has three major ramifications. First, the relatively small area affected suggests that it would be an excellent site for a detailed study of the specific causes of the increases as well as for basic studies of precipitation processes. Secondly, it illustrates the detailed information that can be gleaned from climatological records as well as how this information can be used to detect spatial and temporal changes in weather and climate. Finally, the results prove that man is capable of producing sizeable increases in convective precipitation, in thunderstorms, and in hailstorms; and furthermore, the temporal agreement shown between these phenomena suggests that if convective precipitation is purposefully increased, more hail and lightning will result. Conversely, this finding could mean that hail suppression may be accompanied by a comparable reduction in precipitation.

Acknowledgments

This research has been performed under the general direction of William C. Ackermann, Chief of the Illinois State Water Survey, and under the direct supervision of Glenn E. Stout, Head of the Atmospheric Sciences Section. Harold Danford assisted in the synoptic analysis, and Robert A. Ward offered considerable useful information. Considerable credit is due to Herbert Link, weather observer at La Porte since 1927, for his exceptional observing and current cooperation. L. A. Schaal, State Climatologist for Indiana, aided the field research. F. A. Huff and Mrs. J. L. Ivens reviewed the manuscript and offered many valuable suggestions.

References Cited

Changnon, S. A., 1957: Thunderstorm-precipitation relations in Illinois. Urbana, Illinois State Water Survey Report of Investigation 34, 24 pp.

———, 1967a: Precipitation climatology of Lake Michigan Basin. Urbana, Illinois State Water Survey Bulletin 52, 100 pp.

———, 1967b: Method of evaluating records of hail and thunder. *Mon. Wea. Rev.,* **95,** 209–212.

Conrad, V., and L. W. Pollak, 1950: *Methods in Climatology.* Cambridge, Mass., Harvard University Press, 459 pp.

Falconer, R. E., and B. Vonnegut, 1948: Smoke from smelting operations as a possible source of silver-iodide nuclei. Schenectady, New York, Project Cirrus Occasional Report 4, 3 pp.

Huff, F. A., 1960: Relations between summer hailstorms in Illinois and associated synoptic weather. Chicago, Crop-Hail Insurance Actuarial Association Research Report 5, 35 pp.

——— and S. A. Changnon, 1959: Hail climatology of Illinois. Urbana, Illinois State Water Survey Report of Investigation 38, 36 pp.

Kurtyka, J. C., 1953: Precipitation measurements study. Urbana, Illinois State Water Survey Report of Investigation 20, 177 pp.

Landsberg, H. E., 1956: The climate of towns. *Man's Role in Changing the Face of the Earth.* Chicago, University of Chicago Press, 584–603.

Lyons, W. A., and J. T. Wilson, 1967: Some effects of a lake upon summertime cumulus and thunderstorms. Paper presented at Tenth Conference on Great Lakes Research, Toronto, 40 pp.

Stout, G. E., 1962: Some observations of cloud initiation in industrial areas. Air Over Cities, Cincinnati, SEC Technical Report A62-5, 147–153.

Telford, J. W., 1960: Freezing nuclei from industrial processes. *J. Meteor.,* **17,** 676–679.

U.S. Department of Commerce, 1947: Thunderstorm rainfall. Vicksburg, Miss., Weather Bureau Hydrometeorological Report 5, 331 pp.

ADDITIONAL REFERENCES

Atkinson, B. W. 1968. A preliminary examination of the possible effect of London's urban area on the distribution of thunder rainfall 1951–1960. *Trans. Inst. Brit. Geog.* 44:97–118.

Changnon, S. A., Jr. 1969. Recent studies of urban effects on precipitation in the United States. *Bulletin of the American Meteorological Society* 50:411–421.

Lear, J. 1968. Home-brewed thunderstorms of La Porte, Indiana. *Saturday Review,* April 6, pp. 53–55.

Malone, T. F. 1967. Weather modification: implications of the new horizons in research. *Science* 156(3777):897–901.

Newsweek Editors. 1968. Heavy industry in Chicago means more rain in La Porte. News Focus, *Newsweek,* April 19, p. 2.

Schaefer, V. J. 1969. The inadvertent modification of the atmosphere by air pollution. *Bulletin of the American Meteorological Society* 50(4):199–206.

13
SELECTION

"ALL OTHER FACTORS BEING CONSTANT . . ."—
THEORIES OF GLOBAL CLIMATIC CHANGE

REID A. BRYSON

The extent of man's impact on the atmosphere is now global. We have inadvertently changed the composition of air not just within cities, or regions, or countries. There is now good evidence that air pollution is associated with certain changes in global climate. There is no proof, however, because of our inadequate understanding of the complexities of climate. Yet the coincidences are close enough to convince many people.

In this selection Reid Bryson discusses the processes by which man's alteration of two atmospheric components, carbon dioxide and dust, may be changing the earth's climate. From the 1880s to the 1940s the average temperature of the world rose by at least 0.7°F. This warming may be a consequence of the increased carbon dioxide content of the atmosphere which, during the same period, rose by about 11 percent. The mechanism is the so-called greenhouse effect, explained here.

However, after 1940 the world began to cool off, and by 1960 had cooled about 30 percent of the previous rise, even though carbon dioxide concentration continued to increase. Bryson suspects that the increased reflectivity of the earth caused by increased dustiness has caused enough cooling to override the previous warming trend.

Additional mechanisms of climatic change by pollution, not treated in this selection, may also operate at the global scale. Increased cloud cover caused by pollutants acting as condensation nuclei (see comment on Selection 12) might cause cooling by increasing reflectivity. Contrails from jet planes are one such type of man-made cloud. Contrails in

Reid A. Bryson (b. 1920) is professor of meteorology and geography and director of the Institute for Environmental Studies at the University of Wisconsin, where he has been on the faculty since 1946. He has received degrees from Denison (B.A., 1941) and the University of Chicago (Ph.D., 1948). Widely known as a teacher and scholar, he has published numerous papers in a variety of disciplines, including geomorphology, paleoclimatology, tropical and dynamic meteorology, and plant geography.

This selection originally appeared in *Weatherwise*, volume 21, pp. 56–61, 94, 1968, under the title "'All Other Factors Being Constant . . .'; A Reconciliation of Several Theories of Climatic Change." It is reprinted with the permission of the journal's editor and the author.

the stratosphere, produced by supersonic planes, may be especially persistent and climatically dangerous.

The consequences for man of marked climatic change would be far-reaching. The agricultural potential for a given region probably would change. Most importantly, resulting changes in sea level would affect coastal culture, resources, and erosion—including our largest cities.

(Editor's comment)

"Something is wrong with the weather" is the title of a recent article in *U. S. News and World Report* (1967), and an article in *Saturday Review* (1967) asks, "Is man changing the climate of the earth?" The layman, and the nonspecialist on reading these articles and the many others in the newspapers will probably be convinced that the climate *is* changing, for the accumulating evidence is considerable. He will probably be confused also, for the reasons given for the change are as varied as the authors. One author will blame the change on sunspots, another on the consumption of fossil fuels producing an increase in the carbon dioxide content of the atmosphere. Still another author will suggest air pollution as a significant cause, and another maintains that a complicated feedback of energy between sea and air is sufficient to produce irregular climatic fluctuations. On the other hand, the man next door *knows* that it is due to all those atom bombs, or the cloud seeders, or automobiles, etc.

Who is right? Which of these answers is the correct one? These are questions that I am frequently asked by my colleagues and friends. These questions can only be answered by saying that none are and all are! All are at least partly right, because each of the factors does contribute to climatic change in larger or smaller measure, contributing to rising or falling world temperatures. All are at least partly wrong in failing to emphasize that there is more than one factor.

There is really no good reason why this confusion should exist, for the various factors fit into a quite well-known basic relationship. The principle is that the heat supplied to the earth's surface by the sun and from the interior of the earth must be disposed of or the surface will get hotter and hotter. This heat income is balanced by infrared radiation from the earth to space.

Neglecting the very small flow of heat from the earth's interior, this basic relationship may be expressed by a simple equation

$$ScA = KeT^4 \text{ (4c)}$$

or in words:

"The intensity of the sunlight arriving at the earth (S), times the cross-sectional area of the earth (c), times the fraction of that radiation which is absorbed (A) is equal to a constant (K), times the "effective emissivity" of the earth (c), times the average temperature of the earth raised to the fourth power (T^4), this outward heat radiation flowing from the entire surface of the earth (4c). In still plainer English this says that the sunlight is absorbed on the cross-section "target area" of the earth, but lost by heat radiation over the whole surface. This heat radiation is proportional to the fourth power of the temperature and to an "effective emissivity" of the earth (i.e., how good the earth is as a radiator). With this simple equation the various theories of climatic change may be related.

Numbers may be put into this simple equation to test it. The intensity of the solar beam reaching the earth is about 2 calories per square centimeter per minute. The fraction of the radiation absorbed by the earth, which must then be re-radiated away, is 60 to 65%. The amount of energy which must be lost by each square centimeter of the earth's surface, on the average, must then be 0.30 to 0.325 calories per minute.[1] This is about what the artificial satellite measurements show,—a fact which gives us some confidence in the equation! (Figure 13.1) If the earth were a perfect radiator, however, this value for the outward radiation would require a mean world temperature of 22 to 26 degrees celsius below freezing, or −7 to −15 degs. F. Fortunately, near the ground the temperature averages something on the order of 60° F. Most of the solar heat is absorbed at or near the surface, because the air is nearly transparent to the wavelengths of solar radiation. The earth emits infrared radiation, to which the air is quite opaque, mostly due to water (clouds), water vapor, and carbon dioxide in it. Some of the solar heat absorbed at the surface heats the air by conduction, and then the atmosphere itself must radiate some of the heat away, but about half of this atmospheric radiation is back downward. Even that which is radiated upward is partly absorbed by higher layers of air unless one goes high enough for most of the water vapor, clouds, and carbon dioxide to be left behind. At this level the temperature is well below freezing. In essence, the equation says that the atmosphere acts as though it were radiating perfectly from some upper level where the temperature is minus 22 to minus 26 celsius.

In order to get the heat from the surface up to where it is finally lost by radiation there must be a temperature difference. In effect this temperature difference is on the order of 40 to 50 degrees celsius, the surface where we live averaging that much warmer. Vive l'atmosphère! This is the so-called "greenhouse effect," which is simulated in the simple equation by throwing in an "effective emissivity."

At this point we must digress momentarily to consider what the average temperature of the earth is. For the purposes of the present discussion it is the temperature averaged over the whole earth and whole year, measured near the surface of the earth. All other factors being constant, the effect of increasing sun intensity is to raise the average temperature of the earth. It is this effect that is being singled out by those meteorologists who maintain the fluctuating solar output, per-

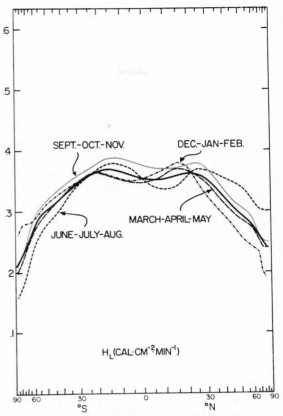

FIGURE 13.1 Infrared radiation leaving the earth, as measured from meteorological satellites, averaged along latitudes. Abscissa is latitude compressed to allow for the smaller area of the earth at higher latitudes, and the ordinate is langleys/minute. The average value agrees quite well with the known values of the solar constant and earth albedo. (From Vonder Haar, Ph.D. thesis, Dept. of Meteorology, Univ. of Wisconsin, 1967.)

haps related to sunspots, is responsible for the ups and downs of the climate over the past few centuries. Hurd Willet of M.I.T. represents this group. A one per cent increase in the solar intensity would raise the average temperature of the earth about 0.8° C. or 1.4° F.

All other factors being constant, the effect of changing the fraction of the sunlight absorbed by the earth is to change the average temperature of the earth. The absorptivity[2] of the earth depends on such things as the amount of snow and ice on the ground, the amount of cloud, the dustiness of the atmosphere, and the nature of the ground cover. Any change which makes the earth a brighter planet, that is, which results in more of the sunlight being reflected, lowers the mean temperature of the earth. Increased cloudiness, snow cover, or dustiness of the atmosphere makes the earth a brighter planet. In fact, the "dark" side of the moon at new moon is less dark when there is much cloud on the sunlit side of the earth or much dust in the air—it is illuminated by sunlight "reflected" by the clouds and dust—and becomes faintly visible.

An increase of one per cent in the normal reflectivity or "albedo" of the earth from perhaps 37% to 38% would lower the mean temperature of the earth about 1.7° C. or 3.1°F.

Proponents of variation in cloudiness, volcanic dust, and man-made dust as factors causing climatic change emphasize this factor. I am one of these.

All other factors being constant, an increase of the "effective emissivity" of the earth for infrared radiation will result in a cooler earth. This is the rather complicated factor discussed in a previous paragraph which involves the mechanism by which the solar heat absorbed at the surface of the earth works its way up to the levels in the atmosphere from which it is finally lost to interstellar space. Part of this "greenhouse effect" is due to the carbon dioxide, clouds, moisture, dust, and ozone in the atmosphere. Those scientists who say that the rising world temperature observed between 1880 and 1940 was due to the observed increase of carbon dioxide in the atmosphere during that time are emphasizing a change of one part of the "effective emissivity."

A one per cent increase in the "effective emissivity" from say 55% to 56% would lower the mean world temperature by about 1.2° C. or 2.2°F. A one per cent change in carbon dioxide would give a much smaller change.

So far the story is simple and straightforward. Change one of the three factors—solar intensity, reflectivity, and "effective emissivity"—and the mean temperature of the earth changes. However true this may be, most of us are concerned with local temperature, not the annual average for the whole world. In general, the local climatic change is not the same as the average, but differs from it by an amount dictated by the circulation patterns of the atmosphere. These patterns do not change in a simple way as the solar intensity, absorptivity, and "emissivity" change.

We do know that one of the most important relations is that which exists between the *differential* heating of the atmosphere and the circulation pattern. It is not the average temperature of the earth which counts so much as the equator to pole contrast of temperature which determines the circulation pattern of the atmosphere, and thus the local climate change. This is why summer circulation patterns are not like those of winter. Just how the pattern changes is quite complicated, but it is sufficient at this point to say that a change in temperature contrast from equator to poles will generally change the pattern of circulation to a *different* pattern.

In general, changes in sunshine intensity, absorptivity, and "emissivity" will change both the average annual temperature of the earth *and* the circulation pattern because the equator to pole contrast is changed. Changing radiation or circulation patterns may also change the distribution of sea temperatures which in turn further modifies the climate. This gets to be so complicated that for purposes of this discussion we will stick to considerations of the mean annual temperature of the earth.

Now the really sticky question is, "Which of these factors is the more important?" Framed in a different way the question is whether the observed variations of sunshine, absorptivity, and "emissivity" give equal effects. According to J. Murray Mitchell, Jr., the increase in world mean annual temperature from the 1880's to the 1940's was about 0.7° F. From the figures given above one can see that this could be due to an increase in the intensity of the solar radiation reaching the earth of about half a per cent, a decrease of reflectivity of about a quarter of a per cent, or a decrease of "effective emissivity" of about a third of a per cent. None of these factors can be measured with this precision!

This leaves us in the unfortunate position of not being able to resolve the question of relative importance at present. In theory it should be possible to measure the sunlight intensity as it reaches the earth, the reflectivity of the earth, and earth's back-radiation to space from artificial satellites. It is likely that these measurements will soon be made with sufficient accuracy. To establish, however, whether the variations with time are enough to explain climatic fluctuations will probably require decades of observations, which doesn't help us answer the question now.

Still, we might be able to throw some light on some of the questions which have been raised concerning climatic change if we consider whether the observed changes go in the right direction. Let us assume that the number of sunspots varies with the solar heat output. If a small increase in solar heat output means a large increase in sunspots, then perhaps observed increase in sunspots since about 1900 might indicate the presence of a small but unmeasurable increase in solar intensity.

An increase of carbon dioxide in the atmosphere increases the "greenhouse effect" and thus decreases the "effective emissivity." Since carbon dioxide provides only a small part of the "greenhouse effect" an easily measurable change in carbon dioxide content of the atmosphere would be necessary to change the "emissivity" by the required amount. The carbon dioxide content of the atmosphere has increased by about 11 per cent since 1870.

Except for seasonal changes, the reflectivity of the seas and land seems to be quite constant, the largest variations being due to cloud and dust in the atmosphere itself. Whether the cloud cover varies from decade to decade is simply not known—the observational system is inadequate. There is better information on dust in the atmosphere, though it is less than needed. Fortunately, dust gets well mixed in the atmosphere so that measurements at a point are often more representative than those of clouds. Robert A. McCormick and John H. Ludwig (1967),

of ESSA, have shown that the turbidity of the air (roughly the "dustiness") increased 57% over Washington, C. C., in about 60 years, and 88% over Davos, Switzerland, in about 30 years. They concluded that while perhaps two-thirds of the Washington increase was local, there was a significant increase in worldwide "dustiness" (see Figure 13.2). My own studies suggest a turbidity increase of 30% per decade over the Mauna Loa Observatory in Hawaii, far from sources of pollution (Figure 13.3). A turbidity change of 3–4%, averaged over the world, appears

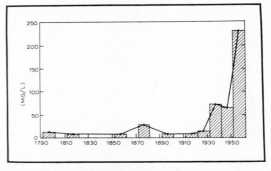

FIGURE 13.2 Dust fall trapped in the firn of the glaciers of the high Caucasus according to F. Davitaya. He believes that the rapid increase in recent decades is due to human activity.

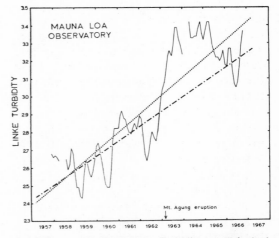

FIGURE 13.3 Trend of Linke Turbidity coefficient at Mauna Loa Observatory, Hawaii, with mean annual variation removed. The dotted line represents the line of least-squares best fit to all the data, and the dash-dot line is for the data with the three years following the Mt. Agung eruption omitted. (Compiled by Mr. James Peterson.)

to be adequate to change the world mean temperature by 0.7° F. Certainly the observed fluctuations in turbidity are large enough to explain the climatic change. The question is whether it is in the right direction.

J. Murray Mitchell, Jr. (1961) has published a diagram which makes it possible to at least see whether the proposed causes of climatic change work in the right direction. (Figure 13.4). He showed that from the 1880's to the 1940's the mean temperature of the world rose by 0.7° F. as mentioned above. His diagram also shows the increase of sunspots during that time and the increase of carbon dioxide in the atmosphere over the same time. These changes are in the right direction to produce the observed change of world temperature. However, Mitchell's diagram shows that after 1940 the world began to cool off, and by 1960 had cooled about 30% of the previous rise—yet the sunspots and carbon dioxide continued to increase. This diverging trend has continued into the 1960's and hints strongly that something other than sunspots and carbon dioxide is more important.

Mitchell suggested in 1961 that this other factor might be dust from volcanic eruptions, such as Mt. Spurr in Alaska in 1953 and Mt. Bezymyannaya, Kamchatka, in 1956, but concluded that the volcanic activity was insufficient to explain the recent cooling. There have been other dusty eruptions since, such as Agung on Bali, which produced easily measurable increases in atmospheric turbidity. I believe that the increasing turbidity of the air due to these volcanic eruptions *plus human activity*, which Mitchell ignored, is now overshadowing the increase of carbon dioxide and sunspots and is now causing a worldwide cooling.

All other factors being constant, an increase of solar output, which may be indicated by increased sunspot activity, will produce increased world temperature—but recent cooling of the earth while the sunspots increased suggests that other factors were operative.

All other factors being constant, an increase of atmospheric carbon dioxide, by decreasing the ease with which radiant energy leaves the earth's surface, should cause world temperatures to rise—but they have been falling while the carbon dioxide continued to rise. Some other factor must be more important and varying.

All other factors being constant, an increase of atmospheric turbidity ("dustiness") will make the earth cooler by scattering away more incoming sunlight. A decrease of dust should make the earth warmer. Mitchell's diagram shows that volcanic activity, as a source of atmospheric dust, varied in the right direction to produce warming from the 1880's to the 1940's followed by cooling. The continued rapid cooling of the earth since World War II is also in accord with the increased global air pollution associated with industrialization, mechanization, urbanization, and an exploding population, added to a renewal of volcanic activity.

Though changes in solar intensity, earth reflectivity, and "effective emissivity" may

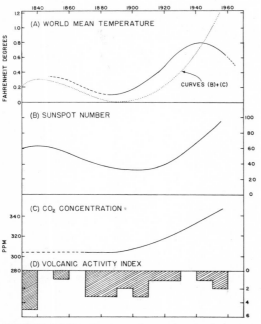

FIGURE 13.4 Trends of world mean temperature, sunspot index, carbon dioxide, and volcanic activity. (After Mitchell, 1961.) The curve for temperature has been extended to include data available since Mitchell constructed the diagram.

each produce climatic change alone, it appears that there is a complex interplay of factors, some dominating at one time, others dominating at other times. I believe that increasing global air pollution, through its effect on the reflectivity of the earth, is currently dominant and is responsible for the temperature decline of the past decade or two.

It has been suggested that the increase of carbon dioxide over the past century is due to human activity also—the burning of fossil fuels since the Industrial Revolution. If this were the case then the carbon dioxide increase and the air pollution increase might balance each other in terms of effect on

climatic change in the future. However, radiocarbon assays by Hans Suess, of the Scripps Institution of Oceanography, have shown that most of the carbon dioxide increase is not from the burning of fossil fuels, but must come from the modern plant materials, such as the slow oxidation of peat bogs or the slash-and-burn clearing of farm fields would produce (Revelle and Suess, 1967). Edward Deevey, Jr., of Yale, believes that peat bogs and soil humus are the source (1958). Perhaps, then, the increased carbon dioxide is the effect of increased temperature rather than its cause.

The atmospheric balances and complexities rival those of politics!

Note

[1] One-fourth of 2 times 0.60 or 2 times 0.65, because the area of the earth is four times the cross-sectional area. The income is on the cross-section, but the loss is over the whole surface.

[2] Meteorologists normally measure the reflectivity, the fraction reflected, rather than the fraction absorbed or absorptivity. The reflectivity is called the *albedo*.

References Cited

Deevey, E. S., Jr. 1958. Bogs. *Sci. Am.* 199(4):114–122.

McCormick, R. A., and J. H. Ludwig. 1967. Climate modification by atmospheric aerosols. *Science* 156(3780):1358–1359.

Mitchell, J. M., Jr. 1961. Recent secular changes of global temperature. *Annals New York Academy of Science* 95:235–250.

Revelle, R., and H. E. Suess. 1957. Carbon dioxide exchange between atmosphere and ocean and the question of an increase of atmospheric CO_2 during the past decades. *Tellus* 9:18–27.

Saturday Review, April 1, 1967, p. 52.

U.S. News and World Report, July 10, 1967.

ADDITIONAL REFERENCES

Bryson, R. A., and J. T. Peterson. 1968. Atmospheric aerosols: increased concentrations during the past decades. *Science* 162:120–121.

Davitaya, F. F. 1965. On the possible influence of atmospheric dust cover on the diminution of glaciers and the warm-up of climate. *Transactions of the Soviet Academy of Science,* Geographical Series 2, pp. 3–22, English translation.

Gunn, R. 1964. The secular increase of worldwide fine particle pollution. *Journal of Atmospheric Science* 21:168–181.

Lamb, H. H. 1966. Climate in the 1960's: Changes in the world's wind circulation reflected in prevailing temperatures, rainfall patterns and the levels of the African lakes. *Geographical Journal* (London) 132:183–212.

Mitchell, J. M., Jr., ed. 1968. *Causes of climatic change.* Met. Monogr. Volume 8, Number 30. Boston: American Meteorological Society. 160 pp.

Nuessler, V. D., and R. W. Holcomb. 1970. Will the SST pollute the stratosphere? *Science* 168:1562.

Plass, G. N. 1957. The carbon dioxide theory of climatic change. Pp. 81–92 in *Recent research in climatology,* by Committee on Research in Water Resources, University of California, La Jolla.

President's Science Advisory Committee, Environmental Pollution Panel. 1965. *Restoring the quality of our environment.* Pp. 112–133.

Rand Corporation. 1969. Weather-modification progress and the need for interactive research. Staff, The Weather Modification Research Project. *Bulletin of the American Meteorological Society* 50:216–243.

Rohrman, F. A., B. J. Steigerwald, and J. H. Ludwig. 1967. Industrial emissions of carbon dioxide in the United States: a projection. *Science* 156:931–932.

Singer, S. F., ed. In preparation. *Global effects of atmospheric pollution.* Dordrecht, Netherlands: Reidel Publishing Company.

NOISE—SOUND WITHOUT VALUE

COMMITTEE ON ENVIRONMENTAL QUALITY,
U.S. FEDERAL COUNCIL FOR SCIENCE AND TECHNOLOGY

Noise is a growing environmental problem in industrial societies, especially in cities. Noise assaults modern man outdoors, indoors, and on the job. This selection surveys, in easily understandable terms, the variety and complex effects of noise.

As implied by the title, noise may be defined as any sound that is undesired by the recipient (Wilson, 1963). Hence, noise is subjective, based on personal evaluation. Sounds in a bustling city may be music for one person but unbearable noise for another. The physical properties of a sound may have little relation to whether it is an annoying noise—witness the drip, drip, drip of a water faucet. Noise that permeates our environment to the extent that it irritates the general public may be termed "noise pollution."

Julius Caesar was forced by public opinion to alleviate noise pollution in Rome. He banned chariots from the streets during daylight hours as a safety precaution, but as a result night traffic created considerable noise. Vehicles subsequently were prohibited from the city. Today the problem is much less easily solved. The necessary activities of urban life may inevitably seem to produce noise. However, designers can greatly reduce noise if the general public is willing to pay the price (Harris, 1957; Beranek and Miller, 1967; Bredin, 1968). The noise effects of some activities may outweigh the social benefits—thus dictating that the activity should cease. For example, sonic booms generated by supersonic transport planes (SST) may overbalance their positive virtues,

In 1967 Donald F. Hornig, director of the U.S. Office of Science and Technology, suggested that the Federal Council for Science and Technology's Committee on Environmental Quality consider the problem of noise in the environment. The committee established an eleven-man study group, representing ten federal departments or other offices, with Donald R. King as chairman. The objective of the study group was an exposition of the dimensions of the noise problem and a proposal for federal programs to elucidate the effects of noise on man and his environment and to develop means for abating the problem.

This selection, emphasizing the first part of the study-group's objective, is extracted from the committee's final report of the same title, U.S. Government Printing Office, September 1968, 56 pp.

which is mainly national status in the world (Shurcliffe, 1967; Accoustical Society of America, 1966; Anthrop, 1969).

As the physical and psychological consequences of noise become better known (e.g., Alexander, 1968; Cohen, 1968, 1969), legal sanctions against this sort of environmental degradation should increase (Young, 1969).

(Editor's comment)

Introduction

Man has been lulled since time beyond reckoning by the sound of wind in the trees and murmuring brooks. He created music in response to some deep inner need for beauty of expression. An society advanced, he thrilled to the hunting horn, and later, dreamed of faraway places when a distant train whistle penetrated the night.

Unusual silence or unusual sounds also served a useful purpose in man's history. Both cautioned him to beware of unwanted intrusions in his environment. We are still uncomfortable in sound-proof rooms, and still react to unaccustomed noise.

But gradually, apparently inexorably, a new world of whining air conditioners, whirring engines, pneumatic hammers, and the neighbor's radio have intruded on our peaceful world in a rising tide of unwanted sound: noise, long considered an inevitable by-product of our modernizing society.

It is unlikely that one needs more than a reflection on self-experience to be convinced of the problem. The proliferation of machinery as a substitute for toil has brought new and louder sources of noise. In some cases, we have equated noise production with power and delight in both. Uninhibited scooters, motor bikes, motorcycles, and some sports cars are illustrations of this phenomenon. In others, we have accepted noise as a necessary accompaniment to progress. Construction, demolition, maintenance and repair of structures, roads and utilities have been aided by the compressor and air hammer, the pile driver, the earth mover, excavation machinery, power saws, chippers and derricks which unfortunately contribute to our racket. The noise of the handsaw and the blow of a hammer driving a nail were really not bad compared to construction noise today.

Nostalgic sounds of earlier days have been replaced by more insistent, more strident noises. The cry of the huckster of perishables has been stilled by the mechanical refrigerator but the ice cream chime brings joy only to the child with ten cents to spend. The hurdy-gurdy and the German band have been replaced by the radio and the record player. The radio and television have effectively quieted the newsboys' cry of "Extra, Extra, Read All About It" that ruined sleep and tensed nerves when an event of special importance occurred. The neighbors' radio and television speakers are with us always, however.

These sounds are intensified as people concentrate in large centers of population where the building and rebuilding of urban areas never ceases. As these concentrations grow, more people are disturbed as traffic and aircraft noise increases in intensity. Areas that are temporarily "suburban" do not really escape. To most of us, shouting children and barking dogs are comforting evidence of a secure and familiar environment. But banging garbage cans, clanging milk bottles, air conditioners that operate at all hours during warm weather, and power lawn mowers that shatter the peace on a summer Sunday morning are another story.

The products of our technology, which have freed us from the problems of day-to-day survival, have been accompanied by noise as the "price of progress." We have been subjected to increasing noise levels in our environment until we recognize only the most blatant violations.

But is it all inevitable? The answer lies

not only in improving our scientific capability to meet the problem, but also in a public conviction that the quality of our environment is everyone's responsibility and must be considered along with technological and economic development. The alternative is tacit acceptance of a deteriorating situation. This does not imply that progress should be sacrificed for silence. Airplanes, typewriters, and vacuum cleaners are essential to our society. Rather, we must bring technology to bear on the problems that progress creates.

One of the more comprehensive publications on the problem of noise compares the results of successive surveys on the reaction of individuals in Europe to noise that arose outside the home (1). The percentage of people so disturbed increased from 23% in 1948 to 50% in 1961. The report also stated that "whether people live in noisy or quiet places does not affect the proportion of them who are seriously disturbed."

But annoyance is not the only piper we must pay. There is also a price in human health and efficiency. Prolonged exposure to intense noise produces permanent hearing loss. Increasing numbers of competent investigators believe that such exposure may adversely affect other organic, sensory and physiologic functions of the human body (2). Although by no means conclusive, some evidence indicates that prolonged exposure to intense noise or vibration at ultrasonic frequencies (above the hearing range) (3), as well as at infrasonic frequencies (below the hearing range) (4), also presents a potential threat to health. In short, growing numbers of researchers fear that the dangerous and hazardous effects of intense noise on human health are seriously underestimated. We have no appropriate yardstick yet for measuring the effects of noise on mental health. Repeated or consistent exposure may create stresses of which we are unaware.

The dangers of exposure to intense noise are found not only in heavy industrial and aircraft operations but also in light industrial, commercial, and business areas. Noise levels in dwellings, particularly in kitchen areas, are beginning to approach those in factories.

While it is true that a person's tolerance of noise produced within the family circle is quite high and can be controlled by curtailing domestic activities, the fact remains that noises generated within a typical dwelling are much more disturbing than need be.

Although the "annoyance factor" of domestic noise is high, another frequently overlooked consideration is the psychological and social stresses suffered by the occupants of buildings which lack acoustical privacy. Most apartment dwellers naturally are under considerable constraint if they are aware that their next door neighbors can hear them. Living under such conditions can be trying for the occupants because any careless outburst of speech or activity may cause them embarrassment or discomfort.

Although there is no conclusive evidence that moderate, normally encountered domestic or social noise produces any apparent physiological effects on most people, such noise is capable of preventing sleep, inducing stress and interfering with concentration, communication, and recreation. Of all these effects, repeated interference with sleep and relaxation is least to be tolerated.

Noise may also disrupt job performance by interfering with speech communication, distracting attention, and otherwise complicating the demands of the task. Such disruption could cause losses in overall efficiency or require increased effort and concentration to cope with the work situation. With regard to the latter, there appears to be a close relationship between bodily fatigue and noise exposure. Noise also has been implicated as a causative factor in industrial accidents. While plausible, there are few data to support this claim. Some examples of typical noise levels to which we are subjected are presented in Table 14.1.

The adverse effects of noise are usually defined in terms of the reactions of the "average person." This concept of the "average person" is interesting and deserves further discussion. It implies that a substantial fraction of the individuals subjected to stress are affected by it in varying degrees. There is an intriguing question concerned

TABLE 14.1 Typical over-all sound levels.
The levels noted in this table reflect sound energy found in the frequency range 20 to 10,000 Hz (cycles per second) as measured on a sound level meter using the flat or C-scale network. Other measures for describing sound levels such as perceived noise level in decibels (PNdB) or loudness level in phons represent values which are frequency weighted and subject to combination procedures designed to reflect the manner in which the ear responds to sound. These latter weighted values are used for annoyance ratings of sound and are not to be confused with the flat or C-scale determinations above.

Decibels
RE 0.0002 Microbar

	Decibels	
	140	Threshold of pain
Hydraulic press (3′)	130	
Large pneumatic riveter (4′)		
Pneumatic chipper (5′)		Boiler shop (maximum level)
	120	
Overhead jet aircraft—4 engine (500′)		
Unmuffled motorcycle		Jet engine test control room
	110	Construction noise (compressors and hammers) (10′)
Chipping hammer (3′)		Woodworking shop
Annealing furnace (4′)		Loud power mower
Rock and roll band	100	
Subway train (20′)		
Heavy trucks (20′)		Inside subway car
Train whistles (500′)		Food blender
	90	
10-HP outboard (50′)		Inside sedan in city traffic
Small trucks accelerating (30′)		
		Heavy traffic (25′ to 50′)
	80	Office with tabulating machines
Light trucks in city (20′)		
Autos (20′)		
	70	
Dishwashers		Average traffic (100′)
		Accounting office
Conversational speech (3′)		
	60	
	50	Private business office
		Light traffic (100′)
		Average residence
	40	
	30	
		Broadcasting studio (music)
	20	
	10	
	0	

with the point in the variableness of the population at which we should disregard those individuals who are excessively prone to the adverse effects of noise. Should we arbitrarily decide that a percentage of people, say 5 or 10% (or perhaps even as few as 1 in 1,000 or 1 in 10,000) who are particularly disturbed by noise, should be obliged to seek solace in quieter surroundings? This may seem a reasonable expedient to keep the cost of noise abatement at acceptable economic levels. Undoubtedly, we will never be able to eliminate each sound that is objectionable to any individual, but we do need to consider very small minorities. The problem is compounded by the fact that human desires are enormously variable; sounds, such as ringing church bells, which appeal to some people are noise to others.

Excessive noise within buildings as well as in the outdoor environment adversely affects property values. The purchase of an acoustically inferior hotel, motel, office or apartment building may be an exceedingly poor investment. High tenant-turnover may require unfortunate building owners to convert very desirable and expensive rental space into storage space to satisfy occupant complaints of the lack of privacy and noise control; to make expensive acoustical modifications in their buildings; or to sell their property at a loss.

Noise also may affect man indirectly through its effects on domestic animals, wildlife, and structures. Available evidence, however, suggests that some animals become habituated to noise very rapidly and exhibit no readily apparent physiological or behavioral changes (5, 6, 7).

Some concern has been expressed that shock waves from such sources as sonic booms may affect archeological structures or delicate geological formations. However, the expected pressures of sonic booms seem, for the most part, to be below levels that will damage such structures.

It is apparent from the foregoing discussion that excessive noise is an undesirable contaminant of our environment. The alleviation of the noise problem is predicated on defining the degree of control we wish to achieve. As in other situations of this nature, a balance must be struck between what we would ultimately like our environment to be and what it presently is. Typically this relationship is established by weighing as many considerations as are available, and arriving at specific limiting levels of contamination. These "standards" then serve as bases for maintaining or improving the quality of our environment.

The effects of excessive noise may extend far beyond the situation in which the source is located. These "externalities" should be evaluated in assessing requirements. For example, a noisy industrial plant near a residential area may cause property values to decline. Higher noise levels might be permitted if the same plant were in an industrial park, or relatively isolated on a larger piece of land.

As another example, preventing hearing loss due to occupational noise may have far greater benefits than merely reducing the number of compensatory claims filed. The intangible benefit of maintaining adequate hearing ability is important to each worker whether he files a claim or not. Since these benefits are not easily assessed, it may be necessary to rank hearing loss prevention with other more easily quantifiable alternatives.

Outdoor Noise

AIRCRAFT NOISE

The rapid growth of the air transportation system has resulted in a wave of public reaction to aircraft noise on and near major airports around the world. The problem also is becoming serious at many smaller airports.

The severity of the situation is illustrated by a 1967 article in the Los Angeles Times: "36 Million Claims Filed Against City Over Airport Noise." Among complaints were these: "Children have been deprived of the use of their schools for proper educational activities . . . ," ". . . subjected to loud noise," ". . . complained of anxiety, loss of sleep, hearing . . . ," ". . . suffered permanent hearing damage and emotional disturbance from jets."

The possible adverse effects of aircraft noise have been recognized for years. In 1952, the Doolittle Report alerted us to the growing aircraft noise problem (8). In recent years the problem has grown to such a magnitude that immediate positive action is essential. The Doolittle Commission pointed out that "positive efforts should be continued by both Government and industry to reduce or control aircraft noise nuisance to people on the ground and that substantial reduction of such noise is practicable."

The problem can be characterized as one of conflict between two groups—those who benefit from air transportation services and people who (individually and collectively) live and work in communities near airports. The conflict exists because social and economic costs resulting from aircraft noise are imposed upon certain land users in the vicinity of airports who receive no direct benefits. It is important that this situation be rectified in an equitable manner consistent with the public welfare and the orderly development of air commerce (9).

The airport noise problem has continued to grow during the last several years not only because jet aircraft have been and still are inherently noisy, but also because large numbers of people live and work in the large industrial, commercial-office complexes which have developed around airports.

The anticipated use of supersonic aircraft has heightened public concern. The United States government is proceeding with development of the supersonic transport plane (SST), after careful consideration of the problems it creates, on the assumption that the present SST model will be used on overwater routes. However, the sonic boom phenomenon is considered in this report as a possible transportation noise of the future.

Economic aspects. The most rational approach to resolving the conflict caused by aircraft noise is to reduce the adverse effect of noise to the lowest practicable level with an equitable allocation of costs.

From an economic viewpoint, airport noise is an "external" cost. By definition, an external cost exists when the production of a commodity or service by one economic entity imposes an unfavorable or unwanted effect on another entity, for which payment is not provided. If some of the external costs of airport noise are not to be borne by the industry—then air transportation production has an advantage over some other industries. The unfairness of this situation leads to the conclusion that the services provided by the air transportation industry should include external costs. This means imposing the costs of new programs to alleviate airport noise on the industry and ultimately on the public.

The question of how the public benefits from air transportation is important. One of the arguments raised against charging air transport users for noise alleviation is that the air transportation industry provides economic and non-economic benefits to the entire nation. Such widespread benefits, it is claimed, justify the use of Federal funds to pay at least a portion of airport noise costs. There is little question that air transportation benefits the majority of the population of the United States, whether or not they have ever flown. In effect, a modern air transportation system is a national requirement. What the net value is of the air transportation system is a major question yet to be addressed. The answer is not clear unless we know the value obtained as well as the value sacrificed to obtain it (10).

Some conception of the cost of noise reduction may be gained from the following example. Prior to the introduction of jet-powered commercial aircraft, an estimated $50 million was spent on research and development by the industry to perfect in-flight sound suppressors for jet powerplants.

By 1965, the industry had invested an estimated $150 million in installation of in-flight noise suppressors (11).

Subsequently suppressor-equipped jet engines were replaced by newly developed turbofan engines at a cost of approximately $1 million per aircraft. This change-over improved operating efficiency and partially reduced noise output.

The SST may be a special case. Frequent commercial SST transcontinental operations would expose millions of people each day to an impulse noise which would be startling and cause various degrees of human annoyance. There would also be allegations of damage to property caused by the boom: principally for broken glass and damaged plaster. The magnitude of these anticipated claims is unknown, but has been estimated to be millions of dollars per year depending upon flight path and frequency.

Sonic boom research. Subsonic aircraft and sonic boom noise research programs are now being addressed simultaneously by the Interagency Aircraft Noise Abatement Program. The Federal Government has conducted extensive research programs to determine the effects of the sonic boom on people, animals, and structures as a basis for establishing criteria for sonic boom acceptability (13, 14). At the present time, early prospects for important reductions in the intensities of sonic boom are not apparent.

In summary, considerable additional effort will have to be addressed to control of the aircraft noise problem. More research will be needed on methods for reducing noise at its source and prediction techniques; effects on people, property and other values; and cost allocation mechanisms. The establishment of aircraft noise standards and abatement regulations as well as comprehensive planning approaches will be required to significantly reduce the public noise problem.

SURFACE TRANSPORTATION NOISE

Noise radiation from vehicular traffic and railroads is a major source of complaint among urban and suburban dwellers (16, 17, 18, 19). Of the two sources, vehicular traffic, especially highway noise, is the more serious offender. However, the development of high-speed jet or turbine engine trains will increase the railroad noise problem substantially.

Generally speaking, traffic noise radiating from the freeways and expressways and from mid-town shopping and apartment districts of our large cities probably disturbs more people than any other source of outdoor noise. Although aircraft noise is much more intense, the exposure time is substantially less than that of round-the-clock, continuous highway noise.

The generation and intensity of traffic noise is dependent chiefly upon (a) the kind, number and speed of vehicles, (b) the character of the vehicle/roadbed interface, and (c) the type of environment—mid-city, suburban, rural—in which the problem exists.

Of all the types of vehicles travelling on our expressways, the trailer truck is perhaps the most notorious noise producer. At expressway speeds, a single truck may generate sound levels exceeding 90 decibels; while a long line of truck traffic may produce noise levels in excess of 100 decibels. Because expressway truck traffic generally is heavy during the night, when ambient background noise levels are low, the noise seems to be much louder than during the daytime. This is one of the major reasons why residents frequently complain about truck traffic disturbing their sleep and relaxation. Following trucks in a descending order of noise annoyance are buses, motorcycles, sport cars, and passenger automobiles.

The effective control of traffic noise involves:

(a) reduction of the noise radiated by the vehicle itself,
(b) improved design, construction and location of expressways and traffic arteries,
(c) increasing the efficiency of traffic flow by improved automated control devices, particularly in central city and suburban areas; and
(d) adoption and enforcement of antinoise ordinances.

A vehicle is a complex noise generator containing a multitude of sources. For example, the overall noise radiated by a truck might be generated by the exhaust system, the engine, the transmission, brakes, horn, tires, and loose chains, pins and cargo.

Although some effort has been made recently to reduce the noise levels within passenger automobiles, very little has been done by truck and automobile manufacturers to suppress noise radiation by the vehicle itself, aside from some improvement in muffler design and more recently tire tread design. The current trend toward producing larger and more powerful trucks, raising speed limits on our expressways and expanding the volume of truck traffic will greatly increase traffic noise, unless effective countermeasures are quickly taken.

Improved planning, design, construction and location of peripheral expressways and of main arteries in urban and suburban areas would lead to a noticeable reduction of traffic noise. Highway planners and engineers should make maximum use of natural acoustical barriers that the topography might offer such as depressions, hills, and heavily wooded areas. The routing of expressways or main traffic arteries near residential areas should be avoided where feasible.

In city traffic, the most disturbing noise is caused by the acceleration, deceleration or braking of trucks and buses at traffic lights or intersections. Any plan, system or device which permits an uninterrupted flow of traffic in such areas will invariably help alleviate the noise problem. Similar measures should be used in the design of expressway interchanges and exit or entrance ramps.

To date, highway engineers and city planners have given little consideration to the effects of traffic noise on a community. They tend to excuse the routing of highways through quiet residential areas, next to schools, churches and hospitals or across peaceful recreational parks as "the price of progress." The design and location of the highway is usually dictated by such socio-economic factors as minimum route mileage, least land acquisition cost, safety, public benefit, and toll charges or other cost-defrayment or cost-allocation schemes.

While these are valid considerations, other important economic factors should be considered; namely, the value depreciation of property along noisy expressways and the high cost of sound-proofing apartments, schools, churches, and houses located near expressways.

In summary, efforts undertaken at the national level to control traffic and rail transportation noise are insignificant in terms of the scope, magnitude and severity of the existing problem.

OTHER OUTDOOR NOISE

Although the characteristics of traffic noise have been identified, relatively little effort has been devoted to other sources of noise in the community. Studies have disclosed that the degree of annoyance from a given noise source is dependent upon the intensity of the radiated noise relative to that of the background noise, and upon the pitch, duration, intermittency or impulsive characteristics of the radiated noise.

Construction sources. Building construction and demolition, road building and repair, and installation and repair of underground utilities and services have increased at a phenomenal rate since World War II. The inconvenience these activities cause is largely unavoidable. They also have been accompanied by the production of noise emerging from pneumatic drills, generators, compressors, bulldozers, pile drivers, ditch diggers, concrete mixers, and earth-moving and demolition equipment. Some of this, of course, cannot be helped, but some improvements can be made to reduce annoyance levels.

Courses of corrective action include (1) moratoria on operation of noisy equipment during the night and in the early morning, (2) installing noise prevention devices such as mufflers and hoods on engines and compressors where possible, (3) using alternative, less noisy equipment such as vibrating pile drivers, and electro-mechanical street drills, (4) locating noisy equipment away from particularly sensitive areas such as hospitals and schools, and (5) screening of demolition and construction noise producers.

Industrial sources. The sources of occupational noise discussed elsewhere in this report are also problems with which we must contend in the surrounding community. Although noise produced by these sources is likely to have less drastic effects on the housewife or her baby than on the factory or farm worker immediately associated with them, it is nerve-wracking and can reduce the desirability of property ownership in the area.

Again there are actions that can be taken, many of them at comparatively little expense. Machinery in factories can be properly designed, mounted and enclosed, buildings can be located and designed in advance to prevent excessive noise radiation outside, and reasonable noise level criteria can be prescribed for the boundaries of plant premises. Noisy farm power equipment such as tractors and power saws also can be muffled.

Commercial and residential sources. Many of our annoying noise problems occur within the areas in which we seek peace and quiet. Symbols of affluence such as go-carts, shopping centers and canned music contribute to these problems. Metal garbage cans, lawn mowers, motor boats, portable radios, and musical instruments may protect our health, enhance the appearance of our homes, provide relaxation or educate our children, but they also may be annoying. Hoards of starlings or blackbirds—or the devices we use to prevent their congregation—as well as barking dogs also are irritating on occasion.

Abatement of these kinds of problems rests in a variety of approaches. Muffling power equipment and advancing technology can cure many of these problems. For others, greater respect for the comfort and well-being of neighbors especially during the "quiet hours" is perhaps the key to greatest progress.

Indoor noise

The problem of noise in buildings did not emerge suddenly but grew almost imperceptibly over the years with the advancing industrialization and mechanization of society.

Many of the old-fashioned dwellings of 40 or 50 years ago, by virtue of their more massive construction, larger rooms, numerous doors, hand operated appliances, and heavy sound-absorbent furnishings, were comparatively quiet places in which to live. In contrast, the modern dwelling with its lightweight construction, open plan design and multitude of noise makers provides very little protection from noise generated within or intruding from the clamorous outdoors. With few exceptions, similar contrasts can be drawn relative to modern hotels and office buildings and their counterparts of yesteryear.

Although the building industry takes pride in its achievements, the fact remains that conventional building techniques have produced some of the noisiest buildings in existence. As a consequence, there is a strong and increasing public demand for noise control action in residential housing, particularly in multifamily dwellings.

Major property management firms report that noise transmission is one of the most serious problems facing managers and owners of apartment buildings throughout the country. They readily admit that market resistance is not only increasing as a result of excessive noise transmission, but that lack of both acoustical privacy and noise control are the greatest objections to apartment living. Similar concern is expressed by owners of hotels, motels, and office buildings which lack adequate sound insulation and noise control. Now even the individual home owner is protesting about the excessive noisiness of his home.

From a technological and economic point of view, the fundamental causes of the noise problem in buildings are:

(a) *mechanization:* increasing use of noisy high-pressure heating, cooling and plumbing systems, power plants and automated domestic appliances. Progress in mechanization is outrunning advances in machinery noise control.

(b) *poor acoustical design*: open-space layout without regard to separating noisy areas from those requiring quiet or privacy.

(c) *light-frame construction:* increasing use of thin wall and floor constructions and hollow-core doors which are poor noise barriers,

(d) *poor workmanship:* careless work by builders in sealing holes, cracks and noise leaks and installing equipment.

(e) *high rise buildings*: greater concentration of families in smaller areas result in noisier indoor and outdoor environments and increasing interfamily annoyance.

(f) *higher costs of sound insulated construction*: the increased cost of constructing a sound insulated building might range from 2% to 10% of the total cost of the building, depending on geographic area, labor market and other economic factors. Builders and owners of buildings are in a highly competitive market; therefore they are reluctant to adopt new features which may result in higher building costs or jeopardize their competitive positions and profit margins.

(g) *the lack of mandatory acoustical criteria and enforcement:* until acoustical criteria are made mandatory and enforced by law, builders will continue to ignore them

Occupational noise

Noise-induced hearing loss looms as a major health hazard in American industry. Noise surveys in assorted industries have revealed that a multitude of machines generate noise levels believed potentially harmful to hearing (20, 21, 22). Audiometric studies have shown that noise-exposed factory workers usually have poorer hearing than groups with minimum occupational noise exposures, e.g. office workers (23, 24, 25). The number of United States workers experiencing noise conditions unsafe to hearing is estimated to be in excess of six million and may be as high as 16 million (26, 27). With some exceptions, verification of the prevalence of hearing loss in different occupations has been difficult owing to management's fears that such tests might precipitate an avalanche of compensation

claims. Unions have not pressured for such surveys either.

Major industries where significant noise-hearing loss hazards exist or are suspected include iron and steel making, motor vehicle production, textile manufacturing, paper making, metal products fabrication, printing and publishing, heavy construction, lumbering and wood products and mechanized farming. Specific Armed Service occupations which can be added to this group include flight line and carrier deck operations, engine test cell and weapons firing, armor operations and assorted repair and maintenance work.

Recognition of the noise-hearing loss problem has prompted research aimed at defining noise exposure criteria safeguarding hearing. Numerous proposals for safe noise exposure exist, some of which have been incorporated in the occupational health regulations of a few states (28–31). Further adoption of such criteria is frustrated by discrepancies in the noise limits proposed, and the fact that existing data permit only "tentative" noise-hazard judgments for certain types of occupational exposures, e.g., impact noise, narrow-band noise and intermittent noise (36, 38). Despite numerous efforts by professional standards and criteria committees, e.g., United States of America Standards Institute, a national hearing conservation standard governing allowable or safe exposures remains to be established.

The differences in proposed noise exposure reflect, in part, differences in protection goals (32). How much of the exposed population should be protected? How much hearing ability should a criterion be designed to protect? Bearing on these issues, the relationships between levels of noise exposure and incidence of hearing impairment in various worker groups are being formulated to identify the risks associated with different proposed noise standards for hearing conservation (33). Hearing impairment is defined in these formulations as losses which cause difficulty in everyday speech reception. All noise criteria are designed to minimize losses at sound frequencies essential to understanding speech but there is some question as to what constitutes the "critical speech frequencies" (34). Manifestations of the latter controversy also occur in compensation formulae used to appraise disability claims for industrial hearing loss (35).

Aside from hearing loss, noise may cause cardiovascular, glandular, respiratory, and neurologic changes, all of which are suggestive of a general stress reaction (2, 36–38). These physiologic changes are produced typically by intense sounds of sudden onset, but also can occur under sustained high level, or even moderately strong, noise conditions. Whether such reactions have pathologic consequences is not really known and may be unlikely in view of the body's capacity to adapt to prolonged or recurring forms of sound stimulation including those of fairly high level. However, there are growing indications, mainly in foreign scientific literature, that routine exposures to intense industrial noise may lead to chronic physiologic disturbances. A German study, for example, has shown a high incidence of abnormal heart rhythms in steel workers exposed to high noise level in their workplaces (37). Neurological examinations of Italian weavers, also exposed daily to intense noise, have shown their reflexes to be hyperactive (38). A study reported in the Russian literature shows that workers in noisy ball-bearing and steel plants have a high incidence of cardiovascular irregularities such as bradycardia (2). Subjective complaints of extreme fatigue, irritability, insomnia, impaired tactile function and sexual impotence also have been made by workers repeatedly exposed to high level industrial noise (37). All of these disturbances appear marginal in nature and may be difficult to relate causally to noise. Other factors in the work situation or in the specific group under study might have been responsible for the observed problems. In any case, corroboration of these findings is needed and a broad-scale survey of non-auditory disorders among workers in noisy industries might prove illuminating.

Noisy conditions in work areas can interfere with speech reception and impair worker performance on jobs requiring reliable voice communication (38, 39). Noise effects on performance not dependent on voice communication are uncertain. Available information suggests that workers devoting constant attention to detail (e.g., quality inspection, console monitoring) may be most prone to distraction (40). Noise may mask auditory warning signals and thereby cause accidents or generate reactions of annoyance and general fatigue. With reference to the latter, it has been stated that man must work harder under noisy conditions than in quiet to attain the same job output (40).

ECONOMIC ASPECTS

The potential cost of compensation for industrial hearing loss is alarmingly large. One estimate is $450 million which assumes that only 10% of those eligible for hearing loss compensation will file a claim and that the average award per claim is $1000 (41). In actuality, hearing loss awards average $2000. While more and more hearing loss claims are being processed each year, the total number is still relatively small. Indications are that fewer than 500 cases were settled in 1966 (42).

There are various reasons for the small number of claims. Many afflicted workers do not know that their hearing loss is compensable. Compensation laws in some states honor claims for total deafness but not partial loss of hearing, the usual result of excessive occupational noise exposure. Workman's compensation provisions in other states cover partial loss of hearing due to noise but require the claimant to be six months away from the job before settlement can take place (35). Reflecting to some extent noise-hearing loss problems in the military, the Veteran's Administration spends $65 million annually in rehabilitation programs for 90,000 war veterans with service-connected hearing disorders (43).

The cost of controlling noise hazards in industry is difficult to compute. In one company, noise control programs utilizing preplacement and periodic audiometric examinations plus personal ear protection cost about $2 per worker annually. Taking the lower estimate of six million workers exposed to unsafe noise conditions, it would require $12 million yearly to provide this population with hearing conservation measures. For several reasons, the number of workers covered by these types of programs is believed to be quite small. For example, small factories which employ over 80% of the total work force lack the medical safety staffs usually needed for successful program implementation. Further, personal ear protection programs as a means of controlling hearing damage by industrial noise have had a high mortality rate because of negative worker and management attitudes. Improving source/path noise control techniques are a more positive remedy but are also more expensive. Estimated costs for engineering noise control in one industry average $26 per decibel reduction per employee. That is, reducing the noise level by 10 decibels in a work area of 100 people would cost $10 \times 100 \times \$26$ or $26,000. Actually, the cost of engineering noise control would be decreased significantly if such provisions were made in the early planning stages of plant layout or in the design of industrial machinery. Needed modifications at this point would not be expected to exceed 5% of the total development cost.

Conclusions and Recommendations

The noise problem in our environment is increasing. The problem is broad in scope; it affects almost every facet of daily living and not only affects the health and well-being of our citizens but also has broad socio-economic implications.

Immediate and serious attention must be given to the control of this mushrooming problem, since the over-all loudness of environmental noise is doubling every ten years in pace with our social and industrial progress. If the noise problem is allowed to go unchecked, the cost of alleviating it in future years will be insurmountable.

Modern man can no longer escape from noise; he is surrounded by a multitude of noise sources in his home, office and place of work, which in turn are under the constant bombardment of noise from aircraft, traffic and scores of other outdoor sources. Indeed, the roar of the jet plane, expressway traffic and power mower follows him to the countryside and seashore and invades the solitude and privacy of these secluded vacation retreats.

The public is becoming increasingly aware of the noise problem. Evidence of this attitude is exemplified by: (a) public concern about jet aircraft noise, particularly sonic booms, (b) complaints of apartment dwellers about the lack of sound insulation, privacy and noise control in their dwellings, (c) the growing number of noise related news items and advertising appearing in newspapers, magazines, and journals throughout the country, (d) complaints from civic associations throughout the country relative to aircraft, expressway and industrial noise intrusion into residential areas, and (e) the emergence of organizations such as Citizens for a Quieter City, Inc., and the Citizens League Against the Sonic Boom. In short, the public is becoming increasingly sophisticated in its appreciation of the benefits noise control can provide. Therefore, it expects and demands more privacy and greater protection from the intrusion of noise from all sources.

Despite this public concern, the development of noise abatement measures has not received the attention it warrants by governmental and code authorities or by the scientific and engineering community. Some governmental authorities in a number of areas have managed to enact noise control ordinances. There is wide variation and poor correlation among such ordinances, which range from being overly restrictive and impractical to completely ineffectual. This is largely due to the lack of effective coordination among the various code authorities drafting noise-control legislation and the basing of such legislation on misleading, erroneous and inadequate data or information. Many of these ordinances, which frequently are weakly phrased and open to ambiguous interpretation, deal with a limited number of common noise violations but often overlook or completely ignore control of the major noise producers such as aircraft, traffic and rail transportation systems. These ordinances are difficult to enforce because of economic, social or political considerations and the problems associated with detection or proof of violation.

There is no doubt that recognition of the noise problem in America has arrived late. With the exception of aircraft noise, the United States is far behind many countries in noise prevention and control. Consequently, there is need for focusing serious attention on abatement measures. An ultimate goal should be the achievement of a desirable environment in which noise levels do not interfere with the health and well-being of man or adversely affect other values which he regards highly. The Federal Government must play a major role in achieving this objective. The problem is a public concern, and its alleviation frequently will require actions that transcend political boundaries within the nation.

Research on noise has been conducted over a long period of time. As a result our technology has reached the stage where, with few but important exceptions, we can cope with almost any indoor or outdoor noise problem provided that we are willing to go to sufficient lengths to do it.

Unfortunately, the state of our knowledge is such that these lengths frequently are impractical or uneconomic, with the possible exception of building design. Consequently, more information is needed in the application of noise abatement techniques to transportation; building methods and materials; appliance, machinery and equipment design and construction; and the substitution of quiet alternate approaches for noisy methods of accomplishing tasks. Additional information is also needed on the non-auditory effects of noise on humans and animals.

References Cited

1. Wilson, Sir Alan. Noise, Final Report. Committee on the Problem of Noise, July 1963, CMND 2056 Her Majesty's Stationery Office, London, England.
2. Shetalov, N. N., Sartausv, A. O. and Glotova, K. V. On the State of the Cardiovascular System Under Conditions of Exposure to Continuous Noise. Labor Hygiene and Occupational Diseases (in Russian) 6, 10–14, 1962.
3. Gorslikov, S. I., Gorbunov, O. N. and Antropov, S. A. Biological Effects of Ultrasound. Medicina, p. 169, Moscow 1965.
4. Gavreau, V., Condat, R. and Saul, H. Infra-Sounds: Generators, Detectors, Physical Properties, Biological Effects. C.N.R.S. 31. Chemin Joseph-Aiguier, Marseille, France.
5. Stadelman, William J. Observations With Growing Chickens on the Effects of Sounds of Varying Intensities. Poultry Science 37:776, 1958.
6. Stadelman, William J. The Effect of Sounds of Varying Intensity on Hatchability of Chick Egg. Poultry Science 37:166, 1958.
7. Jeannoutot, Don W. and Adams, John L. Progesterone vs. Treatment by High Intensity Sound as Methods of Controlling Broodiness of Broad-Breasted Bronze Turkeys. Poultry Science 40:517, 1961.
8. Anon. The Airport and Its Neighbors. Report of the President's Airport Commission, 1952.
9. Anon. Investigation and Study of Aircraft Noise Problems. House Report No. 36, 88th Congress 24, 1963.
10. Dygert, P. K. Allocating the Costs of Alleviating Subsonic Jet Aircraft Noise. ITTE, University of California, 1967.
11. Anon. Report of Proceedings. National Aircraft Noise Symposium—Jamaica, New York. II–I, 1965.
12. Anon. Alleviation of Jet Aircraft Noise Near Airports. Report of the Jet Aircraft Noise Panel. Office of Science and Technology. p. 83, 1966.
13. Anon. Proceedings of the Sonic Boom Symposium. Acoustical Society of America, 1965.
14. Anon. Sonic Boom Experiments at Edwards Air Force Base. Stanford Research Institute, 1967.
15. Anon. Report on Generation and Propagation of Sonic Boom. National Academy of Sciences, Committee on SST-Sonic Boom, Subcommittee on Research, October 1967.
16. Bonvallet, G. L. Levels and Spectra of Traffic, Industrial, and Residential Area Noise. J. Acoust. Soc. Am. 23:4, pp. 435–9, 1956.
17. Goodfriend, Lewis S. Control of Highway Noise, Sound and Vibration, Vol. 1, No. 6, June 1967.
18. Bateman, W. F. and Ackerman, E. Some Observations on Small-Town Noise. Noise Control 1:6, 1955.
19. Ostergaard, Paul B. and Donley, Ray. Background

Noise Levels in Suburban Communities. J. Acoust. Soc. Am. 36, pp. 435–9, 1964.

20. Karplus, H. B. and Bonvallet, G. L. A Noise Survey of Manufacturing Industries, American Industrial Hygiene Association Quarterly *14*, pp. 235–85, 1953.

21. Christman, R. P., Jones, H. H. and Bales, R. E. Sound Pressure Levels in the Wood Products Industry. Noise Control 2, 33–38, 1956.

22. Yaffee, C. D. and Jones, H. H. Noise and Hearing—Relationship of Industrial Noise to Hearing Acuity in a Controlled Population, U.S. Public Health Service Publication No. 850. Government Printing Office, Washington, D.C.

23. Anon. Relations of Hearing Loss to to Noise Exposure, Z24–X–2 Report, American Standards Association, New York, New York 1954.

24. Kylin, B. Temporary Threshold Shift and Auditory Trauma Following Exposure to Steady-State Noise, Acta Oto-laryngol 51, No. 6, Suppl. 152, 1960.

25. Taylor, W., Mair, A. and Burns, W. Study of Noise and Hearing in Jute Weaving, J. Acoust. Soc. Amer. *38*, pp. 113–20, 1965.

26. Glorig, A. Noise and Your Ear. Grune and Stratton Co., Inc. New York, p. 133, 1958.

27. Anon. We Don't Have to Go Deaf on the Job. Popular Mechanics pp. 123–27, Nov. 1964.

28. Kryter, K. D., Ward, W. D., Miller, J. D. and Eldredge, D. H. Hazardous Exposure to Intermittent and Steady-State Noise. J. Acoust. Soc. Amer. *39*, pp. 451–64, 1966.

29. Glorig, A. Damage Risk Criteria and Noise-Induced Hearing Loss, et. al. Arch. Otolaryngol *74*, pp. 413–23, 1961.

30. Cohen, A. Damage Risk Criteria for Noise Exposure: Aspects of Acceptability and Validity. Amer. Indust. Hyg. Assoc. J. *24*, pp. 227–38, 1963.

31. Anon. Noise Control Safety Orders, Division of Industrial Safety, State of California, 1963.

32. Eldredge, D. H. The Problems of Criteria for Noise Exposure. Working Group 22 Report, Armed Forces NRC Committee on Hearing and Bioacoustics. National Academy of Science, Washington, D. C., 1960.

33. Anon. Guidelines for Noise Exposure Control, Amer. Indust. Hygiene Assoc. Jour. *28*, pp. 418–24, Sept.–Oct. 1967.

34. Kryter, K. D., Williams, C. and Green, D. M. Auditory Acuity and the Perception of Speech, J. Acoust. Soc. Amer. *34*, pp. 1217–23, 1962.

35. Anon. Background for Loss of Hearing Claims. Amer. Mutual Insurance Alliance, Chicago, Illinois. 1964.

36. Kryter, K. D. The Effects of Noise on Man. J. Speech and Hearing Disorders. Monograph Supplement # 1, 1950.

37. Grandjean, E. Physiologische and Psychophysiologiche Wirkingen des Larms. *Menschen Umwelt*, No. 4, 1960. (in German)

38. Bell, A. Noise, an Occupational Hazard and Public Nuisance, Public Health Paper No. 30. World Health Organization. Geneva, Switzerland, 1966.

39. Carpenter, A. Effects of Noise on Performance and Productivity in "Control of Noise," National Physical Laboratories. Her Majesty's Stationery Office. London, England. pp. 297–310, 1962.

40. Broadbent, D. Effects of Noise on Behavior. Chapter 10, Handbook of Noise Control (edited by C. M. Harris) McGraw-Hill Book Co., 1957.

41. Glorig, A. The Problem of Noise in Industry. Amer. Jour. of Public Health, *51*. pp. 1339–46, 1961.

42. Anon. Work Injury Cases Settled. Dept. of Industries, Labor and Human Relations, State of Wisconsin, November 1967.

43. Maas, R. Audiometric Aspects of Industrial Hearing Conservation. Audecibel *6–7*, Sept.–Oct. 1962.

ADDITIONAL REFERENCES

Acoustical Society of America. 1966. Proceedings of the Sonic Boom Symposium. *J. Acoust. Soc. Am.* 39(5), part 2.

Alexander, Walter. 1968. Some harmful effects of noise. *Can. Med. Assoc. J.* 99(1):27–31.

American Industrial Hygiene Association, Noise Committee. 1966. *Industrial noise manual*, 2d edition. Detroit, Michigan: American Industrial Hygiene Association. 171 pp.

Anthrop, D. F. 1969. Environmental noise pollution: A new threat to sanity. *Bulletin of the Atomic Scientists*, May 1969, pp. 11–16.

Bell, Alan. 1966. *Noise: An occupational hazard and public nuisance.* Geneva: World Health Organization. 131 pp.

Beranek, L. L., ed. 1960. *Noise reduction.* New York: McGraw-Hill. 752 pp.

Beranek, L. L. 1966. Noise. *Sci. Am.* 215(6):66–74, 76.

Beranek, L. L., and L. N. Miller. 1967. Design for quiet: The anatomy of noise. *Machine Design* 39(21):174–183.

Bredin, Harold. 1968. City noise: Designers can restore quiet, at a price. *Prod. Eng.*, November 18, 1968, pp. 29–35.

Burns, William. 1968. *Noise and man.* London: John Murray. 336 pp.

Carter, L. J. 1970. SST: Commercial race of technology experiment? *Science* 169:352–355.

Cohen, A. 1968. Noise effects on health, productivity, and well-being. *Trans. N. Y. Acad. Sci.* 30(7):910–918.

Cohen, A. 1969. Effect of noise on psychological state. *Am. Soc. Safety Eng. J.* 14:11–15.

Gavreau, V. 1968. Infrasound. *Science Journal,* January, pp. 32–37.

Glorig, A., Jr. 1958. *Noise and your ear.* New York and London: Grune & Stratton. 152 pp.

Harris, C. M., ed. 1957. *Handbook of noise control.* New York: McGraw-Hill. 1 vol. Comprehensive handbook by various authors on various sources of noise and their control.

Mechlin, J. M. 1970. Its time to turn down all that noise. Pp. 131–148 in *The environment,* by the Editors of Fortune. New York: Perennial Library.

National Physical Laboratory Symposium on the Control of Noise. 1962. London: H.M.S.O. 434 pp.

Shurcliff, W. A. 1970. *SST and sonic boom handbook.* New York: Friends of the Earth and Ballantine Books.

Ward, W. D., and J. E. Fricke. 1969. Noise as a Public Health Hazard, Proceedings of the Conference on. Washington: The American Speech and Hearing Association, ASHA Reports 4. 384 pp.

Wilson, Sir Alan. 1963. *Committee on the problem of noise: Final report.* London: H.M.S.O.

Woodlief, C. B. 1969. Effect of random noise on plant growth. *Acoust. Soc. Am. J.* 46:481–482, part 2.

Young, H. A., Jr. 1969. Legal aspects of noise pollution. *Plant Eng.* 23:66–67.

FOUR MAN'S IMPACT ON THE WATERS

"One of our priceless treasures, fresh water, is changed as civilization draws near. Its quality usually becomes poorer; it is seldom improved by man. Communities locate on the water's edge to use navigation routes, irrigate land, and develop power. As a result the water courses are heated, polluted, and fertilized; the levels fluctuate, and new biological pests are introduced."

Dead alewives on a Chicago lakefront beach. Reprinted with permission from the Chicago Sun-Times.

INTRODUCTION

Water is a vital resource for all forms of life and its importance has long been recognized by man. Given a supply of water, we are primarily concerned with its quality.

Man's earliest and major concern with water quality was its suitability for drinking; it must be free of excess salt concentrations and bacterial contamination. The productivity of water—especially fishes and their supporting food chains—is of great interest. We are concerned too with the fitness of water for agricultural, municipal, and industrial uses. And increasingly we care about the esthetic qualities of water (such as odor and visible pollutants) and its suitability for recreational use.

How has man changed the earth's waters? Water supplies are not running out. Despite regional maldistribution of water, nearly all countries, with rational management, would have adequate supplies. Time is running short to stem the waste of water and the destructive uses of water. Wastage and pollution are primarily problems of economics.

Basic knowledge of the distribution of the world's estimated supply of water is useful (from Nace, 1960):

LOCATION	SURFACE AREA (THOUSANDS OF SQ MI)	VOLUME OF WATER (THOUSANDS OF CU MI)	PERCENTAGE OF TOTAL WATER
World (total area)	197,000	—	—
Land area	57,500	—	—
Surface water on the continents			
Polar icecaps and glaciers	6,900	7,300	2.24
Fresh-water lakes	330	30	.009
Saline lakes and inland seas	270	25	.008
Average in stream channels	—	.28	.0001
Total surface water	7,500	7,360	2.26
Subsurface water on the continents			
Root zone of the soil	50,000	6	0.0018
Ground water above depth of 2,640 ft	—	1,000	.306
Ground water, depth of 2,640 to 13,200 ft	—	1,000	.306
Total subsurface water	50,000	2,000	.61
World's oceans	139,500	317,000	97.1
Total water on land	—	9,360	2.87
Atmospheric moisture	—	3.1	0.001
Total, world supply of water		326,000	100

Thus, most of the world's water is oceanic brine. Of the waters on land, most is frozen in Antarctica and Greenland. Only a small portion of continental water is available for use. The discharge of rivers into the oceans is a close measure of the availability of useful liquid water.

Water, of course, circulates through the hydrological cycle, moving from place to place and frequently changing its state. Hence, it is important to consider its temporal distribution as well as its spatial distribution. The following annual budget within the hydrological cycle (from Nace, 1967) reveals the small amounts that are circulated:

	VOLUME OF WATER (THOUSANDS OF CU MI)	PERCENTAGE OF TOTAL WATER
Annual evaporation:		
From world ocean	85	0.026
From land areas	17	.005
Total	102	0.031
Annual precipitation:		
On world ocean	78	0.024
On land areas	24	.007
Total	102	0.031
Annual runoff to oceans from rivers and icecaps	9	0.003
Ground-water outflow to oceans	.4	.0001
Total	9.4	0.0031

The amount of ground water underlying land areas is vast compared with the amount running off in streams which is available for use. The hydrological cycle has operated long enough in modern climatic regimes for the large amounts of water stored underground to be in quasi-equilibrium with water in other parts of the cycle. Man should recognize that ground water is essentially a nonrenewable resource because it is the principal regulator of natural stream flow. Heavy withdrawal of ground water by man causes less water to be available from streams.

In the United States the average total water supply is 1.2 trillion gallons per day—the average daily discharge of streams. Total water use in 1960 was about 270 billion gallons per day, or 22 percent of the total supply. But *consumption* of water (i.e., water not returned after use) was only about 61 billion gallons daily, or 5 percent of the total supply. How can this be squared with claims of a water shortage and a water crisis? One answer is the pollution of water. The United States use 95 percent of its aquatic assets as a conveyor belt for sending waste products out to sea, and the pattern is similar in Europe and other highly developed areas. As R. L. Nace (1967) has said, "The problem is not whether water supplies are running out, but whether people are outrunning the supplies. Water supplies have finite limits, but the demands of people on the supplies have no known limit."

The main water problem, then, is that of maintaining good

water quality. The selections in this part deal primarily with man's impact on the quality of waters. For convenience of discussion most selections concern water quality in a given part of the hydrological cycle—urban streams (Selection 16), ground water (Selection 18), lakes (Selection 19), estuaries (Selection 21), and oceans (Selection 22). In reality, of course, these environments are all interrelated through the hydrological cycle; many of the selections wisely stress such interactions. Two selections discuss special kinds of water pollutants: heat (Selection 17) and aquatic weeds (Selection 20). The introductory selection in this part (Selection 15) discusses the complexities of intensive human use of water in a populous industrial society and technological attempts to treat water pollution. The concluding selection (Selection 23) is the only one that focuses on man's alterations of water supply and its broad consequences, rather than on changes in water quality.

FURTHER READINGS

Bradley, C. C. 1962. Human water needs and water use in America. *Science* 138:489–491.

Cain, S. A. 1969. Ecology: Its place in water management. *Water Spectrum* 1(1):10–14.

Gram, A. L., and D. L. Isenberg. 1969. Waste water treatment. *Science Journal* 5(3):77–81. Excellent general discussion of various methods of treating waste water, including biological techniques.

Hill, G. 1965. The Great and Dirty Lakes. *Saturday Review*, October 23, pp. 32–34.

Holcomb, R. W. 1970. Waste-water treatment: The tide is turning. *Science* 169:457–459.

Klein, L. 1962. *River pollution. Vol. II. Causes and effects*. London: Butterworths. 456 pp. A detailed and broad account.

Marsh, G. P. 1864. The waters. Pp. 281–381 in *Man and nature*, 1965 edition by D. Lowenthal. Cambridge, Mass.: Belknap Press of Harvard University Press.

Meinzer, O. E. 1942. *Hydrology*. New York: Dover. 712 pp.

Nace, R. L. 1960. Water management, agriculture and groundwater supplies. *U.S. Geological Survey Circular* 415. 11 pp.

Nace, R. L. 1967. Are we running out of water? *U.S. Geological Survey Circular* 536. 7 pp.

Nace, R. L. 1967. Water resources: A global problem with local roots. *Environmental Science and Technology* 1(7):550–560.

Nace, R. L. 1969. Arrogance toward the landscape: A problem in water planning. *Bulletin of the Atomic Scientists* 25(10):11–14.

National Research Council. Committee on Water. 1966. *Alternatives in water management*. Publication 1408. National Academy of Sciences. Washington, D.C. 52 pp.

Overman, Michael. 1969. *Water; Solutions to a problem of supply and demand*. Garden City, New York: Doubleday. 192 pp. An excellent popular, yet substantive, treatment of water problems and technological solutions.

Turekian, K. K. 1968. *Oceans*. Englewood Cliffs, New Jersey: Prentice-Hall. 120 pp.

U.S. Department of Agriculture. 1955. *Water*. Yearbook of Agriculture, 1955. Washington, D.C.: U.S. Government Printing Office. 751 pp.

THE LIMITED WAR ON WATER POLLUTION

GENE BYLINSKY

What are the processes of water pollution in a technological society and how can they be controlled or countered? Man is using more and more water in more and more ways. Although lakes, rivers, and oceans have considerable ability to purify themselves by biological action, the quantities of wastes discharged into water by man now frequently exceed this natural self-cleansing ability. In addition, industry and agriculture now contribute large amounts of nondegradable pollutants.

This selection explains the prevalent processes of water pollution in the United States and suggests methods of avoiding and treating water pollution.

The situation concerning domestic sewage will illustrate the magnitude of water problems in the United States. Only two-thirds of the population is served by domestic sewers; the rest of the people discharge their wastes into septic tanks or directly into the ground or water. Of the wastes carried in domestic sewers, one-tenth is discharged raw and one-quarter after only primary treatment. In addition, combined sewers (which transport both domestic sewage and storm water) frequently dump untreated sewage into rivers and lakes. The net effect of these systems is that the total sewage discharge in the United States corresponds to raw sewage from 50 million people.

"Water pollution" is a relative term. For example, chemicals in water may make it unfit for drinking but not for certain industrial uses and certainly not for street cleaning. In 1961 a conference in Geneva on water quality broadly defined water pollution: "A water is considered polluted when its composition or state is directly or indirectly modified by human activity to an extent such that it is less suitable for purposes it could have served in its natural state."

(Editor's comment)

Gene Bylinsky has been an associate editor of *Fortune* magazine since 1966. He has written articles on a variety of scientific subjects for magazines, including *New York Times Magazine, New Republic,* and *Science Digest*.

This selection is reprinted from *Fortune*, February, 1970, pp. 102–107, 193–195, 197, courtesy of Fortune Magazine, © 1970 Time, Inc.

To judge by the pronouncements from Washington, we can now start looking forward to cleaner rather than ever-dirtier rivers. The Administration has declared a "war" on pollution, and Secretary of the Interior Walter J. Hickel says, "We do not intend to lose." Adds Murray Stein, enforcement chief of the Federal Water Pollution Control Administration: "I think we are on the verge of a tremendous cleanup."

The nationwide campaign to clean up ravaged rivers and lakes does seem to be moving a bit. For the first time since the federal government got into financing construction of municipal sewage plants in 1956, Congress has come close to providing the kind of funding it had promised. There are other signs that the war is intensifying. Under the provisions of the Water Quality Act of 1965 and the Clean Water Restoration Act of 1966, federal and state officials are establishing water-quality standards and plans for their implementation, to be carried out eventually through coordinated federal-state action. Timetables for new municipal and industrial treatment facilities are being set, surveillance programs are being planned, and tougher federal enforcement authority is being formulated. Without waiting for these plans to materialize, Interior is talking tough to some municipal and industrial polluters, with the possibility of court action in the background.

Even with all this, however, the water-pollution outlook is far from reassuring. Although the nation has invested about $15 billion since 1952 in the construction of 7,500 municipal sewage-treatment plants, industrial treatment plants, sewers, and related facilities, a surprising 1,400 communities in the U.S., including good-sized cities like Memphis, and hundreds of industrial plants still dump untreated wastes into the waterways. Other cities process their sewage only superficially, and no fewer than 300,000 industrial plants discharge their used water into municipal sewage plants that are not equipped to process many of the complex new pollutants.

Since the volume of pollutants keeps expanding while water supply stays basically the same, more and more intervention will be required just to keep things from getting worse. Within the next fifty years, according to some forecasts, the country's population will double, and the demand for water by cities, industries, and agriculture has tended to grow even faster than the population. These water uses now add up to something like 350 billion gallons a day (BGD), but by 1980, by some estimates, they will amount to 600 BGD. By the year 2000, demand for water is expected to reach 1,000 BGD, considerably exceeding the essentially unchanging supply of dependable fresh water, which is estimated at 650 BGD. More and more, water will have to be reused, and it will cost more and more to retrieve clean water from progressively dirtier waterways.

Just how bad water pollution can get was dramatically illustrated in the summer of 1969 when the oily, chocolate-brown Cuyahoga River in Cleveland burst into flames, nearly destroying two railroad bridges. The Cuyahoga is so laden with industrial and municipal wastes that not even the leeches and sludge worms that thrive in many badly polluted rivers are to be found in its lower reaches. Many other U.S. rivers are becoming more and more like that flammable sewer.

Even without human activity to pollute it, a stream is never absolutely pure, because natural pollution is at work in the form of soil erosion, deposition of leaves and animal wastes, solution of minerals, and so forth. Over a long stretch of time, a lake can die a natural death because of such pollution. The natural process of eutrophication, or enrichment with nutrients, encourages the growth of algae and other plants, slowly turning a lake into a bog. Man's activities enormously speed up the process.

But both lakes and rivers have an impressive ability to purify themselves. Sunlight bleaches out some pollutants. Others settle to the bottom and stay there. Still others are consumed by beneficial bacteria. These bacteria need oxygen, which is therefore vital to self-purification. The oxygen that sustains bacteria as well as fish and other organisms is replenished by natural aeration from the atmosphere and from life processes of aquatic plants.

Trouble starts when demand for dissolved oxygen exceeds the available supply. Large quantities of organic pollutants such as sewage alter the balance. Bacteria feeding upon the pollutants multiply and consume the oxygen. Organic debris accumulates. Anaerobic areas develop, where microorganisms that can live and grow without free oxygen decompose the settled solids. This putrefaction produces foul odors. Species of fish sensitive to oxygen deficiency can no longer survive. Chemical, physical, and biological characteristics of a stream are altered, and its water becomes unusable for many purposes without extensive treatment.

Pollution today is very complex in its composition, and getting more so all the time. In polluted streams and lakes hundreds of different contaminants can be found: bacteria and viruses; pesticides and weed killers; phosphorus from fertilizers, detergents, and municipal sewage; trace amounts of metals; acid from mine drainage; organic and inorganic chemicals, many of which are so new that we do not know their long-term effects on human health; and even traces of drugs. (Steroid drugs such as the Pill, however, are neutralized by bacteria.)

A distinction is often made between industrial and municipal wastes, but it is difficult to sort them out because many industrial plants discharge their wastes into municipal sewer systems. As a result, what is referred to as municipal waste is also to a large extent industrial waste. By one estimate, as much as 40 percent of all waste water treated by municipal sewage plants comes from industry. Industry's contribution to water pollution is sometimes measured in terms of "population equivalent." Pollution from organic industrial wastes analogous to sewage is now said by some specialists to be about equivalent to a population of 210 million.

The quality of waste water is often measured in terms of its biochemical oxygen demand (BOD), or the amount of dissolved oxygen that is needed by bacteria in decomposing the wastes. Waste water with much higher BOD content than sewage is produced by such operations as leather tanning, beet-sugar refining, and meatpacking. But industry also contributes a vast amount of non-degradable, long-lasting pollutants, such as inorganic and synthetic organic chemicals that impair the quality of water. All together, manufacturing activities, transportation, and agriculture probably account for about two-thirds of all water degradation.

Industry also produces an increasingly important pollutant of an entirely different kind—heat. Power generation and some manufacturing processes use great quantities of water for cooling, and it goes back into streams warmer than it came out. Power plants disgorging great masses of hot water can raise the stream temperature by ten or twenty degrees in the immediate vicinity of the plant. Warmer water absorbs less oxygen and this slows down decomposition of organic matter. Fish, being cold-blooded, cannot regulate their body temperatures, and the additional heat upsets their life cycles; for example, fish eggs may hatch too soon. Some scientists have estimated that by 1980 the U.S. will be producing enough waste water and heat to consume, in dry weather, all the oxygen in all twenty-two river basins in the U.S.

How clean do we want our waterways to be? In answering that question we have to recognize that many of our rivers and lakes serve two conflicting purposes—they are used both as sewers and as sources of drinking water for about 100 million Americans. That's why the new water-quality standards for interstate streams now being set in various states generally rely on criteria established by the Public Health Service for sources of public water supplies. In all, the PHS lists no fewer than fifty-one contaminants or characteristics of water supplies that should be controlled. Many other substances in the drinking water are not on the list, because they haven't yet been measured or even identified. "The poor water-treatment plant operator really doesn't know what's in the stream—what he is treating," says James H. McDermott, director of the Bureau of Water Hygiene in the PHS. With more than 500 new or modified chemicals coming on the market every year, it isn't easy for the understaffed PHS bureaus to keep track of new pollutants. Identification and detailed analysis of pollutants is just beginning as a systematic task. Only recently has the PHS established its first official committee to evaluate the effects of insecticides on health.

Many water-treatment plants are hopelessly outmoded. They were designed for a simpler, less crowded world. About three-fourths of them do not go beyond disinfecting water with chlorine. That kills bacteria but does practically nothing to remove pesticides, herbicides, or other organic and inorganic chemicals from the water we drink.

A survey by the PHS shows that most waterworks operators lack formal training in treatment processes, disinfection, microbiology, and chemistry. The men are often badly paid. Some of them, in smaller communities, have other full-time jobs and moonlight as water-supply operators. The survey, encompassing eight metropolitan areas from New York City to Riverside, California, plus the State of Vermont, has revealed that in seven areas about 9 percent of the water samples indicated bacterial contamination. Pesticides were found in small concentrations in many samples. In some, trace metals exceeded PHS limits. The level of nitrates, which can be fatal to babies, was too high in some samples. Earlier the PHS found that nearly sixty communities around the country, including some large cities, could be given only "provisional approval" for the quality of their water-supply systems. Charles C. Johnson Jr., administrator of the Consumer Protection and Environmental Health Service in the PHS, concluded that the U.S. is "rapidly approaching a crisis stage with regard to drinking water" and is courting "serious health hazards."

Clearly, there will have to be enormous improvement in either the treatment of water we drink or the treatment of water we discard (if not both). The second approach would

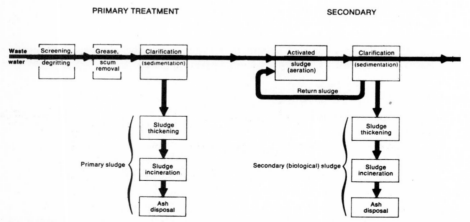

FIGURE 15.1 **How to take out of water some of what people put in.** Advanced techniques that remove more subtle pollutants are in use in only a few places in the U.S., and most such plants are still experimental. The operation of one advanced facility, a 7,500,000-gallon-a-day plant at Lake Tahoe in California, is schematically shown above. The waste water passes through three stages, the first two of which generally correspond to the forms of treatment commonly used in the U.S. Metal screens stop large objects such as sticks and rags from entering the plant. The sewage then passes into a grit chamber where sand and small stones settle to the bottom. Next stop is the sedimentation tank, where speed of flow is reduced and suspended particles sink to the bottom, forming sludge. By itself, this primary treatment removes only about 30 percent of oxygen-consuming organic matter in sewage. In secondary

have the great advantage of making our waterways better for swimming and fishing and more aesthetically enjoyable. And it is more rational anyway not to put poisons in the water in the first place. The most sensible way to keep our drinking water safe is to have industry, agriculture, and municipalities stop polluting water with known and potentially hazardous substances. Some of this could be accomplished by changing manufacturing processes and recycling waste water inside plants. The wastes can sometimes be retrieved at a profit.

A great deal of industrial and municipal waste water now undergoes some form of treatment (Figure 15.1). So-called primary treatment is merely mechanical. Large floating objects such as sticks are removed by a screen. The sewage then passes through settling chambers where filth settles to become raw sludge. Primary treatment removes about one-third of gross pollutants. About 30 percent of Americans served by sewers live in communities that provide only this much treatment.

Another 62 percent live in communities that carry treatment a step beyond, subjecting the effluent from primary processing to secondary processing. In this age of exact science, secondary treatment looks very old-fashioned. The effluent flows, or is pumped, onto a "trickling filter," a bed of rocks three to ten feet deep. Bacteria normally occurring in sewage cover the rocks, multiply, and consume most of the organic matter in the waste water. A somewhat more modern version is the activated sludge process, in which sewage from primary settling tanks is pumped to an aeration tank. Here, in a speeded-up imitation of what a stream does naturally, the sewage is mixed with air and sludge saturated with bacteria. It is allowed to remain for a few hours while decomposition takes place. Properly executed secondary treatment will reduce degradable organic waste by 90 percent. Afterward, chlorine is sometimes added to the water to kill up to 99 percent of disease germs.

Secondary treatment in 90 percent of U.S. municipalities within the next five years and

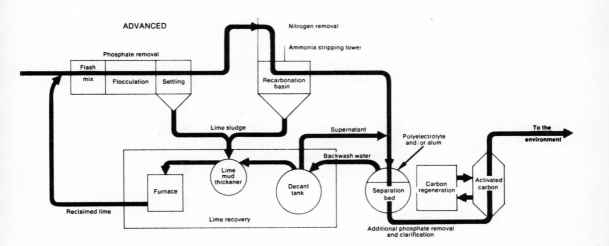

treatment, most of the remaining organic matter is consumed by bacteria. Aeration speeds up, or "activates," the process. Advanced treatment at Lake Tahoe removes both phosphate and nitrogen, undesirable nutrients that cause proliferation of algae. Phosphate is removed with the help of lime ("flash mix" refers to the rapidity of mixing). Nitrogen, which occurs in sewage mostly as ammonia, is more difficult to eliminate. At Tahoe, the effluent is passed through a stripping tower where ammonia is extracted in a process that involves blowing large amounts of air through the sewage. The effluent then undergoes additional cleansing in passing through separation beds (where chemicals remove more phosphate) and finally through activated carbon. The result is water that's almost good enough to drink.

its equivalent in most industrial plants is a principal objective of the current war on pollution. The cost will be high: an estimated $10 billion in public funds for municipal treatment plants and sewers and about $3.3 billion of industry's own funds for facilities to treat wastes at industrial plants.

But today that kind of treatment isn't good enough. Widespread use of secondary treatment will cut the amount of gross sewage in the waterways, but will do little to reduce the subtler, more complex pollutants. The effluents will still contain dissolved organic and inorganic contaminants. Among the substances that pass largely unaffected through bacterial treatment are salts, certain dyes, acids, persistent insecticides and herbicides, and many other harmful pollutants.

Technical "tunnel vision," or lack of thinking about all the possible consequences of a process, has often been the curse of twentieth-century science and technology. Today's sewage plants generally do not remove phosphorus and nitrogen from waste water, but turn the organic forms of these nutrients into mineral forms that are *more* usable by algae and other plants. As one scientist has noted, overgrowths of algae and other aquatic plants then rot to "recreate the same problem of oxygen-consuming organic matter that the sewage plant was designed to control in the first place." The multibillion-dollar program to treat waste water in the same old way, he says, is "sheer insanity."

Yet the U.S. has little choice. Most of the advanced treatment techniques are either still experimental or too costly to be introduced widely. To wait for those promising new methods while doing nothing in the meantime could result in a major pollution calamity.

The pollutants that secondary treatment fails to cope with will increase in volume as industry and population grow. Phosphates, for instance, come in large amounts from detergents and fertilizers, and from human wastes. Phosphorus has emerged as a major pollutant only in recent years. Nitrogen, the other key nutrient for algal growth, is very difficult to control because certain blue-green algae can fix nitrogen directly from the air. Since phosphorus is more controllable, its removal from effluents is critically important to limiting the growth of algae.

A few years ago, when it looked as if America's streams and lakes were to become highways of white detergent foam, the manufacturers converted the detergent base from alkyl benzene sulphonate to a much more biologically degradable substance, linear alkylate sulphonate. That effectively reduced the amount of foam but did almost nothing to reduce the amount of phosphates in detergents. The mountains of foam have shrunk, but green mats of algae keep on growing. The developers of detergents failed to consider the possible side effects; such lack of systematic thinking and foresight is precisely what has led to today's environmental abuses. It might be possible to substitute nonphosphorus bases in detergent manufacture—and work is in progress along those lines.

There is little prospect of substituting something else for the phosphate in fertilizer. It's hard to visualize a fertilizer that is a nutrient when applied to land and not a nutrient when it enters the water. One way to reduce water pollution from farmlands would be to reduce the amounts of chemical fertilizers farmers apply to their fields—it is the excess fertilizer, not absorbed by plants, that washes into streams or percolates into groundwater. Through some complex of social and economic arrangements, farmers might be persuaded to use less fertilizer and more humus. By improving the texture of soils, as well as providing slowly released nutrients, humus can reduce the need for commercial fertilizer to keep up crop yields. The U.S. produces enormous quantities of organic wastes that could be converted to humus. Such a remedy for fertilizer pollution, of course, might seem highly undesirable to the fertilizer industry, already burdened with excess capacity.

Even if phosphorus pollution from fertilizers and detergents were entirely eliminated—an unlikely prospect—phosphates from domestic and industrial wastes would still impose a heavy load upon rivers and lakes. As population and industry grow, higher and higher percentages of the phosphorus will have to be removed from effluents to keep the algae problem from getting worse. The conventional technology being pushed by the federal water-pollution war cannot cope with phosphorus, or with many other pollutants. But there are advanced technologies that can. Advanced water treatment, sometimes called "tertiary," is generally aimed at removal of all, or almost all, of the contaminants.

One promising idea under investigation is to dispense with the not always reliable bacteria that consume sewage in secondary treatment. Toxic industrial wastes have on occasion thrown municipal treatment plants out of kilter for weeks by killing the bacteria. "We've found that we can accomplish the same kind of treatment with a purely physical-chemical process," says a scientist at the Robert A. Taft Water Research Center in Cincinnati.

In this new approach, the raw sewage is clarified with chemicals to remove most suspended organic material, including much of the phosphate. Then comes carbon adsorption. The effluent passes through filter beds of granular activated carbon, similar to that used in charcoal filters for cigarettes. Between clarification and adsorption, 90 percent or more of the phosphate is removed. The carbon can be regenerated in furnaces and reused. Captured organic matter is burned. Carbon adsorption has the great additional advantage of removing from the water organic industrial chemicals that pass unhindered through biological secondary treatment. The chemicals adhere to the carbon as they swirl through its complex structure with millions of pathways and byways.

Other treatment techniques are under study that make water even cleaner, and might possibly be used to turn sewage into potable water. One of these is reverse osmosis, originally developed for demineralization of brackish water. When liquids with different concentrations of, say, mineral salts are separated by a semipermeable membrane, water molecules pass by osmosis, a natural equalizing tendency, from the less concentrated to the more concentrated side to create an equilibrium. In reverse osmosis, strong pressure is exerted on the side with the greater concentration. The pressure reverses the natural flow, forcing molecules of pure water through the membrane, out of the high-salt or high-particle concentration. Reverse osmosis removes ammonia nitrogen, as well as phosphates, most nitrate, and other substances dissolved in water. Unfortunately, the process is not yet applicable to sewage treatment on a large scale because the membranes become fouled with sewage solids. Engineers are hard at work trying to design better membranes.

New techniques are gradually transforming sewage treatment, technically backward and sometimes poorly controlled, into something akin to a modern chemical process. "We are talking about a wedding of sanitary and chemical engineering," says David G. Stephan, who directs research and development at the Federal Water Pollution Control Administration, "using the techniques of the chemical process industry to turn out a product—reusable water—rather than an effluent to throw away." Adds James McDermott of the Public Health Service: "We're going to get to the point where, on the one hand, it's going to cost us an awful lot of money to treat wastes and dump them into the stream. And an awful lot of money to take those wastes when they are going down the stream and make drinking water out of them. We are eventually going to create treatment plants where we take sewage and, instead of dumping it back into the stream, treat it with a view of recycling it immediately—direct reuse. That is the only way we're going to satisfy our water needs, and second, it's going to be cheaper."

Windhoek, the capital of arid South-West Africa, has gained the distinction of becoming the first city in the world to recycle its waste water directly into drinking water. Waste water is taken out of sewers, processed conventionally, oxidized in ponds for about a month, then run through filters and activated-carbon columns, chlorinated, and put back into the water mains. Windhoek's distinction may prove to be dubious, because the full effects of recycled water on health are unknown. There is a potential hazard of viruses (hepatitis, polio, etc.) being concentrated in recycling. For this reason, many health experts feel that renovated sewage should not be accepted as drinking water in the U.S. until its safety can be more reliably demonstrated.

Costs naturally go up as treatment gets more complex. While primary-secondary treatment costs about 12 cents a thousand gallons of waste water, the advanced techniques in use at Lake Tahoe, for instance, bring the cost up to 30 cents. About 7½ cents of the increase is for phosphorus removal. Reverse osmosis at this stage would raise the cost to at least 35 cents a thousand gallons, higher than the average cost of drinking water to metered households in the U.S. Whatever new techniques are accepted, rising costs of pollution control will be a fact of life.

Ironically, these new treatment techniques, such as removal of phosphorus with chemicals, will intensify one of the most pressing operational problems in waste-water treatment—sludge disposal. Sludge, the solid matter removed from domestic or industrial waste water, is a nuisance, highly contaminated unless it's disinfected. The handling and disposal of sludge can eat up to one-half of a treatment plant's operating budget. Some communities incinerate their sludge, contributing to air pollution. "Now in cleaning the water further we are adding chemicals to take out phosphorus and more solids," says Francis M. Middleton, director of the Taft Center. "While we end up with cleaner water, we also end up with even greater quantities of sludge."

Chicago's struggle with its sludge illustrates some of the difficulties and perhaps an effective way of coping with them. With 1,000 tons of sludge a day to dispose of, the metropolitan sanitary district has been stuffing about half of it into deep holes near treatment plants, at a cost of about $60 a ton. The other half is dried and shipped to Florida

and elsewhere where it is sold for $12 a ton to citrus growers and companies producing fertilizers—a nonprofit operation. Vinton W. Bacon, general superintendent of the sanitary district, says this state of affairs can't continue. "We're running out of land. Not only that, but the land we're using for disposal is valuable. And even it will be filled within two years."

Bacon is convinced he has an answer that will not only cut costs but also solve disposal problems indefinitely while helping to make marginal lands bloom. Bacon's scheme, tested in pilot projects in Chicago and elsewhere, is to pump liquid sludge through a pipeline to strip mines and marginal farmland about sixty miles southwest of Chicago. "We put the sludge water through tanks where it's digested," Bacon says. "Then it can be used directly without any odor or health dangers. It's the perfect marriage. That land needs our sludge as much as we need the land. Most astounding, even acquiring the required land at current market prices, taking in the cost of a twenty-four-inch, sixty-mile-long pipeline, the pumps, reservoirs, irrigation equipment, and manpower, the cost would still come to only $20 a ton. We could build a pipeline 200 miles long and still not run higher costs than with our present system."

An aspect of water pollution that seems harder to cope with is the overflow of combined sewers during storms. A combined system that unites storm and sanitary sewers into a single network usually has interceptor sewers, with direct outlets to a stream, to protect the treatment plant from flooding during heavy rains. But in diverting excess water from treatment plants, interceptor sewers dump raw sewage into the waterways. Obviously, this partly defeats the purpose of having treatment plants.

So bad are the consequences of sewer overflow that some specialists would prefer to see part of the federal money being channeled into secondary treatment go into correction of the combined-sewer problem instead. But more than 1,300 U.S. communities have combined sewers, and the cost of separating the systems would be huge. The American Public Works Association estimated the cost of total separation at $48 *billion*. The job could be done in an alternative fashion for a still shocking $15 billion, by building holding tanks for the overflow storm water. Still another possibility would be to build separate systems for sewage and to use existing sewers for storm water. The federal war on water pollution discourages construction of combined sewers but strangely includes no money (except for $28 million already awarded for research and development) to remedy the problem of existing combined-sewer systems.

The General Accounting Office recently surveyed federal activities in water-pollution control and found some glaring deficiencies. The G.A.O. prepared its report for Congress and therefore failed to point out that in some of the deficiencies the real culprit was Congress itself. Still largely rural-oriented, Congress originally limited federal grants for construction of waste-treatment facilities to $250,000 per municipality. The dollar ceiling was eventually raised, but was not removed until fiscal 1968. In the preceding twelve years about half of the waste-treatment facilities were built in hamlets with populations of less than 2,500, and 92 percent in towns with populations under 50,000.

In drafting the legislation that provides for new water-quality standards, Congress again showed limited vision, leaving it up to the states to decide many important questions. Each state is free to make its own decisions on pollution-control goals in terms of determining the uses to which a particular stream or lake will be put. Each state is to decide on the stream characteristics that would allow such uses—dissolved oxygen, temperature, etc. Finally, each state is to set up a schedule for corrective measures that would ensure the stream quality decided upon, and prepare plans for legal enforcement of the standards.

It would have been logical to set standards for entire river basins since rivers don't always stay within state boundaries. What's more, there were already several regional river-basin compacts in existence that could

have taken on the job. But with the single exception of the Delaware River Basin Commission, of which the federal government is a member, the government bypassed the regional bodies and insisted that each state set its own standards. Predictably, the result has been confusion. The states submitted standards by June 30, 1967, but by the end of 1969 Interior had given full approval to only twenty-five states and territories. It has now become the prickly task of the Secretary of the Interior to reconcile the conflicting sets of standards that states have established for portions of the same rivers.

Some states facing each other across a river have set different standards for water characteristics, as if dividing the river flow in the middle with a bureaucratic fence. Kentucky and Indiana, across the Ohio from each other, submitted two different temperature standards for that river: Kentucky came up with a maximum of 93° Fahrenheit, while Indiana wants 90°. Similarly, Ohio sets its limit at 93°, while West Virginia, across the same river, chose 86°. One reason for such differences about river temperature is that biologists don't always agree among themselves about safe temperatures for aquatic life. At one recent meeting in Cincinnati, where federal and state officials were attempting to reconcile the different figures for the Ohio, the disagreement among biologists was so great that one exasperated engineer suggested, "Maybe we should start putting ice cubes at different points in the river."

The biggest deficiency in the federal approach is its lack of imagination. Congress chose the subsidy route as being the easiest, but the task could have been undertaken much more thoughtfully. A regional or river-valley approach would have required more careful working out than a program of state-by-state standards and subsidies, but it would have made more sense economically, and would have assured continuing management of water quality.

A promising river-valley program is evolving along the Great Miami River in Ohio. The Great Miami runs through a heavily industrialized valley. There are, for instance, eighteen paper mills in the valley. Dayton, the principal city on the river, houses four divisions of General Motors and is the home of National Cash Register. To finance a three-year exploratory program for river management, the Miami Conservancy District, a regional flood-control agency, has imposed temporary charges, based on volume of effluent, on sixty plants, businesses, and municipalities along the river. These charges amount to a total of $350,000 a year, ranging from $500 that might be paid by a motel to $23,000 being paid by a single power-generating station.

With this money, plus a $500,000 grant from the Federal Water Pollution Control Administration, the district has been looking into river-wide measures that will be needed to control pollution even *after* every municipality along the river has a secondary treatment plant. (Dayton already has one.) The district's staff of sanitary engineers, ecologists, and systems analysts has come up with suggested measures to augment the low flood of the river as an additional method of pollution control. The Great Miami's mean annual flow at Dayton is 2,500 cubic feet a second, but every ten years or so it falls to a mere 170 cubic feet a second. To assure a more even flow, the Miami District will build either reservoirs or facilities to pump

groundwater, at a cost of several million dollars. The cost will be shared by river users. District engineers are also exploring in-stream aeration, or artificial injection of air into the river, to provide additional dissolved oxygen. The state has set an ambitious goal for the Great Miami—to make the river usable "for all purposes, at all places, all the time."

To meet this goal, the district will introduce waste-discharge fees, which will probably be based on the amount of oxygen-demanding wastes or hot water discharged. Will these amount to a charge for polluting the river? "No," says Max L. Mitchell, the district's chief engineer. "Charges will be high enough to make industry reduce water use."

Federal money would do a lot more good if it were divided up along river-basin lines instead of municipality by municipality or state by state, with little regard for differences in pollution at different points in a basin. To distribute federal funds more effectively, Congress would have to overcome its parochial orientation. Also, Congress should be channeling more funds into new waste-treatment technologies and ways of putting them to use. Unless pollution abatement is undertaken in an imaginative and systematic manner, the "war" against dirty rivers may be a long, losing campaign.

THE HYDROLOGIC EFFECTS OF URBAN LAND USE

LUNA B. LEOPOLD

Cities cause local but severe changes in the hydrologic cycle. The pavement and roofs of urbanization greatly increase the percentage of the land's surface which is impervious to water. Rather than infiltrate into the ground, a high proportion of precipitation runs off into streams, causing greater flooding than in the country. Urban land use promotes erosion and produces large quantities of sediment.

Urbanization also decreases the quality of water in two ways. First, waste materials, including dissolved solids, pathogenic bacteria, and heat are added to the water. Second, the high flood peaks and low rate of infiltration lower the recharge of ground water, and this decreases the amount of water normally flowing in streams. Hence, there is less water available for such uses as municipal supply and safely diluting discharges of sewage.

Finally, urbanization commonly causes streams to lose their attractiveness. Increased floods cause scoured or muddy stream channels. Trash in the channels adds to the disfigurement. Reduced oxygen content and reduced water flow alter aquatic life and contribute to turbid, slimy, smelly streams.

In this selection Luna Leopold explains and elaborates on these changes. It is interesting to note that despite the considerable amount of research done on urban hydrology, there are many gaps in our understanding. Leopold is one of the few modern scientists to evaluate and quantify the esthetics of landscape (Leopold, 1969). Streams flowing through cities, especially, could enhance the quality of urban life if they were properly understood and managed, although the variety and complexity of urban effects on hydrology appear to work against this.

(Editor's comment)

Luna B. Leopold (b. 1915) is a senior research hydrologist with the U.S. Geological Survey in Washington. He has worked for the Geological Survey since 1950 and formerly was Chief Hydrologist of the Water Resources Division. Educated at Wisconsin, U.C.L.A., and Harvard (Ph.D. in geology, 1950), his research has included studies in climatology, geomorphology, soils, hydrology, and, more recently, the esthetics of landscape.

This selection is extracted, with the permission of the author, from "Hydrology for Urban Land Planning—A Guidebook on the Hydrologic Effects of Urban Land Use." *U.S. Geological Survey Circular* 554, 18 pp., 1968.

This circular attempts to summarize existing knowledge of the effects of urbanization on hydrologic factors. It also attempts to express this knowledge in terms that the planner can use to test alternatives during the planning process.

Planning Procedures and Hydrologic Variables

Of particular concern to the planner are those alternatives that affect the hydrologic functioning of the basins. To be interpreted hydrologically, the details of the land-use pattern must be expressed in terms of hydrologic parameters which are affected by land use. These parameters in turn become hydrologic variables by which the effects of alternative planning patterns can be evaluated in hydrologic terms.

There are four interrelated but separable effects of land-use changes on the hydrology of an area: changes in peak flow characteristics, changes in total runoff, changes in quality of water, and changes in the hydrologic amenities. The hydrologic amenities are what might be called the appearance or the impression which the river, its channel and its valleys, leaves with the observer. Of all land-use changes affecting the hydrology of an area, urbanization is by far the most forceful.

FLOW REGIMEN

Runoff, which spans the entire regimen of flow, can be measured by number and by characteristics of rise in streamflow. The many rises in flow, along with concomitant sediment loads, control the stability of the stream channel. The two principal factors governing flow regimen are the percentage of area made impervious and the rate at which water is transmitted across the land to stream channels. The former is governed by the type of land use; the latter is governed by the density, size, and characteristics of tributary channels and thus by the provision of storm sewerage. Stream channels form in response to the regimen of flow of the stream. Changes in the regimen of flow, whether through land use or other changes, cause adjustments in the stream channels to accommodate the flows.

The volume of runoff is governed primarily by infiltration characteristics and is related to land slope and soil type as well as to the type of vegetative cover. It is thus directly related to the percentage of the area covered by roofs, streets, and other impervious surfaces at times of hydrograph rise during storms.

A summary of some data on the percentage of land rendered impervious by different degrees of urbanization is presented by Lull and Sopper (1966). Antoine (1964) presents the following data on the percentage of impervious surface area in residential properties:

LOT SIZE OF RESIDENTIAL AREA (SQ FT)	IMPERVIOUS SURFACE AREA (PERCENT)
6,000	80
6,000–15,000	40
15,000	25

The percentage decreases markedly as size of lot increases. Felton and Lull (1963) estimate in the Philadelphia area that 32 percent of the surface area is impervious on lots averaging 0.2 acre in size, whereas only 8 percent of the surface area is impervious on lots averaging 1.8 acres.

As volume of runoff from a storm increases, the size of flood peak also increases. Runoff volume also affects low flows because in any series of storms the larger the percentage of direct runoff, the smaller the amount of water available for soil moisture replenishment and for ground-water storage. An increase in total runoff from a given series of storms as a result of imperviousness results in decreased ground-water recharge and decreased low flows. Thus, increased imperviousness has the effect of increasing flood peaks during storm periods and decreasing low flows between storms.

WATER QUALITY

The principal effect of land use on sediment comes from the exposure of the soil to storm runoff. This occurs mainly when bare ground is exposed during construction. It is well known that sediment production is sensitive to land slope. Sediment yield from urban areas tends to be larger than in unurbanized areas even if there are only small and widely scattered units of unprotected soil in the urban area. In aggregate, these scattered bare areas are sufficient to yield considerable sediment.

A major effect of urbanization is the introduction of effluent from sewage disposal plants, and often the introduction of raw sewage, into channels. Raw sewage obviously degrades water quality, but even treated effluent contains dissolved minerals not extracted by sewage treatment. These minerals act as nutrients and promote algae and plankton growth in a stream. This growth in turn alters the balance in the stream biota.

Land use in all forms affects water quality. Agricultural use results in an increase of nutrients in stream water both from the excretion products of farm animals and from commercial fertilizers. A change from agricultural use to residential use, as in urbanization, tends to reduce these types of nutrients, but this tendency is counteracted by the widely scattered pollutants of the city, such as oil and gasoline products, which are carried through the storm sewers to the streams. The net result is generally an adverse effect on water quality. This effect can be measured by the balance and variety of organic life in the stream, by the quantities of dissolved material, and by the bacterial level. Unfortunately data describing quality factors in streams from urban versus unurbanized areas are particularly lacking.

HYDROLOGIC AMENITIES

Finally, the amenity value of the hydrologic environment is especially affected by three factors. The first factor is the stability of the stream channel itself. A channel, which is gradually enlarged owing to increased floods caused by urbanization, tends to have unstable and unvegetated banks, scoured or muddy channel beds, and unusual debris accumulations. These all tend to decrease the amenity value of a stream.

The second factor is the accumulation of artifacts of civilization in the channel and on the flood plain: beer cans, oil drums, bits of lumber, concrete, wire—the whole gamut of rubbish of an urban area. Though this may not importantly affect the hydrologic function of the channel, it becomes a detriment of what is here called the hydrologic amenity.

The third factor is the change brought on by the disruption of balance in the stream biota. The addition of nutrients promotes the growth of plankton and algae. A clear stream, then, may change to one in which rocks are covered with slime; turbidity usually increases, and odors may develop. As a result of increased turbidity and reduced oxygen content desirable game fish give way to less desirable species. Although lack of quantitative objective data on the balance of stream biota is often a handicap to any meaningful and complete evaluation of the effects of urbanization, qualitative observations tend to confirm these conclusions.

Availability of Data and the Technique of Analysis

Basic hydrologic data on both peak flow and volume of runoff may be expressed in terms of the characteristics of the unit hydrograph, that is, the average time distribution graph of flow from a unit or standard storm. The unit hydrograph shows the percentage of the total storm runoff occurring in each successive unit of time. The standard storm may be, for example, a typical storm which produced 1 inch of runoff (Figure 16.1). Such data are derived from the study of individual storms and the associated runoff graphs measured at gaging stations.

One factor stating the relation between the

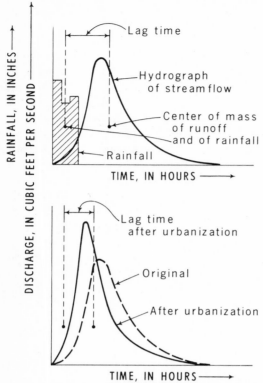

FIGURE 16.1 Hypothetical unit hydrographs relating runoff to rainfall, with definitions of significant parameters.

storm and the runoff is lag time. This is defined as the time interval between the center of mass of the storm precipitation and the center of mass of the resultant hydrograph. Lag time is a function of two basin parameters—the mean basin slope and the basin length. These factors empirically correlate with lag time if expressed in the form of the basin ratio (basin length L divided by the square root of the mean basin gradient, s). This basin ratio is also related to drainage area. As drainage area increases, the basin length increases and the average value of slope generally decreases. Thus, natural basin characteristics can be translated into flood-flow characteristics.

Lag time may be materially altered by the effects of urbanization on the basin surface. Water runs off faster from streets and roofs than from natural vegetated areas. This tends to decrease the lag time. The con-

struction of artificial channels, especially storm sewers, also decreases lag time. As the time required for a given amount of water to run off shortens, the peak rate of runoff (flood peak) increases.

In addition to the basin ratio and lag time, the regimen of a stream, however, can be described in many other ways, including flood frequency, flow duration, mean annual flood, discharge at bankfull stage, and frequency of bankfull stage. This is evidenced in past studies of the effects of urbanization on the hydrology of an area. Many different techniques of relating rainfall to runoff have been used, along with various parameters to measure the degree of urbanization. In order to evaluate our present knowledge, it is necessary to express the results of these studies in some common denominator.

Effect of Urbanization on Increasing Peak Discharge

In a slight modification of a method previously used by several investigators, especially D. G. Anderson (1968) and L. D. James (1965), the percentage of an area sewered is plotted against the percentage of the area rendered impervious by urbanization; isopleth lines (lines of equal value of the ratio) on the graph show the ratio of peak discharge under urbanized conditions to the peak discharge under rural or unurbanized conditions. Such a graph will be different for different drainage area sizes and for different flow frequencies.

Table 16.1 is an interpretation and summary of the effects of urbanization on peak discharges based on previous studies. Results of the studies were interpreted and extrapolated to a common denominator of 1 sq mi (square mile), a practical unit of size for planning. Although the interpretations were necessary to express the degree of urbanization in quantitative terms, there is considerable agreement among the data.

As an indication of the change in impervious area resulting from urbanization, Harris and Rantz (1964) showed that an area near Palo

TABLE 16.1 Increase in discharge as a result of urbanization in a 1-square-mile area

[Discharge is mean annual flood; recurrence interval is 2.3 years. Data are expressed as ratio of discharge after urbanization to discharge under previous conditions. Data from James (1965) have no superscript]

PERCENTAGE OF AREA SERVED BY STORM SEWERAGE	PERCENTAGE OF AREA MADE IMPERVIOUS			
	0	20	50	80
0	1.0	[1]1.2	[1]1.8	[1]2.2
		[2]1.3	[2]1.7	[2]2.2
		1.3	1.6	2.0
20	1.1	[3]1.9	1.8	2.2
		1.4	—	—
50	1.3	[4]2.1	[1]3.2	[1]4.7
		[1]2.8	2.0	2.5
		[5]3.7	—	—
		[6]2.0	2.5	[3]4.2
		1.6	—	—
80	1.6	1.9	—	3.2
100	1.7	[1]3.6	[1]4.7	[4]5.6
		2.0	2.8	[1]6.0
		—	—	3.6

[1] Anderson (1968).
[2] Martens (1966).
[3] Wilson (1966).
[4] Carter (1961).
[5] Wiitala (1961).
[6] Espey, Morgan, and Masch (1966).

Alto, Calif., changed from 5.7 percent to 19.1 percent impervious in a 10-year period.

Data from Table 16.1 have been transposed into the graph shown in Figure 16.2. The ratios of peak discharge of urbanized to rural areas are presented for different percentages of sewerage and impervious area; lines of equal values of the ratio are drawn through the data. Briefly, these data show that for unsewered areas the differences between 0 and 100 percent impervious will increase peak discharge on the average 2.5 times. For areas that are 100 percent sewered, peak discharge for 0 percent impervious will be about 1.7 times the mean annual flood and the ratio increases to about eight for 100 percent impervious areas. Figure 16.2, then, reduces the basic data to the same units applicable to a 1-sq-mi drainage basin and to the mean annual flood.

A basin produces big flows from large and intense storms and smaller flows from less

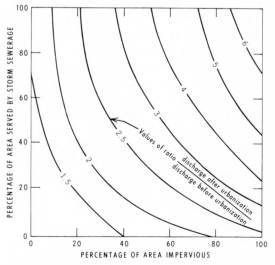

FIGURE 16.2 Effect of urbanization on mean annual flood for a 1-square-mile drainage area. (Based on data from Table 16.1.)

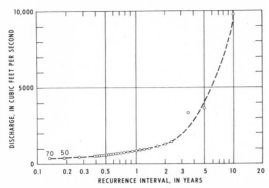

FIGURE 16.3 Flood-frequency curve for partial-duration series, West Branch Brandywine Creek at Coatesville, Pa., based on data for 1942, 1944–51.

intense but more frequent storms. The great or catastrophic event is rare, and the storm of ordinary magnitude is frequent. These events can be arranged in order of magnitude and counted. For example, all discharge events exceeding 400 cfs (cubic feet per second) can be tabulated from the record at a stream-gaging station and arranged in order of magnitude; the values in the array can be plotted as a discharge-frequency curve. This has been done for the gaging station on West Branch Brandywine Creek at Coatesville, Pa., for 9 years of record (Figure 16.3). The theory and practice of constructing such flow-frequency curves is well known. The plotting position or frequency often used is defined as

$$R = \frac{n + 1}{m}$$

where R is the recurrence interval in years, n is number of years of record, and m is the rank of the individual event in the array.

Note in Figure 16.3 that the largest flow in the 9-year record was nearly 10,000 cfs. The number 50 printed on the graph means that there were 50 flows equal to or exceeding 500 cfs. Once a year, on the average, a discharge value of about 900 cfs will be equalled or exceeded.

Studies of river channels have shown that rivers construct and maintain channels which will carry without overflow a discharge

somewhat smaller than the average annual flood. In fact the recurrence interval of the bankfull stage in most rivers is a flow having a recurrence interval of about 1.5 to 2 years.

Urbanization tends to increase the flood potential from a given basin. The channel then will receive flows which exceed its capacity not just once in 1.5 to 2 years on the average but more often. It is now proposed to estimate how much more often and to indicate the effect of this increased frequency on the channel itself.

Effect of Urbanization on Increasing Frequency of Overbank Flow

The effect of urbanization on the average annual flood is shown in Figure 16.2, which shows the increase in average annual flood for different degrees of urbanization as measured by the increase in percentages of impervious area and area served by storm sewers. For convenience these are tabulated as follows:

PERCENTAGE OF AREA SEWERED	PERCENTAGE OF AREA IMPERVIOUS	RATIO TO AVERAGE ANNUAL FLOOD
0	0	1
20	20	1.5
40	40	2.3
50	50	2.7
80	60	4.2
100	60	4.4

The average annual flood of 75 cfs was then multiplied by these ratios and plotted as shown in Figure 16.4 at the 2.3-year interval. These values form the basis of a series of frequency curves for combinations of sewered area and impervious area. The shapes of the curves are guided by the principle that the most infrequent floods occur under conditions that are not appreciably affected by imperviousness of the basin.

The most frequent flows are therefore increased by smaller ratios than would be the average annual flood. Also, the most frequent flows are decreased in number because low flows from an urbanized area are not sustained by ground water as in a natural basin. The curves representing urbanized conditions therefore converge at low flow values.

Obviously the frequency curves in Figure 16.4 are extrapolations based on minimal data and require corroboration or revision as additional field data become available.

The flood-frequency curve under original (unurbanized) condition passes through a value of 67 cfs at a recurrence interval of 1.5 years. At bankfull condition natural channels generally can carry the flow having that recurrence interval. If one assumes that this flow approximates the capacity of the natural channels, the intersection of the estimated curves for different degrees of urbanization with the discharge value of 67 cfs can be used to estimate the increase in number of flows equal to or exceeding natural channel capacity. An auxiliary scale is shown at the top of Figure 16.4 to facilitate this.

For example, under natural conditions it is expected that a 10-year record would show about seven flows equal to or exceeding 67 cfs, or channel capacity. But if the average annual flood were increased 1.5 times (from 75 to 112 cfs) corresponding to 20 percent sewered and 20 percent impervious, the new frequency curve indicates that 14 flows of 67 cfs or greater would occur in a 10-year period, or a twofold increase in number of flows. Similarly, the ratio of number of flows exceeding bankfull capacity was read from the intersection of the other curves in Figure 16.4 with the ordinate value of 67 cfs to obtain the ratios plotted in figure 16.5.

Figure 16.5 shows that with an area 50 percent sewered and 50 percent impervious, for example, the number of flows equal to or exceeding bankfull channel capacity would, over a period of years, be increased nearly fourfold.

Sediment Production

EFFECT OF LAND USE

The basic data available for analyzing the effect of urbanization on sediment yield,

though sparse, have been summarized to some extent in the literature. Expecially valuable is the report by Wolman (1964) who summarized not only the data obtained from sediment sampling stations in streams in Eastern United States but also studied the sediment yield from building construction activities. Sediment yields from urbanized

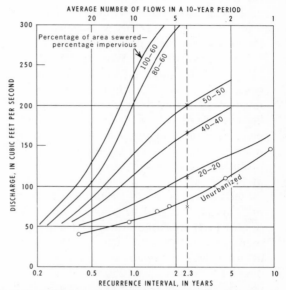

FIGURE 16.4 Flood-frequency curves for a 1-square-mile basin in various states of urbanization.

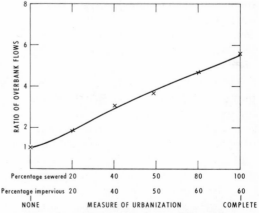

FIGURE 16.5 Increase in number of flows per year equal to or exceeding original channel capacity (1-square-mile drainage area), as ratio to number of overbank flows before urbanization, for different degrees of urbanization. (Derived from Figure 16.4.)

or developing areas ranged from 1000 to more than 100,000 tons per square mile per year.

It should be recognized that sediment yield per square mile decreases with increasing drainage area, but nevertheless it is apparent that unurbanized drainage basins yield 200 to 500 tons per square mile per year, on the average. These figures are slightly higher for the farmed Piedmont lands, which may be expected to produce sediment yield of 500 tons per square mile per year, such as the Watts Branch basin near Rockville, Md.

For very small areas, Wolman (1964) said, "Because construction denudes the natural cover and exposes the soil beneath, the tonnage of sediment derived by erosion from an acre of ground under construction in developments and highways may exceed 20,000 to 40,000 times the amount eroded from farms and woodlands in an equivalent period of time."

The data measured or estimated by Wolman (1964) in small urbanizing, developed or industrial areas show clearly that the sediment yield is larger by 10 to 100 times that of rural areas. Guy and Ferguson (1962) observed an increase of 250 times in an area near Kensington, Md.

Keller (1962) compared the sediment rating curves for Northwest Branch of Anacostia River near Colesville, Md., a relatively unurbanized basin, and the Anacostia River basin near Hyattsville, Md., which is partly urbanized. He found the sediment production to be about four times greater in the urbanized area.

Most sediment carried by a stream is moved by high flows. In Brandywine Creek, for example, about 54 percent of the total sediment transported annually by the river (drainage area 312 sq mi) is carried by flows that occur, on the average, about 3 days each year.

In the tabulation below, a comparison is made between sediment yield from Watts Branch, a rural landscape, and Little Falls Branch, an urban one. These basins are of the size and type represented in East Branch Brandywine Creek.

	DRAINAGE AREA (SQ MI)	TONS PER YEAR	TONS PER YEAR PER SQ MI
Watts Branch in Rockville, Md. (rural)	3.7	1,910	516
Little Falls Branch near Bethesda, Md. (urban)	4.1	9,530	3,220

Wark and Keller (1963) related the average annual sediment discharge in the Potomac River basin to percentage of forest cover and, separately, to the percentage of land in crops. Average annual sediment yield increased from 50 to 400 tons per square mile per year, or eightfold, as forest cover in the basin declined from 80 percent to 20 percent. Sediment yield increased from 70 to 300 tons per square mile per year, or fourfold, as land in crops increased from 10 to 50 percent.

EFFECTS OF INCREASED PEAK FLOWS

If the number of flows above bankfull stage is increased by urbanization, the banks and bed of a channel in erodible material will not remain stable, but the channel will enlarge through erosion. Computation indicates the seriousness of this factor.

For example, assume that a channel is capable of carrying 55 cfs at bankfull stage. In the Brandywine area this represents a channel draining a basin slightly less than 1 sq mi in area. The channel necessary to carry 55 cfs at bankfull stage would probably have a velocity of slightly less than 2.5 feet per second and would be about 2 feet deep and 11 feet wide. In Figure 16.2, urbanization might cause a flow of this frequency to increase 2.7 times, to 150 cfs. If this channel had to adjust itself to carry a flood of 150 cfs at bankfull stage, it is estimated that the new velocity would be about 2.5 feet per second, and the necessary depth and width would have changed respectively to about 3 feet and 20 feet. In other words, this stream would deepen about 50 percent and increase in width a little less than twice its original size. If such erosion takes place through at least one-fourth mile of channel length in a drainage basin of 1 sq mi, the amount of sediment produced by this erosion would be 50,000 cubic feet. At 100 pounds per cubic foot, this amounts to 2,500 tons.

This amount can be compared with the mean annual sediment yield for Watts Branch, an unurbanized area near Rockville, Md. Annual sediment yield of Watts Branch is 516 tons per square mile. Thus, the channel erosion alone under the assumptions made would produce as much sediment as 5 years' usual production from an unurbanized area of the same size. Therefore, one can visualize that as urbanization proceeds, not only does construction activity have the potential of increasing sediment loads many thousands of times while construction is in progress, but also the result of the urbanization through its increase in peak flow would produce large amounts of sediment from channel enlargement as well.

Water Quality

There is little doubt that as urbanization increases, particularly from industrial use of land and water, the quality of water decreases. However, quantitative data to support this observation are sparse. There are two principal effects of urbanization on water quality. First, the influx of waste materials tends to increase the dissolved-solids content and decrease the dissolved-oxygen content. Second, as flood peaks increase as a result of the increased area of imperviousness and decreased lag time, less water is available for ground-water recharge. The stream becomes flashier in that flood peaks are higher and flows during nonstorm periods are lower.

A recent study on the Passaic River at Little Falls, N.J., by Anderson and Faust (1965) provides quantitative data on the effect of urbanization and industrialization on water quality. Seventeen years of data for the flow and chemical quality of the 760-sq-mi drainage basin were analyzed. During these 17 years, diversions of water for domestic and industrial supplies increased more

than 30 percent between 1950 and 1963. Returns of waste waters into the basin became as much as 10 percent of the water withdrawn. Analysis of the data showed that at relatively low discharge the dissolved-solids content increased about 10 ppm (parts per million) between 1948 and 1955 but increased 75 ppm between 1955 and 1963. That is, during the period of greatest population growth the dissolved-solids content increased nearly 40 percent in a period of 8 years.

A long-term change in the average content of dissolved oxygen was also noted. Between 1950 and 1964 the dissolved-oxygen content dropped from an average of 78 percent of saturation to 62 percent of saturation. Further, the analysis demonstrated that these average changes in water quality occurred in all seasons of the year.

An aspect of population growth not generally appreciated is the large segment of population using septic tanks for disposal of sewage. In a given area this segment often becomes large before community water and sewerage systems are built. For the planner it should be important to know how septic-tank installations can affect water quality in streams and in the ground. In the upper East Branch of Brandywine Creek, a basin of 37 sq mi, the population in 1967 was 4,200. As of that date, there were no community water or sewerage systems; all the population was served by individual wells and septic tanks. Population projections indicate that the basin will have 14,000 persons by the year 1990. During the initial part of this projected growth at least, the number of wells and septic tanks can be expected to increase materially.

The soil, containing as it does a flourishing fauna of micro-organisms, tends to destroy or adsorb pathogenic bacteria. Effluent draining from the seepage field of a septic tank tends therefore to be cleansed of its pathogens.* McGauhey and Krone (1954) showed that the coliform count was reduced by three orders of magnitude in moving from

---

*See discussion by McGauhey in Selection 18.

an injection well a distance of 50 feet through sand and gravel. In 100 feet the count was reduced to a small number. As for rate of movement, Mallmann and Mack (1961) showed that bacteria introduced into a permeable soil by a septic-tank seepage field moved 10 feet in 2 days and 20 feet in 3 days and appeared in a well 30 feet away after 10 days.

Both the rate and effectiveness of the process of pathogen reduction depend on the type of soil as has been summarized by Olson (1964), who emphasized that position of the ground-water table is a critical factor in the transmission of pollutants.

Studies by Wayman, Page, and Robertson (1965) of the changes in primary sewage effluent through natural materials in conditions of saturated flow showed that "most soils removed over 90 percent of the bacteria from sewage within a few feet of travel . . . [but there was] severe clogging in the finer-grained soils." They found, however, that "dissolved solids moved through the columns [of soil] virtually unaffected. . . ."

The same authors report on infiltration of polluted river water through sandy loam. "ABS [synthetic detergent] and coliform bacteria are significantly reduced by infiltration through the unsaturated zone; dissolved solids do not seem to be removed. . . . Once a pollutant gets into the ground (saturated flow) little additional change in removal of ABS or dissolved solids, even for movement over extensive horizontal distances, is to be expected. This result is in agreement with the data . . . for flow of sewage effluent through various soil columns (saturated flow)."

The data are not definitive regarding the minimum distance a septic-tank seepage field should be separated from a stream channel, but the application of data cited above with general principles does indicate some tentative rules of thumb which might be useful to the planner. A perennial stream represents the intersection of the saturated zone (water table) with the earth's surface. The observations indicate that, for soil cleansing to be effective, contaminated water must move through unsaturated soil at least 100 feet. Owing to the gentle gradient of the water table near the perennial stream and the fact that seepage water moves vertically as well as toward a nearby channel, it would seem prudent that no septic tank should be as close to a channel as about 300 feet, if protection of the stream water quality is to be achieved. The distance should probably be greater from a perennial than from an ephemeral channel. (An ephemeral stream is one which contains flowing water only in storm periods.) In general, it might be advisable to have no source of pollution such as a seepage field closer than 300 feet to a channel or watercourse.

Even this minimum setback does not prevent the dissolved materials (nitrates, phosphates, chlorides) from enriching the stream water and thus potentially encouraging the proliferation of algae and otherwise creating a biotic imbalance.

The only detailed study of the effect of urbanization on water temperature is that of E. J. Pluhowski (1968), some of whose results are summarized here.* He chose five streams on Long Island for detailed analysis and found that streams most affected by man's activities exhibit temperatures in summer from 10° to 15°F above those in an unurbanized control. Connetquot River, the control stream, flows through one of the few remaining undeveloped areas of central Long Island. Temperatures in reaches most affected by ponding, realinement, or clear cutting of trees are significantly higher in summer, but winter temperatures are 5° to 10°F colder than those observed in reaches unaffected by man.

Solar radiation is the predominant factor in the energy balance determining a stream's thermal pattern. The more solar energy a stream absorbs, the greater its temperature variation diurnally as well as seasonally. By greatly increasing the surface area exposed to the sun's radiation, the construction of ponds and lakes has profoundly affected

---

* For further discussion of thermal pollution in general see Selection 17.

stream temperature regimen. On Long Island, Pluhowski found that ponds having mean depth of about 2 feet or less substantially increase downstream diurnal temperature fluctuations whereas ponds deeper than 2 feet exhibit a dampening effect on daily temperatures. For example, during the period October 31 to November 2, 1967, the mean daily range of temperatures at Swan River, in south-central Long Island, varied from 9°F in a reach immediately below a shallow pond (mean depth, 0.5 foot) to 3°F below Swan Lake (mean depth, 3 feet). In reaches unaffected by man's activities, the mean daily temperature fluctuation was about 4°F.

Under natural conditions, less than 5 percent of the streamflow on Long Island originates as direct surface runoff. With the conversion of large areas of western Long Island from farmland to suburban use during the last 20 years, the proportion of streamflow originating as surface runoff has increased sharply. As a direct consequence, streams most affected by street runoff may exhibit temperature patterns that are markedly different from those observed in streams flowing through natural settings. During the period August 25 to 27, 1967, a series of heavy rainstorms overspread Long Island. Throughout this period, temperatures at each of the five observation sites on Connetquot River showed little day-to-day change. In contrast, temperatures in the upper reaches of East Meadow Brook, which drains highly urbanized central Nassau County, increased steadily in response to the relatively warm street runoff. Pluhowski found that by August 27, water temperatures had risen 10° to 12°F above prestorm levels and were 15°F higher than concurrent temperatures in the control stream.

Selected References

Anderson, D. G., 1968, Effects of urban development on floods in northern Virginia: U.S. Geol. Survey open-file rept., 39 p., 5 figs.

Anderson, Peter W., and Faust, Samuel D., 1965, Changes in quality of water in the Passaic River at Little Falls, New Jersey, as shown by long-term data, *in* Geological Survey research 1965: U.S. Geol. Survey Prof. Paper 525-D, p. D214–D218.

Antoine, L. H., 1964, Drainage and best use of urban land: Public Works [New York], v. 95, p. 88–90.

Carter, R. W., 1961, Magnitude and frequency of floods in suburban areas, *in* Short papers in the geologic and hydrologic sciences: U.S. Geol. Survey Prof. Paper 424-B, p. B9–B11.

Espey, W. H., Morgan, C. W., and Masch, F. D., 1966, Study of some effects of urbanization on storm runoff from a small watershed: Texas Water Devel. Board Rept. 23, 109 p.

Felton, P. N., and Lull, H. W., 1963, Suburban hydrology can improve watershed conditions: Public Works, v. 94, p. 93–94.

Guy, H. P., and Ferguson, G. E., 1962, Sediment in small reservoirs due to urbanization: Am. Soc. Civil Engineers Proc., HY 2, p. 27–37.

Harris, E. E., and Rantz, S. E., 1964, Effect of urban growth on streamflow regimen of Permanente Creek, Santa Clara County, California: U.S. Geol. Survey Water-Supply Paper 1591-B, 18 p.

James, L. D., 1965, Using a computer to estimate the effects of urban development on flood peaks: Water Resources Research, v. 1, no. 2, p. 223–234.

Keller, F. J., 1962, The effect of urban growth on sediment discharge, Northwest Branch Anacostia River basin, Maryland *in* Short papers in geology and hydrology: U.S. Geol. Survey Prof. Paper 450-C, p. C129–C131.

Lull, H. W., and Sopper, W. E., 1966, Hydrologic effects from urbanization of forested watersheds in the northeast: Upper Darby, Pa., Northeastern Forest Expt. Sta., 24 p.

McGauhey, P. H., and Krone, R. B., 1954, Report on the investigation of travel of pollution: California State Water Pollution Control Board Pub. 11, 218 p.

Mallmann, W. L., and Mack, W. N., 1961, Biological contamination of ground water: Robert A. Taft Sanitary Eng. Center Tech. Rept. W61-5, p. 35–43.

Martens, L. A., 1966, Flood inundation and effects of urbanization in metropolitan Charlotte [North Carolina]: U.S. Geol. Survey open-file rept., 54 p.

Olson, G. W., 1964, Application of soil survey to problems of health, sanitation, and engineering: Cornell Univ. Agr. Expt. Sta. Mem. 387, 77 p.

Pluhowski, E. J., 1968, Urbanization and its effect on stream temperature: Baltimore, Md., Johns Hopkins Univ., Ph.D. dissert. (in preparation).

Swenson, H. A., 1964, Sediment in streams: Jour. Soil and Water Conserv., v. 19, no. 6, p. 223–226.

Wark, J. W., and Keller, F. J., 1963, Preliminary study

of sediment sources and transport in the Potomac River Basin: Interstate Comm. on Potomac River Basin, Washington, D.C., Tech. Bull. 1963–11, 28 p.

Wayman, C., Page, H. L., and Robertson, J. B., 1965, Behavior of surfactants and other detergent components in water and soil-water environments: Federal Housing Adm. Tech. Studies Pub. 532, 136 p.

Wiitala, S. W., 1961, Some aspects of the effect of urban and suburban development upon runoff: U.S. Geol. Survey open-file rept., 28 p.

Wilson, K. V., 1966, Flood frequency of streams in Jackson, Mississippi: U.S. Geol. Survey open-file rept., 6 p.

Wolman, M. G., 1964, Problems posed by sediment derived from construction activities in Maryland—Report to the Maryland Water Pollution Control Commission: Annapolis, Md., 125 p.

Wolman, M. G., and Schick, P. A., 1967, Effects of construction on fluvial sediment, urban and suburban areas of Maryland: Water Resources Research, v. 3, no. 2, p. 451–462.

ADDITIONAL REFERENCES

Brater, E. F. 1968. Steps toward a better understanding of urban runoff processes. *Water Resources Research* 4(2):335–347.

Leopold, L. B. 1969a. Quantitative comparison of some aesthetic factors among rivers. *U.S. Geological Survey Circular* 620. 16 pp.

Leopold, L. B. 1969b. Landscape esthetics; how to quantify the scenics of a river valley. *Natural History*, pp. 37–44. October.

Leopold, L. B., M. G. Wolman, and J. P. Miller. 1964. *Fluvial processes in geomorphology.* San Francisco: Freeman. 522 pp.

McGuinness, C. L. 1967. Urbanization—can we live with it? *Water Resources Bulletin* 3(1): 17–20.

Rantz, S. E. 1970. Urban sprawl and flooding in southern California. *U.S. Geological Survey Circular* 601-B. 11 pp.

Spieker, A. M. 1970. Water in urban planning, Salt Creek basin, Illinois. *U.S. Geological Survey Water-Supply Paper* 2002. 147 pp.

Stall, John B. 1966. Man's role in affecting the sedimentation of streams and reservoirs. Pp. 79–95 in *Proceedings Second Annual Water Resources Conference,* American Water Resources Association, Urbana, Illinois.

Tholin, A. L., and C. J. Keifer. 1960. Hydrology of urban runoff. *Trans. Amer. Soc. Civil Engineers* 125:1308 ff.

Thomas, H. E., and W. J. Schneider. 1970. Water as an urban resource and nuisance. *U.S. Geological Survey Circular* 601-D. 9 pp.

THERMAL POLLUTION

LAMONT C. COLE

use →

"Man is on a collision course with disaster if he tries to keep energy production growing by means that will impose increased thermal stress on the earth." So concludes the eminent author of this selection after studying the effect of man on the earth's heat budget.

Increased thermal stress is inevitable when we burn fossil fuels or generate electricity by nuclear or thermonuclear reactions. Though the global effects of such energy conversion to heat are not immediately threatening, heat from industrial plants causes deleterious changes locally. Great amounts of heat are produced by industries that need water for cooling. After being used for cooling, warmed-up water is usually returned to the nearest waterway, raising the temperature of the river, lake, or estuary.

About three-fourths of the waste heat discharged into United States waters results from generating electricity. By 1980, the annual production of electricity is expected to reach 2,000 billion kilowatt-hours, which will require nearly 250 billion gallons of water per day for cooling. About 200 billion gallons of this will be fresh water; this is one-fifth of the average daily fresh water runoff in the United States. For each kilowatt-hour (3,412 British thermal units) generated in a modern, coal-powered plant, about 6,000 Btu must be dissipated by water used to cool heat exchangers. Commonly the temperature of cooling water after use, when it is put back into streams or lakes, is 11° to 17°F higher. Nuclear power plants are even less efficient, wasting approximately 10,000 Btu per kilowatt-hour generated (Davidson and Bradshaw, 1967). Furthermore, most nuclear plants are much larger than fossil-fuel plants, amplifying local problems of thermal pollution.

LaMont C. Cole (b. 1916) is a professor in the Division of Biological Sciences at Cornell University, where he has been a member of the faculty since 1948. He earned a master's degree at Utah and bachelor's and doctoral degrees (1944) from the University of Chicago. He is a former president of the American Institute of Biological Sciences (1970) and of the Ecological Society of America. He has advised numerous governmental agencies on environmental affairs. Much of his research has centered on the ecology of animal populations.

Reprinted with permission from *BioScience*, Volume 19, pp. 989–992, 1969.

The effects of adding heat to water are very complex, but a temperature increase of only three or four degrees can, under certain conditions, seriously affect fish and other aquatic life (e.g., see Novotny, 1967, Clark, 1969, and Krenkel and Parker, 1969). With increased water temperature, metabolism increases and organisms require more oxygen; but there is less oxygen available at higher temperatures because water is less able to retain dissolved oxygen. As temperature rises, nuisance plants and rough fish may flourish, while useful life first loses capability to reproduce and then dies.

Various technological schemes, including cooling towers, have been introduced or proposed as alternatives for dissipating waste heat (Clark, 1969). Other people have suggested beneficial uses for the thermal energy (Mihursky, 1967, Bacher and Swickler, 1967). Heated water from a reactor in Sweden is used to warm a village in winter. All these are only short-term, local solutions, however, which avoid the longer-run problems of earth heating discussed here by LaMont Cole.

(Editor's comment)

There are etymological objections to the expression "thermal pollution," but it is gaining adoption and I shall here accept it without comment as a descriptive term for unwanted heat energy accumulating in any phase of the environment.

Any isolated body drifting in space as the earth is must either increase continuously in temperature or it must dispose of all energy received from external sources or generated internally by one of two processes. The energy may either be stored in some potential form or it must be reradiated to space.

In the past the earth has stored some of the energy coming to it from outside. This was accomplished by living plants using solar energy to drive endothermic chemical reactions, thereby creating organic compounds some of which were ultimately deposited in sediments. This process had two very important effects; in protecting the organic compounds from oxidation it created a reservoir of oxygen in the atmosphere; and it also eliminated the necessity for reradiating to space the heat energy that would have been released by the oxidation of those compounds. Part of the stored organic matter gave rise to the fossil fuels, coal, oil, and natural gas, which we are so avidly burning today—and now the earth must at last radiate

that heat energy back to space, or its temperature will increase.

Many of the most important problems currently facing man are ecological problems arising from the unrestrained growth of the human population and the resultant increasing strains being placed on the earth's life support system. Our seemingly insatiable demand for energy is one important source of strains on the earth's capacity to support life, and I propose here to examine it in very elementary terms.

The Earth's Sources of Energy

Well over 99.999% of the earth's annual energy income is from solar radiation and this must all be returned to space in the form of radiant heat. This has gone on forever, so to speak, and conditions on earth, since before the advent of man, have reflected the necessity of maintaining this balance of incoming and outgoing radiation. A ridiculously small proportion of the sunlight reaching us is used in photosynthesis by green plants. This energy powers all of the earth's microorganisms and animals and is converted to heat by their metabolism. In addition, man can obtain useful heat energy by burning organic matter in such forms as wood, straw, cattle dung, and garbage and other refuse. This is "free" energy in the sense that the earth would have reradiated it as heat even if man had not obtained useful work from it in the meantime. Physical labor performed by man and the work done by domestic animals are also means of utilizing this solar energy.

In addition, it is solar radiation that keeps the atmosphere and hydrosphere in motion. To the extent that man can utilize the energy of the winds, of falling water and of ocean currents, or can make direct use of sunlight, he can do so without imposing increased thermal stress on the total earth environment.

The earth has some other minor sources of energy that contribute to its natural radiation balance. The tides can be used to obtain useful energy and a plant in France is now producing electricity from this source. Also, tidal friction is very gradually slowing the rotation of the earth, thereby converting kinetic energy to heat which plays a small role in maintaining the earth's surface temperature before it is radiated to space. Heat is also emerging from the interior of the earth and current concepts attribute this heat to natural radioactivity. In some local areas this heat flux is concentrated, and in a few countries man utilizes it for such purposes as heating buildings and generating electricity. Italy generates more than 400,000 kw of electricity from geothermal heat and in the United States about 85,000 kw are derived from a geyser field north of San Francisco.

This then is the inventory of energy sources available to man without affecting the surface temperature of the earth or the quantity of heat energy that it must dispose of by radiation. It is important to note this because, at least in the "developed" nations, we actually seem to be regressing from the use of these natural energy sources. Certainly windmills, animal power, and manual labor are much less in evidence today than they were during my childhood, and useful work done by sailboats seems to be a thing of the past in our culture. When we burn fossil

fuels or generate electricity by nuclear or thermonuclear reactions, we must inevitably impose an increased thermal stress on the earth environment and, to the extent that this heat is undesirable, it constitutes thermal pollution.

The Earth's Radiation Balance

I assume the mean temperature of the earth's surface to be 15 C or 288 K; this may be a degree too low or too high. In order to keep the discussion sufficiently simple-minded, I shall introduce three simplifications.

First, I shall treat the earth as though its entire surface was at a uniform temperature equal to its average value, thus ignoring temperature differences due to latitude, altitude, season, and time of day. The effect of this simplification is less drastic than one might expect. It is true if one measures radiation from several bodies at different temperatures and infers the mean temperature of the surfaces from the radiation, he will obtain values that are slightly too high. For example, if we have two otherwise identical areas, one at 0 C and the other at 50 C, the average of their combined radiation will equal that which would be given off by such an area at 28 C rather than at the true mean temperature of 25 C. For the earth as a whole, the error from this source is not likely to amount to even one degree, and the other two simplifications I shall make tend to cause small errors in the opposite direction.

Second, I assume that the earth radiates as a blackbody or perfect radiator. This is probably nearly correct; and, in any case, the assumption is conservative for our purposes here. If the earth is actually a gray body rather than a black one, it will have to reach a somewhat higher temperature to dispose of the same amount of heat energy.

Finally, I assume that the earth radiates its energy to outer space which is at a temperature of 0 K. This is not quite correct because the portions of the sky occupied by the sun, moon, stars, and clouds of interstellar matter are at temperatures above absolute zero, and the earth's surface must therefore be very slightly warmer than it would otherwise be.

Accepting these simplifications, we can now turn to the Stefan-Boltzmann law of elementary physics which states that radiation is proportional to the fourth power of the absolute temperature, and easily calculate the amount of energy radiated from the earth to space.[1] At a temperature of 15 C (288 K) the total radiation from the earth turns out to be 2×10^{24} ergs/sec.

Or, looked at the other way around, if we know the quantity of heat that the earth's surface must get rid of by radiation, we can calculate what its surface temperature must be for it to do so. For example, various students of the subject have concluded that the mean temperature difference between glacial and ice-free periods is quite small, probably no more than 5 C (e.g., see Brooks, 1949). If we can assume that we are now about midway between these climatic types, then a rise of 3 C might be expected to melt the icecaps from Antarctica and Greenland thereby raising sea-level by some 100 m. This would drastically alter the world's coastlines as, for example, by putting all of Florida under water, and drowning most of the world's major cities. To do this would require a 4.2% increase in the earth's heat budget (an increase of 8.44×10^{22} ergs/sec). By the same reasoning, a 4.1% decrease in the energy budget could be expected to bring on a new ice age. As we shall see presently, however, these things are not really quite so simple and predictable.

Man's Effect on the Heat Budget

The amount of energy now being produced by man, I take to be 5×10^{19} ergs/sec or 25/1000 of 1% of the total radiated by the earth. Strangely enough, I am quite happy with this perhaps brash attempt to estimate a difficult quantity. Putnam (1953) estimated the fuel burned by man 16 years ago at 3.3×10^{19} ergs/sec. If he was correct then,

and if energy demand then had been growing at the rate it is now growing, man would now be using twice what I have estimated. Kardashev (1964) estimates the energy now produced by civilization at "over 4×10^{19} ergs per second" which is consistent with my estimate.

There is another way of getting at the figure. The rate of combustion of fossil fuels in the United States is accurately known, as is our rate of generating electricity. Our electrical production as of 1966 corresponds to one-fifth of our fossil fuel consumption. If we assume the same ratio for the entire earth, for which we do have credible figures on electrical generation, the world energy production turns out to be 4.4×10^{19} ergs/sec. With this many independent estimates converging, I am happy with the figure of 5×10^{19} ergs/sec.

This is such a tiny part of the earth's output of energy that it is evident that the heat released by man now has an absolutely insignificant direct effect on the average temperature of the earth's surface. Will this be true if we go on increasing our demands for power? I have been hearing utility company officials assert that we must keep electrical generating capacity growing by 10% per year, but a more common projection is about 7%, which rate the capacity would double every 10 years. I am confident that nonelectrical uses of fuel for such purposes as heating, industry, and transportation are growing at least as rapidly, and I am told that the "developing" countries are going to continue to develop. Let us examine the consequences of an energy economy that continues to grow at 7% per year.

Waggoner (1966) considers it at least possible that a warming of 1 C would cause real changes in the boundaries between plant communities. For this to occur, the earth's energy budget would have to increase by about 3×10^{22} ergs/sec. How long would it take man to cause this at an increased energy production of 7% per year? The answer is 91 years.

As already mentioned, a rise of 3 C could, in the opinion of competent authorities, melt the ice caps and produce an earth geography such as has never been seen by man, and on which there would be much less dry land for man. This would take about 108 years to achieve by present trends. Let us rejoice that the United States Civil War did not embark on an energy-releasing spree as we are now doing.

The highest mean annual temperature of any spot on earth is believed to be 29.9 C (302.9 K) at Massawa on the Red Sea in Ethiopia. I think it is safe to assume that if the average temperature of the whole earth was raised to 30 C, it would become uninhabitable. This would take 130 years under our postulated conditions—the time from the start of the Victorian Age to the present.

These calculations, rough as they are, make it clear that man is on a collision course with disaster if he tries to keep energy production growing by means that will impose an increased thermal stress on the earth. I have here ignored the fact that the fossil fuels, and probably uranium and thorium reserves also, would be exhausted before these drastic effects could be attained. The possibility exists, however, that a controlled fusion reaction will be achieved and bring these disastrous effects within the realm of possibility.

How can we avoid the consequences of the trends we are following? My answer would be to determine what level of human population the earth can support at a desirable standard of living without undergoing deterioration and then to move to achieve this steady state condition. I would like to see increased energy needs met by the direct utilization of solar energy. There are, however, visionary scientists, and policy makers who will listen to them, who will grasp at any straw to keep man's exploitation of the earth forever growing. In my mind I can hear them planning to air condition part of the earth for man and for whatever then will supply his food, while the rest of the earth is allowed to radiate the excess heat by attaining a very high temperature. They will consider putting generating plants and factories on the moon and other planets and reducing the heat stress on earth by reflecting

solar radiation back to space. This latter possibility brings us to consideration of some secondary effects of our expanding energy budget.

Side Effects of Energy Use

The combustion of fuel releases not only heat but also frequently smoke and various chemicals, the most important of which are water and carbon dioxide, into the environment.

Smoke and other particulate matter in the atmosphere scatters and absorbs incoming solar radiation, thus reducing the amount of energy absorbed by the surface. It has little effect on the outgoing longwave radiation, so the net effect is a tendency to cool the earth's surface. Several large volcanic eruptions within historic times have caused a year or so of abnormally low temperatures all over the earth. Perhaps the most striking case was the mighty eruption of Mt. Tomboro in the Lesser Sunda Islands in 1815. The following year, 1816, was the famous "year without a summer," during which snow fell in Boston every month. Actual measurements following the 1912 eruption of Mt. Katmai in the Aleutians showed a reduction of about 20% in the solar radiation reaching the earth.

Water vapor and carbon dioxide have an effect opposite to that of smoke; they are transparent to sunlight but absorb the longwave radiation from the earth and, by reradiating some of it back to earth, tend to raise the surface temperature. Man's combustion of fossil fuels has caused a measurable increase in the CO_2 content of the atmosphere, and now increasing numbers of jet airplanes are releasing great quantities of both water vapor and CO_2 at high altitudes. This would tend to raise the earth's temperature. However, a phenomenon of increasing frequency is the coalescence of the contrails of jet airplanes into banks of cirrus clouds which will reflect some of the incoming solar radiation back to space. Obviously, we cannot now be certain of the ultimate effects of the materials we are releasing to the atmosphere, but

save for end

they certainly have the potential for changing climates.

On a more local scale, we are using prodigious quantities of water for cooling industrial plants, especially electrical generating plants, and this use is expected to increase at least as rapidly as our energy use grows[2]—perhaps more rapidly because nuclear plants waste more heat per kilowatt than plants burning fossil fuels. When heated water is discharged at a temperature above that of the air, we must expect an increase in the frequencies of mist and fog and, in winter, icing conditions.

Biological Effects of Thermal Pollution

The first and most obvious biological effect one thinks of is that bodies of water may become so hot that nothing can live in them. It is true that there are a few bacteria and blue-green algae that can grow in hot springs but even these are very unusual in water above 60 C. I know of only one case of a green alga living above 50 C—a species of *Protococcus* from Yellowstone Park. A few rotifers, nematodes, and protozoa have been found at above 50 C, and some, in a dried and encysted state, will survive much higher temperatures. In general, no higher organisms are to be expected actively living in water above about 35 C. I find it difficult to reconcile the data with the conclusion of Wurtz (1968, p. 139): "Water temperature would have to be increased to about 130 F (54.4 C) to destroy the microorganisms that are responsible for the self-purification capacity of a lake or stream." This statement is certainly incompatible with the recommendation of the National Technical Advisory Committee (1968) that: "All surface waters should be capable of supporting life forms of aesthetic value."

Another factor to be considered is the effect of temperature on the types of organisms present. Fish of any type are rare above 30 C. Diatoms, which are important members of aquatic food chains, decrease as temperature rises above 20 C, and they are gradually replaced by blue-green algae which are not important as food for animals, are often toxic, and are often the source of water blooms which kill the biota and make the water unfit for domestic use. Typically at about 30 C, diatoms and blue-greens are about equally represented and green algae exceed both. At 35 C, the diatoms are nearly gone, the greens are decreasing rapidly, and the blue-greens are assuming full dominance.

So far as animals are concerned, a body of water at a temperature of 30–35 C is essentially a biological desert. The green algae, which are well above their optimum temperature, can support a few types of cladoceran, amphiphod, and isopod crustaceans; bacteria and blue-green algae may abound; and mosquito larvae may do very well; rooted plants may grow in shallow regions; and a few crayfish, carp, goldfish, and catfish may endure. Largemouth bass can survive and grow at 32 C but they do not reproduce above about 24 C. A few other forms such as aquatic insects may inhabit the water as adults but may or may not be able to complete their life cycles there. Desirable game fishes such as Atlantic salmon, lake trout, northern pike, and walleyes require water below 10 C for reproduction.

Another effect of raising the temperature of water is to reduce the solubility of gases. The amount of oxygen dissolved in water in equilibrium with the atmosphere decreases by over 17% between 20 C and 30 C. At the same time, the need of organisms for oxygen increases. As a rule of thumb, metabolic rate approximately doubles for a 10 C increase in body temperature, although the effect is sometimes greater. Krogh (1914) found that the rate of development of frog eggs is about six times as great at 20 C as at 10 C. Similar effects have been noted in the rate of development of mosquitos.

Dissolved oxygen is often in critically short supply for aquatic organisms and increased temperature aggravates the situation. This may be partially compensated by more rapid diffusion of oxygen from the air and, during daylight hours, by photosynthesis. On the other hand, decay of organic matter and other oxidative processes such as the rusting of iron are more rapid at high temperatures.

In polluted water the effect of biochemical oxygen demand (BOD) is more severe at high temperatures. The addition of heat to estuaries may be more critical than in bodies of freshwater because saltwater has a slightly lower specific heat and because oxygen is less soluble in saltwater.

In contrast to the situation with gases, salts become more soluble in water as the temperature increases. Chemical reactions become more rapid and increased evaporation may further increase the concentration of dissolved salts. At the same time the rate of exchange of substances between aquatic organisms and the medium increases. Toxins are likely to have greater effects, and parasites and diseases are more likely to break out and spread. In general, water at a temperature above the optimum places a strain on metabolic processes that may make adaptation to other environmental factors more difficult. For example, the Japanese oyster can tolerate a wider range of salinity in winter than in summer (Reid, 1961, p. 267).

In addition, if the water contains plant nutrients, objectionable growths of aquatic plants may be promoted by increased temperature—extreme cases leading to heavy mortality of fishes and other animals. It has been reported that polluted water from Lake Superior which does not support algal blooms there will do so if warmed to the temperature of Lake Erie.

Still other factors come into play when a body of water is thermally stratified. In a deep cold lake such as Cayuga where we are currently threatened with a huge nuclear generating plant, the lake water mixes, usually in May, so the entire lake is well oxygenated. As the surface warms, the lake stratifies with a level of light, warm water (the epilimnion) floating with no appreciable mixing on a mass of dense cold water (the hypolimnion) in which the lake trout, their food organisms, and other things are living and consuming oxygen. This continues until the lake mixes again, usually in November, by which time the oxygen supply in the hypolimnion is seriously depleted. The power company plans to pump 750 million gallons per day from the hypolimnion at a temperature averaging perhaps 6 C and to discharge it at the surface at a temperature of about 21 C. They plan this despite a recommendation of the National Technical Advisory Committee (1968, p. 33) that: " . . . water for cooling should not be pumped from the hypolimnion to be discharged to the same body of water." The effect of this addition of heat on the average temperature of the lake will be trivially small, but the biological consequences can be out of all proportion to the amount of heating.

The heat will delay fall cooling of the epilimnion and hasten spring warming, so that the length of time the lake is stratified each year will be increased. The water from the hypolimnion is rich in available plant nutrients, and by warming it and discharging it in the lighted zone, the amount of plant growth will be increased. This means more organic matter sinking into the hypolimnion and using up oxygen when it decays. The threat to the welfare of the lake is very real.

Finally, we should comment on fluctuating temperatures. Many organisms can adapt to somewhat higher or lower temperatures if they have time. The water in reservoirs behind hydroelectric dams often becomes thermally stratified, and when it is released at the base of the dam, a stretch of cold stream is produced which can support a cold water fauna even in warm regions. But when water is only discharged during peak electrical generating hours, the stream becomes subject to severe temperature fluctuations that will exclude many sensitive organisms. Similarly, if fishes or other organisms acclimate to the warm discharge from a factory or power plant and congregate near it, they will be subjected to temperature shocks when the plant is shut down for maintenance or refueling.

Conclusion

Man cannot go on increasing his use of thermal energy without causing degradation of his environment, and if he is persistent enough, he will destroy himself. There are other energy sources that could be used, but no source can support an indefinitely growing population. As with so many other things, it is man's irresponsible proliferation in numbers that is the real heart of the problem. There is some population size that the earth could support indefinitely without undergoing deterioration, but people do not even want to consider what that number might be. I suspect that it is substantially below the present world population. One would think that any rational creature riding a space ship would take care not to damage or destroy the ship, but perhaps the word "rational" does not describe man.

Notes

[1] I take the surface area of the earth as 5.1×10^{18} cm^2 and the value of the Stefan constant as 5.67×10^{-5} erg cm^{-2} deg^{-4} sec^{-1}.

[2] Thermally more efficient electrical generating plants are considered possible; e.g., the "magnetohydrodynamic" generator (see Rosa and Hals, 1968).

References Cited

Brooks, C. E. P. 1949. *Climate Through the Ages*. Rev. ed. McGraw-Hill Book Co., New York.

Kardashev, N. S. 1964. Transmission of information by extraterrestrial civilizations. In: *Extraterrestrial Civilizations*, G. M. Tovmasyan (ed.). Trans. by National Aeronautics and Space Administration, Washington, D.C.

Krogh, A. 1914. On the influence of temperature on the rate of embryonic development. *Z. Allg. Physiol.*, **16**: 163–177.

National Technical Advisory Committee. 1968. Water quality criteria. Report of the National Technical Advisory Committee to the Secretary of the Interior. Federal Water Pollution Control Administration, Washington, D.C.

Putnam, P. C. 1953. *Energy in the Future*. D. Van Nostrand Co., New York.

Reid, G. K. 1961. *Ecology of Inland Waters and Estuaries*. Reinhold Publishing Co., New York.

Rosa, R. J., and F. A. Hals. 1968. In defense of MHD. *Ind. Res.*, June 1968: 68–72.

Waggoner, P. E. 1966. Weather modification and the living environment. In: *Future Environments of North America*, F. F. Darling and J. F. Milton (eds.). Natural History Press, Garden City, N.Y.

Wurtz, C. B. 1968. Thermal pollution: The effect of the problem. In: *Environmental Problems*, B. R. Wilson (ed.). J. B. Lippincott Co., Philadelphia.

ADDITIONAL REFERENCES

Bacher, A. A., and S. A. Swickler. 1967. Ecological significance of waste heat utilization. Pp. 197–221 in *Ecological technology; Space-earth-sea*, ed. by E. B. Konecci, A. W. Petrocelli, and A. J. Shiner. Transference of Tech. Ser. No. 1, College of Business Administration, University of Texas, Austin.

Bibliography on Thermal Pollution. 1967. *Proc. Amer. Soc. Civil Engineers, Journal of Sanitary Engineering Division* 93(SA3):85–113.

Clark, J. R. 1969. Thermal pollution and aquatic life. *Sci. Am.* 220(3):18–27.

Davidson, B., and R. W. Bradshaw. 1967. Thermal pollution of water systems. *Environmental Science and Technology* 1(8):618–630.

Glaser, P. E. 1969. Beyond nuclear power—the large-scale use of solar energy. *Trans. N. Y. Acad. Sci.* 31(8):951–967.

Krenkel, P. A., and F. L. Parker, eds. 1969. *Engineering aspects of thermal pollution*. Nashville, Tenn.: Vanderbilt Univ. Press. 351 pp.

Mihursky, J. A. 1967. On possible constructive uses of thermal additions to estuaries. *BioScience* 17(10):698–702.

Morris, J. C. 1968. The problem of thermal pollution. Pp. 123–130 in *Environmental problems; Pesticides, thermal pollution, and environmental synergisms*, ed. by B. R. Wilson. Philadelphia and Toronto: Lippincott.

Novotny, A. J. 1967. *The effects of temperature change on salmon, trout, and competing fishes*. U.S. Bureau of Commercial Fisheries, Biological Laboratory, Seattle, Washington.

Radford, E. P., and others. 1969. Statement of concern. *Environment* 11(7):18–27. A group of Johns Hopkins University scientists discusses the problems presented by heated water and radioactive wastes from nuclear power plants on Chesapeake Bay.

MANMADE CONTAMINATION HAZARDS TO GROUND WATER

P. H. MCGAUHEY

Most of the fresh water in the habitable parts of the world is ground water—water in the saturated zone beneath the ground surface. Ground water reservoirs hold 60 to 70 times more water than is present in lakes and streams at any one time. Unfortunately, in many places (especially drier regions) man is withdrawing ground water much faster than it is being replaced naturally. We are rapidly depleting an essentially *non*renewable resource (Thomas and Leopold, 1964).

Elsewhere, because of the extremely slow movement of ground water (usually only several tens of feet per year), we treat the ground and ground water as a sump for our wastes. Injected contaminants do not appear soon in distant water supplies. But, by the same token, ground water is extremely slow to cleanse itself of nondegradable pollutants. We are trading future high-quality water for immediate convenience in waste disposal.

In this selection McGauhey discusses different processes by which man is contaminating subsurface waters and the dangers of each. Water infiltrating the soil may carry wastes from man's life processes, his industrial activity, or his use of water in agriculture. Fortunately, particulate matter, including bacteria and viruses, does not move far with water percolating in soil. The chemical products of biodegradation of organic wastes, however, generally move quite freely and hence reach ground water. The effect is to increase (sometimes greatly) the concen-

Percy H. McGauhey (b. 1904) has been director of the Sanitary Engineering Research Laboratory, University of California, Berkeley, since 1957. He holds degrees from Oregon State University, Virginia Polytechnic Institute, and the University of Wisconsin. He was on the faculty of Virginia Polytechnic Institute from 1927 to 1951, except for two years as professor of sanitary engineering at the University of Southern California. McGauhey has received many professional awards, including the Water Works Association's Fuller Award and the Water Pollution Control Federation's Eddy Award. He has investigated and written on problems of waste water reclamation, organic clogging of soils, effects and removal of detergents from water, economic evaluation of water, and solid wastes management.

This selection appeared in *Ground Water* 6(3):10–13, 1968, entitled "Manmade Contamination Hazards." Permission to republish has been granted by *Ground Water*, the technical journal of the National Water Well Association, Dr. Jay H. Lehr, editor and executive director.

tration of salts normally present in such waters. Hazardous industrial chemicals include metal ions, phenols, tar residues, brines, and exotic organics. These may contaminate ground water through accident, carelessness, or waste-water discharge. Leaching from solid waste landfills can yield chemicals, iron, and various earth minerals. Agriculture produces pesticide residues and soluble chemical nutrients applied as fertilizers. The most serious hazard to ground water quality is the buildup of dissolved solids.

Other important sources of ground water contamination, not discussed in this selection, include radioactive waste burial grounds and nuclear testing (Committee for Environmental Information, 1969, p. 43), disposal wells (Selection 31, Walker, 1961, and Mechem and Garrett, 1963), coal mining and processing operations (see Selection 26), oil field operations, highway salting (see Selection 30), and salt water encroachment near marine coasts due to pumping of fresh water (Parker, 1955).

(Editor's comment)

The activities of man upon the earth may affect the quality of ground water in two major ways: (1) by accelerating the rate of buildup of compounds or ions normally found in ground water, and (2) by adding or increasing the concentration of dissolved solids during beneficial use of water. The first results from plowing of fields, denuding of forest lands, construction of highways, and similar actions which expedite the normal movement of water into soils containing soluble compounds. The second results from discharging to the water which may infiltrate the soil, or to the land through which water may move, inorganic chemicals, biological agents, and organic compounds associated with municipal, industrial, and agricultural use of water. For the purpose of this discussion, only this second type of activity is considered as producing "manmade" hazards; hence specific attention is directed to the significance to ground-water quality of the natural and synthetic fractions which appear in:

1 Wastes from human life processes.
2 Wastes from industrial processes.
3 Agricultural return flows or percolates.
4 Solid residues resulting from the use of resources or industrial products.

Wastes from Human Life Processes

By far the greatest concern for contamination of ground waters has been directed to human wastes in the form of municipal sewage. Curiously enough, such concern has not generally been expressed over septic tank effluents discharged directly underground. At least such concern is so recent in origin that ground-water quality considerations did not prevent the use of septic tanks in urban subdivisions in the past 25 years on a scale sufficient to run the total of persons served by such systems to more than 30 million. However, from the viewpoint of contamination hazards from human wastes it matters little whether the percolating liquid comes from subsurface leaching fields or from operations involving surface application of sewage effluents, as will presently be noted.

In the practical case municipal sewage contains both domestic and industrial waste products. From the domestic fraction comes wastes from the human body, grease, ground garbage, and residues from commercial products such as soap and detergents. The industrial fraction normally includes a variety of biochemically unstable organic matter and a wide spectrum of common chemicals as well as more exotic organics and toxic ions, generally in concentrations below that critical to waste treatment processes. Therefore, in evaluating contamination hazards involved in municipal sewage the fate of several kinds of material in soil systems must be considered.

For purpose of discussion these materials may be divided into such general classes as:

1 Organic and inorganic particles, other than living organisms.
2 Microorganisms, including bacteria and viruses.
3 Chemical products of degradation of organic matter.
4 Chemicals from industrial wastes or from industrial products in commercial use.
5 Leachings from landfills.

Of this group the organic degradation products may be generated under either aerobic or anaerobic conditions and so develop a variety of intermediate products. All of the group are generated or commonly discarded by man at the earth's surface, with a few rare exceptions, and hence are initially separated from the ground water by the soil mantle of the earth. They are further separated from the user of ground water by the extent of aquifer between the point of possible entry of contaminants and point of outcrop or withdrawal of water. Further, the soil mantle of the earth is biologically active. Under these circumstances the question of manmade hazards to the ground water involves two basic considerations:

1 The nature of contaminants in each of the general classes of material.
2 The fate of each contaminant in water percolating downward through the biologically active mantle of the earth; or in water translated laterally as ground water in saturated aquifer sands and gravels.

To these may be added the question of contaminants in water moving through fractured strata or dissolution channels. However, in this latter case the "hazards" of manmade pollution may be directly assumed

from the nature of the contaminants in five classes of material listed, for while phenomena such as sedimentation adsorption, time-decay, and the like may reduce the concentration of contaminants, the hazard remains. Hazard prevention, therefore, is related to management of wastes above ground—a subject beyond the scope of this paper.

Therefore we turn to the nature of contaminants in the previously mentioned five arbitrary classes of man's wastes, and to their movement with percolating water. In this, more attention is given to what fractions get through than to the scientific aspects of removal, which is discussed elsewhere (McGauhey and others, 1966).

Organic and Inorganic Particles

The fact that ground water is derived from rain falling through an atmosphere containing dust particles and bacteria, passing through a soil mantle containing bacteria and organic and inorganic particles, and yet historically has been notable for its clarity, tells us that suspended matter is not a ground-water contaminant to be expected from man's activities. Such, indeed, is shown to be the case in numerous experiments with soils and waste waters from cities, industries and agriculture.

Micoorganisms

Bacteria: Not only has ground water resulting from percolation or moving through aquifer sands been noted for its clarity, its traditional purity is also well known. This does not mean that all ground water is uncontaminated, because the microgeology of the earth is not always favorable. Certainly, bacteria will flow with water in fissures just as readily as in pipes at similar velocities, although gravity and time are against bacterial contamination of an outcropping ground water. Thus contamination with pathogenic bacteria must always, but not in all situations, be considered as a "hazard" to ground-water quality if nondisinfected sewage effluents are carelessly managed. However, where a protective mantle of soil is involved, bacteria behave as other particulate matter and are removed by such forces as sedimentation, entrapment, and adsorption. Studies of the movement of bacteria with percolating water have been widely reported in the literature. For example, the historic work of A. M. Rawn and associates (McGauhey and others, 1966, pp. 157–158) in Los Angeles County found bacteria in sewage removed in from 3 to 7 feet of quite coarse soil. Pilot infiltration ponds at Lodi, California (McGauhey and others, 1966, p. 42) gave the same results for a fine soil. More recently, the well known Santee Project at San Diego reported the removal of coliform bacteria in 200 feet of travel of water in quite coarse gravel.

When injected directly into a water-bearing stratum, coliform organisms have been found (McGauhey and others, 1966, p. 135 and p. 180) to travel only limited distances—less than 100 feet at Richmond, California. These are but a fraction of the references that support the conclusion that under any circumstances where normal soil bacteria do not reach the ground water, man's activities do not pose a bacterial "hazard" to groundwater quality. However, where fractures or dissolution channels reach the soil surface and transport water underground, sewage disinfection is necessary if released waters are with certainty to pose no hazard to groundwater quality.

Viruses: Viruses are known to be present in sewage but until quite recent years there was no evidence in the literature relative to their movement with percolating water. Being more resistant to chlorine than are enteric bacteria, the possibility of viral contamination of ground water has long been entertained. Recently, however, studies at the Santee Project (McGauhey and others, 1966, pp. 164–165 and pp. 194–195) have shown viruses to be removed in less than 200 feet of flow through a gravel bed. These and other (McGauhey and others, 1966) data support the conclusion that viral contamination of ground water is no more of a hazard than bacterial contamination.

Chemical Products of Biodegradation

Organic solids in sewage, whether from ground garbage, vegetable and meat trimmings, or from the human body, differ from the natural contribution of organic matter to the soil only in that they are associated with man's activities and may reach the soil in varying degrees of degradation. Fundamentally they are proteinaceous in nature and under aerobic conditions oxidize to normal nitrates, sulfates, carbonates, phosphates, etc. Along the way there may be ammonia, nitrites, and similar unoxidized compounds. Under anaerobic conditions degradation products include amino acids and a considerable spectrum of intermediate compounds of notable fragrance and unpleasant taste. Organic molecules themselves are heavily adsorbed on many soils (McGauhey and others, 1966, p. 109 and p. 197); hence they behave very much as particulate matter and there is little likelihood of contamination of ground water by migrating undegraded organic matter of sewage origin. The question is then one of the degree of degradation occurring in a soil system and the nature of the products produced.

Biodegradable organic solids applied to a soil quickly develop a heavy growth of bacteria in the top centimeter or so of the soil. This serves as a reactor in which biostabilization of compounds occurs. It also acts as a clogging zone to limit the rate of infiltration. Under aerobic conditions oxidized compounds result. If it becomes anaerobic, ferric sulfide is also produced, which as a particulate matter, helps to clog the soil completely. Therefore, infiltration is essentially precluded and intermediate compounds which might cause tastes and odors and bacterial aftergrowths cannot reach the ground water.

In high rate direct injection experiments at Richmond, California, partially degraded soluble organic compounds were forced into an aquifer beyond the bacterially active zone and traveled with ground water to support bacterial life when again pumped to the surface (McGauhey and others, 1966, p. 180). Protection against such migration in soil, however, is the normal situation. For example, measurements of degradable material passing through sand and gravel columns reported by Robeck (McGauhey and others, 1966, p. 211) showed that from a septic tank effluent all BOD and 90 percent of the COD was removed.

Of the decomposition products, ammonia is notably adsorbed on soil, where it displaces calcium, magnesium, sodium and potassium ions which are then carried away by percolating water. Later the ammonia is oxidized to nitrates by microbial activity and so becomes soluble and free to move with water. Phosphates too are adsorbed and taken out in the top horizons of soil. Numerous data show that when sewage is applied to a soil the result is simply an increase in the sulfates, bicarbonates, nitrates and other anions and cations normally found in ground water. Thus in summary it may be said that contamination of ground water by degradable organics is largely confined to an increase in concentration of normal ground-water ions.

Dissolved Chemicals of Industrial and Commercial Origin

Chemicals of industrial and commercial origin may reach the earth with municipal sewage, industrial wastes, agricultural fertilization, and the use of pesticides and herbicides for a number of purposes. Prior to 1965, ABS was the principal example of commercial products used in the household which might reach the ground water with domestic sewage effluents. Although degradable in soil systems, its residence time was not always adequate to prevent migration with percolating water. Adoption of the more degradable LAS, however, removed this problem of contamination. Hence from a commercial formulation the phosphates might be expected to be adsorbed on soil and the detergent bio-degraded to an inorganic sulfate, which will travel with percolating water or with moving ground water.

Of the agricultural chemicals, commercial fertilizers are perhaps the most significant. Recently (San Francisco Chronicle, January 25, 1967) the State Health Department of California reported concentrations of nitrate of 176 mg/l in ground waters in California's San Joaquin Valley and warned against its use for young babies. The recommended (P.H.S.) maximum of 45 mg/l has been observed elsewhere (Tucker and others, 1961) in recent years to produce intoxication of livestock on high nitrogen diets.

The effect of fertilization of land can therefore involve both the displacement of alkaline ions by ammonia and the subsequent migration of nitrates derived from residual ammonia or direct application of nitrates.

Perhaps the most serious effect of man's use of water is a buildup in concentration of the salts normally found in surface waters, soils and ground water. Above all others, this seems to be the greatest of manmade hazards to ground-water quality. It begins perhaps with the concentration of salts by evaporation of water from reservoirs, canals, and industrial cooling, plus regeneration of water softeners, water distillation, etc. This concentrate is then applied to the land in irrigation where it leaches out more salts. Percolating downward or flowing as return flows in open channels, some of it percolates to the ground water. Heavy use of ground water recycles an appreciable amount of water and the net result in the semi-arid West is a continuous increase of the salinity of the ground-water resource. The hazard of manmade contamination here is that although we have learned how to prevent the poisoning of land from our irrigation practice, we may go the way of Mesopotamia by poisoning the water instead.*

In addition to the buildup of normal salts, industrial wastes contribute a hazard to ground-water quality by delivering a vast and ever changing spectrum of ions and compounds which move with percolating water. Some of the most commonly deplored are phenols, picric acid, metal ions such as Fe, Mn, Cr, oil field brines, oils, tar residues, weed killer wastes, and a host of miscellaneous chemicals. Instances of long dis-

---

* See "Salt and Silt in Ancient Mesopotamian Agriculture," Selection 28.

tance travel of such materials are to be found in the literature. Control of discharges is the normal method of preventing ground-water contamination with industrial wastes, but it must be recognized that the wastes from many industrial processes always represent a hazard to ground water through accidental spill, carelessness, or deliberate discharge, as well as through ignorance of the behavior of the waste from some newly developed processes.

Commercial use of industry's products presents a varied picture. Attention has already been called to detergents and commercial fertilizers. Of much concern today are the so-called exotic organics—the refractory compounds—of which pesticides and herbicides are the most cited example. While a great deal of speculation exists concerning the ability of pesticides to move with percolating water, and most of the literature deals with surface-water contamination, there is some evidence of hazard to ground waters. Walton (Proceedings, National Conference on Water Pollution, 1960) of the U.S.P.H.S. noted a case near Henderson, Colorado, where ground water contaminated by 2, 4-D from arsenals traveled 3 miles in eight years to affect crops and eventually seriously affect some 60 square miles. At Montebello, California, seepage of 2, 4-D from a manufacturing plant persisted in water for five years after the plant ceased operation.

Leachings from Solid Waste Fills

When the soil mantle of the earth is looked upon as the infiltrative surface from which ground water derives, it is evident that the necessary concentration of solid wastes in landfills creates a local pocket of potential infection overlying the ground water. Therefore, man's activity in managing his solid wastes must be examined in relation to ground-water contamination.

A hazard to ground-water quality might be created by landfill both directly and indirectly. A direct hazard exists, except in unusual geological situations, in the disposal of old cylinder oil, cleaning fluid, and miscellaneous liquid chemicals within a dump. Although good practice, and local ordinances, prohibits such discharges, one need not become particularly familiar with dump operation to observe that it does occur.

Assuming that contact between ground water and fill material is prohibited—a quite generally valid assumption—an indirect hazard exists in most landfill operations. This is the possibility that poor operation will permit rain water or flood waters to enter the fill and so dissolve soluble dry chemicals which might be present, leach iron and various earth minerals from incinerator ashes, pick up soluble fractions of organic degradation and transport them to the ground-water table. Good operation, involving surface drainage of the finished fill, is unfortunately not enough to remove this indirect threat. Cracking of the fill cover due to shrinkage of the fill, poor maintenance of the finished fill during the first decade or two after its completion, and seismic disturbances are among the ways in which avenues of entry of water may be opened with time.

More recent studies (In-situ investigation of movements of gases produced from decomposing refuse, 1966) of diffusion of gases from fills into the surrounding soil show the possibility of carbon dioxide from the decomposing fill material becoming dissolved in percolating water and so increasing its aggressiveness to the primary rocks from which the content of calcium and magnesium bicarbonates in ground water is normally derived.

Summary

Ground water may derive a wide variety of materials from man's waste producing activities. Chemicals characteristic of normal ground waters may be increased in concentration from the degradation of organic solids in human and industrial wastes, and from the storage, transport, and use of water, particularly in irrigation and industry. Similar compounds might come from leaching of a solid waste landfill. Toxic, odorous, and bad tasting compounds may reach the ground water with industrial wastes, or with municipal effluents containing such wastes or the residues of industrial products used in commerce. The variety of such wastes is endless but includes all types of liquid or soluble chemicals. Particular concern is felt for the pesticide residues. Chemical residues of various nature may come also from their illegal disposal in landfills or dumps. Disease producing bacteria or viruses are no particular hazard, nor is particulate matter which might produce turbidity. However,

if fractures or fissures bypass the biologically active mantle of the earth and lead water directly from the surface to the ground water or spring, microorganisms may join the soluble chemicals as contaminants.

In general, all of man's waste producing activities would create "manmade hazards" to ground water if accident, carelessness, or lack of vigilance and constraint were permitted to prevail. The most serious current hazard of man's activities lies in the buildup of salinity of the ground water to levels inimical to all beneficial uses to which such water is put.

References Cited

In-Situ investigation of movements of gases produced from decomposing refuse. 1966. Fifth and Final Report. Engineering-Science, Inc., prepared for State Water Quality Control Board, November.

McGauhey, P. H., R. B. Krone and J. H. Winneberger. 1966. Soil mantle as a wastewater treatment system: review of literature. SERL Report 66-7. Sanit. Eng.

Research Lab., Univ. of Calif., Berkeley, September.

Proceedings, National Conference on Water Pollution. 1960. USPHS, Washington, D. C., December 12-14.

Tucker, J. M., D. R. Cordy, L. J. Berry, W. A. Harvey and T. C. Fuller. 1961. Nitrate poisoning in livestock. Circular 506. California Agricultural Experiment Station Extension Service, Univ. of Calif.

ADDITIONAL REFERENCES

Bergstrom, R. E. 1968. Disposal of wastes; scientific and administrative considerations. *Illinois Geological Survey, Environmental Geology Notes,* No. 20. 12 pp. Reviews the impact of various kinds of waste disposal on ground water.

Committee for Environmental Information, Scientific Division. 1969. Underground nuclear testing. *Environment* 11(6):2-13, 41-53.

Horton, J. H., and R. H. Hawkins. 1965. Flow path of rain from the soil surface to the water table. *Soil Science* 100:377-383.

Mallman, W. L., and W. N. Mack. 1961. Biological contamination of ground water. *R. A. Taft Sanitary Engineering Center Technical Report* W61-5, pp. 35-43.

McGuinness, C. L. 1963. The role of ground water in the national water situation. *U.S. Geological Survey Water-Supply Paper* 1800. 1121 pp.

Mechem, O. E., and J. H. Garrett. 1963. Deep injection disposal wells for liquid toxic waste. *Proc. Amer. Soc. Civil Engin., Jour. Construction Division,* pp. 111-121.

Mink, J. F. 1962. Excessive irrigation and the soils and ground water of Oahu, Hawaii. *Science* 135:672-673.

Muckel, D. C. 1955. Pumping water so as to avoid overdraft. Pp. 294-301 in *Water, Yearbook of agriculture, 1955.* U.S. Department of Agriculture.

Nace, R. L. 1960. Water management, agriculture, and ground-water supplies. *U.S. Geological Survey Circular* 415. 12 pp.

Navone, R., J. A. Harmon, and C. F. Voyles. 1963. Nitrogen content of ground water in Southern California. *J. Am. Water Works Assoc.* 55:615-618.

Parker, G. G. 1955. The encroachment of salt water into fresh. Pp. 615-635 in *Water, Yearbook of agriculture, 1955.* U.S. Department of Agriculture.

Piper, A. M. 1969. Disposal of liquid wastes by injection underground—neither myth nor millennium. *U.S. Geological Survey Circular* 631. 15 pp.

Stewart, B. A., F. G. Viets, Jr., and G. L. Hutchinson. 1968. Agriculture's effect on nitrate pollution of groundwater. *Journal of Soil and Water Conservation* 23(1):13–15.

Thomas, H. E.   1951.   *Conservation of ground water.* New York: McGraw-Hill.   321 pp.

Thomas, H. E.   1955.   Underground sources of our water. Pp. 62–78 in *Water, Yearbook of agriculture, 1955.* U.S. Department of Agriculture.

Thomas, H. E.   1956.   Changes in quantities and qualities of ground and surface waters. Pp. 542–563 in *Man's role in changing the face of the earth,* ed. by W. L. Thomas, Jr.   Chicago: University of Chicago Press.

Thomas, H. E., and L. B. Leopold.   1964. Ground water in North America. *Science* 143(3610):1001–1006.

Todd, D. K.   1959.   *Ground water hydrology.* New York: Wiley.   336 pp.

Walker, T. R.   1961.   Ground water contamination in the Rocky Mountain Arsenal area, Denver, Colorado. *Geol. Soc. Amer. Bull.* 72:489–494.

EUTROPHICATION OF THE ST. LAWRENCE GREAT LAKES

ALFRED M. BEETON

Most of man's effects on rivers and ground water, discussed in the previous four selections, do not simply disappear downstream or underground. Rather, pollutants—and with them problems—commonly accumulate in lakes or estuaries that receive the contaminated water.

Nearly all lakes naturally change from a nutrient-poor ("oligotrophic") to a nutrient-rich ("eutrophic") condition gradually through time. But water pollution by man can greatly accelerate this aging process of eutrophication. Lake Erie has become a classic example. Much of the nitrate which is applied as inorganic nitrogen fertilizer on the 30,000 square miles of farmland in the Lake Erie basin washes into the lake. The lake also receives phosphates at a rate of 20,000 pounds daily, 8,000 pounds from the Detroit area alone. Household detergents and road salt additives are major sources of the phosphates. The nitrates and phosphates are important plant nutrients and their present quantities overfertilize the lakes. One pound of phosphates can grow 700 pounds of algae, provided other nutrients are available too. Huge masses of algae bloom in Lake Erie each year. When the algae die they sink to the bottom, consuming oxygen in the water as they decay and releasing nutrients for another cycle of plant growth. In late summers a 2,600 square-mile area of the lake has no oxygen available within 10 feet of the bottom for other aquatic life. This fertilization, decrease in oxygen, and increase in temperature have helped to bring about gross changes in the other aquatic life, including important commercial and sports fishes (see Selection 44).

Alfred M. Beeton (b. 1927) has been professor of zoology and associate director of the Center for Great Lake Studies at the University of Wisconsin, Milwaukee, since 1966. He holds three academic degrees from the University of Michigan (Ph.D., 1958). Beeton's major research interests and publications have focused on the limnology of the Great Lakes, including their eutrophication, and on the behavioral physiology of crustaceans.

This selection is abridged by permission of the author and reprinted by permission from *Limnology and Oceanography* 10(2):240–254, 1965; it is based on a presentation at the symposium on "Recent trends in ecological research in the Great Lakes," sponsored by the Ecological Society of America, American Association for Advancement of Science meetings, Cleveland, December 27, 1963.

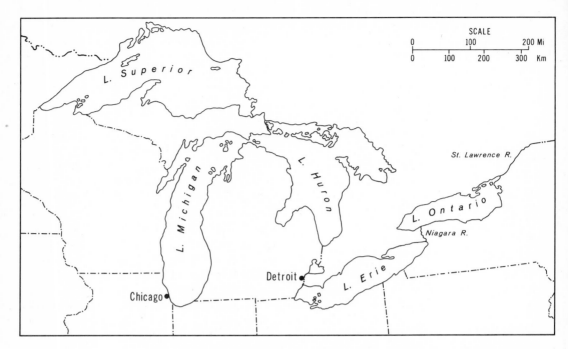

This selection examines how man's activity has changed the physical, chemical, and biological characteristics of Lake Erie and the other Great Lakes. Several changes commonly associated with eutrophication in small lakes now are evident in all of the Great Lakes except Lake Superior. There has been a progressive increase in the concentrations of various major chemical ions and total dissolved solids in all of the lakes except Lake Superior. Taken together, the data demonstrate that, after Lake Erie, Lakes Ontario and Michigan are most threatened. Scientists think that the physiochemical deterioration is largely reversible. If all pollution was stopped, the flush of incoming water provided in the hydrologic cycle would nearly cleanse Lake Erie in five to six years—the shortest time of any of the lakes. Lakes Michigan and Superior would require the longest time, about 100 years, with Lakes Ontario and Huron needing several decades to cleanse.

However, the future for these lakes and others with densely settled watersheds is not bright. Technological advances frequently impose new environmental stress. For example, thermal pollution, especially from nuclear reactors, is burgeoning. Another example demonstrates that even Lake Superior, with its sparsely settled basin, is not immune to new pollutants; the Reserve Mining Company has been dumping 60,000 tons of waste rock into the lake north of Duluth each day for the last fifteen years (*New York Times*, February 15, 1970). This rock is waste that remains after taconite has been crushed and flakes of iron have been removed. Twenty years ago the development of the process for extracting iron from taconite revived the entire Mesabi Iron Range. But the mining waste has clouded the lake's water and covered part of its bottom, affecting fish and the natural beauty of the lake.

(Editor's comment)

Evidence of appreciable change in the biota and physicochemical conditions in Lake Erie (Beeton 1961) and speculation on possible changes in the other lakes, stemming from increases in total dissolved solids (Ayers 1962; Rawson 1951), have directed attention to eutrophication of the Great Lakes. The question does not concern the existence of eutrophication, because all lakes are aging and there is no reason to believe that the Great Lakes are exceptional. Of greatest consequence is the possibility of detection and perhaps even measurement of the rate of eutrophication of these large lakes. Important also is the effect of mankind on the normal rate of eutrophication.

Accelerated rates of aging due to man's activity have been detected in a number of lakes (Hasler 1947). The classic example is the Untersee of Lake Zürich, which urban effluents have changed from an oligotrophic to an eutrophic lake in a relatively short time. Recently, studies of Lake Washington at Seattle (Edmondson, Anderson, and Peterson 1956), and Fure Lake, Denmark (Berg et al. 1958) have demonstrated that these relatively large lakes are undergoing accelerated eutrophication due to man's influence. None of these lakes, however, is large in comparison with any of the St. Lawrence Great Lakes.

Present Trophic Nature of the Great Lakes

The meaning of eutrophication seems to vary according to the special interests of the individual. Limnologists agree that eutrophication is part of the aging of a body of water and implies an increase in the nutrient content of the waters. Most lakes change gradually from a nutrient-poor, *oligotrophic*, to a nutrient-rich, *eutrophic*, condition. At this point agreement ends in arguments on lake classification. Although the terms eutrophic, mesotrophic, and oligotrophic are used freely by limnologists and are well established in the literature, it is difficult to determine precisely what is meant by them. Various in-

vestigators have attached considerable significance to one or more of the following criteria in classifying lakes: abundance or species of plankton or both; benthic organisms; chemical characteristics; sediment types; distribution of dissolved oxygen; productivity; fish populations; and morphometry and morphology of the lake basin. Lake classification has been closely related to regional limnology and has been developed primarily from observations on small lakes. It is not surprising, then, to find that the Great Lakes do not fit readily into the various classification schemes that have been proposed. Rawson (1955, 1956) reviewed the problem of classifying large lakes and considered certain characteristics of the St. Lawrence Great Lakes.

Despite the troublesome problems of lake classification, an attempt should be made to classify the Great Lakes for discussion of their eutrophication and to facilitate comparison with other lakes. A better classification surely is needed since Lake Erie, for example, has been called oligotrophic, mesotrophic, and eutrophic by various investigators over the past 30 years.

PHYSICOCHEMICAL CONDITIONS

Morphometry, transparency, total dissolved solids, conductivity, and dissolved oxygen content of the water appear to be useful in lake classification. On the basis of these five physical and chemical factors, two of the lakes would be classified as oligotrophic, one as tending toward the mesotrophic, and two as eutrophic. The low specific conductance and total dissolved solids, and the high transparency and dissolved oxygen of Lakes Huron and Superior agree with the commonly accepted characteristics of oligotrophy (Table 19.1). Lakes Erie and Ontario have the high specific conductance and total dissolved solids and, of special significance, the low concentration of dissolved oxygen in the hypolimnion [i.e., water below the lake's thermocline that is of nearly uniform temperature] characteristic of eutrophic lakes. Data were not available on the oxygen content of

TABLE 19.1 Physical and chemical characteristics of the Great Lakes*

LAKE	MEAN DEPTH (M)	TRANSPARENCY (AVERAGE SECCHI DISC DEPTH, M)	TOTAL DISSOLVED SOLIDS (PPM)	SPECIFIC CONDUCTANCE (μMHOS AT 18C)	DISSOLVED OXYGEN
Oligotrophic	> 20	High	Low: around 100 ppm or less	< 200	High, all depths all year
Superior	148.4	10	60	78.7	Saturated, all depths
Huron	59.4	9.5	110	168.3	Saturated, all depths
Michigan	84.1	6	150	225.8	Near saturation, all depths
Eutrophic	< 20	Low	High: > 100	> 200	Depletion in hypolimnion: < 70% saturation
Ontario	86.3	5.5	185	272.3	50 to 60% saturation in deep water in winter
Erie, average for lake	17.7	4.5	180	241.8	
Central basin	18.5	5.0	—	—	< 10% saturation, hypolimnion
Eastern basin	24.4	5.7	—	—	40 to 50% saturation, hypolimnion

* Criteria designating lake types are based primarily on factors considered important by Rawson (1960); specific conductance limits from Dunn (1954); dissolved oxygen criteria, Thienemann (1928). Data from Bureau of Commercial Fisheries except transparency and dissolved oxygen for Lake Ontario (Rodgers 1962).

the hypolimnetic waters of Lake Ontario, but it is even more significant that the deep waters had a low percentage saturation of dissolved oxygen under essentially isothermal conditions. The transparencies of Lakes Erie and Ontario are not especially low in comparison with many small lakes, but in comparison to Lakes Huron and Superior, their average transparencies are indeed low. Lake Michigan falls between the other lakes from the standpoint of specific conductance, total dissolved solids, and transparency. The dissolved oxygen content of Lake Michigan water is near saturation, however, at all depths. On occasion, water in the deeper areas has a saturation between 70 and 80%, but these low values are infrequent.

BIOLOGICAL CHARACTERISTICS

The biological characteristics of all the Great Lakes, except Lake Erie, may place them in the oligotrophic category (Table 19.2). This classification surely holds for Lakes Huron, Michigan, and Superior, but is uncertain for Lake Ontario, where recent and detailed information is lacking on benthos and plankton.

Oligotrophic lakes of the north have been considered salmonid lakes. It is not implied that salmonids* do not occur in eutrophic lakes, but, when present, they are not the dominant fishes and usually they have a restricted bathymetric distribution. Salmonids dominate the fish populations in all of the lakes except Lake Erie, although in Lake Ontario ictalurids [catfish] and percids [includes perch and perch pike] are almost as important in the commercial fishery as salmonids (Table 19.2). Three native species (formerly four) of salmonids occur in Lake Erie, but during most of the year they are restricted to the eastern basin. Warmwater fishes dominate the fish fauna of Lake Erie now, including the eastern basin.

Considerable controversy exists over the value of plankton in lake classification. Rawson's (1956) ranking of algae in order of their occurrence from oligotrophy to eutrophy has been used, in part, in Table 19.2, since he worked on lakes similar in many ways to the St. Lawrence Great Lakes. On the basis of plankton abundance and the dominant species of phytoplankton, Lakes Huron, Michigan, and Superior would be

* A suborder of fish that includes salmon and trout.

considered oligotrophic and Lake Erie eutrophic.

The combined biological, chemical, and physical characteristics of Lakes Huron and Superior clearly are those of oligotrophy. The biota and the high dissolved oxygen content of the deep hypolimnetic waters characterize Lake Michigan as oligotrophic but contrariwise, the high content of total dissolved solids indicates a trend toward mesotrophy. Lake Ontario, as a mesotrophic lake, retains the biota of an oligotrophic lake, but the physicochemical characteristics are those of eutrophy. The chemical content of the waters of Lake Ontario is closely similar to that of Lake Erie, since the main inflow to Lake Ontario is from Lake Erie via the Niagara River. The trophic nature of On-

TABLE 19.2 Biological characteristics of the Great Lakes*

LAKE	BOTTOM FAUNA AND DOMINANT MIDGES	DOMINANT FISHES	PLANKTON ABUNDANCE
Oligotrophic	*Orthocladius-Tanytarsus* type (*Hydrobaenus-Calopsectra*)	Salmonids	Low
Superior	*Pontoporeia affinis* *Mysis relicta* *Hydrobaenus*	Salmonids	Very Low
Huron	*Pontoporeia affinis*‡ *Mysis relicta* *Hydrobaenus* *Calopsectra*	Salmonids	Low
Michigan	*Pontoporeia affinis*§ *Mysis relicta* *Hydrobaenus*	Salmonids	Low
Ontario	*Pontoporeia affinis* *Mysis relicta*	Salmonids, ictalurids, percids	—
Eutrophic	*Tendipes plumosus* type	Yellow perch, pike, black bass	High
Erie Central basin	*Tendipes plumosus*	Yellow perch, smelt, freshwater drum	High
Eastern basin	*Pontoporeia affinis* few *Calopsectra*	Yellow perch, smelt, few salmonids	High

* Criteria for lake types as follows: tendipedid larvae, Brundin (1958); fish and plankton abundance, Welch (1952); dominant phytoplankton, Rawson (1956).
‡ Data from Teter (1960).
§ Data from Merna (1960).
‖ Refers to *Melosira islandica-ambigua* type.

tario has been determined to a large extent by the chemical history of Lake Erie waters. Lake Ontario, and perhaps Lake Michigan, would be eutrophic except for the large volumes of deep waters. Even in Lake Erie, the eastern basin has components of a fauna associated with oligotrophy and sufficient deep, cold, oxygenated water to maintain this fauna. These conditions exist despite the highly eutrophic nature of the central basin (flow through the lake is from west to east).

Evidence of Eutrophication

The present trophic nature of the Great Lakes is to a considerable degree the result of their gradual aging since formation. Evidence is accumulating, however, which indicates that human activity is greatly accelerating the eutrophication of all of the lakes but Lake Superior. This evidence is most spectacular for Lake Erie. A difficult problem is one of finding acceptable indices of change.

Various criteria have been used by different investigators to demonstrate eutrophication. Hasler (1947) compiled information on 37 lakes affected by enrichment from domestic and agricultural drainage. Among the changes in many of these lakes were: the dramatic decline and disappearance of salmonid fishes and increases in populations of coarse fish; changes in the species composition of plankton; and blooms of blue-green algae. As the Untersee of Lake Zürich changed from a salmonid to a coarse-fish lake, plankton abundance increased, different species became dominant in the plankton, transparency decreased, and the dissolved oxygen content of the deep waters decreased. At the same time, the concentrations of chlorides and organic matter increased (Minder 1918, 1938, 1943). Minder (1938) attributed the increase and changes in the plankton to the growing amount of phosphorus and nitrogen from domestic sources. Declines in the hypolimnetic oxygen, decrease in transparency, and increases in the abundance of plankton were cited by

Edmondson, Anderson, and Peterson (1956) as evidence of eutrophication of Lake Washington. They held this increased productivity to be the result of growing discharges of treated sewage into the lake. Similar changes were observed in Fure Lake by Berg et al. (1958). Species composition of the phytoplankton changed, transparency decreased, dissolved oxygen concentrations became low in the hypolimnion, and conductivity rose. These changes have occurred during the last 40 to 50 years. Berg (Berg et al. 1958, p. 176) stated, "The cause is an increased introduction of material with the sewage."

Our knowledge of the limnology of the Great Lakes in earlier years is seriously deficient. Observations useful for tracing changes in the Great Lakes are mostly limited to water-quality data, commercial fishing records, and a few observations on plankton. The fishing records and chemical data have the longest history and are the most reliable.

CHEMICAL CHARACTERISTICS

Chemical data representative of the lakes proper were compiled from many sources [see References]. Data on magnesium are not included because no significant change in concentration could be detected in any of the lakes. Broadly speaking, there has been no significant change in Lake Superior. Other lakes in order of increasing chemical change are Huron, Michigan, Erie, and Ontario.

Lake Superior. The indicated slight downward trend in total dissolved solids in Lake Superior is not significant and concentrations have remained at approximately 60 ppm throughout the years (Figure 19.1). Calcium, chloride, and sulfate concentrations also have remained the same since 1886 (Figure 19.2). The close agreement among analyses of Lake Superior water by various individuals using different methods and techniques is unusual. The slight decrease in the sodium-plus-potassium content of the water probably is not real, because present analytical methods differ substantially from former ones. The uniformity in the chemical analyses here lends confidence to the reliability of the chemical data for the other lakes.

Lake Huron. The slight increase in total dissolved solids in this lake is probably real, since about 30% of the inflow to Lake Huron is from Lake Michigan, where dissolved solids have risen significantly (Figure 19.1). The sodium-plus-potassium content has remained about the same over the years of record. Some rather low values were reported for these ions during the 1930's, but the 1890–1910 data agree with recent determinations (Figure 19.2). An increase of 3 ppm in chloride appears to have occurred during the past 30 years. The major source of chlorides within the Lake Huron watershed is in the Saginaw Valley, where considerable quantities of brine are pumped to the surface in the oil fields and for use in the chemical industry. The increased influx of brine during the past 30 years may account for most of the increase in chloride in the lake. Sulfate concentrations have increased 7.5 ppm in the past 54 years.

Lake Michigan. Total dissolved solids have increased about 20 ppm since 1895 (Figure 19.1). Calcium has remained constant (Figure 19.2). The greatest increase in any ion in Lake Michigan has been that of sulfate, which has risen 12 ppm since 1877. The chloride concentrations have risen slowly but steadily by 4 ppm. The sodium-plus-potassium content has not changed since 1907 but it exceeds that extant in 1877–1900. The determinations before 1907 may be too low, since they are below those reported for Lakes Huron and Superior. If, however, these early determinations are reasonably accurate, the increase that occurred between 1877 and 1907 may be attributed to population growth in the Chicago area. The population of Chicago exceeded 1 million in 1890 and the Chicago Sanitary Canal, to divert sewage from the lake, was not completed until 1900. Consequently, during these early years

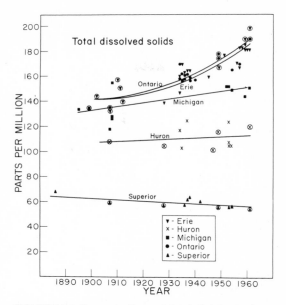

FIGURE 19.1 Concentrations of total dissolved solids in the Great Lakes. Circled points are averages of 12 or more determinations. Data are from sources presented in the bibliography.

considerable amounts of raw sewage entered the lake at Chicago.

Lake Erie. Total dissolved solids, calcium, chloride, sodium-plus-potassium, and sulfate all increased significantly in Lake Erie during the past 50 years. Total dissolved solids have risen by almost 50 ppm (Figure 19.1). Increases of approximately 8, 16, 5, and 11 ppm have taken place in the concentrations of calcium, chloride, sodium-plus-potassium, and sulfate, respectively (Figure 19.2).

Lake Ontario. The rate of increase in total dissolved solids in Lake Ontario has been the same as in Lake Erie. This rate was similar to that occurring in Lake Michigan prior to the late 1920's but has been higher than in Lake Michigan since about 1930 (Figure 19.1). Close agreement of chemical data for Lake Ontario for 1854 and 1884 with those for 1907 indicates that the chemical characteristics of the water were altered little during this period (Figure 19.2). Calcium, chloride, and sodium-plus-potassium increased to the same extent as noted in Lake Erie since 1910. Sulfate concentrations in-

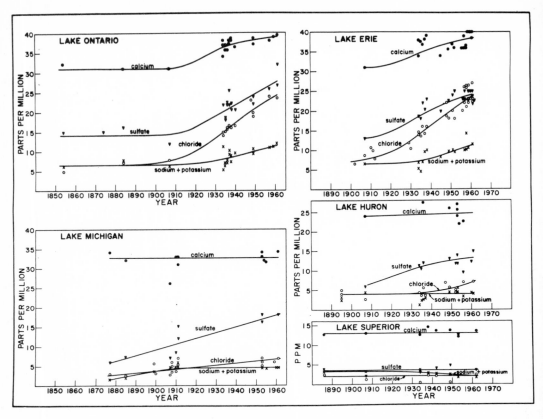

FIGURE 19.2 Changes in the chemical characteristics of Great Lakes waters. Data for Lake Erie, 1958; Lake Huron, 1956; Lake Michigan, 1954, 1955, 1961; Lake Ontario, 1961; Lake Superior, 1952, 1953, 1961, 1962 are from the Ann Arbor Biological Laboratory, U.S. Bureau of Commercial Fisheries. Other data are from sources presented in the bibliography.

creased by 13 ppm, which is somewhat higher than in Lake Erie.

Summary of chemical changes. Changes in the chemical characteristics of Lake Ontario have closely paralleled those in Lake Erie. Prior to 1910 the chemical characteristics of the two lakes were similar and conditions in Lake Erie were probably the same as indicated by 1854 and 1884 analyses of Lake Ontario water. Concentrations of calcium, chloride, sodium-plus-potassium, and sulfate have been somewhat higher in Lake Ontario than in Lake Erie during the past 50 years. The greater concentrations of salts in Lake Ontario probably can be attributed to growth of the Toronto, Hamilton, and Rochester metropolitan areas and the in-

dustrial expansion along the upper Niagara River.

Lakes Erie and Ontario are the only lakes in which calcium increased materially. Increases in sulfate have been significant in all of the lakes except Superior. The 11 ppm and 13 ppm increases in Lakes Erie and Ontario have taken place in 30 years, whereas the rise of 12 ppm in Lake Michigan has been more gradual over a period of 84 years. The sulfate change in Lake Huron parallels that in Lake Michigan and may have resulted largely from the inflow of Lake Michigan waters. The degree of change in the chloride content of Lakes Erie and Ontario is similar to that for sulfate, but chloride has not increased as much as sulfate in Lakes Huron and Michigan.

PLANKTON

Few plankton data are available for Lakes Huron, Ontario, and Superior, especially for earlier years. Some rather extensive plankton data do exist, however, for Lakes Erie and Michigan.

Lake Michigan. Studies of Lake Michigan phytoplankton by Briggs (1872), Thomas and Chase (1886), Eddy (1927), Ahlstrom (1936), Damann (1945), and Williams (1962) show that the diatom species dominant 90 years ago have maintained their importance. The relative abundance and occurrence of individual species give no evidence of change in the phytoplankton.

Lake Erie. Some significant changes have been observed in the plankton of Lake Erie. Evidently copepods and especially cladocerans have shown a marked increase in abundance since 1939 (Bradshaw 1964). A copepod *Diaptomus siciloides*, which was reported as "incidental" in Lake Erie plankton in 1929 and 1930 (Wright 1955), is now one of the two most abundant diaptomids (Davis 1962).

Changes in Lake Erie

Several important changes in Lake Erie have not been detected in the other lakes; all indicate an accelerated rate of eutrophication.

FISH POPULATIONS*

The abundance of several commercially important fishes in Lake Erie has changed markedly during the past 40 years (statistical data below are from Baldwin and Saalfeld, 1962). The fish populations of all of the lakes have changed but most changes, except in Lake Erie, have been the direct or indirect consequence of the build-up in sea lamprey populations (Smith 1964). The sea lamprey has not been

* Selection 44 discusses changes in the Great Lakes fisheries in detail, and offers further explanations (*editor's note*).

important in Lake Erie, where few of the tributaries offer suitable spawning conditions.

The lake herring or cisco contributed around 20 million pounds (9 million kg) annually and as much as 48.8 million pounds (22.1 million kg) to the commercial catch (U.S. and Canada) prior to 1925. In 1925, the production declined to 5.8 million pounds (2.6 million kg) and continued to decrease. The take has amounted to a fraction of that since the early 1930's, except for landings of more than 2 million pounds (about 1 million kg) in 1936 and 1937 and a production of 16.2 million pounds (7.4 million kg) in 1946. The total production was only 7,000 pounds (3,200 kg) in 1962.

The whitefish fishery has been at an all-time low since 1948. The 1962 catch was 13,000 pounds (6,000 kg), whereas production had been 2 million pounds (1 million kg) or more for many years.

The sauger was contributing 1 million pounds (500,000 kg) or more to the commercial production prior to 1946. The catch has not reached 0.5 million pounds (0.22 million kg) since 1945 and has declined progressively since 1952. Production has been only 1 to 4 thousand pounds (450–1,800 kg) in recent years.

The walleye production increased during the 1940's and 1950's to reach 15.4 million pounds (7 million kg) in 1956. Production has decreased since 1958 and recently it has amounted to less than 1 million pounds (450,000 kg).

The commercial catch of blue pike has dropped disastrously. The production fluctuated around an average of about 15 million pounds (6.8 million kg) for many years. The landings dropped to 1.4 million pounds (640,000 kg) in 1958, to 79,000 pounds (36,000 kg) in 1959, and to only 1,000 pounds (450 kg) in 1962. Of the few blue pike caught in 1963, most were more than 10 years old.

The total production of all species in Lake Erie continues to be around 50 million pounds (22.7 million kig), but only because more freshwater drum (sheepshead), carp, yellow perch, and smelt are being caught than in the past. The major factor in the decline in the commercial catch of the more desirable species has been their failure to reproduce.

BOTTOM FAUNA

The changes in the species composition of the bottom fauna of the area west of the islands in Lake Erie have been sweeping. Carr and Hiltunen [1965] have shown that few of the formerly abundant mayfly nymphs (*Hexagenia*) now inhabit this area and that tubificids [sludge worms] are far more abundant now than 30 years ago (Figure 19.3).

Midge larvae and tubificids have increased and mayflies have decreased also among the

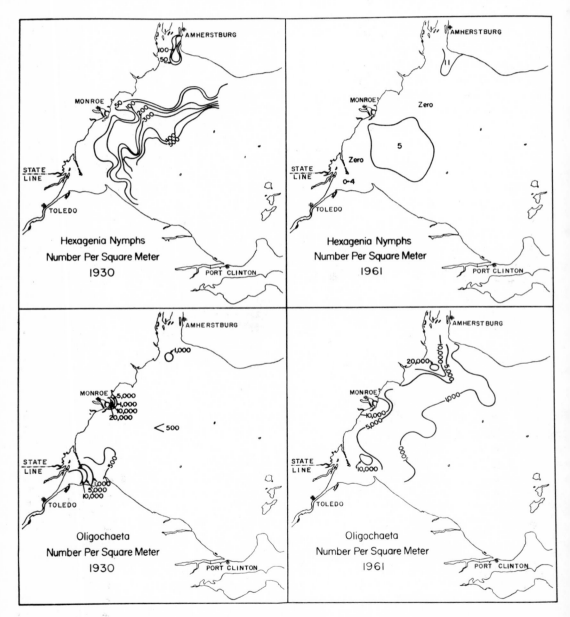

Figure 19.3 Distribution and abundance of *Hexagenia* [mayfly] nymphs and oligochaetes [sludge worms] in western Lake Erie, 1930 and 1961.

islands and in the western part of the central basin (Beeton 1961).

DISSOLVED OXYGEN

Synoptic surveys of Lake Erie in 1959 and 1960 have demonstrated that low dissolved oxygen concentrations (3 ppm or less) appear in about 70% of the hypolimnetic waters of the central basin during late summer (Beeton 1963). Scattered observations of some relatively low dissolved oxygen concentrations have been made during the past 33 years. The information we have indicates that the severity of depletion is more frequent and greater now than in the past and probably affects a more extensive area (Carr 1962).

Conclusion

The chemical content of the water in all of the Great Lakes except Lake Superior has changed in some measure. The biota also has changed in Lake Michigan and especially Lake Erie. These changes, remarkable for such large lakes, are those characteristic of eutrophication in smaller lakes and have come about over the relatively short time of 50 to 60 years. Man's activities clearly have

accelerated the rate of eutrophication. This rate has been greatest in Lakes Erie, Ontario, and Michigan and these lakes have had the largest population growth within their drainage areas. An indication of the growth of population comes from census data for the northeast central states; the population there increased from 4.5 million to 16 million between 1850 and 1900, and by 1960 the population was 36.3 million. The rate of population growth increased sharply after 1910. The substantial increases in the chemical content of the waters of Lakes Erie and Ontario also have appeared since 1910. The increases have been greatest for chloride and sulfate, both of which are conspicuous in domestic and industrial wastes, whereas magnesium concentrations have not changed measurably. Most of the magnesium comes from the limestones in the Lake Michigan basin; the stability of magnesium concentrations, therefore, indicates no appreciable change in the erosion of these deposits. The population along Lake Superior always has been sparse. The population along Lake Huron has been far less than on Lakes Michigan, Erie, and Ontario. Most changes in the open-lake waters of Lake Huron have resulted from the inflow of Lake Michigan water.

References

Ahlstrom, E. H. 1936. The deep-water plankton of Lake Michigan, exclusive of the Crustacea. Trans. Am. Microscop. Soc., **55:** 286–299.

*Allen, H. E. 1964. Chemical characteristic of south-central Lake Huron. Great Lakes Res. Div., Inst. Sci. and Tech., Univ. Mich., Publ. No. 11, p. 45–53.

Ayers, J. C. 1962. Great Lakes waters, their circulation and physical and chemical characteristics. Am. Assoc. Advan. Sci., Publ. No. 71, p. 71–89.

*Bading, G. A. 1909. Water conditions at Milwaukee. Lake Michigan Water Comm., Rept. No. 1, p. 36–39.

Baldwin, N. S., and R. W. Saalfeld. 1962. Commercial fish production in the Great Lakes 1867–1960. Great Lakes Fish. Comm., Tech. Rept. No. 3. 166p.

*Barnard, H. E., and J. H. Brewster. 1909. The sanitary condition of the southern end of Lake Michigan,

bordering Lake County, Indiana. Lake Michigan Water Comm., Rept. No. 1, p. 193–266.

*Bartow, E., and L. I. Birdsall. 1911. Composition and treatment of Lake Michigan water. Lake Michigan Water Comm., Rept. No. 2, p. 69–86.

Beeton, A. M. 1961. Environmental changes in Lake Erie. Trans. Am. Fisheries Soc., **90:** 153–159.

_____. 1963. Limnological survey of Lake Erie 1959 and 1960. Great Lakes Fish. Comm., Tech. Rept. No. 6. 32 p.

*_____, J. H. Johnson, and S. H. Smith. 1959. Lake Superior limnological data. U.S. Fish Wildlife Serv., Spec. Sci. Rept. Fisheries No. 297. 177 p.

Berg, K., K. Andersen, T. Christensen, F. Ebert, E. Fjerdingstad, C. Holmquist, K. Korsgaard, G. Lange, J. M. Lyshede, H. Mathiesen, G. Nygaard, S. Olsen, C. V. Otterstrøm, U. Røen, A. Skadhauge, E. Steemann Nielsen. 1958. Investigations on Fure Lake

* Sources of data used in preparing Figures 19.1 and 19.2.

1950–54. Limnological studies on cultural influences. Folia Limnol. Scandinavica, 10(1958). 189 p.

*Birge, E. A., and C. Juday. No date. The organic content of the water of Lake Erie. Supplemental data to "A limnological survey of western Lake Erie with special reference to pollution," by Stillman Wright. Ohio Div. Wildlife. Unpublished manuscript. 281 p.

*Bowles, J. T-B. 1909. Investigation of typhoid fever epidemic at Sheboygan, Wisconsin. Lake Michigan Water Comm., Rept. No. 1, p. 90–95.

Bradshaw, A. S. 1964. The crustacean zoo-plankton picture: Lake Erie 1939–49–59; Cayuga 1910–51–61. Verhandl. Intern. Ver. Limnol., 15: 700–708.

Briggs, S. A. 1872. The Diatomaceae of Lake Michigan. The Lens, 1: 41–44.

Brundin, L. 1958. The bottom faunistical lake type system. Verhandl. Intern. Ver. Limnol., 13: 288–297.

Carr, J. F. 1962. Dissolved oxygen in Lake Erie, past and present. Great Lakes Res. Div., Inst. Sci. and Tech., Univ. Mich., Publ. No. 9, p. 1–14.

Carr, J. F., and J. K. Hiltunen. 1965. Changes in the bottom fauna of western Lake Erie from 1930 to 1961. Limnol. Oceanog. 10(4):551–569.

Chandler, D. C. 1940. Limnological studies of western Lake Erie. I. Plankton and certain physical-chemical data of the Bass Islands Region, from September, 1938, to November, 1939. Ohio J. Sci., 40: 291–336.

* Collins, W. D. 1910. The quality of the surface waters of Illinois. U.S. Geol. Surv., Water Supply Papers, 239. 94 p.

*Clarke, F. W. 1924. The composition of the river and lake waters of the United States. U.S. Geol. Surv., Profess. Papers, No. 135. 199 p.

Damann, K. E. 1945. Plankton studies of Lake Michigan. I. Seventeen years of plankton data collected at Chicago, Illinois. Am. Midland Naturalist, 34: 769–796.

Davis, C. C. 1962. The plankton of the Cleveland Harbor area of Lake Erie in 1956–1957. Ecol. Monographs, 32: 209–247.

*Dole, R. B. 1909. The quality of surface waters in the United States. Part I. Analyses of waters east of the one hundredth meridian. U.S. Geol. Surv., Water Supply Papers, 236. 123 p.

Dunn, D. R. 1954. Notes on the bottom fauna of twelve Danish lakes. Vidensk. Medd. Dansk Naturhist. Foren., 116: 251–268.

Eddy, S. 1927. The plankton of Lake Michigan. Illinois Nat. Hist. Surv. Bull., 17: 203–232.

*_____. 1943. Limnological notes on Lake Superior. Proc. Minn. Acad. Sci., 11: 34–39.

Edmondson, W. T., G. C. Anderson, and D. R. Peterson. 1956. Artificial eutrophication of Lake Washington. Limnol. Oceanog., 1: 47–53.

*Erie, Pennsylvania, Bureau of Water. 1956. Ninetieth annual report, 1956. 63 p.

*_____. 1957. Ninety-first annual report, 1957, 63 p.

*_____. 1959. Ninety-third annual report, 1959. 56 p.

*Fish, C. J. 1960. Limnological survey of eastern and central Lake Erie, 1928–1939. U.S. Fish Wildlife Serv. Spec. Sci. Rept. Fisheries, No. 334. 198 p.

Hasler, A. D. 1947. Eutrophication of lakes by domestic drainage. Ecology, 28: 383–395.

*Hunt, T. S. 1857. The chemical composition of the waters of the St. Lawrence and Ottawa Rivers. Phil. Mag., Ser. 4, 13: 239–245.

*International Joint Commission. 1951. Report of the International Joint Commission United States and Canada on pollution of boundary waters. Washington and Ottawa. 312 p.

*Jackson, D. D. 1912. Report on the sanitary conditions of the Cleveland water supply. Cleveland. 148 p.

*Kramer, J. R. 1961. chemistry of Lake Erie. Great Lakes Res. Div., Inst. Sci. and Tech., Univ. Mich., Publ. No. 7, p. 27–56.

*_____. 1962. Chemistry of western Lake Ontario. Great Lakes Res. Div., Inst. Sci. and Tech., Univ. Mich., Publ. No. 9, p. 21–28.

*Lake Michigan Water Commission. 1909. Comparative analysis of samples of water from Lake Michigan. Rept. No. 1, p. 103–105.

*Lane, A. C. 1899. Lower Michigan waters: a study into the connection between their chemical composition and mode of occurrence. U.S. Geol. Surv. Water-supply Irrigation Papers, 31. 97 p.

*Lenhardt, L. G. 1955. Water quality and water usage of the Great Lakes public water supplies. The Great Lakes and Michigan. Great Lakes Res. Inst., Univ. Mich., p. 13–15.

*Leverin, H. A. 1942. Industrial waters of Canada. Can. Dept. Mines Resources, Mines Geol. Branch, Rept. 807. 112 p.

*_____. 1947. Industrial waters of Canada. Can. Dept. Mines Resources, Mines Geol. Branch, Rept. 819. 109 p.

*Lewis, S. J. 1906. Quality of water in the upper Ohio River basin and at Erie, Pa. U.S. Geol. Surv. Water-supply Irrigation Papers, 161. 114 p.

*Mangan, J. W., D. W. Van Tuyl, and W. F. White, Jr. 1952. Water resources of the Lake Erie shore region in Pennsylvania. U.S. Geol. Surv. Circ., 174. 36 p.

Merna, J. 1960. A benthological investigation of Lake Michigan. M.S. Thesis, Michigan State Univ. 74 p.

*Michigan Water Resources Commission. 1954. Great Lakes water temperatures. Unpublished manuscript. 50 p.

Minder, Leo. 1918. Zur Hydrophysik des Zürich u. Walensees, nebst Beitrag zur Hydrochemie u. Hydrobakteriologie des Zürichsees. Arch. Hydrobiol., 12: 122–194.

_____. 1938. Der Zürichsee als Eutrophierungsphänomen. Summerische Ergebnisse aus fünfzig Jahren Zürichseeforschung. Geol. Meere Binnengewässer, 2: 284–299.

_____. 1943. Neuere Untersuchungen über den Sauerstoffgehalt und die Eutrophie des Zürichsees. Arch. Hydrobiol., 40: 279–301.

*Ohio, State of. 1953. Lake Erie pollution survey, supplement. Ohio Div. Water, Final Rept., Columbus, Ohio. 39 tables, 125 p.

Rawson, D. S. 1951. The total mineral content of lake waters. Ecology, **32:** 669–672.

———. 1955. Morphometry as a dominant factor in the productivity of large lakes. Verhandl. Intern. Ver. Limnol., **12:** 164–174.

———. 1956. Algal indicators of trophic lake types. Limnol. Oceanog., **1:** 18–25.

———. 1960. A limnological comparison of twelve large lakes in northern Saskatchewan. Limnol. Oceanog., **5:** 195–211.

*Reade, T. M. 1903. The evolution of earth structure. Longmans, Green, New York. 342 p.

Rodgers, G. K. 1962. Lake Ontario data report. Great Lakes Inst., Univ. Toronto, Prelim. Rept. No. 7. 102 p.

Smith, S. H. 1964. Status of the deepwater cisco population of Lake Michigan. Trans. Am. Fisheries Soc., **93:** 209–230.

Teter, H. E. 1960. The bottom fauna of Lake Huron. Trans. Am. Fisheries Soc., **89:** 193–197.

Thienemann, A. 1928. Der Sauerstoff im eutrophen und oligotrophen See. Die Binnengewässer, Band 4, Schweizerbart, Stuttgart. 75 p.

*Thomas, F. J. F. 1954. Industrial water resources of Canada. Upper St. Lawrence River-central Great Lakes drainage basin in Canada. Can. Dept. Mines Tech. Surv., Water Surv. Rept. No. 3, Mines Branch Rept. 837. 212 p.

Thomas, B. W., and H. H. Chase. 1887. Diatomaceae of Lake Michigan as collected during the last sixteen years from the water supply of the city of Chicago. Notarisia, Commetarium Phycologium, **2:** 328–330.

*U.S. Geological Survey. 1960. Quality of the surface waters of the United States. U.S. Geol. Surv., Water Supply Papers, 1520. 641 p.

*U.S. Public Health Service. 1961. National water quality network. Annual compilation of data October 1, 1960–September 30, 1961. U.S. Public Health Serv. Publ. 663. 545 p.

Welch, P. S. 1952. Limnology. McGraw-Hill, New York. 538 p.

Williams, L. G. 1962. Plankton population dynamics. U.S. Public Health Serv. Publ., 663. 90 p.

*Wright, Stillman. 1955. Limnological survey of western Lake Erie. U.S. Fish Wildlife Serv., Spec. Sci. Rept. Fisheries, 139. 341 p.

ADDITIONAL REFERENCES

Bowen, D. H. M. 1970. The great phosphorus controversy. *Environmental Science and Technology* 4(9):725–726.

Dean, A., S. P. Hart, and J. A. Jones. 1969. The economic and social impact of environmental changes in the Great Lakes region. *Lake Erie Environmental Studies Public Information Report No. 1,* State University College, Fredonia, New York. 76 pp.

Edmondson, W. T. 1968. Water quality management and lake eutrophication: the Lake Washington case. Pp. 139–178 in *Water resources management and public policy,* ed. by T. H. Campbell and R. O. Sylvester. Seattle: University of Washington Press.

Harlow, G. L. 1966. Major sources of nutrients for algae growth in western Lake Erie. *University of Michigan, Great Lakes Research Division, Publication No. 15,* pp. 389–394.

Hasler, A. D., and B. Ingersoll. 1968. Dwindling lakes. *Natural History* 77(9):8–19.

Hutchinson, G. E. 1957. *A treatise on limnology. Vol. I. Geography, physics and chemistry.* New York: Wiley. 1015 pp. A comprehensive scientific survey of physical characteristics of lakes.

Powers, C. F., and A. Robertson. 1966. The aging Great Lakes. *Sci. Am.* 215(5):95–100.

Prat, Jean, and A. Giraud. 1964. *The pollution of water by detergents.* Paris: Organization for Economic Cooperation and Development. 86 pp.

20
SELECTION

AQUATIC WEEDS

L. G. HOLM, L. W. WELDON,
AND R. D. BLACKBURN

As eutrophication of lakes, rivers, and estuaries proceeds, populations of aquatic plants growing there commonly "explode." Moderate numbers of these plants are beneficial, but in large quantities they may have numerous harmful effects. In recent years aquatic plants have become overabundant in an increasing number of lakes and streams, paralleling trends in water enrichment. As we have already seen, domestic and industrial wastes, urban drainage, and agricultural runoff are primary sources of plant nutrients.

As the expanding plants are usually introduced from foreign regions, they lack native predators to keep them in check (see Part 6). In many areas these ruinous plants have been purposely introduced for their ornamental quality.

This selection offers several striking examples to show the rampant quality of aquatic weeds and the threats they present. Aquatic weeds may foul water supplies by creating odors, tastes, or colors. Waterways used for supply, such as irrigation canals, may become almost completely clogged. Esthetic values and recreational uses (boating, swimming, fishing, etc.) may be impaired. Water lost by evapotranspiration from water hyacinth may be eight times as great as the loss from a normal water surface in arid areas. There are other commercial, economic, and health effects as well.

Some of the measures discussed in this selection for controlling aquatic

L. G. Holm (b. 1917) is a professor of horticulture at the University of Wisconsin, where he has been on the faculty since receiving his Ph.D. in 1949, with the exception of periods abroad as an exchange professor to the U.S.S.R. and as a member of the staff in Rome of the United Nations Food and Agricultural Organization. Professor Holm has investigated the physiology of crop growth regulators and the chemical control of weeds, and he is inventorying all the world's principal weed and crop species. Lyle W. Weldon (1934–1970) was accidentally drowned while working as a research agronomist for the Crops Research Division, Agricultural Research Service, U.S. Department of Agriculture, in Fort Lauderdale, Florida. Educated at Oregon State College and the University of Wyoming (Ph.D., 1959), he had concentrated his research on the effects of herbicides on plant growth. Robert D. Blackburn is a botanist with the Crops Research Division, Fort Lauderdale.

This selection is reprinted from *Science* 166(3906):699–709, 1969, by permission of the authors and the American Association for the Advancement of Science. Copyright 1969 by the AAAS.

weeds nicely illustrate the conflict, which is so frequently presented by "technological fixes," between various benefits and further environmental costs. For example, herbicides may reduce aquatic weeds but also may kill fish or make water undrinkable. Biocontrol, by introducing predaceous organisms including disease, is dangerous for other nontarget plants (again, see discussions in Part 6). Like terrestrial weeds, many aquatic weeds are adapted for persistence; vegetative reproduction may make removal by mowing hopeless, and many seeds are long-lived. Aquatic weeds have become a serious symptom and a result of our failure to manage our water resources.

(Editor's comment)

In the evolution of the city as a habitat, in the conversion of virgin lands to intensified farming, and in the alteration of watercourses with locks, dams, and reservoirs, man is the interloper. At his behest the natural order of things is set aside. As a result of his activities and their byproducts, new species and numbers of weeds, rodents, insects, and diseases appear where they could not, or did not, exist before. One of our priceless treasures, fresh water, is changed as civilization draws near. Its quality usually becomes poorer; it is seldom improved by man. Communities, planned and unplanned, locate on the water's edge to use navigation routes, irrigate land, and develop power. As a result the watercourses are heated, polluted, and fertilized; the levels fluctuate, and new biological pests are introduced because of man's commerce and mobility.

Several "explosions" of aquatic weeds in the great rivers and lakes of the warm regions of the world have forced us to recognize the power of such infestations. They destroy fisheries, interfere with hydroelectric and irrigation schemes, stop navigation, and bring starvation and disease problems to riverine communities. The rapid growth of weed infestations has been both spectacular and frightening, and the publicity devoted to several of these problems in the past decade has made us aware that something is wrong.

Aquatic weeds obstruct water flow, increase evaporation, cause large losses of water through transpiration, and prevent proper drainage of land. Weeds may interfere with navigation, prevent fishing and recreation, depress real estate values, and present health hazards. In the western United States, Timmons (1) showed that 17 states lost 1,966,000 acre-feet of irrigation water annually because of aquatic and ditchbank weeds. This water, valued conservatively at $20 per acre-foot, is worth $39,230,000 (2). This is enough water to irrigate 132,000 to 315,000 hectares of cropland. In the United States there never has been an evaluation of the total nonagricultural losses due to aquatic weeds. It is certain that this loss, too, would be very high.

The aquatic environment is complex and is of interest to scientists in several disciplines. The management of aquatic vegetation is not a new science, but rather an old field of botany that has been recently revitalized because of increased demand on our fresh waters and the exponential growth in problems caused by aquatic vegetation.

Water Hyacinth

The scourge of some of the world's major rivers is water hyacinth, *Eichhornia crassipes* (Mart.) Solms in the family *Pontederiaceae* (Figure 20.1). A native of South America, it is now widely distributed over the warm regions of the earth (Figure 20.2). The plant is free-floating, has very fine roots, and produces stolons and viable seeds. The leaves are 10 to 15 cm across, bright green, shiny,

FIGURE 20.1 The flowers of water hyacinth *Eichhornia crassipes* (Mart.) Solms.

and, because they are upright, serve as sails before the wind. The lovely flowers are pale lilac or mauve with a yellow patch at the center. Because of his admiration for the flowers, man has assisted the spread of this plant by cultivating it in his pools and gardens. His carelessness toward the cleanliness of his commercial and pleasure craft on land and sea has also contributed to the movement of the plant. For example, charcoal is made in the bush in Africa; and holes in the sacks used for transport are sometimes plugged with water hyacinth plants that may survive a very long journey. Large plants are used as cushions for sitting and kneeling in native canoes, to be thrown away at any place where the plant ceases to be useful. The plants catch on the sides and bottoms of river craft and thus move with the commerce of the region. Natural forces and events have also been important in the spread of water hyacinth. From the nurseries in the swamps and backwaters, great islands of the weed are flushed into the mainstream at flood time.

Water hyacinth populations increase rapidly by vegetative reproduction. In one ex-

periment two parent plants produced 30 offspring after 23 days, and 1200 at the end of 4 months. A plant may flower at the age of 26 days and will normally produce viable seeds. Seed production varies from a few to as many as 5000 seeds per plant. The seeds sink to the bottom and may remain viable for at least 15 years. Movement of seeds between watercourses must surely take place in the mud on furbearing animals and on the legs of birds. Recent reports of the long-distance dispersal of seed by waterfowl and shore birds suggest a possibility that has never been taken seriously. These migrating birds can carry seed several thousand kilometers in one season (3). In the face of such vectors, once the seed of a species is on a continent, there may be little that man can do to prevent its spread.

An account of the spread of water hyacinth in the Congo and Nile rivers will illustrate the immensity of the task we face. The species had been introduced at the delta of the Nile and in Natal, South Africa, at the beginning of the century. Europeans who settled in South Rhodesia in 1937 reported

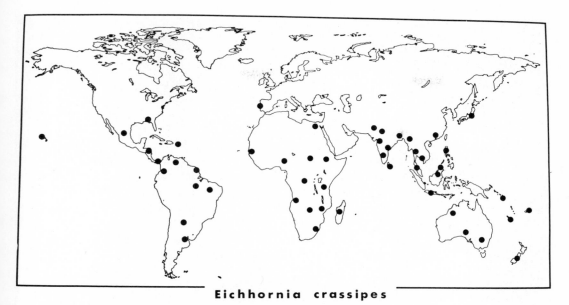

Eichhornia crassipes

FIGURE 20.2 The distribution of water hyacinth.

the presence of water hyacinth. It is now generally distributed in Africa. In spite of the losses and human suffering caused by this plant, it was still available in 1965 for purchase as an ornamental in the street markets of Senegal. In the United States, federal law prohibits interstate shipment of water hyacinth, but it is offered for sale in the catalogs of many distributors of water garden plants.

Water hyacinth was first reported in the Congo River in 1952 and in less than 3 years it had spread 1600 kilometers from Leopoldville up to Stanleyville. In 1954 it had already begun to block transportation. Buoys were submerged and navigation channels were hidden. Fish spawning areas were blocked. Many fishing grounds were destroyed by darkness and lack of oxygen as the weed cover became more dense, and, as a result, the riverine communities were denied their principal source of protein. Using herbicides applied from ships, planes, and helicopters, by 1957 Belgian scientists had directed the cleanup of more than 1600 kilometers of the river at a cost of $1,000,000. In spite of this massive effort, Le Brun reports

that in the same year water hyacinth was still floating past Leopoldville on the way to the sea at the rate of 136 metric tons per hour (4). During the turbulent years following independence, the Congo government services could not maintain the weed control program, and the Congo River is again badly infested.

The history of the infestation of the upper White Nile is equally tragic. The first report of the weed in the White Nile was in 1958. Again, the multiplication and spread took place so quickly that even the best efforts of the Sudan government could not organize a campaign in time to contain the weed. A staff of 200 workers equipped with ships, planes, and land vehicles was organized to keep the river and the harbors open. During the early 1960's, the water hyacinth team of Sudan was able to keep the weed under control in the most critical areas with herbicides. At one time the cost of this operation was $1.5 million per year (5).

In addition to all of the usual hardships caused by the weed, men now began to see the impact of its uncontrolled growth on clogged irrigation pumps and hydroelectric schemes. Some river villages that were regularly supplied with food by boat began to starve because they could not be reached. Insect vectors of human and animal diseases seek harbor in the mats of water hyacinth; so do dangerous snakes and crocodiles. In recent years the political difficulties in the south of the country have prevented workers from spraying many of the nurseries and sources of infestation in the upper White Nile. The region is again in serious difficulty. Figures 20.3 and 20.4 depict the change that took place between 1958 and 1965 above the dam at Jebel Aulia on the White Nile near Khartoum.

The people of Sudan deserve much credit for preventing the spread of water hyacinth from the White to the Blue Nile. The confluence of the two rivers is at Khartoum, and above this point a quarantine system, including many vehicle checkpoints, has been organized and is efficiently administered. By preventing the spread of the weed from the White to the Blue Nile, the Sudanese have protected the great irrigated Gezira cotton scheme.

Water hyacinth is present in the sloughs and backwaters of the Amazon River. It seldom appears to be a problem in the Amazon, perhaps due to lesser demands on utilization of this waterway, or to the presence of natural factors such as insects or plant diseases that limit growth of the weed. It does interfere with man's activities in many lakes, streams, and reservoirs of Central and South America. Many large reservoirs such as Brokopondo in Surinam, Lake Apanas in Nicaragua, and Lake Rio Lempa in El Salvador are threatened with economic disaster if dense stands of water hyacinth are allowed to develop.

The benefit of these reservoirs is dependent upon the amount of available water. However, water hyacinth consumes and wastes tremendous quantities of water through the leaves. The loss of water through evapotranspiration from the leaves has been measured as 3.2 to 3.7 times greater than free evaporation from a surface. This accounted for a loss of more than 6 acre-feet of water in a 6-month period due to a water hyacinth cover. In the dry atmosphere of India, the loss of water through water hyacinth was 7.8 times that of open water (6). Only a partial coverage of water hyacinth on a reservoir can result in the entire river inflow being wasted back into the atmosphere. Thus, the water is not available for hydroelectric power and irrigation.

Water hyacinth is distributed generally in Asia where it may be found in India, throughout the countries of Southeast Asia, and in the Philippine Islands. In East Pakistan some of the farming areas are covered with massive deposits of water hyacinth as the floods come down from the hills in the rainy season. The weed is in Australia and New Zealand as well.

Water hyacinth was reportedly introduced into the United States in 1884 as part of a horticultural exhibit. It spread rapidly and by 1897 was creating enough havoc to navigation to prompt an investigation. Funds for control of the weed became available in 1899. A number of mechanical removal procedures were used initially to control the water hyacinth, but these have largely been replaced with herbicide programs because of the great saving in time and money. Intensive control programs are being conducted by federal, state, and local agencies, drainage districts, and private interests. In spite of this large combined effort water hyacinth caused an annual loss of almost $43,000,000 in Florida, Alabama, Mississippi, and Louisiana in 1956. The types of losses are similar throughout the world (7).

We have indicated some of the navigational problems in Africa. The navigation of rivers and waterways in the southern United States would be just as difficult without proper control of the water hyacinth. Many rivers have to be closed to boat traffic periodically if effective control procedures have not been followed. Fishing camps and marinas are often closed, and many are forced into bankruptcy by inaccesibility.

A cover of water hyacinth on canals with a cross section of 36 to 72 centares may reduce the flow of water by half. The flow in smaller laterals and farm ditches may be almost completely stopped. Many canal

FIGURE 20.3 The dam on the White Nile at Jebel Aulia near Khartoum, Sudan. The area was clean when photographed in October, 1958. [Courtesy E. Buyckx]

FIGURE 20.4 The same area seen in Figure 20.3, showing the accumulation of water hyacinth above the dam in October, 1965.

systems have to be enlarged 50 percent or more to compensate for retarded flow. An additional problem is the constant accumulation of debris from decaying water hyacinth on the canal bottom. During periods of active growth, the lower leaves and roots of water hyacinth are constantly decaying and being replaced. This debris that falls to the canal bottom may amount to more than 30 centimeters per year. If the extensive water hyacinth cover is not prevented, mechanical removal of the debris becomes necessary—at a cost of $400 to $640 per kilometer (6, 8).

Salvinia

Some of the man-made lakes constructed in this century are so large that they are included on world maps. Lake Kariba, on the Zambesi River in Southern Africa, is an interesting example of the frustration which comes with massive efforts to arrange great alterations in the environment. The relocation of 50,000 people to make way for this lake caused considerable human suffering. The biological consequence of impounding such a large stream is in part illustrated by the story of the weed problem that later developed.

The Kariba Dam was closed late in 1958. The maximum water level was reached in July 1963, 4½ years later. Lake Kariba now covers more than 4200 square kilometers, has a maximum depth of 115 meters, and extends up to the foot of beautiful Victoria Falls.

In May 1959, floating mats of the water fern, *Salvinia auriculata* Aublet, were reported in the center of the lake. The mats grew in size and moved about with the wind. Before the end of the year a significant portion of the water near the shore was covered with *Salvinia* plants, as they lodged in branches of partially submerged trees and continued to multiply. By this time, *Pistia stratiotes* L. was associating with *Salvinia* in some of the mats. During 1960, less than 2 years after the dam was closed, it was estimated that the rafts of *Salvinia* had covered 420 square kilometers or 10 percent of the surface area (9). By 1965 the infestation had subsided slightly but was still estimated at 8 percent of the lake's surface (Figures 20.5 and 20.6).

Figure 20.5 A harbor on Lake Kariba completely choked with *Salvinia*. Only very powerful boats can penetrate the mat of weeds (photo taken October, 1965).

Figure 20.6 A permanent mat of Salvinia in a bay of Lake Kariba. The weed mat closes in the wake of boats and ships which try to enter.

The water fern has floating leaves 3 cm long and submerged leaves so finely divided that they have a feathery appearance. In some areas the plant produces spores when it is crowded, but until 1965 only vegetative reproduction had been observed on Lake Kariba. Before formation of the lake, large infestations of *Salvinia* were present in the Upper Zambesi where they sometimes interfered with the fishing of the local people. The weed was also far up the Chobe River, a tributary which feeds into the Zambesi above Victoria Falls. In 1949, Dr. O. West collected *Salvinia* just a short way above Victoria Falls. Boughey (9) assumed that the weed was already present in that portion of the Zambesi River which was flooded by the lake. The records show that warnings were given about the potential weed problem at the time the lake was being planned. Not until 1960 and 1961 were serious research efforts made toward control measures that would be feasible and safe for the lake (10). As a result of political turmoil in the area, no important measures for control or eradication have ever been taken.

Salvinia auriculata, first described as from Guiana, has spread over a wide area in Central and South America, from Cuba to Argentina. It is known to be in the Cape area of South Africa, in the Congo River and the Cameroons on the West Coast, and in some of the countries of Southeast Asia. It first "exploded" and became a serious problem in Ceylon in the period before 1955 (11). At that time *Salvinia* had covered an estimated 8800 hectares of rice fields and 800 hectares of canals and other waterways within about 12 years.

Could the disaster at Lake Kariba have been avoided? The infestations of *Salvinia* in Ceylon were well known. Scheduled inspections of the shore line where weeds build up and prompt treatment of early infestations seem the only way to prevent massive explosions of vegetation which may by then be too expensive or too dangerous to treat. When man-made lakes are constructed, vegetation management must be integrated with the work of all bureaus and agencies concerned with maintenance of the watershed, the lake, and the dam. Recently, an infestation of *Salvinia* was found on Lake Naivasha in Kenya, and it was dealt with promptly and effectively with herbicides applied from aircraft and boats. Constant vigilance has kept the weed under control.

Water Lettuce

Lake Volta in Ghana deserves special mention. The dam was closed in 1964. When filling is completed, the lake will cover 8125 square kilometers. It will be the largest man-made lake in the world. By 1965 great rafts of water lettuce, *Pistia stratiotes*, some many kilometers long, could be seen floating on the surface. Extensive fringes of the weed covered scores of kilometers of the lake's edge and filled the inlets of small rivers entering the lake.

Water lettuce, very widely distributed in the world, is one of the free-floating aquatic plants that must be viewed with concern. It has pale green leaves which are broad and softly pubescent on both sides. The leaves occur in rosettes, beneath which are long fibrous roots, and the plants are connected by stolons. There is a tendency to overlook the potential danger from water lettuce on large water bodies such as Lake Volta because, presumably, it cannot tolerate action from large waves.

The most important problem caused by water lettuce is that of disease and the nuisance associated with mosquitoes. Water lettuce serves as a preferred host site for larvae of several species of mosquitoes. One or more of these species of mosquitoes serve as principal vectors of each of several forms of encephalomyelitis and of rural filariasis. The *Mansonia* larvae obtain their oxygen directly from the roots of water lettuce and never surface. The only way to control these mosquitoes is to remove water lettuce (12).

In an interesting experiment in which herbicides were used to destroy a 120-hectare infestation of water lettuce, there was also complete control of *Mansonia* mosquitoes for 4 months. Only an occasional mosquito of this species was trapped in the year following treatment (13). Demonstrations such as this suggest that suitable methods of destroying water lettuce may provide a means of controlling diseases that affect large numbers of people.

All of the foregoing species of plants are free-floating. There are many more, but perhaps the ones that deserve special mention are those of the duckweed family Lemnaceae L. A single frond may be the size of a pinhead, and there are no stems or true leaves. Members of this family propagate vegetatively by producing new individuals at the edge of the frond. They can cover the surface of an entire pond in a few weeks. Duckweeds are a nuisance in rice fields and cause trouble in irrigation systems by entering siphon tubes and pumps and by collecting on trashracks.

The free-floating species have drawn much attention if only because massive infestations are spectacular and also frightening when they begin to move. But these are by no means the most difficult of the aquatic weed problems.

Submersed Weeds

Submersed weeds are perhaps the most serious of all aquatic weed problems, because they cannot readily be sprayed with herbicides and do not easily lend themselves to clearance by machines. Herbicidal treatments must be made to the entire volume of water, depending upon sorption of the chemical by the undesirable species to achieve control. It must be obvious that the submersed weeds drastically reduce the rate of water flow. It is as though the water must pass through an infinite series of inverted combs that create friction and turbulence.

Of all aquatics, submersed weeds cause the greatest problems in the United States. The most troublesome in the west and north are the genera *Potamogeton* and *Elodea*, and in the east include these genera and *Myriophyllum*. In the south, *Najas* and *Ceratophyllum* are the most common. In addition to these, *Egeria* is widespread throughout the United States. The filamentous and branched algae are almost always present. Also present in the United States, but important on a world basis as well, are members of the genera *Ranunculus, Vallisneria,* and *Utricularia.*

Submersed weeds also have a history of rapid invasion of new sites. Many of the waterways of Europe were blocked by *Elodea canadensis* when it was introduced in the 18th century. One of the most alarming plant invaders is eurasian watermilfoil, *Myriophyllum spicatum* L. The plant, apparently in the United States since the 19th century, has become a problem only during the past 10 years. In that period it has invaded more than 80,000 hectares in the Chesapeake Bay, 2000 hectares in the Tennessee Valley Authority reservoirs, and 26,800 hectares in Curituck Sound.

The weed causes large losses in commercial fishing, smothers shellfish beds, hinders navigation, depresses real estate values, interferes with recreational use, provides mosquito breeding sites, and clogs water intake systems. This is a perennial submersed plant that spreads very rapidly by vegetative reproduction and probably by seed. The leaves are finely dissected, and the flowering spike, without leaves, may extend 10 centimeters above the water. The plant can tolerate salinities up to as much as one-third that of seawater and can thus invade most fresh and estuarine waters. Large acreages in the TVA reservoirs have been treated with 2,4-D (2,4-dichlorophenoxyacetic acid). The chemical has been safely applied at rates of 22 to 44 kilograms per hectare. The results have varied from excellent control in protected embayments to poor control in moving water in these impoundments. The varied results of this work and the inadequacy of the control methods indicate the lack of knowledge to cope with the problem. The need is for concerned public agencies to contain new troublesome plants wherever they are first reported. In one area of Florida,

eurasian watermilfoil spread from 80 to 1200 hectares in 2 years; there was no attempt to control the plant or limit it to the infested area (14).

The story of the invasion by eurasian watermilfoil is still another example of a species that multiplied rapidly after having been in a certain area for a long time. We do not know whether plant material was moved to a more favorable environment, or whether the habitat was altered to make it more suitable for the spread and growth of plants already present.

Submersed weeds are a menace to irrigation systems. Thousands of freshwater reservoirs, large and small, have been constructed throughout the world in the past two decades, and with them have come large new irrigation schemes. Several of these command more than 400,000 hectares. India, for example, the leading producer of three of the world's major crops, has more kilometers of irrigation canals than any other country. As people occupy and farm the land, the effluent from villages, barns, and animal yards, together with the runoff of fertilizers added to the fields, enriches the waters of the canals and reservoirs. Because the distributaries are often shallow, clear, and slow-moving, the added nutrients ensure the growth of weeds. When the weeds enter the system, water can no longer move at the design rate of flow, with the result that the fields most distant from the reservoir cannot be irrigated on schedule. The reduced rate of flow also encourages seepage from canals, and the losses from evaporation are significantly increased. These are matters for serious concern, because they directly affect food production in an already hungry world. The management of aquatic vegetation for an entire irrigation system may be the most complex of all water weed problems. These include reserves of water held in rivers, ponds, and lakes, a network of canals, and a drainage system. Frequently, the water is used for men, animals, and crops.

It is estimated that over a million additional hectares of arable land will be placed under irrigation before the end of the cen-

FIGURE 20.7 A flood control canal 80 feet wide and 22 feet deep completely filled with *Hydrilla* retarded flow by 90 percent.

tury. One example may serve to illustrate the futility of planning irrigation systems without, at the same time, making preparations to protect them from aquatic weeds. In one of the countries of Asia, an irrigation scheme with a command area of 560,000 hectares was completed in this decade. One main arm of the canal system is 400 kilometers long and, with its distributaries, totals more than 1600 kilometers. The discharge at the head is equal to that of the Seine River as it flows through Paris. Within 5 years after the system was opened submersed aquatic weeds had cut the flow of water in the main canal by 80 percent.

Man's efforts to increase food production in the United States have resulted in treatment of 105,833 kilometers of irrigation and drainage channels for aquatic weed control in 17 western states (1). This represents about 55 percent of the infested channels and about 45 percent of the total length in use. Greater world pressure for food production will increase the demand for even more efficient control of vegetation which interferes with water flow.

Man's quest for beauty and recreation has brought about some of the most catastrophic of our weed problems. Exotic and beautiful aquarium species are transported throughout the world. *Egeria, Cabomba, Elodea,* and *Hydrilla* are examples of submersed plants that have been carried from one country to another with dire consequences (Figures 20.7 and 20.8). The problem is twofold. First, in the United States and most other countries there are no limitations on the importation of aquatic plants. Second, most of the aquatic plant dealers grow and harvest the plants in public waters. When a grower desires another species, he simply imports it, places it in several streams or lakes, and then harvests it as it is needed. Many submersed weeds have been introduced in this manner. Failure to restrict their movement has allowed wide distribution of some species.

FIGURE 20.8 This $900,000 resort motel and marina was built on the banks of a crystal-clear river famous for fishing and scuba diving. An invasion of *Hydrilla* prevented the use of the waterway and forced the motel into bankruptcy 18 months after opening.

Emersed Weeds

Emersed aquatic weeds have their roots beneath the water and their stems and leaves above the surface. Many are familiar, including the bulrushes, *Scirpus*; cattails, *Typha*; water lily, *Nymphaea*; spatterdock, *Nuphar*; rushes, *Juncus*; arrowhead, *Sagittaria*; and alligatorweed, *Alternanthera*. Where water levels fluctuate these species may survive for short periods as terrestrial plants. Many are the first to invade newly flooded areas, and they will prosper in the backwater areas which are intermittently wet. Emersed weeds are especially troublesome in irrigation and drainage systems. They choke canals, increase silt deposition, and impede water flow. Frequently, the design rate of flow can never be achieved because of encroachment of plants on the shoreline and the water lost through transpiration.

Phreatophytes

These are the plants that grow at the water's edge or with their roots reaching into the capillary zone overlying the water table. It is as difficult to determine limits for the species which should be in this group as it is to define the shoreline in a swamp. Woody plants, perennial grasses, and broad-leaved plants are prominent in this group. There are an estimated 6 million hectares of stream channels, canals, reservoirs, and river flood plains infested with these weeds in the western part of the United States, and they waste 25 million acre-feet of water annually. It would be practical to save 25 percent of this wasted water by maintenance of stream channels and effective weed control (15).

The most common woody plants are salt cedar, *Tamarix pentandra*; willows, *Salix* spp.; cottonwood, *Populus* spp.; baccharis, *Baccharis* spp.; buttonbush, *Cephalanthus occidentalis* L.; velvet mesquite, *Prosopis juliflora*; and grease wood, *Sarcobatus vermiculatis*.

Floating Island Weeds

In accord with many natural growth cycles, large masses of floating dead aquatic vegetation may support progressively larger types of vegetation. As these enter the final phase of this ecological succession, woody species become established. Large islands bearing trees several feet in circumference are impossible to cope with when they lodge in the channels of main streams, for example.

One of the most dangerous and dreaded weeds of the African waterways is papyrus, *Cyperus papyrus* L., of the sedge family Cyperaceae. It is feared because it may encroach on open water by extending from the banks. It is one of the principal plants in the formation of sudd which is a mass of free-floating vegetation. The plant grows upright to a height of 4 to 5 meters. The rhizomes by which it spreads vegetatively are woody and strong and may reach far out into open water or may quickly travel over weed mats or penetrate through them and thus knit them together. These massive and sturdy floating islands of vegetation, when loosed on a river at any season, can be a menace to navigation. Sudd formation in two of Africa's largest swamps, the Okavango in Botswana and the great swamp in the White Nile above Malakal, are dominated by papyrus. A study of the papyrus sudd of the White Nile revealed that 50 percent of the water entering the river was lost through evaporation and transpiration as a result of the activity of this weed and its associated vegetation.

Vossia cuspidata (Roxb.) W. Griff., a robust member of the grass family Gramineae is frequently mixed with the islands of associated plants. The weed is sometimes called hippo grass, because it is grazed by the hippopotamus as well as by cattle. It can have floating or submersed stalks which grow rapidly for considerable distances under favorable conditions. The aerial portion of the stem is strong and erect and may reach a height of 2 meters. The grass is widely distributed in Africa and Asia. The irrigation canals of the Gezira cotton scheme along the Blue Nile are sorely troubled with this grass because it impedes the flow of water.

Chemical Control

Many selective herbicides have been developed to combat aquatic weeds. Some have such a narrow range of specificity that one species of a genus may be controlled without affecting other species of the same genus. Thus certain problem species can be controlled without adversely affecting the desirable flora and fauna in a waterway. Formerly, large quantities of toxic chemicals, such as sodium arsenite, were used indiscriminately; but today the herbicides used in our waters must pass rigid tests on efficacy, toxicity to fauna and flora in and near the waterway, residues in irrigated crops, and many other hazards.

Chemical control of several floating weeds is possible. Water hyacinth is "managed" and kept under control in the United States with 2,4-D (2,4-dichlorophenoxyacetic acid). At one time the infestations of this weed on the White Nile and the Congo rivers in Africa were controlled with the same herbicide, but now political turmoil and economic problems have made it impossible to continue the control operations.

If sensitive crops are grown in agricultural areas adjacent to infested waterways, some herbicides may not be used because of the danger from volatility and spray drift. Recent development of invert emulsion (water in oil) formulations of 2, 4-D, water thickening agents, and new innovations in spraying equipment (such as the microfoil boom) give the applicator new tools to control placement of the chemical. Diquat (6,7-dihydrodipyrido [1, 2-*a*:2′, 1′-*c*] pyrazidiinium dibromide) has proven effective on water hyacinth at 1.7 kilograms per hectare and can be used with greater safety around ornamentals and crop plants that are very sensitive to 2, 4-D. Two applications of diquat usually give about the same control of this weed as would be expected from four treatments with 2, 4-D. In Australia, amitrole-T (3-amino-1, 2, 4-triazole + ammonium thiocyanate) has been used effectively on water hyacinth (16).

Diquat is also effectively used to control water lettuce at the same rates as it is used to control water hyacinth. As these two plants often grow together, a single application of diquat can be used to control both species (Figure 20.9).

The chemical control of submersed weeds, much more difficult, is achieved through the use of chemicals with several different modes of action. Large quantities of emulsified xylene and other aromatic solvents are used for contact control of vegetation in irrigation canals. The xylene is usually released into the flowing canal, over a 30-minute period, at 6 to 10 gallons per cubic foot per second of flow. As the chemical moves down the canal, the plants absorb lethal doses, the treated portion of the water is spilled into a waste area, and the untreated flowing water is then available for immediate use. The treatment kills the vegetation back to the bottom mud, but regrowth may occur in a few weeks.

Acrolein (acrylaldehyde) is applied in flowing water in the same manner as aromatic solvents (17). In static water sites such as lakes, acrolein (7 parts per million by volume) is injected directly into the water. *Hydrilla* has been controlled with this method for 8 to 16 weeks in both the United States and Australia. Generally two to four treatments are required per year for satisfactory weed control.

Knowledge of the plant cycle has an important bearing on the control of submersed weeds. Sago pondweed, *Potamogeton pectinatus*, and *Hydrilla* produce hydrosoil propagules. In canals that can be dewatered, fenac (2,3,6-trichlorophenylacetic acid) and dichlobenil (2, 6-dichlorobenzonitrile) can be applied to the dry canal bottom. The chemical is then leached into the surface soil and released into the water as growth begins. *Hydrilla* also produces large numbers of hydrosoil turions that sprout as soon as the topgrowth is killed. In areas that cannot be dewatered, successive treatments with fatty acid amino salts of endothall (3,6-endoxohexahydrophthalic acid) and diquat reduce the number of these propagules to the point where regrowth is minimum (18).

Foliar treatments with dalapon (2,2-dichloropropionic acid), at 5.6 to 22.4 kilograms per hectare, will afford quite satisfactory control of most aquatic grasses, cattails, and rushes. Often two or more treatments are required in a growing season.

Amitrole-T is another selective herbicide that is effective on grasses. The response of shore weeds to these two herbicides provides us with an example of the interrelation of stage of development and herbicidal activity. Dalapon is most effective on cattails before they flower, while amitrole-T is more effective in the fall, after flowering. A combination or mixture of these two herbicides is often used as a single application that may be effective for several months and which may cover a broader spectrum of weeds. A mixture of dalapon and 2,4-D is sometimes used where control of both grass and broad-leaved species is necessary (19).

There are still many troublesome species for which there are no mechanical, chemical, or biological controls. For most of these we lack information on the physiology and the stages of growth and development. The pace has quickened in the search for ideas, chemicals, and methods for the selective control of aquatic vegetation. Modern herbicides may also be used safely to keep our waterways productive and useful. However, application of most herbicides to potable water is restricted. Some are toxic to fish. Information is needed on the disposition and effects of herbicides in water, in crops irrigated with treated water, and in fish. Because the

FIGURE 20.9 Diquat was applied at 1.7 kilograms per hectare to control water lettuce (left) and resulted in complete control within 30 days (right).

cost is generally only 10 to 20 percent of other control methods, there is frequently no other practical way to manage the vegetation in a stream, a lake, or a power system.

We do not know whether we shall be able to restore our water resources. It is certain that we shall continue to use them, and many of them are destined to be misused for some time to come. Some types of aquatic vegetation will flourish; we shall find it disagreeable, and sometimes we shall be overwhelmed by its luxuriant growth. Until we have become wise enough to appreciate our water, and until we have come to respect it as one of the most precious of all the gifts of nature, aquatic herbicides will be needed—for they will be one of the few tools that we can afford in the selective management of the vegetation in our waterways. In many places in the world there will be no other choice.

Biocontrol

Natural forces affect aquatic plant growths. These forces are used by man in his biological control programs (biocontrol). Biocontrol, which turns nature against herself, may be the most economical method for the control of portions of this perplexing world problem. Biocontrol has certain advantages, for example, relatively low program costs, ready supply sources, ease of application of techniques which often require no special equipment, minimal training of unskilled personnel, and relative permanence of treatments because of the ability to resist weed reinfestations (20). In this age of emphasis on chemical and mechanical control of aquatic weeds, most people are unaware of the progress being made in biocontrol. Emphasis on this area of weed control has increased rapidly during the last decade.

Biocontrol works best with agents of foreign origin. Scientists have traveled to the native homes of certain species of aquatic plants to collect various organisms that attack the plants. Frequently, in its native habitat, the plant never presents the problem that it does in other parts of the world. The reason for this is that certain natural agents, such as insects, diseases, and the chemistry of the water, have controlled the plant. For this reason the biocontrol of aquatic vegetation should not be confused with aquatic plant eradication. The plant and the biocontrol agent are part of the aquatic ecosystem.

In nature, a balance is maintained in the aquatic flora through plant-feeding insects, diseases, nematodes, fungi, bacteria, viruses, fish, snails, and mammals. When a biocontrol agent is selected it must be thoroughly investigated before introduction into a new area. It must not be released if it will attack desirable plants or other organisms.

A large freshwater snail *Marisa cornuarietis* has freed small ponds in the southern United States and Puerto Rico of submersed weeds (Figure 20.10). *Marisa* carries no diseases of man and has been used as food in Puerto Rico. The indiscriminate feeding habits of *Marisa* have also made it a biocontrol agent for disease-carrying snails. A major disadvantage is its sensitivity to temperatures below 6°C. It may feed upon certain desirable plants such as rice, watercress, and water chestnuts which are growing in the water. A second freshwater snail, *Pomacea australis*, shows promise as a biocontrol for submersed and floating aquatic weeds. This large ampullarid is widely distributed in Brazil (21).

Mammals with aquatic weed-cleaning ability are rare, but the sea cow or manatee, *Trichechus manatus latirostris*, has shown its taste for many types of aquatic weeds. Unofficial reports collected from all areas of the world indicate that this mythological mermaid has no peer in the biological world for the volume of aquatic weeds which can be consumed by one animal. There is only limited use of the manatee because of the

FIGURE 20.10 A freshwater snail, *Marisa,* feeding on *Hydrilla.*

scarcity of animals, and an increase in population is uncertain because of the lack of knowledge about its reproduction (22).

In contrast to the indiscriminate feeding of snails and manatees is the fastidious taste of the alligatorweed beetle, *Agasicles* sp. In nature this small beetle feeds only on alligatorweed and will starve in its absence. No control technique could be simpler than the release of a handful of beetles into an infestation of alligatorweed. Recent laboratory research has also shown that *Salvinia* may be controlled by a wingless aquatic grasshopper *Paulinia acriminate. Paulinia* is now being evaluated in field trials at Lake Kariba. Investigations are also underway to search for natural enemies of the water hyacinth in its native South American home (23).

Certain freshwater fish consume large quantities of aquatic vegetation. The common carp, *Cyprinus carpio*; Chinese grass carp or white amur, *Ctenopharyngodon idella*; tilapia, *Tilapia* sp.; and silver dollar fish,

Metynnia sp., are used for control of aquatic vegetation in many areas of the world. Many of these species are sensitive to cold weather and, in colder climates, must be over-wintered in temperature-control tanks. The most promising of this group is the white amur. Ponds choked with *Hydrilla* in India were cleared of the weed in 2 months after they were stocked with 350 white amur per hectare (24). Russia, Poland, Czechoslovakia, China, and other countries have used the white amur as a biocontrol for aquatic weeds.

Ducks, geese, and swans can remove small amounts of vegetation, and they are especially effective in small ponds for the control of duckweed. Controlled grazing of cows, horses, and goats may be used to hold down vegetation along lake shorelines and canal banks (25).

Diseases, viruses, fungi, bacteria, and nematodes have received very little attention in aquatic weed biocontrol research. Two diseases are considered to be the cause of the decrease in eurasian watermilfoil in the United States (26). The diseases have not been identified and may be only an indirect cause of the decline in the milfoil. A disease was the direct cause of the decline of eel grass along the Atlantic Coast of the United States in the 1930's.

Low-growing species of aquatic plants, several centimeters in height, have been planted in canals to compete with the more undesirable species that may attain lengths of several meters. Removal of nutrients from the water environment by partitioning agents is also being considered as a biocontrol agent. Some success has been obtained in controlling submersed aquatic weeds with selective dyes or black plastic that filter out all, or selective portions of, the sunlight in water.

The employment of biocontrol agents in our aquatic weed programs offers a new approach to the solution of an old and aggravating problem. Combinations of biocontrol agents with chemical and mechanical methods of control may someday be the answer to aquatic vegetation management.

Mechanical Removal

The first effort to control aquatic weeds was with hand tools. Since 1900, many machines have been designed to perform such work, and some are so large that several barges are required for flotation. In the United States today there are still many canals and drainage systems maintained by power shovels and draglines, but these machines work slowly and maintenance costs are high. Emersed weeds are sometimes controlled with the use of underwater mowing machines (27). All of these types of mechanical equipment can bring temporary relief from weed infestations and sometimes provide channels through portions of an otherwise inaccessible waterway. When water is used for human or animal consumption, or when valuable crops are in the immediate area, there may be no practical way to control aquatic weeds

except by mechanical removal. The ratio of costs for these methods as compared to approved herbicidal methods may be on the order of ten to one (8).

Because large quantities of nutrients accumulate in the tissues of some aquatic weeds, the removal of a heavy stand may be beneficial to the waterway. The yield of such massive quantities of green vegetation raises the question of its value for food, for food amendments, or for improvement of soils. But such questions have already been raised, again and again, as to unwanted terrestrial plants (such as woody species that might be used for lumber and wood products) or as to perennial grasses that might be used for pasture. There are many reports of analytical work on water hyacinth and several other aquatic weeds (28). There is no shortage of information on percent dry matter, crude fiber and protein content, or carotene and other special constituents of these plants. Why, then, have aquatic weeds not been more widely used? The answer is that we lack economical ways of harvesting and processing large masses of plants with a very high water content. In certain countries the weed nurseries and other important sources of infestation are almost inaccessible. Add to this the probable cost of transport of a finished product over long distances and it becomes easy to see why public and private agencies have not accepted these risks.

Summary

The great focal points of civilization placed their roots along streams and in sheltered harbors because man needed to be near water for navigation and housekeeping and because it provided protection. There was little thought of caring for the bountiful supplies of water which seemed endlessly renewable. Within living memory the supplies of fresh water in the beautiful streams and lakes of North America were legendary. But suddenly in the 20th century we have at last begun to sense that both the water and soil of the earth are limited. We now realize that we cannot run off to a clean new place each time we have fouled our nest. We shall have to learn to manage our affairs and our immediate environment. We are sickened by the spectacle of the trash and refuse of our own activity. We become uncomfortable in our role as stewards of this wonderful resource, for we do not understand how we may both use and protect it.

While we have been engaged elsewhere, the rampant growth of aquatic weeds has come to be one of the symptoms of our failure to manage our resources. We assign values to the depreciation of property, to the pollution of municipal water supplies, to the loss of navigable streams, and to the failure of irrigation and power systems because of aquatic weeds. But we must also judge the worth of clean water for man in other, quite different ways. Some of the loveliest places on earth are at the water's edge. These may be the sites of our dwellings or the places that we choose for rest and renewal. As we spoil these, one by one, we shall know that

we have surrendered a great part of our humanness, and we shall be anxious because we cannot trust ourselves.

Now we must abandon our view that streams and lakes are great self-cleansing reservoirs that can receive our wastes forever and return to us always as cool, clear water. Many of the watercourses of Asia and Africa, and of Wisconsin and Florida, are now so fertile and so well innoculated with aquatic weeds that they can no longer correct themselves. In many of these places, it is now too late to talk about an equilibrium or the balance of nature. Human activity and neglect have driven the equation far to the right. Within the combinations of mechanical, biological, and chemical methods of aquatic weed control we can find the tools to help with their restoration. We can keep the waterways open so that they can be useful to man and so that he may enjoy them. We can buy the time we need to learn to manage not only the vegetation but each of the resources in an entire watershed.

References and Notes

1. F. L. Timmons, *U.S. Dep. of Agr. ARS–34–14* (1960).
2. N. Wollman *et al.*, *The Value of Water in Alternative Uses* (Univ. of New Mexico Press, Albuquerque, 1962).
3. C. A. Evans, *New Sci.* **19**, 666 (1963); L. J. Mathews, *Pest Art. News Abstr.* **13**, 7 (1967); V. Proctor, *Science* **160**, 321 (1968).
4. J. Lebrun, *Bull. Agr. Congo* **50**, 251 (1959).
5. E. T. Heinen and Salah el Din Hassan Ahmed, *Publication of the Information Production Center* (Dept. of Agriculture, Khartoum, Sudan, 1964).
6. C. E. Timmer and L. W. Weldon, *Hyacinth Contr. J.* **6**, 34 (1967); W. T. Penfound and T. T. Earle, *Ecol. Monogr.* **18**, 447 (1948); R. R. Das, *Proc. Indian Sci. Congr.* **6**, 445 (1969).
7. W. E. Wunderlich, *Hyacinth Contr. J.* **1**, 14 (1962); *U.S. House of Representatives, Document No. 91, Water Hyacinth Obstructions* (55th Congress, Third Session, 1899); *U.S. House of Representatives, Document No. 37, Water Hyacinth Obstructions in the Waters of the Gulf and South Atlantic States* (85th Congress, First Session, 1957).
8. D. B. Bogart, *Proc. Soil Sci. Soc. Fla.* **9**, 32 (1948); J. C. Stephens, R. D. Blackburn, D. E. Seaman,

L. W. Weldon, *Proc. Amer. Soc, Civil Eng. J. Irrig. Drainage Div.* **89**, 31 (1963).
9. A. S. Boughey, *Adansonia* **3**, 49 (1963).
10. E. R. Hattingh, *Weed Res.* **1**, 303 (1961).
11. R. H. Williams, *Trop. Agr.* **33**, 145 (1956).
12. J. A. Mulrennan, *Mansonia Mosquitoes*, mimeographed report (Div. of Entomology, Florida State Board of Health, Tallahassee); R. W. Chamberlain, W. D. Sudia, J. D. Gillett, *Amer. J. Hyg.* **70**, 221. (1959); M. W. Provost, *Mansonia Studies in Leesburg in 1949* (Div. of Entomology, Florida State Board of Health, Tallahassee, 1949); W. D. Sudia and R. W. Chamberlain, personal communication; E. L. Seabrook, *Rep. Annu. Meet. Fla. Antimosquito Ass.* **21**, 1 (1950); C. Chow, *Preliminary Note on Herbicides for Pistia Clearance as a Rural Filariasis Control Measure in Ceylon* (World Health Organization, Geneva, 1953).
13. L. W. Weldon and R. D. Blackburn, *Weeds* **15(1)**, 5 (1967).
14. G. F. Beaven, *Summary of the 1962 Interagency Research Meeting on Eurasian Watermilfoil* (Natural Resources Institute, Univ. of Maryland, 1962); T. E. Crowell, J. H. Steenis, J. L. Sincock, *Proc. S.*

Weed Conf. **20,** 348 (1967); G. E. Smith, *ibid.* **15,** 258 (1962); L. W. Weldon, R. D. Blackburn, D. S. Harrison, *U.S. Dep. Agr. Handb. No. 352* (1969); R. D. Blackburn and L. W. Weldon, *Hyacinth Contr. J.* **6,** 15 (1967).

15. H. C. Fletcher and H. B. Elmendorf, *Yearbook of Agriculture 1955* (U.S. Government Printing Office, Washington, D.C., 1955), pp. 423–429; F. L. Timmons and D. C. Klingman, in *Water and Agriculture*, R. D. Hockensmith, Ed. (AAAS, Washington, D.C., 1960), p. 157.

16. L. W. Weldon, R. D. Blackburn, H.' T. DeRigo, R. T. Mellen, *Hyacinth Contr. J.* **5,** 12 (1966); D. S. Harrison, R. D. Blackburn, L. W. Weldon, J. R. Orsenigo, G. F. Ryan, *Univ. Fla. Agr. Ext. Serv. Circ. No. 219B* (1966); W. T. Parsons, *U.S. Dep. Agr. Vermin Noxious Weeds Destruction Board Bull. No. 3a* (1967).

17. R. D. Comes, R. R. Yeo, B. F. Bruns, J. M. Hodgson, F. L. Timmons, L. W. Weldon, T. R. Bartley, W. D. Boyle, N. E. Otto, D. D. Suggs, *U.S. Dep. Agr. ARS 34–57* (1963); V. F. Bruns, R. R. Yeo, H. F. Arle, *U.S. Dep. Agr. Tech. Bull. No. 1299* (1964); F. L. Timmons, *Proc. Tex. Annu. Indust. Weed Contr. Conf.* **2,** 1 (1967).

18. P. A. Frank, *J. Exp. Bot.* **17,** 546 (1966); P. A. Frank, R. H. Hodgson, R. D. Comes, *Weeds* **11,** 124 (1963); R. D. Blackburn, L. E. Bitting, L. W. Weldon, *Hyacinth Contr. J.* **5,** 36 (1966).

19. F. L. Timmons, L. W. Weldon, W. O. Lee, *Weeds* **6,** 406 (1958); J. M. Hodgson, V. F. Bruns, F. L. Timmons, W. O. Lee, L. W. Weldon, R. R. Yeo, *U.S. Dep. Agr. Prod. Res. Rep. No. 60* (1962); F. L. Timmons, V. F. Bruns, W. O. Lee, R. R. Yeo, J. M. Hodgson, L. W. Weldon, R. D. Comes, *U.S. Dep. Agr. Tech. Bull. No. 1286* (1963).

20. J. B. Butler and F. F. Ferguson, *Proc. S. Weed Conf.* **21,** 304 (1968).

21. R. D. Blackburn and T. M. Taylor, *Abstr. Weed Sci. Soc. Amer.* (1968), p. 51; F. F. Ferguson and J. R. Palmer, *Amer. J. Trop. Med. Hyg.* **7,** 640 (1958); F. F. Ferguson, J. Oliver-Gonzales, J. R. Palmer, *ibid.,* p. 491; Anonymous, *Agr. Res.* **16,** 8 (1968).

22. W. H. L. Allsopp, *Nature* **188,** 762 (1960); G. C. L. Bertram and C. K. R. Bertram, *ibid.* **196,** 1329 (1962); P. L. Sguros, T. Monkus, C. Phillips, *Proc. S. Weed Conf.* **18,** 588 (1965).

23. L. A. Andres, *Abstr. Weed Sci. Soc. Amer.* (1968), p. 51; F. D. Bennett, *Proc. S. Weed Conf.* **19,** 497 (1966); *Pest Art. News Sum. Sec. C* **13,** 304 (1967).

24. J. W. Avault, *Proc. S. Weed Conf.* **18,** 145 (1965); M. T. Philipose, *Indian Livestock* **1(2),** 20, 34 (1963).

25. J. Levett, *World Crops* **12,** 58 (1960).

26. S. Bayley, H. Rabin, C. H. Southwick, *Chesapeake Sci.* **9(3),** 173 (1968).

27. W. E. Wunderlich, *Hyacinth Contr. J.* **1,** 14 (1962); C. F. Zeiger, *ibid.,* p. 16; M. E. Grinwald, *ibid.* **7,** 31 (1968); W. D. Boyle and D. D. Suggs, *U.S. Dep. Interior Reg. I. Bur. of Reclam. Misc. Publ.* (1960); G. C. Klingman, *Weed Control: As a Science* (Wiley, New York, 1961), pp. 323–324.

28. E. Little, *Publication No. PL:CP/20* (Crops Protection Branch, Food and Agricultural Organization of the United Nations, Rome, 1968).

29. Contribution from Department of Horticulture, University of Wisconsin, Madison; and cooperative investigations of the Crops Research Division, Agricultural Research Service, U.S. Department of Agriculture; the Central and Southern Florida Flood Control District; and the University of Florida Agricultural Experiment Station, Fort Lauderdale. Journal Series 3262.

ADDITIONAL REFERENCES

Fogg, G. E.   1969.   The physiology of an algal nuisance. *Proc. Roy. Soc. London,* Ser. B, 173(1031):175–189.

Fremling, C. R.   1964.   Mayfly distribution indicates water quality on the upper Mississippi River. *Science* 146:1164–1166.

Hasler, A. D., and B. Ingersoll.   1968.   Dwindling lakes. *Natural History* 77(9):8–19.

Taft, C. E.   1965.   *Water and algae: World problems.*   Chicago: Educational Publishers.   236 pp.

THE ROLE OF MAN IN ESTUARINE PROCESSES

L. EUGENE CRONIN

Estuaries are places of dynamic interaction, where rivers meet the sea and deposit their wastes, where fluvial and oceanic processes interact—a complex interface. The qualities of estuaries are of extreme importance to man because they also are foci of human interaction and settlement. Of the world's thirty-two largest cities, twenty-two border on estuaries, including the four largest—Tokyo, London, New York, and Shanghai.

This review highlights the multitude of human and natural processes affecting the estuarine environment and shows the complexity of their interaction. Sedimentation, urbanization, chemical contamination, and a host of other processes are at work here. Despite the considerable resiliency of this environment the increasing effluents of modern man now exceed many estuaries' capacities to absorb them. Man's impact there is intensifying and spreading. This is another example of the principle that huge concentrations of people inevitably cause extreme modification of environment. Also, around such a point of intensifying change the impact spreads outward and the variety of repercussions increases.

Clearly, estuaries and the ocean can no longer be considered as an infinite sump for our garbage. The sewage produced by New York City—1,300 million gallons a day, including 360 million gallons of raw sewage—has created a large "dead sea" 12 miles off the harbor (*New York Times,* February 25, 1970). In Europe, dredged-up mud that was dumped offshore from Rotterdam has been diffused 100 miles north-

L. Eugene Cronin (b. 1917) is research professor and director of the Chesapeake Biological Laboratory, Natural Resources Institute, University of Maryland. He holds a Ph.D. degree in zoology (1946) from Maryland and formerly directed the Maryland State Department of Research and Education. Cronin's present research interests center on comprehension of the nature of estuaries, enhancing their utilization through aquaculture, and protection of important characteristics by understanding and minimizing destructive environmental changes in the coastal areas.

eastward by currents, where numerous seabirds have been killed by constituent pesticides (*New York Times,* February 22, 1970). And in the Mediterranean Sea, the continental shelf of France is becoming a sterile stretch of black muck as a result of pollution by oil, detergents, pesticides, and other wastes from the cities of Marseilles and Nice (*New York Times,* January 18, 1970).

(Editor's comment)

Vulnerability to human influence is a characteristic of estuaries. They lie in proximity to man's terrestrial habitat, produce large quantities of his food supply, and are doorways between the oceans and the land masses. Each receives the impact of many human activities throughout an entire watershed, and many are subjected to the most intensive levels of use applied to any marine water areas. It is, therefore, appropriate to identify and consider the past effects of man on the fundamental processes in estuaries and to contemplate future beneficial and detrimental influences on these fascinating, complex, and important waters.

Man's historical development has been closely linked with the estuaries. Humans have always exhibited a natural affinity for water and these bays and river mouths often present unique advantages. They are semi-enclosed and therefore provide natural harbors; they are effective nutrient traps and therefore are rich in food; they connect the oceans and the inland rivers so that they are natural transportation centers; and their often high rates of flux and flush permit disposal of great quantities of waste. The history of exploration, colonization, and settlement of the coasts of the North American continent illustrates the use of estuaries in the development of new populations and cultures.

The effect of human activity on these estuaries was probably unimportant prior to about 1850, and was limited to the effects of silt erosion from agricultural areas and the disposal of human wastes. The enormous expansion during the last century in industrial activity, production and use of power, diversity of manufactured materials,

transportation, fishing intensity, and human population have all placed diverse and increasing pressures on these waters. They all affect the processes of the estuaries and their capacity for future use.

The uses of estuaries are described by others in this volume, but additional examples can be added:

1. The Rhine River, according to Bolomey (1959), is heavily polluted by the 40 million people who live along its course, as well as by the great industrial centers like the Ruhr and the Saar. The need to eliminate this pollution is so great that an international commission has been established. The estuarine areas near Rotterdam receive the net product.

2. In Baltimore Harbor, near the head of Chesapeake Bay, the equivalent of about 400 tons of concentrated sulfuric acid is released daily from a single large industrial operation (Stroup *et al.,* 1961).

3. The city of Washington, D.C., uses the upper Potomac Estuary as the final stage in its sewage treatment process (Auld, 1964). Brehmer (1964) has pointed out that this is a present average daily addition of 22,700 pounds of phosphorous and 68,100 pounds of nitrogen. This annual release of eight million pounds of phosphorous and 25 million pounds of nitrogen will nearly double by the year 2000, as treatment plant effluent increases from 200 million gallons a day to 360 million gallons a day. Brehmer further emphasizes that present knowledge of the effects of this pollution is insufficient to predict the effects on the estuary or even to establish rational limits.

4. Of the ten largest metropolitan areas in the world, seven border estuarine areas

(New York, Tokyo, London, Shanghai, Buenos Aires, Osaka, and Los Angeles). They contain over 55 million people and enormous industrial activity. One-third of the population of the United States lives and works close to estuaries.

5. Bulkheading, dredging, and filling to create waterfront real estate have already permanently changed the nature of some estuaries. The Branch of River Basin Studies of the U.S. Department of the Interior reviews and comments on federal projects which would affect fish and wildlife resources. They have reported on 426 different projects in five years which would affect coastal areas. They expect to start 100 more projects this year, 15 for flood control, 20 for navigation, 20 for beach erosion or hurricane protection projects, and 50 for private proposals.

6. Without waiting for inexpensive nuclear energy, man has begun to engineer vast estuarine changes. The 2,700 km² Zuider Zee has been enclosed for 32 years, essentially fresh for 27 years, and largely converted to sub-sea-level agricultural land. Holland has also begun to transform salt and brackish waters into lakes in the great Delta Project of southwest Holland (Vaas, 1963).

7. More than a billion pounds of biocidal chemicals have been used in the United States, and Butler et al. (1962) point out that many of these substances and their oxidation products reach the coastal waters and the estuaries. Cottam (1960) reported that 35 million pounds of arsenical salts, 45 million pounds of copper sulfate, six million pounds of organic phosphates, and 130 million pounds of chlorinated insecticides and fungicides were used in one year. Six thousand brand-name biocidal materials are now available and almost unrestricted in use. Rachel Carson (1962) has cited specific and vivid examples of the results of application of control chemicals in the areas of the Miramichi in Canada, in the Indian River of Florida, in New Jersey, and at other sites.

These brief examples of the effect of human activities are further evidenced by experience in various parts of the world. They serve as reminders, not as an adequate review.

The future will bring very rapid increase in all the present uses of estuaries, and entirely new pressures and modifications are already taking shape: (1) California is studying alternate plans for damming, diverting, filling, and vastly modifying large areas in the Sacramento-San Joaquin region and elsewhere (Jones et al., 1963). There is a well-advanced plan to divert the waters of the Sabine River, the Neches, the Trinity, the Brazos, the Colorado, and the Nueces from east Texas to west Texas. No water would escape to the coastal estuaries (Thompson, 1961).

The development of inexpensive sources of power in unprecedented quantities may make these seem like mere practice sessions. In this compilation to assemble and assess our knowledge, constructive perspective can be gained by reviewing the effects of man on estuaries.

This review is presented to single out the most significant estuarine processes which man affects, to offer summary and partial assessment of the location and nature of human effects, to suggest the present bennefits and losses from these effects, and to consider the future role of man in the estuaries.*

No attempt will be made here to stress their importance in human welfare, or the economic and social values which they provide. The enormous diversity of systems, which results in highly significant individuality, is assumed. So, too, is the inherent dynamism of most estuaries. We must consider generalized effects by specific examples, and the net effects superimposed on vigorous rhythmic systems.

These are no physical, chemical, or biological processes unique to the estuary, but many are typical of this complex and distinctive mixture of sea and river. In the cases and

---

* Most portions of the paper concerning the future role of man in estuaries, including discussion of the tools for management, have been deleted in this abridged version (*editor's note*).

discussions which follow, primary attention will be given to these questions:

1. What physical, chemical, and biological processes are unusually significant in the estuary and may be modified by man?

2. How have human activities affected these processes beyond the normal range of variation present in the virgin estuary?

3. What are the possibilities for future management of estuarine processes for optimal achievement of human values from estuaries?

The literature of estuaries contains many research reports, administrative summaries, and discussions dealing with specific problems, and many of these will be cited later. No previous general review was located, but several contributions have been especially helpful and stimulating.[1]

The topics presented here are numerous and diverse, ranging from upland erosion to invertebrate toxicity and estuarine hydrography. The pertinent literature is, therefore, represented by illustrative examples rather than by exhaustive inclusion.

Certain processes have been chosen for emphasis here because they meet two criteria: (1) each is significant in many or most estuaries, at least of the coastal plain type; (2) each is now subjected to substantial (i.e., beyond normal range) modification by man.

The physical attributes which will receive emphasis are salinity, temperature, river flow, and basin shape.

Chemical modifications which will be discussed include the addition of biocides, nutrient chemicals, pulp mill wastes, and certain exotics.

Geologically, only silt and siltation are considered.

Among the highly varied modifications of biological processes, human predation (more commonly called fishing!) and the introduction of new species have been chosen as illustrations.

The lists could be very long, but these may serve to summarize present knowledge and provide guidelines for the future.

Activities in the Watershed

Since the estuary is the recipient of effects from changes throughout the watershed, a review of the pertinent human activities along the contributory waterways can be helpful. They vary and are important in the estuarine processes.

MODIFICATION OF RIVER FLOW

Many human activities affect the quantity of inflow of fresh water, its temporal distribution, and its contents. River flow can be reduced, especially by diversion of river water for human consumption (Nelson, 1960; Jones *et al.*, 1963; Ketchum, unpublished ms.; Thompson, 1961), for the vast increases in artificial irrigation of agricultural land (Mansueti, 1961), and by the intentional or accidental use of spillways or breaks in levees (Gunter, 1952, 1956). Conversely, flow can be significantly increased in the basins receiving the diversion. More frequently, increase in the total annual output is the result of denuding the watershed by removing vegetation and by other activities that decrease the insoak and subsurface retention. This is especially vivid in the paved urban areas (Renn, 1956) and along highways where as much as 30 acres per mile is paved or carefully sloped to maximize runoff. These also increase the flashiness of rivers, with greater flooding in high-flow periods and drought in low-flow seasons. Counteracting forces do exist, however, in the increasing number of small and large dams, many of which are specifically designed for moderation of the river flow and long-term release, and in improved general conservation practices.

Gross effects. The gross estuarine effects of changed river flow are rather well understood, although more subtle effects have infinite local variation. The most pervasive effect is on the general hydrographic structure and behavior of the estuary. River flow is a prime factor in the determination of salinity distribution in the estuary (Ketchum, 1951a, c) and of the vertical and horizontal physical structure of the estuary (Pritchard, 1955). Pritchard has shown that increased river flow converts a homogeneous-type estuary through moderate stratification to strong and persistent stratification. Cronin *et al.* (1962) showed that this conversion occurs in the Delaware, following runoff variation. Pritchard (personal communication) has provided additional evidence of the power of flow. During most summers, the deeper waters of the central Chesapeake are severely depleted of oxygen as they are transported up-estuary. Stratification of cooler, saltier, denser deep water under warmer, fresher, lighter surface water may be very strong, and an increase in river flow during this period enhances stratification, enlarges the area of depleted oxygen, and may do extensive damage to estuarine organisms (Carpenter and Cargo, 1957).

More specific estuarine effects of change in river flow have been shown by Beaven (1946), Gunter and Hall (1963), Nelson (1960), and by others. Beaven documented the control by the Susquehanna River over salinity in the upper Chesapeake Bay, and provided excellent evidence that all major oyster mortalities recorded for the upper Bay from 1907 to 1946 were associated with and probably the direct result of periods of high runoff of the river.

Biological effects. The intermittent controlled release of fresh water from Lake Okechobee to the St. Lucie Estuary in Florida has probably enhanced the fisheries by nutrient supply, and may benefit croaker, mullet, anchovy, and menhaden, according to Gunter and Hall (1963). A better pattern of release could be of increased benefit to the fisheries.

Nelson (1931), in reviewing the arguments relating to diversion of Delaware River water to New York City in the Hudson River basin, cited many estimates of the ecological and biological effects. As an example, he predicted an up-bay movement of oyster drills,

Urosalpinx cinerea, to invade several excellent oyster seed beds previously protected by low salinities. In more general terms, salinity is known to limit the distribution of oysters and many other estuarine species (Gunter, 1955; Galtsoff, 1960; Korringa, 1952). Davis (1958) and others have demonstrated from laboratory experiments that the eggs and larvae of clams, *Mercenaria* (*Venus*) *mercenaria*, and oysters (*Crassostrea virginica*) have optimal salinity requirements for development and growth, and the optimal salinity for the eggs of the oyster may be governed by the degree of salinity at which the parent oysters develop gonads.

Additional biological effects of flow change are known. Diversion may disturb the migratory patterns of fish. Gaussle and Kelley (1963) found that flow reversal in the San Joaquin River, because of exportation of water through a power plant, has apparently affected salmon runs, presumably because "home stream" water was not present to stimulate ascent and spawning. The degree of dilution affects the decrease of bacteria in polluted estuaries, although Ketchum *et al.* (1952) found this to be a much smaller factor than the bactericidal effect of sea water. Ketchum (1954) also showed that the vigor of estuarine circulation, which is greatly affected by river flow, determines the reproductive rate necessary for maintenance of plankton populations. Pritchard (1951) suggested that the upstream movement of deep water, also affected by river flow, may transport young croaker, *Micropogon undulatus*, from the spawning ground (off Chesapeake Bay) upstream at .2-.4 knots, or 130 miles in less than 20 days. Our later experience in the Bay suggests that this is a primary and essential method of dispersion for the young of weakfish (*Cynoscion regalis*), spot (*Leiostomus xanthurus*), blue crab (*Callinectes sapidus*), and other species. Pritchard has also shown (1952) that similar movements may provide oyster larvae for the greatest seed oyster area of the world, in James River of Virginia. Bousefield (1955) vividly related such flow-dominated circulation to the distribution of barnacles in the Miramichi Estuary. Odum and Wilson (1962) expressed the possibility that bays with little flushing may develop higher productivity and more effective regeneration of nutrients. Low river flow would obviously favor these effects.

Chemical effects. Flow modification also affects the chemical content of waters entering the estuarine system. Carpenter (1957) found that the calcium content of the Susquehanna is broadly, but imprecisely, related to flow. Renn (unpublished), in preliminary scanning of the distribution of ABS (alkyl benzene sulfonate), principal ingredient of the non-biodegradable detergents, observed the effective reduction caused by dilution. Laundry outfalls showed levels up to 140 ppm ABS, which was reduced by dilution, absorption, blow-off of foam, and degradation (about 5 percent per week) to .2-.3 ppm in rivers and estuaries. Agricultural or silvicultural pesticides would be similarly affected.

Siltation. Siltation in estuaries is caused by both natural and human factors. Deforestation, flashing runoff, and poor agricultural practices contribute. Burt (1955) showed that river discharge affects the distribution of the inorganic suspended load in the Chesapeake, as many others have seen from other estuaries. Wolman *et al.* (1957) calculated that 60 million cubic feet of silt per year are deposited in the estuary of the Potomac River near Washington. Mansueti (1961) estimated that half of the former upper estuary spawning areas for fish and shellfish beds for oysters have been destroyed or shifted downstream by sediments in the Chesapeake. He also pointed out the progressive filling of deeper channels by such silt. Gunter (1956) summarized the soil transport of the Mississippi River as 730 million tons of soil per year into the Gulf of Mexico—38 thousand acres, three feet deep. He deplores the narrow canalization of this transport, which formerly overflowed the basin.

Human countermeasures are again available, but not well utilized, in this country at least. Soil conservation is progressing.

Small watershed dams and larger reservoirs also retain silt effectively.

ENRICHMENT

Organic enrichment of tributaries is an ancient problem. In direct relation to estuaries, Jeffries (1962) has described the nutritional contribution to Raritan Bay of nitrate-nitrogen and phosphate from sewage in the Raritan River and the resultant dense phytoplankton blooms. Renn (1956) cites human organic loading as being .4 lb/person/day. The quantities reaching the estuary will obviously vary greatly with distance, river flow, loading, and many other factors, so that generalizations here are inappropriate.

DAMS AND BARRIERS

Physical barriers in tributary streams create very special and important effects. Hynes (1960) and Mansueti (1961) pointed out that dams absolutely block anadromous fish migrations and may eliminate important runs unless fishways are provided. A series of dams on the Susquehanna has cut off migrations of the white shad (*Alosa sapidissima*) and reduced the spawning area of the striped bass (*Roccus saxatilis*). Others have blocked herrings and other species. Whitney (1961) pointed out that, in addition to physical blockage, dams create reservoirs which differ greatly in circulation, temperature, and currents from the original stream, so that anadromous fish may not be successful even if they pass the wall. Fishways also introduce an artificial but effective factor for genetic selection. In addition, reservoir water can become depleted of oxygen, modified in temperature, and changed in other ways (Whaley, 1960). The common practice of drawing relatively deep water through turbines can release undesirable conditions into the upper estuary. An aged fisherman pointed out other modifications in the upper Chesapeake. Before dams, the upper Bay was subject to annual ice scour alternating with heavy siltation. Dams prevent the ice movement, trap the silt, and produce much greater stability of the bottom. Heavy vegetation grows where it once could not.

SELECTED CASES

To illustrate the range and magnitude of watershed effects on estuaries, four vivid examples, past and future, will be briefly described. They are the leveeing of the lower Mississippi River, operation of the Bonnet Carré Spillway, plans for water management of the Potomac River, and diversion from the Delaware River to the Hudson River.

Levees. Gunter (1952, 1953, 1956, 1957a) describes the development of levees in the lower portion of the 1,257,000 square mile Mississippi basin (Fig. 21.1). First construction was in 1717, and a broader program was inaugurated in 1735 by private interests. The State of Louisiana assumed responsibility in 1828, the Mississippi Valley Commission in 1879, and the U.S. Army Corps of Engineers in 1928. Levees are now up to 35 feet high. Among the many results, runoff is faster and peakier; velocity increase transports more silt; alluviation, sedimentation, and flooding of the swamps, marshes, and estuaries have virtually ceased; and enormous quantities of silt are directly deposited in the Gulf of Mexico. These have brought serious, and usually detrimental, changes to the estuarine areas of Louisiana. Drainage of nutrients from land is reduced; salinity is increased and stabilized; island erosion is increased; and bays may move inland. Species appear to be responding to these changes and some oyster reefs are disappearing.

Bonnet Carré Spillway. In the same system, a great spillway, 7,700 feet wide, was completed in 1933 (Figure 21.1). It was designed to protect New Orleans from Mississippi River floods, and can carry 250 thousand cubic feet per second (cfs). It diverts water into Lake Pontchartrain, thence through Lake Borgne and Mississippi Sound, and eventually to the Gulf of Mexico. Gunter (1953) describes the results of openings in 1937, 1945, and 1950. Since all of the receiving area is estuarine, the effects are of interest here. In Lake Pontchartrain, motile organisms are driven out, and many nonmotile forms are killed by low salinities. A small area is covered by mud. Most or all of the oysters in certain beds are destroyed, with lower loss over a wider area, although oyster pests and predators are killed out. Nutrient is added to the area, estimated in 1950 as 40 thousand tons. Following return to normal salinities, unusually great production of shrimp and other marine life is observed. In Gunter's opinion, the total beneficial economic effect out-weighs the partial oyster mortalities which occur in some years.

The Potomac. The Potomac is a very flashy river. With an average flow at Washington, D. C., of 11,000 cfs, it has an observed range from 800 cfs to 500,000 cfs. Droughts, floods, heavy siltation, massive enrichment, and increasing needs for sustained water supply all present problems in its control and use. Many partial or complete answers have been proposed (Wolman *et al.*, 1957), but the most recent suggestion is a dramatic example of efforts to manage a river and control its effects on an estuary.

The U. S. Army Corps of Engineers has developed four alternate plans, with primary

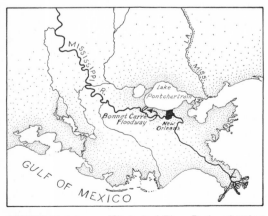

FIGURE 21.1 Lower Mississippi River Basin, showing relation of Bonnet Carré Spillway to the estuarine areas bordering the Gulf of Mexico.

interest in flood control, recreation, water supply, and water quality control (U. S. Army Engineer District, Baltimore, N. Atl. Div., 1963). The one recommended would include establishment of 418 headwater small reservoirs, 16 major reservoirs, 3 small flood control projects, and a general program of land management and conservation. The cost is estimated at $498 million, and it could be completed about 2010; the plan is now being reviewed.

Estuarine effects have been only partially estimated. Augmentation of low summer and fall flow is the obvious, and reduction of spring maxima is inevitable. Uncontrolled low-flow averages about 1,100 cfs, and would normally be expected to decline in 50 years to 800 cfs because of upstream irrigation and other consumptive uses. If the plan is effected, minimal flow would be about 4,700 cfs, which is 42 percent of the annual average. Specific projection of all the effects of this change on the dynamics, populations, and character of the Potomac Estuary offers challenging problems. It has not even been attempted. It is already clear, however, that the upper estuary, at least, would be significantly and permanently different, especially during summer months. Physical circulation, nutrient availability, and biotic communities would all be significantly modified.

The Delaware diversion. New York City, on the Hudson River, has long sought to obtain water from the Delaware River watershed. Delaware Bay, principally through the State of New Jersey, fought such diversion in 1929–1931 and 1952–1954, primarily on the grounds that estuarine productivity would be decreased. Nelson championed this position and has summarized the estuarine argument (1960). Despite evidence which was more precise than usual, the Supreme Court allowed a diversion of 1,240 cfs (800 mgd). Part of this is already in effect. Part of the pattern provided will guarantee minimal flows at Trenton during low-flow periods. Nelson argued that the minimal flows would be ineffective in combating oyster drills, that drills would penetrate farther on to produc-

tive seed beds with higher average salinities, and that the nutrient loss would be especially damaging.

Ketchum was asked to predict the effects, and provided estimates of channel salinities under normal flows and under diversion with controlled summer minima. The near future will test his precision, but his predictions provide an excellent example of the nature of the effects of intentional flow modification on estuarine conditions (Ketchum, unpublished).

The river in 1952 had a mean flow of 11,700 cfs, with usual lows near 2,000 cfs and highs near 29,000 cfs. With stipulated augmentation of flow at Trenton, and diversion of 1,240 cfs, Ketchum predicts that mean flow will be reduced from 11,700 to 10,530 cfs, low flow increased from 2,157 to 2,893 cfs, and high flow reduced from 28,900 to 21,950 cfs. Salinity will increase at mean flow a maximum of .85 ‰,* decrease at low flow a maximum of 1.08 ‰, and increase at high flow a maximum of 3.2 ‰. Range would thus be reduced, with a maximum at the center of the estuary, where annual range of 16.46‰ would become 12.85‰, a difference of 4.61‰. Isohalines would be moved upstream, except during augmented flow. Biologically, the important conditions which limit the viability or success of populations are generally the extreme conditions to which the populations are exposed. The proposed diversions should, therefore, be beneficial to the populations within the estuary.

At the hearings, other biologists expressed broad concern about the detrimental effects, but were unable to make and substantiate specific predictions of those effects.

It is interesting to compare these projections with the report of Segerstraale (1951) that average changes of .5—.75 ‰ produced significant changes in the effective distribution of estuarine species.

Apparently, no one has made an effort to predict the effects of the addition of 1,240 cfs of water to the Hudson Estuary, perhaps

* The symbol, ‰, means per mille, or parts per thousand (*editor's note*).

because no one objects to the addition, or because the lower Hudson at New York City seems to be beyond reclamation.

Activities in the Estuary

PHYSICAL PROCESSES

With increasing frequency and intensity, human activities are changing the physical conditions and processes in estuaries.

Thermal addition.* One dramatic and growing group of effects arises from the addition of heat on a continuous basis. The most important sources have been generating plants for electricity, using great quantities of water to cool condensers. Research on thermal effects in fresh water has been extensive, permitting summary by Ingram and Towne (1959), Hynes (1960), and others for the fluvial situation, where physical effects and the biological sequence produced are reasonably predictable. This is not so for estuaries, where tidal flux and the presence of a different community of animal and plant species introduce complicating factors. Pannell *et al.* (1962) reported observations which illustrate the difficulties of predicting effects, and the types of effects which may occur. Specific predictions were used in designing the release of 26 million gallons per hour with a rise from intake to outfall of 12°F. The prediction was that warmed water would spread thinly on the surface. It was observed, however, that an area 1,000 feet in radius is warmed at least 5°, but most of it is between 3 and 9 feet below the surface, and the plume swings with tidal action.

It was predicted that little heat would be absorbed by the main body of the estuary, and observed that virtually all heat dispersion is by mixing. The most interesting observation was that most warmed water remained below cooler but fresh water and above cooler salt water. The interplay of salinity and temperature produced this unexpected vertical series, with salinity dominant.

* See Selection 17 also (*editor's note*).

Biologically, the heat appears to have extended the local breeding season of the boring gribble, *Limnoria*, and increased the incidence of the shipworm, *Teredo*. These sessile forms were affected, but no significant change in zooplankton was detected. Other effects remain to be evaluated.

In the United States, a valuable experiment may be provided by the construction of a 670 MW steam generating plant on the Patuxent Estuary, a tributary of the Chesapeake. The plant is now under construction and will warm 500,000 gallons per minute by 11.5°F. in warm months and half that quantity by 23°F. in winter. This volume is about 50 percent more than the average freshwater input of the watershed above this point, so that the estuary will be used as a tidal cooling lagoon. Fortunately, intensive studies are preceding and following the construction of the plant. The Chesapeake Biological Laboratory has established a research team and developed cooperation from about 40 scientists in a dozen institutions and agencies for pre- and post-operative studies of circulation, salinity, oxygen and thermal distribution, phytoplankton abundance and productivity, zooplankton distribution, bacterial density, fouling rates and species, benthic community composition, fish egg and larval distribution, adult fish distribution and migration, crab abundance, and other aspects of the area. Perhaps this will permit improved prediction and rational regulation of such activities. Present projections of the need for electric power call for demand to increase in this country from 60 billion gallons per day (bgd) in 1955, to 131 bgd in 1975, to 200 bgd in the 1980's (Picton, 1956). Against these figures, consider the estimates of total dependable surface runoff, 385 bgd at present increased to 630 bgd by 1975 or 1980. Power demand in this country and many others grows even more rapidly than populations, and increasing pressure to use estuaries for cooling is inevitable.

Otto Kinne at Helgoland has recently provided an excellent and valuable review of the effects of temperature on marine and brackish-water animals (1963) as part one of a survey of the effects of both temperature and salinity. The biological effects of thermal change, affecting all chemical and biological rates and processes, are profound. Kinne devotes portions of his review to temperature tolerance and lethal limits, effects on metabolism and activity, reproductive success, distribution, organism size, meristic characters and shape, and biotic adaptation to temperature.

Comprehension of these effects will be invaluable in efforts to prevent estuarine damage or to utilize heat to obtain optimal benefits.

Changed salinity. Human activities in the estuary occasionally affect salinity. Examples are provided by pumpage of large volumes of fresh water into the estuary (Wolman *et al.*, 1957) or by engineering changes affecting the fundamental pattern of circulation, such as major modifications of channel depth.

The great Dutch conversion of an estuarine area of the Zuider Zee to a freshwater lake was completed in 1932, when an enclosure dike was completed (Figure 21.2), cutting off 2700 km² of rich, warm, shoal water with a salinity of 10–15 ‰ in the inner portion and 15–25 ‰ in the outer portion. The results, described and discussed by Havinga (1935,

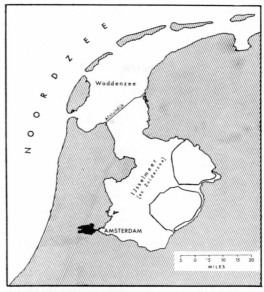

FIGURE 21.2 The old Zuider Zee, cut off by an enclosure dike or "Afsluitdijk" to convert an estuary to a lake and dry land.

1936, 1941, 1949, 1959), show a vivid example of man's impact.

Salinity decreased as the flow of the IJssel River continued while ocean water was almost completely prevented from entering (Figure 21.3). Stability was attained about 1937, and subsequent salt intrusion is limited

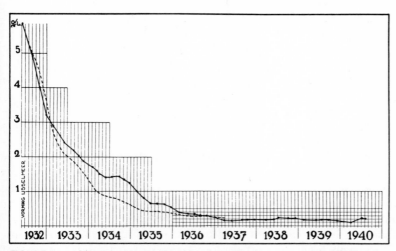

FIGURE 21.3 Chlorinity in the IJsselmeer following enclosure. The broken line indicates the calculated chlorinity level. The solid line shows the observed level (After Havinga, 1941).

to the water near two locks in the dike. The mero-estuarine species which had provided a large fishery (herrings, anchovy, and shrimp) and various non-commercial species were quickly and vastly reduced. Herring were seen in great numbers at the dike, but were unable to reach the low-salinity water. Anchovy sought a different estuarine condition, relatively high temperature, and were equally frustrated. Stenohaline marine and polyhaline organisms were killed, and eventually their predators starved. With varying periods of endurance, the edible mussel, *Mytilus edulis*; the soft-shell clam, *Mya arenaria*; the green crab, *Carcinus maenas;* and other forms (*Cardium edule, Tellina balthica, Corophium* sp., *Heteropanope tridentata, Gobius minutus*, and others) died out. Eventually, the predators dependent on intolerant forms also disappeared.

Most of the euryhaline forms passed out of existence more slowly in the IJsselmeer, but some survived. *Neomysis vulgaris* was highly successful in the new environment, and provides much of the food for larger species. Limnetic species spread slowly but effectively; the motile forms achieved wide dispersion.

As a result, the older fishery has been entirely replaced by freshwater production of pikeperch, bream, roach, and others. A striking survivor is the eel, *Anguilla vulgaris*, which thrives as the principal commercial species. It is aided by nighttime locking of young elvers into the lake when they appear along the dike.

Havinga points out that the result is faunistic poverty, marked by adaptations and intrusions, although total human values have been greatly enhanced. Fish production of 16 million kilograms per year was replaced by 1959 with 7 million kg of fish plus 70 million kg equivalent of pork on the reclaimed land. This may treble when all the potential *polder* reclamation is completed.

The Netherlands has embarked on a second great program for modifying brackish-water areas (Figure 21.4). Primarily for the control of highly destructive floods, they have begun the "Delta Plan" at the mouths of the Rhine, Meuse, and Scheldt Rivers, to be completed in 1978. Three arms of the sea will be cut off and a series of additional dams will modify flow and convert salt and brackish areas to fresh water. Thorough hydrographic study before, during, and after construction is being accompanied by intensive and extensive biological surveys (Hartog, 1963; Vaas, 1962). Present predictions of the effects are stimulating and instructive, in view of Dutch experience in other locations. Tidal action will cease for most of the region, and be reduced throughout the area. Salinity will decrease rapidly, modified by leaching of salt from *polders*, and is not expected to fall below .3 ‰. Stenohaline marine organisms will perish, although euryhaline species will persist for a long period and a brackish-water population will develop, then be succeeded by limnetic species.

Hartog has defined the euhalinicum, polyhalinicum, mesohalinicum, oligohalinicum, and freshwater conditions under the present regime, and published on some of the Amphipoda. Other studies are covering Hirundinea, Isopoda, Gastropoda, Gammaridae, turbellarians, fish, plankton, and vegetation.

Human safety will be gained, but it is most regrettable that part of Holland's import mussel industry and all of her Zeeland oyster industry may be sacrificed. Korringa (1958) described the threat to these industries, in which cultivation and management have been brought to a high and intensive level. He pointed out that it might theoretically be possible to determine the allowable range of salinity, silt content, sand transport, current velocity, plankton, and other requirements and seek new oyster areas, but he was not optimistic. Artificial culture of seed would be required, and this is still a difficult technique, without demonstrated economic justification on a large scale.

Modifications of basins. The shape of the basin of an estuary has many effects on hydrographic dynamics and, as a result, on other processes. Pritchard has expressed the effect of modification (1955) by pointing out that conversion from marked stratification to

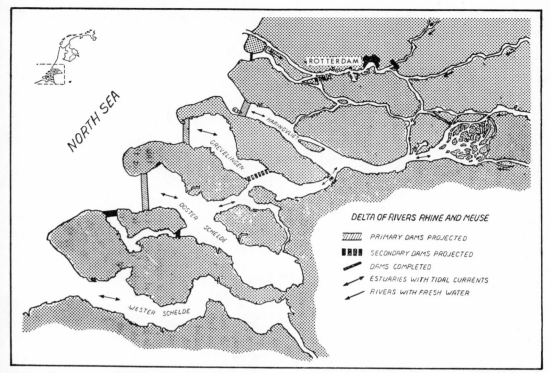

FIGURE 21.4 The "Delta Plan" for modifying estuaries in southwest Netherlands (After Havinga, 1959, modified to show works completed by mid-1964).

vertical homogeneity is favored by increasing the width and opposed by increasing the depth. Shore erosion, siltation, channel dredging and spoil deposition would all have local effects. Skyes (1965) has noted that the establishment of cities on the shore is usually followed by an expanding pattern of reclamation, fills, causeways, and bridges, permanently altering the entire area. The premium which is placed on waterfront residences creates dramatic changes in basins by a pattern of dredging and filling for housing and for industry. Thompson (1961) summarized the usual estuarine effects as reduction in the water area; denudation of the bottom as fill is removed; modification of currents and tidal exchange; alteration in salinity, temperature, and perhaps oxygen content; and sediment dispersion.

Boca Ciega Bay, on the west coast of Florida, is a clear example of the present and future magnitude of these changes (Figure 21.5). Hutton *et al.* (1956) felt that the com-

bined effects of sedimentation and basin change in Boca Ciega Bay might be to reduce or eliminate fishing, destroy breeding and nursery grounds, and create low oxygen areas. Woodburn has provided a guide (1963) for reviewing proposals to change shorelines, and suggests principles to be followed.

Comprehension of the relationships between the shape of the basin and various processes can be put to highly constructive uses. Scale models have been used in many parts of the world to study physical patterns of circulation and to test new possibilities. Simmons (1959) is enthusiastic about the potentials of using models in estuarine research. By using such techniques as single slug and continuous release, methylene blue chloride and other dyes, and artificial roughening, he is confident that models can produce accurate integration of the tidal, density, and freshwater forces that affect dispersion, dilution, and flushing of introduced materi-

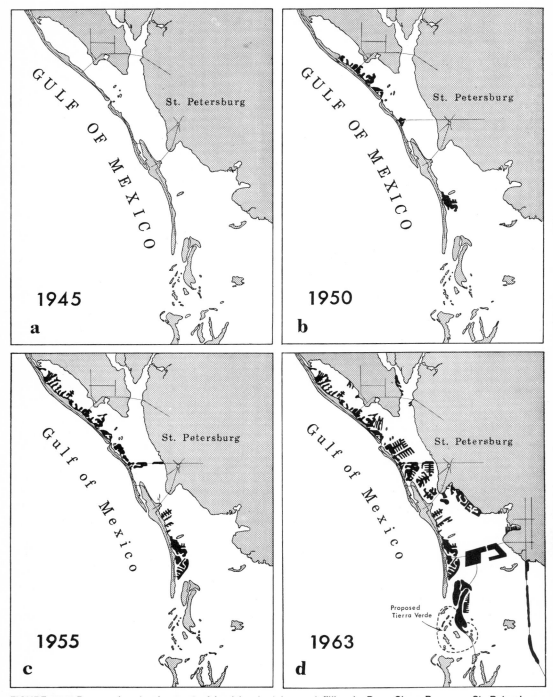

FIGURE 21.5 Progressive development of land by dredging and filling in Boca Ciega Bay near St. Petersburg, Florida (Courtesy Mr. James Sykes and the U.S. Bureau of Sport Fisheries and Wildlife).

als. However, present estuarine models usually cannot scale non-conservative, or interacting, or time-related materials and processes. Pritchard (1960) has called attention to possible limitations in model studies of processes involving diffusion phenomena. Present estuarine models include the Delaware Estuary, San Francisco Bay, Puget Sound, Thames Estuary, New York Harbor, Matagordo Bay, Galveston Bay, Narragansett Bay, and others. Additional models are planned.

Man has created a rather special change in the "shape" of estuaries by removing a portion of the land mass between them. In this country an intercoastal waterway allows water, aquatic organisms, and people to move freely between bays along the entire East Coast and much of the Gulf Coast. The great canal systems of Europe and other areas provide similar interchanges. The greatest effects will probably involve biological exchanges and extensions.

CHEMICAL METHODS

Biocides. Many chemical compounds inhibit vital biological processes. Most compounds do so in excessive concentrations. In recent years, great industrial effort has gone into the development of compounds which could be used in small quantities to interfere with life processes in specific target species. The results are variously called weedicides, herbicides, bactericides, fungicides, and pesticides. Miss Carson has correctly termed the group "biocides" because of their fundamental effect. They destroy life. Advantages and disadvantages from their use are both very great. These, and toxic substances never intended for use in control work, are present in estuaries in increasing amounts.

The U. S. Fish and Wildlife Service has been especially concerned with biocidal effects, and very valuable work has been done on two broad problems. What are the effects of these materials on estuarine species other than the original target? Can biocides be used constructively in the management of

estuarine organisms? This research provides valuable guidance. It is, however, most regrettable that there has as yet been little support for research on the fundamental physiological mechanism of biocides, and on the effects of known toxins on the broad spectrum of noncommercial species.

Davis investigated the effects of 31 pesticides on the eggs and larvae of the oyster and clam (1961). He reported great variation in toxicity within each group of chemicals, ranging from 90 percent mortality of oysters in .05 ppm DDT to improved growth of clams in 5 ppm of lindane. Several apparently beneficial materials may have reduced bacterial action. Reduction in growth rate was identified as a useful indicator of toxicity. Davis felt that it will eventually be possible to select materials for highly specific control.

The effect of toxins on growth was more fully developed by Butler et al. (1962). They observed that change in growth rate provides a sensitive bioassay technique, allowing detection of differences in one or two days. Chlordane, heptachlor, and rotenone were observed to be inhibitory within 24 hours in concentrations as low as .01 ppm. All of the common agricultural pesticides tested were toxic, but there was some indication that they are released from internal storage in organisms when environmental concentration drops.

In efforts to utilize biocides constructively, Loosanoff (1960) and his associates have screened hundreds of compounds in a search for effective methods for controlling green crabs (*Carcinus maenas*) and other arthropod predators on molluscan shellfish. They identified a large number of effective compounds, which can also kill shrimp, prawns, copepods, and other crustaceans. Perhaps it is suggestive of the complexity and difficulties of this field to note that my own professional interest in the blue crab (*Callinectes sapidus*) and the copepods of the estuaries makes me regard this new knowledge with conflicting feelings. Loosanoff also reported that many of the materials tested adversely affect molluscs. 1.0 ppm of DDT caused the death of oyster larvae, and .025 ppm interfered with growth. He suggested combinations which might be effective chemical barriers to minimize the invasion of shellfish beds by arthropods, and urged thorough evaluation of every such possibility prior to use.

Additional efforts in the control of undesired species have been reported recently. Hanks (1963) learned that baitfish could be soaked in lindane solution to reduce green crab populations and reduce crab immigration. Lindsay (1963) tested several materials for the control of ghost shrimp, *Callianassa* sp., and Japanese drills, *Ocinebra japonica*, in Puget Sound. Shrimp could be controlled and drills could be prevented from entering experimental plots, but Lindsay urged that the methods be avoided until long-term effects and public health problems could be fully understood. The use of DDT on oyster cultch to control barnacles (*Elminius*) was tested for the effects on oysters (Waugh and Ansell, 1956). This control technique had been discovered by Loosanoff and tested by others. The set of oysters doubled, initial growth was somewhat inhibited but followed by excellent growth, to reach 40 percent greater size than controls in 2½ months.

With reference to plants, estuarine research on biocides is extremely limited. 2,4-D was effective in killing Eurasian milfoil in the upper Chesapeake Bay (Rawls, 1964), and Beaven *et al.* (1962) showed that the effective concentration had no acute effects on crabs, oysters, clams, and fish. A secondary mortality occurred, however, when the dense mat of killed plants decayed on the bottom, producing anaerobic and toxic conditions.

An excellent summary of the results of research on pesticides has been prepared by Butler and Springer (1963). The specific capacities of organisms to concentrate pesticides are poorly known, but may be extremely important because oysters concentrated 96 percent of available DDT within two days and retained much of this for substantial periods.* The possibilities of recy-

* The biological concentration of DDT residues in an eastern U.S. estuary is detailed in Selection 40.

cling and build-up were noted, citing freshwater experience in which original applications of .014–.02 ppm of TDE (DDD) eventually produced concentration of 2,500 ppm in fish and 1,600 ppm in fish-eating birds. The eventual use of chemicals which are specific for target species and non-toxic to all others is cited as the most promising future avenue of effort.

During March, 1964, the British Government ordered withdrawal of the chlorinated hydrocarbons, aldrin and dieldrin, from use. Action was apparently based on evidence of accumulative contamination, and also on some uncertainty of the physiological human effects. Also in March, 1964, the U. S. Public Health Service and the State of Louisiana established endrin used for cane borers as the probable cause of the killing of 10 million fish in the Mississippi River basin, including brackish waters of the Gulf of Mexico. As compared with environmental concentrations, fish blood showed a thousandfold increase, and fatty tissue a ten-thousandfold accumulation.

In the estuarine studies which have been conducted, these chlorinated hydrocarbons are all dangerous to important estuarine species, but so are many others. Revelations of damage and restrictions on use are not yet ended.

Intensified attention to pesticides should not obscure the ever-present possibilities of other toxic elements and compounds. The paucity of such research in estuaries is impressive in view of the great industrial growth of recent years and the consequent threat to inshore waters. Alexander *et al.* (1936) illustrated one type of effect in that low levels of cyanide showed linear increase in toxicity with temperature, but nearly logarithmic increase in toxicity with decrease in oxygen concentration. Olson *et al.* (1941) and Davis (1948) explained the effects of flocculent copperas pollution on diatoms, and learned that precipitating particles carry some diatoms from the water. This would decrease productivity, although Davis found no evidence of substantial loss. Galtsoff (1960) observed that the precipitate can be dealt with by oysters, but suspects that it may be harmful to larvae. He also notes the absorption and storage of copper, mercury, lead, and arsenic by oysters and other bivalves.

Ideally, research on the effects of chemical additions to the estuary should precede or parallel industrial development, new brand production, and chemical process modification. Regrettably, this is not the present practice. Therefore, new damage and danger remain as continuous and growing threats in coastal waters.

Nutrient chemicals. Human wastes, or their degradation products, are universally placed in the river, the estuary, or the sea (see Koch, 1959, for a comprehensive European summary), and provide a continuous source of nitrogen and phosphorous in various combinations, plus a variable and imperfectly understood mixture of many substances. The great human preference for concentrating near estuaries makes the impact even greater at that site. Nitrogen and phosphorous are essential for photosynthetic elaboration, and availability sometimes limits production, so that they must receive principal discussion.

Before examining some of the effects of human waste, it is of interest to note that other potential mixtures of waste are added to estuaries in significant quantities. Ryther (1954) and others of the staff of the Woods Hole Oceanographic Institution (Ryther *et al.*, 1958a; Guillard *et al.*, 1960) have studied the remarkable growth of algae in Great South Bay and Moriches Bay, on Long Island, New York. Broad study of hydrography, chemistry, and biology has demonstrated that heavy pollution from surrounding duck farms, with high organic nitrogen but unusually low N:P ratio, combines with the topography and hydrography of these bays to yield a very dense population of small algae, dominated by *Nannochloris atomus* and a species of *Stichococcus*. These have seriously reduced the oyster-producing capacity of these estuaries by unbalanced overenrichment.

Effects of nutrient addition, rather than tables of the prevailing quantities, are of interest here. Hynes (1960) has provided a valuable condensation of knowledge of the fluvial and lacustrine effects of organic pollution, and demonstrates that processes are rather well established (see also Ingram and Towne, 1959). Of about 45 pages on the biological effects of organic matter, Hynes was able to devote only two to estuaries because "there is little detailed information on the biological consequences of estuarine pollution". He cites tidal activity and rapid environmental changes as complicating factors. However, the general pattern of dense algal blooms, often accompanied by esthetically undesirable appearance and odor is very familiar (Bartsch, 1961).

Rational attempts must be made to understand these effects, in view of the certain growth of coastal populations. E. P. Odum (1961a) provides a constructive point of departure when he recognizes that the addition of large amounts of organic waste into natural waters creates a new ecosystem, and that an effective response to it is most likely to be found in studying the fundamental principles and processes involved. He includes a helpful analysis of the energy flow involved and the nutrient cycling which occurs, and suggests avenues of attack when the results are inconsistent with human wishes. Krause (1961) and others have outlined the fundamentals of algal physiology, and have urged a basic approach to these highly practical problems.

The distinctive problems and potentials of estuarine enrichment have already received attention. Mansueti (1961) stresses the widespread estuarine tendency to act as a nutrient trap, with tidal cycles and slow flushing to enhance the availability of nutrients for chemical or biological use. Pritchard (1959b) reviewed the physical mechanisms affecting the distribution of conservative materials introduced, and showed that: (a) oscillatory tidal motion produces longitudinal spread; (b) non-tidal dispersion will respond to the density of the material and the pattern of net motion in the estuary (vertically homogeneous, two-layer, three-layer, etc.); (c) net flushing will occur, and usually be predominantly along the right side of the estuary; and (d) entrapment by lateral indentures can provide important reservoirs. He predicted that computation may eventually be feasible for predicting the distribution of conservative contaminants, but that nonconservative materials will be much more difficult. I would add that biological processes and sequences in estuaries rarely permit such broad-scale projections with useful accuracy as yet, although they merit continued effort.

Artificial enrichment has been essayed, but it is expensive because of the cost of fertilizers and of accompanying research. Pratt (1949) found that the addition of superphosphate could elevate phosphate levels in a salt pond, although not by calculated amounts. Repeated addition held levels well above pretreatment concentrations. Nitrate additions, on the other hand, produced short spurts to predicted levels, but these could not be held. A net increase in the standing crop was obtained, and it lasted for a significant period. Earlier large-scale study of changes in a fertilized sea-loch by Raymont (1949) and others showed that plankton production increased, bottom fauna was enhanced, and fish production eventually responded favorably. Use of sewage for enrichment of freshwater ponds is an ancient technique.

Development of practical methods for profitable management of the enormous quantities of fertilizing materials available to estuaries offers a challenging field for further research and for contribution to human welfare. At present, these vast quantities are released in undirected patterns, without using their great potential for profitable selected improvement.

The specific effects at sewage outfalls into estuaries also need further study. Through the tidal cycle, the release plume will swing upstream and downstream, and cover a central area twice or continuously. Effects on planktonic and nektonic species may be ephemeral, and the best record of effect is often made on the benthic community. The affected zones are oval, circular, or simicircular, in contrast with the more linear fluvial

effects noted by Gaufin and Tarzwell (1956), Hynes (1960), and Ingram and Towne (1959). Estuarine patterns have been observed by Blegvad (1932), Fraser (1932), Filice (1954a, b), Reish (1959a, b), and McNulty (1961). Successive zones away from the outfall may include an area of sludge or soft muck with no macroinvertebrates; a poor zone which may have characteristic species present, sometimes dwarfed; a relatively rich zone with heavy populations of molluscs, worms, diatoms, and other species; and normal communities. Effects of local circulation, substrate, salinity, and other variables would produce almost infinite variations. In broader terms, McNulty saw a small damaged area surrounded by a much larger enriched area, and could distinguish indicator organisms and communities for both. Galtsoff (1956), however, reported that sludge from domestic sewers has almost completely smothered the formerly productive shellfish beds in the vicinity of large cities, including New York, Boston, and Norfolk. Hynes cited the reports of Pentelow (1955) that sewage causes severe deoxygenation in some estuaries like the Thames to promote a condition which blocks the upstream and downstream migration of sea trout and salmon so that these runs have become extinct. There is need for additional research on the effects of sewage—and much room for improvement in handling it.

Radioactive wastes. Radioactive wastes are entering coastal waters in increasing quantities from such activities as research, munitions, industry, and medicine. The estuaries are likely to receive, and retain, greater concentrations than the oceans. These are of concern because they may cycle and recycle until they enter human food supplies in significant quantities, and they may also affect the genetic structure of aquatic organisms.

Chipman (1958, 1960) has cited the complexity of obtaining complete answers, since the fate of radionuclides is dependent on many physical, chemical, and biological processes. Pritchard (1960) stated that the principal factors involved will usually be the form of the contaminant, dilution, advective transport, turbulent diffusion, uptake on sediments, and extraction by the biota from solution or from the sediments. Chipman and his associates (Chipman *et al.*, 1958) reported on a series of experiments designed to establish uptake rate of various probable radionuclides by common species and to track these materials through major food chains. Of all the suggested fates, Donaldson (1960) found biological activity to be the most important factor in the distribution and localization of radioactive products at Eniwetok. He found no evidence of biological effects of these products, probably because competition quickly eliminates injured individuals. The applicability of these generalizations to estuaries has not been tested. Extreme local situations may be dangerous and important, but apparently the total effect is not yet great.

Pulp wastes. The wastes from plants that process wood into cellulose products by various processes are released into many estuarine areas. A great deal has been written which contains many conflicting observations and opinions. As an example, in 1947 Galtsoff *et al.* were satisfied that pulp-mill waste was the principal cause of decline of the productivity of oyster bars in the York River of Virginia. In a very different area, Waldichuk (1959) described a variety of releases in British Columbia, and noted that chemical and biological degradation may or may not be present, depending largely on the mechanics of release. The report offered by Gunter and McKee to the Washington Pollution Control Commission in 1960 appears to contain a rational summary: (1) sulfite waste is exceedingly complex, varying with species of wood, treatment, and digestion chemicals; (2) effects have been erratic and mixed, with investigational results including both stimulation and depression of the biota; (3) physical dispersion and dilution are important aids in disposal; (4) interim regulations should be established; and (5) research is essential to study the effects of the liquor and methods of rendering it non-destructive.

Exotic chemical effects. Wherever large quantities of chemicals are placed in estuaries, they cause change. Each case is local and specific. Some special instances are, however, potentially instructive and important.

Stroup *et al.* (1961) commented on the effects of adding large quantities of acid to the carbonate-buffered waters of Baltimore Harbor. They found that pH is decreased, and the partial pressure of CO_2 is increased. This increase in CO_2 tension may be significantly favorable to photosynthesis but unfavorable to the fauna.

Galtsoff (1960) emphasized the capacity of many organisms to concentrate elements and compounds from the environment. Bivalve molluscs, for example, absorb copper, mercury, lead, and arsenic near industrial areas. Oysters, clams, and scallops can contain concentrations of zinc over 100 thousand times that of surrounding waters (Chipman *et al.*, 1958).

Oil, motor exhaust fumes, ship bilge, unusual industrial wastes, garbage dumping, and a limitless variety of special chemical additions exist, and require comprehension and control where they are important.

Pollution-control efforts are universal, but extremely variable. It is improbable, however, that understanding and effectively controlling chemical pollution will ever catch up in the race against new products and processes. In most cases, regulations are created after damage occurs rather than with intelligent foresight.

GEOLOGICAL PROCESSES*

Man has directly influenced geological processes, principally by changing silt production and distribution. Within the estuary, this is usually the result of shoreline construction (Sykes, 1965), dynamiting (Gunter, 1957b), cutting of waterways and canals, or certain specialized fishing operations such as hydraulic dredging for soft shell clams (Man-

---

* The physical effects in estuaries that are caused by man's activities elsewhere along coasts are discussed further in Selection 25.

ning, 1957). Manning described the Maryland gear, developed since 1950; it jets a trench in the bottom about 30 inches wide and up to 18 inches deep. Heavy materials drop rapidly, but clams and other coarse materials are conveyed by belt to the surface; the fine silts and clays are dispersed, usually to no more than 50 feet on either side of the cut. Most material returns to the trench.

Effects of silt handling are usually relatively local, although Hellier and Kornicker reported in 1962 that hydraulic canal dredging deposited silt as deep as 27 cm, and as far as .5 mile s from the dredge. Many factors affect dispersion. Bartsch (1960) has identified the sources and results of silt in fresh water. Turbidity obviously interferes with light transmission and photosynthesis, and usually increases oxygen demand (Odum and Wilson, 1962). After heavier materials settle quickly, turbidities rarely exceed the natural levels caused by wind. Galtsoff (1960) included sedimentation as one of the negative factors in the environment of the oyster, since even the capacity of this remarkably silt-tolerant species can be overcome by smothering loads. Although severe special cases exist, Gunter's comment seems to have general application—deleterious effects are real but localized, and nutrient release may offset the damage done.

BIOLOGICAL PROCESSES

All the modifying activities considered in earlier sections affect biological processes. They operate through effects on photosynthetic production, nutrient cycling, changed food supply, altered activity patterns, direct maiming or killing, and many other pathways in the ecosystem. None of these effects of man are understood fully for estuarine areas. Our basic knowledge of effect on biological processes is limited and most of our information is clustered around the economically important species. Two areas of human activity offer dramatic evidence that we are as powerful in influencing these effects as we are in causing physical and chemical changes. Fishing and the transplanting of species into new aquatic communities are stimulating examples for review.

Human predation (fishing). In the Chesapeake Bay and the immediate coastal waters, about 500 million pounds of aquatic organisms are stripped anually from the total estuary-dependent biota by human predation. Sykes (1964) reports 1,104,000,000 pounds in 1960 for the north portion of the Gulf of Mexico. This is a very specialized predation, which is highly selective by species and by size; it is seasonal in its effects, and does not return the captured nutrients directly into the system. Not all the effects on the biological processes are yet known, but many can be cited or suggested.

The species preyed upon by humans in the estuaries of the Middle Atlantic coast of North America can be grouped into three categories: wild resident species, wild transient species, and cultured species. Man's predation has different effects on each of these groups, but there are several general effects which apply to all.

The wild resident species, which spend virtually all their life history in the estuary, were, obviously, present in the estuary prior to man's intensive use. Consider the oyster bed communities, soft shell clams, and striped bass of the Chesapeake: early harvest was light, with inefficient gear; power boats, nylon nets, better dredges, navigational aids, increased experience, and more efficient predatory techniques have placed increased pressure on these and other residents. Four known and possible changes could be made. First, the structures of the community can be substantially altered: for example, all utilized oyster beds could be changed in species composition, size, distribution for oysters, and physical structure. Secondly, the total abundance and distribution of the prey species can be substantially changed. (Maryland's oyster catch is about 10 percent of earlier levels, despite gear improvement and high price. Many old beds are barren, without oysters or their usual associates.) The size and age composition of prey species can be modified, which appears to have occurred in striped bass, where human predation is heaviest on young fish. A fourth possibility is that growth rates, distribution, and spawning success might be enhanced. (Soft shell clams may be growing more rapidly and densely on worked beds than on undisturbed areas.)

The transient wild species like shad, herrings, etc., which move into or through the estuary to breed or to feed, are exposed to intensive inshore predation for only part of their lives, but it may be under highly vulnerable circumstances. A principle of fishery biology was expressed by an experienced fisherman when he told me that "Fish are fairly safe from over-fishing unless we can get at them in a bottleneck that they must pass through. Then, we can really murder them." Although increased fishing efficiency also contributes to the decreases, the bottlenecks, like migration to limited spawning areas, offer the greatest opportunities for the depletion of stocks by overfishing and for a significant genetic selection. The sturgeon appears to be depleted, for example, but critical studies are lacking; it is rare in this area, and extirpation is imaginable. Significant genetic selection can be effected by size limits, net-mesh regulations, and controlled seasons if the entire stock is regularly exposed to selective predation. Fishways interposed on essential spawning migrations may select to favor strains which can pass ladders.

The cultured and semi-cultured species are particularly vulnerable to change. Complete culture, involving production of young or seed from selected parents and supervision until harvesting, apparently is not now possible for any estuarine species on a commercial scale. *Crassostrea virginica, Ostrea edulis, Mytilus edulis, Chanos chanos,* and *Penaeus setiferus* are all partially cultured, and these and others will probably be fully controlled in the future. Several important steps can be taken on behalf of these species, including provision of effective substrate for larvae of oysters and clams, transportation and concentration in favorable growing areas, partial or complete protection from other predators, feeding, and intensive and thorough harvesting. All of these are violent modifications of the natural biological processes of the estuary, and may result in improved growth rate, survival and condition of the cultured species. Oysters on planted cultch, for example, when transplanted to good growing areas where food is more plentiful and natural predators absent, show improved survival and growth. Genetic selection may also result, as in the case of oysters which may have been modified by culture and by very widescale transplanting along the entire Atlantic coast—the potentials in this field will be enormously enhanced when artificial breeding becomes practicable. Still another result may be increased parasitic and natural predator damage; planted oyster beds can be wiped out by cow-nose rays, oyster drills decimate seed beds, and the intensive populations in planted beds may be more severely parasitized by microparasites.

The capture and permanent removal of large quantities of any of these species is in itself a radical interruption of biological processes. Under undisturbed conditions, each animal would compete, die, be consumed and digested, pass into the nutrient sequence, and continue as recycled elements and compounds. The only net losses to the system would come from flushing and sedimentation. When we extract large chunks of organized organic materials, it seems likely that the total production of the prey species is probably increased because the removal of some organisms provides space and food for their competitors; a substantial quantity of organic material leaves the estuary, at least temporarily, although much may return as sewage and industrial waste; species competing with the prey species are favored; and a broad spectrum of modifications affects the unused species, including those that feed the species directly captured, its parasites, natural predators, and the rest of the ecosystem.

Far too little attention has been directed to research on these effects of human activity in the estuary. Many of the possibilities have not been tested. The speculative comments here are only indications of the actions and reactions that are modified, and suggest some challenging avenues for future investigation.

Artificial introduction of species.* Each species attains a distribution which balances its needs and its environment. Distributions normally change slowly, accompanied by constant adjustments in that balance. Man, however, has often violently disrupted this leisurely pattern by transplanting species to new areas. This has sometimes been done intentionally in estuaries to increase or improve yields of food, and it has often been done inadvertently, carrying species along with transplants, on ship hulls, or by carelessness.

Great benefit is possible from introductions. The oyster fishery on the west coast of North America depends primarily on seed transplanted each year from Japan. Four hundred thirty-five striped bass (1879–81) and 15 thousand white shad fry (1871) were carried laboriously from the East Coast to the West Coast; both are widely established, with substantial benefits and no known damage to the receiving waters.

On the other side of the economic balance are the parasites, predators, and competitors of species which have food value. The Portugese oyster, *Gryphea* (*Crassostrea*) *angulata*, was introduced to the coast of France, where it gradually drove out some of the superior *Ostrea edulis* (Galtsoff, 1946). The voracious screw borer, *Urosalpinx cinerea*, one of the worst of the oyster drills, was accidentally carried into English waters with American oysters, and is a serious and extensive predator (Korringa, 1952). *Urosalpinx* has also been taken to the Puget Sound area, where it joined another immigrant, *Tritonalia japonica*, an oriental species which is considered to be the most destructive drill of the area (Korringa, 1952). The extensive transplantations of oyster stocks among waters of the Atlantic and Gulf Coasts have been suggested as suspected mechanisms for introducing to new areas the fungus, *Dermocystidium marinum*, the microparasite called MSX, and other parasites. Oyster competitors have been observed to create serious problems in new waters. A mudworm, *Poly-*

* See Selection 20 for further discussion of the consequences of introducing aquatic plants.

dora ciliata, was introduced into Australia about 1870 (Nelson, 1946). It changed the industry, forcing oyster culture off the bottoms and onto stakes or stone slabs. A small slipper limpet, *Crepidula fornicata*, was taken to Europe from America. It grows to giant size there and has spread over many areas, especially in Holland and England (Korringa, 1952). It increased so vigorously that it actually threatened to replace the Dutch oyster. Korringa believes that it is a space competitor, harbors a serious shell disease as it decays, and destroys great numbers of oyster larvae.

The barnacle, *Elminius modestus*, accidentally brought from the Southern Hemisphere to England (Korringa, 1952), competes vigorously with oyster larvae for setting space and probably destroys larvae. As reported earlier, DDT applications appear to be useful in its control. The shell of an oyster provides a habitat for a remarkable variety of probryozoans, snails, and the eggs and spores of tozoans, algae, sponges, worms, coelenterates, other species. It is possible that the transplantation of oysters, oyster shells, and seed has modified the distribution of more aquatic species than any other human activity.

The drama and problems associated with artificial introductions in estuaries are not, however, limited to invertebrates. Like the starling and the English sparrow on land, carp, goldfish (*Carassius auratus*), the walleye or yellow pike perch (*Stizostedion vitreum*), catfish, and others have entered the Middle Atlantic area and other waters (Mansueti, 1961). The effects are not yet measured, but the carp and goldfish are regarded with serious concern.

Water chestnut, *Trapa natans*, was imported into the United States as a handsome ornamental plant. Accidental release near Washington, D. C. produced, within ten years, beds covering 10,000 acres (Rawls, 1964). It blocked navigation, provided a breeding site for mosquitoes, and produced devilish "caltrops" or hard-spined seed cases. Expensive mowing, handpicking and chemical treatment have reduced it to a controlled threat.

Eurasian watermilfoil, *Myriophyllum spicatum*, is widely distributed in Europe, Asia, and Africa, where it is a modest member of the flora. In Chesapeake Bay, however, it has recently become a serious menace to many interests, blocking navigation, preventing boating and swimming, interfering with seafood harvesting, increasing siltation, and encouraging mosquitoes. It thrives over a wide salinity range from 0 ‰ to 15 ‰, and can tolerate 20 ‰, reproduces effectively by fragmentation, and survives in all depths less than about 9 feet. At least 100 thousand acres are infested, and new tributaries are invaded each year. Control has been effective on an expensive local basis, applying 2, 4-D in clay pellets. This, in turn, opens serious questions about the dangers of the control method. Beaven *et al.* (1962) showed that standard applications have no acute effects on clams, crabs, oysters, or some fish, but the possibilities of chronic effects, residues, accumulation, and human intake are not yet resolved. Perhaps all this unfinished story began with the emptying of a fish bowl containing this attractive plant.

These varied instances of introduction without comprehension of natural controls and without effective restraint convey their own point. One need only add that each is likely to be an irreversible act, with permanent effects.

Activities in the Ocean

The sea is still beyond man's control, and the strenuous efforts he makes to change his terrestrial environment still seem puny in comparison with oceanic forces. He can, however, successfully block the sea from its tributary bays, with results that are important to the estuary.

Pritchard and many others have stressed the power and importance of tidal currents, which provide the energy for horizontal translation and for mixing throughout the estuary. He showed in 1955, for instance, that increased tidal velocity tends to convert a stratified estuary to vertical homogeneity. When ocean barriers are constructed or re-

moved, the change will have far greater importance than merely reducing or encouraging the intrusion of salt and of marine species. Ryther *et al.* (1958), in considering the algal problem in Great South Bay and Moriches Bay, attributed improvement in the entire area to the reopening of Moriches Inlet to restore effective exchange with the sea.

Hundreds, perhaps thousands, of coastal inlets and harbors have been modified by engineering efforts to stabilize, improve, or protect them for various human endeavors. Groins, breakwaters, channel dredging, bulkheading, and filling all change the natural patterns and processes. Each inlet is a specific and local case, and the concept that engineering changes should always be preceded by thorough consideration of all the physical, chemical, and biological results to be effected should be encouraged. This has not been the usual sequence, and most inlet engineering appears to have been single-purpose modification. Improved comprehension of the total effects of altering relations between ocean and estuary is desirable and will be increasingly valuable.

Important special problems appear when nearshore ocean waters are used for waste disposal. Wastes can be translocated into the estuaries by such mechanisms as the regular migrations of anadromous fish and the great inflow of oceanic water with tidal currents. Ketchum, in an unpublished paper, reviewed pertinent data for one area, the mouth of Delaware Bay. He concluded that discharge would be undesirable at any site within five miles of the coast, but showed the great variation in waste-receiving capacity at different locations. Further, he stressed the necessity for specific on-site studies prior to selection of waste sites. Pritchard (1960) effectively outlined the steps necessary in evaluating sites for disposing of radioactive wastes. He also stressed that this inshore environment comes into more intimate contact with man than any other marine waters. Therefore, it is most likely to receive wastes and, simultaneously, most in need of protection from excess wastes. He discussed many of the factors which influence the fate of these wastes. As understanding of estuarine processes grows, the probabilities of irreparable and massive damage from ignorance in waste disposal should decline.

On the Resiliency of Estuaries

The reading necessary for the preparation of this review has deepened and clarified my personal concern with the future welfare of estuaries. It is clear that many destructive forces are being applied widely, that pressures are increasing at a very rapid rate, but that intelligent planning and control of estuarine changes are rare. Fundamental and practical understanding of estuaries is now · increasing at an impressive rate, but this growth appears to be dangerously slow in comparison with the increase in disruption of estuarine systems.

Several of the characteristic physical, chemical, and biological features of the estuary provide an interesting and valuable resistance to change. Scars often heal quickly. The factors aiding resiliency have not yet been adequately investigated, but several illustrative and stimulating examples are known:

1. The vigor of the rhythmic and turbulent circulation pattern continuously and endogenously renews the supply of water, food, larvae, and other essential elements to any small damaged area. This aids in recovery and protects long-term net stability patterns.

2. The substantial buffering capacity of estuaries, usually operating through the carbonate system, is another element which resists changes imposed on estuaries. It is not so great as the buffering capacity of the open ocean, but it is greater than most rivers, and is enormously important in the estuaries where pollution is received.

3. Exogenous renewal is also normally continuous, because estuaries receive continuous input from rivers and from the ocean. Since the river-sourced and ocean-sourced populations are substantial components of the estuarine biomass, the addition of organisms from these sources is important in normal estuarine sequences and in recovery from damaging or toxic change.

4. Many species have biological characteristics which provide special advantages in estuarine survival. These characteristics usually protect the species against the natural violence of estuaries, and they are often helpful in resisting external forces, like man.

Additional examples of contributors to estuarine resiliency include the oyster, the blue crab and the striped bass. The oyster, for instance, has been cited by Galtsoff (1960) for great tolerance to temperature (0°C. to about 35°C.), salinity (about 5 ‰ to 35 ‰), and for its remarkable ability to hermetically seal the valves of its shell to isolate the animal from unfavorable conditions for as long as three weeks. Nelson (1938) described the oyster's complex and effective mechanisms for dealing with the high silt content of coastal waters. The blue crab uses the net upstream flow of deep waters in estuaries to provide annual redistribution of juveniles to all the tributaries and upstream areas of the Chesapeake Bay. Mansueti (1961) stressed the remarkable resiliency of the striped bass in surviving the increased pressures and damages in the Chesapeake system. He suggested that the specific gravity of the eggs of this species may be crucially important to survival, since the semi-buoyant eggs released in nearly fresh water are buoyed by turbulence as the embryos develop, and protected from silt smothering. When the larvae emerge, they have been carried downstream by net surface flow to waters of higher salinity, past the zone of maximum turbidity, so that they can feed. A last example can be drawn from the copepod populations of estuaries. The mechanisms which permit maintenance of large planktonic populations in these turbulent and flushed systems are not yet fully understood but appear to be complex and effective. They may include vertical migrations (which could move populations downstream at night and upstream by day), reservoirs in marginal areas, and other attributes or patterns of individual or population behavior (Rogers, 1940; Bousefield, 1955; Barlow, 1955; Cronin *et al.*, 1962).

These resilient forces, and the others which certainly exist, are welcome allies in the efforts to achieve optimal balance between man's effects on estuaries and their capacities.

On Positive Thinking

Much of this review has described the destructive, or at least uncomprehended, estuarine changes through man's efforts. However, the cited literature also contains suggestions for the positive and profitable manipulation of rivers, bays, marshes, and other coastal areas. Some of these proposals are well supported by experiments or field evidence, and others will require rigorous investigation prior to acceptance and improvement. The following suggestions do not by any means exhaust these ideas, but they indicate the directions and vitality of some of the recognized possibilities.

Chemical additions could protect or enrich estuaries, if they were used intelligently to offset undesirable conditions or to supplement limiting elements. Hynes (1960) has pointed out that the most outstanding problem in disposing of sewage is the appalling waste of nutrients. Brehmer (1964) noted that the District of Columbia area spends $2.1 million annually in the unmanaged release of $3.2 million worth of fertilizing materials. Constructive techniques are not fully developed, but Føyn (1959), for instance, has learned to remove phosphorous from wastes entering the Oslo Fjord by electrolytic precipitation. E. P. Odum (1961a) pointed out six ways by which phytoplankton blooms might be controlled. No problem here is likely to be beyond the capacity of industrial ingenuity, if economic incentives become sufficiently high. An interesting example may be provided in the case of the detergents. Widespread public reaction against visible suds and reported detergent residues in natural waters produced serious possibilities of strict prohibitive legislation and regulations. Pertinent industries have made massive investment in the discovery and development of "biodegradable" and other degradable cleansing compounds, and now promise that the problem will be effectively solved. If the competitive interest of such industrial giants can be focused on other estuarine problems, magnificent achievements may result.

Thermal additions might be constructively used. Spawning of all species and photosynthetic production are controlled by temperature, and offer tantalizing opportunities for management. Huntsman (1950) suggested the use of warmed water in controlling the movement of fish to concentrate populations, or for other purposes. The present increase in attention to research on many thermal effects should suggest some desirable possibilities. Imaginative engineering and improved biological understanding might be fruitful partners in achieving useful hot spots.

Improved races and species can be selected and introduced. Galtsoff (1956) has pointed out some of the variation that exists among races of oysters and the possibility of selection for desirable characteristics under intensive cultivation. Provenance research has been so widely successful in forestry and agriculture that its potentials are beyond question. The successful introduction of new species presents greater difficulties and requires very thorough preparation and, perhaps, a share of good luck. Korringa (1952) has, however, pointed out that success might sometimes be encouraged and accelerated by simultaneous importation of natural control mechanisms. The literature contains many records of introduction, with both successes and failures, available to guide future efforts. A peculiar blending of conservative concern and imaginative daring may be necessary in improving upon present races and species.

Management—the intentional modification of the factors determining production by a species—can be carried to higher levels than have yet been achieved in estuaries. Maximum culture of oysters, clams, and other usable herbivores may offer the greatest potentials, since they are nutritionally supported near the broad base of the food chains. For instance, Glude (1951) outlined the sequence of seed production, predator control, mortality prevention, fattening, and controlled harvest which might increase oyster production substantially. Similar concepts of population comprehension and management should eventually be possible, not only for the species of fish and shellfish directly utilized, but also for the supporting zooplankton species, phytoplankton, and all the necessary parts of the complex biota of estuaries.

The gross ecology of the estuary can be manipulated to advantage. Present and probable engineering capacities are so great as to require new thinking about potential use of these capacities as well as the more usual effort to resist their application. It may, in some circumstances, be found desirable to store and release river water; divert huge volumes; radically alter channels, currents, and tides; or in other ways introduce major alterations. Those who oppose such suggestions are often expressing fear of the unpredictable consequences, and might alter their position if sufficient knowledge existed to permit accurate prediction and evaluation of all the results.

Note

This paper is Contribution No. 269, Natural Resources Institute of the University of Maryland.

Valuable assistance was received from the following individuals who sought out and sent me original information on estuaries, or material which is difficult to obtain: James E. Sykes and Seton H. Thompson of the U.S. Fish and Wildlife Service, Clair Idyll of the University of Miami, Robert Ingle of the Florida State Board of Conservation, Gordon Gunter of the Gulf Coast Research Laboratory, P. Korringa of the Netherlands Institute for Fisheries Research, and J. E. G. Raymont of the University of Southampton. Their deep interest in the problems discussed here is especially welcome. Mrs. A. J. Mansueti and Arie de Kok of the Chesapeake Biological Laboratory provided illustrations and translations which have been valuable. Mrs. Leone H. Williams performed the essential typing chores with competence, and she and others provided constructive editorial review.

[1] They include the series of reports on estuarine hydrography by Pritchard (1951, 1952, 1955, 1959a, b, 1960); on flushing and biological effects by Ketchum (1950, 1951a, b, c, 1954); on the grand-scale effects of enclosing the Zuider Zee (Havinga, 1935, 1936, 1941); on the biology of pollution by Hynes (1960); on biological aspects of estuaries by Hudgpeth (1957); on physical and chemical aspects by Emery and Stevenson (1957); Mansueti (1961) on the nature of man's effects; Nelson (1947) on enrichment; H. T. Odum and his students (1958, 1962) on estuarine processes; Rounsefell (1963) on the choices of management objectives; Sykes (1965) on multiple usage; and E. P. Odum (1961b) on imaginative and constructive approaches to new potentials. Baughman's valuable bibliography (1948) contains many pertinent annotations. Sverdrup et al. (1942) continues to serve as a splendid general reference.

References Cited

Alexander, W. B., B. A. Southgate, and R. Bassindale, 1936. Survey of the River Tees. II. The estuary—chemical and biological. *J. Marine Biol. Assoc. U. K.:*717–724.

Auld, D. V., 1964. Waste disposal and water supply. In *Problems of the Potomac Estuary;* pp. 13–18. Proc. Interstate Comm. Potomac River Basin, Washington, D.C.

Barlow, J. P., 1955. Physical and biological processes determing the distribution of zooplankton in a tidal estuary. *Biol. Bull., 109*(2):211–225.

Bartsch, A. F., 1960. Settleable solids, turbidity, and light penetration as factors affecting water quality. In *Biological problems in water pollution. Trans. 1959 Seminar, Robert A. Taft Sanitary Eng. Center Tech. Rept., W60-3:*118–127.

Bartsch, A. F., 1961. Introduced eutrophication, a growing water resource problem. In *Algae and Met-* ropolitan Wastes. *Trans. 1960 Seminar, Robert A. Taft Sanitary Eng. Center Tech. Rept., W61-3:*6–9.

Baughman, J. L., 1948. *An annotated bibliography of oysters with pertinent material on mussels and other shellfish and an appendix on pollution.* Texas A. and M. Res. Found., Agr. and Mechanical College of Texas, College Station, Texas.

Beaven, G. F., 1946. Effect of Susquehanna River stream flow on Chesapeake Bay salinities, and history of past oyster mortalities on upper Bay bars. *Third Ann. Rept., Maryland Bd. Nat. Resources:*123–133.

Beaven, G. F., C. K. Rawls, and G. E. Beckett, 1962. Field observations upon estuarine animals exposed to 2,4-D. *Proc. N. E. Weed Contr. Conf., 16:*449–458.

Blegvad, H., 1932. Investigations of the bottom fauna at outfalls of drains in the Sound. *Rept. Danish Biol. Sta., 37:*5–20.

Bolomey, J. G. W., 1959. Effect of the Rhine on Netherlands beaches. *Proc. First Intern. Conf. on Waste Disposal in the Marine Environment:* 164–174.

Bousefield, E. L., 1955. Ecological control of the occurrence of barnacles in the Miramichi estuary. *Bull. Natl. Museum Can., 127:* 1–69.

Brehmer, M. L., 1964. Nutrient enrichment in the Potomac estuary. In *Problems of the Potomac Estuary;* pp. 47–50. Proc. Interstate Comm., Potomac River Basin, Washington, D.C.

Burt, W. V., 1955. Distribution of suspended materials in Chesapeake Bay. *J. Marine Res., 14(1):* 47–62.

Butler, P. A., and P. F. Springer, 1963. Pesticides—A new factor in coastal environments. *Trans. 28th N. Am. Wildlife and Natl. Resources Conf.:* 378–390.

Butler, P. A., A. J. Wilson, Jr., and A. J. Rick, 1962. Effect of pesticides on oysters. *Proc. Natl. Shellfisheries Assoc., 51:* 23–32.

Carpenter, J. H., 1957. A study of some major cations in natural waters. *Chesapeake Bay Inst. Tech. Rept., 15:* 1–75.

Carpenter, J. H., and D. G. Cargo, 1957. Oxygen requirement and mortality of the blue crab in the Chesapeake Bay. *Chesapeake Bay Inst. Tech. Rept., 13:* 1–22.

Carson, R., 1962. *Silent Spring.* Houghton Mifflin Co., Boston.

Chipman, W. A., 1958. Biological accumulation of radioactive materials. *Proc. First Ann. Texas Conf. Utilization Atomic Energy, Misc. Publ. Texas Eng. Exp. Sta.,* 36–41.

Chipman, W. A., 1960. Accumulation of radioactive pollutants by marine organisms and its relation to fisheries. In *Biological Problems in Water Pollution. Trans. 1959 Seminar, Robert A. Taft Sanitary Eng. Center Tech. Rept., W60-3:* 8–14.

Chipman, W. A., T. R. Rice, and T. J. Price, 1958. Uptake and accumulation of radioactive zinc by marine plankton, fish, and shellfish. *U.S. Fish and Wildlife Serv., Fishery Bull., 135:* 279–292.

Cottam, C., 1960. A conservationist's view of the new insecticides. In *Biological problems in Water Pollution. Trans. 1959 Seminar, Robert A. Taft Sanitary Eng. Center W 60-3:* 42–45.

Cronin, L. E., J. C. Daiber, and E. M. Hulburt, 1962. Quantitative seasonal aspects of zooplankton in the Delaware estuary. *Chesapeake Sci., 3(2):* 63–93.

Davis, C. C., 1948. Studies of the effects of industrial pollution in the lower Patapsco River area. II. The effect of copperas pollution in plankton. *Maryland Dept. Res. and Education, Chesapeake Biol. Lab. Publ., 72:* 1–12.

Davis, H. C., 1958. Survival and growth of clam and oyster larvae at different salinities. *Biol. Bull., 114(3):* 296–307.

Davis, H. C., 1961. Effects of some pesticides on eggs and larvae of oysters, *Crassostrea virginica,* and clams, *Venus mercenaria. Com. Fisheries Rev., 23(12):* 8–23.

Donaldson, L., 1960. Radiobiological studies at the Eniwetok test site and adjacent areas of the western

Pacific. In *Biological problems in water pollution. Trans. 1959 Seminar, Robert A. Taft Sanitary Eng. Center Tech. Rept., W60-3:* 1–7.

Emery, K. O., and R. E. Stevenson, 1957. Estuaries and lagoons. I. Physical and chemical characteristics. *Geol. Soc. Am., Mem. 67, 1:* 673–749.

Filice, F. P., 1954a. An ecological survey of the Castro Creek area in San Pablo Bay. *Wasman J. Biol., 12(1):* 1–24.

Filice, F. P., 1954b. A study of some factors affecting the bottom fauna of a portion of the San Francisco Bay estuary. *Wasman J. Biol., 12(3):* 257–292.

Føyn, E., 1959. Chemical and biological aspects of sewage discharge in inner Oslofjord. *Proc. First Intern. Conf. Waste Disposal in the Marine Environment:* 279–284.

Fraser, J. H., 1932. Observations on the fauna and constituents of an estuarine mud in a polluted area. *J. Marine Biol. Assoc., 18(1):* 69–84.

Galtsoff, P. S., 1946. Comment on the importation of foreign shellfish. *Com. Rept., Natl. Shellfisheries Assoc.*

Galtsoff, P. S., 1956. Ecological changes affecting the productivity of oyster grounds. *Trans. 21st N. Am. Wildlife Conf.,* 408–419.

Galtsoff, P. S., 1960. Environmental requirements of oysters in relation to pollution. In *Biological Problems in Water Pollution. Trans. 1959 Seminar, Robert A. Taft Sanitary Eng. Center Tech. Rept., W60-3:* 128–133.

Galtsoff, P. S., W. A. Chipman, Jr., J. B. Engle, and H. N. Calderwood, 1947. Ecological and physiological studies of the effect of sulfate pulp mill wastes on oysters in the York River, Virginia. *U. S. Fish and Wildlife Serv., Fishery Bull., 51:* 58–186.

Gaufin, A. R., and C. M. Tarzwell, 1956. Aquatic macroinvertebrate communities as indicators of organic pollution in Lytle Creed. *Sewage Ind. Wastes, 28:* 906–924.

Gaussle, D., and D. W. Kelley, 1963. The effect of flow reversal on salmon. *Ann. Rept. Delta Fish and Wildlife Protection Study. Append. A, A1–A16.*

Glude, J. B., 1951. The effect of man on shellfish populations. *Trans. 16th N. Am. Wildlife Conf.:* 397–403.

Guillard, R. R. L., R. F. Vaccaro, N. Corwin, and S. A. M. Conover, 1960. Report on a survey of the chemistry, biology, and hydrography of Great South Bay and Moriches Bay, conducted during July and September 1959, for the townships of Islip and Brookhaven, New York. *Woods Hole Oceanog. Inst. Ref.,* 60–15.

Gunter, G., 1952. Historical changes in the Mississippi River and the adjacent marine environment. *Univ. Texas, Publ. Inst. Marine Sci., 2(2):* 119–139.

Gunter, G., 1953. The relationship of the Bonnet Carré Spillway to oyster beds in Mississippi Sound and the "Louisiana Marsh" with a report on the 1950 opening. *Univ. Texas, Publ. Inst. Marine Sci., 3(1):* 17–71.

Gunter, G., 1955. Mortality of oysters and abundance of certain associates as related to salinity. *Ecology,* 36:601–605.

Gunter, G., 1956. Land, water, wildlife and flood control in the Mississippi Valley. *Proc. Louisiana Acad. Sci.,* 19:5–11.

Gunter, G., 1957a. Wildlife and flood control in the Mississippi Valley. *Trans. 22nd N. Am. Wildlife Conf.,* 189–196.

Gunter, G., 1957b. How does siltation affect fish production? *Natl. Fisherman, 38(3):*18–19.

Gunter, G., and G. E. Hall, 1963. Biological investigations of the St. Lucie estuary (Florida) in connection with Lake Okeechobee discharges through the St. Lucie Canal. *Gulf Res. Repts., 1(5):*189–207.

Gunter, G., and J. E. McKee, 1960. A report on oysters, *Ostrea lurida* and *Crassostrea gigas,* and sulfite waste liquors. *Spec. Consultants Rept. to Pollution Control Comm., State of Washington,* February 1960. Olympia, Washington.

Hanks, R. W., 1963. Chemical control of the green crab, *Carcinus maenas* (L.). *Proc. Natl. Shellfisheries Assoc., 52:*75–86.

Hartog, C. den., 1963. The amphipods of the deltaic region of the Rivers Rhine, Meuse and Scheldt in relation to the hydrography of the area. I. Introduction and hydrography. *Neth. J. of Sea Res., 2(1):*29–39.

Havinga, B., 1935. Het Zuiderzeegebied in zijn huidige phase van ontwikkeling. *Vakblad voor Biologen, 17(4):*64–73.

Havinga, B., 1936. De veranderingen in den hydrographischen toestand en in de macrofauna van Zuiderzee en IJselmeer gedurende de jaren 1931–1935. *Mededeelingen van de Zuiderzee-Commissie, 4:*1–26.

Havinga, B., 1941. De veranderingen in den hydrographischen toestand en in de macrofauna van het IJsselmeer gedurende de jaren 1936–1940. *Mededeelingen van de Zuiderzee-Commissie, 5:*1–18.

Havinga, B., 1949. The enclosing of the Zuyder Zee and its effect on fisheries. *U. N. Sci. Conf. Conserv. and Util. of Resources.* (*Wildlife 1(a)/5; Water 7(c)/3*)

Havinga, B., 1959. Artificial transformation of salt and brackish water into fresh water lakes in the Netherlands and possibilities for biological investigations. *Arch. Oceanog. Limnol., 10:*47–52. (Suppl.)

Hedgpeth, J. W., 1957. Estuaries and lagoons. II. Biological aspects. In *Treatise on marine ecology and paleoecology;* vol. 1, Ecology. *Geol. Soc. Am. Mem., 67:*693–729.

Hellier, T. R., Jr., and L. S. Kornicker, 1962. Sedimentation from a hydraulic dredge in a bay. *Univ. Texas, Publ., Inst. Marine Sci., 8:*212–215.

Huntsman, A. G., 1950. Population dynamics in estuaries. In *A Symposium on Estuarine Ecology.* Atl. Estuarine Res. Soc. Yorktown, Virginia.

Hutton, R. F., B. Eldred, K. D. Woodburn, and R. M. Ingle, 1956. The ecology of Boca Ciega Bay with special reference to dredging and filling operations. *Florida Marine Lab., Tech. Ser. 17:*1–86.

Hynes, H. B., 1960. *The biology of polluted waters.* Liverpool Univ. Press, Liverpool.

Ingram, W. M., and W. W. Towne, 1959. Stream life below industrial outfalls. *Public Health Repts., 74(12):*1059–1070).

Jeffries, H. P., 1962. Environmental characteristics of Raritan Bay, a polluted estuary. *Limnol. Oceanog., 7:*21–31.

Jones, R. L., D. W. Kelley, and L. W. Owen, 1963. Delta fish and wildlife protection study. *Ann. Rept. No. 2.* Resources Agr. Calif., Sacramento, California.

Ketchum, B. H., 1950. The exchanges of fresh and salt waters in tidal estuaries. *Proc. Colloq. Flushing of Estuaries, Office of Naval Res.:*1–23.

Ketchum, B. H., 1951a. The flushing of tidal estuaries. *Sewage Ind. Wastes, 23(2):*198–209.

Ketchum, B. H., 1951b. The dispersion and fate of pollution discharged into tidal waters, and the viability of enteric bacteria in the sea. Progress Rept. Res., Grant No. 1249 (C2), Period Dec. 1, 1949 to Feb. 1, 1951. *Woods Hole Oceanog. Inst. Ref. No. 5–11.*

Ketchum, B. H., 1951c. The exchanges of fresh and salt waters in tidal estuaries. *J. Marine Res., 10:*18–38.

Ketchum, B. H., 1954. Relation between circulation and planktonic populations in estuaries. *Ecology, 35:*191–200.

Ketchum, B. H., J. C. Ayers, and R. F. Vaccaro, 1952. Processes contributing to the decrease of coliform bacteria in a tidal estuary. *Ecology, 33(2):*247–258.

Kinne, O., 1963. The effects of temperature and salinity on marine and brackish water animals. I. Temperature. *Oceanog. Marine Bio. Ann. Rev., 1:*301–340.

Koch, P., 1959. Discharge of waste into the sea in European coastal areas. *Proc. First Intern. Conf. Waste Disposal in the Marine Environment:*122–130.

Korringa, P., 1952. Recent advances in oyster biology. *Quart. Rev. Biol., 27:*303, 339–365.

Korringa, P., 1958. The Netherlands shellfish industry and the Delta plan. *Intern. Council Explor. Sea, C. M., Shellfish Comm., No. 60.*

Krause, R., 1961. Fundamental characteristics of algal physiology. In *Algae and Metropolitan Wastes. Trans. 1960 Seminar, Robert A. Taft Sanitary Eng. Center Tech. Rept., W61–3:*40–47.

Lindsay, C. E., 1963. Pesticide tests in the marine environment in the State of Washington. *Proc. Natl. Shellfisheries Assoc., 52:*87–97.

Loosanoff, V. L., 1960. Some effects of pesticides on marine arthropods and mollusks. In *Biological Problems in Water Pollution. 1959 Seminar, Robert A. Taft Sanitary Eng. Center Tech. Rept., W60–3:*89–93.

Manning, J. H., 1957. The Maryland soft shell clam industry and its effects on tidewater resources. *Maryland Dept. Res. and Education Resource Study Rept., No. 11.*

Mansueti, R. J., 1961. Effects of civilization on striped bass and other estuarine biota in Chesapeake Bay and tributaries. *Proc. Gulf Caribbean Fisheries Inst., November 1961:*110–136.

McNulty, J. K., 1961. Ecological effects of sewage

pollution in Biscayne Bay, Florida: Sediments and the distribution of benthic and fouling macroorganisms. *Bull. Marine Sci., Gulf Caribbean, 11(3):*393–447.

Nelson, T. C., 1931. Expert testimony in *New Jersey vs. New York et al.;* Master hearings, U. S. Supreme Court, 283 U.S. 336, No. 16, original. Argued April 13–15, 1931.

Nelson, T. C., 1938. The feeding mechanism of the oyster. I. On the pallium and the branchial chambers of *Ostrea virginica, O. edulis,* and *O. angulata,* with comparisons with other species of the genus. *J. Morph., 63:*1–61.

Nelson, T. C., 1946. Comment on the importation of foreign shellfish. *Com. Rept. Natl. Shellfisheries Assoc.*

Nelson, T. C., 1947. Some contributions from the land in determining conditions of life in the sea. *Ecol. Monographs, 17:*337–346.

Nelson, T. C., 1960. Some aspects of pollution, parasitism and inlet restriction in three New Jersey estuaries. In *Biological Problems in Water Pollution. Trans. 1959 Seminar, Robert A. Taft Sanitary Eng. Center Tech. Rept., W60–3:*203–211.

Odum, E. P., 1961a. Factors which regulate primary productivity and heterotrophic utilization in the ecosystem. In *Algae and metropolitan wastes. Trans. 1960 Seminar, Robert A. Taft Sanitary Eng. Center Tech. Rept., W61–3:*65–71.

Odum, E. P., 1961b. The role of tidal marshes in estuarine production. *The Conservationist, 15(6):*12–15.

Odum, H. T., 1959. Analysis of diurnal oxygen curves for the assay of reaeration rates and metabolism in polluted marine bays. *Proc. First Intern. Conf. Waste Disposal in the Marine Environment:*547–555.

Odum, H. T., and C. M. Hoskin, 1958. Comparative studies on the metabolism of marine waters. *Univ. Texas, Publ. Inst. Marine Sci., 5:*16–46.

Odum, H. T., and R. F. Wilson, 1962. Further studies on reaeration and metabolism of Texas bays. *Univ. Texas, Publ. Inst. Marine Sci., 8:*23–55.

Olson, R. A., H. F. Brust, and W. L. Tressler, 1941. Studies of the effects of industrial pollution in the Lower Patapsco area. I. Curtis Bay region, 1941. *Chesapeake Biol. Lab. Publ., 43:*1–40.

Pannell, J. P. M., A. E. Johnson, and J. E. G. Raymont, 1962. An investigation into the effects of warmed water from Marchwood power station into Southampton water. *Proc. Inst. Civil Engrs., 23:*35–62.

Pentelow, F. T. K., 1955. Pollution and fishes. *Verhandl. Intern. Ver. Limnol., 12:*768–771.

Picton, W. L., 1956. Water use in the United States, 1900–1975. Water and Sewerage Industrial and Utilities Div., *U. S. Dept. Commerce, Bus. Serv. Bull., 136,* Washington, D. C.

Pratt, D. M., 1949. Experiments on the fertilization of a salt water pond. *J. Marine Res., 8:*36–59.

Pritchard, D. W., 1951. The physical hydrography of estuaries and some applications to biological problems. *Trans. 16th N. Am. Wildlife Conf.:*365–375.

Pritchard, D. W., 1952. The physical structure, circula-

tion, and mixing in a coastal plain estuary. *Chesapeake Bay Inst., The Johns Hopkins Univ. Tech. Rept. 3, Ref. 52–2.*

Pritchard, D. W., 1955. Estuarine circulation patterns. *Proc. Am. Soc. Civil Engrs., 81:*1–11.

Pritchard, D. W., 1959a. Computation of the longitudinal salinity distribution in the Delaware estuary for various degrees of river inflow regulation. *Chesapeake Bay Inst., The Johns Hopkins Univ. Tech. Rept. 18, Ref. 59–3.*

Prtichard, D. W., 1959b. The movement and mixing of contaminants in tidal estuaries. *Proc. First Intern. Conf. Waste Disposal Marine Environment:*512–525.

Pritchard, D. W., 1960. Problems related to disposal of radioactive wastes in estuarine and coastal waters. In *Biological Problems in Water Pollution. Trans. 1959 Seminar, Robert A. Taft Sanitary Eng. Center Tech. Rept., W60–3:*22–32.

Rawls, C. K., 1964. Aquatic plant nuisances. In *Problems of the Potomac Estuary;* pp. 51–56. Proc., Interstate Comm. Potomac River Basin. Washington, D.C.

Raymont, J. E. G., 1949. Further observations on changes in the bottom fauna of a fertilized sea loch. *J. Marine Biol. Assoc., 27(1):*9–19.

Reish, D. J., 1959a. An ecological study of pollution in Los Angeles-Long Beach Harbors, California. *Occasional Paper, Allen Hancock Foundation, 22:*1–119.

Reish, D. J., 1959b. The use of marine invertebrates as indicators of water quality. *Proc. First Intern. Conf. Waste Disposal in the Marine Environment:*91–103.

Renn, C. E., 1956. Man as a factor in the coastal environment. *Trans. 21st N. Am. Wildlife Conf.:*470–473.

Rogers, H. M., 1940. Occurrence and retention of plankton within the estuary. *J. Fisheries Res. Bd. Can., 5(2):*164–171.

Rounsefell, G. A., 1963. Realism in the management of estuaries. *Marine Resources Bull. No. 1, Alabama Marine Res. Lab.* Dauphin Island, Alabama.

Ryther, J. H., 1954. The ecology of phytoplankton blooms in Moriches Bay and Great South Bay, Long Island, New York. *Biol. Bull., 106:*198–209.

Ryther, J. H., R. F. Vaccaro, E. M. Hulburt, C. S. Yentsch, and R. R. L. Guillard, 1958a. Report on a survey of the chemistry, biology and hydrography of Great South Bay and Moriches Bay conducted during June and September, 1958, for the townships of Islip and Brookhaven, Long Island, New York. *Woods Hole Oceanog. Inst. Ref., No. 58–57.*

Ryther, J. H., C. S. Yentsch, E. M. Hulburt, and R. F. Vaccaro, 1958b. Dynamics of a diatom bloom. *Biol. Bull., 115:*257–268.

Segerstraale, S. G., 1951. The recent increase in salinity off the coast of Finland and its influence upon the fauna. *J. Conseil Intern. Exploration Mer., 17:*103–110.

Simmons, H. B., 1959. Application and limitations of estuary models in pollution analyses. *Proc. First*

*Intern. Conf. Waste Disposal in the Marine Environment:*540–546.

Stroup, E. D., D. W. Pritchard, and J. H. Carpenter, 1961. Final report, Baltimore Harbor study. *Chesapeake Bay Inst., The Johns Hopkins Univ. Tech. Rept. 26, Ref. 61–5.*

Sverdrup, H. U., M. W. Johnson, and R. H. Fleming, 1942. *The Oceans.* Prentice-Hall, Inc., Englewood Cliffs, New Jersey.

Sykes, J. E., 1964. Requirements of Gulf and South Atlantic estuarine research. *Proc. 16th Ann. Session, Gulf and Caribbean Fish. Inst., 1963:*113–120.

Sykes, J. E., 1965. Multiple utilization of Gulf Coast estuaries. *Proc. Southeast Game and Fish Comm., 17th Ann. Conf. 1963:*323–326.

Thompson, S. H., 1961. What is happening to our estuaries? *Trans. 26th N. Am. Wildlife and Nat. Resources Conf.,* 318–322.

U. S. Army Engineer District, Baltimore, N. Atlantic Div., 1963. *Potomac River Basin Report. Summary, 1–43.*

Vaas, K. F., 1963. Annual report of the Delta Division of the Hydrobiological Institute of the Royal Netherlands Academy of Sciences for the years 1960 and 1961. *Neth. J. Sea Res., 2(1):*68–76.

Waldichuk, M., 1959. Effects of pulp and papermill wastes on the marine environment. *2nd Seminar Biol. Problems in Water Pollution, Robert A. Taft Sanitary Eng. Center.*

Waugh, G. D., and A. Ansell, 1956. The effect, on oyster spatfall, of controlling barnacle settlement with DDT. *Annals Applied Biology, 44:*619–625.

Whaley, R. C., 1960. Physical and chemical limnology of Conowingo Reservoir. *Chesapeake Bay Inst., The Johns Hopkins Univ. Tech. Rept. 20, Data Rept. 32, Ref. 60–2:*1–140.

Whitney, R. R., 1961. The Susquehanna fishery study, 1957–1960: A report of a study on the desirability and feasibility of passing fish at Conowingo Dam. *Maryland Dept. Res. and Education Contrib., 169:*1–81.

Wolman, A., J. C. Geyer, and E. E. Pyatt, 1957. A clean Potomac River in the Washington metropolitan area. *Interstate Comm. Potomac River Basin, October 1957,* Washington, D. C.

Woodburn, K. D., 1962. A guide to the conservation of shorelines, submerged bottoms and saltwaters with special reference to bulkhead lines, dredging and filling. *Marine Lab., Florida Board Cons., Educ. Bull., 14:*1–8.

ADDITIONAL REFERENCES

Hamilton, D. H., Jr., D. A. Flemer, C. W. Keefe, and J. A. Mihursky. 1970. Power plants: Effects of chlorination on estuarine primary production. *Science* 169:197–198.

Howells, G. P., T. J. Kneipe, and M. Eisenbud. 1970. Water quality in industrial areas: profile of a river. *Environmental Science and Technology* 4(1):26–35. Discusses tidal area of the lower Hudson River.

McCrone, A. W. 1966. The Hudson River estuary: hydrology, sediments and pollution. *Geograph. Rev.* 56(2):175–189.

Mihursky, J. A. 1967. On possible constructive uses of thermal additions to estuaries. *BioScience* 17(10):698–702.

Niering, W. A. 1970. The dilemma of the coastal wetlands: conflict of local, national, and world priorities. Pp. 143–156 in *The environmental crisis,* ed. by H. W. Helfrich, Jr. New Haven and London: Yale University Press.

OIL POLLUTION OF THE OCEAN

MAX BLUMER

As world population explodes we are looking more and more toward the oceans to supply man's increasing demands for food and other resources. However, many experts believe that the oceans will not prove to be a panacea for our future resource problems—the useful biological productivity is not as great as often supposed and extensive mineral extraction may be prohibitive (Ricker, 1969; Cloud, 1969; Marx, 1967). Ignorance yet hopefulness also characterize man's idea that the oceans can indefinitely absorb everything we want to dispose of. Recognition is just dawning to the fact that although the ocean covers most of the world's surface it may not forever be a self-renewing cesspool.

Previous selections (especially Selection 21) in this part have mentioned some of man's impacts which are ultimately sustained by the seas—accumulation of biocides and other exotic chemicals, for example. Besides dumping conventional sewage and wastes into the oceans (Rawn, 1966), we also discharge radioactive wastes (Parker, 1967; Templeton, 1965), heat, and oil and oil products.

"The serious consequences of oil pollution of . . . waters need little comment. Careless disposal of oil or oily mixtures is a menace to property, health, comfort and safety. In our harbors, it has created a fire hazard to land structures and shipping. On our beaches it has destroyed opportunities for healthful recreation. It has worked serious injury to marine and wild life. The problem must and can be solved." So stated the chairman of an international conference on oil pollution in 1926. Despite this assessment, the frequency and size of oil spills on the seas have increased dangerously. Thus, oil pollution is not new, but the magnitude of the problem is.

Max Blumer (b. 1923) is an organic geochemist and senior scientist at the Woods Hole Oceanographic Institution, Woods Hole, Massachusetts. Born in Switzerland, he earned a Ph.D. degree in chemistry at Basel University in 1949. Before going to Woods Hole in 1959 he held a fellowship at the University of Minnesota and positions with Scripps Institution of Oceanography, Royal Dutch Shell Company, Shell Development Company, and CIBA, Ltd. Blumer's research has included studies of comparative biochemistry and natural hydrocarbons and pigments.

This article is reprinted by permission from *Oil on the Sea*, edited by David P. Hoult, New York and London: Plenum Press, 1969, pp. 5–13. Copyright 1969 by Plenum Press.

In this selection Max Blumer briefly discusses the extent, nature, and effects of oceanic oil pollution today. Lumps of oil-tar residue, several inches in diameter, now abound near the middle of the North Atlantic Ocean. Thor Heyerdahl in his 1970 crossing of the North Atlantic Ocean was rarely out of sight of such lumps or some other man-made garbage. Blumer estimates that the influx of oil to the ocean by shipping losses alone is 0.1 percent of the total oil shipped, or more than 2 billion pounds each year.

The effects of oceanic oil pollution have been dramatized and publicized by the wreck of the *Torrey Canyon* off the coast of Cornwall in 1967 (e.g., Smith, 1968; Gill and others, 1967; Cowan, 1968, Petrow, 1968) and the Santa Barbara drilling leakages beginning in 1969 (e.g., Holmes, 1969; MacDonald and Ross, 1969). Oil is lethal to many marine birds and toxic to a number of other marine organisms, especially shore life. Decline of the sturgeon and of the production of natural caviar in the Caspian Sea is probably related to the growing oil pollution there (Abelson, 1970). Recreational and esthetic qualities of beaches may also be severely affected. Blumer gives insight into the biological action of different oil fractions and possible long-term consequences of oil contamination of marine ecosystems. Detergents used to clean oily beaches following the *Torrey Canyon* spillage had worse biological effects than the oil itself had. In Cornwall 10,000 tons of detergents were used to treat 14,000 tons of oil. The detergents killed limpets, which normally would browse over rocks on the beach and, as a result, would help to remove the oil.

A thin film of oil may now persist over great expanses of ocean and may interfere with important exchanges of moisture and energy between sea and air.

Hence, oil pollution is an excellent example of how we are deteriorating, rather than enhancing, the oceans' productivity, and there is virtually no sign of reversing this trend soon. The scale of oil operations is increasing because of an ever-increasing demand for energy. Environmentally dangerous drilling from offshore rigs on the continental shelf is proliferating. The total capacity of tank ships has increased six-fold in the last twenty years—but, more important, the likely effect of any given spill is becoming more catastrophic each year with the construction of larger and larger supertankers. Maximum tanker size has burgeoned from less than 20,000 deadweight tons in 1930 to a projected 800,000 dwt sometime in the early 1970s (Cooke, 1969).

(Editor's comment)

The Extent of Marine Oil Pollution

Oil pollution is the almost inevitable consequence of the dependence of a rapidly growing population on a largely oil-based technology. The oil reserves which have accumulated in the earth during the last 500 million years are being depleted rapidly and will be exhausted within a few hundred years. The use of oil or of other natural resources without losses is impossible; losses occur in production, transportation, refining and use. The immediate effects of large scale spills in coastal areas are well known but only through the recent introduction of marine surface sampling tools have we become aware of the degree of oil pollution of the open ocean. Thus, during a recent cruise of R/V *CHAIN* of the Woods Hole Oceanographic Institution to the southern Sargasso Sea, many surface "Neuston" net hauls were made to collect surface marine organisms. These tows were made between $32°N–23°N$ latitude (corresponding to a distance of 630 miles) at a longitude of $67°W$. Inevitably, during each tow, quantities of oil-tar lumps, up to 3 inches in diameter were caught in the nets. After 2–4 hours of towing, the mesh became so encrusted with oil that it was necessary to clean the nets with a strong solvent. On the evening of 5 December 1968, between 1835–2240 R hours at $25° 40'N$, $67° 30'W$, the nets were so fouled with oil and tar material that towing had to be discontinued. It was estimated that there was 3 times as much tar-like material as Sargasso Weed (on a volume basis) in the nets.[1] Similar occurences have been reported worldwide by observers from this as well as from other Institutions.

In order to arrive at a figure for the total oil influx into the ocean from various sources, we need figures for the total amount of oil produced, shipped and for the fraction lost in shipping and handling. The world oil production stands near $1.8 × 10^{15}$ grams/year. Of this amount at least 60% or 10^{15}g/year is transported across the ocean. Much of the transport is concentrated in restricted shipping lanes; thus, 25% of the world production passes through the English Channel!

A minimum estimate of the fraction of oil lost can be calculated from the extent of single large accidents and from operating records of oil ports. Thus, the tanker, *Torrey Canyon*, alone carried and lost 10^{11}g or 0.01% of the annual oil transport across the sea. The recent accident at Santa Barbara has introduced into the ocean 10^{10}g of crude oil. Reliable figures about oil losses in port are available from Milford Haven, a relatively new oil English port, adjacent to a national park. There, great efforts have been made

to control and prevent oil pollution and to keep a record of the size of any spills. In 1966 the annual turnover at Milford Haven was $3 × 10^{13}$g. The losses in the same time period amounted to $2.9 × 10^{9}$g or 0.01% of the total amount handled. A single accident (the tanker, *Chrissi P. Goulandris*) contributed between 10 and 20% of this total;[2] and the other losses are attributed to design faults, breakages, and mechanical failures, losses in transfer and human error.[3] This figure does not include losses outside the port due to accidents in shipping (e.g. the *Torrey Canyon*) and from numerous other sources such as ballasting and flushing of the bilges, etc. With the less stringent operation of many other ports and the additional losses on the high sea, the loss in transport alone may amount to 0.1% of the total oil shipped. The actual oil influx to the ocean is higher, since the figures above do not include accidents in production (e.g. Santa Barbara) return to the ocean of petroleum products (fuels and spent lubricants) in untreated municipal wastes and incomplete combustion of marine fuels.

Therefore, the oil influx to the ocean from shipping losses only is about 10^{12}g/year; other causes like influx from sewage and incomplete combustion may add substantially higher amounts.

Oil Composition and Biological Effects

In order to assess the biological effects of the oil pollution we should discuss the composition of crude oil and the relative toxicity of its fractions. Crude oil is one of the most complex mixtures of natural products, extending over a very wide range of molecular weights and structures. The *low boiling saturated hydrocarbons* have, until quite recently, been considered harmless to the marine environment. However, it has now been demonstrated that these hydrocarbons produce at low concentrations anaesthesia and narcosis and at greater concentration cell damage and death in a wide variety of lower animals and that they may be especially damaging to the larval and other young forms of marine life.[4] *Higher boiling saturated hydrocarbons* naturally occur in many marine organisms and are, probably, not directly toxic though they may interfere with nutrition and possibly with the reception of the chemical clues which are necessary for communication between many marine animals. *Olefinic hydrocarbons* probably are absent from crude oil, but they are abundant in oil products, e.g. in gasoline and in cracking products. They are also produced by many marine organisms, and may serve biological functions, e.g. in communication. However, their biological role is poorly understood. *Aromatic hydrocarbons* are abundant in petroleum; they represent its most dangerous fraction. Low boiling aromatics (benzene, toluene, xylenes, etc.) are acute poisons for man as well as for all other organisms. It was the great tragedy of the *Torrey Canyon* accident, that the detergents which were then used to disperse the oil spill had been dissolved in low boiling aromatics. Their application multiplied the damage to coastal organisms. It should be pointed out, however, that poisoning of marine life *will occur* even with non-toxic detergents or dispersants which are applied in non-toxic solvents, because they disperse the toxic materials of crude oil. This exposes organisms to these poisons through contact and ingestion. The *high boiling aromatic hydrocarbons* are suspected as long term poisons. Current research on the carcinogenic hydrocarbons in tobacco smoke has demonstrated, that the carcinogenic activity is not—as was previously thought—limited to the well known 3.4-benzopyrene. A wider range of alkylated 4- and 5-ring aromatic hydrocarbons can act as potent tumor initiators.[5] While the direct carcinogeneity of crude oil and crude oil residues has not yet been conclusively demonstrated, it should be pointed out that oil and residues contain alkylated 4- and 5-ring aromatic hydrocarbons similar to those in tobacco tar. In their behavior and toxicity the *nonhydrocarbons* of crude oil (nitrogen, oxygen, sulfur and metal compounds) closely resemble the corresponding aromatic compounds.

Oil Analysis and Law Enforcement

The great complexity of crude oil has an interesting consequence: The variety in the composition of different crude oils and oil products is so great that every oil has its own compositional features which are typical and persistent like a fingerprint. Great efforts have been expanded by many oil companies in utilizing this characteristic for correlating or distinguishing oils produced from different oil bearing horizons or for correlating oils with their source sediments. This fingerprinting technique is now becoming available to the public and will lead to improved and often conclusive correlation of an oil spill with oil from a particular oil field or from a particular vessel.[6,7] The analytical techniques are simple and should be a great aid to law enforcement.

Long Term Effects of Oil Pollution

The immediate, short term effects of oil pollution are obvious and well understood in kind if not in extent. The coastal fouling and damage to bird populations has been documented abundantly. As mentioned above, fouling on the high seas is just now being recognized, even though the amount of tar at the sea surface already exceeds the amount of surface plant life. The short term toxicity has been discussed above for individual petroleum fractions. In contrast to this, we are rather ignorant about long-term and low level effects of crude oil pollution. I fear that these may well be far more serious and long lasting than the more obvious short-term effects. I wish to discuss long-term toxicity and low level interference of oil pollution with marine ecology.

In combination, the great complexity of the marine food chain and the stability of the hydrocarbons in marine organisms, lead to a potentially dangerous situation. The food chain of those *terrestrial* organisms, which are important for human nutrition, is simple. Man either eats plant material or meat products from animals that have been raised on plant food. *Human food* derived *from the sea* is much more remote from its origin in plants. Few marine plants are directly used for human nutrition and, except for shellfish, we consume few marine animals that have fed directly on marine plants. Most larger marine animals derive their food from other marine animals that are already remote from the original plant source. We have studied the fate of organic compounds in the marine food chain and have found that hydrocarbons, once they are incorporated into a particular marine organism, are stable, regardless of their structure, and that they may pass through many members of the marine food chain without alteration.[8,9] In fact, the stability of the hydrocarbons in marine organisms is so great that hydrocarbon analysis serves as a tool for the study of the food sources of marine organisms. In the marine food chain hydrocarbons may not only be retained but they can actually be concentrated. This is a situation akin to that of the chlorinated pesticides which are as refractory as the hydrocarbons. These pesticides are concentrated in the marine food chain to the point where toxic levels may be reached. It is likely that the treatment of oil spills with detergents or dispersants, or the natural dispersion of oil in storms, produces oil droplets of a particle size range that is ingested and assimilated by many marine organisms. Once assimilated, this oil passes through the marine food chain, and eventually reaches organisms that are harvested for human consumption. One consequence will be the incorporation into food of materials which produce an undesirable flavor. A far more serious effect is the potential accumulation in human food of long-term poisons derived from crude oil, for instance of carcinogenic compounds.

Another concern is the possible long term damage by pollution to the marine ecology. Many biological processes which are important for the survival of marine organisms and which occupy key positions in their life processes are mediated by extremely low concentration of chemical messengers in the sea water. We have demonstrated that marine predators are attracted to their prey by organic compounds at concentrations below the part per billion level.[10] Such chemical attraction—and in a similar way repulsion—plays a role in the finding of food, the escape from predators, in homing of many commercially important species of fishes, in the selection of habitats and in sex attraction. There is good reason to believe that pollution interferes with these processes in two ways: by blocking the taste receptors and by mimicking for natural stimuli; the latter leads to false responses. Those crude oil fractions likely to interfere with such processes are the high boiling saturated and aromatic hydrocarbons and the full range of the olefinic hydrocarbons. It is obvious that a very simple—and seemingly innocuous—interference at extremely low concentration level may have a disastrous effect on the survival of any marine species and on many other species to which it is tied by the marine food chain.

Countermeasures Against Large Oil Spills

It must be obvious from this discussion that I do not consider the use of detergents or dispersants, toxic or nontoxic, as a solution for pollution problems. The introduction by dispersants of the toxic components of crude oil into the sea and the marine food chain constitutes a risk that should not be taken lightly.

Sinking of an oil spill by treatment with hydrophobic minerals (e.g. chalk treated with stearic acid or refractories treated with silicones) may be preferred; however, we do not know whether the oil remains on the sea floor or whether it will return to intermediate or shallow waters where it can enter the food chain. Also, we do not know enough about the effect of oil on bottom communities. Sedimentation rates in the open ocean are quite low, and oil that has been sunk will remain exposed for very long periods of time. In my opinion, burning of the oil where possible or containment and rapid recovery are the only acceptable solutions for managing large spills.

The Long-Term Outlook

Mankind is depleting the natural oil reserves rapidly. Therefore, it is unlikely that oceanic oil transport will increase by several orders of magnitude. In spite of this there are several good reasons to anticipate an increase in the seriousness of the marine oil pollution. Marine oil transport through more hazardous waters will increase (e.g. transport of the Alaskan oil through the Bering Straits). Oil production will shift increasingly to the continental shelves and oil reserves in very deep water (e.g. Sigsbee Deep, Gulf of Mexico) may be tapped. Both will lead to an increasing risk of accidents. Oil products and synthetic oil (coal hydrogenation products, shale oil), which are more toxic than crude oil, will make up a larger fraction of the oil transported, used and spilled.

We are convinced of the great value of oceanic food production for mankind. In the future, a larger fraction of human nutrition must be derived from the sea. Farming of the sea (aquaculture) will become an important pursuit for man. However, if we do not take care of the present biological resources in the sea, we may do irreversible damage to many organisms, to the marine food chain and we may eventually destroy the yield and the value of the food which we hope to recover from the sea.

Note

Our work on the fate of hydrocarbons in the sea has long been supported by ONR (present grant: N00 14-66-contract CO-241) and by NSF (present grant: GA-1625). Present work is also supported by a grant from FWPCA (18050 EBN). Contribution No. 2336 of the Woods Hole Oceanographic Institution.

References

1. V. E. Noshkin and J. E. Craddock, Event Information Report, Smithsonian Institution. 17 December 1968, Event #66–68.
2. D. R. Arthur, The Biological Problems of Littoral Pollution by Oil and Emulsifiers—A Summing Up, Field Study Council, Suppl. Vol. 2 (1968), 159.
3. G. Dudley, The Problem of Oil Pollution in a Major Oil Port, Field Study Council, Suppl. Vol. 2 (1968), 21.
4. R. J. Goldacre, Effects of Detergents and Oils on the Cell Membrane, Field Study Council, Suppl. Vol. 2 (1968), 131.
5. E. L. Wynder and D. Hoffman, Experimental Tobacco Carcinogenesis, Science, *162* (1968), 862.
6. J. V. Brunnock, D. F. Duckworth and G. G. Stephens, Analysis of Beach Pollutants, J. Inst. Petroleum, *54* (1968), 310.
7. S. J. Ramsdale and R. E. Wilkinson, Identification of Petroleum Sources of Beach Pollution by Gas Liquid Chromatography, J. Inst. Petroleum, *54* (1968), 327.
8. M. Blumer, Hydrocarbons in Digestive Tract and Liver of a Basking Shark, Science, *156* (1967), 390.
9. M. Blumer, "Zamene", Isomeric C., Monoolefins from Marine Zooplankton, Fishes and Mammals, Science, *148* (1965), 370.
10. K. J. Whittle and M. Blumer, Chemotaxis in Starfish, Symposium on Organic Chemistry of Natural Waters, University of Alaska, Fairbanks, Alaska, 1968 (in press).

ADDITIONAL REFERENCES

Abelson, P. H.   1970.   Shortage of caviar. *Science* 168(3928):199.
Carthy, J. D., and D. R. Arthur, eds. 1968. *The biological effects of oil pollution on littoral communities.* Proceedings of symposium, Pembroke, Wales, February 1968. Field Studies Council, London, 1968. (Distributor, Classey, Hampton, Middlesex.)
Cloud, Preston. 1969. Mineral resources from the sea. Pp. 133–155 in *Resources and man,* by Committee on Resources and Man, Division of Earth Sciences, National Academy of Sci-

ences/National Research Council. San Francisco: Freeman.

Conference on Oil Pollution of Navigable Waters, Washington, D.C. 1926. *Preliminary conference on oil pollution of navigable waters, Washington, June 8–16, 1926.* Washington: U.S. Government Printing Office. 449 pp.

Cooke, R. F. 1969. Oil transportation by sea. Pp. 93–102 in *Oil on the sea,* ed. by D. P. Hoult. New York and London: Plenum Press.

Cowan, E. 1968. *Oil and water; The Torrey Canyon disaster.* Philadelphia: Lippincott. 241 pp. A popular account.

Cruickshank, M. J. et al. 1969. Environment and technology in marine mining. *Journal of Environmental Science* 12:14–22. April.

Edwards, M. N. 1969. The role of the federal government in controlling oil pollution at sea. Pp. 103–112 in *Oil on the sea,* ed. by David P. Hoult. New York and London: Plenum Press.

Fonselius, S. H. 1970. Stagnant sea. *Environment* 12(6):2–11, 40–48. Discusses repercussions of pollution in the Baltic Sea.

Gill, C. F. Booker, and T. Soper. 1967. *The wreck of the Torrey Canyon.* Great Britain: David & Charles (Publishers) Limited. 128 pp. A popular account.

Hedgpeth, J. W. 1970. The oceans: World sump. *Environment* 12(3):40–47.

Holcomb, Robert. 1969. Oil in the ecosystem. *Science* 166:204–206.

Holmes, R. W. 1969. The Santa Barbara oil spill. Pp. 15–28 in *Oil on the sea,* ed. by David P. Hoult. New York and London: Plenum Press.

Hoult, D. P., ed. 1969. *Oil on the sea.* New York and London: Plenum Press. 114 pp.

International conference on oil pollution of the sea. Report of proceedings, Rome, October 1968. Available from Secretary, British Advisory Committee on Oil Pollution of the Sea, Natural History Museum, London. 416 pp. Paper 405.

Korringa, Pieter. 1968. Biological consequences of marine pollution with special reference to the North Sea fisheries. *Helgolander wiss.*

Meeresunters 17:126–140.

MacDonald, Ross, and Robert Easton. 1969. Santa Barbarans cite an 11th commandment: "thou shalt not abuse the earth." *The New York Times Magazine.* October 12.

Marx, Wesley. 1967. *The frail ocean.* New York: Ballantine Books. 274 pp.

Marx, Wesley. 1969. How not to kill the ocean. *Audubon* 71:27–35.

Nelson-Smith, Anthony. 1968. The effects of oil pollution and emulsifier cleansing on shore life in southwest Britain. *J. Appl. Ecol.* 5(1): 97–107.

Olson, T. A., and F. J. Burgess, eds. 1967. *Pollution and marine ecology.* Proceedings of Conference, Galveston, Texas, March, 1966. New York: Interscience (Wiley). 364 pp.

Parker, F. L. 1967. Disposal of low-level radioactive wastes into the ocean. *Nuclear Safety* 8(4):376–382.

Petrow, Richard. 1968. *In the wake of Torrey Canyon.* New York: David McKay Company, Inc. 256 pp. A popular account.

Rawn, A. M. 1966. Fixed and changing values in ocean disposal of sewage and wastes. Pp. 6–11 in *First international conference on waste disposal in the sea.* New York: Pergamon Press.

Ricker, W. E. 1969. Food from the sea. Pp. 87–108 in *Resources and man,* by Committee on Resources and Man, Division of Earth Sciences, National Academy of Sciences/National Research Council. San Francisco: Freeman.

Smith, J. E., ed. 1968. *"Torrey Canyon" pollution and marine life; A report of the Plymouth Laboratory of the Marine Biological Association of the United Kingdom.* Cambridge: University Press. 196 pp. Substantive scientific account.

Templeton, W. L. 1965. Ecological aspects of the disposal of radioactive wastes to the sea. Pp. 65–67 in *Ecology and the industrial society.* Fifth Symposium, British Ecological Society.

ZoBell, C. E. 1964. The occurrence, effects and fate of oil polluting the sea. *Adv. Wat. Poll. Res.* 3:85–118.

SOVIET PLANS TO REVERSE THE FLOW OF RIVERS: THE KAMA-VYCHEGDA-PECHORA PROJECT

PHILIP P. MICKLIN

Thus far all of the selections about man's impact on the waters have emphasized inadvertent changes and changes in water quality. We conclude by carefully considering one human scheme for transferring water on a massive scale. None of man's other feasible plans for controlling nature involve such vast construction and cost. The powerful motive is to adjust the supply of water in time and in space to meet the water demands of industry, cities, agriculture, and transporation.

This selection evaluates in detail the kinds of costs of Soviet plans to divert massive quantities of water by building dams and canals. Considerable detail is given for those who are interested. However, the selection exemplifies two major points: First, the complexity of considerations—technical, economic, cultural, political, and environmental—in planning or as consequences of massive water transfers. Second, the similarity of the problems involved in such projects in the many countries where they are being tried or proposed. Although a Soviet example is analyzed, the lessons are widely applicable.

The Kama-Vychegda-Pechora (KVP) Project would provide the following benefits: halt the declining water-level and increasing salinity of the Caspian Sea; provide deep-water transportation routes into northern European Russia; allow economic development, especially logging; and provide fish in reservoirs. But these virtues must be weighed against the following drawbacks: extensive land (130,000 acres) lost by flooding behind dams; land over gas- and oil-bearing fields flooded; threat of water pollution; postulated climatic change over 60,000 square kilometers; soils and vegetation affected by raised water table induced by reservoirs; disruption by dams of some existing transportation; blockage by dams of salmon and whitefish from spawning grounds; and inundation

Philip P. Micklin is an assistant professor of geography at Western Michigan University. He currently is completing the writing of a Ph.D. dissertation (at the University of Washington) concerning the fall in level of the Caspian Sea during the last four decades.

This selection originally appeared in *The Canadian Geographer* 13(3):199–215, 1969, and is reprinted by kind permission of the author and the journal.

of prime wildlife range. The trade-offs between all these factors are obviously complex.

These considerations closely resemble those involved in the NAWAPA (North American Water and Power Alliance) plan for water diversion in North America (Moss, 1966; Nace, 1966; Sewall, 1967; Quinn, 1968). Many of the same elements reappear in connection with smaller water projects elsewhere, for example ones involving the Aral Sea (Shul'ts, 1968), the Nile River (Brady, 1966), Kariba Dam (Scudder, 1969), and the Amazon River (Panero, 1969). In other words, much the same arguments are made to justify different projects—adequate water supply for arid regions, large increase in electric power production, creation of transportation routes, etc.

And the same sorts of adverse consequences result, because typically they are conceived within the same narrow framework of direct economic gains and technical feasibility. Environmental and economic repercussions are inadequately considered. The author of this selection concludes that "When as much weight is placed on the protection of environmental and delicate ecologic systems as on the meeting of economic needs, alternative, less spectacular solutions to water problems not entailing radical modifications of nature may prove to be the wisest course in the USSR and elsewhere." But of course this would not prove to man his dominance over nature!

It should be noted that a modest version of the KVP project was finally approved at the end of 1969 by the State Planning Committee (Gosplan) of the U.S.S.R. Some details of the latest version were published in the Moscow water transport newspaper *Vodny Transport*, December 4, 1969. The project now calls for construction of a dam with a 40-meter head in the upper reaches of the Pechora River. From the southern end of the reservoir formed by this dam, a canal would run 117 kilometers southward to a tributary of the Kama, eliminating the Vychegda element. The revision thus reduces the area to be flooded as well as the amount of water to be diverted from the Pechora to the Kama. The project approved by Gosplan also envisages a future second stage, with construction of a dam at Ust-Voya. With this second dam, the project would approximate the two-dam modification discussed in the selection. (From a letter by Theodore Shabad to *The Canadian Geographer.*)

(Editor's comment)

Grandiose projects aimed at radically altering the natural environment to meet the needs of an industrial society have been seriously contemplated in the Soviet Union for more than three decades. These so-called "nature transformation" schemes have been formulated almost wholly by engineers and, to a lesser degree, by physical scientists. Consequently, although highly imaginative, they have been conceived within a narrow framework of technical and economic feasibility and have either eschewed consideration of the environmental, ecologic, and economic side-effects of their implementation or have given these matters inadequate attention.[1]

This paper will investigate one such project, the purpose of which is the diversion of massive quantities of water from two Arctic flowing rivers of European Russia, the Pechora and Vychegda, into the Kama, a southward-draining stream, to meet a variety of needs in the central and southern regions of the country. The aim here is not only to present the technical aspects and claimed benefits of the proposed undertaking (although these are certainly quite interesting), but, more important, to point out the likely adverse consequences of this unique endeavour. A number of considerations make the project worthy of investigation. In the first place, it is not some engineer's dream; on the contrary, it is technically quite feasible and has been seriously proposed for construction. Secondly, a wealth of detailed information is available on nearly all aspects of the scheme. Finally, the project, although much smaller in scale, resembles the much discussed NAWAPA (North American Water and Power Alliance) plan for water diversion on our continent; hence it should be of more than passing interest to those concerned with the latter.

The Project

According to reliable Soviet sources, the first detailed plan for diversion of water from northward-flowing rivers into the southern regions of the USSR was formulated in 1933–4 by the Institute of Waterway Design (*Gidrovodtrans*) as part of a comprehensive development plan for the water resources of the Volga and its major tributary the Kama.[2] The scheme called for the transfer of four billion cubic metres annually from the Pechora and Vychegda into the Kama. The primary purpose was transporation improvement through the creation of a single reservoir linking the three rivers while the shift of water was of incidental importance.

Numerous other proposals involving diversions of up to 150 billion cubic metres a year via a number of routes to the south were concocted over the next several decades.[3] The most promising of these was put forward by the Leningrad Affiliate of the Hydro-Planning Institute (*Gidroproyekt*) in a

memorandum to the Ministry of Electric Stations dated June 17, 1955.[4] It involved the creation of a huge reservoir linking the Pechora, Vychegda, and Kama for the purpose of annually diverting forty-two billion cubic metres of water by gravitational flow from the first two rivers into the third. This variant along with several others was subjected to technical and economic feasibility studies by *Gidroproyekt* between 1955 and 1958.[5] Further research confirmed the Kama-Vychegda-Pechora (KVP) scheme in a somewhat modified form as the most economical in terms of capital investment required per unit of water transferred (1.2 new kopecks—approximately 1.3 cents per cu. m.).[6] This revised plan then served as the basis for the formulation of a final, and one would assume "officially" sanctioned, scheme which was promulgated in 1961.[7]

The final plan was the same as the preliminary scheme submitted by *Gidroproyekt* in 1955 as regards the number of dams to be built and canals dug. On the other hand, there had been some significant changes: the hydro complex on the Kama had been moved approximately fifty kilometres downstream to a more favourable site, the amount of water to be diverted had been reduced to thirty-eight billion cubic metres, and the reservoir's surface area considerably lessened; the height and length of impounding structures (with one exception) had been significantly scaled down leading to a lessening of required earth and concrete work for them; the total amount of power generation equipment to be installed rose significantly; and, finally, the length and depth of the proposed connecting canals underwent a substantial increase, as did the planned excavation work on them. According to the most recent detailed information, the revised project will require erection of the following structures (the numbers in brackets correspond to the numbers on Figure 23.1:[8]

(a) An earthen dam on the upper Pechora near Ust-Voya [1]. This huge structure, over twelve kilometres in length and eighty metres in height, will require the placing of 110 million cubic metres of fill. Interestingly

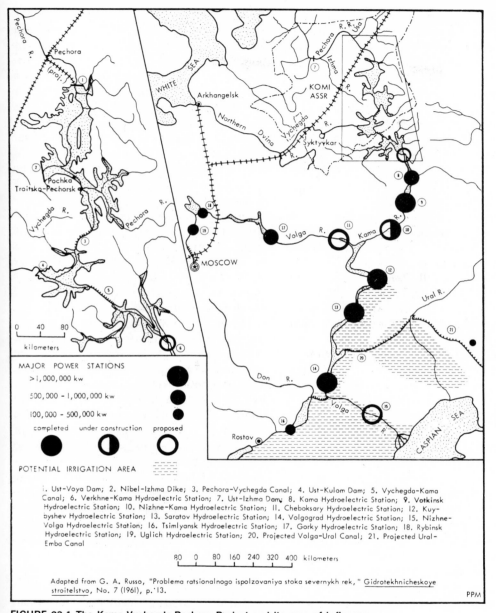

MAJOR POWER STATIONS

>1,000,000 kw

500,000 - 1,000,000 kw

100,000 - 500,000 kw

completed   under construction   proposed

POTENTIAL IRRIGATION AREA

1. Ust-Voya Dam; 2. Nibel-Izhma Dike; 3. Pechora-Vychegda Canal; 4. Ust-Kulom Dam; 5. Vychegda-Kama Canal; 6. Verkhne-Kama Hydroelectric Station; 7. Ust-Izhma Dam; 8. Kama Hydroelectric Station; 9. Votkinsk Hydroelectric Station; 10. Nizhne-Kama Hydroelectric Station; 11. Cheboksary Hydroelectric Station; 12. Kuybyshev Hydroelectric Station; 13. Saratov Hydroelectric Station; 14. Volgograd Hydroelectric Station; 15. Nizhne-Volga Hydroelectric Station; 16. Tsimlyansk Hydroelectric Station; 17. Gorky Hydroelectric Station; 18. Rybinsk Hydroelectric Station; 19. Uglich Hydroelectric Station; 20. Projected Volga-Ural Canal; 21. Projected Ural-Emba Canal

80   0   80 160 240 320 400 kilometers

Adapted from G. A. Russo, "Problema ratsionalnogo ispolzovaniya stoka severnykh rek," Gidrotekhnicheskoye stroitelstvo, No. 7 (1961), p. 13.

PPM

FIGURE 23.1 The Kama-Vychegda-Pechora Project and its area of influence.

enough, no water release facilities are planned for the dam and thus it will entirely cut off the flow of the upper section of the Pechora.

(b) An earthen dam on the lower Pechora somewhat below the entrance into it of the Izhma River [7]. The main purpose of this construction is to ameliorate the effects of the flow loss caused by the Ust-Voya Dam on river navigation through the creation of a reservoir all the way back to the latter. A sizable power station of one million kilowatts is part of the project. The dam is to be eighty metres high and will require earthwork totaling 120 million cubic metres (including both excavation and placement of

material.)   Whether this dam would be constructed simultaneously with the structures
for the main impoundment or some years
afterward is unclear.[9]

(c) An earthen dam on the upper Vychegda near the village of Ust-Kulom [4].
This structure will have a height of thirty-four
metres, a length of nearly two kilometres, and
will require approximately six million cubic
metres of fill.   A small power station of
46,500 kilowatts and a device for passing logs
from the reservoir to the river below the dam
will also be constructed here.

(d) An earthen dike on the water divide
between the Nibel and Izhma rivers [2].   This
structure is necessary not only to raise the
reservoir to the desired head but to prevent
the flooding of an extensive, low, swampy
area lying to the west of the Ust-Voya section
of the impoundment.   The barrier is to be
sixteen kilometres long, nine metres high, and
will contain 2.2 million cubic metres of material.

(e) An earthen dam on the upper Kama
above Solikamsk [6].   It will be five kilometres long, thirty metres high, and require
twenty million cubic metres of fill.   A substantial power station of 700,000 kilowatts,
water release facilities, and navigation locks
are also part of this complex.

(f) Two canals, 62.5 and 99 kilometres in
length respectively, to connect the reservoirs
formed on the Pechora, Vychegda, and Kama
into a single water body [3, 5].   The shorter
canal linking the Pechora and Vychegda will
have a depth of eighteen metres while the
longer canal between the Vychegda and
Kama is to be twenty-one metres deep.
These canals will require the excavation of
523.7 million cubic metres of earth and rock.

Soviet engineers estimate that seven years
will be required to complete all the structures
except the Ust-Izhma Dam.   During this
period, 536 million cubic metres of material
will be excavated, 142.5 million cubic metres
placed, and 1.96 million cubic metres of concrete poured.   A single construction project
of this scale has never before been undertaken in the USSR or, for that matter, anywhere else in the world.   For example, the

largest of the three dams, the Ust-Voya structure, will require almost 20 per cent more
soil than did the world's largest earth fill dam
at Fort Peck, Montana.   To construct the
connecting canals, over two-and-a-half times
more excavating work will be required than
in the digging of the Panama Canal.   Indeed,
the canal construction is to be on such a
massive scale that unique floating suction
dredges of an unprecedented size (70 m. long)
have been designed to facilitate the operation.

The single reservoir created by the dams
on the Pechora, Vychegda, and Kama and
by the linking canals will be immense (Table
23.1).   Its surface area of 15,500 square kilometres would be only 15 per cent less than
that of Lake Ladoga—the largest fresh water
body in European Russia.   Viewing it from
another angle, the impoundment of 235 billion cubic metres will be the largest artificial
water body in the world in terms of volume—more than 30 per cent greater than the
USSR's largest reservoir behind the Bratsk
Dam in Eastern Siberia.   It is estimated that
70.1 billion cubic metres of water will accumulate in the reservoir annually.   Of this,
2.6 billion will be released to the Vychegda
to preserve its log-floating capability and
sanitary condition below the Ust-Kulom
Dam while the lion's share of 64 billion cubic
metres will be released to the lower Kama
through control gates and the penstocks at
the Verkhne-Kama installation.[10]   Approximately thirty-eight billion cubic metres of the
latter flow will be water that formerly trav-
elled northward to the Arctic.

Filling of the reservoir is slated to begin
during the second year of work on the project
rather than after completion of all the dams
and canals.   Hence, filling is to be stretched
over a five-year period and will be finished
simultaneously with the impounding structures.   On the other hand, water diversion,
say the Soviets, can be initiated during the
fifth year of work, two years before the reservoir is full.

Since the reservoir is to be located in the
virgin taiga, much of its proposed expanse
is covered by valuable forests (chiefly stands

TABLE 23.1 Some characteristics of the combined Kama-Vychegda-Pechora Reservoir*

Characteristic	Unit of measure	Total	Sections of the reservoir		
			Pechora	Vychegda	Kama
Surface area	km²	15550	9950	2910	2690
	%	100	64	18.7	17.3
Total capacity	km³	235	184.5	34.5	16.0
	%	100	78.5	14.7	6.8
Usable capacity	km³	56.5	33.7	11.4	11.4
	%	100	59.5	22.25	22.25
Ratio of usable to total capacity	%	24	18.5	32	76
Mean annual flow at dam sites	km³	70.1	34.1	8.3	27.7
Ratio of total capacity to flow	%	336	541	416	59
Ratio of usable capacity to flow	%	81	99	137	41
Population to be resettled	—	60000	20000	13000	27000
Agricultural land to be flooded					
cultivated	ha.	13500	1400	4300	7800
hayland	ha.	35300	5300	15600	14400
pastures	ha.	4400	1000	1000	2400
Reserves of commercial timber to be flooded	000's m³	79000	52000	18500	8500

* S. L. Vendrov, "Geograficheskiye aspekty problemy perebroski chasti stoka Pechory i Vychegdy v basseyn r. Volgi," *Izvest. Akad. Nauk SSSR, ser. geog.,* no. 2 (1963), 37.

of fir and pine). Consequently, the Soviet government is faced with the task of removing the commercial timber (estimated at seventy-five million cubic metres). The situation is complicated by the lack of railroads or roads into the future reservoir area. The solution proposed for this problem is unique: the use of floating sawmills that will cut the timber beneath the water and then raise it onto their decks for further processing.[11] Thus, filling of the reservoir need not be delayed until it has been cleared since this work can be accomplished simultaneously with the impoundment process.

A number of cost estimates are available for the project. The original plan promulgated by *Gidroproyekt* in 1955 had a price tag of 1.2 billion new rubles, roughly 1.3 billion US dollars at the official exchange rate (see n. 6). The figure did not include the cost of the compensating dam which is supposed to be built below the Ust-Voya structure nor expenses accruing to reservoir preparation—it covered only the cost of the structures necessary to create the main impoundment. A revised figure was published in 1959.[12] Although the new estimate included allocations for reservoir preparation, at 935 million new rubles it was significantly lower than the earlier forecast. This trend continued into the early 1960s; the expenditures, again including reservoir costs, for the final scheme (1961) were estimated at only 530 million new rubles.[13] However, this downward tendency may have been reversed in recent years as there is one passing reference to a new figure, prepared by *Gidroproyekt* sometime after 1961, of approximately one billion new rubles for the project.[14]

Given the inconsistency of the above data and the arbitrary nature of the Soviet pricing system, one should be wary of placing great faith in any of the estimates. The great decline in estimated project costs between 1955 and 1961 is particularly curious. It is true that refinement of the 1955 scheme, as mentioned earlier, led to substantial reduction of the expected volume of earth and concrete work on the impounding structures, but, at the same time, there was a marked increase in required excavation operations for the linking canals. Thus, over-all, there was a slight decline from the original to the final scheme in total earth work (750 to 678.5 million cubic metres) and a more substantial decline in concrete work (3.5 to 1.96 million cubic metres). Perhaps this, along with innovations in large-scale construction techniques, could have led to the more than 50 per cent reduction in estimated costs by the early 1960s (particularly if digging canals is much cheaper than building dams.) But then it must be remembered that the later figures include allocations for reservoir costs which presumably would significantly erase savings realized from project refinement and technological innovation. Moreover, it is difficult to reconcile the 1961 estimate with costs incurred on recently completed water resource development projects of smaller scale in the USSR. For example, the Bratsk Hydroelectric Project in Eastern Siberia cost over 800 million new rubles while the Kuybyshev Hydroelectric Project on the Volga ran to over 1.2 billion new rubles.

It may very well be true that the engineers charged with preparing the cost forecasts have been far too optimistic; after all, the lower the required expenditures, the more attractive the project becomes to the government and the more likely it is to be constructed. Indeed, it would not be surprising, if the project is built, to see direct costs run much higher than 530 million new rubles, especially if the compensation dam on the lower Pechora (which seems a necessity) is also built.[15] This conclusion appears to be borne out by the report that the 1961 figure has been approximately doubled, although exactly what now is included as part of the necessary expenditures is not spelled out.

Benefits

The arguments put forward to justify the project are much the same as those used by proponents of our own NAWAPA scheme.

Assurance of an adequate water supply for arid southern regions, a large increase in electric power production, stabilization of an interior water body's level, and the creation of new transportation routes have all been proclaimed as major benefits of the undertaking. Some less important positive consequences ascribed to the diversion are better sanitary conditions on the rivers receiving supplementary water and the formation of new fish-breeding areas in the huge reservoir created behind the dams.

The supplying of more water to the arid southern areas of the European part of the USSR has for some years been a major concern of the Soviet government. For although the heavy-flowing Volga passes through this region, no more water can be withdrawn from it without causing a worsening of the so-called "Caspian Sea problem" as well as the lessening of electric power generation at some of the large Volga hydropower stations. Hence, the addition of thirty-eight billion cubic metres of water from the Pechora and Vychegda, amounting to almost a 17 per cent increase in the Volga's flow, is viewed as necessary to meet the growing needs not only of industry and population, but also of agriculture. Indeed, it is estimated that the diversion would free an additional 8–10 billion cubic metres of water for agriculture and lead to an increase in irrigated lands of 2.5 million hectares.[16]

On the other hand, the supplementary electric power that could be produced by the diverted waters is cited as justifying the major part of the project's capital investment.[17] The yearly increase in power output at the completed, under construction, and planned installations on the Volga and Kama would amount to eleven billion kilowatt hours— equal to the generation at the largest active station of the Kama-Volga hydropower system. In addition, through careful seasonal regulation of water releases from the KVP reservoir to the Kama River, the firm power capacity (i.e. installed capacity operable throughout the year) of the cascade could be increased by one million kilowatts. The additional hydropower provided by the diversion, it is claimed, would eliminate the necessity for future construction of some thermal plants and result in the saving of five million tons of standard fuel annually.[18]

Its many other claimed benefits notwithstanding, unquestionably the chief rationale for the project is to alleviate the Caspian Sea problem.[19] By this is meant the rapid lowering of the level of the Caspian Sea, the largest internal water body in the world, over the last thirty-eight years with concomitant destruction of spawning grounds, shallowing of harbours, and increased salinity of the water. The disastrous fall in the water level, which amounted to 2.65 metres between 1929 and 1963, has been almost entirely caused by a sizable reduction of the discharge from the Volga which accounts for approximately 76 per cent of the surface inflow to the sea. This reduction is ascribed in large measure to a general warming of the climate,[20] but it also is a result of man's action in building huge reservoirs on the Kama and Volga as well as making large consumptive withdrawals from the latter river for irrigational, municipal, and industrial purposes. Thus one well-known hydrologist cites data showing that for the period 1956–60 the surface discharge into the Caspian was reduced by approximately 12 per cent (188 billion cubic metres) solely by human means.[21]

The introduction of thirty-eight billion cubic metres of water annually into the Kama-Volga river system would no doubt be of great help in solving this pressing problem. Yet, that this diversion alone would stabilize the Caspian's level is questionable. For one thing, a sizable portion of the introduced flow would never reach the sea because of losses to evaporation, filtration, and new consumptive withdrawals (primarily to expand the irrigated acreage). Moreover, even if all the introduced flow were to reach the water body it would just make up for the average reduction of normal inflow caused by man in recent years, to say nothing of the naturally occurring deficiency. On the other hand, the shrinkage of the sea's area by approximately 12 per cent over the last thirty years has somewhat reduced evapora-

tion; therefore, less inflow is now required to bring the Caspian's water budget into balance. Also, a change in climatic conditions in the Caspian's basin, leading to more precipitation and, consequently, greater river flow, is expected in the near future; hence, the reduction of flow due to natural causes could lessen or entirely disappear.[22]

Furthermore, other measures to improve the Caspian's situation are contemplated. These would involve, for example, such actions as the diversion of an additional fifteen to twenty billion cubic metres of water to the Volga annually and the blocking off of the Kara-Bogaz-Gol Gulf from the Caspian to reduce evaporation and thereby "save" ten billion cubic metres of water a year.[23] The implementation of such auxiliary measures along with the original diversion could result in the stabilization of the Caspian's surface at a height somewhat above its present level in spite of estimated future consumptive withdrawals from its tributaries of fifty to fifty-five billion cubic metres a year. Such a prediction, of course, rests heavily on the expected improvement of climatic conditions in the Caspian's drainage basin. At any rate, if the sea's level is raised and stabilized, the resultant savings for the period 1970–2000, it is estimated could amount to 563 million new rubles, with the greatest benefits accruing first to fisheries and second to maritime transportation.[24]

Another consequence of the project of major significance is the creation of a deep-water transportation route into the heart of the northern European part of the Soviet Union. The claim is that the huge reservoir created as part of the scheme will "open up" this presently inaccessible area to much greater economic development, as well as provide a shortcut for the movement of raw materials from more northerly areas to some of the major industrial regions of the country.

Economic development, for the most part, will consist of the establishment of logging and, concomitantly, wood processing on a large scale adjacent to the reservoir. According to recent estimates, there is 800–1,000 million cubic metres of commercial timber available in the middle and upper reaches of the Pechora, Vychegda, and Kama, only about 10 per cent of which will be inundated by the reservoir. After cutting, this timber could be floated via the reservoir to proposed wood-processing centres on its shores at Troitsko-Pechorsk and Ust-Kulom. However, a majority of the timber, according to the latest plans of the State Planning Institute for the Paper Industry (*Giprobum*), will be floated along the reservoir and down the Vychegda to Sktyvkar for processing, and then even farther down to the Northern Dvina River and along it to Arkhangelsk, the leading wood-processing centre in the USSR.[25] It is also contemplated to direct large amounts of timber via the Kama-Volga system to the wood-deficient regions along the Volga, in the south, and in the centre of European Russia. Such movements, it is stated, could replace the long-distance, high-cost transportation of wood from Siberia and save ten to twelve million new rubles yearly.[26]

One serious drawback to these optimistic plans is the threat of serious water pollution, particularly in the Ust-Voya portion of the reservoir. The water exchange here would be very slow (5.6 years for complete replacement) and thus industrial effluent from the envisioned Troitsko-Pechorsk Wood Processing Combine would rapidly accumulate as would bark and wood fibres from log rafting. The situation would be worsened by the greater density of effluent water compared to pure reservoir water, resulting in a rapidly thickening layer of concentrated pollution on the reservoir's bottom. This, according to one study, could wipe out all fish life in the Ust-Voya sector of the impoundment and might even add to pollution problems on the Kama and Volga as well as in the Caspian Sea.[27] Of course, purifying installations would be constructed at all the wood-processing combines on the reservoir, but if past Soviet experience in this field is any guide, the outlook for the purity of the reservoir's water is not too sanguine.[28]

The primary raw material whose movement the reservoir is seen as facilitating is coal from the Pechora fields. This high-grade energy source is shipped by rail primarily into northwestern European Russia where it is converted into coke or burned in thermal power stations. With the completion of the diversion project, it will supposedly also be economical to send large amounts of this coal, for use in electric stations, into the Volga basin area via the water short cut across the new reservoir.[29] Opinion on this matter is not unanimous; some leading scholars at the Institute of Geography of the Academy of Sciences hold that Pechora coal will still be too expensive to compete with cheap oil and gas from the Volga fields. Nevertheless, they do admit that in the more distant future the use of northern coal for coking purposes in the northern Volga region is a distinct possibility.[30]

Finally, there are claims of two other less important, albeit still significant, project benefits: improved sanitary conditions on the Kama-Volga river system and an opportunity to develop an important fishery in the new reservoir. To what degree the annual addition of thirty-eight billion cubic metres of northern waters would reduce the locally serious pollution on the Volga and Kama is a moot question, although it could result in substantial improvement since the major part of the yearly water release is scheduled during late summer and early fall—a critical low-flow period for both rivers. However, if the forecasts of serious pollution of reservoir water in connection with wood processing is correct, diversion would worsen, not improve, water quality. On the other hand, Soviet pisciculturists have had good results in introducing fish into artificial water bodies; hence fishing might very well become an important industry for the population residing around the proposed KVP reservoir. Again, this predicted benefit could be abrogated by serious water pollution caused by adjacent industrial development.

Adverse Consequences

In the Soviet Union, as in the United States and Canada, large-scale water resource development measures have been formulated and promoted by organizations dominated by engineers. Therefore, benefit-cost and other feasibility studies have been carried out within a rather strict technical-economic framework and, in the main, have failed to consider and/or give appropriate weight to the environmental, ecologic, and less glaring economic side effects of such schemes. This is true of the well-known NAWAPA plan for water diversion in North America, and it certainly is characteristic of the Kama-Vychegda-Pechora Project. On the other hand, just as in the United States and Canada, non-engineers in the USSR with a professional interest in the resources field have forcefully pointed out the possible harmful consequences of such "nature transformation" projects and have called for delay in their construction until detailed scientific study can ascertain all the possible ramifications.[31]

Expressions of concern about the possible injurious effects of the KVP project have come from various quarters. The most thorough and thoughtful work, however, has been done by Soviet geographers, who in recent years have tended to take a broad, complex view of resource management questions, and by a variety of specialists (e.g., geographers, natural scientists, economists) on the Komi ASSR, the republic which would suffer most from the harmful consequences. Among the most articulate of these individuals have been two geographers: S. L. Vendrov, whose interest is hydrology with an emphasis on the influence of large reservoirs on the natural environment, and N. I. Shiskin, an expert on the economic geography of the Komi ASSR. Vendrov, Shiskin, and other researchers see a number of deleterious effects of the project. Most of these are connected with the enormous size of the proposed reservoir while the rest are results of drastically modifying the natural characteristics of the Pechora River—the main source of the diverted water.

The most obvious negative effect of the reservoir would be its inundation of a vast area. The project designers were well aware of this fact but claimed the resultant economic losses "minimal."[32] Other investigators are not so certain. Shiskin makes the point that much of the best agricultural land (i.e., land under cultivation, in fallow, and in pasture) within the Komi ASSR lies in the flood plains of the Pechora and Vychegda and will be lost (see Table I). This would not only cause serious problems for the present local population which is heavily dependent on flood plain agriculture for milk, meat, potatoes, and vegetables, but could also put a brake on future population increase and economic development within the republic by hindering agricultural expansion. Of course, the lost land is to be compensated for by opening new agricultural areas in the surrounding unflooded territory. But, according to estimates of experts from the Komi Republic, this would cost 3,500–3,800 new rubles per hectare—4 to 4.5 times the *Gidroproyekt* forecasts. Shiskin also asserts that population resettlement from the reservoir area will be much more expensive than has been the case with large reservoirs in the steppe regions of southern European Russia since it requires the costly opening of virgin lands in the northern forests.[33]

Of more economic consequence than the above, however, would be the flooding by the Ust-Voya section of the reservoir of part of the important Timan-Pechora gas- and oil-bearing province. Although the field produced only two million tons of oil and a small but unspecified amount of gas in 1965, annual extraction is slated to reach eight to ten million tons of oil and ten billion cubic metres of natural gas by 1972 and much more than this in the longer run. The reservoir would not prevent extraction of oil and gas but would make it much more expensive because of the need for special equipment and techniques. Reliable estimates place the extractible reserves that would be inundated at 160 billion cubic metres of gas and 179 million tons of oil. However, Soviet geologists, on the basis of recent exploratory drillings, are confident that the actual extractible reserves of both fuels in the area of the proposed reservoir are much greater than the above figures. At any rate, based on these conservative calculations, the estimated increase in capital investment and operational costs for the gas and oil industry because of the reservoir would amount to 2,587 million new rubles over the period 1970–2000. Moreover, if the damages to the industry are included in the cost of the KVP project, then, it is stated, the real cost will be more than double *Gidroproyekt's* recent estimate of one billion new rubles. Further complicating the situation is the fear that oil extraction from the lake bottom because of leakage and spillage would add to the water pollution problem discussed earlier.[34]

It has been recommended that the flooded area be significantly reduced to lessen economic damage. One proposal to this end that would not reduce the project's effectiveness is to dike off the shallow areas of the reservoir (which are very extensive, particularly in the Ust-Voya sector) while simultaneously deepening the connecting canals between the reservoir's three parts in order to raise the ratio of useful to total water volume. However, addition of these refinements to the plan would significantly raise costs.[35]

A second method of limiting the inundated area has received more serious consideration. This variant involves switching from one high dam (Ust-Voya) to two lower dams on the upper Pechora. One of the structures would be located at Ust-Voya and the other approximately 250 kilometres upstream near the village of Pochka. In this plan, the normal surface elevation of the reservoir behind the Ust-Voya Dam would be 100 metres as compared to 125 metres for the single dam variant. The upper reservoir surface would be at an elevation of 132 metres. As part of this scheme, water would be pumped from the lower to the upper reservoir.[36] Although the flooded area would be significantly reduced from 15.5 thousand to ten thousand square kilometres in the two-dam arrangement as compared to the single-dam plan, the same amount of agricultural land would be lost and the number of people to be resettled would even increase slightly. It would, however, cut the estimated damage to the oil and gas industry nearly in half (from 2,587 to 1,408 million new rubles for the period 1970–2000) and this is apparently its real

justification. Total concrete and earth work for the variant, as well as cost, would drop considerably from the one-dam arrangement, but so would the amount of water able to be diverted to the Kama-Volga system (from 38 to 18 million cubic metres annually.) Thus, in terms of transferred water, the cost would rise from 1.2 to 1.4 new kopecks per cubic metre from the old to the new plan.[37]

Although the economic losses associated with the reservoir have primary importance, there is also deep concern about the more subtle environmental and ecological consequences of creating a huge water body in a northern area. Detailed studies, including an analysis of data on existing reservoirs, carried out by the Department on Methods of Nature Transformation of the Institute of Geography of the Academy of Sciences (est. 1961), indicate the impoundment would have a decided effect not only on the climate but also on soils and vegetation over a sizable adjacent area.

Research on possible climatic changes was carried out by the method of analogues, that is, by examining such changes as have occurred due to the constructing of smaller reservoirs in similar environmental zones and then extrapolating to the probable effects of the proposed Pechora-Vychegda-Kama Reservoir.[38] The conclusions reached were (1) the area whose climate would be affected by the reservoir to one degree or another is approximately 60,000 square kilometres, or nearly four times the area of the water body itself; (2) the affected zone would be cooled by the water at the beginning of the warm season but warmed by it at the end; however, the influence of the reservoir on plant growth conditions, and consequently on agriculture, would be negative because of a net loss of heat available to plants during the growth season; and (3) the reservoir would reduce the continentality of the climate with winters becoming less severe and summers becoming both shorter and more humid.[39]

Serious effects on soil and vegetation, on the other hand, are predicated on a rise in groundwater induced by the reservoir. It is feared the heightened water table will result in water-logging of the soil over large areas, leading to its deterioration and the subsequent destruction of vegetation existing upon it. This problem would be especially widespread in the Pechora watershed where large areas which are not to be included in the reservoir are only slightly above groundwater level and, in addition, are underlain by permeable sands and rocks. Indeed, one estimate is that the above conditions would bring about the rapid destruction of forests surrounding the water body equal in area to the reservoir itself.[40]

To mitigate these serious ecologic side effects, it is again recommended that the surface area of the reservoir (especially the Pechora section) be greatly reduced. Furthermore, Vendrov has proposed that in addition to calculating the cost of reservoir preparation and flooding, the designers of the project should investigate destruction of natural resources in the area adjoining the impoundment and state how these losses are to be compensated.[41]

Two modifications of the Pechora's natural condition are viewed as having serious economic and ecologic implications: the diversion of a significant part of the river's flow southward and the blocking of its channel by two huge dams.

About 25 percent (33 billion out of a total 130 billion cubic metres) of the Pechora's average annual flow would be diverted southward. According to *Gidroproyekt*, the project's designer, such a flow reduction will not cause any significant damage below the reservoir.[42] To say the least, this contention is not widely accepted. In the first place, evidence accumulated from study of the effects of flow reduction of the Don River on the character of the Azov Sea suggests the removal of so much water will cause an increase in the salt content and a radical change in the temperature regime of the Pechora's estuary. This in turn could have a very adverse influence on feeding and possibly even spawning conditions of the fish population.[43] Secondly, the diversion of the river's warmest waters could negatively affect the local economy by prolonging the period the

part of the river below the Ust-Voya Dam is frozen and hence delaying the start of shipping and log-rafting operations in the spring.[44]

Thirdly, to get the required amount of water for diversion southward, given the present arrangement and design of structures for the KVP project, necessitates that no significant quantity of water pass the Ust-Voya Dam. Thus it is designed, according to the Soviets, "to cut off fully the flow" of the Pechora.[45] The practical effect of this would be to reduce the river's flow to a trickle, composed of water from small tributaries and leakage through the dam, for 229 kilometres downstream until the influx of a large tributary, the Usa. The adverse effects of this on riverine biota let alone river transportation would be substantial. To cite one example, a primary spawning grounds for the important food fish the *nelma* (whitefish) lies within this stretch of the Pechora; marked reduction of flow here would undoubtedly destroy these grounds and consequently cause significant harm to the *nelma*.

To be sure, the Soviets say a compensating dam will be built to rectify the situation by creating a reservoir back to the Ust-Voya Dam. But, as mentioned earlier, there is no assurance that it would be built simultaneously with the main part of the project. Moreover, this structure, as we shall see, is a mixed blessing as it could create as many problems as it solves vis-à-vis fisheries and transportation.

Even more serious problems could result from blocking of the Pechora by the Ust-Voya and Ust-Izhma Dams than from diversion of part of its flow. Firstly, these structures, unless equipped with locks, will make the shipping of goods along the Pechora more expensive by necessitating transhipment at the dam sites. Although freight movement on this river is not of great volume (2,242.3 thousand tons in 1965), for some settlements it is of critical importance as the only means of mass commodity supply.[46] Thus, it is a certainty such transportation would have to be maintained even if very costly. On the other hand, if locks were to be built at both dams, transportation would be greatly facilitated since a deep-water through route would then exist from the mouth of the Pechora to the Volga basin.

However, when and even if navigation facilities would be installed is uncertain. It is true locks for both dams have been mentioned or hinted at in some reports on the KVP project, but their installation is supposed to follow construction of the dams themselves when economic conditions warrant.[47] Furthermore, the experience in this regard at some other hydroprojects is not encouraging. For example, navigation locks were included in the technical plans for both the Irkutsk and Bratsk hydroelectric stations on the Angara River. Nevertheless, they were not installed at either dam; the same holds true for the Krasnoyarsk project on the Yenisey River. This is easy to understand since such facilities are quite expensive, particularly for high dams. Thus, unless there is an overriding economic imperative to provide them (as at the Volga stations), Soviet engineers have tended to postpone their installation indefinitely.

Secondly, and possibly of greater consequence, is the harm the dams could cause to the runs of anadromous and semi-anadromous fish (most importantly *semga*—Atlantic salmon and *nelma*—whitefish) by blocking access to their spawning grounds on the middle and upper Pechora and its tributaries. The average yearly catch of *semga* in the Pechora is 5,200 centners (one centner = 100 kg) and of *nelma* 1,215. If only the Ust-Voya structure is erected the catch of the former, it is estimated, would drop by 70 per cent, and of the latter by 25 while the construction of both dams would reduce the catch of each by 90 per cent.[48] Fish ladders could be installed at these structures to ameliorate the situation, of course, but they would be expensive and complicated considering the height of the two dams (80 m each.) As far as can be told fish ladders are not planned for either structure.

The loss of fish due to the dams is to be compensated for by constructing fish hatcheries for migratory species and by the increased production of non-migratory varieties in the proposed reservoirs. There is great doubt the first of these measures can produce enough fish to replace those lost even if only the Ust-Voya Dam is constructed, let alone both structures. Thus, regardless of ameliorative measures, the harvest of all migratory fish as a result of building both dams is expected to decline by more than 40 per cent.[49] On the other hand, the production of nonmigratory varieties with commercial value in the reservoirs behind the dams would be much greater than is now the case in the Pechora. Because of this the total annual take of fish along the Pechora after the filling of the reservoirs is expected almost to double (from 38.6 to 75.6 thousand centners.) However, much more of the total catch would be composed of low-value varieties; consequently, the value of the catch would increase only slightly from 6.2 to 6.9 million new rubles.[50] Moreover, as discussed earlier, the fish population of the Ust-Voya section of the main reservoir could be entirely destroyed by pollution from wood-processing mills and log rafting; this would undoubtedly lower total catches of fish for the whole Pechora much below their present level.

The envisioned compensation measures for both the Ust-Voya and Ust-Izhma projects would be more costly than the estimated economic damage each would cause the migratory fish, with the disparity between costs and benefits particularly great for the latter dam (18.8 to 8.6 million new rubles.)[51] In light of these data, one wonders if even the modest effort required to reduce economic damage to a 40 per cent decline in the annual catch of migratory fish would be made or whether their numbers would be allowed to drop to insignificance. This would be, if not an economic disaster, certainly an ecologic one since the Pechora is one of the most important spawning areas left for the dwindling schools of Atlantic salmon and whitefish.

Finally, although not mentioned by Soviet writers, there would appear to be at least one other serious adverse consequence of the KVP project: the inundation of a prime wildlife range—the flood plains of the Kama, Vychegda, and Pechora. A diversity of tundra and taiga fauna lives here including the moose, brown bear, European sable, ermine, and lynx.[52] Certainly, it is not unreasonable to expect damage to them equal to that (which many consider would be of disastrous proportions) forecast for the wildlife of the Yukon River in connection with the proposed Rampart Dam.

Conclusions

The evidence presented in this paper indicates that the proposed Kama-Vychegda-Pechora Project, along with its substantial benefits, could have a number of very adverse economic, environmental, and ecologic effects. Although a rigorous comparison of benefits and costs for the scheme is beyond the scope of this paper, a tentative conclusion would be that the latter are much greater than the former, particularly if environmental and ecologic costs are included along with the more tangible economic variety. In addition, the project's positive and negative ramifications would be polarized on a regional basis with the gains accruing to the southern areas of the country where the water is to be sent (areas along the Volga and around the Caspian) while the losses would be borne by the northern territories (chiefly the Komi ASSR) where the dams and reservoir are to be located. Hence, it is no great wonder that very strong opposition to the undertaking has come from people concerned with the future of the latter areas. These individuals have called for a clear presentation of how each negative effect in the north is to be balanced by a positive one in the south.[53]

It is quite clear that the project planners within *Gidroproyekt* have conceived the endeavour very narrowly. Their engineering bias has tended to make them concentrate on the technical aspects of the scheme and

its positive economic consequences. On the other hand, they failed to give sufficient attention to its negative economic effects—most notably the flooding of a valuable oil and gas field—and worried even less about possible environmental and ecologic harm to wildlife. Whether this oversight was the result of design or ignorance is hard to determine; probably it was an amalgam of both. At any rate, this narrow view of the project was in part responsible for a serious underestimation of costs for the construction of the dams and canals and the preparation of the reservoir alone.

There is no question that the furor raised over the project has postponed and possibly even permanently shelved it. Available evidence suggests that by 1961[54] the Soviet government had decided to implement the scheme; however, widespread opposition to this decision from respected scholars concerned about possible harmful consequences evidently caused official second thoughts. Indeed, the case against the scheme appears strong enough to preclude its execution.*

Nevertheless the project is still being discussed in favourable terms by Soviet writers with only a cursory knowledge of it. These authors leave the distinct impression that the project is to be constructed sometime in the future.[55] Furthermore, *Gidroproyekt*, in light of the criticism levelled at the scheme, held a planning meeting on the subject toward the end of 1966. What modifications, if any, were made to the 1961 plan are not known in any detail, but evidently the variant discussed earlier, involving the placing of two dams on the upper Pechora instead of one, was given serious consideration. A plan was also put forward to divert water at first only from the Pechora and then from the Vychegda,[56] but the proposals have not satisfied the project's opponents who still call for much more research into possible adverse effects. Moreover, far from being satisfied with piecemeal changes in the project to make it more palatable, they want it completely re-

---

* See editorial comments preceding text.

viewed.[57]   But if the KVP project can undergo sufficient modification, if not to satisfy its opponents, at least to win government approval, it may yet be built.

One would hope, however, that the Soviet government, before proceeding with this project would ponder it with the greatest care. This consideration should be more than seeking ways to eliminate the worst features through design improvements or even through some fantastically elaborate benefit-cost equation which would balance all positive and negative economic conse-

quences in order to decide whether or not to implement the plan.   It would also need to take account of the environmental and ecologic ramifications which are often intangible and always difficult to express in monetary terms.   Indeed, when as much weight is placed on the protection of environmental and delicate ecologic systems as on the meeting of economic needs, alternative, less spectacular solutions to water problems not entailing radical modifications of nature may prove to be the wisest course in the USSR and elsewhere.

Notes and References

1. A popular version of the Soviet approach to the transformation of nature is presented in two recent English-language publications from the USSR: Rusin, N. and A. Flit, *Man Versus Climate* (Moscow, no date); Adabashev, I., *Global Engineering* (Moscow, 1966).
2. Russo, G. A., "Problem ratsionalnogo ispolzovaniya stoka severnykh rek," *Gidrotekhnicheskoye stroitelstvo* (hereafter cited as *G-s*), no. 7 (1961), 11. Sarukhanov, G. L., "Skhema perebroski stoka rek Pechory i Vychegdy v basseyn r. Volgi," *Materialy vsesoyuznogo soveshchaniya po probleme Kaspiyskogo morya*, ed. by B. A. Apollov, K. K. Gyul, and V. G. Zavriyev (Baku, 1963), p. 36.
3. Sarukhanov, pp. 36–8.
4. The text of the memorandum was published in 1961 after the plan, in somewhat modified form, had received official blessing. See "Nam teper eto po plechu," *Ekon. gaz.*, Feb. 21, 1961, p. 3.
5. Sarukhanov, pp. 38–40. Akad. Nauk SSSR, Komi filial, *O vliyanii perebroski stoka severnykh rek v basseyn Kaspiya na narodnoye khozyaystvo Komi ASSR*, ed. by L. A. Bratsev, V. A. Vityazeva, and V. P. Podoplepov (Leningrad, 1967), p. 13.
6. Russo, p. 12. All Soviet monetary figures cited in this paper are in terms of the new ruble adopted in 1961. One new ruble equals ten old ones and is equivalent to $1.11 (US) at the official exchange rate.
7. Akad. Nauk SSSR, Komi filial, p. 13.
8. Sarukhanov, G. L., "Gidrotekhnicheskiye sooruzheniya v skheme perebroski stoka Pechory i Vychegdy v Volgu," *G-s*, no. 7 (1961), 17–20; and "Pechora-Kaspiy, reki severa potekut na yug," *Priroda*, no. 7 (1961), 56–7. Petrov, G. D., "Osobennosti proizvodstva rabot pri osushchestvleniy perebroski stoka Pechory i Vychegdy v Volgu," *G-s*, no. 7 (1961), 21–7.

9. See Shiskin, N. I., "On the Diversion of the Vychegda and Pechora Rivers to the Basin of the Volga," *Sov. Geogr.: Rev. and Transl.* (*SGRT*), 3, no. 5 (1962), 54; Sarukhanov (1963), p. 40.
10. The remaining 3.5 billion m^3 of yearly storage will be lost via evaporation from the reservoir's surface and filtration.
11. Sarukhanov (1961), p. 57.
12. Dmitriyev, G. V., "Skhema perebroski stoka severnykh rek v basseyn rek Kamy i Volgi," *Problemy Kaspiyskogo morya*, trudy Okeanograficheskoy Komissii, v (Moskva, 1959), 40. This figure, however, applies to the project as envisioned in 1956.
13. Sarukhanov (1963), p. 42.
14. Akad. Nauk SSSR, Komi filial, p. 192.
15. One authority estimates the cost of this dam will be 480 million new rubles. Dmitriyev, p. 42 (Table 2).
16. Sarukhanov (1961), p. 55; Shiskin, p. 50.
17. Russo, pp. 13. 15.
18. Standard fuel is an evaluation measure of the energy producing capability of coals in the USSR. One ton of standard fuel gives off 7 million calories of heat.
19. There is a vast amount of literature in Russian on this subject. Among many, see above, Apollov *et al.* (eds.), and *Problemy Kaspiyskogo morva* (above).
20. Vasilyev, M., *I reki vspyat potekut* (Moskva, 1962), pp. 39–40.
21. Lvovich, M. I., *Chelovek i vody* (Moskva, 1963), p. 498 (Table 129). The flow deficiency owing to man's actions for the period 1956–60 breaks down as follows: (1) losses due to various water retaining agricultural practices—23.8 billion m^3 (13 per cent of total), (2) losses from irrigation—45 billion m^3 (24 per cent of total), (3) losses associated with the creation of ponds—5 million m^3 (3 per cent of the total), and (4) losses due to filling of reservoir dead

storage—114 billion m³ (60 per cent of the total). Filling of reservoir dead storage is, of course, a non-repetitive water loss; with the completion of the Kama-Volga hydropower cascade (late 1970's ?) it will cease to be a significant factor contributing to man-caused surface flow losses for the Caspian.

22. Vendrov *et al.*, p. 32. Afanasyev, A. N., *Kolebaniya gidrometerologicheskogo rezhima na territorii SSSR* (Moskva, 1967), pp. 208–15. The latter work relates the climatic change to cyclic alterations in solar activity.

23. Russo, p. 14. Vendrov, S. L., *et al.*, "The Problem of Transformation and Utilization of the Water Resources of the Volga River and the Caspian Sea," *SGRT*, 5, no. 7 (1964), 32.

24. Volkov, L. N., "Vliyaniye perebroski stoka rek Pechory i Vychegdy v basseyn rek Kamy i Volgi na narodnoye khozyaystvo prikaspiyskikh rayonov," *Materialy*, p. 256 (Table 11). However, some sectors of the Caspian economy, particularly the oil industry, could suffer from raising and stabilizing of the sea's level.

25. Akad. Nauk SSSR. Komi filial, pp. 75–6.

26. Russo, p. 16.

27. Akad. Nauk SSSR, Komi filial, pp. 49–51.

28. See Micklin, Philip P., "The Baykal Controversy: A Resource Use Conflict in the USSR." *Nat. Resources J*, 7, no. 4 (1967), 486–98.

29. Russo, p. 16.

30. Buyanovskiy, M. S., and M. I. Lvovich, "Volgo-Akhtubinskaya poyma i delta Volgi," *Priroda*, no. 6 (1961), 57–8.

31. A most interesting attack on poor planning and insufficient study regarding modification of the natural environment (including a discussion of the Kama-Vychegda-Pechora Project) recently appeared in *Literaturnaya Gazeta* (July 12, 1967, p. 11) under the name of Academician N. Melnikov, head of the Commission for the Study of Productive Forces and Natural Resources of the Academy of Sciences.

32. Sarukhanov (1961), p. 57. However, this author in his calculations cleverly combined the Komi ASSR with Perm Oblast, which makes the losses appear relatively much smaller than if only the Komi Republic, in which most of the flooding would occur, is considered.

33. Shiskin, p. 54. Akad. Nauk SSSR, Komi filial, p. 190.

34. Akad. Nauk SSSR, Komi filial, pp. 7, 9, 51, 77–89, 188–9.

35. Shiskin, pp. 54–5. Vendrov, S. L., "Geographical Aspects of the Problem of Diverting Part of the Flow of the Pechora and Vychegda Rivers to the Volga Basin," *SGRT*, 4, no. 6 (1963), 32, 40.

36. Akad. Nauk SSSR, Komi filial, p. 87.

37. Sarukhanov (1963), p. 39. Akad. Nauk SSSR, Komi filial, p. 89 (Table 21).

38. The reservoirs used as analogues were the Rybinsk on the upper Volga, the Volkhov near Leningrad, and the Kama on that river's upper reaches.

39. Vendrov (1963), 36–8. Shiskin (1962), p. 53.

40. Vendrov (1963), pp. 38–9. Other conditions resulting from the creation of the reservoir that would promote water-logging are more sluggish runoff and increased atmospheric humidity.

41. *Ibid.*, p. 39.

42. Sarukhanov (1961), p. 57.

43. Vendrov (1963), p. 40.

44. Shiskin (1962), p. 53.

45. Sarukhanov (1963), p. 40. Since no water is supposed to get by the dam, it has been designed, as far as this author can discern, without water release facilities. If so, this would appear to be a serious mistake on the part of project planners. A cycle of "wet years" would produce a substantial rise in river flow on the Kama, Vychegda, and Pechora. This in turn would lead to greatly increased runoff into the reservoir. Given such a situation, there would have to be a substantial increase in the quantity of water released from here. The question is, where would this surplus water be sent? Of course, it could be released through the locks and penstocks of the Ust-Kulom complex on the Vychegda and by the same means at the Verkhne-Kama Station on the Kama. But such action might result in flooding along the Vychegda and also on the Volga and Kama, if they were running high, as well as lead to an undesirable rise in the level of the Caspian Sea. Indeed, if the Kama and Volga are in a heavy flow cycle, the project design calls for a reduction or cut-off of diversion and not its increase. In light of the above, water release facilities at the Ust-Voya Dam would appear to be an absolute necessity to remove surplus water from the KVP reservoir during years of above normal runoff into it.

46. Akad. Nauk SSSR, Komi filial, p. 162.

47. Dmitriyev, p. 40.

48. Akad. Nauk SSSR, Komi filial, pp. 138 (Table 33), 143 (Table 36).

49. *Ibid.*, pp. 144–5, 159 (Table 46).

50. *Ibid.*, pp. 157–9.

51. *Ibid.*, p. 160.

52. Davydova, M. I., *et al.*, *Fizicheskaya geografiya SSSR* (Moskva, 1966), p. 256.

53. Akad. Nauk SSSR, Komi filial, pp. 186–7.

54. See "Nam teper eto po plechu," *Ekon. gaz.*, Feb. 21, 1961, p. 3 and *Pravda*, June 22, 1962, p. 6.

55. Davydova *et al.*, pp. 109–10. Askochenskiy, A. N., *Orosheniye i obvodneniye v SSSR* (Moskva, 1967), p. 164. Kunin, V. N., "Chto proizoydet c nashimi vnutrennimi moryami?" *Priroda*, no. 1 (1967), p. 40.

56. Akad. Nauk SSSR, Komi filial, p. 192.

57. *Ibid.*, p. 193.

ADDITIONAL REFERENCES

Brady, T. F. 1966. Marine famine feared in Mediterranean as Nile Dam bars nutrients' flow. *New York Times,* March 20.

Idyll, B. C. P. 1969. The Everglades: A threatened ecology. *Science Journal* 5A(2):66–71.

Lowe-McConnell, R. H., ed. 1966. *Man-made lakes.* London: Academic Press. 218 pp.

Moss, F. E. 1966. NAWAPA; A bold water plan. Pp. 11–13 in *Highlights of Second International Water Quality Symposium.* Sponsored by Water Conditioning Association International, August 25 and 26, 1966, Montreal.

Nace, R. L. 1966. Water in flatland. Pp. 2–6 in *Highlights of Second International Water Quality Symposium,* Montreal. (Also in *Bull. Amer. Meteor. Soc.* 47(11):850–856, 1966.) Discussion of various impacts of man on water.

Panero, R. B. 1969. A dam across the Amazon. *Science Journal* 5A(3):56–60.

Quinn, Frank. 1968. Water transfers: Must the American West be won again? *Geograph. Rev.* 58(1):108–132.

Scudder, Thayer. 1969. Kariba Dam; the ecological hazards of making a lake. Pp. 68–72 in *The unforeseen international boomerang,* ed. by M. T. Farvar and J. Milton. Supplement to *Natural History Magazine.*

Sewell, W. R. D. 1967. NAWAPA: a continental water system; pipedream of practical possibility. *Bulletin of the Atomic Scientists* 23(7):8–13.

Shul'ts, V. L. 1968. The Aral Sea problem. *Transactions of the Central Asian Hydrometeorological Scientific Research Institute (Trudy SANIGMI),* No. 32(47), pp. 3–7. English translation in *Soviet Hydrology: Selected Papers,* Issue No. 5, 1968, pp. 489–492.

Storch, W. V., and R. L. Taylor. 1969. Some environmental effects of drainage in Florida. *American Society Civil Engineers Proceedings* 95:43–59.

FIVE MAN'S IMPACT ON LAND AND SOILS

FIVE MAN'S IMPACT ON LAND AND SOILS

"Throughout geologic time the earth has been subjected to a continuing cycle of orogeny, erosion, transportation, and deposition. Natural land disturbances are neither new nor intrinsically bad; but to these natural phenomena a new dimension has been added—man. He literally has moved mountains, and some of his surface excavations are so vast as to resemble craters on the moon."

Open pit mining, Bingham Canyon, Utah. Photo from Kennecott Copper Corporation.

INTRODUCTION

Man is basically a terrestrial animal, dependent on the land in many ways. The nature and growth of any human culture depends in considerable part upon the amount and quality of its land resources. The land is an important source of water and our primary source of minerals and energy resources such as coal, gas, and oil. By far most of our food is grown on land. We also use land for living space, for cities, for transportation, and for disposal of our wastes (particularly solid wastes). Further, the quality of land is an important determinant of vegetation and water quality.

Man's activities naturally lead to considerable modification of the land. In a variety of ways he shapes the earth's surface and alters the physical and chemical qualities of the ground. Such changes are the theme of this part.

How do our impacts on land and soils compare with those on the atmosphere and the waters? Human effects on the land are more obvious to more people. More importantly, though, these changes of land and soil are more characteristically fixed in space, with less spreading effects—for the material constituting landforms and soils is less mobile than air and water. Hence, most landforms and soils have an apparent temporal stability as well, with the consequence that once man has changed them, the alterations are not soon erased by "natural" processes. Geologic systems and (but to a lesser degree) soil systems normally are not self-correcting or self-cleansing within the short time periods that man appreciates, in contrast to the atmospheric and hydrologic systems and many ecosystems.

Aided by modern technology, man is now beginning to operate at the same order of magnitude as "natural" geologic forces (Selection 24). Despite this, geologists and geomorphologists have generally neglected the transforming influence of man's activities. A recent 1,200-page encyclopedia of geomorphology, for instance, typically devotes less than two pages of text to the role of man in geomorphology (Fairbridge, 1968). A new book by Flawn (1970) is an exception.

The selections that follow discuss by example some influences on land of man's coastal activities, mining, agriculture, highway construction and use, and waste disposal.

Landforms made by man are at least as old as agriculture. Selection 24 discusses the scale and intensity of agricultural terracing and mounding, mining, man-induced erosion and deposition of sediments, dredging, and urban bulldozing.

The world's coastal regions are extensively altered by harbor and channel construction, land reclamation, and beach protection measures (Selection 25). Natural processes acting on coasts have been modified by both coastal and inland activities of man. Direct reclamation is especially noteworthy along the North Sea. Stabilization, habitation, fishing, recreation, and pollution induce other changes along shores.

Surface mining, mostly for coal and sand and gravel, has disturbed more than 3 million acres in the United States alone (Selection 26). Surface mining also pollutes water and the air and causes other problems.

Removal of oil, gas, and water from beneath the surface of the ground has unintentionally caused marked subsidence of the surface. The ground at Long Beach, California, has subsided as much as 27 feet, causing damage amounting to 100 million dollars, because of oil pumping. In the San Jaoquin Valley, also in California, 3,500 square miles of land are sinking at rates up to 1 foot per year because of intensive pumping of underground water for irrigation. Selection 27 discusses several examples of land subsidence, the physical processes involved, and various solutions to the problem.

The effects of agriculture on environment have contributed to the downfall of previous societies. Selection 28 suggests that several successive cultures in Mesopotamia have risen and fallen depending on the abilities of their technological and social systems to cope with progressive changes in soil salinity and sedimentation.

Selection 29 shows the complexity of other soil changes wrought by man's agriculture, including breakdown in soil structure, increased erosion, excessive drainage, reduction of soil fertility, increased soil temperatures, and altered soil biota. One consequence is decreased quality per unit of agricultural output (e.g., lowered protein content).

The environmental impacts of highways, discussed in Selection 30, include the massive conversion of land from other purposes, regrading of the earth, pollution of air with exhausts and noise, accelerated sedimentation, increased runoff of storm water, road salting, and littering.

The final selection, 31, illustrates some unwanted consequences of injecting liquid wastes deep into the ground. This action has triggered earthquakes in the vicinity of Denver, Colorado. The process may be irreversible, for earthquakes there continue, even though the injection has stopped.

This survey of processes by which man modifies land and soils is broad but not all-inclusive. The depletion per se of mineral resources (National Academy of Sciences, 1969) and the disposal on land of solid wastes (National Academy of Sciences, 1966; U.S. President's Science Advisory Committee, 1965) are two important and growing problems that recently have been reviewed in depth by United States government groups. Similarly, the reshaping of land by means of nuclear excavation devices has lately been discussed elsewhere (Werth, 1969; Committee for Environmental Information, 1969; also see Selection 35). The landforming effects of warfare, such as cratering by bombs, are also of great significance in places;

detonation in 1952 of the first American thermonuclear device completely removed Elugelab Island from the Eniwetok chain in the Pacific and left a crater over 1 mile wide (Hewlett and Duncan, 1969). In Vietnam, bombs have produced millions of craters that make parts of the country look like the surface of the moon (Orians and Pfeiffer, 1970).

FURTHER READINGS

Banks, A. L., and J. A. Hislop. 1956. Sanitation practices and disease control in extending and improving areas for human habitation. Pp. 817–830 in *Man's role in changing the face of the earth*, ed. by William L. Thomas, Jr. Chicago and London: The University of Chicago Press.

Coleman, E. 1953. *Vegetation and watershed management.* New York: Ronald Press. 412 pp.

Committee for Environmental Information, Scientific Division Report. 1969. Underground nuclear testing. *Environment* 11(6):3–13, 41–53. Includes discussion of proposed nuclear excavation projects.

Ellison, L., and J. E. Coaldrake. 1954. Soil mantle movement in relation to forest clearing in southeastern Queensland. *Ecology* 35:380–388.

Fairbridge, R. W., ed. 1968. *The encyclopedia of geomorphology.* Encyclopedia of Earth Sciences Series, vol. III. New York: Reinhold Book Corp. 1295 pp.

Flawn, P. T. 1970. *Environmental geology; Conservation, land-use, and resource management.* New York: Harper & Row. 313 pp.

Frye, J. C. 1968. Geological information for managing the environment. *Texas Quarterly* 11(2):55–68.

Gutkind, E. A. 1956. Our world from the air: Conflict and adaptation. Pp. 1–44 in *Man's role in changing the face of the earth*, ed. by William L. Thomas, Jr. Chicago and London: The University of Chicago Press.

Hewlett, R. G., and F. Duncan. 1969. *Atomic shield, 1947/1952.* Volume 2 of a History of the United States Atomic Energy Commission. University Park, Pennsylvania: Pennsylvania State University Press. 718 pp.

Jahns, R. H. 1968. Geologic jeopardy. *Texas Quarterly* 11(2):69–83.

Kaye, C. A. 1968. Geology and our cities. *Trans. N. Y. Acad. Sci.* 30:1045–1051.

Ludwig, H. F., and R. J. Black. 1968. Report on the solid waste problem. *J. Sani. Eng. Div.*, Proc. of Am. Soc. Civil Engrs. 94(SA2):355–370.

National Academy of Sciences—National Research Council, Committee on Resources and Man. 1969. *Resources and man; A study and recommendations.* San Francisco: W. H. Freeman. 259 pp.

Pecora, W. T. 1968. Searching out resource limits. *Texas Quarterly* 11(2):148–154.

Sherlock, R. L. 1922. *Man as a geological agent.* London, H. F. & G. Witherby. 372 pp.

Spencer, J. E., and G. A. Hale. 1961. The origin, nature, and distribution of agricultural terracing. *Pacific Viewpoint*, pp. 1–40.

Strahler, A. N. 1956. The nature of induced erosion and aggradation. Pp. 621–638 in *Man's role in changing the face of the earth*, ed. by William L. Thomas, Jr. Chicago and London: The University of Chicago Press.

United States Department of Agriculture. 1938. *Soils and men.* Washington, D.C.: Government Printing Office. 1232 pp.

U.S. President's Science Advisory Committee, Environmental Pollution Panel. 1965. Solid wastes. Pp. 134–156 in *Restoring the quality of our environment.*

Werth, G. C. 1969. Planned applications of peaceful nuclear explosives. Pp. 31–61 in *Biological implications of the nuclear age*, U.S. Atomic Energy Commission.

Wolman, A. 1956. Disposal of man's wastes. Pp. 807–816 in *Man's role in changing the face of the earth*, ed. by William L. Thomas, Jr. Chicago and London: The University of Chicago Press.

LANDFORMS MADE BY MAN

BERL GOLOMB AND HERBERT M. EDER

With increasing ease, man sculptures the earth's surface. Landforms are molded for such varied purposes as growing crops, extracting minerals, facilitating transportation, and constructing ceremonial monuments.

The variety of landforms made by man and their modes of formation are surveyed in this selection, which emphasizes an historical approach. Later selections in this part expand on several processes which are mentioned here—coastal land reclamation, mining, agriculture, and so forth. Man's geomorphic activities have received inadequate attention from geomorphologists (many of whom are geologists), who usually consider erosion, transport, and deposition of earth material by "natural" processes only. It is obvious that man's growing role as a geomorphic agent should receive greater recognition and study, for the resulting changes have broad environmental and economic repercussions.

(*Editor's comment*)

The activities of humankind, whose numbers now exceed three billion, constitute an increasingly important agency of landscape change. Unlike other organisms, man adapts to different environments less through direct biological modification than through specialized developments of his culture.[1] Our species has thus been able to inhabit and to exert varied ecological influences over the greatest range of environments. Human modification ranges over a complex interplay of extension and intensity, from faint but noticeable pollution of all the world's oceans to the highly localized but wholly artificial

Berl Golomb (b. 1930) is a geographer on the faculty of the University of California at Santa Barbara. He was educated at Mexico City College and the University of California at Los Angeles (Ph.D., 1965). The cultural and historical geography of Latin America, especially Mexico, are the focus of Golomb's research. Herbert M. Eder (b. 1936) is associate professor of geography at California State College, Hayward. He holds three degrees from the University of California, Los Angeles (Ph.D., 1963). Eder's research interests continue on the relationship between folk cultures and their resources, with field investigation of Indian and Mestizo cultures in highland and coastal Oaxaca, in southern Mexico.

This article is reprinted by permission from *Landscape* 14(1):4–7, 1964. The notes and references, generously provided by the authors, are published here for the first time.

environment of a space capsule in orbit—with temporary clearings of bush for shifting cultivation in the tropics, permanently defrosted agricultural landscapes of the mid-latitudes, or the artificial landscapes of cities distributed appropriately on the continuum. The modifications may involve the micro-climate, the eco-climate, the biological balance of species, geologic weathering processes[2] and even the creation of artificial landforms.

Many of man's activities result in modifications of the actual earth surface. Where such modifications become perceptible, they may be considered man-made landforms. The exact compass of the term "landform" admits debate. The present discussion holds to a limited definition, restricting landforms to features of soil and rock. Even so, man-made landforms cover an ever-larger area of the surface of the earth. The Netherlands, where more than a thousand square miles of land have been reclaimed since Roman times, may be one of the largest deliberately fashioned man-made landforms.[3] Millions of tons of earth have been moved in creating the agricultural terraces of eastern Asia during the past several thousand years. Elsewhere in the world extensive plains have been corrugated into hills and hummocks in the construction of agricultural mounds. The embayments called by the English "broads," by the French "claires," and by the Dutch "meers," are flooded coastal depressions created by the excavation of peat.[4] The examples of landform creation and modification by man are highly varied in form, in scale and in process of formation.

In terms of the amount of work done, man is just now beginning to operate at the same order of magnitude as "natural" forces. In the mine dumps of the Witwatersrand, some 165,000 tons are accumulated daily. At the Ruth open pit mine near Ely, Nevada, 100,000 tons of rock are moved each day. Some 118,000 tons a day were excavated from the Mesabi Range in 1962. In the Rhineland coal fields brown-coal extraction reaches 150,000 tons per day.[5] These examples compare favorably—or alarmingly—with the 700,000 tons of silt the Colorado River

deposits each day in the Lake Mead reservoir behind Hoover Dam. In any one day, over an area comparable to that of its watershed, the Colorado undoubtedly far outstrips man in amount of earth-moving. And the Colorado is far from being the world's major river. Nature, however, generally operates through steady accumulation of small amounts of work over large areas. The sediment deposited in Lake Mead may represent only minute lowering of the average ground surface over thousands of square miles. In contrast, man's work is locally concentrated. The surface of the ground is scraped out, filled, pushed or otherwise molded far more noticeably than would result from comparable expenditure of energy by "natural" forces.

An interesting problem here is the satisfactory distinction of directly and indirectly created landforms. Accelerated erosion in a gully or a landslide along Los Angeles' Pacific Palisades may be as much due to human activity as a roadcut along a freeway. But while the latter was purposely created, the former were accidental and undesired. Landforms indirectly created by man are formed by natural processes to which man has contributed only the initial, triggering force. These examples of indirect morphogenesis are a link between the landforms of "natural" geomorphology and those of artificial "anthropogeomorphology."

If the indirectly created landforms qualify as "man-made," man's geomorphic scope is of greater magnitude than previously described. Erosion initiated by human activity must account for a large share of the 2,000,000 tons of sediments daily swept out by the Mississippi to its mouth, to say nothing of the tonnage deposited enroute.[6] Since around 3000 B.C., the head of the Persian Gulf has receded nearly 150 miles, and some 2000 square miles formerly under water are now alluvial land. A large if undeterminable part of this alluviation resulted from intensive agricultural activity in Mesopotamia, accompanied by over-grazing and deforestation of the upper Tigris and Euphrates watersheds.[7] These relations hold for the vast Hwang Ho delta, where the river has frequently shifted course and alluviated an area of several thousand square miles, transforming the Shantung island into a peninsula within historic times. A similar development, though at a smaller scale, has taken place at the head of the Adriatic Sea, attributable at least in part to human activity within the Po River's watershed. Diversion of waters for irrigation have converted some 10,000 square miles of the Aral Sea into dry land. Irrigation and diversion of waters for navigation canals have taken their toll of the Caspian Sea. Some 15,000 square miles formerly under water have become dry land, and shoals have developed throughout the northern Caspian as water level dropped some six feet.[8]

Taken in gross, no one would deny that these developments are "anthropogene," caused by human activity. But if the wholes are "anthropogene," what about the parts? Are the shoals of the Caspian, the mudbars of the Hwang Ho or the Venetian *lido* to be considered man-made landforms? They match the typical "natural" landforms, and differ markedly from landforms which man has deliberately shaped, such as road cuts, strip and open-pit mines or agricultural terraces. Herein lies a conceptual problem still to be resolved.

Among the surfaces deliberately fashioned by man, agricultural landforms are the most venerable, the most extensive and in many ways the least known and the most ignored. Certainly among the most spectacular are the terraced landscapes of the world. Over thousands of square miles in the Orient, the earth surface has been worked into terraces—flat-lying flood plains, broad, gentle interfluves and steeply sloping rugged hillsides are terraced. The intricately delicate terracing of the Ifugao in the rugged mountains of northern Luzon is the common textbook example. Other such landscapes are characteristic of the Western Andes or of the Mediterranean Basin. In a pioneer paper in *Pacific Viewpoint*, J. E. Spencer and G. Hale[9] have recently called attention to the importance of terracing as a human imprint on the surface of the earth, and offered a tenfold classification of forms. The geomor-

phic significance of terraces varies with the environment of the terraced landscape. As well as transforming the natural slopes, terracing may alter patterns of natural drainage, modify the development of soil profiles, interrupt natural cycles of erosion and alter rates of weathering. An abundance of other agricultural landforms, modern as well as ancient, await study.

Since urban areas are foci of human activity, intensive landform modifications are often characteristic of city sites. The Los Angeles Basin and the San Francisco Bay Area are replete with excellent examples. In both regions, man is cutting, leveling and filling for residential, industrial, recreational and communication purposes. In the Hollywood Hills, spurs are terraced for house sites. Artificial residential islands are built up out of fill in the salt marshes of Seal Beach. On sloping hillsides, houses are built on compacted artificial scree-cones. Earth sculpturing is carving high-rise building sites out of the hills of San Francisco, and leveling pads for "ticky-tacky" tract housing all around the Bay. The transportation function produces a variety of forms. Raised freeway beds twist through the lowlands like artificial eskers and great freeway cuts truncate mountain spurs like fault scarps. Need for sheltered harbors and increased docking space resulted in dredging basins in Southern California or a ship canal in the Bay. San Pedro's important Terminal Island is an artificial bar created from the accumulation of dredgings. Artificial flats of dredgings are shoreside features of Mission and San Francisco Bays. In response to the demands of recreation, great sand beaches have been artificially accumulated along the shores of Santa Monica Bay. Provision of recreational facilities has led to the formation of pocket embayments in the several marinas. Mining activities have also left their mark on the surface of coastal Central and Southern California. Expressions vary from borrow pits opened for gravel, clay and diatomaceous earth to the inexorable industrial erosion of a limestone hill for the cement mills of Colton. Destruction by gold-dredging of the alluvial landscape on the margins of the Sacramento Valley is a large scale example of surface alteration by mining. With efforts to combat air pollution restricting incineration, burial has gained importance as a means of refuse disposal in the Los Angeles and San Francisco Bay regions. Open pit mines are being filled, and whole canyons are being leveled. San Francisco Bay is being constricted; human accretion in the form of "sanitary fill" has been advancing toward the center of the bay at an estimated rate of one foot per year.

Like any other phenomena, man-made landforms may be studied through a variety of approaches. At least three systems of classification can be suggested:

First, man-made landforms could be classified descriptively in terms of the forms they assume, or in terms of similarity to natural landforms that they approximate. For example, embankments, terraces, fills and cuts could constitute classes. This descriptive approach of form analysis would avoid consideration of the underlying generative processes.

Second, man-made landforms could be grouped genetically, according to the agency that formed them. The analogy with "natural" geomorphology would be classification of landforms created by agents such as moving water, wind or mass wasting. In the case of man-made landforms, the agents would be tools and machines. The term "bulldozo-genesis" has often been used informally in the U.C.L.A. Geography Department to refer to the dynamic impact of the bulldozer in creating and destroying landforms throughout the Los Angeles Basin. Many similar terms come to mind, although with less felicitous results. With the application of nuclear technology as in the Atomic Energy Commission's "Project Plowshare," new tools and new terms may develop. The genetic approach has been the most fruitful in geomorphology, but it does not seem promising for the study of man-made landforms. This is, by and large, a result of our burgeoning technology and the proliferation of machines and techniques. Furthermore, given machines are capable of causing a large variety of morphologic expressions on the landscape.

Third, man-made landforms could be classified in terms of the major functions or human activities that led to their formation. Major categories of man-made landforms would be associated with functions such as transportation, shelter, agricultural activity, mineral extraction, etc. A second order of classification could comprise the purposes the individual landforms serve. This approach may permit more meaningful analysis than the other two systems.

The study of man-made landforms need not be limited to the geomorphic aspect or to cataloguing and identification. Historical and comparative studies are certainly of interest, and can shed light on problems in adjacent fields of knowledge. Middens, often imposing topographic features, are associated with settlement sites in human archeo-geography; their study has yielded knowledge of the home environments of early man. Middens, incidentally, are still being formed, whether as "sanitary fill" or as non-sanitary municipal dumps, such as Lima's notorious "El Monton." Less obviously, changes in the space-time pattern of Meso-american earthmounds, the terraced landscape of the Rhine Graben, the earthworks of the Mojos Savannas of northeastern Bolivia, would tell much about regional changes in nature and culture. These may be speculative jobs, but challenging and rewarding to those of inquisitive bent. Problems in the more usual areal-and time-perspective of historical geography abound in the wake of our modern mining activity and urban expansion.[10] Refinement of problems in a cultural-geographic orientation could result from a comparative line of inquiry. Tools, techniques, attitudes and motivations are cultural variables. Comparable man-made landforms in various culture regions might show significant differences. Have Southeast Asian and West Andean terraced landscapes been compared? Or Polynesian taro pits and the mulch-pits of coastal Peru? And might not a scheme of classification be devised to encompass landforms such as the *chinampas* in permanently inundated marsh in the Mexican basin, the "earthworks" of the seasonally flooded Mojos, and the canal-ringed cultivation plots of the arid Viru Valley?[11] Such a scheme would parallel classification of terraces but involve landforms designed for control of moisture rather than slope. Schemes of landforms for other functions, as well as problems of overlap and multifunctional forms, can be expected.

Given its scale, variety and intensity, the importance of man's landforming activity is obvious. A geomorphic agent of such significance deserves study as much as do wind, ice and moving water. In effect, man's activities approximate the gamut of "natural" agents. These processes and their resulting landforms may come to be studied as something distinct from but equally as important as "natural" geomorphology.

Study of man-made landforms has had a curious history. Comments on environmental and land-surface alterations by man have been recorded since classical antiquity. In the early 19th Century, Alexander von Humboldt commented on the force of habit that made Spaniards recreate the arid landscape of Castile in the initially lacustrine environment of the basin of Mexico.[12] In 1864 came publication of *Man and Nature*, George Perkins Marsh's study of man's alterations of landscape and of the impact of human activity on physical geography.[13] Recognition of man's importance as an environmental modifier has accompanied the rapid increase in technologic capabilities. The 1955 symposium called by the Wenner-Gren Foundation led to the compilation of a thousand-page volume, *Man's Role in Changing the Face of the Earth*.[14] Man's impact on environmental resources has become alarming in many quarters.[15] Awareness of the magnitude and pace of change is now apparent in popular discussions, and the mixed feelings toward this change are reflected in Richard Armour's short verse:

Out with trees and don't lament;

Fill the valleys with cement.

A considerable volume of literature has thus accumulated on the subject. Most of the contributions have been of an ecological orientation, focused on the disturbance in the balance of nature that human activities have brought upon the impact on the general environment of man's increasing numbers and expanded enterprises. Only a relatively small part of this literature has stressed man's role as a geomorphic agent, exerting a noticeable effect on the earth's crust. Geologists seem to have been the principal contributors to this geomorphic orientation.[16]

On the whole, specific attention to this geomorphic rather than ecologic aspect has been neglected. This relative neglect is true even of the aforementioned symposium volume itself.[17] The study of man's geomorphic activities, then, is one of the paradoxical "recognized yet unrecognized subjects," to use the phrase P. L. Wagner and M. W. Mikesell applied to cultural geography.[18]

Should geomorphic study of man-made landforms prove useful, it may justify a distinctive name. Of currency, especially in Europe, is "anthropogene geomorphology," as used by Edwin Fels.[19] A closer parallel to Ratzel's "anthropogeographie" is the polysyllabic "anthropogeomorphology." However, a name is simply a mnemonic tag, called for only if a delimiting or unifying device is needed. As indicated above, there is still no conceptual definition or methodological consensus. The bridge of nomenclature can be crossed in good time.

At a time when many of us are involved with hypothetical distributions and non-real spatial models, the study of man-made landforms has an earthy appeal. And certainly, if it is the aim of geographers to describe and explain features of the surface of the earth, man's geomorphic activity cannot be neglected.

Note

We wish to express our thanks to those who assisted at various stages in formulating these ideas. Especially constructive help was given by John D. Passerello, at U.C.L.A., and by Ronald Horvath. J. E. Spencer indirectly provided constant stimulus. Errors of concept, fact, or formulation are, of course, our own.

Notes and References

1. Biological modifications are apt to follow cultural developments that permit tools to take over functions formerly performed by body organs. For example, Loring Brace (*Current Anthropology*, Vol. 5, No. 1, Feb., 1964, p. 3–19) has commented on possible effects of cutting tools in the reduction of human incisors and anterior dentition, with resulting changes in shape of the face.

2. For example, waste from duck farms washing into Long Island's Great South Bay is reported to have changed the quality and quantity of oysters, stimulated intense increase of *Chlorella*, and affected the sediments deposited in the bay (Davis, "Influence of Man upon Coast Lines," *Man's Role in Changing the Face of the Earth*, pp. 504–519 [Selection 25 this book]).

3. Cf. Johan Van Veen, *Dredge, Drain, Reclaim: The Art of a Nation*, The Hague, 5th Edition, 1962.

4. See Bloch, M. R., "The Social Influence of Salt," *Scientific American*, July, 1963, pp. 88–96.

5. Sources, respectively, are: McLaughlin, Donald H., "Man's Selective Attacks on Ores and Minerals" (*Man's Role in Changing the Face of the Earth*, pp. 851–861); "Snow Nor Cold Halts Mining, But Those 'Ski Gals' Might," *New York Times*, Sunday, February 16, 1964; U.S. Bureau of Mines, *Minerals Yearbook 1962*, Vol. 1, p. 688; and Edwin Fels, personal communication dated September 4, 1963.

6. Estimated by Richard J. Russell. See: *Lower Mississippi Delta. Reports on Plaquemines and Saint Bernard Parishes*. La. Dept. Conserv. Geol. Bull. No. 8, 2936.

7. Davis, in *Man's Role in Changing the Face of the Earth*.

8. Taskin, G. A., "The Falling Level of the Caspian Sea in Relation to Soviet Economy," *Geographical Review*, Vol. 44, No. 4, 1954, pp. 508–527.

9. Spencer, J. E. and G. A. Hale, "The Origin, Nature and Distribution of Agricultural Terracing," *Pacific Viewpoint*, Vol. 2, No. 4, March, 1961 (Wellington, New Zealand).

10. See recent works by Deasy, George F., and Phyllis R. Griese, "Coal Strip Mine Reclamation," *Mineral Industries*, Vol. 33, No. 1, October, 1963, pp. 1–7; Thomas, Trevor M., "Wales: Land of Mines and Quarries," *Geographical Review*, Vol. 46, No. 1, 1956, pp. 58–81. Or from an aesthetic viewpoint, see Bowden, Kenneth L. and Richard L. Meier, "Shall We Design New Badlands?" *Landscape Architecture*, Vol. 51, No. 4, July, 1961, p. 225–229.

11. For description of the Mojos "earthworks," see William Denevan's Additional Comments on the Earthworks of Mojos in Northeastern Bolivia," *American Antiquity*, Vol. 28, No. 4, 1963, pp. 540–545; also Plafker, George, "Observations on Archaeological Remains in Northeastern Bolivia," *American Antiquity*, Vol. 28, No. 3, 1963, pp. 163–182. For Viru Valley forms, see Willey, Gordon R., *Prehistoric Settlement Patterns in the Viru Valley, Peru*. Bureau of Ethnology Publication No. 135, Washington, 1953.

12. Humboldt, Alexander von, *Political Essay on the Kingdom of New Spain*.
References to the basin of Mexico in Volume 2 of Robredo Edition, Mexico, 1941. There were many prior observations on the subject, from Andreossi observations on deforestation along the Canal du Midi and Enrico Martinez's on artificially accelerated sedimentation in the basin of Mexico to Plato's *The Critias*.

13. Marsh, George Perkins, *Man and Nature; or Physical Geography as Modified by Human Action*. New York, Scribners; London, Sampson Low, 1864.

14. Thomas, Jr., William L. (ed.), *Man's Role in Changing the Face of the Earth*. Chicago, University of Chicago Press, 1956.

15. See the publications of the Conservation Foundation; Fairfield Osborn's *Our Plundered Planet* (Boston, Little, Brown, 1948); William Vogt's *Road to Survival* (New York, William Sloane, 1948); or Rachel Carson's *The Silent Spring* (Boston, Houghton Mifflin, 1962).

16. The Introductory Section of *Man's Role in Changing the Face of the Earth* lists Fischer, Ernest, "Der Mensch als Geologisher Faktor" (Zeits. Deutscher Geolog. Gessell. Vol. 61, 1915, pp. 106–148); Sherlock, Robert Lionel, *Man as a Geologic Agent* (London, H. F. & G. Witherby, 1922); Pawlowski, Stanislaw, "Modifications apportees par l'homme . . ." (*Przeglad Geograficzny*, Vol. 4, 1923, pp. 48–64). A number of studies by nongeologists such as Edwin Fels, Paul Schultze-Naumburg, and Aldo Sestini may share in part this geomorphic approach. See *Man's Role in Changing the Face of the Earth*, pp. xxxvii-xxxviii.

17. Three papers totaling 43 pages of the total 1,100 or so pages of *Man's Role in Changing the Face of the Earth* are directly devoted to the geomorphic aspects of human activity: John H. Davis, "Influence of Man upon Coast Lines" (pp. 504–521); Arthur N. Strahler, "Nature of Induced Erosion and Aggradation" (pp. 621–638); and Luna B. Leopold, "Land Use and Sediment Yield" (pp. 639–647).

18. Wagner, Phillip L., and Marvin W. Mikesell, *Readings in Cultural Geography*, Chicago, University of Chicago Press, 1962.

19. Fels, Edwin, *Die Umgestaltung der Erde durch Den Menschen; Fragenkriese fur die Obserstufe der hoheren Schulen*. Munich. Bluteburg Verlag; Paderborn, Schonin, Verlag, June, 1962.

ADDITIONAL REFERENCES

Denevan, W. M. 1970. Aboriginal drained-field cultivation in the Americas. *Science* 169: 647–654.

Holz, R. K. 1969. Man-made landforms in the Nile Delta. *Geogr. Rev.* 59(2):251–269.

Nelson, J. G. 1966. Man and geomorphic process in the Chemung River Valley, New York and Pennsylvania. *Annals Assoc. Amer. Geogr.* 56:24–32.

Parsons, J. J., and W. A. Bowen. 1966. Ancient ridged fields of the San Jorge River floodplain, Colombia. *Geogr. Rev.* 56(3):318–343.

25
SELECTION

INFLUENCES OF MAN
UPON COAST LINES

JOHN H. DAVIS

The world's coasts—where sea and land meet—are naturally dynamic zones of great importance to man. This classical paper examines in fascinating detail the coastal relations between man and nature. Our multiple uses of coastal areas have led to many conflicting demands and influences. Waste disposal, food production, recreation, transportation, defense—all must be reconciled in wise coastal management (Beller, 1970; also see Selection 21 for consideration of problems in one coastal environment: estuaries).

(Editor's comment)

Coastal regions are the most continually changing zones of the earth. In them many ceaseless and great forces and processes of nature are at play on a large scale, and man for all his efforts has had relatively little effect on them. He has, however, promoted some coastal modifications by indirect influences upon a number of natural processes and accomplished some direct modifications, of which the reclamation of land from the sea has been the most notable.

Many geologic processes are involved in the coastal conflict zone between the land and the sea, such as degradation and aggradation, diastrophic uplift and depression, faulting, slipping and thrusting, glaciation, vulcanism, and eustatic changes in sea level. Animals, such as corals and shellfish, and plants, such as mangrove-swamp forests and dune grasses and shrubs, take part in the struggle. The atmosphere joins in the fray by processes of slow weathering and the impact of violent storms that hurl the sea at the land. Many currents in the sea, tides

John H. Davis (b. 1901) was professor of botany and plant ecology at the University of Florida from 1946 to 1969. After earning a Ph.D. degree from the University of Chicago in 1929, he taught at several colleges before joining the Florida Geological Survey as a research associate (1941–1946). Davis served as a visiting professor for a year or more each in New Zealand, Burma, and Formosa. His publications include "The Ecology and Geologic Role of Mangroves in Florida," *The Natural Features of Southern Florida*, and *The Peat Deposits of Florida*.

This selection is reprinted by permission of the author and the original publisher from *Man's Role in Changing the Face of the Earth*, edited by William L. Thomas, Jr., The University of Chicago Press, pp. 504–521. With the author's permission Figure 25.4 replaces the original, a similar photograph, which was unavailable for reprinting. Copyright © The University of Chicago, 1956.

that ebb and flow, and even the salinity and temperature of the water affect the coast. Rivers from the vast interiors of the continents bring down loads of sediments, glaciers gouge out shores, and many materials are dumped into the sea in great volume by these and other agents. Therefore, these tremendous forces and processes need review before considering the influences of man upon coast lines.

Geologic Features and Processes

The term "coast line" as used here includes features of both the coast and the shore line. "Coast" usually designates wide zones involving both land and water, across which shifts the shore line, as the active narrow zone of contact between the land and the sea. "Coast" includes in its seaward part the tidal, littoral areas and some of the shallow, shoal-water areas and in its landward part the strand and some other parts of the coastal plain.

Many types of coasts have been distinguished and classified on the bases of their form and development. Some familiar ones are advancing coasts compared to retreating coasts; submerging coasts compared to emerging coasts; and drowned coasts compared to uplifted coasts. Processes of marine erosion or retrogradation contrast with processes of deposition, progradation, or aggradation. These are stressed in some classifications of types, such as by Cotton (1954), who proposed three main kinds: (1) retrograding; (2) prograding by alluviation; and (3) prograding by beach-building. Many clifftype retreating coasts are good examples of the first type, delta coasts are examples of the second, and strand coasts with beaches and dunes are examples of the third. But any one of these types may change to one of the others, and cycles of change are the rule over long periods. In addition to these, there are compound coasts that combine the features of two or more of these three types, and there are coasts termed "neutral" that occur where very slow or no particular processes seem in progress.

In general, there is a geomorphic cycle of coastal development during which depositional and erosional forms develop through a sequence. Spits and bars are typical depositional features, and cliffs, some headlands, and many deep-water embayments are erosional features. The littoral and continental shelf sediments also shift about in cycles.

Some coasts have been classified (Price, 1954) as high-energy coasts, where the wave, tide, wind, and other factors are intense and processes of change are rapid. In contrast, other such coasts are classified as low-energy coasts, where forces are moderate or small. The high-energy type produces either a high relief retrograding coast or a dune-forming prograding coast. The low-energy type is generally of low relief with shallow lagoons and embayments.

There are also a few distinctive type coastal forms, such as coral-reef coasts, volcanic coasts, and glacial coasts. The coral-reef coasts are very extensive in the tropical regions; the glacial, in the polar regions. The retrograding and prograding features of any of these are very complex.

Other complexities of the coastal processes are the factors of uplift and of depression of the land. Both are usually due to active diastrophism that is very difficult to determine, especially when eustatic changes in sea level occur at the same time. The uplifting process is taking place in parts of northern Europe and North America, where there is postglacial rebound due to the diminishing of glacial ice; and a downward depression of land is in progress in some regions, such as in parts of New Zealand.

Man has been associated with most of these coastal forms and processes, has modified a few forms, and has influenced a few processes. He has not been very effective along the high-energy coasts. In general, most of his effectiveness has been along the prograding, outbuilding coasts in regions of low coastal energy, where the changes have been slow and where he could cope with the other forces of nature. On some of the degrading, retrograding, and submerging coasts man has built strong structures, such as port and channel establishments, lighthouses, and forts, but only a few of these along high-energy coasts have withstood for long the ravages of the sea.

During the whole Pleistocene period there were four or five major glacioeustatic oscillations in sea level, resulting particularly in rises during interglacial periods, which have been estimated by geologists and other scientists (Cooke, 1938; Russell, 1940). Paleolithic man was probably associated with one of these periods of sea-level change, and modern man has, since the last glacial period, encountered a slow but sure sea-level rise. This rise has not been continuous but has been interrupted by stillstands or slight recessions. At present the rate of rise seems relatively greater (Anonymous, 1952, p. 11) than at other postglacial times, probably owing to a recently accelerated increase in the melting of glaciers. This was the case, for instance, during the Peorian interglacial period of the "Pamlico Sea," when a rise of about 25 feet occurred.

Without being fully aware of it, man has been combating the eustatic rise of sea level in many areas. He also has encountered land uplift or depression in a number of regions. But, in general, such changes have been so slow that they would not have influenced his activities even if he had been aware of them. The recent period of rise of the sea and its very slow invasion of the land should, however, be taken into consideration when estimating the long-term effects of man upon coast-line changes in some regions; and it is possible that man may have actively to combat sea-level changes, if they become more rapid, in future land reclamations from the sea that he may undertake.

Biologic and Other Features and Processes

Life in the intertidal, littoral zone and over shoal-water areas is very abundant and varied, as is also life on the strand dunes, cliffs, and similar areas above the tides. All these organisms are of some effect in coastal processes, but some, such as the shellfish and corals of the shallow-sea areas and the plants of the strand dunes and salt marshes or mangrove swamps, are particularly important. The dune-forming and dune-holding plants play an important role over extensive areas of land, and the corals build enormous reefs and actively form new land areas. Even the algal growth, most significant as the initial part of the sea's food chain of productivity of organisms, is important in some regions in both coastal processes.

Man has used or influenced these organisms in many ways, especially the shellfish that have been a part of his food supply for ages. He has for various purposes changed the coastal marshes and mangrove swamps, reclaiming many of the former for agricultural purposes. He has used plants to stabilize dunes, and recently he has dumped waste and other polluting materials into the sea in such large quantities that these have had influences on the local fauna and flora.

The atmosphere has been influential mainly through violent storms that in a few short hours have undone the efforts of man over centuries. Winds, alternating cold and warm conditions creating ice and then its melting, and the slow weathering processes of the atmosphere have all been significant. These and other factors will not be enumerated further.

The Human Factor

Our present concern is the relatively small role of man as one of the biologic factors. Although insignificant as compared to much greater natural processes, man has been influential upon some coast-line areas and upon some processes which are in many instances very important to him. Man is also partly a product of the complex environment of coastal regions, along which he has engaged in many varied activities for thousands of years. In his relation to the coasts, sea, and land he may be classified into three ecological types, each of which in some way affects differently from the others the coastline processes and forms, namely, (1) *maritime* men; (2) *coastal* men; and (3) *inland* men.

Maritime men are similar to pelagic animals because they are dependent mainly upon the open sea for their livelihood. Their use of coastal land areas has been mainly as domiciles and ports, and some of the structures of their great ports have persisted for centuries. In some cases their establishments have aided in the stabilization and enlargement of areas upon which they were built, especially the lighthouses and forts. These port, channel, and other structures erected by maritime men are discussed more fully by Klimm in the chapter that follows.

Coastal men are those who claim and use both the land near the sea and the shallow-water areas of the sea. Their commerce and fishing are usually near shore. They catch fish, gather shellfish, and build towns and villages on the strand and in small embayments. Their coastal activities have been so numerous and varied that their total effect has been significant. One of their most persistent activities has been the building of shell mounds, which are large piles chiefly of refuse resulting from various uses of shellfish. These mounds are so extensive on the Atlantic coast from Newfoundland to Florida and on the coast of the Gulf of Mexico that in some parts they occur along as much as 10 per cent of the shore line. They also occur in many other parts of the world. Many of these mounds have been instrumental both in holding the coast line against retrogression and in aiding progression. Coastal men also engage in some agriculture, particularly in conjunction with inland men crowded toward the sea by population pressure. These two have carried out some of the great projects of land reclamation from the sea.

Inland men have been afraid of the sea because it was strange to them, and the term "landlubber" suits them admirably. However, they have sought the sea or been forced toward it for a number of reasons—for pleasure, recreation, commerce, and agriculture. Their activities near or at the sea have grown in proportion with increases of population

and with increased desire for recreation, made possible by rising standards of living. They have built cottages and fashionable hostelries along some coasts to avoid the heat of summer or the cold of winter, and such activities have become very extensive in areas such as Florida, California, and the Mediterranean. These structures often rest on dunes or on filled-in areas of the tidelands, and numerous groins, jetties, sea walls, and other devices have been constructed to protect this valuable property from the erosive forces of the sea (Figure 25.1). The agricultural activities of inland men have impelled them to undertake some great land reclamations, especially in the Low Countries of Europe. For thousands of years they have taken advantage of good soils of delta regions and have influenced delta development at the mouths of many great rivers, such as the Tigris-Euphrates, Nile, Po, and Ganges.

FIGURE 25.1 Miami Beach, Florida. To the left are numerous resort hotels on the dune-strand areas and the groins built to control beach erosion; to the right of the lagoon is the area of homes that are built on land reclaimed from littoral mangrove swamps.

Direct and Indirect Influences

Many of the efforts by these three ecological types of men to improve their lot on the earth have had both direct and indirect influence on coast-line changes. Direct efforts have been made mainly toward harbors and channels, some agricultural reclamation developments, and the retardation of erosion along beach and dune areas. In these connections some of the progradational geologic processes that were present have been encouraged, but in most cases man has merely fought back the retrograding activities of the sea. Since the ancient past, maritime and coastal men have been most instrumental in these direct influences, but recently inland men have increased their direct efforts, especially in agriculture and in the prevention of beach and dune erosion.

In general, the indirect influences have been so well integrated with, or submerged in, the geologic and other processes of nature that they are very obscure and difficult to calculate quantitatively. They include some activities of inland men that occur far inland, such as deforestation, farming, and mining in the drainage basins of the rivers that enter the sea. Such activities result in soil erosion, which is reflected by increases in river sedimentation and the extension of coasts at the mouths of many rivers; but the amount of such increases is very difficult to estimate. Fishing activities, for both shellfish and swimming fish and including the culture of fish, have had mainly an indirect influence. Pollution of waters by urban and manufacturing developments has greatly increased since the industrial revolution, particularly in areas of Western civilization, and some effects are apparent in coastal changes. For example, perhaps the most indirect effects are seen in the few cases of radical upset of the biological balance in nature, such as disturbance of coastal shellfish and bird life.

Man, in fact, is part of the total of natural forces, and he acts within a complexly integrated whole of natural processes. For this reason many of his activities indirectly affect numerous conditions along the coasts. Farming in the flood-plain and delta areas has had both direct and indirect effects, but how and how much is uncertain. We know little of the total or multiple effects of all these indirect activities, and it will be difficult to predict some of the future influences. We might expect that the large-scale use of atomic, fissionable materials would upset many of the biological balances in nature as well as have some direct topographic effect on such particular areas as those in the Pacific, where bomb tests have recently been made. The following descriptions exemplify types of human activities that have either directly or indirectly modified coast lines of particular areas.

Some Regions of Prolonged Changes

Some of the oldest continuous civilizations have flourished along rivers where sediments in their valleys and at their deltas furnished alluvial materials useful for both agriculture and urban development. Some notable examples are the Mesopotamian region of the Tigris and Euphrates rivers, the Po River Delta region of Italy, the Nile Valley and Delta, the Ganges Valley and Delta, and the Hwang Ho, or Yellow River, Valley. The civilizations of the Volga, Danube, Rhone, and Rhine rivers in Europe and of the Mississippi in America have in some cases been of relatively short duration, but they also have affected sedimentation at the river mouths. Of these, the greatest continued changes probably have occurred in the Mesopotamian region, which involves the Persian Gulf as well as the two rivers and their valleys. Shorter-term changes are noticeable in northern Italy along the Adriatic Sea.

MESOPOTAMIA AND THE PERSIAN GULF

Lowland areas that lie between and flank the Tigris and Euphrates rivers inland from the head of the Persian Gulf have been the home of a number of ancient and modern civilizations. The coast line in this region has changed during recorded history (Figure 25.2), and the civilizations have had some effects on these changes.[1] The main human influences have been canal irrigation, drainage, and farming systems along and between these two rivers, which have affected the alluviation and other changes in the region and at the mouths of the rivers entering the Persian Gulf. This region has supported large populations that have done much construction and farming.

Geologic evidence shows that the Persian Gulf shore line, during an interglacial period, was probably above Ramadi at Hit on the Euphrates River and above Baghdad on the Tigris River. At this time human activity had little effect on it. However, during the Sumerian culture period, perhaps as early as 4000 B.C., the development of irrigation canals began, and records of the shore line of the Persian Gulf during the second and third millenniums B.C. indicate that the mouth of the Euphrates was located near Eridu and Lagash, probably before 3000 B.C. Pliny and other historians noted that the Euphrates had a separate mouth to the gulf until about the seventh century B.C. and that the men of Erech dammed this mouth. Ur is noted in some old descriptions as the chief seaport of the Sumerians.

The present, single river, the Shatt-al-Arab, that takes the waters of both the Tigris and the Euphrates to the Persian Gulf, is about 123 miles long, and the combined river flood plain and delta region from ancient Ur and Lagash to the present delta mouth covers more than 2,000 square miles. The Shatt-al-Arab Delta in modern times, between 1793 and 1833, extended itself near Fao at the rate of 53 feet per annum, according to Rawlinson (1854). Other estimates of Mesopotamian delta increase indicate a linear extension of nearly 180 miles from the ancient mouth of the Euphrates River to the present mouth of the Shatt-al-Arab during a period of about forty-five hundred years. The rate of the extension of the delta now seems to be about a mile per seventy years, which is

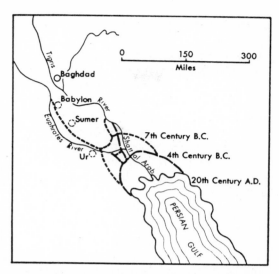

FIGURE 25.2 Changes in the mouths of the Tigris and Euphrates rivers and in the Persian Gulf area since the seventh century B.C. (After Putzger, 1931, and other atlases.)

slower than the older rate of change if 180 miles of land were added in forty-five hundred years.

Although all these distances, areas, and time intervals are but approximate estimates, nevertheless the total land area developed in the ancient embayment of the Persian Gulf has been great. Progressive delta and river deposition, mainly by alluviation, has been responsible for most of the great plain of Mesopotamia, covering some 35,000 square miles and with a gradient of only some 100 feet from Baghdad to the sea. This plain is below sea level over large areas that are now inland from the delta, and many marshes and lakes occur on it. The two rivers have shifted their courses over the plain, in some instances encouraged or made by man, such as the shift accomplished by King Rim-sin when he straightened a few miles of the Euphrates. The Tigris has changed less than the Euphrates. Both rivers almost converged just south of Baghdad when early irrigation by canals was begun, and the canals probably extended between the two rivers. The Euphrates has progressively shifted west and southwest since that time. It has the greater load of sediments and has built up the larger riverine deposits.

In addition to this ancient type of irrigation farming and city development, there were upland, inland activities that had their indirect effects. The hills and mountains of northern Iraq and Iran and adjacent countries were denuded of their forests, and grasslands deteriorated over many centuries of use and exploitation by numerous civilizations. Erosion over these uplands increased the sedimentary loads of the rivers, and this probably increased the alluviation in the plain of Mesopotamia, especially by floods, which at present occur between February and June, when melting snow and rains convey heavy loads of red mud to the rivers. There is some evidence that these annual floods formerly did not occur. In the old records and legends of Sumeria and Babylonia there are no references to floods, which suggests that floods probably followed the advent of intensive settlement and agriculture that led to eroded uplands.

Some effects of canals and irrigation in retarding sediment at the delta mouths of these rivers are shown for three periods in the history of Mesopotamia. From the beginning of the Christian Era to about the ninth century A.D. the canal systems were neglected; the few records of this period indicate a greater formation of delta than before the canal systems were extensively used. During the five-century period of the caliphate that followed, canals and cultivation were extensively developed; delta formation, together with coastal extension, decreased. The Mongol invasions abruptly ended this period with the destruction of most of the irrigation system; ever since, the rate of the coastal extension has been greater than during the caliphate period.

It seems, therefore, that a complex of many direct and indirect activities has affected the long-term development of Mesopotamian coastal extension. The direct effects have been very few, and, while some of the canal and other agricultural activities have indirectly retarded rather than accelerated the natural processes of progradation of land into the sea, inland devastation has accomplished an increase in this progradation.

THE ITALIAN–ADRIATIC SEA COASTAL REGION

The Italian coast from south of Ravenna north and eastward almost to Trieste has been extending itself into the Adriatic Sea for at least twenty centuries (Putzger, 1931). This region was described at about the time of Christ by the Greek geographer Strabo (1917–50, pp. 309, 313–15) as follows: "Now this whole country is filled with rivers and marshes. . . . Of the cities here, some are wholly island, while others are only partly surrounded by water." He noted about the ancient city of Ravenna that "at tides the city receives no small portion of the sea, so that, since the filth is all washed out by these . . . the city is relieved of foul air." Today this city is 6 miles inland, and most of the other ancient coastal cities, such as Adria and Aquileia, are also inland. Brown reports (1910–11) that the encroachment of land on the sea has been at the rate of about 3 miles in a thousand years, which amounts to approximately 200 square miles of increase in land area along this coast since about 200 B.C.

As noted by Brown (*ibid.*, p. 995), "a strong current sets round the head of the Adriatic from east to west. This current catches the silt brought down by the rivers and projects it in long banks, or *lidi*, parallel with the shore. In process of time, as in the case of Venice, these banks raised themselves above the level of the water and became the true shoreline, with lagoons behind them."

Most of this Italian coastal extension has been by the action of this Adriatic Sea current on the sediments brought down by the rivers, particularly the Po, which has helped fill in the lagoons formed behind the barrier *lidi*— and has built deltas. The activities of man on the upland watersheds drained by these rivers have been long, and his intensive agriculture, causing denudation and increasing the sediments of the rivers, has promoted progradation. In this way man has indirectly aided in extending the Italian coast line.

OTHER CHANGES IN DELTA REGIONS

Many other delta regions in Asia and Europe have been affected, but reliable information about most of them is very fragmentary. There has probably been some extension of the Nile Delta: archeological evidence indicates that man has occupied it since before the dynasties, and cultivation in the delta has been intensive and of long duration. Since the building of the city of Alexandria, just prior to the Christian Era, all but two of the seven distributaries of the Nile over this delta have become filled or nearly filled, though no appreciable extension of the coast has been recorded recently.

The Mississippi River Delta has probably accelerated its extension since the advent of European man into the mid-continent areas of North America. Inland deforestation, soil erosion, straightening of the river channel, and pollution have been indirect causes of increased sedimentation at the delta mouths. The construction of levees and jetties in the delta has been a direct cause of land extension. But the extension so caused has been only a few miles at most.

Direct Reclamation

Most of the continuous, extensive, and direct reclamation has been in Europe, especially in the Low Countries along the North Sea, where the deltas, estuaries, embayments of many kinds, and lagoon areas between the barrier islands and the mainland have been modified by many kinds of engineering and agricultural endeavors. The most extensive of these has been the building of a system of dikes and canals which inclose various drained areas known as "polders." Other lowland, coastal regions have experienced a less direct type of reclamation, of which the fen-type marsh development in England is an example. Both of these will be described briefly. Both are the result mainly of the combined efforts of inland and coastal men driven to the necessity of developing land from the sea.

LOW COUNTRIES POLDER-DEVELOPMENT RECLAMATION

The early, partly civilized peoples of the Low Countries built mounds in the moorland marsh and swamp areas for probably a thousand years before their successors began building dikes about A.D. 900. Since that time dike-building and polder development by drainage, dredging, and pumping have increased until the total area claimed from the sea is probably a million acres of farm land, pastures, and sites for towns and cities.[2] Most of these areas are in Belgium and in the Netherlands (Figures 25.3 and 25.4). Reclamation is now even more intensely pursued, and very extensive projects, such as the Zuider Zee development, will add over a million and a half acres to these regions by about 1980.

Part of this development is in a region where delta channels of the Rhine, Maas, and Scheldt rivers bring in fluvial clays and where marine deposits accumulate back of barrier islands. Organic materials, especially peats and mucks, also accumulate in the moor-type marshes. Fresh-water lakes, some natural and some artificial, are present. The whole region is being drowned both by the eustatic rise of sea level and by the downward movement and settling of deposits and soils. As a consequence of these geologic changes and of the retrograding activities of the sea, including such violent storms as that of February, 1953, many of the reclaimed areas have been lost. Also, incorrect engineering in the building of dikes and the dredging of channels has caused the loss of some areas. The cumulative total of these losses has been estimated at nearly two-thirds of the total area claimed from the sea. But now most of the former polders have been restored. These, together with new projects, such as the Zuider Zee and Wadden, will increase the total area far beyond that of all the former reclamations.

Construction of the outer or watcher dikes formerly was slow and accomplished mainly by the use of willow mats and clay. Now, many improvements have hastened con-

FIGURE 25.3 Zuider Zee Dam, The Netherlands. Twenty miles long, the dam separates the Wadden Sea, on the left, from the fresh-water lake, on the right. Polders, like those in the foreground, will be developed from this lake by drainage and pumping, as shown in Figure 25.4. (From Van Veen, 1948; photograph KLM Aerocarto n. v., The Hague.)

struction and made the dikes stronger—stakes, fitted basalt blocks, bricks, and concrete—and with modern machinery much larger projects are being undertaken. Many of the dikes are massive and in some parts wide enough for villages and towns. The inclosures behind the dikes are subdivided by secondary dikes and canals and are drained by electrical and engine-type pumps that have replaced the old, picturesque windmills. Dredging has become more efficient and important; canals and rivers are kept deep enough to carry off flood waters better than formerly. Much of the recent reclamation has been attained by pumping dry the lakes formed behind the watcher dikes, and the watcher dikes are now better protected from erosion by a series of heavy groins.

The soils of the polders are usually drained,

FIGURE 25.4 Outer, or watcher, dike, near Petten, North Holland. This dike, built against the sea and replacing dunes (top and bottom), protects the polders to the left. Strong groins protect the dikes against excessive marine erosion. (Photo KLM Aerocarto n. v., The Hague.)

reflooded with fresh water, and variously tilled to lessen their salinity and make them suitable for many different crops. In some areas the calcium deficiency of the soils is overcome by using gypsum. Outer dike construction is the chief means of extending this reclamation farther and farther out into the sea.

This coastal reclamation has notably affected the ethnic group known as the Frisians, who for centuries were typical coastal men living along the sea front of nearly all the Low Countries. These people, refusing to become agriculturists, have moved away from many reclamation areas and now reside mainly on the northern border of the Netherlands and in Denmark.

FEN-TYPE RECLAMATION

Marshy vegetation areas are known in England and in a few other countries as fens. Some of them near coasts have been variously drained to transform their flooded, wet-land character for farming and industrial uses (Darby, 1940, 1952). In many other places this reclamation has been applied to inland areas, and no coastal areas have been directly influenced. But in one large fen area in the eastern part of England, adjoining the North Sea embayment known as the Wash, fen reclamation has been so extensive and of such long duration that some increase of land into the Wash has resulted.

This fen region of nearly 1,200,000 acres was not in any part reclaimed until work began in it about 1640. Some canals for draining small areas had been constructed during the Roman occupancy before the fifth century A.D., but these canals had fallen into disuse. Reclamation, after the seventeenth-century beginning, was slow and covered only small areas until the last century and a half, during which most of the fen drainage finally was accomplished. The main method of reclamation has been to convert the many small rivers of the region into canals by improving their banks and channels so that they drained the marshes more efficiently. Gravity drainage was first used; later, dikes, field drains, canals, and pumps were established.

The native, coastal-type people of these fens were fishermen, fowlers, and sod-gathers, who led an almost amphibious life, and it was because of their resistance to the drainage projects that no well-co-ordinated development occurred until the king's government began some of the reclamation.

That there has been some extension of land area into the Wash embayment is due to increases in sedimentation at the mouths of the rivers used in the reclamation project. New land thus added to the Wash since the eighteenth century is computed at about 90,000 acres, principally in the areas between Welland and the Great Ouse. Most of this type of modification is due to indirect rather than to direct efforts.

Foreshore, Beach, and Dune Protection

Beaches, dunes inland from them, and the shallow foreshore areas to seaward are becoming increasingly important for recreation and for vacation homes. Some forest and pasture development also is occurring in some dune areas. Man's efforts are concerned mainly with protection of the strand from excessive erosion, the stabilization of the beaches and dunes, and, in some favorable places, the seaward extension of the strand areas. Mechanical means are employed in the foreshore waters and along the lower parts of the beaches, but both mechanical and vegetational means are used on the upper beaches and on the dunes or other inland parts of the strand.

ENGINEERING DEVICES

Mechanical methods of protection and enlargement of the strand have not proved very successful, mainly because many of the projects were started after the onset of retrograding processes, and these processes have not been appreciably curbed. In fact, as stated in an engineering bulletin (Anonymous, 1952, p. 1), "Too many of the things men do to improve beach-fronting property merely increase these rates of erosion—valuable sea beaches have almost disappeared due to the harmful effect of certain unwise improvements." Man has thus changed the coast line by direct action but not in the manner that he planned.

Some of the engineering devices used for protection are heavy sea walls and light bulkheads located on or near the upper beach and the seaward face of the strand scarp, dune, or bluff. Revetments also are used to hold the upper or sloping faces of these structures and as surfacing over the dunes and bluffs near them. In some areas a number of foreshore, shallow-water structures, such as groins, pilings, and jetties, are continuous with onshore structures.

Sea walls frequently caused a depletion of beach sands, because the high-wave action against them pulls the sands away from the base of the walls. This process and the enhanced pounding of violent storm waves often cause sea walls to be undermined or breached. The less heavily constructed bulkheads are usually used along coasts of low energy and are especially effective where mud sedimentation occurs. The methods of building and maintenance of these structures usually improve as the areas protected increase in value, and these practices are leading to better-managed erosion control, often resulting in some coastal extension.

Groins (Figures 25.1 and 25.4) and jetties are the two types of foreshore and onshore structures most used either alone or in conjunction with shore structures. Jetties are usually the more massive and ordinarily are employed along channels and harbors. Groins are extensively used to slow beach erosion and to build beaches. They are designed to take advantage of the longshore currents that drift the sediments along the beach, and they vary in height, length, materials used, and angle of set toward the beach. Groins usually are developed in a series, so that their spacing, length, and height form a tapering system. However, there is disagreement as to whether the direction of taper of the series should be toward or away from the currents—a disagreement which is caused by the dissimilarity of coastal situations. It is difficult also to predict the amount of beach drift so as to build the groins in anticipation of this drift. Consequently, these groins often fail to check erosion or to extend a beach. Some of the best-built, heavy groins are used in connection with the Low Countries system of dikes. The great value of the dikes they protect has warranted their extensive development.

Revetments of many types are used behind sea walls, dikes, and jetties, or on their tops, to prevent the erosion of their sloping faces or upper surfaces. Riprap, brush mats, clay, asphalt, and concrete are employed. As coastal protection becomes more and more necessary, the types of revetments are improved.

DUNE AND UPPER-BEACH STABILIZATION

Stabilization of the dunes and upper beaches is important because they are "the savings account of the beach, deposits made in time of surplus to be drawn out in time of need" (*ibid.*, p. 11). Mechanical methods, such as some retaining walls and revetments, are employed, but most effective have been the use of the natural vegetation and the development of plantings of herbs, shrubs, and trees. In addition the numerous buildings, such as homes, hotels, and motels, constructed mainly by inland men, have served as factors for stabilization.

The natural vegetation is improved mainly by promoting, in accordance with some of the principles of plant ecology (Kurz, 1942), the progress of plant-community succession on the dunes, so that the normal change toward a climax forest or scrub type of vegetation is more rapidly developed. Some conditions are also made better for the pioneer, dune-forming herbs and shrubs, so that they may begin dune stabilization more rapidly and intensely.

The planting method (Chapman, 1949; Van der Burgt and Bendegorn, 1949) is widely practiced from areas bordering the Baltic Sea to the Ninety-Mile Beach in New Zealand. Foreign species and favorable native species are both used, one of the most common choices being the marram grass, *Ammophila arenaria.* A hybrid *Spartina* grass, *S. townsendi,* is also employed in dune swales and over tidal areas. Woody plants are extensively used, and in some cases useful forests are developed. Among the many species of conifers are *Pinus maritima, P. austriaca, P. nigra corsicana,* and *Picea falcata sitchensis*; among the hardwoods are species of *Betula, Quercus, Populus, Alnus,* and *Salix,* which are planted mainly in the damper, swale parts of the strand. Wattles, fences, stakes, and other mechanical means are used in conjunction with the plantings to stop some movement of sands, especially in Germany and Algeria.

Most of the plantings are either line or group plantings, the choice usually depending upon the mode of growth of the species used. Most of the grasses grow in lines or rows by rhizomes, and the lupines grow in groups. The systems of planting are also related to the topography, wind, and drift character of the sands. In some cases these plantings have actively promoted the extension of the dunes and the beaches outward into the sea.

As economic importance of the strand areas increases, these methods of dune and beach protection and stabilization are becoming extensively and intensively used to insure the maintenance of increasingly valuable property. Co-operative efforts of engineers, plant ecologists, agronomists, and foresters have been necessary, because the problem of dune management is complex. The utilization of dune areas for pasturage and forests probably will increase as better methods of handling the vegetation and plantings are developed. But the most intensive use of strand areas is in some recreational regions where the habitations and other real estate improvements have, in many cases, acted in favor of dune stabilization.

HABITATIONS ALONG COAST LINES

Extensive developments of coastal area property for recreation and vacation living have greatly increased recently, particularly along the Florida and California coasts. In Florida many hotels have been built near the beaches since 1946. The total development of coastal property in Florida is now over 150,000 acres of both the strand and the littoral areas. Some of these areas, such as part of Miami Beach, have been reclaimed from the littoral, mangrove swamps and salt-water marshes, but most of them are developments of strand dunes, such as those near the St. Augustine and Daytona beaches.

The houses, hotels, motels, and other constructions help hold the dunes by their presence, which aids in keeping the sands in place. The lawns, gardens, walks, and road-paving associated with these buildings also contribute to dune stabilization. Both the well-sodded lawns and the hard-surfaced roads are important factors, because they usually cover more area than do the buildings. In many instances the ornamental shrubs and trees used to landscape the property have proved even more effective than the original vegetation in holding the dunes or the filled littoral areas. In general, as real estate values increase, the newer beach property developments are better landscaped than the older ones, thus increasing their efficiency in dune protection.

Some Inland Sea and Lake Changes

Some of the inland seas and lakes have recently been the scene of extensive human activity which has had notable effects upon coast lines. Among these are the changes in the offshore areas and coasts of the Caspian and Aral seas owing to large-scale developments of dams for power and irrigation on the rivers supplying water to these seas (Taskin, 1954; Field, 1954).

The Caspian Sea is shrinking in volume, and the coasts are now extending into it much more rapidly than formerly because of engineering activities on the rivers entering it, particularly the Volga.* An evidence for the effect of power dam and irrigation projects is that, soon after 1932, when these projects began, the water level in the Caspian Sea

* See Selection 23.

fell progressively each year. There had been fluctuations in this water level before 1932, but records show that these have been most intensive since that date. Very good evidence of the effects of the dams is the fact that lowering of the water level was definitely retarded during the period of World War II, when dam construction halted; since then a further increase in dam construction has caused the rate of lowering to increase.

A similar and potentially more extensive lowering of water level is beginning in the Aral Sea Basin with the development of irrigation projects on the Amu Darya and Syr Darya, which supply most of the water to this sea. It is the aim of these projects eventually to divert for irrigation most or all of the waters of the rivers from entering the sea. It has been calculated that within twenty-five years the water area of this sea will shrink to half the size that it was in 1940, when the irrigation projects began. This would bring about an increase of nearly 13,000 square miles of land area.

Other navigation, power, and irrigation projects on all continents have variously affected the coastal areas around lakes and inland seas. In many cases the bodies of water have been enlarged, and in some cases new bodies of water have been created. In the Great Lakes region of North America the main efforts have been to keep the water levels stable, with the result that coastal changes have been minor.

Additional Examples of Influences

FISHING ACTIVITIES

One of the general and long-term activities of coastal men has been the gathering of shellfish for food and other purposes. As a result of this, numerous shellfish mounds have been left along many coasts, and they have aided progradational processes in a number of instances. Some of them are large and have been effective in holding their areas against erosion, helping to form headlands or capes in some places. These and many smaller mounds are so numerous along parts

of the Atlantic coast of North America that they occur over nearly 10 per cent of some areas, such as parts of the Florida coast, and, consequently, their total effect in stabilizing coasts and as progradational agents has been great. Many of them are old structures, dating back a few thousand years.

Recently shellfish have been cultivated as well as gathered, especially in the Orient. This activity has increased sedimentation in some littoral and shoal-water areas, such as Manila Bay, and in this way has promoted progradation of coast lines in a few places.

Only a few of the numerous methods of catching fish have in the past had any appreciable effect on coasts, but one of these, the construction of long stone weirs to trap fish in some Pacific areas, has influenced sedimentation. However, the cultivation of fish in tidal basins and other pools (McIntyre, 1954) has recently been increasing and is causing some coastal changes. This practice is common in the Philippines, China, and other parts of the Orient, where the growing populations have increased the demand for food. The fish are raised in built-up inclosed pools at or near the coast, and the construction and maintenance of these pools have locally influenced coastal extension.

COASTAL SWAMPS AND MARSH CHANGES

The tidal-zone mangrove forests and thickets along many low-energy, tropical coasts have been great progradational agents, causing appreciable extension of the coast line (Davis, 1940). Man has variously used these mangrove plants (Watson, 1928) for poles, lumber, charcoal, tannin materials, and firewood, and in some cases his exploitation of these forests has altered the rate of progradation, causing a decrease in coastal extension and even active erosion. Recently man has increased the drainage of a few mangrove swamps by digging ditches to reduce breeding areas for mosquitoes, and this activity has had a small effect on rates of progradation.

Tidal-zone salt and brackish-water marshes have been deliberately changed by many agricultural and other uses to which they have been put. The greatest alterations have been by direct reclamation, which has been described. But some such marshes have been drained or flooded for wildlife purposes, while others have been drained as health projects to reduce mosquito and other insect populations. These activities are now increasing and may become more important factors of coastal changes.

BIOLOGICAL AND POLLUTION CHANGES

Coastal bird life has been disturbed in many ways, such as obtaining guano from areas where great rookeries of sea birds occur, and this activity has caused some local increases in erosion. Protection of bird life has in some instances influenced land changes. An example of this occurred in the Dry Tortugas island group west of Key West, Florida, where a common practice had been the seasonal collection of eggs and birds, which kept their numbers reduced. Conservation people prohibited this activity, and the bird population increased, causing overcrowding and a consequent loss of vegetation that held the island against erosion. The end result was a complete loss of one of the islands.

The collection of seaweeds, mainly algae, in large quantity along some coasts has altered some processes slightly. Similarly, slight changes in coral-reef biota and in their activity as progradational agents have been effected, mainly by pollution or by increases in sedimentation onto reefs due to dredging and other harbor or channel improvements.* The recent A- and H-bomb tests in the Pacific Ocean had direct effects on coral areas, and anyone may speculate as to how many more such violent changes will occur in the future.

In the Gulf of Mexico along the coast of Florida there has recently occurred a series of large "blooms" of microscopic sea organisms, causing what are known as "red tides" that kill many fish. The dead fish have washed up on some beaches and into marshes

in large quantity, and their bodies have in a small way altered normal processes of land change. These blooms seem to be partly the result of recently increased washing of phosphate materials into the gulf, owing to mining operations in the interior; if this is the case, the red tides are caused by an inland human activity.

An example of a more definite effect of pollution is in Great South Bay on Long Island, New York (Lackey, 1952), where the bay waters and shellfish have been altered by excessive mineral and organic excreta from duckfarm areas that drain into this bay. The quality and quantity of the oysters have been changed, and the plankton has been increased, causing intense blooms of *Chlorella*. This biological alteration may have affected the sediments and size of the bay.

A number of other types of pollution are also probably instrumental in causing local coastal changes, especially the industrial wastes brought down by rivers. These will increase with increases in manufacturing and mining, but they are seldom very extensive.

Summary

In terms of total effect on coast lines, the indirect influences of numerous activities of both inland and coastal men have probably been more important than the direct influences of man. Evidences of extensive and prolonged coast-line changes indicate that many agricultural and other soil-altering pursuits of both inland and coastal men have indirectly altered rates of progradation, especially in delta and lagoon regions.

Direct claiming of land from the sea is increasing, and improved methods are insuring more effectiveness in the future. But reclamation is dependent upon numerous fluctuating economic and population factors, such that prediction concerning it is difficult to make.

In some areas, such as Florida, rapidly increasing demand for various recreational establishments along coasts is promoting ac-

* See Selection 43.

tivities directly aimed at stabilizing and extending the coast line. Probably, with increased economic well-being of inland men, these activities will become more intensive and extensive.

Other generally less important human activities variously affect coast-line changes, some of which activities, such as pollution and agriculture in marsh areas, may become more influential in the future.

Notes

[1] Many sources have been used for history and changes in Mesopotamia, among which are: Strabo (1917–50), Ritter (1843), Rawlinson (1854), Putzger (1931), Hogg (1910–11), and personal correspondence (1954) with Youseph al-Jebori of Baghdad.

[2] Most of the information about reclamation in the Low Countries is derived from Van Veen, 1948.

References

Anonymous
  1952 *Information on Beach Protection in Florida.* (Water Survey and Research Paper No. 8.) Tallahassee: State of Florida, Division of Water Survey and Research. 41 pp.
Brown, H. F.
  1910–11 "Venice," *Encyclopaedia Britannica* (11th ed.), XXVII, 995–1007.
Chapman, V. J.
  1949 "The Stabilization of Sand-Dunes by Vegetation," pp. 142–57 in *Proceedings of Conference on Biology and Civil Engineering.* London: Institute of Civil Engineers.
Cooke, C. W.
  1938 *Scenery of Florida.* (Florida Geological Survey Bulletin No. 17.) Tallahassee. 118 pp.
Cotton, C. A.
  1954 "Deductive Morphology and Genetic Classification of Coasts," *Scientific Monthly,* LXXXVIII, 163–81.
Cressey, G. B.
  1936 "The Fenghsien Landscape," *Geographical Review,* XXVII, No. 3, 396–413.
Daly, R. A.
  1934 *The Changing World of the Ice Age.* New Haven, Conn.: Yale University Press. 271 pp.
Darby, H. C.
  1940 *The Medieval Fenland.* Cambridge: Cambridge University Press. 200 pp.
  1952 "Fens," *Encyclopaedia Britannica,* IX, 161–64.
Davis, J. H.
  1940 "The Ecology and Geologic Role of Mangroves in Florida," pp. 303–414 in *Papers from Tortugas Laborory,* Vol. XXXII. (Carnegie Institution of Washington Publication No. 517.) Washington, D.C.
Field, N. C.
  1954 "The Amu Darya: A Study in Resource Geography," *Geographical Review,* XLIV, No. 4, 528–42.
Hogg, W. W.
  1910–11 "Mesopotamia," *Encyclopaedia Britannica* (11th ed.), XVIII, 179–87.

Johnson, D. W.
  1919 *Shore Processes and Shoreline Development.* New York: John Wiley & Sons. 584 pp.
  1938 "Offshore Bars and Eustatic Changes of Sea Level," *Journal of Geomorphology,* I, 273–74.
Kurz, H.
  1942 *Florida Dunes and Scrub, Vegetation and Geology.* (Florida Geological Survey Bulletin No. 23.) Tallahassee. 154 pp.
Lackey, J. B.
  1952 "The Rehabilitation of Great South Bay." Gainesville: University of Florida. 27 pp. (Mimeographed.)
Lobeck, A. K.
  1939 *Geomorphology.* New York: McGraw-Hill Book Co. 731 pp.
McIntyre, W. E.
  1954 "Philippine Fish Culture," *Scientific Monthly,* LXXVIII, No. 2, 86–93.
Martens, J. H. C.
  1931 "Beaches of Florida," pp. 19–119 in *Florida Geological Survey, 21st–22nd Annual Report.* Tallahassee.
Price, W. A.
  1954 "Shorelines and Coasts of the Gulf of Mexico," *Fishery Bulletin,* No. 89, pp. 39–65. Washington, D.C.: U.S. Department of Interior.
Putzger, F. W.
  1931 *Historischer Schul-Atlas.* 50th Anniversary Edition, ed. Velhagen and Klasing. Bielefeld and Leipzig: Max Pehle & Hans Silberboth.
Rawlinson, Sir Henry
  1854 *Notes on the Early History of Babylonia.* London: J. W. Parker. 45 pp.
Ritter, C.
  1843 "West Asien," *Die Erdkunde,* VII, 3–277.
Russell, R. J.
  1940 "Quaternary History of Louisiana," *Bulletin of the Geological Society of America,* LI, 1199–1234.
Strabo
  1917–50 *The Geography of Strabo,* Vol. II, Book v.

Greek text and trans. from the Greek by H. L. Jones. London: William Heinemann.

Taskin, G. A.
1954 "The Falling Level of the Caspian Sea in Relation to Soviet Economy," *Geographical Review*, XLIV, No. 4, 508–27.

United States Congress
1948 *Palm Beach, Florida, Beach Erosion Study.* (80th Cong., 2d sess. [House Document No. 77].) Washington, D.C.: Government Printing Office. 36 pp. (plus 9 maps).

Van der Burgt, J. H., and Bendegorn L.
1949 "The Use of Vegetation to Stabilize Sand-Dunes," pp. 158–70 in *Proceedings of Conference on Biology and Civil Engineering.* London: Institute of Civil Engineers.

Van Veen, J.
1948 *Dredge Drain Reclaim: The Art of a Nation.* The Hague: Trio Printers. 165 pp.

Watson, J. G.
1928 *Mangrove Forests of the Malay Peninsula.* (Malayan Forest Records No. 6.) Singapore: Federated Malay States. 275 pp.

ADDITIONAL REFERENCES

Beller, W. S. 1970. Gearing up for coastal zone management. *Environmental Science & Technology* 4(6):482–486. Plans for treating Hawaii's coastal problems.

Klimm, L. E. 1956. Man's ports and channels. Pp. 522–541 in *Man's role in changing the face of the earth*, ed. by William L. Thomas, Jr. Chicago: The University of Chicago Press.

Renn, C. E. 1956. Man as a factor in the coastal environment. *Trans. 21st N. A. Wildlife Conf.*, pp. 470–473.

IMPACT OF SURFACE MINING ON ENVIRONMENT

U.S. DEPARTMENT OF THE INTERIOR

Man's carving of the earth's surface to obtain minerals is increasingly vigorous. By the mid-1960s 3.2 million acres of land, 5,000 square miles, had been disrupted by surface mining in the United States alone.

This accelerating disturbance is largely a result of our increasing technological demands and capabilities. Modern industries are consuming greater and greater quantities of raw materials, including coal for fuel, that have been surface-mined. Underground mining predominated until about two decades ago, but now about four-fifths of the United States' total production of ore and solid fuels is from surface mines. The development of gigantic tools has allowed this expansion—there are now shovels that can move 185 cubic yards of earth in one bite, and trucks that can haul 100 tons in one load.

Although more than fifty minerals are produced by surface mining in the United States, two-thirds of the disturbed area has resulted from extraction of coal and sand and gravel. Quarries and open-pit mines account for 35 percent of the disturbed area. In these operations the amount of overburden covering the useful ore is slight; some open-pit mines are ½ mile deep. Strip mining, mainly for coal, has disturbed 56 percent of the affected surface. In this type of mining, large amounts of waste material that must be scraped off the ore are usually cast downslope.

The results of surface mining are destruction of vegetation and drastic reshaping of the land surface, including alteration of surface and subsurface drainage patterns. Further: "Square miles of land may be

This selection is from *Surface Mining and Our Environment,* by the Strip and Surface Mine Study Policy Committee, U.S. Department of the Interior, 1967, 124 pp. The Appalachian Regional Development Act, passed by Congress in 1965, directed the Secretary of the Interior to make a survey and study of strip and surface mining operations and their effects in the United States and to recommend a program for rehabilitating affected areas. A policy committee of twelve men from the Interior Department was supported by a working committee whose members were drawn from the Departments of Interior, Agriculture, Commerce, Defense, and Health, Education and Welfare, and from the Appalachian Regional Commission and the Tennessee Valley Authority. This working committee and its staff used questionnaires to survey the operators of approximately 18,000 surface mines and examined a random sample of 693 sites. The final report of the policy committee, in addition to the subjects discussed in the extracts comprised in this selection, also treats legal aspects of surface mining, goals of reclamation, and a list of specific recommendations for dealing with the many problems of surface mining.

turned over to a depth of 100 feet or more. Massive landslides have blocked streams and highways, waters have been polluted by acid and sediment, land areas isolated, and economic and esthetic values seriously impaired." This selection examines these effects and others, and their causes.

Such damage may not be easily remedied. Banks of debris, or "spoil," produced by strip mining commonly contain so much acid (pH of 3) that trees and most other plants cannot grow there. And ridges are so large and steep that regrading is prohibitively expensive. Since technology and economics, which have fostered destruction by surface mining, have not been held accountable, they have not been intensively applied toward avoiding or correcting the damage.

(Editor's comment)

Surface Mining: Its Nature, Extent, and Significance

Stated in the simplest terms, surface mining consists of nothing more than removing the topsoil, rock, and other strata that lie above mineral or fuel deposits to recover them. In practice, however, the process is considerably more complex.

When compared with underground methods, surface mining offers distinct advantages. It makes possible the recovery of deposits which, for physical reasons, cannot be mined underground; provides safer working conditions; usually results in a more complete recovery of the deposit; and, most significantly it is generally cheaper in terms of cost-per-unit of production. Surface mining is not applicable to all situations, however, because the ratio between the thickness of the overburden that must be moved in order to recover a given amount of product places a definite economic limitation upon the operator. While this ratio may vary widely among operations and commodities owing to differences in the characteristics of the overburden, types and capacities of the equipment used, and in value of the material being mined, it is nonetheless the factor that primarily determines whether a particular mining venture can survive in a competitive market.

The procedure for surface mining usually consists of two steps: Prospecting, or "explo-

ration,"—to discover, delineate, and "prove" the ore body—and the actual mining or recovery phrase. Topography and the configuration of the deposit itself strongly influence both. Exploration techniques generally employed consist of either drilling to intersect deeper-lying ore bodies, or excavating shallow trenches or pits to expose the ore. Although drill sites or excavations associated with exploration are usually small, their large number constitutes a serious source of surface disturbance in some of the Western States. Surface methods employed to recover minerals and fuels are generally classified as (1) open pit mining (quarry, open cast); (2) strip mining (area, contour); (3) auger mining; (4) dredging; and (5) hydraulic mining.

Open pit mining is exemplified by quarries producing limestone, sandstone, marble, and granite; sand and gravel pits; and, large excavations opened to produce iron and copper. Usually, in open pit mining, the amount of overburden removed is proportionally small compared with the quantity of ore recovered. Another distinctive feature of open pit mining is the length of time that mining is conducted. In stone quarrying, and in open pit mining of iron ore and other metallics, large quantities of ore are obtained within a relatively small surface area because of the thickness of the deposits. Some open pits may be mined for many years—50 or more; in fact, a few have been in continuous operation for more than a century. However, since coal beds are comparatively thin—the United States average being about 5.1 feet for bituminous coal and lignite strip mined in 1960—the average surface coal mine has a relatively short life.

Area strip mining usually is practiced on relatively flat terrain. A trench, or "box cut," is made through the overburden to expose a portion of the deposit, which is then removed. The first cut may be extended to the limits of the property or the deposit. As each succeeding parallel cut is made, the spoil (overburden) is deposited in the cut just previously excavated. The final cut leaves an open trench as deep as the thickness of the overburden plus the ore recovered, bounded on one side by the last spoil bank and on the other by the undisturbed highwall. Frequently this final cut may be a mile or more from the starting point of the opera-

tion. Thus, area stripping, unless graded or leveled, usually resembles the ridges of a gigantic washboard (see Figures 26.1 and 26.2). Coal and Florida phosphate account for the major part of the acreage disturbed by this method, although brown iron ore, some clays, and other commodities are mined in a similar manner.

Contour strip mining is most commonly practiced where deposits occur in rolling or mountainous country. Basically, this method consists of removing the overburden above the bed by starting at the outcrop and proceeding along the hillside. After the deposit is exposed and removed by this first cut, additional cuts are made until the ratio of overburden to product brings the operation to a halt. This type of mining creates a shelf, or "bench," on the hillside. On the inside it is bordered by the highwall, which may

FIGURE 26.1 Area strip mining for coal, P & M Colonial mine, Paradise, Kentucky. (Division of Forestry, Fisheries, and Wildlife Development, Tennessee Valley Authority.)

range from a few to perhaps more than 100 feet in height, and on the opposite, or outer, side by a rim below which there is frequently a precipitous downslope that has been covered by spoil material cast down the hillside. Unless controlled or stabilized, this spoil material can cause severe erosion and landslides. Contour mining is practiced widely in the coal fields of Appalachia and western phosphate mining regions because of the generally rugged topography. "Rim-cutting" and "benching" are terms that are sometimes used locally to identify workbenches, or ledges, prepared for contour or auger mining operations.

Anthracite strip mining in Pennsylvania is conducted on hillsides where the coal beds outcrop parallel with the mountain crests. Although most of the operations are conducted on natural slopes of less than 10 de-

grees, the beds themselves vary in pitch up to 90 degrees. Beds that are stripped are thicker than in the bituminous fields, most varying from 6 to 20 feet, and can be mined economically to much greater depths. Because of the angles at which the beds lie, the methods employed may not be correctly identified either as contour or area mining, but rather as a combination of both. In a few instances, the operations may resemble open pits and quarries, while others are long, deep narrow canyons.

Auger mining is usually associated with contour strip mining. In coal fields, it is most commonly practiced to recover additional tonnages after the coal-overburden ratio has become such as to render further contour mining uneconomical. Augers are also used to extract coal near the outcrop that could not be recovered safely by earlier under-

FIGURE 26.2 Area strip mining for coal, western Kentucky. (Division of Forestry, Fisheries, and Wildlife Development, Tennessee Valley Authority.)

ground mining efforts. As the name implies, augering is a method of producing coal by boring horizontally into the seam, much like the carpenter bores a hole in wood. The coal is extracted in the same manner that shavings are produced by the carpenter's bit. Cutting heads of some coal augers are as large as seven feet in diameter. By adding sections behind the cutting head, holes may be drilled in excess of 200 feet. As augering generally is conducted after the strip-mining phase has been completed, little land disturbance can be directly attributed to it. However it may, to some extent, induce surface subsidence and disrupt water channels when underground workings are intersected.

Dredging operations utilize a suction apparatus or various mechanical devices, such as ladder or chain buckets, clamshells, and draglines mounted on floating barges. Dredges have been utilized extensively in placer gold mining. Tailing piles from gold dredging operations usually have a configuration that is similar to spoil piles left by area strip mining for coal. Dredging is also used in the recovery of sand and gravel from stream beds and low-lying lands. In the sand and gravel industry most of the material (volume) produced is marketed, but in dredging for the higher-priced minerals virtually all of the mined material consists of waste that is left at the mine site. Some valuable minerals also are recovered by dredging techniques from beach sands and sedimentary deposits on the continental shelf.

In *hydraulic mining* a powerful jet of water is employed to wash down or erode a bank of earth or gravel that either is the overburden or contains the desired ore. The ore-bearing material is fed into sluices or other concentrating devices where the desired product is separated from the tailings, or waste—by differences in specific gravity. Hydraulic mining was extensively used in the past to produce gold and other precious metals, but is practiced only on a limited scale today. As both hydraulic mining and dredging create sedimentation problems in streams, some States exercise strict controls over these techniques, either through mining or water-control regulations.

Regardless of the equipment used, the surface mining cycle usually consists of four steps: (1) Site preparation, clearing vegetation and other obstructions from the area to be mined, and constructing access roads and ancillary installations—including areas to be used for the disposal of spoil or waste; (2) removal and disposal of overburden; (3) excavation and loading of ore; and (4) transportation of the ore to a concentrator, processing plant, storage area, or directly to market.

Reclamation may not be considered by a majority as an integral component of the mining cycle. Experience here and abroad has demonstrated, however, that when reclamation of the land is integrated into both the pre-planning and operational stages, it can be done more effectively and at a lower cost than as a separate operation. This is particularly true because much of the machinery used in the mining operation can be easily used in reducing peaks of spoil piles, segregating toxic materials, and establishing controlled drainage from the site.

The rapid expansion of surface mining since World War II may be attributed primarily to the development of larger and more complex earth-moving equipment. Equipment used today includes bulldozers, loaders, scrapers, graders, trucks up to 100-ton capacity, and a miscellany of other devices. A shovel is now working that can handle 185-cubic yards in one "bite," with a monster having a 200-cubic yard bucket on the engineers' drawing boards. Draglines of up to 85-cubic yard capacity are in operation and larger ones are being planned. Clamshells and wheel excavators are used where conditions permit. There are floating dredges, tower excavators, drag scrapers, and augers; and to move the overburden and ores beyond the reach of the basic excavating machines, tram or rail cars, conveyor belts, overhead cable buckets, and pipelines.

EXTENT

An estimated 3.2 million acres of land, 5,000 square miles, had been disturbed by surface mining in the United States prior to January

TABLE 26.1 Land disturbed by strip and surface mining in the United States as of January 1, 1965, by commodity and state (acres)

STATE	CLAY	COAL (bituminous, lignite and anthracite)	STONE	SAND AND GRAVEL	GOLD	PHOSPHATE ROCK	IRON ORE	ALL OTHER	TOTAL
Alabama[1]	4,000	50,600	3,900	21,200	100	—	52,600	1,500	133,900
Alaska[2]	—	500	—	2,000	8,600	—	—	—	11,100
Arizona[1]	2,700	—	1,000	7,200	1,200	—	—	20,300	32,400
Arkansas[2]	600	10,100	900	2,600	—	—	100	8,100	22,400
California[2]	2,700	20	8,000	19,900	134,000	—	900	8,500	174,020
Colorado[1]	2,000	2,800	6,200	15,500	17,100	—	25	11,400	55,025
Connecticut[1]	—	—	100	16,100	—	—	—	100	16,300
Delaware[2]	200	—	200	5,200	—	—	100	10	5,710
Florida[1]	13,200	—	25,300	3,900	—	143,600	—	2,800	188,800
Georgia	[e]1,300	[e]300	[e]6,800	[e]1,200	—	—	[e]100	[e]12,000	[1]21,700
Hawaii[2]	—	—	—	—	—	—	—	10	10
Idaho[2]	500	—	700	11,200	21,200	3,100	35	4,200	40,935
Illinois[2]	1,400	127,000	5,700	9,000	—	—	—	—	143,100
Indiana[2]	1,500	95,200	10,200	18,000	—	—	—	400	125,300
Iowa[1]	1,300	11,000	12,200	17,600	—	—	6	2,300	44,406
Kansas	[1]1,100	[2]45,600	[1]7,500	[1]5,100	—	—	—	[1]200	59,500
Kentucky	[1][2]2,400	[1][2]119,200	[1]3,900	[1]1,700	—	—	—	[1]500	127,700
Louisiana[1]	900	—	100	29,700	—	—	50	—	30,750
Maine[1]	400	—	4,400	28,200	12	—	100	1,700	34,812
Maryland	[1][2]1,200	[2]2,200	[1]2,200	[1]18,800	—	—	[1]20	[1]800	25,220
Massachusetts[1]	700	—	1,200	36,400	—	—	1,100	900	40,300
Michigan[2]	600	—	7,700	25,200	—	—	2,200	1,200	36,900
Minnesota[1]	600	—	3,900	41,600	3	—	67,700	1,600	115,403
Mississippi[2]	2,700	—	400	26,500	—	—	30	—	29,630
Missouri[2]	6,600	31,800	8,400	3,800	—	—	200	8,300	59,100
Montana[2]	—	1,500	10	[e]13,500	5,600	100	10	6,200	26,920
Nebraska[2]	900	—	4,300	23,700	—	—	—	—	28,900
Nevada[1]	100	—	1,600	5,500	5,600	—	600	19,500	32,900
New Hampshire[2]	—	—	100	8,000	—	—	—	200	8,300
New Jersey[2]	1,400	—	2,000	27,600	—	—	1,000	1,800	33,800
New Mexico[2]	13	1,200	100	400	40	—	100	4,600	6,453
New York[1]	1,700	—	12,500	42,200	5	—	700	600	57,705
North Carolina[1]	5,800	10	6,000	18,400	2,200	300	100	4,000	36,810
North Dakota	[1]800	[2]7,700	[2]300	[1]26,100	—	—	—	[1]2,000	36,900
Ohio	[1]10,200	[2]212,800	[1]21,000	[1]28,100	—	—	[1]4,000	[1]600	276,700
Oklahoma[2]	—	23,500	—	[e]2,500	—	—	—	1,400	27,400
Oregon[2]	100	—	300	1,300	6,300	—	10	1,400	9,410
Pennsylvania	[1]10,400	[2]302,400	[1]24,400	[1]23,800	[1]2	—	[1]8,800	[1]400	370,202
Rhode Island[1]	—	—	20	3,600	—	—	—	—	3,620
South Carolina[1]	10,900	—	1,400	10,400	200	8,100	100	1,600	32,700
South Dakota	[2]2,000	[2]900	—	[e]28,000	—	—	—	[2]3,300	34,200
Tennessee[2]	2,700	29,300	4,400	18,400	—	27,000	5,300	13,800	100,900
Texas[1]	6,800	2,900	21,900	122,300	—	—	9,600	2,800	166,300
Utah[2]	600	—	200	2,200	—	10	500	2,000	5,510
Vermont	—	—	[2]2,300	[1]4,000	—	—	—	[2]400	6,700
Virginia	[1][2]1,100	[2]29,800	[1]4,300	[1]13,100	[1]600	[1]100	[1][2]7,700	[1][2]4,100	60,800
Washington[2]	500	100	1,300	5,700	400	—	20	800	8,820
West Virginia[2]	300	192,000	2,800	300	—	—	100	—	195,500
Wisconsin[2]	100	—	9,000	26,400	5	—	49	—	35,554
Wyoming	[1][2]3,500	[2]1,000	[1][2]300	[1][2]200	—	[2]800	[1][2]300	[2]4,300	10,400
Total	108,513	1,301,430	241,430	823,300	203,167	183,110	164,255	162,620	3,187,825

[e] Estimate.
[1] Data obtained from Soil Conservation, U.S. Department of Agriculture.
[2] Data compiled from reports submitted by the States on U.S. Department of the Interior form 6-1385X.

1, 1965. This total includes only the excavation, or pit, and areas required to dispose of waste or spoil from the mining operation alone. An additional 320,000 acres have been affected by mine access roads and exploration activities. About 95 percent of the acreage disturbed by surface mining is attributable to but seven commodities: Coal for approximately 41 percent of the total; sand and gravel, about 26 percent; stone, gold, clay, phosphate, and iron, together, about 28 percent; and, all others combined, 5 percent. The acreage affected is shown, by States, in Table 26.1.

Harmful off-site effects are also an important component of the surface mining picture. These effects include stream and water-impoundment pollution from erosion and acid mine water; isolation of areas by steep highwalls; and, the impairment of natural beauty by the creation of unsightly spoil banks, rubbish dumps, and abandoned equipment. All of these add appreciably to the total that must be considered as being adversely "affected" by surface mining.

Unreclaimed acreage. The total acreage needing reclamation can only be approximated because definitions of two key words, "reclamation" and "adequacy," are a matter of individual judgment. Professionals in many scientific disciplines can agree on certain essential elements, but the many variables involved preclude a general agreement on a definition of "adequate reclamation" that would be applicable at any given time and for every geographic location. From a survey conducted by the Soil Conservation Service and data submitted by certain States it is concluded that probably only one-third of the total acreage disturbed by surface mining has been adequately reclaimed—either by natural forces or by man's own effort. Thus, approximately two-thirds of the acreage (about 2.0 million) still require some remedial attention. Estimates obtained by the Soil Conservation Service are given in Table 26.2. These estimates are substantiated to some extent by the random-sampling program and an independent survey con-

ducted by the Bureau of Sport Fisheries and Wildlife. Reports submitted to the bureau by State fish and game departments indicated that about two-thirds of the fish and wildlife habitat disturbed could be classified as being severely or moderately affected.

Annual increase in disturbed acreage. The annual increment to the total disturbed acreage is not known exactly, but can be calculated roughly. Based on data reported by producers to the U. S. Department of the Interior, it is estimated that 153,000 acres of land were disturbed in 1964 by strip and surface mining. Sand and gravel accounted for 60,000 acres; coal, 46,000; stone, 21,000; clay and phosphate rock, each 9,000; and the remaining minerals accounted for 8,000 acres. This annual rate of disturbance is expected to increase in future years with an increased demand for minerals and solid fuels and a further diminution in the grade of mineral deposits available for exploitation. Indicative of this trend is the fact that surface mining production of all metals and non-metals increased from 2.5 billion net tons of crude ore (including waste) in 1960 to 3.0 billion in 1965. Strip-mine production of coal (anthracite, bituminous, and lignite) increased from 138 million net tons to 185 million over the same period.

SIGNIFICANCE

The economic potential of any nation is founded primarily upon its soil, its waters, and its mineral deposits. Where these are deficient, the economic wellbeing of the nation will depend upon the ability of its people to import raw materials required to manufacture and compete successfully in world trade.

The United States is blessed with a wealth of natural resources, needing only to import a small portion of its total mineral requirements.* Tens of thousands of firms are engaged in the production of semi- and finished goods. These industries are supported, in

* With mineral consumption rising exponentially this is rapidly changing (see Lovering, 1969). (*Editor's note*)

TABLE 26.2 Status of land disturbed by strip and surface mining in the United States as of January 1, 1965, by state (Thousand acres)

STATE	LAND REQUIRING RECLAMATION[1]	LAND NOT REQUIRING RECLAMATION[1]	TOTAL LAND DISTURBED[2]	STATE	LAND REQUIRING RECLAMATION[1]	LAND NOT REQUIRING RECLAMATION[1]	TOTAL LAND DISTURBED[2]
Alabama	83.0	50.9	133.9	Nebraska	16.8	12.1	28.9
Alaska	6.9	4.2	11.1	Nevada	20.4	12.5	32.9
Arizona	4.7	27.7	32.4	New Hampshire	5.1	3.2	8.3
Arkansas	16.6	5.8	22.4	New Jersey	21.0	12.8	33.8
California	107.9	66.1	174.0	New Mexico	2.0	4.5	6.5
Colorado	40.2	14.8	55.0	New York	50.2	7.5	57.7
Connecticut	10.1	6.2	16.3	North Carolina	22.8	14.0	36.8
Delaware	3.5	2.2	5.7	North Dakota	22.9	14.0	36.9
Florida	143.5	45.3	188.8	Ohio	171.6	105.1	276.7
Georgia	13.5	8.2	21.7	Oklahoma	22.2	5.2	27.4
Hawaii	(3)	(3)	(3)	Oregon	5.8	3.6	9.4
Idaho	30.7	10.3	41.0	Pennsylvania	229.5	140.7	370.2
Illinois	88.7	54.4	143.1	Rhode Island	2.2	1.4	3.6
Indiana	27.6	97.7	125.3	South Carolina	19.3	13.4	32.7
Iowa	35.5	8.9	44.4	South Dakota	25.3	8.9	34.2
Kansas	50.0	9.5	59.5	Tennessee	62.5	38.4	100.9
Kentucky	79.2	48.5	127.7	Texas	136.4	29.9	166.3
Louisiana	17.2	13.6	30.8	Utah	3.4	2.1	5.5
Maine	21.6	13.2	34.8	Vermont	4.2	2.5	6.7
Maryland	18.1	7.1	25.2	Virginia	37.7	23.1	60.8
Massachusetts	25.0	15.3	40.3	Washington	5.5	3.3	8.8
Michigan	26.6	10.3	36.9	West Virginia	111.4	84.1	195.5
Minnesota	71.5	43.9	115.4	Wisconsin	27.4	8.2	35.6
Mississippi	23.7	5.9	29.6	Wyoming	6.4	4.0	10.4
Missouri	43.7	15.4	59.1	Total	2,040.6	1,147.2	3,187.8
Montana	19.6	7.3	26.9				

[1] Compiled from data supplied by Soil Conservation Service, U.S. Department of Agriculture.

[2] Data compiled from reports submitted by the States on U.S. Department of Interior form 6-1385X, from Soil Conservation Service, U.S. Department of Agriculture, and estimates.

[3] Less than 100 acres.

turn, by a wide variety of extractive and processing activities and services. The extractive industries are the primary source of metallic ores and non-metallic minerals and fuels—with agriculture and forestry contributing a wide range of products. Our population, with its varied skills, completes the design and confirms an old truth: Man creates nothing—it is only through his ability to produce crops, convert; process, and synthesize that his civilization flourishes.

The importance of surface mining to the extractive industries is easily measured. In 1965, for example, surface mining accounted for about four-fifths of the total ore and solid fuels produced. Economists recognize that the extractive mineral industries are primarily suppliers of basic materials rather than producers of end products. Some appreciation of the extent to which other industries depend upon the mineral industries can be obtained through an examination of the Input-Output table prepared by the Office of Business Economics, U. S. Department of Commerce, which divides the national economy into 82 industrial sectors and shows the interchange of good among them. Although the data are not current, the patterns have not changed appreciably. For example, the table indicates that 76 percent of all coal mined is used directly (almost entirely as an energy source) by 56 industries to produce other products. The remaining 24 percent represents exports, consumption by individual and public establishments, and intra-company transfers.

Although the relationship of coal to other industrial activities is quite clear, the influence of some other minerals is not always so direct and easily recognized. Examples of indirect, but equally important influences, can be found in iron and ferroalloy ore mining. Over 81 percent of all the iron and ferroalloy ore mined is consumed by the primary iron and steel industry. Yet, output of this industry is used as direct input for 55 of the 82 industrial categories. It is evident that the real value to our economy of the minerals and fuels obtained by surface mining can be measured only by adding to

their prices as crude materials the "value added by manufacturing," a concept that entails an evaluation of their contribution to a finished product.

More than 50 minerals are produced by surface mining in the United States. In this report it is impossible to present either a detailed discussion of the economic significance of each, or its effect upon the land. However, coal, sand and gravel, stone, clay, iron ore, and phosphate rock are responsible for the vast majority of the land disturbed by surface mining.

Impact on Environment

Environment is defined as "the surrounding conditions, influences, or forces which influence or modify." The environment is ever-changing. Throughout geologic time the earth has been subjected to a continuing cycle of orogeny, erosion, transportation, and deposition. Natural land disturbances are neither new nor intrinsically bad; but to these natural phenomena a new dimension has been added—man.

Surface mining frequently shocks the sensibilities, not so much by what is done as by the sheer magnitude of man's accomplishments. He literally has moved mountains, and some of his surface excavations are so vast as to resemble craters on the moon. Surface mining destroys the protective vegetative cover, and the soil and rock overlying the mineral deposit is frequently left in massive piles cast onto adjoining land. The result is a drastic reshaping of the surface, an alteration of normal surface and sub-surface drainage patterns. Square miles of land may be turned over to a depth of 100 feet or more and valleys rimmed by mile after mile of contour benches. Massive landslides have blocked streams and highways, waters have been polluted by acid and sediment, land areas isolated, and economic and esthetic values seriously impaired.

Our derelict acreage is made up of tens of thousands of separate patches. In some regions they are often close together. Where one acre in ten is laid waste, the whole land-scape is disfigured. The face of the earth is riddled with abandoned mineral workings, pocked with subsidence, gashed with quarries, littered with disused plant structures and piled high with stark and sterile banks of dross and debris, and spoil and slag. Their very existence fosters slovenliness and vandalism, invites the squatter's shack and engenders a "derelict land mentality" that can never be eradicated until the mess itself has been cleared up. Dereliction, indeed, breeds a brutish insensibility, bordering on positive antagonism, to the life and loveliness of the natural landscape it has supplanted. It debases as well as disgraces our civilization.

Although the preceding paraphrased excerpts from "Derelict Land" (1964) were written to describe conditions in Great Britain, they are equally relevant to certain mining districts in the United States. To many individuals, natural beauty may exist only in a particular national monument, mountain, forest, park, lake, or well-remembered scenic view. However, this narrow concept is giving way to an awareness that natural beauty is everywhere and in everything.

There is no question that many surface-mining operations blight the landscape. Nearly 60 percent of the more than 690 surface mine sites examined could be observed from public-use areas. Where the sites contrasted with greener surroundings, they could be considered unsightly, or even repellent. In arid, or desert, areas public concern is less evident because of the sparse population and the mine sites are somewhat similar in appearance to the surrounding areas.

It was found in the majority of cases (78 percent), that no abandoned structures or equipment had been left on the site of the operation; however, about one-third of the areas visited were being used illegally by the public to discard garbage, rubble, junked vehicles, and construction materials. Such misuse endangers public health and safety and destroys the appearance of an area. In addition mine fires, which cost the Nation millions of dollars annually, are often started by burning trash and other materials in abandoned coal strip pits.

As yet, only a small percentage (about 0.14 percent) of the total land area of the United States has been disturbed by surface mining. But the effects are evident in every State (see Figure 26.3), varying from small prospecting trenches in the West to the widespread disturbances of Appalachia. Effects of such mining upon the environment also vary widely, depending upon the steepness of the terrain, amount of precipitation, temperature, chemical characteristics of the mineral, and method of mining.

RESHAPING THE SURFACE

Of the approximate 3.2 million acres disturbed by surface mining in the United States, open-pit mining accounts for about 35 percent, strip mining for about 56 percent, and all other types for the remainder (see Figure 26.4). It is estimated that roads built to service mining operations occupy an additional 320,000 acres. Table 26.3 presents estimated data on the acreage disturbed in the United States, by commodity and mining method.

Quarry and open-pit mining. These types of operation range from a few feet to as much as one-half mile in depth. Only about one-fourth are driven horizontally into hillsides. In either case, the amount of overburden handled is usually small in proportion to the tonnage of ore recovered. Some mines classified as open pit are difficult to distinguish from strip mines; brown iron ore mines in Alabama and Georgia and some clay mines fall into this category.

Sand and gravel pits account for approximately 26 percent of the total acreage disturbed by surface mining. These pits usually are located within, or near, urban centers where land values are relatively high. They are not a source of chemical pollution, and most of the fine-grained material produced can be retained in the mined area or settled-out in basins or ponds. However, some operations located in or near streams may

FIGURE 26.3 U.S. acreage disturbed by surface mining, by state (as of January 1, 1965).

contribute significantly to the sediment load. Wind-blown dust, unsightly appearance, and noise are problems, and precipitous banks, subject to slides, can be dangerous. Because of their proximity to urban areas, a large number of sand and gravel pits are reclaimed and sold at premium prices because of the growing competition for land.

Stone quarries are numerous, varied, and widely distributed. They may be steep-walled pits excavated downward from level terrain or workings that are driven horizontally into a hill or mountainside. Whether producing limestone, granite, or other stone, these operations do not ordinarily cause chemical pollution. Erosion and sedimentation frequently can be controlled with minimum effort but do present problems in some areas. The steep walls are hazardous and, in mountainous terrain, the cliff-like high-walls are often considered unsightly.

Iron-ore open pits extend over large areas and usually reach considerable depths. The Mesabi Range of Minnesota is an iron ore formation 120 miles long and about 3 miles wide. In the next hundred years the Range could become a giant canal or lake. The minerals in the formation are chemically inert and the terrain is flat; thus the mining operations cause little or no water pollution.* Many of the pits have steep highwalls which, in places, are dangerous and impede the movement of wildlife and humans. The tremendous piles of low-grade, or "lean" ore that dot the countryside may either be considered an attractive feature in an otherwise monotonous landscape or as unsightly, depending upon one's viewpoint.

Copper pits are large, amphitheater-like openings, few in number, and are generally found in arid or semi-arid regions of the West. The pits are sometimes a mile or more in diameter and hundreds of feet deep. The sides of the pits are cut into giant steps, or benches, having heights and widths exceeding 50 feet.† Also, piles of overburden and

---

* Contrary to this statement, the tailings are a serious pollutant in Lake Superior—see editorial comment for Selection 19.

† See photograph on opening page of Part Five.

mine waste (plus mill tailings) generally occupy a greater surface area than the pits and may be sources of sediment and dust unless preventative measures are taken.   Rainfall is limited in most of the copper-producing areas and the exposed sulfide ores do not appear to pose a chemical pollution problem.   This problem can become acute, however, where low-grade ores and waste piles are "leached" to recover their copper content.   In one locality it is known that leaching has made underground water unsuitable for domestic uses.   In another, the quality of well water used for domestic and irrigation purposes is deteriorating slowly because of its dissolved-mineral content.

Strip mining.   Coal strip pits account for 41 percent of the land disturbed by surface mining in the United States.   About one-half of the coal acreage mined has been by the contour method.   Although this method is used to some extent in extracting other minerals, it is estimated that 87 percent of the acreage contour stripped is to recover coal.   In this type of operation, the waste material (overburden) cast down the outslope is on a steeper angle of repose than the natural slope upon which it rests—and extends downhill varying

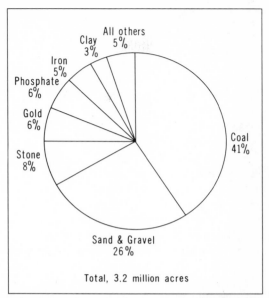

FIGURE 26.4 Percentage of U.S. land disturbed by surface mining of various commodities (as of January 1, 1965).

distances—depending on the steepness of the terrain.   On the 25,000 miles of contour bench, spoil material is stacked on the outer edge for about 18,000 miles and pushed entirely off the bench on the remaining 7,000 miles.   Spoil stacked at the outer edge of

TABLE 26.3 Land disturbed by strip and surface mining in the United States, as of January 1, 1965, by mineral and type of mining[1] (Thousand acres)

MINERAL	STRIP MINING			QUARRY-OPEN PIT			Dredge, hydraulic, and other methods	Grand total[2]
	Contour	Area	Total	Into hillside	Below ground level	Total		
Coal[3]	665	637	1,302	—	—	—	—	1,302
Sand and gravel	38	258	296	82	371	453	74	823
Stone	6	8	14	100	127	227	—	241
Gold	—	8	8	1	3	4	191	203
Clay	10	26	36	22	44	66	7	109
Phosphate	28	49	77	13	93	106	—	183
Iron	7	31	38	30	96	126	—	164
All Other	11	12	23	59	81	140	—	163
Total	765	1,029	1,794	307	815	1,122	272	3,188

[1] Data by method of mining estimated on basis of information obtained by random sampling survey.

[2] Data compiled from reports submitted by the States on U.S. Department of the Interior form 6-1385X, from Soil Conservation Service, U.S. Department of Agriculture, and estimates prepared by the study group.

[3] Includes anthracite, bituminous, and lignite.

a bench, unless properly drained, causes water to accumulate on the bench between the spoil and the highwall. This accumulated water often becomes polluted and may overflow at the lowest point along the shoulder of the spoil bank during heavy storms, resulting in washouts, erosion, and stream pollution.

On the steeper slopes (in excess of 20 degrees), stabilizing the spoil material is difficult. It has been calculated from the sample data collected that approximately 1,700 miles of outslope are affected by massive slides, some of which occurred after the areas had been reclaimed. Loose spoil absorbs large quantities of water, which not only act as a lubricant between the spoil and the original surface, but add an increased load on unstable slopes. The resulting slide not only covers trees and other vegetative cover, but may block highways and stream channels, and destroy valuable farmland and surface improvements.

About 20,000 miles of highwalls were created by coal mining in Appalachia alone and, in some cases, the walls completely isolate entire mountaintops. However, this condition is not confined to Appalachia, as precipitous highwalls are found throughout the Nation. A graphic example is found in the phosphate mining areas of southeastern Idaho, where the deposits lie along a mountaintop which bisects the elk and mule deer migration route between their winter and summer ranges. The migrating herds are forced to cross the mining area at a few places, thus limiting their range and concentrating hunters at these points.

Area strippings create spoil piles or ridges with crests 50 or more feet high, 50 to 100 feet apart, and with side slopes that vary between 17 and 39 degrees. While the rate of erosion on these spoil banks is comparable to that of contour mining, a large percentage of the sediment is retained in depressions on the site. Thus streams and adjoining lands are not affected as severely as in contour stripping areas. Dredge tailings from past gold mining operations, though mined by a different method, have approximately the same conformation as spoil piles at area strippings. Gold-dredge tailings occupy some 200,000 acres, mostly in California and Alaska; but some dredging has been conducted for gold in Montana, Idaho, Oregon, and Colorado.

Large areas of woodland that helped to retard run-off in the anthracite region of northeastern Pennsylvania have been destroyed, particularly during the last two decades. Material washed from the spoil banks has covered vegetation in adjoining downhill areas and choked many stream channels. Much of the surface water pooled in low places behind spoil banks, or trapped in strip pits, has become acid. Samples taken during the survey indicate that most of the spoil material and ponds formed in the pits have pH values ranging from 3.1 to 5.0, and that about one-half of the receiving streams are similarly affected. In many instances, water from strip pits and broken stream beds seeps into underlying mines, where it not only contributes to the volume discharged but also increases pollution from that source.

Phosphate is mined in Florida from bedded deposits comprised of a loosely consolidated "matrix" containing approximately equal parts of clay, sand, and phosphate. Overburden may range from a few feet to as much as 100 feet thick. Generally, the mining operations are conducted in low-lying areas, and may involve prior drainage of swampy land. The matrix is relatively thick in comparison with the overburden and when it is removed, the overburden is usually insufficient to completely backfill the pits.

The matrix is loaded into "sumps" where it is disintegrated by powerful water jets to form a slurry, which is then pumped to separation plants as much as 7 or 8 miles distant. By proper disposal of the overburden and sand returned from the concentrators, desirable land and lakes may be formed. A large portion of the land mined for phosphate is being developed for citrus groves, building sites, parks, and other uses. Thus, except for the possible loss of wet-lands for wildlife use, the mining operations apparently are not serious detrimental to the environment.

Dredge mining. Dredging minerals from natural lakes, estuaries, and stream bottoms, particularly for sand and gravel, is extensively practiced throughout the United States. In many areas, stream bed gravels are the main source of aggregate. Dredging results in a complete upheaval of the stream bottom, and brings large quantities of sediment into suspension. Aquatic flora and fauna are destroyed at the site and further damage is caused downstream. Suspended sediment also may have far-reaching effects on the nature and biota of a stream by reducing light transmittance, blanketing the stream bottom, and by absorbing organic matter and other substances that create unfavorable bottom conditions. The removal of sand and gravel also may destroy spawning sites for fish, widen stream channels (affecting stream velocity and water temperature), and adversely affect municipal water supplies.

The removal of shell deposits (calcium carbonate) for use as construction aggregate was reported by Louisiana as exerting a slight adverse effect on 250 natural lakes (100,000 surface acres of water). Shell mining has also adversely affected fresh-water sport fish, shrimp, and other shellfish of commercial value. In many marshy coastal regions, fill material for industrial and residential development is obtained by dredging adjacent areas. This frequently results in damage to terrestrial and aquatic habitats.

Hydraulic mining. This mining method also presents a significant threat to downstream plant and animal life and general water use because of the large volumes of sediment produced. At the turn of the century, hydraulic mining for gold caused untold damage in California. Lands were regularly inundated by floods caused by river channels that had filled with sediment. Shoals developed in San Francisco Bay and a large bar that formed outside of the Golden Gate strait created serious navigational hazards. A California Debris Commission was established, which attempted to control the sediment problem by building retention barriers. Hydraulic mining is not widely practiced today;

however, a few operations are being conducted in Alaska, California and Oregon, and the potential for expanded hydraulic mining still exists.

BASIC DISTURBANCES

Surface mining affects the environment in three ways. To some degree, it influences the quality of our air, land, and water; and, through these, animal and plant life.

Air. Although air pollution is one of our more serious environmental problems, surface mining, per se, cannot be considered a major contributor.* However, the dust and vibrations resulting from blasting and movement of equipment during mining operations can be annoying and, in densely populated areas, a public nuisance. Some abandoned surface mines and waste piles also may be a source of air-borne dust.

Land. Two factors that are essential to the establishment of vegetation on surface-mined areas are the physical and chemical characteristics of the spoil. The spoil material was considered suitable for agricultural use at only 25 percent of the sites observed during the random-sampling survey. Where excessive stoniness exists (at about 20 percent of the sites inspected) the possibility of getting a quick, vigorous cover is hampered by the rapid run-off and lack of soil. Most of the remaining 55 percent might be receptive to tree or herbaceous type plantings if climatological conditions are favorable.

There were no serious erosion problems at about 60 percent of the areas examined primarily because some vegetation had been established and the slope of the land was relatively gentle before and after mining. Most of the remaining sites showed evidence of erosion in the form of gullies less than one-foot deep; but, at 10 percent of the sites gullies were found that exceeded this depth. Sediment deposits were found in 56 percent

---

* Primary processing of surface-mined materials, however, commonly produces serious air pollution—see Selection 37.

of the ponds and 52 percent of the streams on or adjacent to the sample sites.

Spoil bank materials which have a pH of 4.0 or less are lethal to most plants. A pH of 7.0 is neutral; values higher than 7.0 indicate alkalinity. Free acid may be leached enough in 3 to 5 years to permit planting, but the leaching process will not improve soil conditions if erosion is allowed to expose more sulfuritic minerals in the spoil. Although some plants achieve successful growth in spoil with a pH range under 5.0, most plants require a less acid environment for successful growth. Of the measurements taken on spoil banks, 1 percent showed a pH of less than 3.0 and 47 percent, a range between pH 3.0 and 5.0.

About 15 percent of the spoil banks are covered with vegetation sufficient to provide adequate site protection. Another 15 percent have fair to good cover which, with more time and some spot planting, should suffice to protect the areas and speed renewal of the soil. Twenty percent will require direct seeding, seedlings, and fertilization. About 30 percent of the sites inspected had little, or no, cover and will, therefore, require extensive treatment. On the remaining 20 percent of the sites examined, vegetation will be extremely difficult to grow because of excessive stoniness or toxic conditions. It was also observed that wide variations occur in the rate at which natural revegetation takes place because of differences in physical and chemical characteristics of the spoil, and proximity to seed sources.

It was assumed for the random-sampling survey that, generally, mined land had been used prior to mining for purposes similar to those on adjoining tracts, and that, if left untreated by man, the mining site would eventually regain the same types of cover. Field observations made during the survey showed this to be largely untrue, however, because only about one-half of the areas assumed to have been forested had returned to forest and land classified as idle had increased almost fourfold. Land which had been devoted to crops and human occupancy, of course, had not voluntarily returned to these uses. Curiously, most land assumed to have been grassland had returned to grass. Clearly then, in most cases, natural forces will need a strong assist from man if mined sites are to be brought back to their former uses.

When natural vegetation is removed by exploration and mining activities, the area becomes virtually useless for wildlife because it becomes barren of food, nesting, and escape cover. Even in the most arid areas of the country, erosion eventually follows removal of vegetation, and the resulting silt and sediment may affect fish and wildlife habitat. Thus, except in a few limited areas of the Midwest, poorer soils and vegetative cover resulting from surface mining create less favorable wildlife habitat. However, the rough broken ground found at many sites does afford protection from hunters for some species.

Water. Although basic to human existence, water is perhaps America's most abused resource. The surface mining industries are not the major contributor to the degradation of our water supplies on a national basis, yet in many areas such as Appalachia, they are a significant source of pollution.

Chemical pollution of water by surface mines takes many forms. The polluted water may be too acid, too alkaline, or contain excessive concentrations of dissolved substances such as iron, manganese, and copper. High concentrations of dissolved minerals may make the water unsuitable for certain purposes, but not for others; for example, water unsuitable for domestic use because of chemical content may often be used by industry, and some forms of aquatic life may flourish in it.

Sulfur-bearing minerals are commonly associated with coal, and are a major cause of water pollution. When exposed to air and water, they oxidize to form sulfuric acid. This acid may enter streams in two ways: (1) Soluble acid salts formed on the exposed spoil surfaces enter into solution during periods of surface run-off, and (2) ground water, while moving to nearby streams, may be altered chemically as it percolates through spoil, or waste dumps.

Acid drainage is but one of several adverse chemical effects caused by surface mining. Even in minute concentrations, salts of metals such as zinc, lead, arsenic, copper, and aluminum are toxic to fish, wildlife, plants, and aquatic insects. Indirectly associated with acid drainage are the undesirable slimy red or yellow iron precipitates ("yellow boy") in streams that drain sulfide-bearing coal or metal deposits. Of the streams receiving direct run-off from surface mine sites, 31 percent of those examined contained noticeable quantities of precipitates. Water discoloration was recorded at 37 percent of the streams adjacent to the sites observed, suggesting chemical or physical pollution. The discoloration occurred most frequently in connection with the mining of coal, clay, sand and gravel, peat, iron, stone, and phosphate rock.

Streams are also polluted by acid water from underground mines, preparation plants, and natural seepage from unworked coal and other pyritic material. Because of the intermingling of effluents from these sources, it is difficult, if not impossible, to determine the quantity of acid that comes from surface mining alone. Many authorities believe, however, that not more than 25 percent of the acid load created by coal mining can be attributed directly to surface operations. Many streams in the Appalachian region are affected to various degrees by acid drainage from both surface and underground mines. Altnough acid conditions are associated with coal mining conducted elsewhere, the problems are not usually so severe because the topography is not as rugged, rainfall is less profuse, pyritic materials oxidize more slowly, and, in some cases, limestone formations act as a neutralizing agent. Where acidity is neutralized by alkaline water, or limestone, the concentration of certain dissolved substances still may remain high and the water may not be usable without treatment.

Acid mine drainage affects fish and wildlife in several ways Acid changes the water quality of streams into which it is discharged and, although the concentration may not be lethal to fish or wildlife, it may bring about changes in their physical condition and rate of growth. However, acid may be present in such concentration as to be directly lethal to fish or tend to suppress or prevent reproduction of the most desirable species.

The Bureau of Sport Fisheries and Wildlife reported that in the United States some 5,800 miles of streams (about 57,000 acres) and 29,000 surface acres of impoundments and reservoirs, are seriously affected by surface coal mining operations. The Bureau reported that, in 1964, 97 percent of the acid mine pollution in streams and 93 percent in impoundments, resulted from coal mining operations. Similar data were obtained by a United States Geological Survey reconnaissance conducted in 1965, which disclosed that water quality at 194 of 318 sampling sites in Appalachia was measurably influenced by acid mine drainage. None of these data, however, reflect the percentage of damage that can be attributed to surface mining alone.

Access roads built of pyritic waste material may also be sources of acid water. In past years, some highway departments have hauled waste from the mines for road building purposes. This practice is not generally followed today, and is forbidden in some states; however, roads built of this material continue to acidify rainwater passing over them—despite long periods of leaching. In addition, some privately constructed mine-access roads are being built of pyritic material.

Roads opened on National Wildlife Refuges by prospectors frequently result in broken levees; interfere with controlled burning; increase human activity, which interferes with the nesting and breeding of birds and animals; and, restrict animal movements. The distance that each species, or even individual animals, will place between themselves and the disturbance varies greatly, but some species will leave an area entirely when their natural habitat is invaded by people and equipment.

Physical pollution is most serious in areas

typified by high-intensity storms and steep slopes, particularly during and shortly after mining. In areas undisturbed by strip mining within the Appalachian region, the average annual sediment yield ranges from about 20 to 3,000 tons per square mile of watershed, depending upon land use. Research conducted in Kentucky indicated that yields from coal strip-mined lands can be as much as 1,000 times that of undisturbed forest. During a four-year period, the annual average from Kentucky spoil banks was 27,000 tons per square mile while it was estimated at only 25 tons per square mile from forested areas (see Figure 26.5).

Erosion and sedimentation problems from surface mining are less severe in arid regions; however, even in such areas, storms do occur during which large quantities of sediment are discharged from mine workings, spoil heaps, and access roads. At some idle surface mines in arid country, the effects of wind and water erosion are still evident on steep spoil banks that were abandoned many years ago.

One of the major causes of sedimentation problems is the failure to control surface run-off following rainstorms. In areas outside Appalachia, 86 percent of the surface-mined areas investigated were found to have adequate run-off control. Areas lacking sufficient control were confined almost exclusively to the surface mining of coal, phosphate, manganese, clay, and gold.

Some 7,000 miles of stream channels have had their normal storm-carrying capacity reduced according to the Bureau of Sport Fisheries and Wildlife. It was observed that the normal water-carrying capacity of about 4,500 miles of these streams had been moderately to severely affected. The remaining

FIGURE 26.5 Stream choked with sediment from strip mining for coal. (Photo by W. M. Spaulding, Jr., Fisheries and Wildlife, U.S. Department of the Interior.)

2,500 miles had been affected only slightly (debris reducing channel by less than one-third of capacity). Sediment generally was not a significant problem on small streams located more than two miles from the sample site.

Substandard access and haulage roads, and others built in connection with prospecting activities, are a major source of sediment. Based on the sample data, 95 percent of these roads were less than 3 miles long, but the proximity of many to natural stream channels had considerably increased their potential for sedimentation damage. The roads were fairly passable in the majority of cases; however, approximately 15 percent were eroded to a point that would make them difficult to traverse by ordinary vehicles.

BENEFICIAL EFFECTS OF SURFACE MINING

When massive rocks are fragmented during surface mining, the resulting piles of material contain considerably more void space than existed in the fractures, partings, and pore spaces of the undisturbed rock. As a result, certain desirable hydrologic effects may occur. The danger of floods is diminished because a significant portion of the rainfall is trapped in depressions and behind the spoil banks where it sinks into the earth to augment ground-water supplies, rather than running off rapidly to nearby streams. Because water stored in the banks moves slowly, drainage will continue for a long time before the water level declines to that of adjacent streams. Thus, streams near surface-mined areas often maintain a longer sustained flow during dry weather than those draining undisturbed ground. This phenomenon was verified through field studies conducted in the Midwest by the Indiana University Water Research Center, but it occurs less frequently in most of Appalachia because of the rapid run-off.

In the Western United States, some surface mines have exposed ground-water sources and made water available where none existed before. This water has proved invaluable to livestock and wildlife. At some surface mining operations along mountainsides, the pits impound surface run-off from torrential rains, minimize the sediment load of streams draining the area, and effect considerable ground water recharge as well.

In California, piles of dredge tailings are quite permeable. However, because of their irregular conformation, they undoubtedly inhibit surface run-off to a greater degree than the original slopes, thus making some contribution to flood control and ground-water recharge. In Alaska, dredge mining for gold has destroyed the permafrost and the resulting tailings and mined areas are considered premium property for residential and industrial development.

Many mine-access roads, when properly repaired and maintained, can be of considerable value since they may be used to promote the multiple-land-use potential of extensive areas. Accessibility for fire protection, recreation, and management activities, can mean the difference between use and isolation. For example, by improving fire protection, investments can be made more safely in growing timber, and hazards to human and wildlife considerably reduced. Where massive equipment was used in the mining process, the access roads were usually well constructed, and the cost of repairing and maintaining them would be low. By converting some of these roads to public use, tourism might also be encouraged because many of the sites examined (33 percent) were located in areas that afforded spectacular views of mountains, valleys, and lakes.

Surface mining has created many opportunities to develop recreational areas where none existed before. Water in the form of small ponds or lakes, and the spoil piles themselves, frequently provide a pleasant topographic change in areas of virtually flat land. Examples may be found in flat coastal areas and in such states as Kansas, Illinois, Indiana, Ohio, and California.

Related Problems

Although on-site and some off-site conditions associated with strip and surface mining are discussed, this report does not cover waste materials resulting from processing mineral ores and preparing solid fuels for market. Neither does it explore problems associated with waste brought to the surface from underground operations, mine fires, surface subsidence, acid drainage from underground mines, possible accumulations of spent oil shale, seepages of oil and brine, mining on the continental shelf, and conflicting land uses. However, some of these problems are discussed briefly in the following sections to alert the reader to their significance, and to outline some of the efforts being taken to resolve them.

BUREAU OF MINES SOLID WASTE DISPOSAL PROGRAM

Under Public Law 89-272, the Solid Waste Disposal Act, the Secretary of the Interior has delegated responsibility to the Bureau of Mines for a study of problems associated with the disposal, or use, of solid wastes resulting from the extraction, processing, or utilization of minerals or fossil fuels. To discharge this responsibility, the Bureau has initiated two types of projects:

a. Economic and resource-evaluation investigations aimed at identifying the causes of waste disposal problems in the mineral and fossil fuel industries; and

b. scientific and engineering research to develop methods of utilizing, or otherwise disposing of, a variety of inorganic waste materials.

The economic and resource-evaluation studies are directed toward determining the magnitude, nature, and location of solid waste piles; identifying problems in terms of priority; appraising the effectiveness of current disposal practices, including costs and possible profits that might accrue from further beneficiation or treatment; and, estimating the quantity of waste that may accumulate from future operations. A series of case studies will be included that will attempt to evaluate specific waste piles from the standpoint of public health and safety (such as burning culm banks) and the extent to which they retard industrial or urban development. In addition to wastes that may still contain some mineral values, slag dumps and tailings

will be investigated to determine whether they are potential sources of road materials and lightweight aggregates.

The current research program includes projects at Bureau research installations, grants-in-aid to universities and colleges, and one contract to private industry. Research by the Bureau includes projects designed to produce a clean steel scrap from automobile bodies; to develop technically- and economically-feasible methods of recovering and utilizing the metal content of redmud residues at the alumina industry; to use auto scrap and nonmagnetic taconite ores for the production of marketable magnetic iron oxide concentrates; to develop new or improved methods of salvaging metal from municipal wastes; and, to devise processes for the production of marketable products therefrom.

Grants-in-aid include studies on grass and other plants that might flourish on waste piles; use of mine and mill wastes in manufacturing bricks, lightweight block, structural clay products, or as aggregates for concrete; potential uses for spent oil shale; recovery of valuable products from mine dumps; and, removing contaminating metals from automobile scrap. The private contract is for the purpose of developing techniques to remove and recover copper from auto scrap melted in a cupola. Iron ingots suitable for use in iron or steel foundries will be produced and copper recovered from the slag, thus providing from auto scrap two metals which have well-established markets.

MINE FIRES AND SUBSIDENCE

A coal formation is a vast bed of combustible fuel. Mining makes oxygen available and all that is required to initiate combustion is a source of heat. One of the most common causes of coal mine or waste bank fires is the practice of burning trash or rubbish in strip pits or near the banks. Mine fires not only have a demoralizing effect upon a community, they pose a menace to public health and safety by emitting noxious gases and fumes, endanger surface lands and property, and destroy valuable resources. Of the more than 200 mine fires located in the United

States in 1964, many had been burning for years, a few for several decades. These fires, with nearly 500 waste bank fires, thus exert a considerable adverse effect upon the environment in certain areas. An insidious aspect of these types of fire is that, because of their proximity to each other, a mine fire may ignite a culm bank and vice versa.

Underground mining removes that part of the surface support supplied by the mineral extracted. Regardless of the type of mining and roof support used, subsidence usually occurs when the ore body, or coal seam, is relatively near the surface. Surface subsidence* resulting from underground mining has caused loss of life and millions of dollars of damage to buildings, streets, water mains, and sewage lines in built-up areas. In addition, subsidences disrupt drainage patterns and permit surface water to infiltrate underground mine workings, thus frequently creating enormous underground impoundments in abandoned mines. Where the water is acid, its return to the surface, either by pumping or gravity flow, presents a serious problem in the receiving streams.

DISPOSAL OF SPENT OIL SHALE

About one-half barrel of oil may be recovered from a ton of oil shale by a number of retorting processes. It is estimated that, for a 50,000 barrel-per-day operation, the disposal problem would involve 100,000 tons of spent shale per day. "High-grading" and unwise plant practices could waste large amounts of oil shale, resulting in enormous spoil piles of low-grade shale, and create stream and air pollution problems. Underground mining could induce surface subsidence that might adversely affect the recovery of minerals that lie above the oil shale deposits in some places.

OIL SEEPAGE AND BRINES

Leaks in well casings and the disposal of brines and other wastes seriously contaminate fresh water supplies in many of the older

* Land subsidence is the subject of Selection 27.

oil fields. Leaks that allow brines to percolate downward to the ground water reservoir and the presence of permeable sands beneath some disposal pits are two of the major sources of contamination. Another major problem lies in locating oil wells which may be contaminating ground water. After they are found, the procedure is to clean and cement them from the bottom to seal off permeable formations. However, the problems mentioned require continued study.

OCEAN FLOOR MINING

Ocean floor mining is emerging as a source of future mineral supply. Though in its infancy, commercial operations are being conducted for (1) shells off the coast of Iceland, in San Francisco Bay, and in the Gulf of Mexico; (2) tin off the coasts of Indonesia and Thailand; (3) diamonds off South-West Africa; (4) aragonite in Florida; and (5) iron sand in Ariaka Bay, Kyushu, Japan. Oil and sulfur have long been recovered from offshore deposits, and gold dredging in offshore areas of Alaska is being actively investigated. Effective disposal of the tailings (waste) without seriously impairing the utilization of other marine resources and creating objectionable on-shore waste piles appears to be the most important problem so far encountered.

CONFLICTING MINERAL LAND USE PROBLEMS

Surface mining often disturbs other resources. In many instances, timber is removed, wildlife habitat disrupted, natural streams diverted or contaminated, roads are built in undisturbed areas, and holes drilled. There is also the question of whether the initial mining operation will reduce our mineral-resource base by interfering with or precluding entirely the ultimate recovery of other underlying minerals. The demand for land to support both urban growth and mineral development (particularly sand and gravel) also creates serious social and political questions in densely-populated areas. In addition, when reclamation is contemplated, disagreements often occur as to the type of land use that will contribute most to society.

A nationwide study by the Bureau of Mines (1967) is aimed at determining the effect of mineral extraction on land values. Although primary efforts are directed toward urban centers and scenic and recreational areas, other locales are included. The study attempts to delineate problems of land rehabilitation and end-use following various types of mining such as strip, open pit, quarrying, and underground. Conditions under which mined-out land may enhance in value as well as some of the factors that lead to deterioration of value also are determined. A special feature deals with methods of handling future, or potential, land conflicts in order to maximize the utilization of the Nation's mineral resources and yet minimize the objectionable economic and sociologic after-effects of mining.

References

Hundreds of reports have been published on many aspects of surface mining and mined-land reclamation. The subject matter varies widely, ranging from technical details of a single problem in a small watershed to in-depth studies of problems in areas the size of Appalachia. Because of the sheer volume and diversity of the subject matter covered by the literature, no attempt has been made to compile a comprehensive list of references. Rather, to assist those who might wish to delve further into pertinent writings, the following bibliographies are presented:

Berryhill, Louise R. Bibliography of the U. S. Geological Survey Publications Relating to Coal, 1882-1949. U. S. Geol. Survey Circ. 86, Jan. 1951, 52 pp.

Bituminous Coal Research, Inc., for the Coal Research Board, Commonwealth of Pennsylvania, Mine Drainage Abstracts. A Bibliography, 1910-63. 1964.

Bowden, Kenneth L. A Bibliography of Strip Mine Reclamation, 1953-60. Dept. of Conserv., The Univ. of Mich., 1961, 19 pp.

Funk, David T. A Revised Bibliography of Strip Mine Reclamation. U. S. Forest Service. Central States Forest Expt. Sta. Misc., Release 35, 20 pp.

Lorenz, Walter C. Progress in Controlling Acid Mine Water: A Literature Review. U. S. Bur. Mines Inf. Circ. 8080, 1962, 40 pp.

Pacific Southwest Inter-Agency Committee. Annotated Bibliography on Water Quality in Pacific Southwest Inter-Agency Committee Area, 1950-63. Dec. 1965, 94 pp.

U. S. Department of Agriculture, Forest Service. Annotated List of Publications, Central States Forest Expt. Sta., Jan. 1965-Mar. 1966, 18 pp.

The following publications include comprehensive lists of references that are directly related to the subject matter indicated in the titles.

Averitt, Paul. Coal Reserves of the United States—A Progress Report, January 1, 1960. U. S. Geol. Survey Bull. 1136, 1961, 116 pp.

Bauer, Anthony M. Simultaneous Excavation and Rehabilitation of Sand and Gravel Sites. Nat. Sand and Grav. Assoc., Silver Spring, Md., 1965, 60 pp.

Biesecker, J. E., and J. R. George. Stream Quality in Appalachia as Related to Coal-Mine Drainage, 1965. U. S. Geol. Survey Circ. 526, 1966, 27 pp.

Brooks, David B. Strip Mine Reclamation and Economic Analysis. Natural Resources J. v. 6, No. 1, Jan. 1966, pp. 13-44.

Derelict Land, A study of industrial dereliction and how it may be redeemed. Civic Trust, 79 Buckingham Palace Road, London S.W. 1, 1964, 70 pp.

Federal Water Pollution Control Administration, Region VIII. Disposition and Control of Uranium Mill Tailings Piles in the Colorado River Basin. U. S. Dept. of H. E. W., Mar. 1966, 36 pp. and 28 p. Appendix.

Forest Service, Eastern Region and the Soil Conservation Society of America. Strip Mine Reclamation (a digest). U. S. Dept. Agr., Rev., 1964, 69 pp.

Johnson, Craig. Practical Operating Procedures for Progressive Rehabilitation of Sand and Gravel Sites. Nat. Sand and Grav. Assoc., Silver Spring, Md., 1966, 75 pp.

Kinney, Edward C. Extent of Acid Mine Pollution in the United States Affecting Fish and Wildlife. U. S. BuSport Fish. and Wildlife Circ. 191, 1964, 27 pp.

Ministry of Housing and Local Government, Her Majesty's Stationery Office. New Life for Dead Lands, Derelict Acres Reclaimed. Brown, Knight and Truscott, Ltd., London and Tonbridge. 1963, 30 pp.

Research Committee on the Coal Mine Spoil Revegetation in Pennsylvania. A guide for Revegetating Bituminous Strip-Mine Spoils in Pennsylvania. 1965, 46 pp.

The Council of State Governments. Proceedings of a Conference on Surface Mining, Roanoke, Virginia, April 1964. Surface Mining—Extent and Economic Importance, Impact on Natural Resources, and Proposals for Reclamation of Mined-Lands. 1964, 64 pp.

Udall, Stewart A. Study of Strip and Surface Mining in Appalachia. In Interim Report to the Appalachian Regional Commission. U. S. Dept. of the Int. June 1966, 78 pp.

ADDITIONAL REFERENCES

Council of State Governments. 1964. *Surface mining—extent and economic importance, impact on natural resources, and proposals for reclamation of mined lands.* Proceedings of a Conference on Surface Mining, April 13-14, 1964. Chicago.

Deasy, G. F., and P. R. Greiss. 1961. Stripped and breaker-waste lands of the anthracite region. *Proc. Penn. Acad. Sci.* 35:129-136.

Doerr, A., and L. Guernsey. 1956. Man as a geomorphological agent: the example of coal mining. *Ann. Assoc. Am. Geogr.* 46:197-210.

Fund, D. T. 1962. *A revised bibliography of strip-mine reclamation.* Central States Forest Experiment Station, Misc. Release No. 35. Columbus, Ohio.

Lovering, T. S. 1969. Mineral resources from the land. Pp. 109-134 in *Resources and man,* by the Committee on Resources and Man, of the Division of Earth Sciences, National Academy of Sciences/National Research Council. San Francisco: W. H. Freeman.

Meiners, R. G. 1964. Strip mining legislation. *Natural Resources Journal* 3:442-469.

Miller, E. W. 1949. Strip mining and land utilization in western Pennsylvania. *Science Monthly* 69:94-103.

Ross, W. G. 1967. Encroachment of the Jeffrey Mine on the town of Asbestos, Quebec. *Geogr. Rev.* 57(4):523-537.

Sherlock, R. L. 1922. *Man as a geological agent.* London: H. F. & G. Witherby. 372 pp.

Walsh, John. 1965. Strip mining: Kentucky begins to close the reclamation gap. *Science* 150: 36-39.

LAND SUBSIDENCE DUE TO
WITHDRAWAL OF FLUIDS

J. F. POLAND AND G. H. DAVIS

Thus far, the selections in this part have treated the intentional shaping of the earth's surface by man, which has a considerable history. Within the last century, however, some of man's activities have begun to inadvertently produce geological effects of considerable magnitude and human consequence. Geological subsidence, or the sinking of land, is one serious geological effect which may result from any of several causes.

Land may sink naturally because of such processes as (1) underground solution or erosion of rocks; (2) lateral flow of some earth materials (such as clay) under loading; (3) compaction of sediments by loading, drainage, wetting, or vibration; (4) tectonic movements of the earth, such as earthquakes; and (5) volcanic activity (Allen, 1969). Human activities can simulate or promote all these processes except the last, hence causing land to subside. The past few years have even seen man's advent as a tectonic agent, as underground nuclear blasts cause subsidence (Houser and Eckel, 1962; also see Selection 31).

Underground mining of solid minerals has long been recognized as a major cause of collapse of the ground surface (Hull, 1883; Young and Stoek, 1916; Crane, 1929; and Wallwork, 1956 and 1960). To cite another mechanism, draining of peat land in the Florida Everglades

Joseph F. Poland (b. 1908) has been a research geologist and hydrologist with the Ground Water Branch of the U.S. Geological Survey since 1956. Before that he was a geologist (1940–1946) and a district geologist for California (1946–1956) in the same organization. Since 1956 he has been project chief for studies of land subsidence by the U.S. Geological Survey; he is also chairman of several interagency committees on land subsidence and a consultant to UNESCO. Poland's current research interests continue to deal with problems of worldwide land subsidence, with special attention to the development of predictive techniques and remedial measures. He earned a bachelor's degree from Harvard University and a master's degree from Stanford University (1935). George H. Davis (b. 1921) has been a research hydrologist with the U.S. Geological Survey, Washington, D.C., since 1948. He studied at the University of Illinois and the University of California, Los Angeles. Davis has been applying isotope techniques in hydrology since 1966, when he joined the International Atomic Energy Agency in Vienna for two years. He also maintains an active interest in land subsidence and is editor of *Water Resources Research*.

This selection is extracted from a much longer review with the same title, with the kind permission of the authors and The Geological Society of America, from the society's *Reviews in Engineering Geology*, vol. 2, pp. 187–269, 1969.

has caused oxidation and soil shrinkage above the water table. After forty years of drainage, the soil there has subsided at a rate of about 1 foot every eight to twelve years; the peat formed at a rate of 1 foot in 400 years. If the subsidence continues, farming will soon be impractical because the peat overlies bedrock into which drainage ditches would have to be deepened (Stephens, 1956). Application of water, usually to irrigate crops, also has caused widespread and alarming subsidence elsewhere (Lofgren, 1969). Numerous other sorts of human activities which cause land subsidence are discussed by Allen (1969).

This selection discusses a principal cause of subsidence: the withdrawal of underground fluids—water and oil and gas—by man. The Wilmington oil field, which underlies Long Beach, California, is a fascinating example. Subsidence there had reached 27 feet and caused damage amounting to more than 100 million dollars before remedial measures began to take effect in the early 1960s. Salt water is now injected into the ground, at a rate of 1,000,000 barrels a day since 1965, to repressure the oil zones. This action has arrested subsidence and even caused a 6 to 15 percent rebound of the land, but at considerable expense.

The Mexico City area is discussed as an area in which the removal of ground water from beneath has caused remarkable subsidence. Most of the land in the old city has sunk at least 13 feet since 1891 and spots have subsided as much as 25 feet! Sewer lines now slope into rather than away from the city and visitors now walk downstairs rather than upstairs into the cathedral.

(Editor's comment)

Introduction

Principal causes of land-surface subsidence are removal of solids or fluids from beneath the land surface, either naturally or artificially; solution; oxidation; compaction of soil or sediments under surface loading, vibration, or wetting; and tectonic movement. This paper discusses subsidence believed to have been caused chiefly, if not wholly, by fluid withdrawal by man. Land-surface subsidence due to the withdrawal of fluids by man has become relatively common in the United States since 1940 and has been described at several places throughout the world.

The two types of fluid withdrawal by man that have caused noticeable subsidence under favorable geologic conditions are (1) the withdrawal of oil, gas, and associated water and (2) the withdrawal of ground water. The withdrawal of steam for geothermal power

has caused subsidence; also, the withdrawal of brines, reportedly, has caused subsidence.

Regardless of the nature of the fluid removed, the principles involved are the same; therefore, the separation of subsidence phenomena due to fluid withdrawal into those caused by exploitation of oil and gas fields and those caused by pumping of ground water may seem highly arbitrary. On the other hand, there are marked differences in the character and dimensions of the two types of reservoirs and in the magnitude of man-made stresses involved. Oil and gas commonly are produced from rocks that are older, at greater depth, more consolidated, and have lower permeability and porosity than most ground-water reservoir rocks. Also, oil and gas come from fields of relatively small extent, mostly from 1 to 50 square miles; whereas ground-water reservoirs may be many hundreds of square miles in area. Fluid pressures in deep oil- or gas-producing zones in a fully exploited field may be reduced as much as 2000-4000 pounds per square inch, from initial hydrostatic to approximately atmospheric pressure. Rarely has the fluid pressure in a ground-water reservoir been reduced more than 200 pounds per square inch (about 460 feet).

Fuller (1908, p. 33) was the first to theorize that withdrawal of fluids and decrease of fluid pressure cause sinking of the land surface (because of the removal of the hydrostatic support). The first published descriptions of subsidence, by Minor (1925) and Pratt and Johnson (1926) were for the Goose Creek oil field in Texas. The first specific observation of subsidence due to groundwater withdrawal—that in the Santa Clara Valley in California—was published in 1933 (Rappleye). Most of the major subsidences due to withdrawal of fluids have developed as a result of intensified withdrawal of resources during and since the Second World War in order to satisfy the needs of the burgeoning world population. Thus, most of the problems and damage due to subsidence have developed in the past two decades; these have spurred several intensive investigations of causes and possible remedial measures. Still more intensive and widespread exploiting of fluid resources, especially ground water, in the future will multiply the incidence of subsidence. Therefore, it appears particularly appropriate at this time to summarize available information on subsidence due to fluid withdrawal.

Subsidence of Oil and Gas Fields

Major subsidence of three oil fields has been reported in the literature. These are Goose Creek oil field in Texas (Pratt and Johnson, 1926); the Wilmington oil field in the harbor area of Los Angeles and Long Beach, California; and oil fields on the shore of Lake Maracaibo in Venezuela. Although the Lake Maracaibo subsidence has been known since the early thirties (Kugler, 1933, p. 758, discussion, p. 769), little has been published on that subsidence. Each of these

subsiding areas is at sea level, and the subsidence was obvious because of submergence of the land surface.

Minor subsidence has been noted at several California oil fields, such as Venice-Playa del Rey (Grant, 1944, p. 136) and Long Beach (Signal Hill), Huntington Beach, and Santa Fe Springs (Gilluly and Grant, 1949, p. 525–527). Undoubtedly, many oil fields away from the ocean or other large water bodies have subsided as much as several feet, but without repeated precise leveling such subsidence may pass unnoticed.

Gas fields at Niigata, Japan (Aki, 1959), and in the Po Delta, Italy, experienced rapid subsidence in the late fifties. The Niigata field is at sea level, and the Po Delta field borders the sea. Many other gas fields above sea level and not subject to inundation probably have experienced subsidence, but with no marked deleterious effects; thus, they have not been publicized.

WILMINGTON, CALIFORNIA

A spectacular and costly land subsidence, first noticeable in 1940 and 1941, has occurred at the Wilmington oil field in the harbor area of Los Angeles and Long Beach, California. By August 1962, the subsidence had increased to 27 feet at its center and included an area of about 25 square miles that had subsided 2 feet or more (Figure 27.2). Much of the subsiding area initially was only 5–10 feet above sea level and is intensively industrialized, containing many costly structures, such as port facilities, industrial plants, oil wells, pipe lines, and a major naval shipyard.

The subsidence at the Wilmington oil field is particularly noteworthy for three reasons: (1) the vertical settlement of 27 feet at the center is the greatest subsidence due to fluid withdrawal known to have occurred to date anywhere in the world; (2) many fields yielding oil from deposits of similar age and from an equivalent depth range, of approximately similar lithology, and with comparable decrease in fluid pressure have *not* experienced subsidence of more than a few feet; and (3) corrective remedial action taken since 1958 by repressuring of the oil zones had stopped the subsidence in much of the field by the end of 1962.

The first major published reports describing the subsidence (Harris and Harlow, 1947; Gilluly and Grant, 1949), both based on consulting reports made in 1945, concluded that it was caused primarily by the decrease in fluid pressure in the oil zones, due to removal of oil, gas, and water, which increased the grain-to-grain load and caused compaction. Those reports have been followed by many others, chiefly of the consulting type and reproduced in relatively few copies. To the authors' knowledge, the subsequent reports have concurred with the findings of the initial reports on the primary cause, which has been proven incontrovertibly by the results of the periodic casing collar logs and the repressuring briefly discussed later in this paper.

Geology. The Los Angeles-Long Beach harbor area is underlain by sediments of Recent to Miocene age about 6000 feet thick that unconformably overlie a basement schist of pre-Tertiary age.

Seven productive oil zones have been developed. They extend from a depth of about 2500 feet to 6000 feet.

The Wilmington field is a gently arched anticlinal fold plunging to the northwest. Five main faults that trend roughly north and south divide the oil field into six structural blocks. The faults divide the oil zones into semiseparate pools because of the barrier effect to movement of fluids although the effectiveness of the faults as barriers is reported to be highly variable. The per cent of sand in the several zones ranges from 23 to 70; and the average porosity ranges from 24 to 34 per cent (Murray-Aaron and Pheil, 1948, p. 11).

Development of the field. Oil production began in 1936 (Bartosh, 1938, p. 1052), reached a peak average rate of about 140,000 barrels a day in 1951, and declined to about 70,000 barrels a day by 1959. By March 1962, however, production increased to 82,000 barrels per day, due to the repressuring by water flood. Cumulative production through December 1962 was 913 million barrels of oil, 484 million barrels of water, and 832 million MCF of gas (data from Long Beach Harbor Dept.; gas volume at atmospheric pressure; MCF = 1000 cu. feet). The developed productive area is about 10 square miles, but an undeveloped part of the field extends several miles to the southeast beneath the harbor.

Land subsidence. The subsidence of the Wilmington oil field began in 1937 (Gilluly and Grant, 1949, pp. 464, 479) but was first definitely recognized in the summer of 1941.

Because of the problems caused by the accelerating subsidence, the Long Beach Harbor Department established almost 300 bench marks in 1945, and since 1946 the Department has made level surveys to these marks every 3 months. In 1948, the U. S. Navy began quarterly surveys on a net of bench marks on the Naval base on Terminal Island; these surveys have been continued to date. The data from these surveys have been utilized by the Long Beach Harbor Department in preparing maps each year showing total and annual subsidence. (These surveys are the basis for the lines of equal subsidence on Figures 27.2 and 27.3.)

Figure 27.1 shows the yearly rate of sub-

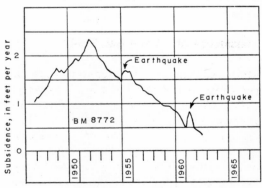

FIGURE 27.1 Subsidence rate at center of subsidence at Wilmington oil field, California. For location of BM 8772, see Figure 27.3. (Data from Long Beach Harbor Department.)

sidence from 1947 to 1962 at the east end of Terminal Island. The rate increased rapidly from 1 foot a year early in 1947 to 2.37 feet a year in November 1951. Since 1951, the rate has decreased about 0.2 foot per year on the average, except for disturbances associated with two local earthquakes that relieved stress and caused a temporary increase in the subsidence rate. From August 1961 to August 1962, this bench mark subsided 0.4 foot, and by August 1962, the annual rate was less than 0.3 foot per year. The oil withdrawal from the Wilmington field reached its maximum rate of 140,000 barrels a day in 1951, the year of maximum subsidence. There is a general correlation between subsidence and oil production, both in time and rate.

The volume of subsidence from 1928 to August 1962 for the entire Wilmington field (beyond the extent shown on Figures 27.2 and 27.3) within the 2-foot subsidence line is 3.07 billion cu. feet or 550 million barrels. Neglecting the gas, the volume of oil and water produced to December 1962 is 1397 million barrels (data from Long Beach Har-

bor Dept.); thus, the volume of subsidence within the 2-foot subsidence line is equivalent to 39 per cent of the oil and water (at atmospheric pressure) removed. The volume of subsidence outside the 2-foot subsidence line is not known.

Horizontal movement. The vertical subsidence has been accompanied by horizontal movement directed inward toward the center of subsidence. In 1951, when subsidence at the center was 16 feet, horizontal movement since 1937 had been as much as 6.2 feet (Grant, 1954, Fig. 1). By 1962, some points on the east end of Terminal Island had moved as much as 9 feet, according to the Long Beach Harbor Department.

The compressional and tensional stresses and the horizontal movements caused by the bending of the sedimentary plate overlying the compacting oil zones have resulted in failure of many surface structures (Shoemaker, 1955; Shoemaker and Thorley, 1955; Neel, 1957). Sheared bridge columns of a lift bridge and buckled railroad tracks and pipe lines are representative examples.

FIGURE 27.2 Subsidence, 1928–1962, of Long Beach area, California. The subsidence in upper right is due to fluid withdrawal from Long Beach (Signal Hill) oil field. The major subsidence in foreground is due to withdrawal from Wilmington oil field. (Photograph and lines of equal subsidence, in feet, courtesy of Long Beach Harbor Department.)

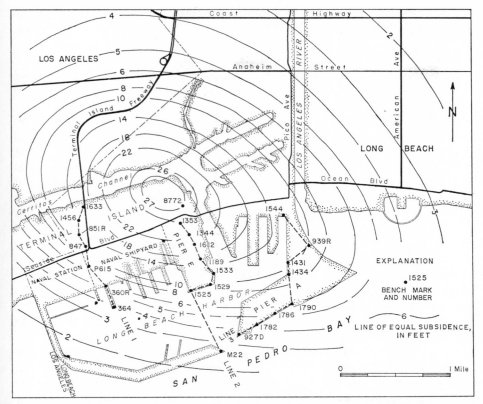

FIGURE 27.3 Subsidence from 1928 to August 1962 and location of selected bench marks at Long Beach Harbor area, California. (Lines of equal subsidence from Long Beach Harbor Department.)

Remedial measures. Extensive remedial measures have been necessary to keep the sea from invading the subsiding lands and structures (Shoemaker, 1955; Coxe, 1949). These measures have been chiefly in the form of construction of levees, retaining walls, fill, and raising of structures. Methods of repairing the sheared, deformed, or collapsed oil-well casings have been described by Frame (1952) and Allen (1959). The cost of remedial work to maintain structures and equipment in operating condition and to repair the several hundred ruptured oil wells had exceeded $100 million by 1962. This remedial work was necessary in order to keep facilities operating; it did not reduce the subsidence or eliminate the cause.

Repressuring. Estimates of ultimate subsidence of 30–45 feet made in the middle

1950's spurred joint constructive action directed toward active remedial work. Findings of consulting reports in 1957 that repressuring of the oil zones by water injection would not only control subsidence but also increase oil recovery by about one half billion barrels furnished both a method and economic justification. Many difficult legal, economic, and engineering problems had to be overcome before water injection could be done on a field scale. Probably the greatest of these was unitization of the 117 producers (Anonymous, 1959b). By concerted action, most of these problems have been solved, and repressuring, which had been initiated on a pilot scale in 1953 by the City of Long Beach, was undertaken on a large scale in 1958.

Injection water is obtained from supply wells tapping shallow aquifers. In large part,

TABLE 27.1 Rebound to 1963 of seven bench marks in Wilmington oil field that recovered from 6 to 15 per cent of their initial subsidence.

Bench mark	Approximate subsidence* (feet)	Rebound to May 1963 (feet)	Rebound in per cent of subsidence
Line 1			
364	4.0	0.49†	12
360R	5.7	.40†	7
Line 2			
M 22	2.7	.40†	15
1525	8.0	.45†	6
Line 3			
927D	3.7	.39	11
1786	5.3	.53	10
1790	6.0	.54	9

* Interpolated from map of subsidence, 1928–1960
† Rebound to August 1963

it has essentially the composition of ocean water and in general is chemically compatible with the oil-zone waters. It is treated chemically to inhibit corrosion and prevent bacterial growth. Then, it is injected into the oil zones at casing-head pressures ranging from 850 to 2000 pounds per square inch (Anonymous, 1960). By August 1960, the rate of repressuring was 370,000 barrels per day through 136 injection wells; by October 1962, the rate had increased to about 530,000 barrels per day through 203 injection wells, and total injection had been about 575 million barrels. The Long Beach Harbor Department has estimated that a total of 300 injection wells and an injection rate of at least 1 million barrels per day will eventually be required. The estimated cost of the repressuring installations is about $30 million (Anonymous, 1959a).

Effects of repressuring on subsidence. The initial repressuring was concentrated largely in the southern part of the field for the purpose of slowing down and arresting subsidence in the waterfront area. In order to show the effect of repressuring on subsidence, the relative change of elevation has been plotted for bench marks along three north trending lines, shown on Figure 27.3.

The bench marks at the southern end of

each line have experienced appreciable rebound. Table 27.1 shows the approximate rebound to May (or August) 1963 of seven bench marks that have recovered from 6 to 15 per cent of their initial subsidence. The maximum rebound has been 0.54 foot at bench mark 1790 (line 3), equivalent to about 9 per cent of the over-all subsidence at that place.

Subsidence Due to Ground-Water Withdrawal

For many years, major subsidence of the land surface has been observed in certain areas of intensive ground-water withdrawal. Areas of major subsidence in California are the San Jose area in the Santa Clara Valley (Poland and Green, 1962) and the Los Banos-Kettleman City, Tulare-Wasco (Poland and Davis, 1956), and Arvin-Maricopa areas (Lofgren, 1963) in the San Joaquin Valley (Poland, 1960). Elsewhere, the best-known subsidences are in Mexico City, Mexico, and the Houston-Galveston area of Texas (Winslow and Doyel, 1954; and Winslow and Wood, 1959). All of these areas are underlain by confined aquifers, and in all, the artesian head has been drawn down at least several tens of feet by heavy withdrawal. Doubtless, subsidence has occurred in many other ground-water basins, but it has gone undetected because of lack of repeated leveling.

MEXICO CITY, MEXICO

Mexico City is in southeastern Mexico, in the west central part of the Valley of Mexico, a closed basin at an elevation of about 7500 feet surrounded by high mountains. The relatively flat part of the valley underlain by alluvial deposits is about 100 km long (north–south) and 15–40 km wide (Mooser, 1961, unnumbered geologic map). Many small rivers flow into the valley, and under natural conditions, the rivers formed a series of shallow lakes, the largest of which was Lake Texcoco.

Roberto Gayol (1929) presented the first specific evidence on the subsidence of Mexico City and pointed out the need for continuing observation. By 1959, subsidence exceeded

4 m (13 feet) beneath all the old city (extent of city in 1891) and was as much as 7.5 m (25 feet) in the northeast part (Figure 27.4). This great and long-continued sinking has caused many problems in water transport, drainage, and in the construction of buildings and other engineering structures in the heart of a great and growing city; consequently, this subsidence has been studied more intensively in its soil-mechanics aspects than has any other subsidence due to ground-water withdrawal.

Geology. Logs of water wells show that sand and gravel containing some interbeds of clayey silt occur almost continuously from a depth of 50–60 m to more than 500 m. They constitute the highly productive aquifer underlying Mexico City (Zeevaert, 1949, Ph.D. thesis, Univ. of Illinois). This aquifer is overlain chiefly by soft fine-grained lake deposits of late Pleistocene age—volcanic ash and water-transported sediments.

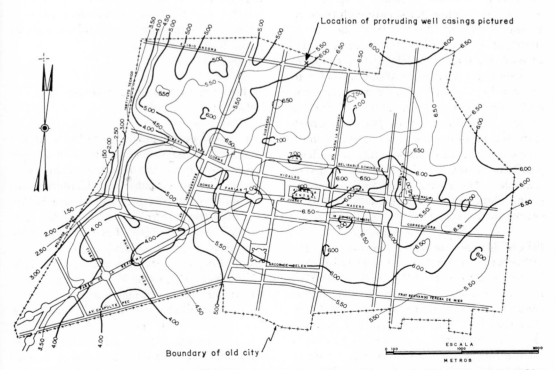

Figure 27.4 Subsidence, 1891–1959, of Mexico City, Mexico. Lines of equal subsidence in meters. (After Comision Hidrologica de la Cuenca del Valle de México, 1961, p. 47.)

The depositional units from the land surface to the top of the productive aquifer at about a depth of 50 m vary in thickness from place to place in the city. However, their character and thickness can be generalized as follows: artificial fill and water-laid silt and sand from the land surface to a depth of 6 m; then an upper soft bentonitic and diatomaceous silty clay about 30 m thick; then a coarse cemented sandy bed about 5 m thick; and then a second bentonitic silty clay 5–10 m thick, stiffer than the upper clay bed. Both of the bentonitic clay beds are highly compressible.

In the upper bentonitic clay, the natural water content ranges from 200 to as much as 500 per cent of the solids by weight, depending on location and loading history. The average value is about 300 per cent. The void ratio ranges from about 5 to 9; the average value is about 7. Thus, the porosity of this upper clay ranges from 84 to 90 per cent; the average is about 88 per cent. In the lower bentonitic clay, the natural water content is 200–300 per cent by weight. The void ratio generally is 4–5, indicating an average porosity of about 82 per cent.

Hydrology. Until the last few years, most of the water supply for Mexico City has been obtained from wells within the city. As early as 1854, 140 artesian wells had been constructed. According to Loehnberg (1958), water was supplied from 3000 privately owned wells 30–100 m (100–325 feet) deep and from about 220 municipal wells 100–300 m (325–1000 feet) deep in 1957. Private wells yielded about 2.5 m³/second (90 cubic feet per second), and municipal wells yielded about 6.5 m³/second (230 cubic feet per second). This discharge of these wells far exceeded the natural recharge. The great increase in demand for water was a result of the rapid increase in population, which grew from about one half million in 1895 to 1 million in 1922 and to 5 million people by 1960.

The artesian head in deep wells initially was a few feet above the land surface, but by 1959, the pressure at 50 m depth (at the top of the main aquifer) had decreased 20–35 m (65–110 feet) (Comision Hidrologica de la Cuenca del Valle de México, 1961, p. 338).

Land subsidence. Local subsidence first occurred owing to loading by the large Aztec structures and later by Spanish buildings. The principal subsidence, however, began in the late 1800's as a result of development of artesian water, the consequent decline of artesian head, and the increase in effective stress.

Between 1898 and 1938, subsidence was not defined by leveling; it probably was not uniform, but the average rate was about 4 cm per year (Marsal, and others, 1952, p.3). The rate of subsidence increased sharply in 1938 and again in 1948, presumably as a result of increased withdrawal from municipal wells beginning in those years. From 1938 to 1948, the rate of sinking was about 15 cm per year; from 1948 to 1952, the rate increased to 30 cm (1 foot) per year in the central part of the city and to 50 cm per year locally (Marsal and Sainz-Ortiz, 1956, p. 3). After 1952, the rate decreased slightly to about 25 cm per year. The total subsidence of the four bench marks from 1898 to 1956 was 5-7 m (16–23 feet).

Figure 27.4 shows the magnitude and distribution of subsidence in the old city from 1891 to 1959 as determined by leveling. Maximum subsidence was 7.5 m (25 feet), and subsidence exceeded 4 m (13 feet) in all but the western edge of the old city.

From 1952 to 1957, subsidence was about 1 m on the average although it reached 1.5 m at a few centers, possibly areas of large building load. Thus, in this period, the average subsidence was about 0.2 m a year. In some areas of recent urbanization, beyond the extent of the old city shown in Figure 27.4, subsidence in the fifties occurred at a more rapid rate, but maps are not available to show the full areal extent and magnitude of the subsidence.

Protrusion of well casings is a common occurrence in the subsiding area and is a graphic demonstration of the decrease in thickness (compaction) of the sediments within the casing depth. The protrusion indicates that here most of the subsidence has resulted from compaction of the deposits within the first 100 m below land surface.

Cause of the subsidence. Investigators of the subsidence in the Mexico City area agree that the principal cause of the regional subsidence is the reduction in artesian pressure that has occurred—most rapidly since 1938.

Estimates of the proportion of subsidence caused by compaction of the upper 50 m of deposits range from about two-thirds to 85 per cent, depending partly on location and the increase in effective stress (Zeevaert, 1953). Evidence from the protruding casings suggests that at some places, at least, the compaction of the top 100 m of sediment is about equal to the subsidence.

Recognizing that the artesian-head decline can be stopped only by reducing the local ground-water draft, comprehensive plans have been made for importing water to the city. Since 1952, several new projects have been completed to bring water into the city, and others are under construction. In addition, reservoirs and recharge wells have been constructed for the purpose of injecting flood waters into the aquifer system. According to Quintero (1958), 13 recharge wells have been installed since 1953, and others are planned.

AREAS IN CALIFORNIA

Development of ground water has been intensive in California. Most of the water is withdrawn for irrigation although ground water is also pumped extensively for domestic and industrial supply. In 1955, about 13 million acre-feet of ground water was pumped for irrigation from ground-water basins in California, slightly more than one-third of the total pumpage for irrigation in the United States.

The ground-water withdrawals in California are chiefly from intermontane basins in which the valley fill of late Tertiary and Quaternary age is chiefly alluvial deposits but also, in places, is of lacustrine and shallow

marine origin. In many of the basins, the water bodies tapped are semiconfined or confined below depths ranging from 100 to 600 feet, and, thus, much of the withdrawal is from confined aquifer systems.

The intensive and long-continued pumping has drawn down water levels more than 100 feet in many of the basins—maximum drawdown of 400-500 feet has been on the west side and in the southern end of the San Joaquin Valley. Thus, in California, substantial lowering of water level has occurred in young, unconsolidated, compressible deposits that contain extensive semiconfined to confined aquifer systems. It is not surprising, therefore, that land subsidence due to ground-water withdrawal has developed in many areas. Subsidence in all areas shown on Figure 27.5, except for those in the Wilmington oil field and in the Sacramento-San Joaquin Delta, is due to ground-water withdrawal and decline of artesian head. Subsidence in most of these areas has been described briefly by Poland (1958). About 11,000 square miles (7 million acres) of land in California is irrigated, and nearly two-thirds of this is irrigated wholly or in part by ground water. Of this 11,000 square

FIGURE 27.5 Areas of land subsidence in California. Major subsidence due to fluid withdrawal shown in black; subsidence in Delta caused by oxidation of peat.

miles, at least 30 per cent has subsided 1 foot or more due to artesian-head decline. Doubtless, many other areas in addition to those shown on Figure 27.5 have subsided at least a few tenths of a foot, but leveling control is not available to define the magnitude and extent of subsidence in most of these.

The peat lands in the Sacramento-San Joaquin Delta have subsided as much as 15 feet in the last century as a result of drainage (lowering of the water table) for cultivation (Poland, 1958, p. 1774-1775). The primary cause of this subsidence, however, is oxidation of the peat (Weir, 1950), rather than compaction of an aquifer system due to increase in effective overburden load (Allen, 1969).

Summary

(1) Decrease in hydrostatic pressure in confined systems, such as oil and gas zones or artesian aquifers, results in increased grain-to-grain load on the sediments. The sediments compact in response to the added load, and the land surface subsides.

(2) Damage from subsidence and compaction has totaled hundreds of millions of dollars throughout the world and takes many forms. In tidal areas, flooding by sea water has been a major problem. Changing gradients have seriously affected the capacity of canals, drains, and sewers, and even the channel capacity of streams has been changed materially. Structural failure of buildings, pipe lines, railroads, and other engineering structures at the land surface has occurred due to tensional or compressional stresses caused by flexure of the sediments. Compaction and flexure of sediments at depth have caused extensive damage by compressional or shear failure of oil- and water-well casings. In compressible aquifers, such as micaceous sand, the loss of groundwater storage capacity through compaction is a subtle but, in part, a permanent damage.

(3) Subsidence of the surface can be measured by precise leveling from stable reference points and, in tidal areas, by observing the change with respect to sea level. Compaction at depth can be measured by the use of anchored cables or pipes and by surveys in wells of reference points, such as casing collars and radioactive markers. Protrusion of well casings indicates that compaction has occurred but supplies only a minimum value for subsidence, not an absolute measure.

(4) The ratio of subsidence to head change depends upon the thickness and lithologic character of the compacting sediments. Chief controlling factors are the number, thickness, compressibility, and permeability of fine-grained interbeds and confining beds, clay mineralogy, geochemistry of pore fluids in aquifers and aquitards, initial porosity, previous loading history, and cementation. The most compressible materials are loosely consolidated, clayey sediments of Tertiary and Quaternary age, particularly those of volcanic provenance, that contain montmorillonite as the predominant clay mineral. In subsidence areas overlying these sediments, the range in ratio where known is about 0.01-0.2. The only known marked exceptions are at London, England, and Savannah, Georgia, where water is produced from soft marine carbonate sediments associated with clays. In both of these areas, the ratio of subsidence to head decline is relatively small (less than 0.005).

(5) Continuous measurements of compaction indicate quick response to pressure changes in many areas although, commonly, some residual compaction or lag due to slow drainage of clays may continue long after the pressure decline has ceased.

(6) Subsidence problems have been or are being alleviated in several ways: (1) cessation of withdrawal of petroleum, gas, or water due to depletion of the supply, legal action, or replacement with substitute supply; (2) increase or restoration of reservoir pressure due to reduction in production rate or to increase in recharge (water); (3) repressuring by injection of water. The last method has been highly successful in the Wilmington, California, oil field where it has stopped subsidence and has caused some rebound of the land surface.

References Cited

Aki, Kooichi, 1959, Notes on the investigation of earth level subsidence in Niigata, Japan: Japan Nat. Res. Bur., Sci. Technology Board, 27 p.

Allen, Alice S., 1969, Geologic settings of subsidence: Geol. Soc. Amer., Rev. in Engin. Geol., v. 2. pp. 305–342.

Allen, Dennis, 1959, Wilmington subsidence problems: Houston, Tex., World Oil, v. 149, no. 2, p. 86–88.

Anonymous, 1959a, Water buoys land that sank as oil was removed: Eng. News-Rec., v. 163, no. 20, p. 26–27.

_____ 1959b, Wilmington unitization is moving fast: Tulsa, Okla., Oil and Gas Jour., v. 57, no. 18, p. 94–95.

_____ 1960, The world's largest water flood: Western Oil and Refining Mag., v. 57, no. 1, 8 p.

Bartosh, E. J., 1938, Wilmington oil field, Los Angeles County, California: Am. Assoc. Petroleum Geologists Bull., v. 22, no. 8, pp. 1048–1079.

Comision Hidrologica de la Cuenca del Valle de México, 1961, Boletin de Mecanica de Suelos, no. 3, June 1956-June 1959: Secretaria de Recursos Hidraulicos, Oficina de Estudios Especiales, 344 p.

Coxe, L. C., 1949, Long Beach Naval Shipyard endangered by subsidence: Civil Eng., v. 19, no. 11, p. 44–47, 90.

Frame, R. G., 1952, Earthquake damage, its cause and prevention in the Wilmington oil field, *in* Summary of Operations, California Oil Fields: California Dept. Nat. Res., Div. Oil and Gas, v. 38, no. 1, p. 5–15.

Fuller, M. L., 1908, Summary of the controlling factors of artesian flows: U.S. Geol. Survey Bull. 319, 44 p.

Gayol, Roberto, 1929, Breves apuntes relativos a las obras de Saneamiento y Desagüe de la Capital de la República de las que, del mismo género, necesita con grande urgencia: Mexico, D. F., Rev. Mexicana de Ingeniería y Arquitectura, v. 7.

Gilluly, James, and Grant, U.S., 1949, Subsidence in the Long Beach Harbor area, California: Geol. Soc. America Bull., v. 60, p. 461–530.

Grant, U.S., 1944, Subsidence and elevation in the Los Angeles Region, p. 129–158 *in* Science in the University, by members of the faculties of the University of California: Berkeley and Los Angeles, California Univ. Press, 332 p.

_____ 1954, Subsidence of the Wilmington oil field, California, p. 19–24 *in* Jahns, R. H., *Editor*, Geology of Southern California: California Dept. Nat. Res., Div. Mines Bull. 170, 700 p.

Harris, F. M., and Harlow, E. H., 1947, Subsidence of the Terminal Island-Long Beach area, California: Am. Soc. Civil Engineers Proc., v. 73, no. 8, p. 1197–1218.

Kugler, H. G., 1933, Contribution to the knowledge of sedimentary volcanism in Trinidad (with discussion): Inst. Petroleum Technologists Jour., v. 19, p. 743–772.

Loehnberg, Alfred, 1958, Aspects of the sinking of Mexico City and proposed countermeasures: Am. Water Works Assoc. Jour., v. 50, no. 3, p. 432–440.

Lofgren, B. E., 1963, Land subsidence in the Arvin-Maricopa area, California: U.S. Geol. Survey Prof. Paper 475-B, art. 47, p. B171–B175.

Marsal, R. J., and Sainz-Ortiz, I., 1956, Breve descripción del hundimiento de la Ciudad de México [Short description of the sinking of Mexico City]: Bol. Soc. Geol. Mexicana, p. 1–11.

Marsal, R. J., Hiriart, Fernando, and Sandoval, L. Raúl, 1952, Hundimiento de la Ciudad de México, observaciones y estudios analíticos [Sinking of the City of Mexico, observations and analytical studies]: Ingenieros Civiles Asociados, S. A. de C. V., Serie B Ingenieria Experimental, no. 3, 26 p.

Minor, H. E., 1925, Goose Creek oil field, Harris County, Texas: Am. Assoc. Petroleum Geologists Bull., v. 9, no. 2, p. 286–297.

Mooser, Federico, 1961, Informe sobre la geologia de la cuenca del Valle de México y zonas colindantes [Report on the geology of the Valley of Mexico and adjacent area]: Comision Hidrologica de la Cuenca del Valle de México, Oficina de Estudios Especiales, 38 p.

Murray-Aaron, E. R., and Pfeil, A. W., 1948, Recent developments in the Wilmington oil fields. *in* Summary of Operations. California oil fields: California Dept. Nat. Res., Div. Oil and Gas, v. 34, no. 2, p. 5–13.

Neel, Charles H., 1957, Surface subsidence and remedial measures at the Long Beach Naval Shipyard, Long Beach, California: Rept. to Long Beach Naval Shipyard, 90 p.

Poland, J. F., 1958, Land subsidence due to ground-water development: Am. Soc. Civil Engineers Proc., Jour. Irrigation and Drainage Div., Paper 1774, v. 84, no. IR3, 11 p.

_____ 1960, Land subsidence in the San Joaquin Valley, California, and its effect on estimates of ground-water resources: Internat. Assoc. Sci. Hydrology, Comm. Subterranean Waters. Pub. No. 52. p. 324–335.

Poland, J. F., and Davis, G. H., 1956, Subsidence of the land surface in the Tulare-Wasco (Delano) and Los Banos-Kettleman City areas, San Joaquin Valley, California: Am. Geophys. Union Trans., v. 37, no. 3, p. 287–296.

Poland, J. F., and Green, J. H., 1962, Subsidence in the Santa Clara Valley, California—A progress report: U.S. Geol. Survey Water-Supply Paper 1619-C, 16 p.

Pratt, W. E., and Johnson, D. W., 1926, Local subsidence of the Goose Creek field: Jour. Geology, v. 34, no. 7, p. 577–590.

Quintero, Andres Garcia, 1958, Recharge wells in Mexico City, Mexico: The Texas Engineer, v. 28, no. 2, p. 6–10.

Rappleye, H. S., 1933, Recent areal subsidence found in releveling: Eng. News-Rec., v. 110, p. 848.

Shoemaker, R. R., 1955, Protection of subsiding waterfront properties: Am. Soc. Civil Engineers Proc., v. 81, no. 805, p. 805-1–805-24.

Shoemaker, R. R., and Thorley, T. J., 1955, Problems of ground subsidence: Am. Water Works Assoc. Jour., v. 47, no. 4, p. 412–418.

Weir, W. W., 1950, Subsidence of peat lands of the Sacramento-San Joaquin Delta, California: Hilgardia, California Univ. Agr. Expt. Sta., v. 20, no. 3, p. 37–56.

Winslow, A. G., and Doyel, W. W., 1954, Land-surface subsidence and its relation to the withdrawal of ground water in the Houston-Galveston region, Texas: Econ. Geology, v. 49, no. 4, p. 413–422.

Winslow, A. G., and Wood, L. A., 1959, Relation of land subsidence to ground-water withdrawals in the upper Gulf Coast region, Texas: Mining Eng., v. 11, no. 10, p. 1030–1034.

Zeevaert, Leonardo, 1953, Pore pressure measurements to investigate the main source of surface subsidence in Mexico City: Switzerland, 3rd Internat. Conf. on Soil Mech. and Found. Eng. Proc., v. 2, 299–304.

ADDITIONAL REFERENCES

Berbower, R. F., and C. F. Parent. 1964. Effects of ground surface subsidence in Long Beach Harbor District. *Amer. Soc. Testing Mater. Proc.* 64:903–921.

Crane, R. W. 1929. Subsidence and ground movement in the copper and iron mines of the Upper Peninsula of Michigan. *U.S. Bureau of Mines Bulletin No. 295.* 66 pp.

Dawson, R. F. 1963. Land subsidence problems. *Am. Soc. Civ. Eng. Proc.* 89(SU2):1–12.

Houser, F. N., and E. B. Eckel. 1962. Possible engineering uses of subsidence induced by contained underground nuclear explosions. *USGS Professional Paper No. 450-C.* pp. 17–18.

Hull, Edward. 1883. On the recent remarkable subsidences of the ground in the salt districts of Cheshire. *Royal Dublin Soc. Sci. Proc. 3,* new ser. 381 pp.

Lockwood, M. G. 1954. Ground subsides in Houston area. *Civil Eng.* 24(6):48–50.

Lofgren, B. E. 1961. Measurement of compaction of aquifer systems in areas of land subsidence. *USGS Professional Paper No. 424-B.* pp. 49–52.

Lofgren, B. E. 1968. Analysis of stress causing land subsidence. *USGS Professional Paper No. 600-B.* pp. 219–225.

Lofgren, Ben. E. 1969. Land subsidence due to the application of water. *Geol. Soc. Am. Reviews in Engineering Geology* 2:271–303.

Lofgren, B. E., and R. L. Klausing. 1969. Land subsidence due to ground-water withdrawal, Tulare-Wasco area, California. *USGS Professional Paper.* pp. B1–B103.

Marsden, S. S., Jr., and S. N. Davis. 1967. Geological subsidence. *Sci. Am.* 216(6):93–100.

Roll, J. R. 1967. Effects of subsidence on well fields. *Am. Water Works Assoc. J.* 59(1):80–88.

Stephens, J. C. 1956. Subsidence of organic soils in the Florida Everglades. *Soil Sci. Soc. Am. Proc.* 20(1):77–80.

Wallwork, K. L. 1956. Subsidence in the mid-Cheshire industrial area. *Geograph. J.* 122:40–53. Discusses subsidence due to salt mining.

Wallwork, K. L. 1960. Some problems of subsidence and land use in the mid-Cheshire industrial area. *Geograph. J.* 126:191–199.

Young, L. E., and H. H. Stoek. 1916. Subsidences resulting from mining. *University of Illinois Engineering Experiment Station Bulletin No. 91.*

SALT AND SILT IN ANCIENT MESOPOTAMIAN AGRICULTURE

THORKILD JACOBSEN AND ROBERT M. ADAMS

Although this book concentrates on the environmental effects of modern man, some past civilizations also have had pronounced influence on the landscape. The historical case study presented here is of special significance today because the processes of environmental change that it describes have recurred in the past and are occurring widely at present. Man's failures of yesterday should be lessons for today.

Irrigation for agriculture has caused progressive changes in soil salinity and sedimentation which have contributed to the decline of past civilizations. Cycles of salinization and land abandonment span a 6,000-year period in the valleys of the Tigris and Euphrates Rivers in Iraq. Cultural innovations, mainly in irrigation technology and government, allowed these successive eras of agriculture. This selection describes three ancient occurrences of marked siltation and salinization in the basin of the Diyala River, a Tigris tributary. Although an elaborate and extensive system of irrigation canals was constructed, maintenance of the system was dependent on a strong central authority, which failed. Silt choked canals; salts from irrigation water accumulated in soils and poisoned them for crops. Today the Iraqi government is once again trying to reclaim and repopulate the area, which has been a desert since the twelfth century.

Irrigation, and with it harmful salinization, is increasing in the world today (UNESCO, 1961). Irrigation water continuously adds soluble salts

Thorkild Jacobsen (b. 1904) has been director of the Diyala Basin Archaeological Project (on which this selection reports in part) since 1957. He holds doctoral degrees from the University of Chicago (Ph.D., 1929) and the University of Copenhagen (Dr. Phil., 1939). He formerly was on the University of Chicago faculty, as chairman of the Department of Oriental Languages and Civilizations and as director of the Oriental Institute (1946–1948) and as dean of the Division of Humanities (1948–1951). Jacobsen later was professor of Assyriology at Harvard University (1962–1966) and, more recently, has been a Guggenheim Fellow (1969). He is currently completing a book about ancient Mesopotamian religion and is preparing results of the Diyala Survey for publication. Robert M. Adams (b. 1926) is dean of social sciences at the University of Chicago. He earned three degrees from Chicago (Ph.D., 1956) and since 1955 has been a member of the faculty and on the staff of the university's Oriental Institute (director, 1962–1968). Adams is author or editor of several books and numerous articles concerning the development of culture and the evolution of urbanization in the ancient Near East.

This selection is reprinted by permission of the authors and *Science* from vol. 128, pp. 1251–1258, November 21, 1958.

to the soil. No irrigation scheme can persist for long unless it provides for the continuous removal of salts from the root zone of the crops. The major deleterious effect of excess salts is to reduce the ability of the plants to absorb water. Increasing levels of salinity cause increasing water stress in the plants. Furthermore, in hot, arid areas where irrigation is fast developing transpiration rates are highest and hence the effects of a given salt concentration are even more adverse.

The general approach to controlling salt is to use water with a low salt content and to flush accumulations of salt into the groundwater, which ideally should be at least 6 feet below the soil surface. But the concentration of salt in irrigation water typically increases greatly as it flows downstream through the irrigation system, as water is evaporated or transpired. For example, increasing irrigation in the upper basin of the Colorado River has increased the salinity of water in the lower part of the river by 30 percent in the last twenty years—to 1.3 tons of salt per acre-foot of water, or about 1,000 parts of salt per million parts of water. The 250-million-dollar annual agricultural empire in California's 500,000-acre Imperial Valley depends almost entirely on this water for irrigation. Salt concentrations are causing thousands of once-fertile acres to be abandoned and are causing soaring costs to keep the remaining acres temporarily suitable for farming.

As the water becomes more salty, more water must be used to flush salts into the subsoil. Attempts to economize water under such conditions, as by wetting only the top several feet of soil, inevitably lead to increased salt concentrations. "Success" in flushing salts into the groundwater also has its price; in parts of California, for example, nitrates have built up in the groundwater to such an extent that the water is toxic to man and livestock. The application of inorganic fertilizers frequently aggravates the situation even further.

The kind of salts found in the soil is also important. Sodium and boron, for example, are toxic to many crops even at low concentrations. Sodium, calcium, and chlorine commonly accumulate to toxic levels along roadsides that have been salted in winter to melt ice (see Selection 30).

(Editor's comment)

Under the terms of a farsighted statute, 70 percent of the oil revenues of the Iraqi Government are set aside for a program of capital investment which is transforming many aspects of the country's predominantly agricultural economy. As compared with the subsistence agriculture which largely has characterized Iraq's rural scene in the past, new irrigation projects in formerly uninhabited deserts are pioneering a rapid increase in land and labor productivity through crop rotation, summer cultivation in addition to the traditional winter-grown cereals, and emphasis on cash crops and livestock.

But these and similar innovations often have disconcerting effects in a semiarid, subtropical zone—effects which cannot be calculated directly from the results of experiment in Europe and America. At the same time, old canal banks and thickly scattered ruins of former settlements testify to former periods of successful cultivation in most of the desert areas now being reopened. The cultural pre-eminence of the alluvial plains of central and southern Iraq through much of their recorded history provides still further evidence of the effectiveness of the traditional agricultural regime in spite of its prevailing reliance on a simple system of fallow in alternate years. Accordingly, the entire 6000-year record of irrigation agriculture in the Tigris-Euphrates flood plain furnishes an indispensable background for formulating plans for future development.

At least the beginnings of a comprehensive assessment of ancient agriculture recently were undertaken on behalf of the Government of Iraq Development Board. In addition to utilizing ancient textual sources from many parts of Iraq which today are widely scattered in the world's libraries and museums, this undertaking included a program of archeological field work designed to elucidate the history of irrigation and settlement of a portion of the flood plain that is watered by a Tigris tributary, the Diyala River (1). Here we cannot report all the diverse findings of the project and its many specialists, but instead will outline some aspects of the general ecological situation encountered by agriculturalists in the Mesopotamian alluvium which seem to have shaped the development of irrigation farming. And, conversely, we hope to show that various features of the natural environment in turn were decisively modified by the long-run effects of human agencies.

Historical Role of Soil Salinization

A problem which recently has come to loom large in Iraqi reclamation planning is the problem of salinity. The semiarid climate and generally low permeability of the soils of central and southern Iraq expose the soils to dangerous accumulations of salt and exchangeable sodium, which are harmful to crops and soil texture and which can eventually force the farmer off his land.

For the most part, the salts in the alluvial soils are presumed to have been carried in by river and irrigation water from the sedimentary rocks of the northern mountains.

In addition, smaller quantities may have been left by ancient marine transgressions, or borne in by winds from the Persian Gulf. Beside the dominant calcium and magnesium cations, the irrigation water also contains some sodium. As the water evaporates and transpires it is assumed that the calcium and magnesium tend to precipitate as carbonates, leaving the sodium ions dominant in the soil solution. Unless they are washed down into the water table, the sodium ions tend to be adsorbed by colloidal clay particles, deflocculating them and leaving the resultant structureless soil almost impermeable to water. In general, high salt concentrations obstruct germination and impede the absorption of water and nutrients by plants.

Salts accumulate steadily in the water table, which has only very limited lateral movement to carry them away. Hence the ground water everywhere has become extremely saline, and this probably constitutes the immediate source of the salts in Iraq's saline soils. New waters added as excessive irrigation, rains, or floods can raise the level of the water table very considerably under the prevailing conditions of inadequate drainage. With a further capillary rise when the soil is wet, the dissolved salts and exchangeable sodium are brought into the root zone or even to the surface.

While this problem has received scientific study in Iraq only in very recent years, investigation by the Diyala Basin Archeological Project of a considerable number and variety of ancient textual sources has shown that the process of salinization has a long history. Only the modern means to combat it are new: deep drainage to lower and hold down the water table, and utilization of chemical amendments to restore soil texture. In spite of the almost proverbial fertility of Mesopotamia in antiquity, ancient control of the water table was based only on avoidance of overirrigation and on the practice of weed-fallow in alternate years. As was first pointed out by J. C. Russel, the later technique allows the deep-rooted *shoq* (*Proserpina stephanis*) and *agul* (*Alhagi maurorum*) to create a deep-lying dry zone against the rise of salts through capillary action. In extreme cases, longer periods of abandonment must have been a necessary, if involuntary, feature of the agricultural cycle. Through evapotranspiration and some slow draining they could eventually reduce an artificially raised water table to safe levels.

As to salinity itself, three major occurrences have been established from ancient records. The earliest of these, and the most serious one, affected southern Iraq from 2400 B.C. until at least 1700 B.C. A milder phase is attested in documents from central Iraq written between 1300 and 900 B.C. Lastly, there is archeological evidence that the Nahrwan area east of Baghdad became salty only after A.D. 1200.

The earliest of these occurrences particularly merits description, since it sheds light on the northward movement of the major centers of political power from southern into central Iraq during the early second millennium B.C. It seems to have had its roots in one of the perennial disputes between the small, independent principalities which were the principal social units of the mid-third millennium B.C. Girsu and Umma, neighboring cities along a watercourse stemming from the Euphrates, had fought for generations over a fertile border district. Under the ruler Entemenak, Girsu temporarily gained the ascendancy, but was unable to prevent Umma, situated higher up the watercourse, from breaching and obstructing the branch canals that served the border fields. After repeated, unsuccessful protests, Entemenak eventually undertook to supply water to the area by means of a canal from the Tigris; access to that river, flowing to the east of Girsu, could be assured without further campaigning against Umma to the northwest. By 1700 B.C. this canal had become large and important enough to be called simply "the Tigris," and it was supplying a large region west of Girsu that formerly had been watered only by the Euphrates. As a result, the limited irrigation supplies that could be drawn from the latter river were supplemented with copious Tigris water. A corresponding increase undoubtedly occurred in seepage, flooding, and overirrigation,

creating all the conditions for a decisive rise in ground-water level.

Several parallel lines of evidence allow the ensuing salinization to be followed quantitatively:

1) Beginning shortly after the reign of Entemenak, the presence of patches of saline ground is directly attested in records of ancient temple surveyors. In a few cases, individual fields which at that time were recorded as salt-free can be shown in an archive from 2100 B.C. to have developed conditions of sporadic salinity during the 300 intervening years of cultivation.

2) Crop choice can be influenced by many factors, but the onset of salinization strongly favors the adoption of crops which are more salt-tolerant. Counts of grain impressions in excavated pottery from sites in southern Iraq of about 3500 B.C., made by H. Helbaek, suggest that at that time the proportions of wheat and barley were nearly equal. A little more than 1000 years later, in the time of Entemenak at Girsu, the less salt-tolerant wheat accounted for only one-sixth of the crop. By about 2100 B.C. wheat had slipped still further, and it accounted for less than 2 percent of the crop in the Girsu area. By 1700 B.C., the cultivation of wheat had been abandoned completely in the southern part of the alluvium.

3) Concurrent with the shift to barley cultivation was a serious decline in fertility which for the most part can be attributed to salinization. At about 2400 B.C. in Girsu a number of field records give an average yield of 2537 liters per hectare—highly respectable even by modern United States and Canadian standards. This figure had declined to 1460 liters per hectare by 2100 B.C., and by about 1700 B.C. the recorded yield at nearby Larsa had shrunk to an average of only 897 liters per hectare. The effects of this slow but cumulatively large decline must have been particularly devastating in the cities, where the needs of a considerable superstructure of priests, administrators, merchants, soldiers, and craftsmen had to be met with surpluses from primary agricultural production.

The southern part of the alluvial plain

appears never to have recovered fully from the disastrous general decline which accompanied the salinization process. While never completely abandoned afterwards, cultural and political leadership passed permanently out of the region with the rise of Babylon in the 18th century B.C., and many of the great Sumerian cities dwindled to villages or were left in ruins. Probably there is no historical event of this magnitude for which a single explanation is adequate, but that growing soil salinity played an important part in the breakup of Sumerian civilization seems beyond question.

Silt and the Ancient Landscape

Like salt, the sources of the silt of which the alluvium is composed are to be found in the upper reaches of the major rivers and their tributaries. Superficially, the flatness of the alluvial terrain may seem to suggest a relatively old and static formation, one to which significant increments of silt are added only as a result of particularly severe floods. But in fact, sedimentation is a massive, continuing process. Silt deposited in canal beds must be removed in periodic cleanings to adjoining spoil banks, from which it is carried by rain and wind erosion to surrounding fields. Another increment of sediment accompanies the irrigation water into the fields themselves, adding directly to the land surface. In these ways, the available evidence from archeological soundings indicates that an average of perhaps ten meters of silt has been laid down at least near the northern end of the alluvium during the last 5000 years.

Of course, the rate of deposition is not uniform. It is most rapid along the major rivers and canals, and their broad levees slope away to interior drainage basins where accumulated runoff and difficult drainage have led to seriously leached soils and seasonal swamps. However, only the very largest of the present depressions seem to have existed as permanent barriers (while fluctuating in size) to cultivation and settlement for the six millennia since agriculture began in the northern part of the alluvium. More commonly, areas of swamp shifted from time to time. As some were gradually brought under cultivation, others formed behind newly created canal or river levees which interrupted the earlier avenues of drainage.

As the rate of sedimentation is affected by the extent of irrigation, so also were the processes of sedimentation—and their importance as an agricultural problem—closely related to the prevailing patterns of settlement, land-use, and even sociopolitical control. The character of this ecological interaction can be shown most clearly at present from archeological surveys in the lower Diyala basin, although other recent reconnaissance indicates that the same relationships were fairly uniform throughout the northern, or Akkadian, part of the Mesopotamian plain (2). To what degree the same patterns occurred in the initially more urbanized (and subsequently more saline) Sumerian region further south, however, cannot yet be demonstrated.

The methods of survey employed here consisted of locating ancient occupational sites with the aid of large-scale maps and aerial photographs, visiting most or all of them—in this case, more than 900 in a 9000-square-kilometer area—systematically in order to make surface collections of selected "type fossils" of broken pottery, and subsequently determining the span of occupation at each settlement with the aid of such historical and archeological crossties as may be found to supplement the individual sherd collections (3). It then can be observed that the settlements of a particular period always describe networks of lines which must represent approximately the contemporary watercourses that were necessary for settled agricultural life. For more recent periods, the watercourses serving the settlements often still can be traced in detail as raised levees, spoil banks, or patterns of vegetation disturbance, but, owing in part to the rising level of the plain, all of the older watercourses so far have been located only inferentially.

A number of important and cumulative, but previously little-known, developments emerge from the surveys. By comparing the over all pattern of settlement of both the early

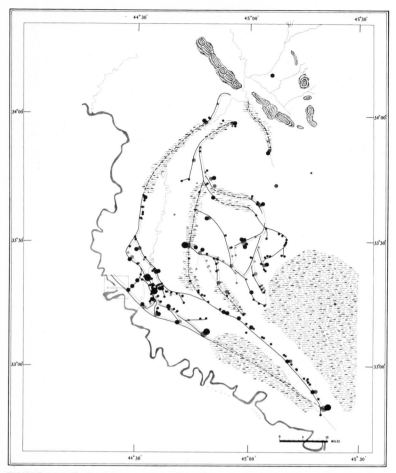

FIGURE 28.1 Early watercourses and settlements in the Diyala region. The system shown in grey was in use during the Early Dynastic period, about 3000–2400 B.C. Sites and watercourses shown in black, slightly displaced so that the earlier pattern will remain visible, were occupied during the Old Babylonian period, about 1800–1700 B.C. In this and subsequent figures, size of circle marking an ancient settlement is roughly proportional to the area of its ruins. Modern river courses are shown in grey.

third and early second millennium B.C. (Figure 28.1) with the prevailing pattern of about A.D. 500 (Figure 28.2) these developments can be seen in sharply contrasting form. They may be summarized conveniently by distinguishing two successive phases of settlement and irrigation, each operating in a different ecological background and each facing problems of sedimentation of a different character and magnitude.

The earlier phase persisted longest. Char-

acterized by a linear pattern of settlements largely confined to the banks of major watercourses, it began with the onset of agricultural life in the Ubaid period (about 4000 B.C.) and was replaced only during the final centuries of the pre-Christian era. In all essentials the same network of watercourses was in use throughout this long time-span, and the absence of settlement along periodically shifting side branches seems to imply an irrigation regime in which the water was not drawn great distances inland from the main watercourses. Under these circumstances, silt accumulation would not have been the serious problem to the agriculturalist that it later became. The short branch canals upon which irrigation depended could have been cleaned easily or even replaced without the necessary intervention of a powerful, centralized authority. Quite possibly most irrigation during this phase depended simply on uncontrolled flooding through breaches cut

in the levees of watercourses (like the lower Mississippi River) flowing well above plain level.

It is apparent from the map in Figure 28.1 that large parts of the area were unoccupied by settled cultivators even during the periods of maximum population and prosperity that have been selected for illustration therein. An extended, historical study of soil profiles would be necessary to provide explanations for these uninhabited zones, but it is not

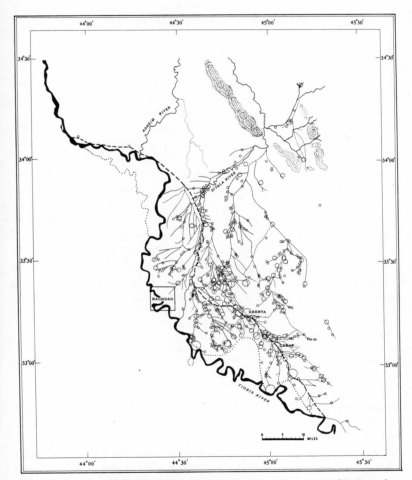

FIGURE 28.2 Maximum extent of settlement and irrigation in the Diyala region. All canals shown by lines with minute serrations were in use during the Sassanian period, A.D. 226–637. However, expansion to the full limits came only with construction of the Nahrwan Canal (shown as a dashed black line) late in the period. Settlements shown as black circles are also of Sassanian date. The different course probably followed in places by the Tigris River during the Sassanian period is suggested by black dotted lines.

unreasonable to suppose that some were seasonal swamps and depressions of the kind described above, while others were given over to desert because they were slightly elevated and hence not subject to easy flooding and irrigation. Still others probably were permanent swamps, since it is difficult to account in any other way for the discontinuities in settlement that appear along stretches of some watercourses. One indication of the ecological shift which took place in succeeding millennia is that permanent swamps today have virtually disappeared from the entire northern half of the alluvium.

Considering the proportion of occupied to unoccupied area, the total population of the Diyala basin apparently was never very large during this long initial phase. Instead, a moderately dense population was confined to small regional enclaves or narrow, isolated strips along the major watercourses; for the rest of the area there can have been only very small numbers of herdsmen, hunters, fishermen, and marginal catch-crop cultivators. It is significant that most of the individual settlements were small villages, and that even the dominant political centers in the area are more aptly described as towns rather than cities (4).

An essential feature of the earlier pattern of occupation, although not shown in a summary map like Figure 28.1, is its fluctuating character. There is good historical evidence that devastating cycles of abandonment affected the whole alluvium. The wide and simultaneous onset of these cycles soon after relatively peaceful and prosperous times suggests that they proceeded from sociopolitical, rather than natural, causes, but at any rate their effects can be seen clearly in the Diyala region. For example, the numerous Old Babylonian settlements shown in Figure 28.1 had been reduced in number by more than 80 percent within 500 years following, leaving only small outposts scattered at wide intervals along watercourses which previously had been thickly settled. An earlier abandonment, not long after the Early Dynastic period that is shown in gray in Figure 28.1, was shorter-lived and possibly affected the

main towns more than the outlying small villages. Village life in general, it may be observed, remains pretty much of an enigma in the ancient Orient for all "historical" periods.

Under both ancient and modern Mesopotamian conditions, a clear distinction between "canals" and "rivers" if frequently meaningless or impossible. If the former are large and are allowed to run without control they can develop a "natural" regime in spite of their artificial origin. Some river courses, on the other hand, can be maintained only by straightening, desilting, and other artificial measures. Nevertheless, it needs to be stressed that the reconstructed watercourses shown in Figure 28.2 followed essentially natural regimes and that at least their origins had little or nothing to do with human intervention. They were, in the first place, already present during the initial occupation of the area by prehistoric village agriculturalists who lacked the numbers and organization to dig them artificially. Secondly, the same watercourses persisted for more than three millennia with little change, even through periods of abandonment when they could not have received the maintenance which canals presuppose. Finally, the whole network of these early rivers describes a "braided stream" pattern which contrasts sharply with the brachiating canal systems of all later times, which are demonstrably artificial.

Specific features of the historic geography of the area are not within the compass of this article, but it should be noted that the ancient topography differed substantially from the modern. Particularly interesting is the former course of the Diyala River, flowing west of its present position and joining the Tigris River (apparently also not in its modern course) though a delta-like series of mouths. A branch that bifurcated from the former Diyala above its "delta" and flowed off for a long distance to the southeast before joining the Tigris has been identified tentatively as the previously unlocated "River Dabban" that is referred to in ancient cuneiform sources.

The pattern of occupation illustrated in

Figure 28.2 began to emerge in Achaementian times (539–331 B.C.), after nearly 1000 years of stagnation and abandonment. Perhaps the pace of reoccupation quickened with the conquest of Mesopotamia by Alexander, but the density of population reached during much older periods was attained again, and then surpassed, only in the subsequent Parthian period (about 150 B.C.-A.D. 226). New settlements large enough to be described as true cities, on the other hand, were introduced to the area for the first time by Alexander's Macedonian followers—demonstrating, if doubt could otherwise exist, that the onset of urbanization depends more on historical and cultural factors than on a simple increase in population density.

A central feature of this second phase of settlement is the far more complete exploitation of available land and water resources for agriculture. There is some evidence that the irrigation capacity of the Diyala River was being utilized fully even before the end of the Parthian period, and yet both the proportion of land that was cultivated and the total population rose substantially further, reaching their maxima in this area, for any period, under the Sassanian dynasty (A.D. 226–637) that followed. A rough estimate of the total agricultural production in the area first becomes possible with records of tax collections under the early Abbasids, perhaps 300 years after the maximum limits of expansion shown in Figure 28.2 had been reached. From a further calculation of the potentially cultivable land it can then be shown that (with alternate years in fallow and assuming average yields) virtually the entire cultivable area must have been cropped regularly under both the Sassanians and early Abbasids.

Increased population, the growth of urban centers, and expansion in the area of cultivation to its natural limits were linked in turn to an enlargement of the irrigation system on an unprecedented scale. It was necessary, in the first place, to crisscross formerly unused desert and depression areas with a complex—and entirely artificial—brachiating system of branch canals, which is outlined in Figure 28.2. Expansion depended also on the construction of a large, supplementary feeder canal from the Tigris which, with technical proficiency that still excites admiration, and without apparent regard for cost, brought the indispensable, additional water through a hard, conglomerate headland, across two rivers, and thence down the wide levee left by the Dabban River of antiquity. Enough survives of the Nahrwan Canal, as the lower part of this gigantic system was called, even to play a key part in modern irrigation planning. Excavations carried out by the Diyala Basin Archeological Project at one of several known weirs along the 300-kilometer course of this canal provided a forceful illustration not only of the scale of the system but also of the attention lavished on such ancillary works as thousands of brick sluice gates along its branches. In short, we are dealing here with a whole new conception of irrigation which undertook boldly to reshape the physical environment at a cost which could be met only with the full resources of a powerful and highly centralized state (5).

In spite of its unrivaled engineering competence, there were a number of undesirable consequences of the new irrigation regime. For example, to a far greater degree than had been true earlier, it utilized long branch canals which tended to fill rapidly with silt because of their small-to-moderate slope and cross-sectional area. Only the Nahrwan Canal itself—and that only during the first two centuries or so of its existence—seems to have maintained its bed without frequent and costly cleaning. Salt banks left from Parthian, Sassanian, and Islamic canal cleaning are today a major topographic feature not only in the Diyala region but all over the northern part of the Mesopotamian alluvium; frequently they run for great distances and tower over all but the highest mounds built up by ancient towns and cities. Or again, while massive control installations were essential if such a complex and interdependent system was to operate effectively, they needed periodic reconstruction at great cost (six major phases at the weir excavated by the Divala Project) and practically continuous maintenance. Moreover, the provi-

sion of control works of all sizes acted together with the spreading networks of canal
branches and subbranches to reduce or eliminate flood surges which otherwise might
have contributed to the desilting process.

None of these consequences, to be sure,
vitiated the advantages to be obtained with
the new type of irrigation *so long as there
remained a strong central authority committed
to its maintenance.* But with conditions of
social unrest and a preoccupation on the part
of the political authorities with military adventures and intrigues, the maintenance of
the system could only fall back on local communities ill equipped to handle it. These
circumstances prevailed fairly briefly in late
Sassanian times, leading to a widespread but

temporary abandonment of the area. After
an Islamic revival, they occurred again in the
11th and 12th centuries A.D., accompanied
by such storm signals of political decay as
the calculated breaching of the Nahrwan
during a military campaign. On this occasion there was no quick recovery; it still
remains for the modern Iraqis to re-establish
the prosperity for which the region once was
noted.

A closer look at the role of sedimentation
along the Nahrwan during the years of political crisis under the later Abbasids is given
in Figure 28.3. In the first illustrated phase,
in late Sassanian times, irrigation water was
drawn from the Nahrwan at fairly uniform
intervals and applied almost directly to fields

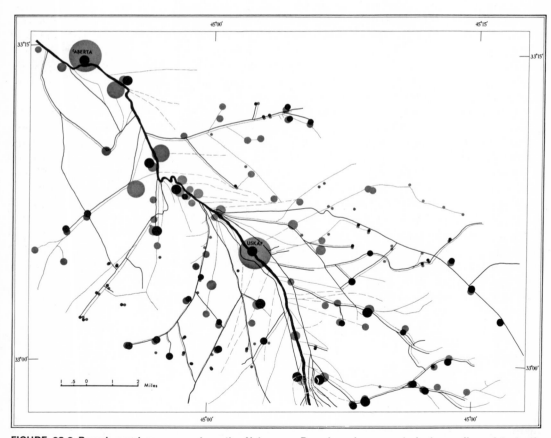

**FIGURE 28.3 Branch canal sequence along the Nahrwan. Branches shown as dashed grey lines date to the
later Sassanian period (about A.D. 500–637). Settlements shown as grey circles and branch canals shown as
continuous grey lines belong to the Early Islamic and Samarran periods, prior to about A.D. 900. Settlements and
branch canals shown in black are those in use during the final phase of irrigation in the lower Nahrwan district,
about A.D. 1100. The weir excavated by the project was located at the junction of numerous branch canals
northwest of the city of Uskaf.**

adjoining its course. During a second phase, roughly coinciding with the rise of the Abbasid caliphate, irrigation water tended to be drawn off further upstream from the field for which it was destined. This is best exemplified by the increasing importance of the weir as a source for branch canals serving a considerable area. For some distance below the weir the level of the Nahrwan apparently no longer was sufficient to furnish irrigation water above the level of the fields.

By the time of the final phase, soon after A.D. 1100, practically all irrigation in the very large region below the weir had come to depend on branch canals issuing from above it; it is worth noting that two of the largest and most important of these branches simply paralleled the Nahrwan along each bank for more than 20 kilometers. The same unsuccessful struggle to maintain irrigation control is shown by the shrinkage or disappearance of town and city life along the main canal and the depopulation of the initial 5 to 10 kilometers along each major branch issuing from it, while lower-lying communities at the distal ends of the branches continued to flourish.

This cumulative change in the character of the system probably was a consequence of both natural and social factors. On the one hand, silt deposition had raised the level of the fields by almost 1 meter over a 500-year period. Since the natural mechanisms for maintaining equilibrium between the bed of a watercourse and its alluvial levee were largely inoperative in such a complex and carefully controlled system, this rise in land surface may have reduced considerably the level of water available for irrigation purposes. At the same time, inadequate maintenance and subsequent siltation of the Nahrwan's own bed in time sharply reduced its flow and surely also reduced the head of water it could provide to its branches. But whatever the responsible factors were, the result was an especially disastrous one. At a time when the responsibility of the central government for irrigation was eroding away and when population had been reduced substantially by warfare and by prolonged disruption of the water supply, the heavy burden of desilting branch canals remained constant or even increased for the local agriculturalist. If the accumulation of silt was no more than a minor problem at the beginning of irrigation in the Diyala basin 5000 years earlier, by the late Abbasid period it had become perhaps the greatest single obstacle that a quite different irrigation regime had to deal with.

With the converging effects of mounting maintenance requirements on the one hand, and declining capacity for more than rudimentary maintenance tasks on the other, the virtual desertion of the lower Diyala area that followed assumes in retrospect a kind of historical inevitability. By the middle of the 12th century most of the Nahrwan region already was abandoned. Only a trickle of water passed down the upper section of the main canal to supply a few dying towns in the now hostile desert. Invading Mongol horsemen under Hulagu Khan, who first must have surveyed this devastated scene a century later, have been unjustly blamed for causing it ever since.

References and Notes

1. The Diyala Basin Archeological Project was conducted jointly by the Oriental Institute of the University of Chicago and the Iraq Directorate General of Antiquities, on a grant from the First Technical Section of the Development Board. It was directed by one of us (T. J.), with the other (R. M. A.) and Sayyid Fuad Safar, of the Directorate General of Antiquities, as associate directors. Excavations were under the supervision of Sayyid Mohammed Ali Mustafa, also of the Directorate General of Antiquities. Field studies of paleobotanical remains were undertaken in association with the project by Dr. Hans Helback, of the National Museum, Copenhagen, Denmark. Intensive study of the cuneiform and Arabic textual sources on agriculture was made possible through the collaboration of scholars of many countries. Especial thanks for assistance to the field program in Iraq, and for advice in the interpretation of its results, are due to Mr. K. F. Vernon, H. E. Dr. Naji al-Asil, Dr. J. C. Russel, and Sayyid Adnan Hardan.

2. R. M. Adams, *Sumer*, in press.
3. A preliminary application of this approximate methodology to conditions prevailing in Iraq was introduced by one of us (T. J.) in the Diyala basin in 1936–37, and the results of that earlier survey have been incorporated in the present study. Fortunately for the archeologist, there is sufficient disturbance from routine community activities (for example, foundation, well, and grave digging, and mud-brick manufacture, and so forth) for some traces of even the earliest of a long sequence of occupational periods to be detected on a mound's surface.
4. Partial town plans for the political capital of the region at Tel Asmar (ancient Eshnunna) and for two other slightly smaller centers are available from extensive Oriental Institute excavations carried out in the Diyala region between 1930 and 1937. See P. Delougaz, *The Temple Oval at Khafaja* [Oriental Inst. Publ. 53 (Univ. of Chicago Press, Chicago, 1940)]; P. Delougaz and S. Lloyd, *Pre-Sargonid Temples in the Diyala Region* [Oriental Inst. Publ. 58 (Univ. of Chicago Press, Chicago, 1942)]; and H. Frankfort, *Stratified Cylinder Seals from the Diyala Region* [Oriental Inst. Publ. 72 (Univ. of Chicago Press, Chicago, 1955), plates 93–96. For recent general overviews of the history and culture of the earlier periods, see A. Falkenstein "La cité-temple Sumérienne" [*Cahiers d'Histoire Mondiale* 1 (1954)] and T. Jacobsen, "Early political developments in Mesopotamia" [*Z. für Assyriologie* (N.F.) 18 (1957)].
5. General accounts of political, social, and cultural conditions in Mesopotamia during the Persian dynasties and under the Caliphate are to be found in R. Ghirshman, *Iran* (Pelican, Harmondsworth, Middlesex, England, 1954) and P. K. Hitti, *History of the Arabs* (Macmillan, London, ed. 6, 1956).

ADDITIONAL REFERENCES

Boyko, H., and E. Boyko. 1964. Principles and experiments regarding direct irrigation with highly saline and sea water without desalination. *N. Y. Acad. Sci., Trans.*, ser. 2, 26:1087–1102.

Cantor, L. M. 1970. *A world geography of irrigation*. New York: Praeger. 252 pp.

Eaton, F. M. 1935. Boron in soils and irrigation waters and its effects on plants with particular reference to the San Joaquin Valley of California. *U.S. Department of Agriculture, Technical Bulletin* 448:1–131.

Glymph, L. M., and H. C. Storey. 1967. Sediment—Its consequences and control. Pp. 205–220 in *Agriculture and the quality of our environment*, ed. by N. C. Brady. Washington, D.C.: Amer. Assoc. Adv. Sci., Publ. 85.

Leopold, L. B. 1956. Land use and sediment yield. Pp. 639–647 in *Man's role in changing the face of the earth*, ed. by William L. Thomas, Jr. Chicago and London: The University of Chicago Press.

Longenecker, D. E., and P. J. Lyerly. 1959. *Some relations among irrigation water quality, soil characteristics and management practices in the Trans-Pecos area*. Texas Agricultural Experiment Station, Miscellaneous Publication 373.

Marsh, G. P. 1864. *Man and nature*. Irrigation and its climatic and geographical effects, pp. 311–325 in 1964 edition, ed. by David Lowenthal. Cambridge, Mass.: Belknap Press.

Mink, J. F. 1962. Excessive irrigation and the soils and ground water of Oahu, Hawaii. *Science* 135:672–673.

Navone, R., J. A. Harmon, and C. F. Voyles. 1963. Nitrogen content of ground water in Southern California. *J. Am. Water Works Assoc.* 55:615–618.

Russell, E. W. 1961. *Soil conditions and plant growth*. 9th edition. New York: Wiley. See especially chapter 23, The management of irrigated and saline and alkali soils, pp. 603–619.

Stewart, B. A., F. G. Viets, Jr., and G. L. Hutchinson. 1968. Agriculture's effect on nitrate pollution of groundwater. *Journal of Soil and Water Conservation* 23(1):13–15.

Thorne, D. W., and H. B. Peterson. 1954. *Irrigated soils, their fertility and management*. 2d ed. New York: The Blakiston Co. 392 pp.

Thorne, W., and H. B. Peterson. 1967. Salinity in United States waters. Pp. 221–240 in *Agriculture and the quality of our environment*, ed. by N. C. Brady. Washington, D.C.: Amer. Assoc. Adv. Sci., Publ. 85.

UNESCO. 1961. *Salinity problems in the arid zones. Proceedings of the Teheran symposium*. Paris: UNESCO. Arid Zone Research, 14. 395 pp.

U.S. Salinity Laboratory. 1954. Diagnosis and improvement of saline and alkali soils. *U.S. Department of Agriculture, Handbook 60*.

Wittfogel, K. A. 1956. The hydraulic civilizations. Pp. 152–164 in *Man's role in changing the face of the earth*, ed. by William L. Thomas, Jr. Chicago and London: The University of Chicago Press.

PHYSICAL, CHEMICAL, AND BIOCHEMICAL CHANGES IN THE SOIL COMMUNITY
WILLIAM A. ALBRECHT

Man is the most important product of soils—indirectly through our food chains. Man also profoundly changes the substratum on which he depends. Many of these changes make the soil less useful and productive. Despite a long human history of soil modification, both destructive and constructive, soil scientists have only recently begun to study the importance of man as an agent of soil change (e.g., Bidwell and Hale, 1965; Yaalon and Yaron, 1966). Rather, soil has generally been considered to be the product of five "natural" factors of formation (parent material, climate, vegetation, topography, and time), excluding man's activities.

The importance of soil to man lies in its functions as a reservoir of nutrients and as a medium of nutrient exchange. These nutrients, which include air and water, are essential for plant growth. Any action that impedes or prevents the provision of useful soil nutrients to crops is detrimental to agriculture. Types of physical interference by man include acceleration of soil erosion (Leopold, 1956), siltation over productive soils (see Selection 28), and removal of land from agriculture for urbanization, roads, airports, rights-of-way, etc. Each year the United States loses about 1 million acres (much of it first-class farmland) to these uses, while gaining 2 to 3 million domestic consumers of agricultural products.

Man-induced chemical changes in soils include excess salt accumulation from irrigation water (see Selection 28), from fertilizer use, and from air pollution (see Selection 37), and contamination by foreign

William A. Albrecht (b. 1888) is emeritus professor of soils and former chairman of the department of soils at the University of Missouri, where he has been a member of the faculty since 1916. He holds four degrees from the University of Illinois (Ph.D., 1919). In addition to his soils studies in the United States, he has conducted research in Europe and Australia. Many of Albrecht's publications have stressed the relation of soil fertility to human nutrition and the need for proper soil treatment to ensure healthy life. Still active in research, his current interest is desert soils and the problem of their calcium deficiency for plant nutrition.

substances.   The variety, and in most cases amounts, of soil pollutants have increased in recent years: pesticides to kill both plants and animals (see Selections 38 to 42), polyethylene and petroleum mulches, radionuclides, and toxic elements.   Radioactive fallout is of concern because of its possible eventual incorporation in human food, although the amounts have declined greatly since the reduction of atmospheric atomic detonations in the early 1960s.   Radionuclides are washed from the atmosphere into soil by precipitation.   Strontium-90 and cesium-137 are most threatening because of their sizable quantities, longer half-lives (twenty-eight years and twenty-seven years, respectively), and incorporation into food chains.   Strontium-90 acts like calcium and is taken up by plants and, from them, by the human body.   Similarly, cesium-137 behaves like potassium and becomes incorporated in human muscle. Toxic nonradioactive elements may be inadvertently introduced into soil with fertilizers.   Superphosphates, for example, often contain traces of harmful substances, such as arsenic, boron, fluorine, and uranium, which may concentrate in soil and in plants.

Many of these effects of man on the soil community have become pronounced only in the last few years and hence do not receive much emphasis in this selection, written fifteen years ago.   However, this selection by an eminent soil scientist reveals and explains the complex, interwoven fabric of relations between man's agricultural practices and physical, chemical, and biochemical changes in the soil system.   Albrecht documents the processes which have led him to conclude that "American agriculture is producing bulk and sacrificing quality, and we are paying for it in our own health as well as in the health of our plants and animals."

(Editor's comment)

For generations, the conquest of Nature has been accepted as man's prerogative.   But man is a part of Nature, it being his essential environment, and unless he can find his rightful place in it he has poor hope of survival.   Man's present behavior often resembles that of an over-successful parasite which, in killing its host, accomplishes also its own death.

Man's environment is the whole natural scene, the earth with its soil and water, its plants and its animals.   In many places these have reached a natural balance which man disturbs at his peril.   C. L. Boyle, "Mother Earth," *Journal of the Soil Association*, VIII (1954), 3.

Introduction

If we accept a state of natural balance, or a kind of momentary equilibrium, in the soil community at that date in its geological de-velopment when man arrived on any particular virgin scene, then man may well be viewed as a force upsetting that equilibrium. Since the soil is a temporary interlude for rocks and minerals on their way to solution and to the sea—in suspension if not in solution—man's activities in working the soil hasten the traverse by rocks from their higher potential energies and chemical dynamics to lower ones.

INCREASING POPULATIONS AND SOIL CONSERVATION—A PARADOX

Man's survival in a situation in which he can be fed only by means of rocks and minerals en route to the sea appears to be a paradox. Those rocks must be put into solution.   Their nutrient elements must be extracted from stable mineral forms.   They must be brought into ionic activity in solutions if they are to be adsorbed into the soil colloidal complex and to be held there for exchange to the roots of plants upon which animals and men feed. Yet, in our concern with conservation, especially of the soil, we are apt to believe that rocks should not be allowed to weather and thus go into solution and into the sea. However, only by this dynamic behavior of rocks and minerals can life-forms survive on earth. This is a fact that cannot be gainsaid.

Soil conservation, to some degree, can reduce excessive movements to the sea of the nutrient elements after they enter into the ionic activities of solution. Under virgin conditions the minerals weathering within the soil are not moved hastily to the sea. Instead, they are quickly taken up by soil microbes and by plant roots. The accumulated organic matter resulting within and on top of the soil serves as a microbial diet of excess energy food, holding the microbial population down to the levels of the supplies of more soluble inorganic elements and nitrogen. Soluble inorganic elements are always quickly taken out of solution and made insoluble in the microbial and plant cells. Thereby, not much of the virgin soil and of

its active chemical contents is on its way to the sea. Continuous plant cover, even in the humid regions with much water going into the soil, does not result in speedy soil depletion (Figure 29.1). Neither is there a rapid soil erosion. The rates of solubles and suspensions going to sea are low.

Man must increase the rate of mineral solution if he is to feed himself. But his neglect of conservation of those soluble elements has increased the rate of their passage into the sea through erosion, sewage disposal, and other ways. Man, in changing the face of the earth, has altered the soil community by moving it, both directly and indirectly, more rapidly into the sea. It is in this respect that "man's . . . behavior . . . resembles that of an oversuccessful parasite." While exploiting his soils, man is destroying his host and accomplishing slowly his own death.

The speed of these changes in the soil community brought on by man is astounding. As Sears puts it (1954, p. 959):

> The earth as a separate planet is at least 2000, perhaps 3000, million years old.* The species

---

* Isotopic dating now indicates that the age of the earth's crust is c. 4,500 million years (*editor's note*).

FIGURE 29.1 Excessive erosion—man-wrought. Erosion is a symptom of a fertility level of the surface soil too low to grow cover equal to the stresses and strains of the falling rain and runoff water.

of mammal to which we belong has been present for only the last 30 seconds of the 24th hour of the earth's existence, while modern power technology based on fossil fuel compares with a very fast instantaneous snapshot. For the first time in earth history, a single species has become dominant, and we are it. The power and intensity of our pressure upon environment is without precedent. Our numbers increase at the net rate—conservatively—of 1 per cent a year.* This means a net gain of more than 50,000 a day, doubling in a generation. This also means increasing demand for space in which to live and move, and increasing demand for food and other necessities from the space that is left.

Physical Changes Due to Man's Activities

MORE SOIL FOR SITE VALUE, LESS FOR FOOD SERVICES

Urban man—85 per cent of the population in the United States—now uses much soil exclusively for sites on which to live and move. The remaining space on which to produce food and other biotic necessities for everyone is occupied by only 15 per cent of that population—the rural folk. In the recent shift from a rural family to an urban crowd, man has lost sight of the significance of the biological behavior and services of the soil community as our food source. With emphasis on economics, technologies, and industries, he has built big cities on soil and so exploited its site value only. The soil community has had the attention of agricultural and chemical technologies to make it more highly productive per farm operator or to hasten the rocks and minerals into solution, so as to be potentially creative of more crops and more livestock. The higher agricultural efficiency per farm worker has, in turn, made possible the urban congestion where, as the Indian said, "You ought to put a town here; nothing will grow here." Now we must soon face the dilemma of feeding ourselves on paved streets, because the rural soil community is about to be the dead victim of a

* Probably closer to a 2 percent yearly increase at present (see Selection 4). (*Editor's note*)

parasitic, technical soil exploitation that has failed to appreciate the biological aspect of the soils in the creative business of feeding all of us. It is time that more of us paid attention to the physical, chemical, and biochemical changes wrought by man in the soil community, for soils represent either assets or liabilities for man's survival.

Physical changes which cultivated soils undergo are not sudden and readily recognized, save for occasional landslides or natural flooding-in of sands or of deposits of clay on top of the soil. Such coverings add new horizons to the top of the profile, making for abrupt transitions in texture and other properties between the top horizons. These are decided hindrances to plant root-feeding and to root penetration, and they put much soil out of cultivation. The physical changes in soils over long periods of cultivation by man are not so sudden. Rather, the changes are more insidious, with no suddenly visible symptoms of the transformation.

Man has been covering soil not only with cities but with connecting highways of concrete, to remove much soil entirely from potential food production. Alongside the soil covered by concrete, there is the right of way serving as shoulders and as drainage ditches. When a two-lane highway parallels a railroad, as is common when the railroad's location represents past experience in judicious grade selections, a strip of land as much as 25 rods wide is taken out of food production by agriculture. This represents 50 acres for every mile of such transportation facilities.

Much of our soil area is also being blotted out of service in food production by expanding urbanization. Urbanites are moving into rural areas around the cities to an increasing extent, owing to the automobile, which makes possible long commuting distances. This expansion does not represent a "back to the soil" movement aimed toward independent agricultural production by families contributing to city food supplies as well as providing their own. On the contrary, covering the soil by more urban expansion, more parking spaces, more airports, more military reservations, more defense plants, more industrial developments, and more superhighways represents a decided physical change in the soil community brought on by man. Instead of growing vegetation, loading itself with organic matter, and breaking down its rock content—the whole forming the active assembly line of food creation—the soil is shorn of this biological service and represents no more than site value. This physical change of the soil community is now one of geometric dimension and no longer one of arithmetic dimensions only.

TILLAGE MEANS LESS CONSTRUCTION, MORE DESTRUCTION OF THE SOIL

Putting virgin soil under cultivation initiates a breakdown of what may be called the "body" of the soil. Virgin soil, when plowed, takes on a granular body which only slowly slakes out under successive rains. The granular units of soil have a remarkable stability. They do not pack together under machinery traveling over the soil. The entrance of air in consequence of tillage starts microbial decay action. There is an increase in the carbon dioxide released. Runoff of rain water is slow and, instead, the rainfall filters in readily. Significant amounts of water are stored in the greater depths of the profile to support vegetative growth over extended rain-free periods.

It was this character of granular yet stable body by which the pioneer judged the potential productivity of the land when he took a handful of soil, allowed it to run between his fingers, and said, "This will be a good place to farm."

The shift in our soils to a body which rainfall disperses readily is a major physical change in the soil community. Continuously cultivated soils, when plowed and mechanically put under granular form by tillage machinery, are quickly hammered by the rainfall into surface slush. This seals the pores and prevents rapid infiltration of water. Water that would be beneficial were it stored in the soil is compelled to run off and represents not only loss of water but also a force for

serious erosion of the surface, the very place where maximum returns and additions of organic residues are always made by nature to maintain potential productivity. Thus the advent of increased erosion, about which we have recently become concerned, is merely evidence of the previous breakdown of the soil body (Figure 29.2).

This breakdown or degeneration of the soil body is not, however, a physical change alone. Rather it is the physical manifestation of chemical and bio-chemical changes which the soil suffers under tillage. It is the reverse of the soil construction under virgin conditions. The chemical force bringing about granulation of significant stability is exercised by salts of the divalent cations like calcium and magnesium, or even by the trivalent and multivalent ones. The monovalent ones, like hydrogen, sodium, potassium, and others adsorbed on the clay colloid, have quite the opposite effect, that is, they are dispersing agents rather than granulating and flocculating ones. The loss of fertility salts through crop removal, and by water percolating through the soil where increased decay under tillage has given more carbon dioxide and more acidity for their removal, represents more dispersion. Thus, granulating agencies are replaced by dispersing ones, and the soil is consequently shifted from a physically stable body to an unstable one and from one that takes water and has little erosion to one taking little water and having much erosion.

Another chemical change acting as cause for the decreasing physical stability of the granular structure is the loss of much of the organic matter originally in the virgin soil. Tillage of the soil serves to fan the microbial fires burning out carbon and leaving instead inorganic ash of past generations of dead plants. This seasonal provision of ash by decay is the means for growing large crops. A rising delivery rate of such ash, running parallel with the advance of the growing season and with the mounting temperatures, is nature's way of providing more nourishment for the growing crop in synchronization with its increasing demands. This represents a uniquely co-ordinated set of processes.

FIGURE 29.2 Unreplenished cultivated soil contrasted with soil regularly replenished. Man's continuous cropping breaks the soil down chemically and physically to where nature fails to grow cover (upper right), and a single rain puts the plowed soil into slush (lower right). Similar cropping and manure returned regularly give the soil winter cover (upper left) and a granular structure holding the plow-turned form under rain (lower left).

This inorganic part of the soil organic matter must continue in its cycle of decay, incorporation into the new growing plants, return to the soil, and then decay again if crops are to be grown continually.

We could not expect to keep virgin organic matter preserved in the soil indefinitely. Its decay is a requisite for agricultural production. But more organic matter must always be returned and incorporated if production is to be maintained. Organic matter manifests pronounced physical effects on the soil in bringing about granular structure, but these are the results of chemical effects by both the inorganic and the organic components of the soil. The desirable physical condition of the soil is a matter not only of a fine physique. Rather is it also one of nutrition of the plants grown on that soil, of nutritional support for the fungal and bacterial crops within the soil, of the suite of inorganic nutrient elements required by the growing vegetation, and of the regular incorporation of organic matter into the soil by which alone this condition is maintained.

A physical change, this one consequent on cultivation, in the soils of humid regions is the increase in clay content of profiles when the top of the profile is truncated by erosion and when the successive cultivations cut more deeply into the lower horizon of higher clay concentrations. As a result of the truncation of the profile the physical condition gradually shifts to one of more clay (Figure 29.3). Since the deeper horizons, or the more acid sub-soils, are less fertile in both inorganic and organic essentials, the top layer gradually becomes not only less tillable because of the high clay content but also less productive. If this increase in clay content were an addition of a more fertile or less weathered clay, then the gradual change would be an asset rather than a liability (Figure 29.3). Potentially, the more clay, the more active fertility than can be held. It was on the fertile clay soils of some parts of the Old World, intrac-

FIGURE 29.3 Rate of soybean growth in soils containing varying amounts of clay. More clay (left to right in sand in glass containers) with more adsorptive capacity to hold calcium for the soybean roots gave more and healthier plants. Soils "heavy" in clay have supported crops longest under cultivation.

table and difficult to cultivate though they may have been, that agricultures survived longest (Figure 29.4).

SOIL MOISTURE REQUIRED FOR IONIC ACTIVITIES THAT NOURISH PLANTS

One of the physical conditions of the soil required for its proper tillage is the presence of water. Water is required in a physico-chemical setting for the ionic activities of the nutrient elements and for their entrance into the plant roots, into the microbial cells, and into the other living forms within the soil. It is in the aqueous atmosphere, or the very thin film of water, surrounding the colloidal clay particles that the chemodynamics of the nutrient elements occur. It is in that limited area that the positively charged elements like calcium, magnesium, potassium, sodium, hydrogen, and others—when once broken out of the rock and put into solution—are held rather than lost to the water passing through the soil. It is within that atmosphere,

FIGURE 29.4 Tillage of clay soils in France. Heavy clay soils in the Old World (France) require much power for tillage but have supported agriculture over the many years.

blended into the corresponding colloidal atmosphere of the root hair enshrouded by its hydrogen carbonate, that the root exchanges its very active hydrogen for any of the list of the clay's nutrient cations just cited. Water is then the ionizing medium required in any fertile soil so that its nutrient salts may be active suites of many essentials serving in proper nutrition of different plant species.

Fertile soils must contain the salts in the presence of water if the electrical performances of exchange between the root and the soil are to occur. As an interesting and suggestive illustration, there is in the United States a close similarity between the areas of maximum concentration of farming and of high efficiency of radio reception (Figure 29.5). Areas of excessive soil moisture are neither good for farming nor good for radio reception. Such soils are too highly developed, and their fertility salts are too nearly washed out. While arid soils contain plenty of salts for radio reception—though not necessarily in the proper combination for concentrated general farming—they do not contain enough moisture to serve together with air to complete an electrical circuit when the radio switch is turned.

DROUGHTS ARE BECOMING MORE DISASTROUS

Man has changed decidedly the high degrees of fluctuation against which the moisture content of the surface soils was once maintained. For the pioneer farmer in the eastern United States, water in excess, or standing water, was the problem. He concerned himself seriously with drainage, in order to allow air to enter the soil and the sun's heat to raise its temperature for crop production. Now that we have cleared the land so that little permanent plant cover is left to hold the water where it falls, we have unwittingly moved into excessive drainage. Hasty runoff by water cuts small rills into our barren soils, and each is soon the equivalent of a drainage ditch. Our land areas, now cut up into smaller units, make each owner thereof an opponent of standing water,

scarcely permitting it to stand long enough for infiltration sufficient to provide water for crops from one rain to the next.

Our hydrophobia is exhibited by the drainage ditch alongside every highway and roadway draining each unit of land area. All-weather roads to fulfil automobilist demands have encircled about every section, however small, of productive land. Those drainage ditches, dug to depths of three or more feet around a square mile, have lowered the water table to nearly that extent. They have literally lifted the soil that much higher out of contact with the water table. This is desiccating our soil and our country. Roots are not nourished by a dry soil, and we are bringing the deserts around ourselves by hastening the drying of the surface soil. Unfortunately, that soil layer so highly dried is also the soil horizon to which both man and nature are most regularly adding and returning the fertility elements so as to maintain production.

Man's excessive drainage and change of soil conditions under which less water enters the profile to store itself are the reasons why there is less water to evaporate and so hold down summer temperatures, which, consequently, rise to record-breaking figures year by year. Our drought disasters have pushed themselves eastward into the national treasury, while the western deserts are on a rapid march eastward, too.

SHORTAGE OF STORED WATER IS INCREASING

That the deserts are on the march, because man has been changing the earth to absorb less water from rainfall, is a physical phenomenon with significant chemical and biochemical consequences. Temperature falls when the evaporation of a gram of water spends 540 calories of heat, but that reduction of temperature fails to take place when there is no soil water to evaporate. Consequently, the thermometer climbs to the disaster point for plants and animals. This amounts to giving us record-breaking heat waves, commonly characterized by the broad term "drought," as if it were a matter wholly

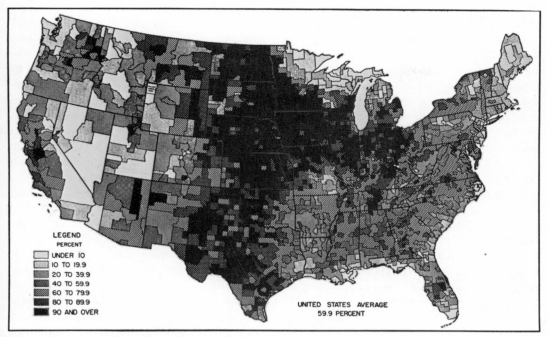

FIGURE 29.5a Land in farms in the United States, 1945.

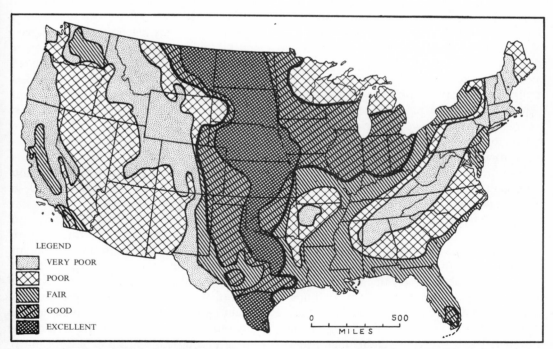

FIGURE 29.5b Ground conductivity in the United States. The higher concentration of farms in the mid-continent and the higher efficiency of radio reception there are both the result of the higher concentration of chemical dynamics in the soil by which, respectively, larger crops are grown and the soil is a better conductor.

of weather when we are bringing it on ourselves.

Droughts are not just rain-free periods. They cannot be defined from standard meteorological observations, since the intensity and the length of the drought depend on characteristics of crops, soil water, and soil-fertility conditions as well as on meteorological parameters. Consequently, we need to recognize the soil as a major factor in those disturbances to crops which we call "droughts." These are in reality dry periods that bring about crop disaster through chemical and biochemical irregularities.

Since water's services to plants are exercised mainly after rain water has entered the soil, the soil should be considered more than merely a water reservoir. The many services of water to crops need to be understood before we use water shortage as the alibi for poor crops.

CONTINENTAL EFFECTS OF CLIMATE ARE BECOMING MORE SEVERE

The areas between the humid and the semiarid soil regions are the climatic settings for most droughts. In general, these are regions of mineral-rich soils, since low rainfall has not developed them excessively or removed the calcium and other minerals of similar soil behavior from the profile to replace them by hydrogen. These are the soils where agriculture grows protein-rich forages, where soils are windblown, and where animals grow readily on what are apt to be called "the prairie and the plains soils."

Droughts are also geographically located in the midst of larger land areas where the effects of what is called "continentality" are pronounced. This represents the degree of variability of the weather or the daily meteorological condition. The larger the body of land, that is, the more continental the area, the more the weather or the daily condition will vary from the climate or average. This is the "law of continentality" in brief. Droughts, then, are "continental" manifestations and may be expected more commonly in the mid-continent of the United States.

Columbia, Missouri, for example, is reported to have an annual rainfall of 39.33 inches. This mean annual rainfall from records covering nearly a half-century says nothing about how high or how low the amount for any single year may be. Because of the continentality of Missouri—it being located a thousand miles from any seacoast—Columbia, according to recorded data, has a continentality effect of 50 per cent. That is, while the rainfall is reported to average 40 inches, it actually varies over a range of 50 per cent, namely, 25 per cent, or 10 inches, below 40; and 25 per cent, or 10 inches, above 40. Precipitation ranges, then, from a low of 30 inches to a high of 50 inches in different years.

But that figure, once established for continentality, is the fact no longer. The record was broken in 1953, when the annual rainfall was but 25.12, rather than 39.33 inches, or 36.1 per cent below the mean. This is a continentality effect of twice 36.1, or 72.2 per cent.

If one considers the rainfall for only the summer months of 1953—May to September, inclusive—when the effects of the extended rain-free period on vegetation were exaggerated by high temperatures, then Columbia, Missouri, suffered under a continentality effect amounting to 86 per cent. This was a most severe disaster to an agricultural area devoted extensively to livestock and heavily dependent on grass for their feed. The law of climatic averages applied to Missouri may leave us content, but the law of continentality is disturbing, yet revealing, when droughts such as that of 1953 are experienced in record-breaking dimensions.

We have, to repeat, been bringing our droughts, as they represent shortage of supplies of soil water, upon ourselves. Droughts are disastrous in terms of deficiency of that liquid mineral in the soil and, thereby, of the food it grows. The more fertile, high-protein–producing soils are exhibiting the more serious droughts. Man is thus pushing himself off the soils which are best for nutrition. He is crowding himself into areas of higher rainfall and onto soils yielding feeds and foods of high-fattening rather than high-feeding values. He has not noticed this, since hidden hunger is registering all too slowly. But now that he is crowding himself out of drink, which registers more quickly, since thirst is more speedily lethal than hunger, droughts take on more meaning. Droughts, moreover, are moving from the country to the towns and to the cities, where they are known as water shortages. They register as thirst disasters, regardless of whether humans or vegetation are concerned.

FERTILITY SHORTAGES ARE CONFUSED WITH WATER SHORTAGES

The shortage of plant nutrition for our crops has too commonly been mistaken for water shortage. When the farmers said, "The drought is bad, since the corn is 'fired' for four or five of the lower leaves on the stalk," they were citing the plant's translocation of nutrients, especially nitrogen, from the lower, older, nearly spent leaves in order to maintain the upper, younger, and growing leaves. Now that we can apply fertilizer nitrogen along with other nutrient elements, we know that in the confusion about plant nutrition we made too much of the drought as a direct shortage of liquid for the plants, at the expense of the more common deficiency of nitrogen to be synthesized into protein and all that compound represents in crop production.

In this case the shortage of nutrition in the soil and not of water was responsible for what was called "drought." With the drying-out of a fertile surface soil underlain by an acid, infertile clay horizon, the roots of the crops were compelled to leave the surface horizon that originally provided both fertility and water and to penetrate into the subsoil, which had wqter but no qualities of fertility. That shallow surface layer was dried not only by the sun's heat but also by the roots of the growing crop—corn, for example, being estimated to take from 0.15 to 0.25 of an inch of water per day by transpiration alone (Decker, 1954). Some hold that 0.10 inch of water is transpired daily by a corn crop,

and so they define a drought for corn as rainfall of less than an inch every ten days. This gives no consideration to the soil fertility concerned. When the lower leaves of a cornstalk "fire," we need only to note the growing tip of the stalk, which will be wilted too if water shortage is responsible. The growing tip will not commonly be wilted, since the roots, going deeper into the subsoil, are delivering water to maintain that active plant part (Albrecht, 1954a).

Data from the Soil Conservation Research project at McCredie, Missouri, compiled during the drought of 1953, showed the corn crop exhausting the soil moisture to a depth of 3.5 feet where the soil was well fertilized. The equivalent of only 1.04 inches of water remained in that entire depth. Where the soil was not fertilized, the crop dried the soil to a lesser depth, leaving the equivalent of 4.5 inches of water in the upper 3.5 feet. On the unfertilized corn, which took a total of 14 inches of water from the soil, the yield was only 18 bushels per acre. It required 26,000 gallons of water to make a bushel of grain. On the fertilized soil, with a yield of 79 bushels, only 5,600 gallons of water per bushel were required. The drought was a case of plant hunger rather than one of plant thirst (Albrecht, 1954c).

SOIL'S PHYSICAL AND CHEMICAL CHANGES ARE BECOMING BIOCHEMICALLY INTOLERABLE

That water shortage in the soil is detrimental to biochemical activities in the crops and in the animals was demonstrated in the mid-continental drought of 1954. The effects of that disaster on the different levels of soil fertility of the plots on Sanborn Field, at the Missouri Agricultural Experiment Station, suggested forcefully that drought disturbs plant processes because of high temperatures. It suggested also a more severe injury to plant tissues according as the higher soil fertility represented more actively growing plants (ibid.).

Where corn had been grown continuously since 1888 with crop removal and no soil treatment, the plants remained the greenest of all corn plots on the entire field. Only the lower two leaves on the stalks were "fired." The other eight leaves, though much rolled, showed no visible irregularities. The stalks were tasseled but were without shoots. This was about the customary "short" crop which that plot has been producing for many years.

On the adjoining plot, where 6 tons of manure per acre annually have been used, the much taller and heavier stalks had the lower five leaves badly "fired." The remaining six leaves were rolled, but they were not visibly injured. The stalks were well tasseled, but the plants were without shoots, suggesting no grain production.

The physiological strain on these dioecious plants by the heat seemingly did not disrupt the masculine efforts of the plant to reproduce but eliminated the female contribution to the survival of the species. This suggests that the female phase of reproduction is a much heavier physiological load or a more extensive integration of biochemical processes than is the male phase.

On another near-by plot where heavy crop residues are turned under and the soil given full fertilizer treatment—including nitrogen—only a single lower leaf per plant was "fired." The other thirteen or more leaves were closely bunched on the shortened stalk. The tassel had not emerged. Neither were there any shoots or signs of ears. More significant, however, was the fact that the leaves were badly bleached from their tips back to almost their mid-length. This part of the leaf tissue was dead. Save for its widely different appearance, the damage duplicated the pattern of the leaf area involved when the plant suffers from nitrogen deficiencies in the soil. It suggested death in the area where the extra nitrogen was involved in rapid growth rather than where there was a deficiency of it.

Since the more vigorous plant growth for seed production involves more physiological functions than growth for fodder production only, it seems reasonable that high temperatures might be more disturbing to the living processes centered in the expectably higher protein content of the cells than to those in plants growing less vigorously and doing little more than making the minimum of carbohydrates. Processes of growth and life are activated by enzymes, compounds resembling proteins in some respects. They are decidedly thermolabile, or are killed by temperatures going above 45°C. (113°F.). The proteins of vigorously growing plants may not be very widely different in their responses to high temperatures from fertile eggs under incubation. Eggs give a good hatch when the temperature is held at 100°F. But a few hours at 10°F. above that temperature will ruin the hatch even if the egg protein is not coagulated or coddled. No signs of injury are visible until the egg dies and processes of decomposition have had time to give the evidence. In the case of the corn leaf, time was also required for the disturbed plant metabolism to reveal itself.

HIGH TEMPERATURES DISRUPT BIOCHEMICAL
PROCESSES AND RESULT IN DEATH OF
PLANTS AND ANIMALS

This disruption of the metabolic processes in the leaves of corn plants was not corrected by the next rain, which moved nitrogen, for example, as nitrate from the revived soil into the corn plants. Also, this nitrate was not reduced significantly. Nor did it move well up into the plant and become changed into organic forms of nitrogen. Instead, it accumulated toward the lower part of the stalk. Those concentrations were high enough to be lethal to the cattle consuming the fodder. More than two hundred head of cattle were reported killed in the state of Missouri as a result of this biochemical irregularity in the corn plants due to the disruption of physiological processes when the air temperatures went above 110°F.—and this because there was not enough water stored in the soil.

Some other biochemical disturbances resulted from the high temperatures. The heat wave in Missouri in 1954 was disastrous to animals as well as to plants, killing both poultry and rabbits. The correlation of increasing temperatures with increasing deaths of experimental rabbits fed on wheat in conjunction with hay grown on soil of different treatments suggested that the nutrition of the animal and not the high temperature per se was the responsible factor in the fatalities associated with the heat.

Seven lots of nine rabbits each, separated from the larger original group, were fed on wheat of a single lot and timothy hays grown on soil given different treatments: (1) full fertilizer treatment; (2) this supplemented by copper; (3) by boron; (4) by cobalt; (5) by manganese; (6) by zinc; and (7) by all these trace elements.

With the mounting temperatures of the heat wave, many of the experimental rabbits died, and, at the weighing dates after each fortnight, replacements were made from those remaining in the original group (which had suffered no heat fatalities) fed on the same wheat as the experimental rabbits, but on the roughage of green grass growing on soil fertilized with rabbit manure. During the period June 11–July 17, 1954, a total of fifty-seven rabbits (70 per cent) died on the timothy-wheat ration, while in the same room there were no deaths among the original group remaining on their wheat-grass ration and tolerating the same heat wave. This represented maxima ranging from 88° to 113°F. and a mean maximum of 99.4°F. during the fortnight closing July 17.

On that date the wheat–timothy hay ration was supplemented with 10 grams per rabbit per day of commercial, dried skim-milk powder. No more deaths occurred during the extension of the experiment for nine days, where maximum daily temperatures ranged from 89° to 111°F., with a mean high of 98.2°F.

A repeat of this test was started on July 26, using corn, oats, and wheat in equal parts by weight along with the same timothy hays. This trial exhibited again the fatalities with the high temperatures until August 23, when the feeding of the timothy hay was discontinued and red-clover hay subsituted. No deaths occurred during the extension of this test with red-clover hay from August 23 to September 6, during which the maxima of temperatures ranged from 79° to 102°F., with a mean maximum of 97.6°F. for those fourteen days. For the fortnight preceding the date of change to red clover, the maxima ranged from 70° to 98°F., with a mean maximum of 82.°F. At the close of this test there still remained all eight rabbits of the original group kept on the wheat-grass ration during the entire summer.

These deaths of the experimental rabbits represent differing fatalities according to nutrition of the animal. They were merely another part in the reaction chain of many biochemical processes pointing to man's manipulations of the soil community to his own detriment, whereas, ultimately, the soil must give the nutrition of all life (Figure 29.6).

FIGURE 29.6 The difference in quality between legumes seeded in manured soil and those seeded in soil without manure. Sixty years of cropping resulted in chemical and biochemical effects differing according to a six-year rotation with manure (Plot 12, left) and without manure (Plot 13, right), as illustrated by the difference in emergence of newly seeded legume.

Chemical Changes Due to Man

MAN'S SURVIVAL DEMANDS RECONSTRUCTIVE
CHANGES IN THE SOIL COMMUNITY

Man has pulled down the levels of virgin-soil fertility to the point where those predatory acts will not continue to feed him and his growing numbers. He must now change his soil communities physically, chemically, and biochemically by construction instead of by continued destruction. Instead of exploiting nature's work, he must now cooperate in re-establishing that work.

We may well observe the principles un-derlying natural conservation and be guided by them toward wiser soil management (Figure 29.7). The study of man's exploitation of soil under agricultural cropping reveals resulting chemical soil conditions similar to those where excessive development has resulted naturally under higher rainfall. Our exploitation of soils under higher rainfall and lower temperatures was less rapid than that of soils under similar rainfall and higher temperatures. Virgin soils in the northeastern United States, with clays of high exchange capacity and much acidity, suffered less exploitation under cultivation than that by virgin soils of equal clay content, less

FIGURE 29.7 The development of mesquite as a result of soil exploitation. Soil exploitation by livestock removal and reduced return of organic matter brought in the mesquite (lower photo, 1943) where forty years previously there had been a cattleman's paradise (upper photo, 1903).

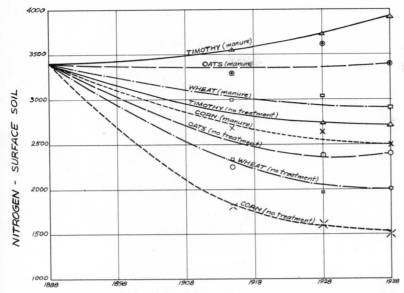

FIGURE 29.8 Some declines in the total nitrogen of the soil during fifty years of continuous cropping with and without manure.

exchange capacity, and less acidity but developed under similar rainfall and higher temperatures in the southeastern United States. Soils farther west, developed under corresponding longitudinal temperatures but under lower rainfalls, like those near the mid-continent, soon approach (under exploitation) the fertility array illustrated in soils farther east but naturally more highly developed under higher rainfalls (Albrecht, 1951b, p. 384). When man uses the soil under rainfalls generous enough for large crop yields, he depletes the fertility rapidly. He encourages leaching to enlarge its toll. He brings the soil to a much higher degree of development and more rapidly than nature would under his absence in that climatic setting (Figure 29.8). Its depletion leads him to believe that the climate (average of weather) has become worse in terms of the contrast between the nutritional quality of the present vegetation and of that which was virgin in the area. The vagaries of the weather are much more disastrous to his agriculture via poorer soil as poor nutrition than they once were. Nutrition in the fullest sense must, then, be declining along with the fertility of

the soil and with the successive harvests of crops.

Successive stages of increasing soil development under higher rainfall give decreasing soil fertility under natural conditions. The increasing rainfall (temperatures constant) in the United States as we go east toward the Atlantic from the soils that once grew proteins for the bison's body makes for a decreasing supply of the total essential elements coming from the soil as nutrition for microbes, plants, animals, and men. However, the relative decrease in supply of calcium, which element the soils must give generously for the production of protein-rich forages (illustrated by lime for legumes and better grasses), is much greater than the decrease in potassium, which serves in the plant's production of carbohydrates. Thus, with increasing soil development, the fertility supporting the plant's biosynthetic processes of converting the carbohydrates into protein is lost first (relatively high calcium loss from the soil), while the fertility supporting the photosynthesis of carbohydrates continues to give crops of considerable vegetative bulk (illustrated by sufficient potassium).

FIGURE 29.9 Field of soybeans spotted by streaks of better crops where calcium compounds were supplied. Liming the soil serves the crop because it fertilizes with calcium (or magnesium) and not because it reduces soil acidity. Streaks of better crops of soybeans resulted (right to left) from (a) calcium chloride, (b) calcium nitrate, and (c) calcium hydroxide because they all provided calcium and not because each (a) made the soil more acid, (b) made it more acid, or (c) made it less acid.

The changing ratio between amounts of calcium and potassium shifts the ecological pattern from the grasses and legumes of high nutritional value per acre (providing proteins along with carbohydrates for the original herds of bison) eastward to deciduous forests able to support only a few browsing animals and then to the coniferous forests on which even such life cannot survive. This is a principle of soil fertility in relation to the climatic pattern of natural soil development that controls the ecological patterns of different life-forms via protein production by the soil. It tells us to expect the nutritional values to dwindle as we intensify the soil's use without concern about maintaining fertility adequate for the plant composition and the food values we expect the soil to deliver. This principle is basic in outlining the rebuilding of the soil now that almost every corner of the earth has been exploited.

MANAGED AGRICULTURE DEMANDS UPLIFT AND INTEGRATION OF MORE SOIL FACTORS THAN THE LIMITING ONE

Attempts to offset exploitation of the soil have brought on the practice of using chemical and mineral fertilizers. A major practice is the liming of the soil (originally to remove soil acidity) in order to restock it with calcium and magnesium (Figure 29.9). These two elements are required in the highest active amounts within the soil for exchange to the plant roots. Phosphorus has been used both as the natural mineral and in chemically treated forms. Others, like potassium, serving among the cations in smaller active amounts in the soil, are now more commonly required as treatment if soils are to produce. Nitrogen, a fertilizer of the crop more than of the soil, and available now as the result of advances in chemical processing of this inert gaseous element from the atmosphere, is serving extensively as a soil treatment. It has two alternatives: (1) offsetting soil exploitation when we purposely use nitrogen to build up the organic matter in the soils at the same time that the crop production is increased and (2) increasing soil exploitation for increased crop production in disregard of the need to rebuild soils in both their organic and their inorganic essentials (Figure 29.10).

In line with the latter view of increased production by soil treatments, research in soil chemistry and plant nutrition has made progress in its efforts to offset soil exploitation in the inorganic essentials. Experimental studies using colloidal clay as the medium for well-controlled plant nutrition have demonstrated that differences in the ratios of the several inorganic fertility elements active on this soil fraction bring about differences in both the proteins and the carbohydrates as plant composition. Thus, by different ratios, or variable balance, of calcium and potassium, we can grow either much plant bulk mainly of high carbohydrate with low protein content or, vice versa, less bulk of higher protein concentration and low carbohydrate content. By varying the fertility ratio in only these two cations in the soil, there are brought about not only different amounts of carbohydrates but also differences in the sugars, starches, hemicelluloses, etc., composing them. Likewise, the ratios of the different amino acids composing the proteins, and the amino nitrogen, as part of the total nitrogen, will be variable according as the ratios and amounts of inorganic fertility are varied for movement into the root as plant nourishment from the soil (Reed, 1953).

Up to this moment the operation in agriculture of this basic principle of soil fertility in relation to crop production has exemplified itself in (1) the introduction of crops mainly for increased yields of carbohydrates and in (2) managed crop composition and improved yield under the program of testing of soils for the appropriate application of inorganic fertility. While the introduction of the corn hybrids covered itself with some semblance of glory, their yield increase comes at the loss of their power to procreate themselves by their own seed. They suffer also in being of lesser value in animal nutrition because of their reduced concentration of crude protein and its deficiency in certain required amino acids, notwithstanding their reputation as the crop giving high farm income.

More particularly, the principle of the ratios to one another of the many active inorganic fertility elements in the soil for control of the biosynthetic services by crops has offered decided promise when applied

in relation to increased protein production along with the carbohydrates. Thus we can use the soil to grow more nearly balanced nutrition. It has given us the concepts of (1) specific ratios of active fertility elements for production of plants of certain nutritional value in their proteins in balance with their carbohydrates as well as (2) generous total yields of them mainly as carbohydrates per acre *(ibid.).*

As a result, 75 per cent of the soil's exchange capacity might well be saturated by calcium; 7.5–10 per cent by magnesium; and 2.5–5 per cent by potassium for the growth of forages rich in protein and carrying also the quota of the many other inorganic elements—the vitamins, enzymes, hormones, and other essential compounds associated with proteins and required for proper animal nutrition. Thus, via soil management, there becomes possible the production of crops with nutritional purposes in mind. By such management soil moves into the food-creating category rather than growing only filler feeds for fattening values (Albrecht, 1954*b*).

While man has been bringing about destructive chemical changes in his soil community, he has also learned much about constructive soil management. This is the

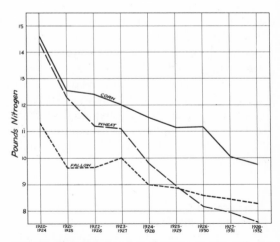

FIGURE 29.10 Biochemical activities in the soil, as illustrated by the level of nitrate nitrogen during the growing season for advancing five-year means, show serious decline under soil exploitation by tillage without soil restoration.

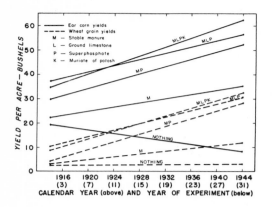

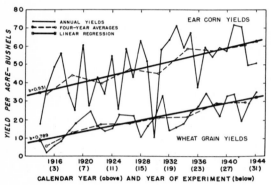

FIGURE 29.11 Trends of yields of corn and wheat under various treatments with "nothing" returned to the soil (above), compared with yields where manure, limestone, phosphate, and potash were combined (below).

FIGURE 29.12 The effects of different chemical fertilizers on the growth quality of plants. Chemical fertilizers manifest wide differences in their chemical and biochemical effects at the same rates of application: ammonium sulfate (above) and superphosphate (below).

exception rather than the rule in practice. It is hoped that constructive soil management will dominate, so that improved soil communities will result in better nutritional support of man. Research evidence from soil study has outlined many essentials, pointed out hazards, and suggested the high costs of maintaining a soil community for the continued nutrition of sedentary man (Figures 29.11 and 29.12).

Biochemical Changes in the Soil Community via Man

When the soil community is viewed as a biochemical entity, we recognize within it many microscopic living forms and their life-processes, including the use by the plant roots of the sunlight on the plant top to derive energy. Plant roots bring a stream of carbon dioxide down into the soil by way of the respiration. To this, there is added what comes from the microbial forms oxidizing the returned organic remains. Consequently, the soil air represents a concentration of 1 per cent of carbon dioxide, to give a high acid concentration along with all the other decomposition products of both catabolic and anabolic origin. The exploitation of the soil in disregard of a generous return of organic matter represents biochemical destruction of the virgin soil much in advance of, and in a higher degree than, that under chemical and physical exploitation. Unfortunately, our observations on the biochemical changes of the soil community have been few. The tools for their recognition and critical inventory have not yet been so plentifully designed. When inorganic chemistry has developed as a phase of soil science so late, we should not be surprised that organic chemistry has not yet turned its light more strongly on plant physiology as modified by the organic aspects of the soil.

Because we can grow certain plants in water cultures of purely chemical salts, the erroneous conclusion has been drawn that plants do not therefore take organic compounds from the soil for their physiological service. Plant studies have demonstrated that a great variety of organic compounds is absorbed by the plant root from the soil, since their soluble amounts within the soil may represent as high a concentration as that of the inorganic compounds (Miller, 1938, p. 297). A long list of carbohydrates has been assembled from tests, showing them taken up by the roots and serving the plant as an energy source in the absence of light.

With the addition of certain vitamins to sterile, mineral-nutrient solutions, excised root tips have been grown over long periods of time in the dark with sugars, via root absorption, supplying the energy (Robbins and Schmidt, 1938). Organic acids are also absorbed by plant roots. Nitrogen in organic compounds is no exception when the extensive list of amino acids may serve as well as many other organic nitrogenous compounds. These experiments suggest that organic substances very commonly supplement, but in few cases replace, the inorganic nitrogenous salts. But, when man and his herds have been so closely associated and interdependent on soils (Albrecht, 1952a), the return of the animal manure may have been more significant in terms of organic compounds returned for crop production than we commonly recognize. Manures suggest fertility values transcending those represented by their ash contents only.

Observations are accumulating to suggest that, in the synthesis by plants of the proteins complete in all the essential amino acids for man and his livestock, some organic compounds must be returned to the soil or kept in cycle. It seems a logical theory that, for the synthesis of the more complex amino acids by the plants, some complex organic compounds must be absorbed from the soil as starter compounds (Albrecht, 1952b). For example, this seems a suitable theory in regard to that very commonly deficient amino acid—tryptophan. The indole ring seems to be a requisite when bean plants have demonstrated their absorption of this compound from the soil and have deposited it into the seed, with the fecal odor of the indole detectable there. It is also significant when the indole ring is so much of the indoleacetic acid and related compounds serving as the major growth hormone of plants (Thimann, 1954).

The significance of indole as a fecal waste, resulting from the digestion of the amino acid tryptophan, impressed itself in some observations on the volunteer weed crops and the planted bean crops in the sand of abandoned, experimental cat pens (Figure 29.13). The cats had buried their dung during two years while being kept under study for differential development because of a cooked diet in which milk was the only variable. The cats were segregated in pens according as they were fed on (1) condensed, (2) evaporated, (3) pasteurized, and (4) raw milk. No other soil treatment or fertilizer was used (Pottenger, 1946).

The weeds, showing wide differences in amount of growth, were removed, and each of the pens (male cats separate from the female) planted with two rows of a "dwarf" bean, all from the same lot of seed. Wherever the cat's diet contained the heated milks, the plant growth characters were those of what one would call the "bush" or the "dwarf" kind of bean. But, where the dung from the cats fed the raw milk was the fertilizer, the plants were "pole" beans, with vines climbing the screened sides as high as 6 feet.

Since the indole odor was present in the seeds of the dwarf-bean plants and no such odor was detectable in the seeds of the pole-bean plants, there is the suggestion that intake of the cooked milk led to excretion of indole by the cats, its absorption by the roots of the bean plants, and its mobilization without change into the seed, where the protein would be the expected deposit guaranteeing survival of the plant species. There is the suggestion that drinking the raw milk also

FIGURE 29.13 The effects derived from controlled diets on the growth quality of a weed and a bean crop. Cat dung, buried in sand during two years of experimental feeding of male cats on evaporated milk (left) and raw milk (right), when all else in the diet was cooked and constant, brought differences in the volunteer weed crop (upper photos) and shifted the "dwarf" bean to a "pole" bean (lower photos).

led to indole excretion, but there followed its later synthesis into indoleacetic acid as a hormone to shift the "dwarf" growth characters of the ancestor beans into the "pole" growth characters. There may have followed the synthesis of some of the indole into tryptophan and its deposition into the seed, for which no tests were made.

All this points up that there are some biochemical behaviors in the soil related to plant nutrition and to animal nutrition in a degree of refinement we have not yet envisioned. It raises the question whether man did not bring on serious disturbances in the nutritional values of his foods coming via animals, plants, microbes, and the soil when he put the plow ahead of the cow to the point where he has now almost forgotten the cow. This question is all the more challenging, since the nomad had the cow ahead of the plow as a kind of perambulating soil-tester for its health and reproduction, to say nothing

of the nomad's, and since prevailing degenerative human diseases are now suggesting that we ought to expect such troubles in accepting in our nutrition almost any foods on caloric values alone and "crude" proteins in our nutrition in place of the complete array of required amino acids (Figures 29.14 and 29.15).

Man has become aware of increased needs for health preservation, interpreted as a technical need for more hospitals, drugs, and doctors, when it may be simply a matter of failing to recognize the basic truth in the old adage which reminded us that "to be well fed is to be healthy." Unfortunately, we have not seen the changes man has wrought in his soil community in terms of food quality for health, as economics and technologies have emphasized its quantity. Man is exploiting the earth that feeds him much as a parasite multiplies until it kills its host. Slowly the reserves in the soil for the support

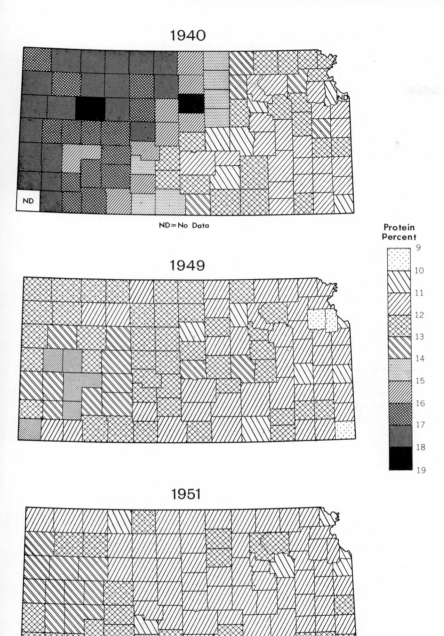

FIGURE 29.14 The concentration of crude protein in the wheat of Kansas, by county averages, has been declining during successive years of sampling.

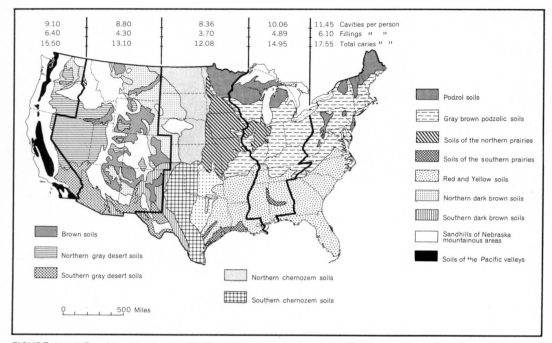

9.10	8.80	8.36	10.06	11.45	Cavities per person
6.40	4.30	3.70	4.89	6.10	Fillings " "
15.50	13.10	12.08	14.95	17.55	Total caries " "

Podzol soils

Gray brown podzolic soils

Soils of the northern prairies

Soils of the southern prairies

Red and Yellow soils

Northern dark brown soils

Southern dark brown soils

Sandhills of Nebraska mountainous areas

Soils of the Pacific valleys

Brown soils

Northern gray desert soils

Southern gray desert soils

Northern chernozem soils

Southern chernozem soils

0 _____ 500 Miles

FIGURE 29.15 Results of teeth examinations of Navy inductees related to respective soil regions. The above numbers revealed cavities, fillings, or total caries per inductee, as a mean, of 69,584 inductees into the Navy in 1942 from respective soil regions. These were lowest in the mid-continent of moderate development of the soil according to the climatic forces but were higher to the west, with underdevelopment under low rainfall, and higher also to the east, with overdevelopment and higher rainfall. (Soils groups after Marbut, 1935.)

of man's nutrition are being exhausted. All too few of us have yet seen the soil community as the foundation in terms of nutrition of the entire biotic pyramid of which man, at the top, occupies the most hazardous place.

Summary

The physical, chemical, and biochemical changes in the soil community brought about by man have represented soil destruction so much more than soil construction that they have brought into sharp focus the problem of food for population numbers mounting geometrically. This focus is all the sharper when land areas are not only shrinking as areas but in food quality per unit produced.

Man has changed the soil to reduce its services in the absorption and storage of rainfall. These changes have increased our droughts. Those are now starting—from the soil—a set of chain reactions amounting to near-national emergencies. The soil exploitation, destructive of that creative resource, is lowering the quality per unit of agricultural output. Lowered protein content of crops grown is the major single, summarized report of what man has brought about via the several soil changes.

When the population pressures on the soil give it no rest for natural reconstruction, and when the farmer's economic entanglements similarly preclude such rest, the depletion of the fertility of the soil, by which it gives biochemical as well as chemical activities in food service, must push this service to a lower and lower potential.

Science, having given so much to technology, has not yet collected and organized enough knowledge of biology for us to manage conservatively all the natural phenomena via agricultural soils. In consequence, continued soil exploitation must eventually be recognized as causative of many biotic manifestations which are simply hidden hungers originating in the deficiencies of the soil. As the shrinkage of the supporting soil areas under each of us continues, or as more of our lifelines back to the soil are shortened and severed, we hope we shall gather sufficient knowledge soon enough to balance increased population against the pressure of

increased food output, while still maintaining the productivity of the soil. For that, knowledge gained from our past soil destruction may well contribute some principles of wise management for sustained soil construction.

The Moving Finger writes; and, having writ,
Moves on: nor all your Piety nor Wit
Shall lure it back to cancel half a Line,
Nor all your Tears wash out a Word of it.
Rubáiyát of Omar Khayyám,
trans. FitzGerald

References

Albrecht, W. A.
  1951a "War: Some Agricultural Implications," *Organic Farmer,* LXXXII, 36 ff.
  1951b "Nutrition via Soil Fertility According to the Climatic Pattern," pp. 384–97 in *Proceedings, Special Conference in Agriculture on Plant and Animal Nutrition in Relation to Soil and Climatic Factors, Australia, 1949.* London: H.M. Stationery Office. 490 pp.
  1952a "The Cow Ahead of the Plow," *Guernsey Breeders' Journal,* LXXXIV, 1173–77.
  1952b "Protein Deficiencies via Soil Deficiencies. II. Experimental Evidence," *Oral Surgery, Oral Medicine and Oral Pathology,* V, 483–99.
  1954a "Droughts: The Soil as Reasons for Them," pp. 42–55 in *Proceedings of the Eleventh Annual Meeting of the American Institute of Dental Medicine, Palm Springs, California, November, 1954.* 185 pp.
  1954b "Soil and Nutrition," pp. 24–40, *ibid.*
  1954c "Drought," *Better Crops with Plant Food,* XXXVIII, No. 9, 6–9.
Boyle, Lt. Col. C. L.
  1954 "Mother Earth," *Journal of the Soil Association,* VIII, 3.
Decker, Wayne L.
  1954 "Sixth Annual Progress Report of the Missouri

Climatological Research Project." (University of Missouri in co-operation with the U.S. Weather Bureau.) Columbia, Mo.: U.S. Department of Commerce. 21 pp. (Mimeographed.)
Miller, Edwin C.
  1938 *Plant Physiology.* New York: McGraw-Hill Book Co. 1,201 pp.
Pottenger, Francis M.
  1946 "Effect of Heat Processed Foods and Metabolized Vitamin D Milk on Dento-facial Structures of Experimental Animals," *American Journal of Orthodontics and Oral Surgery,* XXXII, 467–85.
Reed, Lester W.
  1953 "Biosynthesis in Plants as Influenced by the Nutrient Balance in the Soil." Unpublished Ph.D. thesis, Department of Soils, University of Missouri. 190 pp.
Robbins, W. J., and Schmidt, Mary Bartley
  1938 "Growth of Excised Roots of the Tomato," *Botanical Gazette,* XCIX, 671–728.
Sears, Paul B.
  1954 "Human Ecology: A Problem in Synthesis," *Science,* CXX, 959–63.
Thimann, Kenneth V.
  1954 "The Physiology of Growth in Plant Tissues," *American Scientist,* XLII, 589–606.

ADDITIONAL REFERENCES

Albrecht, W. A. 1957. Soil fertility and biotic geography. *Geogr. Rev.* 47:86–105.
Alexander, M. 1967. The breakdown of pesticides in soils. Pp. 331–342 in *Agriculture and the quality of our environment,* ed. by N. C. Brady. Washington, D.C.: Amer. Assoc. Adv. Sci., Publ. 85.
Bidwell, O. W., and F. D. Hole. 1965. Man as a factor in soil formation. *Soil Sci.* 99:65–72.

Bormann, F. H., G. E. Likens, D. W. Fisher, and R. S. Pierce. 1968. Nutrient loss accelerated by clear-cutting of a forest ecosystem. *Science* 159:882–884.
Buckman, H. O., and N. C. Brady. 1960. *The nature and properties of soils.* 6th edition. New York: MacMillan. 567 pp.
Bugher, J. C. 1956. Effects of fission material on air, soil, and living species. Pp. 831–848 in *Man's role in changing the face of the earth,*

ed. by William L. Thomas, Jr. Chicago and London: The University of Chicago Press.

Bunting, B. T. 1965. *The geography of soil.* Chicago: Aldine. 213 pp.

Commoner, B. 1968. Nature unbalanced; How man interferes with the nitrogen cycle. *Scientist and Citizen* 10(1):9–13, 28.

Dale, T., and V. G. Carter. 1955. *Topsoil and civilization.* Norman, Oklahoma: University of Oklahoma Press.

Dimbleby, G. W. 1962. *The development of British heathlands and their soils.* Oxford Forestry Memoires 23. Oxford: Claredon Press. 120 pp.

Edwards, C. A. 1969. Soil pollutants and soil animals. *Sci. Amer.* 220(4):88–92, 97–99.

Iverson, L. G. K. 1967. Monitoring of pesticide content in water in selected areas of the United States. Pp. 157–162 in *Agriculture and the quality of our environment,* ed. by N. C. Brady. Washington, D.C.: Amer. Assoc. Adv. Sci., Publ. 85.

Jacks, G. V. 1956. Influence of man on soil fertility. *The Advancement of Science* 13(50): 137–145.

Koch, C. R. 1960. William Albrecht sums up a career in soil research. *The Farm Quarterly* 14(4):64–65, 112, 114, 116.

Lagerwerff, J. V. 1967. Heavy-metal contamination of soils. Pp. 343–364 in *Agriculture and the quality of our environment,* ed. by N. C. Brady. Washington, D.C.: Amer. Assoc. Adv. Sci., Publ. 85.

Marbut, C. F. 1925. The rise, decline, and revival of Malthusianism in relation to geography and character of soils. *Ann. Assoc. Amer. Geog.* 15:1–29.

Mohr, E. C. J., and F. A. van Baren. 1954. *Tropical soils.* New York: Interscience Publishers, Inc. 498 pp.

Nikiforoff, C. C. 1959. Reappraisal of the soil. *Science* 129:186–196.

President's Science Advisory Committee, Environmental Pollution Panel. 1965. *Restoring the quality of our environment.* Washington, D.C.: Government Printing Office.

Reitemeier, R. F., H. Hollister, and L. T. Alexander. 1967. The extent and significance of soil contamination with radionuclides. Pp. 269–282 in *Agriculture and the quality of our environment,* ed. by N. C. Brady. Washington, D.C.: Amer. Assoc. Adv. Sci., Publ. 85.

Russell, E. W. 1961. *Soil conditions and plant growth.* 9th ed. New York: Wiley. 688 pp. The standard reference on the relationships between soils and crops.

Shaler, N. S. 1891. The origin and nature of soils. *U.S.G.S. Twelfth Annual Report,* Part I, Geology, pp. 213–345.

Sheets, T. J. 1967. The extent and seriousness of pesticide buildup in soils. Pp. 311–330 in *Agriculture and the quality of our environment,* ed. by N. C. Brady. Washington, D.C.: Amer. Assoc. Adv. Sci., Publ. 85.

Smith, G. E. 1967. Fertilizer nutrients as contaminants in water supplies. Pp. 173–186 in *Agriculture and the quality of our environment,* ed. by N. C. Brady. Washington, D.C.: Amer. Assoc. Adv. Sci., Publ. 85.

Stout, P. R., and R. G. Burau. 1967. The extent and significance of fertilizer buildup in soils as revealed by vertical distributions of nitrogenous matter between soils and underlying water reservoirs. Pp. 283–310 in *Agriculture and the quality of our environment,* ed. by N. C. Brady. Washington, D.C.: Amer. Assoc. Adv. Sci., Publ. 85.

Treshow, M. 1970. *Environment and plant response.* New York: McGraw-Hill. 422 pp.

United States Department of Agriculture. 1938. *Soils and men.* Washington, D.C.: Government Printing Office. 1232 pp.

Yaalon, D. H., and B. Yaron. 1966. Framework for man-made soil changes—an outline of metapedogenesis. *Soil Sci.* 102:272–277.

ENVIRONMENTAL EFFECTS OF HIGHWAYS

MELVIN E. SCHEIDT

Roadways consume a significant portion of the land removed from agricultural and other uses. In the United States, for instance, there are 3.6 million miles of roads and streets—one mile of road for every square mile of land. About 24,000 square miles are covered by roads and their rights-of-way, equal to the area of the state of West Virginia (Mowbray, 1969, p. 12). Freeways consume twenty-four acres of land per mile and eighty acres of land per interchange.

During and after construction, highways have many pollutional effects on the surrounding environment. These effects are the subject of this selection. Many of them also are treated in other parts: air pollution (Selections 8, 9, and 37), noise (Selection 14), runoff (Selection 16), and herbicides (Selection 38). Many of the effects of roadways generally decline exponentially with distance, depending on barriers and other factors such as wind. Accumulated concentrations of lead (from tetraethyl lead in gasoline) in vegetation and soil provide an example (Cannon and Bowles, 1962). Salt concentrations, from salt applied on roads to melt ice, are another example, mentioned here but amplified by Berthouex (1968). More than 6 million tons of salt were used on highways in 1966–1967, an increase of 400 percent since 1954. In Connecticut 20 tons per mile are applied to some principal highways each year (Berthouex, 1968).

Even after their use for transportation ceases, the environmental influence of roadways may continue for millennia. In France a very distinctive strip of vegetation extends through the forest between Orléans and Sens. The 60-foot-wide band of forest reflects the path of an

Melvin E. Scheidt (b. 1900) is a civil engineer who, until recently, was program advisor and director of water supply and pollution control for the U.S. Public Health Service, Washington, D.C. His work for a number of public agencies has mainly concerned public works, water resources, and recreation and park development.

This article is reprinted from the *Journal of the Sanitary Engineering Division, Proceedings of the American Society of Civil Engineers,* vol. 93, no. SA5, pp. 17–25, October, 1967. Copyright 1967 by the American Society of Civil Engineers.

ancient Roman road.   Limestone slabs used in its construction have formed an alkaline soil (pH 7.3 to 8.0), contrasting with acid podzolic soils (pH 3.0 to 4.5) elsewhere in the area (Milleret, 1963).

(Editor's comment)

The pollutional effects of highways on the environment are described primarily from a sanitary engineering point of view. Highways, of course, also have important esthetic, economic and sociological effects upon the environment, but these will not be considered herein.

Pollutional Effects of Highways

The pollutional effects of highways are varied and appear at several stages in the life of the highway. First, erosion during construction of the highway produces troublesome sediment. Pollution may also occur from oils, chemicals, and other substances used during the construction process. Secondly, pollution can result from operation and maintenance of the highway. Involved are such things as flooding, pollution of adjacent land and water areas by chemicals used to melt ice, and the effects of herbicides and other spray materials used to control roadside vegetation. Finally, pollution can result from use of the highway itself, including for example, accidental spills of chemicals, oils and other materials in transport, roadside litter and debris thrown or blown from vehicles, pollution of the air from engine exhausts, and oils, greases and other substances deposited on the road surface in the normal use of the highway by motor vehicles.

SEDIMENTATION

Sedimentation caused by erosion of soil exposed during construction is one of the most serious detriments to the environment caused by highways. This erosion not only damages the contractor and owner in terms of costly regrading, but the resulting sediments cause substantial damage downstream from the construction area. Not all of the eroded material reaches the main stream channels, of course. Some, to the detriment of the owners, is spread on adjacent properties or is deposited in the smaller watercourses. But a substantial amount does reach the major channels, where it covers the stream beds, fills navigation channels, reservoirs, and lakes, and has a deleterious effect on aquatic life.

Some idea of the sediment loads and damages involved is provided by studies in the Potomac and Patuxent river basins in Maryland. Rural areas in these basins, under normal conditions, contribute less than 200 tons of sediment per sq mile per year. Land undergoing development in this same region has been found to contribute from 1,010 to 121,000 tons per sq mile per year (1). In general, erosion from land undergoing urban development may be 10 to 50 times greater than from rural areas. Divided lane highways, which require exposure of 10 acres per mile to 35 acres per mile during construction, have been found to produce 3,000 tons of sediment per mile (2). Damages caused by these sediments are correctable only at great cost, and some, such as destruction of fish life, are not readily correctable at all. On this latter point, the Congressional Record in recent years has contained numerous references to destruction of the trout fishery in Western streams, caused by uncontrolled erosion and sedimentation from construction of highways parallelling the streams. Studies by the U.S. Fish and Wildlife Service suggest that, once the benthic life has been destroyed because of sediments covering the stream bottom, it may take many years to reestablish the ecological balance in the stream.

In the case of the Potomac River, of the

2,500,000 tons of sediment dumped into the tidal estuary every year, something on the order of 25% is produced in the immediate Washington Metropolitan area, which represents only about 2% of the total drainage area of the basin. Erosion from highway construction contributes considerably to this locally produced sediment load. Annual dredging is required to keep the navigation channel open, but the remainder of the estuary is slowly becoming a shallow mud flat which, if nothing is done, will eventually become esthetically unattractive and of little use to anyone (4).

A classic example of damage produced by erosion from construction sites is that of Lake Barcroft in Fairfax County, Va., adjacent to the District of Columbia. Here the lake, which is the center and focal point for a fine residential development, has, in recent years, been almost filled with sediments from developments upstream, much of it from highways and roadside ditches. The community has had to resort to continuous and expensive dredging to maintain the lake in reasonably useful condition (3).

There is also the familiar case with the highway construction sites where extensive soil areas have remained uncovered and unprotected for months, with continuous and expensive erosion damage. Such long exposure of raw earth to the elements is not essential to the construction operation. The slopes of excavation and fill areas can and should be brought to final grade and protected in a relatively short time, long before the pavement is installed. This can be done at little if any additional cost and, in many instances, with substantial savings to the contractor in costs of regrading after storms. The writer recently observed several highway construction operations where this was done with great benefit to all concerned. However, the writer has also seen situations where the exposed soil remained untreated for 18 months or more, and where regrading was repeated as many as five times before seeding and mulching finally stabilized the slopes.

Fortunately, the United States Bureau of Public Roads has recognized the need to correct this situation. Operating under the authority of a Presidential executive order calling for the correction, control, and abatement of water pollution caused by Federal activities, the Federal Highway Administrator recently issued instructions calling for the adoption of appropriate measures for the correction of sedimentation and other water pollution resulting from construction of Federal and Federally aided highways (5).

The directive required that, as soon as feasible, but not later than January 1, 1967, the plans, specifications, and estimates for direct Federal and Federally aided highway construction projects shall contain provisions that will keep pollution of all waters by highway construction to an achievable, reasonable minimum. Such specifications will require the scheduling and conducting of construction operations to prevent when necessary, and otherwise to minimize, pollution of streams, lakes, and reservoirs with sediment or other harmful materials. In most situations this is to be accomplished by specifying that the areas of land that can be exposed to erosion by construction operations at any one time shall be subject to approval by the project engineer, and that the exposure be of as short a duration as practicable. Erosion control, including sediment traps, seeding, mulching, and other measures, is to be practiced concurrently with other work and initiated at the earliest practicable time. Disturbance of lands and waters outside the staked-out construction limits is to be prohibited except as may be found necessary and ordered by the project engineer. The specifications will state the controls required in the location, operation, and final condition of borrow pits, including assurance that erosion of the pit after completion of the work will not result in water pollution. Contractors must also provide adequate sanitation facilities on all construction projects.

Applying and enforcing such provisions on all highway construction, whether Federally financed or not, can materially reduce sedimentation from this source. For complete control of this situation, however, local ordinances and State laws imposing these same requirements on all subdivision and other construction are required.

STORM WATER RUNOFF

Storm water flowing off completed highways and adjacent areas requires adequate drains and channels if danger to the travelling public and damage to adjacent lands and properties are to be avoided. This requirement would seem to be obvious. Yet the increased area of impervious surface which results from highway construction, and changes in land slope can substantially shorten the runoff time and increase the amount of storm water runoff from an area, as compared with pre-construction conditions. Stream channels or storm sewers which were adequate for the runoff under earlier conditions may thus prove inadequate after completion of the facility. Also, some of the modern interchanges are of such "complex" nature that even greater care must be exercised to ensure that adequate facilities for carrying off the water are provided at the time of construction. For, once the project is completed, the cost of constructing corrective facilities becomes almost prohibitive. Similarly, culvert and bridge openings must be adequate to permit passage of flood waters under the increased surface imperviousness which will prevail after urbanization and development, induced by the construction of the highway, takes place on adjacent lands.* Failure to foresee these changes that may come in the wake of highway construction can result in costly flood damage. Also, culverts placed too high to permit proper drainage of lands adjacent to highways may transform these lands into swamps and wet lands, with extensive damage to forests or reduction of the agricultural value of the land (6).

ROAD SALTING

The application to highway surfaces of common salt, calcium chloride, and other chemi-

* Increased flooding due to urbanization is discussed in Selection 16.

cals for the purpose of melting or preventing formation of ice has become almost a universal practice. In addition to corroding vehicles and highway structures, these materials can also damage trees and vegetation, and may have a polluting effect on adjacent streams, lakes, and ground waters. These effects have not been given the wide study they would appear to deserve, but investigations in Connecticut, Michigan, and elsewhere have indicated that pollution from this source is significant.

For example, tastes and odors in a Connecticut municipal water supply were attributed to the presence of sodium ferrocyanide which was added to salt in storage piles in the amount of 250 ppm to prevent caking. A reduction in dosage to 50 ppm was proposed to limit the possible amount of free cyanide in any waters which could be affected. Covers for the storage piles were also recommended.

The brine from a rapid thaw can cause local pollution problems in small receiving streams, both because of the salt and the sodium bichromate and other chemicals sometimes added to reduce the corrosive effects of the salt.

In Michigan, ground water recharged by melted snow which was contaminated by de-icing salt is reported to have contaminated roadside wells. In another case, litigation resulted from claims that leachings from salt piles contaminated shallow aquifers in limestone beds.

Another instance in Connecticut cited rock salt stored in piles as the source of pollution of wells serving four families, causing corrosion damage to plumbing and heating equipment as well as reducing the potable quality of the water. The cause of the pollution was indicated to be rainwater washing off the piles, which seeped into the ground water supplying the wells.

Evidences were also found in Connecticut of damage to roadside vegetation from salt solution seeping into the ground. Sugar maple trees along the highways were found to have a significant increase in sodium and chloride ions which depressed the intake of nutrient ions, thereby causing a slow degeneration of the trees. Elsewhere, in New Hampshire, maple trees in roadside drainage areas showed the presence of higher-than-normal sodium levels in leaves and twigs (7, 8, 9, 10).

HERBICIDES

Damage to crops, shrubs, and trees on private property, caused by herbicides used to control roadside vegetation, has been cited in a number of instances. The damage results from the sprays being carried by the wind. Excessively applied herbicides can also be carried into streams by heavy runoff and, in some instances, can be damaging to fish. Extreme care should be taken to ensure that these chemicals are carefully applied by experienced personnel under suitable atmospheric conditions, and only in recommended amounts (11).

This whole matter of the use of chemicals in highway management needs more study before a full understanding of their polluting significance can be reached.

AIR POLLUTION

Probably the most discussed environmental effect of the vehicular use of highways is that of air pollution. The newspapers and technical journals are replete with articles and discussions concerning the smogs and other objectionable and damaging effects on the atmosphere of the exhaust gases from the internal combustion engine. Water pollution caused by fallout from leaded gasoline vapors is also attributed to this source and objectionable odors are caused by the incomplete combustion of fuels. These effects stem, of course, from the vehicle itself, rather than from its use of the highway as such. The problem is of direct concern to the Air Pollution Division of the Public Health Service, and is being intensively researched in a number of directions. Reports from time to time of new or improved engine types suggest that we will eventually lick this problem.

This must be done, if we are to continue to occupy our cities in comfort and health.

ACCIDENTAL SPILLS

Pollution arising from the transporting of commodities presents a different kind of problem. This is the problem of spills of deleterious substances caused by accidents. Accidental spills are not peculiar to highways, of course. They occur on railroads, on the inland waterways and on pipelines as well. But the spill from a highway accident can directly involve or affect other persons concurrently using the highway, as well as residents adjacent to the scene of the accident, and others along water courses which may be polluted by the substances spilled. Substances transported on highways which can be dangerous to humans or cause serious damage if spilled include such items as explosives, flammable petroleum products, various poisonous gases, radioactive materials, or chemicals which can in any way have deleterious effects upon either people, animals, or properties.

Petroleum products and chemicals are the principal commodities germane to this discussion. The 68,000,000 tons of petroleum products carried annually by trucks is over 2.5 times the amount of these products carried by railroads, and chemicals of all kinds transported over the highways total over 6,000,000 tons. While the volume of chemicals thus carried is only 0.1 that of petroleum products so carried, it is a significant portion of the chemical tonnage transported by all means. Chemical spills pose much greater danger than other commodities because of the nature of some of the chemicals. The release of certain gases, such as chlorine, can be highly dangerous to persons in the vicinity. Phenols, caustic soda, and other chemicals can pollute a nearby stream or river, causing difficulties for downstream water users unless forewarned. Insecticides endanger birds, fish, and other animals. Other chemicals can cause fish kills, or damage vegetation. Still others, such as inflammable gases, are fire and explosion hazards.

The damaging effects upon the environment resulting from highway accidents is, of course, relatively small in comparison to environmental degradation from all causes. Because of the large number of highway stream crossings, and because commodities are carried on highways in a large number of separately controlled units, the potential is high for accidental spills on highways which can cause water pollution. A single truck can carry up to 20,000 gal, and this amount of oil or chemicals, spilled into a stream, can cause considerable difficulty for downstream water users and aquatic life.

Here are some recent examples of damaging spills originating with highway accidents:

A transport company discharged 3,900 gal of diesel oil from a wrecked truck. In this case, the company was fined $500.

A truck wreck at a bridge caused 1,000 lb of pesticides to spill into a stream.

Four separate motor truck accidents resulted in the discharge of oils and chemicals to adjacent streams, causing fish kills and coating the stream beds.

Pollution of the environment as a result of highway accidents is, of course, just one part of the larger problem of pollution from accidental spills occurring in all forms of transportation. This problem has been made the subject of a Congressional inquiry, and an Interagency Committee of the Federal Government is currently attempting to develop methods for dealing with it. One of the Committee's most important considerations is the devising of a suitable reporting system, so that adequate precautions can be taken to protect persons and properties against the effects of accidental spills of hazardous materials.

If transport companies were required, for example, to immediately report all accidents which might cause the release of any polluting substances (not just dangerous cargo) to water pollution control authorities, downstream water users might be warned in time to prevent harm. The question of whom to call in any particular geographic location poses a problem, however. Thus it might be desirable to have a central place to receive calls reporting accidents, the reports to include time and location of occurrence, materials involved, person in charge and how he can be reached. This information then could be relayed by phone to the proper authorities in the State having responsibility for the control of pollution in the waters involved.

The Public Health Service has an emergency information service for use when poisons are accidentally introduced into public water supplies. Water works and public health officials who have need of such emergency information may call the Chief, Poison Control Branch, Division of Accident Prevention, Washington, D. C., at telephone number WO-3-7312, furnish name, organization, position, telephone number, and information concerning the pollution, and can expect to obtain help within 3 hr.

Fortunately, this service is not needed often—but it has been useful in a few cases of accidental pollution of drinking water supplies. In the matter of water, however, this service is concerned only with potable supply sources and problems of human toxicity. This clearinghouse should be expanded to cover spills which might be detrimental to industrial or agricultural users. The coverage should probably also include spills affecting any part of the environment. The release of poisonous gas to the atmosphere, for example, can be quite dangerous to people and animals, unless evacuation or other protective measures can be quickly invoked in the area involved.

Much of the apprehension and the damages caused by pollution resulting from transportation accidents could be prevented through an organized plan of action such as the one just described, requiring immediate reporting of all such accidents. This national clearing house service should, in turn, be supplemented by appropriate organizational arrangements establishing clear cut lines of responsibility in each State (12).

OTHER POLLUTANTS

Surface runoff from streets and highways contains a variety of polluting substances which are harmful to humans and animal life or render the receiving waters unfit for many uses. These substances derive from the filth and rubbish which accumulate on highway surfaces, from the wear and tear on tires, and from oils, greases and gasoline leaking from vehicles, which in turn leach or dissolve other substances from the asphaltic binders used in paving materials. Studies have shown that urban runoff contains various chemicals, such as salt, calcium chloride, hexavalent chromium, phenols, picric acid, fuel oil, gasoline, fertilizers, and a variety of other substances; it also contains organic wastes and bacteria of human and animal origin, in sufficient numbers to clearly indicate a danger to human health. Thus, runoff from paved surfaces is a serious pollutant of surface waters, and can also seep into and contaminate ground waters.

Probably little can be done to reduce the amounts of most of these materials that are deposited on highway surfaces. They are inherent in modern highway traffic. We are taking a look at the resulting polluted storm water, however, especially in urban areas, to determine what might be done to treat it before discharging it to the stream or lake. Various proposals are being made, involving detention and clarifying basins, chemical treatment and disinfection. So far, only a few facilities of limited capability for handling polluted storm water have been constructed. This is so largely because of the huge volumes of water which must be handled during a relatively brief period. But as emphasis on the abatement of pollution in our environment continues to increase, we can expect greater attention to this problem (13, 14, 15, 16).

ROADSIDE LITTER

Roadside litter is a direct outgrowth of the development of the modern highway and of rapid automobile transportation. The most prevalent and significant item in roadside litter is the ubiquitous "no deposit, no return" beverage container. Originally developed to dispense beer, it is now used also for various

other beverages and is rapidly replacing all returnable containers. Roadside vending machines and the sale of these commodities at every service station, tavern, and store, coupled with the easily-opened top, make it convenient for the motorist to acquire and consume as he travels, whatever pre-cooled refreshment he may desire. The empty container is readily disposed of through the car window.

Unsightly roadside litter is increasing. It not only seriously diminishes the esthetic qualities of the immediate roadside, but presents a problem for adjacent property owners and added expense to county or state governments for periodic clean-up. Broken glass containers are also hazardous to automobile tires on the highway itself and to livestock which often incur serious hoof cuts on areas parallelling the highways.

Most states have laws setting forth fairly severe penalties for discarding rubbish along roads and highways, but arrests are few and the penalties seldom imposed. The travelling public appears to be little concerned and not much deterred by the existence of these laws. Campaigns to educate the traveller to deposit his rubbish in service station receptacles and elsewhere appear to be equally fruitless.

Coors Brewery in Golden, Colo., is sufficiently concerned about this problem and the association of its commodity and name with the problem, that it offers $0.01 for the return of each Coors container, which in the case of its aluminum cans, is salvageable. About half of its containers are reported to be returned (17).

In another such effort, a liquor store proprietor in the District of Columbia recently offered $0.01 for each bottle or beer can brought to his store. In 1 hr, 2,750 containers were turned in, and many times this number for the whole day. He reported that, in a walk around the neighborhood at the end of the day, he could find not one bottle or can.

These are steps in the right direction, but they are hardly enough; and apparently the antilitter laws are not going to eliminate this blight. Accordingly, the writer suggests a more positive approach, somewhat along the lines of what Coors is doing, but to be undertaken by the State under appropriate legislation. The writer would, by law, impose a surcharge of something like $0.03 to $0.05 on every nonreturnable beverage container, to be redeemed upon presentation of the container either to the vendor or to a collection station operated by the state or the local government. Excess funds left over from unredeemed containers could be turned over to the local governments to cover expenses they now incur in cleaning up this roadside mess. However, the writer suspects that, if the surcharge is at the level suggested, the local governments might well be relieved of this burden by youngsters, and some not so young, interested in making an extra dollar or two by gleaning discarded containers from the roadsides.

Summary

In summary, then, the polluting effects of highways upon the environment and the measures required to deal with them are:

1. The control of sediment resulting from soil erosion at highway construction sites causes considerable damage downstream, the correction of which requires careful application of the measures called for in the directive of the Bureau of Public Roads and the extension of similar measures to non-Federal highway and other construction through appropriate action by state, county, and other local governments.

2. Additional study of the detrimental effects of chemicals used to melt ice and control roadside vegetation is needed.

3. Air pollution from automobile engine exhausts is of a serious nature and a major effort must be made to correct it.

4. A center for the reporting of highway accidents involving the spilling of hazardous commodities should be established as a means of providing aid, rapid control, and warnings concerning possible polluting effects.

5. The polluting effects of runoff from paved surfaces can be detrimental to recreational bathing areas and other water uses and users and requires a great deal more attention.

6. The problem of roadside litter, especially the "no return" beverage containers, requires more direct action by state governments than mere prohibitory laws and penalties. A redeemable surcharge or penalty imposed on each such container is suggested.

References Cited

1. "Report on Patuxent River Basin, Maryland," The Johns Hopkins University, Baltimore, Md., June, 1966.
2. Wolman, M. Gordon, "Problems Posed by Sediment Derived from Construction Activities in Maryland," Maryland Water Pollution Control Commission, Jan., 1964.
3. Finley, Stewart, "Exploring Lake Barcroft with Dragline and Ten Wheeled Truck," Small Sanitary District, Fairfax County, Va.
4. "Preliminary Study of Sediment Sources and Transport in the Potomac River Basin," Interstate Commission on the Potomac River Basin, Washington, D. C., 1963.
5. *Instructional Memorandum No. 20-3-66,* Bureau of Public Roads, U. S. Department of Commerce, June 7, 1966.
6. *Better Roads Magazine,* Aug., 1966.
7. Weiner, Daniel J., Unpublished report, Robert A. Taft Sanitary Engineering Center, Cincinnati, Ohio, Aug., 1966.
8. Button, E. F., "Influence of Rock Salt Used for Highway Ice Control on Mature Sugar Maples at One Location in Central Connecticut,"
9. Button, E. F., "The Effect of Rock Salt Upon Roadside Sugar Maples in Connecticut,"
10. "Maple Decline in New Hampshire," *Phytopathology,* Vol. 54, No. 1, Sept., 1964.
11. *Better Roads Magazine,* Aug., 1966.
12. Burke, George, "Transportation Accidents and Water Pollution," paper presented at the 19th Annual Industrial Waste Conference, at Purdue University, Lafayette, Ind., May, 1964.
13. Burn, R. J., Krawczyk, D. F., Harlow, G. L.,

"Chemical and Physical Comparison between Combined and Separate Sewer Discharges in Southeastern Michigan" (unpublished report).

14. Weibel, S. R., Weidner, R. B., Christianson, A. G., and Anderson, R. J., "Characterization, Treatment and Disposal of Urban Stormwater," 3rd International Conference on Water Pollution Research.

15. Palmer, C. L., "The Pollutional Effects of Stormwater Overflows from Combined Sewers," *Sewage and Industrial Wastes,* Vol. 22, p. 154.

16. "Ground Water Contamination and Legal Controls in Michigan," *Water Supply Paper 1691,* Geological Survey, U. S. Department of the Interior, 1963.

ADDITIONAL REFERENCES

Berthouex, P. M. 1968. Environmental effects of highways. (Discussion.) *J. San. Eng.* 94(SA2):440–443.

Cannon, H. L., and J. M. Bowles. 1962. Contamination of vegetation by tetraethyl lead. *Science* 131:1733–1734.

Demaree, A. T. 1970. Cars and cities on a collision course. Pp. 90–104 in *The environment,* by the Editors of Fortune. New York: Perennial Library.

Lagerwerff, J. V., and A. W. Specht. 1970. Contamination of roadside soil and vegetation with cadmium, nickel, lead, and zinc. *Environ. Sci. and Tech.* 4(7):583–586.

Middleton, J. T., and W. Ott. 1968. Air pollution and transportation. *Traffic Quarterly,* April, 1968.

Milleret, Claude. 1963. La forêt d'Orléans. *Annales de Géographie;* no. 392, pp. 426–458.

Motto, H. L., et al. 1970. Lead in soils and plants: Its relationship to traffic volume and proximity to highways. *Environ. Sci. and Tech.* 4(3):231–237.

Mowbray, A. Q. 1969. *Road to ruin.* Philadelphia: J. B. Lippincott Co. 240 pp.

THE DENVER EARTHQUAKES

J. H. HEALY, W. W. RUBEY, D. T. GRIGGS, AND C. B. RALEIGH

Man now triggers earthquakes by upsetting geologic equilibrium deep under ground. In trying to dispose of some of the noxious wastes which modern technology produces we have subscribed to the foolish principle, "Out of sight, out of mind." Liquid wastes are being disposed of by pumping them into subsurface space—either pores and joints in rocks or man-made cavities. Normally all deep space below the water table is already filled with fluids, but wastes injected under high pressure can force existing fluids to move out, depending on the permeability of the rock. Major kinds of liquid wastes disposed of in this way are salt water (often abundant with oil from oil wells), chemicals, and radioactive wastes.

This selection discusses the disposal of waste chemical fluids by injection into a deep well and the earthquakes it has triggered near Denver, Colorado. This case is an outstanding example of man's actions causing unintended and unforeseen environmental consequences which circle back on him.

John H. Healy (b. 1929) and Cecil B. Raleigh (b. 1934) are geophysicists with the U.S. Geological Survey's National Center for Earthquake Research in Menlo Park, California. Healy has been with the Geological Survey since he earned his Ph.D. degree at the California Institute of Technology in 1951. His present research includes studies of earthquake triggering by nuclear explosion as well as earthquakes related to fluid injection. Raleigh holds a Ph.D. (geology, 1963) from the University of California, Los Angeles. He is continuing, with Healy, experiments in Colorado at the Rangely oil field to determine the physical mechanism of earthquake triggering by fluid injection in a well-controlled environment. William W. Rubey (b. 1898) is emeritus professor of geology and geophysics at the University of California, Los Angeles. Before going to U.C.L.A. in 1960 he was a geologist with the U.S. Geological Survey for thirty-six years. He has been honored by doctoral degrees from Missouri, Villanova, Yale, and California. He also is director of the Lunar Science Institute, a member of the National Academy of Sciences (Council, 1965–1968; Space Science Board, 1968–), the Geological Society of America (president, 1950; Penrose Medal, 1963), and was on the National Science Board from 1960 to 1966. He has received the National Medal of Science (1965). Rubey has served on several federal panels investigating earthquake generation. His recent research interests have extended to space science, including lunar geology and exploration. David T. Griggs (b. 1911) has been a professor of geophysics at the University of California, Los Angeles, since 1948. He is a member of the National Academy of Sciences, was chief scientist for the United States Air Force, and has advised numerous governmental groups, including the Atomic Energy Commission. Subjects of Griggs' research have included nuclear energy and deformation of rocks under high pressure.

This selection is abridged with permission of the authors from *Science* 161(3848):1301–1310, September 27, 1968. Copyright 1968 by the American Association for the Advancement of Science.

The nature and dangers of the waste itself, barely mentioned in this selection, are of interest.   Since 1942 the Rocky Mountain Arsenal, located a few miles northeast of Denver and operated by the Chemical Corps of the United States Army, has manufactured chemical weapons. Until 1961 the contaminated waste water from this operation was allowed to evaporate from open-air reservoirs (Scopel, 1964).   However, wastes seeped into the ground, contaminating the groundwater supply and endangering crops (Walker, 1961).   The army then decided to drill an injection disposal well to dispose of the wastes; it was completed at a total depth of 12,045 feet in September, 1961, with the lowermost 75 feet in highly fractured Precambrian gneiss (Evans, 1966a).

Injection of fluids began in March 1962.   The next month small earthquakes began to occur in the vicinity of the arsenal.   The frequency of earthquakes was closely correlated with the volume of fluid injected into the well, until early 1966 when the injection of wastes was halted. Since then, however, the earthquakes have continued and have become even more severe, with some likelihood of a really destructive earthquake occurring in the Denver area.

The immediate cause of an earthquake is the sudden fracturing with movement (or "faulting") of rocks that have been stressed beyond the limit of their strength.   Simply stated, the authors hypothesize that in this case the injected fluid has released stored strain in the rocks by reducing their frictional resistance to faulting.   Some details of the proposed mechanism are given here for readers who are interested; more are presented in the original article.

Fluids are being injected into the ground in many other places also, sometimes with the same physical consequence—earthquakes.   The nearness of cities to such places increases the human consequences of waste disposal in injection wells.   In the Los Angeles area, salt water is being injected into the ground to counter land subsidence resulting from the withdrawal of oil (see Selection 27).

Underground nuclear explosions are an additional mechanism by which man causes earthquakes, although there is uncertainty about the magnitude and the extent in space and time of the effects (Healy and Marshall, 1970; Werth, 1969).   Breaks in rock caused by such explosions normally are not visible from the surface, although a test in Nevada in 1968 (ironically named the Faultless test) created a long surface fault with a vertical displacement of 15 feet (Committee for Environmental Information, 1969, p. 47).   At present the hazard of earthquakes from such tests probably is less than the danger of accidental releases of radiation to the outside air through holes.

In summary, injected wastes and underground nuclear explosions may be out of sight, but because of the earthquakes that they trigger they certainly are not out of mind.   A more visible and direct danger is presented by one of the Rocky Mountain Arsenal's primary products—deadly nerve gas for warfare.   In 1968 Colorado citizens complained about nerve gas being stored in the open directly under the flight path into Denver's International Airport (Nelson, 1970).

(Editor's comment)

Scientists and public officials are seriously considering the question of whether removal of fluid from a deeply buried reservoir will reduce the likelihood of a destructive earthquake near Denver, Colorado. The question at issue in the discussions is not so absurd as it might seem. It is widely, though not unanimously, held that injection of chemical-waste fluid into the reservoir in the Denver basin triggered the earthquakes. We attempt here to present the statistical evidence for correlating the two events—fluid injection and earthquakes—and to develop a hypothesis relating the two as cause and effect.*

In 1961 a deep disposal well was completed for the U.S. Army at the Rocky Mountain Arsenal, northeast of Denver, Colorado. The well was drilled through 3638 meters of nearly flat-lying sedimentary rocks in the Denver basin into Precambrian crystalline

* Details of the explanatory physical model are deleted in this abridgement (*Editor's note*).

rocks; its depth at completion was 3671 meters. The disposal of waste fluids from chemical-manufacturing operations at the arsenal had been a difficult problem, for which the deep well appeared to be an ideal solution. Injection of fluids on a routine basis was begun on 8 March 1962 and continued through 30 September 1963 at an average rate of about 21 million liters per month. No fluid was injected from October 1963 to August 1964. Then for a time fluid was put into the well under gravity flow at an average rate of about 7.5 million liters per month. Gravity flow was continued until 6 April 1965, when injection under pressure was resumed, at an average rate of 17 million liters per month. On 20 February 1966 injection of fluid was stopped because of a suggested connection between the well and earthquakes in the Denver area.

Two seismograph stations were operating in the Denver area in 1962, one by the Colorado School of Mines, at Bergen Park, about 34 kilometers west of Denver, the other

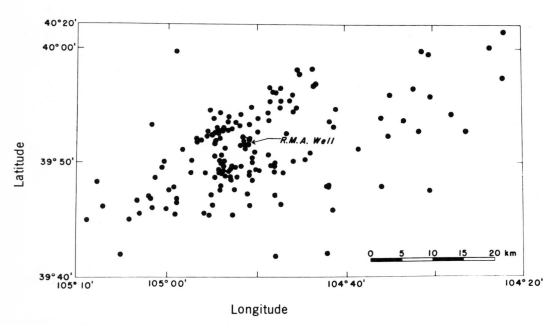

FIGURE 31.1 Observations on which David Evans in 1965 based his theory of the relation between fluid injection and earthquakes at the Rocky Mountain Arsenal, Denver, Colorado. (Above) Epicenters (solid circles) of earthquakes as calculated by Wang using data from the Bergen Park and Regis College stations and from temporary U.S. Geological Survey stations. (Right) Correlations, by Evans, between the number of earthquakes and the volume of fluid injected.

at Regis College in Denver. Both stations began to record earthquakes from the region northeast of Denver, starting on 24 April 1962. As the sequence continued, the U.S. Geological Survey established several additional stations, and Yung-Liang Wang, a graduate student at the Colorado School of Mines, undertook a study of all the available seismic recordings. He located many of the earthquakes (*1*) within a region about 75 kilometers long, 40 kilometers wide, and 45 kilometers deep (Figure 31.1, left). It was pointed out later that most of the earthquakes located by Wang were within 8 kilometers of the disposal well.

Father Joseph V. Downey, director of the Regis College Seismological Observatory, was among the first to suggest the possibility of a relationship between the disposal well and the earthquakes. In November 1965 David Evans (*2*), a consulting geologist in Denver, showed a correlation between the volumes of fluid injected into the well and the number of earthquakes detected at Bergen Park, and publicly suggested that a direct relation did exist (Figure 31.1, right).

The proximity of the earthquakes to the Denver metropolitan area created considerable public interest and concern. A number of the larger earthquakes, of Richter magnitude between 3 and 4, were felt over a wide area, and minor damage was reported near the epicenters. The sudden appearance of seismic activity close to a major city posed serious questions, and the possibility that the earthquakes were caused by operations at the Rocky Mountain Arsenal had to be evaluated as quickly as possible.

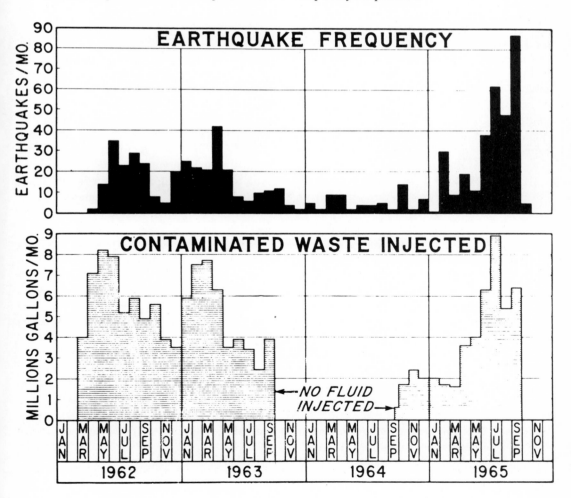

The Preliminary Program

The U.S. Army Corps of Engineers was called upon for technical support and advice, and the U.S. Geological Survey, in cooperation with the Corps of Engineers, began a program of investigation to evaluate the Evans theory. The Colorado School of Mines played a major role in those investigations, with support from the State of Colorado, the Corps of Engineers, and the Environmental Science Services Administration.

A search of the available instrumental and historical records was one of the first investigations undertaken. Any earthquakes that had occurred before the start of fluid injection would lessen the correlation between water injection and earthquake occurrence. The seismograph station at Bergen Park began operation only a few months before the start of water injection, and no earthquakes were recorded from the Denver area during that period. The station at Regis College had been in operation since 1909, but it is located in an area of high background noise and, for most of its history, was operated at low magnification. Thus, earthquakes of small magnitude could have escaped detection by the local stations and the regional networks.

Between 1954 and 1959 a short-period seismograph station was operated by Warren Longley at the University of Colorado, Boulder. A search of the records from that station (3) revealed 13 events that might have been earthquakes in the Denver area, but all had occurred during normal working hours and were probably the result of construction blasting or disposal of explosives at the arsenal.

Hadsell (4), in a search of newspaper accounts and other historic records, uncovered reports of a number of earthquakes in Colorado in historic times. None had epicenters near the zone of current activity, with the possible exception of an earthquake in 1882 that was felt in the Denver-Boulder area as well as at other, widely separated points in Colorado. It appears that there is no evidence of seismic activity before 1962 similar to the earthquakes that have occurred since 1962.

A very dense network of seismic stations was established by the U.S. Geological Survey in the vicinity of the arsenal well, to obtain accurate locations of earthquake hypocenters. Slightly modified explosion seismology equipment was used, in eight small arrays. Each array consisted of six vertical seismometers at half-kilometer intervals, arranged in an L-shaped pattern, and two horizontal seismometers located at one of the vertical-seismometer positions. This special network was operated during January and February of 1966 for about 6 hours each day. During this 2-month period, between one and five earthquakes large enough to be located occurred each day during the hours of recording. A survey of the seismic velocities of the rocks penetrated by the well and a nearby seismic refraction profile were used to determine a velocity-depth function (5). The dense net of seismic stations and the unusually good control on seismic velocities made it possible to locate small earthquakes with a high degree of accuracy. Well-recorded earthquakes were located with a precision of 0.3 kilometer in the horizontal plane and 0.5 kilometer in the vertical plane. Not all the earthquakes were so well recorded, but all of the calculated locations are thought to be within 1 kilometer of the true locations.

Sixty-two earthquakes for which accurate locations could be obtained occurred in a roughly ellipsoidal zone about 10 kilometers long and 3 kilometers wide, which includes the disposal well (Figure 31.2, top). The long axis of the zone trends N 60°W. The depths of the earthquakes ranged from 4.5 to 5.5 kilometers.

Following completion of the preliminary program, the Colorado School of Mines installed additional short-period seismograph stations and the U.S. Geological Survey installed a 17-element array over the zone of hypocenters. These networks are continuing to record earthquakes.

Change in the Pattern of Activity

Injection of fluids in the disposal well was terminated in February 1966, but earthquakes have continued at a rate varying from 4 to 71 per month, as indicated at the Bergen Park Observatory. During that period, hundreds of very small earthquakes were detected on the U.S. Geological Survey network centered on the hypocentral zone. On 10 April 1967, the largest earthquake of the series to that date shook the Denver area. Its magnitude was estimated at 5.0 by Maurice Major (6), on the basis of the Bergen Park Observatory records. The U.S. Geological Survey network located the hypocenter within the zone of previous activity. In fact, all the earthquakes located fell within or close to the bounds defined by the 2-month preliminary study (Figure 31.2, top). A number of aftershocks of the 10 April earthquake define a linear pattern which trends about N 60°W (7) (Figure 31.2, bottom), as the earlier earthquake locations did. From the statistics for the frequency and magnitude of the entire sequence, the large earthquake of 10 April might reasonably have been expected. But there was more to come. On 9 August there was a second large earthquake of magnitude between 5¼ and 5½, and on 26 November there was a third, of magnitude 5.1 (Figure 31.2, bottom). The three large earthquakes, with their foreshocks and aftershocks, introduce a dramatic change in the pattern of activity.

Some seismologists have argued that the magnitude-frequency plot, a histogram of the common logarithm of the number of earthquakes relative to their magnitude, can be used to establish the level of seismicity in an area and to predict the rates of recurrence of large earthquakes over a period of years. A considerable number of data support this view, but there are some startling exceptions (8).

With the exception of the Los Angeles Basin, the magnitude-frequency histograms for all the southern California regions studied can be fitted with a straight line having a

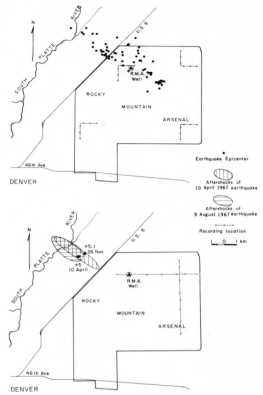

FIGURE 31.2 (Top) Epicenters of earthquakes located in January and February of 1966 by means of a dense network of temporary seismic stations. The locations are accurate to within 1 kilometer. (Bottom) Location of (i) the earthquake of 10 April 1967 and its aftershocks; (ii) aftershocks of the event of 9 August 1967; and (iii) the epicenter of the 26 November 1967 earthquake.

slope between −0.8 and −1.02. The average for southern California is −0.86.

The magnitude-frequency relationship for earthquakes in Denver was determined first by Yung-Liang Wang (1), who obtained a value of −0.78 for the slope. A recent determination of −0.82 was made by Major and Wideman (9), on the basis of data obtained through April 1967.

Only the data from the Bergen Park Observatory were used in determining magnitudes for the Denver earthquakes, because it is the only station that has been in operation at high magnification throughout the period of activity.

TABLE 31.1 Magnitude and frequency of occurrence of Denver earthquakes.

| YEAR | MAGNITUDE* | | | | | | | TOTAL† |
	1.5—1.9	2.0—2.4	2.5—2.9	3.0—3.4	3.5—3.9	4.0—4.4	4.5—4.9	5.0—5.4	
1962	72	29	4	2	1	1			189
1963	89	34	9	3	1	1			284
1964	26	8	6						72
1965	168	64	25	6	4				550
1966	61	18	3	2	1				186
1967	62	29	15	4	4	2		3	306
Total	478	182	62	17	11	4		3	1584
Average‡	83.2	30.5	9.4	2.6	1.4	0.4			

* To the nearest 0.1-magnitude unit.
† Total includes all earthquakes reported.
‡ Average yearly activity 1962–66.

Recently, Ruth Simon at the Colorado School of Mines has reexamined all the Denver earthquake seismograms and has prepared a new list of earthquakes for the entire period of earthquake activity (6). These data were used in preparing the mag-nitude-frequency plots given here. The data on magnitude and frequency, by year, are given in Table 31.1.

The yearly plots (Figure 31.3a) reveal a remarkably consistent pattern from 1962 through 1966, with the possible exception of

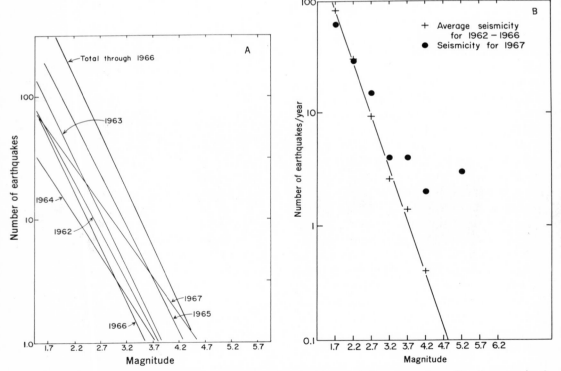

FIGURE 31.3 (A) Frequency-magnitude relationships for the Denver earthquake series. The lines are least-squares fits to histograms for each year and for the total period. The histograms were prepared in 0.5-magnitude units. **(B)** Comparison of the frequency-magnitude relationship (seismicity) for 1967 with the average for the preceding 5 years.

1964, for which the slope is somewhat lower. The number of earthquakes recorded in 1964 is too small to provide an adequate measure of the seismic acitivty.

The average for the data for the years 1962 through 1966 suggests that one earthquake with a magnitude of about 4.5 could be expected within a 5-year period, the total period of earthquake activity. The rate of recurrence for earthquakes of magnitude between 6.0 and 6.4 is more than 100 years. The occurrence of a single earthquake in April 1967 having a magnitude of 5.0 was not in serious conflict with expectation. However, the two succeeding earthquakes of magnitude greater than 5 in 1967 clearly showed that the earthquakes were not following this statistical pattern, established from 1962 to 1966, which predicts about three such earthquakes in 60 years (Figure 31.3b).

When the frequency-magnitude relationship for 1967 is examined more closely, it becomes clear that a significant change has occurred. The data for earthquakes smaller than magnitude 4.5 are best fitted by a straight line having a slope of -0.61, which is substantially smaller than the magnitude-frequency slope for other years (Figure 31.3b). However, because of the occurrence of three earthquakes with magnitude between 5.0 and 5.5, with no earthquakes in the magnitude range 4.5 to 4.9, it is not possible to fit all the points for 1967 with a straight line.

The significance of this change in the earthquake pattern is more clearly revealed if we consider the seismic energy radiated as a function of magnitude. Richter (*10*, p. 366) gives the following relationship between energy, E, and magnitude, M: log $E = 11.4 + 1.5\,M$. From this relationship, a graph of cumulative energy release for each 6-month period was prepared (Figure 31.4).

Because the energy of earthquakes increases by a factor of about 31 for each 1-unit increase in magnitude, the three earthquakes with magnitude greater than 5 that occurred in 1967 account for almost all of the energy released in the earthquake series. It seems clear that something new is happening, with unknown portent for the future.

Correlation of Earthquakes with Fluid Injection

What is the probability that an earthquake sequence such as that at Denver could occur by pure chance close to the time and place of the injection of fluids into the basement rock? The occurrence of swarms of small earthquakes in Colorado is probably a more common event than most people recognize. During the course of our work, several groups of earthquakes were noted that might have been similar to the Denver earthquakes. An earthquake sequence is occurring near Ranggely, Colorado; another is occurring some distance to the north of Denver, perhaps in Wyoming; and others may be occurring in the San Juan Mountains of southern Colorado. Most of this activity was detected by only a few stations and has not been studied in detail. It is probable that most of these areas are somewhat less active than the area near Denver. Hadsell's (*4*) list of Colorado earthquakes shows 70 earthquakes between December 1870 and January 1967. The list for the years prior to 1962 is based on reports of felt earthquakes. The list for 1962 and subsequent years includes all earthquakes in Colorado, exclusive of the Denver area, of magnitude greater than 3.0 and all earthquakes in the Denver sequence of magnitude greater than 3.1. Of the 70

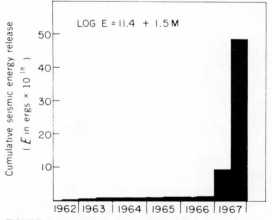

FIGURE 31.4 Cumulative seismic-energy release in Denver earthquakes, by 6-month periods.

earthquakes, 28 were in the Denver sequence. We can say conservatively that not more than ten earthquake swarms similar to the Denver swarm are occurring in Colorado at any one time. Colorado has an area of 270,000 square kilometers. The accurately located earthquakes in the Denver sequence are all contained in an area of less than 65 square kilometers. The probability of finding a swarm in a randomly selected 65-square-kilometer area is therefore 1 in 4150.

What is the probability that an earthquake swarm would start within 7 weeks of the beginning of a fluid-injection program? The only known possibly similar seismic activity near the disposal well is an earthquake that occurred in 1882. The location of this earthquake is given in Hadsell's list as Vail Pass, but it was felt in the Denver area, so it may possibly have occurred near the present location of the disposal well.

If one assumes that the earthquake of 1882 occurred near Denver rather than at Vail Pass and that the recurrence rate for this activity was 80 years, the probability that an earthquake swarm would start within 7 weeks of the beginning of fluid injection in the disposal well is 1 in 600. The joint probability that the earthquakes would be so closely associated in both time and space, with the disposal well is $1/600 \times 1/4150 = 1/2,500,000$. The occurrence of a natural earthquake swarm so closely related to the disposal well would thus be an extremely unlikely coincidence.

Since shallow earthquakes are caused by movements along faults, seismic activity at the level of the Denver earthquake sequence will, if repeated at frequent intervals through geologic history, probably result in large tectonic displacements. These displacements should produce recognizable deformation of the sedimentary rocks overlying the earthquake zone. A seismic-reflection survey of the epicentral region of the Denver earthquakes revealed no extensive folding or faulting in the sedimentary rocks overlying the earthquakes (*11*). Several small faults, of displacement less than 30 meters, were discovered, and topographic relief over the

area of the survey was less than 60 meters. This evidence suggests that there has been very little seismic activity at this site since Precambrian time.

In a search for clues to the earthquake mechanism, the original pressure charts were reexamined and, wherever possible, the average daily wellhead pressure and the volume of fluids injected were redetermined. The daily data (Figure 31.6a) were used to determine an average pressure for each month, and these averages were plotted against the number of earthquakes per month (Figure 31.6b). Figure 31.6 shows that there is a strong correlation between fluid pressure and the level of seismic activity for the years 1962–66, but the increase in seismic activity in 1967 appears to rule out any simple direct relationship between these parameters.

Mechanism of the Earthquakes

An understanding of the mechanism of these earthquakes is of great importance, not only for controlling the current sequence at Denver but also for predicting where other such sequences might occur. It now seems clear that, contrary to some early conjecture, the energy released by the earthquakes was stored in the basement rock as nonhydrostatic elastic strain. The evidence pointing to a tectonic origin for the elastic strain energy released is twofold.

1) The frequency-magnitude relationship for the early earthquakes is similar to that for tectonically active areas such as southern California.

2) The seismic-radiation patterns are consistent with right-lateral strike-slip motion on vertical fault planes aligned with the trend of the seismic zone. The prolongation of the epicentral zone in a west-northwestern direction parallel to one of the two possible fault-plane sets (Figure 31.5) strongly suggests that a zone of vertical fractures existed along the trend prior to the injection of fluid. Examination of core from the basement rock has shown the presence of vertical fractures prior to such injection (*12*). These observations

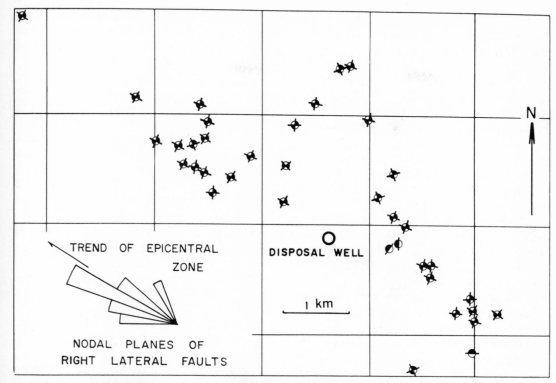

FIGURE 31.5 Seismic radiation patterns of first arrivals from epicentral locations. Black quadrants: compressional first motions; crosses: azimuthal orientations of the near-vertical nodal planes, one of which is the fault plane for the event. The compass rose diagram at lower left gives azimuthal orientations of right-lateral strike-slip faults.

suggest that the earthquakes are produced by a regional stress field of tectonic origin.

From this evidence we consider it highly probable that the release of the stored tectonic strain was triggered by the injection of fluid into the basement rock. This hypothesis has a rational basis established theoretically by Hubbert and Rubey (*13*) and tested experimentally by several workers.

The distribution of the Denver earthquakes in space and time has two features which at first glance seem anomalous but in fact are consistent with the Hubbert-Rubey theory.

1) Although there is a net migration of epicenters away from the well consistent with the advance of a pressure front during the period of fluid injection (*14*), earthquakes appear to have been occurring over the whole of the existing epicentral zone at the end of the pumping period (Figure 31.2, top).

2) Since the cessation of fluid injection in February 1966, earthquake activity has continued despite reduction of pore pressure in the reservoir at the well to 311 bars in April 1968. Seismic activity near the well has ceased, but earthquakes of larger magnitude than those that occurred during the injection period have occurred near the northwesterly terminus of the epicentral zone (Figure 31.2, bottom).

We assume that the rocks in the fault zone contain a large number of cracks that vary in length and have a normal distribution of orientation about the trend of the fault zone. Furthermore, the cracks parallel to the fault zone are assumed to have the most favorable orientation for propagation. In the cracks where τ/σ_n exceeds the coefficient of sliding friction, irregularities along the fracture surface and the crack terminations may be considered lock points restricting move-

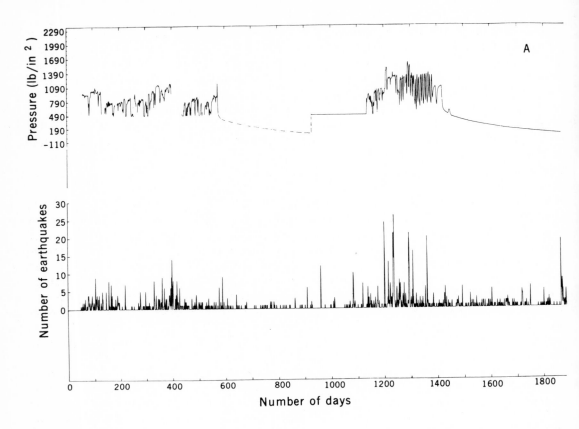

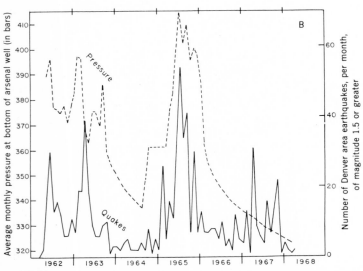

FIGURE 31.6 (A) Daily pressure plotted relative to number of earthquakes. The dashed portions in the pressure curve are interpolated where only data on the volume of fluid injected were available. (B) Comparison of number of earthquakes and pressure, on a monthly basis.

ment. At the time of an earthquake, when one of these lock points fails, the break may propagate until it is inhibited by a stronger lock point along the fracture surface. The crack would also tend to arrest as it passed from a region of higher into a region of lower pore pressure.

A relation between the length of a fault rupture and the magnitude of the associated earthquake has been established from data on faults which break the surface (*15*). If this relation holds for the Denver earthquakes, our conceptual model, as outlined above, would predict a predominance of earthquakes of greater magnitude following cessation of fluid injection, when only the longer cracks are capable of propagation. Moreover, faulting near the well would diminish, in comparison with that during the injection period, when seismic activity would be more evenly distributed over the entire epicentral zone and greater numbers of earthquakes of smaller magnitude would occur.

Conclusions

Most investigators working on the Denver earthquakes have concluded that the injection of fluid triggered the seismic activity. However, some investigators believe that the earthquakes might have occurred even if the well had not been drilled, and there is a wide range of opinion on the advisability of attempting to terminate the earthquake sequence by removing fluid from the well (*16*).

We consider the possibility of a coincidental occurrence of earthquakes with the onset of fluid injection at Denver to be remote. Furthermore, there is now evidence that fluid injection and swarms of earthquakes occur together at other locations (*17*). The mechanism by which fluid injection triggered the earthquakes is the reduction of frictional resistance to faulting, a reduction which occurs with increase in pore pressure. Other mechanisms, including reduction in the strength of the rocks, due to chemical alteration, have been investigated,

but so far none of these appear to explain the seismicity adequately. The implication of the pore-pressure mechanism—that the rocks were stressed to near their breaking strength before the injection of fluid—is in accord with the available data. Faulting is predominantly right-lateral strike-slip on faults which are parallel to the epicentral zone, an observation which also suggests release of tectonic stress rather than disturbances produced by fluid injection alone.

Prior to 1967, the frequency of occurrence of earthquakes of different magnitudes in the Denver area was such that the likelihood of a really destructive earthquake could reasonably be considered remote. In view of the 1967 earthquakes, however, there is no longer any assurance that a destructive earthquake will not occur. Hence, the question of what might be done to lessen the earthquake hazard now confronts those earth scientists who have been studying the problem.

In our view, it might be possible to reduce the size and number of the earthquakes by removing substantial quantities of fluid from the reservoir. If the Hubbert-Rubey pore-pressure effect is the cause of the earthquakes (and, to our knowledge, it is the only mechanism yet demonstrated to explain them adequately), reducing the pore pressure should effectively strengthen the reservoir rocks and thus reduce the size and number of the earthquakes.

Despite the theoretical attractiveness of this approach, the engineering difficulties and costs involved in removing sufficient quantities of fluid from the reservoir to reduce significantly the occurrence of earthquakes may prove prohibitively expensive. Early withdrawal tests conducted before fluid injection was begun indicated a reservoir with very low transmissibility. If this low transmissibility is characteristic of the reservoir today, the removal of fluid would probably be impractical. One technique used successfully to increase the production of oil from reservoirs having low transmissibility is the propping open of fractures with coarse sand.

Steps are now being taken to evaluate the properties of the reservoir and to design preliminary tests to determine the feasibility of removing the fluids (*18*).

Given sufficient time, the pore pressure in the focal zone will dissipate naturally, and it is hoped that, as the zone of high pressure spreads outward from the well, the maximum pressures in the reservoir will fall below the level required to trigger seismic activity. Unfortunately we do not have precise measurements of the original static pressure in the reservoir and, therefore, we cannot tell how much excess pressure remains in the reservoir rock. Because the level at which the fluid stands in the disposal well is still falling, we know that a substantial overpressure must still exist and that therefore the zone of high pressure is still moving out from the well. There is no reason to believe that the excess pressure will dissipate naturally before the epicentral zone is extended by further faulting and attendant large earthquakes. It appears that, unless the removal of fluid can be shown, either theoretically or by pumping tests, to constitute a real hazard, every reasonable effort should be made to remove fluids from the reservoir in order to reduce the reservoir pressures and minimize the earthquake hazards. To best achieve this goal and to test the hypothesis presented here, we favor removal of fluid by means of a second well drilled into the currently active focal zone.

References and Notes

1. Y. Wang, thesis, Colorado School of Mines (1965).
2. D. Evans, *Mountain Geologist* 3, No. 1, 23 (1966).
3. H. L. Krivoy and M. P. Lane, in "Geophysical and Geological Investigations Relating to Earthquakes in the Denver Area, Colorado," *U.S. Geol. Surv. Open File Rep.* (1966), pt. 2.
4. F. Hadsell, "History of Earthquake Activity in Colorado," *Colorado School of Mines Rep.* (1967).
5. J. H. Healy, W. H. Jackson, J. R. Van Schaack, in "Geophysical and Geological Investigations Relating to Earthquakes in the Denver Area, Colorado," *U.S. Geol. Surv. Open File Rep.* (1966), pt. 5.
6. M. Major and R. Simon, *Quart. Colorado School of Mines* 63, 9 (1968).
7. The location of the earthquake of 10 April and of its aftershocks was determined by D. B. Hoover of the U.S. Geological Survey.
8. The nature of the magnitude-frequency plots for southern California, together with a good discussion of the pros and cons of using these curves for predicting large-magnitude earthquakes, is given by C. Allen, P. St. Amand, C. Righter, and J. Nordquist [*Bull. Seismol. Soc. Amer.* 55, 753 (1965)].
9. M. Major and C. Wideman, "Seismic Study of Derby Earthquakes," *Colorado School of Mines Rep.* (1967).
10. C. Richter, *Elementary Seismology* (Freeman, New York, 1958).
11. D. B. Hoover, unpublished manuscript.
12. D. M. Sheridan, C. T. Wrucke, R. E. Wilcox, in "Geophysical and Geological Investigations Relating to Earthquakes in the Denver Area, Colorado," *U.S. Geol. Surv. Open File Rep.* (1966), pt. 4.
13. M. K. Hubbert and W. W. Rubey, *Bull. Geol. Soc. Amer.* 70, 115 (1959).
14. M. Major, personal communication, 1967.
15. D. Tocher, *Bull. Seismol. Soc. Amer.* 48, 147 (1958).
16. It would be extremely difficult to summarize all of the opinions that have been expressed regarding the Denver earthquakes. Many investigators who have worked on the problem have not published their contributions, and most of the people working on it have modified their views as additional evidence has become available. The current views of workers at the Colorado School of Mines are summarized by J. C. Hollister and R. J. Weimer in *Quart. Colorado School of Mines* 63, No. 1, 2 (1968).
17. One example that has been studied is at Rangely oil field in western Colorado; see J. H. Healy, C. B. Raleigh, J. M. Coakley, paper presented before the 64th annual meeting of the Seismological Society of America, 1968.
18. Pumping tests were initiated at the arsenal well on 1 September 1968.
19. Publication of this article (publication No. 679 of the Institute of Geophysics and Planetary Physics) has been approved by the director of the U.S. Geological Survey. The work described has been supported in part by NSF grant G.A. 277. We thank M. Major and R. Simon of the Colorado School of Mines for providing us with a list of the times of occurrence and the magnitudes of Denver earthquakes recorded at the Cecil H. Green Observatory, Bergen Park, Colorado; W. H. K. Lee for making his spectral analysis program available to us; and M. K. Hubbert for discussions on hydraulic fracturing.

ADDITIONAL REFERENCES

Caswell, C. A. 1970. Underground waste disposal: Concepts and misconceptions. *Environ. Sci. and Tech.* 4(8):642-647.

Committee for Environmental Information, Scientific Division Report. 1969. Underground nuclear testing. *Environment* 11(6):3-13, 41-53. Includes a discussion (1) of earthquakes and faulting caused by underground testing and (2) of proposed nuclear excavation projects.

Evans, D. M. 1966a. The Denver area earthquakes and the Rocky Mountain Arsenal disposal well. *The Mountain Geologist* 3(1):23-36.

Evans, D. M. 1966b. Man-made earthquakes in Denver. *GeoTimes* 10(9):11-18.

Galley, J. E., ed. 1968. Subsurface disposal in geologic basins—A study of reservoir strata. *Am. Assoc. Petrol. Geol., Memoir 10,* 253 pp.

Healy, J. H., and P. A. Marshall. 1970. Nuclear explosions and distant earthquakes: A search for correlations. *Science* 169:176-177.

Interstate Oil Compact Commission. 1968. *Subsurface disposal of industrial wastes.* 109 pp.

Mechem, O. E., and J. H. Garrett. 1963. Deep injection disposal wells for liquid toxic waste. *Proc. Am. Soc. Civil Engrs., J. Construct. Div.,* pp. 111-121.

Nelson, B. 1970. Colorado environmentalists: Scientists battle AEC and Army. *Science* 168: 1324-1328.

Piper, A. M. 1969. Disposal of liquid wastes by injection underground—neither myth nor millennium. *U.S. Geological Survey Circular 631.* 15 pp.

Scopel, L. J. 1964. Pressure injection disposal well, Rocky Mountain Arsenal, Denver, Colorado. *The Mountain Geologist* 1(1):35-42.

Simon, R. B. 1969. Seismicity of Colorado: Consistency of recent earthquakes with those of historical record. *Science* 165:897-899.

Walker, T. R. 1961. Ground water contamination in the Rocky Mountain Arsenal area, Denver, Colorado. *Geol. Soc. Am. Bull.* 72:489-494.

Walker, W. R., and R. C. Stewart. 1968. Deepwell disposal of wastes. *Proc. Am. Soc. Civil Engrs., J. Sanit. Engr. Div.* SA5:945-968.

Warner, D. L. 1967. Deep wells for industrial waste injection in the United States—Summary of data. Federal Water Pollution Control Administration, *Water Pollution Control Research Series,* publication no. WP-20-10. 45 pp.

Werth, G. C. 1969. Planned applications of peaceful nuclear explosives. Pp. 31-61 in *Biological Implications of the Nuclear Age,* U.S. Atomic Energy Commission.

Rabbits, introduced by man into Australia. Photo from Australian News and Information Bureau.

THE SPREAD OF ORGANISMS BY MAN

"The history of introductions and invasions of plants and animals as a result of human interference has, as often as not, been fraught with disaster. . . . These introductions frequently lead to ecological explosions."

INTRODUCTION

We now turn to man's impacts on the living landscape, on other organisms. For convenience, this part and the next three parts of the book are broadly divided according to *how* man has affected his biological environment: the importation of strange organisms into new lands (Part 6); the destruction of the land's vegetative cover (Part 7); the contamination, destruction, and extinction of animals (Part 8); and finally the formation by man of new kinds of plants and animals (Part 9). Excluded from consideration here is man's direct influence on his fellowmen. However, nearly all the biological impacts treated here have implications for human welfare.

This part deals with the environmental disruption that occurs when species that have lived apart and evolved in isolation are brought together by man. As Charles Elton has noted in his classical synthesis, *The Ecology of Invasions* (1958), resulting ecological explosions "are really happening much more commonly; indeed they are so frequent nowadays in every continent and island and even in the oceans, that we need to understand what is causing them and try to arrive at some general viewpoint about the whole business."

The introductory chapter from Elton's book, reprinted as Selection 32 here, beautifully illustrates by brief examples a variety of mechanisms, both deliberate and accidental, and consequences of plant and animal invasions. The remaining selections delve further into three examples, revealing the concerted, complex interactions that typically occur when groups of exotic organisms are introduced into a new environment. The three selections present case studies of continental, insular, and marine invasions, respectively.

Selection 33 traces the rapid and profound ecological changes in the American Southwest caused by changes in land use and the spread of a small number of woody plant species. Some of these species are native shrubs which are expanding their ranges; others are aliens, like tamarisk or saltcedar from Eurasia. Human settlement in the last century has led to increased seed dispersal, overgrazing, and the suppression of grass fires, all of which have favored the invasion of grassland by woody plants.

The ecosystems of isolated islands are especially vulnerable to change by invaders because of their relative biological simplicity and their lack of native species adapted to conditions produced by man. Selection 34 surveys the biological changes that man has brought about in the world's southern temperate and sub-Antarctic islands and explains why island floras and faunas are so sensitive to disruption. Man has directly destroyed wild vegetation in the southern temperature and sub-Antarctic islands by cutting, burning, and cultivation; but our indirect actions—through the introduction of grazing and predatory animals—have produced the most radical changes.

Finally, Selection 35 discusses the potential biological catastrophe presented by a planned sea-level canal across Central America. Fresh water between the locks of the existing Panama Canal serves as an effective barrier to the mixing of Atlantic and Pacific marine organisms. We must look beyond the mere technological feasibility and economic utility of a new sea-level canal to its wider ecological and environmental implications.

Selection 20 gives additional examples of the invasion of alien aquatic plants into new waters.

Thus, the subject of the spread of organisms by man is approached here by considering their impact on continental, insular, and marine environments. The ecological effects of invasions on these three types of environment commonly differ somewhat. The dispersal of plants and animals by man has more often been classified according to the purposefulness and actual mechanism of dispersal, rather than the nature of the receiving habitat (e.g., Ridley, 1930; Bates, 1956). First, is the introduction deliberate or accidental? Accidental dispersals of plants may be by (1) adhesion to moving objects, (2) dispersal among crop seed, (3) dispersal among other plants (such as packing materials or drugs), and (4) dispersal among minerals (such as soil or ship's ballast). Regardless of why or exactly how organisms are introduced, however, our primary concern is usually to understand the *effects* of invasions; this understanding is independent of such classifications of introduction. (Knowledge of the mode of invasion is useful, though, in controlling the spread of organisms.)

The beneficial aspects of introducing useful plants and animals for agriculture have long been recognized and exploited (e.g., see Theophrastus, fourth century B.C., de Candolle, 1886). Most details of agricultural origins and movements remain a mystery, even though there is no shortage of speculation concerning them. It is clear, however, that these purposeful dispersals of organisms by man essentially predate the last century. Since then, both the number and speed of international contacts have been greatly accelerated, at first by ships and more recently by planes. Inadvertent introductions of plant and animal pests are an inevitable consequence of this travel. Ironically, the successes of modern agriculture, which have resulted in part form the earlier introductions, have fostered unstable agricultural populations of plants and animals that are especially susceptible to the new pests. Crop monoculture—the extensive growing of one crop alone—has been stimulated further by mechanized farming and modern chemical fertilizers and pesticides. This ecological simplification invites explosions of new or latent pests, just as simple island biotas have been vulnerable. (See Selections 42 and 50 for discussions of the unstabilizing effects of pesticides.)

One last aspect concerning the spread of organisms by man is worth noting: the initial diffusion around the world of man himself, thousands of years ago. There is evidence to indicate that as man invaded new lands he may have overhunted (to extinction) numerous populations of large animals. The self-introduction of man and its consequences on the biological landscape is discussed later, in Selection 45.

FURTHER READINGS

Ackerknecht, E. H. 1965. *History and geography of the most important diseases.* New York: Hafner. 5-224 pp.

Bates, Marston. 1956. Man as an agent in the spread of organisms. Pp. 778-804 in *Man's role in changing the face of the earth,* ed. by William L. Thomas Jr. Chicago and London: Univ. of Chicago Press.

de Candolle, A. P. 1886. *Origin of cultivated plants.* 2d ed. Reprinted 1964 by Hafner, New York and London. 468 pp.

De Vos, A., R. H. Manville, and G. Van Gelder. 1956. Introduced mammals and their influence on native biota. *Zoologica* 41:163-194.

Ingersoll, J. M. 1964. The Australian rabbit. *Am. Scientist* 52:265-273.

King, L. J. 1966. *Weeds of the world: Biology and control.* London: Leonard Hill; New York: Interscience (Wiley). 564 pp.

Ratcliffe, Francis. 1959. The rabbit in Australia. In Biogeography and ecology in Australia. *Monog. Biol.* 8:545-564.

Ridley, H. N. 1930. *The dispersal of plants throughout the world.* Ashford, Kent: L. Reeve. 744 pp. See especially chapter 9, "Dispersal by human agency," pp. 628-659.

Salisbury, E. J. 1961. *Weeds and aliens.* London: Collins. 384 pp.

Sauer, C. O. 1952. *Agricultural origins and dispersals.* Bowman Memorial lectures, Series 2. Am. Geog. Soc. 110 pp.

Theophrastus. Fourth century B.C. *Enquiry into plants.* English transl. by Sir Arthur Hort, 1916. 2 volumes. London: Loeb Classical Library.

Zinsser, Hans. 1935. *Rats, lice and history.* Boston: Little, Brown and Co. 301 pp. Discusses the history of dispersal of human diseases.

THE INVADERS

CHARLES S. ELTON

Ecological explosions have resulted from the introduction by man of foreign plants, animals, or diseases into new environments. This selection briefly discusses seven cases that illustrate a variety of modes of introduction, rates of spread, and ecological effects: (1) entry of the African malaria mosquito into South America, (2) chestnut blight from Asia into forests of the eastern United States, (3) spread of the starling from Eurasia to three new continents, (4) diffusion of the muskrat over Europe after its introduction from North America, (5) cord grass (a hybrid of an American and an English species), now abundant along both coasts of the English Channel, (6) invasion of the sea lamprey into the Great Lakes, and (7) introduction of the Chinese mitten crab from the rivers of northern China to those of Europe.

Viewed in the context of evolutionary time such biological mixing, in which man is the catalyst, is indeed "one of the great historical convulsions in the world's fauna and flora."

(Editor's comment)

Nowadays we live in a very explosive world, and while we may not know where or when the next outburst will be, we might hope to find ways of stopping it or at any rate damping down its force. It is not just nuclear bombs and wars that threaten us, though these rank very high on the list at the moment: there are other sorts of explosions, and this book is about ecological explosions. An ecological explosion means the enormous

Charles S. Elton (b. 1900) was director of Oxford University's Bureau of Animal Population in the Department of Zoological Field Studies from 1932 to 1967. He also was senior research fellow, Corpus Christi College, Oxford (1936-1967), and is now an honorary fellow. He graduated in zoology from New College, Oxford, in 1922. This eminent ecologist is a fellow of the Royal Society (since 1953), recipient of the Linnean Society Gold Medal (1967), and is a foreign honorary member of the American Academy of Arts and Sciences (1968). He is author of numerous books on the ecology of animals, including the now-classical *Animal Ecology* (1927) and, most recently, *The Pattern of Animal Communities* (1966).

This selection is reprinted from chapter 1 (pp. 15-32) of *The Ecology of Invasions by Animals and Plants*, 1958, published by Methuen & Co., Ltd., London.

increase in numbers of some kind of living organism—it may be an infectious virus like influenza, or a bacterium like bubonic plague, or a fungus like that of the potato disease, a green plant like the prickly pear, or an animal like the grey squirrel. I use the word 'explosion' deliberately, because it means the bursting out from control of forces that were previously held in restraint by other forces. Indeed the word was originally used to describe the barracking of actors by an audience whom they were no longer able to restrain by the quality of their performance.

Ecological explosions differ from some of the rest by not making such a loud noise and in taking longer to happen. That is to say, they may develop slowly and they may die down slowly; but they can be very impressive in their effects, and many people have been ruined by them, or died or forced to emigrate. At the end of the First World

War, pandemic influenza broke out on the Western Front, and thence rolled right round the world, eventually, not sparing even the Eskimos of Labrador and Greenland, and it is reputed to have killed 100 million human beings. Bubonic plague is still pursuing its great modern pandemic that started at the back of China in the end of last century, was carried by ship rats to India, South Africa, and other continents, and now smoulders among hundreds of species of wild rodents there, as well as in its chief original home in Eastern Asia. In China it occasionally flares up on a very large scale in the pneumonic form, resembling the Black Death of medieval Europe. In 1911 about 60,000 people in Manchuria died in this way. This form of the disease, which spreads directly from one person to another without the intermediate link of a flea, has mercifully been scarce in the newly invaded continents. Wherever plague has got into natural ecological communities, it is liable to explode on a smaller or larger scale, though by a stroke of fortune for the human race, the train of contacts that starts this up is not very easily fired. In South Africa the gerbilles living on the veld carry the bacteria permanently in many of their populations. Natural epidemics flare up among them frequently. From them the bacteria can pass through a flea to the multimammate mouse; this species, unlike the gerbilles, lives in contact with man's domestic rat; the latter may become infected occasionally and from it isolated human cases of bubonic plague arise.[4] These in turn may spread into a small local epidemic, but often do not. In the United States and Canada a similar underworld of plague (with different species in it) is established over an immense extent of the Western regions (Figures 32.1 and 32.2), though few outbreaks have happened in man.[22] Here, then, the chain of connexions is weaker even than in South Africa, though the potentiality is present. Although plague-stricken people and plague-infected rats certainly landed from ships in California early this century, it is still possible that the plague organism was already present in North America. Professor Karl Meyer, who started the chief

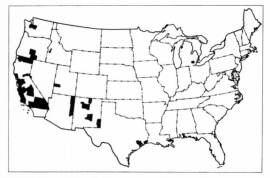

FIGURE 32.1 Counties in the United States where plague has occurred in man. (From V. B. Link, 1955.)

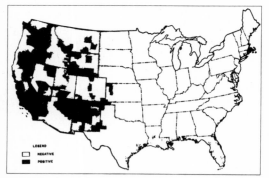

FIGURE 32.2 Counties in the United States where plague has occurred in rodents. (From V. B. Link, 1955.)

ecological research on sylvatic plague there, says: "The only conclusion one can draw is that the original source and date of the creation of the endemic sylvatic plague area on the North American Continent, inclusive [of] Canada, must remain a matter of further investigation and critical analysis."[24]

Another kind of explosion was that of the potato fungus from Europe that partly emptied Ireland through famine a hundred years ago. Most people have had experience of some kind of invasion by a foreign species, if only on a moderate scale. Though these are silent explosions in themselves, they often make quite a loud noise in the Press, and one may come across banner headlines like 'Malaria Epidemic Hits Brazil', 'Forest Damage on Cannock Chase', or 'Rabbit Disease in Kent'. This arrival of rabbit disease—myxomatosis—and its subsequent spread have made one of the biggest ecological explosions Great Britain has had this century, and its ramifying effects will be felt for many years.

But it is not just headlines or a more efficient news service that make such events commoner in our lives than they were last century. They are really happening much more commonly; indeed they are so frequent nowadays in every continent and island, and even in the oceans, that we need to understand what is causing them and try to arrive at some general viewpoint about the whole business. Why should a comfortably placed virus living in Brazilian cotton-tail rabbits suddenly wipe out a great part of the rabbit populations of Western Europe? Why do we have to worry about the Colorado potato beetle now, more than 300 years after the introduction of the potato itself? Why should the pine looper moth break out in Staffordshire and Morayshire pine plantations two years ago? It has been doing this on the Continent for over 150 years; it is not a new introduction to this country.

The examples given above point to two rather different kinds of outbreaks in populations: those that occur because a foreign species successfully invades another country, and those that happen in native or long-established populations. This book is chiefly about the first kind—the invaders. But the interaction of fresh arrivals with the native fauna and flora leads to some consideration of ecological ideas and research about the balance within and between communities as a whole. In other words, the whole matter goes far wider than any technological discussion of pest control, though many of the examples are taken from applied ecology. The real thing is that we are living in a period of the world's history when the mingling of thousands of kinds of organisms from different parts of the world is setting up terrific dislocations in nature. We are seeing huge changes in the natural population balance of the world. Of course, pest control is very important, because we have to preserve our living resources and protect ourselves from diseases and the consequences of economic dislocation. But one should try to see the whole matter on a much broader canvas than that. I like the words of Dr. Johnson: 'Whatever makes the past, the distant, or the future, predominate over the present, advances us in the dignity of thinking beings.'[16] The larger ecological explosions have helped to alter the course of world history, and, as will be shown, can often be traced to a breakdown in the isolation of continents and islands built up during the early and middle parts of the Tertiary Period.

In order to focus the subject, here are seven case histories of species which were brought from one country and exploded into another. About 1929, a few African mosquitoes accidentally reached the north-east corner of Brazil, having probably been carried from Dakar on a fast French destroyer. They managed to get ashore and founded a small colony in a marsh near the coast—the Mosquito Fathers as it were. At first not much attention was paid to them, though there was a pretty sharp outbreak of malaria in the local town, during which practically every person was infected. For the next few years the insects spread rather quietly along the coastal region, until at a spot about 200 miles farther on explosive malaria blazed up and continued in 1938 and 1939, by which time the mosquitoes were found to have moved a further 200 miles inland up the Jaguaribe River valley (Figure 32.3). It was one of the worst

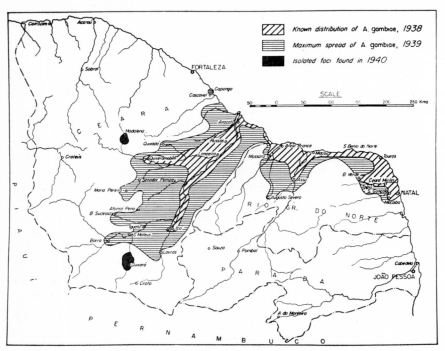

FIGURE 32.3 Distribution areas of the African malaria mosquito, *Anopheles gambiae*, in Brazil in 1938, 1939, and 1940. Eradication measures had made it extinct in South America after this. (From F. L. Soper and D. B. Wilson, 1943.)

epidemics that Brazil had ever known, hundreds of thousands of people were ill, some twenty thousand are believed to have died, and the life of the countryside was partially paralysed. The biological reasons for this disaster were horribly simple: there had always been malaria-carrying mosquitoes in the country, but none that regularly flew into houses like the African species, and could also breed so successfully in open sunny pools outside the shade of the forest. Fortunately both these habits made control possible, and the Rockefeller Foundation combined with the Brazil government to wage a really astounding campaign, so thorough and drastic was it, using a staff of over three thousand people who dealt with all the breeding sites and sprayed the inside of houses. This prodigious enterprise succeeded, at a cost of over two million dollars, in completely exterminating *Anopheles gambiae* on the South American continent within three years.[28]

Here we can see three chief elements that recur in this sort of situation. First there is the historical one—this species of mosquito was confined to tropical Africa but got carried to South America by man. Secondly, the ecological features—its method of breeding, and its choice of place to rest and to feed on man. It is quite certain that the campaign could never have succeeded without the intense ecological surveys and study that lay behind the inspection and control methods. The third thing is the disastrous consequences of the introduction. One further consequence was that quarantine inspection of aircraft was started, and in one of these they discovered a tsetse fly, *Glossina palpalis,* the African carrier of sleeping sickness in man, and at the present day not found outside Africa.[28]

The second example is a plant disease. At the beginning of this century sweet chestnut trees in the eastern United States began to be infected by a killing disease caused by a fungus, *Endothia parasitica,* that came to be known as the chestnut blight. It was brought from Asia on nursery plants. In 1913 the parasitic fungus was found on its natural host in Asia, where it does no harm to the chestnuts. But the eastern American species, *Castanea dentata,* is so susceptible that it has almost died out over most of its range. This species carries two native species of *Endothia* that do not harm it, occurring also harmlessly on some other trees like oak; one of these two species also comes on the chestnut, C. *sativa,* in Europe.[27] As the map shows (Figure 32.4), even by 1911 the outbreak, being through wind-borne spores, had spread to at least ten states, and the losses were calculated to be at least twenty-five million dollars up to that date.[23] In 1926 it was still spreading southwards, and by 1950 most of the chestnuts were dead except in the extreme south; and it is now on the Pacific coast too. So far, the only answer to the invasion has been to introduce the Chinese chestnut, *C. mollissima,* which is highly though not completely immune through having evolved into the same sort of balance with its parasite,[31] as had the American trees with theirs; much as the big game animals of Africa can support trypanosomes in their blood that kill the introduced domestic animals like cattle and horses. The biological dislocation that occurs in this trypanosomiasis is the kind of thing that presumably would have happened also if the American chestnut had been introduced into Asia. The Chinese chestnut is immune both in Asia and America. Already by 1911 the European chestnuts grown in America had been found susceptible.[23] In 1938 the blight appeared in Italy where it has exploded fast

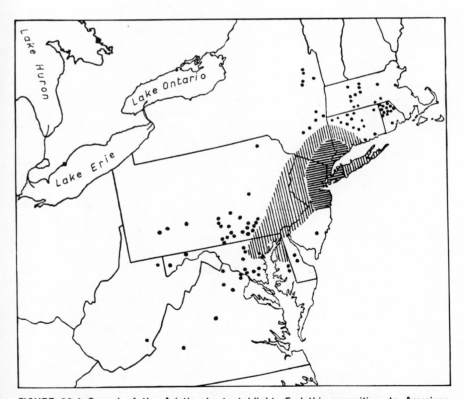

FIGURE 32.4 Spread of the Asiatic chestnut blight, *Endothia parasitica,* to American chestnuts, *Castanea dentata,* in ten states. Horizontal hatching: majority of trees already dead; vertical hatching: complete infection generally; dots: isolated infections, many of which had been eradicated. (From H. Metcalfe and J. F. Collins, 1911.)

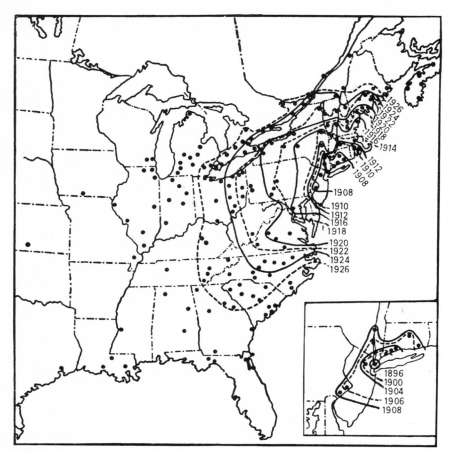

FIGURE 32.5 Spread of the breeding range of the European starling, *Sturnus vulgaris,* in the United States and Canada from 1891 to 1926. Dots outside the 1926 line are chiefly winter records of pioneer spread. (From M. T. Cooke, 1928.)

and threatens the chestnut groves that there are grown in pure stands for harvesting the nuts; it has also reached Spain and will very likely reach Britain in the long or short run.[8] Unfortunately the Chinese chestnut will not flourish in Italy, and hopes are placed solely on the eventual breeding of a resistant variety of hybrid.

The third example is the European starling, *Sturnus vulgaris,* which has spread over the United States and Canada within a period of sixty years. (It has also become established in two other continents—South Africa and Australia, as well as in New Zealand.) This subspecies of starling has a natural range extending into Siberia, and from the north of Norway and Russia down to the Mediter-

ranean. We should therefore expect it to be adaptable to a wide variety of continental habitats and climate. Nevertheless, the first few attempts to establish it in the United States were unsuccessful. Then from a stock of about eighty birds put into Central Park, New York, several pairs began to breed in 1891. After this the increase and spread went on steadily, apart from a severe mortality in the very cold winter of 1917–18. But up to 1916 the populations had not established beyond the Allegheny Mountains. Cooke's map of the position up to the year 1926 (Figure 32.5) shows how the breeding range had extended concentrically, with outlying records of non-breeding birds far beyond the outer breeding limits, which had moved beyond the Alleghenies but nowhere westward of a line running about southwards from Lake Michigan.[3] By 1954 the process was nearly reaching its end, and the starling was to be found, at any rate on migration outside its breeding season, almost all over the United States, though it was not fully entrenched yet in parts of the West coast states. It was penetrating northern Mexico during migration, and in 1953 one starling was seen in Alaska.[17] This was an ecological explosion indeed, starting from a few pairs breeding in a city park; just as the spread of the North American muskrat, *Ondatra zibethica* over Europe was started from only five individuals kept by a landowner in Czechoslovakia in 1905 (Figure 32.7). The muskrat now inhabits Europe in many millions, and its range has been augmented by subsidiary introductions for fur-breeding, with subsequent establishment of new centres of escaped animals and their progeny (Figure 32.8). Since 1922, over 200 transplantations of muskrats have been started in Finland, some originally from Czechoslovakia in 1922, and the annual catch is now between 100,000 and 240,000.[1] Independent Soviet introductions have also made the muskrat an important fur animal in most of the great river systems of Siberia and northern Russia, as well as in Kazakstan.[18] In zoogeographical terminology, a purely Palaearctic species (the starling) and a purely Nearctic species (the muskrat) have both become Holarctic within half a century (Figure 32.6).

The fifth example is a plant that has changed part of our landscape—the tall strong-growing cord-grass or rice-grass, *Spartina townsendii,* that has colonized many stretches of our tidal mud-flats.[14] It is a natural hybrid between a native English species, *S. maritima,* and an American species, *S. alterniflora,* the latter brought over and established on our South coast in the early years of the nineteenth century. The strong hybrid, which breeds true, was first seen in Southampton Water in 1870, and for thirty years was not particularly fast-spreading. But during the present century it has occupied great areas on the Channel coast, not only in England but also on the North of France. It has also been planted in some other places in England, and has been introduced into North and South America, Australia and New Zealand. The original American parent has largely been suppressed or driven out by the hybrid form. Here is a peculiar result of the spread of a species by man: the creation of a new polyploid hybrid species, from parents of Nearctic and Palaearctic range, which then becomes almost cosmopolitan by further human introduction. And it is on the whole a rather useful plant, because it stabilizes previously bare and mobile mud between tide-marks, on which often no other vascular plant could

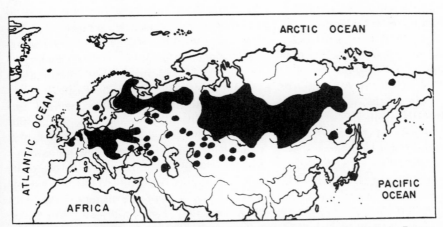

FIGURE 32.6 Distribution of the North American muskrat, *Ondatra zibethica,* **in Europe and Asia. (From A. De Vos, R. H. Manville and R. G. Van Gelder, 1956.)**

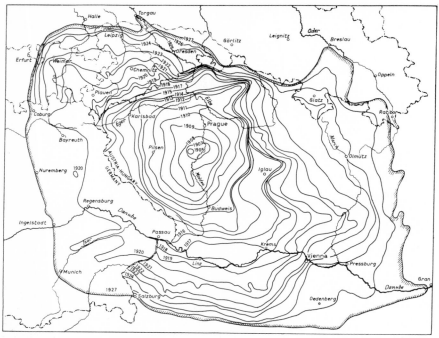

FIGURE 32.7 Spread of the muskrat, *Ondatra zibethica*, up to 1927, from five individuals introduced into Bohemia in 1905. (After a coloured map in J. Ulbrich, 1930.)

grow, helps to form new land and often in the first instance provides salt-marsh grazing. Its effects upon the coastal pattern are, however, not yet fully understood by physiographers and plant ecologists; but Tansley remarks that 'no other species of salt-marsh plant, in north-western Europe at least, has anything like so rapid and so great an influence in gaining land from the sea'.[29]

Changes of similar magnitude have been taking place in fresh-water lakes and rivers, as a result of the spread of foreign species. The sixth example given here concerns the sea lamprey, *Petromyzon marinus*, in the Great Lakes region of North America.[7] * This creature is a North Atlantic river-running species, mainly living in the sea, and spawning in streams. But in the past it established itself naturally in Lake Ontario, as well as in some small lakes in New York State. But Niagara Falls formed an insurmountable barrier to further penetration into the inner Great Lakes. In 1829 the Welland

Ship Canal was completed, providing a bypass into Lake Erie. But it was a further hundred years or so before any sea lampreys were observed in that lake. Then the invasion went with explosive violence. By 1930 lampreys had reached the St Clair River, and by 1937 through it to Lake Huron and Lake Michigan, where they began to establish spawning runs in the streams flowing to these lakes. In 1946 they were in Lake Superior. Meanwhile the lampreys were attacking fish, especially the lake trout, *Salvelinus namaycush*, a species of great commercial importance. The sea lamprey is a combination of hunting predator and ectoparasite: it hangs on to a fish, secretes an anticoagulant and lytic fluid into the wound, and rasps and sucks the flesh and juices until the fish is dead, which may be after a few hours or as long as a week. The numbers of lake trout caught had always fluctuated to some extent, and the statistics of the fishery since 1889 have been thoroughly analysed. But never before the recent catastrophe had the catch collapsed so rapidly: in ten years after the lamprey invasion began to take effect, the

---

* See Selection 44 for more recent information about the sea lamprey and its effects on Great Lakes fisheries.

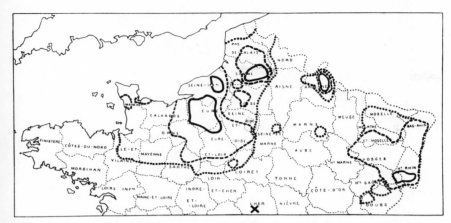

FIGURE 32.8 Spread of the muskrat, *Ondatra zibethica*, in France. Unbroken line, 1932; dashed line, 1951; dotted line, 1954. Cross, one muskrat caught, extent of occupation unknown. (From J. Dorst and J. Giban, 1954.)

numbers of lake trout taken in the American waters of Lake Huron and Lake Michigan fell from 8,600,000 lb. to only 26,000 lb. On the Canadian side things were little better.[12] This was not caused by change in fishing pressure. Other species besides the lake trout have also been hard hit. Among these are the lake whitefish, burbot, and suckers, all of which declined in numbers. So, the making of a ship canal to give an outlet for produce from the Middle West has brought about a disaster to the Great Lakes fisheries over a century later. But in Lake Erie lampreys did not multiply, partly because there are not many lake trout there, but probably also because the streams are not right for spawning in.[19]

The seventh example is the Chinese mitten crab, *Eriocheir sinensis,* a two-ounce crab that gets its name from the extraordinary bristly claws that make it look as if it was wearing dark fur mittens. At home it inhabits the rivers of North China, and it has been found over 800 miles up the Yang Tse Kiang. However, it breeds only in the brackish estuaries, performing considerable migrations down-stream for the purpose. The females don't move so far away from the sea as the males, and they can lay up to a million eggs in a season, which hatch into a planktonic larva whose later Megalopa stage migrates up-river again.[26] It is not really known how they got from East to West; they were first seen in the River Weser in 1912. The most likely explanation is that the young stages got into the tanks of a steamer and managed to get out again on arrival. Two large specimens were actually found in the sea-water ballast tanks of a German steamer in 1932, having, it is thought, got in locally from Hamburg Harbour. But these tanks are normally well screened. In the last forty-five years, mitten crabs have colonized other European rivers from the Baltic to the Seine (Figure 32.9). Those that invaded the Elbe have arrived as far as Prague, like Karel Čapek's newts. This crab has not yet taken hold in Britain, though it may very likely do so some day, as one was caught alive in a water-screen of the Metropolitan Water Board at Chelsea in 1935.

These seven examples alone illustrate what man has done in deliberate and accidental introductions, especially across the oceans. Between them all they cover the waters of sea, estuary, river, and lake; the shores of sea and estuary; tropical and temperate forest country, farm land, and towns. In the eighteenth century there were few ocean-going vessels of more than 300 tons. Today there are thousands. A Government map made for one day, 7 March 1936, shows the position of every British Empire ocean-going vessel all over the world. There are 1,462 at sea and 852 in port; and this map does not include purely coasting vessels. Some idea of

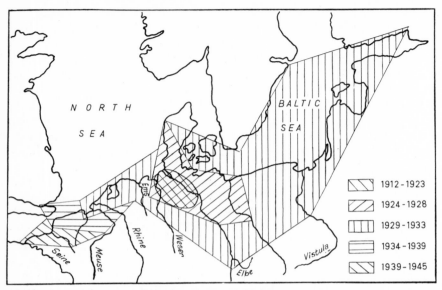

FIGURE 32.9 Zones of spread of the Chinese mitten crab, *Eriocheir sinensis,* in Europe, 1912–1943. (From H. Hoestlandt, 1945.)

what this can mean for the spread of animals can be got from the results of an ecological survey done by Myers, a noted tropical entomologist, while travelling on a Rangoon rice ship from Trinidad to Manila in 1929. He amused himself by making a list of every kind of animal on board, from cockroaches and rice beetles to fleas and pet animals.[25] Altogether he found forty-one species of these travellers, mostly insects. And when he unpacked his clothes in the hotel in Manila, he saw some beetles walk out of them. They were *Tribolium castaneum,* a well-known pest of stored flour and grains, which was one of the species living among the rice on the ship.

A hundred years of faster and bigger transport has kept up and intensified this bombardment of every country by foreign species, brought accidentally or on purpose, by vessel and by air, and also overland from places that used to be isolated. Of course, not all the plants and animals carried around the world manage to establish themselves in the places they get to; and not all that do are harmful to man, though they must change the balance among native species in some way. But this world-wide process, gathering momentum every year, is gradually breaking

down the sort of distribution that species had even a hundred years ago.

To see the full significance of what is happening, one needs to look back much further still, in fact many millions of years by the geological time-record. It was Alfred Russel Wallace who drew general public attention to the existence of great faunal realms in different parts of the world, corresponding in the main to the continents. These came to be known as Wallace's Realms, though their general distribution had already been pointed out by an ornithologist, P. L. Sclater. Wallace, however, did the enormous encyclopaedic work of assembling and classifying information about them. He supposed these realms to have been left isolated for such long periods that they had kept or evolved many special groups of animals. When one was a child, this circumstance was very simply summed up on books about animals. The tiger lives in India. The wallaby lives in Australia. The hippopotamus lives in Africa. One might have learned that the coypu or nutria lives in South America. A very advanced book might have speculated that this big water rodent was evolved inside South America, which we now know to be so. But nowadays, it would have to add a footnote to later editions, saying that the coypu is also doing quite well in the States of Washington, Oregon, California, and New Mexico;[11] also in Louisiana (where 374,000 were trapped in one year recently); in southeast U.S.S.R.;[32] in France;[6] and in the Norfolk Broads of East Anglia.[20] In the Broads it carries a special kind of fur parasite, *Pitrufquenia coypus,* belonging to a family (Gyropidae) that also evolved in South America.[9] These fur lice have antennae shaped like monkey-wrenches, which perhaps explains how they managed to hang on so well all the way from South America.

But in very early times, say 100 million years ago in the Cretaceous Period, the world's fauna was much more truly cosmo-politan, not so much separated off by oceans, deserts, and mountains. If there had been a Cretaceous child living at the time the chalk was deposited in the warm shallow seas at Marlborough or Dover, he would have read in his book, or slate perhaps: 'Very large dinosaurs occur all over the world except in New Zealand; keep out of their way.' Or that water monsters occurred in more than one loch in the world. In fact, zoogeographically, it would have been rather a dull book, though the illustrations and accounts of the habits of animals would have been terrifically inter-esting. There would have been much less use for zoos: you just went out, with suitable precautions, and did dinosaur-watching wherever you were, and made punch-card records of their egg clutch-sizes. But the significance of these dinosaurs for the serious historical evidence is that you couldn't then get an animal the size of a lorry from one continent to another except by land; there-fore the continents must have been joined together, at any rate fairly frequently, as geological time is counted.

This early period of more or less cosmo-politan land and fresh-water life was about three times longer than that between the Cretaceous Period and the present day. It was in the later period that Wallace's Realms were formed, because the sea, and later on great obstructions like the Himalaya and the Central Asian deserts, made impassable bar-riers to so many species. In fact the world had not one, but five or six great faunas, besides innumerable smaller ones evolved on isolated islands like Hawaii or New Zealand or New Caledonia, and in enormous remote lakes like Lake Baikal or Tanganyika. Man was not the first influence to start breaking up this world pattern. A considerable amount of re-mixing has taken place in the few million years before the Ice Age and since then: two big factors in this were the emer-gence of the Panama Isthmus from the sea, and the passage at various times across what is now Bering Strait. But we are artificially stepping up the whole business, and feeling the manifold consequences.

For thirty years I have read publications about this spate of invasions; and many of them preserve the atmosphere of first-hand reporting by people who have actually seen them happening, and give a feeling of ur-gency and scale that is absent from the drier summaries of text-books. We must make no mistake: we are seeing one of the great his-torical convulsions in the world's fauna and flora. We might say, with Professor Chal-lenger, standing on Conan Doyle's 'Lost World', with his black beard jutting out: 'We have been privileged to be present at one of the typical decisive battles of history—the battles which have determined the fate of the world.' But how will it be decisive? Will it be a Lost World? These are questions that ecologists ought to try to answer.

References Cited

1. Artimo, A. 1949. [Finland a profitable muskrat land. Preliminary report.] *Suom. Riista,* 4:7-61.
2. Cabrera, A., and Yepes, J. 1940. *Historia natural ediar. Mammiferos Sud-Americanos (vida, costumbres y descripcion).* Buenos Aires.
3. Cooke, M. T. 1928. The spread of the European starling in North America (to 1928). *Circ. U.S. Dep. Agric.* 40:1-9.
4. Davis, D. H. S. 1953. Plague in Africa from 1935 to 1949. A survey of wild rodents in African terri-tories. *Bull. World Hlth Org.* 9:665-700.
5. De Vos, A., Manville, R. H., and Van Gelder, R.

G. 1956. Introduced mammals and their influence on native biota. *Zoologica, N.Y.* 41:163–94.

6. Dorst, J., and Givan, J. 1954. Les mammifères acclimatés en France depuis un siècle. *Terre et la Vie,* 101:217–29.

7. East, B. 1949. Is the lake trout doomed? *Nat. Hist.,* N.Y. 58:424-8.

8. Forestry Commission. 1950. Chestnut blight caused by the fungus *Endothia parasitica. Bookl. For. Comm.* 3:1–6.

9. Freeman, R. B. 1946. *Pitrufquenia coypus* Marelli (Mallophaga, Gyropidae), an ectoparasite on *Myocastor coypus* Mol. *Ent. Mon. Mag.* 82:226–7.

10. Gravatt, G. F., and Marshall, R. P. 1926. Chestnut blight in the Southern Appalachians. *Dep. Circ. U.S. Dep. Agric.* 370:1–11.

11. Harris, V. T. 1956. The nutria as a wild fur mammal in Louisiana. *Trans. 21st N. Amer. Wildl. Conf.:* 474–86.

12. Hile, R., Eschmeyer, P. H., and Lunger, G. F. 1951. Decline of the lake trout fishery in Lake Michigan. *Fish. Bull., U.S. Fish & Wildlife Service,* 52 (No. 60):77–95.

13. Hoestlandt, H. 1945. Le crabe chinois (*Eriocheir sinensis* Mil. Ed.) en Europe et principalement en France. *Ann. Epiphyt.* N.S. 11:223–33.

14. Hubbard, C. E. 1954. *Grasses.* Harmondsworth, Middlesex.

15. Johnson, C. E. 1925. The muskrat in New York: its natural history and economics. *Roosevelt Wild Life Bull.* 24:193–320.

16. Johnson, Samuel. 1775. *A journey to the western islands of Scotland.* London.

17. Kalmbach, E. R. 1954. Pigeon, sparrow and starling control. *Pest Control,* 22(5):9–10, 12, 31–2, 54.

18. Kuznetzov, B. A. 1944. [VIII. Order Rodents, Ordo Rodentia.] In Bobrinskii, N. A., and Kuzyakin, A. P. [*Key to the mammals of the U.S.S.R.*] Moscow. (In Russian.)

19. Langlois, T. H. 1954. *The western end of Lake Erie and its ecology.* Ann Arbor.

20. Laurie, E. M. O. 1946. The coypu (*Myocastor coypus*) in Great Britain. *J. Anim. Ecol.* 15:22–34.

21. Lennon, R. E. 1954. Feeding mechanism of the sea lamprey and its effect on host fishes. *Fish. Bull., U.S. Fish & Wildlife Service,* 56 (No. 98):247–93.

22. Link, V. B. 1955. A history of plague in the United States of America. *Publ. Hlth Monogr.,* Wash. 26:1–120.

23. Metcalfe, H., and Collins, J. F. 1911. The control of the chestnut bark disease. *Farmers' Bull. U.S. Dep. Agric.* 467:1–24.

24. Meyer, K. F. 1942. The known and the unknown in plague. *Amer. J. Trop. Med.* 22:9–36.

25. Myers, J. G. 1934. The arthropod fauna of a rice-ship, trading from Burma to the West Indies. *J. Anim. Ecol.* 3:146–9.

26. Peters, N., and Panning, A. 1933. Die chinesische Wollandkrabbe (*Eriocheir sinensis* H. Milne-Edwards) in Deutschland. *Zool. Anz.* 104 (Suppl.): 1–180. (Abstract by C. Elton (1936) in *J. Anim. Ecol.* 5:188–92.)

27. Shear, C. L., Stevens, N. E., and Tiller, R. J. 1917. *Endothia parasitica* and related species. *Bull. U.S. Dep. Agric.* 380:1–82.

28. Soper, F. L., and Wilson, D. B. 1943. Anopheles gambiae *in Brazil 1930 to 1940.* New York.

29. Tansley, A. G. 1939. *The British Islands and their vegetation.* Cambridge.

30. Ulbrich, J. 1930. *Die Bisamratte: Lebensweise, Gang ihrer Ausbreitung in Europa, wirschaftliche Bedeutung and Bekampfung.* Dresden.

31. Ulm, A. 1948. The Chinese chestnut makes good. *Amer. Forests,* 54:491, 518, 520 and 522.

32. Vereshchagin, N. K., 1941. [Establishment of the nutria (*Myocastor coypus* Mol.) in west Georgia.] *Trav. Inst. Zool. Acad. Sci. R.S.S.G.* 4:3–42. (In Russian.)

ADDITIONAL REFERENCES

Audy, J. R. 1956. Ecological aspects of introduced pests and diseases. *Med. J. Malaya* 2: 21–31.

Brown, R. C., and Sheals, R. A. 1944. The present outlook on the gypsy moth problem. *J. Forestry.* 42:393–407.

Coppel, H. C., and Leius, K. 1955. History of the larch sawfly, with notes on origin and biology. *Canad. Ent.* 87:103–11.

Craighead, F. C., et al. 1949. Insect enemies of Eastern forests. *U.S. Dep. Agric. Misc. Publ.* 657:1–679.

Phillips, J. C. 1928. Wild birds introduced or transplanted in North America. *U.S. Dep. Agr. Tech. Bull.* 61:1–63.

Salaman, R. N. 1949. *The history and social influence of the potato.* Cambridge: Cambridge Univ. Press. 685 pp.

Smith, M. R. 1936. Distribution of the Argentine ant in the United States and suggestions for its control and eradication. *U.S. Dep. Agr. Circ.* 387:1–39.

RECENT PLANT INVASIONS IN THE ARID AND SEMI-ARID SOUTHWEST OF THE UNITED STATES [1]

DAVID R. HARRIS

Man not only brings alien plants to new continents, he often aids the spread and growth of some of them by drastically disturbing native vegetation. In the American Southwest, for example, several woody plant species have invaded disturbed grassland and altered river valleys on a massive scale within the last century.

Mesquite and one-seed juniper (native species, but formerly restricted in habitat) have spread because of grazing and browsing by domestic livestock and cessation of recurrent grassland fires (among other factors). Tamarisk or saltcedar, an alien species from Eurasia, now chokes many water courses where dams control flooding.

Saltcedar provides a vivid example of serious environmental repercussions that plant introductions can bring (Robinson, 1965). Since saltcedar was introduced into the United States more than 100 years ago it has spread quickly from one stream valley to another, especially in the last 40 years or so. The shrub now grows in fifteen of the seventeen states and has increased from about 10,000 acres in 1920 to almost 1 million acres in the early 1960s. The density of growth also has increased — in many places it has entirely replaced the native vegetation. A detrimental consequence of saltcedar growth is its consumption of water. The plants are "phreatophytes"; that is, they use ground water, not just soil moisture. They can tap this water supply even where the water table is 25 feet deep. Because the plants have almost no economic value, the water used by them is essentially wasted. And the consumption of ground water by saltcedars is probably the highest of all phreatophytes—commonly 5 to 9 feet of water per unit of area that they cover, annually. This loss of water by evapotranspiration is huge compared

David R. Harris (b. 1930) is a member of the geography department at University College, London. He has earned three degrees from Oxford and a Ph.D. degree from the University of California (1963). His major research interests are in the ecology and evolution of agricultural systems, particularly those of tropical America. He has worked principally in the Caribbean and northern South America, but also in Greece and North Africa. Harris is preparing a book on the origins of agriculture and the evolution of paleotechnic agricultural systems.

This selection is reproduced by permission of the author and publisher from the *Annals* of the Association of American Geographers, 56(3): 408–422, 1966.

with the approximately 1 foot of yearly precipitation that falls on most of this region. Streams whose flood plains have been invaded by salt-cedar suffer three further consequences: depletion of streamflow, increase in the area inundated by floods (because the shrubs choke overflow channels), and substantial deposition of sediment (by reducing the velocity of floodwater).

Many additional continental invasions by plants and animals are discussed by Elton (1958), who notes that in the United States the work of the Office of Plant Introduction has resulted in the introduction of nearly 200,000 named species and varieties of plants from all over the world (Fairchild, 1945, in *op. cit.*). Thus, man is mixing the floras and faunas of the different continents, and thereby breaking down the distinctive biogeographic realms that millions of years of evolution and ecological adjustments have created.

(Editor's comment)

The most remarkable phenomenon in the vegetational history of the arid and semi-arid Southwest during the last hundred years is the extent to which pre-existing plant communities have suffered large-scale invasion by both native and alien species. The chief invaders have been native woody species, such as mesquite *(Prosopis juliflora)* and one-seed juniper *(Juniperus monosperma)*, but certain introduced aliens, notably tamarisk or saltcedar *(Tamarix pentandra)*, have also spread explosively. The scale and speed of these changes in distribution and dominance imply a high degree of environmental instability and pose the question as to whether this is owing mainly to natural or to cultural factors. In this paper it will be argued that the invasions were initiated by changes in land use that followed occupation of the area by American settlers, but that their magnitude was increased by the arid and semi-arid environment in which they occurred.

The area subject to major plant invasions extends from the Colorado River in the west to beyond the Rio Grande and Pecos rivers in the east. Southward it crosses the international boundary into Mexico and northward it is limited by the high country of the Colorado Plateau and the southern Rocky Mountains. The area coincides closely with those parts of Arizona, New Mexico, and Texas that experience arid and semi-arid conditions as defined by Thornthwaite's

moisture index of 1948 (Figure 33.1). Plant invasion has taken place mainly on the flatter surfaces which, in the form of elevated plateaus, lowland plains, intermontane basins, and valley floors, occupy most of the region. Invasion has been much less extensive within the mountainous areas of rugged relief and more abundant rainfall.

Two types of grassland have long occupied these lower and flatter surfaces, and it is they that have been most subject to large-scale invasion by woody plants. The desert grassland is found at lower elevations, from about 3,000 to 5,000 feet, whereas the plains grassland occurs between about 4,500 and 6,500 feet. Overlapping both these grass communities and extending from about 4,500 to 7,500 feet is the piñon pine-juniper woodland, much of which has also been transformed by plant invasion in recent decades (Figure 33.2). The remaining major vegetation types of the Southwest (ponderosa pine and other coniferous forests above the piñon-juniper woodland and desert shrub communities below the desert grassland) have not suffered large-scale invasion. Stream channels and flood plains, as well as disturbed areas along roads and elsewhere, have been effectively occupied by invading species.

In an attempt to elucidate the factors chiefly responsible for these invasions the spread of three of the principal invaders, mesquite, one-seed juniper, and tamarisk,

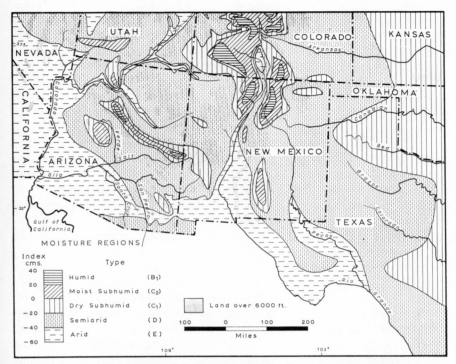

FIGURE 33.1 The arid and semi-arid Southwest. Moisture regions after C. W. Thornthwaite, "An Approach toward a Rational Classification of Climate," *Geographical Review*, Vol. 38 (1948), Plate I A, p. 94.

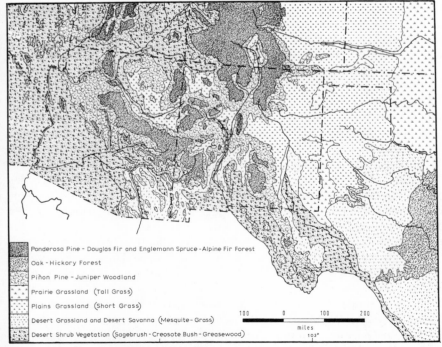

FIGURE 33.2 Major vegetation types of the Southwest. Modified from H. L. Shantz and R. Zon, *Atlas of American Agriculture Natural Vegetation* (Washington, D.C.: U.S. Department of Agriculture, 1924), Fig. 2.

will be reviewed. Each has spread extensively within a different type of habitat and pre-existing plant community.

The Mesquite Invasion

TAXONOMY AND ECOLOGY OF MESQUITE

The mesquites of the Southwest comprise a variable group of spiny, deciduous trees and shrubs assigned to a single species, *Prosopis juliflora* (Swartz) DC.,[2] of the Leguminosae family. Three intergrading varieties are distinguished on the basis of differences in their geographical distribution and in the size, shape and hairiness of the leaflets. Honey mesquite *(Prosopis juliflora* var. *glandulosa* [Torr.] Cockerell) is a shrub or tree with long, smooth leaflets and is most abundant in Texas; western honey mesquite (*P. juliflora* var. *torreyana* L. Benson), which usually grows as a shrub, has smaller, somewhat hairy leaflets and is common in westernmost Texas and southern New Mexico; and velvet mesquite (*P. juliflora* var. *velutina* [Woot.] Sarg.) is usually a medium-sized tree, has short hairy leaflets, and is restricted to southern Arizona. Another species of *Prosopis,* the screw bean or tornillo (*P. pubescens* Benth.), grows in the Southwest but it has not spread beyond drainage courses where it forms dense thickets.

The growth habit of all three varieties varies with edaphic, climatic, and other factors. In moist valley bottoms they grow into large trees with well-defined trunks up to forty feet or more in height, but in dry, sandy areas they form low, many-stemmed shrubs only two or three feet high. Over most of the area occupied by mesquite, where soils remain compact and dry for much of the year, intermediate forms of shrub and small tree are usual.

The root system also varies with soil type and moisture. Young mesquites develop strong tap roots which sometimes penetrate twenty-five feet or more into the moist alluvial soil of valley bottoms. Mature plants also develop extensive lateral root systems.[3]

A root spread of fifty feet from the stem can occur in medium-textured soils and lateral roots over seventy-five feet long have been recorded. Such root systems enable mesquite to survive long periods of drought by utilizing deep reserves of soil moisture, and they also enable the species to compete successfully with other species by depriving their seedlings of moisture over large areas.

The seeds of mesquite are contained in fleshy pods which, unlike those of other members of the Leguminosae, do not split open when ripe. Their dispersal is, however, greatly assisted by animals. The pods contain a sweetish pulp and are frequently browsed by cattle with the result that many seeds pass unharmed through the digestive tract and are widely distributed in dung.[4] The seeds are also eaten and disseminated by birds, rodents, and other animals. Colonization by mesquite is very much favored by such animal-assisted dispersal, combined with the ability of the hard seeds to remain viable in the soil for long periods until conditions are right for germination.

Mesquite reproduces chiefly by seed, but its stems will take root if covered by wind- or water-transported soil and it has a remarkable ability to sprout from the base of the stem after being felled. This is owing to the presence of buds just below the soil surface which remain dormant, beneath the bark, until the stem above ground is injured or destroyed, when they sprout vigorously.[5] Cutting does not, therefore, normally kill mesquite, and a plant can only be eliminated if all stem tissue within the bud zone is either dug out or poisoned.

PRESENT AND PAST DISTRIBUTION OF MESQUITE

The range of mesquite in the Southwest is shown in Figure 33.3. The northern limit of occurrence is apparently controlled by winter temperatures. Mesquite only flourishes at elevations below about 5,000 feet where the frost-free growing season lasts 200 or more days. Above 5,500 feet in the mountains, and at lower elevations near its northern limit on the Great Plains of Kansas and

Colorado, it is often killed back to the base of the stem by winter frost. Rainfall does not appear to exert any direct control over its floristic range. Mesquite tolerates variation in mean annual rainfall from over thirty inches, as in parts of Texas, to three inches, as at Yuma, Arizona. Edaphic factors may limit its growth eastward but in the Southwest it flourishes on all but the most saline soils.[6]

Figure 33.3 also indicates the areas in which the vegetation is now dominated by mesquite. It is these areas that have suffered massive invasion during the last hundred years and all three varieties of the plant are involved. In southern Arizona velvet mesquite has increased particularly in the Colorado, Gila, Santa Cruz, and San Pedro valleys; in southern New Mexico western honey mesquite has done so in the Rio Grande valley south of Albuquerque and in the dry Tularosa valley to the east; and in western Texas honey mesquite has spread in its tree form over an enormous area of the

southern Great Plains. It is not possible to assess precisely the total area affected by recent invasion, because the nineteenth century distribution of mesquite is not sufficiently well known, but there is no doubt that the total area now amounts to well over seventy million acres. Invasion has been most extensive within the desert grassland but it has also affected areas of plains grassland, especially in northwest Texas. Large expanses of both types of grassland, which were formerly dominated by perennial and annual grasses such as grama (*Bouteloua* spp.), mesquite grass (*Hilaria* spp.), and three-awn (*Aristida* spp.), and had only a scatter of shrubs and trees chiefly along watercourses, have given way to continuous mesquite woodland in which the grasses are reduced to impoverished stands between the trees.

The studies by Humphrey, Malin, and others, of nineteenth century descriptions of the Southwest[7] suggest that, prior to its en-

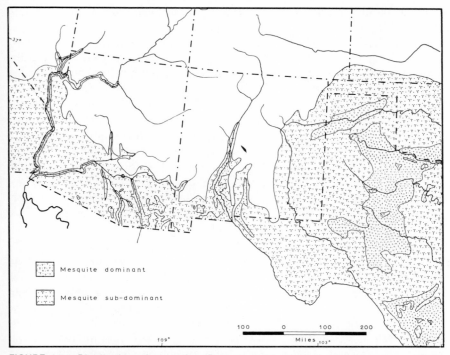

FIGURE 33.3 Distribution of mesquite (*Prosopis juliflora*) in the Southwest, ca. 1950. Based on K. W. Parker and S. C. Martin, "The Mesquite Problem on Southern Arizona Ranges," *U.S. Department of Agriculture Circular*, No. 908 (1952), Fig. 3.

croachment on these grasslands, dense groves of mesquite were present only on valley floors and along drainage courses, although there were considerable areas of mesquite savanna on the higher ground. By 1900, however, many observers had commented on the increase of mesquite thickets in grassland areas, particularly in western Texas. In a few areas it is possible to compare previous and present conditions directly because of the existence of early photographs taken from known points. Such comparisons indicate that woody species, chiefly mesquite, have become noticeably denser and have partly replaced grasses.[8]

In 1943 Bell and Dyksterhuis reported, on the basis of a comprehensive survey by the Soil Conservation Service, that about forty-five million acres in Texas had a conspicuous cover of mesquite,[9] and continuation of the survey suggested that about fifty-five million acres were affected by 1949.[10] When Parker and Martin reported in 1952 on the mesquite problem in southern Arizona they estimated that, in addition to the area affected in Texas, some nine or ten million acres in New Mexico and over nine million acres in Arizona were dominated by mesquite.[11] No more recent general estimates are available but mesquite has continued to spread in many areas so that well over seventy million acres of range land in the Southwest are now affected, a major part of which is the result of mesquite invasions that have occurred during the last hundred years.

CAUSES OF THE MESQUITE INVASION

Since the magnitude of the mesquite invasion first became apparent there has been little agreement as to its causes. Most investigators, however, have regarded one or more of four inter-related factors as primarily responsible for the plant's spread. These four factors are:

1 grazing and browsing by domestic livestock,
2 the effects of rodents and other wild animals,
3 short-term climatic fluctuations, and
4 the cessation of recurrent grassland fires.

Several workers have attributed the spread of mesquite entirely or in part to overgrazing by domestic livestock.[12] There is no doubt that seed dissemination has been aided by livestock depositing viable seeds in their droppings and that the dung provides a favorable medium for germination.[13] Mesquite invasion is most favored where grazing is exceptionally heavy, because the more numerous animals browse a higher proportion of the seed crop, leave a greater number of droppings, and overgraze the range so that mesquite seedlings suffer less competition from grasses. The progressive fencing of former open range has thus intensified mesquite invasion by restricting cattle movements and forcing animals to remain on ranges already overgrazed. However, livestock do not appear to have a direct effect on the continued growth of mesquite after the seedlings are well established. Glendening and others have shown that, once the seedling stage is passed, mesquite continues to increase rapidly at the expense of grass regardless of whether the area is grazed heavily, lightly, or not at all.[14] This is probably owing to the ability of the mesquite plants, once they are sufficiently large and numerous, to develop root systems capable of using all or most of the available soil moisture so that the grass cover thins out and is eventually almost eliminated, regardless of the intensity of grazing. It seems, therefore, that the presence of large numbers of livestock in the Southwest since the mid-nineteenth century has greatly increased the rate of mesquite invasion of grassland, by the wide dissemination of seeds and by favoring the establishment of seedlings, but has not had an appreciable effect on the continued growth of mesquite in areas already invaded. A further indirect effect of livestock that has favored mesquite invasion is the removal by grazing of dry grass that formerly provided fuel for range fires.

Rodents and other wild animals have also contributed to the spread of mesquite by disseminating viable seeds.[15] Reynolds and

Glendening have shown that mesquite seeds are a favorite food of the kangaroo rat (*Dipodomys merriami merriami* Mearns) which collects and stores them in shallow underground caches where they often germinate.[16] As a result the number of mesquite trees increases, stands of grass decrease, and the habitat for kangaroo rats is improved so that they in turn multiply and the spread of mesquite proceeds still more rapidly. Overgrazing of the grass cover by domestic livestock may also result in the explosive increase of kangaroo rat populations and thus indirectly favor the further spread of mesquite. Many other rodents, particularly jackrabbits, facilitate mesquite colonization by consuming grasses that hinder the establishment of seedlings.[17]

It has often been suggested that competition for moisture is a factor of primary importance in preventing the establishment of mesquite and other shrubs in grassland areas. Glendening and Paulsen, in a study of velvet mesquite in southern Arizona, concluded that establishment of seedlings was "markedly curtailed by the perennial grasses" and that "survival through the first spring drought was rare on well-grassed sites."[18] Conversely ranges with a thin cover of grass are invaded by mesquite much more rapidly than those that are well-grassed. The reduction of competition from grasses, which may result from overgrazing by domestic livestock, or rodents, or from prolonged drought, appears therefore to be a factor of considerable, but secondary importance favoring the spread of mesquite.

Invasion by mesquite and other woody species has sometimes been ascribed, in part at least, to recent climatic fluctuations towards intensified drought.[19] However, analysis of the longest available records of precipitation, which reach back well into the nineteenth century,[20] does not indicate any progressive increase of aridity since the instrumental record began.[21] Annual and seasonal rainfall totals for individual stations do show sequences of years with below- and above-average precipitation,[22] but these minor fluctuations are not synchronous over the whole Southwest and do not reveal any statistically significant trend towards drier or wetter conditions that might be correlated with the spread of woody plants. On the other hand, Leopold's analysis of changes in the frequency of large and small daily rains at four long-record stations in New Mexico does indicate that a statistically significant shift occurred in the proportion of large to small rains towards the end of the nineteenth century.[23] If, as Leopold suggests, a "decrease of the small rains of summer which provide the main moisture for grasses . . . would weaken that portion of the vegetal cover"[24] then it is reasonable to suppose that the spread of mesquite and other deep-rooting species was favored when this shift in rainfall decreased competition from grasses. Although, in its seedling stage, mesquite is as vulnerable to drought as are grasses,[25] once it is established its extensive root system enables it to draw on reserves of soil moisture over a wide area and thus to deprive the grasses of much of their moisture supply. Even prolonged drought seldom causes the death of whole mesquite plants but it is capable of killing perennial grasses, particularly in areas already invaded by mesquite, and so opens up fresh areas to colonization by seedlings.

The idea that the cessation of recurrent grassland fires is the primary factor responsible for mesquite invasion goes back to the earliest observations of this phenomenon in the Southwest. Most of the nineteenth and early twentieth century investigators, who observed the early stages of invasion, attributed it primarily to the fact that since livestock ranchers and other white settlers had occupied the region the frequent fires that formerly swept the grasslands and killed mesquite seedlings had largely ceased.[26] That this belief was current before 1850 is indicated by Josiah Gregg's comments on the earliest stage of invasion.[27]

> Indeed there are parts of the southwest now thickly set with trees of good size, that, within the remembrance of the oldest inhabitants, were as naked as the prairie plains; and the appearance of the timber in many other sections in-

dicates that it has grown up within less than a century . . . It is unquestionably the prairie conflagrations that keep down the woody growth upon most of the western uplands . . . In fact, we are now witnessing the encroachment of timber upon the prairies, wherever the devastating conflagrations have ceased their ravages . . . Yet may not the time come when these vast plains will be covered with timber?

By the turn of the century Gregg's prophecy had already become a reality over such large tracts of the Southwest that Bray, describing the vegetation of western Texas, could only speculate on the former extent of open grassland and the role of fire in maintaining it.[28]

> Regarding the establishment of woody vegetation, it is the unanimous testimony of men of long observation that most of the . . . mesquite covered country was formerly open prairie . . . Apparently under the open prairie régime the equilibrium was maintained by more or less regular recurrence of prairie fires . . . It was only after weakening the grass floor by heavy pasturing and ceasing to ward off the encroaching species by fire that the latter invaded the grass lands.

In 1910, following a seven-year study of the effect of complete protection from livestock grazing of part of the Santa Rita Experimental Range in southern Arizona, Griffiths concluded that "The probability is that neither protection nor heavy grazing has much to do with the increase of shrubs here, but it is primarily the direct result of the prevention of fires."[29] Subsequent attempts to measure the effectiveness of grass fires in killing mesquite and other shrubs have produced results that vary from a fifty-two percent kill of seedlings (compared with eight-to-fifteen percent for mature trees)[30] to a fifty-to-seventy-five percent kill of all age classes of mesquite.[31]

Although fire may be only partially effective as a means of eliminating established stands of mesquite now, in the past, before the grass cover had been impoverished by overgrazing and when there was a sufficient annual accumulation of dead grass to support recurrent, destructively hot fires, there can be little doubt that fire was very effective

in preventing mesquite establishment. Furthermore if, as early accounts suggest, most grassland areas in the Southwest were burned over at least once every few years, then such seedlings as did succeed in establishing themselves would be prevented from achieving sufficient maturity to produce seed. If not actually killed by fire they would be maintained indefinitely in an immature, non-fruiting condition by recurrent burning. The potential supply of new plants available for colonization would thus be severely curtailed. By contrast perennial grasses commonly set seed the year they germinate and so are well adapted to withstand frequent burning. Also, unless they are killed completely by an exceptionally hot fire, perennial grasses lose only one season's growth when they are burned (most of which may already have died back) and they are able to resume normal growth the following year.

It is apparent from this review of the causes of the mesquite invasion that all four factors discussed have contributed to the spread of the plant. They are related variables, the effectiveness of any one of which may be modified by one or more of the others. However, it appears that the combined effect of two factors, the suppression of grassland fires and the introduction of domestic livestock, was primarily responsible for initiating invasions. Until fire ceased to sweep the desert and plains grasslands at fairly frequent intervals it was impossible for mesquite seedlings to become generally established; and without the wide dissemination of seeds by domestic animals, invasion could never have affected so large an area in so short a time. Although considerable numbers of livestock were introduced by the Spanish, to west Texas and New Mexico from the late sixteenth century and to southern Arizona during the eighteenth century, it was not until grassland fires were effectively checked in the nineteenth century that the dispersal of seeds by the animals could result in large-scale mesquite invasions. Overgrazing has also assisted mesquite establishment by reducing competition from grasses and removing much of the fuel that formerly sustained grass fires. The remaining two factors appear to have been of only secondary or local importance. Rodents and other wild animals have encouraged the dispersal and establishment of mesquite on a small scale; short-term climatic fluctuations towards greater aridity have, by intensifying competition for moisture, favored mesquite at the expense of grasses.

The spread of mesquite, within the last hundred years, across such extensive tracts of desert and plains grassland in the Southwest casts doubt on the common assumption that these grasslands are the "natural" vegetation of the flatter surfaces that lie at intermediate elevations between the woodland communities of the lower mountain slopes and the shrub communities of the desert proper. It seems likely that these grasslands were maintained in pre-European times by recurrent burning and it is most improbable that lightning was the principal cause of the frequent fires mentioned by early travellers, many of whom indeed ascribed them to burning by the aboriginal population. It is known that the non-agricultural Indians of the southern Great Plains deliberately burned the grassland both to promote fresh growth that would attract game animals and to drive them during communal hunts. It appears to have been the destruction of this aboriginal mode of life by European settlers, combined with the settlers' fear of losing their homes and livestock in range fires, that resulted in the suppression of regular burning and so allowed the mesquite invasion to get under way. Definite knowledge of the ecological status of the desert and plains grasslands at the time of European settlement awaits fuller investigation of the post-Pleistocene history of vegetation in the Southwest, by pollen analysis and other means; but meanwhile it is reasonable to suppose that they were secondary or "disclimax" communities derived from a former cover of woody vegetation in which mesquite may well have been an important element. If so, then the spread of mesquite should be seen not as an invasion of natural, primary grassland but as part of the re-occupation by woody plants of areas in which secondary grass communities had attained dominance as a result of human interference.

The Juniper Invasion

Five species of juniper occur in the Southwest but only two of them, Utah juniper (*Juniperus oteosperma* [Torr.] Little) and one-seed juniper (*J. monosperma* [Engelm.] Sarg.), are abundant at lower elevations within the semi-arid and arid areas. The chief invading species is one-seed juniper which grows widely throughout the Southwest. It is most commonly associated with piñon-juniper woodland but it also extends downslope into areas of plains and desert grassland and upslope into ponderosa pine forest (Figure 33.2). The recent spread of one-seed juniper has taken place both within the woodland and into adjacent grassland areas. There are no reliable estimates of the total area affected but it is very much less than that invaded by mesquite. Juniper has spread chiefly between 4,500 and 6,500 feet in the Colorado Plateau and southern Rocky Mountain regions of northern Arizona and northern New Mexico and, to a lesser extent, on the southern Great Plains of western and central Texas between 1,000 and 3,000 feet. Its extension has taken the form of increases in the density of open juniper stands and establishment on grassland areas within, and adjacent to, piñon-juniper woodland, rather than the wholesale invasion of pure grasslands.[32]

One-seed juniper is a hardy small tree or shrub, which, like mesquite, develops an extensive root system and is capable of withstanding prolonged drought. It is evergreen with small scale-like leaves and single seeds each contained in a succulent berry. These fruits are relished by many native animals and birds, as well as by domestic livestock, and the seeds are widely dispersed by each of them. However, it is doubtful whether the dissemination of seed by livestock has been of such critical importance in initating juniper invasion as it has been in the spread of mesquite. It is difficult to postulate lack of seed dispersal in the past in areas now subject to juniper invasion because, unlike mesquite, the juniper fruit is adapted to dispersal by many different native birds and animals.[33] Its fruits are neither as accessible nor as attractive to livestock as those of mesquite and fewer domestic animals have been grazed within areas of piñon-juniper woodland than on the open grasslands. Browsing by livestock and the deposition of seeds in dung has probably accelerated invasion in some areas, but it does not appear to have been of major importance in the spread of juniper. Domestic animals have, however, assisted the establishment of juniper seedlings by reducing competition from grasses through overgrazing and trampling. This observation is supported by the fact that as juniper spreads it is the forage grasses that are reduced or eliminated first.[34]

Although overgrazing has favored juniper invasion in this way it is not the only factor involved because juniper continues to spread even in areas from which livestock have long been excluded. It is necessary, therefore, to consider the role of recent climatic fluctuations and the cessation of grassland fires in initiating and accelerating juniper invasion.

The spread of juniper, as of mesquite, cannot be ascribed directly to the minor and irregular fluctuations in rainfall that have occurred over the Southwest during the last hundred years. Young juniper seedlings are as vulnerable to drought as are grasses, but once well established they can withstand drought better and it is therefore probable that juniper invasion has been accelerated, though not initiated, by periods of below-average rainfall when competition from grasses is reduced.

The cessation of recurrent fires, which formerly affected areas of grassland within as well as adjacent to piñon-juniper woodland, has probably been primarily responsible for initiating juniper invasion. Many areas into which juniper has spread since the late nineteenth century are characterized by a scatter of large, old trees on rocky sites where the ground cover was probably always insufficient to sustain a grass fire. Conversely there are some grassland areas within the woodland that have been largely exempt from fire and have not been invaded by juniper despite overgrazing.[35] It seems, therefore, that the suppression of fire has been the essential trigger factor responsible for the spread of juniper, as of mesquite, and that both overgrazing by domestic livestock and the occurrence of periods of greater aridity have accelerated the process by reducing competition from grasses.

The Tamarisk Invasion[36]

TAXONOMY AND ECOLOGY OF TAMARISK

The genus *Tamarix* comprises a large and variable group of alkali-tolerant trees and shrubs of the Old World family Tamaricaceae. Some ninety species have been recognized but their taxonomy is very confused.[37] In particular it is difficult to classify a group of deciduous forms with very small flowers that contain five petals, sepals, and stamens. This pentamerous group includes the species that has spread with explosive speed through the drainage systems of the Southwest during the past fifty years. It has been provisionally identified as five-stamen tamarisk (*Tamarix pentandra* Pall).[38] No other species of tamarisk has become widely naturalized in the United States although several have been introduced. Most striking of these is a graceful evergreen species from northern Africa, *T. aphylla* (L.) Karst., which is commonly planted as an ornamental in the Southwest. It is propagated from cuttings and does not reproduce by seed.

Five-stamen tamarisk is well adapted to growth on wet or moist sites within arid and semi-arid areas. It draws its supply of moisture from the ground water reservoir or the capillary fringe above it and is, therefore, classed as a phreatophyte.[39] Its root system sometimes extends twelve or more feet down to the water table but lacks the extreme power of penetration of mesquite. For this reason, and because seedlings require wet soil for successful establishment, tamarisk is restricted to stream sides and flood plains where the water table is always relatively close to the surface. Its remarkable ability to colonize such areas results from the fact that large numbers of wind-dispersed seeds are produced through a long flowering season that lasts from April to September. Seeds lose their viability rapidly, but any falling on wet soils or water surfaces usually germinate within 24 hours. Seedlings can germinate in water and, if stranded at the water's edge, often become established there. Ideal conditions for tamarisk germination and establishment are created when receding floods or falling reservoir levels gradually expose large expanses of bare, moist ground in late spring or summer. Then, provided the soil remains saturated for several weeks, a dense cover of seedlings will appear.[40] Falling water levels following winter floods do not result in tamarisk invasion because of the absence of viable seed. The natural flood regime of rivers in the Southwest, which is characterized by receding snowmelt flows in late spring and early summer, is therefore ideally suited to colonization by tamarisk.

INTRODUCTION AND SPREAD OF TAMARISK

Five-stamen tamarisk is native to Eurasia and the date of its earliest introduction to North America is not definitely known. This or related species may first have reached the New World with the Spanish and subsequently been introduced to the Southwest from Mexico, but there appear to be no authentic references to tamarisk in accounts of the early Spanish expeditions into the Southwest, and the sparsity of herbarium specimens of tamarisk collected in Mexico also argues against this possibility. It is much more likely that the first introduction of tamarisk took place in the nineteenth century. In the 1820's and 1830's tamarisk was listed among plants for sale by several nurseries in the eastern United States and by

the 1850's it was also available from nurserymen in California.[41] It is probable that seedlings distributed in this way and planted as ornamentals in parks and gardens formed the original stock of tamarisk in the Southwest. In the late nineteenth and early twentieth centuries several different species of tamarisk, including *T. pentandra*, were imported by the U.S. Department of Agriculture and their use for erosion control and as windbreaks was recommended.[42] As a result tamarisk was planted experimentally along stream courses and boundaries on many farms and it is from such nuclei that the present invasion of Southwestern drainage systems mainly derives.

The earliest definite record of tamarisk in the Southwest is a herbarium specimen collected at Galveston, Texas, in 1877.[43] The plant was already naturalized in the area, and a few other specimens were collected, chiefly in Texas, in the late nineteenth century. After 1920, however, frequent collections were made from most of the major drainage systems of the Southwest indicating that the tamarisk invasion was well under way by that time.

The speed and scale of the invasion is suggested by records of the spread of tamarisk in the Pecos valley in New Mexico. The plant was first reported in the valley in 1912 when a few seedlings were observed on alluvial deposits above the McMillan Reservoir which had been created by damming the Pecos between Carlsbad and Artesia. By 1915 seedlings covered 600 acres and from this nucleus they spread both up and down stream. By 1925 tamarisk covered 12,300 acres, by 1946 26,200 acres, by 1955 41,000 acres, and by 1960 about 50,000 acres.[44] Today the whole Pecos valley from its junction with the Rio Grande northward to beyond Santa Rosa is infested with tamarisk. Tamarisk has spread with comparable speed through much of the Rio Grande valley, the Colorado drainage system and the upper reaches of the rivers that cross the Great Plains in western Texas (Figure 33.4). The total area occupied by tamarisk in the

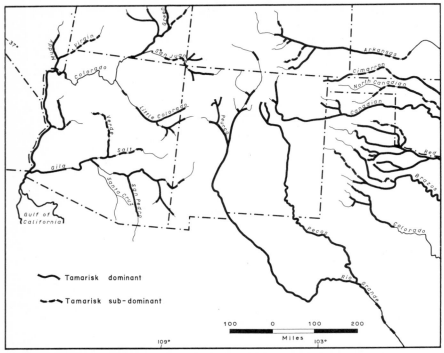

FIGURE 33.4 Distribution of tamarisk *(Tamarix pentandra)* in the Southwest, 1961. Based on T. W. Robinson, "Introduction, Spread and Areal Extent of Saltcedar *(Tamarix)* in the Western States," *U.S. Geological Survey Professional Paper,* **No. 491-A (1965), Plate 1.**

Southwest in 1961 was approximately 723,000 acres, about 450,000 of which were in Texas, 155,000 in New Mexico and 118,000 in Arizona.[45]

CAUSES OF THE TAMARISK INVASION

It is unlikely that tamarisk would have become more than a minor element in the riparian vegetation of the Southwest if stream regimes had not been drastically altered by man and much of the riparian vegetation itself removed from many drainage channels. In areas where native phreatophytes, such as cottonwood (*Populus* spp.), willow (*Salix* spp.), baccharis (*Baccharis* spp.), rabbitbrush (*Chrysothamnus* spp.), and greasewood (*Sarcobatus vermiculatus* [Hook.] Torr.) are well established, tamarisk, if present, is only a subordinate member of the community and shows no sign of replacing the native species. But where the construction of dams has resulted in the control of seasonal floods and the accumulation of alluvium upstream, pure stands of tamarisk, from which most native species are excluded, have developed rapidly. These stands reach their greatest extent and density on the aggrading flood plains or "deltas" which have formed above the largest reservoirs, such as the Avalon and McMillan reservoirs on the Pecos, and the Caballo and Elephant Butte reservoirs on the Rio Grande. There, dense jungles of tamarisk have sprung up, to reach 30 or 40 feet in height. The ground is covered by a thick litter of dead leaves and no shrubs or grasses can establish themselves beneath the canopy layer. Cattle, which do normally browse young tamarisk shoots,[46] are excluded by the dense growth and these jungles have little use as ecological or recreational reserves. Their nuisance value is increased by the fact that tamarisk transpires large quantities of precious water. Comparisons of water loss by evapotranspiration from tamarisk and Bermuda grass (*Cynodon dactylon* [L.] Pers.) show that it is at least twice as great from tamarisk-covered as from grass-covered areas.[47] Tamarisk has also spread downstream from reservoirs, but in these areas it seldom forms extensive stands as there are no large accumulations of moist alluvial soil awaiting colonization. With the prevention of natural floods below the dams tamarisk has, however, occupied the margins of many stream channels that were formerly kept clear of vegetation by seasonal flooding.

The tamarisk invasion is thus seen to be the result of the fortuitous introduction into an arid and semi-arid environment of a phreatophyte species particularly well adapted to the rapid colonization of areas of fresh alluvial deposition with little or no cover of vegetation. The program of dam building in the Southwest, which began soon after 1900, progressively modified the natural drainage regime and, by causing alluviation upstream and by preventing seasonal flooding downstream of the reservoirs, created ideal conditions for the explosive spread of tamarisk.

The partial or complete clearance by settlers of riparian vegetation from many drainage channels in the Southwest must also have contributed to the tamarisk invasion by reducing competition from native species. By the mid-nineteenth century it could be said of New Mexico that[48]

> On the water-courses there is little timber to be found except cottonwood, scantily scattered along their banks. Those of the Rio del Norte [Rio Grande] are now nearly bare throughout the whole range of the settlements, and the inhabitants are forced to resort to the distant mountains for most of their fuel.

Likewise the rivers of the southern Great Plains were reported denuded of vegetation:[49]

> The Cimarron river for more than a hundred miles is absolutely without timber; and the Arkansas, for so large a stream, is remarkably scant . . . The banks of the Canadian are equally naked . . . in fact there is scarce anything else but cottonwood, and that very sparsely scattered along the streams throughout most of the far-western prairies.

As a result of continued exploitation for building timbers, fence posts, and fuel, the vegetation of many drainage channels was still impoverished at the beginning of the twentieth century,[50] and the consequent reduction in competition from native species increased the opportunity for tamarisk to spread.

It seems likely that, with the completion of large reservoirs on all the major rivers, the tamarisk invasion of the Southwest has already passed its peak. However, limited extensions of tamarisk can be expected upstream from any new reservoirs and also following exceptionally high spring or summer floods along natural stream channels. On the other hand the area occupied by tamarisk is likely to decrease wherever lowered water tables and marked increases in salinity result from irrigation. Ambitious programs of clearance have also been carried out in parts of the most thickly infested valleys and attempts are being made to replace tamarisk with a grass cover in some areas.

Other Recent Invasions

Although mesquite, juniper, and tamarisk provide the most dramatic examples of recent plant invasion in the Southwest they are by no means the only species involved. Many native shrubs have shared in the woody invasion of grassland areas. Chief among them are big sagebrush (*Artemisia tridentata* Nutt.), which has spread most extensively in semi-arid areas of plains grassland, as for example in north-central and northwestern New Mexico;[51] and creosote bush (*Larrea divaricata* Cav.), snakeweed (*Gutierrezia* spp.), burroweed (*Haplopappus* spp.), and cholla (arborescent cacti of the genus *Opuntia*), which have invaded large tracts, particularly of desert grassland.[52] All these plants are relatively unpalatable to livestock and some, such as burroweed, can cause actual poisoning. They are only browsed when more palatable forage is lacking and there is little doubt that overgrazing has, by reducing competition from grasses and other palatable plants, been primarily responsible for their spread. The cessation of recurrent grass fires has also been an essential prerequisite for the spread of these shrubby species into areas of grassland.

The invasion of Southwestern drainage systems, too, has involved species other than tamarisk. Although none has proved as effective as tamarisk in the colonization of the open alluvial habitats created by reservoir construction, a limited number of phreatophytes have recently spread quite extensively. Conspicuous among them is the silvery-leaved Russian olive (*Elaeagnus angustifolia* L.) from Eurasia which now grows, alone or in association with tamarisk, along many stream channels in the Southwest. In addition roadsides and other severely disturbed habitats throughout the region have been colonized in recent decades by many weedy species. These include a number of introduced aliens, notably the ubiquitous Russian thistle (*Salsola kali* L.), an annual "tumbleweed" from central Asia.

Conclusion

A review of the course and causes of recent plant invasions in the Southwest shows how rapidly man may bring about drastic ecological change in arid and semi-arid environments. His impact on pre-existing plant communities is likely to be most far-reaching when new systems of land use are introduced, as when the first American settlers brought large-scale livestock ranching to the Southwest and when reservoir construction began to transform the drainage systems of the region. Major changes in plant distribution may also be accentuated by short-term climatic fluctuations, but they are unlikely to be initiated by them. Plant invasion usually involves partial or complete replacement of pre-existing species by the invaders, as with the spread of mesquite and other woody plants at the expense of grasses. But sometimes it involves only addition, with little or no replacement. This may occur if man creates a new habitat, or ecological niche, which is then occupied by the invading species, as has happened with tamarisk on areas of fresh alluvium upstream from reservoirs.

One of the most significant aspects of ecological change induced by man is that it is usually unintentional. Large-scale plant invasions, which often result in great losses of actual or potential productivity, commonly develop indirectly and unexpectedly from changes in land use;[53] and when attempts are made to plan future agricultural development it is important to try to anticipate and prevent undesirable plant invasions such as have occurred in the Southwest.[54] Thus the retrospective study of vegetation change can refine and deepen our understanding not only of the origins of the present landscape but also of its economic potential.

There are few parts of the world's deserts and semi-deserts where plant and animal life have escaped modification by man. Indeed most arid areas have felt the impact, whether in the distant past or more recently, of the fundamental changes in land use that often accompany shifts in cultural dominance, such as that from Indian hunter to American settler in the Southwest. The recency of this cultural mutation enables us to perceive some of its effects on plant distributions, but to explore through time the relationship between changes of culture and of vegetation elsewhere in the dry lands, especially in those Old World deserts which have been occupied by man for millennia, is immeasurably more difficult.[55] Seen in this perspective the plant invasions that have taken place recently in the Southwest appear as a minor but revealing incident in the obscure ecological history of the world's dry lands, most of which remains undeciphered.

Notes and References

1. Field observations on which this paper is based were carried out in 1962–63 when the author was Visiting Assistant Professor at the University of New Mexico, Albuquerque. His grateful thanks are offered to Dr. Y-Fu Tuan, then of the Department of Geography, University of New Mexico, for reintroducing him to the sunlit landscapes of the Southwest. A preliminary version of this paper was presented at a meeting of the Arid Zone Commission of the 20th International Geographical Congress in London on 24 July, 1964.

2. In this paper botanical nomenclature follows usage adopted in T. H. Kearney and R. H. Peebles, *Arizona Flora* (Berkeley and Los Angeles: University of California Press, 1951). For discussion of the taxonomy of the mesquites see M. C. Johnston, "The North American Mesquites: *Prosopis* section Algarobia (Leguminosae)," *Brittonia*, Vol. 14 (1962), pp. 72–90.

3. W. A. Cannon, "The Root Habits of Desert Plants," *Carnegie Institution of Washington Publication,* No. 131 (1911), pp. 80–81.

4. K. W. Parker and S. C. Martin, "The Mesquite Problem on Southern Arizona Ranges," *U.S. Department of Agriculture Circular,* No. 908 (1952), p. 16.

5. C. E. Fisher, J. L. Fults and H. Hopp, "Factors Affecting Oils and Watersoluble Chemicals in Mesquite Eradication," *Ecological Monographs,* Vol. 16 (1946), pp. 112–18.

6. J. T. Peacock and C. McMillan, "Ecotypic Differentiation in *Prosopis* (Mesquite)," *Ecology,* Vol. 46 (1964), pp. 35–51.

7. R. R. Humphrey, "The Desert Grassland; a History of Vegetational Change and an Analysis of Causes," *The Botanical Review,* Vol. 24 (1958), pp. 198–217; J. C. Malin, "Soil, Animal, and Plant Relations of the Grassland, Historically Reconsidered," *Scientific Monthly,* Vol. 76 (1953), pp. 213–17; M. C. Johnston, "Past and Present Grasslands of Southern Texas and Northeastern Mexico," *Ecology,* Vol. 44 (1963), pp. 456–66; L. C. Buffington and C. H. Herbel, "Vegetational Changes on a Semidesert Grassland Range from 1858 to 1963," *Ecological Monographs,* Vol. 35 (1965), pp. 139–64. See also a map showing presumed spread of mesquite across western Texas between 1600 and 1923 in V. E. Shelford, *The Ecology of North America* (Urbana: University of Illinois Press, 1963), p. 357.

8. Humphrey, *op. cit.,* footnote 7, p. 218; see also R. R. Humphrey, "The Desert Grassland, Past and Present," *Journal of Range Management,* Vol. 6 (1953), Fig. 1; and L. B. Leopold, "Vegetation of Southwestern Watersheds in the Nineteenth Century," *Geographical Review,* Vol. 41 (1951), pp. 310–16.

9. H. M. Bell and E. J. Dyksterhuis, "Fighting the Mesquite and Cedar Invasion on Texas Ranges," *Soil Conservation,* Vol. 9 (1943), p. 111.

10. B. W. Allred, "Distribution and Control of Several Woody Plants in Texas and Oklahoma," *Journal of Range Management,* Vol. 2 (1949), p. 19.

11. Parker and Martin, *op. cit.,* footnote 4, p. 10.

12. For example, J. J. Thornber, "The Grazing Ranges of Arizona," *Arizona Agricultural Experiment Station Bulletin,* No. 65 (1910); C. J. Whitfield and H. L. Anderson, "Secondary Succession of the Desert Plains Grassland," *Ecology,* Vol. 19 (1938), pp. 171–80; L. Ellison, "Influence of Grazing on Plant Succession of Rangelands," *The Botanical Review,* Vol. 26 (1960), pp. 19–23; and Buffington and Herbel, *op. cit.,* footnote 7.

13. G. E. Glendening and H. A. Paulsen, Jr., "Recovery and Viability of Mesquite Seeds Fed to Sheep Receiving 2, 4-D in Drinking Water," *Botanical Gazette,* Vol. 111 (1950), pp. 486–91; Parker and Martin, *op. cit.,* footnote 4, p. 16.

14. G. E. Glendening, "Some Quantitative Data on the Increase of Mesquite and Cactus on a Desert Grassland Range in Southern Arizona," *Ecology,* Vol. 33 (1952), pp. 319–28.

15. H. G. Reynolds, "Relation of Kangaroo Rats to Range Vegetation in Southern Arizona," *Ecology,* Vol. 31 (1950), pp. 456–63.

16. H. G. Reynolds and G. E. Glendening, "Merriam Kangaroo Rat a Factor in Mesquite Propagation on Southern Arizona Range Lands," *Journal of Range Management,* Vol. 2 (1949), pp. 193–97.

17. See, for example, C. T. Vorhies and W. P. Taylor, "Life History and Ecology of Jackrabbits, *Lepus alleni* and *Lepus californicus,* in Relation to Grazing in Arizona," *Arizona Agricultural Experiment Station Technical Bulletin,* No. 49 (1933).

18. G. E. Glendening and H. A. Paulsen, Jr., "Reproduction and Establishment of Velvet Mesquite as Related to Invasion of Semidesert Grasslands," *U.S. Department of Agriculture Technical Bulletin,* No. 1127 (1955), p. 35.

19. For example W. A. Price and G. Gunter, "Certain Recent Geological and Biological Changes in South Texas, with Consideration of Probable Causes," *Proceedings and Transactions of the Texas Academy of Science,* Vol. 26 (1942), p. 154; and B. L. Branscomb, "Shrub Invasion of a Southern New Mexico Desert Grassland Range," *Journal of Range Management,* Vol. 11 (1958), pp. 129–32.

20. The longest continuous record in the Southwest, at Santa Fe, dates from 1850. Many other stations have records dating back to the 1870's and 1880's.

21. C. W. Thornthwaite, C. F. S. Sharpe, and E. F. Dosch, "Climate and Accelerated Erosion in the Arid and Semi-arid Southwest, with Special Reference to the Polacca Wash Drainage Basin, Arizona,"

U.S. Department of Agriculture Technical Bulletin, No. 808 (1942), pp. 43–46.

22. See, for example, Yi-Fu Tuan and C. E. Everard, "New Mexico's Climate: the Appreciation of a Resource," *Natural Resources Journal,* Vol. 4 (1964), pp. 293–97; W. D. Sellars, Precipitation Trends in Arizona and Western New Mexico," *Proceedings of the 28th Annual Meeting of the Western Snow Conference,* Vol. 81 (1960); G. F. Von Eschen, "Climatic Trends in New Mexico," *Weatherwise,* Vol. 11 (1958), pp. 191–95; and J. Leighly, "Dry Climates: their Nature and Distribution," *Desert Research,* Research Council of Israel Special Publication No. 2 (Jerusalem, 1953), pp. 11–15. For an investigation of climatic variation in the Southwest based on tree-ring analysis rather than the instrumental record see E. Schulman, *Dendroclimatic Changes in Semiarid America* (Tucson: University of Arizona Press, 1956). With reference to the drainage basins of the Colorado and Gila rivers Schulman distinguishes two recent phases of below-average precipitation, one from 1870 to 1904 and the other from 1931 onwards, separated by a wet interval (p. 64), but these phases are not apparent in the instrumental record.

23. L. B. Leopold, "Rainfall Frequency: An Aspect of Climatic Variation," *Transactions of the American Geophysical Union,* Vol. 32 (1951), pp. 347–57.

24. Leopold, *op. cit.,* footnote 23, p. 351.

25. E. R. Bogusch, "Brush Invasion in the Rio Grande Plain of Texas," *Texas Journal of Science,* Vol. 4 (1952), p. 89.

26. For example J. Gregg, *Commerce of the Prairies: or, the Journal of a Santa Fé Trader, During Eight Expeditions Across the Great Western Prairies, and a Residence of Nearly Nine Years in Northern Mexico* (New York: Henry G. Langley, 1844), Vol. 2, pp. 200–02; H. L. Bentley, "A Report upon the Grasses and Forage Plants of Central Texas," *U. S. Department of Agriculture Division of Agrostology Bulletin,* No. 10 (1898), p. 8; J. G. Smith, "Grazing Problems in the Southwest and How to Meet Them." *U. S. Department of Agriculture Division of Agrostology Bulletin,* No. 16 (1899), p. 18; W. L. Bray, "The Ecological Relations of the Vegetation of Western Texas," *Botanical Gazette,* Vol. 32 (1901), pp. 99–123, 195–217, 262–91; O. F. Cook, "Change of Vegetation on the South Texas Prairies," *U. S. Department of Agriculture Bureau of Plant Industry Circular,* No. 14 (1908), pp. 1–5; D. Griffiths, "A Protected Stock Range in Arizona," *U. S. Department of Agriculture Bureau of Plant Industry Bulletin,* No. 177 (1910), pp. 22–23; and J. H. Foster, "The Spread of Timbered Areas in Central Texas," *Journal of Forestry,* Vol. 15 (1917), pp. 442–45.

27. Gregg, *op. cit.,* footnote 26, p. 202.

28. Bray, *op. cit.,* footnote 26, p. 289.

29. Griffiths, *op. cit.,* footnote 26, p. 22.

30. Glendening and Paulsen, *op. cit.,* footnote 18, p. 44.

31. R. R. Humphrey, "Fire as a Means of Controlling Velvet Mesquite, Burroweed, and Cholla on Southern Arizona Ranges," *Journal of Range Management,* Vol. 2 (1949), pp. 178–79.

32. The spread of juniper has been discussed by many twentieth century observers. See, for example, Foster, *op. cit.,* footnote 26, pp. 443–44; F. H. Miller, "Reclamation of Grasslands by Utah Juniper on the Tusayan National Forest, Arizona," *Journal of Forestry,* Vol. 19 (1921), pp. 647–51; A. Leopold, "Grass, Brush, Timber, and Fire in Southern Arizona," *Journal of Forestry,* Vol. 22 (1924), pp. 2–8; F. W. Emerson, "The Tension Zone Between the Grama Grass and Pinon-juniper Associations in Northeastern New Mexico," *Ecology,* Vol. 13 (1932), pp. 347–58; Bell and Dyksterhuis, *op. cit.,* footnote 9, p. 111; Allred, *op. cit.,* footnote 10, p. 20; A. A. Nichol, "The Natural Vegetation of Arizona," *University of Arizona Agricultural Experiment Station Technical Bulletin,* No. 127 (1952), pp. 197–200; E. F. Castetter, "The Vegetation of New Mexico," *New Mexico Quarterly,* Vol. 26 (1956), pp. 270–72; T. N. Johnsen, Jr., "One-seed Juniper Invasion of Northern Arizona Grasslands," *Ecological Monographs,* Vol. 32 (1962), pp. 187–207; and D. A. Jameson. "Effects of Burning on a Galleta-Black Grama Range Invaded by Juniper," *Ecology,* Vol. 43 (1962), pp. 760–63.

33. Johnsen, *op. cit.,* footnote 32, pp. 191, 203.

34. J. F. Arnold, "Effects of Juniper Invasion on Forage Production and Erosion," *University of Arizona Agricultural Extension Service Special Report,* No. 2 (1958), pp. 17–18.

35. Johnsen, *op. cit.,* footnote 32, pp. 190, 204–05.

36. I wish to thank T. W. Robinson of the Water Resources Division, U. S. Geological Survey, Menlo Park, California, for providing me with a prepublication copy of his map of tamarisk distribution in the western United States. I am grateful both to him and to J. S. Horton of the U. S. Forest Service at Arizona State University, Tempe, for their generous response to my requests for information.

37. See L. H. Shinners, "Salt Cedars (*Tamarix,* Tamaricaceae) of the Soviet Union, by S. G. Gorschkova: Translation and Commentary," *The Southwestern Naturalist,* Vol. 2 (1957), pp. 48–73; and M. Zohary, "The Genus *Tamarix* in Israel," *Tropical Woods,* Vol. 104 (1956), pp. 24–60.

38. See J. S. Horton and J. E. Flood, "Taxonomic Notes on *Tamarix pentandra* in Arizona," *The Southwestern Naturalist,* Vol. 7 (1962), pp. 23–28; and E. McClintock, "Studies in California Ornamental Plants 3. The Tamarisks," *Journal of the California Horticultural Society,* Vol. 12 (1951), pp. 76–83. *Tamarix pentandra* is apparently equivalent to the Russian species *T. ramosissima* Ledeb. described by Gorschkova, and it is often confused with *T. gallica* L. which, in the western United States, appears to be confined to saline soils near the Texan coast.

39. T. W. Robinson, "Phreatophytes," *U. S. Geological Survey Water-Supply Paper,* No. 1423 (1958), pp. 70–75.
40. J. S. Horton, F. C. Mounts and J. M. Kraft, "Seed Germination and Seedling Establishment of Phreatophyte Species," *U. S. Department of Agriculture Forest Service Rocky Mountain Forest and Range Experiment Station Paper,* No. 48 (1960), p. 16.
41. T. W. Robinson, "Introduction, Spread and Areal Extent of Saltcedar (*Tamarix*) in the Western States," *Geological Survey Professional Paper,* No. 491-A (1965), pp. 3–4; J. S. Horton, "Notes on the Introduction of Deciduous Tamarisk," *U. S. Department of Agriculture Forest Service Research Notes,* No. RM-16 (1964), p. 2.
42. Imports of tamarisk are recorded in, for example, *U. S. Department of Agriculture Bureau of Plant Industry Inventory,* Nos. 26 and 27 (1912), 34 (1915), 41 (1917) and 42 (1918).
43. Robinson, *op. cit.,* footnote 41, pp. 4–5.
44. T. W. Robinson, "The Phreatophyte Problem. Definition, Major Species, Areal Extent of Infestation, Consumptive Waste of Water, Potential Salvage," *Pacific Southwest Inter-Agency Committee,* Minutes of the 61-4 Meeting (Las Vegas, Nevada, 1961, processed), p. 9.
45. Robinson, *op. cit.,* footnote 41, p. 8.
46. H. L. Gary, "Utilization of Five-Stamen Tamarisk by Cattle," *U. S. Department of Agriculture Forest Service Rocky Mountain Forest and Range Experiment Station Research Notes,* No. 51 (1960), pp. 1–4.
47. J. P. Decker, W. G. Gaylor and F. D. Cole, "Measuring Transpiration of Undisturbed Tamarisk Shrubs," *Plant Physiology,* Vol. 37 (1962), p. 394.

48. Gregg, *op. cit.,* footnote 26, Vol. 1, p. 159.
49. Gregg, *op. cit.,* footnote 26, Vol. 2, pp. 201–02.
50. For example the upper Rio Grande valley as described by J. R. Watson, "Plant Geography of North Central New Mexico," *Botanical Gazette,* Vol. 54 (1912), p. 199. See also C. J. Campbell and W. A. Dick-Peddie, "Comparison of Phreatophyte Communities on the Rio Grande in New Mexico," *Ecology,* Vol. 45 (1964), pp. 492–502.
51. Castetter, *op. cit.,* pp. 269–70.
52. See, for example, R. S. Campbell and E. H. Bomberger, "The Occurrence of *Gutierrezia sarothrae* on *Bouteloua eriopoda* Ranges in Southern New Mexico," *Ecology,* Vol. 15 (1934), pp. 49–61.
53. For a case study of the relationship between plant invasion and changes of land use in a tropical environment see D. R. Harris, "The Invasion of Oceanic Islands by Alien Plants: an Example from the Leeward Islands, West Indies," *Transactions and Papers of the Institute of British Geographers,* No. 31 (1962), pp. 67–82.
54. A warning on the possible uncontrolled spread of tamarisk in Australia has recently been sounded by C. F. Cooper, "Tamarix as a Potential Noxious Shrub," *Journal of the Australian Institute of Agricultural Science,* Vol. 29 (1963), pp. 178–81.
55. Much that is relevant to this theme can be gleaned from three recent publications in the Unesco Arid Zone Research series: *Plant Ecology Reviews of Research,* Arid Zone Research VI (Paris: Unesco, 1955); L. D. Stamp (Ed.), *A History of Land Use in Arid Regions,* Arid Zone Research XVII (Paris: Unesco, 1961); and D. H. K. Amiran (Ed.), *Land Use in Semi-Arid Mediterranean Climates,* Arid Zone Research XXVI (Paris: Unesco, 1964).

ADDITIONAL REFERENCES

Clark, Andrew H. 1956. The impact of exotic invasion on the remaining New World mid-latitude grasslands. Pp. 737–762 in *Man's role in changing the face of the earth,* ed. by William L. Thomas, Jr., Chicago and London: Univ. of Chicago Press.

Elton, Charles S. 1958. *The ecology of invasions.* London: Methuen. See especially chapter 3, "The invasions of continents," pp. 50–76.

Hastings, J. R., and R. M. Turner. 1965. *The changing mile.* Tuscon, Arizona: Univ. of Arizona Press. 328 pp. Photographic documentation of historical vegetational changes in the Sonoran Desert.

Parsons, J. J. 1970. The Africanization of the New World tropical grasslands. *Tübinger Geographische Studien,* Heft 34 (Sonderband 3), Beiträge zur Geographie der Tropen und Subtropen.

Robinson, T. W. 1965. Introduction, Spread, and Areal Extent of Saltcedar (*Tamarix*) in the Western States. *U. S. Geol. Surv. Professional Paper 491-A.* 12 pp.

Rousseau, Jacques. 1966. Movement of plants under the influence of man. Pp. 81–99 in *The evolution of Canada's flora,* ed. by Roy L. Taylor and R. A. Ludwig. Toronto: Univ. of Toronto Press.

THE INFLUENCE OF MAN ON THE FLORAS AND FAUNAS OF SOUTHERN ISLANDS

M. W. HOLDGATE AND N. M. WACE

Distance and isolation have been slight barriers to man and his accompaniment of animal and plant invaders. Once reached, "Island floras and faunas are far more vulnerable to human interference than those to be found in a continental region of comparable terrain and climate. To a large extent this reflects their isolation and consequent species-poverty; their simple ecosystems are far less well 'buffered' against change."

This selection explains how and why island biotas differ from those of continents and the reasons for their vulnerability to invading species. Generalizations are supported and enlivened by the histories of plant and animal destruction on fifteen islands and island groups in the southern temperate and sub-Antarctic oceans. In contrast with the previous two selections, this selection deals with the total impact of all invaders, not just single species.

The significance of this selection extends well beyond the minor islands on which it concentrates. As patches of vegetation or populations of animals anywhere — "biological islands" — are made smaller and simpler by man's activities, they become more unstable, more easily disrupted. This fact argues forcefully for conserving complexity in our ecosystems.

Hawaii and New Zealand are other areas, more famous and well understood, that have been drastically altered by alien organisms. As

Martin W. Holdgate (b. 1931) is presently in the Office of the Secretary of State for Local Government and Regional Planning, London, coordinating government research and activity in the field of environmental pollution in Britain. Holder of a Ph.D. degree from Cambridge (1955), his past appointments have been lecturer in zoology at the University of Durham (1957–1960), assistant director of research at the Scott Polar Research Institute, Cambridge (1960–1963), senior biologist with the British Antarctic Survey (1963–1966), and deputy director for research for the Nature Conservancy. Holdgate's major professional interests are pollution, management of the environment, and Antarctic and southern temperate zone ecology and biogeography. He edited the book *Antarctic Ecology* (1970). Nigel M. Wace is a senior lecturer in the department of geography at the University of Adelaide, Australia. He has earned bachelor's and master's degrees from Oxford and a doctoral degree in plant ecology from Queens University, Belfast (1961). He has studied the plant life on several southern islands.

This selection is reprinted from *Polar Record,* 10 (68): 473–493, 1961.

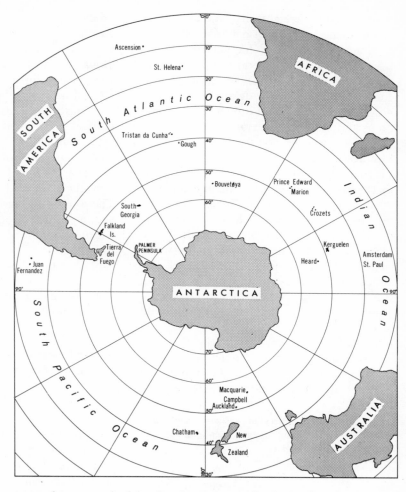

on most other oceanic islands, the most radical changes have been wrought by grazing, browsing, and predatory mammals — such as deer, goats, rabbits, and opossums. The steady stream of invaders continues. A number of the Additional References discuss these island examples.

(Editor's comment)

Introduction

Most of the world's tropical and subtropical oceanic islands were settled by man, and their floras and faunas modified by his activities, some centuries before the development of any scientific interest in them. The original vegetation and fauna of islands like Ascension, the Azores, Bermuda, St Helena or Mauritius cannot now be described with any degree of certainty, while the native communities of many others have been markedly changed. Consequently the few remaining undisturbed oceanic islands are of great scientific importance, and many of these lie in the southern temperate and sub-Antarctic zones.

While the southern temperate and sub-Antarctic islands have not altogether escaped human interference, their chief inhabitants have, until recently, been explorers, sealers, and whalers whose visits were of short duration. During the eighteenth and nineteenth centuries most of them also harboured parties of shipwrecked sailors, for periods varying from a few days to several years. Absence of written records makes it impossible to chronicle these visits in detail, but all these groups had a significant influence on insular floras and faunas. Sealers largely destroyed the once immense populations of southern Fur Seals, greatly reduced the numbers of Elephant Seals and took a toll of penguins; there must have been consequent changes in the biological equilibrium of extensive coastal regions. Whalers and sealers together were responsible for liberating domestic stock, especially pigs, goats, and rabbits on many islands. Expeditions and shipwrecks also added involuntarily to the influx of alien species; the importation of rats to several islands can be traced to the running aground of ships.

Only the Chatham Islands, the Falkland Islands,[1] and Tristan da Cunha[2] have been settled successfully by farming communities. Abortive attempts at colonization were made on the islands of Auckland,[3, 4,] Campbell,[3] and Amsterdam,[5, 6] while some livestock has been kept on Îles Kerguelen,[5, 7, 8] and Marion,[9, 10] Gough[11] and Inaccessible Islands.[12] Since 1945 their value as sites for weather stations has led to the establishment of semi-permanent bases on Amsterdam,[5, 6, 13] Campbell,[3] Gough,[11] Kerguelen,[5, 6] Macquarie,[14] and Marion Islands.[9, 10] Heard Island was occupied from 1947 until 1954[15] and Auckland between 1941 and 1945,[3] while stations on Bouvetøya[16] and Îles Crozet[5] and projected. There is a danger that this occupation will accelerate the disappearance of those features which render the islands especially interesting to biologists. The object of this paper is to explain why island floras and faunas are especially vulnerable, and to catalogue the changes which man has so far brought about in the southern temperate and sub-Antarctic islands.

General Features of Island Floras and Faunas

POVERTY IN NUMBERS OF NATIVE SPECIES

Most oceanic islands are isolated volcanoes which have arisen in mid-ocean and have never been connected to the continents by land. To colonize them, their native animals and plants have had to cross wide expanses of sea, and since most species are poorly adapted for this kind of long-range dispersal very few reach remote islands. In general, the more remote an island is from a continent, and the shorter the period for which it has existed, the more impoverished its flora and fauna will be. Many sub-Antarctic islands are not only extremely remote, but were subjected to glacial or peri-glacial conditions in the Quaternary and have therefore offered suitable conditions for life for a much shorter period than their geological age. Consequently their floras and faunas are strikingly impoverished as compared with mainland areas. Table 34.1 illustrates this by showing the numbers of flowering plants and beetles (two of the best-collected groups) recorded from some of the better known sub-Antarctic areas.

TABLE 34.1. The numbers of vascular plants and beetles recorded from certain sub-Antarctic and southern temperate regions

ISLAND	NUMBER OF NATIVE SPECIES	
	Vascular plants	Coleoptera
(a) Continental areas		
Tierra del Fuego	440[17]	100[18]
New Zealand, S. Island	1430[19]	
(b) Continental shelf islands		
Falklands	160[20]	49[21]
Auckland	150[17]	64[22]
Campbell	116[23]	26[22]
South Georgia	20[24]	7[21]
(c) Oceanic islands		
Amsterdam and St Paul	33[24]	4[21]
Gough	59[24]	7[25]
Heard	8[17]	6[21]
Kerguelen	28[26]	20[21]
Macquarie	35[17]	3[21]
Marion	14[27]	4[21]
Tristan group	69[24]	21[28]

THE ABSENCE OF IMPORTANT ANIMAL AND PLANT GROUPS

Because of the difficulties of long-range dispersal across the oceans, many important groups of animals and plants do not reach the remotest islands at all. Land vertebrates (apart from birds), the dominant element in the fauna of the world as a whole, are absent as natives from all sub-Antarctic islands.[29] So are gymnosperms (including the Podocarpaceae) and the Fagaceae (including *Nothofagus* spp., the southern beeches) which provide the most characteristic dominant trees of the southern temperate continental forests. Many important invertebrate groups are similarly lacking; Gough Island, for example, has no known native slugs, millipedes, centipedes, grasshoppers, ants, bees, wasps, carabid beetles, mayflies, stoneflies, dragonflies or caddis flies, while other important groups are represented by a single species only.[25] Even the marine fauna shows analogous features: barnacle and mussel bands, which are characteristic of temperate continental sea shores are probably absent from all the sub-Antarctic islands except Îles Kerguelen and the New Zealand shelf islands.[30]

Conversely, the absence of predatory ground vertebrates has permitted the development of the enormous populations of ground-nesting seabirds which are such a prominent feature of southern islands. It has probably also allowed the evolution of flightless land birds such as the rails of Inaccessible and Gough Islands and formerly also of Tristan da Cunha,[12] and the famous Dodo of Mauritius and the Solitaire of Rodriguez Island. The absence of herbivorous mammals has similarly permitted the development of types of vegetation highly sensitive to grazing, such as the coastal tussock grass formation which is so characteristic of the southern islands.[24]

MODIFIED ECOLOGICAL BEHAVIOUR OF SPECIES

Because there are so few species on remote islands, and so many important groups are lacking, some ecological niches remain untenanted, or are filled by species which would be excluded from them in the greater competition of a continental area. Up to 40 per cent of the freshwater fauna of oceanic islands have colonized this habitat directly from the sea; on Gough Island two out of six aquatic animals have this history and have invaded the new environment almost certainly because of the absence of better-adapted competitors.[31] Lack of competition also allows species to broaden their ecological range in an accustomed habitat, developing what is termed a 'high ecological amplitude'. Many plants on Tristan da Cunha and Gough Island appear to range much more widely there than they do on the continents, occurring at almost all altitudes and in all vegetation types.[32]

EVOLUTION OF ENDEMIC SPECIES

Because of their isolation, insular species are cut off from interbreeding with continental parent stocks, and since they are subjected to different conditions, are likely to diverge from them. Peculiar 'endemic' species thus arise as adaptations to island conditions. In archipelagos an early colonizing species which spreads over several islands in which conditions are slightly different may similarly diverge in time into separate species on each island. This has happened with birds of the genera *Nesopiza* and *Nesocichla*,[12] and also with weevils[33] in the Tristan da Cunha group, although to a less spectacular degree than in the celebrated finches of the Galapagos Islands or the sickle-bills of Hawaii.[34]

In addition, the isolation of the islands and the low level of competition there may have a protective effect, allowing species to survive when their continental relatives have been eliminated by competition or environmental change. This produces a second type of endemic species, in this case a relict which originally evolved elsewhere and may be of considerable age. Several plant genera of the southern Indian Ocean islands (*Pringlea, Lyallia*) and of the New Zealand shelf islands (*Pleurophyllum*) probably come into this category, as do certain insect groups.

Islands may thus harbour endemic species either because those species are newly arisen, or because they are relict, and some sub-Antarctic and southern cold temperate islands have mixtures of both these types. But because most of these islands have experienced Pleistocene glaciation or recent volcanicity, few relicts have survived upon them, and there has been insufficient time for the evolution of many new endemic species. For these reasons their floras and faunas are less peculiar and less diverse than those of the older tropical islands.[33]

The Causes of Vulnerability

It is obvious that most of the peculiar features of insular floras and faunas result from their isolation, and since man's action in introducing alien species (deliberately or accidentally) breaks that isolation down it is not surprising that major changes ensue.[35]

EFFECT OF SELECTION PRIMARILY FOR TRANSOCEANIC DISPERSAL

Because the species inhabiting remote islands have been selected primarily for their dispersal capacity, they have not necessarily been dominant or even highly successful in their original continental setting. Consequently, if man later imports mainland species to an island, these may well prove more vigorous and efficient as competitors than those which arrived by natural means. It is therefore easy for them to establish themselves and spread into the native communities where they may supplant the native species or greatly restrict their range.

It is probably a valid generalization that the more dominant a species is in a continent, the more rapid and catastrophic will be its effect when imported to an island of comparable terrain and climate. Land mammals are the dominant faunistic element over all the world's continents to-day, and it is not surprising that their impact on the communities of isolated islands is especially profound. The importation of predators like cats, rats, or dogs has in many cases caused the extermination of flightless birds

which have evolved in their absence, and the radical reduction of the populations of ground nesting sea birds. The introduction of herbivores like cattle, sheep, goats or rabbits has caused the devastation and wholesale disappearance of the most vulnerable vegetation types, like tussock grassland.

SIMPLICITY OF THE ECOSYSTEM

In any one habitat on an oceanic island very few species are involved in the complex interacting network termed the ecosystem. This inevitably leads to diminished stability.[35] for when one species suffers from an attack by a predator or parasite or grazing mammal there may be no others which can take over its role in the community. This is well illustrated by the fate of the tussock grasslands of Macquarie Island, whose single dominant, *Poa foliosa,* is extremely susceptible to rabbit grazing and is the only native species capable of stabilizing the soil on steep slopes. Where it is attacked the whole community of some twenty-three species breaks up and widespread erosion follows.[17, 36]

LACK OF INDIGENOUS SPECIES ADAPTED TO CONDITIONS PRODUCED BY MAN

Man disturbs natural vegetation by cutting, burning, and cultivation, and indirectly by stocking the land with grazing animals. As a result communities are rendered more open, and plants characteristic of early seral stages (therophytes) spread. On remote islands therophytes are absent or very scarce,[37] and there are often no native species capable of rapidly recolonizing the disturbed areas. Patches of bared ground which would quickly be clothed with vegetation on a continent may remain exposed long enough for erosion to begin. On the other hand, the plant species commonly introduced by man include many therophytes adapted to these conditions, and they quickly exploit the cleared areas. Many common weeds of the north temperate zone (Table 34.2) are now widespread as introduced species in the sub-Antarctic and southern temperate islands.

The effects of human interference are therefore additive: burning or grazing not only checks the native vegetation but accelerates the spread of alien plants.

The Destruction of Insular Floras and Faunas

ATLANTIC ISLANDS

Tristan da Cunha. Until its occupation by settlers in 1810, the lower levels of Tristan da Cunha, including the north-western coastal plain, were covered in dense thickets of the low-growing tree *Phylica arborea,* interspersed with ferns, tree-ferns, and tussock grasses. The steeper slopes probably supported dense tussock grassland. Higher up the 6,760 ft. volcanic cone there were a variety of bog, wet heath, and feldmark formations.[32] Great colonies of ground-nesting petrels and shearwaters were a feature of the island, and albatrosses and an endemic flightless rail (*Porphyriornis nesiotis*) were also abundant.[11, 12, 38]

Burning, grazing, and the cutting of wood have since eliminated the natural vegetation from the entire north-western coastal plain, and the other smaller lowland plains on the east and south of the island. Extensive burning of tussock grassland is recorded in 1824.[39] The bush and grassland have been replaced by a heavily grazed turf incorporating many introduced species.[32] Overgrazing by semi-wild cattle at free range has caused erosion on the southern areas of lowland plain, at Cave Point and Stony Beach, and the areas of unstable sand near the main landing place in the north-west may once have been covered by tussock. The small tussock grass, *Poa flabellata,* does not now occur on Tristan da Cunha, but it is possible it has been eliminated by grazing and formerly grew on the large sections of the main cliff-slopes that now support fern-sward. Higher up the Peak a whole vegetational zone is now dominated by the introduced species *Holcus lanatus* and *Rumex acetosella,* and this too may once have been dominated by native grasses.

Goats were probably landed by the Portuguese and were numerous in 1790,[2] and pigs had run wild by 1824,[39] but neither species is recorded as a major pest and both have now been exterminated. Cattle, sheep, goats and pigs were on the island in 1829.[40] At the present time cattle and sheep are the main grazing animals (both being only partly confined by fences), while there are donkeys, pigs, geese and fowl near the Settlement.[2, 11] Rabbits are said to have occurred in 1829,[40] but to have been extinct in 1873.[41]

The principal feral predatory mammals on Tristan da Cunha are rats and cats. The rats came ashore from a ship wrecked in 1882, but since two sub-species are present, may well have been reinforced by later introductions.[42] They have almost certainly been responsible for the extermination of the endemic flightless rail and the great reduction in the petrel colonies.[12] Cats were brought to the island by the early settlers and soon ran wild; today, though widely distributed, they are not numerous. Human slaughter of many bird species for food has contributed greatly to the decline of the petrel, penguin, and albatross populations and caused the extinction of the Wandering Albatross as a breeding species.[12]

Numerous alien plants are established on Tristan da Cunha. In 1937, forty-four out of seventy-four known flowering plants were believed to have been introduced, and the total is certainly larger today.[32, 43] Many of these have spread throughout the natural vegetation, and the same is true of imported invertebrate animals like slugs, millipedes, and some snails.[33]

Of the minor islands in the Tristan group, Nightingale has suffered little human interference apart from the annual harvest of some thousands of younger Greater Shearwater (*Puffinus gravis*), a number of penguin eggs, and a few other birds.[12] Inaccessible Island once supported goats, which had dwindled to a small remnant by 1873, and feral pigs.[41] These were not recorded by a shipwrecked party in 1822 but were abundant in 1873.[41, 44] They are described as damaging tussock grasses and other plants, but feeding

TABLE 34.2 A summary of human influence on certain southern islands

MAN	ANIMALS INTRODUCED BY MAN (THOSE NOW EXTINCT ON THE ISLAND IN PARENTHESES)	NATIVE ANIMALS NOW EXTINCT ON THE ISLAND, OR MUCH REDUCED (THOSE EXTINCT IN PARENTHESES)	AGGRESSIVE INTRODUCED PLANTS (I.E. SPREADING INTO NATIVE VEGETATION)	NATIVE PLANTS NOW EXTINCT OR MUCH REDUCED (THOSE EXTINCT IN PARENTHESES)
Tristan da Cunha 1506 discovered; thereafter visited; 1790's sealing gangs ashore; 1810 settled. (Present population about 300.)	(Before 1790—goats) (Before 1810—pigs) c. 1810—cats Before 1824—cattle Before 1824—dogs Before 1824—sheep Before 1824—poultry (Date unknown)—mice Before 1867—donkeys 1882—rats	(*Arctocephalus gazella*) *Diomedea chlororhynchus* (*D. exulans dabbenena*) *Eudyptes crestatus* (*Macronectes giganteus*) (*Mirounga leonina*) (*Nesospiza achunhae achunhae*) *Phoebetria fusca* (*Porphyrionis nesiotis*) *Procellariideae*	*Agrostis stolonifera* *Anthoxanthum odoratum* *Cerastium caespitosum* *Holcus lanatus* *Poa annua* *Rumex acetosella* *Sonchus oleraceus*	*Phylica arborea* (*Poa flabellata*)?? *Spartina arundinacea*
Nightingale Island 1506 discovered; thereafter visited; now visited annually by Tristan islanders	None recorded	*Arctocephalus gazella* *Mirounga leonina*	*Holcus lanatus* *Poa annua* *Sonchus oleraceus*	None recorded
Inaccessible Island 1506 discovered; visited thereafter, several shipwrecks; 1871–73 two residents; 1938 abortive farming	(Between 1882 and 1883—pigs) (Between 1882 and 1883—goats) (1938—sheep) (Occasionally—dogs)	*Arctocephalus gazella* *Diomedea exulans dabbenena* *Eudyptes crestatus?* *Mirounga leonina*	*Aira caryophyllea* *Cerastium caespitosum* *Poa annua* *Sonchus oleraceus*	None recorded
Gough Island ?1505 discovered; visited occasionally thereafter, shipwreck recorded in 1867; 1955 weather station established	Before 1887—mice 1956—poultry 1956—sheep (1958—goats) 1959—dogs	*Arctocephalus gazella* *Mirounga leonina*	*Agrostis stolonifera* *Holcus lanatus* *Poa annua* *Sonchus oleraceus* *Rumex obtusifolius*	None

TABLE 34.2 (continued)

Island				
Macquarie Island 1810 discovered; sealed intensively thereafter by gangs living ashore; 1948 weather station established	c. 1820—mice c. 1820—rats c. 1820—cats (Before 1821—dogs) c. 1880—*Gallirallus australis* c. 1880—rabbits (Before 1923—horses) (1947—goats) 1947—sheep	*Arctocephalus forsteri* *Aptenodytes patagonicus* (?*Anas gibberifrons*) (*Cyanoramphus novaezelandiae*) *Diomedea exulans* (*Hypotaenidia philippensis*) At least nine species burrowing petrels	*Cerastium triviale* *Poa annua* *Stellaria media*	*Pleurophyllum hookeri* *Poa foliosa* *Poa hamiltonii* *Polystichum vestitum* *Stilbocarpa polaris*
Campbell Island c. 1890–1927 settled and farmed; 1908–14 whaling and sealing visits	c. 1890—sheep (1883—goats) (1883—pigs) (1883—rabbits) (?—game birds) (?—guinea fowl) Before 1883—rats	*Arctocephalus forsteri*	*Cerastium vulgatum* *Poa annua* *Sagina procumbens* *Stellaria media*	*Danthonia flavescens* *Pleurophyllum hookeri* *Poa foliosa* *Poa litorosa*
Auckland Island 1806 discovered; 1841–56 settled; occasional stock-raising attempts later	1807—pigs (1849—cattle) (?—sheep) Before ?1866—goats ?—cats (1895—cattle) Before 1866—rabbits	*Arctocephalus forsteri* (*Hypotaenidia muelleri*) *Nesonetta aucklandica* Many ground nesting birds } Rose and Enderby Islands only		*Danthonia?* *Poa foliosa?* *Stilbocarpa polaris*
Kerguelen 1772 discovered; thereafter whaling and sealing visits; 1908–14 and 1921–32, shore-based whaling and sealing; 1949 base established (110 men in 1960)	Before 1874—mice Before 1874—cats 1874—rabbits Before 1900—rats ?—dogs (doubtful) 1909—sheep 1949—mules 1950—pigs 1950—horses 1950—cattle 1955—reindeer	*Arctocephalus gazella* *Calopteryx moseleyi* *Mirounga leonina* And probably many species of penguins and other sea birds breeding on the island	*Cerastium glomeratum* *Myosotis versicolor* *Poa annua* *Sagina procumbens* *Stellaria media* *Taraxacum* sp. (?*erythrospermum*)	*Azorella selago* *Lyallia Kerguelensis* *Poa cookii* *Pringlea antiscorbutica* and all vegetation where rabbits most abundant

chiefly on birds and their eggs: a penguin rookery on the south coast is said nearly to have been exterminated by them. In 1938 however only one pig was present, and about seven sheep,[12] and probably no such animals survive there today. Inaccessible Island has also been damaged by fires, one of which, lit among tussock grass in 1909, is said to have burned for a month.[12] Rats and cats were absent from Inaccessible and Nightingale Islands in 1938 and probably are still, but occasional dogs have been left there by Tristan Islanders.

Gough Island. Gough Island resembles Tristan de Cunha in its vegetation and fauna, but remains in a virtually natural state. Until 1956 no grazing animals had been imported. In that year about ten sheep were landed to provide meat for the South African Weather Station,[11] and since then the number has fluctuated, but remained below thirty. The sheep have been confined to part of the Glen and above Capsize Sands, and have attacked the *Poa flabellata* tussocks selectively, reducing the abundance of this species in these areas.[45] One or possibly more, goats were landed in 1958, but their destruction was immediately ordered by the Tristan da Cunha Administration. A few domestic fowls are kept.

The only predatory animal on Gough Island (in 1960) is a single pet dog, and mice are the only other introduced mammals. Twelve alien plants are recorded out of a total vascular plant flora of seventy-one, but only a few of these have so far become established in native vegetation (Table 34.2).[45] The number of alien invertebrate animals is also much smaller than on Tristan de Cunha.[33]

Falkland Islands. Cattle were introduced to the Falkland Islands in 1764, and soon ran wild, as did horses and rabbits. Sheep were imported later, and farmed extensively. The onslaught of these mammals, and destructive burning by early settlers, has caused the native tussock grass, *Poa flabellata,* to disappear almost everywhere except on small off-lying islets.[1, 46]

South Georgia. South Georgia is virtually an Antarctic island, with permanent snow above 2000 ft., and a highly impoverished flora and fauna. Only twenty species of vascular plant are recorded; of these *Poa flabellata* is the largest and dominates large areas of coastal tussock grassland. Inland there is a tundra meadow of grasses, sedges, and *Acaena adscendens.*[47] There are large colonies of breeding sea birds and two endemic land birds, a pipit *(Anthus antarcticus)* and a teal *(Anas georgica).*

Rabbits were introduced to South Georgia in 1872, but failed to establish themselves then or later. A small population survived on Jason Island, off Cumberland Bay, in 1930.[47] Sheep have also been imported without success. Horses, imported in 1905, died out after a while, but reindeer, introduced in 1911 and 1912, have established themselves and number some hundreds, ranging over a small part of the island.[47] The effect of these animals is uncertain.

Rats were brought to the island by sealers in about 1800 and are numerous and widespread in the coastal grasslands, causing serious destruction of the smaller petrels. Man has greatly reduced the populations of Fur Seal *(Arctocephalus gazella),* Wandering Albatross, and the endemic teal.

INDIAN OCEAN ISLANDS

Île Amsterdam. Like Tristan da Cunha and Gough Island, the lower levels of Île Amsterdam support thickets of *Phylica arborea,* while the upper parts are covered in wet heath and bog. The native vegetation and fauna has yet to be described in detail.[5, 6] Wild hogs were abundant on the island in 1823 and there were a few goats also.[48]

From 1843 until 1853 a fishing industry operated around this island and Île St Paul, but no shore-based installations were erected.[5, 6, 7] In 1871 a farm was established in the north-east, only to be abandoned 8 months afterwards. Cattle introduced at this time have run wild and now increased to 1000–2000 head. They have eliminated the trees from much of the northern part and check regeneration by biting off young saplings.[6] On the south and west, however, dense thickets remain in the least accessible places.[5] Much of the open country between the woodlands seems (judging by photographs)[49] to have been converted into a close-cropped grassland which has been terraced by trampling on the steeper slopes. The number of cattle is probably now regulated by winter starvation, and the higher mortality of cows and calves is said to be responsible for the remarkable sex ratio of four bulls per cow.[5] Goats were introduced by early visitors but seem to have diminished; in 1957 only one old male was reported. A small flock of sheep also existed in 1957. No soil erosion has been described, but a large scar on the side of a secondary crater cone, conspicuous in photographs,[49] may owe its origin partly to the activities of man and his stock.

Predatory mammals include cats and rats, and the former are stated to have caused damage to the bird populations.[6] An attempted reduction of the cat population is alleged to have caused a compensating rise in the numbers of rats and mice, and so to have been abandoned.[5]

Many plants were introduced by the early colonists, and some at least have invaded native vegetation, but the number and status of these is uncertain.

Île St Paul.

Unlike Amsterdam, the smaller and lower island of St Paul lacks woody vegetation and is largely covered by tussock grassland dominated by *Spartina arundinacea.* There is an abundant sea bird population.[5, 6]

Île St Paul was the centre of a fishing industry from 1843 until 1853 and intermittently thereafter until 1914.[7] In 1927 a crawfish fishery was based on the island, and about 120 people took up residence; after forty deaths from beri-beri and scurvy in 1931 the venture was abandoned in 1932.[7, 8] The fishery was revived in 1937–38, and since 1948 has been operated from ships; there are no shore installations at present.[5]

Wild pigs were abundant on the island in 1823[48] and goats were liberated by fishermen in the nineteenth century, but these were exterminated to provide meat and had disappeared by 1874.[8] Sheep have only recently been imported and are not numerous.[5] Rabbits were released at some time in the last century and increased rapidly, devastating the vegetation and almost certainly causing erosion. Latterly they have decreased, probably through disease, and in 1957 it was stated that the recolonization of the bared ground by vegetation was nearly complete.[5]

Cats and rats were both numerous on Ile St Paul in 1874, subsisting alike on the birds.[8] Mice also flourished. The cats have since died out but rats and mice remain numerous: the effect of the former on the bird colonies is unknown.

A number of alien plants certainly occur, but the lists and descriptions are inadequate to estimate their status. The greater part of the terrestrial invertebrate fauna is stated to consist of introduced species.[8]

Îles Kerguelen.

The Kerguelen archipelago is colder and more barren than Amsterdam and St Paul, and has a very poor native flora. Tussock grassland of *Poa cookii* probably once grew on steep coastal slopes, and the famous 'Kerguelen cabbage', *Pringlea antiscorbutica,* dominated a unique vegetation type which was widespread elsewhere. The two other main vegetation types, both important in inland areas are dominated by cushions of *Azorella selago* and mats of *Acaena adscendens.*[5, 6, 7, 8, 26, 50, 51, 52, 53, 73]

The distribution of all these plant communities has been greatly modified by the effect of rabbits, liberated on the island in 1874 by a British Transit of Venus expedition, in an area where the Kerguelen cabbage was abundant and seemed likely to provide suitable food for them.[54] "Now it is the rabbit that has become abundant, and the cabbages have disappeared with many other plants whose absence has altered the appearance of the central part of the archipelago to an extent unbelievable to one who has not seen it with his own eyes."[5] The plant community dominated by *Pringlea* has become restricted to small rabbit-free islets and to cliffs,[8, 51, 53] while the tussocky *Azorella* heathland has been invaded by *Acaena*.[51, 52] The heavy grazing of all types of vegetation has broken the plant mat and allowed severe erosion by wind and water; in many places the underlying peat and soil have been stripped away and rock and moraine exposed.[55] The elimination of the native vegetation has been accompanied by the loss of the remarkable invertebrate fauna associated with it.[8, 56]

Sheep were imported in 1908 to Île Longue[7] and, in 1911, 1000 were liberated on Presque'île Bouguet de la Grye.[7, 8] A small staff of five or six shepherds maintained the flocks, largely for the benefit of the seasonal staff of the whaling station at Port Jeanne d'Arc. This venture, interrupted between 1914 and 1921, was recommenced at Port Couvreux and Île du Corbeau, but abandoned in 1932. In 1949 a staff of about fifty men occupied a new weather station and base at Port aux Français;[5] today the personnel there number 110.[57] A wide range of livestock has been imported. In 1952 sheep were landed on Ile Mussel, and later on another small rabbit-free island.[5] Proposals to establish them on other islets would certainly lead to the further reduction of the native vegetation. Mules were imported in 1949, the last being killed in 1953,[58] and Shetland ponies, pigs, and cattle are all kept around the main base.[5] Rabbit grazing is too intense to permit stock raising on any scale on the main island, but if these pests can be destroyed the present intention is to replace them with sheep. Reindeer were imported in 1955 (2 pairs) and 1956 (1 male and 5 females) and seem to be establishing themselves since the rabbits do not compete with them for the lichens which form their main food.[5]

Wild dogs have been reported from Îles Kerguelen, and reputed to descend from sledge dogs abandoned by the *Gauss* expedition of 1902,[8, 50] but this has been denied[59] and the very existence of the animals doubted.[5] Cats were present on Île du Chat in 1874.[54] Rats were introduced by whalers in the nineteenth century and occur around Port Jeanne d'Arc and perhaps elsewhere.

Mice were abundant in 1875.[54] Dogs and cats from the base at Port aux Français have been stated to constitute a threat to nearby bird and seal colonies and to need control,[60] but on the whole no predator is widely dispersed and abundant over the whole island. It is rumoured that the introduction of mink is now contemplated, and this predator may cause severe damage to bird populations.

Several alien plants had become widespread in natural vegetation on Îles Kerguelen by 1903 (Table 34.2).[26] Recent experiments, which involve the attempted establishment of species, will certainly increase the number.[61] They will also add to the list of alien invertebrates of which several are known to be numerous around sites of human settlements.[8]

The Kerguelen archipelago is so large and complex that good examples of the natural flora and fauna almost certainly remain in the outlying and smaller islets and less frequented parts of the group. A detailed study of these is much to be desired.

Heard Island. Only small areas of Heard Island are ice-free and the vascular plant flora numbers seven or eight species only. There are large sea bird colonies. So far as is known there are no established alien mammals or plants.[15]

Îles Crozet. Like Îles Kerguelen, the Îles Crozet are covered, up to about 1200 ft., by a dense herbaceous vegetation of tussock grasses, *Azorella*, *Acaena* and *Pringlea antiscorbutica*.[5] Unlike Îles Kerguelen they remain in a relatively natural state. Pigs were established on Île aux Cochons before 1820, and by that year had become numerous and fierce.[48] They fed partly on tussock grass roots and partly on sea birds, and caused great damage in the penguin rookeries, for which reason they were exterminated in the mid- or late nineteenth century. Rabbits were said to be abundant in 1873,[41] probably in Île de la Possession where *Pringlea* apparently grazed by them was noticed in 1938:[8] in 1959, however, none were seen on this island.[62] Goats were also reported from the group in 1875 but no details are available.[54]

Marion and Prince Edward Islands.

Like the Îles Crozet, this group has a vegetation and fauna allied to that of Îles Kerguelen,[42, 63] and this has been little disturbed by man. Permanent occupation was only begun in 1947,[9] since which year the South African Weather Bureau has maintained a staff of 12 to 15 men.[10] A few sheep were imported in 1947 but failed to establish themselves, and a supply is now brought annually to the island and killed for meat when required.[10] Fowls have been kept in confinement with success. No introduced predators are reported, nor are any alien plants known to be established in the vegetation. A large number of alien bushes and trees have, however, been planted, many in soil brought from the Cape, so that the probability of inadvertent introduction of therophytes and alien invertebrates is high.

ISLANDS SOUTH OF NEW ZEALAND AND AUSTRALIA

Macquarie Island.

Macquarie Island originally supported tussock grassland dominated by *Poa foliosa* on the steeper slopes up to 1000 ft., with herbfield (in which *Pleurophyllum hookeri* is characteristic), bog, and fen on the flatter ground and feldmark in the highest and most exposed places.[17]

Sealers were active about the island throughout the nineteenth century, and one firm introduced rabbits in 1880.[64] Until about 1930 these were not abundant, but were noted as attacking the 'Macquarie Island cabbage' *Stilbocarpa polaris*.[64] Subsequently they have invaded all except the northern quarter of the island and virtually eliminated tussock grassland from many of the steep coastal slopes.[17, 36] Widespread erosion has been caused and unless some natural check occurs (like that reported from St Paul)[5] the elimination of all this vegetation and its replacement by scree seems likely. Grazing is also affecting the upland herbfields and gullying is going on.[36]

The island was reported as suitable for sheep in 1915,[64] but was not stocked until 1947, since which year a flock of about fifteen has been kept.[17] Two horses were present in 1923.[65]

Dogs were wild on the island in 1821,[66] but later died out; they certainly caused some destruction of the native fauna. Cats were also introduced by sealers before 1821[66] and were abundant in 1890–94, when they probably caused the extermination of the parakeet and banded rail which took place between 1880 and 1894.[64, 65] Cats were 'not numerous' in 1930[64] but were common over the whole island in 1955.[17] Rats are numerous and widespread, and were probably also brought by sealers.[64] One alien bird, the Weka *(Gallirallus australis)* is also abundant on Macquarie Island, having been introduced in about 1879.[64, 65] Some authors state that it has little effect on native vegetation or fauna,[17, 64] but in fact it is certainly destructive of ground-nesting birds and has probably been a major cause of the decline of nine species of resident petrel.[65, 67] Man himself has almost exterminated the Fur Seal and reduced the populations of King Penguin and Wandering Albatross.[67]

Only three species of alien plant are listed from Macquarie Island, and all these are established in native vegetation (Table 34.2).[17] Experimental cultivations were carried out on the island in 1915, but none of the species tested seems to have become established.[64]

Campbell Island.

Campbell Island lies on the New Zealand shelf and has a fairly rich flora with close neozelanic affinities. Tussock grassland covers steep slopes, especially around the coasts. Various scrub formations (dominated by *Dracophyllum* and *Coprosma* with *Suttonia*) occur low down, while peat bogs occur on both lowlands and uplands. The uplands have a wet heath dominated by *Rostkovia* and a discontinuous vegetation covers the highest rocks.[23]

Sheep farming was carried out on Campbell Island from the 1890's until 1927, the stock reaching 8000 head, and a shore-based whaling station was operated between 1908 and 1914.[3, 68, 69] About 1500 wild sheep remained in 1950,[23] and some 950 survive today. They have grazed the tussock grasslands selectively, causing the almost complete disappearance of the grasses *Danthonia flavescens* and *Poa foliosa* which were once dominant.[23] *P. litorosa* is now the main species, and is also grazed. "The sheep have probably been responsible for the exposure of patches of peat which are like ugly scars . . . patches which are ever enlarging as the roots of the tussock become exposed and normal erosive forces become operative."[23] However, in contrast to Macquarie, the richer flora of Campbell Island includes a species *(Chrysobactron rossii)* which is unpalatable to sheep and which is spreading locally on the grazed cliffs. The alien grass *Poa annua* is also increasing. Sheep grazing is affecting most of the larger and most interesting herbs on the island, and *Pleurophyllum hookeri,* perhaps the most interesting, is becoming confined to inaccessible rocks.

At various times goats, pigs, game birds, and guinea fowl have been released on Campbell Island, but none is established today. Rats infest part of the island, especially near the abandoned sheep-farm buildings.[3]

Forty-eight species of alien plants have been recorded from Campbell Island, making about one-third of the total flora.[23] Most are confined to coastal areas, but almost all are spreading and some, notably *Poa annua, Stellaria media, Cerastium vulgatum,* and *Sagina procumbens,* are widespread. The checking of the native vegetation by sheep is greatly assisting this invasion by aliens.

Auckland Island. Auckland lies nearer to New Zealand than Campbell, but resembles it in its general features. The main scrub vegetation is dominated by the New Zealand myrtaceous shrub *Metrosideros lucida* and the flora is richer.[68, 70]

The island was settled by about seventy Maoris in 1841,[4] and a larger colony founded by the Enderby Brothers in 1849 as a shore-based whaling settlement.[3,4] This was abandoned in 1852[4] and the whole population had left by 1856;[3] since then there have been intermittent sheep farming attempts. Cattle were imported in 1849 but killed off later by sealers. Others were landed in 1895 on the small Rose and Enderby Islands and by 1916 the population had overgrazed its range and was suffering from starvation. A small number survive today. Sheep and goats have both been imported, but the sheep have vanished. Goats are still frequent in the north of the island. Pigs were imported in 1897[4] and have run wild causing considerable local damage to the vegetation and making serious inroads on the colonies of ground-nesting birds. Rabbits abound on Enderby and Rose Islands, but not on the mainland, and have caused severe damage to the vegetation. On Rose Island the population appeared diseased in 1942 and may have been undergoing a check similar to that reported from Île St Paul.

Wild cats are numerous and reported to be destructive of birds, but rats and other predators have not been reported.[3] There are numerous alien plants, but their detailed status is unknown.

TWO SOUTHERN SUB-TROPICAL ISLANDS

Although lying outside the southern temperate region, the islands of the Juan Fernandez group and St Helena present such well documented cases of the human destruction of native floras and faunas that they are worth considering here for the principles they illustrate.

Juan Fernandez.[71] The three islands of this group were discovered in 1574, and Más-á-tierra was soon afterwards settled by its discoverer, who introduced goats, pigs and donkeys. The goats thrived on the luxuriant sub-tropical native vegetation, and became such an important source of meat to the buccaneers of the seventeenth century that the Spaniards introduced mastiffs in 1686 to control them. After this the goat population declined sharply, but the dogs increased to such an extent that they became a danger to humans, and were exterminated by 1830.

After this the goats multiplied again and were estimated to number 3000 in 1877. They have had a devastating effect on the native vegetation on Más-á-tierra and also on Más-afuera (where they were plentiful in 1866), and severe soil erosion has ensued, especially on the steep slopes of Más-afuera.

Several introduced species of plant were early noticed as aggressive weeds of Más-á-tierra. Oats (*Avena barbata*) and radishes (*Rhaphanus sativus*) covered large areas in 1740, and bramble (*Rubus ulmifolius*), macal (*Aristotelia maqui*), and *Acaena argentea*, which were imported later, have also spread widely. Their success illustrates the ease with which alien species invade a disturbed native vegetation, and the history of the islands as a whole shows how difficult it is to restore an equilibrium once it has been upset.

St Helena.   St Helena provides a most striking case of the complete and catastrophic destruction of a whole flora by a single grazing mammal. The following account comes from the classic work of Wallace.[72]

> When first discovered, in the year 1501, St Helena was densely covered with a luxuriant forest vegetation, the trees overhanging the seaward precipices and covering every part of the surface with an evergreen mantle. This indigenous vegetation has been almost wholly destroyed, and although an immense number of foreign plants have been introduced and have more or less completely established themselves, yet the general aspect of the island is now so barren and forbidding that some persons find it difficult to believe that it was all once green and fertile. The cause of the change is however easy to explain. The rich soil formed by the decomposed volcanic rock and vegetable deposits could only be retained on the steep slopes so long as it was protected by the vegetation to which it in great part owed its origin. When this was destroyed the heavy tropical rains soon washed away the soil and left a vast expanse of bare rock and sterile clay. This irreparable destruction was caused in the first place by goats, which were introduced by the Portuguese in 1513 and increased so rapidly that in 1588 they existed in thousands. These animals are the greatest foes to trees, because they eat off the young seedlings and thus pre-

vent the natural restoration of the forest. They were however aided by the reckless waste of man.

> In 1709 the Governor of the island complained that the timber was rapidly disappearing, and asked that the goats be destroyed, to preserve the woods and because the island was suffering from droughts. The reply was "the goats are not to be destroyed, being more valuable than ebony." In 1809 the Governor reported the total destruction of the forests, and that in consequence the cost of importing fuel for Government use in the one year had been £2729-7-8d. About this time large numbers of European, American, Australian, and South African plants were imported and many of these ran wild and increased so fast as to drive out and exterminate much of the relics of the native flora!

Summary and Conclusions

Man has altered the flora and fauna of southern islands both by the direct destruction of native species and by the introduction of aliens. Direct destruction has greatly reduced populations of seals and nesting sea birds on many islands, and vegetation has been modified by cutting and burning. But by far the most radical changes have been produced by the human importation of grazing and predatory animals. Goats have irreparably damaged St Helena and Juan Fernandez; in the colder southern islands however their influence has been less marked and they are perhaps not perfectly adapted to the cold and wet climates prevailing there. Cattle similarly have caused damage only on Tristan da Cunha and Île Amsterdam, both among the warmer islands considered here. Sheep, pigs, and especially rabbits, have been most destructive in the southern temperate and sub-Antarctic regions. The most vulnerable vegetation type in the islands is undoubtedly maritime tussock grassland, but fern-bush, wet heath, and feldmark formations have all been affected severely where grazing pressure is high. There is no doubt that in the most extreme cases the biological productivity of large tracts of land has been permanently reduced owing to the exposure of the ground to erosion and the washing of much of its soil into the sea.

The native island fauna, especially the smaller ground-nesting birds, have been severely damaged by rats, cats and pigs, and indirectly by the destruction of the habitat by grazing mammals. No endemic flightless land-birds have survived on any island into which cats or rats have been imported, and on no island has the ground nesting petrel population remained large after the establishment of these animals.

Disturbance of the native vegetation by man and his stock has greatly assisted the spread of alien plants. In some cases these could probably establish themselves even in undamaged communities, but there is no doubt that grazing and burning contribute greatly to the wholesale replacement of indigenous species by imported ones.

In general, therefore, it is evident that island floras and faunas are far more vulnerable to human interference than those to be found in a continental region of comparable terrain and climate. To a large extent this reflects their isolation and consequent species-poverty; their simple ecosystems are far less well 'buffered' against change. It is also evident that if such native floras and faunas are to be preserved for scientific study almost all normal human 'farming' activities must be excluded. Grazing and predatory mammals are totally incompatible with natural island ecosystems, and even the cultivation of vegetables inevitably increases the rate of establishment of alien plants through the impossibility of guaranteeing weed-free seed.

There are now only a few southern islands which are sufficiently undamaged to be worth preserving by such rigorous measures, which must inevitably impose added discomfort on the personnel of weather stations and other bases established there. Nightingale, Inaccessible, and especially Gough Islands in the Atlantic; Prince Edward Island, the Îles Crozet, and some of the smaller outliers of the Îles Kerguelen in the Indian Ocean; and some of the outlying islets in the New Zealand sub-Antarctic groups alone fall into this category. In the other islands research should aim at recording as far as possible the native floras and faunas before they are lost, and studying the natural experiments that are going on through the activities of introduced species.

References Cited

1. V. F. Boyson. *The Falkland Islands*, Oxford, 1924.
2. P. A. Munch, The sociology of Tristan da Cunha. *Results of the Norwegian Scientific Expedition to Tristan da Cunha, 1937–38*, No. 13, 1945.
3. A. W. Eden. *Island of Despair*. London, 1955.
4. T. Musgrave. *Castaway on the Auckland Islands . . .* , London, 1866.
5. X. N. Reppe. *L'aurore sur l'antarctique*, Paris, 1957.
6. E. Aubert de la Rue. *Les terres australes*, Paris, 1955.
7. E. Aubert de la Rue. *Terres Françaises inconnues*, Paris, 1930.
8. R. Jeannel. *Au seuil de l'antarctique*, Paris, 1941.
9. J. Marsh. *No pathway here*. Cape Town, 1948.
10. J. J. la Grange. The South African Station on Marion Island 1948–55. *Polar Record*, Vol. 7, No. 48, 1954, p. 155–58.
11. M. W. Holdgate. *Mountains in the Sea*, London, 1958.
12. Y. Hagen. Birds of Tristan da Cunha. *Results of the Norwegian Scientific Expedition to Tristan da Cunha, 1937–38*, No. 20, 1952.
13. M. Aubert. L'établissement de la Nouvelle Amsterdam. *T.A.A.F.* No. 6, p. 5–20.
14. P. G. Law *and* T. Burstall. Macquarie Island. *A.N.A.R.E. Interim Reports*, No. 14, 1956.
15. P. G. Law *and* T. Burstall. Heard Island. *A.N.A.R.E. Interim Reports*, No. 7, 1953.
16. SCAR Bulletin. No. 3. *Polar Record*, Vol. 9, No. 63, 1959, p. 589–608.
17. B. W. Taylor. The flora, vegetation and soils of Macquarie Island. *A.N.A.R.E. Reports*, Series B. Vol. II, Botany, 1955.
18. G. Enderlein. Die Insekten des Antarcto-Archiplata Gebietes. Beitrag zur kenntnis der Antarktischen Fauna 20. *Kungl. Svenska Vetenskapsakademiens Handlingar*, Vol. 48, No. 8, 1911.
19. L. Cockayne, G. Simpson *and* J. Scott Thomson. The vegetation of South Island, New Zealand. *Vegetationsbilder*, Vol. 22, 1931–32, p. 1–17.
20. C. Skottsberg. A botanical survey of the Falkland Islands. *Kungl. Svenska Vetenskapsakademiens Handlingar*, Vol. 50, No. 3, 1913.
21. J. L. Gressitt *and* N. A. Weber. Bibliographic in-

troduction to Antarctic-subantarctic entomology. *Pacific Insects,* Vol. 1, No. 4, 1959, p. 441–80.

22. A. E. Brookes. The coleptera of the Auckland and Campbell Islands. *Cape Expedition Series,* Bulletin 5, 1951.

23. R. L. Oliver *and* J. H. Sørensen. Botanical investigations on Campbell Island. *Cape Expedition Series,* Bulletin 7, 1951.

24. N. M. Wace. Botany of the southern oceanic islands. *Proceedings of the Royal Society,* B, Vol. 152, 1960, p. 476–90.

25. M. W. Holdgate. *The fauna of Gough Island.* In preparation.

26. P. Cour. A propos de la flore de l'archipel de Kerguelen. *T.A.A.F.,* 4 and 5, 1958, p. 10–32.

27. W. B. Hemsley. *Challenger Reports,* Botany, Vol. 1, 1885.

28. P. Brinck. Coleoptera of Tristan da Cunha. *Results of the Norwegian Scientific Expedition to Tristan da Cunha, 1937–38,* No. 17, 1948.

29. P. J. Darlington. The zoogeography of the southern cold temperate zone. *Proceedings of the Royal Society* B, Vol. 152, 1960, p. 659–668.

30. G. A. Knox. Littoral ecology and biogeography of the southern oceans. *Proceedings of the Royal Society* B, Vol. 152, 1960, p. 577–624.

31. M. W. Holdgate. The fresh water fauna of Gough Island (South Atlantic). *Journal of the Linnean Society of London (Zoology)* (in the Press), 1961.

32. N. M. Wace *and* M. W. Holdgate. The vegetation of Tristan da Cunha. *Journal of Ecology,* Vol. 46, 1958, p. 595–620.

33. M. W. Holdgate. The fauna of the mid-Atlantic islands. *Proceedings of the Royal Society* B, Vol. 152, 1960, p. 550–67.

34. D. Lack. *Darwin's Finches,* Cambridge, 1947.

35. C. S. Elton. *The Ecology of Invasions by Animals and Plants,* London, 1958.

36. A. B. Costin *and* D. M. Moore. The effects of rabbit grazing on the grasslands of Macquarie Island. *Journal of Ecology,* Vol. 48, 1960, p. 729–39.

37. J. D. Hooker. A lecture on insular floras. *Gardiner's Chronicle and Agricultural Gazette,* 1867, p. 6, 7, 27, 50, 51, 75, 76.

38. D. Carmichael. Some account of the Island of Tristan da Cunha and of its natural productions. *Transactions of the Linnean Society,* Vol. 12, 1817, p. 483–513.

39. A. Earle. *A Narrative of Nine Months' Residence in New Zealand in 1827, with a Journal of Residence in Tristan da Cunha,* London, 1832.

40. B. Morrell. *A Narrative of Four Voyages . . . ,* New York, 1832.

41. H. M. Moseley. *Notes by a Naturalist on H.M.S. "Challenger",* London, 1892.

42. J. E. Hill. Rats and mice from the islands of Tristan da Cunha and Gough, South Atlantic Ocean. *Results of the Norwegian Scientific Expedition to Tristan da Cunha, 1937–38,* No. 46, 1959.

43. E. Christophersen. Plants of Tristan da Cunha. *Scientific results of the Norwegian Antarctic Expeditions, 1927–28,* Vol. 2, No. 16, 1937.

44. J. G. Lockhart. *Blenden Hall,* London, 1930.

45. N. M. Wace. *The Vegetation of Gough Island.* In preparation.

46. W. Davies. *The Grasslands of the Falkland Island,* London, 1939.

47. L. Harrison Matthews. *South Georgia,* Bristol. 1931.

48. C. M. Goodrich. *Narrative of a Voyage to the South Seas and the Shipwreck of the "Princess of Wales" Cutter, with an Account of Two Years' Residence on an Uninhabited Island.* Exeter, 1843.

49. E. Aubert de la Rue. Les îles Saint Paul et Nouvelle Amsterdam. *Geographia* (Paris) 1954, p. 38–43.

50. D. Mawson. The Kerguelen archipelago. *Geographical Journal.* Vol. 83, No. 1, 1934, p. 1–12.

51. E. Aubert de la Rue. Notes sur une récente reconnaissance dans l'est des Îles Kerguelen. *Compte rendu sommaire des séances, Société de Biogéographie,* No. 231, 1950, p. 32–37.

52. E. Aubert de la Rue. La flore des Kerguelen. *Naturalia,* Octobre, 1954, p. 33–39.

53. R. Jeannel. Les milieux biologiques des îles Kerguelen. *Compte rendu sommaire des séances, Société de Biogéographie.* Vol. XVII, 1940, No. 141, p. 1–9.

54. J. H. Kidder. Contributions to the natural history of Kerguelen Island. *Bulletin of the United States National Museum.* No. 2, 1876, p. 1–122.

55. E. Aubert de la Rue. Phénomènes periglaciares et actions eoliennes aux îles de Kerguelen. *Memoires de l'Institut Scientifique de Madagascar Série D,* Vol. 9, 1959, p. 1–21.

56. P. Paulian. Les biotypes entomologiques des îles Kerguelen. *L'Entomologiste,* Vol. 9, No. 3, 1953, p. 33–42.

57. SCAR Bulletin No. 5. *Polar Record,* Vol. 10, No. 65, 1960, p. 172–79.

58. A. Migot. *The lonely south,* London, 1956.

59. E. Von Drygalski. Hunde auf Kerguelen. *Zeitschrift der Gesellschaft für Erdkunde,* No. 1/2, 1935.

60. P. Paulian. Compte-rendu d'une mission aux îles Kerguelen et Amsterdam 1950–52. *Bulletin du Muséum National d'Histoire Naturelle.* 2nd Série, Vol. 24, No. 5, 1952, p. 455–59.

61. J. Breheret. Les possibilités de culture aux terres australes. *T.A.A.F.,* No. 3, 1958, p. 19–26.

62. H. W. Tilman. A voyage to the Crozet Islands. *Geographical Magazine,* Vol. 33, No. 7, 1960, p. 391–95.

63. R. Jeannel. Croisière du Bougainville aux îles australes françaises. *Mémoires du Muséum National d'Histoire Naturelle, Nouvelle Série,* Vol. 14, 1940.

64. D. Mawson. Macquarie Island, its geography and geology. *Scientific Report of the Australian Antarctic Expedition, 1911–14,* Series A, Vol. 5, 1943.

65. R. A. Falla. Birds. *B.A.N.Z. Antarctic Research Expedition,* Series B, Vol. 2, 1937, p. 1–304.

66. F. F. Bellingshausen. *The voyage of Captain Bel-*

lingshausen to the Antarctic Seas, 1819–1821 (*Ed.* F. Debenham), London, 1948.

67. R. Carrick. The wildlife of Macquarie Island. *Australian Museum Magazine,* Vol. 12, No. 8, 1957, 255–60.

68. L. Cockayne. The ecological botany of the sub-antarctic islands of New Zealand. *Subantarctic islands of New Zealand (Ed.* Chilton) Vol. 1. Article 10, 1909, p. 182–235.

69. R. M. Laing. The chief plant formations and associations of Campbell Island. (*Ed.* Chilton) *Subant-*

arctic Islands of New Zealand, Vol. 2, Article 21, 1909, p. 482–92.

70. L. Cockayne. The vegetation of New Zealand. *Die Vegetation der Erde.* Vol. 14 (*ed.* Engler & Drude), Leipzig, 1928.

71. C. Skottsberg, *Ed. The Natural History of Juan Fernandez and Easter Island,* Uppsala, 1952–65.

72. A. R. Wallace, *Island Life,* London, 1902.

73. A. Chastain. La flore et la végétation des îles Kerguelen. *Mémoires du Muséum National d'Histoire Naturelle,* Série B, Botanique, Vol. 11, 1958, p. 1–136.

ADDITIONAL REFERENCES

Abbot, R. T. 1949. March of the giant African snail. *Nat. Hist.* 30:68–71.

Allan, H. H. 1946. Indigene versus alien in the New Zealand plant world. *Ecology* 17:187–93.

Carrick, R. 1964. Problems of conservation in and around the Southern ocean. In *Biologie Antarctique: Antarctic biology,* ed. by R. Carrick, M. W. Holdgate, and J. Prévost. Paris: Hermann.

Clark, A. H. 1949. *The invasion of New Zealand by people, plants and animals: The South Island.* New Brunswick, New Jersey: Rutgers Univ. Press. 465 pp.

Darlington, P. J., Jr. 1965. Biogeography of the southern end of the world. Cambridge, Mass.: Harvard Univ. Press. 236 pp.

Dorst, J., and P. Milon. 1964. Acclimation et conservation de la nature dans les îles subantarctiques française. In *Biologie Antarctique: Antaractic biology,* ed. by R. Carrick, M. W.

Egler, F. E. 1942. Indigene versus alien in the development of arid Hawaiian vegetation. *Ecology* 23:14–23.

Elton, C. S. 1958. *The ecology of invasions.* London: Methuen. See especially chapter 4, "The fate of remote islands," pp. 77–93.

Gulick, A. 1932. Biological peculiarities of oceanic islands. *Quart. Rev. Biol.* 7:405–27.

Harris, D. R. 1962. The invasion of oceanic islands by alien plants: an example from the Leeward Islands, West Indies. *Trans. and Papers,* Institute of British Geography, pp. 67–82.

Harris, D. R. 1965. *Plants, animals, and man in the Outer Leeward Islands, West Indies.* Berkeley, Calif.: Univ. of California Press. 194 pp.

Holdgate, M. W. 1968. The influence of introduced species on the ecosystems of temperate oceanic islands. *Proc. Int. Union Cons. Nat. 10th Tech. Meeting,* I.U.C.N. Publ., New Ser., No. 9, pp. 151–176.

Holdgate, M. W., ed. 1970. *Antarctic ecology.* Vol. 1. Based on a symposium, Cambridge, England, 1968. New York: Published for the Scientific Committee on Antarctic Research by Academic Press. 604 pp.

MacArthur, R. H., and E. O. Wilson. 1967. *The theory of island biogeography.* Princeton, N. J.: Princeton Univ. Press. 199 pp.

Murphy, R. C. 1951. The impact of man upon nature in New Zealand. *Proc. Am. Phil. Soc.* 95(6):569–582.

Paterson, C. R. 1953. The establishment and spread in New Zealand of the wasp *Vespa germanica. Proc. 7th Pacific Sci. Congr., 1949,* 4:358–62.

Seaman, G. A. 1952. The mongoose and Caribbean wildlife. *Transactions of the 17th North American Wildlife Conference* 17:188–197.

Thompson, C. M. 1922. *The naturalization of plants and animals in New Zealand.* London and New York: Cambridge Univ. Press. 607 pp.

Tomich, P. Q. 1969. *Mammals in Hawaii. A synopsis and notational bibliography.* Honolulu: Bishop Museum Press. 240 pp.

Wace, N. M. 1968. Alien plants in the Tristan da Cunha Islands. *Proc. Int. Union Cons. Nat. 10th Tech. Meeting,* I.U.C.N. Publ., New Ser., No. 9.

Weber, P. W. 1956. Recent introductions for biological control in Hawaii. *1st Proc. Hawaiian Entomol. Soc.* 16:162–164.

Wodzicki, K. A. 1950. Introduced mammals of New Zealand: An ecological and economic survey. *Bull. D.S.I.R., N.Z.* 98:1–255.

CENTRAL AMERICAN SEA-LEVEL CANAL: POSSIBLE BIOLOGICAL EFFECTS

IRA RUBINOFF

Canals built by man have obvious economic effects; they also have more subtle environmental consequences, including biological exchange between the connected waters. The exchange of marine organisms through the Suez Canal is increasing as the salinity of the Bitter Lakes (part of the canal) decreases. Since the canal was opened in 1869 at least twenty-four species of fishes have passed from the Red Sea to the Mediterranean (Ben-Tuvia, 1966). In the present Panama Canal the fresh water of Gatun Lake is an effective barrier to similar migration from one ocean to another.

However, a proposed sea-level Panamanian Canal would allow large-scale invasions, probably with catastrophic biological consequences, because the Atlantic and Pacific Oceans and their biotas are so different, as this selection illustrates. Another author has advanced even more dire predictions than those given here (Briggs, 1969), stating that mass extinctions (numbering in the thousands of marine species) would seem inescapable.

Other environmental arguments have also been advanced against exercising our new-found competence to blast a sea-level canal, using nuclear explosives, across Central America. Radioactive contamination, for example, should be an important consideration (Charnell, et. al, 1969;

Ira Rubinoff (b. 1938) is assistant director for marine biology at the Smithsonian Tropical Research Institute, Panama Canal Zone, where he has worked since 1965. He holds a Ph.D. degree in zoology from Harvard University (1963). Rubinoff's research has focused on the evolution of reproductive isolating mechanisms in Panamanian inshore marine fishes. He currently is evaluating the antipredator mechanisms of the yellow-bellied sea snake, *Pelamis platurus,* a venomous species that is absent from the Atlantic Ocean but which might be introduced through a sea-level canal. He notes that his research is "not directly designed to answer sea-level canal problems, but by increasing our basic knowledge of behavior and evolution of Central American organisms we are frequently in a favorable position to make reasoned predictions of the implications of such large-scaled environmental manipulation."

Tamplin, 1969). Again, the greater our environmental manipulation, the greater are the likely complexity, variety, and extent of the consequences of which we must be wary.

(Editor's comment)

Balboa discovered the Pacific Ocean 455 years ago, after a brief journey across the Isthmus of Panama. The possibility of constructing an interoceanic canal in Central America was raised almost immediately. Preliminary studies ordered by Charles V were made before 1530, and in 1534 he ordered an investigation of the feasibility of using the Chagres River valley as a route (*1*). Nothing was done, but the idea remained of interest to the Spanish crown until the early 19th century when independence movements in the colonial empire generally reduced the importance of such a waterway to Spain. Since then, canal projects have been a matter of more or less serious preoccupation to Panama and other Central American republics, Colombia, England, France, and the United States (beginning in the administration of Jefferson).

Although alternative routes were considered from time to time through the centuries, the Chagres valley was selected by the first French Canal Company, the first organization actually to attempt construction. The Chagres valley also was adopted by their American successors. The Panama Canal, in which locks are used, was completed in 1914. It was a great success, but now it is becoming increasingly inadequate and probably will not be able to cope with either the increased number or the size of the ships which will attempt to use it in the future (*2*). Thus, the need for a new canal is obvious, and a sea-level canal, without locks, would be the most desirable replacement. Many of the problems raised by the prospect of a sea-level canal are similar to those discussed 50 to 75 years ago. Will the cost of the project be justified in terms of benefits to shipping or to hemispheric defense? Can satisfactory diplomatic arrangements be made with the host country? The only new

factor is the possibility of using nuclear cratering techniques, and the necessity for evaluating the consequences.

Since World War II, there have been a series of studies concerned with both the problems of converting the Panama Canal to sea level by conventional means and of finding alternative sea-level routes. An investigation authorized by the 79th Congress (1947) considered 30 different routes from the Isthmus of Tehuantepec in Mexico south and east to northwest Colombia. In 1960, a report by the president of the Panama Canal Company included five routes suitable for nuclear excavation (Tehuantepec, Mexico; Nicaragua-Costa Rica; San Blas and Sasardi Morti in Panama; and Atrato-Truando in Colombia) (Figure 35.1).

In 1965, President Johnson established the Atlantic-Pacific Interoceanic Canal Study Commission whose members he authorized to call upon any department or agency of the executive branch for advice and assistance in collecting and evaluating technical data necessary to determine the feasibility of constructing a sea-level canal. In addition to engineering problems, pertinent political, military, and economic problems related to location, construction, and operation of a sea-level canal were to be analyzed. Extensive studies have been and are being carried out by the commission and its contractors. These include: engineering studies of problems such as flood control, sedimentation, and channel hydraulics; studies of radioactivity, ground shock, and air blast; as well as studies in other areas including meteorology, geology, navigation, and medicine. Bioenvironmental studies, exclusive of literature surveys, have been restricted to analyses of the dangers to human ingestion of organisms which may become contaminated with radionuclides. In the ocean, the cycling of radionuclides is particularly complicated. In inshore environments there is a continuous exchange between the sediments, bottom filter feeders, and free-swimming organisms. Most direct human contact with radionuclides would come from this system. In the open sea, radionuclides can be distributed over large areas by ocean currents and migratory organisms. However, the dangers involving larger geographical areas are somewhat offset by dilution effects.

The Major Problem

It might therefore be supposed that the problems inherent in a sea-level canal were known and that complete and thorough efforts were being made to provide the information necessary to assay all the possibly dangerous consequences. Unfortunately, this is not true. One major aspect of the situation has been almost completely ignored. There will

be major biological effects of a sea-level canal regardless of the site selected or the methods of construction used.

At present, the lock canal appears to be quite effective as a barrier to the migration of marine organisms from one ocean to another (3). The crucial factor is not the physical interposition of locks but the fresh water of Gatun Lake between the locks. A few euryhaline fishes transit the lake occasionally, but only one species is known to have gone from one ocean to the other and established a breeding population there (4). Sessile invertebrates of various types can effect interoceanic invasion as fouling attached to the bottom of ships, and planktonic forms might possibly transit in ballast tanks, but they certainly have not colonized new areas on a major scale.

The proposed sea-level canal will be a different matter. It will remove the barrier and will permit intermingling of large parts of the Atlantic and Pacific biotas. In effect, there will be a whole series of nearly simulta-

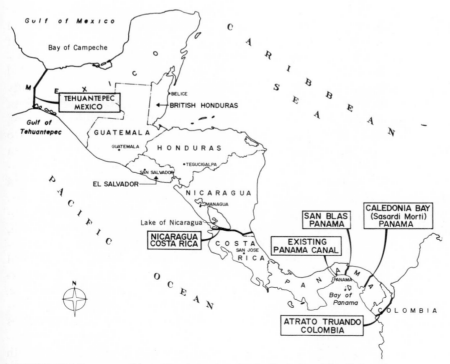

FIGURE 35.1 Some possible sea-level canal routes in Central and South America.

neous invasions and introductions of species into new areas.

The only other man-made connection of great bodies of water is the Suez Canal connecting the Mediterranean and Red seas. The situation of this sea-level canal is not similar to that planned for a Central American site. The Bitter Lakes, incorporated into the Suez Canal, represent a high-salinity barrier to migrations of most tropical organisms of the Red Sea and to most subtropical organisms of the Mediterranean. The salinity of the Bitter Lakes, however, has gradually decreased (from 68 to 45 per mille) since 1869, and the migrations of organisms through the canal has been facilitated. Over 150 species occurring in the eastern Mediterranean originated in the Red Sea, and possibly two species are reverse immigrants. Some of these immigrants are economically important, and nine of the commercially exploited species of the Mediterranean coast of Israel are of Red Sea origin (5).

The history of introductions and invasions of plants and animals as a result of human interference has, as often as not, been fraught with disaster. Elton (6) says these introductions frequently lead to ecological explosions. That is, "an enormous increase in numbers of some kind of living organism—it may be an infectious virus like influenza, or a bacterium like bubonic plague, or a fungus like that of the potato disease, a green plant like the prickly pear, or an animal like the grey squirrel. I use the word 'explosion' deliberately, because it means the bursting out from control of forces that were previously held in restraint by other forces."

One of the most notorious examples (and most pertinent in this connection) of an environmental manipulation leading to a population explosion is the construction of the Welland Canal which permitted the sea lamprey to invade the western Great Lakes. It took approximately 100 years for the population explosion of the sea lampreys to occur, but when it did, it resulted in the decimation of the whitefish and lake trout fisheries. In the last 12 years the United States and Canada have contributed approximately $16

million for control measures and research of this problem (7). This figure does not include the millions lost by the fishing industry of this region or the contributions of the various state conservation and fishery research programs. Other examples of outbreaks of populations after introductions into the United States include: Japanese beetles (*Popillia japonica*); European gypsy moth (*Porthetria dispar*); South American fire ant (*Solenopsis saevissima*); and the Asiatic chestnut blight (*Endothia parasitica*), the latter completely eliminating the domestic chestnut trees (8).

Spectacular as some of these cases may have been, they are minor by comparison with what would be expected to result from the construction of a sea-level canal in Central America. The mutual invasions of Atlantic and Pacific organisms should be much more extensive, numerous, and rapid, and their ultimate consequences should be quite incommensurable with any biological changes ever recorded before.

History of the Isthmus and Environments

The precise date at which an uninterrupted isthmian landbridge emerged is not known. The isthmus while acting as a barrier to marine organisms has been a landbridge for the exchange of North and South American terrestrial fauna. This landbridge had certainly been in full operation throughout the Pleistocene (9), and the water gap probably was finally closed during the latter part of the Pliocene (10). This would mean that the eastern Pacific and western Atlantic marine populations have remained separated for at least 3 or 4 million years.

Because the interruption of the Atlantic and Pacific oceans in this area has been geologically recent, there are still many similar forms of vertebrates and invertebrates on the opposite coasts. In a few cases, these Atlantic and Pacific populations are indistinguishable, although most have evolved minor differences and some have changed profoundly since they became isolated by the rise of the isthmus. The more closely related allopatric species have been referred to by a number of designations including: "species pairs," "geminate species," and "amphi-American species" (*11*).

Such divergence as has occurred may be largely a result of adaptations to the dissimilar environments on the respective coasts. The waters along the Atlantic and Pacific coasts of the isthmus at certain times of the year differ greatly in temperature, salinity, transparency, degree of tidal fluctuation, and, most important, in the biota which they support.

The Atlantic coast consists of a series of sandy beaches and extensive mangrove swamps, interspaced with and overlapping long fringing coral reefs. The tops of these reefs are frequently exposed at low tides. There is some exposure of volcanic rocks along the Atlantic coast, although it does not constitute nearly as extensive an inshore habitat as it does along the Pacific coast.

The most outstanding topographical feature of the Pacific coast is the presence of numerous lava flows extending into the Pacific at frequent intervals along the coast. In some areas, these lava flows extend into the Pacific for almost a mile and many tide pools are formed in the irregular surfaces. The shoreline between these flows consists of muddy or sandy beaches and mangrove swamps.

The Atlantic water conditions adjacent to the isthmus are relatively constant. The differences between maximum and minimum recorded water temperatures at Cristobal are only about 6°C (Figure 35.2). The difference between maximum and minimum tide at Cristobal is well under 0.5 meter, with the mean daily range averaging less than 0.3 meter (Figure 35.3). The tides here are mixed diurnal, varying from two lows and two highs each day to one low or one high with intermediate conditions also being exhibited. The rainfall along the Atlantic slope is greater than along the Pacific slope, and the temporary dilution of the surface waters at the height of the rainy season along the

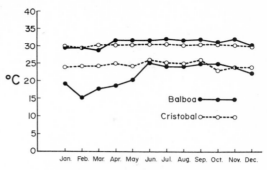

Max. & Min. Recorded Temp. 1907–1963

FIGURE 35.2 Maximum and minimum sea-surface temperatures recorded at Balboa (Pacific) and Cristobal (Atlantic) 1907–1963. [Compiled from data collected by the Panama Canal Company, Meteorological and Hydrographic Branch.]

Caribbean may be higher than that along the Pacific coast.

Compared to the relatively constant conditions found along the Atlantic coast, the Pacific waters are variable. The differences between recorded maximum and minimum temperatures at Balboa are as much as 18°C and the tidal amplitude in a single day can exceed 6 meters. From January through April (occasionally including periods of December and May) the Gulf of Panama is influenced by strong northeast trade winds. These winds drive the upper water mass offshore and produce upwellings of water from below 100 meters which is colder, more

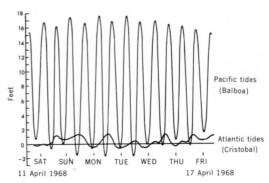

FIGURE 35.3 Comparison of Balboa (Pacific) and Cristobal (Atlantic) tides, 11 to 17 April 1968 (1 foot ~ 0.3 meter). [Drawn from data in tide tables compiled by Coast and Geodetic Survey, U.S. Department of Commerce (1968).]

saline, and richer in nutrients than the water it replaces (*12*).

A striking contrast between the Atlantic and Pacific coasts is provided by the absence of coral reefs and a sparsity of attached algae along the Pacific mainland. This absence of coral reefs in the eastern Pacific is attributed to the periodic cold upwellings which frequently approach the lower physiological limit ascribed to reef corals. Other conditions, such as the lack of transparency of the water column and the prolonged desiccation due to the great tidal amplitude, undoubtedly also contribute to the general hostility of this region for corals. The turbidity of the water during flood tides may interfere with light transmission enough to inhibit photosynthesis in adherent algae as well as in coralline commensals.

Possible Consequences

The possible general biological effects have been mentioned above. It may be useful, however, to consider some of the possible effects in more specific detail.

Theoretically, the results of sudden mixing of two formerly isolated populations can be predicted according to well-known genetic and ecological principles (*13*). Thus, for example, the potential for interbreeding between the newly intermixing populations depends upon whether or not they have diverged genetically during their isolation in ways that made them reproductively incompatible. Isolating mechanisms can be inherent in populations that have not diverged morphologically or may be absent in isolated populations that have diverged morphologically. However, the levels of morphological divergence and isolating mechanisms are usually correlated.

Not all allopatric populations have necessarily completed speciation, and it is expected that some of these populations might successfully fuse if the geographical barrier were removed. Depending upon the level of reproductive isolating mechanisms that have been evolved in allopatry, the effects of pop-

ulations coming into contact with one another may be classified into the following not necessarily exclusive categories. (i) If during the period of allopatry no isolating mechanisms were developed, the populations may freely interbreed, producing a viable hybrid swarm. This swarm may eventually include the complete range of variability of both parental populations, or it may be limited to a narrow hybrid belt. The extent of such a hybrid belt will be determined by the ability of the hybrids to adapt ecologically to the geographical ranges of both parental populations. (ii) The newly sympatric populations may freely interbreed but if their genetic constitutions are not sufficiently similar (because of chromosomal rearrangements such as fusions or inversions) then swarms containing adaptively inferior individuals may result because of meiotic malorientations (*14*), and these could lead to the extinction of both populations. (iii) If the development of reproductive isolating mechanisms between two populations was begun but not completed in isolation, then occasional matings between individuals of the populations may be expected. These matings may be sterile, or the progeny may be inviable or sterile. In this case, those individuals whose behavior insures their mating only with others of their kind will be reproductively more successful, and isolating mechanisms will become more prevalent throughout the population. Selection will act to improve efficiency of some of the isolating mechanisms so that the two populations continue to remain separate. If, however, the occasional crossings between two populations do not produce adaptively inferior progeny, the two populations may react as in the first category, but somewhat more slowly. (iv) If the isolated populations have completed speciation before they mingle, they may coexist without interbreeding for part or all of their ranges, or competition between the two forms may cause replacement or extinction of one species by the other.

From the various degrees of divergence exhibited by the amphi-American species of shore fishes we have studied, one would expect that different groups will behave in all the ways enumerated above. Our laboratory is examining the degree of genetic isolation achieved in various groups of inshore fishes. Studies with two groups of Atlantic and Pacific marine gobies (*Bathygobius* and *Lophogobius*) indicate that many allopatric species are still interfertile and are not reproductively isolated at the gametic level. Experiments designed to test whether ethological isolating mechanisms have evolved demonstrated that allopatric species of these genera are reluctant to interbreed in "no choice" mating experiments. This result was unexpected since other investigators have frequently been able to break down behavioral isolation between various related species by performing mating experiments with unbalanced sex ratios or by completely eliminating any choice of conspecific mates. We discovered that although it was difficult to induce heterospecific spawnings in experiments with one male of one species with one female of another (conspecific controls in adjacent aquariums were breeding regularly), such spawnings could be achieved if five or six males of one species were placed with five or six females of another. Some sort of social facilitation seems to be operating, and presumably a greater level of stimulation is necessary for successful heterospecific courtship and mating. Groups of individuals are the normal condition—the type of situation to be expected when a sea-level canal is completed. Whether or not there is a quantitative level of discrimination when both conspecific and heterospecific mates are available in equal numbers can be determined by "choice" experiments. At the same time, the relative viability and fertility of hybrids formed by heterospecific spawnings in the above groups (*15*) should be studied.

The principal ecological effects involve competition for different resources; for example, food, space to live and breed, and so forth. Interference may be direct—by the activities of one species against another—or indirect—through the influence of parasites or diseases of one species upon the other. We can anticipate that certain extant species will enlarge their niches owing to the removal of a competitor or some other species whose presence was restricting.

The construction of a sea-level canal may also change the physical environments on the respective coasts. It is conceivable, for instance, that a layer of warm Caribbean water could be spread through many miles in the eastern Pacific (*16*). The possible consequences of such developments are difficult to anticipate. At the very least, the resident populations and the new immigrants will have to make rapid adaptations. The influx of new organisms could upset the balance of populations, and certainly would change the nature of the selection to which organisms were subjected; we can expect an increase in turnover, the process of extinction of some species and their replacement by others. The population dynamics of some commercially important species may be disrupted by these changes.

Physical changes will probably have only local influence, their extent depending upon the volume of interoceanic flow and on the accompanying differentials in temperature, salinity, and silt. Biological results, by contrast, may have chain effects influencing the ecology of areas thousands of miles from the canal site.

Furthermore, the extinction occurring as a result of the mixing of the two biotas may involve forms that have either not been described yet or are still very rare in collections. Their disappearance before being studied would be a great loss to scientific knowledge and would effectively remove a potentially important historical base for biological oceanography of the future.

What Should Be Done?

The sea-level canal can provide a unique opportunity to advance our scientific understanding of evolutionary and ecological processes. In order to realize this potential it is necessary to treat the whole situation as an experiment in which case the necessary "control" is the pre-canal situation. If this is not thoroughly understood, then a large part of the contribution to knowledge that this engineering feat would afford will be lost forever.

Several types of biological studies should precede the construction of a sea-level canal if we are to have any hope of predicting the general consequences with any degree of adequate accuracy. A committee containing various marine systematists, ecologists, oceanographers, and statisticians should be convened and charged with the specific responsibility of organizing and operating a long-term quantitative and qualitative survey of the Atlantic and Pacific Central American region. They should be concerned with describing what is there, with what abundance, and with what seasonal, annual, and long-term fluctuations in densities (17). This committee should also be responsible for the critical task of organizing and executing the post-canal monitoring of the regions to assay what the canal-related changes are.

Analytical and experimental work should be initiated in a number of key groups to establish how Atlantic and Pacific species may interact genetically, ecologically, and behaviorally. Tests should be made of relative physiological, pathological, and parasitological tolerances of representative groups. It is not an impossible task to place samples of related populations from the Atlantic and Pacific oceans together experimentally, to learn how they compete for elements such as substrate, food, nest sites, or to challenge species experimentally with one another's parasites, or to test their physiological tolerances to hydrographic conditions on the opposite coast. Studies such as these will put predictions of the possible effects of Atlantic and Pacific intermingling on a sound basis of scientific data.

Concluding Remarks

It is no longer possible to permit only regional considerations and private interest groups to effect changes of wide-ranging implications.

John F. Kennedy remarked to the National Academy of Sciences in October 1963:

> I would mention a problem which I know has greatly concerned many of you —that is, our responsibility to control the effects of our own scientific experimentation. . . . In the past the problem of conservation has been mainly the problem of inadvertent human destruction of natural resources. But science today has the power for the first time in history to undertake experiments with premeditation which can irreversibly alter our biological and physical environments on a global scale.

> The problem is difficult because it is hard to know in advance whether the cumulative effects of a particular experiment will help or harm mankind. . . .

> The government has the clear responsibility to weigh the importance of large-scale experiments to the advance of knowledge or to national security against the possibility of adverse and destructive effects. The scientific community must assist the government in arriving at rational judgments and in interpreting the issues to the public (18).

The necessary support must be provided to conduct adequate studies of the biological effects of a sea-level canal. Modern science can identify significant processes, quantify the relations of many oceanographic complexities, and resolve them in predictable patterns.

I believe that a control commission for environmental manipulation should be established and that this commission should be given broad powers of approving, disapproving, or modifying all major alterations of the marine or terrestrial environments in the United States, or any place where United States government or private contractors might be active. This commission should be multidisciplinary, independent of any single government agency, bureau, university, or private research institution, and it should have adequate funding to support its own investigations (19). Such a commission should be in operation before a sea-level canal is built, and its decisions should be made with the benefit of comprehensive biological investigations.

References and Notes

1. D. A. Arosemena, *Documentary Diplomatic History of The Panama Canal* (Imprenta Nacional, Panama, R.P., 1961).
2. Atlantic-Pacific Interoceanic Canal Study Commission, *A Plan For Study of Engineering Feasibility of Alternate Sea-Level Canal Routes Connecting the Atlantic and Pacific Oceans* (Atlantic-Pacific Interoceanic Canal Study Commission, Washington, D.C., 1965), 61 pp.
3. S. F. Hildebrand, *Sci. Mon.* 44, 242 (1937); *Zoologica* 24, 15 (1939).
4. R. W. Rubinoff and I. Rubinoff, *Nature* 217, 476 (1968).
5. A. Ben-Tuvia, *Copeia* 1966, 254 (1966).
6. C. S. Elton, *The Ecology of Invasions by Animals and Plants* (Methuen, London, 1958), p. 15.
7. U.S. Fish and Wildlife Service, personal communication.
8. D. Pimental, *Science* 159, 1432 (1968).
9. W. P. Woodring, *Proc. Amer. Phil. Soc.* 110, 425 (1966).
10. J. J. Lloyd, in *Backbone of the Americas* (American Association of Petroleum Geologists, Tulsa, Okla., 1962), p. 88.
11. A. Günther, *Trans. Zool. Soc. London* 6, 377 (1869); C. H. Gilbert and E. C. Starks, *Mem. Calif. Acad. Sci.* 4, 1-304 (1904); S. Ekman, *Zoogeography of the Sea* (Sidgwick and Jackson, London, 1953), pp. 30-55.
12. W. S. Wooster, *Amer. Mus. Natur. Hist. Bull.* 118, 119 (1959); M. B. Schaefer, Y. M. M. Bishop, G. V. Howard, *Bull. Inter-Amer. Trop. Tuna Comm.* 3, 79 (1958); E. D. Forsbergh, *ibid.* 7, 1 (1963); T. J. Smayda, *ibid.*, p. 191.
13. E. Mayr, *Animal Species and Evolution* (Harvard Univ. Press, Cambridge, Mass., 1963), 797 pp.; I. Rubinoff, *Natur. Hist.* 74, 69 (1965).
14. M. J. D. White, *Science* 159, 1065 (1968).
15. I. Rubinoff and R. W. Rubinoff, in preparation.
16. C. O'D. Iselin, personal communication.
17. It is commonly believed that population fluctuations in tropical species are minimum, but this certainly is not true of reptiles (O. Sexton, in press); mammals and birds (M. Moynihan, personal communication); at least some groups of insects (R. Dressler, personal communication); and it is my impression that the fluctuations in marine fishes are at least as great as in land animals. It is important to recognize that population studies should begin at least 10 to 20 years before a canal is completed if normal long-term population fluctuations are to be mapped. Without these data a canal may be "blamed" for sudden reduction or disappearance of species which might just coincidentally be at a density nadir.
18. New York *Times* (23 October 1963), p. 24.
19. For a recent discussion of federal activities in environmental control, see *Environmental Quality*, Hearings before the House Subcommittee on Science Research and Development, Jan.-Mar., 1968, Emilio Q. Daddario, chairman (U.S. Government Printing Office, Washington, D.C., 1968).
20. Based in part on research supported by NSF grant GB-3450 and grants from the Smithsonian Research Foundation. I thank W. Aron, S. Galler, P. Glynn, E. Mayr, R. Menzies, M. Moynihan, R. Rubinoff, N. Smith, R. Topp for criticizing the manuscript.

ADDITIONAL REFERENCES

Ben-Tuvia, Adam. 1966. Red Sea fishes recently found in the Mediterranean. *Copeia* 2:254–275.

Bishop, M. W. H. 1951. Distribution of barnacles by ships. *Nature* 167:531.

Bishop, M. W. H., and D. J. Crisp. 1957. The Australasian barnacle, *Elminius modestus*, in France. *Nature* 179:482–3.

Briggs, J. C. 1968. Panama's sea-level canal. *Science* 169(3853):511–513.

Briggs, J. C. 1969. The sea-level Panama canal: Potential biological catastrophe. *BioScience* 19(1):44–47.

Charnell, R. L., T. M. Zorich, and D. E. Holley. 1969. Hydrologic redistribution of radionuclides around a nuclear-excavated sea-level canal. *BioScience* 19(9):799–803.

Chesher, R. H. 1968. Transport of marine plankton through the Panama Canal. *Limnol. Oceanogr.* 13(2):387–388.

Hildebrand, S. F. 1939. The Panama Canal as a passageway for fishes, with lists and remarks on the fishes and invertebrates observed. *Zoologica* 24:15–45.

Tamplin, A. R. 1969. Estimation of the maximum dose to man from the contamination of an aquatic ecosystem with radionuclides. Pp. 75–94 in *Biological implications of the nuclear age*, U.S. Atomic Energy Commission. An assessment of some radioactive hazards of sea-level canal construction.

Logging in Redwood National Park, near Orick, California.   Photo by Martin Litton.

SEVEN

DESTRUCTION OF VEGETATION BY MAN

"The changes induced in native vegetation by man range from simple modification through severe degradation to complete destruction and replacement. All these changes in plant cover are accompanied by changes in the environment within and adjacent to the affected vegetation."

INTRODUCTION

It is vegetation that largely gives character to the landscape. Nature's mountains or urban piles of stone, steel, and glass may prevail locally, but at the usual scale of our awareness the land's mantle of plants predominates. Many regions are distinguished by their vegetation—the form, size, and variety of plants and their grouping, color, and seasonal aspect. For centuries man has wondered how vegetation affects human sensibility, but firm answers have been few. Without principles for planning the vegetative landscape, economics and happenstance have unfortunately governed our treatment of the plant cover.

Though the influence *of* our vegetative environment remains unexplained, our influence *on* vegetation is quite clear. The spread of crop plants and the development of intensive agriculture have done most to transform the landscape. Alexander von Humboldt, in 1805, succinctly described the process and its effect: "Man plays favorites with newly-introduced plants in cultivating them, and makes them dominant over indigenous ones; but this preponderance, which makes the European landscape look so monotonous, affects only that small part of the globe where civilization is at its peak." Today, with many more people and with modern agricultural technology, greater regions are covered by fields of crops. The present threat of extensive monoculture must be recognized as being more than just monotony—the principal danger is *ecologic simplification*, with inherent instability and vulnerability to explosive changes.

Man's destruction of wild vegetation for cropland is, more and more, being followed by a second step: the conversion of cropland for cities and suburbs. The first selection in this part (Selection 36) focuses on the history and consequences of these two stages of vegetational change in mid-latitude forest and grassland regions (especially in North America). Further information on the history of vegetational changes wrought by man can be found in works by Iverson (1949), Marsh (1864), Darby (1956), and Sauer (1938). Sustained fertility and dense human populations have brought more continued as well as more intensive changes in the mid-latitudes. Shifting cultivation and grazing, typical in areas of tropical forest and desert respectively, are other major land uses affecting the plant cover elsewhere in the world (see, for example, Bartlett, 1956; Gourou, 1956; Conklin, 1963; Budowski, 1956 and 1966; Halwagg, 1962; Sears, 1966).

Other human activities may destroy vegetation indirectly. The serious and growing damage to plants by air pollutants, which is the subject of Selection 37, is an outstanding example of man's environmental repercussions. Scientific studies in the last several decades have clearly identified industrial and automotive air pollution (see Part 3) as a menace to organisms. Vegetation is also the inadvertent object of change by other activities, including watershed management (Colman, 1953; Stone and Vasey, 1968), foraging by domesticated animals (Darling, 1956), burning (Guthrie, 1936; Stewart, 1956), and war.

Since the Second World War, technology has developed chemical plant killers ("herbicides") that can wreck vegetation with unprecedented ease. Chemical weed killers have provided well-known gains (at least in the short run) in agricultural production. However, herbicides further simplify crop ecosystems and may have other deleterious environmental consequences (perhaps endangering them to disease in the long run; Yarwood, 1970; also see Selection 42). The use and ecological effects of plant killers and defoliants in the Vietnam war, discussed in Selection 38, provide a chilling example. Defoliants have been sprayed from the air over several million acres to prevent concealment of troops and supplies and to destroy food crops. Known inadvertent or indirect effects include killing of rubber trees in plantations, altering the composition of forests, retarding regeneration of some forests for decades, threatening some animal species with extinction, and contaminating soil with arsenic and other toxic compounds. Many other environmental consequences are suggested, but unsubstantiated as yet. Clearly, war involves more than politics, economics, and morals—environmental considerations (including many not specified here) are also important. Most of man's larger problems—the war in Southeast Asia, social injustice, hunger, and environmental crises—are symptoms of his basic refusal to recognize the complex web of interconnections between all components on this finite earth.

FURTHER READINGS

Bartlett, H. H. 1956. Fire, primitive agriculture, and grazing in the tropics. Pp. 692–720 in *Man's role in changing the face of the earth,* ed. by William L. Thomas, Jr. Chicago and London: Univ. of Chicago Press.

Budowski, Gerardo. 1956. Tropical savannas, a sequence of forest felling and repeated burnings. *Turrialba* 6(1–2):23–33.

Budowski, Gerardo. 1966. Middle America: The human factor. Pp. 144–155 in *Future environments of North America,* ed. by F. Fraser Darling and John P. Milton. Garden City, New York: Natural History Press.

Colman, E. 1953. *Vegetation and watershed management.* New York: Ronald Press.

Conklin, H. C. 1963. *The study of shifting cultivation.* Pan American Union, Department of Social Affairs Studies. 185 pp.

Darby, H. C. 1956. The clearing of the woodland in Europe. Pp. 183–216 in *Man's role in changing the face of the earth,* ed. by William L. Thomas, Jr. Chicago and London: Univ. of Chicago Press.

Darling, F. Fraser. 1956. Man's ecological dominance through domesticated animals on wild lands. Pp. 778–787 in *Man's role in changing the face of the earth,* ed. by William L. Thomas, Jr. Chicago and London: Univ. of Chicago Press.

Fowells, H. A., ed. 1965. *Silvics of forest trees of the United States.* Division of Timber Management Research, Forest Service, U.S. Department of Agriculture, Handbook No. 271. 762 pp.

Gourou, Pierre. 1956. The quality of land use of tropical cultivators. Pp. 336–349 in *Man's role in changing the face of the earth,* ed. by William L. Thomas, Jr. Chicago and London: Univ. of Chicago Press.

Graham, Edward H. 1956. The re-creative power of plant communities. Pp. 677–691 in *Man's role in changing the face of the earth,* ed. by William L. Thomas, Jr. Chicago and London: Univ. of Chicago Press.

Guthrie, John D. 1936. *Great forest fires of America.* U.S. Department of Agriculture, Washington, D.C.

Halwagg, R. 1962. The impact of man on semi-desert vegetation in the Sudan. *J. Ecol.* 50:163–273.

Haden-Quest, S., J. K. Wright, and E. Teclaff, eds. 1956. *World geography of forest resources.* New York: Ronald Press.

Hepper, F. N. 1969. The conservation of rare and vanishing species of plants. Pp. 353–360 in *Wildlife in danger,* by James Fisher, Noel Simon, and Jack Vincent. New York: Viking Press.

Iversen, J. 1949. The influence of prehistoric man on vegetation. *Danmarks Geol. Under-*

spegelse, Series IV, vol. 3, no. 6, Copenhagen.

Marsh, George Perkins. 1864. The woods. Pp. 113–280 in *Man and nature,* 1965 ed. by D. Lowenthal. Cambridge, Mass.: Harvard Univ. Press.

Mikesell, Marvin W. 1960. Deforestation in northern Morocco. *Science* 132(3425):441–448.

Moore, J. J. 1963. Summary Report of the International Symposium on Anthropogeneous Vegetation held at Stolzenau/Weser, 27–30 March. *Vegetatio* 11:136–139.

Sauer, Carl O. 1938. Theme of plant and animal destruction in economic history. *J. Farm Econ.* 20:765–775. (Reprinted in *Land and life,* Univ. of California Press paperback 132.)

Sears, Paul B. 1966. Vegetational changes in Sonoran Desert. *Science* 153:919–920.

Stewart, Omer C. 1956. Fire as the first great force employed by man. Pp. 115–133 in *Man's role in changing the face of the earth,* ed. by William L. Thomas, Jr. Chicago and London: Univ. of Chicago Press.

Stone, Edward C., and Richard B. Vasey. 1968. Preservation of coast redwood on alluvial flats. *Science* 159:157–161.

Treshow, Michael. 1970. *Environment and plant response.* New York: McGraw-Hill. 422 pp. Especially see Part 4, "Pollution in the environment," pp. 145–397, for recent and broad discussion of the effects of air pollutants and pesticides on plants.

Yarwood, C. E. 1970. Man-made plant diseases. *Science* 168:218–220.

36
SELECTION

THE MODIFICATION OF MID-LATITUDE GRASSLANDS AND FORESTS BY MAN

JOHN T. CURTIS

The forests and the grasslands of the earth's populous mid-latitudes have each undergone similar changes under the hand of man. This selection puts these changes in historical perspective. In general the sequence of forest-land use has been from hunting and trapping (with slight direct effect on the vegetation), to exploitation of special forest products, to cutting of wood for building material and fuel, to increased clearing of the land for agriculture, and finally to urbanization. In forests that are cut or burned, species of trees that can sprout from stumps or roots following these impacts are favored, and the balance between various species (or forest composition) shifts. Repeated cutting of a regenerated forest, like repeated grazing of grassland, allows plants with "pioneer" tendencies (such as an ability to withstand great climatic extremes) to proliferate at the expense of species that are less resistant to the particular pressures. The expanding species commonly are alien plants.

Contrary to Curtis' closing suggestion, it might be argued that repetitious forest cutting, or frequent grassland grazing, has created unprecedented stability of the vegetation. In the forest, for instance, man has virtually eliminated several former processes of disruption—for example, fire and windthrow (trees are now cut before they are big enough to be toppled by the wind). However, there are probably many other environmental repercussions, like soil-nutrient loss following clear-cutting (Bormann, et. al., 1968), still to be determined before a balanced conclusion concerning man's impact on the forest is possible.

(Editor's comment)

John T. Curtis (1913–1961) was a professor of botany at the University of Wisconsin and research director of the University Arboretum (1941–1961). He was educated at Carroll College and the University of Wisconsin (Ph.D. in botany, 1937) and was twice a Guggenheim Fellow (1942 and 1956). Curtis has written *The Vegetation of Wisconsin* (1959) and numerous papers on plant ecology, especially on the continuum concept of community relationships.

Reprinted from *Man's Role in Changing the Face of the Earth,* edited by William L. Thomas, Jr., The University of Chicago Press, pp. 721–736. Copyright © The University of Chicago, 1956.

Man's actions in modifying the biotic composition of mid-latitude grasslands and forests can best be studied by separating them into two groups of processes. In the first group are the effects induced by pioneer cultures in areas peripheral to main population centers. These areas may be peripheral because the main population has not had time to spread out over the entire region, as was the case during the European settlement of North America, or they may be peripheral because the severity of the environment more or less permanently prohibits the development of intensive civilization, as in rugged mountains, deserts, or taiga. In either case the exploiting peoples have economic ties with the main population in the sense that the latter furnishes both the tools for exploitation and a market for the products.

The second group of effects is composed of those that are produced by the intensive utilization of land for agricultural and urban purposes within the regions of high population. These typically follow the pioneer effects in time and are influenced by the earlier changes. Most of the available evidence on the nature of the changes induced by man is concerned with impact of European man on his environment, but it is probable that both older civilizations and aboriginal cultures exerted similar effects whenever their populations were sufficiently high.

Modifications of Mid-latitude Forests

The mid-latitude forests are typified by the deciduous forest formation, although several kinds of conifer forests are also to be found within the strict geographical boundaries of the mid-latitudes. In the interests of simplicity, this discussion will be concerned almost solely with the deciduous forest.

PERIPHERAL EFFECTS

Ordinarily, the first products of a peripheral wilderness to be exploited by an adjoining civilization are derived from the animal members of the community, especially the fur-bearers. The French *voyageurs*, the Hudson's Bay Company, and John Jacob Astor and his fur-trading competitors are familiar agents of such exploitation in America. Ecologically, the effects were not very great, since the rather minor population changes brought about in the animal species concerned were not radically different from those experienced in natural fluctuations. Of far greater significance was the utilization of the forest for its timber. The first stages in this utilization were concerned with the harvest of products of high value, such as shipmasts, spars, and naval timbers in general, followed by woods of importance in construction of houses and furniture. When the tree species suitable for these needs were common and especially when they grew in nearly pure stands, as was the case with the white pine in eastern North America, the impact of the exploitation was great. This was true both of the magnitude of the changes and of the relative size of the area affected. White pine was a favorite goal of the early American lumberman and was ruthlessly harvested far from the scenes of its ultimate use.

Some forest types were composed mostly of trees of lesser value, such as the oaks and maples. These were commonly by-passed, or their more valuable members, used as cabinet woods, were selectively logged. This emphasis on special products rather than on complete utilization was mainly a feature of young expanding cultures whose demands were small relative to the size of the resource base in the peripheral area. The phenomenon is present in current times, as exemplified by the utilization of only a few of the host of tropical species for special veneers and by the selective harvest of spruce in the conifer forests of Canada and the nonutilization of the equally abundant balsam fir and other species.

All these exploitations were and are dependent upon certain definite physical properties of the wood as it occurs in the trunks of natural trees produced under natural conditions. These properties are commonly unrelated to the ecological behavior of the species in the sense that no special growth habits or reproductive capacities are concerned. The primitive exploiter was not worried about whether or not a second or continuing crop of the species would be available. In many respects, the selective harvest resembled mining in that it was the utilization of a non-renewable resource or at least was treated as such.

As the economic demands of the main population centers grew and especially as the population centers spread out in area, the utilization of the peripheral resources became more intense. In non-industrial civilizations or non-industrial stages in the development of any culture, the forest is called on to produce a considerable share of the fuel used by that culture. This might be in the form of firewood or in the form of charcoal. Even in those countries or stages where coal was used for fuel, the forest was a source of timber for mine props and for ties or sleepers on the railroads used for hauling the coal. All these uses were more or less dependent upon a near-by source of supply. The biological significance of this lies in the fact that the harvesters now became desirous of gathering more than one crop from the same land. The ecological behavior of the species thus came to be of greater importance than the physical structure of the wood. Species were utilized regardless of behavior, but only those which possessed the ability to resprout or otherwise to reproduce themselves remained in the forest. Firewood, charcoal, and mine props all utilize small-dimension stock by preference, and thus a premium was placed on those species which could quickly return to a merchantable size. The technique of coppicing, so widely used in Eurasia, is a direct result of this situation.

In many places in the world the more intensive utilization of the trees in the sub-peripheral areas was accompanied by the introduction of grazing animals to the forest community. The wood-choppers, charcoal-makers, and lime-burners were more permanent inhabitants of a region than the earlier lumbermen, and they commonly broadened the base of their economy by the use of cattle, sheep, or goats. These animals were allowed to roam the woods on free range and to make use of such forage and browse as might be available there. The livestock pressure was rarely as great as that which accompanied the agricultural economies of subsequent times, but its effects cannot be overlooked (Steinbrenner, 1951). In addition to the growth behavior patterns selected by the harvesting techniques, the successful species were also those best able to withstand the effects of grazing.

Thus we find in the areas peripheral to major population centers a gradually increasing intensity of utilization, either in space or in time, from a negligible pressure with little effect on the biotic composition of the forest to a severe pressure which selectively favored species with particular behavior patterns and eliminated other species which did not conform.

Let us now inquire into the actual nature of the changes that accompanied this increase in utilization. The earlier stages in the process are best studied by examples from the United States, since these stages occurred so long ago in Asia and Europe as to have left almost no record. In the United States the fur-trapping stage was roughly a seventeenth- and eighteenth-century phenomenon, while the lumber-harvest stage was most prominent in the nineteenth century.

The later, more intensive stages began in the latter half of the 1800's in the eastern portion of the United States. In much of Europe the intensive utilization began in the 1200's and continues in marginal areas up to the present. Thus, in England, extensive forests were utilized chiefly for hunting purposes through the period of Norman domination. Later timber-harvesting resulted in such a severe depletion of suitable trees that large-scale imports from the Baltic region were required by 1300. Widespread utilization of the forests for pasturage of swine and cattle, combined with intensive cutting of fuelwood, made further inroads on the peripheral areas. By 1544 a series of laws was passed regulating the procedures by which a coppiced woods should be managed (Tansley, 1939). In the Balkans utilization of the forests for construction timber and marine products was active in the 1200's, with many areas depleted by 1620. Intensive utilization for firewood, charcoal, and lime-burning still continues in the more mountainous regions (Turrill, 1929). In China peripheral exploitation is much older and has long since been completed in all but the most rugged and inaccessible terrain. Clearing of forests for agricultural purposes was widespread during the Shang dynasty beginning in 1600 B.C. (Needham, 1954).

The most obvious biotic change in the forest is the great shift in species composition, both qualitative and quantitative. This is best seen today in the northern states of the United States, where the original forest was a mosaic of patches of hardwoods with a few conifers and patches of conifers with a few hardwoods (Brown and Curtis, 1952). Those portions of the northern forests originally covered with hardwoods underwent a relatively slight alteration. They were composed of a mixture of species, none of which was ever in great economic demand. Large areas, therefore, were rarely cut over in anything like the intensity so common in the neighboring pine forests. In addition, fires were much less frequent and usually not so severe as those in the coniferous area. Many of the component species had the ability to resprout after cutting, like the maple and the beech, and most of them had very efficient means of reproduction, so that a stand was able to regenerate itself following partial destruction. Here and there, selective pressure reacted against one or more species. Millions of board feet of hemlock were cut in the region solely for the bark, which was used in the tanning industry. The logs were allowed to rot where they fell after they had been peeled (Goodlett, 1954). In more recent times, yellow birch has been intensively exploited because of its value as a veneer wood, and a few other species have experienced similar selective pressures. The major change resulting from all this has been an increase in the relative importance of sugar maple (*Acer saccharum*) in the remaining stands. This species is ecologically the most vigorous of all. The normal subordinate rank of the other species, accentuated by the added pressure from man, has resulted in their gradual disappearance in favor of the maple.

In contrast to this shift in relative importance of one member of the hardwood forest at the expense of others, the pine forests suffered a much more severe alteration. The march of the lumbermen from Maine in the late 1700's, to New York in 1850, to Michigan in 1870, to Wisconsin in 1880, and finally to Minnesota in 1890 was primarily a quest for white pine (*Pinus strobus*). This species, like the majority of pines, is a "fire tree" and was found in essentially pure stands in large blocks on lands subject to widespread burns. Profitable harvesting enterprises could be centered in regions where such blocks were common and where adequate facilities for transportation by river driving were available. In such regions the initial harvest obviously made great changes in forest composition by the removal of 90 per cent or more of the dominant trees. Of even greater importance were the frequent fires which broke out in the slash following the lumbering operations. These fires were allowed to burn unchecked and were often actually encouraged. White pine is adapted to seeding-in following a fire but has no mechanism for sprouting from a burned stump. The first fire, therefore, often produced a new crop of pine seedlings, but a second fire before the trees had matured destroyed the entire population. The land became covered with weedy tree species like the aspens, birches, and oaks and with shrubs like the hazelnut, all of which could resprout following fire and thus remain in control of the ground. Excessive burning sometimes produced the so-called "barrens"—desolate tracts almost devoid of large woody plants, such as occupy extensive portions of Michigan and Wisconsin.

Accompanying the changes in species composition have been changes in the micro-environment within the forest. Selective logging or other mild harvesting practices result in an opening-up of the canopy of the forest, a breaking of the former more or less complete cover. The openings thus created possess a very different microclimate from the remaining portions of the forest. The most significant change is an increase in the rate of evaporation, and this increase is proportional to the intensity of the harvest, reaching maximum values in clear-cut and particularly in cut and burned woods.

With the exception of those lightly harvested forests containing sugar maple in which the net result is an increase in maple, practically all the environmental changes induced by the peripheral harvesting sequence are in the direction of a more xeric habitat, with greater light, more variable temperatures, more variable moisture, and much greater transpirational stress. The internal, stabilizing mechanisms of the community that lead toward homeostasis are upset or destroyed. The new environment tends to resemble that normally found in adjacent, hotter and drier regions (the "pre-climax conditions" of Clements, 1936). Such conditions are most suitable for the ecologically pioneer plants of the region, which are those species that grow vigorously under the unstable climatic conditions and that possess adaptations to make use of the high light intensities. Ordinarily, such species possess highly effective means of reproduction and dispersal and, in addition, are likely to survive under severe disturbance, as by cutting or fire, through the ability to sprout from stumps or roots. The initial invaders of the disturbed areas, therefore, tend to be the pioneer species. Subsequent harvesting, as by coppicing, favors the persistence of these species and the gradual elimination of those with more climax tendencies. Thus, the original mixed forests come to be replaced by large areas of scrub oaks, aspen, box elder, sassafras, and similar species. The final selection under grazing pressure may eliminate or depress some of these, since there are very few species in the biota with the necessary combination of attributes to resist all the decimating influences. A fertile field for future investigation would be the study of the characteristics of various plants which enable them to survive under the conditions just outlined.

AGRO-URBAN EFFECTS

As the main centers of populations expanded into the peripheral areas, a considerable change in the land-use pattern followed. In the mid-latitudes, with their generally favorable climate during the growing season, agriculture became the dominant feature. The forests, already modified by peripheral utilization, were cleared to make room for fields with an initial selection of the best sites, followed by gradual encroachment onto less favorable land types. The actual nature of the best sites naturally varied from place to place, but the ideal appeared to be a large area of level or gently rolling land, with well-drained soils of high fertility. Frequently, the land was chosen on the basis of indicator species, black walnut being a favorite of the American settler, as it grew in rich forest stands well supplied with moisture and available nutrients. On these preferential sites the trees were killed by girdling or cutting, the logs and tops burned, the stumps pulled, blasted, or otherwise removed, and the ground plowed. Any member of the original community which persisted under the treatment was subsequently eradicated by the clean cultivation practices employed on the fields. The impact of man on these agricultural fields was thus one of total destruction with respect to the original community.

Marginal lands which were remote, difficult of access, or topographically unsuited for crop agriculture were commonly employed for intensive grazing. A continuing pressure was also exerted on them for lumber and firewood harvest. The distinction between peripheral and central activities is least clear at this stage, which is usually rather short in duration. With long-term occupancy of the land by an agro-urban culture, the remnants of the original forest come to be restricted to sites which are totally unusable for agriculture, such as cliffs, rocky ground, barren sands, ravines, or swamps. These habitats all differ markedly from the bulk of the land in their physical environment and hence also in their community composition. For various reasons, successional development is retarded in these extreme sites, and they retain a very high proportion of ecologically pioneer species. Consequently, they are less subject to drastic change by man's disturbance, since this disturbance usually leads to an increase in pioneers which are here the natural dominants.

The rate and the extent of the destruction of original cover by agricultural clearing are well demonstrated by a case history covering the first century of use of a township of land in Green County, Wisconsin, along the Wisconsin-Illinois border. The vegetation in 1831 before agricultural settlement began, as derived from records of the original Government Land Survey, was mostly upland deciduous forest, dominated by basswood, slippery elm, and sugar maple except for an area of oak-hickory forest in the northwest. A small portion of prairie with surrounding oak savanna was present in the southwest corner. The extent of forest cover in 1882 and 1902 was mapped by Shriner and Copeland (1904), while that in 1935 was recorded by the Wisconsin Land Economic Survey. The present condition was determined from aerial photos taken in 1950 and from personal inspection. The changes are shown in Figure 36.1 and in Table 36.1. While the very first clearings may have been confined to the best lands, by 1882 the most evident factor influencing the pattern of land clearing was

the unfortunate system of land survey which resulted in square landholdings independent of terrain. Not until the forest had been reduced to less than 10 per cent of its original extent did the remaining wood lots begin to reflect the topography. Currently, the majority of the remnant forests still have one or more straight boundaries, although most of them are confined to rocky outcrops and thin-soil hilltops. The statistics for the township show a reduction in forest cover to 29.6 per cent of the original by 1882, to 9.6 per cent by 1902, to 4.8 per cent by 1936, and to 3.6 per cent by 1954. The existing forests are used by their owners as sources of firewood and occasional saw timber. In addition, 77 per cent of the present wooded area is heavily grazed by cattle to the point where no regeneration of the trees is taking place. Thus only 0.8 per cent of the land under forest cover in 1831 is still in what might be called a seminatural state, and this tiny portion is broken up into even more minute fragments, widely scattered throughout the area.

Concomitant with the reduction in forest cover in a presumed cause-and-effect relation was a decrease in total length of the streams draining the area. The permanently flowing streams had decreased by 26 per cent in 1902 and by 36 per cent in 1935. This was due largely to the drying-up of springs in their original headwaters, thus reflecting a decrease in subsoil water storage from the reduced infiltration on agricultural fields and pastured wood lots.

A number of important changes occur in

Table 36.1 Change in Wooded Area, Cadiz Township, Green County, Wisconsin (89°54′W., 43°30′N.), from 1831 to 1950

	1831	1882	1902	1935	1950
Total acres of forest	21,548	6,380	2,077	1,034	786
Number of wood lots	1	70	61	57	55
Average size of wood lot in acres	21,548	91.3	34.0	18.2	14.3
Total wooded area as a percentage of 1831 condition	100	29.6	9.6	4.8	3.6
Total periphery of wood lots in miles		99.0	61.2	47.2	39.8
Average periphery per wooded acre in feet		82	155	241	280

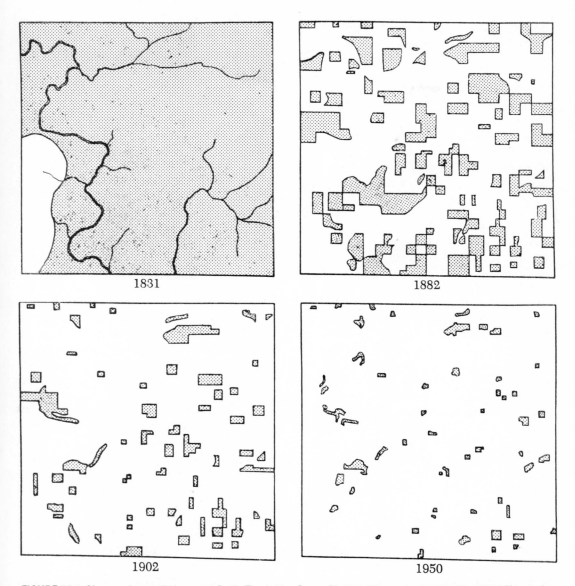

FIGURE 36.1 Changes in wooded area of Cadiz Township, Green County, Wisconsin (89°54′W., 43°30′N.), during the period of European settlement. The township is six miles on a side and is drained by the Pecatonica River. The shaded areas represent the land remaining in, or reverting to, forest in 1882, 1902, and 1950.

forested regions under the impact of agriculture aside from the obvious destruction of most of the forest. Under aboriginal use or peripheral exploitation, fire was a common occurrence, with large areas involved at each burn, since both the means and the desire to stop the fires were absent. Following the dissection of the landscape and the inter-polation of farm land between remnant forest stands, fires were more or less automatically stopped by the bare fields or were consciously suppressed by the farmers. In consequence, the forests that escaped clearing received a degree of protection far greater than they had normally experienced. In addition, the high cost of fencing wood lots in many instances prevented their use for grazing animals. As a result of these two influences, the forest, although gradually reduced in size and contiguity, actually improved in structure, with an increased density of trees per acre and an increase in cover and hence in humidity. On many marginal sites which had been reduced to brush by recurrent presettlement fires, mature forests subsequently developed. Since the species which were able to persist through the fires were the extremely vigorous pioneers, the first forests that developed were dominated by these pioneer species. In much of the central United States, where the recovery of marginal and remnant sites has been under way for about a century, the natural processes of succession are just beginning to convert the forests to a more climax condition (Cottam, 1949).

The conversion frequently is hastened in regions where mixed forests are present by the selective utilization of the mature pioneer members of the community for farm timber and firewood. Species of oaks are most commonly involved in the process in the United States and in Europe, although other pioneer species of high economic value are sometimes important. Since these trees are removed only a few at a time as the farmer needs them, environmental conditions are not greatly altered. The major result is a liberation of the understory layer of climax species like maple, beech, and basswood and the consequent repression of regeneration of the original pioneer trees.

The early period in the agro-urban utilization of forest land, therefore, presents the anomaly of severe reduction in total amount of forest but considerable improvement in the stands that did survive. These remnants commonly suffered severe damage from grazing at a later date.

Another change accompanying agricultural occupation of forested land is in what might be called the physiognomic result. Instead of an essentially continuous forest cover, with infrequent meadow-like openings along watercourses or small grasslands where fires had been unusually severe, the landscape now presents the aspect of a savanna, with isolated trees, small clumps or clusters of trees, or small groves scattered in a matrix of artificial grassland of grains and pasture grasses, unstable and frequently devoid of plant cover as a result of regular plowing. The physical conditions of the intervening "grasslands" are such as to prevent the successful growth of practically all members of the forest biota. A few of the plant members persist along fence rows and other places of relatively infrequent disturbance, and a very few are sufficiently weedlike actually to compete in the farmer's fields, especially in the permanent pastures (bracken fern, hazelnut, etc.).

Among the animal members of the community is a group that normally made use of the original forest edges. Some birds, for example, nested within the forest but sought their food in the open places and in the tangle of vines and shrubs that commonly bordered the openings. Such animals were greatly benefited by the increased "edge" provided by the fragmented wood lots, and their relative populations increased accordingly. As shown in Table 36.1, the average length of the periphery per acre of forest increased from 82 feet in 1882 to 280 feet by 1950.

The artificial savanna condition provided a suitable habitat for a number of species which originally occurred in grasslands and natural savannas on the dry margin adjacent to the mid-latitude forests. A number of birds, like the prairie horned lark (Forbush, 1927, pp. 336–70) and the western meadow lark, extended their range well into the original forest country of the eastern United States. Aggressive prairie plants, like ragweed, black-eyed Susan, and big bluestem similarly advanced far beyond their original areas of prominence and became conspicuous features of the vegetation along roadsides and in agricultural fields. Similar migrations of steppe plants westward into the forests of Central Europe are known (Oltmanns, 1927, pp. 104–56). These migrations resulted in a partial blending of the components of two or more major biotic communities and served to lessen their inherent differences.

Within the remnant forest stands, a number of changes of possible importance may take place. The small size and increased isolation of the stands tend to prevent the easy exchange of members from one stand to another. Various accidental happenings in any given stand over a period of years may eliminate one or more species from the community. Such a local catastrophe under natural conditions would be quickly healed by migration of new individuals from adjacent unaffected areas (the "gap phase" concept of Watt, 1947). In the isolated stands, however, opportunities for inward migration are small or nonexistent. As a result, the stands gradually lose some of their species, and those remaining achieve unusual positions of relative abundance.

The lack of interchange of plant individuals also applies to plant pollen. Those members of the community which are regularly or usually cross-pollinated no longer have the opportunity of crossing with a wide range of individuals. It is probable, therefore, that opportunities for evolution of deviant types by random gene fixation will be increased in the future, as the isolating mechanisms have longer times in which to operate. In heavily utilized stands selection pressures engendered by the frequent disturbance, together with the shift toward pioneer conditions resulting directly from the small size of the stands, would tend to favor those ecotypes which have pioneer tendencies and to reject the more conservative climax strains. The study of this micro-evolution should be one of the most fertile fields for future investigations.

Effects on Mid-latitude Grasslands and Savannas

PERIPHERAL EFFECTS

The plant members of the mid-latitude grasslands for the most part are of no direct use to man. Their main value comes after they have been converted to high-protein foods in the form of animals. The earliest utilization of grasslands, therefore, was by hunting cultures or by peripheral exploitation for the benefit of a remote agro-urban civilization. The slaughter of the bison on the prairies of mid-continental North America is a familiar example of this process (Garretson, 1938). In the absence of adequate information as to the influence of the bison on the structure of the remainder of the grassland community, little of value can be said about the effects of their removal. In any case, such effects would have been temporary, for intensive agricultural use of much of the eastern area followed quickly afterward, while domesticated cattle were introduced in the drier ranges to the west and began to exert an effect of their own.

The nature of the changes induced by cattle were probably different from those formerly resulting from the bison. The cattle were kept on limited ranges, so that the vegetation was subject to pressure over a long season, year after year. The bison, on the other hand, may have exerted an even greater pressure for brief periods, but a recovery period of several years commonly intervened before the wandering herd revisited any particular area. The longterm effects of the two types of grazing animals thus were very different.

Cattle begin to utilize the prairie grasses as soon as growth starts in the spring. Utilization of regrowth occurs during the summer and is particularly damaging when the reproductive stems begin to elongate in the later months. The continual reduction in photosynthetic area due to leaf removal results in a decreased storage of reserves in the underground organs. At the same time, the normal control of dormant buds by growth hormones is upset by the removal of stem tips, with a resultant stimulation of new growth which further depletes the stored reserves. The bluestems (*Andropogon* sp.), Indian grass (*Sorghastrum nutans*), and switch grass (*Panicum virgatum*) are typical species which respond in this way, and the gradual weakening leads to their eventual elimination and replacement by others. The replacing forms, under normal circumstances, are grasses which are recumbent, with their stems on or near the ground surface and with a large proportion of their leaves in a similarly protected position. They accordingly escape destruction by cattle, which do not graze closely. The grama grasses (*Bouteloua* sp.) and buffalo grass (*Buchloe dactyloides*) are good examples. In the absence of competition from the former dominants, these forms rapidly increase their populations. In range parlance, they are said to be "increasers" as opposed to the species which decline under grazing, which are called "decreasers" (Dyksterhuis, 1949). Both types were present in the prairie before grazing began, but the decreasers, because of their erect habit and greater size, were dominant over the increasers.

When the carrying capacity of the grasslands is greatly exceeded, either by too many cattle per unit area or by a reduction in productivity of the grasses due to drought, then the increasers themselves begin to suffer. Their decline results in a breaking of the continuous plant cover. The bare soil thus exposed becomes available for invasion by weedy annuals, which were formerly excluded from the closed community. In the American grasslands these newcomers, termed "invaders," are frequently exotics which originated in similar situations in the grasslands of the Old World, like cheat grass, Russian thistle, and halogeton. Native invaders are typically plants indigenous to the drier shrub deserts toward the west and are frequently unpalatable as a result of spines and thorns, like prickly poppy and prickly-pear cactus. Continued overgrazing results in the almost complete eradication of the original prairie flora and its replacement by an unstable community of annuals and thorny perennials.

The entire degradation process involves a shift from climax to pioneer plants and from mesic to xeric conditions. The upgrading effects of the original flora with respect to organic-matter accumulation in the soil, to nutrient pumping, and to water-entrance rates and other constructive activities are greatly lessened or reversed. The soil becomes compacted, less easily penetrated by rain, and much more subject to erosion, especially by wind.

Accompanying these direct effects of cattle on the plant community are a number of important secondary effects deriving from the disruption of the animal community. Misguided efforts at predator removal in the form of wolf and coyote bounties and other more direct means allow the rodent populations to get out of balance. Mice, pocket gophers, prairie dogs, and jack rabbits frequently reach epizootic levels and further add to the already excessive pressures on the plants. Control by extensive campaigns of rodent poisoning is usually temporary in effect and often serves to accentuate the unbalanced condition and to make return to stability more difficult.

In the more humid eastern portion of the grasslands in North America, the better sites were soon used for crop agriculture rather than for grazing, but marginal lands on thin soils, steep hills, or rocky areas frequently remained in use as pastures. In this region the decreasers behaved in the same manner as those farther west, and a few of the same increasers were also present. The major difference, and a very important one for the economy of large sections of the country, was the fact that the most important increaser was in reality an invader—Kentucky bluegrass (*Poa pratensis*). This species has a growth habit similar to the grama grasses and the buffalo grass of the western plains but thrives under a humid climate. It differs from the usual invaders in that it does not require bare soil or a broken cover to become established and is neither an annual nor an unpalatable perennial. The time and conditions of its origin in Eurasia are unknown. In all probability it developed under the influence of man and his pastoral habits, since it is found in the Old World in those regions where grazing has been practiced for long periods. In America it demonstrates a vigor scarcely exceeded by any other plant of similar size and has come to dominate most of the unimproved pasturages in the eastern half of the continent. This domination is virtually total in many areas, so that the original grassland species are completely lacking. The forbs and the few other grasses that do accompany bluegrass (dandelion, white clover, oxeye daisy, quack grass, timothy, etc.) are themselves exotic and serve to replicate on this continent a man-made community that is very widespread in Europe. In fact, this great expansion of the world range of a particular community under the unintentional influence of man is one of the most powerful examples of man's role as the major biotic influence in the world today. Investigation of the origin of the component species and intensive studies of the dynamics of the assemblage in its new environment should be highly rewarding.

AGRO-URBAN EFFECTS ON GRASSLANDS

The extensive utilization of the major mid-latitude grasslands for crop agriculture was restricted to those portions adjacent to the deciduous forest where the rainfall, although irregular, was usually sufficient for grain crops. The most favored places were those grasslands which had been extended into the forest during the postglacial xerothermic period (Sears, 1942) and which had subsequently been maintained by fire when the climate again favored forest. The Corn Belt in the prairie peninsula of the United States and the European breadbasket in the steppes of the Ukraine and in the *puzta* of Hungary are outstanding examples. In the climatically suitable areas utilization of the grassland for crops instead of for pasture was dependent upon the development of the steel plow for subjugation of the tough prairie sod. The invention and widespread manufacture of such an instrument occurred in the second quarter of the nineteenth century. Hence we find that the American prairies and the European steppes were both converted to cropland at about the same time (Conard, 1951), although the inhabitants of the former were scarcely past the stage of a hunting economy, while the latter had been used for grazing for centuries or millenniums.

The conversion from grassland to cropland was far more complete than the equivalent conversion from forest.In large part this was a result of the fact that the grasslands were flat or gently rolling and presented far fewer topographical obstacles to the plow than did the forest. The destruction of the entire prairie community by clean cultivation over extensive tracts of land means that remnants of the original vegetation are very rare. The major agency preventing complete eradication in much of the American prairie is the railroad system which was extended throughout the area contemporaneously with the advance of the settler (Shimek, 1925). The railroad right of way in many instances was laid on grade and was protected by fences. The tracks themselves were placed in the middle of the right of way, thus leaving a strip of virgin grassland on either side. The only maintenance operations which affected the vegetation was an occasional burning. Since this merely continued the normal practices of aboriginal times, these linear strips of prairie have been maintained in more or less primeval condition except for the random destruction of certain species and their failure to re-enter (Curtis and Greene, 1949).

Contrary to the case of the forest remnants, these railside prairies are not necessarily on pioneer or otherwise deviant sites but rather sample the full range of environment originally present. This is indeed fortunate, since over millions of acres of middle western prairie the only prairie plants to be found are on these railroad prairies. The much-needed research on prairie ecology has been and will continue to be conducted there.

The savannas between the grasslands and the surrounding forests are physiognomically intermediate between the two major formations. In the mid-latitudes they are largely the result of repeated advances and retreats of the prairie-forest border. Along the prairie peninsula of the United States, the characteristic savanna was the oak opening, a community of widely spaced orchard-like oak trees with an understory of prairie plants and a few forest shrubs. All available evidence indicates that these savannas were created by an advance of the prairie into the forest under the driving force of fire. Their maintenance was similarly effected by recurrent fires set by the Indians. They were but little used during the peripheral period except by the early hunters. A very brief period of open-range grazing was quickly followed by agricultural settlement. The potential yields of timber were so low and the quality of the gnarled oaks so poor that no extensive lumbering was ever practiced.

Within a decade or two of settlement, the remnant oak openings that escaped the ax and plow suddenly began to develop into dense, closed-canopy forests. In large part, this rapid increase in number of trees was due to the liberation of previously suppressed "grubs" or oak brush which had been repeatedly killed to the ground by fire and which had persisted through production of adventitious buds from underground rootstocks (Cottam, 1949). One of the major tribulations of the early settler on the savannas was the laborious hand removal of these underground growths which effectively stopped the best plow and the strongest oxen.

Agricultural occupation of the oak openings thus resulted in two very different effects. On the one hand, the majority of the land was cleared and cultivated, thus destroying the entire community. On the other, the remnant portions rapidly changed over from savanna to forest under the influence of fire protection. Those few areas which continued to be kept open by fire or other means were ordinarily thus treated so that they might be used as pasture, with consequent destruction of the understory vegetation. As a result, an oak savanna, with its full complement of original vegetation, is one of the rarest vegetation types in the United States today.

A similar release of woody vegetation by excessive fire protection has produced the mesquite stands now so common on the savannas of the southwestern range land (Humphrey, 1953).

General Consequences of Man's Utilization

CHANGES IN ENVIRONMENT

The changes induced in native vegetation by man, either through peripheral, pioneer, or primitive utilization or through more intensive agro-urban occupation, range from simple modification through severe degradation to complete destruction and replacement. All these changes in plant cover are accompanied by changes in the environment within and adjacent to the affected vegetation.

Whether or not widespread deforestation can influence the amount or distribution of rainfall has been debated for decades. No satisfactory proof that such influence exists has appeared so far, but the question remains unresolved. The most convincing arguments concerning the influence of vegetation removal on over-all regional climate are those connected with the energy balance as it is influenced by the albedo or reflecting power of the earth's surface. The value of this factor is very similar for any green vegetation, whether it be forest, prairie, or corn crop. In deciduous forests it may drop during the winter, especially in regions without a permanent snow cover. In grasslands, on the other hand, it actually increases during the winter, owing to the light color of the dead and matted grasses. When the grasslands are plowed, particularly where the land is fallowed or fall-plowed, the dark prairie soils cut down reflection tremendously. The absorption of solar energy is thereby increased, with a possible appreciable change in the total energy increment and hence in the local temperature. This could be of major significance in the spring months in the northern grasslands.

The soil factor of the environment has also been altered by man's activities. Trampling and other disturbances incident to the harvesting operation, combined with activities of livestock, tend to compact the soil, destroying its loose structure and impeding the free entrance of water from rainstorms. The amount of surface runoff is thereby increased. The partial or total absence of tall trees reduces the amount of subsoil water which would normally be lost by transpiration. The excess finds its way to the stream system of the region by way of springs. The initial result of forest-cutting is an increase in the total volume of streamflow, but the complete destruction of the forest, as by fire, greatly increases the flash-flood potential of the watershed and decreases its usable water-producing abilities.

One of the major consequences of the agricultural utilization of mid-latitude forests and prairies has been the very great decrease in soil stability. The resultant soil erosion, both by water and by wind, reached terrifying proportions in many sections of the United States before concerted efforts were made to bring it under control. For the most part, this erosion is unrelated to the previous vegetation and is largely due to the misguided attempt to apply an agricultural system developed under one set of environmental and economic conditions to a totally different situation. The current severe "nutrient erosion" now accelerating in the Corn Belt under the influence of hybrid grains is another example of a faulty socioeconomic farm philosophy and is unrelated to the original prairie vegetation except in so far as the inherited soil richness, which hides the folly of the system, is a result of millenniums of prairie activity.

GENERAL CHANGES IN COMMUNITY COMPOSITION

In those cases where man's utilization has not completely destroyed the original biotic community, whether under peripheral conditions or in remnants within agricultural areas, it is possible to detect a recurrent pattern in the compositional changes that have occurred. In both forest and grassland the more conservative elements of the vegetation (the "upper middle class" and the "aristocrats" of Fernald, 1938) have tended to disappear. These are the plants that are most demanding in their requirements, with low tolerance of fluctuations in moisture, with high nutrient requirements, and with low ability to withstand frequent disturbance. They commonly have only limited powers of vegetative reproduction and usually have specialized requirements for germination. They make up the most advanced communities of a given region from the standpoints of degree of integration, stability, complexity,

and efficiency of energy utilization (Sears, 1949). They are "climax" plants in the basic sense of the word.

Under the impact of man these climax plants tend to decline in numbers and importance. Their retrogression leads to decreased stability and to disorganization of the community pattern. The environmental changes accompanying the decline are in the direction of more xeric, lighter, and more variable conditions. These encourage the expansion of less conservative plants with such pioneer tendencies as the ability to withstand greater fluctuations in temperature and available moisture, the capacity for resisting disturbance through production of proliferating shoots or adventitious buds, and the possession of efficient means of rapid population increase. Particular harvesting techniques of man, either directly through logging and coppicing or indirectly through the medium of grazing animals, tend to exert a selective influence on the pioneer plants which do succeed. A premium is placed on those species which can resist the particular pressure and still maintain their populations. All others tend to decline or disappear.

This reduction in species complement increases in proportion to the intensity and duration of the utilization. In the final stages the communities completely dominated by man are composed of a small number of extremely vigorous, highly specialized weeds of cosmopolitan distribution, whose origin and distribution are in themselves man-induced phenomena. The subfinal stages are a mixture of these weeds and the most aggressive elements of the native flora. The relative proportion of indigenous and exotic elements varies with the climate, those regions most like the ancient centers of agricultural development (semidesert or Mediterranean climates) having a vegetation which is more completely exotic than that of the cool humid regions.

The highest vegetational product of evolution is the tropical rain forest. In the mid-latitudes the climax deciduous forest as found in the southern Appalachians and in the mountains of China is the ultimate in complexity, stability, and integration. Large numbers of species grow in intimate inter-relationship, with maximum capture and reutilization of incident energy consistent with the seasonal nature of the climate. Many niches exist, and each has its adapted species with the necessary modifications in nutritional, growth, or photosynthetic habit to enable it to make the most of its specialized opportunities. Not only is energy capture at a maximum in this highly organized community but normal processes of peneplana-tion are reduced to a minimum. Indeed, there may be a decrease in randomness of the local habitat due to intake of highly dilute mineral elements from the subsoil or bedrock by tree roots and their subsequent accumula-tion in the humus-rich topsoil. In the sense that entropy means randomness or "mixed-up-ness" in the universe as a result of highly probable events, the climax deciduous forest may be said to possess a very low entropy, since it is an incomprehensibly improbable phenomenon existing in a dynamic steady state.

Man's actions in this community almost entirely result in a decrease in its organization and complexity and an increase in the local entropy of the system. His activity in reduc-ing the number of major communities, climax or otherwise, and in blurring the lines of demarcation between them by increasing the range of many of their components likewise reduces the non-randomness of his surround-ings. Man, as judged by his record to date, seems bent on asserting the universal validity of the second law of thermodynamics, on abetting the running-down of his portion of the universe. Perhaps the improbability of the climax biotic community was too great to be sustained, and man is the agent of readjustment. Let us hope his new powers for total entropy increase are not employed before the readjustments can be made.

References Cited

Brown, R. T., and Curtis, J. T.
1952 "The Upland Conifer-Hardwood Forests of Northern Wisconsin," *Ecological Monographs,* XXII, No. 3, 217–34.

Clements, F. E.
1936 "Nature and Structure of the Climax," *Journal of Ecology,* XXIV, No. 1, 252–84.

Conard, H. S.
1951 *The Background of Plant Ecology.* Ames, Iowa: Iowa State College Press. 238 pp.

Gottam, Grant
1949 "The Phytosociology of an Oak Woods in Southern Wisconsin," *Ecology,* XXX, No. 3, 171–287.

Curtis, J. T.
1951 "Hardwood Woodlot Cover and its Conser-vation," *Wisconsin Conservation Bulletin,* XVI, No. 1, 11–15.

Curtis, J. T., and Greene, H. C.
1949 "A Study of Relic Wisconsin Prairies by the Species-Presence Method," *Ecology,* XXX, No. 1, 83–92.

Dyksterhuis, E. J.
1949 "Condition and Management of Range Land Based on Quantitative Ecology," *Journal of Range Management,* II, No. 3, 104–15.

Fernald, M. L.
1938 "Must All Rare Plants Suffer the Fate of Frank-linia?" *Journal of the Franklin Institute,* CCXXVI, No. 3, 383–97.

Forbush, E. H.
1927 *Birds of Massachusetts and Other New England States.* 2 vols. Boston: Massachusetts Department of Agriculture.

Garretson, M. S.
1938 *The American Bison.* New York: New York Zoological Society. 254 pp.

Goodlett, J. C.
1954 *Vegetation Adjacent to the Border of the Wiscon-sin Drift in Potter County, Pennsylvania.* (Harvard Forest Bulletin No. 15.) Petersham, Mass.: Harvard Forest. 93 pp.

Humphrey, R. R.
1953 "The Desert Grassland, Past and Present," *Journal of Range Management,* VI, No. 3, 159–64.

Kittredge, Joseph
1948 *Forest Influences.* New York: McGraw-Hill Book Co. 394 pp.

Needham, Joseph
1954 *Science and Civilization in China,* Vol. I. Cam-bridge: Cambridge University Press. 318 pp.

Oltmanns, F.
1927 *Das Pflanzenleben des Schwarzwaldes.* Frei-burg: Badischen Schwarzwaldverein. 690 pp.

Sears, P. B.
1942 "Xerothermic Theory," *Botanical Review,* VIII, No. 10, 708–36.
1949 "Integration at the Community Level," *Ameri-can Scientist,* XXXVII, No. 2, 235–42.

Shimek, B.
  1925   "The Persistence of the Prairies," *University of Iowa Studies in Natural History,* XI, No. 5, 3–24.
Shriner, F. A., and Copeland, F. B.
  1904   "Deforestation and Creek Flow about Monroe, Wisconsin," *Botanical Gazette,* XXXVII, No. 2, 139–43.
Steinbrenner, E. C.
  1951   "Effect of Grazing on Floristic Composition and Soil Properties of Farm Woodlands in Southern Wisconsin," *Journal of Forestry,* XL, No. 12, 906–10.
Tansley, H. G.
  1939   *The British Islands and Their Vegetation.* Cambridge: Cambridge University Press.   930 pp.
Turrill, W. B.
  1929   *The Plant-Life of the Balkan Peninsula.* London: Oxford University Press.   487 pp.
Watt, A. S.
  1947   "Pattern and Process in the Plant Community," *Journal of Ecology,* XXXV, No. 1, 1–22.

ADDITIONAL REFERENCES

Bormann, F. H., G. E. Likens, D. W. Fisher, and R. S. Pierce. 1968. Nutrient loss accelerated by clear-cutting of a forest ecosystem. *Science* 159:882–884.

Dinsdale, E. M. 1965. Spatial patterns of technological change: The lumber industry of northern New York. *Econ. Geography* 41:252–274.

Larson, F. D. 1957. Problems of population pressure upon the desert range. *J. Range Management* 10:160–161.

Maxwell, H. 1910. The use and abuse of forests by the Virginia Indians. *William and Mary Quarterly Historical Magazine* 19:73–103.

Sauer, Carl O. 1950. Grassland climax, fire, and man. *J. Range Management* 3:16–21.

Stearns, F. W. 1949. Ninety years change in a northern hardwood forest in Wisconsin. *Ecology* 30:350–358.

Van Eimern, J., R. Karschon, L. A. Razumova, and G. W. Robertson. 1964. *Windbreaks and shelterbelts.* World Meteorological Organization Technical Note No. 59. 188 pp.

DAMAGE TO FORESTS FROM AIR POLLUTION

GEORGE H. HEPTING

Air pollution is a modern disease of forests and other crops which may cause an insidious decline of whole populations of plants. It has risen with industrialization to the point that, in many parts of the world, it now does more damage to agriculture than do insect or climatic pathogens. Losses to American agriculture are estimated at more than 500 million dollars a year (U.S. Department of Health, Education, and Welfare, 1968). Until a few years ago damage to vegetation from air pollution generally was localized to neighborhoods where oxides of sulfur or fluoride (associated with ore reduction) were produced. In recent years damage is resulting from air pollution associated with our enormous urban development, with gases from new industrial processes, and with greatly increased emissions of stack gases from industrial plants using coal and oil at rates much higher than only a few years ago.

This selection briefly surveys the processes, extent, and trends of damage to forests by various air pollutants. Abundant recent research shows that the situation has generally worsened since this article was written in 1964. Sulfur dioxide continues to be a major menace (Dreisinger, 1966; Brandt and Heck, 1968), as do fluoride (Crocker, 1965; Jacobson, et al., 1966; McCune and Daines, 1969) and smog (Bobrov, 1955; Thomas, 1969). Synergistic effects of several pollutants frequently compound the casualty (e.g., Menser and Heggestad, 1966). A number of recent studies have demonstrated damage to roadside vegetation by automobile exhaust (e.g., Darley, et al., 1963) and both roadside and regional contamination of plants and soils with various heavy metals (Rühling and Tyler, 1969; Purves and MacKenzie, 1969; Lagerwerff and

George H. Hepting (b. 1907) is principal research scientist, Forest Disease Research, U.S. Forest Service, Asheville, North Carolina. He earned two degrees at Cornell University, including a Ph.D. in plant pathology in 1933. He has worked for the U.S. Department of Agriculture since 1931. Hepting's research interests, in addition to air pollution damage to forests, include decays of timber, wilt diseases, and diseases of southern pines and hardwoods.

This article is reprinted by special permission from the *Journal of Forestry*, 62(9):630–634, September 1964.

Specht, 1970), especially lead (Cannon and Bowles, 1962; Rühling and Tyler, 1968; Motto, et al., 1970). Radiation and radionuclides are additional modern threats to vegetation (Woodwell and Rebuck, 1967; Menzel, 1967).

Trees and crops are not the only plants afflicted by air pollution. Lichens are especially sensitive. The effects of the urban environment on these small plants have been recognized for over a century and widely studied in recent decades (e.g., Skye, 1968; Fenton, 1964). For example, New York City detrimentally influences the lichen flora on Long Island up to 40 miles away; city-induced drought (see Selection 11) is regarded as acting on pollution-tolerant lichens close to a city center with air pollution acting to decrease lichen diversity and cover at much greater distances (Brodo, 1966). Hence, the costs of air pollution include considerable esthetic, as well as economic, losses by plant damage. Such indirect and almost unwitting destruction and contamination of vegetation demands wide recognition and abatement.

(Editor's comment)

The Clean Air Act (*10*), passed by the 88th Congress in December 1963, states "that the growth in the amount and complexity of air pollution brought about by urbanization, industrial development, and the increasing use of motor vehicles, has resulted in mounting dangers to the public health and welfare, including injury to agricultural crops and livestock, damage to and the deterioration of property, and hazards to air and ground transportation."

This recognition by Congress of the hazards imposed by the various forms of air pollution to our health and welfare indicate that they can no longer be ignored and no longer be considered local problems with which public agencies need not become involved. Until recent years most of our streams were treated as common sewers into which virtually any liquid waste could be dumped. This situation resulted in a multitude of health, wildlife, and other water use problems that have led to the widespread adoption of strong measures for stream pollution abatement. The public has been slower to recognize the dangers of polluting the atmosphere. So long as acute impacts remained isolated cases, dealt with locally, settled by agreement or litigation, or considered the result of meteorological acts of God, the air has been widely used in the "common sewer" sense with respect to gaseous emissions.

In recent years, however, there has been a slow but steady increase in public awareness of the chronic buildup of pollution levels in many parts of the world. This has been due in part from episodes like the Donora Pennsylvania, fumigation of 1948, the London acute smog of 1952, the smog effects of the Los Angeles area, and from the clear evidence of chronic damage, not only to health but to property, to products of many kinds including paint and rubber, and to agriculture and forestry.

The current literature on the causes and effects of air pollution is enormous and new periodicals on the subject have been appearing at a rapid rate. Good summaries of our air pollution problems were presented by McCabe in 1952, who assembled the contributions to the deliberations of the United States Technical Conference on Air Pollution (*24*), by Stern, who edited an excellent compendium (*35*), by several authorities in the monograph "Air Pollution," released by the World Health Organization in 1961 (*40*), and by the Proceedings of the two National Air

Pollution Conferences (*37, 38*). The possible effects of ionizing radiations on plants are not included in the present review.

Information on the many types of air pollution damage to economic plants has been brought together recently by Thomas (*36*), Middleton (*25*), and others (*1, 20*). In the past the principal pollutants have been oxides of sulfur from industrial sources and from London-type smog, and fluorine mainly from ore reduction and the preparation of phosphate fertilizers. Today many additional constituents of polluted air are known to contribute to plant damage, particulary ozone and peroxidized compounds such as peroxyacetyl nitrate (PAN), which are the main elements of Los Angeles-type smog that are toxic to plants and animals. Ozone and PAN result from photochemical reactions between oxides of nitrogen and organic vapors mostly derived from the incomplete combustion of petroleum. In addition to the four principal pollutants already mentioned (sulfur dioxide, fluoride, ozone, and PAN), plant damage has been caused by many other gases including ethylene, chlorine, ammonia, hydrogen chloride, hydrogen sulfide, and others (*36*). While nitrogen oxides are essential to the formation of photochemical smog, and can themselves be toxic to plants (*26*), some consider it questionable that they occur in the atmosphere in concentrations high enough to cause injury directly (*36*).

Virtually all of the principal types of agricultural crops have suffered important damage from air pollution. A few examples among nonforest crops might be mentioned (*36*). Alfalfa, cotton, and lettuce have been readily injured by sulfur dioxide at field levels; gladiolus, azalea, and vaccinium are among the most sensitive plants to fluorine; ozone produces weather fleck in tobacco (*13*); ethylene ruins orchid blooms; and a recent report of the University of California states that the photochemical smog from Los Angeles has reduced the production of citrus fruit in the main California citrus area south of that city by 20 to 25 percent in the past 15 years (*4*).

Past Air Pollution Impacts to the Forest

Scheffer and Hedgcock (*32*), in their bulletin on injury to northwestern forest trees by sulfur dioxide from smelters, give a brief literature review of air pollution damage to forests and state that sulfur dioxide discharged from smelters had been the major cause of gas injury to forest trees. The National Research Council of Canada in 1939 released a 447-page report (*29*) on the effects of sulfur dioxide on vegetation, and damage to coniferous trees from smelting was a major feature of this report. Katz (*19*), in Canada, further described damage to coniferous forests from sulfur dioxide, and later Linzon (*21*) measured and documented heavy damage to white pine from sulfur dioxide released in connection with ore smelting in the Sudbury, Ontario, area. Gordon and Gorham (*12*) reported on extensive forest changes attributed to sulfur dioxide around an iron-sintering plant at Wawa, Ontario, where white pine failed to appear on test plots leeward of the plant for a distance of over 30 miles, indicating that this species was the most readily injured of the 30 woody plants recorded. The sensitivity of this tree to the fumes was again pointed up by these authors when white pine showed up for the first time on plots 16 miles leeward from another source, thus making it also the most sensitive of the woody plants recorded in connection with this source.

The Scheffer and Hedgcock study (*32*) cites the losses from mortality, growth reduction, lack of reproduction, and other impacts to many species of forest trees in the upper Columbia River valley south of the Trail, British Columbia, smelter before corrective measures were taken in 1931. Appreciable damage to conifers extended over 40 miles down the river from the smelter. These authors also cite the heavy damage to timber around the Washoe smelter in the vicinity of Anaconda, Montana, revealed by field studies made in 1910 and 1911.

Before corrective measures were instituted, the smelting operations in the Copper Hill,

Tennessee, area, early in the century, had laid waste an area of 17,000 acres and damaged another 30,000 acres of timberland (*18*), mostly hardwoods. Much of the area is still virtually bare and eroding severely.

In 1949 an intensive investigation was started of the browning and dying of ponderosa pine within a 50-square-mile area around an aluminum ore reduction plant near Spokane, Washington. In this case the characteristic browning and banding was related to fluoride (*34*). Adams and his co-workers (*2, 3*) have given us much information on the susceptibility of ponderosa pine foliage, particularly when immature, to fluoride, and their work indicates a higher sensitivity of ponderosa pine and lodgepole pine to fluoride than western white pine, Douglas-fir, or Engelmann spruce.

These acute cases of smelter fume injury, while severe, have been fairly local and not numerous. For the most part highly toxic stack emissions from ore reduction have been controlled by various engineering devices and a major bonus of byproduct recovery has followed air pollution reduction measures in many cases. Yet sulfur dioxide and fluoride damage are still problems around a great many sources.

Present Air Pollution Damage to the Forest

Since the rate of growth of forest stands and the vigor and appearance of individual trees are influenced by so many site factors, including soil type, moisture, temperature, drainage, competition, etc., alien impacts not identifiable with known diseases or insects, can go unrecognized unless very severe damage is done. Partly for this reason we have recognized some measure of air pollution damage in the past only where the cause of such damage was obvious. Within recent years, however, injury to and death of trees over large areas, have been attributed to atmospheric insults not related to smelting (*16*). The pollution scientist's term, "atmospheric insult," is used advisedly here, instead

of "air pollution," because it is not at all certain that the high oxidant levels that result in some injuries, such as the burning of the tips of eastern white pine needles result, mainly, from man's activities.

It is interesting to note that in four of the cases of forest tree damage recently either proven or considered likely to be caused by atmospheric constituents; namely, thermal power plant stack gas injury to white pine (*7*), ozone injury to white pine (emergence tipburn [*6*]), chlorotic dwarf of white pine (*9*), and chlorotic decline of ponderosa pine (*30*), pathologists spent years eliminating other, more conventional, possible causes before new knowledge and new techniques led the investigators to a consideration of aerological factors.

The loss of individual shade trees is seldom blamed on the atmosphere unless a direct relation to the source of the pollutant is almost self-evident. Cases of killing obviously related to such sources include the blighting of trees in close proximity to automobile exhaust, toxic gas leaks, waste burners, or burning municipal dumps. No one knows the extent of loss of city and highway trees resulting from urban smogs, whether of the reducing (London) type or the oxidizing (Los Angeles) type, but when such data become available they will undoubtedly show that many of our tree species have a low tolerance to urban air. In a general way such tolerance in the East ranges from high, as with the rugged Norway maple and the exotic gingko, to very low as with the sensitive balsam fir (*8*).

Recent research on the four pine problems already alluded to in connection with atmospheric impacts illustrates that the techniques and fields of knowledge employed in the solution of such problems are quite different from those conventionally used in working with parasites.

Chlorotic Decline of Ponderosa Pine

A condition called chlorotic decline, or X-disease, first noted in the early 1950's has affected ponderosa pine over thousands of acres in the San Bernardino Mountains of California (30). Other intermixed conifers of several genera and species have been unaffected. The decline is characterized by reduction in growth; loss of all but the current year's needles; yellowing, mottling, and stunting of needles; and death of trees. Fumigation experiments and air sampling data in the affected area (28) suggest that photochemical smog, aggravated by drought, is probably the principal cause of the decline of ponderosa pine in this area, in spite of the elevation (4,000 to 5,000 feet above the valley floor) and a distance of over 50 miles from Los Angeles.

Lodge (23) discusses our country's tendency to move from the reducing sulfur dioxide type of urban pollution toward the oxidizing "ozone" pollution as we move from solid to liquid and gas fuels. The particulate matter in smoke tends to reduce photochemical smog through the reduction in light intensity reaching the polluted air. Thus, an increase in oil and gas consumption plus a reduction in smoke can bring us new high levels of oxidant emanating from cities and certain types of industrial activities.

In southern California PAN has apparently been the most destructive smog constituent, while in the East ozone appears to be causing most of the oxidant damage to plants (31). With respect to the recent changes in types of pollution, Rodenhiser (31) emphasizes that whereas fluoride and sulfur dioxide, which are still major pollutants, are usually traceable to a limited number of large industrial plants, smog comes from "millions" of sources throughout our highly mechanized society.

Reaction of White Pine to Certain Atmospheric Constituents

Recently Berry and Ripperton (6) reported on studies indicating that one of the long-known needle blights of white pine, investigated by many pathologists since the turn of the century, is due to atmospheric oxidant,

probably ozone. Berry (5) first attributed the term "emergence tipburn" (ET) to this trouble, and pointed out that in 1961, when an unusual wave of ET hit the Southeast, an unusual wave of tobacco weather fleck, also an ozone-induced disorder, was reported by North Carolina State College.

When field oxidant concentrations, expressed as ozone, reached 6.5 p.p.h.m. (parts per hundred million) tipburn occurred on susceptible white pine clones. When the ambient air was filtered through an activated carbon filter, thus removing any oxidant, no tipburn occurred. Finally, when susceptible clones were fumigated with ozone at 6.5 p.p.h.m., on the basis of the Mast recorder, tipburn occurred apparently identical in symptoms with the tipburn occurring naturally in the field.

Heggestad and Menser (14) produced tobacco weather fleck at concentrations of ozone, as measured by the Mast recorder, and exposure times almost the same as those used by Berry and Ripperton (6) in tipburning white pine. Thus ET appears to be the pine analogue of tobacco weather fleck, and an explanation is afforded to a perennial pine problem of previously undetermined cause.

Emergence tipburn is probably one of the commonest white pine troubles that have long been known to us, that occurs in increasing intensity going northward from the southern Appalachian Mountains into New England and Canada, and that is seemingly unrelated to pathogen attack (22). A relation to weather, as brought out by Berry (5) in connection with ET, by Linzon (22) for the same or a similar trouble, and as implied in the term weather fleck of tobacco, is a common denominator in these troubles. The rises in atmospheric ozone, leading to these troubles, whether resulting from natural sources (36) or from polluted air (39), appear to be related to certain weather patterns.

Another baffling stunting of white pine, called chlorotic dwarf, that occurs solely in the Northeast and Central States is being investigated by Dochinger and Seliskar (9). Their recent report, based on grafting experiments and other studies, suggested that the trouble results "from a causal agent that acts directly on the foliage," and no virus, fungus, or other pathogen appeared to be implicated. Regarding the cause, some atmospheric impact has been suggested as a strong possibility.

A third decline of white pine related to one or more atmospheric constituents has occurred within about a 20-mile radius of some soft-coal-burning power plants. Berry and Hepting (7) have shown that while fume damage symptoms of the acute sulfur dioxide type, together with elevations in foliar content of sulfate in white pine needles, may occur immediately around a plant of this type, damage of a different kind may extend for 20 or more miles, depending on wind, terrain, and other local conditions. The latter, more extensive type of injury, is at least temporarily being called post-emergence chronic tipburn (PECT) to differentiate it from emergence tipburn (ET). While ET, a type of oxidant (probably ozone) injury, starts and ends during the period of shoot elongation and needle growth, PECT may start any time of year, typically showing up first in the winter. PECT is also characterized by a gradual change from a brown tip to a green base, often with mottling or banding in between. The separation of these two troubles from some fungus diseases of white pine is described by Hepting and Berry (17).

PECT results in needle blight, a casting of older needles, growth reduction, and often in early death. In the case of all three of the eastern white pine troubles described here, as well as the smog damage to ponderosa pine in the San Bernardino Mountains of California, and fluoride damage to ponderosa pine in Washington (2), there is striking tree-to-tree variability in susceptibility. Normal trees and trees in the last stages of decline may occur side by side, indicating a genetic difference in resistance. These characteristics of resistance or susceptibility are retained in scions after they are grafted on stock trees of the opposite susceptibility tendency. Steps have already been taken to establish a seed orchard of eastern white pine

clones resistant to the PECT type of stack gas injury.

When ramets (vegetative reproductions) of a PECT-susceptible clone of white pine were taken from an unpolluted area to an area eight miles from a coal-burning power plant, growth was checked. They lost needles and the remaining needles developed typical PECT symptoms. Ramets of the same clone, in plastic buckets of the same soil, that were left in the unpolluted area remained normal. The trees exposed to pollution for seven months that survived the exposure developed normal foliage within two years after being returned to the unpolluted area (7).

PECT of eastern white pine was observed around several thermal power plants in the Appalachian region although the offending gas or gases are still unknown. Although only white pine showed obvious symptoms once away from the immediate environs of the stacks, we have reasons for being concerned with the effects of the increasing output of power plant and industrial stack gases on our forest acreage (16).

Trends in Air Pollution as They Affect Trees

An impressive list of crops damaged by photochemical smog from urban pollution can be compiled (26, 36), including those in the categories of field, flower, fruit, and vegetable crops, as well as forest trees. Unless measures now being taken by various public and private agencies, and spearheaded on a national basis by the U. S. Public Health Service, can successfully combat this problem in the near future, we can expect increasing damage to orchard, forest, and shade trees. As brought out during the last five years, we will also likely be recognizing certain kinds of damage to trees as caused by air pollution that we have not known the cause of before.

Damage from urban smog can take many forms and extend considerable distances. Parmeter, Bega, and Neff (30) point out that the San Bernardino ponderosa pine case involves thousands of acres of land important not only for timber, but for valuable watershed needs, and as a recreational area that attracts more than 4 million visitors each year. Scurfield (*33*) relates how the British National Pinetum had to be moved from Kew, near London, to an area in Kent because of urban air pollution.

Changes in our climate that have been taking place in the past 70 years have been described as probably affecting the incidence of many of our forest diseases (*15*), including both those caused by parasites and by physiogenic influences. Certainly we would expect that climate effects would not only influence the concentration or dissipation of man-made smog and the amount of light energy available for photochemical reactions but also, through subsidence, turbulence, or other meteorologic phenomena, could affect the amount of stratospheric ozone that reaches the troposphere, which is the zone in which we and our plants live. In investigating the possible causes of decline in a number of forest tree species in the Northeast, notably sugar maple, ash, black walnut, oak, and birch, the influence of climatic changes must be considered (*15*). The possible effects of high oxidant levels and other atmospheric impacts are additional influences related to weather that may play a part in these unresolved problems. We must study our trees in relation to their total environment, and polluted air can be an important, and often ignored, part of the environment.

Another upward pollution trend, in addition to urban pollution, is related to thermal power production and it, also, is a source of some concern. Frankenberg (*11*) depicts the growth in large power units of this type. Up to 1954 we had no plants with a boiler capacity of 2 million pounds of steam per hour. By 1962 over 60 percent of our power was generated in such huge new plants. More plants and larger plants, many using lowgrade soft coal, mean far greater stack gas emissions. Since the problem of controlling these complex stack gases, which include

among other gases sulfur dioxide, fluoride, and oxides of nitrogen, has only been partly solved, we must learn much more than we now know about the impact of the increasing number of such large-capacity, soft-coal-burning industrial units on the surrounding forest vegetation.

Most people today read and hear much about our own and British urban air pollution problems, especially with regard to human health. From our point of view as foresters, it is interesting to note a 1962 Associated Press dispatch from Rome, Italy, that "a special study commission says many of Rome's pine trees are drying up (sic) largely because of gases in the air." It urged city officials to take steps to limit air contamination caused by industrial fumes, smoke from homes and automobile exhaust fumes.

Scurfield (*33*) presents, under the title "Air Pollution and Tree Growth," an impressive compendium, including 258 references, of information on sources of air pollution around the world, and gives examples of damage to different tree species by these pollutants in parts of Germany, England, Russia, the United States, Portugal, Tasmania, South America, South Africa, India, and New Zealand. The more important earlier investigations demonstrating air pollution damage to farm and forest crops was done in Germany as an outgrowth of their industrial expansion starting about a century ago. How individual trees or individual species react to different gases is interesting and important, but it is also important that we determine the expected impact of the many major sources of pollution on our forest and shade tree resources in terms of how much they reduce timber and other forest production, and recreational and civic improvement values. I have tried to show; first, that we have had notable but scattered cases of severe air pollution damage to forests in the past; second, that we are being subjected to new forms of air pollution, as part of our urban and industrial growth, which have already severely damaged certain tree species over considerable areas in the United States; and third, that as our research facilities, knowledge, and techniques improve, we are finding tree declines due to air pollution that were either erroneously ascribed to other causes or to no cause at all.

Air pollution authorities point out that we have gone beyond strictly urban problems, in the sense of Pittsburgh, St. Louis, or Los Angeles, to regional problems as in southern California, the East Coast, and other industrialized areas. We are finding that we must manage our air as we do our land, water, and forests.

References Cited

1. Adams, D. F. 1956. The effects of air pollution on plant life. Amer. Med. Assoc. Arch. Indus. Health 14: 229–245.

2. _____, C. G. Shaw, and W. D. Yerkes, Jr. 1956. Relationship of injury indexes and fumigation fluoride levels. Phytopathology 46:587–591.

3. _____, J. W. Hendrix, and H. G. Applegate. 1957. Relationship among exposure periods, foliar burn, and fluorine content of plants exposed to hydrogen fluoride. Agric. and Food Chem. 5:108–116.

4. Anonymous. 1964. Citrus study under way: smog answer sought. Air in the News 1(9):12.

5. Berry, C. R. 1961. White pine emergence tipburn, a physiogenic disturbance. U. S. Forest Service, Southeastern Forest Expt. Sta. Paper 130. 8 pp.

6. _____, and L. A. Ripperton. 1963. Ozone, a possible cause of white pine emergence tipburn. Phytopathology 53:552–557.

7. _____, and G. H. Hepting. 1964. Injury to eastern white pine by unidentified atmospheric constituents. Forest Sci. 10:2–13.

8. Collingwood, G. H., and W. D. Brush. 1947. Knowing your trees. The American Forestry Assoc., Washington, D. C.

9. Dochinger, L. S., and C. E. Seliskar. 1963. Susceptibility of eastern white pine to chlorotic dwarf. (Abst.) Phytopathology 53:874.

10. Eighty-Eighth Congress. 1st Session. 1963. An act to improve, strengthen, and accelerate programs for the prevention and abatement of air pollution. Public Law 88–206, 88 Cong., II. R. 6518. 10 pp. Dec.

11. Frankenberg, T. T. 1963. Air pollution from power plants and its control. Combustion 34:28–31.

12. Gordon, A. G., and E. Gorham. 1963. Ecological aspects of air pollution from an iron-sintering plant at Wawa, Ontario. Canadian Jour. Bot. 41:1065–1078.

13. Heggestad, H. E., and J. T. Middleton. 1959. Ozone in high concentrations as cause of tobacco leaf injury. Science 129:208–209.

14. _____, and H. A. Menser. 1962. Leaf spot-sensitive tobacco strain Bel W-3, a biological indicator of the air pollutant ozone. (Abst.) Phytopathology 52:735.

15. Hepting, G. H. 1963. Climate and forest diseases. Ann. Rev. Phytopath. 1:31–50.

16. _____. 1963. [Statement in discussion of agricultural, natural resource, and economic considerations.] *In* Proceedings of the National Conference on Air Pollution of 1962. U. S. Public Health Service. P. 200.

17. _____, and C. R. Berry. 1961. Differentiating needle blights of white pine in the interpretation of fume damage. Internatl. Jour. Air and Water Pollut. 4:101–105.

18. Hursh, C. R. 1948. Local climate in the Copper Basin of Tennessee as modified by the removal of vegetation. U. S. Dept. Agric. Cir. 774. 38 pp.

19. Katz, M. 1952. The effect of sulfur dioxide on conifers. *In* U. S. Tech. Conf. on Air Pollution Proc. 1952:84.

20. _____, and V. C. Shore. 1955. Air pollution damage to vegetation. Jour. Air Pollut. Control Assoc. 5:144.

21. Linzon, S. N. 1958. The influence of smelter fumes on the growth of white pine in the Sudbury region. Ontario Dept. Lands and Forests and Ontario Dept. Mines, Toronto, Ontario. 45 pp.

22. _____. 1960. The development of foliar symptoms and the possible cause and origin of white pine needle blight. Canadian Jour. Bot. 38:153–161.

23. Lodge, J. P. 1957. [Discussion statements.] *In* Proceedings of the Air Pollution Research Planning Seminar of 1962. U. S. Public Health Service. Pp. 32–33.

24. McCabe, L. C. 1952. Air pollution, U. S. Technical Conference on Air Pollution Proceedings 1950. McGraw-Hill Book Co., New York.

25. Middleton, J. T. 1961. Photochemical air pollution damage to plants. Ann. Rev. Plant Physiol. 12:431–448.

26. _____, and A. O. Paulus. 1956. The identification and distribution of air pollutants through plant responses. Amer. Med. Assoc. Arch. Indus. Health 14:526–532.

27. _____, D. F. Darley and R. F. Brewer. 1957. Damage to vegetation from polluted atmospheres. Amer. Petrol. Inst. Sect. III, Refining, Proc. 8 pp.

28. Miller, P. Robert, J. R. Parmeter, Jr., O. C. Taylor, and E. A. Cardiff. 1963. Ozone injury to the foliage of Pinus ponderosa. Phytopathology 53:1072–1076.

29. National Research Council of Canada. 1932. Effect of sulfur dioxide on vegetation. Ottawa. Publ. 815.

30. Parmeter, J. R., Jr., R. V. Bega, and T. Neff. 1962.

A chlorotic decline of ponderosa pine in southern California. U. S. Dept. Agric. Plant Dis. Rptr. 46:269–273.

31. Rodenhiser, H. A. 1962. Effects of air pollution on crops and livestock. *In* Proc. of the National Conf. on Air Pollution of 1962. U. S. Public Health Service. Pp. 175–178.

32. Scheffer, T. C., and G. G. Hedgcock. 1955. Injury to northwestern forest trees by sulfur dioxide from smelters. U. S. Dept. Agric. Tech. Bul. 1117. 49 pp.

33. Scurfield, G. 1960. Air pollution and tree growth. Forestry Abst. 21:1–20.

34. Shaw, C. G., G. W. Fisher, D. F. Adams, and M. F. Adams. 1951. Fluorine injury to ponderosa pine. (Abstr.) Phytopathology 41:943.

35. Stern, A. C., Editor. 1962. Air pollution. 2 volumes. Academic Press, New York.

36. Thomas, M. D. 1961. Effects of air pollution on plants. *In* Air pollution. World Health Organ. Monog. Series 46. Pp. 233–278.

37. U. S. Public Health Service. 1958. Proceedings of the National Conference on Air Pollution of 1958. 526 pp.

38. ———, 1963. Proceedings of the National Conference on Air pollution of 1962. 436 pp.

39. Wanta, R. C., W. B. Moreland, and H. E. Heggestad. 1961. Tropospheric ozone: an air pollution problem arising in the Washington, D. C., metropolitan area. Monthly Weather Rev. 89:289–296.

40. World Health Organization. 1961. Air pollution. Monog. Series 46. 442 pp.

41. Zimmerman, P. W. 1952. Effects on plants of impurities associated with air pollution. *In* Air Pollution. U. S. Tech. Conf. on Air Pollution Proc. 1950:127–139.

ADDITIONAL REFERENCES

Bobrov, R. A. 1955. Use of plants as biological indicators of smog in the air of Los Angeles County. *Science* 121:510–511.

Brandt, C. S., and W. W. Heck. 1968. Effects of air pollutants on vegetation. Pp. 401–443 in *Air pollution*, 2nd ed., vol. I, ed. by A. C. Stern. New York: Academic Press. Excellent detailed review.

Brodo, I. M. 1966. Lichen growth and cities: A study on Long Island, New York. *Bryologist* 69(4):427–449.

Cannon, H. L., and J. M. Bowles. 1962. Contamination of vegetation by tetraethyl lead. *Science* 131:1733–1734. Lead from gasoline is concentrated in vegetation along highways as a function of distance from the road, traffic volume, and wind direction.

Crocker, T. D. 1965. In Polk and Hillsborough Counties, Florida. *Bull. Atomic Scientists* 21(6):17–19.

Crowther, C., and A. G. Ruston. 1911. The nature, distribution and effects upon vegetation of atmospheric impurities in and near an industrial town. *J. Agr. Science* 4:25–55.

Daines, R. H., I. A. Leone, and E. Brennan. 1967. Air pollution and plant response in the northeastern United States. Pp. 11–31 in *Agriculture and the quality of our environment*, ed. by N. C. Brady. Washington, D. C.: Am. Assoc. Advan. Sci. Publ. 85.

Darley, E. F., et al. 1963. Plant damage by pollution derived from automobiles. *Arch. Environ. Health* 6:761–770.

Dreisinger, B. R. 1966. The impact of sulphur dioxide pollution on crops and forests. In *Background papers prepared for the National Conference on Pollution and Our Environment*, 31 Oct.–4 Nov. 1966, vol. 1.

Fenton, A. F. 1964. Atmospheric pollution of Belfast and its relationship to the lichen flora. *Irish Nat. J.* 14:237–245.

First European Congress on the Influence of Air Pollution on Plants and Animals, Proceedings of. 1969. *Air pollution.* The Netherlands: Centre for Agricultural Publishing and Documentation, Wageningen.

Hansbrough, J. R. 1967. Air quality and forestry. Pp. 45–55 in *Agriculture and the quality of our environment*, ed. by N. C. Brady. Washington, D.C.: Am. Assoc. Advan. Sci. Publ. 85.

Hedgecock, G. G. 1912. Winter-killing and smelter-injury in the forests of Montana. *Torreya* 12:25–30.

Heggestad, H. E. 1968. Diseases of crops and ornamental plants incited by air pollutants. *Phytopathology* 58:1089–1097.

Hepting, G. H. 1968. Diseases of forest and tree crops caused by air pollutants. *Phytopathology* 58(8):1098–1101.

Jacobson, J. S., et al. 1966. The accumulation of fluorine by plants. *J. Air Pollution Control Assoc.* 17:38–42.

Katz, M. 1949. Sulfur dioxide in the atmosphere and its relation to plant life. *Ind. Eng. Chemistry* 41:2450–2465.

Katz, M., and A. W. McCallum. 1952. The effect of sulfur dioxide on the conifers. Chapter 8 in *Air pollution,* ed. by L. C. McCabe. New York: McGraw-Hill.

Lagerwerff, J. V., and A. S. Specht. 1970. Contamination of roadside soil and vegetation with cadmium, nickel, lead, and zinc. *Environ. Sci. and Technol.* 4(7):583–586. Concentrations of these contaminants (from gasoline, motor oil, and car tires) decrease with distance from traffic.

McCune, D. C., et al. 1967. The concept of hidden injury in plants. Pp. 33–44 in *Agriculture and the quality of our environment,* ed. by N. C. Brady. Washington D.C.: Am. Assoc. Advan. Sci. Publ. 85.

McCune, D. C., and R. H. Daines. 1969. Fluoride criteria for vegetation reflect the diversity of plant kingdom. *Environ. Sci. and Technol.* 3:720–732.

Menser, H. A., and H. E. Heggestad. 1966. Ozone and sulfur dioxide synergism: Injury to tobacco plants. *Science* 153:424–425.

Menzel, Ronald G. 1967. Airborne radionuclides and plants. Pp. 57–75 in *Agriculture and the quality of our environment,* ed. by N. C. Brady. Washington, D.C.: Am. Assoc. Advan. Sci. Publ. 85.

Middleton, J. T. 1964. Trends in air pollution damage. *Arch. Environ. Health* 8:27–31. Survey of damage to crops in California by various air pollutants.

Motto, Harry L., et al. 1970. Lead in soils and plants: Its relationship to traffic volume and proximity to highways. *Environ. Sci. and Technol.* 4(3):231–237.

Mukammal, E. I., C. S. Brandt, R. Neuwirth, D. H. Pack, and W. C. Swinbank. 1968. *Air pollutants, meteorology, and plant injury.* World Meteorological Organization Technical Note No. 96. 73 pp. Review of sources of various contaminants and variations in plant susceptibility to air pollution. Extensive bibliography.

Pearson, Lorentz, and Erik Skye. 1965. Air pollution affects pattern of photosynthesis in *Parmelia sulcata,* a corticolous lichen. *Science* 148:1600–1602.

Purves, D., and E. J. MacKenzie. 1969. Trace element contamination of parklands in urban areas. *J. Soil Sci.* 20(2):288–290.

Rao, D. N., and Fabius Le Blanc. 1967. Influence of an iron-sintering plant on corticolous epiphytes in Wawa, Ontario. *Bryologist* 70(2):141–157.

Rühling, Ake, and Germund Tyler. 1968. An ecological approach to the lead problem. *Botan. Notiser* 121:321–342. A study showing temporal and spatial variations of lead in different plants in Sweden.

Rühling, Ake, and Germund Tyler. 1969. Ecology of heavy metals—a regional and historical study. *Botan. Notiser* 122:248–259. Differences in heavy metal concentrations in vegetation are related to location with respect to industrial regions.

Skye, Erik. 1968. Lichens and air pollution. *Acta Phytogeographica Suecica* 52. 123 pp.

Thomas, M. D. 1951. Gas damage to plants. *Ann. Rev. Plant Physiol.* 2:293–322.

Thomas, M. D. 1961. Effects of air pollution on plants. Pp. 233–278 in *Air pollution,* by World Health Organization. New York: Columbia Univ. Press. Detailed account with colored photographs and bibliography.

Thomas, M. D. 1969. Reactivities of smog components are central issue in setting control standards. *Environ. Sci. and Technol.* 3:629–633.

Toumey, J. W. 1921. Damage to forests and other vegetation by smoke, ash and fumes from manufacturing plants in Naugatuck Valley, Conn. *J. Forestry* 19:267–273.

Treshow, Michael. 1968. The impact of air pollutants on plant populations. *Phytopathology* 58(8):1108–1113.

U.S. Department of Health, Education, and Welfare. 1968. *The effects of air pollution.* U.S. Public Health Service Publ. 1556. 18 pp.

Webster, C. C. 1967. *The effect of air pollution on plants and soil.* London: Agr. Res. Council. 53 pp.

Wood, Francis A. 1968. Sources of plant-pathogenic air pollutants. *Phytopathology* 58(8):1075–1084.

Woodwell, G. M., and A. L. Rebuck. 1967. Effects of chronic gamma radiation on the structure and diversity of an oak-pine forest. *Ecol. Monogr.* 37:53–69.

38
SELECTION

DEFOLIATION IN VIETNAM

FRED H. TSCHIRLEY

Modern science has provided today's politicians and ideologists with tools for ecological warfare. This selection reviews some known effects of plant killers in Southeast Asia. Significantly, many more environmental consequences (particularly effects extended in time) can only be speculated about. Characteristically, man once again acts massively to change the environment for a very limited, short-run purpose (primarily to remove vegetation as a visual barrier) without understanding extended impacts on the ecosystem. The full consequences of the use of herbicides in Southeast Asia—although this use was greatly reduced by 1970—will not be clear until future effects are measured.

The evaluation of other knowledgeable scientists concerning the ecological consequences, including the effects on man, of defoliation in Vietnam (and also of bombing and other military activities) is even more jolting (e.g., Heilands, 1970; Orians and Pfeiffer, 1970). Other, still-leashed chemical and biological weapons have much greater potential for upsetting biological systems (see, for example, Langer, 1967; McCarthy, 1969; Rose, 1969).

More beneficial uses of herbicides—to eliminate weeds for instance—are widely recognized and described (e.g., National Academy of Sciences, 1965; Hull, 1967; Niering and Goodwin, 1963; Niering, 1968); although here again there are often hidden deleterious consequences such as ecologic simplification and soil contamination.

(Editor's comment)

Fred H. Tschirley (b. 1925) is assistant chief of the Crops Protection Research Branch, Crops Research Division, Agricultural Research Service, U.S. Department of Agriculture, Beltsville, Maryland, and has been with the Crops Research Division since 1954. He holds two degrees from the University of Colorado and a Ph.D. degree from the University of Arizona (1963). Tschirley's primary research interests are physiological ecology and the control of woody plants. The assessment and report on which this article is based were prepared when he served as an advisor to the U.S. Department of State.

The article is reprinted from *Science* 163 (3869): 779–786, 1969. Copyright 1969 by the American Association for the Advancement of Science.

An assessment of ecologic consequences of the defoliation program in Vietnam was undertaken at the request of the U.S. Department of State. This article is based on a report made as a part of an overall review of the defoliation and crop destruction programs in Vietnam.

The timetable for completion of the policy review required submittal of a report 1 month after my arrival in Vietnam on 15 March 1968. The period from mid-March to mid-April was the end of the dry season when many tree species are naturally defoliated. This added to the difficulty of determining the effects of herbicides on vegetation.

The dry season, the short time available, and the difficulty of making on-the-ground observations were restrictive for an ecologic evaluation. Thus, this report is not a detailed analysis, but an assessment based on the observations that were possible and on discussions with foresters and others knowledgeable about the local situation. The observations were supported by scientific reports and personal research experience in ecology and the effect of herbicides on vegetation in temperate and tropical America.

There were no constraints placed on what I was permitted to see in Vietnam nor on what I reported. Some areas and vegetative types could not be visited because there was not adequate time, or because safety could not be assured in areas of military activity. In other areas, inspections were limited to aerial observations because the sites were not sufficiently secure to permit ground assessments. Civilian and military elements of the U.S. mission in Vietnam gave me all the help and cooperation that was possible. The military provided aircraft for aerial surveys of defoliated and nondefoliated forests, arranged transport to Special Forces camps and a security force for observations from the ground, arranged briefings on all aspects of the defoliation program, and made available whatever records I wished to see on where and when forests were sprayed with defoliants. Civilian elements of the U.S. mission provided background information based on

their experiences in Vietnam, aircraft for additional aerial surveys, introductions to Vietnamese foresters, and background material needed for writing my report. Probably the best indication of the lack of constraints on my activities was that the report which I prepared was released, without a word having been changed, by the U.S. mission in Saigon.

This article is essentially the same as the report I prepared in Vietnam. Some material has been deleted because of space limitations, but my observations and conclusions do not differ from the original report.

Defoliated Areas Surveyed

Time did not permit a survey of all the defoliated areas in Vietnam. Therefore, my observations were limited to those areas where large blocks of forest had been sprayed with herbicides. The ecologic consequences of the defoliation program would be expected to be most evident and most readily definable in such areas.

The most intensive defoliation treatments in the mangrove vegetational complex have been applied in the Rung Sat Special Zone, an area that surrounds the shipping channel into Saigon. Defoliation of the mangrove was started in 1966, but most of the defoliation flights were made after June 1967. A block of about 460 square kilometers had been treated by the end of January 1968. The Rung Sat Special Zone was surveyed from a helicopter ranging in height from treetop level to about 1000 feet. Mangrove on the Ca Mau peninsula was surveyed from a C-123 flying at about 2000 feet. This flight also permitted a survey of a 1962 herbicidal treatment of mangrove on both sides of the Ong Doc River.

The most intensive defoliation treatments on upland semideciduous forest have been applied in war zones C and D and in the Demilitarized Zone. My efforts were limited to war zones C and D. War zone C is northwest of Saigon between the Song Be River and the Cambodian border; war zone D is northeast of Saigon between the Son Be and Song Dong Nai rivers. Blocks of about 920 and 1920 square kilometers have been sprayed in war zones C and D, respectively. Some areas within those blocks have received two to four treatments. Defoliation in the semideciduous forest was observed from two relatively high-level flights in fixed-wing aircraft, six high- and low-level flights in helicopters, and observations from the ground in forests surrounding the four Special Forces camps of Thien Ngon, Katum, Tong Le Chon, and Bo Dop. Several hours were spent in the forest at each location to assess defoliation, refoliation, successional patterns, and to get an idea of the possible effects of the defoliation on wildlife. In addition to my own observations, men at the camps were questioned regarding the effect of defoliation on their operation, their impressions about the relative difficulty of human movement in the forest (a rough measure of the density and composition of the understory vegetation), and sightings they had made of wildlife.

Effect of Defoliation on Climate

Not uncommonly one hears that large-scale modification of vegetation (forest to savanna or grassland, for example) or the vegetative denudation of an area will cause a change of climate, particularly in the amount of rainfall. The theory behind this statement is that as forest is converted to grassland or the soil is bared of vegetation, the evapotranspirational surface is reduced, and thus there is less moisture released to the atmosphere for subsequent precipitation. The fallacy of the theory is readily apparent when one considers the vast scale of atmospheric air flow, with the moisture it contains, and the relatively insignificant reduction in moisture that might be caused by reduced evapotranspiration from a small area. Some simple calculations point out the fallacy of the theory more explicitly.

By applying the reasoning used for an arid area (1), let us apply some simple calculations

to a forested area that is 100 kilometers on a side. If we assume, conservatively I think, that the total moisture in a vertical column of the atmosphere above the area has a depth of 3 centimeters and the air mass is moving over the area at a rate of 5 kilometers per hour, we can calculate that moisture is passing over the area at a rate of 4.17×10^9 grams per second. Now let us further assume that our hypothetical forest has been entirely denuded of vegetation and we reasoned that it may have been contributing 10 percent to the total atmospheric moisture. In other words, we expect a 10-percent decrease of rainfall after the vegetation is removed. Ten percent of the total atmospheric moisture would be 4.17×10^8 grams per second. In other words, our hypothetical forest would have to be contributing moisture to the atmosphere at a rate of 1.1×10^5 gallons per second. Such a figure is unreasonable. If we carry this calculation further and consider one tree with its branches in the upper or middle canopy for each 10 square meters, the evapotranspiration from each such area would have to be 417 milliliters per second. That is far beyond the measurements that have been made for salt cedar (*Tamarix pentandra*), one of the heaviest users of water (2).

The work of Ohman and Pratt (3) also lends itself to this discussion. They measured dew point over and downwind from a desert irrigation project covering some 100,000 acres near Yuma, Arizona [annual precipitation about 3 inches]. Despite application of annual totals of from 5 to 10 feet of irrigation water on this area extending some 20 miles parallel to prevailing winds for the summer months studied, all influence of the irrigated fields upon crop-level dew points became immeasurably small only 100 feet to the lee of the downwind edge of the entire area. And at 12 feet (3.6 meters) above the crop level, dew points were not measurably increased even at points inside the irrigated acreage. These measurements were made under midday conditions in July and August when monthly totals of irrigation varied between about 0.7 and 1.5 feet of applied water. These measurements show the small effect that artificial measures have on atmospheric moisture content.

My conclusion is that defoliation in Vietnam has no significant measurable effect on atmospheric moisture and thus would have no effect on precipitation.

Another point that refutes the evapotranspiration-precipitation theory is that water molecules are not motionless in the atmosphere. Sutcliffe (4) estimated that the average time between a water molecule's evaporation into and its precipitation from the atmosphere was about 10 days. Thus, from consideration of the mean wind speed, the average water molecule must drift several hundred miles before it is precipitated.

Extensive defoliation would be expected to change temperature patterns through a forest profile simply because there would be less shielding of direct solar radiation. In addition, the average wind speed would be greater in a defoliated than in an undefoliated forest. These two factors probably would not have a great effect on higher plants and animals, but might temporarily affect lower life forms that are more dependent on specific microclimatic niches for growth and survival.

Effect of Defoliation on Soils

One of the principal fears about exposing soil in the tropics is the possibility of increased laterization. The term laterite generally refers to an indurated concretionary deposit, high in iron or aluminum oxide content, which has formed in place by the weathering of rocks. True laterite hardens irreversibly. Laterite has been found to be best developed when the following conditions exist (5). (i) The climate must have high rainfall and uniformly high temperatures. (ii) The topography must have been fairly gentle, peneplain in nature. (iii) A well-drained soil must have been present. This is usually an alluvial soil, but soils high in iron content may be an exception. (iv) There must have been a uniformly fluctuating water table

which had a definite low level during the dry season. (v) Stable geological conditions must have existed for a long time.

About 30 percent of the soils of Vietnam have a potential for laterization (5). Many of the red soils of Vietnam (often confused with laterite) dry out and become hard but soften again when wet. The soft doughy laterite, which hardens to a rocklike material when exposed to alternate wetting and drying, is not found in significant amounts in Vietnam.

Two kinds of laterite are found in Vietnam. Wormhole laterite is generally consolidated and occurs as massive beds, commonly at the bottom of a 1- to 30-foot layer of well-drained soil. It is red to brown in color, and has a slaggy appearance due to numerous holes, often interconnecting, and thus facilitate the passage of groundwater. Wormhole laterite occurs throughout most of the Mekong Terrace region, in soils of both forested and cultivated areas.

Pellet laterite is unconsolidated and occurs as small pellet-like concretions in an iron- or aluminum-rich soil. The hard concretions are usually surrounded by fine-grained material that is generally clayey when moist. The coarser particles in this fine-grained material are commonly iron-stained quartz sand. Pellet laterite occurs on the iron-rich basalt plateau soils of the Mekong Terrace, the basalt plateau of Ban Me Thuot, the extreme western edge of the high plateau west of Pleiku, and in a small area around Quang Ngai. Pellet laterite has been observed forming on the metamorphic rocks near Bong Son and on some of the rocks near Qui Nhon. It is likely that wormhole and pellet laterite could occur in the northeastern coastlands, but this has not been substantiated by field studies.

Laterization under natural conditions is a long-term process. The process is accelerated when soil is exposed to direct solar radiation and wind. I do not find it reasonable to conclude that the defoliation program in Vietnam would hasten the laterization process significantly because bare soil does not result from defoliation. It is possible, however, that laterization will be accelerated around base and Special Forces camps where the soil is maintained free of vegetation.

The amount of erosion that occurs as a consequence of defoliation depends on soil type, topography, relative degree of vegetative cover, and amount and intensity of rainfall. In general, erosion is greatest on steep slopes of bare soil, decreasing as slope decreases and as vegetation becomes more dense. It was not possible to examine defoliated forest in mountainous terrain for evidence of accelerated erosion. I did not detect such evidence during flights over the defoliated areas. Gully and sheet erosion were noted around camps where there was little or no vegetation, regardless of whether or not those areas were sprayed.

The possibilities of flooding or of changes in the water table as a result of defoliation are subjects that need careful consideration. The replacement of woody vegetation with grass in the southwestern United States has resulted in perennial flow of streams that were only intermittent before and also in the flow of springs that had been dry for many years. There are cases where harvesting trees increased stream flow (6) and where clearcutting resulted in a marshy condition unsuitable for desirable timber species (7). I mention these points because they have occurred elsewhere and could conceivably occur in Vietnam. But I do not know the local situation well enough to make a reasonable assessment of that probability.

Microorganisms are an essential feature of the soil system. A herbicide that killed the microorganisms would have a severe effect on soil ecology. What are the possibilities of destroying the microbial population in the soil with the chemicals being used for defoliation in Vietnam?

The code names for the defoliants used in Vietnam are Orange and White. The constituents of Orange are the normal butyl esters of (2,4-dichlorophenoxy)-acetic acid and (2,4,5-trichlorophenoxy)acetic acid, better known as 2,4-D and 2,4,5-T, respectively, in a 1:1 ratio. The constituents of White are triisopropanolamine salts of 2,4-D and picloram (4-amino-3,5,6-trichloropicolinic

acid) in a 4:1 ratio. There seems to be no danger that any of the three chemicals will kill microorganisms. Actually, numbers of soil microorganisms capable of inactivating 2,4-D apparently increase when 2,4-D is present in the soil. Thus, repeated applications of 2,4-D were less persistent in soil than the initial application (8). There are no reports suggesting that the effect of 2,4,5-T on microorganisms is significantly different from that of 2,4-D. Picloram does not destroy soil microorganisms, but neither is the microbial population enriched as a result of picloram application. Thus, picloram cannot be considered a good energy source for microorganisms. The decomposition of picloram is an incidental process in the breakdown of soil organic matter, requiring the loss of approximately 10,000 to 100,000 pounds of organic matter per pound of herbicide (9).

Effect of Defoliation on Plant and Animal Populations

The chemicals 2,4-D and 2,4,5-T are highly selective herbicides, but picloram is somewhat less selective. Not all plant species react similarly to them. The differential susceptibility may be a function of such factors as time of treatment, nature of the leaf surface, variable capacity for absorption and translocation of the herbicide, biochemistry of the plant, or the nature of the herbicide itself. Some established annual and perennial grasses are tolerant to rates of application used in the Republic of Vietnam (RVN). Thus, in any vegetative type, one would expect that some species would not be killed; some would be killed easily; others with difficulty. Most species in the mangrove association are highly susceptible to the herbicides being used for defoliation in Vietnam, and thus represent an exception to the general rule. For that reason, and because the mangrove association presents a different set of ecological considerations than the semideciduous forest does, each will be discussed separately.

MANGROVE FOREST

Botanical considerations. The mangrove association is relatively simple floristically. The principal species include: *Avicennia marina, A. intermedia, Rhizophora conjugata, Bruguiera parviflora, B. gymnorhiza, Ceriops candolleana, Nipa fruticans, Phoenix* spp., *Lumnitzera coccinea, Sonneratia acida, Melaleuca leucadendron, Excoecaria agallocha, Carapa obovata,* and *Acronychia laurifolio.*

Other plant species are represented in the mangrove type, but they are of lesser importance. Bamboo was not observed in the mangrove association.

Susceptibility to herbicides. The mangrove species seem to be almost uniformly susceptible to Orange and White, the herbicides used for their control in Vietnam. An exception is *Nipa fruticans,* which is reported to be resistant to White. Strips of mangrove on both sides of the Ong Doc River, sprayed with Orange in 1962, were of particular interest. The treated strips were still plainly visible. Thus, one must assume that the trees were not simply defoliated, but were killed.

Successful aspects. The mangrove type in the Republic of Vietnam occurs on about 2800 square kilometers (*10*). *Avicennia marina* is the pioneer species of the mangrove type, colonizing on the clay accretion areas at the sea face. At the 5th and 6th year *Rhizophora conjugata, Bruguiera parviflora,* and *Ceriops candolleana* will develop where there has been partial stabilization of the soil. At about the 20th year *Rhizophora* and *Bruguiera* will dominate the site. From that point on, further succession depends on the degree of silting and the consequent decrease of water circulation. As organic matter accumulates, conditions are created for the advent of other species into the mangrove complex. The final stage in the mangrove type is the cajeput (*Melaleuca leucadendron*), found on the highest, most stable soil above high tide.

Seed production of mangrove species is annual and abundant to prolific, with seeds viviparous or otherwise, of high germinability and capable of remaining viable for long periods (*11*). Germination and rooting are usually rapid and successful. In some locations, when the seeds are able to settle as a result of favorable water conditions, natural regeneration may become successfully established in less than a year. The movement of the water, however, may not only bring in seeds but may also carry them away before they can take root.

The most serious animal pest is the crab, which may entirely prevent regeneration by attacks on seedlings (*12*). In Malaya two species of *Acrostichum* (a fern) may hinder the establishment of waterborne seedlings. The fern grows and spreads rapidly when the tree cover is removed. McKinley (*10*) mentions two ferns (Choai, a creeping form; Don, an erect form) as occurring in the climax mangrove, but does not comment on their possible interference with regeneration.

Ecological considerations. According to the timetable discussed by McKinley, about 20 years are required for the establishment of a dominant *Rhizophora-Bruguiera* association. That timetable was established for a situation in which newly silted areas were colonized by *Avicennia* and then were replaced by *Rhizophora-Bruguiera.* It is not unreasonable to suspect that the same timetable might apply to areas in which the trees had been killed by herbicides. Dead trees do not hold soil as well as living trees do. The amount of soil removed would depend on the rapidity of tidal recession, which is unknown to me. The greater the amount of soil removed, the greater would be the time required for regeneration of a mangrove stand similar to the original.

The regeneration of mangrove since the 1962 treatments along the Ong Doc River was observed from an aircraft flying at 2000 feet (600 meters). Regeneration was apparent as fingers extending into the treated strip, but I could not determine whether regeneration had occurred across the entire breadth of the treated strip.

In the mangrove areas treated in 1962, trees of the colonizing species were not yet

TABLE 38.1 The total catch, in metric tons, for the past 3 years in the Republic of Vietnam

YEAR	FISH		OTHERS*
	Freshwater	Marine	
1965	57,000	289,000	29,000
1966	64,710	287,450	28,340
1967	54,300	324,700	31,700

* Including cuttlefish, mollusks, shrimp, crabs, and the like.

discernible from 600 meters on all the treated area. Thus, if the information provided by McKinley is extrapolated, 20 years may be a reasonable estimate of the time needed for this forest to return to its original condition.

There is little information available on the effect of killing mangrove on animal populations. In that regard, I considered the food chain among aquatic organisms. Although it was not possible to obtain information on the many links in the food chain, phytophagous and carnivorous fish would be near the top of the food chain. Disruption of lower links in the chain might be expected to reduce fish populations.

Information on fish populations is based on fish catch statistics provided by the Fisheries Branch of U.S. Agency for International Development (AID) (Table 38.1). Fish catch appears to have been increasing. The drop for freshwater fish in 1967 was at first a cause for concern. But the assistant chief of inland fisheries explained that the reduction was due to an absence of flooding in the Mekong Delta in 1967. When flooding does occur, fish are trapped in rice paddies and fishermen have no trouble catching them.

The statistics on the fish catch give a strong indication that the aquatic food chain has not been seriously disturbed. Data comparable to those available for fish were not available for birds and other animals.

The application of herbicide in strips or in a checkerboard pattern rather than large-area treatment would have an ecologic advantage. The trees remaining in untreated strips would provide a seed source for refor-estation as well as a habitat for animals and lower plant forms. The ecological effects in large treated areas would be greater and recovery would probably be slower.

SEMIDECIDUOUS FOREST

The Republic of Vietnam has a total area of 172,540 square kilometers, of which about 30 percent is forested *(10)* (Table 38.2). Some coniferous forest may have been treated in strips along roads, but I have no specific information on that point. I am sure that no large areas of coniferous forest have been treated.

Botanical considerations. I will not attempt to characterize all of the vegetation types of the Republic of Vietnam. There are different forest types, but except for the pine forest, the differences are ones of degree rather than substance. My discussion of the forests in III Corps can be extrapolated to other semideciduous forests of RVN. It cannot be extrapolated to the pine forests or to the small area of rain forest that probably exists in a small area of the northwestern part of RVN, along the Laotian border.

The forests of war zone C are, for the most part, secondary forests with an admixture of bamboo, and semideciduous forest of *Lagerstroemia* and legumes (General Forest Map of RVN, Phan Thuong Tuu, 1966). The forests of war zone D are moist forest

TABLE 38.2 The types of forest, their area of coverage, and the approximate area treated for defoliation in the Republic of Vietnam

VEGETATION TYPE	COVERAGE (km²)	AREA TREATED (km²)
Open forest (semideciduous forest)	50,150	8,140
Flooded area		
Mangrove	2,800	960
Other aquatic plants	2,000	0
Coniferous forest		
Three-leaved pine	900	0
Two-leaved pine	350	0

over most of the area, and semideciduous forest of *Lagerstroemia* and legumes over the reminder.

There are obvious differences among the three forest types. The differences are taxonomic for the most part. Physiognomically, they are similar. In terms of ecologic considerations, therefore, they will be discussed collectively.

The three forests are similarly characterized by having members of the family Dipterocarpaceae as dominant trees in the upper canopy. This does not mean necessarily that dipterocarps are numerically superior. Other well-represented families include the Leguminosae, Meliaceae, Lythraceae, Guttiferae, and Sterculiaceae (*10, 13, 14*). Botanical composition, taxonomically and numerically, varies from one location to another.

The difficulty of a botanic description of the forest may be appreciated with the knowledge that about 1500 woody species occur in RVN (*10*). Moreover, I saw the forests at a time when identification was most difficult. Many species are normally deciduous during the dry season; many that are normally evergreen had been defoliated by herbicides or by fire.

The period from mid-March to mid-April was not an ideal time to assess the ecologic impact of the defoliation program on the semideciduous forests of the Republic of Vietnam. The combination of natural defoliation, defoliation by herbicides, and defoliation by many, many fires (civilian and military caused) made the determination of the causes of defoliation difficult. A careful delineation of the causative factors within a 1-month period was not possible. An observer making an ecologic assessment during the middle or latter part of the rainy season would not have to contend with the confounding influences of natural defoliation and fire.

Susceptibility to herbicides. Trees in the semideciduous forests of Vietnam are almost uniformly susceptible in terms of initial defoliation. But when refoliation and the percentage of plants killed are considered, the average susceptibility of the vegetative type is unknown. The best estimate I can obtain is an extrapolation of data developed in Thailand by Darrow *et al.* (*15*) and in Puerto Rico by Tschirley *et al.* (*16*).

Darrow's tests in Thailand were conducted in a semievergreen monsoon forest having an annual precipitation of about 40 inches. Two hundred twenty plant species were identified from two test sites totaling 3400 acres, so species diversity was high. Darrow found that two or more gallons of Purple (same as Orange except that 20 percent of the 2,4,5,-T is an isobutyl ester rather than *n*-butyl ester) caused defoliation greater than 60 to 65 percent for a period of 6 to 8 or 9 months.

My collaborators and I worked in a semievergreen forest in Puerto Rico (*16*) having an annual precipitation of about 85 inches. Species diversity was high; 106 woody species were recorded on 2.4 acres, in an area adjacent to the aerial test plots. We also worked in a tropical rain forest in Puerto Rico having an annual precipitation of about 120 inches (*16*). About 88 woody species were recorded for the rain forest site. Defoliation of the semievergreen forest treated with 3 gallons of Purple was 61 percent 6 months after treatment. In the rain forest, an equivalent rate of Orange provided 66 percent defoliation 6 months after treatment and 55 percent 1 year after treatment.

Thus, the defoliation obtained in taxonomically distinct forests in opposite parts of the world was similar. It is justifiable, then to expect that average defoliation in the semideciduous forests of Vietnam would be about the same. Actually, I would expect defoliation in Vietnam to be somewhat lower because applications are made from greater height than was the case for the experimental work in Thailand and Puerto Rico.

Multiple treatments were not made in Thailand or Puerto Rico, so the effects of two and three treatments in war zones C and D can only be inferred from extensive experience in woody plant control in temperate zones and from my experience in tropical

America, instead of being extrapolated from actual research data. But the inference is necessary because the ecologic impact becomes greater with each succeeding treatment.

A single treatment with 3 gallons of Orange or White would not be expected to have a great or lasting effect on a semideciduous forest in Vietnam. Some trees would be killed, and the canopy would be less dense temporarily. But within several years the canopy would again be closed, and even a careful observer would be hard pressed to circumscribe the treated area. A second application during the period of recovery would have a wholly different effect.

Research on a two-storied oak-yaupon forest in Texas showed that the top canopy intercepted about 72 percent of the spray droplets and the understory intercepted an additional 22 percent. Only 6 percent of the droplets reached the ground *(16)*. Thus, one would expect that the principal effect from an initial treatment would be on trees of the top canopy. As the density of the top canopy is reduced, subsequent treatments will kill more trees in the top canopy and have a far greater effect on the understory, regenerating vegetation.

The theoretical response to multiple herbicide applications was supported by my observations on the ground. The area visited at Thien Ngon was sprayed with Orange on 19 December 1966; the area at Katum was treated with White on 9 November 1966 and with Orange on 28 October 1967. Two areas were visited at Tong Le Chon; one was treated with Orange on 23 September 1967, and the other was treated with White on 7 November 1966. There were more dead trees and a higher percentage of defoliation at Katum than at any other site. Granting the inadequacy of the sample at each location, the difference between Katum and the other sites was obvious. Despite more defoliation and more dead trees at Katum, the ground was not bare. Many established grasses are tolerant to the herbicides used. In addition, grasses, sedges, and vines quickly occupy areas that have been defoliated.

Grasses were abundant in all defoliated areas observed on the ground.

Successful aspects. I can think of no better introduction to this section than a quotation from Richards *(17)*.

> The process of natural regeneration in tropical forests is no doubt exceedingly complex, and though its practical importance to the forester is obvious, surprisingly little is known about it. Much of what has been written about the so-called "natural regeneration" of rain forest refers to the reproduction of a few economic species under conditions rendered more or less unnatural by the exploitation of timber. Before regeneration under these artificial conditions can be understood or controlled scientifically, we need to know what happens under undisturbed conditions, and information about this is extremely scanty.

I must emphasize the last sentence of the quotation. Data on regeneration of tropical forests is indeed scanty—and particularly scanty for Vietnam!

There is general agreement that the usual successional series in a terrestrial tropical forest is grass—shrub—secondary forest—primary forest *(14, 17, 18)*. The same successional series could be applied equally well to deciduous forests in temperate zones.

Because of the inadequacy of data about forest regeneration in Vietnam, perhaps an example in a different situation would be instructive. The island of Krakatau presents a good example of ecologic succession. Richards described the island as follows *(17)*.

> Krakatau is one of a group of small volcanic islands situated between Java and Sumatra. Early in 1883 it was about 9 km long and 5 km broad, rising to a peak 2,728 ft (822 m) above sea level. At this date the whole island was covered with luxuriant vegetation. About the nature and composition of this vegetation next to nothing is known, but there is every reason for supposing that it was mostly tropical rain forest similar to that now existing in the neighboring parts of Sumatra. In May 1883, the volcano which had long been regarded as extinct began to be active and the activity gradually increased until it reached a climax on

August 26 and 27. On these two days occurred the famous eruption, the sound of which was heard as far away as Ceylon and Australia. More than half the island sank beneath the sea, the peak being split in two, though its highest point still remained. The surviving parts of Krakatau were covered with pumice stone and ash to an average depth of about 30 m and a new marginal belt 4.6 km² in area was added to the southern coast. During the period of volcanic activity the bulk of the vegetation was certainly destroyed.

For a while the island remained without any vegetation. The only living thing a visitor saw in May 1884 was one spider. In 1886 there was already a considerable amount of vegetation on the island and the succeeding seral stages have developed quite rapidly (Figure 38.1).

In 1964 Richards wrote about the ecology of Krakatau,

The development of vegetation on Krakatau has not yet reached a stable climax stage, but the general course of future changes can be predicted with some confidence, at least for the middle and upper regions of the island. In the former it may be expected that the *Macaranga-Ficus* woodland will develop by a series of changes into a stable climax rain forest to some extent similar to the mixed primary rain forest of the neighboring parts of Sumatra and Java. How long this development will take is difficult to guess, but the study of secondary successions suggests that it will be much longer than from the great eruption to the present day.

The example of Krakatau cannot, and should not, be applied to the semideciduous

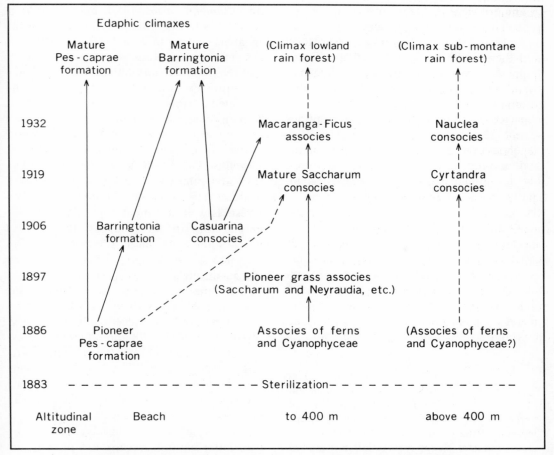

FIGURE 38.1 Diagram of successions on Krakatau since the eruption of 1883 (15).

forests of Vietnam for at least three reasons. (i) Defoliation does not destroy all vegetation; (ii) it does not cover the soil with pumice stone and ash; and (iii) RVN is not an island. Krakatau is merely an example of the relative time needed for the development of a mature forest when it must start from nothing. That is not the case in Vietnam.

There are a few records available for tree ages in tropical forests that give an indication of the time required for regeneration of a mature forest. An average individual of *Parashorea malaanonan* in the Philippine dipterocarp forest reaches a diameter of 80 centimeters in 197 years *(19)*. The average maximum age of *Shorea leprosula* in Malaya is 250 years *(2)*. Both are primary forest species. The fastgrowing trees characteristic of secondary forest have a shorter life than do primary forest species.

The principal ecologic danger imposed by repeated treatments with herbicides is that saplings and poles present in the lower story, and then seedlings, may be killed. If that happens in large areas, natural reseeding may be a problem. Dipterocarp seeds are disseminated by the wind and thus would be expected to be among the first tree species to repopulate an area. Seeds of other species, dependent on dissemination by small mammals and rodents and by birds, would probably not spread as rapidly. Seeds of some species would undoubtedly remain viable in the soil and would germinate after the last in a series of multiple treatments. Many species in the family Leguminosae have that capability. Less is known about seed characteristics in other families. Turrill *(21)* reported it has been proved at Rothamstead that seeds of arable weeds remained viable in soil under pasture after 300 years in one area and 30 to 40 years in others.

Little is known of the time scale of secondary successions in the tropics. Chevalier (1948) states that the forest on the site of the ancient town of Angkor Vat in Cambodia, destroyed probably some five or six centuries ago, now resembles the virgin tropical forest of the district, but still shows certain differences. In general, it seems clear that the longer the period between the destruction of the primary forest and the onset of the secondary succession and the greater the modification of the soil and the environment in general during this period, the longer the time needed for the re-establishment of the climax *(17)*.

The paragraph quoted does not apply to the forests being defoliated in Vietnam because the Vietnamese forests were not primary, but secondary, at the time of treatment. The time required for the establishment of a secondary forest is much less than for a primary forest.

The greatest danger resulting from repeated defoliation treatments in Vietnam is that such areas will be invaded by bamboo. The presence of bamboo is the most constant feature of the semideciduous forests I saw in Vietnam. Species of large bamboo (the most common being *Dendrocalamus strictus* and *Bambusa arundinacea* according to a local RVN forester) are particularly apparent in areas where the "rail" (slash and burn) system of agriculture has been practiced. But bamboo is not limited to areas that were previously cleared of trees. A small-stemmed bamboo is present as an understory in many forested areas and can be seen frequently where trees have been defoliated. In addition, the small bamboo *Schizostachyum sollingeri,* 10 to 15 feet high, was present in the forest at all of the camps I visited. The presence of bamboo in Asian forests is well documented *(17, 22)*. Aerial observations in RVN suggest that it first invades new areas along routes of more favorable moisture supply. From there it can spread throughout the forest.

While making ground observations at the four Special Forces camps, I attempted to evaluate the relative density of seedling and sapling tree species in bamboo-infested sites. Although I have no quantitative data, seedlings were rare in dense bamboo, but frequent to numerous where there was no bamboo. Probably of more importance is the fact that saplings were rare in dense bamboo.

The length of time that bamboo might retard the natural successional progression is unknown, but I am certain it would cause a retardation. The following statement by Ahmed (23) may be cause for concern: "A bamboo will be the first member to colonize on a new site in a seed year and will be the last to leave it. Once established on a soil it is difficult to eradicate it."

The life history of different bamboo species varies, but usually culms die after flowering. The germination to flowering cycle may be from 30 to 50 years (17, 24). Flowering is gregarious (whole populations flowering in 1 year) in some species and sporadic in others. Most bamboo species have very efficient vegetative reproduction from buds on creeping rhizomes.

Seedling mortality of tree species is naturally high in tropical forests. A study of *Euterpe globosa*, a palm found in the American tropics, showed that the mortality of seedlings was 95 percent, of established seedlings 12 percent, and of shrubs 64 percent. Thus, only 1.6 percent of the seedlings survived to become trees (25). Another study (25) showed the average half-life of all seedlings in test plots to be 6 months.

If it were not for the probable invasion by bamboo of severely defoliated areas in the forests of Vietnam, I am reasonably certain that the successional progression to a secondary forest would proceed without undue retardation. A reason for feeling so is based on data I obtained from plots in Puerto Rico that were treated at the rate of 3, 9, and 27 pounds per acre as follows: picloram, 5-bromo-3-*sec*-butyl-6-methyluracil [bromacil], 3,6-dichloro-*o*-anisic acid [dicamba], 3-(3,4-dichlorophenyl)-1,1-dimethylurea [diuron], (2,3,6-trichlorophenyl)acetic acid [fenac], and 2,4-bis(isopropylamino)-6-(methylthio)-*s*-triazine [prometone] applied to the soil. Two years after treatment, the plots were examined for the presence of seedlings. Many of the secondary forest species and several primary forest species were present as seedlings. In addition, there was no apparent differential effect of the six herbicides.

The presence of seedlings on plots treated with such high rates of herbicides is an important point. Several of the herbicides, particularly fenac and picloram, persist in soil. There is no doubt that highly susceptible plant species would be affected by herbicide residues in the soil. But experience has shown that species commonly present in forests are not so susceptible that regeneration would be prevented. The small experimental plots in Puerto Rico were treated with 27 pounds per acre of picloram; one treatment with White in Vietnam would apply only 1.5 pounds of picloram per acre.

In conclusion, the time scale for succession in a semideciduous forest in RVN is unknown. Single treatments with defoliants should not cause severe successional problems, but multiple treatments probably will because of site dominance by bamboo.

Ecologic considerations. The ecologic considerations as they apply to plant populations were discussed in the previous section of this article. The effect of defoliation on animal populations is truly unknown.

Men stationed at Special Forces camps have told me of seeing deer (two reports), birds (many reports), tiger (one sighting, several sound identifications), elephant (two reports), monkey (numerous reports), and coldblooded vertebrates (numerous reports). I saw a tiger track in the road at Katum. There were no reports of bovines. It is possible that such bovines as the kouprey, gaur, and banteng, reported to be rare (26), are no longer present in the defoliated areas in war zones C and D. But I suspect that bombing, artillery, fire, human presence, and hunting have had a far greater effect than has defoliation.

TOXICITY OF HERBICIDES

A discussion of ecologic effects would hardly be complete without mentioning the relative toxicity of the herbicides being used for defoliation and crop destruction. The herbicides used in Vietnam are only moderately toxic to warm-blooded animals. None deserves a lengthy discussion except for Agent Blue (cacodylic acid), which contains arsenic. Inorganic arsenicals such as arsenic trioxide,

TABLE 38.3 The LD_{50} (dose in milligrams per kilogram of body weight needed to kill 50 percent of test animals) for the herbicides used in RVN and for several other chemical compounds are as follows (29)

CHEMICAL	LD_{50}
Sodium arsenite	10—50
Paraquat*	150
2,4,5-T	100—300
2,4-D	300—1000
Cacodylic acid†	830
Aspirin	1775
Picloram	8200

* 1,1'-dimethyl-4,4'-bipyridinium salt.
† Active ingredient of Agent Blue.

sodium arsenite, lead arsenate, calcium arsenate, and Paris green are extremely toxic. Organic arsenicals, such as Blue, have a low mammalian toxicity. Two series of organic arsenicals are used as herbicides. The arsonic acid series is formed by a single organic group combined directly to arsenic; the arsinic acid series has two organic groups. By varying the organic group in either series, a wide range of phytotoxicities can be obtained in products with a relatively low level of mammalian toxicity *(26)* (Table 38.3).

Toxicity studies for White have shown the oral dose needed to kill 50 percent of test animals to be (LD_{50}) 3080 milligrams per kilogram for rats, 2000 for sheep, and more than 3163 for cattle *(27)*. The oral dose for Blue is 2600 milligrams per kilogram for rats *(28)*. There is no evidence to suggest that the herbicides used in Vietnam will cause toxicity problems for man or animals.

Summary and Conclusions

If my assignment had been simply to determine if the defoliation program had an ecologic effect, the answer would have been a simple "yes," and a trip to the country would not have been necessary. But to assess the magnitude of the ecologic effect is an entirely different matter.

One must realize that biologic populations, even those remote from man, are dynamic. Seasonal changes, violent weather events,

fire, birth, maturation, senescence, and death cause a continuing ecologic flux. Normally, the ecologic flux operates within narrow limits in a climax community. It is only catastrophic events that cause an extreme ecologic shift and reduce the community to a lower seral stage.

The defoliation program has caused ecologic changes. I do not feel the changes are irreversible, but complete recovery may take a long time. The mangrove type is killed with a single treatment. Regeneration of the mangrove forest to its original condition is estimated to require about 20 years.

A single treatment on semideciduous forest would cause an inconsequential ecologic change. Repeated treatments will result in invasion of many sites by bamboo. Presence of dense bamboo will then retard regeneration of the forest. The time scale for regeneration of semideciduous forest is unknown. Available information is so scanty that a prediction would have no validity and certainly no real meaning. Most of the defoliation treatments in the semideciduous forests have been made in strips along lines of communication. The ecologic effect of defoliation in those areas would not be as severe as in areas where large blocks have been treated.

The effect of defoliation on animals is not known, but it does not appear to have been extreme. I hasten to add that I know far less about animals than about plants. Fish catch has increased during a period of intensive treatment for defoliation, which surprised and pleased me. Actual data were not available for population trends of other forms of animal life. Large mammals have been seen recently in war zones C and D, the areas of greatest defoliation activity. Included were tiger, monkey, elephant, and deer.

Recommendations

1) The desirability of ecologic research in Vietnam after the war ends cannot be overemphasized. The research should be admin-

istered through an institution that will provide continuity and breadth for the research program.   The opportunity of establishing ecologic research under the International Biological Program should be explored.

2) Continuing assessment of the defoliation program as it affects forestry and watershed values should be made.   Ground observa-

tions are most desirable, but aerial surveys during various seasons of the year will contribute much good information.

3) From an ecologic point of view, the concept of defoliating in strips or in a checkerboard pattern has great merit.   Undefoliated areas would serve as a seed source for regeneration and as habitat for wildlife.

References Cited

1. J. E. McDonald, *Weather* 17, 1 (1962).
2. J. P. Decker, *Plant Physiol.* 37, 393 (1962).
3. H. L. Ohman and R. L. Pratt, "The daytime influence of irrigation upon desert humidities," *Tech. Rep. No. EP-35* (U.S. Army Quartermasters R & D Command, 1956).
4. R. C. Sutcliffe, *Quart. J. Meteorol. Soc.* 82, 394 (1956).
5. J. F. Taranik and E. J. Cording, "Laterite and its engineering properties," *Mimeo Rep. 579th Engin. Detachment (Terrain)* (U.S. Army, A.P.O. 96491, 1967).
6. G. R. Trimble, Jr., K. G. Reinhart, H. H. Webster, *J. Forestry,* 61, 635 (1963).
7. W. F. Johnston, *ibid.* 66, 566 (1968).
8. T. J. Sheets and L. L. Danielson, "Herbicides in soils," *Tech. Rep. No. ARS-20-9* (U.S. Department of Agriculture, Agricultural Research Service, Washington, D.C., 1960), p. 170.
9. C. R. Youngson, C. A. I. Goring, R. W. Meikle, M. H. Scott, J. D. Griffith, *Biokemia* 1967 (No. 15), 19 (1967).
10. T. W. McKinley, *The Forests of Free Vietnam* (Ministry of Agriculture, Saigon, 1957) (in English and Vietnamese).
11. *Trop. Silviculture* 1, 129 (1958).
12. D. S. P. Noakes, *ibid.* 2, 309 (1957).
13. Thai Cong Tung, *Natural Environment and Land Use in South Vietnam* (Ministry of Agriculture, Saigon, 1967), p. 156.
14. L. Williams, "Vegetation of Southeast Asia—studies of forest types," *Tech. Rep. No. CR-49-65* (U.S. Department of Agriculture, Washington, D.C., 1965).
15. R. A. Darrow, G. B. Truchelut, C. M. Bartlett, "OCONUS defoliation test program," *Tech. Rep. No. 79* (U.S. Army Biology Center, Fort Dietrick, Md., 1966), p. 149.
16. F. H. Tschirley *et al.,* "Response of tropical and subtropical woody plants to chemical treatments," *Tech. Rep. No. CR-13-67* (U.S. Department of Agriculture, Washington, D.C., 1968), p. 197.
17. P. W. Richards, *The Tropical Rain Forest—An Ecological Study* (Cambridge Univ. Press, London, 1964), p. 450.
18. *Trop. Silviculture* 1, 59 (1958).
19. W. H. Brown, cited in *(15)*.
20. J. G. Watson, *Malayan Forester* 6, 146 (1937).
21. W. B. Turrill, *Gardener's Chron.* 142, 37 (1957).
22. L. Williams, "Forests of Southeast Asia, Puerto Rico, and Texas," *Tech. Rep. No. CR-12-67* (U.S. Department of Agriculture, Washington, D.C., 1967), p. 410; anonymous, *Trop. Silviculture* 1, 151 (1958); "Timber trends and prospects in the Asia-Pacific Region," *FAO ECAFE Publ. No. E/CN, 11/533* (Food and Agricultural Organization of the United Nations, Rome, Italy, 1961), p. 224.
23. K. J. Ahmed, *Trop. Silviculture* 2, 287 (1957).
24. F. A. McClure, *The Bamboos, A Fresh Perspective* (Harvard Univ. Press, Cambridge, Mass., 1966), p. 347.
25. H. T. Odum, *Annual Report 1965* (Puerto Rico Nuclear Center, Rio Piedras, 1965) p. 220.
26. W. B. House, L. H. Goodson, H. M. Gadberry, K. W. Docktor, "Assessment of ecological effects of extensive or repeated use of herbicides," *Midwest Research Institute Rep. No. 3103-B* (Midwest Research Institute, Kansas City, Mo., 1967), p. 369.
27. G. E. Lynn, *Down Earth* 20, 9 (1965); J. T. Weimer *et al., Toxicological Studies Relating to the Use of White (Tordon 101) as a Defoliant* (U.S. Army Edgewood Arsenal, Pharmacology Laboratories, Edgewood, Md., 1967).
28. *Book on Organic Arsenicals* (Ansul Chemical Co., Marinette, Wis., 1965).
29. H. M. Hull, *Herbicide Handbook of the Weed Society of America* (Humphrey Press, Geneva, N.Y., 1967), p. 293.

ADDITIONAL REFERENCES

Audus, L. J., ed. 1964. *The physiology and biochemistry of herbicides.* New York: Academic Press. 555 pp.

Crafts, A. S. 1961. *The chemistry and mode of action of herbicides.* New York: Interscience (Wiley). 269 pp.

Epstein, S. S. 1970. A family likeness. *Environment* 12(6):16–25. Discusses ability of common herbicides to produce birth defects.

Fair, S. D. 1963. No place to hide: How defoliants expose the Viet Cong. *Army* 14(2):54–55. (Also in *Armed Forces Chem. J.* 18(1):5–6.)

Gruchow, Nancy. 1970. Curbs on 2,4,5,-T use imposed. *Science* 168:453, 24 April.

Huddle, F. P. 1969. *Technology assessment of the Vietnam defoliant matter: A case history.* U.S. House of Reps., Committee on Science and Astronautics. 73 pp.

Langer, Elinor. 1967. Chemical and biological warfare (II): The weapons and the policies. *Science* 155:299–303, 20 January.

McCarthy, Richard D. 1969. *The ultimate folly; War by pestilence, asphyxiation, and defoliation.* New York: Vintage Books. 176 pp. (See pp. 74–98 for discussion of defoliation.)

Mrak, E. M., et al. 1969. *Report of the secretary's commission on pesticides and their relationship to environmental health.* U.S. Dept. of Health, Education, and Welfare. 677 pp.

National Academy of Sciences. 1965. *Weed control.* Vol. 2. *Principles of plant and animal pest control.* NAS Publ. No. 1597. 471 pp.

Neilands, J. B. 1970. Vietnam: Progress of the chemical war. *Asian Surv.* 10(3):209–229.

Niering, W. A., and R. H. Goodwin. 1963. Creating new landscapes with herbicides. *Conn. Arboretum Bull.* 14:1–30.

Niering, W. A. 1968. The effects of pesticides. Pp. 101–122 in *Environmental problems,* ed. by B. R. Wilson. Philadelphia: Lippincott.

Orians, Gordon H., and E. W. Pfeiffer. 1970. Ecological effects of the war in Vietnam. *Science* 168:544–554, 1 May.

Price, Don K., et al. 1968. On the use of herbicides in Vietnam. *Science* 161:253–256, 19 July. Statements by members of the board of directors of the American Association for the Advancement of Science.

Rose, S., ed. 1969. *CBW: Chemical and biological warfare.* Boston: Beacon. 209 pp. (See especially pp. 62–98.)

Whiteside, Thomas. 1970. *Defoliation.* New York: Ballantine. 168 pp.

Wolfe, Martin. 1969. Using systemic fungicides. *New Scientist,* 11 December. Pp. 551–553.

EIGHT DESTRUCTION AND EXTINCTION OF ANIMALS BY MAN

Bermuda petrel.   Photo by David B. Wingate.

EIGHT DESTRUCTION AND EXTINCTION OF ANIMALS BY MAN

"A very widespread, perhaps worldwide, decline among many species of carnivorous birds is apparent. The pattern of decline is characterized by reduced success in reproduction correlated with the presence of residues of chlorinated hydrocarbon insecticides—primarily DDT. . . . A hundredth of our higher animals have become extinct since 1600 and nearly a fortieth are now in danger . . . It appears that only about a quarter of the species that have become extinct since 1600 may have died out naturally; humans, directly or indirectly, may be responsible for extermination of the rest."

INTRODUCTION

Can man, the animal, survive? This is a question of ultimate interest to everyone reading this book. Many of the kinds of environmental degradation that are documented in this book can, in extreme cases at least, either kill humans directly or make enduring human life impossible.

Stated another way, the question of man's survival is: Will we change our environment to the point that conditions generally exceed our environmental tolerance? All organisms have a range of environmental conditions which must be satisfied or they die. The very young, the old, and the infirm individuals of any population generally are most apt to be killed by environmental extremes, exemplified by the effects on man of intense air pollution episodes. If enough members of a population are killed or reproduction is insufficient, the population will fall below a certain viable level and eventually disappear entirely. In this way many species have become extinct.

Extinction is more than death. Death, of course, is a part of life; for every individual animal (except protozoans, which reproduce by fission) death is a natural part of the life cycle. Extinction, however, refers to the dying out or end of a species, the end of a population, the end of a line of evolution that may have developed over millions of years.

This part discusses destruction and extinction of animals. In the present destruction and reduction of animal populations we may be seeing extinction in the process of occurring. We cannot be sure, of course, until the last members of a species' population are snuffed out—the last dodo or the last passenger pigeon (Schorger, 1955). This uncertainty exists because all populations fluctuate in size and because some species may survive as very small populations for an extremely long time (e.g., the tuatara, a reptile that has persisted virtually unchanged for 200,000,000 years). However, the processes of extinction and the processes of destruction are the same. Extinction is merely complete destruction.

Five processes of destruction and extinction of animal populations are outlined by Fisher in Selection 46. In decreasing order of importance they are: (1) hunting (in which I would include war), (2) habitat disruption, usually by humans, (3) natural causes unrelated to man's actions, (4) introduced predators, and (5) other pressures from introduced animals. According to Fisher, three-quarters of the animals that have become extinct or reached the verge of extinction since 1600 have become so because of man (causes 1, 2, 4, and 5 above). To these five causes I would add chemical poisoning as a sixth, man-induced process.

The first four selections in this part illustrate the environmental effects of a major chemical contaminant, the pesticide

DDT. These four selections provide a sequence in tracing four major steps that pesticides may take through the environment and considering the biological effects at each step: *diffusion* of pesticides throughout the world (Selection 39), *concentration* upward in food chains (Selection 40), the *poisonous* (or "toxicological") *effects* of concentrations on animals near the top of food chains (Selection 41), and broader *ecological consequences* of pesticides (Selection 42).

There is an increasing number of other toxic chemicals in the environment which could be discussed here, but they follow many of the same environmental principles exemplified by pesticides—diffusion in the environment, concentration in organisms, and toxic effects at certain levels, for instance. References are given below to the serious environmental effects of contaminants such as mercury (Jernelöv, 1968), lead (Symposium on Lead Contamination, 1965), other heavy metals (Swedish Natural Science Council, 1969), radioactive materials (many references), polychlorinated biphenols (PCBs —Gustafson, 1970), fluorides (Merriman, 1967; Crocker, 1965), and other air pollutants (Catcott, 1961). The environmental importance, especially biological, of many of these substances, has been overlooked until recent years, partly because their presence (and thus their effects) has not even been looked for. The example of mercury is worth brief discussion here. The pervasiveness and insidious biological effects of mercury are now being documented because of a few dramatic events. Fungicides containing mercury are widely applied to grain seed; in the United States alone 800,000 pounds of mercury in pesticides are marketed yearly. In nature most mercurial compounds are finally converted into methyl-mercury, and this may accumulate in fish and shellfish. Human chromosome aberrations and death are consequences directly attributed to consumption of seafoods containing mercury in Sweden and Japan. It is known that mercurial residues can persist up to 100 years in polluted lakes (U.S. Department of Health, Education, and Welfare, 1969, p. 612).

The last four selections in this part treat processes of animal destruction by means other than chemical contamination. Selection 43 describes an interesting and important instance in which habitat destruction by man (blasting and dredging of coral reefs) apparently has triggered a population explosion of a sea star species. In turn, the sea star is a predator of living coral; numerous fringing coral reefs in the Pacific are now being rapidly destroyed. Hence, the complex repercussions of a once seemingly mild alteration of environment are well documented in this study.

Selection 44 excellently shows the complexity both of man's environmental actions and of the responses of fish populations in the Great Lakes. Here all the defined processes of extermination by man operate. Lake sturgeon were over-hunted almost to extinction. In Lake Erie the populations of whitefish, walleye, and some other fish have fallen drastically as water quality has deteriorated through pollution (see Beeton, Selection 19). Stocks of lake trout collapsed following the introduction of the sea lamprey, a vigorous-predator. And another introduced species, the small alewife, has come by competitive advantage to dominate the lakes.

One of the earliest severe modifications of environment by man is now thought to have been the decimation of many large animals by late-Pleistocene hunters. Thus, the foremost cause of extinction has a very long tradition. In Selection 45 Paul Martin presents evidence for this view. The chronology and geographic pattern of prehistoric man's spread throughout the world, used by Martin to support his thesis, also suggests that at this scale of space and time man might best be viewed as a self-introduced predator (process 4 above). Krantz (1970) proposes that habitat destruction (process 2 above) and competition for food supplies (included in 5 above) may have been more important mechanisms than direct overkill.

Although the destruction of vegetation has been widely discussed (see Part 7), the question of extinction of plant species is rarely raised (however, see Hepper, 1969, and Ehrenfeld, 1970, pp. 123–127).

What solutions are there to the problem of threatened species of animals? As Fisher points out in the final selection here, the remedy certainly is not zoos, which many people would advocate. Rather, we must seek to preserve the environmental qualities upon which threatened species depend. But this is becoming more and more difficult because of the increasing spatial scale, intensity, and kinds of man's environmental impacts. Will some contaminant, or combination of contaminants acting with synergistic reinforcement, threaten *us* as a species before we recognize its potence and can neutralize it by technology?

FURTHER READINGS

Abelson, P. H. 1970. Methyl mercury. *Science* 169(3942):237.

Åberg, B., and F. P. Hungate, ed. 1967. *Radio-ecological concentration processes.* Proc. Int. Symp., Stockholm, April 25–29, 1966. London: Pergamon Press. 1040 pp.

Alexander, Peter. 1965. *Atomic radiation and life.* 2d edition. Baltimore: Penguin Books. 296 pp.

American Chemical Society. 1970. *Radionuclides in the environment.* A symposium, San Francisco, April 1968. E. C. Freiling, Symposium chairman. Washington, D.C.: Advances in Chemistry Series, No. 93. 532 pp.

Bell, M. C. 1967. Airborne radionuclides and animals. Pp. 77–90 in *Agriculture and the quality of our environment,* ed. by N. C. Brady. Washington, D.C.: Amer. Assoc. Adv. Sci. Publ. 85.

Bugher, John C. 1956. Effects of fission material on air, soil, and living species. Pp. 831–848 in *Man's role in changing the face of the earth,* ed. by William L. Thomas, Jr. Chicago and London: The University of Chicago Press.

Carson, Rachel. 1962. *Silent spring.* Boston: Houghton-Mifflin.

Catcott, E. J. 1961. Effects of air pollution on animals. Pp. 221–231 in *Air pollution.* World Health Organization Monograph Series No. 46. New York: Columbia University Press.

Cole, L. C. 1964. Pesticides: A hazard to nature's equilibrium. *Journal of Public Health* 54:24–31.

Comar, C. L. 1962. Biological aspects of nuclear weapons. *Am. Sci.* 50:339–353.

Commoner, Barry. 1969. The unforeseen international ecologic boomerang, frail reeds in a harsh world. *Natural History* 78:44–45.

Crocker, T. D. 1965. In Polk and Hillsborough Counties, Florida. *Bull. Atomic Sci.* 21(6):17–19.

Ehrenfeld, D. W. 1970. *Biological conservation.* New York: Holt, Rinehart and Winston. 226 pp.

First European Congress on the Influence of Air Pollution on Plants and Animals, proceedings of. 1969. *Air Pollution.* The Netherlands, April 1968: Centre for Agricultural Publishing and Documentation, Wageningen.

Fisher, James, Noel Simon, and Jack Vincent. 1969. *Wildlife in danger.* New York: Viking Press. 368 pp. Authoritative account with delightful illustrations (many in color) of the animals, birds, and plants of the world that are threatened with extinction (see Selection 46).

Gofman, J. W., and A. R. Tamplin. 1970. Radiation: the invisible casualties. *Environment* 12(3):12–19, 49.

Graham, Frank, Jr. 1970. *Since silent spring.* Boston: Houghton-Mifflin. 334 pp.

Gustafson, C. G. 1970. PCB's—prevalent and persistent. *Environmental Science & Technology* 4(10):814–819.

Hepper, F. Nigel. 1969. The conservation of rare and vanishing species of plants. Pp. 353–360 in *Wildlife in danger,* ed. by James Fisher, Noel Simon, and Jack Vincent. New York: Viking Press.

International Union for the Conservation of Nature and Natural Resources. Survival Service Commission. 1966. *Red data book.* Lausanne, Switzerland. 2 vol. This is the ultimate published resource concerning endangered species; its loose leaves provide continual updating.

Jernelöv, A. 1968. The menace of mercury. *New Scientist* 40:627.

Krantz, G. S. 1970. Human activities and megafaunal extinctions. *Am. Sci.* 58(2):164–170.

Le Cren, E. D., and M. W. Holdgate, eds. 1962. *The exploitation of natural animal populations.* New York: Wiley.

Leopold, A. S. 1966. Adaptability of Animals to Habitat Change. Pp. 66–75 in *Future environments of North America,* ed. by F. F. Darling and J. P. Milton. Garden City, New York: The Natural History Press.

Lofroth, Goran. 1968. Pesticides and catastrophe. *New Scientist* 40:567–568.

Mathews, L. H. 1959. Man and the world's fauna. *The Advancement of Science* 16(62).

Merriman, G. M. 1967. Fluorides and other chemical pollutants affecting animals. Pp. 91–95 in *Agriculture and the quality of our environment,* ed. by N. C. Brady. Washington, D.C.: Amer. Assoc. Adv. Sci. Publ. 85.

Miller, M. W., and G. G. Berg, ed. 1969. *Chemical fallout—current research on persistent pesticides.* Springfield, Illinois: Charles C Thomas.

Miller, Robert W. 1969. Delayed radiation effects among Japanese survivors of the atomic bombs. Pp. 307–317 in *Biological implications of the nuclear age,* U.S. Atomic Energy Commission.

Moore, N. W., ed. 1966. Pesticides in the environment and their effects on wildlife. *Journal of Applied Ecology,* vol. 3 Supplement. 311 pp.

Moore, N. W. 1967. A synopsis of the pesticide problem. Pp. 75–129 in *Advances in ecological research,* volume 4, edited by J. B. Cragg. London: Academic Press (see Selections 42 and 50).

Nelson, Norton. 1969. Some biological effects of radiation in relation to other environmental agents. Pp. 223–230 in *Biological implications of the nuclear age,* U.S. Atomic Energy Commission.

Rudd, R. L. 1964. *Pesticides and the living landscape.* Madison, Wisconsin: University of Wisconsin Press. 320 pp. An excellent documented discussion of pesticides' environmental effects.

Sauer, Carl O. 1938. Theme of plant and animal destruction in economic history. *Journal of Farm Economics* 20:765–775. (Reprinted in *Land and life,* University of California Press, Paperback 132.)

Schorger, A. W. 1955. *The passenger pigeon, its*

natural history and extinction. Madison: University of Wisconsin Press. 424 pp.

Smith, C. L. 1965. Radiation hazard to man and animals from fallout in the Arctic. *Polar Record,* no. 81, pp. 709–716.

Stearns, F. W. 1967. Wildlife habitat in urban and suburban environments. *Trans. N. A. Wildlife and Nat. Res. Conf.* 32:61–69.

Swedish Natural Science Council. 1969. *Metals and ecology.* A symposium, Stockholm, March 1969. Ecological Research Committee, Bulletin No. 5. 69 pp.

Symposium of Environmental Lead Contamination, Washington, D.C. 1965. *Symposium on environmental lead contamination.* Washington: U.S. Department of Health, Education, and Welfare, 1966. Public Health Serivce. 176 pp.

Symposium on Lead. February 1964. *Archives of environmental health.*

U.S. Department of Health, Education, and Welfare. 1969. *Report of the Secretary's Commission on Pesticides and their relationship to environmental health.* Parts I and II. Washington, D.C.: U.S. Government Printing Office. 677 pp.

Van Cleave, H. J. 1935. Man meddles with nature. *Science Monthly* 40:339–348. General, reflects attitudes of 1930s.

Van Der Schalie, Henry. 1969. Man meddles with nature—Hawaiian style. *The Biologist* 51(4):136–145.

Waters, W. R. 1967. Perspectives of radioactive contamination in nuclear war. *Can. Med. Assn. Jour.* 96(4):200–203. Degrees of risk in different situations are compared.

Wolfe, Martin. 1969. Using systemic fungicides. *New Scientist* 44:551–553.

Woodwell, George M. 1967. Toxic substances and ecological cycles. *Sci. Am.* 216(3):24–31.

World Health Organization. 1970. *Health aspects of chemical and biological weapons.* Geneva. (United States distributor, American Public Health Association, New York.)

Ziswiler, Vinzenz. 1967. *Extinct and vanishing animals.* Rev. English ed. by F. and P. Bunnell. New York: Springer-Verlag. 133 pp. An excellent treatment of direct and indirect processes of animal extermination by man; includes lists of threatened and extinct animals.

CHLORINATED HYDROCARBON INSECTICIDES AND THE WORLD ECOSYSTEM

CHARLES F. WURSTER, JR.

Chlorinated hydrocarbon insecticides are now among the world's most widely distributed synthetic chemicals, and they contaminate a substantial part of the biosphere. Although their spread has occurred only since World War II, the degree of pollution continues to worsen because of continued high production and use and because of these chemicals' persistence in the environment.

DDT is among the most notable of pesticides, because of its great usage and potent effects. DDT production in the United States, constituting about one-half of the world production of chlorinated hydrocarbon insecticides, was 103 million pounds in 1967 (U.S. Department of Health, Education, and Welfare, 1969, p. 48). This was a slight decline from the previous few years—largely related to increasing foreign production and increasing resistance of insects to DDT. The latter phenomenon (see Selection 50) has spurred development of new pesticides. There are now in the United States some 900 active pesticide chemicals —including insecticides, herbicides, and fungicides—which are formulated into over 60,000 preparations. Of these, approximately 100 insecticides, or 1,000 formulations, are commonly used. The value of pesticides made in the United States, which produces 50 to 75 percent of all pesticides manufactured in the world, rose from 440 million dollars in 1964 to 12,000 million dollars in 1969 (op. cit., p. 46).

Pesticides are injected into the environment as dusts, sprays, aerosols, granules, pellets, and baits. Chlorinated hydrocarbons and other synthetic organic insecticides kill animals by attacking the nervous system and disrupting the transmission of nerve impulses.

Charles F. Wurster, Jr. (b. 1930), is assistant professor of biological sciences at the State University of New York at Stony Brook and chairman of the Scientists Advisory Committee of the Environmental Defense Fund. He was educated at Haverford College, the University of Delaware, and Stanford University (Ph.D. in organic chemistry, 1957). Before joining the faculty at Stony Brook in 1965, Wurster was a Fulbright Fellow (Innsbruck, 1957-1958), a research chemist at Monsanto Research Corporation (1959-1962), and a research associate at Dartmouth College (1962-1965). Much of his research has involved studies on the effects of DDT on nontarget organisms.

This article is reproduced from Biological Conservation 1(2):123-129, 1969, by courtesy of the author and Elsevier Publishing Company, Ltd.

It has become impossible for virtually all the earth's animals, including man, to avoid assimilation of a variety of pesticides, primarily by ingestion with food. In the United States, chlorinated organic pesticides are present at detectable levels in all human foods except some beverages (op. cit., p. 385). Even human milk has an average content of 0.1 to 0.2 parts of DDT-derived materials per million parts of whole milk; thus it is estimated that the average breast-fed baby ingests daily about 0.02 mg. of DDT-derived materials per kilogram of body weight—twice the acceptable daily intake recommended by the World Health Organization (op. cit., p. 374).

How do pesticides bear directly on human health? A recent inclusive study has concluded that on the basis of present knowledge (which is poor), the only unequivocal consequence of long-term exposure to persistent pesticides (such as DDT), at levels encountered by the general population, is the acquisition of residues in tissues and body fluids. No reliable study has revealed a causal association between the presence of these residues and human disease. But the fact that some pesticides produce cancer and birth defects in experimental mammals indicates cause for concern (op. cit., pp. 234–235). This is another example of man's wide adoption of a new technology before knowing many of the environmental consequences.

This selection is an excellent survey of how some insecticides (especially DDT) have gained their frightening ecological significance—how they are spread around the world, concentrate in food chains, destroy populations of animals, and upset ecological balances. Wurster has summarized: "The chlorinated hydrocarbon insecticides are now among the world's most widely distributed synthetic chemicals. They are dispersed throughout the environment in currents of air and water. The movement through an ecosystem is explained by their solubility characteristics and chemical stability, while their broad toxicity indicates a potential for biological effects on many kinds of organisms. The chlorinated hydrocarbons are seriously degrading biotic communities in many parts of the world." The emphasis in this selection, made largely by examples, is on the great extent to which these dangerous man-made chemicals now permeate the world ecosystem.

(Editor's comment)

During the past quarter-century, Man has subjected the Earth's biota to an increasing variety of chemical insults in the form of pollutants with molecular structures never before encountered by living organisms. Of the host of such contaminants, the chlorinated hydrocarbon insecticides are probably more widely distributed than any other synthetic chemicals, and have become one of the world's most serious pollution problems.

The residues of DDT seem to be almost everywhere: in soils never treated with insec-ticides (Cole et al., 1967); in birds and seals that never leave the Antarctic, even though DDT has never been used on that continent (Sladen et al., 1966); in most other animals and probably all humans (Woodwell et al., 1967; Quinby et al., 1965); in air, even of remote parts of the world (Risebrough et al., 1968); and they even come down in the rain (Abbott et al., 1965). And yet, after 25 years of use, the physiological mechanism of action for DDT is poorly understood, as are some of its other biological and ecological effects.

We are, in a sense, conducting a biological experiment of truly colossal proportions, using the entire world's biota as experimental organisms.

How will it all come out? No one knows! Clearly some parts of the experiment have gone sour, and the flow of bad news seems to increase as the data come in. But not all is mystery about these chemicals—there is also a very great deal that we do know about them.

History and Identities

DDT (1,1,1-trichloro-2,2-bis(p-chlorophenyl) ethane) was first made in 1874, but its insecticidal properties were not discovered until World War II (O'Brien, 1967). With a high toxicity, great persistence, and side-effects that were neither of concern nor well-understood at the time, DDT was the miracle insecticide that played a heroic and glamorous role in the war. After the war it quickly became a panacea for all insect problems, and usage greatly expanded.

Dieldrin came into use shortly after the war. It is a cyclodiene insecticide—a group that also includes Aldrin, Endrin, Isodrin, Telodrin, Heptachlor, and others (O'Brien, 1967). All of these are classified as chlorinated hydrocarbons, in that they contain primarily chlorine, hydrogen, and carbon.

As DDT has been the most widely used and extensively studied of the chlorinated hydrocarbons, and its residues are the most widespread within the environment, this paper will be concerned particularly with DDT and its metabolites; most other chlorinated hydrocarbons have similar properties, however, and should be expected to have comparable ecological effects.

Pertinent Biological, Chemical, and Physical Properties

In order to understand the movement and consequences of these materials within the natural environment, it is first necessary to know something of their properties.

Far from having a toxic action that is limited to the Class Insecta as is popularly supposed, the chlorinated hydrocarbons are highly toxic to a broad spectrum of living organisms. Toxicity is general throughout much of the animal kingdom, including the rest of the Arthropoda (e.g. lobsters, crabs, shrimp), Mollusca, Annelida, and the vertebrates—amphibians, reptiles, fish, birds, and mammals (Butler & Springer, 1963).

The cyclodienes are generally, though not invariably, considerably more toxic than DDT (O'Brien, 1967); all are nerve poisons. Their presence in the vicinity of the nerve axon may cause instability or spontaneous 'firing'; increased concentrations result in tremours or convulsions as the typical symptoms of acute poisoning in a diversity of organisms ranging from houseflies to men. In general, if an organism has nerves, the chlorinated hydrocarbons can kill it. In view of the breadth of their toxicity, these insecticides therefore may appropriately be termed *biocides*.

At sublethal concentrations, organisms show increased nervousness, hyperactivity, and various behavioural abnormalities (O'Brien, 1967; Ogilvie & Anderson, 1965; Warner et al., 1966). Recent studies have revealed another, more subtle mechanism of action—hepatic enzyme induction. The chlorinated hydrocarbons can induce liver enzymes to break down steroid sex-hormones (Conney, 1967; Kupfer, 1967), resulting in a hormonal imbalance that is potentially of very great ecological significance.

In the environment, the chlorinated hydrocarbons are very stable compounds, probably having a half-life of 10 to 15 years (Edwards, 1966; Nash & Woolson, 1967). Mechanisms for effectively metabolizing these exotic materials have apparently not been evolved. Some microorganisms can degrade them, but oxygen inhibits degradation (Guenzi & Beard, 1967). Certain tissues, particularly liver, can bring about gradual breakdown.

DDT is metabolized into DDE and DDD, and eventually into other compounds; unfortunately, DDE and DDD, though less toxic than DDT, are toxic nevertheless, and are also effective enzyme-inducers (Conney, 1967; Kupfer, 1967). Of all the chlorinated hydrocarbons, DDE is the most universally distributed in the environment.

The rates of disappearance of insecticides from treated areas are often studied by measuring their persisting residues (Nash & Woolson, 1967). That which doesn't remain obviously 'disappeared'—decomposed, maybe? Increasing evidence indicates that the materials simply went elsewhere. We shall see later where they went.

SOLUBILITY CHARACTERISTICS

DDT is insoluble in water—almost. Water is saturated with DDT at 1.2 parts per 10^9 (ppb), or a little over one part in a thousand million, making it one of the most insoluble organic substances known (Bowman et al., 1960). Dieldrin is nearly 100 times as soluble as DDT, but still must be considered almost insoluble in water (Edwards, 1966). Conversely, the chemicals are quite soluble in organic solvents (hexane, benzene, etc.) and in lipids (fats and fat-like materials). Other chlorinated hydrocarbons are similar in these respects. They are therefore invariably more soluble in any biological material—living or dead—than in water, as all biological material contains lipids. If we divide the biosphere into the inorganic (non-biological) and the organic (biological), then we must always expect the chlorinated hydrocarbons to 'flow' from the former into the latter.

Dispersal Mechanisms

The residual quality of the chlorinated hydrocarbons adds to their value as insecticides; but unfortunately, much of the material leaves the site of application. Dispersal through the environment is facilitated by a variety of transport mechanisms. Obviously the chemicals can travel about within mobile, living organisms. Despite their low water solubilities and vapour pressures (Edwards,

1966), large amounts can be carried in vast quantities of moving water and air. In addition, they readily form suspensions in both air and water (Bowman et al., 1964; Edwards, 1966). As many application procedures intentionally produce atomized droplets or particles, a substantial amount of the applied material passes into the atmosphere. Less than half the DDT sprayed from a plane may reach the target on the ground (Woodwell, 1961).

Escape into the air is further facilitated by codistillation with water; an aqueous suspension of a few ppb of DDT, for example, may lose more than half of its DDT to the air within 24 hours (Bowman et al., 1964). The compounds also adsorb to particulate matter (Edwards, 1966). Particulates from one water sample in California carried 78 ppm of DDT—at least 100,000 times the concentration within the water itself (J. O. Keith & Hunt, 1966).

It is clear, then, that these insecticides can be carried throughout much of the world by currents of water and air, and by organisms. Air transport is especially rapid; once in the air, these materials can circle the globe in a few weeks. Fallout from the air probably contributes about the same quantity of pesticides to the oceans as do major river systems (Risebrough et al., 1968).

Movement Through the Ecosystem

Because of their solubility characteristics, the chlorinated hydrocarbons will be absorbed from the environment by living organisms throughout the food-chain. This occurs by absorption through the gills of fish, through the skin, from the diet, and from the air via the lungs. Muds and other solids that are able to hold the chemicals by adsorption serve as reservoirs, feeding the chemicals into water as organisms remove them.

Living organisms therefore accumulate these residues and become contaminated—often from an environment that may appear relatively uncontaminated. For this reason some measures of environmental quality are misleading. One must analyze living organisms, rather than water, to monitor contamination of a river, lake, estuary, or ocean. Water and air are the transport media, yet contain only minute amounts of these chemicals.

Once these insecticides get into food-chains, something else happens—the phenomenon of biological concentration, often called biological 'magnification'. Each organism eats many organisms from the next lower trophic level. A robin, for example, eats many earthworms and a large fish eats many smaller fish. The food organisms are digested, metabolized, and excreted, but much of the insecticide is retained. The chemicals tend to stay and accumulate in biological material, the concentration depending on rates of intake and excretion. This concentration factor may vary from two or three to 100 or even 1000 between predator and prey. Chlorinated hydrocarbons are therefore not only funnelled into food-chains, but they are concentrated as they flow up the food-chain from one trophic level to the next. These mechanisms can, and often do, result in carnivorous organisms, especially birds, carrying residues at a concentration which is more than a million times greater than that of their environment (Woodwell et al., 1967).

The importance of chemical stability is that the chlorinated hydrocarbons retain their original broad toxicity even when they become far removed by both time and space from the point of application. Contamination of non-target organisms therefore may be potentially associated with biological effects on them.

Appreciating the properties of the chlorinated hydrocarbons allows some understanding of their behaviour in the environment. The following are some examples of the operation of these mechanisms in practice.

Residues in the Natural Environment

TERRESTRIAL ECOSYSTEMS

Dutch elm disease, DDT, and birds. The use of DDT in attempted control of Dutch elm disease is a clear and relatively simple example of food-chain contamination (D. H. Wurster et al., 1965). DDT is sprayed when the elms are leafless, but only a small fraction remains on the tree. The rest is either lost into the air or settles to the earth. That retained by the tree eventually also reaches the ground. Earthworms and other organisms that work the soil accumulate the DDT and become contaminated. Many species of ground-feeding birds eat the soil organisms, concentrate the DDT further, receive a lethal dose, and die with tremors.

Flying insects also become contaminated by contact with the trees and the soil—especially those emerging from soil-dwelling larvae. Insectivorous birds of the treetops thereby also become involved in this mass mortality. Sometimes American Robin (*Turdus migratorius*) mortality has been virtually complete, and birds of all species have been reduced by 90 per cent (Hunt, 1960). This dismal sequence has been repeated again and again during the past 20 years as hundreds, perhaps thousands, of municipalities in the eastern United States have killed millions of birds in this way.

The most unfortunate part of this story is that DDT is relatively ineffective in preventing the spread of Dutch elm disease. The best record for controlling this fungous disease has been achieved by the process of sanitation, *i.e.* the destruction of dead or dying elm branches and trees, which serve as breeding sites for the bark beetles that spread the Fungus (Matthysse, 1959).

DDT in New Brunswick. Wide areas of the coniferous forests of North America have been sprayed with DDT during the past decade to control the Spruce Budworm—especially in New Brunswick, Canada. This province also has excellent salmon streams, including the Miramichi River. Beginning in 1952, DDT applications caused severe, widespread losses of salmon, trout, and other fishes (Elson, 1967). In 1954, 0.5 lb of DDT/acre (0.56 kg/ha) was applied to the Miramichi watershed; not a single salmon fry was seen that year. Spraying at this dosage in other parts of New Brunswick generally reduced under-yearlings to 2–10 per cent, small parr to 30 per cent, and large parr to 50 per cent, of the numbers found in unsprayed streams. Harmful effects extended 30 or more miles (48 kilometres) below the spray zones.

Delayed mortality followed from four to six months after spraying with the onset of winter cold, killing many of the survivors. Reduced numbers of young salmon were followed in later years by fewer adults taken in fisheries and returning as spawners.

Effects of this programme were not restricted to fish. A single treatment changed the insect ecology of the area for at least three to four years (Ide, 1967). Initially there was a severe reduction in Arthropod stream fauna, including larvae and nymphs on which salmon feed. Small species, especially Blackflies, recovered rapidly, reaching large numbers later in the spray year. Larger species did not recover to their former numbers for several years.

DDT was also accumulated by earthworms, diet of the American Woodcock (*Philohela minor*). Woodcock tissues became contaminated, as did their eggs, and breeding success was inversely correlated with the quantity of DDT applied annually to the habitat (Wright, 1965).

Reproduction in carnivorous birds. Since the chlorinated hydrocarbons are concentrated as they ascend the food-chain, carnivorous birds at the top of this trophic structure reach the highest concentrations and face special problems. Effects may include, but not be limited to, direct mortality. In both Europe and North America there appears to be a pattern of diminished reproductive success among carnivorous birds that coincides with, and is probably caused by, their contamination with chlorinated hydrocarbons— especially DDT (C. F. Wurster, 1968*a*).

Effects that are so far removed in time and space from their cause are much less obvious and more difficult to study than mortality in residential areas, where birds may drop from the trees and Robins die on lawns. Ecologically, however, such sublethal effects may be vitally important to wild popula-

tions. Whole species are involved and they are in serious danger.

In North America, reproductive success of the Osprey (*Pandion haliaetus*) has declined sharply (Ames, 1966). A colony in Connecticut, its general habitat and other factors apparently unchanged, declined from 200 pairs in 1938 to 12 pairs in 1965. Their eggs contained 5.1 ppm of DDT residues, and productivity was 0.5 young per nest. Maryland birds with 3.0 ppm fledged 1.1 young per nest. Normal productivity is 2.2 to 2.5 young per nest. Ospreys are fish-hawks, and DDT residues in the fish eaten by Connecticut Ospreys proved to be from five to ten times higher than in the food of the Maryland birds.

Studies of the Peregrine Falcon (*Falco peregrinus*) in Europe, especially by Ratcliffe (1967) in Britain, reveal a widespread, rapid population decline that began during the early 1950s. The decline was characterized by egg breakage and egg eating by parent birds, abandonment of nests, and other abnormal breeding behaviour, and it coincided geographically and in time with the use of chlorinated hydrocarbon insecticides. Tissues and eggs contained DDE, Dieldrin, and Heptachlor epoxide.

In North America the Peregrine was not studied in this context, but recently it suddenly became evident that the breeding population in the eastern United States had become extinct since 1950 (Hickey, in press). Residue analyses are therefore unavailable, but the decline was also marked by abnormal behaviour (Herbert & Herbert, 1965).

Recently Ratcliffe (1967a) reported a highly significant, sudden, and widespread decrease in eggshell thickness and calcium content during 1946–50 in several British birds of prey, including the Peregrine. Shell thickness and calcium content were stable from 1900 to 1946, then declined by 7–25 per cent within a few years, with no recovery since then. The years of decline coincided exactly with the introduction of DDT into the world environment. Recent measurements of eggshells in museums by Hickey and Anderson (1968) show a similar and simultaneous effect in North America for the Peregrine, Osprey, and Bald Eagle (*Haliaetus leucocephalus*).

But what do eggshells have to do with DDT and reproduction? Probably quite a lot. In birds, increased absorption of calcium from the diet, decreased excretion, and deposition of calcium in bone marrow, are all mediated by estrogen, a steroid sex-hormone (Simkiss, 1961). The calcium in the marrow is then transported to the oviduct, where it becomes part of the eggshell. A subnormal estrogen level interrupts this crucial chain of events in the reproductive cycle. Recently Peakall (1967) showed that DDT and Dieldrin induced liver enzymes to break down steroid sex-hormones in pigeons. If in Nature these chemicals induce the liver of female birds to metabolize their own estrogen, then we can expect various hormonal disturbances and symptoms of calcium deficiency—including abnormal behaviour and thin eggshells. Exactly these symptoms have been observed among many species of carnivorous birds since introduction of the chlorinated hydrocarbons into the world environment.

AQUATIC ECOSYSTEMS

Biological concentration in action. In an aqueous environment the chlorinated hydrocarbons may contaminate virtually all organisms at all levels of the trophic structure. This has happened to the Lake Michigan ecosystem (Hickey *et al.*, 1966). DDT residues in bottom muds averaged 0.014 ppm; Amphipods contained 0.41 ppm, or nearly 30 times that of the mud. Several species of fish carried 3–6 ppm—10 times higher than the Amphipods—and Herring Gulls (*Larus argentatus*), with 99 ppm in muscle tissue, were some 20–30 times higher than the fish.

These gulls showed low breeding success and also behavioural abnormalities (J. A. Keith, 1966). Furthermore, they could not withstand stress. When starved, the birds developed tremors and died of DDT poisoning, whereas less contaminated gulls easily withstood this treatment (J. P. Ludwig, personal communication, 1968). Starvation depletes fat reserves that store DDT residues, thus releasing the toxins into vital tissues.

The Coho Salmon, being top carnivores, also accumulated residues in Lake Michigan, and these were passed into the eggs. Recently almost 700,000 salmon fry died shortly after hatching from these contaminated eggs (Johnson, 1968). The residues were in the egg-yolk, and the fry were poisoned during final absorption of the yolk-sac. Heavy mortality of trout fry occurred similarly in several New York lakes; for several years mortality of fry from Lake George was 100 per cent (Burdick *et at.*, 1964).

Clear Lake, California, offers another classic example of biological concentration. Additions of DDD at 14, 20, and 20 ppb to the water, the last in 1957, were followed by the dying of Western Grebes (*Aechmophorus occidentalis*), reduction of the nesting colony from 1,000 to 30 pairs by 1960, complete nesting failure among survivors for several years, and 500–1500 ppm of DDD in grebe fat (Herman *et al.*, 1968). In 1967, ten years after the last DDD treatment, the grebes still averaged 544 ppm of DDD in their fat, and the colony of 165 pairs still had very poor nesting success.

The base of the food chain. Effects are by no means limited to the top of the food pyramid. A few ppb of DDT in the water can decrease photosynthesis in certain marine phytoplankton (C. F. Wurster, 1968). Such single-celled Algae are the indispensable base of marine food-chains, responsible for more than half of the world's photosynthesis; interference with this process could have profound, worldwide biological implications.

Selective poisoning of certain planktonic Algae, and not others, could lead to an undesirable imbalance within the flora. A 'population explosion' of the favoured species might then occur, encouraged by eutrophication from sewage, runoff of agricultural fertilizers, and other sources of nutrients. This process may in part explain some of the 'unexplained' algal blooms of recent years within certain bodies of water (*e.g.* Lake Erie).

THE OCEANS

Dispersal mechanisms predict a net transfer of chlorinated hydrocarbons from the Earth's treated land areas to its ocean basins, where accumulation and build-up would be expected. Being so insoluble in water, however, we cannot expect them to 'get lost' in the oceans; they will be picked up by living organisms. Recent analyses of fish and birds from both the Atlantic and Pacific Oceans indicate that this process is occurring.

The Bermuda Petrel (*Pterodroma cahow*) is a rare oceanic bird of the North Atlantic that has no contact with any continent or area treated with insecticides. Yet its eggs and chicks averaged 6.4 ppm of DDT residues, and reproductive success has declined significantly since 1958 (C. F. Wurster & Wingate, 1968 [see Selection 41]). Only from its ocean food-chain could this bird become so contaminated.

There are more data from the Pacific, but the story is the same (Risebrough, 1968). Some sea-birds carried higher residues than the Bermuda Petrel. Various marine fish, including hake, mackerel, and tuna, contained 0.2 to 2.0 ppm of DDT residues—actually higher than those in the fish of many lakes with heavily-treated agricultural land in their watersheds. The implication is clear. The failure of salmon and trout to produce viable fry in Lake George and Lake Michigan may soon be repeated among some of the world's major marine fisheries—if it is not already occurring.

ONLY A LITTLE

Although residue concentrations generally are lower, susceptibility often is higher towards the lower end of food-chains. Toxic effects can therefore be anticipated at all levels in the trophic structure. Thus Brine-shrimps are almost unbelievably sensitive to DDT (Grosch, 1967); 39 per cent were killed within three weeks by a concentration of one part per trillion—1/1000th of a drop in a tank-car lot!

Temperature control mechanisms were upset in young salmon by a few ppb of DDT (Ogilvie & Anderson, 1965); this could cause the difference between life and death in a natural, competitive environment of wide temperature fluctuations. Oyster shell-growth was reduced (Butler, 1966), and nervous excitability of fish and amphibians increased, under the influence of chlorinated hydrocarbons that were present in the ppb range (Warner *et al.*, 1966; C. F. Wurster, unpublished). In sunfish, 1.68 ppb of Dieldrin reduced stamina and coordination, and increased oxygen consumption (Cairns & Scheier, 1964).

The Choice: Which Way from Here?

We have examined some of the side-effects of the chlorinated hydrocarbons—which often turned out to be the main effects. There are many more. A small library could be filled with documentation of environmental degradation by these chemicals.

Clearly the chlorinated hydrocarbon insecticides cannot continue to be used in the natural environment without serious degradation of the world ecosystem. Fortunately we have a choice. Many biological control techniques exist (Chant, 1966); numerous other less stable, more specific insecticides are available, particularly among the carbamates and organophosphates (O'Brien, 1967). These alternatives are highly effective. Man's control of pest populations requires ecological sanity. Which way will we go?

References

In the interest of brevity, documentation is far from exhaustive; instead, the reader is primarily guided to recent sources where additional references will be found.

Abbott, D. C., Harrison, R. B., Tatton, J. O'G. & Thomson, J. (1965). Organochlorine pesticides in the atmospheric environment. *Nature, London*, **208**, 1317–8.

Ames, P. L. (1966). DDT residues in the eggs of the Osprey in the north-eastern United States and their relation to nesting success. *J. Appl. Ecol.*, **3** (Suppl), 87–97.

Bowman, M. C., Acree, F. & Corbett, M. K. (1960). Solubility of carbon-14 DDT in water. *J. Agr. Food Chem.*, **8**, 406–8.

Bowman, M. C., Acree, F., Lofgren, C. S. & Beroza, M. (1964). Chlorinated insecticides: fate in aqueous suspensions containing mosquito larvae. *Science*, **146**, 1480–1.

Burdick, G. E., *et al.* (1964). The accumulation of DDT in lake trout and the effect on reproduction. *Trans. Am. Fish. Soc.*, **93**, 127–36.

Butler, P. A. (1966). Pesticides in the marine environment. *J. Appl. Ecol.*, **3** (Suppl.), 253–9.

Butler, P. A. & Springer, P. F. (1963). Pesticides—a new factor in coastal environments. *Trans. 28th North Amer. Wildl. Nat. Res. Conf.*, March. 4–6, pp. 378–90.

Cairns, J. & Scheier, A. (1964). The effect upon the Pumpkinseed Sunfish *Lepomis gibbosus* (Linn.) of chronic exposure to lethal and sublethal concentrations of Dieldrin. *Notulae Naturae*, No. 370, 1–10.

Chant, D. A. (1966). Integrated control systems. *Nat. Acad. Sci. Nat. Res. Council Publ.*, 1402, 193–218.

Cole, H., Barry, D., Frear, D. E. H. & Bradford, A. (1967). DDT levels in fish, streams, stream sediments, and soil before and after aerial spray application for Fall Cankerworm in northern Pennsylvania. *Bull. Environ. Contam. Toxicol.*, **2**, 127–46.

Conney, A. H. (1967). Pharmacological implications of microsomal enzyme induction. *Pharmacol. Rev.*, **19**, 327–66.

Edwards, C. A. (1966). Insecticide residues in soils. *Residue Rev.*, **13**, 83–132.

Elson, P. F. (1967). Effects on wild young salmon of spraying DDT over New Brunswick forests. *J. Fish. Res. Bd. Canada*, **24**, 731–67.

Grosch, D. S. (1967). Poisoning with DDT: effect on reproductive performance of *Artemia*. *Science*, **155**, 592–3.

Guenzi, W. D. & Beard, W. E. (1967). Anaerobic biodegradation of DDT to DDD in soil. *Science*, **156**, 1116–7.

Herbert, R. A. & Herbert, K. G. S. (1965). Behavior of Peregrine Falcons in the New York City region. *Auk*, **82**, 62–94.

Herman, S. G., Garrett, R. L. & Rudd, R. L. (1968). Pesticides and the Western Grebe. *First Rochester Conf. Toxicity, Univ. of Rochester*, 4–6 june.

Hickey, J. J. (Ed.) (in press). *Peregrine Falcon Populations, their Biology and Decline.* Univ. of Wisc. Press, Madison, in press for early in 1969.

Hickey, J. J. & Anderson, D. W. (1968). Chlorinated hydrocarbons and eggshell changes in raptorial and fish-eating birds. *Science*, **162**, 271–3.

Hickey, J. J., Keith, J. A. & Coon, F. B. (1966). An exploration of pesticides in a Lake Michigan ecosystem. *J. Appl. Ecol.*, **3** (Suppl.), 141–54.

Hunt, L. B. (1960). Songbird breeding populations in DDT-sprayed Dutch elm disease communities. *J. Wildl. Mgmt*, **24**, 139–46.

Ide, F. P. (1967). Effects of forest spraying with DDT on aquatic insects of salmon streams in New Brunswick. *J. Fish. Res. Bd Canada*, **24**, 769–805.

Johnson, H. (1968). Press release, Mich. State Univ., Mar. 7.

Keith, J. A. (1966). Reproductive success in a DDT-contaminated population of Herring Gulls. *J. Appl. Ecol.*, **3** (Suppl.), 57–70.

Keith, J. O. & Hunt, E. G. (1966). Levels of insecticide residues in fish and wildlife in California. *Trans. 31st North Amer. Wildl. Nat. Res. Conf.*, Mar. 14–16, pp. 150–77.

Kupfer, D. (1967). Effects of some pesticides and related compounds on steroid function and metabolism. *Residue Rev.*, **19**, 11–30.

Matthysse, J. G. (1959). An evaluation of mist blowing and sanitation in Dutch elm disease control programs. *Cornell Misc. Bull.*, **30**, N. Y. State Coll. Agr., Ithaca, N. Y., 16 pp.

Nash, R. G. & Woolson, E. A. (1967). Persistence of chlorinated hydrocarbon insecticides in soils. *Science*, **157**, 924–7.

O'Brien, R. D. (1967). *Insecticides, Action and Metabolism.* Academic Press, N. Y., 332 pp.

Ogilvie, D. M. & Anderson, J. M. (1965). Effect of DDT on temperature selection by young Atlantic Salmon, *Salmo salar*. *J. Fish. Res. Bd. Canada*, **22**, 503–12.

Peakall, D. B. (1967). Pesticide-induced enzyme breakdown of steroids in birds. *Nature, London*, **216**, 505–6.

Quinby, G. E., Hayes, W. J., Armstrong, J. F. & Durham, W. F. (1965). DDT storage in the U. S. population. *J. Am. Med. Assoc.*, **191**, 175–9.

Ratcliffe, D. A. (1967). The Peregrine situation in Great Britain 1965–66. *Bird Study*, **14**, 238–46.

Ratcliffe, D. A. (1967a). Decrease in eggshell weight in certain birds of prey. *Nature, London*, **215**, 208–10.

Risebrough, R. W. (1968). Chlorinated hydrocarbons in marine ecosystems. *First Rochester Conf. Toxicity, Univ. of Rochester*, 4–6 June.

Risebrough, R. W., Huggett, R. J., Griffin, J. J. & Goldberg, E. D. (1968). Pesticides: transatlantic movements in the northeast trades. *Science*, **159**, 1233–6.

Simkiss, K. (1961). Calcium metabolism and avian reproduction. *Biol. Rev.*, **36**, 321–67.

Sladen, W. J. L., Menzie, C. M. & Reichel, W. L. (1966). DDT residues in Adelie Penguins and a Crabeater Seal from Antarctica: ecological implications. *Nature, London*, **210**, 670–3.

Warner, R. E., Peterson, K. K. & Borgman, L. (1966). Behavioural pathology in fish: a quantitative study of sublethal pesticide toxication. *J. Appl. Ecol.*, **3** (Suppl.), 223–47.

Woodwell, G. M. (1961). The persistence of DDT in a forest soil. *Forest Sci.*, **7**, 194–6.

Woodwell, G. M., Wurster, C. F. & Isaacson, P. A. (1967). DDT residues in an East Coast estuary: a case of biological concentration of a persistent insecticide. *Science*, **156**, 821–4.

Wright, B. S. (1965). Some effects of Heptachlor and DDT on New Brunswick Woodcocks. *J. Wildl. Mgmt*, **29**, 172–85.

Wurster, C. F. (1968). DDT reduces photosynthesis by marine phytoplankton. *Science,* **159,** 1474–5.

Wurster, C. F. (1968*a*). Chlorinated hydrocarbon insecticides and avian reproduction: how are they related? *First Rochester Conf. Toxicity, Univ. of Rochester,* June 4–6.

Wurster, C. F. & Wingate, D. B. (1968). DDT residues and declining reproduction in the Bermuda Petrel. *Science,* **159,** 979–81.

Wurster, D. H., Wurster, C. F. & Strickland, W. N. (1965). Bird mortality following DDT spray for Dutch elm disease. *Ecology,* **46,** 488–99.

ADDITIONAL REFERENCES

Alexander, Martin. 1967. The breakdown of pesticides in soils. Pp. 331–342 in *Agriculture and the quality of our environment,* ed. by N. C. Brady. Washington, D.C.: Amer. Assoc. Adv. Sci., Publ. 85.

Cohen, J. M., and Cecil Pinkerton. 1966. Widespread translocation of pesticides by air transport and rain-out. Pp. 163–176 in *Organic pesticides in the environment.* Advances in Chemistry, Number 60. Washington, D.C.: American Chemical Society.

Edwards, C. A. 1969. Soil pollutants and soil animals. *Sci. Am.* 220(4):88–92, 97–99.

Frost, Justin. 1969. Earth, air, water. *Environment* 11(6):14–33. Reviews evidence for atmospheric transport of chlorinated hydrocarbons.

Iverson, Leo G. K. 1967. Monitoring of pesticide content in water in selected areas of the United States. Pp. 157–162. in *Agriculture and the quality of our environment,* ed. by N. C. Brady. Washington, D.C.: Amer. Assoc. Adv. Sci., Publ. 85.

Sheets, T. J. 1967. The extent and seriousness of pesticide buildup in soils. Pp. 311–330 in *Agriculture and the quality of our environment,* ed. by N. C. Brady. Washington, D.C.: Amer. Assoc. Adv. Sci., Publ. 85.

Stickel, L. F. 1968. Organochlorine pesticides in the environment. *U.S. Department Interior special scientific report wildlife* 119. 31 pp.

Tarrant, K. R., and J. O'G. Tatton. 1968. Organochlorine pesticides in rainwater in the British Isles. *Nature* 219:725–727.

U.S. Department of Health, Education, and Welfare. 1969. *Report of the Secretary's Commission on Pesticides and their relationship to environmental health.* Parts I and II. Washington, D.C.: U.S. Government Printing Office. 677 pp.

Woodwell, G. M. 1968. *Persistent pesticides: The world burden.* Report for National Research Council, Committee on Persistent Pesticides. Washington, D.C. 5 pp.

DDT RESIDUES IN AN EAST COAST ESTUARY

GEORGE M. WOODWELL, CHARLES F. WURSTER, JR.,
AND PETER A. ISAACSON

Man tends not to worry about poisons that become thinly spread out in the environment, diluted over space by cleaner air and water. Will not nature, after all, cleanse itself of them?

Frequently not, for (as pointed out in the previous selection) ecological mechanisms can concentrate persistent insecticides many thousands of times. This selection clearly illustrates by example how DDT and its residues (which are products of the partial breakdown of DDT) can undergo biological magnification in food chains. The authors' studies of a salt marsh on the east coast of the United States show that the higher the level of an organism in the food chain (or "trophic level"), the greater is the concentration. Thus, carnivorous birds near the top of marsh food chains have concentrations of DDT residues about a million times greater than the nearly imperceptible concentrations in the water.

DDT residues in the soil of the salt marsh, located on the south shore of Long Island, averaged 13 pounds per acre. A systematic sampling of various organisms living there showed concentrations of DDT increasing with trophic level from 0.04 part per million in plankton to 75 parts per million in a ring-billed gull. Highest concentrations occurred in scavenging and carnivorous fish and birds, although birds had 10 to 100 times more than fish. These concentrations approach those in animals dying from DDT poisoning, which suggests that many natural

George M. Woodwell (b. 1928), an ecologist, has been associated with Brookhaven National Laboratory since 1961. He holds degrees from Dartmouth College and Duke University (Ph.D., botany, 1958). Woodwell does research on the structure and function of ecosystems, with emphasis on the effects of ionizing radiation and other toxins. Charles F. Wurster, Jr., is a member of the faculty at the State University of New York at Stony Brook (see biographical note on p. 555). Peter A. Isaacson is a technical staff specialist with the Bureau of Sport Fisheries and Wildlife, U.S. Department of the Interior, Washington. He is studying the effects of nuclear and hydroelectric power developments on fish and wildlife.

This selection is reprinted with the kind permission of the authors from *Science* 156(3776):821–824, 1967, where it appeared under the title "DDT Residues in an East Coast Estuary: A Case of Biological Concentration of a Persistent Insecticide." Copyright 1967 by the American Association for the Advancement of Science.

populations in this area are now being affected, possibly limited, by DDT residues. Studies elsewhere report similar concentrations, demonstrating the generality and importance of biological concentration processes.

This selection further provides the reader with insight into how scientists investigate environmental contamination and its effects.

(Editor's comment)

DDT residues (*1*) have become an intrinsic part of the biological, geological, and chemical cycles of the earth (*2*) and are measurable in air (*3*), water (*4*), soil (*5*), man (*6*), and even in animals from the Antarctic, many hundreds of miles from places where DDT has been applied (*7, 8*). While the presence of residues does not prove an effect on living systems, the world-wide distribution of a substance as persistent and broadly toxic as DDT is itself reason to question whether residues are accumulating to toxic levels in certain populations. Accumulation occurs either through direct absorption from the environment or by concentration along food chains, and this latter phenomenon has been documented in several aquatic situations (*9*). Such accumulations have been correlated with recent declines in populations of carnivorous birds (*8, 10*) and other organisms. Residues of persistent pesticides are now so widespread that they must be considered as potentially aggravating the problems of eutrophication by degrading populations of consumers.

We measured residues of DDT in the soils of a brackish marsh on the south shore of Long Island, New York, and in various organisms from the area. Results showed a high concentration of residues in the marsh and a systematic increase in DDT residues with increase in trophic level, thus providing an especially clear example of what has been called "biological magnification." In many cases the concentrations approached those in organisms known to have died of DDT poisoning, which suggests that DDT residues are currently reducing certain animal populations within the estuary.

The marsh from which soil samples were taken was at the mouth of Carmans River

at the eastern end of Great South Bay, Long Island. The area was selected as representative of relatively undisturbed marsh. The marsh along the western side of the river was sampled by a modification of the technique described by Woodwell and Martin (*5*). A "sample" consisted of six subsamples, each subsample being a core 4.8 cm in diameter and either 20 or 40 cm long, taken with a sharpened aluminum tube pressed into the soil. In each area of interest, subsamples were collected systematically about 10 m apart. Seven such samples were taken, four in the *Spartina patens* marsh, two along the margins of drainage ditches dug for mosquito control, and one from the bottom of the estuarine bay a few meters from the edge of the marsh.

For DDT analyses, 2-cm increments from equal depths among the six subsamples were pooled. Analyses were performed on the increments from 0 to 2, 4 to 6, 8 to 10, and 18 to 20 cm, and where deeper samples were taken, 38 to 40 cm. Total residues were calculated on a weight-per-area basis by integrating the area under the curve expressing residues per square meter at the various depths.

Plankton were collected in a No. 6 (0.239-mm mesh) plankton net. All organisms were living when taken except as indicated; fish were netted; birds were shot. Samples were stored frozen until analyzed, and mud samples were oven-dried before analysis. In most cases, whole organisms were analyzed, but feathers, beaks, feet, and wing tips of birds were discarded. Analyses were on 1-g samples of the homogenized organism. Extraction was from Florisil with petroleum ether–diethyl ether as described by Cummings *et al.* (*11*). Analyses of samples to which measured quantities of DDT, DDE, and DDD, individually, had been added prior to extraction indicated recoveries averaging 96 percent. Analyses for DDT, DDE, and DDD were by electron-capture gas chromatography; certain identifications were confirmed by thin-layer chromatography (*11*).

Residues of DDT in the *Spartina* marsh varied widely from less than 3 to more than 32 lb/acre (Table 40.1) The mean concentration of the four samples from this marsh (each a composite of 6 cores) was 13.1 lb/acre. Slightly lower quantities occurred along the ditches, but total residues were still 1 to 5 lb/acre; submerged bay bottom contained 0.28 lb/acre. In all of these samples most of the residues (approximately 90 percent) occurred in the upper 4 cm of the profile. Residues were highly variable in relative proportions of DDT, DDE, and DDD. In general there was an increase in DDT, with increase in depth. In the 0- to 2-cm samples, the mean DDE content was about 25 percent; in the 18- to 20-cm samples it was about 60 percent. Residues in the bottom of the bay contained only traces of DDT and DDD, the principal residue being DDE.

Thirty-nine samples of plants and animals from the vicinity were analyzed. Arrangement of the samples in sequence according to increasing concentration of DDT residues (Table 40.2) shows a progression according to both size and trophic level, larger organisms and higher carnivores having greater concentrations than smaller organisms and organisms at lower trophic levels. Total residues ranged through three orders of magnitude from 0.04 part per million (ppm) in plankton to 75 ppm in a ring-billed gull. Shrimp contained 0.16 ppm; eels, 0.28; insects from the marsh, 0.30; and mummichogs (*Fundulus*), 1.24 ppm. Among fish, the needle-fish, a carnivore, had the highest content, 2.07 ppm, about twice that of *Fundulus,* which forms part of its food. In general, the concentrations of DDT residues in carnivorous birds were 10 to 100 times those in the fish on which they feed. Concentrations

TABLE 40.1 DDT residues (DDT + DDE + DDD) (*1*) in Carmans River marsh and in the bottom mud of Great South Bay, N.Y., August 1966. Each sample was a composite of six subsamples, taken to the depths indicated.

ZONE	SAMPLE NO.	DEPTH (CM)		TOTAL RESIDUES	
				Lb/ acre	Kg/ ha
Spartina mat	1	0–20		2.69	3.01
	2	0–40		9.23	10.3
	3	0–20		7.86	8.81
	4	0–40		32.6	36.5
			Mean	13.1	14.7
Drainage ditch	1	0–20		4.63	5.19
	2	0–40		1.10	1.23
			Mean	2.87	3.21
Bay bottom (submerged)		0–40		0.28	0.31

of DDT in the waters of Great South Bay must be assumed to be less than the 0.0012-ppm saturation limit, a reasonable estimate probably being closer to 0.00005 ppm (*4, 12*). Based on this estimate, birds near the top of these food chains have concentrations of DDT residues about a million times greater than the concentration in the water.

The shift in relative proportions of DDT, DDE, and DDD with progression in trophic level is also conspicuous. Organisms containing high proportions of DDT, as opposed to its metabolites, are common at lower trophic levels; at upper levels, most of the residue is DDE. In most organisms, DDD and DDE are somewhat less toxic than DDT.

The secondary effects of applications of DDT to marshes, streams, and forests are the subject of an extensive literature. Single applications in the range of 0.1 to 0.3 lb/acre have repeatedly caused drastic reductions in populations of crayfish, shrimp, amphipods, isopods, annelids, fish, fiddler crabs, blue crabs, and others, sometimes with no recovery for years (*13*). Aerial spraying with 0.5 lb of DDT per acre in New Brunswick, Canada, caused extremely high mortality of young salmon, reduced salmon food organisms, and

TABLE 40.2 DDT residues (DDT + DDE + DDD) (1) in samples from Carmans River estuary and vicinity, Long Island, N.Y., in parts per million wet weight of the whole organism, with the proportions of DDT, DDE, and DDD expressed as a percentage of the total. Letters in parentheses designate replicate samples.

SAMPLE	DDT RESIDUES (PPM)	PERCENTAGE OF RESIDUE AS		
		DDT	DDE	DDD
Water*	0.00005			
Plankton, mostly zooplankton	.040	25	75	Trace
Cladophora gracilis	.083	56	28	16
Shrimp†	.16	16	58	26
Opsanus tau, oyster toadfish (immature)†	.17	None	100	Trace
Menidia menidia, Atlantic silverside†	.23	17	48	35
Crickets†	.23	62	19	19
Nassarius obsoletus, mud snail†	.26	18	39	43
Gasterosteus aculeatus, threespine stickleback†	.26	24	51	25
Anguilla rostrata, American eel (immature)†	.28	29	43	28
Flying insects, mostly Diptera†	.30	16	44	40
Spartina patens, shoots	.33	58	26	16
Mercenaria mercenaria, hard clam†	.42	71	17	12
Cyprinodon variegatus, sheepshead minnow†	.94	12	20	68
Anas rubripes, black duck	1.07	43	46	11
Fundulus heteroclitus, mummichog†	1.24	58	18	24
Paralichthys dentatus, summer flounder‡	1.28	28	44	28
Esox niger, chain pickerel	1.33	34	26	40
Larus argentatus, herring gull, brain (d)	1.48	24	61	15
Strongylura marina, Atlantic needlefish	2.07	21	28	51
Spartina patens, roots	2.80	31	57	12
Sterna hirundo, common tern (a)	3.15	17	67	16
Sterna hirundo, common tern (b)	3.42	21	58	21
Butorides virescens, green heron (a) (immature, found dead)	3.51	20	57	23
Larus argentatus, herring gull (immature) (a)	3.52	18	73	9
Butorides virescens, green heron (b)	3.57	8	70	22
Larus argentatus, herring gull, brain§ (e)	4.56	22	67	11
Sterna albifrons, least tern (a)	4.75	14	71	15
Sterna hirundo, common tern (c)	5.17	17	55	28
Larus argentatus, herring gull (immature) (b)	5.43	18	71	11
Larus argentatus, herring gull (immature) (c)	5.53	25	62	13
Sterna albifrons, least tern (b)	6.40	17	68	15
Sterna hirundo, common tern (five abandoned eggs)	7.13	23	50	27
Larus argentatus, herring gull (d)	7.53	19	70	11
Larus argentatus, herring gull§ (e)	9.60	22	71	7
Pandion haliaetus, osprey (one abandoned egg)‖	13.8	15	64	21
Larus argentatus, herring gull (f)	18.5	30	56	14
Mergus serrator, red-breasted merganser (1964)‡	22.8	28	65	7
Phalacrocorax auritus, double-crested cormorant (immature)	26.4	12	75	13
Larus delawarensis, ring-billed gull (immature)	75.5	15	71	14

* Estimated from Weaver *et al.* (4). † Composite sample of more than one individual. ‡ From Captree Island, 20 miles (32 km) WSW of study area. § Found moribund and emaciated, north shore of Long Island. ‖ From Gardiners Island, Long Island.

was correlated with reduced reproductive success in woodcock (*14, 15*). Applications of 1 to 5 lb/acre are known to have serious long-term effects on amphibians, fish, and birds (*16–18*).

While it is not true that residues distributed through 4 cm of highly organic soil are continuously available to the biota in the same degree as immediately after spraying, there is little question that residues in soil are leached by water, moved by erosion, and absorbed by mud-dwelling and mud-scavenging organisms. As a result of such processes, DDT residues in a marsh inevitably enter environmental cycles. Deleterious effects on wildlife from 13 lb/acre on the Carmans River marsh might therefore be expected. Detailed long-term observations have shown substantial reductions during the past decade in local populations of shrimp, amphipods, summer flounder, blue crab (*Callinectes sapidus*), spring peeper (*Hyla crucifer*), Fowler's toad (*Bufo woodhousei fowleri*), woodcock (*Philohela minor*), and various other species, known to be sensitive to DDT, that are indigenous to this area (*13–19*). Other aspects of human disturbance unquestionably contribute to degradation of estuaries, but do not offer adequate explanations for all of these declines. This is especially true for declines in populations indigenous to marshes that have been remote from other disturbances (*19*).

The concentration of DDT residues that affect animals in nature is difficult to appraise. Analyses of whole organisms, rather than of specific organs, are most representative of the degree of exposure to DDT, although correlation of such measurements with death is not precise. Nevertheless, broad correlations exist between whole-body concentrations and mortality (*20*) and are useful in appraising the hazards of residues in the estuary we sampled. For instance, fish of several species, known to have been killed by DDT, contained whole-body concentrations of 1 to 26 ppm, commonly averaging 4 to 7 ppm (*18, 21*); the concentrations reported for living fish in Table 40.2 lie between 0.17 and 2.07 ppm, within and somewhat below this apparently lethal region. Birds known to have died of DDT poisoning contained 30 to 295 ppm of DDT residues when analyzed as whole birds, the average for several species being about 112 ppm (*17*); the birds in our sample contained residues ranging from 1 to 75 ppm.

Living birds and fish that were analyzed in this study contained DDT residues that exceed one tenth of the mean concentrations in organisms known to have died of acute exposures to DDT. This in itself implies that concentrations of DDT in this food web are approaching the maximum levels observable in living organisms and now occasionally reach acutely lethal levels in both birds and fish. Two observations lead to this conclusion: (i) the trophic-level effect has been shown to produce concentrations in carnivorous birds and fish that are 10 to 1000 times the concentrations lower in the food web. We must assume that, although we have sampled fish-eating carnivorous birds such as the merganser, carnivorous or scavenging birds feeding on birds would have even higher levels, probably by as much as another 10-fold. Such birds probably would not survive. (ii) Perhaps even more important because it occurs at all trophic levels, great variability characterizes the total amounts of residues in animals from the wild. Differences in the range of 5- to 10-fold can be expected between the minimum and maximum concentrations in birds of a single species killed under similar conditions by DDT (*17*). While the causes of such variability are not clear, its existence implies that mortality from DDT residues is now occurring in these populations through elimination of individuals at the upper end of the range of concentrations. This constant attrition or "cropping" process would be extremely difficult to detect, since it does not produce spectacular "kills," and dead individuals, widely scattered, tend to disappear rapidly (*17, 22*). The probability appears high that not only are the populations of many of the organisms of this sampling now being affected by accumulation of DDT residues, but that other species in the area have already been depleted to the point where study is difficult or impossible.

Acute mortality, however, is but one effect of DDT. Sublethal concentrations, although studied less, may actually have more important effects on populations in nature. In the laboratory, sublethal amounts of DDT reduce reproductive success in bobwhite, ring-necked pheasants, and mice (*23*). Evidence has linked chlorinated hydrocarbon residues with reduced reproduction in field populations of trout (24), osprey, woodcock, bald (25) and golden eagles, peregrine falcon, and others (8, 10, 15). Serious population declines have occurred for some of these species. Minute quantities of chlorinated hydrocarbons affect the patterns of behavior of goldfish and upset temperature-regulating mechanisms in salmon (26). Such sublethal effects might be expected within the populations represented in Table 40.2.

One important conclusion is that analyses of water have limited meaning when evaluating the effects of DDT residues on animal populations. Water can be expected to contain a lower concentration of DDT than other components of an ecosystem—quantities that are usually vanishingly small or "nondetect-able" (4). Even these very low concentrations may be important because natural mechanisms can concentrate residues many thousands of times. A better criterion of hazard from DDT pollution would be analyses of carnivores or other organisms that concentrate the residues.

Concentrations of DDT residues reported here are not unique to this marsh or even to Long Island. Observations from widely scattered fish and bird populations in North America show concentrations approximating those reported here (8, 9), which suggests that DDT residues are moving through the biological, geological, and chemical cycles of the earth at concentrations that are having far-reaching and little-known effects on ecological systems.

References and Notes

1. DDT residues include DDT and its decay products (metabolites), DDE and DDD; DDT, 1,1,1-trichloro-2,2-bis(p-chlorophenyl)ethane; DDE, 1,-1-dichloro-2,2-bis(p-chlorophenyl)ethylene; also known as TDE, 1,1-dichloro-2,2-bis(p-chlorophenyl) ethane.
2. G. M. Woodwell, *Sci. Amer.* **216**, 24 (March 1967).
3. P. Antommaria, M. Corn, L. DeMaio, *Science* **150**, 1476 (1965); G. M. Woodwell, *Forest Sci.* **7**, 194 (1961).
4. L. Weaver, C. G. Gunnerson, A. W. Breidenbach, J. J. Lichtenberg, *Public Health Rep.* **80**, 481 (1965).
5. C. A. Edwards, *Residue Rev.* **13**, 83 (1966); G. M. Woodwell and F. T. Martin, *Science* **145**, 481 (1964).
6. G. E. Quinby, W. J. Hayes, Jr., J. F. Armstrong, W. F. Durham, *J. Amer. Med. Ass.* **191**, 175 (1965).
7. W. J. L. Sladen, C. M. Menzie, W. L. Reichel, *Nature* **210**, 670 (1966); J. L. George and D. E. H. Frear, *J. Appl. Ecol.* **3** (suppl.), 155 (1966).
8. "The effects of pesticides on fish and wildlife," *U.S. Fish and Wildlife Service Circ.* 226 (1965); "Pesticides in the environment and their effects on wildlife," *J. Appl. Ecol.* **3** (suppl.) (1966).
9. E. G. Hunt and A. I. Bischoff, *Calif. Fish and Game* **46**, 91 (1960); J. J. Hickey, J. A. Keith, F. B. Coon, *J. Appl. Ecol.* **3** (suppl.), 141 (1966); J. O. Keith, *ibid.*, p. 71; E. G. Hunt, *Scientific Aspects of Pest Control* (Nat. Acad. Sci.-Nat. Res. Council, Publ. No. 1402, 1966), p. 251.
10. P. L. Ames, *J. Appl. Ecol.* **3** (suppl.), 87 (1966); I. Prestt, *ibid.,* p. 107; S. Cramp, *Brit. Birds* **56**, 124 (1963); J. D. Lockie and D. A. Ratcliffe, *ibid.* **57**, 89 (1964); D. A. Ratcliffe, *ibid.* **58**, 65 (1965); D.

A. Ratcliffe, *Bird Study* **12**, 66 (1965); A. Sprunt, *Audubon Mag.* **65**, 32 (1963).
11. J. G. Cummings, K. T. Zee, V. Turner, F. Quinn, R. E. Cook, *J. Ass. Offic. Anal. Chemists* **49**, 354 (1966); M. F. Kovacs, Jr., *ibid.*, p. 365.
12. M. C. Bowman, F. Acree, Jr., M. K. Corbett, *J. Agr. Food Chem.* **8**, 406 (1960).
13. H. H. Ross and W. Tietz, Jr., *Illinois Nat. Hist. Surv.* (1949) (mimeographed); P. F. Springer, *Proc. 50th Annu. Mtg. N.J. Mosquito Extermination Ass.* (1963), pp. 194–203; P. A. Butler and P. F. Springer, *Trans. 28th North American Wildlife and Natural Resources Conf.* (1963), pp. 378–390; P. F. Springer, *Diss. Abstr.* **22**, 1777 (1961); P. F. Springer and J. R. Webster, *Mosquito News* **11**, 67 (1951); R. A. Croker and A. J. Wilson, *Trans. Amer. Fish. Soc.* **94**, 152 (1965); A. D. Hess and G. G. Keener, Jr., *J. Wildlife Management* **11**, 1 (1947); J. L. George, R. F. Darsie, Jr., P. F. Springer, *ibid.* **21**, 42 (1957).
14. M. H. A. Keenleyside, *Can. Fish Cult. No. 14,* 17 (1959); F. P. Ide, *Trans. Amer. Fish. Soc.* **86**, 208 (1956).
15. B. S. Wright, *J. Wildlife Management* **29**, 172 (1965).
16. B. A. Fashingbauer, *Flicker* **29**, 160 (1957); R. J. Barker, *J. Wildlife Management* **22**, 269 (1958); P. Goodrum, W. P. Baldwin, J. W. Aldrich, *ibid.* **13**, 1 (1949); C. S. Robbins, P. F. Springer, C. G. Webster, *ibid.* **15**, 213 (1951); L. B. Hunt, *ibid.* **24**, 139 (1960); G. J. Wallace and E. A. Boykins, *Jack-Pine Warbler* **43**, 13 (1965); R. B. Anderson and W. H. Everhart, *Trans. Amer. Fish. Soc.* **95**, 160 (1966); R. L. Rudd, *Pesticides and the Living Landscape* (Univ. of Wisconsin Press, Madison, 1964).

17. C. F. Wurster, Jr., D. H. Wurster, W. N. Strickland, *Science* **148**, 90 (1965); D. H. Wurster, C. F. Wurster, Jr., W. N. Strickland, *Ecology* **46**, 488 (1965).

18. K. Warner and O. C. Fenderson, *J. Wildlife Management* **26**, 86 (1962).

19. Long-term field studies by D. Puleston and A. P. Cooley, many of them specifically covering the Carmans River marsh and documented in personal notes kept over more than 20 years, show the decline or disappearance of these and many other populations, including American bittern, *Botaurus lentiginosus,* least bittern, *Ixobrychus exilis,* green heron, and marsh hawk, *Circus cyaneus.* During this period the physical characteristics of the marsh have remained largely unchanged.

20. DDT and its residues are nerve toxins; when DDT is suspected as a cause of death in vertebrates, the best appraisal is by analyses of residue concentrations in the brain [W. E. Dale, T. B. Gaines, W. J. Hayes, Jr., G. W. Pearce, *Science* **142**, 1474 (1963); L. F. Strickel, W. H. Stickel, R. Christensen, *ibid.* **151**, 1549 (1966)]. However, DDT residues can be stored in adipose tissues for long periods without conspicuous effects; symptoms occur when fat reserves are utilized, redistributing the toxin [R. F. Bernard, *Mich. State Univ. Mus. Publ. Biol. Ser.* **2**(3), 155 (1963)]. In many species of birds, for example, fat reserves are utilized during reproduction and migration. Because of the accumulation of residues in other tissues, analyses of whole bodies appears to be a better criterion of exposure to DDT and of its hazard to the organism than analyses of brain tissues alone.

21. A. V. Holden, *Ann. Appl. Biol.* **50**, 467 (1962); F. H. Premdas and J. M. Anderson, *J. Fish. Res. Board Can.* **20**, 827 (1963); D. Allison, B. J. Kallman, O. B. Cope, C. C. Van Valin, *Science* **142**, 139 (1963).

22. W. Rosene, Jr., and D. W. Lay, *J. Wildlife Management* **27**, 139 (1963).

23. J. B. DeWitt, *J. Agr. Food Chem.* **3**, 672 (1955); *ibid.* **4**, 863 (1956); R. E. Genelly and R. L. Rudd, *Auk* **73**, 529 (1956); R. F. Bernard and R. A. Gaertner, *J. Mammal.* **45**, 272 (1964).

24. G. E. Burdick *et al., Trans. Amer. Fish. Soc.* **93**, 127 (1964).

25. On the basis of 61 specimens taken from many parts of the United States, the bald eagle averages 11 ppm of DDT residues in breast muscle, a quantity probably approaching lethal concentrations (*8*).

26. R. E. Warner, K. K. Peterson, L. Borgman, *J. Appl. Ecol.* **3** (suppl.), 223 (1966); D. M. Ogilvie and J. M. Anderson, *J. Fish. Res. Board Can.* **22**, 503 (1965).

27. Supported in part by a grant from the Research Foundation of the State University of New York and in part by Brookhaven National Laboratory under the auspices of AEC.

ADDITIONAL REFERENCES

Åberg, B., and F. P. Hungate, ed. 1967. *Radio-ecological concentration processes.* Proc. Int. Symp., Stockholm, April 25–29, 1966. London: Pergamon Press. 1040 pp.

Cox, James L. 1970. DDT residues in marine phytoplankton: Increase from 1955 to 1969. *Science* 170:71–72.

Risebrough, R. W., D. B. Menzel, D. J. Martin, Jr., and H. S. Olcott. 1967. DDT residues in Pacific sea birds: A persistent insecticide in marine food chains. *Nature* 216:589–590.

Woodwell, George M. 1967. Toxic substances and ecological cycles. *Sci. Am.* 216(3):24–31.

DDT RESIDUES AND DECLINING REPRODUCTION IN THE BERMUDA PETREL

CHARLES F. WURSTER, JR., AND DAVID B. WINGATE

The ultimate hazard of persistent chemical poisons such as DDT residues is their ability to kill species populations of animals. As previous selections have shown, carnivorous animals generally are in the greatest danger of extinction, for they accumulate the highest concentrations of insecticides.

This selection focuses on the relations between DDT residues and the declining population of a rare bird, the Bermuda petrel, or cahow. Residues of DDT average 6.44 parts per million in eggs and chicks of this carnivorous bird. Although the bird itself certainly is unimportant to most people, the phenomena that it exemplifies are important to everyone. This selection illustrates three important aspects of environmental contamination by DDT and other "hard" pesticides:

(1) The destruction of a population or species may be subtle, operating through complex physiological mechanisms which lead to diminished reproduction rather than killing in a more direct way. Reproduction by the petrel has declined during the past ten years at an annual rate of 3.25 percent; and if this decline continues, reproduction will cease completely by 1978. Incidentally, this selection shows the detail of investigation that often must be conducted to understand the indirect (but critical) effects on environment of man.

(2) The DDT in this case comes from far-distant lands, not locally. Today the whole world is sometimes forced to pay the price of ignorant

Charles F. Wurster, Jr., is a member of the faculty at the State University of New York at Stony Brook (see biographical note on p. 555). David B. Wingate (b. 1935) is a zoologist and head of the Conservation Division in the Bermuda government since 1966. Educated in Bermuda and at Cornell University (B.S., 1957), he also has been associated with the Bermuda Department of Agriculture and Fisheries (1957–1959) and the Bermuda Government Aquarium (1959–1966), the latter tenure mainly under a research grant from the New York Zoological Society to develop a conservation program for the Bermuda Petrel. Wingate has been instrumental in establishing several nature reserves and parks in Bermuda and in creating the Conservation Division. He presently is involved in combating problems of pollution and in developing and managing a natural history museum.

local or regional treatment of environment. The islands where the petrel breeds have never been treated with DDT; the oceanic food chain upon which the bird depends is contaminated.

(3) A similar and widespread decline in many other species of birds is apparent—the peregrine falcon (Hickey, 1969), the golden eagle, the bald eagle, the sparrowhawk (Porter and Weimeyer, 1969), and others.

It is interesting to note that man's more direct actions nearly eliminated the Bermuda petrel more than three centuries ago, when early settlers and their introduced pigs hunted the bird for food (Fisher and others, 1969, pp. 173-178). Perhaps modern man will unconsciously and indirectly accomplish the annihilation that earlier men sought.

(Editor's comment)

Many oceanic birds nested on Bermuda in 1609 when the first settlers arrived, the most abundant apparently being the Bermuda petrel, *Pterodroma cahow*. Within 20 years man and his imported mammals virtually exterminated this species; for nearly 300 years it was considered extinct. Several records of specimens since 1900 were followed in 1951 by discovery of a small breeding colony (*1*), and in 1967 22 pairs nested on a few rocky islets off Bermuda. With a total population of about 100 the petrel is among the world's rarest birds.

A wholly pelagic species, *P. cahow* visits land only to breed, breeds only on Bermuda, and arrives and departs only at night. The single egg is laid underground at the end of a long burrow. When not in the burrow the bird feeds far at sea, mainly on cephalopods; when not breeding it probably ranges over much of the North Atlantic (*1*).

Reproduction by *P. cahow* has declined recently. The data since 1958 (Table 41.1) show an annual rate of decline of 3.25 ± 1.05 percent; the negative slope of a weighted regression is significant (*P*, .015; *F* test). If this linear decline continues, reproduction will fail completely by 1978, with extinction of the species. Many recent reports have correlated diminished reproduction by certain carnivorous birds with contamination by chlorinated hydrocarbon insecticides (*2-7*). As the terminal member of a pelagic food chain, presumably feeding over much of the North Atlantic, the petrel may be expected

to concentrate by many orders of magnitude any stable, lipid soluble chemicals, such as chlorinated hydrocarbon insecticides, present in lower trophic levels (*2, 3, 8*). In fact it should serve as an ideal environmental monitor for detection of insecticide contamination as a general oceanic pollutant, rather than contamination resulting directly from treatment of a specific land area (*9*). When we analyzed several specimens of *P. cahow* for chlorinated hydrocarbon insecticides, all samples contained DDT residues (*10*).

TABLE 41.1 Reproductive success of the Bermuda petrel between 1958 and 1967: percentages of established adult pairs under observation whose chicks survived 2 weeks after hatching. Numbers of pairs of unknown success (not included in calculations) appear in parentheses. Data from 1961–7 are believed to represent the total breeding population; earlier, not all burrows had been discovered. The decline in reproductive success follows the linear relation $y = a + bx$ **(y, reproductive success; a, a constant; b, annual percentage decline in success; x, year). The regression, weighted by numbers of pairs:** $y = 251.9 - 3.25x$.

YEAR	PAIRS	CHICKS	SUCCESS (%)
1958	6(1)	4	66.7
1959	5(2)	2	40.0
1960	13(3)	6	46.2
1961	18(1)	12	66.7
1962	19	9	47.4
1963	17(1)	9	52.9
1964	17(1)	8	47.1
1965	20	8	40.0
1966	21	6	28.6
1967	22	8	36.4

TABLE 41.2 Residues of DDT (*10*) in parts per million (wet weight) in eggs and chicks of the Bermuda petrel, collected in Bermuda in March 1967; proportions of DDT, DDE, and DDD are expressed as percentages of the total.

| | | PERCENTAGES | | |
| | RESIDUES | | | |
SAMPLE	(ppm)	DDT	DDE	DDD
A, egg†	11.02	37*	58*	5*
A, egg†§‖	10.71	34*	62*	4*
B, addled egg†	3.61	15	65	20
C, chick in egg‡	4.52	33	64	3
D, chick in egg‡	6.08	33	62	5
D, chick brain‡‖	0.57	30	54	16
E, chick, 1 to 2 days old	6.97	29*	66*	5*
		Averages		
	6.44	31	62	7

* Identity confirmed by thin-layer chromatography (*11*).
† Egg showed no sign of development.
‡ Fully developed chick died while hatching.
§ Analysis 5 months later by Wisconsin Alumni Research Foundation, which also detected dieldrin at 0.02 ppm.
‖ Not included in averages.

During March 1967 five unhatched eggs and dead chicks were collected from unsuccessful petrel burrows and stored frozen. The small size of the population precluded the sampling of living birds. Samples were analyzed for DDT, *o,p*-DDT, DDE, DDD, dieldrin, and endrin by electron-capture gas chromatography; the results are summarized in Table 41.2. No *o,p*-DDT, dieldrin, or endrin was detected, but an independent laboratory detected a trace of dieldrin.

Certain identifications were confirmed by thin-layer chromatography (*11*) as follows: After Florisil cleanup (*12*), the unknown sample was spotted on a thin-layer plate with 1-μg authentic standard samples on both sides. After development, the unknown was masked by a strip of paper, and the standards were sprayed with chromogenic reagent (*11*). When spots were visible following exposure to ultraviolet light, the masking was removed, horizontal lines were drawn between the standard spots in order to locate corresponding compounds in the unknown, and these areas were scraped from the plate and extracted with a few drops of a mixture of hexane and acetone (9:1 by volume). Injection into the gas chromatograph confirmed the presence of DDT, DDE, and DDD by

showing the appropriate single peaks for these compounds. This confirmation procedure was employed because the electron-capture detector is more sensitive than the chromogenic spray reagent in detecting minute amounts of these materials.

Coincidental with diminishing reproduction by the Bermuda petrel is the presence of DDT residues averaging 6.44 parts per million (ppm) in its eggs and chicks. In itself this coincidence does not establish a causal relation, but these findings must be evaluated in the light of other studies. Whereas a healthy osprey (*Pandion haliaetus*) population produces 2.2 to 2.5 young per nest, a Maryland colony containing DDT residues of 3.0 ppm in its eggs yielded 1.1 young per nest, and a Connecticut colony containing 5.1 ppm produced only 0.5 young per nest; the Connecticut population has declined 30 percent annually for the last 9 years (*4*). In New Brunswick, breeding success of American woodcocks (*Philohela minor*) showed a statistically significant inverse correlation with the quantity of DDT applied to its habitat in a given year. Furthermore, during 1962 and 1963, birds from unsprayed Nova Scotia showed breeding success nearly twice as great as did those from sprayed New Brunswick, where woodcock eggs averaged 1.3 ppm of DDT residues during those years (5).

In Britain five species of raptors, including the peregrine falcon (*Falco peregrinus*) and golden eagle (*Aquila chrysaetos*), carried residues of chlorinated hydrocarbon insecticides in their eggs, averaging 5.2 ppm; each of these species has shown a decline in reproduction and total population during recent years. By comparison, residues in the eggs of five species of corvids averaged 0.9 ppm, and breeding success and numbers have been maintained (6). It is noteworthy that during the last decade the peregrine has become extinct as a breeding bird in the eastern United States (13). Residues in bald eagle (*Haliaeetus leucocephalus*) eggs averaged 10.6 ppm, and this species also shows declining reproduction and population (7). Lake Michigan herring gulls (*Larus argentatus*), exhibiting very low reproductive success, averaged 120 to 227 ppm of DDT residues in the eggs (3), the suggestion being that susceptibility varies widely between species.

In most of the above instances, including *P. cahow*, reduced success in breeding resulted primarily from mortality of chicks before and shortly after hatching. Bobwhites (*Colinus virginianus*) and pheasants (*Phasianus colchicus*), fed sublethal diets of DDT or dieldrin, gave similar results (14); a mechanism explaining chick mortality from dieldrin poisoning during the several days after hatching has been presented (15).

From studies of these birds and other avian carnivores a very widespread, perhaps worldwide, decline among many species of carnivorous birds is apparent. The pattern of decline is characterized by reduced success in reproduction correlated with the presence of residues of chlorinated hydrocarbon insecticides—primarily DDT. Our data for the Bermuda petrel are entirely consistent with this pattern.

Observations of aggressive behavior, increased nervousness, chipped eggshells, increased egg-breakage, and egg-eating by parent birds of several of the above species (3, 6, 13) suggest symptoms of a hormonal

disturbance or a calcium deficiency, or both. Moreover, DDT has been shown to delay ovulation and inhibit gonadal development in birds, probably by means of a hormonal mechanism, and low dosages of DDT or dieldrin in the diet of pigeons increased metabolism of steroid sex hormones by hepatic enzymes (16). A direct relation between DDT and calcium function has also been demonstrated, and these endocrine and calcium mechanisms could well be interrelated; DDT interferes with normal calcification of the arthropod nerve axon, causing hyperactivity of the nerve and producing symptoms similar to those resulting from calcium deficiency (17). Dogs treated with calcium gluconate are very resistant to DDT poisoning (18); female birds are more resistant than males (19), perhaps because of the calcium-mobilizing action of estrogenic hormones.

Of major importance, then, was the discovery that a significant ($P < .001$) and widespread decrease in calcium content of eggshells occurred between 1946 and 1950 in the peregrine falcon, golden eagle, and sparrowhawk, *Accipiter nisus* (20). This decrease correlates with the widespread introduction of DDT into the environment during those years, and further correlates with the onset of reduced reproduction and of the described symptoms of calcium deficiency. These multiple correlations indicate a high probability that the decline in reproduction of most or all of these birds, including *P. cahow*, is causally related to their contamination by DDT residues.

Other potential causes of the observed decline for the Bermuda petrel appear unlikely. The bird has been strictly protected and isolated since 1957, and it seems that human disturbance can be discounted. In such a small population, inbreeding could become important, but hatching failure is now consistent in pairs having earlier records of successful breeding, and deformed chicks are never observed. Furthermore, the effects of inbreeding would not be expected to increase at a time when the total population, and probably the gene pool, is still increasing. The population increase results from artificial protection since 1957 from other limiting factors, especially competition for nest sites with tropic birds (*21*).

It is very unlikely that the observed DDT residues in *P. cahow* were accumulated from Bermuda: The breeding grounds are confined to a few tiny, isolated, and uninhabited islets never treated with DDT, and the bird's feeding habits are wholly pelagic. Thus the presence of DDT residues in all samples can lead only to the conclusion that this oceanic food chain, presumably including the plankton, is contaminated. This conclusion is supported by reported analyses showing residues in related seabirds including two species of shearwaters from the Pacific (*22*); seabird eggs (*9, 22*); freshwater, estuarine, and coastal plankton (*2,8,23*); planktonfeeding organisms (*2,8,9,22,23*); and other marine animals from various parts of the world (*8, 22*). These toxic chemicals are apparently very widespread within oceanic organisms (*8, 22*), and the evidence suggests that their ecological effects are important.

References and Notes

1. R. C. Murphy and L. S. Mowbray, *Auk* **68**, 266 (1951); A. C. Bent, *U.S. Nat. Museum Bull. 121* (1922), pp. 112–7.
2. E. G. Hunt and A. I. Bischoff, *Calif. Fish Game* **46**, 91 (1960); E. G. Hunt, in *Nat. Acad. Sci.–Nat. Res. Council Publ. 1402* (1966), p. 251.
3. J. P. Ludwig and C. S. Tomoff, *Jack-Pine Warbler* **44**, 77 (1966); J. A. Keith, *J. Appl. Ecol.* **3**(suppl.), 57 (1966); J. J. Hickey, J. A. Keith, F. B. Coon, *ibid.*, p. 141.
4. P. L. Ames, *ibid.*, p. 87.
5. B. S. Wright, *J. Wildlife Management* **29**, 172 (1965).
6. S. Cramp, *Brit. Birds* **56**, 124 (1963); J. D. Lockie and D. A. Ratcliffe, *ibid.* **57**, 89 (1964); D. A. Ratcliffe, *ibid.* **58**, 65 (1965); *Bird Study* **10**, 56 (1963); **12**, 66 (1965).
7. L. F. Stickel *et al.*, in *Trans. North American Wildlife Natural Resources Conf. 31st* (1966), pp. 190–200; J. B. DeWitt, *Audubon Mag.* **65**, 30 (1963); A. Sprunt, *ibid.*, p. 32.
8. G. M. Woodwell, C. F. Wurster, P. A. Isaacson, *Science* **156**, 821 (1967); G. M. Woodwell, *Sci. Amer.* **216**, 24 (March 1967).
9. N. W. Moore and J. O'G. Tatton, *Nature* **207**, 42 (1965); N. W. Moore, *J. Appl. Ecol.* **3**(suppl.), 261 (1966).
10. Residues of DDT include DDT and its decay products (metabolites) DDE and DDD; DDT, 1,1,1-trichloro-2,2-bis(*p*-chlorophenyl)ethane; DDE, 1,-1-dichloro-2,2-bis(*p*-chlorophenyl)ethylene; DDD (also known as TDE), 1,1-dichloro-2,2-bis(*p*-chlorophenyl)ethane.
11. M. F. Kovacs, *J. Assoc. Offic. Anal. Chemists* **49**, 365 (1966).
12. J. G. Cummings, K. T. Zee, V. Turner, F. Quinn, R. E. Cook, *ibid.*, p. 354.
13. R. A. Herbert and K. G. S. Herbert, *Auk* **82**, 62 (1965); J. J. Hickey, Ed., *Peregrine Falcon Populations, Their Biology and Decline* (Univ. of Wisconsin Press, Madison, in press).
14. J. B. DeWitt, *J. Agr. Food Chem.* **3**, 672 (1955); **4**, 863 (1956); R. E. Genelly and R. L. Rudd, *Auk* **73**, 529 (1956).
15. J. H. Koeman, R. C. H. M. Oudejans, E. A. Huisman, *Nature* **215**, 1094 (1967).
16. D. J. Jefferies, *Ibis* **109**, 266 (1967); H. Burlington and V. F. Lindeman, *Proc. Soc. Exp. Biol. Med.* **74**, 48 (1950); D. B. Peakall, *Nature* **216**, 505 (1967); *Atlantic Naturalist* **22**, 109 (1967).
17. J. H. Welsh and H. T. Gordon, *J. Cell. Comp. Physiol.* **30**, 147 (1947); H. T. Gordon and J. H. Welsh, *ibid.* **31**, 395 (1948).
18. Z. Vaz, R. S. Pereira, D. M. Malheiro, *Science* **101**, 434 (1945).
19. D. H. Wurster, C. F. Wurster, R. N. Strickland, *Ecology* **46**, 488 (1965); L. B. Hunt, unpublished manuscript, University of Wisconsin, 1965.
20. D. R. Ratcliffe, *Nature* **215**, 208 (1967).
21. D. B. Wingate, *Can. Audubon* **22**, 145 (1960).
22. R. W. Risebrough, D. B. Menzel, D. J. Martin, H. S. Olcott, *Nature* **216**, 589 (1967); J. Robinson, A. Richardson, A. N. Crabtree, J. C. Coulson, G. R. Potts, *ibid.* **214**, 1307 (1967); W. J. L. Sladen, C. M. Menzie, W. L. Reichel, *ibid.* **210**, 670 (1966); J. O'G. Tatton and J. H. A. Ruzicka, *ibid.* **215**, 346 (1967); J. O. Keith and E. G. Hunt, in *Trans. North American Wildlife Natural Resources Conf. 31st* (1966), pp. 150–77.
23. P. A. Butler, *ibid.*, pp. 184–9; *J. Appl. Ecol.* **3**(suppl.), 253 (1966).
24. Aided by a grant from the Research Foundation of the State University of New York; transportation by the Smithsonian Institution, Washington, D. C. The Bermuda petrel conservation program was financed by Childs Frick and the New York Zoological Society. We thank G. M. Woodwell for criticizing the manuscript.

ADDITIONAL REFERENCES

Fisher, James, Noel Simon, and Jack Vincent. 1969. *Wildlife in danger.* New York: Viking Press. The extermination of the Bermuda petrel is discussed on pp. 173–178.

Herbert, R. A., and K. G. S. Herbert. 1965. Behavior of peregrine falcons in the New York City region. *Auk* 82:62–94.

Hickey, J. J., ed. 1969. *Peregrine falcon populations—Their biology and decline.* Madison, Wisconsin: University of Wisconsin Press.

Moore, N. W., ed. 1966. Pesticides in the environment and their effects on wildlife. *Journal of Applied Ecology,* Vol. 3 Supplement. 311 pp.

Porter, R. D., and S. N. Weimeyer. 1969. Dieldrin and DDT: Effects on sparrow hawk eggshells and reproduction. *Science* 165:199–200.

Risebrough, R. W., D. B. Menzel, D. J. Martin, Jr., and H. S. Olcott. 1967. DDT residues in Pacific sea birds: A persistent insecticide in marine food chains. *Nature* 216:589–590.

Sladen, William J. L., C. M. Menzie, and W. L. Reichel. 1966. DDT residues in Adelie penguins and a Crabeater seal from Antarctica. *Nature* 210(5037):670–673.

CONCLUSIONS ON PESTICIDE EFFECTS

N. W. MOORE

The importance of pesticides in the environment goes beyond the marked effects on certain species (discussed in the previous selection). The broader ecological effects of pesticides are not the same as their toxicological effects. Pesticides, like invading alien organisms (see Selection 34), usually reduce species diversity within an ecosystem and hence increase its instability. Unlike natural ecological regulators of populations (such as predators), however, most pesticides act independently of population density—every last organism may be killed.

This selection surveys these and other broad implications of pesticides. Viewed in grand historical perspective, pesticides are recognized as an important interactant in developing agricultural systems. Moore shows that the pesticide problem is one of our many environmental problems in which short-term solutions are the enemies of long-term ones.

Biological controls of pests are now being sought and developed as better alternatives to chemical pesticides (Irving, 1970; Holcomb, 1970). These measures include development of resistant crop varieties, release of parasites or predators to control pests, and bred-in sterility of insects; nonpersistent chemicals are also being developed.

Moore also compares the dispersal, concentration, and biological effects of radioactive materials with those of pesticides (a comparison made elsewhere also, e.g., Woodwell, 1970). Environmental contamination by radioisotopes is an important topic, treated only briefly in this book, but a problem whose urgency has declined since the abatement of atmospheric explosions of nuclear devices in the early 1960s.

(Editor's comment)

Norman W. Moore (b. 1923) is head of the Toxic Chemicals & Wildlife Section at Monks Wood Experimental Station (The Nature Conservancy), Abbots Ripton, Huntingdon, England, and has been principal scientific officer of The Nature Conservancy since 1958. He was educated at Cambridge and Bristol University (Ph.D., 1953). Moore has written numerous research articles on ecology and edited *Pesticides in the Environment and their Effects on Wildlife* (1966, *J. Appl. Ecol.* vol. 3, Suppl.).

This selection is extracted from pp. 121–125 in "A Synopsis of the Pesticide Problem," pp. 75–129 in *Advances in Ecological Research*, vol. 4, 1967, edited by J. B. Cragg. Reprinted by permission of the author, the editor, and the publisher, Academic Press, London and New York.

Comparisons with Other Factors

We have seen that pesticides can have many different types of effect but since these are usually independent of density they do not normally control populations in the manner of density-dependent factors like disease and availability of food. Total weed killers, by killing the whole flora and fauna, resemble fire in their general effect. Pesticides which kill all animals resemble freak natural conditions like excessive cold and flooding which kill many or few animals according to severity, but on the other hand leave plants relatively unaffected. Systemic insecticides, like schradan, whose effects are limited to animals that suck plant juices, have no counterpart among "natural" factors. Specific chemicals resemble specific diseases only in the sense that they are specific—there is no equivalent of intraspecific infection.

Persistent pesticides with their attendant phenomena of dispersal, biological concentration and concentration in food chains, share many features with radioactive materials (Odum, 1959; Templeton, 1965). A detailed comparison between the two types of environmental contamination would be valuable but is not attempted here. Like persistent pesticides, radioactive particles become widely distributed over the surface of the earth, they have widely different effects on different organisms (Higgins, 1951), and they become concentrated at different rates in different species of plants and animals. However, radioactive isotopes are not taken up differentially—their concentration rate depends first on the normal uptake of the element concerned and secondly on the proportion of the element in the environment which is radioactive.

The concentration factors of radioisotopes in food chains vary considerably but are comparable to those of persistent insecticides. Pendleton and Hanson (1958) show that plants in an aquatic environment accumulate ^{137}Cs 500 times as much as plants grown in soils, and that animals feeding on aquatic plants accordingly become proportionately more contaminated. The radioactive burdens of predators, unlike organo-chlorine insecticide residues of predators, do not greatly exceed those of prey species. The pattern of concentration factors of radioisotopes with a relatively short half life (e.g. ^{32}P) differs from that of persistent insecticides in that predators carry smaller radioactive burdens than herbivores because there is not time for them to accumulate larger amounts than their prey. Some radioactive substances differ from pesticides in that they occur naturally and are merely increased by man, whereas most pesticides do not occur naturally. There are other important differences: some radioactive materials remain active very much longer than pesticides and the rate of their decay is regular and predictable, whereas the decay of pesticides depends on a number of factors and is not constant. In this connection it should be noted that the term "half life" is sometimes used to describe the likely duration of a pesticide in soils, but it is misleading since it is not equivalent to the half life of a radioactive substance.

Pesticides as Part of a Developing System

One of the aims of this paper is to demonstrate that the ecological effect of a pesticide is not the same as the toxicological effect writ large. Pesticides characteristically affect ecological relationships, and man and his actions are an integral part of the whole—not only has he produced the need for pesticides but he has invented them and controlled their use according to experience of their action in the field: there is a reciprocal reaction. Pesticide control as well as pest control is an essential "ecological factor." Further, all the effects on relationships have to be seen in relation to time since the initial effects produce others which themselves interact. Eventually strong selective pressures cause genetic changes. The evolution of the pest/pesticide relationship is shown schematically in Figure 42.1. The development of the human factor has shown characteristics which are similar to certain ecological developments. In the first place, by growing crops in monocultures man has created simplified

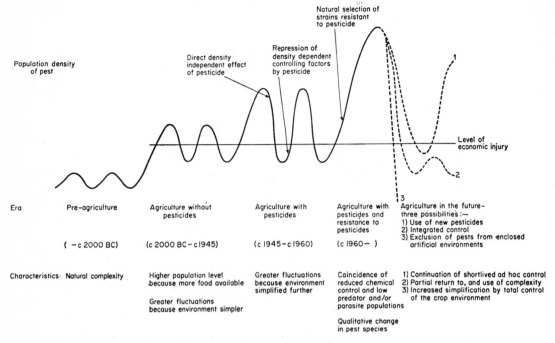

FIGURE 42.1 Diagram illustrating the historical development of pest control and pest fluctuations.

situations in which some species present are likely to become pests. To control them he has used powerful, largely nonspecific chemicals with density-independent effects. His actions have led in some cases to resurgences of pests, the formation of new pests, resistant strains in pests* and varying degrees of damage to beneficial species including himself. As a result man has reacted in different ways:

1 He continues treatments which continue to give successful results (e.g. control of weeds in cereal crops with selective herbicides).
2 He invents new pesticides to replace the old. This postpones pest control problems rather than solves them. It produces a rapidly changing pesticide situation which provides little time for species to adapt.
3 He attempts to exclude pests altogether by growing crops in enclosed places. This process of simplification is impossible in the field.
and

* See Selection 50.

4 He takes the more radical steps of doing ecological research so as to harness naturally occurring beneficial factors, and to refine chemical methods so that pesticides are less toxic and more specific.

This last development results in a more complicated type of pest control in which biological complexity is reintroduced into the system. The pesticide problem is one of many in which short-term solutions are often the enemies of long-term ones. But there are hopeful signs that the human approach to pesticide use is evolving from a simple one with diminishing long-term prospects to a complex one with good long-term prospects. This should be reflected in increasing stability in the ecosystems affected by pesticides. In other words the whole pesticide situation is, to some extent, self-regulatory.

Summary

The pesticide problem is essentially ecological and an interdisciplinary approach to it is essential. Pesticides always affect ecosystems although they are usually applied to control single or very few pest species. Conclusions about pesticide effects on populations must generally remain tentative owing to the lack of information on population dynamics, feeding habits and toxicology. Most pesticides are non-specific in their action and their effects are density-independent. Pesticides vary greatly in their toxicity and persistence and solubility. There are differences of response to one chemical between species, sexes, age groups and individuals. Sublethal effects on reproduction and behaviour are likely to be ecologically significant. Persistence and fat solubility cause organochlorine insecticides to become widely dispersed and concentrated in food chains. Little is known about the ecological effects of pesticide interaction (potentiation). Pesticides have been used for over 200 years but they have only become an important ecological factor during the past 20 years. Existing statistics are inadequate in assessing the amount of pesticides in the environment. A pesticide may affect a species directly by delayed effect and by affecting food species, habitat, competitors and predators. Pesticides usually reduce diversity and since they have differential effects on taxa at different trophic levels they may affect production. Pesticides, like all deleterious density-independent factors, are likely to have a particularly severe effect on predators. This effect is enhanced in the case of organochlorine insecticides by the food chain effect (see above). Pesticides are likely to affect freshwater ecosystems more severely than terrestrial ones. Modifications of succession by pesticides are described. The natural selection of resistant strains by pesticides can cause qualitative changes in species. Pest control and pesticide control are both ecological factors. Some reasons for not taking an ecological approach to pesticide problems are discussed. It is suggested that future trends in pest control will polarize towards two types of system, one involving complete control of very simple systems and others involving integrated control of complex systems. The use of pesticides is to some extent self-regulatory. Pesticides, particularly the more selective ones, have value as tools in ecological research.

References Cited

Higgins, E. (1951). J. Wildl. Mgmt. 15, 1–12.

Odum, E. P. (1959). "Fundamentals of Ecology." Philadelphia and London: Saunders.

Pendelton, R. C., and Hanson, W. C. (1958). In "2nd U.N. Geneva International Conference on the Peaceful Uses of Atomic Energy." London: Pergamon.

Templeton, W. L. (1965). In "Ecology and the Industrial Society." 5th Symp. of the Brit. Ecol. Soc. Oxford.

ADDITIONAL REFERENCES

Conway, Gordon R. 1969. A consequence of insecticides; Pests follow the chemicals in the cocoa of Malaysia. Pp. 46–51 in *The unforeseen international boomerang,* ed. by M. T. Farvar and John Milton. Supplement to *Natural History* magazine.

Holcomb, R. W. 1970. Insect control: Alternatives to the use of conventional pesticides. *Science* 168:456–468.

Irving, G. W., Jr. 1970. Agricultural pest control and the environment. *Science* 168:1419–1424.

Kuenen, D. J., ed. 1961. *The ecological effects of biological and chemical control of undesirable plants and animals.* International Union Cons.

Nature Symposium, 1960, Eighth Tech. Meeting. Leiden: E. J. Brill. 118 pp.

McLean, L. A. 1967. Pesticides and the environment. *BioScience* 17(9):613–617.

Niering, William A. 1968. The effects of pesticides. *BioScience* 18(9):869–875.

Radford, Edward P. 1968. Biological aspects of synergisms. Pp. 160–173 in *Environmental problems,* ed. by Billy Ray Wilson. Philadelphia & Toronto: J. B. Lippincott Company.

Woodwell, George M. 1967. Toxic substances and ecological cycles. *Sci. Am.* 216(3):24–31.

Woodwell, G. M. 1970. Effects of pollution on the structure and physiology of ecosystems. *Science* 168:429–433.

DESTRUCTION OF PACIFIC CORALS BY THE SEA STAR (ACANTHASTER PLANCI)

RICHARD H. CHESHER

The crown-of-thorns starfish or sea star (*Acanthaster planci*) is a coral predator that is undergoing a population explosion in many parts of the Pacific Ocean. In a recent 2½-year period, 90 percent of the coral fringing reefs were killed along 38 kilometers (24 miles) of Guam's shoreline. Observations of feeding rates, population movements, and stages of infestation indicate that narrow, fringing reefs—which protect tropical coasts against erosion—may be killed as rapidly as 1 kilometer per month.

This problem, discussed in this selection, exemplifies an environmental plight in which man's specific role as a causal agent is uncertain. Chesher suggests that the sea-star infestations are triggered by local destruction of reefs by man (as by blasting and dredging), which has provided fresh surfaces for the concentrated establishment of larvae. Other workers have argued, however, that if reef damage is a sufficient initial condition, then reef destruction by typhoons or severe bombing in World War II should have spurred earlier population explosions of the sea star, which were not in evidence (Fischer, 1969; Newman, 1970). Fischer (op. cit.) has suggested that insecticides may have depleted predators of the sea star, which normally would keep populations under control. Whatever the specific causes, it appears likely from the list of places that are suffering serious infestations that some kind of human activity is responsible, because all are areas that have appreciable human settlements. And despite the cause some kind of control action against the sea star appears to be advisable unless man is willing to accept the death of extensive coral reefs and their loss for several human generations (Chesher, 1970).

Populations of other marine organisms are exploding elsewhere in the

Richard H. Chesher is a marine zoologist (Ph.D., biological oceanography) living in Miami, Florida. He has been associated with the Institute of Marine Sciences at the University of Miami, the Museum of Comparative Zoology at Harvard University, and the University of Guam at Agana. His research interests include the systematic zoology of sea urchins.

tropical Pacific. Herbivorous sea urchins have removed formerly luxuriant kelp beds from along the coast of southern California. Even after the kelp is destroyed urchins may persist in densities of fifty per square meter and prevent the reestablishment of kelp beds. North and Pearse (1970) believe that "the persisting high population densities may be the result of (1) destruction of their main predator, sea otters, during the close of the last century, (2) depletion of an important competitor, abalone, during the last few decades, and (3) enrichment of coastal waters with sewage effluent."

(Editor's comment)

Goreau (*1*), in seeking causes for impoverished coral growth in areas of the Red Sea, suggested that predation by a large, sixteen-armed, spiny sea star, *Acanthaster planci* (Linnaeus), the "crown-of-thorns starfish," might be sufficient explanation. Barnes and others (*2*) reported that the same species was destroying large tracts of living coral along the Great Barrier Reef in Australia. Recently *A. planci* was reported from several Pacific islands (*3*). A severe infestation on the reefs of the U.S. Territory of Guam has led to the establishment of a control program under the direction of the University of Guam. Available information indicates that recent population explosions of *A. planci* are occurring almost simultaneously in widely separated areas of the Indo-Pacific Ocean and that these are not short-term population fluctuations of the type reported for numerous other marine invertebrates (*4*).

Although *Acanthaster planci* is a Linnaean species and has been known for a long time, it has been regarded as a great rarity until about 1963, when large swarms were reported by local residents from the Great Barrier Reef near Cairns.

Since 1967 this starfish has killed well over 90 percent of the living coral along 38 km of the coastline of Guam from just below low spring tide level to the depth limit of reef coral growth (about 65 meters). After the death of the coral polyps, the coralla are rapidly overgrown with algae. Most fish leave the dead reefs, with the exception of small, drab-colored, herbivorous scarids and acanthurids.

Other animals feed on coral (*1*), but none

so efficiently as *A. planci*. Caged, starved specimens ate mollusks and other echinoderms, but observations showed scleractinian corals of any configuration as the primary diet of undisturbed specimens. Hydrocorals and octocorals were eaten only after the madreporarian corals were gone. *Acanthaster planci* feeds by everting the gastric sac through its mouth, spreading the membranes over the coral, and digesting the soft tissues in place (*1–3*). The skeleton left behind stands out sharply as a patch of pure white until overgrown with algae. On reefs with low *A. planci* densities, feeding was nocturnal and specimens were cryptic during daylight. On reefs with high densities, many animals were found feeding during the day (Figure 43.1).

FIGURE 43.1 *Acanthaster planci,* normally a nocturnal coral predator, often feeds during daylight in regions of high population densities.

Although *A. planci,* 60 cm in total diameter, were collected, those in the infested areas of Guam averaged 24.2 cm across the arms and 13.8 cm across the disk. The daily feeding rate was observed to be twice the area of the disk. Coral is therefore killed in areas of infestation at a mean rate of 378 cm^2 per animal per day or about 1 m^2 per month. In some localities, with population densities as high as one animal per square meter of reef, all living coral would be eaten in 1 month.

Before 1967, *A. planci* was not common on Guam (*5*). In early 1967, the starfish became abundant on reefs off Tumon and Piti bays (Figure 43.2). They were observed feeding actively at depths of 3 to 10 m. The numbers of sea stars increased rapidly, and they were observed in deeper water. Large parts of the reef were completely stripped of living coral before the sea stars moved to adjacent areas. By spring, 1968, almost all of the coral off Tumon Bay was dead. In September of 1968, *A. planci* had spread

to Double Reef, and in November divers removed 886 animals from 90,000 m^2 of reef at that locality. At that time, half of the coral of this reef was dead. Coral to the north of Double Reef was alive, although *A. planci* was present in limited numbers. Hazardous weather prevented surveillance of this area from December until late March. By then, the reef was dead for another 4 km, and the main concentration of animals had moved to an area extending 3 km southeastward from Ritidian Point.

Strong wave surge along this northern shoreline prevented the sea stars from entering shallow water until late March. The sea stars were observed circumnavigating Ritidian Point in water over 30 m deep, along a flat coralline pavement. During April, the main front of sea stars moved into shallower coral reefs as wave action decreased. In late April, dense concentrations were present at the lower edge of the northern fringing reef at a depth of 20 m. Coral destruction was extensive.

An underwater survey of the entire area between Orote Point and Ritidian Point during April and May showed that over 90 percent of the reef coral was dead from low spring tide level to the limit of coral growth. Living coral was found only along the shallower, more exposed parts of the coastline.

The larger, rounded, massive corals such as *Porites lutea* survived to depths of over 3 m. The tops of these coral heads were alive, but the lower portions were eaten, presumably because *A. planci* apparently could not maintain a hold on the evenly rounded coralla in the face of strong surge movements. Both the coral and the sea star produce mucus during the feeding process (*1*) which decreases the holding power of the asteroid tube feet. Specimens feeding on this type of coral in protected areas or during calm seas were easily dislodged, whereas they are difficult to dislodge when they can wrap themselves around a projection. With the exception of these few corals, the only living reef-building coelenterates were *Millepora* and octocorals, which were attacked only after stony corals had been eaten.

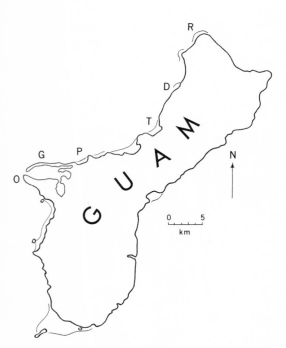

FIGURE 43.2 Diagram of Guam; *R,* **Ritidian Point;** *D,* **Double Reef;** *T,* **Tumon Bay;** *P,* **Piti Bay;** *G,* **Glass Breakwater;** *O,* **Orote Point.**

Specimens of *A. planci* marked with anchor tags (5) moved as far as 250 m per week. However, movement was slower when the starfish were feeding.

Movement of populations is inferred from disappearance, by March 1969, of *A. planci* from Tumon and Piti bays where large numbers had previously been observed and by the appearance of large numbers of adults in previously uninfested areas. After eating most of the coral, the starfish spread north and south, killing the reef as they went. Observations of the advancing "front" showed that the population density was as high as one animal per square meter along a 2.5-km section of coastline (Figure 43.3). Here the starfish were arranged in a relatively narrow, irregular band 5 to 20 m wide parallel to the coastline. Long bands sometimes broke up into groups that moved as amorphous herds of 20 to 200 individuals.

Depth was no barrier to movement, but soft substrates were avoided. Sand, moved by surge action, was an effective obstacle, since patch reefs surrounded by sand in areas of strong wave action were not infested. Sand provides no gripping surface for the tube feet, and the sea stars are easily overturned by water movements. In protected areas or during calm seas, sand is not a barrier.

Estimation of size of population and severity of infestation is difficult because the animals hide in crevices during the day, particularly in reefs with well-developed coral. In areas of poor coral development, animals are easier to count, except when herding. Population size can be estimated from numbers of animals seen during a particular time period. In normal reef environments, a diver observes less than one specimen per hour of search. In infested areas, the number is generally more than five per hour and can be as high as 100 per 10 minutes. In conditions of infestation, several individuals may congregate on a single corallum, and as many as 12 have been found completely covering a coral head.

Reasons for the sudden increase of population are obscure. Depletion by shell col-

FIGURE 43.3 A small portion of the advancing wave of *A. planci* that has eaten almost all coral along the northwestern sector of Guam. Densities as high as this extend along a 2.5-km section of Guam's coral reefs.

lectors of the triton shell *Charonia tritonis,* a predator of *A. planci,* has been implicated as a possible cause of the outbreaks (7). My studies indicate that predation by *C. tritonis* would not result in adequate control of *A. planci* populations. Two specimens of *C. tritonis* (29.5 and 36.8 cm in length of shell) were put together with *A. planci* in a large penned-in area of a living reef. At night, the triton actively sought out sea stars and could detect the presence of its prey from a distance of at least 1 m. When contact was made, the sea stars rapidly moved away, but the triton usually managed to attach itself to the aboral side of the disk with its proboscis and pull itself up onto the sea star. However, often only half of the sea star was eaten, the attached part being autotomized, and the remainder escaped and lived to regenerate lost parts. Regeneration of small functional arms required about 2 months. One triton attacked only one adult sea star per 6 days, even when an unlimited supply was available. *Charonia tritonis* does not prey solely on *A. planci* but also attacks *Culcita novae-guinea* and *Linckia laevigata* when these are available, and the chance of survival of its prey is large.

Even if the triton were abundant, it is doubtful that it could control *A. planci.*

Depletion of other gastropod predators, such as *Murex* and *Cassis,* which might feed on *A. planci* under natural conditions does not seem to be the cause of the infestations. Large populations of the sea stars occur in parts of Palau and Rota which are seldom visited by shell collectors and where these gastropods are common.

In seeking a cause for the sudden appearance of large numbers of adult *A. planci,* early life stages must be considered. The greatest mortality must occur during the larval stages. Shallow-water tropical Pacific substrates, where the larvae can survive after settling, are solidly encrusted with filter feeders (such as corals) capable of eating the larvae. Destruction of reefs by blasting, dredging, and other human activities has provided fresh surfaces, free of filter feeders, for settlement of the larvae. In such areas original populations of several hundred animals, concentrated together, might provide the necessary seed population for an infestation. Such dead coral areas must probably be freshly provided during time of larval settlement (December and January in Guam). Infestations in Guam, Rota, and Johnston Island were first noted near blasting and dredging activities.

For the second phase of infestations we must assume that *A. planci* larvae can, like many marine invertebrate larvae (8), seek out adults near which to settle. Coral recently killed by adult starfish provides excellent settling areas for larvae. Concentrations of adults would provide areas of attraction for larvae, resulting in localized recruitment. Support for this hypothesis was gained by the appearance in March and April 1969 of large numbers of small *A. planci* (3 to 6 cm in diameter) at Double Reef, the northernmost region of infestation during the breeding season of November and December. Juveniles are not abundant elsewhere, indicating either that the larvae are attracted to feeding adults or that areas of feeding adults permit the highest survival of young.

Control of infestations requires that adults be prevented from infesting new coral areas. If infestations are discovered at an early stage, control is simplified because the seed populations are localized and the animals are easy to find. At a later stage topographical zones must be found to establish zones through which the sea stars cannot move. Containment of adults within areas delimited by these zones will result in a natural, rapid decline of the population through starvation. After a period of 1 or 2 years, remaining animals could be removed.

Where suitable zones cannot be set up, sections of the reef may be preserved by extermination in local areas (2). Major reef sections or islands connected by shallow waters to other coral zones could be isolated, if possible, to prevent migration to nearby reefs. Such migrations are most likely to occur after complete destruction of the infested zone. Adults have an estimated life span of about 8 years, but, when deprived of living coral, they starve in about 6 months.

On Guam, where narrow, fringing reefs are common, areas in advance of the population movement were selected, and migration over these zones was prevented by weekly inspections of about 2 km of coastline. Divers were towed behind a boat, and any sea stars found were then killed with Formalin (5-mc injection, full strength).

Acanthaster planci have not been killed between the barriers. The sooner they finish what live coral remains, the sooner death through starvation will occur. It is important that this happen prior to the influx of larvae in the fall, or control activities may have to be extended for an additional year.

Destruction of living coral reefs would be an economic disaster for small isles and atolls of Oceania. Most inhabitants of Oceania derive almost all their protein from marine resources, and destruction of living reefs results in the destruction of fisheries. Eventually, loss of living corals would allow severe land erosion by storm waves.

Information concerning infestations in other areas of the Pacific is urgently needed. Reports of infestations have come from islands off Mersing on the east coast of Malaysia, from Borneo, New Guinea, Fiji Islands, Truk, Palau, Yap, Rota, Sipan, Wake, Johnston Island, the Great Barrier Reef, Midway, and Guam. With the exception of Guam, Australia, and Palau, the extent of the infestations is not known. Guam's infestation began only a little more than 2 years ago. Palau is in an early stage of infestation. Truk has had a heavy infestation for less than a year. Researchers working in the Pacific are requested to notify the author of normal populations or abnormal concentrations of *A. planci* and the degree of coral damage. Pertinent data on recent dredging or blasting activities or dynamiting for fish should be noted.

Long-term control may be possible by monitoring of areas subject to blasting or dredging during periods of larval settlement.

Seed populations can be eliminated before larval settlement in the following year. If, however, the population explosion is due to a basic change in the life history of *A. planci,* control will probably not be possible. Geological records clearly indicate that large groups of animals have become extinct within a relatively short time. Rugose corals offer an excellent example. The appearance of an overly efficient predator might cause such extinction. Wholesale destruction of madreporarian corals has been witnessed during the past few years. This destruction may continue to the point where the coral fauna cannot recover. There is a possibility that we are witnessing the initial phases of extinction of madreporarian corals in the Pacific.

References and Notes

1. T. F. Goreau, *Bull. Sea Fish. Res. Sta. Haifa* 35, 23 (1963).
2. J. H. Barnes, *Aust. Nat. Hist.* **15,** 256 (1966); D. E. Williamson, *Skin Diver* **17** (No. 3), 26 (1968); J. Harding, *Sea Frontiers* **14** (No. 5); 258 (1968).
3. R. H. Chesher, *Skin Diver* **18** (No. 3), **34,** 84 (1969).
4. W. R. Coe, *J. Mar. Res.* **16,** 212 (1956).
5. R. Randall, University of Guam, unpublished field notes.
6. R. Endean, University of Queenland, personal communication.
7. M. B. Dell, *Trans. Amer. Fish. Ass.* **97** (No. 1), 57 (1968).
8. G. Thorson, *Trans. N.Y. Acad. Sci. Ser.* **2** (No. 8), 693 (1956).
9. I thank Capt. Grieve and Capt. Wideman of the U.S. Navy for logistic support during the course of this project, and members of the University of Guam's Division of Marine Studies and Biosciences, and civilian and military scuba divers who provided considerable aid. Support was obtained through Resolution No. 519 (6-S) passed by a special session of the 9th Guam Legislature.

ADDITIONAL REFERENCES

Chesher, R. H. 1970. Letter to *Science* 167:1275.
Dixon, Bernard. 1969. Domesday for coral? *New Scientist* 44:226–227.
Fischer, J. L. 1969. Starfish infestation: Hypothesis. Letter to *Science* 165:645.

Newman, W. A. 1970. Acanthaster: A disaster? *Science* 167:1274–1275.
North, W. J., and J. S. Pearse. 1970. Sea urchin population explosion in southern California coastal waters. *Science* 167:209.

SPECIES SUCCESSION AND FISHERY EXPLOITATION IN THE GREAT LAKES

STANFORD H. SMITH

Lakes are delimited ecosystems in which the complex repercussions of animal exploitation can be seen clearly. The Great Lakes of North America provide an absorbing and important example, for they cover 95,000 square miles and are the largest and most valuable fresh water resource in the world. In this selection, Smith focuses on man's direct exploitation of fishes, although he also recognizes the important biological effects of environmental deterioration (see Selection 19). Complicating the impacts of these two factors are the effects of introduced organisms—notably the sea lamprey and the alewife, which were allowed entry into the lakes by the Welland Canal after 1829. By the mid-1960s alewives alone constituted more than 90 percent by weight of the total fish in Lake Michigan. This population explosion was largely attributable to the removal of larger predatory species by lampreys. Periodic die-offs of the alewives now endanger urban water supplies and impede recreation by their stench (see opening photograph to Part 4, p. 190); Michigan alone lost more than 50 million dollars in tourist business in the summer of 1967.

These successive changes in the Great Lakes fisheries were spurred by two of the basic causes outlined early in this book—increased demand by growing nearby human populations and increased technological ability to exploit the fish populations.

Now the human impacts on the lakes and their biota are accelerating and diversifying. Millions of salmon and other large exotic fish have been planted since 1966. Thermal pollution by nuclear power plants has commenced. DDT and other chlorinated hydrocarbons have contaminated aquatic food chains, with concentrations in herring gulls reaching a deleterious average of 2,441 ppm (Hickey, and others, 1966).

Stanford H. Smith (b. 1920) is a fishery research biologist with the Bureau of Commercial Fisheries, U.S. Fish and Wildlife Service, with which he has been associated since 1944. He holds degrees from Oregon State University and University of Michigan (Ph.D. in zoology, 1954). He has written numerous publications on the limnology and fishery ecology of the Great Lakes.

This selection is from the *Journal Fisheries Research Board of Canada* 25(4):667–693, 1968. Reproduced with the permission of the author and the Queen's Printer for Canada.

Recurrent spills of cyanide, hundreds of gallons at a time, cause repeated fish kills—"But," as the mayor of one town where such a spill occurred remarked, "there is a lot of water out there" (*Ann Arbor News,* April 8, 1970). By 1970 discharges of mercury—as much as 200 pounds a day from one Dow Chemical Company plant alone (*New York Times,* April 19, 1970)—have so contaminated fish in Lake St. Clair, the Detroit River, and western Lake Erie that human consumption of all fish from these waters has been banned indefinitely.

In other lakes and in the oceans overfishing has drastically cut the yields of other favored fish species, including the California sardine (1946), the Northwest Pacific salmon (1950), the Atlantio-Scandian herring (1961), and the Barents Sea cod (1962). Likewise, the history of whaling is a history of overexploitation (McVay, 1966). Even with the development of new sea and fresh water fisheries, fish and other marine organisms will not provide the limitless food energy that some popular writers have pictured. Food production from the sea can probably increase only about 2.5 times that being produced in 1968— to an expected total of 150–160 million metric tons annually. However, even this expected production would supply only about 3 percent of the energy requirements of the six to seven billion people expected by the end of this century (Ricker, 1969).

(Editor's comment)

It was not apparent until recent years that the intensive and selective fishery of the Great Lakes over the past century has been a significant factor in a major modification of fish stocks. A succession of fish species would be expected during the natural aging process of the Great Lakes, but recent progressive changes in species composition have been rapid and obviously accelerated by influences of man, both by enrichment of the environment with wastes and by despoilment of the most abundant or preferred species of fish.

The species composition of fish in the Great Lakes has undergone continual change since the earliest records (Smith and Snell, 1891) but never have changes been more rapid or more drastic than in recent years. Environmental changes in Lake Erie (Beeton, 1961) and the related changes in the composition of the fish population and other aquatic organisms (Smith, 1962) have received considerable publicity in recent years. Modifications of fish stocks in the upper Great Lakes (Superior, Michigan, and

Huron), which are deeper and more oligotrophic, have been equal to or greater than changes in Lake Erie, but appear not closely related to modification of the physical-chemical environment. Although the water quality of the upper Great Lakes has undergone some changes (Beeton, 1965), these have not been the primary cause of what appears, with few exceptions, to be an irreversible succession of the major fish species. Recent changes have led to a state of biological instability in the mid-1960's that is almost unparalleled in the history of fishery science.

Early Changes

Since its beginning over a century ago the fishery of the Great Lakes has always shown preference for species that were abundant and in high demand. Less than a dozen species have been major contributors to the catch and, despite an intensive selective fishery, major changes in these species were few and local until recent years. Those that were influenced greatly by the fishery before the late 1930's were the lake sturgeon (*Acipenser fulvescens*), lake herring (*Leucichthys artedi*[1]), and lake whitefish (*Coregonus clupeaformis*).

LAKE STURGEON

The lake sturgeon was the first species affected by intensive exploitation and the only one that was knowingly depleted by man. Although the commercial value of the sturgeon was not great, they were abundant in all of the Great Lakes before 1900, particularly near shore where fishing for other species was heavy. These large fish frequently damaged gear fished for more valuable species, and were fished heavily to remove them from the fishing grounds (Harkness and Dymond, 1961). The recorded catches of sturgeon in the late 1800's exceeded 1 million lb annually in each of Lakes Michigan, Huron, and Erie, and often reached several hundred thousand pounds in Lakes Ontario and Superior (Baldwin and Saalfeld, 1962). The recorded catches represent an unknown fraction of the total poundage taken; many were killed and thrown back in the lake or left to rot on the beaches. As a consequence of their slow growth and late maturity the accumulated stocks of adult fish were soon reduced to insignificance and became so scarce by the 1920's that sturgeon fishing was prohibited throughout most U.S. waters of Lakes Superior, Michigan, and Huron. Restrictions have been lifted in the State of Michigan waters of these lakes in recent years to permit the fishermen to keep sturgeon which are caught incidental to other fishing.

[1] Some authors include *Leucichthys* (ciscoes) in the genus *Coregonus* (whitefishes). I prefer the separate genera for clarity, and because a recent acrylamide electrophoretic study of blood serum made by Richard Chellevold at the University of Michigan showed that the serum proteins distinctly separate ciscoes and whitefishes of both North America and Europe; that ciscoes and whitefishes each produce identical electrophoretic patterns between the continents; and that differences between ciscoes and whitefishes of Europe are the same as the differences in North America. Thus it is evident that the two groups are genetically distinct; have had separate origins; have attained their circumpolar distribution independently; and deserve generic distinction.

The total production, however, is only a few thousand pounds in any of the lakes.

Partial protection of the sturgeon did not seem to increase its abundance noticeably, nor has an incidental fishery seemed to cause a decline. The only noticeable recent decline has been in Lake Erie, where catches have reached new lows since the mid-1950's, which may reflect recent unfavorable changes in the environment (Carr, 1962; Carr and Hiltunen, 1965; Carr et al., 1965). The lake sturgeon undoubtedly will continue to live in the Great Lakes at low abundance until influenced adversely by the changing environment, or by a fishery for another species that raises the incidental catch above the limit of its biological yield.

LAKE HERRING

The collapse of the lake herring population in Lake Erie in the mid-1920's (Van Oosten, 1930) was the first precipitous change in the fish stocks of the Great Lakes. Historically the lake herring has been very abundant and the most productive species in the Great Lakes—frequently contributing one-third to one-half of the catch of various lakes. In Lake Erie, lake herring were particularly abundant and were larger than in the other lakes. Because of these factors and the proximity of markets in large eastern cities, the fishery was intense. Before the collapse of the population the recorded catches were usually greater than 20 million lb annually and ranged as high as 49 million lb. Actual catches were much greater, however, as large quantities were frequently discarded during periods when catches were heavy and the market was glutted (Van Oosten, 1930).

The cause of the collapse of lake herring stocks in Lake Erie was never settled because detailed biological, ecological, and fishing data were lacking, but there are two pertinent factors that can be considered in retrospect. Fishing was very intense in the years preceding the decline and was particularly intense in the fall of 1924—the year before the decline—due to an unusual concentration of lake herring in the east end of the lake (Van

Oosten, 1930). After initial collapse the lake herring produced only one strong year-class—that hatched in 1944 (Scott, 1951)—although substantial spawning stocks were present until the mid-1950's. If the fishing rate before the decline was near that required for full utilization of the biological potential of the stock, and if recruitment was lowered due to reduction of spawning stocks or to environmental variability in the early 1920's, the catch would have exceeded the maximum sustainable yield. This relation must lead to a swift decline in the stock (Ricker, 1963).

Although intensive exploitation and possible interaction with environmental change may have caused the sharp drop in lake herring stocks in the 1920's, a subsequent decline since the mid-1940's to extreme rarity approaching extinction in the mid-1960's undoubtedly is a response to increasingly unfavorable physical-chemical or biological environmental conditions. Fish collected in 1957 showed average 1st-year growth of lake herring of only 2.7 inches (Scott and Smith, 1962) which is much below the calculated 1st-year growth for lake herring in Lake Superior (4.7 inches; Dryer and Beil, 1964), Green Bay, Michigan (5.2 inches; Smith, 1956), or Saginaw Bay, Lake Huron (6.0 inches; Van Oosten, 1929). The slowest 1st-year growth recorded for the lake herring of 11 other lakes in the Great Lakes region was 3.4 inches (Carlander, 1953). Fish of Lake Erie, however, have been noted for their rapid growth. Examination of scales from Lake Erie lake herring showed that the average 1st-year growth was 7.2 inches—the highest value recorded for this species—for fish collected in 1945. The decline to 2.7 inches in 1957 provides strong evidence that the recent reduction of the lake herring in Lake Erie is more likely a result of environmental stress than a result of the small catches that have continued, and which have been mostly incidental to fishing for other species.

LAKE WHITEFISH

The second collapse of a local fishery during the early period involved the development of a new type of gear—the deep trap net—that was very efficient for capture of lake whitefish in Lake Huron (Van Oosten et al., 1946). These nets were introduced in Lake Huron in 1928 at a time when whitefish abundance was high and apparently increasing. Beginning in 1930 their use expanded rapidly throughout the U.S. waters of the lake (this gear was never permitted in Canada), and the net proved particularly effective in central and southern Lake Huron. Over 4.1 million lb of whitefish were taken from the lake in 1931. As the nets were moved successively into various sections of the lake, local stocks were depleted rapidly. Thus, although stocks in different locations declined sharply, the total production of the lake did not decrease abruptly. The catch had declined to 1.9 million lb in 1935 when restrictions were imposed that prohibited setting trap nets in water deeper than 80 ft, but continued to decline to less than 0.1 million lb in 1942. Predation by the sea lamprey (*Petromyzon marinus*) discussed later may have been responsible in part for this low. Except for progeny of a very successful 1943 year-class that resulted in catches of about 3 million lb in U.S. waters in 1947 and 1948, the catch of lake whitefish has been less than 0.2 million lb in most years after the 1942 low (Baldwin and Saalfeld, 1962). A high mortality of the 1943 year-class and the recent low have been attributed to sea lamprey depredations rather than depletion through overfishing (Hile and Buettner, 1959).

OTHER SPECIES

Although unrelated to exploitation, collapse of another fish stock which took place in the early 1940's should be mentioned briefly. The American smelt (*Osmerus mordax*) was endemic in Lake Ontario but was introduced into the Lake Michigan drainage in 1912 and underwent a population explosion in Lakes Michigan and Huron in the 1930's (Van Oosten, 1937). The smelt population suffered a severe mortality during the fall and winter of 1942–43 probably due to a bacterial or virus disease (Van Oosten, 1947). The commercial production in Lake Michigan, where a thriving fishery for smelt had been established, fell from 4.8 million lb in 1941 to 4500 lb in 1944. The population recovered, however, and contributed to a very productive fishery as it became established in all of the lakes above Lake Ontario. The fishery was particularly productive in Lake Michigan where the catch reached a maximum of 9.1 million lb in 1958, and in Lake Erie where a peak catch of 19.2 million lb was produced in 1962.

A selective fishery for the larger chubs or deepwater ciscoes (*Leucichthys* spp.) influenced the species composition of this closely related group of species during the late 1800's and early 1900's. The early stages of these changes could not be measured because the various species of chubs were taken in the same net and were so similar that they were not sorted by the fishermen or listed separately in the catch statistics. But early records indicate clearly that the two largest species (*L. nigripinnis* and *L. johannae*) did, in fact, decline (Hile and Buettner, 1955). This early decline of certain species of chubs is discussed later in relation to the extreme modification of the chub population in recent years.

Recent Changes

A rapid sequence of catastrophic changes which started in the 1940's led to a major alteration of the fish stocks in the Great Lakes. Until the 1940's the fishery of the Great Lakes as a whole was stable and productive despite loss of the sturgeon and the collapse of a few stocks in certain lakes. All preferred species continued in abundance somewhere in the Great Lakes; although many showed varying degrees of cyclical fluctuation, the composition of the total catch showed no marked changes or trends. The total production had stabilized and fluctuated only slightly around 100 million lb after declining from highs which often exceeded 140 million lb before 1920.

The major events that started in the 1940's involved the upper three lakes (Huron, Michigan, and Superior). The resulting succession of species resembled similar changes that apparently had taken place earlier in Lake Ontario, but which had gone almost unnoticed because the fishery was small and little studied. Changes that were progressing in Lake Erie, and which have accelerated since the 1940's, are not discussed here because both selective exploitation and environmental change were involved and their interactions are not understood.

The most intensive studies in the upper three lakes were made in Lake Michigan which is used here to illustrate similar events in Lakes Huron and Superior. The primary differences among these lakes have been timing and degree—in general, changes in Lake Huron started earlier and appear to have progressed further than Lake Michigan, and in Lake Superior they started later and have not advanced as far. The ultimate outcome may differ among the three lakes—their limnological characteristics differ somewhat, all are undergoing rapid change, and varying types and degrees of management are being imposed when each lake is at a different stage of change.

THE LAKE MICHIGAN FISHERY

The history of fishery exploitation in Lake Michigan was typical of the other Great Lakes. The highest annual production occurred near or before the turn of the century when the fishery had become well established. The catch exceeded 40 million lb in 4 of the 13 years for which statistics were available between 1897 and 1909 (Baldwin and Saalfeld, 1962), and averaged 35 million lb (Table 44.1). In subsequent periods the total catch showed no marked variations or trends (Figure 44.1) and averaged about 25 million lb until 1966 when the catch increased sharply to over 42 million lb due primarily to a greater catch of alewives. Nine species have been major contributors to the catch; they have constituted 95.6–99.8% of the catch in periods for which records of all species are complete (Table 44.1).

TABLE 44.1 Catch of major species and total commercial catch (thousands of pounds) per year in Lake Michigan for various periods.

| Period | Native species | | | | | | New species | | | Total major species | | Other species | Total catch |
	Lake trout	Lake herring	Suckers	Whitefish	Chubs	Yellow perch	Carp[a]	Smelt[b]	Alewife[c]	Pounds	Percentage of total catch		
1898–1909	7,225	16,977	1,810	2,715	2,061	3,866	261	—	—	34,915	—	— d	35,149
1910–1919	6,763	8,642	4,035	1,670	3,525	2,411	247	—	—	27,293	—	— d	27,059
1920–1929	7,001	4,015	2,117	2,111	2,902	1,537	679	—	—	20,362	—	— d	20,477
1930–1934	5,342	4,985	2,258	3,730	4,387	1,199	769	425	—	23,075	98.0	465	23,540
1935–1939	5,038	4,621	2,280	1,201	5,295	2,406	1,605	1,462	—	23,908	98.7	312	24,220
1940–1944	6,579	1,830	2,125	1,351	1,971	2,729	1,702	2,913	—	21,200	97.8	474	21,674
1945–1949	2,675	6,044	1,901	3,756	5,435	1,446	1,319	765	—	23,324	95.6	1,066	24,407
1950–1954	14	8,000	882	1,436	10,482	1,963	1,170	4,384	—	28,334	97.1	848	29,182
1955–1959	<1	3,639	652	105	9,947	3,055	1,785	6,983	568	26,735	97.8	592	27,327
1960	<1	233	767	124	12,695	3,285	1,416	3,267	2,370	24,158	99.4	153	24,311
1961	<1	177	494	412	12,133	4,959	1,842	2,152	3,199	25,370	99.3	189	25,559
1962	<1	116	263	278	11,115	4,050	1,206	1,546	4,742	23,317	99.3	158	23,475
1963	<1	41	299	298	7,460	4,872	1,277	1,203	5,396	20,795	98.9	226	21,021
1964	<1	34	215	788	5,172	5,835	1,320	969	11,744	26,080	99.5	121	26,201
1965	<1	47	168	995	7,441	1,297	2,016	927	14,007	26,900	99.7	94	26,994
1966	<1	49	402	1,422	7,228	654	2,713	1,110	29,002	42,580	99.8	97	42,677

[a] Introduced in the late 1800's.
[b] Introduced into Crystal Lake tributary to Lake Michigan in 1912.
[c] Invaded the upper Great Lakes via the Welland Canal and was first reported in Lake Michigan in 1949.
[d] Data incomplete.

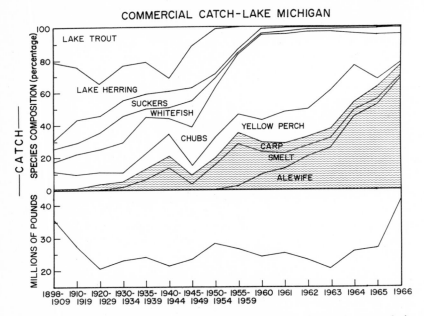

FIGURE 44.1 Contribution of major species (percentage) and total commerical catch (pounds) of Lake Michigan for various periods 1898–1966. Shaded portion indicates exotic species.

At the turn of the century seven major species were represented in the catch (Table 44.1). The lake trout (*Salvelinus namaycush*) and lake herring were the largest contributors, and the carp (*Cyprinus carpio*), which was introduced into the lake in the late 1800's, constituted less than 1% of the catch. Despite increased abundance of carp and the subsequent introduction and establishment of the smelt, the relative contribution of the native species to the catch showed no marked changes or trends until the 1945–49 period when the lake trout catch declined sharply. Subsequent species changes took place in swift succession (Figure 44.1). In 1966, the catch was dominated by the alewife (*Alosa pseudoharengus*) which invaded the lake in the late 1940's (first recorded in 1949; Miller, 1957); exotic species constituted nearly 77% of the catch; and the portion of the catch composed of lake trout, lake herring, suckers (*Catostomus* spp. and *Moxostoma* spp.), and whitefish was only 4.4% as compared with more than 82% in the 1898–1909 period.

Several factors contributed to this extreme change. Much is known about these factors and their interactions although the exact mechanisms that brought about the change are incompletely understood. Unquestionably, predation of the sea lamprey initiated the events that led to the extreme decline of the lake trout in the upper Great Lakes. The resultant pressures of a shifting fishery and a population explosion of the alewife were factors of major significance. How these factors operated is illustrated by examining the changes in the deepwater stocks— lake trout and chubs—which occupy the area most strongly affected by sea lamprey predation, and the changes in the fishery.

DECLINE OF THE LAKE TROUT

The lake trout has provided the most stable fishery of the Great Lakes. It was particularly productive in Lakes Superior, Huron, and Michigan, where catches usually exceeded 4, 5, and 6 million lb, respectively, and had not fluctuated widely before the declines in recent years. Biological information about the early stocks is not available. It is possible, however, as Kennedy (1954) has observed for lake trout stocks in Great Slave Lake, that recruitment was not strongly cyclic and that annual fluctuations of year-class strength were not great.

Lake trout production has been highest in Lake Michigan but the history of the catch was similar for all three lakes even though timing differed somewhat (Hile, 1949; Hile et al., 1951a, b). Catches in Lake Michigan increased in 1879–90 during the development of the fishery on the newly exploited stocks (Figure 44.2). Production was highest during 1890–1911 and was characterized by periods of relative stability in 1912–26 and 1927–39 at slightly lower levels (Hile et al., 1951a). The catch increased briefly in 1940–44, after which it underwent the collapse attributed to sea lamprey predation, and neared extinction by the mid-1950's due to a complete failure of natural reproduction after 1948 (Eschmeyer, 1957).

The collapse of the lake trout populations in the upper Great Lakes stimulated a massive effort to control the sea lamprey (Moffett, 1958). The early research has produced information on sea lamprey abundance during its population explosion that helps to interpret the relation between sea lamprey predation and lake trout decline, and the subsequent upset of the chub stocks. Although the measures of sea lamprey abundance over the longest period for each lake

are based on spawning adults entering only one or a few streams (Table 44.2), their agreement with trends in counts available for shorter periods for other streams at various times suggests that these measures reflect closely the trends of abundance for each of the lakes.

The abundance of sea lampreys was very low in all three of the upper Great Lakes at the time when lake trout stocks started to decline (Figure 44.3). The lake trout were unquestionably the prime prey of the sea lamprey as lake trout were the only abundant species of large fish that inhabited the colder (subthermocline) regions of the lakes preferred by the sea lamprey. Although large burbot (*Lota lota*), which occupied this area were less abundant and suffered the same fate as the lake trout, it can be safely assumed that the trout suffered the brunt of the earliest predation. This predation could not have been great since spawning runs into the larger streams reportedly amounted to less than a hundred individuals before and during the early stages of lake trout decline (Vernon C. Applegate, personal communication).

The decline of lake trout in Lake Michigan was particularly abrupt, however, and may reflect the possible combined effect of increased predation by sea lampreys that were able to move freely from Lake Huron into Lake Michigan, and by the greater exploitation of lake trout by the commercial fishery in the period just before the decline. The

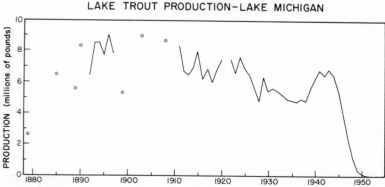

LAKE TROUT PRODUCTION–LAKE MICHIGAN

FIGURE 44.2 Commerical production of lake trout in Lake Michigan for years of records 1879–1955.

TABLE 44.2 Number of sea lampreys counted during spawning runs in various streams in Lakes Huron, Michigan, and Superior, and their abundance index expressed as percentage of the average for the period of counts in each lake.[a]

Year	Lake Huron[b] Ocqueoc River	Abundance	Lake Michigan[c] Hibbards Creek	Three[d] streams	Abundance	Lake Superior[c] Five[e] streams	Abundance
1944	4,488	50	–	–	–	–	–
1945	6,144	68	–	–	–	–	–
1946	8,072[f]	90	125	–	3	–	–
1947	10,000	111	596	–	16	–	–
1948	13,000	145	989	–	27	–	–
1949	24,634	275	1,579	–	43	–	–
1950	18,822	210	5,431	–	148	–	–
1951	19,393	216	12,640	–	345	–	–
1952	9,437	105	3,302	–	90	–	–
1953	11,676	130	9,247	–	252	1,424	24
1954	10,183	113	7,279	–	199	2,614	45
1955	13,683	153	6,395	18,279	164	3,096	53
1956	10,923[f]	122	5,325	19,653	155	8,048	138
1957	8,163	91	6,525	18,175	165	12,983	223
1958	5,465[f]	61	2,563	10,669	80	6,649	114
1959	2,766	31	2,330	8,636	68	8,224	141
1960	7,560	84	–	6,651	52	12,897	221
1961	4,715	53	–	12,886	101	13,305	228
1962	5,205	58	–	8,089	63	2,743	47
1963	4,674	52	–	7,461	59	3,838	66
1964	2,677	30	–	4,593	36	2,250	39
1965	1,390	15	–	3,277	26	2,205	38
1966	3,273	36	–	1,168	9	1,359	23

[a] The abundance for Lake Michigan was obtained by adjusting the total catch of the three streams to equal the catch of Hibbards Creek for the period of overlap (1955–59), averaging the figures for each year during this period, and extending the series based on the 1959 average and the percentage change from year to year for counts of the three streams.
[b] Records supplied by Dr Vernon C. Applegate.
[c] From reports of the Great Lakes Fishery Committee, and meeting reports and annual reports of the Great Lakes Fishery Commission available at the library of the Ann Arbor Laboratory, U.S. Bureau of Commercial Fisheries.
[d] Bark, Cedar, and Sturgeon rivers.
[e] Betsy River, Furnace Creek, Miners River, Sucker River, and Two Hearted River.
[f] No counts made; estimates are means of preceding and following years.

increased catch occurred during the period when lake trout stocks were declining in Lake Huron and may be related in part to greater demand and higher prices at the time. Although the greater production may have been due in part to improvement in stocks since it was not accompanied by increased fishing effort in State of Michigan waters (Hile et al., 1951a), the higher production resulted mostly from the increased catch in Illinois which rose from 259 to 972 thousand lb (275% increase) between the periods 1927–39 and 1940–44. The Illinois catch had never been large and the increased catch of 713 thousand lb must have resulted in part from greater fishing intensity because of proximity to the Chicago market, the strong demand during World War II, and the declining catch in Lake Huron. It is also unlikely that the abundance increased to this degree in Illinois waters alone as sharp fluctuations in abundance were not characteristic of the lake trout and lake trout move freely throughout the lake (Smith and Van Oosten, 1940). This increase alone was more than 13% above the 1927–39 average for Lake Michigan, and if only half of it were attributed to greater fishing effort, it could have initiated a weakening of the lake trout stocks.

If fishing had been near the optimum rate in earlier years, only a small increase in exploitation would have been necessary to start a decline in the stocks. In an example based on biological characteristics similar to those of lake trout, Ricker (1963) determined that a 14% increase in exploitation separated maximum yield and no yield (collapse of the stock), and that half this increase (7%) would initiate a sharp decline. Thus, an increase of only 370–740 thousand lb over the average of about 5.3 million lb for the earlier period of stability during 1927–39 (Hile et al., 1951a) may have been sufficient to initiate the decline of the lake trout stock, which then became weakened further by sea lamprey predation.

INTERACTION OF THE DEEPWATER FISHERIES

Until the establishment of the alewife in recent years, lake trout and chubs were the only species that were abundant in the deepwater area of Lake Michigan and important in the fishery. Although the interactions between the lake trout and chub fisheries were complex (Hile and Buettner, 1955), the two fisheries were essentially alternate; they usually employed the same boats and fished in much the same areas, but differed in the use of large-mesh gillnets for lake trout and small mesh for chubs.

The chub fishery was depressed by reduced effort during the war years in 1940–44, but recovered as the lake trout declined; the change reflected a transfer of effort from lake trout to chubs (Hile and Buettner, 1955). The chub catch reached a record high of 7 million lb in 1949 and increased to a high period of production above 10 million lb during 1951–57 (Table 44.3). It was during these same peak years of chub production that the sea lamprey attained its greatest

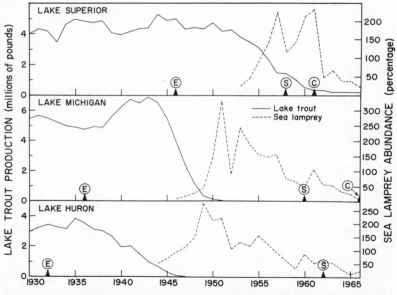

FIGURE 44.3 Production of lake trout and abundance of the sea lamprey in Lakes Superior, Michigan, and Huron, and the time of first sea lamprey record or establishment (E), initiation of chemical control (S), and completion of the initial series of chemical treatment (C) in each Lake.

TABLE 44.3 Production of lake trout, chubs, and alewives, and estimated pounds of fish destroyed by spawning run sea lampreys in Lake Michigan in 1935–66.

| Year | Lake trout | Chubs | | | Alewife | Fish destroyed by sea lamprey[a] |
		Gillnet	Trawl	Total		
		(Thousands of pounds of fish)				
1935	4,873	5,794	–	5,794	–	–
1936	4,763	5,674	–	5,674	–	–
1937	4,988	5,579	–	5,579	–	–
1938	4,906	5,404	–	5,404	–	–
1939	5,660	4,025	–	4,025	–	–
1940	6,266	1,648	–	1,648	–	–
1941	6,787	1,630	–	1,630	–	–
1942	6,484	1,755	–	1,755	–	–
1943	6,860	2,214	–	2,214	–	–
1944	6,498	2,607	–	2,607	–	–
1945	5,437	4,221	–	4,221	–	–
1946	3,974	4,525	–	4,525	–	116
1947	2,425	5,087	–	5,087	–	554
1948	1,197	5,929	–	5,929	–	919
1949	342	7,421	–	7,421	–	1,467
1950	54	9,291	–	9,291	–.	5,046
1951	11	10,301	–	10,301	–	11,744
1952	4	11,098	–	11,098	–	3,068
1953	b	11,151	–	11,151	–	8,591
1954	b	10,568	–	10,568	–	6,762
1955	b	10,895	–	10,895	–	5,576
1956	0	10,913	–	10,913	b	5,275
1957	0	10,546	–	10,546	220	5,622
1958	0	9,583	–	9,583	1,357	2,711
1959	b	6,392	1,404	7,796	1,264	2,313
1960	b	5,530	7,129	12,695	2,370	1,782
1961	b	5,915	6,218	12,133	3,199	3,452
1962	b	6,346	4,769	11,115	4,742	2,167
1963	26	4,050	3,410	7,460	5,396	1,999
1964	b	3,381	1,791	5,172	11,744	1,230
1965	b	6,857	583	7,440	14,007	877
1966	b	6,990	238	7,228	29,002	313

[a] Based upon a proportional expansion of the abundance index (Table 44.2) to reflect the sea lamprey count in 1958 when the maximum number of streams were blocked with counting barriers (Great Lakes Fishery Commission, 1958) which was doubled on the assumption that one-half of the spawning streams were blocked, and that each lamprey killed 37 lb of fish to reach maturity (Packer and Lennon, 1956).

[b] Less than 500 lb. Most lake trout caught since 1953 were hatchery-reared fish planted to measure survival and planting techniques.

abundance. Because the deep waters contained no other prey (lake trout and burbot had both disappeared) the chubs received the impact of sea lamprey predation (Moffett, 1957). The estimated pounds of fish killed by the number of sea lampreys that had survived to spawn exceeded 11 million lb in 1951 and was above 5 million lb until 1957 except for a low of 3 million lb in 1952. These estimates are conservative because they are based on counts of spawning-run sea lampreys and do not account for an unknown amount of predation by lampreys that did not survive to spawn.

The consequence of this extreme pressure of high commercial production and sea lamprey predation on the chub population was severe. Of the seven species of chubs that inhabited Lake Michigan the two largest (*Leucichthys johannae* and *L. nigripinnis*) had become extinct, and the four species of intermediate size (*L. alpenae, L. kiyi, L. reighardi,* and *L. zenithicus*) had been seriously depleted as shown in a survey during 1960–61 (Smith, 1964). The smallest and slowest growing chub, the bloater (*L. hoyi*), was favored during this period and became very abundant. It had been a primary food of the lake trout (Van Oosten and Deason, 1938) and most were too small to be taken profitably in commercial gillnets or serve as suitable prey for the sea lamprey. As the supply of larger chubs declined during the late 1950's, the commercial gillnet catch declined, and the abundance of sea lampreys and their predation decreased (Figure 44.4), but the total chub catch increased to a new high of 12.7 million lb in 1960 (Table 44.3). This increase resulted from the use of trawls which had not been employed in the Great Lakes fishery until they were introduced in the late 1950's to catch the small bloater which had become very abundant by the mid-1950's (Moffett, 1957) and alewives which were starting to become abundant.

Most of the bloaters and the alewife were too small for the human food market, and trawling provided an efficient means of catching them in large quantity at low cost for animal food and fish meal. Markets for alewives were not well established, however, and the population had not increased sufficiently to support heavy production during all seasons. The trawl fishery was restricted to certain species and depths of fishing so that the only abundant species that could be taken by trawling were alewives and chubs. Thus, during the early stages of the trawl fishery bloaters composed the greater part of the catch (Table 44.3) because they were very abundant, available during all seasons, brought a higher price than alewives on the animal-food market, and included some large chubs (about 7% of the catch) that brought a high price on the human-food market.

Even the gillnet fishery became dependent

on bloaters when species of large chubs had become scarce during the late 1950's. The human-food market accepted smaller chubs at lower price, but the bloaters were also becoming larger (Tables 44.4 and 44.5). The average length of bloaters in both southern and northern Lake Michigan increased in every year for which data are available between 1954 and 1966. The mean length in southern Lake Michigan increased almost 2 inches during this period, and the percentage of bloaters large enough for the human-food market (usually > 9 inches) increased from 4.2 to 38.2%. In northern Lake Michigan the length increased about 1 inch between 1955 and 1964, and the bloaters suited for human food rose from 25.0 to 67.0%. Since the average length of bloaters taken in 1960–61 increased from south to north (Table 44.6), it might be assumed that the length increased throughout the lake during the period of 1954–66. Preliminary studies show that this increase in average length reflects both an increase in average age and an increase in growth rate.

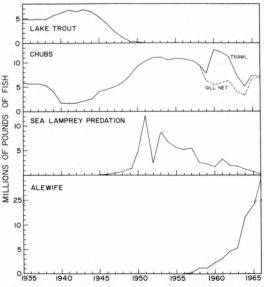

FIGURE 44.4 Production of lake trout, chubs, and alewives, and the estimated pounds of fish destroyed by sea lampreys of the spawning population of Lake Michigan.

TABLE 44.4 Length distribution (percentage) of bloaters taken in trawls in southern Lake Michigan at Grand Haven (1954, 1960) and Saugatuck (1962–66).

Length (inches)	Year						
	1954	1960	1962	1963	1964	1965	1966
2.5–2.9	0.1	–	–	–	–	–	–
3.0–3.4	0.1	–	–	–	–	–	–
3.5–3.9	0.5	–	–	–	–	–	–
4.0–4.4	1.2	T	T	–	T	–	–
4.5–4.9	1.3	T	0.2	–	T	–	0.1
5.0–5.4	1.2	0.1	T	T	–	T	0.3
5.5–5.9	10.8	0.2	0.1	0.1	T	–	0.1
6.0–6.4	22.5	0.8	–	0.1	T	0.1	0.1
6.5–6.9	23.8	3.0	0.6	0.2	0.1	0.1	0.1
7.0–7.4	12.7	20.1	9.2	3.3	3.6	2.0	0.9
7.5–7.9	10.3	32.3	35.0	26.4	25.6	17.7	10.1
8.0–8.4	6.4	19.9	28.4	34.6	32.6	28.4	23.8
8.5–8.9	4.9	11.5	13.8	17.2	19.2	22.9	26.3
9.0–9.4	2.4	7.3	6.8	10.0	10.4	15.9	20.3
9.5–9.9	1.2	3.4	3.8	4.9	5.7	7.5	10.7
10.0–10.4	0.5	1.1	1.6	2.3	1.9	3.7	5.1
10.5–10.9	0.1	0.2	0.4	0.7	0.6	1.3	1.5
11.0–11.4	–	0.1	0.1	0.2	0.2	0.3	0.5
11.5–11.9	–	–	–	–	0.1	0.1	0.1
12.0–12.4	–	–	–	–	–	T	–
Avg length:	6.86	7.98	8.15	8.36	8.38	8.59	8.78
No. of fish:	4,336	16,454	1,745	5,215	8,720	3,055	1,771
Percentage >9.0 inches:	4.2	12.1	12.7	18.1	18.9	28.8	38.2

TABLE 44.5 Length distribution (percentage) of bloaters taken in trawls at Manistique in northern Lake Michigan in various years between 1955 and 1964.

Length (inches)	1955	1961	1964
5.0–5.4	0.8	–	–
5.5–5.9	0.3	–	–
6.0–6.4	1.3	0.1	–
6.5–6.9	1.8	–	–
7.0–7.4	6.7	2.8	0.4
7.5–7.9	13.2	11.5	1.9
8.0–8.4	26.9	28.7	9.9
8.5–8.9	24.0	24.3	20.8
9.0–9.4	12.4	17.0	29.5
9.5–9.9	7.7	10.2	18.7
10.0–10.4	2.8	3.7	11.2
10.5–10.9	1.5	1.3	5.1
11.0–11.4	0.3	0.2	1.7
11.5–11.9	0.3	0.2	0.6
12.0–12.4	–	–	0.2
Avg length:	8.46	8.68	9.30
No. of fish:	387	1635	475
Percentage >9.0 inches:	25.0	32.6	67.0

The combined influence of the new trawl fishery and the increase in size of bloaters which made them better suited for the gillnet fishery resulted in the largest chub catches of record in Lake Michigan in 1960–62. Sea lamprey predation of about 2 million lb or more during this period was also directed primarily at bloaters, many of which had increased to a size more vulnerable to lamprey predation.

The chub fishery declined sharply after this period of record catch (Figure 44.4). Deaths from botulism in October 1963 of several persons who had eaten smoked chubs from the Great Lakes undoubtedly contributed to the low catches in 1963–64, but the catch through September 1963 had already declined 27% from that of the comparable period in 1962. The increase between 1964 and 1965 probably reflects recovery of the market after the botulism scare and the sharp increase in availability of large bloaters (Tables 44.4 and 44.5).

INTERACTION AMONG DEEPWATER SPECIES

There is little question that the selective fishery in the Great Lakes has had a substantial influence on the interaction among various species (Hile, 1954). When ecological relationships are disturbed by selective fishing so that the reduction of some species gives a competitive advantage to others, a population imbalance is created and a rapid succession of species can follow. It is difficult to separate successions induced by environmental changes from those caused by exploitation because both factors are usually involved. The deepwater area of Lake Michigan has had no conspicuous environmental changes except in fish populations, however, and provides a good illustration of the interaction and succession of species influenced primarily by exploitation.

Unexploited stocks. The Great Lakes are young; during less than 10,000 years in their present form they have developed a very simple deepwater fish fauna. The lake trout was the principal climax predator and it fed mostly on the young of six species of large chubs and a small slow-growing chub bloater (Figure 44.5A). Adults of the larger chubs were mostly too large for prey of lake trout and provided a breeding stock that added stability to the predator-prey balance.

The burbot was the only other predator in the deepwater region but it was less abundant than the lake trout. The lake trout and burbot also preyed heavily on the deepwater sculpin (*Myoxocephalus thompsonii*) and to a lesser extent on the ninespine stickleback (*Pungitius pungitius*) in the northern end of the lake (Van Oosten and Deason, 1938). Measures of abundance are not available for the burbot, sculpin, and stickleback and they cannot be included in this discussion, but it can be assumed that the burbot underwent changes similar to the lake trout. There has been no evidence of major change in the abundance of the deepwater sculpin (which occupies a very limited niche close to the bottom in the deeper areas throughout the lake) or of the stickleback (largely restricted to the northern section of the lake).

TABLE 44.6 Length distribution (percentage) of bloaters taken in trawls at various ports in Lake Michigan in 1960 and 1961.

Length (*inches*)	St. Joseph 1960	Milwaukee 1960	Grand Haven 1960	Frankfort 1961	Sturgeon Bay 1961	Charlevoix 1961	Manistique 1961
2.5–2.9	–	–	–	0.1	–	–	–
3.5–3.9	0.1	–	–	–	–	–	–
4.0–4.4	–	–	T	–	–	–	–
4.5–4.9	–	0.1	T	0.1	–	–	–
5.0–5.4	T	T	0.1	0.5	–	–	–
5.5–5.9	0.1	0.1	0.2	0.5	–	–	–
6.0–6.5	0.4	1.0	0.8	0.6	–	0.1	0.1
6.5–6.9	3.1	2.5	3.0	2.0	0.4	0.3	–
7.0–7.4	31.6	20.5	20.1	9.8	5.0	3.6	2.8
7.5–7.9	36.7	37.3	32.3	30.2	24.8	18.3	11.5
8.0–8.4	15.0	23.3	19.9	26.1	36.7	32.4	28.7
8.5–8.9	6.8	8.9	11.5	15.6	22.4	21.7	24.3
9.0–9.4	4.1	4.3	7.3	8.3	8.4	13.0	17.0
9.5–9.9	1.6	1.6	3.4	3.8	2.0	6.1	10.2
10.0–10.4	0.5	0.3	1.1	1.9	0.3	3.3	3.7
10.5–10.9	T	0.1	0.2	0.4	–	1.0	1.3
11.0–11.4	–	T	0.1	0.1	–	0.1	0.2
11.5–11.9	–	–	–	–	–	0.1	0.2
Avg length:	7.74	7.86	7.98	8.14	8.25	8.49	8.68
No. of fish:	3,570	4,228	16,454	2,077	1,039	1,226	1,635

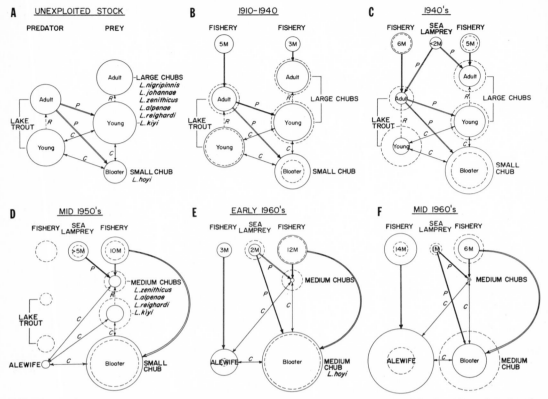

FIGURE 44.5 Interrelations of major deepwater species of Lake Michigan before exploitation (A) and during the following periods: stable exploitation, 1910–40 (B); early influence of the sea lamprey, 1940's (C); maximum abundance of the sea lamprey, mid-1950's (D); maximum abundance of bloaters, early 1960's (E); maximum abundance of the alewife, mid-1960's (F). P = predation; C = food competition; and R = recruitment.

Stable fishery, 1910–40. The introduction of a lake trout fishery which underwent an initial increase and several subsequent levels of stability (Hile et al., 1951a) undoubtedly had the usual effect on a newly exploited stock composed of many age-groups, and reduced the number of older and larger fish (Ricker, 1963). Data are lacking but scattered accounts indicate clearly that the largest lake trout were reduced and became legends by 1927–39 when the catch stabilized at about 5 million lb (Hile et al., 1951a). Since the lake trout experienced no major fluctuations it can be safely assumed that the stocks were not overexploited and that the population underwent the typical adjustment to lower average age, increased growth rate, and more rapid recruitment of young to adults which compensated for the exploitation of the fishery (Figure 44.5B).

A modest fishery for chubs that fluctuated about a usual catch of some 3 million lb had a similar influence on the chub stocks. Two of the largest species of chubs, however, were selected strongly by the fishery and were reduced greatly by the early 1900's (Hile and Buettner, 1955). This reduction was apparently compensated by an increase in the representation of bloaters in the chub stocks as measured during a fishery survey in 1930–32 (Moffett, 1957). The increase in abundance of bloaters would have offset any reduction of young of the larger chubs that served as prey for lake trout, and thus contributed to the stability of the lake trout stock and the lake trout fishery.

Establishment of the sea lamprey, 1940's. The sea lamprey became established in the deep-water population in small but significant numbers during the 1940's. Although the sea lamprey undoubtedly preyed on all large fish in the deepwater area (lake trout, burbot, and adults of large chub species), their effect on the lake trout population was swift and drastic. The estimated pounds of fish killed by the sea lamprey annually in the 1940's was small in comparison with later years and may not have exceeded 2 million lb at the end of the decade (Table 44.3). Sea lamprey predation certainly must have been comparatively small when the lake trout catch started to decline about 1945 (Figure 44.3). The increased exploitation by the fishery during the period immediately preceding the decline of lake trout, however, could have made the lake trout stock of Lake Michigan particularly sensitive to the predation by the sea lamprey.

As the lake trout declined, its predation on small chubs decreased and the sea lamprey predation turned from lake trout to the adults of large chubs. The fishery also transferred to large chubs as lake trout declined (Figure 44.4). Thus the deepwater stocks of Lake Michigan, after supporting a stable fishery since its beginning, entered a period of instability favoring bloaters (Figure 44.5C) which according to complaints of commercial fishermen had started to become a nuisance in their nets by 1950.

Sea lamprey maximum, mid-1950's. Fishery surveys of Lake Michigan during 1950-55 showed that the two largest chubs had become nearly extinct; that the four remaining species of larger chubs were greatly reduced; that bloaters constituted over 75% of the chub population (Moffett, 1957); and that lake trout were near extinction (Eschmeyer, 1957). By the mid-1950's the sea lamprey population had reached maximum abundance; the estimated destruction exceeded 5 million lb of fish per year (Table 44.3), primarily large chubs. In this period of peak abundance, the sea lamprey was also observed more frequently in shallower areas of

the lake where it preyed heavily on whitefish, suckers, and walleyes (*Stizostedion vitreum*), all of which suffered sharp reduction in stocks. The deepwater fishery which had only chubs to catch increased to over 10 million lb during 1951–57, the period of the sea lamprey maximum. The large chubs were preferred by the fishery but were insufficient to fill the demand so the larger bloaters started to enter the catch for the first time and were marketed as a "No. 2 chub" at a lower price.

The events of the mid-1950's produced great instability in the balance of deepwater species, created a strong pressure against the large chubs, and favored bloaters despite the first substantial exploitation of larger bloaters by the fishery (Figure 44.5D). An almost unnoticed but significant event in the early 1950's was the establishment of the alewife which was first reported in 1949. No alewives were taken in extensive experimental trawling in southern Lake Michigan in 1954, but eight alewives were taken during a survey throughout the northern part of the lake in 1955. Over 45,000 and 38,000 alewives were taken in experimental trawls during similar surveys of southern and northern Lake Michigan in 1960 and 1961, respectively.

Bloater maximum, early 1960's. Bloaters dominated the chub population even more strongly according to surveys in 1960–61, when they constituted 93–95% of the chubs taken in experimental gillnets (Smith, 1964). The abundance of bloaters had increased in the latter period at four of the seven locations used for 1954–55 and 1960–61 comparisons. The size of bloaters had increased during this period (Tables 44.4 and 44.5) and, since the largest individuals of the other species of chubs were gone, much of the ecological and fishery significance of size differences among species of chubs had been lost. Also exploitation of all sizes of chubs started with the initiation of trawling, as chubs constituted well over half of the catch taken by trawls in 1960–61 when the total chub catch had reached record highs above 12 million lb (Table 44.3). The larger chubs of all species were still preferred, however, and were exploited heavily by the gillnet fishery. The sea lamprey, which had suffered a population decline as its prey declined, still destroyed more than 2 million lb of fish annually in the early 1960's.

Thus, the pressures had shifted to bloaters but continued heavy on the small populations of the four larger chub species that remained in the lake (Figure 44.5E). The alewife was the only species present in deeper areas of the lake that could be favored by the selection against chubs. It had become well established throughout the lake by the early 1960's and supported an expanding fishery of about 3 million lb.

Alewife maximum, mid-1960's. The competitive advantage of the alewife which resulted from heavy exploitation of chubs of all sizes undoubtedly speeded a population explosion of alewives that gained its greatest impetus in the early 1960's. The number of young-of-the-year alewives taken in comparable trawling during early November in southern Lake Michigan increased 56 times between 1962 and 1964, and the number of adults increased 5 times between 1962 and 1966 (Table 44.7). The small change in abundance of adults, the increase in average age of the adult stock between 1965 and 1966, and the failure of the extremely large 1964 year-class to increase the adult stocks in 1966 indicate clearly that the alewife population was approaching saturation.

The great abundance of alewives and a continuing heavy exploitation of chubs had placed the chubs at a strong disadvantage by the mid-1960's (Figure 44.5F). It is not certain if the fishery for alewives that reached 29 million lb in 1966 was large enough to influence the alewife stocks sufficiently to affect their competitive advantage.

Measures of the abundance of chubs have not been available since 1960–61 but the dominance of bloaters continued to increase, and they constituted 99.2% of all chubs taken in experimental trawls during 1964 (Wells, 1966). Evidence also exists of a biological change of uncertain causes that may reflect

an ecological stress for bloaters. In addition to the marked increase in size of bloaters which reflects the combined effect of faster growth and an increase in average age in recent years, there has also been a continued increase in percentage of females in the population. The proportion of females in the population reached 97–99% during various months in 1966.

An increase in size has accompanied declines in populations of the lake herring, a close relative of the bloater. The size and growth rate of the lake herring of Lake Superior increased during early stages of a recent decline in numbers of fish in the stock in 1950–62 (Dryer and Beil, 1964), and the size has continued to increase as the abundance declined sharply after 1962. A well-documented study of the collapse of a lake herring population in Birch Lake, Michigan, showed that an increase in growth and size of fish in the population, and a strong dominance of females (84–93%) preceded a sharp decline in 1945–46 (Clady, 1967). Although data are lacking, the collapse of lake herring stocks of Lake Michigan in the late 1950's also was accompanied by observations of fishermen and biologists of a progressive increase in the size of fish taken in the fishery. The lake herring of Lake Michigan were presumed to have declined as a result of early establishment of alewives in shallow water (Miller, 1957). Such evidence implies that the recent biological changes of the bloater stocks of Lake Michigan may be indicators of a pending collapse of the population. There is no indication among coregonids that these changes have stopped or reversed until after the population has declined.

ESTABLISHMENT AND DOMINANCE OF THE ALEWIFE

The alewife has been the only fish in the Great Lakes that has occupied all sections of a lake and its bays, estuaries, and tributaries in great numbers. It has become the most abundant and widely distributed species in Lake Michigan where it has displaced all major planktivorous species. Although

TABLE 44.7 Abundance of adult and young-of-the-year alewives in Lake Michigan at Saugatuck, expressed as catch per 10-min trawl tow and as effective catch per unit of effort (CPE) for depths of 3–40 fath during early November in 1962–66.

Depth	Young-of-the-year					Adult				
	Nov. 8, 9, 1962	Nov. 7, 9, 1963	Nov. 4, 1964	Nov. 10, 1965	Nov. 15, 1966	Nov. 8, 9, 1962	Nov. 7, 9, 1963	Nov. 4, 1964	Nov. 10, 1965,[a]	Nov. 15,[b] 1966
3	–	12	1714	2340	0	–	64	18	406	80
5	7	254	1478	2638	4	294	182	176	260	514
7	27	357	2599	2500	42	18	111	28	657	911
10	48	25	107	946	587	80	52	198	803	752
12	–	78	319	925	518	–	62	238	497	429
15	74	299	1591	22	320	12	107	308	507	534
17	30	204	1989	0	462	110	42	204	798	805
20	28	5	5863	0	2	26	74	396	507	529
25	4	3	0	0	2	57	206	106	227	400
30	0	0	0	0	1	76	60	34	232	219
35	0	0	1	0	0	182	14	52	156	84
40	0	0	0	0	0	1	12	56	143	141
Effective CPE[c]	31	137	1740	1562	215	86	82	151	432	450

[a] Percentage age composition: I, 2%; II, 73%; III, 25%.
[b] Percentage age composition: I, 1%; II, 59%; III, 38%; IV, 2%.
[c] Average catch for depths at which fish were taken.

studies are lacking, similar dominance of the lake and other species appears to have occurred in Lakes Ontario and Huron.

The alewife was first recorded in the Great Lakes in Lake Ontario in 1873 and has been abundant there since the late 1800's. Just how the alewife got into Lake Ontario is uncertain. It long had free access to the lake via the St. Lawrence River from its native habitat along the Atlantic Coast. It seems that the alewife would have appeared in Lake Ontario much earlier if it had followed this route. It is more likely that alewives that became established in Lake Ontario were included in shipments of young American shad (*Alosa sapidissima*) that were planted in Lake Ontario in the early 1870's (Woods, 1960).

After its establishment in Lake Ontario, the movement of the alewife to the other Great Lakes was slow. Niagara Falls was a natural barrier to fish migration between Lakes Ontario and Erie before the completion of the Welland Canal in 1829. Contrary to common belief, this canal did not provide an easy route for fish to bypass Niagara Falls. Its many locks, which raise ships 327 ft between Lakes Ontario and Erie, impose partial barriers and the strong downstream currents created as the huge locks are emptied repeatedly, are major deterrents to upstream migration. The sea lamprey, a native of Lake Ontario, took nearly 100 years after the canal was opened to appear in Lake Erie in 1921 (Applegate, 1950), and the alewife did not appear in Lake Erie until 1931—58 years after it was first found in Lake Ontario. When the alewife reached Lake Erie it had free access to all of the other Great Lakes. It was first found in Lake Huron in 1933, in Lake Michigan in 1949, and in Lake Superior in 1954.

The alewife was common in Lake Erie by 1942, but it probably did not become extremely abundant there. The deep water where the alewives concentrate in winter to avoid unfavorably cold water is limited in Lake Erie and the lake has always had a large population of predators. Lake Huron also had a large population of lake trout and

burbot that would have preyed on the alewife when it entered the lake in the 1930's, but these were virtually eliminated from the lake during the mid-1940's by sea lamprey predation. Subsequently the alewife became very abundant by the mid-1950's and increased irregularly until 1964 (Coble, 1967).

The alewife has spread throughout Lake Superior but has not yet become abundant and its future there is uncertain. The lake not only has a large population of predators, but is the coldest of the Great Lakes—and cold does not favor the alewife.

The sea lamprey had almost eliminated the large predators in Lake Michigan when the alewife was first recorded there in 1949. The alewife had strong competitive advantage over other planktivorous species because of its efficient filter-feeding behavior and its characteristic of forming dense schools that occur in all areas of the lake during different seasons.

The alewife increased rapidly in Lake Michigan during the 1950's; it was first noted in abundance in Green Bay in 1953, and was abundant throughout the lake in 1956. During recent years the adult population has more than doubled each year. Obviously this rate of increase could not continue as each new hatch of young encounters an increasingly greater population density and more competition for food and space. Scattered data on age composition indicates that a decreasing percentage of young survived to become adults as the population increased. As this trend continues to a point where the number of adults is so great that it becomes very difficult for young to survive, the number of young reaching adulthood starts to decrease and the population reaches a peak. Evidence indicates that the population had reached this point during 1966–67.

Because the alewife occupies various sections of the lake in dense schools during different seasons, it can influence all other species of the lake. In midwinter the adult alewives are densely concentrated on the bottom in the deepest areas (Wells, 1968), where they seek the warmest waters. This area was occupied by the kiyi (*L. kiyi*), which was abundant as recently as 1954–55 (Moffett, 1957), but had become greatly reduced by 1960–61 (Smith, 1964), and was nearly extinct by 1964 (Wells, 1966).

In late winter and early spring the alewives move toward shore in dense schools that pass through the region occupied by the bloater (Wells, 1968). This region is also occupied by the alewife in the fall as it returns to deep water. Although the bloaters increased greatly during the 1950's (Moffett, 1957; Smith, 1964), their abundance has been decreasing sharply in the 1960's as alewives increased.

During the late spring and summer the adult alewives are concentrated in the shallower areas (Wells, 1968), where they spawn near shore and in rivers and bays during June and July. The lake herring and the emerald shiner (*Notropis atherinoides*), which previously were extremely abundant in the shallow areas and bays of the Great Lakes, decreased sharply in various areas as alewives became established (Miller, 1957) and were very scarce or absent after the alewife reached extreme abundance in Lake Michigan (Wells, 1968).

The yellow perch (*Perca flavescens*) which occupies the inshore area became more abundant as the alewives increased in Lake Michigan. The increase in abundance and resultant stimulation of effort were reflected by an increasing catch of perch during the early 1960's that reached 5.8 million lb in 1964. The increase in yellow perch may have resulted from the greater supply of food that the alewives provided for larger perch. As alewives became very abundant they crowded the shore in dense schools during spring and summer and the yellow perch moved further from shore. The concentration of alewives near shore, and the displacement of yellow perch occurred during the spawning and hatching period of the yellow perch, and as the alewives became very abundant during the early 1960's recruitment of perch must have been affected as the abundance of adult perch dropped sharply. This was reflected by the sharp decline of the catch of yellow perch to 1.3

and 0.7 million lb in 1965 and 1966, respectively.

The American smelt which also occupied the inshore areas of the lakes declined sharply when alewife abundance increased. The smelt production in Lake Michigan declined from a peak of about 9.1 million lb in 1958 to 0.9–1.2 million lb since 1963. Because the American smelt is still abundant in Lake Ontario where the alewife has long been the dominant fish, it seems unlikely that smelt will be influenced as strongly by the alewife as were the chubs, lake herring, and emerald shiners, all of which are very scarce in Lake Ontario.

During the fall and winter after hatching, the young alewives occupy the mid-depths of the lake where they remain until their third summer (age II) before moving to the bottom. The midwater area has also been the zone occupied by the young lake herring, chubs, and American smelt during their first 2 years. Undoubtedly the competition between the young of the alewives and the young of other species was severe as the alewives reached great abundance.

The occupation of various zones of the lake in different periods by dense congregations of alewives has changed greatly the utilization of the invertebrate productivity by fish. The chubs, lake herring, emerald shiners, yellow perch, and American smelt were abundant species that occupied various sections of the lake and were major consumers of invertebrates throughout the year. Under present conditions when the alewife is concentrated inshore in the summer, the deepest zone previously inhabited by the kiyi in great abundance (Hile and Deason, 1947) is essentially unoccupied by an abundant species and the invertebrate food is incompletely used. Similar situations occur during other seasons when sections of the lake vacated by the alewives as they move from zone to zone are left with greatly reduced populations of the species that once occupied each section in great abundance throughout the year. As abundant as the alewife is, and despite its apparent intensive use of the invertebrate food of each zone of the lake during different seasons, I believe it unlikely that the biomass represented by the alewife is equal to the total of all of the previously abundant species that it has displaced.

REESTABLISHMENT OF CLIMAX PREDATORS

The unprecedented instability of fish stocks in Lake Michigan in the mid-1960's at a time when the alewife fishery is continuing to expand and climax predators are being reestablished certainly will result in continued rapid change. Although the alewife catch reached 29 million lb in 1966 and may reach 50 million lb in 1967, processing facilities that exist can handle approximately 100 million lb. Despite the heavy annual die-off of alewives each spring that was the greatest on record in 1967, alewives continued to be plentiful during the summer of 1967. It is uncertain if the fishery approached full exploitation of the alewife stocks at their peak. Early decrease in alewife stocks seems likely, however, due to over-population and a sharp increase in mortality between the end of the 1st year and entry into the adult stocks, as illustrated by the fewer adults that entered the stocks at age II from the very large 1964 year-class (266 in 1966) than from the much smaller 1963 year-class (315 in 1965; Table 44.7).

A vigorous program is underway to reestablish climax predators in Lake Michigan to create a predator-prey balance with the alewife. Sea lamprey control in Lake Michigan was initiated in 1960 and was effective in 1967. Lake trout stocking by the states and federal government started in 1965, has reached nearly 2 million fingerlings annually, and will be continued until natural reproduction is well established. Michigan stocked 660,000 fingerling coho salmon (*Oncorhynchus kisutch*) in Lake Michigan in 1966, and 1,700,000 coho and 800,000 chinook salmon (*O. tshawytscha*) in 1967. The survival of coho salmon as indicated by spawning runs of adults from the 1966 plant and precocious males of the 1967 plant indicate unusual success. Michigan and Wisconsin are increasing their plants of steelhead trout (*Salmo gairdneri*) in Lake Michigan tributaries. The coho salmon are occupying the upper strata of the lake and are feeding heavily on the young alewives that live at mid-depths. This region is apparently where the steelhead trout and chinook salmon will feed most heavily as neither are taken on the bottom in deeper water.

The Province of Ontario has started to make large introductions of splake in Lake Huron and these fish will have free access to Lake Michigan if successful. The splake is a hybrid of lake trout and brook trout (*Salvelinus fontinalis*) that has been selected for several generations to develop a strain that will occupy deep water, grow fast, and mature early. Michigan and Ontario have also initiated experimental introductions of kokanee (*Oncorhynchus nerka*) in the Lake Michigan watershed and in Georgian Bay of Lake Huron. Although it is uncertain where the kokanee will live in the Great Lakes, they will probably compete with the alewife for food.

It seems unlikely that all of these species can be established with equal success as the productivity of Lake Michigan has not changed greatly over the pre-sea lamprey period. The closed ecosystem of a lake differs greatly from the native ocean habitat of the salmon, and competition among the various species of salmon and trout for the available food will undoubtedly become intense as their numbers increase. It is uncertain yet which predators will have a biological or competitive advantage over others, but it does appear that the predator-prey relation will be unstable as long as the alewife remains the single dominant prey species. In fact, it seems likely that the fishery productivity may be lowered from the pre-sea lamprey period because of the instability of the predator-prey balance, and apparent less-efficient use of the invertebrate food of the entire lake by the alewife than by the previous multiple-species complex.

Greater stability and full productivity of Lake Michigan, and other Great Lakes that have been similarly affected by recent events, can only be achieved by careful regulation of the kinds and numbers of predators, and the reestablishment of a multiple-species complex of prey species. Since the greatest stability occurs at low population density, management of the lakes to obtain the highest yield will require continuous surveillance and manipulation of all species to prevent onset of uncontrolled instability and recurrence of extreme imbalances in the future.

To manage the fishery resource for high yield, both recreational and commercial fisheries must be closely regulated and the amounts of various species taken by each must be closely controlled with respect to the potential yield of each species and the expected interactions among competing predator or prey species that are not fished heavily or selectively. It may also be necessary to create or induce fisheries for species not involved directly in the predator-prey balance of the lakes, but which could be favored by short- or long-term changes of the environment.

An essential requirement for successful and continued restoration of a useful fishery balance is uniformity in management approach among the states and Canada which own and manage the fisheries in their respective sections of the various lakes. Management objectives for individual lakes or adjoining lakes must be compatible and regulations and management procedures closely integrated.

The potential of common attack on problems of the Great Lakes is illustrated by the highly successful interstate and international program to control the sea lamprey and rehabilitate the lake trout that has been, in fact, the first step toward the achievement of a new and more favorable ecological balance among fish stocks.

ACKNOWLEDGMENTS: I am particularly grateful for the constructive comments of many colleagues of the U.S. Bureau of Commercial Fisheries that have helped develop the concepts presented in this paper. I wish to express special appreciation to Norman S. Baldwin, Michael D. Clady, Robert G. Ferguson, Shelby D. Gerking, William A. Kennedy, and William E. Ricker for their thorough review of the manuscript and many helpful comments and suggestions.

References

Applegate, Vernon C. 1950. Natural history of the sea lamprey, *Petromyzon marinus,* in Michigan. U.S. Fish Wildlife Serv., Spec. Sci. Rept. Fish. No. 55. 237 p.

Baldwin, Norman S., and Robert W. Saalfeld. 1962. Commercial fish production in the Great Lakes, 1867–1960. Great Lakes Fish. Comm., Tech. Rept. 3. 166 p.

Beeton, Alfred M. 1961. Environmental changes in Lake Erie. Trans. Am. Fish. Soc., **90**(2):153–159.
　　1965. Eutrophication of the St. Lawrence Great Lakes. Limnol. Oceanog., **10**(2):240–254.

Carlander, Kenneth D. 1953. Handbook of freshwater fishery biology. Wm. C. Brown Co., Dubuque, Iowa. 429 p.

Carr, John F. 1962. Dissolved oxygen in Lake Erie, past and present. Proc. 5th Conf. Great Lakes Res. Univ. Mich., Inst. Sci. Technol., Great Lakes Res. Div., Publ. 9. p.1–14.

Carr, John F., Vernon C. Applegate, and Myrl Keller. 1965. A recent occurrence of thermal stratification and low dissolved oxygen in western Lake Erie. Ohio J. Sci., **65**(6):319–327.

Carr, John F., and Jarl K. Hiltunen. 1965. Changes in the bottom fauna of western Lake Erie from 1930 to 1961. Limnol. Oceanog., **10**(4):551–569.

Clady, Michael D. 1967. Changes in an exploited population of the cisco, *Coregonus artedi* LeSueur. Papers Mich. Acad. Sci., **52**:85–99.

Coble, Daniel W. 1967. The white sucker population of South Bay, Lake Huron, and the effects of the sea lamprey on it. J. Fish Res. Bd. Canada, **24**(10):2117–2136.

Dryer, William R., and Joseph Beil. 1964. Life history of lake herring in Lake Superior. U.S. Fish Wildlife Serv., Fish. Bull. No. 63. p. 493–530.

Eschmeyer, Paul H. 1957. The near extinction of lake trout in Lake Michigan. Trans. Am. Fish. Soc., **85** (1955):102–119.

Great Lakes Fishery Commission. 1958. Annual report for the year 1958. 67 p.

Harkness, W. J. K., and J. R. Dymond. 1961. The lake sturgeon: the history of its fishery and problems of conservation. Ontario Dept. Lands Forests. 121 p.

Hile, Ralph. 1949. Trends in the lake trout fishery

of Lake Huron through 1946. Trans. Am. Fish. Soc., **76**(1946): 121–147.

———. 1954. Changing concepts in fishery research on the Great Lakes. Proc. Gulf Caribbean Fish. Inst., 6th Ann. Session. p. 64–70.

Hile, Ralph, and Howard J. Buettner. 1955. Commercial fishery for chubs (ciscoes) in Lake Michigan through 1953. U.S. Fish Wildlife Serv., Spec. Sci. Rept. Fish. No. 163. 49 p.

———. 1959. Fluctuations in the commercial fisheries of Saginaw Bay, 1885–1956. U.S. Fish Wildlife Serv., Res. Rept. No. 51. 38 p.

Hile, Ralph, and Hilary J. Deason. 1947. Distribution, abundance and spawning season and grounds of the kiyi, *Leucichthys kiyi* Koelz, in Lake Michigan. Trans. Am. Fish. Soc., **74**(1944): 143–165.

Hile, Ralph, Paul H. Eschmeyer, and George F. Lunger. 1951a. Decline of the lake trout fishery in Lake Michigan. U.S. Fish. Wildlife Serv., Fish. Bull. No. 52. p. 77–95.

———. 1951b. Status of the lake trout fishery in Lake Superior. Trans. Am. Fish. Soc., **80**(1950): 278–312.

Kennedy, W. A. 1954. Growth, maturity and mortality in the relatively unexploited lake trout, *Cristivomer namaycush,* of Great Slave Lake. J. Fish. Res. Bd. Canada, **11**(6): 827–852.

Miller, Robert R. 1957. Origin and dispersal of the alewife, *Alosa pseudoharengus,* and the gizzard shad, *Dorosoma cepedianum,* in the Great Lakes. Trans. Am. Fish. Soc., **86**(1956): 97–111.

Moffett, James W. 1957. Recent changes in the deepwater fish populations of Lake Michigan. Ibid., **86**: 393–408.

———. 1958. Attack on the sea lamprey. Mich. Conserv., **27**(3): 21–27.

Parker, Phillip S., and Robert E. Lennon. 1956. Biology of the sea lamprey in its parasitic phase. U.S. Fish Wildlife Serv., Res. Rept. No. 44. 32 p.

Ricker, W. E. 1963. Big effects from small causes: two examples from fish populations dynamics. J. Fish. Res. Bd. Canada, **20**(2): 257–284.

Scott, W. B. 1951. Fluctuations in abundance of the Lake Erie cisco (*Leucichthys artedi*) population. Contrib. Roy. Ont. Museum Zool., No. 32. 41 p.

Scott, W. B., and Stanford H. Smith. 1962. The occurrence of the longjaw cisco, *Leucichthys alpenae,* in Lake Erie. J. Fish. Res. Bd. Canada, **19**(6): 1013–1023.

Smith, Hugh H., and Mervin-Marie Snell. 1891. Review of the fisheries of the Great Lakes in 1885, with introduction and description of fishing vessels and boats by J. W. Collins. Appen. Rept. U.S. Comm. Fish. 1887. 333 p.

Smith, Oliver H., and John Van Oosten. 1940. Tagging experiments with lake trout, whitefish, and other species of fish from Lake Michigan. Trans. Am. Fish. Soc., **69**: 63–84.

Smith, Stanford H. 1956. Life history of lake herring of Green Bay, Lake Michigan. U.S. Fish Wildlife Serv., Fish. Bull. No. 57. p. 87–138.

———. 1962. Lake Erie or Lake Eerie? Izaak Walton Mag., **27**(4): 4–5.

———. 1964. Status of the deepwater cisco population of Lake Michigan. Trans. Am. Fish. Soc., **93**(2): 155–163.

Wells, LaRue. 1966. Seasonal and depth distribution of larval bloaters (*Coregonus hoyi*) in southeastern Lake Michigan. Ibid., **95**(4): 388–396.

———. 1968. Seasonal depth distribution of fish in southeastern Lake Michigan. U.S. Fish Wildlife Serv., Fish Bull. (In press.)

Woods, Loren P. 1960. The alewife. Chicago Natural History Museum Bull. Nov. 1960. p. 6–8.

Van Oosten, John. 1929. Life History of the lake herring (*Leucichthys artedi* Le Sueur) of Lake Huron as revealed by its scales, with a critique of the scale method. U.S. Bur. Fish. Bull. No. 44. p. 265–428.

———. 1930. The disappearance of the Lake Erie cisco—a preliminary report. Trans. Am. Fish. Soc., **60**: 204–214.

———. 1937. The dispersal of smelt, *Osmerus mordax* (Mitchill), in the Great Lakes region. Ibid., **66**(1936): 160–171.

———. 1947. Mortality of smelt, *Osmerus mordax* (Mitchill), in Lakes Huron and Michigan during the fall and winter of 1942–1943. Ibid., **74**(1944): 310–337.

Van Oosten, John, and Hilary J. Deason. 1938. The food of the lake trout (*Cristivomer namaycush namaycush*) and the lawyer (*Lota maculosa*) of Lake Michigan. Ibid., **67**(1937): 155–177.

Van Oosten, John, Ralph Hile, and Frank W. Jobes. 1946. The whitefish fishery of Lakes Huron and Michigan with special reference to the deep-trap-net fishery. U.S. Fish Wildlife Serv., Fish. Bull. No. 50. p. 297–394.

ADDITIONAL REFERENCES

Borgstrom, Georg. 1970. The harvest of the seas: How fruitful and for whom? Pp. 65–84 in *The environmental crisis,* ed. by Harold W. Helfrich, Jr. New Haven: Yale Univ. Press. 187 pp.

Borgstrom, Georg. 1967. *The hungry planet.* New York: The Macmillan Company. 507 pp.

See especially Chapter 13, The Soviet fisheries revolution, and Chapter 17, Cultivation of the sea and its present exploitation.

Clark, John R. 1969. Thermal pollution and aquatic life. *Sci. Am.* 220(3): 18–27.

McVay, Scott. 1966. The last of the great whales. *Sci. Am.* 215(2): 13–21.

Hickey, Joseph J., J. A. Keith, and Francis B. Coon. 1966. An exploration of pesticides in a Lake Michigan ecosystem. Pp. 141–154 in N. W. Moore, ed., *Journal of Applied Ecology,* Vol. 3 Supplement.

Marx, Wesley. 1967. *The frail ocean.* New York: Ballantine Books, Inc. 274 pp.

Ricker, William E. 1969. Food from the sea. Pp. 87–108 in *Resources and man: A study and recommendations.* Committee on Resources and Man of the Division of Earth Sciences—National Research Council. San Francisco: W. H. Freeman and Co. 259 pp.

45
SELECTION

PREHISTORIC OVERKILL
PAUL S. MARTIN

Man's severe impact on populations of other large mammals extends back into the past at least 40,000 years. The migration, or "self-introduction," of early man over the earth's surface brought the extinction of numerous animals, directly by killing them and indirectly by destroying their habitat (often by fire) and by competing for food (Krantz, 1970).

A sudden wave of large-animal extinction, involving more than 200 genera, characterizes the late-Pleistocene age. Except on islands, extinction struck only large terrestrial herbivores and their ecologically dependent carnivores and scavengers. The event is not clearly related to climatic change. Rather, recent discoveries show that extinction closely follows the chronology of prehistoric man's spread and his development as a big-game hunter. No continents or islands are known where accelerated extinction certainly predates man's arrival. Overkill alone explains the global extinction pattern.

As the next selection shows, hunting today remains a primary cause of animal extinction.

(Editor's comment)

The end of the Ice Age saw the sudden decline of an extraordinary number of large vertebrates. Unlike the relatively gradual, essentially orderly replacement of new genera seen earlier in the Pleistocene and Tertiary, extinction rates suddenly skyrocketed. New genera did not appear. There was no generic replacement either by immigration or evolution (Martin, 1958, p. 400). As a result,

Paul S. Martin (b. 1928) is a professor of geosciences at the University of Arizona; he was a research associate there from 1957 to 1962 and has been on the faculty since 1962. He has degrees from Cornell University and the University of Michigan (Ph.D., 1956). Martin was a Guggenheim Fellow in 1965-1966. His research interests in Pleistocene biogeography continue, with emphasis on man's effect on large animals throughout the world and on the use of fossil pollen as a tool in paleoclimatic reconstructions.

This selection is abridged by the editor, with kind permission of the author, from a chapter of the same title (pp. 75–120) in *Pleistocene Extinctions: The Search for a Cause*, edited by P. S. Martin and H. E. Wright, Jr., Yale University Press, 1967. Many supporting data, including regional lists of extinct species and radiocarbon dates, have been deleted.

We live in a zoologically impoverished world, from which all the hugest, and fiercest, and strangest forms have recently disappeared . . . yet it is surely a marvelous fact, and one that has hardly been sufficiently dwelt upon, this dudden dying out of so many large Mammalia, not in one place only but over half the land surface of the globe [Wallace, 1876, p. 150].

At the time he wrote, Wallace regarded the cause of extinction as a direct outcome of the wordwide effects of Pleistocene glaciation. But in the voyage of the *Beagle,* Darwin had already shown that extinct Pleistocene fauna occurred in beds younger than the last glaciation. Wallace himself came to reject the effects of the glacial epoch as a sufficient explanation. In the *World of Life* (1911, p. 264), he wrote:

What we are seeking for is a cause which has been in action over the whole earth during the period in question, and which was adequate to produce the observed result. When the problem is stated in this way, the answer is very obvious. It is, moreover, a solution which has often been suggested, though generally to be rejected as inadequate. It has been so with myself, but why I can hardly say.

While crediting it to Lyell, Wallace reached the view that seems to me best supported by subsequent evidence, that no known environmental defects or crises, other than those brought by prehistoric man, can adequately account for the sequence of events. I would depart from Wallace's view in only one regard—he apparently also believed, following Lyell, in certain deep-seated general causes operating to exterminate large animals at the end of each geological era.

I do not consider the intriguing question of accelerated extinction at the end of the earlier geological eras (Bramlette, 1965; Newell, 1966) relevant to the matter at hand. In the late Pleistocene one has a far more detailed stratigraphy and chronology to work with. But the main point is that one finds a totally different pattern in the Pleistocene, one affecting mainly one class of organisms, the Mammalia. There is no upturn in extinction rate among marine organisms, such as typifies the close of Permian, Triassic, and Cretaceous. The phenomenon of accelerated extinction is unknown in the marine Pleistocene. If it had occurred, Lyell's method of dating marine Cenozoic beds would not have been so simple or successful.

The Pattern of Pleistocene Extinction

I shall attempt to sketch salient features of late-Pleistocene generic extinction, with emphasis on North America, revising some interpretations presented in an earlier effort (Martin, 1958, p. 394–413). The reason for concentrating on genera is pragmatic. The generalized ecologic, chronologic, and phylogenetic interpretations for discussing an extinct genus are likely to be speculative enough without entering a taxonomic level in which more than a dozen valid specific names may be available in a group that could not possibly have evolved into as many good biological species. Are we to infer a dozen allopatric species in a genus that is seldom or never known to be represented by two distinct morphological forms in a single fossil horizon? Even in the case of a thoroughly and very skillfully revised group, with much of its synonymy resolved, the critical identification of a species from a carefully dated outcrop of considerable archaeological or paleoecological significance may require presence of diagnostic parts such as horn cores or complete jaws. Ecologists, long subjected to various pressures to study modern communities at the species level whenever possible, may not fully anticipate or appreciate the hazards of trying to study Pleistocene mammals at the species level.

To turn now to the matter of Pleistocene chronology. Although many large extinct animals have yet to be dated by C^{14} and although the method itself continues to present discordant results, especially when applied incautiously, it seems possible to conclude on the basis of both relative and absolute dating that throughout the Americas, in Australia, and on the islands of Madagascar and New Zealand a major wave of generic extinction occurred once only, and at a time within the last 15,000 years. This was not the case in Africa and Southeast Asia, where most generic extinction occurred some tens of thousands of years earlier, essentially beyond the reach of the C[14] dating method.

Apart from small oceanic islands, the animals lost were mainly "big-game" mammalian and avian herbivores of over 50 kg adult body weight. Doomed by the collapse of the herbivores was a retinue of ecologically dependent carnivores, scavengers, commensals, and, presumably, various unknown parasites. One need not assume any narrow predator–prey relationship. In fact, most mammalian predators seek a variety of prey species. One can assume that the loss of thirty-one genera of large herbivores at the end of the last glaciation of North America reduced the variety of carnivores. In other words, while one cannot say that saber-tooth cats disappeared *because* of the extinction of their supposed prey (such as mammoths), one can say that there had to be some feedback, some extinction of carnivores, when various herbivores disappeared. It happened that the saber-tooth was among those lost and the jaguar among those surviving. The fact that prehistoric man would not have hunted and killed saber-tooth cats or other large carnivores is not a valid criticism of the hypothesis of overkill. The question is whether or not he triggered extinction of the herbivores.

Generic extinction did not occur only at the end of the Pleistocene. *Nannippus, Plesippus, Stegomastodon, Titanotylopus, Canimartes, Trigonictis,* and other genera disappear from the United States at the end of the Blancan, over a million years ago. But the adaptive niches for horses, mastodons, camels, and large mustelids continued to be occupied (see Hibbard et al., 1965, p. 520). In contrast, in the late Pleistocene, the life forms lost were not replaced or maintained by related species. Possibly the browsing and grazing niches so suddenly abandoned by large animals in the late Pleistocene were partly refilled by an increase in biomass of small mammals and insects. But in the strict sense, the record is one of extinction without replacement.

Late-Pleistocene extinction must be regarded as imbalanced. It left empty niches in the terrestrial ecosystem, niches previously occupied by a succession of large herbivores through the Neogene. *Only on oceanic islands* were numerous small vertebrate genera obliterated. Among the animals lost were giant marsupials in Australia, moas in New Zealand, giant lemurs and struthious birds in Madagascar, about twenty-eight genera of mammals and one genus of tortoise in North America, and a still poorly known but probably larger number of mammalian genera in South America. Late-Pleistocene generic extinction is less well marked in northern Eurasia. There *Mammuthus* (mammoth), *Coelodonta* (woolly rhino), and *Megaceros* (Irish elk) were the only common late-Pleistocene genera to disappear. Thanks to a refuge in the unglaciated eastern Canadian Arctic, *Ovibos* (musk-ox) survived in the New World. In both Africa and Southeast Asia, a major episode of Pleistocene extinction antedates the late Würm and apparently coincides with the end of the Acheulean cultural stage, ca. 40,000–50,000 B.P. Can the cause of this peculiar pattern be found in its chronology?

Among large genera (50 kg or more in adult body weight), the recent list of Pleistocene distributions for the United States in Hibbard et al. (1965, p. 573) indicates four large mammals lost by the end of the Kansan, three at the end of the Yarmouth, none at the end of the Illinoian, and one at the end of the Sangamon. The spectacular upset comes at the end of the Wisconsin. By the end of the late-glacial, thirty-three genera are going or gone, far more than disappear in the rest of the Pleistocene put together.

North American Mastodons and Mammoths

Haynes (1964) has reviewed the radiocarbon dates and cultural content of some of the best known Early Man–mammoth sites in North America. There is little doubt that Clovis fluted-point hunters pursued the mammoth for a very short period of time in western North America before being replaced after 11,000 B.P. by hunters who used Folsom points and killed *Bison*. Carefully dated extinct bison sites are well known in the postglacial period. There is no question of extinct *Bison* living thousands of years after 11,000 B.P. But what about the mammoth? Haynes (p. 1412) cautiously concludes that the change from Clovis to Folsom may be related to a decline in the mammoth populations. Not only are there no well documented cases of mammoth associated with man in postglacial deposits of the last 10,000 years, there are no well-documented cases of postglacial mammoth sites without him. One possible exception is the Mexico City mammoth of San Bartolo Atepehuacan, found with an obsidian flake and no fewer than fifty-nine small chips of basalt and obsidian. A date on associated carbon fragments was 9,700 B.P. (M-776 Aveleyra, 1964, p. 404). Elsewhere there is every reason to assume that New World mammoths and their hunters had disappeared before 10,000 B.P.

There remains the matter of mastodon extinction, an event that most authors have regarded as postglacial, significantly later than the extinction of other Pleistocene genera and later than the early hunters. If it can be shown that mastodons were little affected by the intrusion of the Clovis hunters and indeed survived them by 4,000 years, as Griffin claims (1965, p. 658), the case for prehistoric man as the major cause of extinction would certainly need to be seriously modified or abandoned. In addition to Griffin, Martin (1958), Hester (1960), Skeels (1962), and most recent authors except Quimby (1960) have accepted a terminal radiocarbon date at about 6,000 B.P.

Is it possible that all postglacial dates on mastodons are overshots? No skeptical archaeologist would consider accepting a radiocarbon date of 6,000 to 8,000 years on an alleged Clovis site before subjecting it to the most minute excavation and examination, without demanding an effort at replication of the date on the critical beds, without considering carefully all the possibilities of intrusion, and without a field demonstration of the evidence to equally critical colleagues.

There are three reasons why cautious second thoughts may now be needed regarding widely accepted claims of postglacial mastodon survival. The first is the radiocarbon dates published in the last few years. With one exception, all the new dates, which are on wood, gyttja, or material other than the bones themselves, are of late-glacial age, ranging between 12,700 and 10,500 B.P. (W-1358, W-1038, Y-460, OWU-126, Pontiac, Michigan; I-586, S-29, S-30, and W-944). In contrast, of four mastodon dates on bone or tusk, three (M-694, M-347, and M-490) are younger than 9,500 B.P. The discrepancy between these and the organic dates may be attributed to inorganic carbonate replacement or to humic acid contamination rather than to a real difference in age of the fossils.

The second is the fact that palynological study of beds containing mastodon and mammoth bones in the northeast indicates an association with spruce–pine pollen zones (Ogden, 1965) and presumably spruce forests. This environment disappears from the Great Lakes with the retreat of Valders ice about 10,500 years ago (Wright, 1964).

The third difficulty in accepting a 6,000-year extinction date for mastodon emerges from study of its fossil distribution (Figure 45.1). This proboscidean is the most common Pleistocene fossil in northeastern United States, so it may have once been as important in vertebrate biomass of the region as *Loxodonta* is in the game parks of central Africa. Skeels (1962) reports 163 records from Michigan alone. She proposes that its extinction there was hastened by its failure to follow the boreal forest environment across the Great Lakes into Canada after deglaciation. But the northern limit of the mastodons in Michigan is not the Straits of Mackinac, as one might imagine if the elephants were trapped in a cul-de-sac south of the Great Lakes. The distribution of the 163 fossils is remarkable (Figure 45.1). Both mastodons and mammoths did not range beyond Osceola and Gladwin counties at the latitude of Saginaw Bay (44° N). Equally remarkable is the distribution of fluted points from surface sites in Michigan. As Quimby (1958,

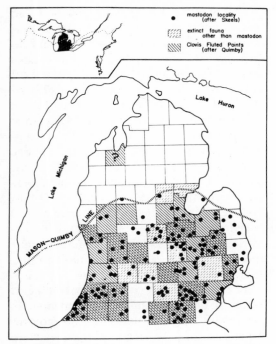

FIGURE 45.1 Distribution of Michigan mastodons (after Skeels, 1962), other extinct Pleistocene genera, and fluted points (after Quimby, 1960).

1960) noted, they are found only in the same part of the state as fossil mastodons—but south of what I have drawn as the "Mason-Quimby Line." One doubtful record, possibly an import, is that of a fluted point in Grand Traverse County (J. B. Griffin, personal correspondence).

The mystery of why fauna and fluted points apparently terminated at the Mason–Quimby Line (Figure 45.1), rather than reaching the Valders ice margin, remains unexplained. But it is a minor matter compared with that of explaining why, if the species survived until 6,000 years ago, mastodons failed to spread throughout the state, and from the beachhead in southern Ontario on into central Canada. Beyond possible interglacial records there are no bones of mastodon north of the fluted-point line of Mason (1962) copied on the inset of Figure 45.1. A more than coincidental association between fluted points and mastodons in the

Southeast is mapped by Williams and Stoltman (1965, p. 677).

Griffin (1965) protests the lack of stratigraphic association between fluted points and extinct fauna in the East. But there are very few stratified fluted-point sites anywhere in mastodon country east of the Mississippi, and fewer in which suitable conditions for bone preservation exist. Unless more substantial documentation is forthcoming, present claims of postglacial mastodon survival based on radiocarbon evidence alone are insufficient. Meanwhile, the Mason-Quimby Line is evidence of the sort to be expected if overkill were the cause of mastodon extinction.

This hypothesis also makes credible some of the peculiar cultural attributes of the Paleo-Indians. Mason (1962, p. 242) concluded:

> It seems more than coincidental that the end of the Paleo-Indian cultural dominance, as measured by radiocarbon and other dating techniques, agrees closely with the demise of the fossil Pleistocene big-game animals; or to put it another way, that it was during the period characterized archaeologically by such artifact types as Folsom and Clovis that the great Pleistocene extinctions were taking place. It would push the limits of credibility to view as likewise coincidental the fact of the emergence of the generalized subsistence basis of the Archaic cultures during the disappearance of the Pleistocene fauna and fluted points. In other words, there is expressed a functional relationship between these culture types and the total ecology of which they are parts.

Müller-Beck (1966) states that "The first invasion of man in the New World for which a reliable archaeological reconstruction seems possible—there could have been earlier invasions—took place about 28,000 to 26,000 years ago." This conclusion is advanced on typological and paleontological grounds, recognizing that there is no indisputable radiocarbon-dated evidence for man in the New World older than that associated with the fluted-point hunters of around 12,000 years ago.

The possibility that *Homo sapiens* spread

into the Americas long before the late-glacial by no means eliminates the hypothesis of overkill. One may assert that the postulated users of core tools, choppers, and perhaps even bone tools were not specialized for killing big game, and thus had little effect on the megafauna, unlike the Clovis hunters of elephants or the Folsom hunters of extinct *Bison*. What would upset the hypothesis of overkill would be clear-cut cases on the continent of many of the extinct animals surviving beyond the time of the big-game hunters, or clear-cut cases of massive unbalanced Pleistocene extinction anywhere before man.

New Zealand

That extinction of a variety of medium to large-sized herbivores can occur within a few hundred years after prehistoric man's initial appearance is shown by the extinction chronology of New Zealand (Fleming, 1962). New Zealand occupies 103,000 square miles, slightly smaller than the State of Colorado. There were no native terrestrial mammals, but twenty-seven species of extinct moas (large flightless birds), including a 10-ft-tall *Dinornis maximus,* have been discovered in astonishing numbers in postglacial deposits, 800 to the acre in Pyramid Valley and that many in a pocket (30 × 20 × 10 ft deep) at Kapua (Duff, 1952). These giant flightless birds can be traced to the late-Miocene (*Anomalapteryx*). Regarding extinction, the orthodox theory was that many were extinct before man arrived, thus most had died out naturally (Duff, 1963a, p. 6). Partly on the basis of radiocarbon dates of moa bones, stomach contents, associated charcoal, and tussock bedding and partly on recent archaeological findings, Fleming (1962) has concluded that such was not the case. Twenty-two of the extinct moa species have now been found in association with prehistoric man (Figure 45.2). Sixteen moas have been dated by radiocarbon analysis of the bone itself, although some of the bone may have been contaminated by younger humates. In addition to the moas, a number of other birds

became extinct in the same general period; half of these have been found in cultural association. Reviewing the last ten years of New Zealand archaeology, Golson and Gathercole (1962) conclude: "Nevertheless one definite result has emerged from this aspect of the decade's work. Possible climatic and genetic factors notwithstanding, man as the moa's first mammalian predator was a prime instrument in its extinction."

Duff (1963a, p.6) has abandoned his hypothesis that moa extinction must have been due largely to natural causes, although he is still concerned with the absence of the giant moa *Dinornis maximus* in most of the moa-hunter camps; he still suggests a considerable reduction in moa numbers before man's arrival.

Fleming (1962) reports little evidence of early and mid-Holocene moa extinction, an extremely important fact in comparing the New Zealand pattern with that of Australia and the Americas. Despite piedmont glaciation and widespread periglacial phenomena on South Island and despite volcanism with the extensive blanketing of North Island by nutrient-poor pumice and ash, no species of the giant birds are definitely known to have disappeared before man's arrival.

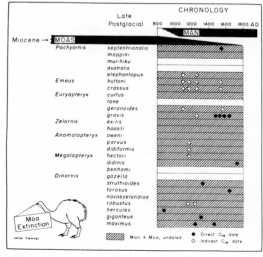

FIGURE 45.2 Carbon-14 dates and extinction of moas in New Zealand (after Fleming, 1962).

Duff (1963b) notes that the moa hunters must have independently developed techniques for seeking their prey; they were of East Polynesian origin and, unlike the Upper Paleolithic cultures, had no tradition of big-game hunting. They developed new techniques fairly rapidly. A simple one was fire, widely used in South Island, to judge by charcoal horizons in the soil. Golson and Cathercole claim that the moa hunters retained their tools even after the birds were largely extinct and marine resources were their main source of food. Retention of hunting tools and persistence of a hunting tradition through the time of minimum numbers of his prey would establish man's role as a superpredator, still selecting big game whenever possible, even after his main food supply came from other sources.

Ultimately, when the Maori arrived in A.D. 1350, most of the giant birds were gone, so when first questioned on the subject a hundred years ago the Maori could provide no convincing accounts of the birds. Less explicable was the initial refusal of New Zealand scientists to regard prehistoric man as the cause for moa extinction. Fleming (1962, p. 116) remarks:

> It seems we are reluctant to blame our fellow men for a pre-historic offense against modern conservation ideals and would rather blame climate or the animals themselves. The simplest explanation is to attribute all late Holocene extinction to the profound ecological changes brought about by the arrival of man with fire, rats, and dogs.

Australia

Although Gill (1963) concludes that aboriginal entry began at least 20,000 years ago, the evidence of man at the time has been questioned by Mulvaney (1964). More convincing dates on prehistoric man are GaK-334 (11,600 B.P.) from Nools, where Tindale recovered a flake assemblage below a microlith assemblage, and those at Kenniff Cave, where Mulvaney (1964) obtained samples dated at 13,000 and 16,000 years (NPL 33

and 68) and associated with a "Tasmanoid" industry.

Younger dates from Lake Menindee, NZ-66 and W-169 of 6,000 and 8,600, respectively, are now thought to be associated with essentially modern faunas (Hubbs et al., 1962). A terminal date for *Nototherium* (not to be confused with the southwestern United States sloth *Nothrotherium*) may be Gx-105, 14,000 B.P., on bone fragments of a jaw. Although all bone carbonate dates are suspect, the age agreed with the collectors' estimate and is also equivalent with Y-170, 13,700 B.P., according to Hubbs et al. (1962), the youngest dating definitely applicable to a varied assemblage of giant marsupials. This is in accord with absence of extinct fauna from Nansump Cave in beds dated at 12,000 B.P. (Lundelius, 1960.)

Thus it appears that both prehistoric hunters and the main wave of extinction swept through Australia slightly before these events occurred in North America. Many additional geochronological data are needed before intercontinental cultural, climatic, and extinction chronologies can be compared more critically. But there is no longer doubt that man and the extinct Australian marsupials coexisted (Gill, 1963).

Tropical America

Although the extinct late-Pleistocene fauna from Central and South America is less well known than that of the United States, it is obvious that the inventory of extinct genera and species exceeds that of higher latitudes. In a preliminary account of a single fauna in Bolivia, Hofstetter (1963) recovered the following extinct genera, far more than are known from any single fossil locality in North America: *Nothropus, Megatherium, Glossotherium, Lestodon, Scelidotherium, Glyptodon, Chlamydotherium, Neothoracophrous, Hoplophorus, Panochthus, Neochoerus, Theriodictis, Arctotherium, Smilodon, Macrauchenia, Toxodon, Cuvieronius, Notiomastodon, Hippidion, Onohippidium, Palaeolama,* and *Charitoceros.* It is apparent that the Pleistocene game range of South America was especially well stocked, as one would expect in a tropical ecosystem. Extinction impoverished the tropical American fauna to a greater degree than that of the temperate regions. Did it occur before, after, or coincidental with extinction in temperate North America?

In South America, sloth dung, one of the best materials for critical radiocarbon dating, indicates survival to just over 10,000 years ago of ground sloth associated with extinct horse at Mylodon Cave and Fells Cave (Sa-49, W-915, C-484). If C-485 (8,639 B.P.) on burned bone from Palli Aike Cave, Chile, and Sa-47 (6,500 B.P.), Ponsomby, Patagonia, are also correctly associated with sloth and horse, a remarkably late survival could be claimed. However, no extinct animal remains were found in somewhat older rock shelters from Minas Gerais, Brazil (P-521, P-519), excavated by W. B. Hurt. For this reason the use of Palli Aike, Ponsomby, and certainly the 3,000-year age on "extinct giant bear" from Minas Gerais (M-354) may be questioned as valid terminal dates for the fauna. If the date of 14,000 B.P. (M-1068) from Falcon, Venezuela, associated correctly with big-game hunters in South America, it would, of course, obliterate the concept of their relatively late (12,000 B.P.) arrival in the New World. Apparently, more dates support the view that extinction in South America coincided with or slightly postdated that in North America, but those who believe in a slow, steady reduction of the late-Pleistocene fauna over tens or hundreds of thousands of years have yet to be confronted with the sort of dating evidence that invalidates this interpretation elsewhere.

In the West Indies, extinct vertebrates were of too small a size to have suffered extermination on the mainland (Martin, 1958, p. 409). Rouse (1964) attributes the extinction of at least some of the twenty-two genera of mammals found in prehistoric middens and cave earth to the arrival of man two to four thousand years ago. Subfossil "giant" species of small or medium-sized terrestrial vertebrates are still being discovered (cf. Ethridge, 1964), and a giant land snail, presumably also extinct, is known from Hispaniola (Clench, 1962). Whereas some of the native West Indian fauna may have disappeared as a result of catastrophic post-Columbian ecologic changes, brought by the introduction of *Rattus,* it appears that more disappeared before the fifteenth century. Here, as elsewhere, the main circumstance pointing toward prehistoric man's role in extinction, without shedding light on details of the process, is the matter of chronology. The fauna survives until man arrives.

On the continent, there is some archaeo-faunal evidence of local extirpation of medium-sized animals in certain intensely occupied areas like the Valley of Mexico, where Vaillant (1944) reported deer (*Odocoileus*) to be virtually exterminated two thousand years ago. The postglacial withdrawal of mule deer and antelope from southern parts of the Mexican Plateau has been attributed to vegetation change (Alvarez, 1964; Flannery, 1966), but overkill by expanding prehistoric populations seems at least equally probable. Peccary, marmot, and porcupine bones are notably scarce or absent in refuse from the more densely inhabited parts of the prehistoric Southwest. Local hunting may have wiped out these mammals during the late Pueblo period. In the Antilles, late prehistoric extinction of the larger lizards, rodents, and sloths probably occurred as a result of intense seasonal search for animal protein, when the relatively numerous prehistoric tribes were not cultivating manioc and maize, their mainstay. A comparable region in which the effect of prehistoric man on extinction of medium- to small-sized animals remains to be determined is the islands of the Mediterranean. The disappearance of *Myotragus* in Minorca seems much more closely timed to the earliest record of human occupation of the island than was once realized (Waldren, personal correspondence).

Africa

The "rose-colored glasses" view of prehistoric man in Africa is well put by Harper (1945,

p. 15): "As long as the African Continent was occupied by primitive savages, without modern weapons, animal life was, in a large sense, in a virtual state of equilibrium." I shall take this opportunity to point out a grave error in the assumptions of various scientists writing on the question of big game and the Pleistocene (e.g. Eiseley, 1943; Mason, 1962, p. 243; Leopold in Talbot and Talbot, 1963, p. 5; and, alas, Martin, 1958, p. 412). These authors failed to realize that Africa, no less than the other continents, suffered its episode of accelerated megafaunal extinction. Perhaps some of them were thinking of the last twenty thousand years, when it is true that practically no extinction occurred (Flint, 1957, p. 277; Butzer, 1964, p. 400). Perhaps others were misled by Theodore Roosevelt's chapter (1910), "A Railroad Through the Pleistocene," where he compares the game of the East African plains with the American Pleistocene fauna. Whatever the reason, they have assumed that the African megafauna survived the Pleistocene unscathed, and Eiseley in particular has used this point as an argument against the hypothesis of New World overkill.

Although its fossil fauna is far from adequately known, roughly fifty genera disappeared during the Pleistocene (see Hopwood and Hollyfield, 1954; Cooke, 1963). Furthermore, in Africa, as in America, most of the surviving large animals are also known as Pleistocene contemporaries of the extinct genera. The living genera of African big game represent only 70 per cent of the middle-Pleistocene complement (Martin, 1966). Thus despite its extraordinary diversity, the living African fauna must be regarded as depauperate, albeit much less so than that of America or Australia.

The time of "middle"-Pleistocene extinction was barely within the range of reliable dating by radiocarbon—i.e. over just forty thousand years ago. Fortunately, the rich archaeological content of many fossil beds aids in age interpretation. Toward the end of the Acheulian, and often associated with the stone bifaces and other tools of these big-game hunters in sites such as Olduvai

(Bed IV) in Tanzania, Olorgesailie and Kariandusi in Kenya, and Hopefield and the Vaal River gravels in South Africa, the following large mammals are last recorded: *Mesochoerus, Tapinochoerus, Stylochoerus, Libytherium, Simopithecus, Archidiskodon* (*Elephas*), and *Stylohipparion*. Eight additional extinct genera of the period are known only from middle, or occasionally late, Pleistocene sites in South Africa (Cooke, 1963, p. 98–101). All are absent from Middle Stone Age sites, and thus were extinct *before* the major depression of African montane vegetation zones of full- and late-glacial age recently reported by pollen stratigraphers (Coetzee, 1964; Livingstone, 1962; Morrison, 1961; Van Zinderen Bakker, 1962).

On stratigraphic and faunal evidence, Leakey (1965) attributes extinction of the Olduvai Gorge genera to drought. Clark (1962) places the evolved Acheulian at about 57,000 B.P., and, on the basis of intercontinental correlation with the Brørup Interstadial, he considers the First Intermediate Period (after the Acheulian) of 40,000 B.P. to have been dry.

If drought decimated the African mainland fauna at the end of the Middle Pleistocene, it managed to leave unscathed the endemic and ecologically vulnerable insular fauna of Madagascar. Seven genera of extinct lemurs, the pigmy hippopotamus, two species of giant tortoise, and two genera of struthious birds occur in very late Pleistocene beds. No earlier episode of extinction is known there. All the animals were contemporaries of prehistoric man, who did not reach the island until remarkably late in the postglacial. One date on charcoal associated with pottery and iron hooks is also a time when the roc, *Aepyornis maximus*, was abundant (GaK-276, A.D. 1100). Unless substantial paleobotanical evidence for a unique drought can be found in the "First Intermediate Period" in Africa, or evidence for a major decline of the Malagasay fauna prior to man's arrival, the evidence for a climatic cause of extinction in Africa suffers from the same ad hoc appeal that has made it an unacceptable explanation for the pattern elsewhere.

Late-Pleistocene extinction in Africa long precedes that in the Americas and Australia, as would be expected in view of man's gradual evolution in Africa. A major point for paleontologists to recognize is that the question "Why no extinction in Africa despite man's antiquity?" is misleading. There was a major wave of generic extinction in Africa although not so intense as in South America. Extinction in Africa seems to coincide with the maximum development of the most advanced early Stone Age hunting cultures, the evolved Acheulian of abundant, continent-wide distribution. The case of Africa neither refutes the hypothesis of overkill nor supports the hypothesis of worldwide climatic change as a cause of extinction (Martin, 1966).

Conclusion

In continental North America, the only major episode of generic extinction in the Pleistocene occurred close to eleven thousand years ago. Provisional ages for the start of major extinction episodes elsewhere are:

South America, 10,000 B.P.; West Indies, mid-postglacial; Australia, 13,000 B.P.; New Zealand, 900 B.P. (Figure 45.2); Madagascar, very late postglacial (800 B.P.); northern Eurasia (four genera only), 13,000 to 11,000 B.P.; Africa and probably Southeast Asia, before 40,000 to 50,000 B.P. Radiocarbon dates, pollen profiles associated with extinct animal remains, and new stratigraphic and archaeofaunal evidence show that, depending on the region involved, late-Pleistocene extinction occurred either after, during, or somewhat before worldwide climatic cooling of the last maximum of Würm–Weichsel–Wisconsin glaciation (Figure 45.3).

While it occurred at a time of climatic change, the pattern appears to be independent of a climatic cause. Outside continental Africa and Southeast Asia, massive extinction is unknown before the earliest known arrival of prehistoric man. In the case of Africa, massive extinction coincides with the final development of Acheulean hunting cultures, which are widespread throughout the continent.

Yet the notion of prehistoric overkill is commonly dismissed out of hand. In his book on extinct and vanishing birds of the last few

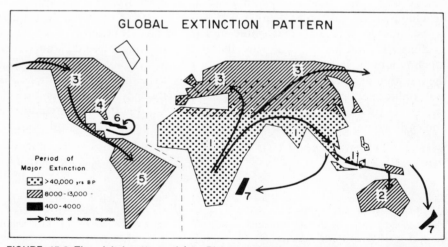

FIGURE 45.3 The global pattern of late Pleistocene extinction in sequence: 1. Africa and southern Eurasia; 2. New Guinea and Australia; 3. Northern Eurasia and northern North America; 4. southeastern United States; 5. South America; 6. West Indies; 7. Madagascar and New Zealand. In each case, the major wave of late-Pleistocene extinction does not occur until prehistoric hunters arrive.

hundred years Greenway (1958, p. 29) suggests that prehistoric men and birds "arranged a means of living together to the end that no birds were extirpated." At least one very perceptive neo-Darwinian evolutionist and humanist probably speaks for many in regarding it as "almost inconceivable that Indians alone put an end to the whole vast horse population of the late Pleistocene over so enormous an area." After considering and discounting all other possible explanations of horse extinction at the end of the Pleistocene, Simpson (1961, p. 200) held:

> This seems at present one of the situations in which we must be humble and honest and admit that we simply do not know the answer. It must be remembered too that extinction of the horses in the New World is only part of a larger problem. Many other animals became extinct here at about the same time. The general cause of extinction then or at earlier times must have been the occurrence of changes to which the animal populations could not adapt themselves. But what precisely were those changes?

Indeed, it is not when horses alone but when the full complement of extinct Pleistocene animals are considered, when all major land masses are included in the analysis, and especially when the chronology of extinction is critically set against the chronology of human migrations and cultural development (as in Figure 45.3) that man's arrival emerges as the only reasonable answer to Simpson's question. To be sure there is much ignorance left to admit. We must beg the question of just how and why prehistoric man obliterated his prey. We may speculate but we cannot determine how moose, elk, and caribou managed to survive while horse,

ground sloth, and mastodon did not. One must acknowledge that within historic time the Bushmen and other primitive hunters at a Paleolithic level of technology have not exterminated their game resources, certainly not in any way comparable to the devastation of the late-Pleistocene. These and other valid objections to the hypothesis of overkill remain. But thus far the hypothesis has survived every critical chronological test. On a world scale the pattern of Pleistocene extinction makes no sense in terms of climatic or environmental change. During the Pleistocene, accelerated extinction occurs only on land and only after man invades or develops specialized big-game hunting weapons.

It seems to me that the chronologic evidence strongly supports the conclusion of an earlier Darwinian who took pains not to dismiss the phenomenon as trivial and who ended a lifetime of study by concluding, in a generally overlooked part of his work, that man must in some way be the destructive agent (Wallace, 1911, p. 261–67).

The thought that prehistoric hunters ten to fifteen thousand years ago, (and in Africa over forty thousand years ago) exterminated far more large animals than has modern man with modern weapons and advanced technology is certainly provocative and perhaps even deeply disturbing. With a certain inadmissible pride we may prefer to regard ourselves, not our remote predecessors, as holding uncontested claim to being the arch destroyers of native fauna. But this seems not to be the case. Have we dismissed too casually the possibility of prehistoric overkill? The late-Pleistocene extinction pattern leaves little room for any other explanation.

I have sought and received stimulating conversation and correspondence on this problem from colleagues, teachers, and students. Without attempting to evaluate the magnitude of their help, or to imply their endorsement of my use of it, my grateful thanks at least are due the following: J. B. Griffin, J. E. Mosiman, L. S. B. Leakey, D. Livingstone, J. G. Clarke, C. V. Haynes, V. M. Bryant, P. J. Mehringer, J. Schoenwetter, M. S. Stevens, J. Elson, C. W. Hibbard, Roger Duff, R. J. Mason, Ruth Gruhn, D. S. Byers, C. Ray, K. P. Koopman, A. Dreimanis, M. K. Hecht, and C. A. Reed. It goes without saying that each contributor to the chapters in this book has greatly added to my efforts at understanding the extinction problem. A final acknowledgment remains, above all, to Marian.

References Cited

Alvarez, T., 1964, Nota sobre restos oseos de mamiferos del Reciente, encontrados cerca de Tepeapulco, Hidalgo, Mexico: *Mexico Inst. Nac. Antrop. Hist., Dept. Prehistoria,* Publ. 15, p. 1–15

Bramlette, M. B., 1965, Massive extinctions of biota at the end of Mesozoic time: *Science,* v. *148,* p. 1696–99

Butzer, K. W., 1964, *Environment and archeology; An introduction to Pleistocene geography:* Chicago, Aldine, 524 p.

Clark, J. D., 1962, *Carbon-14 chronology in Africa south of the Sahara:* Tevoren, Belgium, IV° Congrès Panafricain de Préhistorie et de l'Etude du Quaternaire, Actes, Sect. III, p. 303–11

Clench, W. J., 1962, New species of land mollusks from the Republica Dominica: *Brevoria.,* v. *173,* p. 1–5

Coetzee, J. A., 1964, Evidence for a considerable depression of the vegetation belts during the upper Pleistocene on the Eastern African mountains: *Nature,* v. *204,* p.564–66

Cooke, H. B. S., 1963, Pleistocene mammal faunas of Africa, with particular reference to Southern Africa, p. 65–116, *in* Howell, F. C., and Bourliere, F., Editors, *African ecology and human evolution:* Chicago, Aldine, 666 p.

Duff, R., 1952, *Pyramid valley:* Christchurch, Pegasus Press, 48 p.

———— 1963a, *The problem of* Moa *extinction:* Thomas Cawthron Mem. Lect. 38, Cawthron Inst., Nelson, N.Z., Stiles, 27 p.

———— 1963b, New Zealand archaeology: *Antiquity,* v. *37,* p. 65–8

Eiseley, L. C., 1943, Archaeological observations on the problem of postglacial extinctions: *Amer. Antiq.,* v. *8,* p. 209–17

Ethridge, R., 1964, Late Pleistocene lizards from Barbuda, British West Indies: *Florida State Mus. Bull. Biol. Sci.,* v. *9,* p. 43–75

Flannery, K. V., 1966, The postglacial "readaptation" as viewed from Mesoamerica: *Amer. Antiq.,* v. *31,* p. 800–05

Fleming, C. A., 1962, The extinction of moas and other animals during the Holocene period: *Notornis,* v. *10,* p. 113–17

Flint, R. F., 1957, *Glacial and Pleistocene geology:* New York, Wiley, 553 p.

Gill, E. G., 1963, The Australian aborigines and the giant extinct marsupials: *Austr. Nat. Hist.,* v. *14,* p. 263–66

Golson, J., and Gathercole, P. W., 1962, The last decade in New Zealand archaeology: *Antiquity,* v. *36,* p. 168–74

Greenway, J. C., Jr., 1958, Extinct and vanishing birds of the world: New York Amer. Comm. Inst. Wild Life Protection, Spec. Publ., v. *13,* 518 p.

Griffin, J. B., 1965, Late Quaternary prehistory in the northeastern woodlands, p. 655–67, *in* Wright, H. E., Jr., and Frey, D. G., Editors, *The Quaternary of the United States:* Princeton Univ. Press, 922 p.

Harper, F., 1945, Extinct and vanishing mammals of the Old World: New York Zool. Park Special Publ. no. *12,* 850 p.

Haynes, C. V., Jr., 1964, Fluted projectile points; Their age and dispersion: *Science,* v. *145,* p. 1408–13

———— 1967, Carbon-14 dates and Early Man in the New World, p. 267–268, *in* Martin, P. S., and Wright, H. E., Jr., Editors, *Pleistocene Extinctions:* Yale Univ. Press, 453 p.

Hester, J. J., 1960, Pleistocene extinction and radiocarbon dating: *Amer. Antiq.,* v. *26,* p. 58–77

Hibbard, C. W., 1958, Summary of North American Pleistocene mammalian local faunas: *Michigan Acad. Sci. Papers,* v. *43,* p. 3–32

Hibbard, C. W., Ray, C. E., Savage, D. E., Taylor, D. W., and Guilday, J. E., 1965, Quaternary mammals of North America, p. 509–25, *in* Wright, H. E., Jr., and Frey, D. G., Editors, *The Quaternary of the United States:* Princeton Univ. Press, 922 p.

Hofstetter, R., 1963, La faune Pleistocene de Tarija (Bolivia); Note préliminaire: *Mus. Nat. d'Histoire Naturelle, Bull.,* v. *35,* p. 194–203

Hopwood, A. J., and Hollyfield, J. P., 1954, *An annotated bibliography of the fossil mammals of Africa* (1792–1950): London, British Museum (Natural History), p. 1–194.

Hubbs, C. L., Bien, G. S., and Suess, H. E., 1962, La Jolla natural carbon measurements II: *Radiocarbon,* v. *4,* p. 204–38

Leakey, L. S. B., 1965, *Olduvai Gorge* 1951–1961: Cambridge Univ. Press, 118 p.

Livingstone, D. A., 1962, Age of deglaciation in the Ruwenzori range, Uganda: *Nature,* v. *194,* p. 859–60

Lundelius, E. L., Jr., 1960, Post-Pleistocene faunal succession in western Australia and its climatic interpretation: Internat. Geol. Cong., 21st Session, Nordern, Rept., pt. 4, p. 142–53

Martin, P. S., 1958, Pleistocene ecology and biogeography of North America, p. 375–420, *in* Hubbs, C. L., Editor, *Zoogeography:* Publ. 51, Amer. Assoc. Adv. Sci., 509 p.

———— 1966, Africa and Pleistocene overkill, *Nature,* v. *212,* p. 339–42

Mason, R. J., 1962, The Paleo-Indian tradition in eastern North America: *Current Anthropol.,* v. *3,* p. 227–78

Morrison, M. E., 1961, Pollen analysis in Uganda: *Nature,* v. *190,* p. 483–86

Müller-Beck, H., 1966, Paleohunters in America; Origins and diffusion: *Science,* v. *152,* p. 1191–210

Mulvaney, D. J., 1964, Tasmanoid industry (premicrolith), Kenniff Cave: *Antiquity,* v. *38,* p. 263–67

Newell, N. D., 1966, Problems of geochronology: Acad. Nat. Sci. Philadelphia, *Proc.,* v. *118,* p. 63–89

Quimby, G. I., 1958, Fluted points and geochronology of the Lake Michigan Basin: *Amer. Antiq.,* v. *23,* p. 247–54

_____ 1960, *Indian life in the Upper Great Lakes,* 11,000 B.C. to *A.D.* 1800: Univ. Chicago Press, 182 p.

Roosevelt, Theodore, 1910, *African game trails:* New York, Scribner's, 529 p.

Rouse, I., 1964, Prehistory of the West Indies: *Science,* v. *144,* p. 499–513

Simpson, G. G., 1961, *Horses:* The Natural History Library Edition: Garden City, Doubleday, 323 p.

Skeels, M. A., 1962, The mastodons and mammoths of Michigan: *Michigan Acad. Sci., Arts, Lett., Papers,* v. *47,* p. 101–33

Talbot, L. M., and Talbot, M., 1963, The wildebeest in western Masailand, East Africa: Wildlife Monog. no. *12,* 88 p.

Vaillant, G. T., 1944, *The Aztecs of Mexico:* Middlesex, Penguin Books, 333 p.

Van Zinderen Bakker, E. M., 1962, A late-glacial and post-glacial climatic correlation between East Africa and Europe: *Nature,* v. *194,* p. 201–03

Wallace, A. L., 1876, *The geographical distribution of animals,* Vol. 1: London, MacMillan, 503 p.

_____ 1911, *The world of life:* New York, Moffat, Yard, 441 p.

Williams, S., and Stoltman, J. B., 1965, An outline of southeastern United States prehistory with particular emphasis on the Paleo-Indian era, p. 669–83, *in* Wright, H. E., Jr., and Frey, D. G., Editors, *The Quaternary of the United States:* Princeton Univ. Press, 922 p.

Wright, H. E., Jr., 1964, Aspects of the early postglacial forest succession in the Great Lakes region: *Ecology,* v. *45,* p. 439–48

ADDITIONAL REFERENCES

Cornwall, I. W. 1968. *Prehistoric animals and their hunters.* London: Faber & Faber.

Krantz, G. S. 1970. Human activities and megafaunal extinctions. *Am. Sci.* 58(2):164–170.

Lee, Richard B., and Irven DeVore, eds. 1968. *Man the hunter.* Chicago: Aldine. 415 pp.

Martin, P. S., and H. E. Wright, Jr., eds. 1967. *Pleistocene extinctions; The search for a cause.* New Haven: Yale University Press. 453 pp. A valuable collection of original studies, with various viewpoints concerning the importance of man the hunter.

WILDLIFE IN DANGER
JAMES FISHER

About 1 percent of the earth's higher animals have become extinct since the year 1600; man is responsible for the extermination of three-fourths of these. Another one-fortieth of our higher animals are in grave danger of extinction, and of these four-sixths of the birds and five-sixths of the mammals have been reduced to their present state by man.

This selection surveys the causes and victims of historical extinctions, and the book from which it is reprinted details the stories of extinct and threatened animals. Of all the causes, hunting for "sport" and to supply the whims of women's fashion are among the most despicable. For example, the vicuña, a wild relative of the llama, have been reduced to perhaps 8,000, as poachers and smugglers—driven by prices up to $240 a yard for the wool in rich nations—remain defiant of strict conservation legislation in Peru and Bolivia (*New York Times,* March 1, 1970, p. 20). In 1969, United States fur dealers imported the skins of 13,516 jaguars and 9,556 leopards—a number far larger than some subspecies of these big cats can sustain (Oberle, 1970).

Why worry at all about conserving animal species? Extinctions irreversibly reduce the diversity of ecosystems, making them more susceptible to unwanted change. This stabilizing effect, or ecological buffering, is probably most important. However, we cannot now measure the loss to future generations resulting from fewer forms of life and reduced genetic variability. Man suddenly is truncating lines of evolution and ecological relationships that have developed over millions of years, without respect for *life.*

(Editor's comment)

James M. Fisher (b. 1912) is a renowned zoologist and presently deputy chairman of the Countryside Commission of the United Kingdom. He is also a member of the Survival Service Commission of the International Union for Conservation of Nature (I.U.C.N.) and a council member of the Fauna Preservation Society. Educated at Oxford, Fisher is a medalist of the Zoological Society of London, the Royal Society for Protection of Birds, and the British Ornithological Union. He has written more than twenty books on natural history and is further noted in Great Britain for his many broadcast commentaries.

The Red Data Book of the Survival Service Commission of the International Union for Conservation of Nature and Natural Resources was published in a new, lithographed form in July 1966, and is the guiding intelligence document for workers all over the world in forming their policies for the conservation, and indeed preservation, of endangered species of animals and plants. As it is in loose-leaf form, the batches of new leaves are sent to its subscribers as the status of living things changes (which it does often with alarming rapidity).

The "Red," of course, is for Danger. The S.S.C. has another list, which could be called Black for Death, or rather extinction; organisms extinct since 1600 (or believed to be so) are recorded periodically in the *I.U.C.N. Bulletin.*

The year 1600 might be thought an arbitrary date; but it has been chosen for a good reason. The S.S.C., not surprisingly, has more precise information about the higher vertebrates—the birds and mammals—than about any other organisms. Virtually all the mammals and birds known to have become extinct since 1600 are identified by adequate descriptions or portraits, nearly all of them by skins, and a considerable number also by subfossil bones; all but two that we can critically admit have acceptable Linnean or scientific names.[1] The two will doubtless soon be formally named. The year 1600 is the year after which zoologists know at least the colours (more than less) of the extinct birds and mammals. Of course zoologists know of very many animals extinct in historical times, though before 1600: but only in a few exceptional cases, based on very rare early documentary evidence, do they know the colours of these; and only very exceptionally do they possess their skins, or parts of them. So 1600 is accepted by the S.S.C. as the reckoning date for modern extinction. It is a practical date that happens to coincide with the approximate beginning of the civilized epoch's own special attack on wild nature.

To summarize the erosion of the variety of wild life, whose study and cure is the particular duty of the S.S.C., a simple statement can be made.

In 1600 there were approximately 4,226 living species of mammals. Since then thirty-six (or 0.85 per cent) have doubtless become extinct; and at least 120 of them (or 2.84 per cent) are presently in some (or great) danger of extinction.

In 1600 there were approximately 8,684 living species of birds. Since then ninety-four (or 1.09 per cent) have doubtless become extinct; and at least 187 of them (or 2.16 per cent) are presently, or have very lately been, in danger of extinction. Of the single order Passeriformes (the "higher" singing birds), which with about 5,153 species in 1600 represented nearly three-fifths of the living birds, twenty-eight (0.54 per cent) are now extinct and at least seventy (1.36 per cent) presently in danger; of the rest, about 3,531 species in 1600, sixty-six (1.87 per cent) are now extinct and at least 117 (3.32 per cent) in danger.

To sum up: a hundredth of our higher animals have become extinct since 1600 and nearly a fortieth are now in danger. These figures apply to full species: geographical races—or subspecies—of our higher animals have had a similar fate. Among the mammals whose species survive, at least sixty-four races have become extinct since 1600, and at least 223 races are still surviving but are included in the Red Data Book. Among the birds, 164 races have become extinct and at least 287 are presently endangered.

As will emerge, this is a state of affairs that is quite without parallel in the former span of man's life with nature, that is to say, in his less civilized history before 1600. What has happened to the mammals and birds since 1600?

It is not easy to measure, despite the fact that the files of the Survival Service Commission are much deeper and more complete for the mammals and birds than for any other

---

[1] The expression "Linnean name" is used in celebration of the founder of scientific naming, Linnaeus of Sweden, and in preference to the usual expression "Latin name", not as an exercise in pedantry, but because nearly as many Linnean names are derived from the Greek as from the Latin.

animals or any plants. What we have tried to do is the following.

Every entry in the Red Data Book mentions the causes of the rarity (or extinction) of an animal as completely as the available information warrants. Not all the evidence is of the same value. Some of it is very deep. Some of it is slender. If some of it is obviously guesswork, we have ignored it. But most of our researches and investigations have given us at least leads and pointers, to the extent that in all cases we have been able to identify one or more of five main factors. These are:

Natural causes. Extinction is a biological reality: it is part of the process of evolution. The study of fossils tells us that before man came on the scene the mean life of a bird species was rather over 2,000,000 years, of a mammal species not much over 600,000. No species has yet "lived" more than a few million years before evolving into one or more others, or "dying" without issue. In any period, including the present, there are doomed species: naturally doomed species, bound to disappear through over-specialization, an incapacity to adapt themselves to climatic change or the competition of others, or occasionally some natural cataclysm of earthquake, eruption, flood, or the like.

Hunting. Pressure on species is exerted by the human hunter for food, clothing, sport, or scientific, quasi-scientific, or status-symbol collection, or as a means of "disease," "pest," or "vermin" control; or pressure as a consequence (usually not intended) of the control of other pests, particularly by poisons.

*Introduced predators.** These exist most commonly in areas colonized since 1600, where mammal predators particularly have been introduced (as in the West Indies, Australia, and New Zealand) to "keep down" the explosive populations of other introduced animals (for instance, rats and rabbits) and have readily turned their predatory attention to the native fauna.

Other introduced animals. Among these are species that have become supplanting competitors in the native habitats of the indigenous animals, or even crude habitat-destroyers (goats in Galápagos), or animals that have brought into the habitats diseases against which the native forms have had little or no resistance (for example, in the Hawaiian archipelago and New Zealand).

Habitat disturbance and destruction. These involve the modification, degradation, and sometimes total destruction of habitat, usually by humans, and most particularly through the felling of forests and the drainage of swamps, for timber, farming space, reservoirs, buildings, airfields, and many other purposes, even sometimes including recreation.

To arrive at some assessment of the relative importance of these main factors, we have awarded eight marks to each species on our list, and shared them in a proportion between the five factors based on our common-sense judgment of the evidence available. This has been a somewhat arbitrary process in cases where the evidence is slender; but we could not think of a better. Expressed as percentages of the total marks that fell to each factor, the results are as in Table 46.1.

From this it appears that only about a quarter of the species of birds and mammals that have become extinct since 1600 may have died out naturally: humans, directly or indirectly, may be responsible for the extermination of the rest. Also, about four-sixths of the birds and five-sixths of the mammals presently known to be in danger of extinction may have come to their present state because of man's activities. Most, but by no means all, of these live or lived on islands, whose faunas (and floras) are far more vulnerable than those of continents to the influence of civilized man.*

In 1965 fossil bones were found in Hungary belonging to our (probably) ancestral species, *Homo erectus,* in a deposit that was laid down in a shortish period of relaxation of the second principal advance (the Mindelian advance) of the European ice systems in the Pleistocene Ice Age. Radioactive and astronomical datings agree that this man lived

* See Part 6 for discussion of the effects of introduced animals.

* See Selection 34.

TABLE 46.1 Causes of animal extinction (since 1600 A.D.) and of present rarity

	BIRDS			MAMMALS
	Non-passerine (large)	Passerine (small)	Total	
Cause of extinction	*per cent*	*per cent*	*per cent*	*per cent*
Natural	26	20	24	25
Human				
hunting	54 ⎫	13 ⎫	42 ⎫	33 ⎫
introduced predators	13 ⎬ 74	21 ⎬ 80	15 ⎬ 76	17 ⎬ 75
other introductions	– ⎪	14 ⎪	4 ⎪	6 ⎪
habitat disruption	7 ⎭	32 ⎭	15 ⎭	19 ⎭
	100	100	100	100
Cause of present rarity				
Natural	31	32	32	14
Human				
hunting	32 ⎫	10 ⎫	24 ⎫	43 ⎫
introduced predators	9 ⎬ 69	15 ⎬ 68	11 ⎬ 68	8 ⎬ 86
other introductions	2 ⎪	5 ⎪	3 ⎪	6 ⎪
habitat disruption	26 ⎭	38 ⎭	30 ⎭	29 ⎭
	100	100	100	100

about 470,000 years ago—nearly twice as long ago as the oldest known *Homo sapiens,* the famous Swanscombe fossil from Kent. The Pleistocene period is now generally agreed to have started well over 1,000,000 years ago, and has been characterized by a global climate far more fluctuating than at any time in the previous 10,000,000 years (or so) of Pliocene times. In the northern part of the Northern Hemisphere and in the southern part of the Southern Hemisphere the Pleistocene brought in a series of ice advances and retreats—in the north a succession of four major and up to a dozen minor ice advances, with warmer or even sometimes quite hottish periods in between. Some of these ice advances covered very large areas indeed of the northern continents.

There is no evidence, in fact, that we are "out" of the Ice Ages yet: many geologists think that we are living at present in no more than an "interglacial" period that started about 10,000 years ago and may continue for no more than another 10,000 or so before the ice returns.

Despite the climate's alternation of hot and cold in the Pleistocene, unlike any that had previously occurred (as the rock records show) for millions of years, the mammals and

birds adapted themselves well to it—better than the flowering plants. After a beginning when a number of specialized Pliocene species and groups fell out, the Pleistocene fauna settled down to evolve in its own way, producing all manner of new genera and species, including some specialist forms and even giant species, and one highly successful species whose very success depended on its non-specialist adaptability—man: whose immediate ancestors are now believed beyond any reasonable doubt to have evolved in Africa in the period between the end of the Pliocene about 3,000,000 years ago and the onset of Pleistocene glaciations in the north, with parallel dry and wet periods in Africa, about 1,000,000 years ago.

The stabilized Pleistocene faunas of all the continents are—or were—dominated by highly adapted big land animals, with which big predators and scavengers were associated. Huge elephants and rhinoceroses even became successfully adapted to life in the tundra where the undersoil was permanently frozen.

South America had its huge ground-sloths and glyptodons (super-armadillos); North America its super-elephants, super-bison, super-camels, and super-lions; even Europe its share of elephants and hippos and giant bison. All continents had arrays of giant birds: North America had the vast tera-torns—the biggest birds of prey known to science; Europe had its Maltese super-vulture (last heard of at Monte Carlo 100,000 years ago or so) and a super-swan so big that it must have been flightless. Only Africa to-day—and perhaps for special and complicated reasons—still has a characteristic Pleistocene fauna; and that is now mainly in the national parks and game reserves: big elephants, rhinos, giraffes, vultures, and storks, and a galaxy of magnificent antelopes. The isolated lands had their Pleistocene heyday, too—Australia with giant marsupials; New Zealand with its moa fauna, the tallest (up to 12-foot) birds known; Madagascar with its elephant-bird (the biggest, half a ton) and super-lemur fauna. Even the isolated little Mauritius, Réunion, and Rodriguez islands in the Indian Ocean had their own flourish through (and after) the Pleistocene with their dodos and other curious flightless birds.

By general agreement among geologists and paleontologists (and largely to make definitions and meanings clear), the Pleistocene is considered to have ended "officially" a little over 10,000 years ago. The period we live in is called the Holocene—even if the ice may soon come back (using "soon" in the geological sense), and we may be still in the Pleistocene, in terms of irregular climate-changes. In terms of faunas, the Pleistocene really ended in Europe, perhaps also in most of Asia, more or less at the beginning of the official Upper Pleistocene over 100,000 years ago; in North America about 8,000 years ago; in the West Indies and Central and South America rather later than that; in Australia at the most twenty, but probably only a few, thousand years ago; in New Zealand after A.D. 950. The main reason why the Pleistocene fauna, as characterized by its more exaggerated and highly adapted (and therefore vulnerable) elements, collapsed in these different places at different times seems to be a simple one: the coming of man the hunter, Stone Age man—in the case of the Indian Ocean islands, civilized man.

Now, the Pleistocene fauna has not yet departed from Africa, or rather from the continent south of the Sahara that is the home of the present Ethiopian fauna (this fauna extended sometimes to France up to Miocene times, perhaps 20,000,000 years ago). Yet it was in Africa that man evolved in the Pleistocene period, from higher apes.[*] Is there a paradox here? Probably not. As man evolved, the Pleistocene fauna of Africa evolved with him, and developed defence adaptations as he rather quickly became the most intelligent and skilful hunting animal the world has ever known. Very probably Stone Age man destroyed some large African species; but he did not destroy the Pleistocene fauna. It was when man became an armed invader of new faunal areas that their faunas, without such adaptations, became decimated (in some cases literally so, or more than so).

Sapient man of our own kind was, as we have seen, in Europe about 250,000 years ago. The heavy Pleistocene elements disappeared as his skills improved; the forest elephant and hippopotamus and perhaps the giant vulture about 100,000 years ago; the forest rhino not long afterwards. The bird fauna was already a modern one: of the Pleistocene types, only the French sarus crane and the cave chough lasted until the late Pleistocene times of the sophisticated Magdalenian cave men. The giant deer lasted beyond the official end of the Pleistocene up to the Iron Age. The other last big animals (apart from bison and aurochs) retreated to Siberia, where the last mammoths and woolly rhinos, tundra-adapted, probably survived until the last glaciation, when a warm spell made it too boggy for them to range in the summer.

The impact of man upon the animals of America was much more sudden and sweeping.

The great Rancho la Brea fauna fossilized in the asphalt tarpits of Los Angeles is the

---

[*] Contrary to this statement, man's evolution from less advanced (non-tool-making) hominids extends well back into the Pliocene, and humans and higher apes have evolved from common primate ancestors, not one from the other. (*Editor's note.*)

most complete and the best worked out array of its kind in the world. As we now know from carbon dating, it survived, at least in part, well beyond the official end of the Upper Pleistocene 10,000 years ago. It is now certain that the earliest Amerindians reached North America at least 15,000 and possibly (or even probably) over 30,000 years ago—that is to say, in the Upper Pleistocene—and rather quickly penetrated to what is now the western United States.

Early man in North America encountered a Pleistocene fauna. From the evidence of the Rancho la Brea tarpits, his bones and atlatl darts are associated there with the fossils of early prehistoric or Holocene age.

Now, of fifty-four different species of mammals in the la Brea tarpits of Upper Pleistocene to prehistoric date (at the broadest from a little over 18,000 to a little less than 4,500 years ago), twenty-four, or nearly half, are now extinct; and of 113 fully identified birds twenty-two, or nearly a fifth, are extinct.

Gone now, amongst others, are the huge dire wolf; the short-faced coyote; the vast short-faced bear; the big sabre-toothed cat, *Smilodon;* the giant lion (or jaguar), *Panthera atrox* (the present lion in linear measurements plus a quarter); the super-camel or super-llama, *Camelops,* 7 feet at the withers; the American mastodon (6 feet 3 inches); the imperial (10 feet 8½ inches) and Columbian mammoths; and the greater (huge), middle, and lesser la Brea ground-sloths. Gone these are indeed; but it seems certain that they did not go until after the coming of man.

Gone too are Rancho la Brea's peculiarly Pleistocene birds, many of them also giants. Nearly all the great latest-Pleistocene birds of North America that we know of are represented in the Rancho la Brea fauna, including all the remarkable extinct birds of prey of that time. From the regions in which their fossils have been found, we can be sure that at least a dozen of them survived to early human times. The asphalt stork was evidently the New World representative of our Old World white and black storks, and stood, on slender limbs, about 4 feet 6 inches high. The

extinct la Brea turkey, or ground-fowl, was a robust bird not unlike the surviving ocellated turkey of Mexico that, from the abundance of its bones, must have been the commonest game bird of what is now the Los Angeles district in la Brean times.

Of the great Rancho la Brea raptors, the largest was Merriam's teratorn, which had a 12-foot wingspread and an estimated weight of 50 pounds, and which was doubtless a scavenger on the corpses of the giant mammals. *Teratornis merriami* may have persisted until the tarpit faunas of about 4,500 years ago. Its congener (member of the same genus), the incredible teratorn, *T. incredibilis,* which, with a wingspan of 16 to 17 feet, was the largest soaring bird of prey yet known to have lived, survived not quite so long—in Nevada, until the Upper Pleistocene.

Most important of all among six other birds of prey of Rancho la Brea, for the simple reason that it is (just) with us, and a Red Data Book bird of the Survival Service Commission, was *Gymnogyps.* Males of the California condor (and there are about twenty of them left alive) run to a wingspread of 9 feet 7 inches and a weight of 23 pounds. The California condor, *Gymnogyps californianus,* and what is probably its rather bigger direct ancestor, *G. amplus* (the transition from one species to the other, if separate species they really were, seems to have taken place around the official end of the Pleistocene 10,000 years ago), in Pleistocene years ranged west of the Rocky Mountains from the border of Washington and British Columbia in the north to that of California and Mexico's Lower California in the south; also in a great strip across the southern states from New Mexico through Texas to Florida. By the time the modern Americans had opened up the West, it had retreated west of North America's great Rocky Mountain spine. To cut a story short, it was confined to a few counties of California with a population of about sixty in 1947; by 1963 was nesting and roosting in but two California counties; and between these two main years of survey (on behalf of the National Audubon Society) had been reduced to a world population of only about forty-two.

To bring the story of the California condor up to modern times has been a digression. Only in the last forty years has the Upper Pleistocene presence of man in America been confirmed, and only lately have archaeologists and paleontologists begun to collate his hearths and flints and other remains with the last of the North American mastodons and mammoths, big tortoises and birds. With the success and spread of carbon dating, the collapse of the North American Pleistocene super-fauna has been narrowed down to a period of between 11,000 and 8,000 years ago; which makes it very sudden. Only a few of the big extinct mammals and birds held on longer. The period of "Pleistocene overkill," now recognized as a phenomenon that has occurred at one time or another all over man's realm, which means all over the world, was short in North America, and marches with the development of the sophisticated flints of the Clovis and Folsom cultures, tools quite effective enough to kill and butcher an elephant.

New Zealand's higher vertebrate fauna has naturally consisted almost entirely of birds, which had a remarkable adaptive radiation into mammal niches, the great order of the moas taking the place of big grazers. When the first humans—Polynesians—discovered the main islands and the offlying Chatham Islands in about A.D. 950, they were confronted with an array of classic Pleistocene quality, an indigenous bird fauna that can be guessed, from the evidence of the fossil and living examples, to have been over 150 species. Before Captain Cook's time, the Polynesians had killed off at least twenty species of moas, and shortly after the European discovery the last one was killed, on South Island, in the late eighteenth century. The Polynesians and the Europeans (who helped a little towards the end) killed off about a third of the birds of the islands. The fact that the present nesting fauna of the islands is up to about 147 is the consequence of thirty-five successful introductions of non-native birds by the Europeans, and eight

known natural colonizations in European times. At least forty-three New Zealand species have been globally lost since the Polynesians arrived, nine of them since 1600. Both families of the moas have been totally exterminated, and with them two flightless geese, a great swan, a great eagle, flightless rails, interesting passerines like the extraordinary huia (this, early in the present century). At least a dozen surviving New Zealand birds are in the Survival Service Commission's Red Data Book. A few, like the famous flightless rail, *Notornis,* the takahé, seem to be holding their own under close protection. The very status of others (that is, whether surviving or extinct), like the piopio, or New Zealand thrush, and the New Zealand laughing owl, is still mysterious. New Zealand is blessed with energetic and skilful ornithologists; but it is a rugged country to work over, and the competition of the introduced exotics may be an important cause of the rarity and "pocket isolation" of the ancient indigenous song-birds at least.

In Hawaii, a still further isolated archipelago, even more exotics have been introduced than in New Zealand. Here the old fauna does not seem to have been destroyed by the first Polynesian colonists, who probably arrived there before they discovered New Zealand. But the Westerners who arrived since Captain Cook have brought about the extermination of fourteen species, and have brought perhaps as many more to Red Data Book status. Destruction of habitat has been as powerful as the introduction of disease and competitors. The status of many species now hangs in the balance, despite the efforts of the excellent farming and conservation authorities, and the watchful Hawaiian Audubon Society. There is a triumph here to report, though. The native Hawaiian goose, or néné, with the help of a remarkable programme of captive culture in England at the Wildfowl Trust's Slimbridge and in Hawaii at Pohakuloa, and with the successful release of nearly 200 birds into the wild population, has been restored in numbers from its all-time lowest around fifty just over a decade ago to ten times that. The population of the Hawaiian duck is turning the corner, too; and the Laysan teal is now flourishing both on its isolated home at the western end of the long Hawaiian chain, and in captivity.

Stone Age man, then, has been a fauna-exterminator. If we narrow the period of Pleistocene over-kill in North America to 3,000 years, we can find with some reasons that in or around that time about fifty mammals and forty birds may have been extinguished at most: that is to say, not more than three every century on average. Between the Polynesian colonization of New Zealand in about A.D. 950 and Cook's first voyage there in 1769, about thirty-six species of birds (there were no land mammals save rodents and bats) were extinguished—not more than one every twenty years on average. Since 1769 seven more have gone, or about one every twenty-seven years on average. The world is not comparable with a part of itself; but it seems quite clear that on islands and in other specially vulnerable areas, where most of the modern extinctions have taken place and most of the Red Data Book animals are presently found, modern man has contrived to arrange an extinction rate even higher than that attained by an Old Stone Age community that discovered a fauna hitherto unknown to man. Of the ninety-four birds believed extinct since 1600, only the following became extinct that lived on continents: in Asia the pink-headed duck (1944), the Himalayan mountain quail (1868), Jerdon's courser (1900), and the forest spotted owlet (*c.* 1872); in North America the Labrador duck (1875), Cooper's sandpiper (1833), the passenger pigeon (1914), the Carolina parakeet (1914), and Townsend's bunting (1833). All the others have become extinct on islands large and small, particularly in New Zealand, Hawaii, and others of the South Seas, the Mascarene Islands of the Indian Ocean, and the West Indies. In the West Indies, from fossil and other evidence, we can calculate that the average expectation of total "geological" life of the larger bird species was about 180,000 years, before any humans arrived (much smaller than on the North American continent at the same time, owing to the specially fast natural evolution rate on islands). It was brought down to about 30,000 years by the aboriginal colonists in about 5,000 years of prehistoric times. It was brought down to a bare 12,000 years or so since 1600, after the establishment of the more sophisticated and civilized Western colonists. The pre-man bird species of Mauritius and Rodriguez in the Indian Ocean seem to have had a mean geological life-span of only about 6,000 years, from the fossils and their likely dating; these islands had no Stone Age phase, and their Western discoverers quickly brought the span, after 1600, down to about 1,000 years.

We have already seen that the suppression of fauna by man has been, and is, attained in several ways, and that hunting and habitat destruction are by far the most important and powerful. Hunting is our own society's almost ineradicable link with Old Stone Age times.

Hunting was the living of our species for 250,000 years or more, in which the Old Stone Age peoples learn its art and tradition by trial and error. Masters of tools and fire, and, doubtless early on, of speech and pictorial art, the men of the Old Stone Age became food-gatherers, and skilful hunters of all things of the land and shallow waters, from shellfish to honey, from tubers to fruit, from sparrows to ostriches, from rodents to at least eight kinds of elephants and mastodons, rhinos, tapirs, bison, wild cattle, and huge deer. Hyena, wolf, cave lion, sabre-tooth, cave bear were their rivals at the top, and they learnt to master them, usurp their homes, share space and prey with them, and dominate the hunting-grounds. At some time in their evolution, many Stone Age groups encountered the effects of their own Pleistocene over-kill and developed lore of totem, taboo, and self-denying ordinance, cropping and rationing rules. Inventions, often quite independent, carried them over thresholds of hunting power: bolas, hand-dart, spear-thrower, bow-and-arrow, throwing-stick, boomerang, blowpipe, stalking-horse, deadfall, trap, snare, net, decoy; and the domestication of the faithful dog and horse.

With the invention of methods of polishing and grinding stone to make tools for cutting tree and earth, our neolithic ancestors found it possible to settle, to let the nomadic rhythms of a purely hunting life cease or run down, to carve farms from the forests, plant seed, and become pastoralists. But even with metal, first copper and bronze and later hard iron, they never stopped hunting. Hunting became then a facet of their lives, not the main thing in their lives. Its rules and arts became more complex, and its practice began to have a class structure. In the Dark Ages of the early sophistication of iron, a trend began—to organize hunting as a noble pursuit: parks in the Dark Ages became conservation areas under rules in essence no different from (though cruder than) those that exist in modern African game reserves, or syndicate areas in Britain's pheasant woodlands, or in the hills and fields of Pennsylvania at the opening of the deer season, or the wetlands of Russia when duck-hunting begins. High hunting art, the more interesting because of its relative, and perhaps unconsciously fostered, inefficiency, reached its climax with the invention of falconry, probably in several countries quite independently; in the English Bronze Age; at about the same time, or a little earlier, in China (c. 2000 B.C.); and with a wonderful flourishment in Dark Age Persia and Arabia and Europe.

The painters of magical animals of the chase at Lascaux in France have left us what is doubtless the earliest surviving work of art, including a picture of a rhinoceros that can represent (unless the artist took remarkable liberties) none other than Merck's forest rhinoceros, a very close relation of the Sumatran rhinoceros, which is not known from any fossil deposit younger than about 30,000 years! The Persian kings of old enclosed little wildernesses of hunting land and called them paradises, and the Norman kings of England did the same and called them parks and chases. The Zulu King Dingaan, himself no mean hunter of elephants and trader in ivory, established a protected game park years before the present game-park system was developed in Africa, north of the Umfolozi River, where today the square-lipped rhinoceros still has a headquarters. The Vikings of a thousand years ago or more established a sea-bird hunting culture in St Kilda and other parts of the Hebrides, and in Faeroe and Iceland, which still thrives in much of its old range (still shared by as many—or more—sea-birds), with very strict rules about the cropping season and the size of the "take." The northern world in America and Eurasia is networked with a complex array of public licence systems, and conservation areas both public and private, designed to foster hunting and at the same time the populations of the hunted; and the enlightened emergent nations are learning and copying and adapting the rules and experience with gratifying speed, especially in Africa.

The statements in the previous paragraph may appear to be somewhat disconnected. They have been so arranged deliberately, to show a common thread that runs through the history of hunting, woven from the facts that hunting has its atmosphere as well as its achievement, and that, even when it no longer supplies the main tribal or national protein, it continues to have, or indeed further refines, its complicated rules. It is when the rules are unknown, or lost and forgotten, or (as has happened lately) ruthlessly ignored, that a situation of over-kill develops.

We have seen that Stone Age people all over the globe attained the power to over-kill and extinguish at varying times in the Pleistocene and prehistoric epochs; and our ancestors learnt wisdom from the warning. This wisdom appears to have been widely forgotten again in our later years of post-Renaissance exploration, and particularly since the Industrial Revolution, and the rapid refinement of guns and other hunting tools, in the early nineteenth century. The over-killing of the whales cleared huntable whale populations out of the Northern Hemisphere before that century had finished, and promises to do the same for the Southern Hemisphere before the end of the present century. The modern over-kills are "investment over-kills," with expensive tools and loaned capital behind them. Such investments of money and skill run contrary to the public good and even to the interest of the investments (without mentioning the future of the animal species concerned) unless they can be planned and controlled. In our late historical times such conservation forces as have been available have resembled a weak, unarmed police force in a town where looting is going on. In the past the looters have often looted until there was nothing left worth looting— witness the whale trade, the seal trade, the sea-otter trade, and some fisheries. The bird-plumage trade has been mostly stopped, before any species became badly endangered by it, but was stopped only just in time. Serious over-hunting persists in many parts of Africa and some of Asia and the Americas —not all of it for protein, some in the name of sport: though, in most of the northern world and much of Australasia, the conservation leaders are perhaps more likely than not to be also experienced hunting sportsmen. Many people, especially those brought up in industrial towns, cannot understand that the roles of hunter and conservationist can be compatible, far less that they have proved compatible in some countries for ages, and long before Renaissance thought. Many people still find it hard to understand that the ultimate protection of nature, and all its ecological systems, and all its endangered forms of life, demands a plan, in which the core is a management of the wilderness, and an enlightened exploitation of its wild resources based on scientific research and measurement.

The latest phase of over-hunting is not quite describable as over-kill, since its products are wanted alive. Private aviculture all over the civilized world has multiplied in the last three decades by geometrical progression. There were about 526 zoos in the world in 1965, the number having doubled since 1946! This fantastic increase is largely due to the escalation of roadside menageries, many of which may never attain the standards and rules of the mainstream zoos, whose relation with the Survival Service Commission is ex-

cellent. The wholesale trade in zoo animals, involving illegalities and smuggling on its seamy side, is now turning over millions of pounds annually; and it concerns conservationists and opponents of cruelty to animals very deeply indeed.

Perhaps in the long run the over-kill or the over-capture (for it amounts to over-kill) will be controlled and prevented. That is what the I.U.C.N. is for. But the main battle is now, beyond any doubt, in the ecological field of habitat maintenance. It can of course be truly said that ever since New Stone Age times man has altered his environment deeply, with his power to cut down forests and drain wetlands. When the first men shortly reach the moon, they will probably be able to see the forest slashes of the last century with the naked eye, so accelerated have been the environmental changes of the Industrial Age. Already habitat destruction has contributed a significant share of the extinctions and endangerments of species since 1600. In the future, unless controlled, it may contribute an even greater share. In some tropical forest areas, of which the Philippines and Colombia are examples, lumbering has almost run wild: few scientists have been available to monitor and measure its effects, but insofar as they can be measured they are deplorable.

This book has been compiled from I.U.C.N. files as dispassionately as its compilers could find possible. Confronted with a list of species on the verge of extinction, and the high likelihood that three-quarters of them have become so because of man (and thus avoidably), a certain amount of rage might seem justified. Rage, however, does not cure. We hope that we can arouse righteous indignation with the accounts in this book, which are as true as we, and our many helpful naturalist friends and correspondents, have been able to make them. By the very act of buying it, our readers are supporting the cause of international conservation. We hope that our readers will be able to do more: join their local and national nature conservation societies, if they have not done so already; support their national sections of the International World Wildlife Fund; and help the I.U.C.N. and its Survival Service Commission, beyond the stage where its members and staff have to count the stamps, think twice before telephoning, and hitch-hike to conferences and field programmes. We need more time and power and money to learn, teach, persuade, and dissuade.

ADDITIONAL REFERENCES

Allen, Durward L. 1966. The preservation of endangered habitats and vertebrates of North America. Pp. 22–37 in *Future environments of North America,* ed. by F. Fraser Darling and John P. Milton. Garden City, New York: The Natural History Press.

Allen, Glover M. 1942. *Extinct and vanishing mammals of the Western Hemisphere with marine species of all the oceans.* American committee for international wildlife protection. 620 pp. Detailed account, as of 1942, by family and species; well documented.

Caras, Roger A. 1966. *Last chance on earth; A requiem for wildlife.* Philadelphia: Chilton. 207 pp. Popular account of forty threatened species (mostly mammals and birds) with striking pen-and-ink drawings.

Crowe, Philip K. 1967. *The empty ark.* New York: Scribner. 301 pp. A region-by-region survey of threatened wildlife with many first-hand observations; no references.

Dembeck, Hermann. 1965. *Animals and men.* Transl. from German by R. & C. Winston. Garden City, N.Y.: Natural History Press. 390 pp. The first 148 pages ("The animal as prey") provide a good popular history of hunting, with emphasis on Europe.

Ehrenfeld, D. W. 1970. *Biological conservation.* New York: Holt, Rinehart and Winston Inc. 226 pp.

International Union for the Conservation of Nature and Natural Resources. Survival Service Commission. 1966. *Red data book.* Lausanne, Switzerland. 2 vols. This is the ultimate published resource concerning endangered species; its loose leaves provide continual updating.

McVay, Scott. 1966. The last of the great whales. Sci. Am. 215(2):13–21.

Marshall, S. J., ed. 1966. *The great extermination.* London: Heinemann.

Oberle, M. W. 1970. Endangered species: Congress curbs international trade in rare animals. *Science* 167:152–154.

Schorger, A. W. 1955. *The passenger pigeon; Its natural history and extinction.* Madison: University of Wisconsin Press. 424 pp.

Talbot, Lee M. 1961. *A look at threatened species.* London: Fauna Preservation Society.

Ziswiler, Vinzenz. 1967. *Extinct and vanishing animals.* Rev. English ed. by F. and P. Bunnell. New York: Springer-Verlag. 133 pp. An excellent treatment of direct and indirect processes of animal extermination by man; includes lists of threatened and extinct animals.

NINE MAN AS A MAKER OF NEW PLANTS AND ANIMALS

"What is there about the presence of man that stimulates his plant and animal companions into increased evolutionary activity? Plants and animals have gradually been selected which are adapted to life with each other like pieces of a multidimensional jigsaw puzzle. It is only when man, or some other disruptive agent, upsets the whole puzzle that there is any place where something new and different can fit in. Man, the great weed-breeder, the great upsetter, catalyzes the formation of new biological entities."

Moths on an oak tree, Birmingham, England. Photo by M. Lyster.

INTRODUCTION

Man not only surrounds himself with alien organisms from afar (Part 6) and destroys vegetation and animals wherever he goes (Parts 7 and 8) but also creates new kinds of plants and animals.

Man has stimulated the evolution of both valuable and harmful new organisms. These changes in organisms themselves are an important impact of man on the biological environment, but a neglected one. Edgar Anderson has pointed out the strong tendency to study the plants and animals of "mountaintops and jungles rather than those of dooryards and gardens, to think of plant and animal communities as they must have been in some blissfully innocent era before the advent of man."

What has been man's impact on the courses of organic evolution? How does man alter the stuff that determines the very nature of life itself? This part explores these questions. In general, man makes new organisms in three ways: (1) by artificial selection, (2) by altered natural selection through environmental change, and (3) by differential extermination of portions of populations and thus favoring survivors (a special sort of artificial selection).

Selection 47 explains how the first two of these processes operate in the case of animal domestication. In both plants and animals, evolution occurs by the production of genetic variation and the sifting of these variants by natural selection. Man may alter the sifting process (1) by consciously picking and breeding plants and animals that possess desirable traits (artificial selection) and (2) by modifying the environment, with which all organisms interact to help determine which genotypes (groups of individuals sharing a certain genetic make-up) will survive. The authors contrast these changes that occur in captivity with evolution in wild populations. In both cases the bases for evolution are both genetic and environmental. The creation of domesticated animals and cultivated plants has been called "the oldest and grandest example of experimental biological activity of man" (Epstein, 1955).

Selection 48 discusses man's creation of new plants. Whereas the human-directed evolution of most crop plants occurred during prehistoric times, many other new plants continue to be fostered inadvertently through environmental changes. New natural hybrids are often the best adapted plants in new habitats created by man, such as burns, clearings, fields, pathways, and dumps.

Some very striking evolutionary changes have been stimulated through subtle chains of cause and effect that begin with man's actions. Selection 49 nicely illustrates a fascinating case of animal evolution induced by air pollution—the phenomenon of "industrial melanism." A formerly minor black form of the peppered moth in England now has an advantage in natural selection over light forms in regions where trees have been darkened by air pollutants; the dark moths are notably better camouflaged against predatory birds.

The final selection in this part, Selection 50, briefly shows how selective destruction of insects by pesticides has spurred the development of resistant pests. The author mentions numerous ecological implications of this induced evolution.

Should man now consciously attempt to genetically remake himself, the human animal? This question is now receiving greater serious discussion. Such action is laden with severe moral, social, and political difficulties. Further, the scientific means for controlling human genetics are not yet developed. Part of the argument for considering human genetic manipulation is based on the increasing conflict between man's biological nature, primarily determined in paleolithic times, and man's modern environment. This disharmony is discussed by René Dubos in Part 10 (Selection 51).

FURTHER READINGS

Belyaev, D. K. 1969. Domestication of animals. *Science Journal* 5(1):47–52.

de Candolle, A. P. 1886. *Origin of cultivated plants.* 2d ed. Reprinted 1964 by Hafner, New York and London. 468 pp.

Darwin, Charles. 1868. *The variation of animals and plants under domestication.* 2 vols. London.

Sauer, Carl O. 1952. *Agricultural origins and dispersals.* Bowman Memorial Lectures, Series 2. Amer. Geog. Soc. 110 pp.

Ucko, Peter J., and G. W. Dimbleby, eds. 1969. *The domestication and exploitation of plants and animals.* Chicago: Aldine. 581 pp. A varied and stimulating set of essays which concentrate on the prehistoric origins of domesticated animals and plants.

Zeuner, Frederick E. 1963. *A history of domesticated animals.* New York: Harper & Row. A standard reference on the origins of various domesticated animals. 560 pp.

DOMESTICATION AND ADAPTATION

E. O. PRICE AND J. A. KING

Domestication of animals by man has brought about numerous important changes in the animals. Man has selected, and perpetuated, certain traits mainly for economic reasons. In general, size decreases (excluding modern developments), coloration changes, production of meat and milk increase, and the length and texture of the hair and skin are altered; even the brain is affected, with the centers of sensual perception suffering in some species (Zeuner, 1963, pp. 65–74). For detailed discussion of changes in numerous domesticated animals see works by Zeuner (1963), Epstein (1955), Dimbleby and Ucko (1969), and the early classic by Charles Darwin, *The Variation of Plants and Animals under Domestication* (1868).

This selection discusses domestication as an evolutionary process, including mechanisms by which genotypic—inheritable—changes occur during captivity. The production of variations and the sifting of them in wild populations are described first. Domestication requires adaptation to physical and biological conditions that are much different from those commonly found in nature. Inbreeding, genetic drift, and selection are the genetic mechanisms by which animal evolution in captivity proceeds. This selection provides insight into how man has both consciously and inadvertently created new kinds of animals.

(Editor's comment)

Edward O. Price is an assistant professor at the State University College of Forestry, Syracuse, New York. John A. King (b. 1921) is professor of zoology at Michigan State University, where he has been a member of the faculty since 1961. He holds three degrees, including a Ph.D. (1951), from the University of Michigan. King was associated with the U.S. Public Health Service's Jackson Memorial Laboratory from 1951–1960. His areas of research include sociobiology, mammalian behavior and its evolution, and the effects of early experience.

This selection first appeared as Chapter 3 (pp. 34–45) in *Adaptation of Domestic Animals,* edited by E. S. E. Hafez, Philadelphia: Lea & Febiger, 1968. Reprinted by courtesy of the authors, the editor, and the publisher.

Natural Populations

The diversity of animals and plants prompted the search for the mechanisms of evolution. Lamarck, in the early 1800's, proposed an explanation based on the inheritance of acquired characters, suggesting that environmental modifications of morphologic, physiologic and behavioral characteristics could be inherited. Lamarck was followed by Wagner who proposed a theory based on isolation and DeVries who envisioned evolution as resulting from large mutations.

Weismann's germ-plasm theory was also added to the list of explanations. Even Darwin focused his attention on one causal factor, natural selection, which he viewed as change resulting from a balance of conflicting forces. It was not until the 1930's that the various theories were incorporated into a workable explanation (synthesis) based on the concepts of Darwin's theory and genetics: that variation among animals and plants in nature makes certain individuals better adapted for survival than others. According to the "Modern Synthesis," as Huxley calls it, evolution revolves around two central themes: (*a*) the production of variation, and (*b*) the sifting of these variants by natural selection. The purpose of this chapter is to discuss domestication as an active evolutionary process and to study mechanisms responsible for genotypic changes in species adapting to captive conditions.

THE PRODUCTION OF VARIABILITY

Phenotypic variability. Phenotypic variability (the raw material of selection) is obtained from both genetic variation and differential response to the environment. Behavioral, physiological or morphological characters are the result of an interaction between the environment and the genotype. In the Himalayan rabbit the black pigment of the nose, ears, feet and tip of the tail result from cooler temperatures at the extremities. When a portion of the white fur is removed and the animal is exposed to a low temperature, the new hairs are pigmented black. Conversely, a shaved ear wrapped in bandages to keep it warm grows white hairs where black grew previously.

Genetic variability. Genetic variability is basically dependent on: (*a*) polymorphism (variability due to two or more alleles at a given locus), and (*b*) the frequency of these alleles in the species gene pool. If each locus carried only one allele, all individuals would possess the same genotype and genetic variability would be nonexistent. The maintenance of two or more alleles at a given locus increases genetic variability arithmetically to that locus and makes possible exponential increase of interactions between the alleles at different loci (Chapter 11 in Hafez, 1968).

The source of new genetic material is through mutation. Mutations have appeared in all domestic animals and are of three basic types: (*a*) mutations with visible effects; (*b*) mutations with slight effects (only cumulative effects of many similar ones are recognizable) and (*c*) lethal mutations. All three have had a role in the development of the various breeds of livestock and pets.

NATURAL SELECTION

In natural populations, the frequency of a given gene is determined by its relative contribution in the total adaptation of individuals to their environment. The genotypes of those animals showing the greatest "fitness" (leaving the most descendents) will be perpetuated, while those less adapted to the environment will contribute fewer genes to the population gene pool. This sifting of the adapted and non-adapted is known as natural selection.

Natural selection (in contrast to artificial selection) is not goal oriented. Its influence can only be measured after it has occurred and the adaptations of the animals are observed. All normal individuals are potential breeders and natural selection determines which individuals leave the most descendents. In artificial selection, man selects the breeding population which will produce a desired result. In the former, reproduction

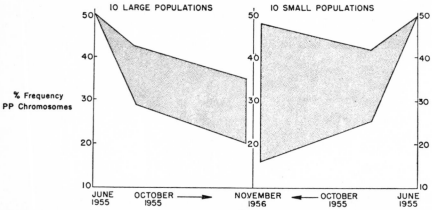

FIGURE 47.1 Variance in frequency of PP chromosomes in 10 populations each founded by 4,000 individuals (left) and 10 populations each founded by 10 individuals (right). Random fluctuations in gene frequencies are maximized in small populations. (From Dobzhansky & Pavlovsky, 1957. *Evolution* 11:311.)

is instrumental in the selection process, whereas in the latter, selection occurs prior to reproduction. Natural selection is not accompanied by artificial selection, but natural selection accompanies artificial selection because individuals of captive populations always show some variation in "fitness."

RANDOM CHANGES IN GENE FREQUENCIES

In large interbreeding natural populations, significant changes in gene frequencies are the result of natural selection. In small populations random changes in gene frequencies occur.

Genetic drift. This term is defined as the "random fluctuation of gene frequencies in effectively small populations." Since the word "drift" has an unidirectional connotation, Mayr refers to this phenomenon as the "founder principle." Genetic drift exists because of three phenomena which act randomly in determining gene frequencies. First, the genotypes comprising the founder population may represent a randomly selected group of genotypes from the parent population. Secondly, the inbreeding prevalent in small isolated groups affects gene frequencies in a random manner. And thirdly, one out of several possible gene combinations of *equal* selective value may be randomly fixed in a small population (genetic indeterminacy).

Whereas genetic drift may contribute little to evolution when natural selection is the primary force, it can affect genetic fixation in small captive populations. Several factors determine the importance of random fluctuations in gene frequency and evolution, namely, the relative contribution to fitness of the genes involved, the size of the population, its isolation and its resistance to outside invasion (Figure 47.1). Since most small isolated colonies usually are only temporarily withdrawn from outside gene exchange, even random fixation is of questionable importance in evolution. On the other hand, most captive populations are small isolated units, maximizing the effects of drift.

Inbreeding. Inbreeding, or the mating of blood-related individuals (brother-sister, father-daughter) also produces random fluctuations in gene frequencies. Inbreeding affects gene frequencies by increasing homozygosity and, thus reducing genetic variability (Figure 47.2). Close inbreeding often results in "inbreeding depression." The latter refers to the lowering of fitness brought about by the effect of many deleterious gene combinations on the phenotype. Inbreeding depression has been demonstrated for egg hatchability, clutch size, milk yield, litter size, growth rate and viability. The harmful effects of many deleterious recessive genes are often not realized in an outbreeding population because heterozygosity prevents phenotypic expression of the recessive genes.

Despite its harmful effects, inbreeding allows for the rapid expression of new genetic material (mutations). A new recessive mutation may be carried in an out-breeding population for some time before it appears in homozygous form. The increased homozygosity produced by inbreeding increases the likelihood for phenotypic expression of the character which can then be selected.

Little is known about the incidence of inbreeding in natural populations. A highly inbred population which has found an adaptive gene combination can do well in a specialized environment but is unable to cope with sudden environmental change. A highly outbred population, on the other hand, is well buffered against the environment at the expense of maintaining many inferior genotypes.

ADAPTIVE VARIATIONS

In the following discussion "adaptation" will refer to the process of obtaining genotypic and phenotypic modifications of morphology, physiology and behavior which enhance the fitness of individuals to their environment.

Adaptation implies changes over successive generations (genotypic adaptations) or changes during the lifetime of an individual (phenotypic adaptations). The potentiality for adaptation is always inherited but some adaptations have both inherited and non-inherited components. Although the environment may influence the development of morphologic characteristics, they are relatively insensitive to environmental modification. Some behaviors, however, (particularly those controlled by the higher brain centers) are extremely sensitive to environ-

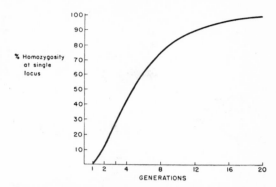

FIGURE 47.2 Probability of homozygosity at a single locus after 20 generations of brother-sister matings (inbreeding). Genetic variability is reduced as homozygosity is increased. (From Green, 1966. *Biology of the Laboratory Mouse.* New York, McGraw-Hill.)

mental stimuli and have a large non-inherited component. Techniques have been devised to measure the relative roles of the genotype and the environment in determining the phenotypic variability of a given character.

The fitness of an individual is determined by its total adaptation to the environment. This includes all aspects of all adaptations, whether morphological, physiological or behavioral. The genetic component of adaptation is guided by natural selection. Those gene combinations fostering the best adapted phenotypes will be "selected for" while inferior genotypes will be eliminated. Given enough time, slight advantages in adaptation per generation can result in major adaptations as attested by adaptive modifications of teeth, feet (Figure 47.3) and limbs.

In an unchanging environment, all characters could be under rigid genetic control with maximum adaptation to the environment. In a changing environment, a certain amount of variability is necessary to ensure that the population will survive each environmental change. This requirement for variability can be fulfilled either genetically, phenotypically or both. In most natural populations a balance exists between the production of a variety of genotypes and individual flexibility.

The capacity of an individual to show flexibility in adjusting to its environment is

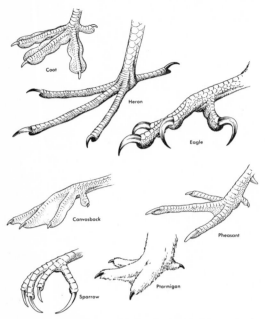

FIGURE 47.3 Adaptive specialization of feet among birds. The coot swims or paddles with its feet, which have lobed toes. The elongate toes in front and in back of the feet of the heron, a tall and large bird, give it a firm base for walking. The eagle is typical of birds of prey in having long talons on each toe with which to grasp its prey. The canvasback duck is a swimmer with fully webbed feet. The pheasant has feet suited to walking and scratching the ground for food. The sparrow is a typical perching bird, with feet equipped for grasping a branch. The ptarmigan, inhabitant of cold regions, has feet stockinged by feathers. (From Simpson & Beck, 1965. *Life: An Introduction to Biology.* New York, Harcourt Brace Jovanovich, Inc.).

genetically controlled. Non-heritable or phenotypic adaptation is the individual's response to the environment with no accompanying changes in the genotype. Phenotypic adaptation can be physical as in callous formation on the hands and feet or behavioral as in the taming of wild animals. Genetically controlled adaptations ensure the species that some adaptive characteristics will be attained by all members. Phenotypic flexibility enables a species to refine its adaptations to environmental change.

Many adaptations of mammals and birds to climatic conditions at different latitudes have become generalized in a large number of genera and species. These adaptations

are known as ecological laws or rules and are often evident in domesticated species bred for climatic tolerances (see Chapter 5 in Hafez, 1968).

A sudden change in the environment, as when a wild animal is placed in captivity, results in a basic reorganization of the factors determining fitness and fosters a host of new genotypic and phenotypic adaptations. The adaptation process becomes unidirectional in that natural selection follows a given trend generation after generation. This is in contrast to the oscillatory nature of adaptation in an unchanging environment, where trends are but short term. Thus, adaptation to a new environment is *directive* rather than *homeostatic* in nature. Although both involve changes in the gene pool, the effects of the former are more profound. Directive adaptation results in evolutionary change, while homeostatic adaptation merely preserves the *status quo*.

Domestication is an example of directive adaptation with two distinguishing characteristics. First, the magnitude of the change from nature to captivity is far greater than most natural environmental changes. Secondly, the course of domestication can be influenced by man through artificial selection. In the next section the natural and captive environments are compared in order to clarify the nature of the change in fitness-determining criteria.

The Process of Domestication

Definite changes in the fitness-determining criteria accompany domestication. Adaptation to the physical and biological features of the captive environment requires a basic reorganization of the species gene pool. In captivity, climate, predation, food and water availability, for example, are of lesser importance for survival. Psychological stresses associated with a reduction in the quantity and quality of space, forced social groupings and interactions with man, take on new importance. The role of directive adaptation in domestication cannot be understood without knowledge of the physical and biological characteristics of the natural and captive environments and problems of survival in each.

THE NATURAL VERSUS CAPTIVE ENVIRONMENTS

Physical environment

In regard to domestication the physical environment may be divided into the components of climate (Chapter 4 in Hafez, 1968), shelter and space.

Climate. Animals living in temperate zones possess a variety of adaptations to temperature fluctuations. Since the wild ancestors of most domesticated animals lived in temperate regions, they are generally better equipped to deal with colder than warmer environments. Most domesticated animals are given protection from the rigors of winter by various types of shelter or natural vegetation. Protection against extreme heat is more difficult. Avoidance of the direct rays of the sun provides only partial relief. Consequently domestic breeds have been developed with high temperature tolerances. Many wild animals can escape temperature extremes by burrowing underground, migrating or otherwise seeking out favorable niches (Chapter 15 in Hafez, 1968). These temperature-regulating behaviors are seldom possible in the relatively barren captive environment and other behavioral and physiological adjustments must be employed.

Shelter. In nature, shelter or cover provides: (a) protection from rigorous climatic conditions; (b) privacy for the rearing of offspring; and (c) a means of escape from predators and aggressive species members. Many of these same problems must be dealt with in captivity. The kind of shelter required by domestic animals is often determined by the type of shelter found in the natural environment of the species. In their natural habitat wild animals have ready access to the shelters provided by their native environments. Domestic animals often lose the tendency to seek shelter in rain and hail. In the absence of shelter, large flocks of domestic sheep often mass together and smother in severe winter storms. Mortality from smothering is highly unlikely among wild mountain sheep which live in rocky environments where natural windbreaks and shelter are provided.

Many animals fail to reproduce or may cannibalize their offspring if not given sufficient privacy from their mates and other animals. In nature, habitat diversity and freedom of movement permits wild animals to find solitude when desired. In captivity, the quantity and quality of space provided and man's constant intervention often permit little privacy for successful reproduction and the rearing of offspring. Although most farm animals have lost this requirement during domestication, female swine are known to cannibalize newly born young when disturbed by squealing pigs or other noises. The breeding requirements of domestic animals are essentially a minimum of space and an acceptable individual of the opposite sex. However, placing two wild animals of opposite sex together is not enough to ensure breeding. Both physiological and psychological readiness must be obtained and nurtured by the proper environment.

Shelter or cover provides wild animals a means of escape from predators and aggressive social interactions. An increase in the quantity or quality of cover permits higher population densities by reducing the incidence of inter- and intra-specific contacts (Jenkins, 1961). In captivity, inter-specific competition and predation are essentially nonexistent and shelter may serve primarily to reduce the likelihood of intra-specific social interactions. The inability to escape more aggressive individuals can change the species social structure. In nature, house mice practice territoriality; whereas in the laboratory, the inability to avoid more dominant individuals results in the establishment of social hierarchies.

Space. The spatial requirements of wild species are determined primarily by the quantity and quality of shelter or cover, food and water availability, and inter- and intra-specific interactions. Animals living in highly diversified, biotically rich environments, such as the tropics, require considerably less space than those living in poorly diversified, resource-poor environments such as arctic and desert areas.

Spatial requirements are also dictated by types of social interactions. In nature, subtle social factors, such as territoriality, may play a greater role in determining population densities than the diversity and richness of the environment. Crowding, by increasing the incidence of intra-specific strife, may have profound effects on endocrine and physiological systems associated with adrenocortical mechanisms and reproduction. Reproductive success is inversely correlated with high densities. Fox and Clayton found that egg production in chickens decreases with higher densities but is not affected by flock size. By increasing the space allotted per adult pig from 0.91 to 1.37m^2, Wingert and Knodt showed that losses due to injuries were considerably decreased.

In captivity, physical limitations of space imposed by cages, fences and other enclosures often foster a uniform and ever-present social environment. These restrictions of behavior coupled with relatively uniform physical environments often result in stereotyped patterns of movement (pacing), hyper-sexuality and increased aggression. This is particularly true for wild and semi-domestic species (animals bred in captivity for many generations) in contrast to domesticated forms which have become well adapted to spatial restrictions.

To summarize, an animal born and reared in its natural habitat possesses the freedom to choose the microhabitat best suited to its needs. In captivity, the physical environment provided by man may be far from the species requirements. Although most farm animals are well adapted to relatively confined, uniform environments, serious problems are obtained by overcrowding.

Biological environment

For purposes of this discussion the biological environment has been divided into the areas of food and water availability, predation, parasitism and disease, and social interactions, including those associated with man.

Food and water availability. In nature, intricate food webs are established whereby both herbivorous and carnivorous species eat and are eaten. A large proportion of a wild animal's time and energy is spent in maintenance activities (procurement of food and water). Wolves and larger carnivores regularly travel great distances in hunting for prey. The sand grouse of Southwest Africa may fly over 81 km. (one way) daily to obtain water. Only under rare circumstances is it necessary for animals in captivity to search for food and water. Man's provision for these requirements may constitute the greatest energy-conserving advantage of life in captivity.

Most wild animals have a varied diet, whereas the food consumed by domesticated species is usually determined by man and often consists of one diet. Wild animals possess a high degree of control over their diet. Although the availability of certain food changes with the seasons, some choice of food items is usually possible. Wild species use mineral "licks" and a variety of food material as determined by stomach analyses. Animals in captivity are faced with a severe reduction in the number and types of foods available and when dietary requirements are not known, deficiencies may result. Eating unusual and unsuitable things such as rubber, cloth, feces and metal objects are often indicative of dietary deficiencies. With the advent of improved diets (feed mixes, vitamin and rare element mixes, feed additives, mineral licks), the health and reproductive success of captive animals has been enhanced.

Predation. Predation is an integral part of the food web found in nature. Survival in the wild is to some extent determined by those morphological and behavioral adaptations which enable organisms to avoid predatory species. Natural selection operates directly on those responses which enable animals to avoid specific detrimental stimuli in their natural environment. On farms and in other captive environments predation is essentially nonexistent. The capacity to avoid predators has been largely lost during domestication. Domestic animals are usually less wary and more tolerant of disturbances than their wild counterparts.

Parasitism and disease. Parasitism and disease are problems faced by both wild and domestic forms. Wildlife biologists have been concerned with these afflictions in game species for some time. Even more is known about the parasites and diseases of domestic animals. The variety of living conditions provided animals in captivity makes it difficult to form generalizations regarding parasites and disease. In situations where animals are maintained at high densities and under unsanitary conditions, parasitism and disease may reach epidemic proportions at a rapid rate. Where animals are given ample space in which to roam, a fresh supply of drinking water, and are relatively free from large accumulations of fecal depositions, the incidence of parasitism and disease may be very low. The artificial situations under which many domestic species are maintained may support a smaller variety of secondary hosts or vectors than the natural environment. Hence, the number of different parasites and diseases infecting domestic animals may represent only a portion of those infecting their wild counterparts.

Social interactions. The social interactions of wild animals aid them in the location of mates, rearing of young, portioning of space and food and protection from predators and severe climatic conditions. Social interactions are not always beneficial to the individual. The conflict over natural resources and mates often results in a waste of energy and lives. Social organizations which tend to reduce agonistic behavior and exert some control over population size are common in natural populations. Territoriality or the defense of a definite area, tends to distribute resources, so that individuals will be assured the minimum necessary for survival and reproduction. Many species of song birds organize territories which they and their mates actively defend in the spring.

Social hierarchy is another type of social organization in which each individual establishes a dominance-submissive relationship with other individuals of the population. A well-established social hierarchy in nature is more stable than a similar system in captivity in that a submissive wild animal can readily retreat from or avoid a dominant individual without being forced into a rank-determining struggle. The relatively high densities of most domestic populations encourages frequent intra-specific contacts and subsequent testing of rank. The inability of subordinate animals to avoid dominant individuals in captivity can change the prevalent social organization.

In captivity, social or group behavior has essentially lost its function in offering protection from predators and climatic stress. The problem of locating mates has been eliminated along with many types of communication necessary for bringing potential mates together. The female receives little or no assistance from the male in the care and defense of the young.

Domesticated species have been bred for non-aggressive characteristics, yet most groups of farm animals are organized by social hierarchies. Basic social organization has been retained during domestication, since it tends to reduce the incidence of aggression and other stress-producing social interactions. As efforts are made to maintain domestic stocks at higher densities, the importance of social organization will increase and efforts will be made to breed aggressive characteristics out of animals in captivity.

Interactions with man. The relative importance of man in the social environment of domestic stocks varies with the species and the intimacy of the relationship. Household pets, dairy cattle, and saddle horses live in close association with man, while range cattle, sheep, and swine are more removed. Nevertheless, through countless generations of selection, man has produced domestic breeds that exhibit little physiological or behavioral disturbance in his presence. This reaction to man is genetically determined, although it is highly modifiable through taming.

Man is seldom encountered in the natural environment of most wild animals. The innate fear of man can lead to serious disturbances when wild animals are placed in captivity. Among zoo animals, unwillingness to eat and breed, and even death through heart failure have been attributed to man's constant presence together with physiological disturbances resulting from isolation. Some wild animals can readily be tamed if reared by man from a very young age. A critical period in the development of many animals enables them to establish lasting social relationships. Once this critical period for socialization has passed, certain wild species (wild rabbits, moose, giraffes, some antelopes) are difficult to maintain in captivity.

In summary, differences between the natural and captive environments concern the availability of food and water, the lack of predation in captivity and the response to man (Table 47.1).

ENVIRONMENTAL INFLUENCES DURING
DOMESTICATION

Although all behaviors have a genetic basis, some are under strict genetic control while other behaviors are highly modifiable by experience (Scott, 1962). The degree of flexibility of behavior can be both advantageous and disadvantageous to the individual and the population and, thus, subject to natural selection (Waddington, 1961).

In higher organisms, nearly all adaptive modifications of behavior involve learning phenomena (Chapter 15 in Hafez, 1968). Animals learn where to find shelter or food and water. They learn which environmental stimuli to approach and which to avoid. In captivity, the taming of wild animals

involves habituation, a simple form of learning. Classical and instrumental conditioning, likewise, play an important role in the adaptation of wild and semidomestic animals to the captive environment. Learning is of lesser importance in the adaptation of long domesticated species to captivity. The taming process is greatly facilitated by breeding for tameability and ease in handling. Furthermore, learning is no longer important for predator avoidance, finding food and water and locating shelter and mates. Yet learning associated with social interactions (*e.g.* individual recognition) may take on greater importance in the ever-present social environment.

Many learned behaviors are established early in life. "Critical periods" for learning may be experienced in certain species as the phenomenon of "imprinting" in birds indicates (Hess, 1959).

Maternal environment. The early environment provided by the mother may affect the later behavior of her offspring. The importance of the natural environment in the development of behavior is best illustrated by monkeys (Harlow & Harlow, 1966).

Female monkeys reared in isolation from other individuals, including their own mothers, showed either indifference or violently abusive behavior toward their own offspring. All monkeys given the opportunity to interact with other individuals during the first half-year of life developed normal adult-type sexual responsiveness even when reared without monkey mothers. The expression of normal maternal affection in monkeys is more dependent on general rather than specific social experiences.

Among wild animals, mother-offspring relationships develop freely. In captivity, mother and young are often separated shortly after birth in accord with certain husbandry practices. Zoo babies are often reared by man and/or foster mothers when abandoned by their natural mothers. Some animals are reared in isolation from other species members. While these practices may be necessary for the survival of the individual, they may

TABLE 47.1. Physical and biological environments of wild and domestic animals: problems of survival in nature and captivity

	NATURE	CAPTIVITY
Physical Environment		
Climate		
1. Temperature	behavioral adaptations: possible-migration; burrowing underground; seeking out favorable microhabitats	uniform environments limits behavioral adaptations; protection from temperature extremes provided by man
2. Humidity	free to seek out favorable microhabitats	little control over environment; adjustment is physiological
3. Radiation	natural protection	shelter and/or natural vegetation provided for shade
Shelter	habitat diversity & freedom of movement permits wild animals to find shelter for (1) protection from rigorous climatic conditions; (2) privacy; (3) escape from predators & aggressive conspecifics	shelter usually provided for protection from rigorous climatic conditions, inter-specific contacts, aggressive conspecifics; quantity & quality of shelter minimal for breeding
Space	space limited only by suitable habitat available; spatial requirements often met by subtle social interactions, territoriality, etc.	available space determined by man; overcrowding leads to serious psychological & physiological disturbances affecting reproduction, mortality
Biological Environment		
Food & Water	considerable time & energy spent in search for food & water; diet usually varied	food & water supplies provided by man; diet less variable; dietary deficiencies common
Predation	essential to food web; ability to avoid predators subject to natural selection	decreased wariness toward unfamiliar stimuli
Parasites & Disease	large variety of parasites & disease present due to diversity of environment	incidence of parasitism & disease dependent on living conditions; unsanitary conditions & high densities foster epidemic levels of parasitism and disease; uniform environment supports smaller variety of secondary hosts, reducing variety of potential parasites & diseases available
Social Interactions	social structure may determine population density; territoriality common; social hierarchy stable; social interaction may be important in group defense, & protection from climatic factors	man, rather than social structure determines population density; territoriality uncommon; social hierarchy unstable; social interactions not important in group defense due to lack of predation
Sexual Interactions	freedom to select mates; male often assists female in care & defense of young	mates usually chosen by man; male seldom assists female in care & defense of young
Man	little or no contact with man	constant presence of man; difficult adjustment for wild animals in captivity

have detrimental effects on the development of normal social relationships.

Place of rearing. Most wild animals are well adapted for life in a given natural environment. Because the "struggle for survival" involves locating food and water, finding mates, avoiding predators and aggressive conspecifics, natural selection has favored those animals which are most sensitive and attentive to stimuli in their environment. When an adult wild animal is taken from

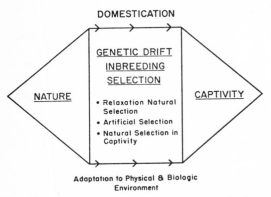

FIGURE 47.4 Genetic influences during domestication. Long-range adaptation to the captive environment includes genetic change. Random changes in gene frequencies are accomplished through *inbreeding* and *genetic drift*. Directional changes are the result of *selection*. Selection during domestication is both independent of and controlled by man (natural and artificial selection, respectively).

its natural habitat and placed in captivity, it is suddenly faced with a barrage of novel environmental stimuli to which it is neither genotypically nor phenotypically adapted. The psychological and physiological stress experienced during the adjustment process is reflected in such phenomena as cessation of feeding.

Wild animals born and/or reared in captivity adjust more readily to man's environment than do adults. Since young animals develop a certain "attachment" to the environment in which they were raised, rearing a wild animal in captivity fosters a host of phenotypic adaptations to this environment not achieved by adult wild animals brought into captivity. A wild animal reared in captivity still retains many genotypically determined characters which retard the adaptation process and make improbable complete adjustment to the captive environment.

In captivity, the need for efficient use of the sensory capacities is largely absent. Problems such as locating food and water, avoiding predators, and finding mates are no longer important for survival. Hence, during domestication, farm animals have lost the sensitivity to environmental stimuli charac-

teristic of their wild ancestors. Movements of domestic animals from farm to farm are accomplished with less difficulty and stress than movements of wild animals.

The ability of domestic animals to adapt to the environment of their wild ancestors is essentially unknown. *Feral* cattle, horses, sheep, dogs, cats are more difficult to approach and handle than those reared in close association with man. Domestic stocks of laboratory rats are difficult to handle after being allowed to "run wild." It appears that the place of rearing and associated early experience may be as important in the behavioral development of domestic species as it is in wild forms.

GENETIC INFLUENCES DURING DOMESTICATION

Domestication is an evolutionary process involving the genotypic adaptation of animals to the captive environment. The genetic changes accompanying domestication are the result of three phenomena: inbreeding, genetic drift and selection (Figure 47.4).

Inbreeding. Inbreeding or line-breeding is often used to maintain a particular desired characteristic, such as in dog breeds used for hunting or show. The practice of breeding large groups of domestic animals from a single sire enhances the possibility of father-daughter inbreeding. Man's control over mating and artificial selection has resulted in a homogeneity and constancy of characteristics among domesticated species unobtainable in wild populations. This loss of variability during inbreeding is regained in captivity by man's ability to preserve those domestic variants that would normally not survive in nature. Thus, inbreeding can be used either to accelerate or slow up the domestication process.

Genetic drift. The relatively permanent isolation of most domestic populations fulfills an initial requirement of genetic drift.

Moreover, most captive stocks of reproducing wild-caught animals are relatively small. For example, all of the golden hamsters (*Microcricetus*) found in laboratories and pet stores are thought to be the descendants of a female and her twelve offspring. The elimination of outbreeding in such populations makes them susceptible to drift. Variants "unfit" for the natural environment of the species may be highly adapted to captive conditions and the special care afforded by man. Each time a daughter colony is established the phenomenon of drift is repeated.

Selection. Where inbreeding and genetic drift produce random change in gene frequencies during domestication, the changes brought about by selection are unidirectional. There are basically three selective phenomena operating on populations undergoing domestication: (*a*) the relaxation of natural selection; (*b*) artificial selection by man; and (*c*) "natural selection in captivity" (selection beyond man's control).

Relaxation of natural selection. The relaxation of selection on certain characteristics is a natural consequence of environmental changes associated with the provision of food, shelter and the protection from predators. Certain adaptations important for survival in nature lose their adaptive significance. For example, natural selection favors those responses which enable wild animals to react appropriately to certain predator-associated stimuli in their environment. MacMillan reports that the postures and movements of a bobcat (*Lynx rufus*) can serve to inform its prey, the cottontail rabbit (*Sylvilagus floridanus*) on the former's intent to feed.

Artificial selection. Man's ability to select for specific characters in captive stocks of animals is well established. Comparison of the dachshund with its wolf-like ancestors clearly demonstrates man's ability to select morphologic characters. Artificial selection may produce desired characters rapidly. Haldane has estimated that natural selection in rapidly evolving species can result in a 1 to 2% change in a quantitative character each million years. However, this estimate is considered low for some species.

"Natural selection in captivity." True artificial selection occurs when all selected individuals are of equal fitness. Practical experiences dictates that this is seldom the case. Selection experiments are usually hampered by breeding failure. Attempts to satisfy man's whims and desires are often accompanied by unwanted side-effects. Selection for the Rex hair color in rabbits has resulted in certain metabolic and endocrine disturbances, increasing mortality and susceptibility to specific diseases (Muntzing, 1959). Factors beyond man's control often determine the efficiency of artificial selection and, thus, are of great importance to domestication. Lerner refers to these factors as representing "natural selection in captivity" in that they mimic the effect of natural selection in nature.

"Natural selection in captivity" begins early in the domestication process. Individuals differ in their capturability. Only when the capture technique is nondiscriminatory can one obtain a representative sampling of a wild population.

"Natural selection in captivity" and artificial selection are most severe in the early stages of domestication. Natural selection acts primarily to eliminate those individuals biologically and/or psychologically incapable of producing offspring. "Fitness" among reproducing individuals is determined primarily by artificial selection. As the species becomes more adapted (genetically) to the captive environment, "natural selection in captivity" exerts a lesser influence. Its effect on population is roughly measured by the incidence of infertility.

References Cited

Anderson, P. K. (1961). Density, social structure and nonsocial environment in house-mouse populations and the implications for regulation of numbers. *Trans. N. Y. Acad. Sci.* (II), *23*, 447–451.

Barnett, S. A. (1958). Experiments on "neophobia" in wild and laboratory rats. *Brit. J. Psych., 49,* 195–201.

Beach, F. A. and Jaynes, J. (1954). Effects of early experience upon the behavior of animals. *Psychol. Bull., 51,* 239–263.

Christian, J. J. and Davis, D. E. (1964). Endocrines, behavior and population. *Science, 146,* 1550–1560.

Denenberg, V. H. (1964). Critical periods, stimulus input, and emotional reactivity: A theory of infantile stimulation. *Psych. Rev., 71,* 335–351.

Falconer, D. S. (1960). *Introduction to Quantitative Genetics,* Edinburgh, Oliver and Boyd.

Hafez, E.S.E., ed. (1968). *Adaptation of Domestic Animals,* Philadelphia, Lea & Febiger.

Harlow, H. F. and Harlow, M. K. (1966). Learning to love. *Amer. Sci., 84,* 244–272.

Hess, E. H. (1959). Imprinting. *Science, 130,* 133–141.

Jenkins, D. (1961). Social behavior in the partridge (*Perdix perdix*). *Ibis, 103,* 155–188.

King, J. A. (1958). Parameters relevant to determining the effects of early experience upon the adult behavior of animals. *Psychol. Bull., 55,* 46–58.

Leopold, A. S. (1944). The nature of heritable wildness in turkeys. *Condor, 46,* 1933–197.

Muntzing, A. (1959). Darwin's views on variation under domestication. *Amer. Sci., 47,* 314–325.

Phillips, R. E. and Tienhoven, A. van (1960). Endocrine factors involved in the failure of pintail ducks (*Anas acuta*) to reproduce in captivity. *J. Endocrin., 24,* 253–261.

Scott, J. P. (1962). Critical periods in behavioral development. *Science, 138,* 949–958.

Spurway, H. (1955). The causes of domestication: An attempt to integrate some ideas of Konrad Lorenz with evolution theory. *J. Genet.,53,* 325–362.

Stodart, E. and Myers, K. (1964). A comparison of behavior, reproduction and mortality of wild and domestic rabbits in confined populations. *CSIRO Wildlife Res., 9,* 144–159.

Waddington, C. H. (1961). Genetic assimilation. *Adv. in Genetics, 10,* 257–293.

Wynne-Edwards, V. C. (1965). Social organization as a population regulator. *Symp. Zool. Soc. (Lond.), 14,* 173–178.

ADDITIONAL REFERENCES

Darwin, Charles. 1868. *The variation of animals and plants under domestication.* 2 vols. London.

Epstein, H. 1955. Domestication features in animals as functions of human society. *Agricultural History* 29:137–146.

Leopold, A. S. 1966. Adaptability of Animals to Habitat Change. Pp. 66–75 in *Future environments of North America,* ed. by F. F. Darling and J. P. Milton. Garden City, New York: The Natural History Press.

Pirchner, Franz. 1969. *Population genetics in animal breeding.* Translated from the German edition (Hamburg, 1964) by Franz Pirchner and Max von Krosigk. San Francisco: Freeman. 274 pp.

Reed, Charles A. 1959. Animal domestication in the prehistoric Near East. *Science* 130: 1629–1639.

Ucko, Peter J., and G. W. Dimbleby, eds. 1969. *The domestication and exploitation of plants and animals.* Chicago: Aldine. 581 pp. A varied and stimulating set of essays which concentrate on the prehistoric origins of domesticated animals and plants.

Zeuner, Frederick E. 1963. *A History of domesticated animals.* New York: Harper & Row. A standard reference on the origins of various domesticated animals. 560 pp.

MAN AS A MAKER OF NEW PLANTS AND NEW PLANT COMMUNITIES

EDGAR ANDERSON

Like the domestication of animals (Selection 47), the origin of cultivated plants has in considerable part been a purposeful activity of man. However, most of our crops are basically products of prehistoric times and their precise modes, places, and periods of origin are poorly known (but often speculated about—see, for example, de Candolle, 1886, and Sauer, 1947). Many crop plants are closely related (genetically) to certain weeds with which they grow in disturbed habitats, suggesting hybridization as a means of producing genetic variation, from which man selected certain plants for cultivation.

In this selection Anderson shows how man, "the great weed-breeder, the great upsetter, catalyzes the formation of new biological entities by producing new and open habitats." In such places new hybrid plants —genetic mixtures of two or more plant species—can grow. These hybrids can endure the disturbed environments much better than the native species which have evolved mutual adaptations over long periods. Anderson cites wild sage, sunflower, iris, and pokeweed as plant groups in which man has favored new hybrids in natural selection by disturbing the environment. Hence, to artificial selection, we must add altered natural selection in disturbed habitats as a second major way in which man makes new organisms.

(Editor's comment)

Edgar Anderson (1897–1969) was a distinguished botanist and geneticist, noted for his research and writing on the role of hybridization in evolution (e.g., *Introgressive Hybridization,* 1949), the evolution of maize, and the role of man in modifying useful plants (e.g., *Plants, Man and Life,* 1952). Educated at Michigan State University and Harvard University (Sc.D., genetics, 1922), he was Engelmann Professor of Botany at Washington University and long associated with the Missouri Botanical Garden (director, 1954–1956). In addition, Anderson has been a Guggenheim Fellow, a fellow at the Center for Advanced Study in Behavioral Sciences, a member of the National Academy of Sciences, and president of the Botanical Society of America.

This selection is reproduced from *Man's Role in Changing the Face of the Earth,* edited by William L. Thomas, Jr., The University of Chicago Press, pp. 763–777. Copyright © The University of Chicago, 1956.

That man changes the face of nature may be noted by any casual observer; not even the ablest and most experienced scholar can yet estimate just how far this has reclothed the world. Whole landscapes are now occupied by man-dominated (and in part by man-created) faunas and floras. This process began so long ago (its beginnings being certainly as old as *Homo sapiens*) and has produced results of such complexity that its accurate interpretation must await reseaarch as yet scarcely begun. Though answers to many basic questions remain unknown, they are by no means unknowable.

The average thoughtful person has little inkling of this reclothing of the world; even professional biologists have been tardy in recognizing that in the last analysis a significant portion of the plants and animals which accompany man is directly or indirectly of his own making. The ordinary American supposes that Kentucky bluegrass is native to Kentucky and Canada bluegrass native to Canada. A few historians and biologists know that these grasses (along with much of our meadow and pasture vegetation) came to us from Europe. The research scholar inquiring critically into the question realizes that some of this vegetation was as much a Neolithic immigration into Europe as it was a later immigration into the New World. Like Kentucky mountaineers, this vegetation has its ultimate roots in Asia and spread into Central and Western Europe at times which, biologically speaking, were not very long ago.

It is obvious that landscapes such as the American Corn Belt have been transformed by man. Other man-dominated landscapes do not betray their origin to the casual observer. Take the grasslands of California, the rolling hills back from the coast, the oak-dotted savannas of the Great Valley. Here are stretches of what look like indigenous vegetation. Much of this mantle is not obviously tended by man; it has the look of something that has been in California as long as the oaks it grows among, yet the bulk of it came, all uninvited, from the Old World along with the Spaniards. Most of it had a long history of association with man when it made the trip. Wild oats, wild mustards, wild radishes, wild fennel—all of these spread in from the Mediterranean, yet over much of the California cattle country they dominate the landscape. Native plants are there, even some native grasses, but it takes a well-informed botanist going over the vegetation item by item to show how small a percentage of the range is made up of indigenous California plants.

For those parts of the tropics where plants grow rapidly it will take careful research before we can have an informed opinion about such questions. Thorn scrub, savannas, bamboo thickets, weedy tangles of quick-growing trees and shrubs are known to have covered vast areas in the last two or three millenniums. Yet Standley, our greatest authority on the vegetation of Central America, digging up a small tree in what appeared to him to be a truly indigenous forest in the Lancetilla Valley, came upon a layer of potsherds (Standley, 1931). What is the relation between the supposedly wild avocados of such a forest and the avocados eaten in the village that once covered that site? We now have various techniques (pollen profiles, carbon-14 datings, chromosome analysis, extrapolated correlates) which can give critical answers, but they are time-consuming, and their application to such problems has just begun.

The total number of plants and animals that have moved in with man to any one spot on the earth's surface is way beyond what even a biologist would estimate until he looked into the problem. There are the cultivated plants both for use and for display, the domesticated animals, the weeds, and their animal equivalents such as houseflies, clothes moths, rats, and mice. A much larger class of organisms is those not purposely introduced by man, which are neither eyesores nor plagues, but which, like weeds, have the capacity to get along in man's vicinity. Such are the daisies and yarrows and buttercups of our meadows. Such in a sense are even those native species that spread under man's influence. Take, for example, the sunflowers of Wyoming. They are certainly native to North America and may possibly in part be prehuman in Wyoming. They line the roadways yet seldom are elsewhere prominent in the native landscape. They appeared along with the road, even though they may have moved in from not so far away. But how did they get into the spot from which they spread, and did pioneers or primitive man have anything to do with making this previous niche? This is the sort of question we are now making the subject of decisive experiments; we do not yet have enough results for decisive answers.

For microorganisms the problem of the species which travel about with man staggers the imagination. Microorganisms seemingly fall into the same general categories as macroorganisms. Brewers' yeasts are as much cultivated plants as the barleys and wheats with which they have so long been associated for brewing and baking. The germs of typhoid and cholera are quite as much weeds as are dandelions or Canada thistles. The microorganisms of our garden soil are apparently the same mixture of mongrel immigrants and adapted natives as our meadow and pasture plants. Soils are good or bad quite as much because of the micro-communities they contain as because of their composition. Man's unconscious creation of new kinds of microorganisms is an important part of his total effect on the landscapes of the world. Think, then, of this total composite mantle of living things which accompanies man: the crops, the weeds, the domesticated animals, the garden escapes such as Japanese honeysuckle and orange day lily, the thorn scrub, the bamboo thickets, the English sparrows, the starlings, the insect pests. Think of the great clouds of alge, protozoa, bacteria, and fungi—complex communities of microorganisms that inhabit our soils, our beverages, our crops, our domesticated animals, and our very bodies.

If we turn to the scientific literature for an orderly summary of where these species came from and how, there is a depressing lack of information. The crop plants and domesticated animals have been somewhat studied, the ornamentals and the weeds scarcely investigated. Even for the crop plants one notes that for those which have been the most carefully studied—wheat (Aase, 1946), cotton (Hutchinson *et al.*, 1947), maize (Mangelsdorf and Reeves, 1938)—there is now general recognition that their origins, relationships, and exact histories are much more complex problems than they were thought to be a generation ago. In spite of these wide gaps in our knowledge, I believe the following generalizations will stand:

1. All the major crops and most of the minor ones were domesticated in prehistoric times. *Modern agriculture, classified solely by the plants it uses, is Neolithic agriculture.*

2. For none of the major crops can we point with certainty to the exact species (or combination of species) from which it was derived: for some we can make guesses; for a number we can point to closely related weeds. This merely complicates the problem. We then have to determine the origin of the crop, the origin of the weed, and the history of their relationships.

The world's knowledge of crop plants, in other words, does not tell us very much. All we know is that we are dealing with man's effects on certain plants in the Neolithic or before. Yet for weeds and ornamental plants even less is known. A few general observations may be offered, parenthetically, about their origins.

1. We can now point to crops which are definitely known to have been derived from weeds. For instance, rye as a crop originated from a grainfield weed (Vavilov, 1926). As barley and wheat spread farther north onto the sandy Baltic plain, the weed gradually replaced the crop. The origin of rye as a weed is a far older and more complex problem. Stebbins and his students are far enough into it to tell us that it is a story with several chapters, most of them unsuspected until recently.

2. We can point to weeds which originated from crop plants. The bamboo thickets that cover whole mountainsides in the Caribbean came from cultivated bamboos. It now seems much more probable that teosinte the

weed was derived from maize the crop than that maize was derived from teosinte.

3. Crop plants and their related weeds frequently have a continuing effect upon each other. We have documented evidence of weeds increasing their variability by hybridizing with crop plants and of crop plants consciously or unconsciously improved through hybridization with weeds. These processes recur repeatedly in the histories of weeds and crop plants. For wheat it is clear that a minor grain was in very early times built up into one of the world's great cereals through the unconscious incorporation of several weeds from its own fields (Anderson, 1952, pp. 57–64).

As a whole, ornamentals (though little studied as yet) provide the simplest keys and the clearest insights into the basic problems of domestication of any class of plants or animals. Some have been domesticated within the last century, the African violet, for instance, but are already distinct from the species from which they arose. Such recent domesticates provide unparalleled experimental material for determining what happens to the germ plasm of an organism when it is domesticated. Others of our garden flowers originated in prehistoric times. They seem to have been associated with magic and ceremony; some of them may have been with us for as long or even longer than our crop plants. Take woad, *Isatis tinctoria,* now known only as a garden flower, though it persisted as a commercial dye plant until Victorian times (Hurry, 1930). When Caesar came to Britain, he found our semisavage ancestors using it to paint their bodies. There are various other ornamentals (*Bixa, Amaranthus, Helianthus*) whose earlier associations were with dyes and body paints. Which is older, agriculture or body painting?

The cultivated grain amaranths (known to the Western world mainly through such bizarre late-summer annuals as love-lies-bleeding) demonstrate that we shall be in for some rude shocks when we make serious studies of these apparently trivial plants. J. D. Sauer found (1950) that this whole group was domesticates, divisible into several different species, none of which could be equated to any wild amaranth; that the whole group was of American origin; and that the varieties cultivated since ancient times in Kashmir, China, and Tibet were not (as had previously been taken for granted) derived from Asiatic amaranths. They are instead identical with those cultivated by the Aztecs and the Incas.

It is now becoming increasingly clear that the domestication of weeds and cultivated plants is usually a process rather than an event. None of them rose in one leap from the brain of Ceres, so to speak. The domestication of each crop or weed went on at various times and places, though by bursts rather than at a regular rate. For many it still continues. Our common weed sunflowers, for example, are at the moment being bred into superweeds. In California, by hybridization with a rare native sunflower, these weeds are increasing their ability to colonize the Great Valley (Heiser, 1949). In Texas (Heiser, 1951), by similar mongrelizations with two native species, they are adapting themselves to life on the sandy lands of the Gulf Coast (see Figures 48.1–48.3).

The story of the American sunflowers is significant because it demonstrates the kinds of processes which went on in the Stone Age and before, when our major crops were domesticated. It is because the domestication of weeds and cultivated plants (using the word "domestication" in its broadest sense) is a continuing process that it came to my professional attention. Thirty years ago I started out to study (and if possible to measure) such evolution as was still going on. As I analyzed example after example, the fact became increasingly clear that evolutionary activity is concentrated in (though by no means confined to) disturbed habitats—to times and places where man's interference with the prehuman order of things has been particularly severe. Post-Pleistocene evolution, it seems, has been very largely the elaboration of weedlike plants and animals.

Now why should this be? What is there about the presence of man that stimulates his plant and animal companions into increased evolutionary activity? A growing body of observational and experimental data bears directly upon that question; rather than summarizing it, let me describe in considerable detail one particularly illuminating example. It concerns the hybridization of two California species of wild sage, *Salvia apiana* and *S. mellifera*. They have been meticulously studied by Epling—in the field (1947), the herbarium (1939), the laboratory, and the experimental plot (Epling and Lewis, 1942). Burton Anderson and I (1954) have made an exhaustively detailed analysis of the variation pattern of several populations, confirming and extending Epling's conclusions.

These two species of sage are so unlike that any ordinary amateur would immediately recognize them as radically different plants; only an occasional botanist would see that they are really quite closely related and that their differences, though conspicuous, are superficial. This was what first drew Epling's attention to them. He found that they hybridized readily when artificially cross-pollinated. The hybrids grew vigorously in an experimental plot and were fertile enough to produce abundant and and variable offspring. In spite of this fertility, hybrids were ordinarily not found in nature or occurred mainly at spots where the native vegetation had been greatly altered by man's activities. Yet on the rocky slopes where they were native, these two kinds of sage frequently grew intermingled. Burton Anderson and I worked with samples of wild populations of both species so intensively that eventually we could distinguish between mongrels, seven of whose great-grandparents were from one species and one from the other, and plants with all eight grandparents from one species. With this yardstick we learned that, though the plants on the mountainside were prevailingly of one species or the other, yet along the pathway from which we collected them we could find a few mongrels. These were mostly plants closely resembling typical *Salvia mellifera* but showing slight indications of *S. apiana* in one character or another. Apparently the very rare hybrids which Epling had found were not completely without issue. Some of them had

crossed back to *S. mellifera*, and, of these three-quarter bloods, a few of those similar to the recurrent parent had been able to fend for themselves.

At one point along the path we found conspicuous hybrids resembling those produced by Epling; careful investigation of this area gave us new understanding. With repeated visits we gradually realized that these bizarre mongrels were limited to a definitely circumscribed plot having a greatly altered habitat. It was at a point where the trail swung down along the slope. Originally a forest of live oaks had abutted on the rocky, sunny slopes where the salvias grow. The oaks had been cut and a small olive orchard planted and then abandoned—abandoned so long ago that native plants had flowed in and the whole site looked quite natural. A collection of salvias made exclusively from among the olives was almost entirely hybrids and hybrid descendants. Though the bulk of the plants looked somewhat like *Salvia apiana*, there was not a single plant which in all its characters agreed exactly with the *apianas* outside this plot. Furthermore, they resembled artificial backcrosses in that their differences from *apiana* were all in the direction of *S. mellifera*. These "sub-*apianas*" graded into plants closely resembling the first-generation hybrids raised by Epling. There were a few "sub-*melliferas*" similar to those we had detected along the pathway on the mountainside and a few plants which on our index scored as typical *melliferas*. However, in the field *none* of them looked quite average. Dr. Anderson and I had to work in St. Louis on pressed and pickled material previously collected in California. Had we been able to go back and add characters such as flower color and flower pattern to our battery of measurable differences between *S. mellifera* and *S. apiana*, I believe we could have demonstrated that the entire plot was colonized with hybrids and mongrels, most of them first or second or third backcrosses from the original hybrids to one or the other species.

These results indicate that hybrids are being constantly produced on this mountainside, but one does not ordinarily find them, because there is no niche into which they can fit. The native vegetation had a long evolutionary history of mutual adaptation. Plants and animals have gradually been selected which are adapted to life with each other like pieces of a multidimensional jigsaw puzzle. It is only when man, or some other disruptive agent, upsets the whole puzzle that there is any place where something new and different can fit in. If a radical variant arises, it is shouldered out of the way before it reaches maturity. In a radically new environment, however, there may be a chance for something new to succeed. Furthermore, the hybrids and their mongrel descendants were not only something new; they varied greatly among themselves. If one of them would not fit into the strange new habitat, another might. Though virtually all of them had been at a selective disadvantage on the mountainside, a few of them (aided and abetted no doubt by the vigor which is char-

acteristic of these and many other hybrids) were now at a selective advantage. They consequently flowed in and occupied the old olive orchard to the virtual exclusion of the two original species.

Furthermore, to take up an important fact about which biology as yet knows very little, the habitat among the olives was not only something new; it was *open*. It was not full of organisms which had been selected to fit together. Remember that for the mountainside, on those rare occasions where a first-generation hybrid plant had been able to find a foothold, virtually none of its highly variable descendants was able to persist. Such species crosses can father hundreds if not thousands of distinguishably different types of mongrel descendants. Only along the pathway had *any* of these been able to find a place for themselves and then only those which differed but slightly from *Salvia mellifera*. Hybridization does not advance in closed habitats.

FIGURES 48.1, 48.2, and 48.3 A diagrammatic and greatly simplified demonstration of the extent to which the domestication of the sunflower as a cultivated plant and its development as a weed are processes rather than events. Data from Heiser (1949, 1951) and personal communications and from my own observations. The history of the cultivated sunflower, complicated though it is shown to be, will be simpler than that of most cultivated plants when these histories have been worked out in accurate and documented detail. Various complications have been ignored altogether to keep the diagram intelligible, as, for instance, the continuing intercrossing between the "camp-follower" weed and the cultivated ornamental and field-crop sunflowers.

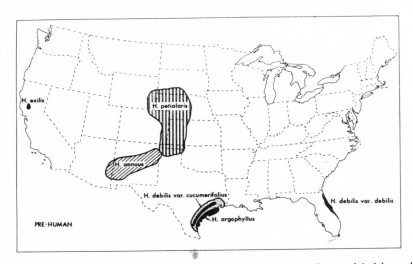

FIGURE 48.1 Annual species of North American sunflowers as presumed to have existed in prehuman times: (1) *Helianthus exilis*, a highly localized endemic in the serpentine areas of California; (2) *H. petiolaris* on bare sandy areas in the western Great Plains; (3) *H. annuus* in playas and other raw-soil habitats of the southwestern deserts; (4) *H. argophyllus* on the sands of the Texas coastal plain; and (5) *H. debilis* in Florida and Texas.

The plants in the olive orchard had no such history of long association. The olives were new to California. The societies of microorganisms in the soil were originally those which go with live oaks, not those accompanying the salvias on the sunny slopes. These must have been greatly changed during the time the olives were cultivated. Fur-

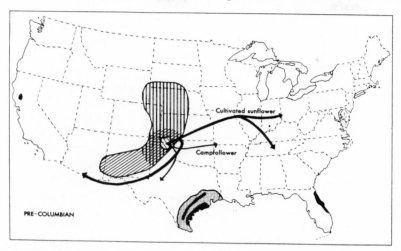

FIGURE 48.2 Hypothetical origin of the North American sunflower as a weed and as a cultivated annual in pre-Columbian times. In the areas where *annuus* and *petiolaris* had begun to introgress, this process is being unconsciously accelerated by the activities of early man.

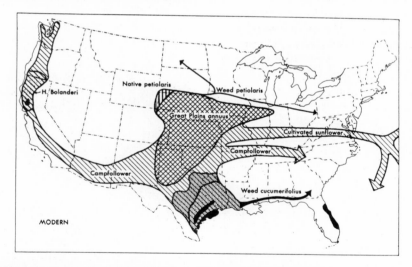

FIGURE 48.3 Spread of annual species of North American sunflowers in modern times. In the Great Plains extensive introgression of *annuus* and *petiolaris* produced the Great Plains race of *Helianthus annuus*, which has spread eastward through the prairies as a somewhat weedy native. The camp-follower weed (sometimes mixed with Great Plains *annuus*) has spread as a weed throughout the East and to irrigated lands in the West. In California, by extensive and continuing introgression with *exilis*, it has created the semiweedy *H. bolanderi*, which is still actively spreading. Similarly on the sands of the Texas coast and the Carrizo ridge, *H. argophyllus* is introgressing actively with *H. annuus* to produce weedier strains. Over an even wider area in Texas extensive introgression of *annuus*, *petiolaris*, and *cucumerifolius* is producing a coastal plain weed sunflower which is actively spreading along the coast. In spots it has already reached the North Carolina coastal plain. Eventually this will react actively with *H. debilis* var. *debilis*, breeding a superweed for the American southeast but, fortunately, a not unattractive one. The Texas and California phenomena have already been documented by Heiser (1949, 1951), and research on other facets of the problem is going forward rapidly.

thermore, the olives, being planted at considerable distances from each other, did not re-create either the fairly continuous shade of the oaks or the open sunshine of the upper slopes. The orchard became the site for evolutionary catch-as-catch-can, and under these circumstances, as we have seen, the new and variable had a decisive advantage.

Now that we know this much about these salvias, it would be interesting to work experimentally with them and the species with which they are associated to determine just what factors allow two different but closely related species to fit together with their associates so perfectly that all hybrid intermediates are excluded. From experience with other similar problems I should predict that among the most important factors would be fairly specific reactions between some of the other associated plants and these two sages. In our experimental work with sunflowers we have discovered that one of the strongest factors in determining where weed sunflowers may or may not grow is their reaction to grass. Many grasses apparently give off a substance highly toxic to weed sunflowers. The various species of weed sunflowers differ in their sensitivity to this poison. When two such sunflowers hybridize, one of the factors affecting the outcome is the grassiness of the site. Such relationships seem to be very general among plants. One the whole, many species grow where they do, not because they really prefer the physical conditions of such a site, but because they can tolerate it and many other organisms cannot.

Generally speaking, the plants which follow man around the world might be said to do so, not because they relish what man has done to the environment, but because they can stand it and most other plants cannot.

Are these salvias weeds? I would put forward the working hypothesis that those in the abandoned olive orchard are on the way to becoming weeds. The small exceptional communities of hybridizing colonies similar to this one, which can be found here and there over southern California, are worth considerably more attention than they have hitherto received. They demonstrate the way

in which man, the great weed-breeder, the great upsetter, catalyzes the formation of new biological entities by producing new and open habitats.

The *Salvia* case is not unique. We now have over a score of similar well-documented studies of the connection between hybridization and weedy, disturbed habitats. This relationship had long been known to observant naturalists, though not until the last few decades was its significance stressed or experimental work undertaken. One other example demonstrates the role of man's operations on the habitat. Riley (1938) studied the hybridization of two species of *Iris* on the lower delta of the Mississippi in a neighborhood where the land-use pattern had produced something as demonstrable and convincing as a laboratory experiment (Anderson, 1949; see Figure 48.4). Property lines ran straight back from the river; the farms were small, only a few hundred yards wide, and very narrow. Under these conditions it was easy to see that the hybrids between these two irises were virtually limited to one farm. They grew in a swale which crossed several of the farms, yet were nearly all on one man's property. On his farm they went right up to the fences and stopped, and this could be demonstrated at either side of his property. Unlike his neighbors, he had kept the swale heavily pastured. His cattle had held in check the grasses which are serious competitors of swamp irises. They had also, tramping about in wet weather, turned the swale into more of a quagmire than existed on any of the neighboring farms. They had at length produced an open environment in which the pasture grasses were at a disadvantage and the resulting hybrid swarm of irises at a very real advantage. Hybrids in various patterns of terra cotta, wine, purple, and blue flooded out into this swale until it had almost the appearance of an intentionally created iris garden.

Though Riley never published the sequel, it might be inserted here, parenthetically, since it points up some kind of a moral. The farmer himself did not remove the irises, even though they interfered seriously with

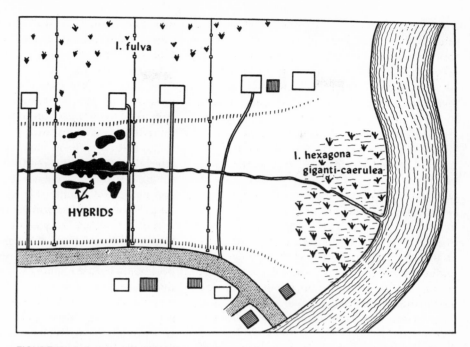

FIGURE 48.4 A demonstration of man's unconscious role in creating new plants. (From Riley, 1938.) At the far right one of the minor bayous of the lower Mississippi Delta. At right angles to it and running nearly across the figure is the abandoned channel of a former stream, now drained by a ditch. The natural levees of the stream are slightly higher than the surrounding country. Their sharp inner edges are indicated on the map by hachures. The road has been run along the lower levee, and houses have been built along the opposite one. The property lines (as in many old French settlements) produce a series of long narrow farms, which for our purposes serve as so many experimental plots. Each farm has its house on a low ridge with a long entrance drive connecting it across a swale to the public road on the opposite ridge. The farms (including a score of others which are out of sight to the left of the figure) were originally essentially similar. At the point where the ditch joins the bayou is a large population of *Iris hexagona giganti-caerulea*. Behind the levee on which the houses were built, *I. fulva* grows on the lower ground as well as farther upstream along the ditch. The key fact to be noted is that the hybrids are on only one farm, that they are abundant there, and that they go up to the very borders of the property on either side. Nature is evidently capable of spawning such hybrids throughout this area, but not until one farmer unconsciously created the new and more or less open habitat in which they could survive did any appear in this part of the delta. (See Anderson, 1949, pp. 1–11, 94–98, for a more complete discussion.)

the carrying capacity of his pasture. The irises were conspicuously beautiful, and garden-club members from New Orleans dug them up for their gardens, at so much per basket, until they were eventually exterminated. The hybridization which nature began in this and other pastures around New Orleans has been continued by iris fans. These Louisiana irises are now established as cultivated plants both in Europe and in America. Until the arrival of the garden-club ladies, they were nascent weeds (Figure 48.5).

A little reflective observation will show that the ways in which man creates new and open habitats, though various, can mostly be grouped under a few headings: (1) dumps and other high nitrogen areas; (2) pathways; (3) open soil; (4) burns. The last is probably the oldest of his violent upsettings of the natural order of things. It must have stimulated evolutionary activity very early—whole

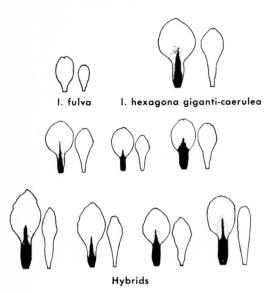

I. fulva   I. hexagona giganti-caerulea

Hybrids

FIGURE 48.5 Sepals and petals of some hybrids of *Iris hexagona giganti-caerulea* and *I. fulva* somewhat diagrammatic but accurately to scale. In each case the sepal (the so-called "fall" of iris fanciers) is shown to the left; the petal, "standard," to the right. *I. fulva* has small lax terra cotta sepals and petals. *I. hexagona giganti-caerulea* has large crisp petals and sepals of bright blue. The sepal has a brilliant yellow signal patch (*shown in black*) surrounded by a white area (*shown by stipples*) shading off into the blue. Note that in the various hybrids the small-sized flowers (characteristic of *I. fulva*) tend to be associated with the lack of a white area (another *fulva* characteristic). Note the variability of the hybrids. In color they varied from deep wine to very pale, light blue.

floras or certainly whole associations must have come to a new adjustment with it here and there; fire should be, of all man's effects upon evolution, the most difficult to analyze. Until valid experimental and exact historical methods deal with this problem, it inevitably must spawn more polemic activity than scientific analysis.

In contrast to fire, the creation of open-soil habitats as a really major human activity belongs much more to the age of agriculture and industry than to prehistory. It may be that is why it seems to be the simplest to analyze. In Europe and eastern North America, in the humid tropics and subtropics, open soil—bare exposed earth—is scarcely part of the normal nature of things. Most of the flora truly native to these areas cannot germinate in open soil or, having germinated,

cannot thrive to maturity. Make a series of seed collections from wild flowers and forest trees and plant them in your garden just like radishes or lettuce. You will be amazed to learn how small a percentage of them ever comes up at all. Make similar collections from the weeds in a vacant lot or from the plants (wanted and unwanted) of your garden. Nearly all of them will come up promptly and grow readily. Where did these open-soil organisms come from in the first place, the weeds of gardens and fields, these fellow-travelers which rush in after the bull-dozer, which flourish in the rubble of bombed cities? Well, they must have come mostly from pre-human open-soil sites. River valleys did not supply all of them, but rivers are certainly, next to man, the greatest of weed-breeders. Our large rivers plow their banks at floodtimes, producing raw-soil areas. Every river system is provided with plants to fill this peculiar niche; all those known to me act as weeds in the uplands. One of the simplest and clearest examples is our common pokeweed, *Phytolacca americana*, native to eastern North America. It will be found growing up abundantly in the immediate valleys of our major rivers (Sauer, 1952; see Figure 48.6). On the uplands it is strictly limited to raw soil, though, once established in such a habitat, it can persist vegetatively for a long time while other kinds of vegetation grow up around it. Being attractive to birds, its seeds are widely scattered. I remember, from my Michigan boyhood, how pokeweed came in when a woodland near our home was lumbered over. We had never noticed this weed in that community, but the birds had been planting it wherever they roosted. When the felling of the big oaks tore lesser trees up by the roots, pokeweed plants appeared as if by magic for the next few years in the new craters of raw soil. Man and the great rivers are in partnership. Both of them breed weeds and suchlike organisms. The prehuman beginnings of many of our pests and fellow-travelers are to be sought in river valleys. River valleys also must have been the ultimate source of some of the plants by which

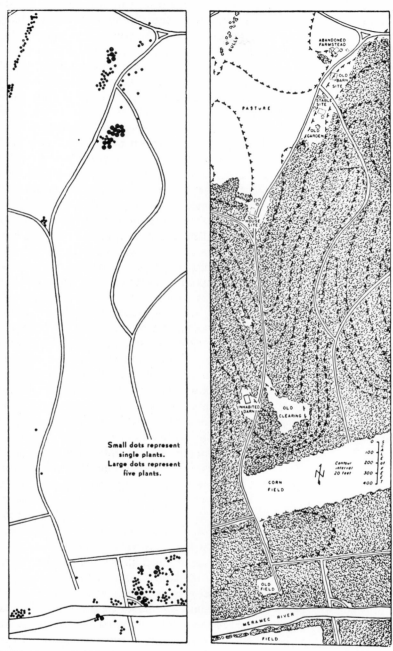

FIGURE 48.6 Occurrence of pokeweed in two different habitats. Pokeweed (*Phytolacca americana*) is an example of a species which is apparently native in the open soil along American rivers but a weed in the open soil of disturbed habitats. (Map from Sauer, 1952.) Small dots represent single plants. Large dots represent five plants. It will be seen that the pokeweed is occurring in two quite different kinds of habitats: in the raw soil of repeatedly flooded woodlands on the immediate banks of the river and as a weed around farm buildings, gardens, and the like. (See Sauer, 1952, for further details and discussion.)

we live: gourds, squashes, beans, hemp, rice, and maize.

The examples of the salvias and irises show how quickly evolution through hybridization can breed out something new and different under man's catalytic influence. What we should most like to know is the extent to which weeds and suchlike organisms, created or at least extensively modified through man's influence, are built up into whole associations. It is clear that such things can happen; the *maqui* vegetation of the Mediterranean, the *shiblyak* and *karst* vegetation of the Balkans, the *carbón* scrub of Central America, are obviously very directly the results of man's interference. One would like to analyze the dynamics of these associations. We must do so if man is to understand his own past or to be the master of his own future. For such purposes we need ways of studying vegetation which are analytical as well as merely descriptive—methods not based upon preconceived dogmas. I should like to suggest that the methods used in analyzing the *Iris* hybrids and the *Salvia* hybrids, if combined with other experimental techniques, would allow us to get a long way into these problems. Let me illustrate what I mean by describing some recent studies of *Adenostoma*, a fire-resistant shrub, which is a common component of the California chaparral (Anderson, 1954).

Between the Great Valley and the Pacific Coast, *Adenostoma fasciculatum* is one of the commonest shrubs in the California landscape. Noting that it varied conspicuously from one plant to the next, I made collections of it near Palo Alto and applied to them the methods of pictorialized scatter diagrams and extrapolated correlates. The details of these techniques need not concern us here, since they have been adequately published elsewhere, both in technical journals and in books for the intelligent public. They allow us (through a meticulous examination of variability in such mongrel complexes as the salvias of the abandoned olive orchard) to determine precisely the good species (or subspecies or varieties) from which these complexes must ultimately have arisen. Fur-

thermore, though it takes considerable hard work, these methods can be used successfully by one with no previous knowledge of the organisms or of the faunas and floras from which they may have come.

Using these methods, I have shown that the common *Adenostoma fasciculatum* of coastal California arose from the hybridization of two very different adenostomas. One of these was *A. fasciculatum* var. *obtusifolium*, a low-growing shrub of the headlands and islands along the California coast. The other is now found in its purest form in the Mother Lode country of the Sierra foothills, a tall, branching shrub which, when in flower, somewhat resembles a small-leaved white lilac. Each of these had its own contributions to make to life in coastal California. The coastal shrub brought in a tolerance of brilliant sunlight and the ability to grow in thin, rocky soil. However, it was accustomed to fog and drizzle even during the dry season. The inland form could go months without a drop of water, but it is used to deeper soil and to less extreme radiation. When these two centers of variation had been identified, it was easy to demonstrate that the common *Adenostoma* is a great, plastic, hybrid swarm, including approaches to these two extremes and many intermediates between them. On dry, rocky ridges in sites which are frequently foggy, one finds plants very close to the island extreme. On deeper soils and in the shade of small oaks are bushes scarcely different from those of the Mother Lode country. Around old ranch buildings and in other peculiar habitats one finds strange and bizarre recombinations of various sorts.

Just as these studies came to a close and it was time for me to leave California, I realized that many of the other plants in the chaparral association were similarly variable. There were swarms of hybrid oaks and hybrid ceanothus and hybrid manzanitas. The entire association seemed to be in a state of flux. Unlike the coastal sages which I had studied in southern California, there was room for hybrid recombinations within the association itself. The entire chaparral seemed to be ecologically in the same general class of disturbed habitat as the abandoned olive orchards.

I do not wish to jump to conclusions from one small experiment. I would merely suggest that these methods are appropriate for the analysis of such problems, particularly if combined with experimental work (for instance, the removal of a single specie or species complex from a small area using modern herbicides followed by measurement of the effect of this removal on the other complexes in the association). Here is a field in which we could very rapidly get down to some of the basic principles concerning closed versus open habitats. In my opinion, the degree to which such associations as the California chaparral are man-made is a better subject for study than for debate. They have certainly been greatly affected by man. To learn to what degree, I should prefer to look for more facts rather than to listen to more opinions.

Even among biologists there has been a strong tendency to avoid such problems—to study the plants and plant associations of mountaintops and jungles rather than those of dooryards and gardens, to think of plant and animal communities as they must have been in some blissfully innocent era before the advent of man. It seems to me far healthier and far more logical to accept man as a part of nature, to concentrate one's attention as a naturalist on man's activities, since he is the one species in the world we most nearly understand. It is because we know from inside ourselves the problems in which man is deeply involved that we appreciate their bewildering complexity; experiments with laboratory insects would not seem so beautifully simple if we knew as much about them as we do about man. The population genetics of garbage-pail flies (Dobzhansky, 1949) would appear more complex if we understood from within what it is like to be a *Drosophila*. The apparently standardized environment of flour in a bottle (Park, 1938) would not seem undifferentiated to any investigator who had once been a flour beetle and who knew at firsthand the complexities of flour-beetle existence. Imagine a non-human investigator of human populations recently arrived from Mars. What could he understand of the relationships of Catholics and Protestants? How long would it take him to discover that, though most of the shortest girls in New York City get married, the very tallest seldom do? Having discovered this phenomenon, how much longer would it take him to understand it? When we attempt to work with laboratory insects, our ignorance of their social complexities makes them seem far simpler material than they really are.

I must confess that when, from being a student of variation in natural populations, I was of necessity led to being a student of man's upsetting effects on his environment, my own thinking was too much colored by this attitude. Only gradually did I come to realize that, though man is now the world's great upsetter, he is not the first. There were others before him, and they played a similar role in evolution. Stebbins and I have recently suggested (1954) that the great bursts of evolutionary activity in the past, the times of adaptive radiation, were caused by such upsets. The formation *de novo* of a great fresh-water lake such as Lake Baikal produced a new and open habitat in which the organisms from various river systems could meet and mongrelize and, under the hand of selection, evolve as rapidly into new paths as did the salvias in the abandoned olive orchard. What must have happened when the first land vertebrates at last arrived on continents whose vegetation had no experience of such beasts? What occurred when the giant reptiles of the Mesozoic churned like gigantic bulldozers through the ferny swamps of that period? Must not the plants of those periods have gone through the same general experiences as are now facing the adenostomas of the California chaparral?

Man has been a major force in the evolution of the plants and animals which accompany him around the world, in the midst of which he largely spends his days. The detailed study of this process (1) should illuminate for us the course of evolution in prehuman times; (2) should be as well one of our truest guides to the history of prehistoric man; (3) most importantly, should enable us at last to understand and eventually to control the living world around us.

References Cited

Aase, Hannah C.
  1946 "Cytology of Cereals. II," *Botanical Review,* XII, No. 5, 255–334.
Anderson, Edgar
  1949 *Introgressive Hybridization.* New York: John Wiley & Sons. 109 pp.
  1952 *Plants, Man, and Life.* Boston: Little, Brown & Co. 245 pp.
  1954 "Introgression in *Adenostoma,*" *Annals of the Missouri Botanical Garden,* XLI, 339–50.
Anderson, Edgar, and Anderson, Burton R.
  1954 "Introgression of *Salvia apiana* and *Salvia mellifera,*" *Annals of the Missouri Botanical Garden,* XLI, 329–38.
Anderson, Edgar, and Stebbins, G. L., Jr.
  1954 "Hybridization as an Evolutionary Stimulus," *Evolution,* VIII, No. 4, 378–88.
Dobzhansky, Th.
  1949 "Observations and Experiments on Natural Selection in *Drosophila,*" pp. 210–24 in Bonnier, Gert, and Larsson, Robert (eds), *Proceedings of the Eighth International Congress of Genetics (July 7–14, 1948, Stockholm).* Lund: Berlingska Boktryckeriet. 696 pp.
Epling, Carl C.
  1938 "The California *Salvias:* A Review of *Salvia,* Section Audibertia," *Annals of the Missouri Botanical Garden,* XXV, 95–188.
  1947 "Natural Hybridization of *Salvia apiana* and *Salvia mellifera,*" *Evolution,* I, Nos. 1–2, 69–78.
Epling, Carl C., and Lewis, Harlan
  1942 "The Centers of Distribution of the Chaparral and Coastal Sage Associations," *American Midland Naturalist,* XXVII, No. 2, 445–62.
Heiser, Charles B., Jr.
  1949 "Study in the Evolution of the Sunflower Species *Helianthus annuus* and *H. bolanderi,*" *University of California Publications in Botany,* XXIII, No. 4, 157–208.

  1951 "Hybridization in the Annual Sunflowers: *Helianthus annuus* × *H. debilis* var. *cucumerifolius,*" *Evolution,* V, No. 1, 42–51.
Hurry, Jameison B.
  1930 *The Woad Plant and Its Dye.* London: Oxford University Press. 328 pp.
Hutchinson, J. B.; Silow, R. A.; and Stephens, S. G.
  1947 *The Evolution of Gossypium and the Differentiation of the Cultivated Cottons.* London: Oxford University Press. 160 pp.
Mangelsdorf, P. C., and Reeves, R. G.
  1938 "The Origin of Maize," *Proceedings of the National Academy of Sciences,* XXIV, No. 8, 303–12.
Park, Thomas
  1938 "Studies in Population Physiology. VIII. The Effect of Larval Population Density on the Post-embryonic Development of the Flour Beetle, *Tribolium confusum* Duval," *Journal of Experimental Zoology,* LXXIX, No. 1, 51–70.
Riley, H. P.
  1938 "A Character Analysis of Colonies of *Iris fulva, I. hexagona* var. *giganticaerulea* and Natural Hybrids," *American Journal of Botany,* XXV, 727–38.
Sauer, Jonathan D.
  1950 "The Grain Amaranths: A Survey of Their History and Classification," *Annals of the Missouri Botanical Garden,* XXXVII, No. 4, 561–632.
  1952 "A Geography of Pokeweed," *ibid.,* XXXIX, 113–25.
Standley, P. C.
  1931 *Flora of the Lancetilla Valley, Honduras.* ("Field Museum of Natural History, Botanical Series," No. 10.) Chicago: Field Museum. 418 pp.
Vavilov, N. I.
  1926 "Studies on the Origin of Cultivated Plants," *Bulletin of Applied Botany and Plant Breeding,* XVI, No. 2, 138–248.

ADDITIONAL REFERENCES

de Candolle, A. P. 1886. *Origin of cultivated plants.* 2d ed. Reprinted 1964 by Hafner, New York and London. 468 pp.
Flannery, Kent V. 1965. The ecology of early food production in Mesopotamia. *Science* 147:1247–1256.

Sauer, Carl. 1947. Early relations of man to plants. *Geograph. Rev.* 37(1):1–25.
Stebbins, G. L., Jr. 1950. *Variation and evolution in plants.* New York: Columbia University Press. 643 pp.

INDUSTRIAL MELANISM IN MOTHS

H. B. D. KETTLEWELL

Among all living things, moths and butterflies provide the most striking evidence of rapid evolutionary change—and that change is an indirect response to man's impact on the environment. Although the evolutionary fate of moths is of no interest to most people, it should be emphasized that "the same laws which govern the adaptation of moths to a changing environment can also be applied to all other living things, including man himself."

Melanism in moths refers to increased dark pigmentation in the wings or other parts of the insect. Usually melanism is controlled genetically; probably over 90 percent of industrial melanics are controlled by a single gene, inherited as a Mendelian dominant (Kettlewell, 1961, p. 253). Industrial melanism is brought about by the indirect effects of industrialization through natural selection.

The phenomenon of industrial melanism was first noted in England about the middle of the last century. In Manchester the black form of the peppered moth was rare in 1848, but fifty years later it comprised 95 percent of the Manchester population; this reflected a 30 percent yearly selective advantage of the melanic form over the light for this period (op. cit., pp. 249–250). By the period 1952 to 1964 typical, light-colored forms of the peppered moth were not found (in 760 moths collected). However, it is interesting to note that within the last few years the percentage of typical moths near Manchester has significantly increased (25 of 972 *B. betularia* collected) as air pollution has been reduced (Cook, Askew, and Bishop, 1970).

H. B. D. Kettlewell is senior research officer in the Sub-Department of Genetics, Department of Zoology, Oxford University, Oxford, England. For several decades his research has focused on the genetics of color variations and the survival mechanism in insects, especially in moths and butterflies. He currently is investigating the antiquity of melanism in Lepidoptera; this research is providing evidence about the origins of industrial melanism which will soon be published as a book, *The Evolution of Melanism: The Study of a Recurring Necessity*. In addition to writing numerous research articles, Kettlewell was coauthor (with Sir Julian Huxley) of *Charles Darwin and His World* (1965).

This selection, slightly edited, is reprinted by courtesy of the author and the Royal Institution of Great Britain from the Institution's *Proceedings*, vol. 36, part 3, no. 164, pp. 616–635, 1957, where it appeared under the full title, "Industrial Melanism in Moths and Its Contribution to Our Knowledge of Evolution."

Industrial melanism is an indirect consequence of air pollution. Air pollutants have killed, and blackened, lichens on tree trunks and boughs. In such a habitat the blackness of melanic moths is of great value in protecting them from predatory birds. This selective advantage has been neatly demonstrated in field experiments, briefly described here. The spreading damage to lichens by air pollutants (see Selection 37) accounts for the wide distribution of industrial melanics over central and eastern England, even down-wind for considerable distances from industrial areas. Industrial melanism is notable elsewhere in Europe and in North America; in the Pittsburg area alone it is probable that more than 100 species of moths and butterflies are in the process of becoming mainly melanic (op. cit., p. 249).

Man should ask: What similar, but subtle and yet undetected, evolutionary changes are occurring in other organisms as a consequence of our changing environment?

(Editor's comment)

The phenomenon of industrial melanism at present taking place before our eyes is undoubtedly the most spectacular evolutionary change which has ever actually been witnessed in any organism, animal or plant. A melanic moth must, by definition, refer to any individual in whom there is either a darkening of the normal complicated wing pattern, or in which the ground colour is replaced by all black coloration. Industrial melanism is a special type and, at the present time, is found among no fewer than 70 of our 780 species of larger moths, the Macrolepidoptera, and each year fresh species are added to the list. This profound evolutionary change has taught us a great deal more than just about the moths themselves which, it must be admitted, play but a small part in the world's economy. It has contributed to our knowledge in the first place of how fast living creatures can adapt themselves to a changing environment: in fifty generations some of our moth populations have turned from white to black. Secondly, and coincidental with this work, we have been able to learn a great deal of the widespread effects of air pollution on the natural history of this country, and also the great distances which smoke fall-out travels.

The same laws which govern the adaptation of moths to a changing environment can also be applied to all other living things, including man himself, whether the countryside is being altered by smoke pollution or, for instance, radioactive fall-out. It is indeed an encouraging thought to know that living things are able to adapt themselves in this way so rapidly to a new situation.

Melanic moths can be classified under the following three headings:

1　Industrial Melanics
2　Recessive Melanics
3　Ancient or Relict Melanics

Industrial Melanics

A polymorphism implies a situation in which more than one form of a species live together at the same time. In most examples in nature, the situation is balanced by the various selective forces involved and a "balanced polymorphism" is established, in which the respective frequencies vary but slightly. In industrial melanism, however, the position is entirely different and the black forms are at present increasing in frequency from decade to decade, and in many species extremely rapidly. This then can be referred to as a "transient polymorphism." The black forms are always perpetuated by inheritance and not as the direct result of the environment on the individual. Genetically, they are nearly always Mendelian dominants and only in one or two exceptions recessive. It is important to note that industrial melanism is, for the most part, confined to those species which depend on camouflage for their protection during the day by sitting motionless on long-established backgrounds, such as lichened tree trunks, boughs, rocks and twigs, and is never found in those species which depend for their survival on other forms of protective coloration such as, for example, "warning."

Recessive Melanics

These are found as extreme rarities in those species which do not depend for their survival on camouflage by day. They probably occur in nature at about the recurrent mutation rate, and are usually physiologically weaker. A recessive state suggests that in the past the gene complex has but rarely found use for the particular mutation and hence, by selection, that it has usually been eliminated from the population. Nevertheless, it must be expected that the environment today, being so very different to that which was found in the past, must from time to time present advantages not previously experienced. Under these conditions, it is not surprising that we occasionally find a recessive melanic at an advantage, probably for the first time in its history. Only two successful recessive industrial melanics are known to me (*Lasiocampa quercus* f. *olivacea*, and *Arctia caja* f. *fumosa*), so that they represent quite exceptional circumstances.

Ancient or Relict Melanics

The Caledonian pine forests are probably the areas least affected by civilization today and have remained unchanged for several thousand years. It is of interest then that in the Black Wood of Rannoch at least five species of Lepidoptera were found by me in 1956 with their melanic forms in an apparent

state of balanced polymorphism. Reference will be made later in this discourse to a possible connection between these relict forms and the modern industrial melanics.

Our present work up to date can be clearly divided into two parts:

Firstly, we have been attempting to ascertain the camouflage efficiency of the black and white forms in both rural and industrial England.

Secondly, we have found that behaviour and physiological differences exist between the black and the white forms.

In regard to the first, Figures 49.1 and 49.2 portray the situation in rural and industrial England in *Biston betularia*, the peppered moth, and its black form *carbonaria*. If we analyze the efficiency of the *typical* form (Figure 49.1), we see that it depends on the presence of lichens and algae on the trunks and boughs of trees on which the species always passes the day. Figure 49.2* depicts an oak trunk near Birmingham, and it will be appreciated that two things have happened: all vegetative lichens have disappeared and the bark has become black, the result of constant washing of the canopy of the tree by rain storms. Experimentally, by releasing known numbers of marked peppered moths, both black and white forms, into the local population at Birmingham, which is about 90 per cent melanic, we were able to recapture a proportion subsequently, and hence assess the selective advantage of one form over the other. Near Birmingham, in fact, in a release of 137 *typical* and 447 *carbonaria*, we recaptured 27.5 per cent of the latter, but only 13 per cent of the *typical* form returned (*1*). Conversely in an unpolluted and heavily lichened wood in Dorset, probably similar to those found throughout England 200 years ago and where the population of the peppered moth is still 100 per cent of the light form, we recaptured only half as many of the black form as of the

---

* **Figure 49.2,** reproduced here as the opening photograph for Part 9 (p. 636), shows *Biston betularia* (the peppered moth) and its melanic form *carbonaria* on an oak trunk in the industrial area of Birmingham. (Photo by M. Lyster.) (*Editor's note.*)

FIGURE 49.1 *Biston betularia* L. (the peppered moth) and its melanic form *carbonaria* Jordan on a lichened oak trunk in Dean End Wood, Dorset.   (Photo by M. Lyster.)

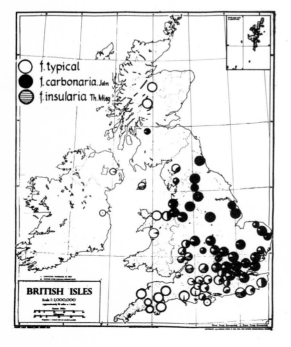

light in a release of 969 insects (*2*).   Furthermore, in each place we were able to show by direct observation that birds were responsible for a selective predation, and we succeeded in filming them taking both forms, but on the majority of occasions the more conspicuous of the two forms was eaten, the better hidden surviving.   We must envisage this highly competitive selection as taking place in every wood and spinney in England and, as the state of the tree trunks is largely decided by the amount (and duration) of the pollution fall out, we may expect to find some correlation between the frequency of the *carbonaria* form and the amount of smoke contamination.   Figure 49.3 shows a map of England giving the frequencies of the black and white forms of the peppered

FIGURE 49.3 Frequency map of *Biston betularia* (the peppered moth) and its melanic forms in Britain.

moth, and is the result of over 20,000 records collected by more than 150 observers living in different parts of Britain. The following points can be established:

Firstly, there is a correlation between the industrial centres and the high frequency of the black form.

Secondly, only in the west of England and North Scotland is the countryside melanic free.

Thirdly, that nowhere down the east coast of England does the *carbonaria* drop below 75 per cent. This, taken in conjunction with leaf washings (to estimate the amount of contamination) and lichen counts, is, in my opinion, the indirect result of air pollution which has been carried scores of miles by the prevailing south westerly winds from central industrial England. It is our failure to recognize the insidious changes which have been taking place over a large part of our countryside, which has made it so difficult for us to understand why these melanic moths so frequently occur at such great distances from industrial areas.

The peppered moth is only one of many species undergoing similar changes in their populations, and Figure 49.4 shows some of these. Melanic *Apatele aceris* L. (nos. 1 and 2) is at a high frequency in the London area, and *A. alni* L. (nos. 3 and 4) and *leporina* (nos. 5 and 6) in Sheffield. The story of *Procus literosa* Haw. (nos. 9 and 10) is somewhat different, however. It failed to survive in its *typical* form in Sheffield and was driven out. Only recently, in fact, has it reoccurred after many years, but now in its melanic form, the black mutation no doubt having taken place somewhere outside Sheffield.

The phenomenon of industrial melanism is not limited to the British Isles, where it was first noted about the middle of the last century. At the same time, it appeared in industrial areas on the Continent. It is widespread in North America, where also it has been for the most part overlooked. Recently, I was able to list over forty species having melanic forms in Canada, and Figure 49.5 shows *Catocala cerogama* Guenée (nos.

FIGURE 49.4 Some British moths with their industrial melanic forms. (In each case the melanic form is shown beneath the typical.)
 1 and 2 Apatele aceris L.
 3 and 4 Apatale alni L.
 5 and 6 Apatele leporina L.
 7 and 8 Deileptenia ribeata Cl.
 9 and 10 Procus literosa Haw.
11 and 12 Abrostola tripartita Hufn.

(Photo by J. Haywood)

1 and 2) which is now about 40 per cent in its melanic form near Montreal. *Amphydasis cognataria* Guenée the American peppered moth (nos. 3 and 4) is also black in many areas, and we are now experimenting with successful crosses between it and its British confrère. The origin of the melanic *Neocleora (Boarmia) tulbaghata* Felder (nos. 5 and 6) is somewhat different to those previously mentioned. I recently found an isolated colony of this species in a valley in the Cape of Good Hope, South Africa, where, as can be imagined, there was no industrial pollution. Following the introduction of Australian wattle, *Acacia* spp. this valley was burnt out at frequent intervals and the tree trunks were black and bare. The dark form

FIGURE 49.5 Examples of melanics occurring outside Britain. (In each case the melanic form is shown beneath the typical.)
1 and 2, Catocala cerogama Guenée; 3 and 4, Amphydasis cognataria Gn; 5 and 6, Boarmia tulbaghata Felder. (Photo by J. Haywood)

had here a great camouflage advantage, though I found it nowhere else in Africa.

So far, I have been discussing the colour efficiency between the melanic and the typical forms, but this is not the whole story. We have recently been investigating behaviour and physiological differences between these two, and have found that they do, in fact, exist. For example, in some *betularia* broods with their origin from industrial areas the larvae of the black form feed up much slower than those of the *typical,* who thereby escape the heavier pollution which is found on leaves later in the year. Again, there appear to be different assembling behaviours between virgin black and white moths, *typical* males coming to *carbonaria* females more freely on warm nights, and to *typical* females on cold ones (3). Several workers have shown that the melanic forms are hardier than the type (4) and, lastly, there is some, but so far insufficient, evidence that the two forms are aware of the backgrounds on which they choose to sit, the melanics selecting the darker portions of a trunk than the light forms (5). All these differences, chemical, physiological, and behavioural, are governed by a single pair of genes and the rest of the gene-complex which has by selection adapted itself to them.

I wish now to discuss the theories of the spread of industrial melanism, and also of its origin. Heslop Harrison has tried to explain both on the grounds of "induced mutation" brought about by a specific "melanogen" present in air pollution (6), and he envisages this as taking place at a prodigious rate, sufficient to be responsible for the origin and spread of industrial melanism. The published figures of his experiments give an 8 per cent mutation rate, yet J. B. S. Haldane has shown that one of the highest known is in haemophilia in man, which is 1 in 50,000 (7). In spite of frequent repetitions of Heslop Harrison's experiments, and using many thousands of moths, no worker has so far succeeded in achieving his results. In fact, all have been completely negative. Personally I prefer to account for the origin and spread of industrial melanism on the existing laws of nature without having to invoke new theory.

It is my contention that in the recent past prior to the Industrial Revolution when melanic mutations took place in areas where deciduous trees were heavily covered with lichens, they were ruthlessly eliminated by natural selection because of their colour disadvantages, and this has been amply borne out in my own experiments. 6,000 years ago, however, the climate was different and much of Britain was covered by large tracts of pine forest similar to those found in certain small areas of Scotland today, where melanic forms occur in conditions very different from those of industrial England. At least two of the black forms found here are similar, if not identical, to those now spreading through polluted England: their method of inheritance is the same, dominant. One of these species, *Cleora repandata* L., I was able to study in some detail. *Repandata* is a trunk sitter, and I was able to observe just under 500 specimens, of which 10 per cent were black. The *typical* form was nearly always most difficult to observe whilst at rest, but the black were scored as conspicuous on most occasions. By labelling the spot where each insect sat at dawn and revisiting the trees later in the day, we were able to show that on some days more than 50 per cent had moved and subsequently we found that, because of disturbance by ants, hot sunshine or some other cause, these had had to take flight to another tree trunk, usually a distance of about 50 yards. I saw large numbers on the wing, and three other observers and I all agreed that the black form was practically invisible over 20 yards, but that the light form could be followed with ease up to a distance of 100 yards, and we did, in fact, see birds catch them on three occasions. A model showing this aerial camouflage has been sponsored by the Royal Institution and there can be little doubt that it reflects the correct situation in these woods, and that the black form is at a greater advantage to the *typical* whilst on the wing, but that the reverse is true when at rest. In fact, this situation may explain, in part, the origin of the balanced polymorphism found here today as, no doubt, it has been for centuries. It demonstrates one of the ways in which melanics have been of use in the past and, though conditions today are very different, these same black forms, or similar ones, are spreading through industrialized England. There is a series of species found throughout England in which a comparable connection possibly exists between the black and light forms to those found in the old Caledonian forests. In each case, the black form occurs in non-polluted districts and, no doubt, has always conferred certain advantages in the past. In the case of *Allophyes oxyacanthae* L. and *Nonagria dissoluta* Tr., the black forms were known and named as early as the beginning of the last century. Nevertheless, the frequency of these melanics in some of these species increases in an industrial and urban environment. In other words, the original melanic form, which has been preserved in a state of balanced polymorphism through the ages, is now being made use of under entirely different conditions today. Recurrent mutation provides the source, and natural selection, as postulated by Darwin, decides its destiny. Melanism, in fact, is not a recent phenomenon but a very old one. It enables us to appreciate the vast reserves of genetic variability which are held within each species, and which are capable of being used when the occasion arises.

The Industrial Revolution brought a cataclysm on us, and our natural history. It is by an evolutionary cataclysm that the moths of this country have had to respond to it, the like of which we may never see again.

References Cited

1. H. B. D. Kettlewell, *Heredity*, **9** Part 3, 323–342 (1955).

2. H. B. D. Kettlewell, *Heredity*, **10** Part 3, 287–301 (1956).

3. H. B. D. Kettlewell, *Proc. Roy. Soc. B.* **145,** 297–303 (1956).

4. E. B. Ford, *Biol. Rev.* **12,** 461 (1937).

5. H. B. D. Kettlewell, *Nature,* Lond. **175,** 943 (1955).

6. J. W. H. Harrison, *Proc. Roy. Soc. B.* **101,** 115–28 (1927).

7. J. B. S. Haldane, *J. Genet.* **31,** 317–26 (1935).

ADDITIONAL REFERENCES

Brodo, I. M. 1966. Lichen growth and cities: A study on Long Island, New York. *The Bryologist* 69(4):427–449.

Cook, L. M., R. R. Askew, and J. A. Bishop. 1970. Increasing frequency of the typical form of the peppered moth in Manchester. *Nature* 227:1155.

Fenton, A. F. 1964. Atmospheric pollution of Belfast and its relationship to the lichen flora. *Irish Nat. Jour.* 14:237–245.

Kettlewell, H. B. D. 1956. Further selection experiments on industrial melanism in the Lepidoptera. *Heredity* 10(3):287–301.

Kettlewell, H. B. D. 1961. The phenomenon of industrial melanism in lepidoptera. *Annual Review Entomology* 6:245–262.

Kettlewell, H. B. D. 1965. Insect survival and selection for pattern. *Science* 148:1290–1296.

Skye, Erik. 1968. Lichens and air pollution. *Acta Phytogeographica Suecica 52.* 123 pp.

PESTICIDES AND EVOLUTION

N. W. MOORE

Selective killing of animals by man—exemplified by the use of insecticides—is a third and recent method by which man makes new organisms (in addition to artificial selection in the usual sense and environmental change, discussed in Selections 47 to 49). And, in the case of evolving insects that are resistant to insecticides, this creation by man is having dire consequences for man.

Resistance in pests is produced by Darwinian selection. As susceptible individuals in a population are killed, the more resistant genotypes remain to reproduce succeeding generations. Most different resistant types are mainly caused by a single gene.

By 1967 resistance had developed in 224 species of insects and ascarines (Brown, 1968), up from 137 species in 1961. Of the former number, 97 are of veterinary or public-health importance and 127 attack field or forest crops or stored products.

Resistance is specific to classes of pesticides: 135 species are cyclodiene-resistant (often called dieldrin-resistant), 91 are DDT-resistant, and 54 are resistant to organophosphorus compounds. Certain pests are now resistant to all the above pesticides—including the house fly, the cattle tick in Australia, and the cotton leafworm in Egypt. Crop after crop, around the world, additional resistant strains of pests evolve each year. And the wider the area covered by an insecticide, the faster insect resistance develops and spreads, since fewer susceptible individuals are left to dilute and compete with the resistant survivors of the applications. Aldrin-resistance in the western corn rootworm spread from one spot in Nebraska into seven states in five years (op. cit.).

This selection discusses additional ecological implications of pesticide resistance. Clearly there is a growing need for new kinds of pest

N. W. Moore is head of the Toxic Chemicals & Wildlife Section, Monks Wood Experimental Station, England (see biographical note on p. 578).

This selection is extracted from pp. 116–117 in "A Synopsis of the Pesticide Problem," pp. 75–129 in *Advances in Ecological Research*, vol. 4, 1967, edited by J. B. Cragg. Reprinted by permission of the author, the editor, and the publisher, Academic Press, London and New York.

control, for measures that are not self-defeating as in the case of many chemical pesticides. Such alternatives are now being sought and developed (see Selection 42; Holcomb, 1970; Irving, 1970).

(Editor's comment)

Pesticides exert strong selective pressure on pest populations. It is not surprising that resistant strains of pests are quickly selected; but the range of preadaptations to pesticides present in pests has been remarkable. By 1940 resistance to pesticides had been recorded in eight insect species (Georghiou, 1965); by 1961 at least 137 species of pest had become resistant to pesticides. For a review of the earlier literature see Brown (1958). Two main types of resistance have been recorded. In some species the resistant strain has a biochemical or physiological property which prevents pesticides damaging the insect, for example a detoxicating enzyme. In others the insect has a behavioural property which reduces contact with lethal doses of the insecticide. Many pests become resistant to several pesticides as a result of exposure to them (multiple resistance) but in addition many cases of cross-resistance are known: in these resistance acquired to one pesticide confers resistance to one or more other pesticides. Frequently cross-resistance is between related chemicals, for example between those of the cyclodiene-derived group, but cross-resistance is also known between organochlorine and organo-phosphorus and carbamate insecticides. Distinct patterns of cross-resistant types are emerging (Winteringham and Hewlett, 1964).

The generation time of arthropods is so much shorter than that of vertebrates that it is not surprising that resistance has been most frequently observed in this group. However, in recent years it has been reported in fish (Vinson *et al.*, 1963) and mammals (Boyle, 1960) and possibly in amphibia (Boyd *et al.*, 1963). Strains which are 1.7 times as resistant to DDT as the controls, have been produced experimentally in mice in nine generations (Ozburn and Morrison, 1962). Cross-resistance has been demon-strated in fish (Boyd and Ferguson, 1964).

The ecologically relevant effects of pesticide resistance are these:

1   It causes a change in spraying pro-grammes and hence in the nature of the pesticide factor. The change may be towards higher doses or to new chemicals.
2   In a sprayed area vertebrate species are unlikely to develop resistance before invertebrate pests.
3   If a species achieves resistance by being able to store more pesticides it would become a more effective biological con-centrator of pesticides, and hence a greater hazard to its predators.
4   Genes conferring resistance may be linked with those conferring other characteristics. These may be advantageous (but are more likely to be disadvantageous).

At the present time it is quite impossible to predict what evolutionary changes will take place as a result of pesticide pressures. In some cases resistance to pesticides is linked with other favourable characters. But in general when pesticide pressure is withdrawn the new genotypes do not survive; in other words those selected by pesticides are less well adapted in general than the original type. All that can be said is that a powerful new type of selective factor is in operation throughout the world and it might eventually have important qualitative effects.

In the course of evolution it has always been disadvantageous to feed on some types of potential food—those that contain poisons and those that transmit disease to the animal. The avoidance of toxic forms is acquired instinctively or by learning. There is often a relationship of reciprocal advantage between prey and predator (aposematic coloration). However, there is no evidence that any species has learnt to avoid individuals which carry disease organisms, while preying on other individuals of the same species which do not carry such organisms. In this respect animals which contain persistent pesticides are like those that carry diseases—it is to the advantage of the predator to be able to distinguish the prey with the pesticide residues and the prey without, but there is no evidence that such discrimination has yet been evolved. Far from avoiding animals showing sublethal effects of pesticides, predators are more likely to prey upon them as they are upon all weak and diseased individuals. A behaviour mechanism which caused the animal to avoid contaminated prey would have to overcome an instinct which under "normal" conditions is effective in preventing starvation. It is unlikely to be evolved in the present pesticide situation.

References Cited

Boyd, C. E., and Ferguson, D. E. 1964. *Mosquito News* 24, 19–21.

Boyd, C. E., Vinson, S. B., and Ferguson, D. E. 1963. *Copeia* 1963, 426–429.

Boyle, C. M. 1960. *Nature, Lond.* 188, 517.

Brown, A. W. A. 1958. *Adv. Pest Control Res.* 2, 351–414.

Georghiou, G. P. 1965. *Adv. Pest Control Res.* 6, 171–230.

Ozburn, G. W., and Morrison, F. O. 1962. *Nature, Lond.* 196, 1009–1010.

Vinson, S. B., Boyd, C. E., and Ferguson, D. E. 1963. *Science, N. Y.* 139, 217–218.

Winteringham, F. P. W., and Hewlett, P. S. 1964. *Chem. Ind.* 1964, 1512–1518.

ADDITIONAL REFERENCES

Babers, F. H. 1949. Development of insect resistance to insecticides. *U.S. Bur. Ent. Plant Quarant.* E-776:1–31.

Babers, F. H., and Pratt, J. J. 1951. Development of insect resistance to insecticides. II. A critical review of the literature up to 1951. *U.S. Bur. Ent. Plant Quarant.* E-818:1–45.

Brown, A. W. A. 1961. Ecological consequences of the development of resistance. Pp. 33–37 in Kuenen, D. J., ed. *The Ecological Effects of Biological and Chemical Control of Undesirable Plants and Animals,* Intern. Union. Cons. Nat. 8th Tech. Meeting.

Brown, A. W. A. 1963. Meeting the resistance problem. *Bulletin World Health Organization* 29:41–50. Suppl., 1963.

Brown, A. W. A. 1968. Insecticide resistance comes of age. *Bulletin of the Entomological Society of America* 14(1):3–9.

Carson, Rachel. 1962. *Silent spring.* Boston: Houghton Mifflin.

Conway, Gordon R. 1969. A consequence of insecticides; pests follow the chemicals in the cocoa of Malaysia. Pp. 46–51 in *The unforeseen international boomerang,* ed. by M. T. Farvar and John Milton. Supplement to *Natural History* magazine.

Ferguson, D. E., D. D. Culley, W. D. Cotton, and R. P. Dodds. 1964. Resistance to chlorinated hydrocarbon insecticides in three species of fresh water fish. *BioScience* 14(11):43–44.

Ferguson, Denzel. 1967. The ecological consequences of pesticide resistance in fishes. *Transactions of the 32nd North American Wildlife and Natural Resources Conference* (March 13–15, 1967):103–107.

Graham, Frank, Jr. 1970. *Since silent spring.* Boston: Houghton Mifflin. 334 pp.

Grant, C. D., and A. W. A. Brown. 1967. Development of DDT resistance in certain mayflies in New Brunswick. *The Canadian Entomologist* 99:1040–1050.

Holcomb, R. W. 1970. Insect control: Alternatives to the use of conventional pesticides. *Science* 168:456–468.

Irving, G. W., Jr. 1970. Agricultural pest control and the environment. *Science* 168:1419–1424.

Kuenen, D. J., ed. 1961. *The ecological effects of biological and chemical control of undesirable plants and animals.* International Union Cons. Nature Symposium, 1960, Eighth Tech. Meeting. Leiden: E. J. Brill. 118 pp.

Labrecque, G. C., and C. N. Smith, eds. 1968.

Principles of insect chemosterilization. New York: Appleton-Century-Crofts. 345 pp.

Rudd, R. L. 1964. *Pesticides and the living landscape.* Madison, Wisconsin: University of Wisconsin Press. 320 pp.

Sanders, H. J. 1969. Chemical mutagens. I. The road to genetic disaster. II. An expanding roster of suspects. *Chemical and Engineering News* 47(21):53–71; 47(23):54–68.

Sax, Karl, and H. J. Sax. 1968. Possible mutagenic hazards of some food additives, beverages and insecticides. *Japanese Journal of Genetics* 43(2):89–94.

Schoff, H. F. 1959. Resistance in arthropods of medical and veterinary importance—1946–1958. *Misc. Publications of the Entomological Society of America* 1:3–11.

U.S. Department of Health, Education, and Welfare. 1969. *Report of the Secretary's Commission on Pesticides and their relationship to environmental health.* Parts I and II. Washington, D.C.: U.S. Government Printing Office. 677 pp.

Vinson, S. B., C. E. Boyd, and D. E. Ferguson. 1963. Resistance to DDT in the mosquito fish, *Gambusia affinis. Science* 139:217–218.

Williams, C. M. 1968. Third-generation pesticides. *Sci. Am.* 217:13–17.

Yarwood, C. E. 1970. Man-made plant diseases. *Science* 168:218–220.

TEN TRENDS AND PROSPECT

Countryside, Aargau, Switzerland. Photo by Thomas R. Detwyler.

TEN TRENDS AND PROSPECT

"In the world of real life men constantly change their ways, and places also change. The solution to environmental problems cannot be found, therefore, in a return to an imaginary Arcadia or in the search for a static Utopia. The most man can do is on the one hand to make sure that the environmental changes he brings about do not outstrip his adaptive potentialities, and furthermore to govern his adaptive responses in such a manner that they do not decrease the qualities of his life."

INTRODUCTION

In this final part we step back from case studies and specifics to look more broadly, yet critically, at the nature of man's relationship to his environment. The major question here is: What are the general characteristics and trends of man's impact on environment and are these induced environmental changes outracing his ability to adapt to them?

As we have seen in Part 9, many organisms recently have evolved adaptations to man-altered environments through natural selection. However, as Dubos states in Selection 51, man the animal "has remained essentially the same since he became differentiated as a distinct biological species late in paleolithic times, some 50,000 years ago." Although man, like other species, can undergo genetic changes enabling him to adapt to new conditions, "Biological (genetic) evolution is far too slow to permit effective adaptation to the rapid changes that commonly occur in the physical environment at the present time." Certain environmental qualities are essential to man's survival because during his development with them in the evolutionary past he acquired a dependence on them that cannot be quickly outgrown by means of genetic changes.

But man has unequaled powers to adjust *culturally*— through technological and social innovations—to environmental changes. Dubos notes that "Modern man is adapting to environmental pollution, to intense crowding, to deficient or excessively abundant diets, to monotonous, ugly, and depressing environments." In fact, "The most polluted, crowded, and traumatic cities are also the ones that have the greatest appeal and where population is increasing most rapidly."

Dubos believes that there is no longer enough time for the orderly and successful operation of the unconscious adaptive processes, either biological or social, that saved man in the past. Rather, man must learn to recognize and carefully plan for his needs. The alternative is self-destruction by upsetting the complex and delicate web of life that includes man.

Man's present desecration of environment is so severe and the trends so unfavorable (Selection 52) that I am gloomy about the prospects of a quality life for future generations, for meaningful survival. Man's only hope is to work hard for basic solutions to the difficult problems. Some solutions are touched upon in Selection 52 (also see many of the following references).

FURTHER READINGS

Burton, Ian, and R. W. Kates, eds. 1965. *Readings in resource management and conservation.* Chicago: The University of Chicago Press.

Carpenter, R. A. 1970. Information for decisions in environmental policy. *Science* 168:1316–1322.

Ciriacy-Wantrup, S. V., and J. J. Parsons, eds. 1967. *Natural resources—quality and quantity.* Berkeley: University of California Press.

Coale, Ansley. 1970. Man and his environment. *Science* 170:132–136.

Cooley, A., and Geoffrey Wandesforde-Smith, eds. 1970. *Congress and the environment.* Seattle: University of Washington Press. 284 pp.

Dansereau, Pierre, ed. 1970. *Challenge for survival; Land, air, and water for man in megalopolis.* New York and London: Columbia University Press. 235 pp.

Darling, F. F., and J. P. Milton, eds. 1966. *Future environments of North America.* Garden City, New York: Natural History Press. 767 pp.

Davies, J. C., III. 1970. *The politics of pollution.* New York: Pegasus. 231 pp.

Eipper, A. W. 1970. Pollution problems, resource policy, and the scientist. *Science* 169-(3940):11–15.

Ewald, W. R., Jr., ed. 1967. *Environment for man: The next fifty years.* Bloomington: Indiana University Press. 308 pp.

Ewald, W. R., Jr., ed. 1968. *Environment and policy: The next fifty years.* Bloomington: Indiana University Press. 459 pp.

Graham, E. H. 1957. Nature protection as·a part of land development. *Proc. 6th Meeting Int. Union Conserv. Nature & Nat. Res.*:194–201.

Hare, F. Kenneth. 1970. How should we treat environment? *Science* 167(3917):352–355.

Kesteven, G. L. 1968. A policy for conservationists. *Science* 160:857–860.

Mumford, Lewis. 1967. *The myth of the machine: Technics and human development.* New York: Harcourt, Brace & World. 342 pp.

Nicholson, Max. 1970. *The environmental revolution; A guide for the new masters of the world.* New York: McGraw-Hill. 366 pp.

President's Science Advisory Committee, Environmental Pollution Panel. 1965. *Restoring the quality of our environment.* Washington, D.C.: Government Printing Office. 317 pp.

Roslansky, J. D., ed. 1967. *The control of environment.* Amsterdam: North-Holland. 124 pp.

Ross, C. R. 1970. The federal government as an inadvertant advocate of environmental degradation. Pp. 171–187 in *The environmental crisis,* ed. by H. W. Helfrich, Jr. New Haven and London: Yale University Press.

Sax, J. L. 1970. The search for environmental quality: The role of the courts. Pp. 99–114 in *The environmental crisis,* ed. by H. W. Helfrich, Jr. New Haven and London: Yale University Press.

Study of Criticial Environment Problems. 1970. *Man's impact on the global environment; Assesment and recommendations for action.* Cambridge, Mass.: M.I.T. Press.

Teilhard de Chardin, Pierre. 1959. *The phenomenon of man.* New York: Harper and Row. 319 pp.

Thomas, W. L., Jr., ed. 1956. *Man's role in changing the face of the earth.* Chicago: University of Chicago Press. 1193 pp. See especially Part III, "Prospect."

U.S. Department of Health, Education, and Welfare, Task Force on Environmental Health and Related Problems. 1967. *A strategy for a livable environment.* Washington, D.C.: Government Printing Office.

U.S. House of Representatives. 1968. Report of the Subcommittee on Science, Research, and Development to the Committee on Science and Astronautics. *Managing the environment.*

U.S. Senate. A Special Report to the Committee on Interior and Insular Affairs. July 11, 1968. *A national policy for the environment.*

Van Dyne, G. M. 1969. *The ecosystem concept in natural resource management.* Based on a symposium, Albuquerque, February, 1968. New York: Academic Press. 386 pp.

Watt, K. E. 1968. *Ecology and resource management.* New York: McGraw-Hill. 450 pp.

51
SELECTION

MAN AND HIS ENVIRONMENT: SCOPE, IMPACT, AND NATURE

RENÉ DUBOS

This brilliant article provides insight into the conflict between modern man and environment. Dubos draws on many of the same environmental examples which are elaborated in previous selections, beautifully integrating them with philosophical and humanistic understanding. The important points are many and diverse, yet unified. This selection speaks for itself.

(Editor's comment)

Air, Water, and Earth

The three words, air, water, and soil, that define the subject matter of this symposium evoke some of the deepest, most ancient, and most lasting emotions of mankind. They symbolize also some of the greatest adventures of the human mind. All primitive people regard air, water, and earth as the very essence of material creation. The early philosophers tried to account for the structure of the universe and of the human body in terms of these primeval principles. Modern man, as we shall see, still regards them as eternal, fundamental, and essentially irreducible values.

In the 5th century B.C. the Greek philosopher Empedocles of Agrigentum wrote a didactic poem entitled "On Nature," in which he asserted that the whole world was made up of four elementary principles: air, water, earth, and fire. According to him and to the Pythagorean school, these elements were indestructible and accounted for every-

René Jules Dubos (b. 1901), an eminent biologist and humanist, has been associated with the Rockefeller University since 1927 and professor of pathology since 1957. Educated at the Institut National Agronomique in Paris (B.S., 1922) and Rutgers University (Ph.D., 1927), he has also received honorary doctoral degrees from Rochester, Harvard, Liège, Rutgers, Paris, Dublin, and the New School for Social Research. Dubos has received numerous professional awards for his work in bacteriology, pathology, and biochemistry and is a member of the U.S. National Academy of Sciences. His books relating man and environment include *Dreams of Reason: Science and Utopias* (1961), *Torch of Life* (1962), *Man Adapting* (1965), *Man, Medicine, and Environment* (1968), *So Human an Animal* (1970), and *Reason Awake: Science for Man* (1970).

This selection is reprinted from *Environmental Improvement (Air, Water, and Soil)*, edited by Ralph W. Marquis, 1966, by permission of the Graduate School Press, U.S. Department of Agriculture, Washington, D.C.

thing that ever was, that is now, and that is to be, including man's body. In his dialogue "Timaeus," Plato applied the same view to medicine. He expounded the doctrine that health requires harmony among these four principles, and that disharmony among them inevitably results in disease. Interestingly enough, a similar doctrine was presented in a classical Chinese anthology entitled "The Golden Mirror of Medicine," published on order of the Emperor Kien Lung.

It may seem farfetched and pretentious to begin a discussion of the environment in the modern world with a reference to such antiquated Greek and Chinese theories. Crude as they are, however, these theories express attitudes and preoccupations having direct relevance to our own lives.

It has long been known, of course, that air, water, and earth are not elementary principles; they constitute immensely complex mixtures which differ profoundly from one place to the other. But despite this knowledge, the words themselves are still associated in the mind of modern man with sensations and physiological effects very similar to those experienced by ancient man. Whereas the scientist deals with air, water, and earth as crude mixtures to be studied analytically, the layman (and the scientist also is a layman emotionally) identifies the words with fundamental values of Nature to which he reacts holistically, with his whole physical and emotional being. These ancient and unchanging aspects of man's relation to nature still constitute essential determinants of his health and happiness.

Throughout ages, and in all climes, man has expressed a reverence for nature and acknowledged his dependence on air, water, and earth, by personalizing them as deities. We still worship Nature, but with a sense of guilt. The very existence of this series of lectures symbolizes a deep collective concern for the fact that industrial and urban civilization threatens to destroy the natural values that have been identified for so long with the richest emotions of mankind. One of the most painful dilemmas of our times is that we still regard nature as the ultimate source of beauty and other fundamental blessings, yet exploit and despoil it for the sake of wealth and power. We place in the parts of it that are not yet economically useful the highest qualities of nature and its beauty, but paradoxically accept the belief that economic profits justify the creation of ugliness. The sense of guilt comes from the knowledge that it is crudely hypocritical to praise the values of the wilderness, while converting the land into a gigantic dump.

To improve the environment has now become national policy [in the U. S.], but it is not easy to formulate a philosophical basis for this policy. The word environment is so vague as to be almost meaningless, and furthermore any environmental change can affect human life in many different ways. At the cost of much oversimplification and arbitrariness, I shall attempt to highlight the complexities of the problem by making some general statements concerning the multifarious effects that air, water, and earth exert on the activities and well-being of man.

Unquestionably, most of the environmental problems in the modern world have their origin in the rapid increase of world population. Population problems are of paramount importance not only in the underdeveloped areas of the world but in the affluent countries as well, and even more. The abundance of food and of manufactured goods made available in our communities by technological achievements should not blind us to the fact that *we* are *already* overcrowded. The phrase "improvement of the environment" really denotes at the present time the hope that it is possible to minimize the further degradations of the environment that are likely to be caused by increasing population densities. It is still questionable that this conservative, and almost negative attitude, can ever be converted into a more positive policy.

All civilizations so far have been built on an orderly system of relationships linking man to nature, but these relations are being disrupted all over the world by technological forces and high population densities. Increasingly, we destroy forests and we flood deserts to create more farmland, factories, houses, and roads. We eliminate all forms of wildlife that compete with us for space and for food. We tolerate animals, plants, and landscapes only to the extent that they serve economic purposes. Highways, factories, and dwellings occupy more and more of the land areas; the use of all natural resources, including water, will soon have to be restricted to utilitarian ends. Disruption of the water cycle is speeding water on its way to the sea and increasing its destructive action on land surfaces. The denudation of the soil is creating dust bowls. Pollution of the air and of water is beginning to upset the biological balance and to damage human health. Man is rapidly destroying all the aspects of the environment under which he evolved as a species, and that have created his biological being.

Modern science is so inventive that it will probably succeed in providing mankind with technologies to compensate for the destruction of natural resources. But this alone will not correct the damage to the environment done by overpopulation and undisciplined technology. Nor will it prevent the damage to physical and mental health caused by rapid environmental changes. Suffice it to mention here that most types of disease are the expressions of man's failure to adapt to his environment, and that adaptation will become increasingly difficult as air, water, and soil are altered more and more rapidly by the new ways of life.

The disturbances in the system of relationship between man and nature are so obvious that they are now creating all over the Western World—and especially in the U.S. —a vague nostalgia for the conditions of the pre-industrial era. This nostalgia takes different forms, depending upon the temperament and past experience of the person involved. The various aspects of it reflect the multiple views that human beings hold of nature.

For most Europeans, nature means beautiful meadows, disciplined forests, daintily tilled farmlands, streams with polished banks, manicured parks and gardens. Such human-ized types of landscape also contribute to the nature scene in this country. But the more common and deeper nostalgia in the American mind is for another type of scenery, wilder and on a much grander scale than that associated with the word nature in the European mind. Words like the Rockies, the Far West, and even the Appalachians still give to the concept of nature a peculiarly American quality.

The sense of collective guilt in the U.S. comes in large part from the awareness that the immense and romantically exciting grandeur of the primeval wilderness is rapidly giving way to an immense ugliness. Brush is overgrowing mountain slopes that were once covered with majestic forests; industrial sewers are sterilizing streams that used to teem with game fish; air pollutants generate opaque and irritating smogs that dull even the most brilliant and dramatic skies. The price of the power symbolized by super-highways and giant factories is a desecration of all aspects of nature.

The waste of natural resources, the threats to health, the annihilation of civilized sceneries, and the destruction of the wilderness all constitute as many different aspects of the environmental problem in the modern world, each with characteristics of its own. But irrespective of their differences, all cause conflicts with some traits that have been woven into man's very fabric during his evolutionary development. Man evolved in association with natural forces, and civilized as he may be the natural world is still essential to his well-being.

For lack of hard, empirical reflection on the subject, it is difficult to harness evolutionary metaphysics to the practical problems of the modern environment. Scientists, like moralists, react to environmental problems with deep and many-sided sensibility and insight, but they have not so far contributed much precise knowledge to their solution. It may be of some help nevertheless to consider the human aspects of the environment from the point of view of evolutionary history. To this end, I shall take in succession two different points of view that reveal two complementary pictures of human needs. One shows that man's fundamental nature and his responses to the environment have not changed significantly since the Stone Age. The other confirms the obvious truth that since human societies are constantly changing, they must endlessly transform the environment in which they function.

Nature and the Unchangeable Aspects of *Homo Sapiens*

Surprising as it may seem, *Homo sapiens* has remained essentially the same since he became differentiated as a distinct biological species late in paleolithic times, some 50,000 years ago. All biological characteristics and needs of modern man, as well as his susceptibilities and mental reactions, are governed by the assembly of genes that governed the life of ancient man when he was a paleolithic hunter or a neolithic farmer. The ways of life have changed, of course, but physiologically and emotionally the fundamental requirements of mankind are still today what they have always been. Ancient art is profoundly meaningful to us and indeed appears timeless precisely because it resonates with the many aspects of man's nature that are unchangeable.

The permanency of man's nature imposes a fundamental pattern on the philosophy of environmental improvement. This philosophy cannot be formulated in the abstract. To be good for man, the environment must be compatible with the unchangeable needs of his nature. There is no doubt, of course, that like other biological species, *Homo sapiens* can undergo genetic changes enabling him to adapt to new conditions. But biological (genetic) evolution is far too slow to permit effective adaptation to the rapid changes that commonly occur in the physical environment at the present time. Fortunately there are certain physiological and psychosocial adjustments that can be made without changing the genetic endowment. These adjustments are often stressful and result in disease, but as least they enable man to

survive and to function in environments that are potentially deleterious.

A century ago, especially under the influence of Lamarck and of the popular science inspired by Herbert Spencer, it was believed that the habits and tolerance engendered by exposure to a new environment were handed on to succeeding generations by biological inheritance, but this belief was erroneous. Many of the so-called "acquired characteristics" are culturally transmitted by the learning process, but most of them are not genetically inherited. Biologically, each generation starts in all essentials not from where its fathers left off, but from where they began.

There are limits furthermore, to the range of adaptation that man can achieve through acquired characteristics. In other words, it is unjustified to hope that man will eventually be able to adjust biologically to all the new conditions created by crowding and technological developments. The frontiers of the environmental changes that man can tolerate will be determined by the frontiers of his adaptive potentialities.

There is widespread awareness that almost any excessive level of pollution of air, water, and soil will have deleterious effects on man because his evolutionary past has not prepared him to cope with modern pollutants. But it is less commonly realized that quality and quantity of emotional stimuli are important in this regard. For lack of precise knowledge concerning such aspects of man's evolutionary nature, two analogies derived from the animal kingdom may help in visualizing the nature of the problem.

Even though the dog has been domesticated since the neolithic period, it still retains many of the behavioral characteristics of the wild species from which it was derived. Likewise, the cat still has a "need" to hunt, even when pampered and well fed in a city apartment. Civilized dog and civilized cat are outwardly very different from their primitive ancestors, but their essential dogness and catness have survived under the veneer of civilization.

In man, also, there persists certain deeply

ingrained psychological needs that have as much force as orthodox physiological requirements. The pathetic exodus to the "country" every weekend and whenever conditions permit obviously means more than the mere search for comfort and quiet. It is an expression of man's biological urge to maintain contact with the kind of environment in which he evolved. There is profound biological truth in the words of Paul the Apostle: "Man is of the earth, earthy." Granted that it is part of man's nature to make him behave at times like a Lucifer, more commonly like a Faust, and now and then like an angel, the fact is that biological man cannot remain healthy very long if he loses all contact with his earthy origins. The ancient Greeks symbolized this truth in the legend of Anteus who lost all his strength as soon as his two feet were simultaneously off the ground.

The knowledge of man's origins is admittedly very incomplete, but it is sufficient nevertheless to leave no doubt that his genetic evolution came almost to a standstill many thousands of years ago. Certain qualities of the environment are essential to his well-being and indeed his survival because he developed in association with them during his evolutionary past and acquired a dependence on them that he can hardly outgrow through genetic changes. In this light, the word recreation becomes much more meaningful when spelled re-creation. For reasons difficult to define scientifically, but nonetheless imperative, man needs now and then, and perhaps often, to reestablish direct contact with the natural environment in order to recover his physiological vitality and psychological sanity.

The Adaptability of Mankind and the Dangers of Adaptation

While the fundamental genetic traits of the species *Homo sapiens* are permanent and universal, it is obvious that the ways of life of human societies are constantly changing. They differ not only with time but from one area to the other because mankind is endowed with a wide range of adaptive potentialities. Through biological and social mechanisms of adaptation that are largely independent of genetic evolution, human beings have been able to establish themselves all over the earth. They can even survive, function, and multiply in environments that appear at first sight almost incompatible with life.

The experience of the historical period suggests that man has remained as adaptable as he was in the ancient past. The rapid increase in population during the 19th century occurred even though the proletariat was then living under conditions that most of us would find almost unbearable. In our own times, human beings are achieving some form of physiological and socio-cultural adjustment to the many forms of stress which they experience in industrial and urban environments. Many of them have managed to function in concentration camps and to survive the frightful ordeal of combat during the war!

Modern man is adapting to environmental pollution, to intense crowding, to deficient or excessively abundant diets, to monotonous, ugly, and depressing environments. All over the world, the most polluted, crowded, and traumatic cities are also the ones that have the greatest appeal and where population is increasing most rapidly. Furthermore, conditions that appear undesirable biologically do not necessarily constitute a handicap for economic growth. Great wealth is being produced by men working under high nervous tension in atmospheres contaminated with chemical fumes, or in crowded offices polluted with tobacco smoke.

Biologically speaking, adaptability is almost by definition an asset for survival. However, the very fact that man readily achieves some form of biological or social adjustment to many different forms of stress is paradoxically becoming a source of danger for his welfare and his future. The danger comes from the fact that this adjustment commonly results in pathological consequences; but these pathological effects are often delayed, and extremely indirect. Consequently it is usually very difficult to relate the damage caused by the environmental insults to its primary cause. Atmospheric pollution in the industrial areas of Northern Europe strikingly illustrates the distant dangers of human adaptability.

Ever since the beginning of the Industrial Revolution, the inhabitants of Northern Europe have been heavily exposed to many types of air pollutants produced by incomplete combustion of coal, and released in the fumes of chemical plants. Such exposure is rendered even more objectionable by the inclemency of the Atlantic climate. However, long experience with pollution and with bad weather has resulted in physiological reactions and in living habits that have adaptive values. This is proved by the fact that Northern Europeans accept almost cheerfully their dismal environment even though it appears almost unbearable to outsiders who experience it for the first time. Adaptive responses to environmental pollution are not peculiar to Northern Europeans. They occur all over the world in the heavily industrialized areas whose inhabitants function effectively despite constant exposure to irritating substances in the air they breathe. It would seem therefore that human beings can readily make an adequate adjustment to massive air pollution. In fact, Gerard Piel recently wrote in *The Bulletin of the New York Academy of Medicine* that there is "no clear connection . . . established between air pollution and health. Abel Wolman, the senior member of the current generation of municipal sanitation engineers, thinks it is principally an esthetic affliction. Wolman observes: 'If exhaust gases emitted by a Diesel bus had a fragrant aroma or, worse yet, led to physiological addiction, not many people would complain about traffic fumes.' "

Air pollution unfortunately is not only an esthetic affliction. Its acceptance results eventually in various forms of physiological suffering and economic loss. Even among persons who seem almost unaware of the fumes and smogs surrounding them, the respiratory tract continuously registers the insult of the various pollutants. The cumulative effects of such exposure commonly become manifest in the form of chronic bronchitis and other pulmonary diseases later in life.

Chronic pulmonary disease now constitutes the greatest single medical problem in Northern Europe, as well as the most costly, and it is becoming increasingly prevalent also in North America. There is good evidence, furthermore, that air pollution also increases the numbers of fatalities among persons suffering from vascular diseases as well as the incidence of various types of cancers. But the long and indefinite span of time that usually separates cause and effect makes it difficult to relate the manifestations of the pathological conditions to the primary physiological insults. It is for this reason, and for this reason only, that so far, "no clear connection has been established between air pollution and health."

One can almost take it for granted that unless social attitudes change, society will become adjusted to the levels of air pollution that do not have gross immediate nuisance value—even though this apparent adaptation will eventually result in much pathological damage and many social burdens. A similar situation will probably develop with regard to other aspects of the environmental pollution problem such as concern water.

Highly effective techniques have been developed to control the acute diseases that used to be caused by the microbial contamination of water. Microbial pathogens can be held in check by chlorination; organic matter content can be minimized by dilution, oxygenation, and other chemical techniques; and water can be made limpid by filtration. But there are no practical techniques for removing the inorganic materials and the various synthetic organic substances that tend to accumulate in water supplies as a result of industrial and domestic usage. Even though clear and free of pathogens, many sources of potable water now contain a variety of chemical substances that may have delayed toxic effects. This constitutes a new kind of threat to health which, though ill-defined, bids fair to become of increasing importance in the near future.

Allowing that the dangers created by modern technologies and environmental changes have been exaggerated, there are many facts which nevertheless justify anxiety for the future. One of the alarming aspects of environmental pollution is that despite all the new powers of science, or rather because of them, man is rapidly losing control over his environment. He introduces new forces at such a rapid rate and on such a wide scale that the effects are upon him before he has a chance to evaluate their consequences and can afford to change his course. For example, the photochemical conversion of hydrocarbons and of nitrous oxides into the toxic products responsible for the Los Angeles type of smog was recognized only after the California economy had become dependent on an excessive concentration of automobiles and industries. The absorption of radioisotopes in the human body became known only several years after the beginning of large scale nuclear testing. The resistance of synthetic detergents to bacterial decomposition began to cause trouble only after their universal use as household items had led to their accumulation in water supplies.

The dangers posed by environmental pollutants are rendered even more difficult to evaluate and to predict by the fact that these substances usually have indirect effects which manifest themselves through a complex chain of reactions. Most biologically active substances act indirectly through other members of the ecological system to which the organism belongs. For example, one of the unexpected findings to emerge from the Chariot project was that lichens have an extraordinary power to concentrate Strontium 90 from fallout. As lichens constitute the main source of food for reindeer, and as these animals in turn constitute an important food for Eskimos and other residents of the Arctic regions, it is obvious that the selective uptake of Strontium 90 by lichens greatly magnifies the hazards of fallout for human beings in the Arctic.

The preceding examples illustrate that immensely complex studies will be required to bring to light the pathological effects created on man by environmental pollutants and other biologically active substances. These studies will have to deal not only with immediate primary effects, but also with secondary effects involving structures and functions other than those primarily affected. Man is part of a complex ecosystem which responds as an integrated whole to each of the forces making up the total environment.

Needless to say, exposure to toxic agents is not a new experience for mankind. It became prevalent as soon as man escaped from the restraints of organic evolution and began civilized life. However, the problems posed by environmental stimuli and insults have acquired a critical urgency. In the past the rate of change was generally so slow that mankind, if not individual persons, could unconsciously make the adjustments necessary for survival. The genetic character of the population became progressively altered; phenotypic modifications helped many individuals to function effectively in their ecological niche; and especially, man learned to achieve better fitness to his milieu through technological and social innovations. In contrast, the rate of technological and social change is now so rapid that it affects almost simultaneously all parts of the world and all economic classes. There is no longer enough time for the orderly and successful operation of the unconscious adaptive processes that were the salvation of mankind in the past. Biologically and socially, the experience of the father is becoming almost useless to the son.

Nature as Human Creation

Many persons are becoming weary and frazzled by the rat race of constant change. Their cry goes up: "Stop the world. I want to get off." They urge that we go back to Arcadia, and live once more in the simple purity of Nature. But Arcadia has never existed except in dreams.

Throughout the ages, true enough, it has been widely believed that mankind could enjoy health and happiness by living in accordance with the ways of nature. This romatic ideal, however, is incompatible with the human condition. Man abandoned the ways of nature in the very process of becoming human, when he began to modify his environment by using fire, cutting down forests, tilling the land, opening roads, covering himself with clothing, building houses for shelter, etc. In fact, the word "nature" does not denote a definable and constant entity when applied to human life. There is not one *nature;* there are combinations of states and circumstances associated with the different ways of life.

Although man can exist only within an extremely narrow range of conditions determined by physiological exigencies, he has learned to manipulate the external world so as to render "natural" many kinds of environments exhibiting an astonishingly wide range of moods. Indeed the word nature means very different things to different men. It is a far cry, for example, from the equatorial jungles to the Great Barrens, from the Sahara Desert to the fogs of Newfoundland, from the depths of Arizona canyons to the high altitudes in the Peruvian Andes. Yet man has managed to live and sustain civilization in all these different places, all of them constituting an equal number of different types of nature. It could almost be said that there is no such thing as "nature" for man; there are only homes. For a particular person, almost everything is "unnatural" outside the home environment to which he has become adapted.

Adaptation, however, does not mean a static equilibrium between man and his environment. The ancient Greek concept of harmonious equilibrium with nature has a Platonic beauty, but it lacks the flesh and blood of real life. It fails to convey the creative quality of human existence.

Homo sapiens probably achieved his biological identity on the shores of some inland sea with a mild climate, but he has moved far from the place of his generic birth in the course of his countless adventures. For thousands of years the "nature" to which he had to adapt included the various climates and soils, plants and beasts, periods of plenty and of famine, and all other factors of his total environment, with which he came into contact and experienced during his long evolutionary journey. For modern man, the word "nature" must now include his urban and industrial creations.

The human saga has been the endless search for new environments; and each new move has required adaptive changes often painful and dangerous. The need for continuous adaptation with all the threats that it implies would disappear only if men could remain stable in a static environment. But in the world of real life men constantly change their ways, and places also change. The solution to environmental problems cannot be found, therefore, in a return to an imaginary Arcadia or in the search for a static Utopia. As man continues to modify nature and to create new civilizations, unexpected dangers will continuously arise. The most man can do is on the one hand to make sure that the environmental changes he brings about do not outstrip his adaptive potentialities, and furthermore to govern his adaptive responses in such a manner that they do not decrease the qualities of his life.

The present series of lectures is focused on air, water, and soil because of the general awareness that these essential environmental factors are most acutely threatened by modern civilization. But while the specific problems are fairly obvious, it is much more difficult to define the meaning of the phrase "improvement of the environment." The difficulty is that quality involves taste and perception, and where these are concerned, individual factors intervene that make consensus all but impossible. Walden Pond as a public bathing and boating place may serve the needs of a public park, but would have no appeal for Thoreau.

Allowing for all the individual differences with regard to quality of the environment, there are a few problems that are not controversial and demand immediate action.

The most immediate is to determine the maximum levels of contamination that can be tolerated from the health point of view. As already mentioned, toxicity must be measured not only in terms of obvious nuisance and of immediate deleterious effects, but also of delayed and indirect consequences.

Some of these indirect and delayed consequences will naturally affect physical health and will therefore be measurable objectively. But others will be concerned with more subtle qualities of human life and will require qualitative value judgments. Because man is so adaptable he can learn to tolerate murky skies, chemically treated waters, and lifeless land. In fact, he may soon forget that some of his most exhilirating experiences have come from direct contact with the freshness, brilliance, and rich variety of unspoiled natural phenomena. Unfortunately, perhaps, starless skies and joyless sceneries are not incompatible with the maintenance of life, or even with physical health. The only measure of their loss may be a progressive decadence in the quality and sanity of the human condition.

It may be difficult to justify economically the cost of maintaining the esthetic quality of the natural environment. The best that can be said on this score is to echo Oscar Wilde's scorn for those who know the price of everything and the value of nothing.

The most important values, unfortunately, are not definable in forms of any specific qualities or characteristics of nature. They involve man's relation to his total environment. The subtle complexity of this relationship has been poetically formulated by the English scientist and writer Jacquetta Hawkes in her book, *A Land*. She expressed in the following words her belief that England had enjoyed during the 18th century a high level of harmony between the human condition and the development of the countryside:

> Recalling in tranquility the slow possession of Britain by its people, I cannot resist the conclusion that the relationship reached its greatest intimacy, its most sensitive pitch, about two hundred years ago. By the middle of the eighteenth century, men had triumphed, the

land was theirs, but had not yet been subjected and outraged. Wildness had been pushed back to the mountains, where now for the first time it could safely be admired. Communications were good enough to bind the country in a unity lacking since it was a Roman province, but were not yet so easy as to have destroyed locality and the natural freedom of the individual that remoteness freely gives. Rich men and poor men knew how to use the stuff of their countryside to raise comely buildings and to group them with instinctive grace. Town and country having grown up together to serve one another's needs now enjoyed a moment of balance.

Appealing as it is, the picture of 18th century England drawn by J. Hawkes cannot serve as a model for solving 20th century environmental problems and reestablishing harmonious relationships between modern man and the external world. But it provides nevertheless a useful lesson for the future.

Our social philosophy is based on the assumption that nature must be "conquered" so that it can be exploited more effectively. However, conquest, or mastery, is not the only nor the best manner to deal with natural forces. Man should try instead to collaborate with them. Ideally, he should insert himself into the environment in such a manner that his ways of life and technologies make him once more part of nature.

Modern ecological studies leave no doubt that almost any disturbances of natural conditions are likely to have a large variety of indirect unfavorable effects because all components of nature are interrelated and interdependent. The different living forms are organized into a highly integrated web which is only as strong as the weakest of its constituent parts. Moreover this web is supported by the physical environment.

Man needs other human beings and must maintain harmonious relationships with the land; he is also indirectly dependent on other creatures—animals, plants, and microbes—with which he evolved and that form part of the integrated patterns of Nature. Unquestionably, he will destroy himself if he thoughtlessly and violently upsets the complex and delicate web of life of which he is a part. It is the interdependence of all living things, and their complex relation to the physical environment, that constitutes the scientific basis of conservation policies.

Conservation means much more than providing amusement grounds and comfortable camps for weekenders. Its ultimate goal should be to help man retain contact with the natural forces under which he evolved and to which he remains linked physiologically and emotionally. Like Anteus of Greek mythology, as already mentioned, man loses his strength when his two feet are off the earth.

Physical and mental well-being here and now are not, however, the only determinants of sanity and happiness. Man is not isolated in time; he needs to relate to the past and the future. In this light, we should give thought to what our own civilization will leave for the generations to come. Where are the monuments of today that will survive two thousand years hence? Where are the gardens, parks, and avenues of trees made of lasting species and planted in a noble style, that could become increasingly poetical and majestic with added centuries? Improving the environment should be a creative collaboration between man and nature.

Only two kinds of landscape are fully satisfying. One is primeval nature undisturbed by man; we shall have less and less of it as the world population increases. The other is one in which man has toiled and created through trial and error a kind of harmony between himself and the physical environment. What we long for is rarely nature in the raw; more often it is an atmosphere suited to human limitations, and determined by emotional aspirations engendered during centuries of civilized life. The charm of the New England or Pennsylvania Dutch countryside should not be taken for granted, as a product of chance. It did not result from man's conquest of nature. Rather it is the expression of a subtle process through which the natural environment was humanized, yet retained its own individual genius.

Air, water, soil—these simple words convey much more than material aspects of nature. They symbolize some of the deepest needs of human life because man is still of the earth, earthy.

Environmental planning has become necessary because man cannot be safely dissociated from the natural forces under which he evolved and that have molded his own unchangeable biological nature. Fortunately, the success of certain highly organized states like Sweden indicates that large scale and environmental planning is possible. The possibility to plan toward esthetic qualities is even more convincing. One needs only evoke the marvelous parks of Europe to realize the usefulness of a long range view in social improvements.

These parks were the creations of artists who had visualized the outcome of their efforts with that extraordinary sense which is peculiar to man, the imaginary vision of things to come. Several books by the great landscape architects of the 18th century show drawings of the European parks as they appeared at the time of their creation, and then a century later when the plantations had reached maturity. It is obvious that the landscape architects had composed the surfaces of water, of lawns and flowers to fit the silhouettes of trees and the masses of shrubbery not as they existed at the time, but as they were to become. And because men could thus visualize the future and plan for it centuries ago, millions of human beings enjoy today the great European parks and classical gardens.

In general, the phrase "social planning" evokes the thought of Utopias—conceived in terms of rigid social institutions. Such utopias are now out of fashion, in part as a result of the progressive erosion of the belief in rational progress and more justifiably because of the general awareness that static institutions are not viable. The regrettable consequence, however, is that 20th century intellectuals are now inclined to caricature the world and to replace utopias by antiutopias. Yet, utopian thinking presents a great intellectual challenge. To formulate alternatives for the present state of affairs is more difficult than simply to protest against evils.

An immense amount of money and effort will certainly be expended in the years to come on programs of environmental control. It is therefore essential that we try, collectively, to imagine the world in which we want to live. The great periods of history have always created such ideal images through their social philosophers and their artists.

Improving the environment should not mean only correcting pollution or the other evils of technological and urban growth. It should be a creative process through which man and nature continue to evolve in harmony. At its highest level, civilized life is a form of exploration which helps man rediscover his unity with nature. In the words of T. S. Eliot,

> We shall not cease from exploring,
> And the end of all our exploring
> Will be to arrive where we started
> And know the place for the first time.

SELECTION 52

SUMMARY AND PROSPECT

THOMAS R. DETWYLER

We have seen that nearly all of nature has been altered by man. From the broad collection of studies presented or referred to, some major points of summary or generalization can be drawn. It is of interest and benefit to attempt to identify both some recent major *trends* and some other *common characteristics* of environmental alteration by man. Environmental *goals* must be defined before we can hope to reverse our detrimental actions and their effects, although the problem of setting goals can only be touched upon here. Then, a brief discussion of *solutions* is in order.

Some Trends and Features of Man's Impact on Environment

The following points must be recognized as tentative because there are so few cases and such difficult problems of measurement. Or, perhaps, they might best be considered as working hypotheses against which evidence may be continually weighed to provide a continuous monitoring of the condition of man's environment. In other words, further study of the real world is needed to test and refine the following points of summary. Trends—recent changes through time—are considered first, because they suggest changes that may occur during the next few years.

Five major *trends* of man's recent impacts are identified:

1. *Increasing variety of impacts.* The number of ways that man affects the environment is proliferating. Nearly all the powerful pesticides have been developed since the Second World War, and new chemical contaminants are being invented yearly (e.g., PCBs). Techniques such as deep-well injection of wastes (Selection 31) are also of recent development.

2. *Intensification of impacts.* At any given place, the frequency and/or magnitude of a given kind of impact is probably increasing. We should expect more frequent and greater environmental catastrophes. Recall, for instance, the increasing severity in many large cities of noise (Selection 14) and of air pollution episodes (Selection 11) or the increasing damage to forests and crops by air pollutants (Selection 37).

3. *Geographical spreading of impacts.* Environmental problems that were once locally confined have become regional problems, and likewise many national problems have assumed international, even worldwide, importance. Air pollution (Selections 9 to 13) and contamination by DDT (Selection 39) are excellent examples.

4. *Increasing complexity and repercussions of impacts.* Numerous indirect effects of man's activities have been cited: changes in

climate (Selections 12 and 13), deterioration of soils (Selection 29), inadvertent triggering of earthquakes (Selection 31), damage to forests from air pollution (Selection 37), and unconscious alteration of animal evolution (Selections 49 and 50).

5. *Increasing per capita impact.* Compounding the effects of greatly expanding populations is a general increase in per capita consumption and environmental impact. This trend is even marked in the developed parts of the world, where per capita impacts are already large. For example, although the United States population is expected to increase by 33 percent between 1967 and 1980, the number of trucks and autos is expected to rise by 40 percent and the yearly consumption of fuel is predicted to increase by at least 50 percent.

Eight additional *common features* of man's alteration of environment may also be noted:

6. *Cities are nodes of greatest environmental impact.* This physical phenomenon parallels the historically important roles of cities as centers of cultural change and diffusion. The intensity of urban effects on climate (Selection 11) and hydrology (Selections 16 and 21) are noteworthy examples.

7. *Many environmental changes are irreversible or persistent for very long periods.* Examples of changes that probably are irreversible are several types of land subsidence (Selection 27), some induced earthquakes (Selection 31), and, of course, animal extinctions (Selections 41, 45, and 46). Other changes are persistent for long periods, even if perhaps ultimately largely reversible —for instance, contamination of ground water (Selection 18), lake eutrophication (Selection 19), some effects of herbicides (Selection 38), and ecological impacts of introduced organisms (Part 6). Reversibility may be claimed, but is not demonstrated, for a number of other effects. In other words, man is trading future environmental quality, and future management options, for present expedience.

8. *Man is simplifying and homogenizing the biological landscape.* Modern agricultural practices, such as monoculture (Selection 29) and pesticide usage (Selection 42), and biological impacts of introduced animals (Selection 34) reduce the complexity of ecosystems; subsequently, simplified systems are more likely to be upset. On a broad scale, the spread of organisms by man has broken down many distinctive qualties of floras and faunas that were previously well differentiated by virtue of their isolation (Part 6). Such biotic homogenization is partly countered locally, in disturbed habitats, by man's inadvertent creation of new hybrid organisms (Selection 48).

9. *Some organisms have greater power than man to adapt by evolution to environmental changes.* Insects especially, but also some other organisms with shorter life cycles than man's, have adapted biologically (genetically) to environmental conditions altered by man (Selections 49 and 50), whereas man biologically remains primarily a Pleistocene animal.

10. *Man's unique ability to adapt culturally to new environmental conditions, although great, may not be sufficient to compensate for new environmental demands on him as an organism.* Some environmental changes induced by man double back and harm him by exceeding his environmental tolerances. Cultural adaptations prevent some such consequences, but only postpone others—making human catastrophe greater when it does come (Selections 2 and 51).

11. *War is an important influence on environment.* A few effects of war are examined in Selection 38. Fortunately the most disastrous effects remain, primarily, potential —the threats of widespread nuclear explosions and radioactive contamination and the use of existing biological and chemical killers. We must also recognize the tremendous expenditure on war and armament, which is a loss of life, material, and finances to mankind. Environment is not only affected directly by the waging of war but also indirectly by the production of war goods and further by the diversion of attention and resources from environmental problems.

12. *Political control has been required to develop and maintain major environmental*

modifications. This has been true of past schemes (e.g., Mesopotamian agriculture, Selection 28), present projects (e.g., Soviet water transfer, Selection 23, and land reclamation, Selections 21 and 25), and prospective alterations (e.g., major canals, Selection 35). As a corollary, *inadvertent* modifications (such as pesticide usage) should be subject to governmental control, because of their frequently far-reaching effects. Most governments are sadly deficient on this count, however (e.g., see Selections 6, 15, 37, 39, and 46).

13. *The same few basic causes of environmental degradation underlie a wide spectrum of impacts.* These causes are extensively discussed in Part 2, but they merit brief retrospective consideration here.

a. *Ignorance.* A great many of the cases cited in this book portray environmental alterations that were initially unanticipated because of our ignorance about environmental systems (e.g., the LaPorte weather anomaly, Selection 12; land subsidence, Selection 27; and invading organisms, Selection 32). In some cases man's role remains poorly understood (e.g., global climatic change, Selection 13, and destruction of coral by the sea star, Selection 43). Each day new environmental repercussions about which we have been blind come to light.

b. *Attitude.* The idea that nature exists only to be used by man and that man will not be held accountable by nature pervades our treatment of environment. Witness our trust that an almost endless stream of wastes can be harmlessly absorbed by the environment—by air (Selections 9 and 10); by streams (Selection 15); by ground water (Selection 18); by the land (Selection 31); and by the biosphere (Selection 39). Numerous additional faults in man-environment relations are also attributable to man's attitudes, notably overemphasis of economic values and a lack of concern as long as consequences do not strike very close.

c. *Population growth.* It is axiomatic that an increase in the number of people increases the magnitude of man's environmental impact. Population growth is an implicit cause

of such changes as increased air pollution (Selection 8) and eutrophication of the Great Lakes (Selection 19). With a growth in population, man has expanded geographically and modified his habitat along the way (e.g., Selections 34 and 45).

d. *Technological development.* The long history of man's cultural development is also a history of increased power to alter environment (Selection 2). An expanding technology largely accounts for numerous modern impacts—landscape transfiguration by surface mining (Selection 26), a succession of forest and grassland exploitations (Selection 36), and contamination by exotic chemicals (Part 8), to name several. Frequently, technological "solutions" to man's problems ("technological fixes") have spawned new environmental repercussions (e.g., injection of wastes in deep wells has triggered earthquakes, Selection 31).

e. *Economics.* Lewis Mumford (1970) has aptly described the dual threat of technology and economics: "The aim of our technology is not to enhance life and to foster the processes of growth and effloresence, but to exploit power and bring ever-larger portions of the environment, and of human life, too, under more and more rigid and regimented modes of control. Expansion, magnification, multiplication, quantification, speed, turnover, profit, 'overkill'—these are the criteria of technical success. In the interests of an expanding economy, we have been settling for a contracted life in which no organic function will be tolerated unless it can be profitably attached to some corporate megamachine and made to conform to its requirements." Environmental assaults are promoted by capitalist and socialist economies alike (Selection 6). Economic exploitation clearly underlies many of the cases studied in this book.

f. *Synergism.* As the variety and degree of environmental impacts mount, the resulting effects will often be greater than the sum of the independent effects (see introduction to Part 2). Blooms of introduced aquatic weeds in nutrient-enriched waters is a good example (Selections 19 and 20).

Setting Environmental Goals

This book, then, presents a broadly painted picture of man's present impact on environment. Current exigency has demanded that concentration be on the present, although past impacts have also been noted (e.g., Selections 2, 28, and 45), particularly as they bear on the present, and prospective alterations have also been touched upon (e.g., Selection 35). Changes of all sorts are occurring so fast and unpredictably that most plans and predictions beyond the 1970s are unreliable. Yet we must develop some coherent views of what the world *should be*. We need goals toward which to strike in order to implement constructive environmental change.

I shall simply state that short-range goals (on a one- to five-year scale) must be developed, without suggesting their substance. Clearly, as René Dubos has said, "To formulate alternatives for the present state of affairs is more difficult than simply to protest against evils." Thus, recognition and protestation of our environmental ills are only necessary first steps.

Some people (including many existentialists) believe that future goals and events, even including such questions as the survival of the human species, are unimportant. Rather, they argue, the present quality of human life is paramount. This attitude has virtue for achieving needed change (if not for specifying what the change should be) because continued concern and action about *today's* conditions should improve *tomorrow's* environment. Preoccupation with tomorrow, on the other hand, too often brings delay today.

Man cannot afford delay. In a perceptive analysis of world crises John Platt (1969) has classified man's major problems by their estimated time to realization and their intensity. He believes that large-scale scientific mobilization may be the only way to avert many crises. Platt lists the problem of "ecological balance" as among man's most serious threats, with an estimated time of five to twenty years until crisis strikes with an intensity just short of total annihila-tion (assuming no major effort is made at anticipatory solution).

Some Basic Solutions

Even without specifying environmental goals, some general features of basic solutions can perhaps be identified. Regarding the threats identified by John Platt, W. D. McElroy (1970), director of the U.S. National Science Foundation, has noted that "The most serious problems listed present a common feature: they will be settled principally by political decision, by economic choice, and by the education of people. If such solutions are to be truly effective, however, they must be buttressed by sound knowledge and understanding. It is precisely at this point that the problems that confront us today differ from those that led to the massive scientific efforts during and following World War II. Thirty years ago much of the basic science was available and was used to devise urgently needed technologies; today, much of the requisite knowledge simply does not exist. We know far too little about the interactions that occur within any ecological system. We do not really understand the dynamics of our environment or the effects of technology upon it."

It is a truism that basic solutions reside in correcting basic causes. We must attack basic causes of environmental degradation, not just symptoms. The inadequacy of the "band-aid" approach is reinforced by the fact that it is deluding—often passing as a cure.

Hence, we must strive to (1) learn and communicate the nature of environmental problems, removing our ignorance, (2) adopt new attitudes which recognize man's mutual dependence on other components of the ecosystem, (3) reduce the human population, (4) abandon blind faith in, and blind use of, technology, and (5) restructure economic systems to *reduce* production and consumption as much as possible (while maintaining adequate capital supplies) and to hold producers responsible for environmental costs.

These basic solutions face great obstacles because they require that man change his life style—especially in developed countries. But this change is necessary. The myth of continued economic growth must be supplanted by an environmental ethic.

At a more personal level, what can you and I do? Numerous specific suggestions for action have been made elsewhere (e.g., Mitchell and Stallings, 1970; Marx, 1970). But worthwhile action is contingent upon understanding the environmental facts and proceeding wisely. Certain groups, which for years have shielded their despoilation of air, water, land, and life, are now trying to capitalize on the increasing public interest in environment to justify continued environmental damage. Industries, especially, are using public relations image-builders to construct façades of righteousness—let the concerned citizen beware!

Let me illustrate such delusions with a specific example. *Recycling* of limited resources is a concept which should generally be put into practice, breaking man's pervasive habit of production/consumption/disuse. However, the current appeal to recycle "noreturn" glass bottles is an environmental sham which unfortunately is being furthered by the glass industry and also by individuals and groups supposedly interested in the quality of our environment. Recycling involves the crushing and melting of once-used bottles and the making of new ones; recycling should not be confused with *re-use* (or refilling) of bottles. There are three major environmental factors involved in the production and consumption of glass bottles. First, the production of throw-aways clearly has provoked problems of solid waste disposal. We are running out of space to dump our solid wastes, which in the United States now average 2,000 pounds per person yearly. Tied to this problem is the more superficial one of "littering." Second, the consumption of raw materials needed to produce a bottle, only to be used once and then discarded, is extremely wasteful. Recognition is growing that we live in a world of finite, not infinite, resources—leading to advocation of recycling,

particularly of our most limited resources. These two factors, now acknowledged by many people, are leading to drives in the United States to recycle rather than throw away beverage bottles.

Unfortunately, a third factor of great importance is rarely recognized. We have limited resources of *energy*—witness the realistic fear of electrical power blackouts in the United States. It is folly to consume this precious energy to crush, melt, and remake glass bottles after only one use. This is the insidious, unrecognized factor. The average returnable deposit bottle is used about twenty times before being broken or discarded. The glass industry is delighted to develop rationale and muster widespread public support for increasing its production twentyfold.

The support given to glass companies by environmentalists only serves to delay a badly needed solution to all three of the environmental problems. The clearest answer is to vigorously promote re-use (not recycling) by legally requiring that all beverage bottles produced in the United States have a meaningful value in the market place, say 15 or 20 cents each. In addition, glass jars as well as bottles should be standardized, greatly reducing the number of shapes and sizes, to facilitate re-use. Such regulations would greatly reduce the present waste of glass and cut by 95 percent the consumption of raw materials and energy to make bottles.

It should also be pointed out that the new glass-recycling procedure does not really do much to alleviate problems associated with the first two environmental factors mentioned above. Without some greater value attached to throw-away bottles, the vast majority of people will simply continue to discard them. Of the 36 billion glass containers produced in the United States yearly (as of 1969), glass companies receive back no more than 2 to 3 percent for recycling. According to the president of the Glass Container Manufacturers' Institute (a euphemism for the disposable bottle lobby, sponsored by all the major glass manufacturers), even at their best "The collection centers will never get above 5 percent" (Bird, 1970). But even at this maximum rate, the collection would barely sustain the yearly growth of new glass containers, which is increasing at a rate of 5 percent annually. Further, the raw material recycling argument is specious in this case because of the great abundance of raw materials (other than energy) used to make glass. Silicon and oxygen, the primary constituents of glass, are the two most abundant elements in the earth's crust, accounting for 47 percent and 28 percent respectively of the crust's weight.

The glass recycling drive is an excellent example of Lord Acton's dictum that "Small reforms are the enemy of great reforms." By enlisting the aid of citizens interested in improved environmental quality, the glass container industry has obscured the needed basic reform, which is to greatly reduce *production* and the waste of energy. Similarly, with other ecological problems too much attention is given to palliatives such as slight reductions of pollutant emissions from internal combustion automobile engines when emphasis should instead be on new power sources, new systems of mass transit, and (in the meantime) on reducing mileage driven in existing vehicles.

All of us—but especially politicians, financiers, and industrialists—must begin to respond to qualities of society and environment, not solely to monetary profits and self-serving news stories. We desperately need to adopt additional value systems, not simply based on money or vanity but recognizing the worth of ecological balance and social harmony. There is frequent conflict between these sets of values. Donald Gray has discerned that economic systems generally aim to maximize short-term gains whereas ecologists strive to minimize longer-term liabilities.

I strongly suspect that several environmental catastrophes must, unfortunately, occur before basic problems are effectively attacked. Meanwhile, most individuals feel overwhelmed and powerless to affect constructive change and most institutions do nothing (except orate). In the final analysis it is we, as individuals, that must change. Our impact on environment results from the kind of people we are and the kinds of societies we have built.

References Cited

Bird, David. 1970. Bottle round-up and image-builder. *New York Times,* November 8, 1970, p. 64.

McElroy, W. D. 1970. A crisis of crises. *Science* 167:9.

Marx, Leo. 1970. American institutions and ecological ideals. *Science* 170:945–952.

Mitchell, J. G., and C. L. Stallings. 1970. *Ecotactics: The Sierra Club handbook for environmental activists.* New York: Pocket Books. 288 pp.

Mumford, Lewis. 1970. Survival of plants and man. Pp. 221–235 in *Challenge for survival; Land, air, and water for man in megalopolis,* ed. by Pierre Dansereau. New York and London: Columbia University Press.

Platt, John. 1969. What we must do. *Science* 166: 1115–1121.

GLOSSARY
OF ENVIRONMENTAL TERMS

Acanthurid. A fish of the large family Acanthuridae, known as surgeonfish because of the hinged "knife" in a groove on the dorsal surface.

Acheulean, or Acheulian, culture. A culture of the Lower Paleolithic period characterized by bifacial stone tools. Named after an archeological site near Saint-Acheul, France, occupied during the second glacial period in Europe.

Acrolein. A toxic liquid which has an acrid odor and irritating vapors.

Adaptive radiation. Diversification of a group of organisms into subgroups as it evolves and spreads in various directions and into various environments it encounters; or, the phenomenon of distantly related organisms evolving similar ecological tolerances, and hence occupying similar niches in similar habitats.

Adiabatic lapse rate. The rate of temperature change with change in elevation of a mass of air without the addition or subtraction of heat. The change results entirely from compression or expansion of the air.

Aggradation. The building up of land by deposition of material, such as by the deposition of detritus by streams where they flow onto a surface of lower gradient.

Albedo. Whiteness; or the proportion of incident light upon a surface or body which is again diffusely reflected from it.

Aldehydes. A class of chemical compounds intermediate between alcohols and acids; most are colorless, volatile fluids with suffocating odors.

Aldrin. A white insecticide containing a chlorinated derivative of naphthalene, $C_{12}H_8Cl_6$. It is especially effective against pests resistant to DDT.

Allele. Either of a pair of genes located at a certain position (locus) on both chromosomes of a pair of chromosomes. If one allele is dominant over the other, it largely determines the character conveyed by the pair of genes.

Allopatric species. Species of organisms living in different geographical areas.

Alluvium. Sediments transported by streams and deposited on land.

Amphipod. An animal having feet for walking and feet for swimming.

Anabolic. Refers to constructive metabolism; opposed to catabolic metabolism.

Anadromous. Fish ascending rivers from the ocean at certain seasons for breeding.

Anaerobic. Living or active in the absence of free oxygen.

Anthropocentric. Considering man to be the central or most significant part of the universe.

Anticline or anticlinal fold. An arched fold of stratified rock in which the sides slope downward in opposite directions from a crest or central axis.

Anticyclone. A mass of air of higher atmospheric pressure than that in adjacent areas, which circulates clockwise in the northern hemisphere, counterclockwise in the southern. An anticyclone commonly advances at 20 to 30 m.p.h. and brings cool, dry weather.

Aposematic. Relating to features of an organism, such as coloration or structure, which serve to ward off enemies.

Aquifer. A porous soil or geological formation in which water may move for long distances and which readily yields ground water to springs and wells.

Aquitard. A geological formation which retards the movement of ground water.

Arthropoda. A phylum of invertebrate animals with jointed limbs and a body divided into similar segments; the body generally is covered with a chitinous shell. Includes crustaceans, insects, and spiders and related forms.

Artificial selection. The process of breeding plants or animals to obtain qualities desired by man.

Atavism. Recurrence in an organism of a form found in ancestors more remote than the parents; usually produced by recombination of ancestral genes.

Atmosphere. The gaseous envelope of air surrounding the earth, commonly including suspended small solid particles.

Atoll. A coral reef rising above the ocean as a low ring-shaped coral island around a shallow lagoon.

Aurochs. The European bison (*Bos bonasus*), or wisent, which is now nearly extinct. It is slightly larger than the American bison and has a more compressed body and less shaggy hair in front.

Autotomize. To cast off, or cause to cast off, an organ, as some animals do when handled or disturbed.

B.P. Before present; commonly used when expressing dates determined by radiocarbon dating, in which case the year 1950 is used as the base (or "present").

Bathymetric. Relating to the measurement of depths of water in the ocean or in lakes.

Benthic. Of, pertaining to, or occurring on the bottom of a sea or lake.

Bentonite. A moisture-absorbing rock composed mainly of clay minerals, formed by the decomposition of volcanic ash.

Bioassay. Determination of the character and strength of a drug or other substance by studying its effects on a laboratory organism.

Biocide. Any agent that kills organisms.

Biomass. The total weight of all living matter in a particular habitat or area.

Biosphere. That part of the world which consists of living things; also, sometimes applied generally to the portion of the earth and atmosphere in which life can exist.

Bocage (or boscage). A wooded landscape broken by patches of shrubs, heath, or small fields.

Bradycardia. An abnormally slow heart rate; usually less than sixty beats per minute in man.

Carbamates. Selective nonpersistent alkaloid insecticides that act through cholinesterase inhibition; include carbaryl or Sevin.

Carbon monoxide. A colorless, odorless, and very toxic gas, CO, with a great toxic potential as an air pollutant in cities, where levels up to 120 ppm have been found.

Carcinogen. A substance that produces cancer.

Catabolic. Pertaining to destructive metabolism involving release of energy.

Celsius. Of or pertaining to a temperature scale on which 0 degrees is the freezing point of water and 100 degrees is the boiling point of water (under normal atmospheric pressure). Commonly called "centigrade." Abbreviated C. The formula for converting a Celsius temperature to Fahrenheit is $C° = 5/9(F° - 32)$.

Cenozoic. The latest era of geologic time, including the Tertiary and Quaternary periods, and characterized by the appearance of mammals and the rapid evolution of birds, grasses, and higher flowering plants. The Cenozoic era began about 70 million years ago.

Cfs. Cubic feet per second, a common measure of water flow.

Chaparral. A dense thicket of shrubs or small trees with thorny or stiff branches or leaves.

Chlordane. A chlorinated hydrocarbon (see) insecticide, $C_{10}H_6Cl_8$. It is a viscous, volatile, amber-colored liquid.

Chlorinated hydrocarbon (or organochlorine) insecticides. Synthetic organic poisons, containing chlorine, hydrogen, and carbon. Since they are highly stable and fat-soluble, they tend to be recycled through food chains, thereby affecting nontarget organisms. They kill by attacking the nervous system. Members include DDT, aldrin, dieldrin, endrin, chlordane, heptachlor, toxaphene, and BHC.

Chlorotic. Refers to a plant that has chlorosis

(the condition of plants when chlorophyll fails to develop); most such plants are yellowish or white and poorly developed.

Cladocera. An order of small crustaceans, the water fleas.

Coelenterata. Radially symmetrical invertebrate animals lacking a true body cavity (including jellyfishes, sea anemones, and corals).

Coliform. Relating to the bacterium *Escherichia coli* and other bacterial species commonly found in the human large intestine, and whose presence in the outside environment usually indicates contamination by human waste.

Commensals. Two or more kinds of organisms that live together, with one or several benefiting and without injury to any.

Concretion. A solid or concrete mass of matter formed by coalescence or cohesion.

Conspecific. Pertaining to individuals or populations belonging to the same species.

Convection (atmospheric). The upward movement of air heated at and near the earth's surface, the warmer air being less dense than adjacent air (which flows downward by gravity to replace it).

Coppice. A grove of trees which are periodically cut, with new stems growing vegetatively from the base into a new crop.

Coregonids. Bony fishes of the family Coregonidae, including whitefishes, ciscoes, and chubs.

Coriolis effect. The deflection of a body in motion (such as currents of air and water) due to the earth's rotation; such deflection is to the right in the northern hemisphere and to the left in the southern.

Culm bank. A heap of slack or refuse from coal screenings.

Cultch. Materials (such as oyster shells and pebbles) dumped into the sea to furnish places of attachment for the larval stage of the oyster (or any other shellfish).

Curie. A unit of radioactivity, specifically the amount of a radionuclide that undergoes 3.7×10^{10} disintegrations per second.

Cyclodiene insecticides. A subgroup of the chlorinated hydrocarbons (see), including chlordane, heptachlor, aldrin, dieldrin, and endrin.

Deciduous. Refers to the losing of parts, such as leaves of trees, at the end of the growing season. Semideciduous: losing some but not all of such parts seasonally.

Deflocculate. To disperse, or break apart, compound masses or aggregations of particles.

Diaptomid. A crustacean of the common freshwater genus *Draptomus*.

Diastrophism. The processes (including bending, folding, and breaking) by which the earth's crust is deformed.

Diatom. Unicellular or colonial algae having cell walls impregnated with silica that persists as a skeleton after death; forms a large proportion of the plankton in both freshwater and seawater.

Dieldrin. A white crystalline insecticide, $C_{12}Cl_6H_8O$, produced by oxidation of aldrin. See chlorinated hydrocarbon group, to which dieldrin belongs.

Dioecious. Pertaining to the occurrence of male reproductive organs in one individual and female in another.

Diurnal. Daily; recurring every day; or, active during the daytime rather than at night.

Echinoderm. A member of the phylum Echinodermata; radially symmetrical coelomate marine animals (such as starfishes and sea urchins).

Ecology. Study of the relationships between organisms and their environments (see p. 4).

Ecosystem. The organisms of a locality, together with their functionally related environment, considered as a unit.

Edaphic. Of or pertaining to soil, especially with regard to its influence on plants and animals.

Eddy. A current of air or water running contrary to main current, especially one having a rotary or whirlpool motion.

Elastic deformation. A nonpermanent deformation, which after the load is released returns to its original configuration.

Elver. A young eel that is found chiefly along shores or in migration up freshwater drainages.

Endemic. Belonging or native to a given geographic region; not introduced or naturalized.

Endothermic. Characterized by or formed with absorption of heat.

Endrin. A very toxic broad-spectrum insecticide and rodenticide, $C_{12}Cl_6H_8O$. See chlorinated hydrocarbon group.

Enteric bacteria. Bacteria that inhabit the intestines, including organisms that may cause infectious diseases such as typhoid.

Environment. The aggregate of external conditions that influence the life of an individual or population, specifically the life of man. Environment ultimately determines the quality and survival of life.

Epicenter. The point on the earth's surface directly above the focus of an earthquake.

Epidemiology. The science that deals with the incidence of disease in a population (as of animals or plants) rather than in a single individual.

Esker. A long, narrow, and often serpentine ridge of glacial drift deposited between walls of stagnant ice by a stream.

Estuary. That portion of a stream near the mouth where the river current meets the tide.

Ethology. The scientific study of animal behavior.

Ethylene. A colorless flammable gas which may damage plants at very low concentrations (e.g., orchids at 0.005 ppm).

Euryhaline. An organism that can tolerate a wide range of salinity.

Eustatic. Relating to worldwide and simultaneous changes of sea level.

Eutrophic. Refers to lakes rich in dissolved nutrients but having an oxygen deficiency (at least seasonally) in the bottom layers of water.

Feral. Refers to plants or animals that are no longer cultivated or domesticated and revert to a wild state.

Ferroalloy. A mixture or alloy of iron and one or more other elements, such as silicon or manganese, used for making alloy steel.

Focus (earthquake). The source of elastic earthquake waves, or true center of an earthquake.

Gene pool. The total genetic information possessed by a given reproducing population.

Genetic drift. Random fluctuation of gene frequencies, which has most evident effects in small populations.

Genotype. A group of individuals possessing the same genetic constitution.

Genus (plural: genera). A group of closely related plant or animal species, marked by one or more common characteristics; each genus is a taxonomic subdivision of a family.

Geomorphology. Study of the form and development of the earth, especially its surface or landscape.

Geosphere. The solid, nonliving portion of the earth, as contrasted with the atmosphere,
hydrosphere, and biosphere; also called lithosphere.

Geostrophic wind. A horizontal wind whose direction and speed are determined by a balance between the force due to the earth's rotation (the Coriolis effect) and the pressure-gradient force.

Geothermal. Of or pertaining to the heat of the earth's interior.

Gravity flow (in atmosphere). Winds due to the effect of gravity, in which dense, cooler air flows downward along a slope (because of radiation cooling at higher elevations); sometimes called katabatic winds.

Greenhouse effect. The effect seen in a garden greenhouse, in which short-wave solar radiation penetrates glass and water vapor but back-radiation from the ground (being of long wavelength) is blocked by the glass and water vapor, thus raising air temperature in the greenhouse. The earth's atmosphere acts similarly, with back-radiation being largely absorbed by water vapor, carbon dioxide, and ozone.

Groin (also groyne). A shore-protection structure built out at an angle to trap sand and reduce erosion by currents, tides, and waves.

Ground water. Water beneath the surface of the ground that is in a saturated zone.

Habitat. The environment of the place that is inhabited by an organism or a population of organisms.

Hectare. A metric unit of area equal to 10,000 square meters or 2.471 acres.

Heptachlor. A solid insecticide, $C_{10}H_5Cl_7$, similar to chlordane. See chlorinated hydrocarbons, to which heptachlor belongs.

Herbicide. An agent, often a chemical, used to kill plants.

Herbivore. An animal that eats plants (e.g., sheep).

Holarctic. The biogeographic region that includes the Nearctic (or temperate and arctic North America and Greenland) and the Palaearctic (or Europe, the northern parts of Africa, the Arabian Peninsula, and Asia north of the Himalayas).

Holocene. The later of the two geologic epochs comprising the Quaternary period; i.e., the time period from the close of the Pleistocene or Glacial epoch (about 10,000 years ago) through the present; synonymous with Recent.

Homeostasis. A tendency toward internal equilibrium in the bodies of higher animals by means of coordinated physiological response of its parts to any disturbing stimulus.

Homozygous. Having identical alleles at corresponding loci on chromosomes, and therefore breeding true to the characteristics determined by that pair of alleles or genes.

Humate. A salt or ester of a humic acid, obtained from humus during the decomposition of organic matter in soils.

Hybrid. The offspring from parents having different genotypes; especially any organism resulting from a cross between parents of different varieties or species.

Hydrocarbon. Any of numerous organic compounds containing only carbon and hydrogen (including, for example, benzene and methane); commonly found in petroleum, natural gas, and coal and as products of the partial combustion of these substances.

Hydrocoral. A colonial marine hydrozoan of the order Milleporina or the order Stylasterina, having a limestone skeleton and resembling the true corals.

Hydrogen fluoride. A gaseous air pollutant toxic to plants.

Hydrogen sulfide. An occasional air contaminant with a smell like rotten eggs. Acute episodes can kill humans (twenty-two died at Poza Rica, Mexico, in 1950).

Hydrograph. A graph of the level of water (as in a stream or well) or the rate of flow of water through time.

Hydrologic cycle. A complex sequence of conditions through which water passes, including the condensation and falling of atmospheric water as precipitation upon land or water surfaces and evaporation back into the atmosphere.

Hydrosphere. The water portion of the earth (including water vapor in the air), as distinguished from the solid, gaseous, and living parts.

Hydrostatic pressure. The pressure exerted by water at rest, at any point within the water body; as, in the case of ground water, the pressure caused by the weight of water in the same zone of saturation above a given point.

Hygroscopic. Readily attracting or absorbing moisture from the atmosphere.

Hypolimnion. The lower layer of water (below the thermocline) in a lake or sea; it is stagnant and of nearly uniform temperature except during the period of overturn.

Indigenous. Native; living naturally in an area, not introduced from outside the particular region or environment.

Indole. A white crystalline compound, C_8H_7N, that is found especially in coal tar and used as a flavoring.

Interfluve. The land area between adjacent streams.

Inversion. A meteorological state in which air temperature rises with increasing altitude (instead of falling as usual), holding down surface layers of air and their pollutants.

Isohaline. A line drawn on a chart or map of an area, indicating points of equal salinity.

Isohyets. A line on a map connecting points receiving equal rainfall during a stated period.

Isopleth (or isarithm). A line on a map connecting points at which given variables have the same numerical value (e.g., topographic contour lines).

Isopod. Any crustacean of the large order Isopoda; these small animals have seven pairs of legs and flattened bodies.

Isotopes. Any of two or more forms of a chemical element with the same number of protons in the nucleus but with a different number of neutrons. Different isotopes of the same element thus have the same atomic number but different atomic weights.

Laterite. A red, highly weathered residual soil characteristic of moist tropical and subtropical regions, rich in oxides of iron and aluminum.

Limnology. The scientific study of physical, chemical, and biological conditions in lakes, ponds, and streams.

Lindane. An insecticide and herbicide consisting of at least 99 percent of the white, water-insoluble powder, $C_6H_6Cl_6$.

Littoral. Relating to or taking place on or near the shore.

Locus. The place occupied in a chromosome by a gene.

Madreporaria. An extensive order of corals known as stony corals that produce an ectodermal calcareous skeleton.

Manioc. Also called "cassava"; a tropical American plant with a large, starchy root used as a staple food in the tropics. Tapioca is also made from the plant's roots.

Megalithic. Relating to the huge stones used by prehistoric man in various types of monuments.

Megalops. A larva or larval state of some crustaceans, such as crabs, in which the eyes are large.

Meiotic malorientation. Process of two sympatric populations interbreeding to produce adaptively inferior individuals because their genetic constitutions are not similar.

Mercaptans. Odorous sulfur compounds produced as a gaseous pollutant by the kraft pulp industry.

Meristic. Divided into parts or segments.

Metempsychosis. The transmigration or passing of souls at death into another animate body.

Methane. CH_4, often called marsh gas; an odorless, flammable gas that is the major constituent of natural gas. It develops in nature from decomposing organic matter.

Midden. A refuse heap, especially of a primitive culture.

Moa. Any large flightless bird of the genus *Dinornis*, native to New Zealand but extinct for several centuries.

Monoculture. The cultivation of a single crop (such as corn or wool) to the exclusion of other land uses.

Morphology. The study of the form and structure, and often including their origin, of organisms or earth features (such as landforms: geomorphology).

Morphometry. A field of geomorphology or limnology that deals with morphologic measurements and analyses of various earth features, such as landforms, stream systems, and lakes.

Mustelid. A small carnivorous mammal of the family Mustelidae, including the mink, otter, and fisher.

Mutation. A basic inheritable change in a gene or in the structure or number of chromosomes.

Myxomatosis. A severe disease of rabbits caused by a virus and marked by fever, inflammation, and often death.

Natural selection. The agent of evolutionary change by which the organisms possessing advantageous adaptations in a given environment produce more offspring than those lacking such adaptations.

Nearctic. Of the biogeographic region that includes Greenland and the northern parts of North America.

Nektonic species. Aquatic animals that swim essentially independently of waves and water currents, ranging in size from microorganisms to whales.

Niche (ecological). The total functional relationships between an organism or population and its environment; or, the site within a habitat that is occupied by an organism and that provides its needs.

Nitrogen oxides. The major air pollutants in this group are nitric oxide and nitrogen dioxide, for which numerous kinds of damage to health have been found (but at concentrations considerably above ambient levels).

Oil shale. Fine-grained shale impregnated with natural hydrocarbons from which crude oil may be produced by distillation.

Olefin compounds. Open-chain hydrocarbons containing at least one double bond.

Oligotrophic. Refers to lakes with a low accumulation of dissolved nutrient salts and usually with considerable dissolved oxygen in the bottom waters (owing to a low organic content).

Ore. A mineral or rock from which a constituent of value, especially a metal, can be profitably extracted.

Organochlorine insecticide. See chlorinated hydrocarbons.

Organophosphates. A diverse group of nonpersistent synthetic chemical poisons which act chiefly through breaking down nerve and muscle response; includes parathion, malathion, and schradan.

Ozone. A triatomic molecule of oxygen, O_3, that is generally unstable because of its high oxidizing power (which is second only to fluorine); it is produced in the air by photochemical reaction of nitrogen dioxide, hydrocarbons and oxygen, by discharge of electricity, and by action of ultraviolet radiation on oxygen.

Palaearctic. Of or relating to the biogeographic region that includes Europe, Asia north of the Himalayas, northern Arabia, and northern Africa.

Paleoecology. The study of relationships between ancient organisms and their environments.

Palynology. The study of pollen and spores, particularly the analysis of the different fossil kinds in a deposit or rock; widely used to interpret past environmental conditions.

Passerine. Refers to the largest order of birds, including more than half of all living birds (chiefly songbirds).

Pathogen. Any organism that produces disease.

Periglacial. Pertains to conditions bordering a frozen or ice-covered region (as a glacier), especially with regard to climatic or geological processes.

Permafrost. Perennially frozen ground.

Peroxyacyl nitrates (PAN). A component of photochemical smog and the primary plant toxicant of "smog" type injury; field levels of 0.01 to 0.05 ppm will injure sensitive plants. Causes eye irritations and other health effects in man.

Phenotype. The characters of an organism due to the interaction of genotypic characters and the environment; or, a group of individuals with the same external appearance.

Philoprogenitive. Producing abundant offspring; prolific.

Photochemical. Pertains to the permanent, chemical effects of the interaction of radiant energy (especially light) and matter.

Phreatophyte. A plant with very long roots that reaches the water table and hence obtains water from the ground water supply.

Phylogeny. The evolution of a group of organisms as distinguished from the development of the individual organism.

Physiognomy. The external aspect or outward appearance of anything, particularly as regards form.

Phytophagous. Refers to animals that feed on plants; i.e., herbivorous.

Phytotoxicant. Poisonous to plants.

Picloram. An extremely toxic plant killer which persists almost indefinitely in soil (an herbicidal analog of DDT, environmentally); contained in Dow's Tordon and in the agent "white" used in Vietnam.

Pico-. One trillionth, 10^{-12}.

Pisciculture. The culture or growing of fish.

Plankton. The marine or freshwater plants and animals that drift with the water containing them or that can swim only weakly; chiefly minute, as diatoms and protozoans.

Pleistocene. The geological epoch preceding the Recent (or Holocene) in the Quaternary period which began about 1 million years ago and lasted until about 10,000 years ago; also called the Glacial epoch and the Ice age.

Polder. A flat tract of land, especially in The Netherlands, lying below the level of the sea or nearby rivers; such lands have been reclaimed by draining and are protected from inundation by dikes or dams.

Pollution. The process of contaminating a medium (air, water, or soil) with impurities to a level of quality that is less desirable.

Polyp. One of two kinds of individuals occurring in many species of coelenterates; it has a cylindrical, elongated body, usually attached at one end and bearing a mouth surrounded by tentacles at the other.

Potable water. Drinkable; suitable for drinking.

Progradation. The process of outward building, into the sea, of a coastline by the deposition of sediment.

Propagule. Any reproductive structure that is capable of developing into an adult organism, such as some buds, shoots, and seeds.

Pyrite. A mineral, FeS_2, which is an important ore of sulfur and looks metallic.

Quaternary. The geologic period beginning at the end of the Tertiary and extending to (and including) the present; it is subdivided into Pleistocene and Holocene (or Recent) epochs.

Radioactivity. The property of certain chemical elements of spontaneously emitting radiation from unstable atomic nuclei. The emitted radiation, including gamma rays, may damage organisms.

Radiocarbon dating. The determination of the age of a substance by the proportion of radiocarbon (the isotope carbon-14) in the carbon it contains. Once an organism dies its radiocarbon breaks down at a known half-life, which allows the determination of ages between several hundred and about 50,000 years.

Radiosonde. An instrument with a radio transmitter which is carried up in the air, usually by balloon, to collect and broadcast meteorological data, such as temperature, pressure, and humidity.

Rebound. The elevation of a part of the earth's surface during or following the removal of an overlying load or the refilling of an underground cavity.

Recessive gene. A gene that has no effect on the appearance of an organism unless it is homozygous (i.e., the dominant gene is not present).

Refractories. Any material, such as silica and alumina, that does not become physically deformed or chemically altered at high temperatures.

Relative humidity. The ratio of the actual amount of water vapor present in a given volume of air to the quantity which would be present when saturated.

Relict. Not functional but originally adaptive; or, geographically, living as a remnant in an area isolated from the main distributional area or as a surviving remnant of an otherwise extinct group of organisms.

Riparian. Living or located at the bank of a water course, such as a river or a stream.

Riprap. A foundation or wall of broken rock thrown together irregularly, as to protect embankments from erosion; or the rock used for such purposes.

Rotenone. A crystalline compound, $C_{23}H_{22}O_6$, that is derived from certain tropical plants and used as an insecticide; it is only slightly toxic to man and quickly breaks down into relatively harmless compounds.

Sauger. A small freshwater fish of North America, of the pike perch group.

Savanna. A grassland with scattered trees or shrubs.

Scree or talus. A heap of coarse rock debris at the base of a cliff; or (of scree only), a sheet of coarse debris on a mountain slope.

Sessile. Permanently attached; stationary; or on a base without a stalk.

Silviculture. The branch of forestry that concerns the establishment, growth, and care of forest trees.

Sonic boom. A loud sound produced by the shock wave of an aircraft traveling at supersonic speed; the shock wave is continuously produced, but sounds explosive at any single point on the ground.

Species. A population of animals or plants whose members have substantially the same structure, habits and range, normally interbreed, and are identified by a systematic biologist under the same binomial name.

Spinney. A thicket or small grove of trees with undergrowth.

Spit. A small point of land or shoal projecting into a body of water from the shore.

Stenohaline. Unable to endure wide variation in salinity of the water.

Strand coast. A prograded plain (see "progradation") continuous along a shoreline for a considerable distance.

Strike slip. The component of a fault displacement that is parallel with the fault strike.

Struthious. Of or resembling ostriches and related birds.

Sudd or sedd. Material composed of decaying vegetable matter (especially roots) matted together with earth, commonly having a consistency of peat.

Sulfur dioxide. A heavy colorless gas, SO_2, that is very toxic to plants and fairly toxic to man; it is produced by burning coal and by smelting and other industrial processes.

Sulfuric acid. A corrosive acid, H_2SO_4; often produced from sulfur dioxide.

Swale. An elongated slight depression in nearly level or gently rolling land; a swale may be wet or marshy but is normally without flowing water.

Sylvatic plague. A plague spread by rodents and their fleas.

Sympatric populations. Applied to populations, events, or distributions occupying coinciding or overlapping areas.

Synonymy. Equivalent scientific names that have been used to designate a species or other taxonomic group.

Synoptic meteorology. The subject dealing with analysis of numerous weather observations taken over a large area and synthesized into recognizable weather patterns.

Taiga. A Russian word applying to the swampy coniferous forest region of subarctic regions.

Tectonic. Of or relating to physical forces that deform the earth's crust or designating the rock structure resulting from such deformation.

Thermal upslope flow (in atmosphere). Winds due to the heating near the ground of air which rises and flows upslope, as in many mountain valleys during the day; sometimes called anabatic winds.

Thermocline. A layer in a thermally stratified body of water separating an upper warmer zone from a lower colder zone.

Therophyte. An annual plant; i.e., a plant that completes its life cycle within one season and survives an unfavorable period as a dormant seed.

Troglodyte. A prehistoric cave dweller.

Tropopause. The boundary between the troposphere (or lower two-thirds of the atmosphere, in which most weather occurs) and the stratosphere, at an altitude of about 10 km (but varying with latitude and season); below the tropopause temperature generally decreases with increasing altitude, whereas above the tropopause temperature either varies slightly or increases with altitude.

Trypanosome. A flagellate protozoan of the genus *Trypanosoma*, parasitic in the blood of vertebrates and in insects, which transmit them. Trypanosomes cause sleeping sickness and other diseases in man, horses, and cattle in Africa.

Turbidity. Refers to the amount of sediment suspended in a fluid (usually water); muddiness.

Turion. A scaly shoot of some water plants that becomes detached, overwinters, and may develop into a new plant.

Viviparous. Refers to an animal that produces living offspring instead of eggs (e.g., nearly all mammals); or, the production by plants of bulbils or small plants instead of (or in addition to) seeds.

Würm. The fourth and last stage of Pleistocene glaciation in Europe.

Xeric. Refers to a dry environment or to biological characteristics supposedly adapted to such conditions.

Xerothermic period. A historical period of warm-dry climate; there has been at least one such period during the Holocene.

INDEX

Page references in **boldface** indicate photographs.

Abrostola tripartita, 671
ABS (*see* Alkyl benzene
  sulfonate)
Acanthaster planci (*see* Sea star)
Accidental spills on highways,
  423–424
Accidents, oil pollution from,
  295–297, 299–300
Accipiter nisus, decline related
  to chlorinated hydrocarbon
  insecticides, 575
Acidity:
  of mine spoil, 362
  of water from mining opera-
    tions, 362–363
Acrolein used to control acquatic
  weeds, 259
Acton, Lord, 700
Adams, Robert M., 383
Adaptation of animals in do-
  mestication, 640–652
Adaptation of bird feet, 644
Adaptation of man to environ-
  ment, 19–20, 684–694
Adaptation to man's impacts, 696
Adaptive variations in natural
  animal populations, 643–644
Adenostoma, 664
Adriatic Sea, 327
  sedimentation in, 338
AEC (*see* U.S. Atomic Energy
  Commission)
Aechmophorus occidentalis, re-
  productive decline related to
  DDT residues, 561
Aerosols (*see* Particulate matter)

Africa, 621
  papyrus in waterways, 258
  pattern of prehistoric extinc-
    tion in, 619–621
  population growth, 38
  salvinia in, 252–254
  spread of water hyacinth in,
    248–250
African malaria mosquito introduced to Brazil, 449–450
Agasicles (*see* Alligatorweed
  beetle)
Agricultural technology, 53
Agricultural terraces, 326–327
Agriculture:
  in California, problem of
    salinization, 384
  clearing of forests for, 511–515
  conversion of land from, in
    U.S., 395
  by early man, 13–15
  effects on grasslands, 516–518
  introduction of organisms for,
    445
  medieval, 31
  in Mesopotamia, problem of
    salt and silt, 383–394
  neolithic, 655
  sedimentation resulting from,
    326–327
  U.S. land in, 403
Air (*see* Atmosphere)
Air Conservation Commission, 81
Air pollution, cost of, in U.S., 55
Air pollution meteorology,
  applied, 106–108

Air quality standards in U.S., 96
Aircraft noise, 175–176, 179–181
Albedo of earth, changes in, 170
Albrecht, William A., 395
Aldehydes, as atmospheric
  pollutants, 87
Aldrin-resistance, 675
Alewife, **190,** 588, 594, 598–599,
  602–608
Algae:
  blooms: in estuaries, 281
    in Lake Erie, 233
    related to selective poisoning,
      561
  growth stimulation by ferti-
    lizers, 200–201
  heat relations, 222–223
  in urban streams, 207
Alkyl benzene sulfonate (ABS),
  271
Alligatorweed beetle, as bio-
  control agent, 262
Amaranths, grain, 657
Amazon River:
  water hyacinth in, 250
  water projects on, 303
Amenities in the hydrologic
  environment, 207
American woodcock, accumulation of DDT by, 560, 574–
  575
Amitrole-T used to control
  aquatic weeds, 259
Amphibia, resistance to pesticides in, 676
Amphydasis cognataria, 671–672

711